THE RESTORATION
AND THE EIGHTEENTH CENTURY

THE OXFORD ANTHOLOGY OF ENGLISH LITERATURE

General Editors: Frank Kermode and John Hollander

Medieval English Literature
J. B. TRAPP, Librarian, Warburg Institute, London

The Literature of Renaissance England
JOHN HOLLANDER, Hunter College;
and FRANK KERMODE, University College London

The Restoration and the Eighteenth Century
MARTIN PRICE, Yale University

Romantic Poetry and Prose
HAROLD BLOOM, Yale University;
and LIONEL TRILLING, Columbia University

Victorian Prose and Poetry
LIONEL TRILLING and HAROLD BLOOM

Modern British Literature
FRANK KERMODE and JOHN HOLLANDER

The Restoration and the Eighteenth Century

MARTIN PRICE
Yale University

New York   OXFORD UNIVERSITY PRESS
London   Toronto   1973

General Editors' Preface

The purpose of the Oxford Anthology is to provide students with a selective canon of the entire range of English Literature from the beginnings to recent times, with introductory matter and authoritative annotation. Its method is historical, in the broadest sense, and its arrangement, commentary, and notes, both analytic and contextual, have benefited not only from the teaching experience of the several editors, but from a study of the virtues and shortcomings of comparable works. A primary aim has been to avoid the insulation of any one section from the influence of others, and more positively, to allow both student and instructor to come to terms with the manner in which English literature has generated its own history. This aim has been accomplished in several ways.

First, a reorganization of chronological phases has allowed the Tudor and Stuart periods to be unified under the broad heading of the English Renaissance, with two editors collaborating over the whole extended period. Similarly, the nineteenth century has two editors, one for the poetry of the whole period, and one for the prose. This arrangement seemed appropriate in every way, especially since neither of these scholars could be called a narrow specialist in "Romantic" or "Victorian," as these terms are used in semester- or course-labels.

Every contributing editor has worked and taught in at least one period or field outside the one for which he is, in this anthology, principally responsible, and none has ever allowed specialization to reduce his broader commitment to humane studies more largely considered. Thus we were able to plan a work which called for an unusual degree of cross reference and collaboration. During a crucial phase in the preparation of the text, the editors held daily discussions of their work for a period of months. By selection, allusion, comparison, by direction and indirection, we contrived to preserve continuity between epochs, and to illuminate its character. At the same time, the close co-operation of the various editors has precluded the possibility of common surrender to any single dominating literary theory; and the teacher need have no fear that he must prepare to do battle with some critical Hydra showing a head on every page.

The method of selecting text was consistent with these principles. In the eighteenth- and nineteenth-century sections it was our general policy to exclude the novel, for obvious reasons of length; but in the twentieth, where short fiction becomes more prominent and more central, we have included entire works of fiction, or clearly defined parts of them—for example, *Heart of Darkness,* "The Dead," the "Nausicaa" episode of *Ulysses,* and *St. Mawr.* On the other hand we were persuaded, after much reflection, that a different principle must apply in the cases of Spenser and Milton, where we waived the requirement of completeness. To have given the whole of one book—say, the First of *The Faerie Queene*—would have been a solution as easy as it is, no doubt, defensible; but it is asking a great deal of students to see that portion of the poem as an epitome of the rest, which is often so delightfully different; and we decided that we must provide selections from the whole poem, with linking commentary. We did the same for *Paradise Lost* though without abandoning the practice of providing complete texts when this was both possible and desirable; for example, *Comus* is reprinted entire, and so is a lesser-known but still very important masque, Jonson's *Pleasure Reconciled to Virtue,* which is interesting not only in relation to *Comus* but as an illustration of the part poetry can play in political spectacle and—more generally—in the focusing of the moral vision. Minor texts have been chosen for their exemplary force and their beauty, as well as to embody thematic concerns. If the teacher wishes, he or she may work, both within and across periods, with recurrent patterns as large as the conception of the Earthly Paradise, or with sub-genres as small but as fascinating as the Mad Song. It will also be evident from certain patterns of selection—*The Tempest* as the Shakesperean play, the very large amount of Blake, the emphasis given to D. H. Lawrence's poems as well as his fiction—that a genuinely modern taste, rather than an eager modishness, has helped to shape our presentation of the historical canon. It is also hoped that the unusually generous sampling of material in certain sections—notably the Renaissance, eighteenth century, and the Romantics—will allow the teacher to use secondary or minor works, if he so chooses, to highlight these newer concerns or to fill in contextual background.

As for the annotations, the editors have never been afraid to be lively or even speculative. They have consistently tried to avoid usurping the teacher's role, as providing standard or definitive readings might do. On the other hand, the commentary goes beyond merely providing a lowest common denominator of information by suggesting interpretive directions and levels along which the teacher is free to move or not; and of course he always has the freedom to disagree. The editors have been neither prudish nor portentous in their tone, nor have they sought—in the interests of some superficial consistency, but with leaden effect—to efface their personal styles.

Texts have all been based on the best modern editions, which happen quite often to be published by the Oxford University Press. Spelling and punctuation have been modernized throughout, save in three instances: portions of the medieval period, and the texts of Spenser and Blake, two poets whose spelling and punctuation are so far from idiosyncrasies to be silently normalized that they constitute attempts to refashion poetic language. In the medieval section, modern verse translations of *Beowulf* (by C. W. Kennedy) and of *Gawain* (by Brian Stone) have been adopted. Glossaries of literary and historical terms in all periods have been provided, sometimes keyed to the annotations, sometimes supplementing the larger headnotes. These, it will be noticed, seek to illuminate the immediate contexts of the literature of a period rather than to provide a dense précis of its social, political, and economic history. Similarly, the reading lists at the end of each volume are not exhaustive bibliographies; in the happy instance where a teacher finds an extensive bibliography advisable, he or she will want to supply one.

A word about the pictures. They are not to be thought of simply as illustrations, and certainly not as mere decorations, but rather as part of the anthologized material, like the musical examples and the special sections (such as the one on Ovidian mythology in the Renaissance and on the Urban Scene in the eighteenth century). Throughout, the reader is introduced to the relations between poem as speaking picture, and picture as mute poem. Aside from contextual and anecdotal illustration, of which there is indeed a good deal, the pictorial examples allow teachers, or students on their own, to explore some of the interrelations of texts and the visual arts in all periods, whether exemplified in Renaissance emblems or in contemporary illustrations of Victorian poems.

Finally, an inevitable inadequate word of acknowledgment. To the English Department of Dartmouth College the editors are deeply indebted for having so generously and hospitably provided a place in which to work together for a sustained period. The staff of the Dartmouth College Library was extraordinarily helpful and attentive.

All of the editors would like to extend a note of gratitude to the many academics throughout the United States who willingly made suggestions as to what should be included as well as excluded. A special note of thanks to Jim Cox of Dartmouth College and Paul Dolan of the State University of New York at Stony Brook for their challenging and always helpful comments.

And finally to the entire staff of the New York branch of the Oxford University Press who have done more than could be humanly expected in connection with the planning and execution of this book. We would especially like to thank our editor John Wright, as well as Leona Capeless and her staff, Mary Ellen Evans, Patricia Cristol, Joyce Berry, Deborah Zwecher, and Jean Shapiro. An unusual but very deserved note of thanks to the Production people, especially Gerard S. Case and Leslie Phillips and to the designer, Frederick Schneider, whose excellent work speaks for itself.

New York   Frank Kermode
September 1972   John Hollander

Contents

* An asterisk indicates that a work does not appear in its entirety.

Eighteenth Century

THE MOCK FORM, 291

Later Eighteenth Century

THE RESTORATION
AND THE EIGHTEENTH CENTURY

The Restoration and
the Eighteenth Century

We may speak of the eighteenth century as the period of the Enlightenment, and the term carries a fairly precise meaning when it is applied to France: secular in spirit, skeptical in matters of knowledge, rationalistic only in its critique of historical institutions, devoted to the idea of justice, and jealously protective of the dignity of human nature. Not all these traits are to be found in every writer, it is true, but they serve well enough to characterize the age. When we turn from France to England, however, the idea of an Enlightenment becomes less clear.

As a predominantly Protestant nation, and one whose established church had turned away from dogmatic and evangelical extremes toward a religion of moral duty, England had less reason to be anticlerical or militantly secular. Deism became a force in the later seventeenth century and persisted as a rationalistic natural religion opposed to all dependence upon revelation; but it never achieved a highly respectable position in England. English political liberties, which served as a model for French reformers, were sufficient to make plausible the Whig trust in slow historical progression and to win loyalty, if not in fact reverence, to constitutional forms. Most of the major writers of the age, from Dryden to Dr. Johnson (and including Swift and Pope), were largely Tory in spirit: distrustful of human nature and devoted to the cause of public order.

Yet one can see a degree of secularization in England. The center of concern has shifted from the institutions that confer legitimate authority to the detached individual, from dogma to the painful quest for balance and tact. Decisions are made by man rather than for him, and they exact a new intensity of self-criticism, a wary resistance to the appeals of partiality and self-interest—a discipline, as the age would have it, of both head and heart. For while there is distrust of the private spirit and of anarchic individualism—usually shown to be based in pride—there is no easy recourse in turn to rule or formula. The distinctive spirit of the age, then, and it might be called Enlightenment, is a critical one—constantly testing through irony, purging with satire, and finding conviction in the poise of an exact antithesis or a delicate balance.

POLITICS AND MORALITY

When the Stuarts returned to the throne in 1660, the changes of two intervening decades of revolution could not simply be reversed, for the experience of power had awakened new capacities and justified new ambitions. At first there was apparent reaction. The Church of England was re-established as the state religion. But it now had to fight and intrigue with Dissenters and Roman Catholics to preserve its authority. There were strong demands for full civil rights by the Puritans, and there were grave fears of what Charles II might grant to the Catholic French monarch, Louis XIV, in return for financial subsidy. The fears of the church were only a reflection of the instability of the King's power. Charles was under constant pressure in his later years from Whig lords (whose alliances were with London merchants, middle-class Dissenters, and former Dutch allies) and from the Tory supporters of his Catholic brother and apparent heir, the Duke of York (later James II). But more fundamentally, the idea of kingship itself was in question.

In his great political work of 1651, the *Leviathan,* Thomas Hobbes had argued the need for a stable and undivided sovereignty. Hobbes opposed the growing myth of the mixed state (a balance of power among King, Lords, and Commons), but his defense of absolute sovereignty was no return to the Stuart doctrine of the divine right of kings ("right divine to govern wrong," as Pope described James I's doctrine). Hobbes based his case on natural expediency; the alternative was intolerable anarchy, in which each man warred against every other. It hardly mattered to Hobbes what form the sovereignty took so long as it could command and maintain power (and Swift, writing after the Glorious Revolution of 1688, declared that Hobbes's essential error lay in making the King rather than the Parliament the ultimate sovereign). John Locke, writing in Charles II's reign what was not to be published until 1690, insisted that the King derived his authority not from the sheer necessity of his subjects but from their active consent; should he destroy their property or enslave them, he would put himself "into a state of war with the people, who are thereupon absolved from any further obedience."

This secularized view of the state left little sanctity to the king, and Charles II was rarely the man to claim it. Urbane and cultivated, with a taste for music and wit, he inspired personal affection and public distrust in equal measure. He lacked moral depth or tenacity of purpose, and, while his love of pleasure was a welcome relief for many from the sober fanaticism of strict Puritans and surly republicans, it encouraged little repose in his strength or reliance on his word. The Marquess of Halifax wrote of Charles after his death: "It must be allowed he had a little over-balance on the well-natured side, not vigour enough to be earnest to do a kind thing, much less to do a harsh one; but if a hard thing was done to another man, he did not eat his supper the worse for it. It was rather a deadness than a severity of nature. . . ." One is struck by how often Halifax recurs to the King's physical well-being: "It may be said that his inclinations to love were the effects of health and a good constitution, with as little mixture of the seraphic part as man ever had; and though from that foundation men often raise their passions, I am apt to think his stayed as much as any man's ever did in the lower region. . . . He had more properly . . . a good stomach to his mistresses than any great passion for them. His taking them from others was never learnt in a romance, and indeed fitter for a philosopher than a knight-errant." If Charles showed no jealousy, it was "love of ease" that prevented it; for "where mere nature is the motive, it is possible for a man . . . to argue that a rival taketh away nothing but the heart and leaveth the rest."

The Glorious Revolution of 1688, which brought William III and Mary to the throne, confirmed the principle of the mixed state, a principle that was to be invoked throughout the century to follow and to be accepted as the Revolution Settlement by all but the few fanatical Jacobites (who remained loyal to James II and his heirs). There was still only a cautious assertion of constitutional changes: the fiction of James's abdication was used to soften the force of Parliament's action, and the limits set to the king's power were left implicit in his oath to govern "according to the statutes in Parliament agreed on." For years to come the full meaning of the changes remained in the process of definition, and the stability to be found in the harmony of a mixed state remained more vision than actuality.

The growth of the electorate gave more power to Commons, and the conduct of protracted wars led to the growth of the court bureaucracy. To support its program the court required more and more recourse to public loans, and with them came an increase both of an administrative cadre and of a moneyed class whose wealth came from investment rather than from rents. This erosion of the landed interest was felt most acutely by the smaller landowners, the country gentry, and they were most suspicious of the centralized power at court. The early years of the eighteenth century were a period of frequent elections and shifts of power, and the efforts of the Whig forces to enlist wider support led to more toleration for Dissenters and more dependence upon the financial power of London.

Much of the energy of the writers of the day was devoted to defending traditional attitudes or to destroying them. Daniel Defoe attacked the landed gentry in behalf of the men of wealth; Swift exposed the increasing power of men whose loyalty was claimed not by tenant and estate but by interest rates and "paper money." But meanwhile these distinctions were breaking down, as men of wealth invested in land (at times buying up the nearly bankrupt estates of small landholders) and as the landed aristocracy, through both investment and intermarriage, allied itself with the "moneyed" men. The political stability dreamed of in the mixed state was attained at last in the 1720's when Sir Robert Walpole strengthened the court by his bold use of patronage to win support, and there arose the serious question of whether the state had become a stable balance or rather a new kind of tyranny under the forms of parliamentary leadership.

If Charles II sets the note of the Restoration period, Walpole does as much for the mid-eighteenth century. Bluff, hospitable, ostentatious, he had a sufficient sense of his own power. "I am certainly at present in a situation that makes me," he said to Lord Hervey, "of consequence to more people than any man ever before me was, or perhaps than any man may ever be again." Hervey reflected on "the double vanity this great man was guilty of in believing what he said, and saying what he believed." Walpole's management of George II through Queen Caroline and of Parliament through a system of patronage made his control of England a formidable substitute for earlier and franker forms of tyranny. Walpole's control of English liberties was far less complete; but the Licensing Act of 1737, which imposed political censorship on the stage, might recall Dryden's words about Augustus, who "conscious of himself of so many crimes which he had committed, thought . . . to provide for his own reputation by making an edict against lampoons and satires."

Walpole achieved stability by freeing the court of the overriding power of Commons. In the process the Whig oligarchy, having attained a one-party system, adopted much of the traditional doctrine of the Tories. It was the so-called Patriots (led by the friend of Swift and Pope, Lord Bolingbroke) who kept alive the idea of an Opposition as a guarantor of freedom, who demanded more frequent elections and more extensive representation, and who sought to free Parliament of its control by place-holders.

In an age where power increasingly followed wealth, the highly paid sinecures that Walpole distributed were not only a reward for obedience, they were a further entrenchment of a self-perpetuating group. More appalling to men like Swift and Pope was Walpole's marshalling of a squad of hireling writers, serviceable men of limited talent, to defend his ministry and discredit his opponents. Royal patronage no longer furthered merit for its own sake but used the forms of distinction to reward subservience and intellectual dishonesty. Pope's *Dunciad* makes Colley Cibber the monarch of the duruces, the epitome of a commercialized and debased culture; he had been elevated to the post of poet-laureate less for talent than for pliability.

The opposition to Walpole was made articulate by men who had loyalties to a landed aristocracy, but those loyalties were neither felt nor expressed in limited economic terms. Rather, they were universalized as the opposition of genuine culture to sham, of free intelligence to prostitute mediocrity. For the stability that Walpole gave England was gained at the cost of moral aspiration. A man might aspire to power or wealth, but he had to leave his integrity behind when he went "to see Sir Robert." This sense of universal corruption was the specter created in the great satires of the age, and in opposition to it a new kind of heroism emerged. It included aristocratic scorn for mercantile zeal that slights honesty and justice; esteem for the "middle state" of man (above brutalizing poverty and below debilitating luxury); disdain for the mindless "mob," whether of the lower classes or the hireling nobles; nostalgia for institutions which embodied principles stabler than individual will or current fashion. One can see this as a rear-guard resistance to growing bourgeois liberalism, as reactionary appeal to a past that could not be restored and perhaps had never truly existed. But from the other end of that cycle of growth we may find it harder to call it reaction; such judgments trust history to settle issues, and history never does so for long.

The aspiration that Walpole and his chosen successors, the Pelhams, failed to satisfy found release in the leadership of the elder William Pitt, Earl of Chatham. The hero of the London merchants, he also fostered a sense of national greatness, presiding over the defeat of France on three continents and her loss of power in both Canada and India. These were triumphs of mercantile expansion which laid the groundwork for the growth of empire abroad and of industry at home; but Pitt infused them with a sense of moral purpose.

In George III, who became king in 1760, moral aspiration reached the throne itself, but his earnestness was marked by obstinacy and his devotion to duty by priggishness. The third George, unlike the first two, cultivated domestic virtues rather than foreign mistresses, and his favor was worthily conferred (with the guidance of ministers) upon such men as Dr. Johnson, Gibbon, and Rousseau. But his rigid and suspicious nature made him declare, with a sense of shock, that he had to "call in bad men to govern bad men." Among the "bad men" to be governed were the American colonists, who completed their successful revolution by 1783, and the political radicals at home, whose sympathy with the colonies was only a prelude to their support of the French Revolution a few years later.

Perhaps the best of the men George chose to govern for him was the younger William Pitt, who became chief minister in 1784 at the age of twenty-five (as Coleridge was to observe, he was "always full-grown," for he "was cast rather than grew"). Pitt had genius in administrative reform; he reduced waste in government offices, revised the tax and customs system, reduced the national debt, and stimulated trade.

These technical achievements were, however, overtaken by the war with France which followed upon the Revolution; and Pitt became, with the threat of invasion from abroad and the fear of subversion at home, all too ready to see political radicalism of any sort as potential treason and to make it so in law. Somewhat as Robert Walpole had been the object of attack by the major poets of the mid-century, so Pitt, for different reasons, was to win the scorn of Blake, Wordsworth, and Coleridge.

THE MIDDLE WAY: WIT AND DRESS

Few moments seem so decisive a break in the continuity of English literature as the Restoration. While in exile in France, the court of Charles II had acquired a new tone of worldliness and self-conscious sophistication that was to affect literary as well as social forms. The fact that Milton's *Paradise Lost* or Bunyan's *Pilgrim's Progress* was published after the Restoration seems incongruous. Yet the new tone was not simply a brittle elegance derived from French manners and turned mockingly upon sober Puritan zeal. It had its own seriousness even when it was most willfully outrageous; and it was marked by deep skepticism. The unlimited claims of religious sects and political causes had produced decades of painful division—within the nation, even within families—and they were now seen with a strong sense of their danger. Extravagant assertions of divine favor by radical Protestants and no less fanatical Royalists seemed frivolous, fevered, and deeply destructive. Skepticism turned to the practical and viable; it tested all claims and assertions for both their meaningfulness and their consequences.

One of the forms of this skepticism was the cultivation of dialectic and banter. Against each unlimited assertion one could place its contrary. Or one could frame dialogues in which the intellectual bankruptcy of the fanatics was exposed by a deadlock between extremists or by an opponent of Socratic modesty and irony. We can see the spirit of this in Dryden's *Essay of Dramatic Poesy* (1668), where four critics assert in turn the superiority of ancient or modern, French or English, literature. It is a dialogue of exceptional amiability, for these men are good-tempered and comparatively flexible; it takes place, moreover, just on the margin of an Anglo-Dutch war, a quiet retreat from public conflicts. Other dialogues were more satirical and reductive; they allowed the "enthusiast" to expand to the utmost before he was punctured and deflated by wit. Enthusiasm itself was a term of reproach; it referred to the delusion of being divinely inspired and to the self-hypnotic rhetoric of those who acted under that delusion. To show them as all the more vehement for their ignorance and superstition was the satirist's device; we see it in Samuel Butler's portrait of the radical Protestant squire Ralpho in *Hudibras* (1663–78). Another method was to study the psychopathology of enthusiasm and to trace its madness to a pride that could not endure the restraints of reason and common truths.

The retreat from public conflicts had led a group of learned men of various allegiances to gather for the discussion of scientific matters at Gresham College in London during the years of Cromwell's Protectorate; out of these meetings (from which the topics of religion and politics were barred) emerged the Royal Society, chartered by the King in 1662. The Royal Society was devoted, in a Baconian spirit, to empirical investigation, and it framed as well an influential conception of language. Joseph Glanvill, for example, could see nothing but "endless disputes and quarrels" come of devotion to the "verbal emptiness of the philosophy of the Schools," that is, the Scholasticism that sought to explain phenomena by multiplying terms: "For what else can be the fruit of a philosophy, made of occult qualities, sympathies, entelechies, elements, celestial influences, and abundance of other hard words and lazy generalities but an arrest of all ingenious and practical endeavour, and a wilderness of opinions instead of certainty and science?" What Glanvill hoped for and at last saw as possible was "a philosophy fruitful in works, not in words, and such as may accommodate the use of life, both natural and moral." And he, like others, drew a parallel for religion: the need to give up endless and insoluble controversy about doctrine, often based upon obscure texts of Scripture, and to concentrate upon the "practical and certain knowledge which will assist and promote our virtue and our happiness."

This reaction against "notion and theory" affected all realms of experience. Sir Isaac Newton boasted, "I do not frame hypotheses," and by that he meant his refusal, in contrast to Descartes, to be seduced by speculation from the essential task of empirical description. In politics and religion the men of "latitude" and moderation tried to forge a method of critical discrimination. It was typically represented as the search for a middle way between extremes. By this was meant not lukewarmness or weak compromise (what the age called "trimming") but a bold rejection of untested dogma. The middle way lacked the support of authority and precedent; it required a delicate judgment of each new situation, a weighing of values without formula, and a readiness to dwell in uncertainties rather than surrender to prejudice or cant.

We can see the theme of the middle way captured in the metaphor of dress that pervaded the writing of the age. Language has often been described as the dress of thought, and rhetoric has been treated as a wardrobe of idioms in which ideas might be clothed. In the Restoration we find a strong reaction against merely verbal wit. The attack could extend to the conceits of the metaphysical poets (and particularly the late, mannered style of a John Cleveland), to the metaphorical flights of baroque sermons, to the jargon of Scholastics or (worse) of pseudo-mystical and alchemi-cal writers, to the "wresting of scriptures" that tortured the text of the Bible until it could serve any prejudice or party. In the realm of manners, the attack (such as we see in Restoration comedy) was turned on the coxcomb who made constant use of the "jerk and sting of an epigram" and who chased the reputation of brilliance through a thousand puns. The would-be wit was always on the stretch to show his cleverness and seldom concerned about whether truth or insight might lie below the dazzling surface. Restoration comedy tended to equate the would-be wit with the fop. The fop, too, disregards "propriety" or "decency," a sense of what belongs or is fitting. He does not dress in a manner appropriate to his rank or to the occasion but seeks only to overwhelm others with his finery. His dress is a collection of unrelated bits of brilliance—"one glaring chaos and wild heap of wit," as Pope described a poem full of conceits—whose only purpose is to dazzle.

What were the alternatives? Was not all dress a form of deception? Some believed so and insisted upon naked nature, as if that were still possible in a world of men. In Restoration comedy, the fop's opponent was often the rake, a man of frankly licentious appetite with the cunning to satisfy it, a cool Machiavellian in the world of sex and money. He enacted the unabashed animal he thought man might better be and gloried in his energy and resourcefulness. Yet neither of these extremes, fop or rake, stood up to scrutiny, for both revealed anarchic pride and self-seeking. The typical response to both was to find a middle way: to recognize the "way of the world" and to dress to meet its demands. For the true wit did not neglect the guises the world would accept; but he used them as a means of preserving his independence and integrity. This was the case of Mirabell in William Congreve's *The Way of the World* (1700), and we can see its deeper implications in Swift's *A Tale of a Tub* (1704).

Swift's allegory presented Christian teaching as a simple garment that, in the course of history, was covered with all the fashionable accessories that the world demanded. Three brothers showed the different ways of treating the garment. Peter (the Roman Catholic Church) first led the others in loading his coat with elaborate ornaments and refused, when they were criticized, to remove any. Jack (the radical Protestant church) condemned Peter's error and, in a fit of enthusiastic reformation, tore his own coat to shreds in the effort to remove whatever Peter had persuaded him to add. Only the third brother, Martin (representing the middle way of the Church of England), recognized the impossibility of restoring his coat to its original purity, accepted those additions whose removal would destroy its fabric, and carefully detached the rest stitch by stitch. Martin was concerned with the coat itself rather than its expression of his own will; and in his rejection of both imposture and brutality he showed an awareness that reached, in effect, a different level rather than lay midway on a single plane. The middle way, for Swift, is not simply a compromise between two errors but a transcendence of the vicious folly that produced both.

AN AUGUSTAN AGE

In his scorn for the verbal sophistries of false wit, the writer of this age often called them barbarous or "Gothic." By contrast he looked back to the grace and lucidity of classical writing and tried to recover its virtues in his own work. The period was one of great translation; not only did Dryden translate all of Virgil, and Pope all of Homer, but there were also the free "imitations" of Horace and Juvenal, from Rochester's early experiments to Dr. Johnson's *Vanity of Human Wishes* (1749). To write in the spirit of the ancients while adapting them to the day is perhaps a greater sign of devotion than the museum-like reproductions that were to follow once historicism, with its sense of the pastness of the past and the distinctiveness of each culture, arose in the late eighteenth century. The earlier revival of the classics was predicated on the view that these writers were more genuinely alive than the eccentric or time-bound authors of the immediate past; it was not the rust of antiquity but its relevance that was esteemed.

The period of the Restoration and early eighteenth century is now often called the Augustan age. The term arose in the period itself, but it was applied tentatively and in more than one sense. London, once called Troynovant or New Troy, came now to be called Augusta, as the heir to imperial Rome. In 1712 John Oldmixon wrote that the age of Charles II "probably may be the Augustan Age of English poetry," and Dr. Johnson applied to Dryden's role in English poetry the words once used of Augustus as the builder of Rome: "He found it brick and left it marble." The term "Augustan" was a tribute to the new urbanity and formal elegance of English verse, and it evoked as well the tradition of a ruler who gave his patronage to and won the sincere respect of his greatest writers. This role could be said to fit Charles II in some measure, but to apply it, as Pope did with brilliant irony, to George I or George II, could be nothing but a gesture of scorn. George II hated poetry and painting alike and allowed politics to dictate patronage.

There were grounds, however, for distrusting the Emperor Augustus as well; his subversion of the freedom of the Roman Republic was a constant theme of historians: Swift alluded to it in 1701, and Gibbon made it the subject of the great third chapter of his *Decline and Fall of the Roman Empire* (1776). The ambivalence felt toward an age that was at once courtly, polished, and servile awakened all the more reverence for republican Rome and praise for the stoical Horace of the Republic rather than the epicurean Horace of the court.

Still, the tribute to Rome served to evoke a common European culture beneath the accidents of time or the changing national and local customs. It was an appeal to values that had won agreement in most times and places and would be confirmed by posterity in turn. For the classical view of history saw man as constant and the accidents of time as repetitive and cyclical rather than progressive. This view provided the Enlightenment with the secular counterpart of those religious values that stood outside the world and could be used to judge it. Whatever the corruptions and blindness of the present, one could see beyond them to permanent truths.

The desire to free the general or the universal in all its grandeur from particular fashion (of dress, of manners, of language) could lead at worst to a vacuous academicism. One might remove all character in order to remove idiosyncrasy. We may recall those white marble statues (for the eighteenth century invented a white antiquity, purified of those colors that had once adorned statues and temples) in classical costume that restored contemporary statesmen (Walpole or Washington) to their universality or a poet like Pope to his role of laurel-crowned *vates*. But at their best, poets and artists achieved a nice balance between the classical form and the substantial actuality. This is most obvious in the "imitation" or in the mock form (such as mock-heroic or mock-pastoral) where the pure form is opposed to the bristling disorder of everyday life. The greatest works of the age play back and forth between the ideal form and the stubborn particular, each criticizing the other.

There is a similar interplay in the architecture of the period. When the Earl of Burlington revived the designs of Andrea Palladio as the most classical and humanistic of Renaissance architects, he was rejecting the baroque freedom of Sir Christopher Wren and in fact restoring a greater Roman severity than he could find in Palladio. Yet the Palladian country house was set in gardens which achieved the natural freedom of landscape rather than geometric formality. House and grounds were set against each other to yield a more complex harmony.

In painting no one caught the vitality and exuberance of urban life so well as William Hogarth, but he was also possessed by the desire to succeed in the high form of history-painting, with its generalized figures of heroic grandeur. Sir Joshua Reynolds, who formulated the doctrine of the grand style in his presidential addresses to the Royal Academy, created in turn witty plays upon the heroic, evoking it in teasing allusions or "quoted" poses, placing children in the heroic stances of prophets or rulers.

SATIRE AND THE NOVEL

Nowhere did the classical forms serve so well as in satire. Satire had never been so central and powerful a form of literature before in England, nor had it ever shown so great a capacity to absorb the tragic and heroic vision as well. The skeptical impetus that discredited false claims to authority found its form by inventing a ludicrous world of mock-grandeur and self-deception, where men pursued the outward forms of greatness with no sense of their meaning or their true cost. In the finest satires of the age the mantle of greatness is placed upon the fool and falls with an overwhelming weight, as if to crush an insect. The heroic vision is essential to the satiric; the satirist shows his anti-hero falling as far below the norms of decency and intelligence as the true hero rises above them. To trap an oaf in the pattern of the heroic is to define his grossness all the more sharply; his high pretensions only serve to measure his contemptible performance.

Yet the heroic works in another way, too. For while the particular object of satire may be ludicrous and transparent, he may serve to reveal a wider and deeper pattern of failure that is more commonplace and less easy to identify in actual men. When Swift embodies the history of the church in the careers of three Restoration fops, the small foreground figures serve to interpret (reductively but with frightening lucidity) vast and complex historical forces. When Pope in *The Dunciad* presents the debased culture of his day as if it were the eclipse of all culture, he is not simply attacking the corruption of the Hanoverian court or of commercialized London. He is attacking "Dulness," the chronic tendency of the mind to relapse into lazy fantasy and to give up its critical powers; the current scene is only the latest instance of a process whose dimensions extend through all history. Satire magnifies as well as reduces; it may reduce man's plausible pretexts to mechanical folly, but it makes the folly in turn a potential tragic failure and a force worthy of heroic resistance.

Once satire gives way to more neutral curiosity, what was seen as failure is regarded with more sympathy and willingness to condone or understand. In the process the very details which were an affront to the high forms of the heroic become the absorbing material of daily life. The marvelous, saintly, and heroic may be transposed to the level of the commonplace. Instead of a lonely Odysseus outwitting vengeful gods we have a sober Robinson Crusoe ingeniously transforming a lonely island into a scene of middle-class enterprise. With the rise of the novel the studied detachment of satire gives way to an exploration of the confusions and inconsistencies seen within the self. In *Robinson Crusoe* (1719) Defoe fused what might have been the material of a Puritan spiritual autobiography with the heroism of mercantile adventure. In *Moll Flanders* (1722) he went on to consider those forms of excess, the ruthlessness of theft and prostitution, that lie at the edge of mercantile zeal, and he treated them with remarkable awareness of the power of their appeal.

Defoe in his first-person narratives and, even more, Samuel Richardson in his epistolary novels, notably *Pamela* (1741) and *Clarissa* (1748), found techniques for giving their stories an air of veracity. The point was not to deceive the reader about their being fictions but to bring him into close involvement with character and event. The novel's slow unfolding and full record of both internal and external realities created a remarkable new opportunity for identification; the letters of the day record the compelling power of the novel upon the reader's feelings. Henry Fielding, particularly in *Joseph Andrews* (1742) and *Tom Jones* (1749), created a new balance between the detached satiric observer, brilliantly artful in his rhetoric, and the closely presented incident. Fielding's formalization is bold and free, and he mocks the very conventions by which the novel asserts its veracity, but he uses them too. In Laurence Sterne's *Tristram Shandy* (1759–67), the self-consciousness of the novel reaches its extreme, veering between circumstantial realism and elaborate contrivance, pushing realism to the point where it frankly topples over into *tour de force*. Sterne also carries sympathy to the point where it becomes sentimentalism, that is, the prizing of feeling and the cultivation of it for its own sake; but he mocks this, too, with a recoil into ironic detachment.

NEW FEELINGS AND FORMS

The growing esteem for sentiment and feeling in the eighteenth century was the culmination of a long process—a movement toward internalization, first from the rationalistic systems of the seventeenth century to the Augustan emphasis on immediate intuition. The Augustans were intensely distrustful of systems; their pursuit of a middle way was a matter of achieving sound feeling as well as true insight, for the two were inextricably related. Pride and self-interest distorted all awareness: the delicate balance of disinterestedness was difficult to attain, and its attainment was as much a moral achievement as an intellectual one. The action of the honest heart was more reliable than any process of reasoning; and it was not a long step to the trust in heart over head. Trust your heart, wrote the third Earl of Shaftesbury, so long as you keep it honest.

In a similar way the grandeur of the general, once derived from a vision of cosmic order, became internalized and identified with what men have generally felt. Generality became a psychological rather than a metaphysical standard. As Reynolds observed, there are illusions that all men share, such as the impression that a medieval castle is older than a classical temple, if only because its origins are more darkly shrouded in a remote but native culture. A century earlier, Sir Christopher Wren had distinguished between natural or geometric beauty and customary beauty (where "familiarity or particular inclination breeds a love to things not in themselves lovely"). Wren has no doubt that natural or geometric beauty is to be preferred; but Reynolds has come to wonder. Reality is becoming what the mind of man creates.

The imaginative power of feeling was given new stress with the doctrine of association of ideas. If men framed an image of the world through repeated and reinforced associations, the linkages were often forged and more often confirmed by the action of the feelings. That seemed true, for David Hume, of our most fundamental conceptions, such as that of causality. Hume showed in his *Treatise on Human Nature* (1739) that the necessary connection of cause and effect was a necessity of our thought rather than an objective natural process. The more distinctive structures of the literary imagination could be traced to the rapid associative movement of genius working under the guidance of strong passion, and the explanation was made complex enough to account for all that was later to be included in the idea of imagination save only conscious artistry and active control. It is interesting, in fact, that Sterne presents man alternately as a victim of his associative processes and as the creator of imagined worlds; an ironic skepticism still surrounds the creative powers of the conscious artist.

In the early stages of this cult of feeling and the exploration of its power of artistry, poetry turned away from the everyday experience that had provided the stuff of Pope's satires or Swift's occasional verse. Instead it cultivated the sublime, images that filled the mind with awe or dread by their very transcendence of its normal scope—images of vastness, of sudden rise or fall, of dark obscurity or blazing light. Before these images were given a theoretical explanation by Edmund Burke in 1757, they had become the characteristic note of such poets of the 1740's as William Collins and Thomas Gray, or of the earlier and most influential poet of the landscape,

James Thomson. These images were, as Burke made clear, supremely realized in Milton's poetry, but they bring to the fore an aspect of Milton given less stress than his moral grandeur in the criticism of Joseph Addison. For the new poetry—as later for the Gothic novel—these images seemed to well up out of the unconscious mind, unrestrained by logic or morality. Their grandeur was not the grandeur of generality, but rather a power to reduce the conscious mind and all its high achievements to triviality. They loom over the ordinary world like towering cliffs or fierce clouds; or they expose the transitoriness of man's control in the images of ruins, the sharp angles of architecture crumbling into organic forms.

Inevitably the sublime and the Gothic provided a form of play-acting, and deliberately created ruins provided a stage for meditation. Yet there was a deeper force at work. To relate man's emotions and unconscious powers to the forms of nature deepened the response to both. Nature became an object of reverence rather than exploitation, a place that both revealed man to himself and imposed limits on his will. On the other hand, the beauty as well as the terror of man's elemental feelings became clear. There were dangers in such a movement toward primitivism; as man's taste opened, it was fed by synthetic products designed to meet it more completely than the natural. If Homer seemed difficult to treat as a primitive bard, the works of the Celtic bard, Ossian, were served up through forgeries that won acclaim throughout Europe. Yet authentic folk poetry was recovered, as in collection of ballads, and the dignity of folk speech or of local dialects began to be credited. All those peculiarities which had been seen as defects of the general now began to seem expressive of a deeper humanity, one that a high culture had suppressed or undervalued.

Another way in which the particular was given new dignity was through the idea of the picturesque. This began as the effort to find (later to create) in natural landscape the designs of the painters of the seventeenth century—Claude Lorrain, Nicolas Poussin, Salvator Rosa. What it came to in time was the rejection of a landscape, however "natural," that was too simple or featureless; the picturesque sought complex relationships of form and color. This was extended from landscape to houses, to villages, to the people who inhabited them. Ironically, bandits were more complex figures—rough, colorful, energetic—than solid tradesmen. There seemed, as often with the sublime, an inverse proportion between the picturesque and the moral. So, too, squalor might provide variety of forms, but the planned town imposed tame uniformity: one might not be content to keep the squalor, but one needed to imitate the slow evolution through time and accident, as in a natural scene, in designing structures or streets. It was better, too, that a cottage reveal its various functions in its surface structure rather than be forced into a pattern of symmetry.

The titanic forces found in the sublime view of nature were found by many in the French Revolution, where oppressive and lifeless forms were thrown off by a people awakened to its own dignity and power. In England some of the enthusiasm which might have turned to revolutionary humanism was captured by Methodism. John Wesley's great evangelical revival had much of the energy of earlier Puritanism, but its anti-intellectualism and political conservatism did nothing to foster the rebellious spirit of an earlier century. Radicalism was largely the product of urban societies of artisans, small merchants, and professional men; their efforts to broaden suffrage and to reform Parliament were blocked by the war with France and the repressive measures undertaken by the younger Pitt. But by the end of the eighteenth century England was clearly moving toward change.

The population of England increased from five and a half million to nine million in the course of the century, and though London maintained its dominance there was rapid growth in the northern areas, where industry developed most rapidly and freely. The concentration of industry in the cities was marked by 1800, but technology was giving all of the landscape a new look: improved turnpikes and canals (including a triumphant aqueduct bearing a canal over a river), new steam-powered pumps for coal mines, large factories for cotton-weaving and pottery-making, and (in 1779) the first iron bridge, over the Severn in Shropshire. To support an increased population required an agricultural as well as an industrial revolution, and this was achieved through the development of new crops (notably root-vegetables), the improved breeding of cattle and sheep (doubling their average weights in the course of the century), and the enclosure of commons so as to make more efficient use of the land. The most controversial developments were the enclosures, and their cost in human displacement was recorded in Oliver Goldsmith's *The Deserted Village* (1770). Hundreds of individual acts of enclosure were approved each year by Parliament from 1760 on, and these were taking place at the time when the growth of factories was destroying the cottage industries that had supplemented farm incomes. The movement toward the towns increased; yet the new agricultural techniques managed, even with a diminished labor force, to add some two million acres of arable land during the century.

By the close of the eighteenth century, English intellectual life had begun to move outside the major cities. We find a provincial painter like Joseph Wright of Derby painting the new industrial landscape as well as portraits of its builders, sublime landscapes and scenes of popular scientific demonstrations such as an experiment with an air-pump. An industrialist like Josiah Wedgwood, properly attentive to the state of roads and canals that served his potteries in Staffordshire, was no less attentive to archaeological discoveries in Pompeii and Herculaneum, from which he adapted designs through the skills of such artists as John Flaxman. Even more, the village and countryside had found poets, and resident poets rather than nostalgic ones, in men like Crabbe, Cowper, and Burns.

SAMUEL BUTLER
1613–1680

Butler first emerged from obscurity at the age of fifty with the publication of *Hudibras*. The poem pleased Charles II and his court, ran through nine printings in a year, and eventually won Butler a royal pension. Born the son of a prosperous Worcestershire yeoman, Butler had served as clerk in several households where he could pursue learning and study painting; and he had acquired a considerable knowledge of law, perhaps as a student at Gray's Inn, London.

As the first great satire to look back upon the Commonwealth, *Hudibras* converts nightmare into farce and sums up an era of fanaticism in the Quixotic career of its Presbyterian knight and his independent or radical Protestant squire. By presenting their adventures as a parody of knight-errantry, Butler catches the preposterous self-importance of two dolts whose smattering of learning is just enough to release them from common sense. Between them they represent many tendencies of the mind to overleap the limits of empirical check: Scholastic logic-chopping; the cult-idiom of sectarians; visionary enthusiasm; and above all, hypocritical self-righteousness. While Hudibras is more Aristotelian and Ralpho, his squire, is more neoplatonic and theosophical, each achieves the absolutism of the private self, a mixture of uncritical superstition and arrogant crusading zeal.

Butler creates this image in large part through literary allusion. In the manner of Paul Scarron, who travestied Virgil's epic by retelling it with low knockabout antics and vulgar speeches (imitated in English by Charles Cotton's *Scarronides*, 1664), Butler accommodates romance forms to the low clowns he creates. But Butler's wit, with its reductive parody of a soaring baroque idiom of paradox, also ridicules man's constant effort to exceed his rational powers. Here the result is self-defeating sophistry, transparently mindless and suggestive of the enthusiastic preaching that followed upon the all-too-easy delusion of being inspired. Enthusiasm was studied in the Restoration (by such men as Henry More and Meric Casaubon) as a typical form of psychopathology, and it was to be analyzed once more in Jonathan Swift's *A Tale of a Tub* (1704). Swift, it was reported, knew much of *Hudibras* by heart; like Matthew Prior, he found new uses for Butler's form of "anti-poetry," the heavily rhymed octosyllabic couplet.

Dr. Johnson explains some of the remarkable power *Hudibras* must have had upon its first appearance:

> The brightest strokes of his wit owed their force to the impression of the characters, which was upon men's minds at the time; to their knowing them, at table and in the street; in short, being familiar with them; and above all to his satire being directed against those whom a little while before they had hated and feared.

As for Butler's wit and learning, Johnson finds them so abundant as at times to be too much, but he asserts that "there is more thinking" in Milton and Butler (the pairing is remarkable) "than in any of our poets." Indeed, he goes on, "If the French boast of the learning of Rabelais, we need not be afraid of confronting them with Butler."

Hudibras°
From Part I   Canto I

THE ARGUMENT
Sir Hudibras his passing worth,
The manner how he sallied forth,
His arms and equipage, are shown;
His horse's virtues and his own.
The adventure of the bear and fiddle
Is sung, but breaks off in the middle.

When civil dudgeon first grew high,
And men fell out, they knew not why;
When hard words,° jealousies, and fears
Set folks together by the ears,
And made them fight, like mad or drunk,
For Dame Religion as for punk;°
Whose honesty they all durst swear for,
Though not a man of them knew wherefore;
When gospel-trumpeter, surrounded
10   With long-eared rout,° to battle sounded;
And pulpit, drum ecclesiastic,
Was beat with fist instead of a stick;
Then did Sir Knight abandon dwelling,
And out he rode a-colonelling.
A wight° he was, whose very sight would
Entitle him Mirror of Knighthood,°
That never bowed his stubborn knee
To anything but chivalry,°
Nor put up blow but that which laid
20   Right Worshipful on shoulder-blade;
Chief of domestic knights and errant,°
Either for chartel° or for warrant;
Great on the bench, great in the saddle,
That could as well bind o'er as swaddle;°
Mighty he was at both of these,
And styled of war as well as peace.
(So some rats, of amphibious nature,
Are either for the land or water.)

Hudibras named for the rash, morose knight who woos the pleasure-hating Elissa in Spenser, *Faerie Queene* II.ii.

hard words not merely harsh words but technical jargon (see ll. 85, 111 below), in this case the cant words ("fears" and "jealousies") by which Puritans described events and motives

punk whore

long-eared rout epic diction for "asses"; applied to Puritans whose short hair (thus Roundheads) made their ears conspicuous and who sometimes cupped their ears with their hands to catch each word of an enthusiastic sermon, in this case a call to rebellion

wight romance diction for "man"

Mirror of Knighthood a chivalric romance admired by Don Quixote

chivalry to the vision of himself as a knight, kneeling to be dubbed by his lord (ll. 19–20)

domestic . . . errant As "domestic" knight, or Justice of the Peace "on the bench," he could issue a "warrant" for arrest and "bind over" a prisoner for future trial; as knight "errant," he could wander in search of righteous battle, i.e. look for vices to suppress.

chartel knightly challenge

swaddle bind up, as in a diaper; but also cudgel

But here our authors make a doubt
30 Whether he were more wise or stout.°
Some hold the one, and some the other;
But howsoe'er they make a pother,
The difference was so small, his brain
Outweighed his rage but half a grain;
Which made some take him for a tool
That knaves do work with, called a fool.
For it has been held by many, that,
As Montaigne, playing with his cat,
Complains she thought him but an ass,
40 Much more she would Sir Hudibras;
(For that's the name our valiant knight
To all his challenges did write).
But they're mistaken very much;
'Tis plain enough he was no such.
We grant, although he had much wit,
He was very shy of using it,
As being loath to wear it out,
And therefore bore it not about,
Unless on holidays or so,
50 As men their best apparel do.
Beside, 'tis known he could speak Greek
As naturally as pigs squeak;
That Latin was no more difficile,
Than to a blackbird 'tis to whistle.
Being rich in both, he never scanted
His bounty unto such as wanted;
But much of either would afford
To many that had not one word.
For Hebrew roots, although they're found
60 To flourish most in barren ground,°
He had such plenty as sufficed
To make some think him circumcised.
And truly so he was perhaps,
Not as a proselyte, but for claps.°
He was in logic a great critic,
Profoundly skilled in analytic;
He could distinguish and divide
A hair 'twixt south and southwest side;
On either which he would dispute,
70 Confute, change hands, and still confute.
He'd undertake to prove by force
Of argument, a man's no horse;

stout bold, brave (although Hudibras is also
"stout" in the modern sense)
barren ground the arid minds of pedants; or,
since Hebrew was believed by some to be the
natural language of man, the completely untutored mind
claps gonorrhea

He'd prove a buzzard is no fowl,°
And that a lord may be an owl;°
A calf° an alderman, a goose a justice,
And rooks° committee-men and trustees.°
He'd run in debt by disputation,
And pay with ratiocination.
All this by syllogism, true
80   In mood and figure,° he would do.
   For rhetoric, he could not ope
His mouth but out there flew a trope;°
And when he happened to break off
In the middle of his speech, or cough,
He had hard words ready to show why,
And tell what rules he did it by.
Else, when with greatest art he spoke,
You'd think he talked like other folk;
For all a rhetorician's rules
90   Teach nothing but to name his tools.
But when he pleased to show it, his speech
In loftiness of sound was rich,
A Babylonish dialect°
Which learnèd pedants much affect.
It was a parti-coloured dress
Of patched and piebald languages;
'Twas English cut on Greek and Latin,
Like fustian° heretofore on satin.
It had an odd promiscuous tone,
100   As if he had talked three parts° in one;
Which made some think, when he did gabble,
They had heard three labourers of Babel,
Or Cerberus himself pronounce
A leash° of languages at once.
This he as volubly would vent,
As if his stock would ne'er be spent;
And truly, to support that charge,
He had supplies as vast and large;
For he could coin or counterfeit
110   New words with little or no wit,
Words so debased and hard, no stone°

fowl domestic bird
owl a bird that may symbolize gravity or stupidity or both
calf fool
rooks crow-like birds, here swindlers
committee-men and trustees appointed by Parliament to confiscate and sell off Church of England property, often high-handed and sometimes dishonest
mood and figure good logical form
trope figure of speech (see Glossary)
Babylonish dialect with a suggestion of the splintering of languages at Babel to undo the building of the tower; a "confusion of languages, such as some of our modern virtuosi [i.e. experimenters and scientific dabblers] use to express themselves in" (Butler)
fustian a coarse cloth in which slashings were made, revealing colorful satin lining
three parts as in rounds, with overtones of trinitarian mystery
leash one for each of the heads of Cerberus, the three-headed dog that guarded the entrance to Hades
stone the touchstone, used to test the purity of metal in coins

Was hard enough to touch them on;
And when with hasty noise he spoke 'em,
The ignorant for current° took 'em—
That, had the orator° who once
Did fill his mouth with pebble stones
When he harangued, but known his phrase,
He would have used no other ways.
    In mathematics he was greater
120 Then Tycho Brahe° or Erra Pater;°
For he by geometric scale
Could take the size of pots of ale;
Resolve by sines and tangents straight
If bread or butter wanted weight;
And wisely tell what hour o' the day
The clock does strike, by algebra.
    Besides, he was a shrewd philosopher,
And had read every text and gloss over;
Whate'er the crabbedest author hath,
130 He understood by implicit faith;
Whatever sceptic could inquire for,
For every why he had a wherefore;
Knew more than forty of them do,
As far as words and terms could go.
All which he understood by rote,
And, as occasion served, would quote;
No matter whether right or wrong,
They might be either said or sung.
His notions° fitted things so well,
140 That which was which he could not tell,
But oftentimes mistook the one
For the other, as great clerks° have done.
He could reduce all things to acts,
And knew their natures by abstracts;
Where entity and quiddity,°
The ghosts of defunct bodies, fly;
Where Truth in person does appear,
Like words congealed in northern air.
He knew what's what, and that's as high
150 As metaphysic wit can fly.
    In school-divinity as able
As he that hight° Irrefragable;°

---

current acceptable as money or meaning
orator Demosthenes
Tycho Brahe (1546–1601) eminent Danish
astronomer
Erra Pater the pseudonymous author of a popular 16th-century almanac and work of astrology,
perhaps William Lilly
notions They "are but pictures of things in the
imagination" (Butler).

clerks men of learning
entity and quiddity Scholastic terms for being
and essence, here treated as real things rather
than as verbal abstractions
hight romance diction for "was called"
Irrefragable irrefutable, applied to the theologian Alexander of Hales (1175?–1245)

A second Thomas,° or, at once
To name them all, another Duns;°
Profound in all the nominal
And real ways beyond them all;
For he a rope of sand° could twist
As tough as learned Sorbonist;°
And weave fine cobwebs, fit for skull
160   That's empty when the moon is full:
Such as take lodgings in a head
That's to be let unfurnishèd.
He could raise scruples° dark and nice,°
And after solve 'em in a trice;
As if divinity had catched
The itch of purpose to be scratched;
Or, like a mountebank,° did wound
And stab herself with doubts profound,
Only to show with how small pain
170   The sores of faith are cured again;
Although by woeful proof we find
They always leave a scar behind.
He knew the seat of Paradise,°
Could tell in what degree it lies,
And, as he was disposed, could prove it
Below the moon, or else above it;
What Adam dreamt of when his bride
Came from her closet in his side;
Whether the devil tempted her
180   By a High Dutch interpreter;°
If either of them had a navel;°
Who first made music malleable;°
Whether the serpent at the Fall
Had cloven feet, or none at all.°
All this, without a gloss or comment,
He could unriddle in a moment,
In proper terms, such as men smatter
When they throw out and miss the matter.
    For his religion, it was fit

Thomas Aquinas, St. (1225–74), who created
the philosophical-theological synthesis called
Thomism after him
Duns John Duns Scotus (1265?–1308), the
Scottish theologian whose name was the source
of "dunce"
rope of sand incoherent argument
Sorbonist a theologian at the University of Paris
scruples objections
nice foolishly oversubtle
mountebank performer at a fair, trickster
Paradise Its location was a subject of fantastic
speculation in the Middle Ages and the Renaissance.
Whether . . . interpreter "Goropius Becanus

endeavors to prove that High-Dutch was the
language that Adam and Eve spoke in Paradise"
(Butler); in fact, he tried to prove that the
Teutonic was the most ancient of languages
If . . . navel "Adam and Eve, being made and
not conceived and formed in the womb, had no
navels, as some learned men have supposed,
because they had no need of them" (Butler)
Who . . . malleable "Music is said to be invented by Pythagoras, who first found out the
proportion of notes from the sounds of hammers
upon an anvil" (Butler)
Whether . . . all learned speculation about the
form of the serpent before it was made to crawl
upon its belly after the Fall (Genesis 3:14)

190 To match his learning and his wit;
'Twas Presbyterian true blue,°
For he was of that stubborn crew
Of errant° saints whom all men grant
To be the true church militant;°
Such as do build their faith upon
The holy text of pike and gun;
Decide all controversies by
Infallible artillery;
And prove their doctrine orthodox,
200 By apostolic blows° and knocks,
Call fire and sword and desolation
A godly, thorough reformation,
Which always must be carried on,°
And still be doing, never done;
As if religion were intended
For nothing else but to be mended—
A sect whose chief devotion lies
In odd perverse antipathies,
In falling out with that or this,
210 And finding somewhat still amiss;
More peevish, cross, and splenetic,
Than dog distract or monkey sick;
That with more care keep holy-day
The wrong,° than others the right way;
Compound for sins they are inclined to,
By damning those they have no mind to;
Still so perverse and opposite,
As if they worshipped God for spite.
The self-same thing they will abhor
220 One way, and long another for.
Free will° they one way disavow,
Another, nothing else allow.
All piety consists therein
In them, in other men all sin.
Rather than fail, they will defy
That which they love most tenderly:
Quarrel with minced-pies, and disparage
Their best and dearest friend, plum-porridge;

true blue emblem of loyalty to the cause, also opposed to Royalist red
errant wandering in search of righteous causes, like "knight errant" (l. 21), but also "arrant" (as in "arrant knave"), i.e. thoroughgoing; "saints" was a term applied to Puritans as the self-styled "elect"
church militant the church fighting the temptation and persecution of the world; but also the contentious and rebellious Puritan sects
apostolic blows the laying on of hands in ordination; but also self-righteous force

carried on from the favorite Puritan cant phrase, "carrying on the work"
The wrong as in turning Christmas from a feast to a fast in 1647. The Puritan often "breaks the sabbath by taking too much pains to keep it" (Butler, Characters).
Free will denied by the Calvinistic doctrine of predestination but insisted upon in radical Protestant claims of inspiration and righteousness. The Puritan "denies free will and yet will endure nothing but his own will in all the practice of his life" (Butler, Characters).

Fat pig and goose itself oppose,
230   And blaspheme custard through the nose.°
The apostles of this fierce religion,
Like Mahomet's, were ass and widgeon,°
To whom our knight, by fast instinct
Of wit and temper, was so linked,
As if hypocrisy and nonsense
Had got the advowson° of his conscience.

. . .

A squire he had whose name was Ralph,°
That in the adventure went his half,
Though writers, for more stately tone,
460   Do call him Ralpho, 'tis all one;
And when we can, with metre safe,
We'll call him so; if not, plain Raph;
(For rhyme the rudder is of verses,
With which like ships they steer their courses).
An equal stock of wit and valour
He had laid in, by birth a tailor.
The mighty Tyrian queen,° that gained
With subtle shreds a tract of land,
Did leave it with a castle fair
470   To his great ancestor, her heir;
From him descended cross-legged° knights,
Famed for their faith° and warlike fights
Against the bloody cannibal,°
Whom they destroyed both great and small.
This sturdy squire had, as well
As the bold Trojan knight,° seen hell;°
Not with a counterfeited pass
Of golden bough, but true gold-lace.
His knowledge was not far behind
480   The Knight's, but of another kind,
And he another way came by't.
Some call it gifts, and some new-light;°
A liberal art that costs no pains
Of study, industry, or brains.

---

through the nose a reference to the nasal drone cultivated by many Puritan preachers
ass and widgeon Mahomet rode to heaven on a milk-white mule, and he kept a pigeon that ate grain from his ear and brought him divine messages; here mule and pigeon are altered into emblems of stupidity, ass and widgeon (a wild duck).
advowson right to fill a vacant office
Ralph perhaps named for the grocer's apprentice who enjoys chivalric exploits in Beaumont and Fletcher's *The Knight of the Burning Pestle* (1608). Neither a Presbyterian nor a man of pseudo-learning like Hudibras, he is a more radical Protestant and probably illiterate.
Tyrian queen Dido, who bought the amount of land she could surround with an ox hide, but cut the hide in thin strips to embrace a large tract (*Aeneid* I.367 ff.)
cross-legged as Knights Templars were supposedly represented on their tombs, and as tailors sat at their work
faith for tailors, credit to customers
cannibal Saracens or (for tailors) lice
Trojan knight Aeneas, who took the golden bough to Proserpina in Hell (*Aeneid* VI.136–41)
hell also the tailor's waste-box for scraps of cloth
gifts . . . new-light cant terms for divine inspiration and revelation, claimed by Puritans at the expense of institutional religion

His wits were sent him for a token,
But in the carriage° cracked and broken;
Like commendation nine-pence° crooked
With 'To and from my love' it looked.
He ne'er considered it, as loath
490 To look a gift horse in the mouth,
And very wisely would lay forth
No more upon it than 'twas worth;
But as he got it freely, so
He spent it frank and freely too:
For saints themselves will sometimes be,
Of gifts that cost them nothing, free.°
By means of this, with hem and cough,
Prolongers to enlightened snuff,°
He could deep mysteries unriddle
500 As easily as thread a needle;
For as of vagabonds we say
That they are ne'er beside their way,
Whate'er men speak by this new-light,
Still they are sure to be in the right.
'Tis a dark lanthorn of the Spirit,°
Which none see by but those that bear it;
A light that falls down from on high,
For spiritual trades to cozen° by;
An *ignis fatuus*° that bewitches,
510 And leads men into pools and ditches,
To make them dip themselves° and sound
For Christendom in dirty pond;
To dive like wild fowl for salvation,
And fish to catch regeneration.
This light inspires and plays upon
The nose of saint, like bagpipe drone,°
And speaks through hollow empty soul,
As through a trunk° or whispering hole,°
Such language as no mortal ear
520 But spiritual eavesdropper's can hear:
So Phoebus° or some friendly Muse

carriage delivery
nine-pence coins bent and sent as love tokens
free a reference to Puritan thrift
snuff candle end, perhaps used to time a sermon.
"[It] is frequent for a single *vowel* to draw
sighs from a multitude; and for a whole assembly of saints to sob to the music of one solitary liquid. . . . Hawking, spitting, and belch-
ing, the defects of other men's rhetoric, are the
flowers, and figures, and ornaments" of the enthusiastic Puritan preacher's (Jonathan Swift,
The Mechanical Operation of the Spirit, 1704)
dark . . . Spirit The dark lantern, whose light
is confined, is set in contrast with the "candle of
the Lord," reason.
cozen cheat

ignis fatuus will-o'-the-wisp
dip themselves referring to the Anabaptist belief
in total immersion, which gave them the popular
name of Dippers
bagpipe drone a reference to nasal sounds, to
Scottish Presbyterianism, and to the literal meaning of "inspiration"; cf. Thomas Hobbes: "A
man enabled to speak wisely from the principles
of nature . . . loves rather to be thought to
speak by inspiration, like a bagpipe" (*Hobbes's
Answer to Davenant's Preface to Gondibert*,
1651)
trunk speaking tube
whispering hole as in the ancient oracle at
Delphi
Phoebus Apollo as god of poetry

Into small poets song infuse,
Which they at second hand rehearse,
Through reed or bagpipe, verse for verse.
   Thus Ralph became infallible
As three or four-legged oracle,°
The ancient cup, or modern chair,
Spoke truth point-blank, though unaware.
   For mystic learning,° wondrous able
530 In magic talisman° and cabal,°
Whose primitive tradition reaches
As far as Adam's first green breeches;°
Deep-sighted in intelligences,
Ideas, atoms, influences;°
And much of *Terra Incognita,*°
The intelligible world,° could say;
A deep occult philosopher,
As learned as the wild Irish° are,
Or Sir Agrippa,° for profound
540 And solid lying much renowned:
He Anthroposophus° and Fludd°
And Jacob Behmen° understood;
Knew many an amulet and charm,
That would do neither good nor harm;
In Rosicrucian° lore as learned
As he that *Vere adeptus*° earned.
He understood the speech of birds

three . . . oracle references to the three-legged stool of the Delphic priestess of Apollo, to the divining cup of Joseph as prophet (Genesis 44:5), and to the four-legged papal throne

mystic learning a reference to the occult philosophy traced back to the legendary Hermes Trismegistus, supposedly a seer contemporary with Moses and author of the *Hermetica,* a body of mystic writings drawn from neoplatonic and Judaic sources; revived during the Renaissance, particularly by Paracelsus and Jacob Boehme

magic talisman metal or stone objects imprinted with symbols of the stars, whose spiritual power they were supposed to command

cabal the mystical and magical doctrines drawn from the *Cabala,* a 13th-century work supposedly based on traditions of Jewish wisdom, part of the large stream of occult thought here likened to radical Protestant "new light"

green breeches the garment of fig leaves (translated as "breeches" in the so-called Breeches Bible of 1557) made after the Fall (Genesis 3:7); also satire on Roman Catholic reliance upon oral tradition as the counterpart of specious claims of occultists and astrologers

intelligences . . . influences technical terms for objects of knowledge too subtle to be received by the senses, such as spirits controlling planets ("intelligences"), platonic "ideas" literalized into angelic forms, "atoms" too refined to

be observed, and astral "influences" upon human character

Terra Incognita the mapmaker's term for unexplored sections of the world

intelligible world "discovered only by the [occult] philosophers, of which they talk, like parrots, what they do not understand" (Butler)

wild Irish "addicted to this occult philosophy" (Butler)

Sir Agrippa Cornelius Agrippa (1486–1535), well-known writer on occult sciences

Anthroposophus Thomas Vaughan (1622–66), twin brother of the poet Henry Vaughan, an occultist and alchemist, author of *Anthroposophia Theomagica*

Fludd Robert Fludd (1574–1637), physician, hermeticist, Rosicrucian, author of a mystical interpretation of creation

Jacob Behmen Jacob Boehme (1575–1624), the German mystic and alchemist, whose influence was strongest in the 18th century in William Law (1686–1761), the tutor of Edward Gibbon's father and aunts

Rosicrucian the mystical secret society with magical rites, whose lore was later used by Alexander Pope for the "epic machinery" of *The Rape of the Lock*

Vere adeptus "truly a master," a title given to those alchemists who had achieved the proper degree of secret wisdom

As well as they themselves do words;
Could tell what subtlest parrots mean,
550　That speak and think contrary clean;
What member° 'tis of whom they talk
When they cry 'Rope,' and 'Walk, knave, walk.'°
He'd extract numbers° out of matter,
And keep them in a glass, like water,
Of sovereign power to make men wise;
For, dropped in blear thick-sighted eyes,
They'd make them see in darkest night,
Like owls, though purblind in the light.
By help of these (as he professed)
560　He had First Matter° seen undressed:
He took her naked, all alone,
Before one rag of form was on.
The Chaos,° too, he had descried,
And seen quite through, or else he lied:
Not that of pasteboard, which men show
For groats at fair of Bartholomew;°
But its great grandsire, first o' the name,
Whence that and Reformation came,
Both cousin-germans,° and right able
570　To inveigle and draw in the rabble.
But Reformation was, some say,
O' the younger house° to Puppet-play.
He could foretell whatsoever was
By consequence to come to pass;
As death of great men, alterations,
Diseases, battles, inundations:
All this without the eclipse of sun,
Or dreadful comet, he hath done
By inward light, a way as good,
580　And easy to be understood;
But with more lucky hit than those
That use to make the stars depose,
Like Knights o' the Post,° and falsely charge
Upon themselves what others forge;
As if they were consenting to

---

member of the fraternity of Rosicrucians or possibly of Parliament
'Rope . . . walk' words commonly taught to parrots
numbers Pythagoreans stressed the numerical structure of the world and endowed some numbers with special virtues; here the abstraction is materialized, as in ll. 133 ff.
First Matter the universal substance, in Hermetic doctrine, out of which all was made; but perceptible in that form only in mystic vision, such as was claimed by Thomas Vaughan

Chaos as in *Paradise Lost,* Book II, the materials out of which God creates cosmos, but perceptible in their original form only by angels
Bartholomew Bartholomew Fair, where puppet shows of the Creation might be seen
cousin-germans first cousins
younger house of later date, born of a younger son; perhaps an imitation, for some doctrines promoted by the Reformation (such as divine inspiration or predestination) might seem to reduce men to puppets
Knights o' the Post hired perjurers

All mischief in the world men do,
Or, like the devil, did tempt and sway 'em
To rogueries, and then betray 'em
They'll search a planet's house° to know
590 Who broke and robbed a house below;
Examine Venus and the Moon,
Who stole a thimble or a spoon;
And though they nothing will confess,
Yet by their very looks can guess,
And tell what guilty aspect° bodes,
Who stole, and who received the goods.
They'll question Mars, and by his look
Detect who 'twas that nimmed° a cloak;
Make Mercury confess, and peach°
600 Those thieves which he himself did teach.°
They'll find in the physiognomies
O' the planets, all men's destinies,
Like him that took the doctor's bill,°
And swallowed it instead o' the pill;
Cast the nativity° o' the question,
And from positions to be guessed on,
As sure as if they knew the moment
Of native's birth, tell what will come on't.
They'll feel the pulses of the stars,
610 To find out agues,° cough, catarrhs,°
And tell what crisis° does divine
The rot in sheep, or mange in swine;
In men, what gives or cures the itch,
What makes them cuckolds, poor or rich;
What gains or loses, hangs or saves;
What makes men great, what fools or knaves;
But not what wise, for only of those
The stars (they say) cannot dispose,
No more than can the astrologians;
620 There they say right, and like true Trojans:°
This Ralpho knew, and therefore took
The other course,° of which we spoke.
    Thus was the accomplished squire endued
With gifts and knowledge perilous shrewd.
Never did trusty squire with knight,
Or knight with squire, jump° more right.
Their arms and equipage did fit,

planet's house that sign of the zodiac where, in
astrology, a planet has greatest influence
aspect in the planet, its astrological position; in
the thief, his countenance
nimmed stole
peach accuse
teach as god of thieves
bill prescription

nativity horoscope
agues fevers
catarrhs sore throats
crisis conjunction of planets
true Trojans good fellows
other course religious rather than astrological
imposture
jump agree, coincide

As well as virtues, parts,° and wit:
'Their valours too were of a rate,°
30   And out they sallied at the gate. . . .

                                    1663

JOHN BUNYAN
1628–1688

Bunyan was born near Bedford into the family of a traveling tinker whose ancestors had once been landholders. Bunyan tended to exaggerate the lowness of his origin and the limits of his education in order to magnify the extent of grace that was shown him, as he does his own guilt in the title of his great spiritual autobiography, *Grace Abounding to the Chief of Sinners* (1666). This is a record of Bunyan's inner life and of his conversion; like many such works of the age, it followed certain formulae (but so, in fact, did life): God's showing of special providences, the imperfect conversion that produced a merely legal Christianity rather than deep conviction, a pattern of temptation and backsliding into doubt and despair, and a final confirmation in faith marked by an intensely emotional vision. "Suddenly," he wrote,

> there was, as if there rushed in at the window, a noise of wind upon me, but very pleasant, as if I had heard a voice speaking, "Didst ever refuse to be justified by the blood of Christ?" and withal my whole life of profession past was in a moment opened to me, wherein I was made to see that designedly I had not; so my heart answered groaningly, "No." Then fell that word of God upon me, "See that ye refuse not him that speaketh" (Hebrews 12:25). This made a strange seizure upon my spirit; it brought light with it and commanded a silence in my heart of all those tumultuous thoughts that did use, like masterless hellhounds, to roar and bellow and make a hideous noise within me.

Bunyan served in the parliamentary army during the Civil War, in a garrison commanded by Sir Samuel Luke, one of the models for Butler's portrait of Hudibras. By 1649 Bunyan was married and had four children by his first wife, who died in 1658; he remarried a year later. He worked, like his father, as a tinker, but his life became increasingly one of religious devotion. He began to preach by 1656 and engaged in strong controversy with the Quakers, whose doctrine of "inner light" seemed to him a rejection of the objective nature of revelation; although he was a dissenter from Anglican doctrine, he was by no means the most radical of Protestants. With the repression of Dissenters that began after the Restoration, Bunyan was imprisoned for his preaching and refused to give assurances that he would stop. He remained in prison at Bedford for most of the eleven years that followed, writing and preaching as he could all the while, and probably completing a good part of *The Pilgrim's Progress*. Upon his release in 1672 he became well known as a preacher, drawing an audience of three thousand on one occasion in London; and he continued to write religious allegories, notably *The Life and Death of Mr. Badman* and *The Holy War*.

The *Pilgrim's Progress* was a great success, and in the ten years between its first publication and Bunyan's death, it ran through twelve editions—no doubt helping him win the offer, which he refused, of a "place of public trust" from the Catholic James II. Bunyan's book is an allegorical dream vision recounting Christian's pilgrimage from the

parts native abilities   **of a rate** well paired

City of Destruction (the present world seen at the point of apocalypse) to the Celestial City. The dreamer, reminiscent of Will Langland in *Piers Plowman,* can only reach in vision what Christian, within the vision, can attain in act, and the poignant final words reflect their difference: "which, when I had seen, I wished myself among them." The book draws upon medieval allegory and upon the chivalric romances that gave the young Bunyan guilty delight; one can see, after reading of Apollyon, why Dr. Johnson remarked, "There is reason to think that he had read Spenser." But the verve of the book is no less strong in the homely adaptation of spiritual experience to realistic scenes; and the satirical accuracy with which it renders the jury of Vanity Fair makes one recognize a kinship (for all the differences of viewpoint) with Dryden's adaptation of the story of David and Absalom or even with Swift's brisk allegory in *A Tale of a Tub.* In an age when so many wrote critically of Puritan zeal and religious enthusiasm, it is good to have so eloquent a spokesman for them and so fine a specimen, as well, of popular literature.

Bunyan's text provides marginal references to Scripture at many points; the most important of these are given in the notes.

From The Pilgrim's Progress

From This World to That Which Is To Come

As I walked through the wilderness of this world, I lighted on a certain place where was a den,[1] and I laid me down in that place to sleep: and as I slept I dreamed a dream. I dreamed, and behold I saw a man clothed with rags, standing in a certain place, with his face from his own house, a book in his hand, and a great burden upon his back.[2] I looked and saw him open the book and read therein; and, as he read, he wept, and trembled; and not being able longer to contain, he brake out with a lamentable cry, saying, What shall I do?

In this plight, therefore, he went home and restrained himself as long as he could, that his wife and children should not perceive his distress; but he could not be silent long, because that his trouble increased. Wherefore at length he brake his mind to his wife and children; and thus he began to talk to them. O my dear wife, said he, and you the children of my bowels, I, your dear friend, am in myself undone by reason of a burden that lieth hard upon me; moreover, I am for certain informed that this our city will be burned with fire from heaven, in which fearful overthrow both myself, with thee, my wife, and you my sweet babes, shall miserably come to ruin, except (the which yet I see not) some way of escape can be found whereby we may be delivered. At this his relations were sore amazed; not for that they believed that what he had said to them was true, but because they thought that some frenzy distemper had got into his head; therefore, it drawing towards night, and they

---

1. Often taken as a reference to the Bedford prison.
2. See Isaiah 64:6: "But we are all as an unclean thing, and all our righteousnesses are as filthy rags"; Psalms 38:4: "For mine iniquities are gone over my head; as an heavy burden they are too heavy for me"; Habakkuk 2:2: "And the Lord answered me, and said, Write the vision, and make it plain upon tables, so that he may run that readeth it."

hoping that sleep might settle his brains, with all haste they got him to bed. But the night was as troublesome to him as the day; wherefore, instead of sleeping, he spent it in sighs and tears. So, when the morning was come, they would know how he did. He told them, Worse and worse. He also set to talking to them again: but they began to be hardened. They also thought to drive away his distemper by harsh and surly carriages to him: sometimes they would deride, sometimes they would chide, and sometimes they would quite neglect him. Wherefore he began to retire himself to his chamber, to pray for and pity them, and also to condole his own misery; he would also walk solitarily in the fields, sometimes reading and sometimes praying: and thus for some days he spent his time.

Now, I saw upon a time, when he was walking in the fields, that he was (as he was wont) reading in his book [3] and greatly distressed in his mind; and as he read, he burst out, as he had done before, crying, What shall I do to be saved?

I saw also that he looked this way and that way, as if he would run; yet he stood still, because, as I perceived, he could not tell which way to go. I looked then, and saw a man named Evangelist [4] coming to him, who asked, Wherefore dost thou cry?

He answered, Sir, I perceive by the book in my hand that I am condemned to die, and after that to come to judgment, and I find that I am not willing to do the first, nor able to do the second.

Then said Evangelist, Why not willing to die, since this life is attended with so many evils? The man answered, Because I fear that this burden that is upon my back will sink me lower than the grave, and I shall fall into Tophet.[5] And, sir, if I be not fit to go to prison, I am not fit to go to judgment, and from thence to execution; and the thoughts of these things make me cry.

Then said Evangelist, If this be thy condition, why standest thou still? He answered, Because I know not whither to go. Then he gave him a parchment roll, and there was written within, 'Fly from the wrath to come.'

The man therefore read it and, looking upon Evangelist very carefully, said, Whither must I fly? Then said Evangelist, pointing with his finger over a very wide field, Do you see yonder wicket-gate? [6] The man said, No. Then said the other, Do you see yonder shining light? He said, I think I do. Then said Evangelist, Keep that light in your eye, and go up directly thereto: so shalt thou see the gate; at which when thou knockest, it shall be told thee what thou shalt do.

So I saw in my dream that the man began to run. Now, he had not run

---

3. The Bible.
4. The name was a term for an itinerant preacher, for any of the authors of the Four Gospels, and, in its literal sense, for the bringer of good news or glad tidings.
5. The name of a refuse dump which became a symbol of damnation; cf. Isaiah 30:33: "For Tophet is ordained of old; yea, for the King it is prepared: he hath made it deep and large: the pile thereof is fire and much wood; the breath of the Lord, like a stream of brimstone, doth kindle it."
6. A small gate for foot-passengers, as opposed to a large gate for horsemen or coaches; cf. Matthew 7:13–14: "Enter ye in at the strait gate: for wide is the gate, and broad is the way, that leadeth to destruction, and many there be which go in thereat: Because strait is the gate, and narrow is the way, which leadeth unto life, and few there be that find it."

far from his own door, but his wife and children perceiving it, began to cry
after him to return; but the man put his fingers in his ears, and ran on, crying,
Life! life! eternal life! So he looked not behind him, but fled towards the
middle of the plain. . . .

[Apollyon]
But now in this Valley of Humiliation poor Christian was hard put to it; for
he had gone but a little way before he espied a foul fiend coming over the
field to meet him; his name is Apollyon.[7] Then did Christian begin to be afraid,
and to cast in his mind whether to go back or to stand his ground. But he
considered again that he had no armour for his back, and therefore thought
that to turn the back to him might give him the greater advantage with ease
to pierce him with his darts. Therefore he resolved to venture and stand his
ground. For, thought he, had I no more in mine eye than the saving of my
life, 'twould be the best way to stand.

So he went on, and Apollyon met him. Now the monster was hideous to
behold; he was clothed with scales like a fish (and they are his pride), he
had wings like a dragon, feet like a bear, and out of his belly came fire and
smoke, and his mouth was as the mouth of a lion. When he was come up to
Christian, he beheld him with a disdainful countenance and thus began to
question with him.

APOL. Whence come you? and whither are you bound?

CHR. I am come from the City of Destruction, which is the place of all
evil, and am going to the City of Zion.[8]

APOL. By this I perceive thou art one of my subjects, for all that country is
mine, and I am the prince and god of it. How is it, then, that thou hast run
away from thy king? Were it not that I hope thou mayest do me more service,
I would strike thee now at one blow to the ground.

CHR. I was born, indeed, in your dominions, but your service was hard, and
your wages such as a man could not live on, for the wages of sin is death;[9]
therefore, when I was come to years, I did as other considerate persons do,
look out if perhaps I might mend myself.

APOL. There is no prince that will thus lightly lose his subjects, neither will
I as yet lose thee; but since thou complainest of thy service and wages, be
content to go back. What our country will afford, I do here promise to give
thee.

CHR. But I have let myself to another, even to the King of Princes; and how
can I, with fairness, go back with thee?

APOL. Thou hast done in this, according to the proverb, changed a bad for
a worse; but it is ordinary for those that have professed themselves his servants,
after a while to give him the slip and return again to me. Do thou so too, and
all shall be well.

7. Literally, the Destroyer or the "angel of the bottomless pit" (Revelation 9:11). His
description is based on the account of Leviathan in Job 41 and of the "great beast" of
Revelation 13, both taken as types of Satan. See also the dragon Sin in Spenser, *Faerie
Queene* I.xi.
8. The New Jerusalem, i.e. the celestial city of Revelation 21:2.
9. Romans 6:23: "For the wages of sin is death, but the gift of God is eternal life through
Jesus Christ our Lord."

CHR. I have given him my faith, and sworn my allegiance to him; how, then, can I go back from this and not be hanged as a traitor?

APOL. Thou didst the same to me, and yet I am willing to pass by all, if now thou wilt yet turn again and go back.

CHR. What I promised thee was in my nonage; and, besides, I count the Prince under whose banner now I stand is able to absolve me; yea, and to pardon also what I did as to my compliance with thee; and besides (O thou destroying Apollyon) to speak truth, I like his service, his wages, his servants, his government, his company, and country, better than thine; and, therefore, leave off to persuade me further; I am his servant, and I will follow him.

APOL. Consider, again, when thou art in cool blood, what thou art like to meet with in the way that thou goest. Thou knowest that, for the most part, his servants come to an ill end, because they are transgressors against me and my ways. How many of them have been put to shameful deaths! And, besides, thou countest his service better than mine, whereas he never came yet from the place where he is to deliver any that served him out of their hands; but as for me, how many times, as all the world very well knows, have I delivered, either by power or fraud, those that have faithfully served me, from him and his, though taken by them; and so I will deliver thee.

CHR. His forebearing at present to deliver them is on purpose to try their love, whether they will cleave to him to the end; and as for the ill end thou sayest they come to, that is most glorious in their account; for, for present deliverance, they do not much expect it, for they stay for their glory, and then they shall have it, when their Prince comes in his and the glory of the angels.

APOL. Thou hast already been unfaithful in thy service to him; and how dost thou think to receive wages of him?

CHR. Wherein, O Apollyon, have I been unfaithful to him?

APOL. Thou didst faint at first setting out, when thou wast almost choked in the Gulf of Despond; [10] thou didst attempt wrong ways to be rid of thy burden, whereas thou shouldst have stayed till thy Prince had taken it off; thou didst sinfully sleep and lose thy choice thing; thou wast, also, almost persuaded to go back at the sight of the lions; and when thou talkest of thy journey and of what thou hast heard and seen, thou art inwardly desirous of vain-glory in all that thou sayest or doest.

CHR. All this is true, and much more which thou hast left out; but the Prince whom I serve and honour is merciful and ready to forgive; but, besides, these infirmities possessed me in thy country, for there I sucked them in; and I have groaned under them, been sorry for them, and have obtained pardon of my Prince.

APOL. Then Apollyon broke out into a grievous rage, saying, I am an enemy to this Prince; I hate his person, his laws, and people; I am come out on purpose to withstand thee.

CHR. Apollyon, beware what you do; for I am in the king's highway, the way of holiness; therefore take heed to yourself.

APOL. Then Apollyon straddled quite over the whole breadth of the way, and said, I am void of fear in this matter: prepare thyself to die; for I swear

---

10. Recalling Christian's earlier temptation to despair and the temporary loss of the parchment roll, "his pass into the Celestial City."

by my infernal den that thou shalt go no further; here will I spill thy soul.

And with that he threw a flaming dart at his breast; but Christian had a shield in his hand, with which he caught it, and so prevented the danger of that.

Then did Christian draw, for he saw it was time to bestir him: and Apollyon as fast made at him, throwing darts as thick as hail; by the which, notwithstanding all that Christian could do to avoid it, Apollyon wounded him in his head, his hand, and foot. This made Christian give a little back; Apollyon therefore followed his work amain, and Christian again took courage and resisted as manfully as he could. This sore combat lasted for above half a day, even till Christian was almost quite spent; for you must know that Christian, by reason of his wounds, must needs grow weaker and weaker.

Then Apollyon, espying his opportunity, began to gather up close to Christian, and wrestling with him, gave him a dreadful fall; and with that Christian's sword flew out of his hand. Then said Apollyon, I am sure of thee now. And with that he had almost pressed him to death, so that Christian began to despair of life. But as God would have it, while Apollyon was fetching of his last blow, thereby to make a full end of this good man, Christian nimbly stretched out his hand for his sword, and caught it, saying, Rejoice not against me, O mine enemy: when I fall I shall arise; and with that gave him a deadly thrust, which made him give back, as one that had received his mortal wound. Christian perceiving that, made at him again, saying, Nay, in all these things we are more than conquerors through him that loved us. And with that Apollyon spread forth his dragon's wings, and sped him away, that Christian for a season saw him no more. . . .

[Vanity Fair]

Then I saw in my dream, that when they [11] were got out of the wilderness, they presently saw a town before them, and the name of that town is Vanity; and at the town there is a fair kept, called Vanity Fair.[12] It is kept all the year long; it beareth the name of Vanity Fair, because the town where it is kept is lighter than vanity; and also because all that is there sold or that cometh thither is vanity. As is the saying of the wise, all that cometh is vanity.

This fair is no new-erected business, but a thing of ancient standing; I will show you the original of it.

Almost five thousand years agone, there were pilgrims walking to the Celestial City, as these two honest persons are: and Beelzebub, Apollyon, and Legion,[13] with their companions, perceiving by the path that the pilgrims made, that their way to the city lay through this town of Vanity, they contrived here to set up a fair; a fair wherein should be sold all sorts of vanity, and that it should last all the year long: therefore at this fair are all such merchandise sold, as houses, lands, trades, places, honours, preferments,[14] titles, countries,

11. Christian has been joined by Faithful.
12. Probably based upon Bunyan's experience of the great annual fair at Stourbridge, near Cambridge; "vanity" in the sense of something empty or worthless, like the cheap or false wares often sold at fairs.
13. Named for the "unclean spirit" or devil, who replies, when asked his name, "My name is Legion; for we are many" (Mark 5:9).
14. Promotions.

kingdoms, lusts, pleasures, and delights of all sorts, as whores, bawds, wives, husbands, children, masters, servants, lives, blood, bodies, souls, silver, gold, pearls, precious stones, and what not.

And, moreover, at this fair there is at all times to be seen juggling, cheats, games, plays, fools, apes, knaves, and rogues, and that of every kind.

Here are to be seen, too, and that for nothing, thefts, murders, adulteries, false swearers, and that of a blood-red colour.

And as in other fairs of less moment, there are the several rows and streets, under their proper names, where such wares are vended; so here likewise you have the proper places, rows, streets (viz. countries and kingdoms), where the wares of this fair are soonest to be found. Here is the Britain Row, the French Row, the Italian Row, the Spanish Row, the German Row, where several sorts of vanities are to be sold. But, as in other fairs, some one commodity is as the chief of all the fair, so the ware of Rome and her merchandise is greatly promoted in this fair; only our English nation, with some others, have taken a dislike thereat.

Now, as I said, the way to the Celestial City lies just through this town where this lusty fair is kept; and he that will go to the City, and yet not go through this town, must needs go out of the world. The Prince of Princes himself, when here, went through this town to his own country, and that upon a fair day too; yea, and as I think, it was Beelzebub, the chief lord of this fair, that invited him to buy of his vanities; yea, would have made him lord of the fair, would he but have done him reverence as he went through the town. Yea, because he was such a person of honour, Beelzebub had him from street to street, and showed him all the kingdoms of the world in a little time, that he might, if possible, allure the Blessed One to cheapen [15] and buy some of his vanities; but he had no mind to the merchandise, and therefore left the town without laying out so much as one farthing upon these vanities. This fair, therefore, is an ancient thing, of long standing, and a very great fair.

Now these pilgrims, as I said, must needs go through this fair. Well, so they did: but, behold, even as they entered into the fair, all the people in the fair were moved, and the town itself as it were in a hubbub about them; and that for several reasons: for—

First, the pilgrims were clothed with such kind of raiment as was diverse from the raiment of any that traded in that fair. The people therefore of the fair, made a great gazing upon them: some said they were fools, some they were bedlams, [16] and some, they are outlandish men. [17]

Secondly, and as they wondered at their apparel, so they did likewise at their speech; for few could understand what they said. They naturally spoke the language of Canaan, but they that kept the fair were the men of this world;

15. To bid or bargain for; referring to the temptation of Christ: "Again, the devil taketh him up into an exceeding high mountain, and showeth him all the Kingdoms of the world. . . . And saith unto him, All these things will I give thee, if thou wilt fall down and worship me" (Matthew 4:8–9).
16. Madmen.
17. Foreigners; emphasizing, in dress as below in speech, the difference of style between the worldly and the devout, the speech of the latter—like Bunyan's prose—often steeped in the idiom of the Bible. See Isaiah 19:18: "In that day shall five cities in the land of Egypt speak the language of Canaan, and swear to the Lord of hosts."

so that, from one end of the fair to the other, they seemed barbarians each to the other.

Thirdly, but that which did not a little amuse the merchandisers, was that these pilgrims set very light by all their wares; they care not so much as to look upon them; and if they called upon them to buy, they would put their fingers in their ears, and cry, Turn away mine eyes from beholding vanity, and look upwards, signifying that their trade and traffic was in heaven.

One chanced mockingly, beholding the carriages of the men, to say unto them, What will ye buy? But they, looking gravely upon him, answered, We buy the truth. At that there was an occasion taken to despise the men the more; some mocking, some taunting, some speaking reproachfully, and some calling upon others to smite them. At last things came to a hubbub and great stir in the fair, insomuch that all order was confounded. Now was word presently brought to the great one of the fair, who quickly came down, and deputed some of his most trusty friends to take these men into examination, about whom the fair was almost overturned. . . .

[A trial is held, in which Faithful is accused by three witnesses, Envy, Superstition, and Pickthank.]

Then went the jury out, whose names were Mr. Blind-man, Mr. No-good, Mr. Malice, Mr. Love-lust, Mr. Live-loose, Mr. Heady, Mr. High-mind, Mr. Enmity, Mr. Liar, Mr. Cruelty, Mr. Hate-light, and Mr. Implacable; who every one gave in his private verdict against him among themselves, and afterwards unanimously concluded to bring him in guilty before the Judge. And first, among themselves, Mr. Blind-man, the foreman, said, I see clearly that this man is a heretic. Then said Mr. No-good, Away with such a fellow from the earth. Ay, said Mr. Malice, for I hate the very looks of him. Then said Mr. Love-lust, I could never endure him. Nor I, said Mr. Live-loose, for he would always be condemning my way. Hang him, hang him, said Mr. Heady. A sorry scrub,[18] said Mr. High-mind. My heart riseth against him, said Mr. Enmity. He is a rogue, said Mr. Liar. Hanging is too good for him, said Mr. Cruelty. Let's despatch him out of the way, said Mr. Hate-light. Then said Mr. Implacable, Might I have all the world given me, I could not be reconciled to him; therefore, let us forthwith bring him in guilty of death. And so they did; therefore he was presently condemned to be had from the place where he was, to the place from whence he came, and there to be put to the most cruel death that could be invented.

They therefore brought him out to do with him according to their law; and, first, they scourged him, then they buffeted him, then they lanced his flesh with knives; after that, they stoned him with stones, then pricked him with their swords; and, last of all, they burned him to ashes at the stake. Thus came Faithful to his end.

Now I saw that there stood behind the multitude a chariot and a couple of horses, waiting for Faithful, who (so soon as his adversaries had despatched him) was taken up into it, and straightway was carried up through the clouds, with sound of trumpet, the nearest way to the celestial gate.

18. Insignificant fellow.

But as for Christian, he had some respite, and was remanded back to prison. So he there remained for a space; but He that overrules all things, having the power of their rage in his own hand, so wrought it about, that Christian for that time escaped them, and went his way. . . .

[Faithful is replaced by the convert, Hopeful.]

[The Celestial City]
. . . I saw in my dream that these two men went in at the gate: and lo, as they entered, they were transfigured, and they had raiment put on that shone like gold. There were also that met them with harps and crowns and gave them to them—the harps to praise withal, and the crowns in token of honour. Then I heard in my dream that all the bells in the city rang again for joy, and that it was said unto them, Enter ye into the joy of your Lord. I also heard the men themselves, that they sang with a loud voice, saying, Blessing and honour, and glory, and power, be unto Him that sitteth upon the throne, and unto the Lamb, for ever and ever.

Now, just as the gates were opened to let in the men, I looked in after them, and, behold, the City shone like the sun; the streets also were paved with gold, and in them walked many men with crowns on their heads, palms in their hands, and golden harps to sing praises withal.

There were also of them that had wings, and they answered one another without intermission, saying, Holy, holy, holy is the Lord. And after that they shut up the gates; which, when I had seen, I wished myself among them. . . .

1678

GEORGE SAVILE, MARQUESS OF HALIFAX
1633–1695

Although his wit was great and indiscreet, leading many to doubt his faith and his principles, Halifax led a life of devoted public service, holding major offices in three reigns. His parliamentary leadership reached its high point in the debate of 1680 over the bill designed to exclude James II from the throne. The bill had passed the House of Commons readily and was championed in the House of Lords by Shaftesbury (the Achitophel of Dryden's satire, as Halifax is the Jotham), with whom Halifax had often sided. On this occasion Halifax met Shaftesbury's powerful oratory with greater eloquence of his own, rising to speak sixteen times over seven hours, and brought the bill to defeat.

He wrote Advice to a Daughter (1688), addressed to the mother-to-be of the famous Lord Chesterfield; a brilliant Character of King Charles II; as well as political pamphlets and maxims. In The Character of a Trimmer he defends himself against the charge of compromise and lukewarmness, redefining a Trimmer as one who, in a boat overbalanced by shifting of sides, conceives "it would do as well if the boat went even, without endangering the passengers. . . ." Elsewhere he remarks that the "best party is but a kind of conspiracy against the rest of the nation," and he expects abuse for his detachment: "Nothing hath an uglier look to us than reason, when it is not of our side." He found Montaigne's Essays "the book in the world I am the best entertained with," admiring that "great man, whom Nature hath made too big to confine himself to the exactness of a studied style," and who "let his mind have its full flight" in "a generous kind of negligence." Halifax's own prose is as good as any of its age. One may contrast his brilliant use of analogy with the desperate chase after bright similitudes of Congreve's Witwoud in *The Way of the World,* and one may compare the nicely antithetic syntax with that of the heroic couplet or of the later prose of Johnson and Gibbon: "Friendship cannot live with ceremony, nor without civility." Or that dazzling construction: "Those who merit because they suffered, are so very angry with those that made them suffer, that, though their services deserve employment, their temper rendereth them unfit for it."

From The Character of a Trimmer

[The Laws]

Our Trimmer, as he hath a great veneration for laws in general, so he hath a more particular for our own. He looketh upon them as the chains that tie up our unruly passions, which else, like wild beasts let loose, would reduce the world into its first state of barbarism and hostility;[1] all the good things we enjoy, we owe to them; and all the ill things we are freed from is by their protection.

God himself thought it not enough to be a creator, without being a lawgiver; and His goodness had been defective towards mankind in making them, if He had not prescribed rules to make them happy too.

All laws flow from that of Nature, and where that is not the foundation, they may be legally imposed, but they will be lamely obeyed. By this Nature is not meant that which fools and madmen[2] misquote to justify their excesses; it is innocent and uncorrupted Nature, that which disposeth men to choose virtue without its being prescribed, and which is so far from inspiring ill thoughts into us, that we take pains to suppress the good ones it infuseth.

The civilized world hath ever paid a willing subjection to laws; even conquerors have done homage to them. . . .

They are to mankind that which the sun is to plants, whilst it cherisheth and preserveth them. Where they have their force and are not clouded or suppressed, everything smileth and flourisheth; but where they are darkened and not suffered to shine out, it maketh everything to wither and decay.

They secure man not only against one another, but against themselves too; they are a sanctuary to which the Crown hath occasion to resort as often as the people, so that it hath an interest as well as a duty to preserve them.

There would be no end of making a panegyric of laws; let it be enough to add that without laws the world would become a wilderness, and men little less than beasts. But with all this, the best things may come to be the worst, if they are not in good hands; and if it be true that the wisest men generally make the laws, it is true that the strongest do too often interpret them. And as rivers belong as much to the channel where they run as to the spring from

1. That is, a state of nature such as Hobbes describes in *Leviathan* I.13; but here conceived as a fallen state in opposition to "innocent and uncorrupted Nature."
2. Perhaps a reference to Hobbes; but cf. also Dryden, *Absalom and Achitophel,* ll. 51–56.

whence they first arise, so the laws depend as much upon the pipes through which they are to pass as upon the fountain from whence they flow.

The authority of a king who is head of the law, as well as the dignity of public justice, is debased when the clear stream of the law is puddled and disturbed by bunglers, or conveyed by unclean instruments to the people.

Our Trimmer would have them appear in their full lustre, and would be grieved to see the day when, instead of speaking with authority from the seats of justice, they should speak out of a grate, with a lamenting voice like prisoners that desire to be rescued. . . .

A judge hath such power lodged in him that the king will never be thought to have chosen well where the voice of mankind hath not beforehand recommended the man to his station; when men are made judges of what they do not understand, the world censureth such a choice, not out of ill will to the men, but fear for themselves.

. . . Men will fear that out of the tree of the law, from whence we expect shade and shelter, such workmen will make cudgels to beat us with, or rather they will turn the cannon upon our properties that were entrusted with them for their defence.

To see the laws mangled, disguised, made speak quite another language than their own; to see them thrown from the dignity of protecting mankind to the disgraceful office of destroying them; and, notwithstanding their innocence in themselves, to be made the worst instruments that the most refined villainy can make use of, will raise men's anger above the power of laying it down again, and tempt them to follow the evil examples given them of judging without hearing, when so provoked by their design of revenge. Our Trimmer therefore, as he thinketh the laws are jewels, so he believeth they are nowhere better set than in the constitution of our English government, if rightly understood and carefully preserved.

It would be too great partiality to say they are perfect or liable to no objection; such things are not of this world; but if it hath more excellencies and fewer faults than any other we know, it is enough to recommend them to our esteem.

The dispute which is a greater beauty, a monarchy or a commonwealth, hath lasted long between their contending lovers, and they have behaved themselves too like lovers (who in good manners must be out of their wits), who have used such figures to exalt their own idols on either side, and such angry aggravations to reproach one another in the contest, that moderate men have in all times smiled upon this eagerness, and thought it differed very little from a downright frenzy. We in England, by a happy use of the controversy, conclude them both in the wrong and reject them from being our pattern, not taking the words in the utmost extent, which is, monarchy, a thing that leaveth men no liberty, and a commonwealth, such a one as alloweth them no quiet.

We think that a wise mean between these barbarous extremes [3] is that

3. This strategy of thinking is characteristic of Halifax, of his age, and of that to follow. We see it in Bishop Simon Patrick's celebration of the Church of England as a happy mean between the "squalid sluttery" of Puritan chapels and the "meretricious gaudiness" of the Church of Rome, or in Halifax's own plea (elsewhere in this work) for a "mean" between the "sauciness of some of the Scotch apostles" (i.e. militant Presbyterians) and "the indecent

which self-preservation ought to dictate to our wishes; and we may say we have attained to this mean in a greater measure than any nation now in being, or perhaps any we have read of, though never so much celebrated for the wisdom or felicity of their constitutions. We take from one the too great power of doing hurt and yet leave enough to govern and protect us; we take from the other the confusion of parity,[4] the animosities, and the license, and yet reserve a due care of such a liberty as may consist with men's allegiance. But it being hard, if not impossible, to be exactly even, our government hath much the stronger bias towards monarchy, which by the general consent and practice of mankind seemeth to have the advantage in dispute against a commonwealth. The rules of a commonwealth are too hard for the bulk of mankind to come up to; that form of government requireth such a spirit to carry it on as doth not dwell in great numbers, but is restrained to so very few, especially in this age, that let the methods appear never so reasonable in paper, they must fail in practice, which will ever be suited more to men's nature as it is than as it should be.

Monarchy is liked by the people for the bells and tinsel, the outward pomp and gilding; and there must be milk for babes, since the greatest part of mankind are and ever will be included in that list; and it is approved by wise and thinking men as the best when compared with others, all circumstances and objections impartially considered. Then it hath so great an advantage above all other forms, when the administration of that power falleth in good hands, that all other governments look out of countenance when they are set in competition with it. Lycurgus[5] might have saved himself the trouble of making laws if either he had been immortal, or that he could have secured to posterity a succeeding race of princes like himself. . . . Such a magistrate is the life and soul of justice, whereas the law is but a body and a dead one, too, without his influence to give it warmth and vigour; and by the irresistible power of his virtue he doth so reconcile dominion and allegiance that all disputes between them are silenced and subdued. And indeed no monarchy can be perfect and absolute without exception but where the prince is superior by his virtues as well as by his character and his power. So that to screw out precedents of unlimited power is a plain diminution to a prince that nature hath made great, and who had better make himself a glorious example to posterity than borrow an authority from dark records raised out of the grave, which, besides their non-usage, have always in them matter of controversy and debate. . . .

But since for the greater honour of good and wise princes, and the better to set off their character by the comparison, Heaven hath decreed there must be a mixture, and that such as are perverse or insufficient, or perhaps both,

---

courtship of some of the silken divines who, one would think, do practice to bow at the altar only to learn to make the better legs at Court." One culmination of this theme is Swift's *A Tale of a Tub*, where the "barbarous extremes" of Peter (the Church of Rome) and Jack (radical Protestantism) are opposed to the "wise mean" of Martin (the Church of England). See also "The Middle Way" in the Introduction to Restoration section.

4. Leveling, as opposed to hierarchy.

5. The Spartan lawmaker (9th century? B.C.), who, once his constitution was accepted, extracted a vow that it would not be changed until he returned; thereupon he left Sparta forever, hoping to preserve his laws inviolate.

are at least to have their equal turns in the government of the world; and besides, that the will of man is so various, and so unbounded a thing, and so fatal too when joined with power misapplied, it is no wonder if those who are to be governed are unwilling to have so dangerous as well as so uncertain a standard of their obedience.

There must be therefore rules and laws; for want of which, or at least the observation of them, it was as capital for a man to say that Nero did not play well upon the lute [6] as to commit treason or blaspheme the gods. And even Vespasian [7] himself had like to have lost his life for sleeping whilst he should have attended and admired that emperor's impertinence upon the stage. There is a wantonness [8] in great power that men are generally too apt to be corrupted with; and for that reason a wise prince, to prevent the temptations arising from common frailty, would choose to govern by rules for his own sake, as well as for his people's, since it only secureth him from errors, and doth not lessen the real authority that a good magistrate would care to be possessed of. For if the will of a prince is contrary either to reason itself, or to the universal opinion of his subjects, the law by a kind restraint rescueth him from a disease that would undo him; if his will on the other side is reasonable and well directed, that will immediately becometh a law, and he is arbitrary by an easy and natural consequence, without taking pains or overturning the world for it.

If princes consider laws as things imposed on them, they have the appearance of fetters of iron, but to such as would make them their choice as well as their practice they are chains of gold; and in that respect are ornaments, as in others they are a defence to them. And, by a comparison not improper for God's vicegerents [9] upon earth, as our Maker never commandeth our obedience to anything that as reasonable creatures we ought not to make our own election, so a good and wise governor, though all laws were abolished would, by the voluntary direction of his own reason, do without restraint the very same things that they would have enjoined.

Our Trimmer thinketh that the king and kingdom ought to be one creature, not to be separated in their political capacity; and when either of them undertake to act apart, it is like the crawling of worms after they are cut in pieces, which cannot be a lasting motion, the whole creature not stirring at a time. If the body have a dead palsy, the head cannot make it move; and God hath not yet delegated such a healing power to princes as that they can in a moment say to a languishing people oppressed and in despair, Take up your bed and walk.[10]

The figure of a king is so comprehensive and exalted a thing that it is a kind of degrading him to lodge that power separately in his own natural person,

6. The Roman emperor (37–68 A.D.) fancied himself as musician and actor.
7. Roman emperor and earlier a military leader under Nero, noted for the frugality and simplicity of his life.
8. "Sportiveness; negligence of restraint" (Samuel Johnson, *Dictionary*).
9. Those deputed by God to exercise His authority in government, as the doctrine of the divine right of kings would maintain.
10. As Christ said to the "sick of palsy": "Arise, take up thy bed, and go unto thine house" (Matthew 9:6).

which can never be safely or naturally great but where the people are so united to him as to be flesh of his flesh and bone of his bone. For when he is reduced to the single definition of a man he shrinketh into so low a character that it is a temptation upon men's allegiance, and an impairing that veneration which is necessary to preserve their duty to him. Whereas a prince who is so joined to his people that they seem to be his limbs, rather than his subjects; clothed with mercy and justice rightly applied in their several places; his throne supported by love as well as by power; and the warm wishes of his devoted subjects, like never-failing incense, still ascending towards him, looketh so like the best image we can frame to ourselves of God Almighty that men would have much ado not to fall down and worship him, and would be much more tempted to the sin of idolatry than to that of disobedience.

Our Trimmer is of opinion that there must be so much dignity inseparably annexed to the royal function as may be sufficient to secure it from insolence and contempt; and there must be condescensions too from the Throne, like kind showers from Heaven, that the prince may look so much the more like God Almighty's deputy upon earth. For power without love hath a terrifying aspect, and the worship which is paid to it is like that which the Indians give out of fear to wild beasts and devils. He that feareth God only because there is a hell, must wish there were no God; and he who feareth the king only because he can punish, must wish there were no king. So that, without a principle of love, there can be no true allegiance; and there must remain perpetual seeds of resistance against a power that is built upon such an unnatural foundation as that of fear and terror. All force is a kind of foul play, and whosoever aimeth at it himself doth by implication allow it to those he playeth with; so that there will be ever matter prepared in the minds of people when they are provoked, and the prince, to secure himself, must live in the midst of his own subjects as if he were in a conquered country. . . . And besides that there can be no lasting radical security but where the governed are satisfied with the governors, it must be a dominion very unpleasant to a prince of an elevated mind to impose an abject and sordid servility instead of receiving the willing sacrifice of duty and obedience. The bravest princes in all times, who were incapable of any other kind of fear, have feared to grieve their own people; such a fear is a glory, and in this sense 'tis an infamy not to be a coward. So that the mistaken heroes who are void of this generous kind of fear need no other aggravation to complete their ill characters.

When a despotic prince hath bruised all his subjects with a slavish obedience, all the force he can use cannot subdue his own fears, enemies of his own creation, to which he can never be reconciled, it being impossible to do injustice and not to fear revenge. There is no cure for this fear but the not deserving to be hurt; and therefore a prince who doth not allow his thoughts to stray beyond the rules of justice hath always the blessing of an inward quiet and assurance as a natural effect of his good meaning to his people; and though he will not neglect due precautions to secure himself in all events, yet he is incapable of entertaining vain and remote suspicions of those of whom he resolveth never to deserve ill. . . .

Our Trimmer thinketh it no advantage to a government to endeavour the suppressing all kind of right which may remain in the body of the people, or to employ small authors in it whose officiousness [11] or want of money may encourage them to write, though it is not very easy to have abilities equal to such a subject. They forget that in their too high-strained arguments for the rights of princes, they very often plead against human nature,[12] which will always give a bias to those reasons which seem to be of her side. . . .

In power, as in most other things, the way for princes to keep it, is not to grasp more than their arms can well hold; the nice [13] and unnecessary inquiring into these things, or the licensing some books and suppressing some others [14] without sufficient reason to justify the doing either, is so far from being an advantage to a government that it exposeth it to the censure of being partial, and to the suspicion of having some hidden designs to be carried on by these unusual methods.

When all is said, there is a natural reason of state, an undefinable thing,[15] grounded upon the common good of mankind, which is immortal, and in all changes and revolutions still preserveth its original right of saving a nation, when the letter of the law perhaps would destroy it; and by whatsoever means it moveth, carrieth a power with it that admitteth of no opposition, being supported by Nature, which inspireth an immediate consent at some critical times into every individual member, to that which visibly tendeth to preservation of the whole; and this being so, a wise prince, instead of controverting the right of this reason of state, will by all means endeavour it may be of his side, and then he will be secure.

Our Trimmer cannot conceive that the power of any prince can be lasting but where 'tis built upon the foundation of his own unborrowed virtue; he must not only be the first mover and the fountain from whence the great acts of state originally flow but he must be thought so to his people that they may preserve their veneration for him; he must be jealous of his power, and not impart so much of it to any about him as that he may suffer an eclipse by it. . . .

Princes may lend some of their light to make another shine, but they must still preserve the superiority of being the brighter planet, and when it happeneth that the reversion [16] is in men's eyes, there is more care necessary to keep up the dignity of possession that men may not forget who is king, either out of their hopes or fears who shall be. If the sun should part with all his

11. Eagerness to serve; meddlesome zeal.
12. That is, by insisting, as Hobbes did, upon the intolerable chaos man's appetitive nature would produce without the commanding power of a sovereign; or more generally, scorning the natural capacities of the people to rule themselves in order to exalt the power of a monarch.
13. Excessively close.
14. The issue earlier discussed by Milton in the *Areopagitica* and later to be renewed with the Licensing Act of 1737, whereby Walpole sought to repress public criticism in the theater.
15. Later in the work Halifax writes: "In order to its preservation there is a hidden power in government which would be lost if it was defined, a certain mystery by virtue of which a nation may at some critical times be secured from ruin; but then it must be kept as a mystery; it is rendered useless when touched by unskillful hands, and no government ever had, or deserved to have that power which was so unwary as to anticipate their claim to it. . . . " Perhaps relevant is one of Halifax's "thoughts": "There is a happy pitch of ignorance that a man of sense might pray for."
16. Right of succession.

light to any other stars, the Indians would not know where to find their God, after he had so deposed himself, and would make the light (wherever it went) the object of their worship. . . .

[Liberty and the Constitution]

Our Trimmer owneth a passion for liberty, yet so restrained that it doth not in the least impair or taint his allegiance; he thinketh it hard for a soul that doth not love liberty ever to raise itself to another world; he taketh it to be the foundation of all virtue, and the only seasoning that giveth a relish to life; and though the laziness of a slavish subjection hath its charms for the more gross and earthly part of mankind, yet to men made of a better sort of clay, all that the world can give without liberty hath no taste. It is true, nothing is sold so cheap by unthinking men; but that doth no more lessen the real value of it than a country fellow's ignorance doth that of a diamond in selling it for a pot of ale. Liberty is the mistress of mankind; she hath powerful charms which do so dazzle us that we find beauties in her which perhaps are not there, as we do in other mistresses. Yet if she was not a beauty, the world would not run mad for her; therefore, since the reasonable desire of it ought not to be restrained, and that even the unreasonable desire of it cannot be entirely suppressed, those who would take it away from a people possessed of it are likely to fail in the attempting, or be very unquiet in the keeping of it.

Our Trimmer admireth our blessed constitution, in which dominion and liberty are so well reconciled; it giveth to the prince the glorious power of commanding freemen, and to the subjects the satisfaction of seeing the power so lodged as that their liberties are secure. It doth not allow the crown such a ruining power as that no grass can grow wherever it treadeth, but a cherishing and protecting power; such a one as hath a grim aspect only to the offending subjects, but is the joy and the pride of all the good ones; their own interest being so bound up in it as to engage them to defend and support it. And though in some instances the king is restrained, yet nothing in the government can move without him; our laws make a true distinction between vassalage [17] and obedience; between a devouring prerogative [18] and a licentious ungovernable freedom; and as of all the orders of building the composite [19] is the best,

---

17. Political dependence (as in the fealty owned a vassal to his lord) as opposed to voluntary "obedience."

18. Those powers of the sovereign unlimited by laws.

19. This refers first to the orders of architecture, each named for its characteristic column, the Doric, Ionic, Corinthian, and (later in Rome) the Tuscan. During the Roman empire elements of the Ionic and Corinthian were fused to form the new Composite order, and the term was more generally applied to a style that mixed elements of various orders. The counterpart to this is the mixed state, which fuses elements to be found in the pure forms of government—monarchy, oligarchy, and democracy; that is, the rule of the One, the Few, or the Many. It was believed by the classical historian Polybius (204–122 B.C.) that a mixed government might prevent the cyclic alternation of the pure forms and thus achieve stability and enduring power. This doctrine was widely revived in the late 17th century and influenced John Locke and others, including the authors of the American Constitution a century later, in promoting a balance of power within the state. Swift's earliest published work, *The Contests and Dissensions of . . . Greece and Rome* (1701) was a defense of this balance against the tyranny of Commons, and Pope was later to celebrate the "according music of a well-mixed state" (*Essay on Man* III.294).

so ours by a happy mixture and a wise choice of what is best in others, is brought into a form that is our felicity who live under it, and the envy of our neighbours that cannot imitate it.

The Crown hath power sufficient to protect our liberties. The people have so much liberty as is necessary to make them useful to the Crown.

Our government is in a just proportion, no tympany, no unnatural swelling either of power or liberty; and whereas in all overgrown monarchies, reason, learning, and inquiry are banished and hanged in effigy for mutineers,[20] here they are encouraged and cherished as the surest friends to a government established upon the foundation of law and justice. When all is done, those who look for perfection in this world may look as long as the Jews have done for their Messiah; and therefore our Trimmer is not so unreasonably partial as to free our government from all objections. No doubt there have been fatal instances of its sickness, and more than that, of its mortality for some time; though by a miracle it hath been revived again; but till we have another race of mankind, in all constitutions that are bounded there will ever be some matter of strife and contention, and, rather than want pretensions, men's passions and interests will raise them from the most inconsiderable causes.

Our government is like our climate. There are winds which are sometimes loud and unquiet; and yet, with all the trouble they give us, we owe part of our health unto them; they clear the air, which else would be like a standing pool, and instead of refreshment would be a disease unto us.

There may be fresh gales of asserting liberty without turning into such storms of hurricane as that the state should run any hazard of being cast away by them. These strugglings, which are natural to all mixed governments, while they are kept from growing into convulsions, do by a mutual agitation from the several parts rather support and strengthen than weaken and maim the constitution; and the whole frame, instead of being torn or disjointed, cometh to be the better and closer knit by being thus exercised. But whatever faults our government may have, or a discerning critic may find in it when he looketh upon it alone, let any other be set against it, and then it showeth its comparative beauty. Let us look upon the most glittering outside of unbounded authority, and upon a nearer inquiry we shall find nothing but poor and miserable deformity within. Let us imagine a prince living in his kingdom as if in a great galley, his subjects tugging at the oar, laden with chains and reduced to real rags that they may gain him imaginary laurels; let us represent him gazing among his flatterers and receiving their false worship, like a child never contradicted and therefore always cozened,[21] or like a lady complimented only to be abused; condemned never to hear truth, and consequently never to do justice; wallowing in the soft bed of wanton and unbridled greatness, not less odious to the instruments themselves than to the objects of his tyranny; blown up into an ambitious dropsy,[22] never to be satisfied by the conquest of other people or by the oppression of his own. By aiming to be more than a man,

20. Cf. Pope's assertion that merely verbal learning thrives in a despotic reign; see *The Dunciad* IV.175–88.
21. Deceived, beguiled, imposed upon.
22. A disease marked by swelling caused by the accumulation of liquids in the body.

he falleth lower than the meanest of them,[23] a mistaken creature, swelled with panegyrics, and flattered out of his senses, and not only an incumbrance, but a nuisance to mankind, a hardened and unrelenting soul; and, like some creatures that grow fat with poisons, he groweth great by other men's miseries: an ambitious ape of the Divine greatness, an unruly giant that would storm even heaven itself, but that his scaling-ladders are not long enough; in short, a wild and devouring creature in rich trappings and with all his pride, no more than a whip in God Almighty's hand, to be thrown into the fire when the world hath been sufficiently scourged with it. This picture laid in right colours would not incite men to wish for such a government, but rather to acknowledge the happiness of our own, under which we enjoy all the privilege reasonable men can desire and avoid all the miseries many others are subject to; so that our Trimmer would keep it with all its faults and doth as little forgive those who give the occasion of breaking it as he doth those that take it. . . .

Our Trimmer is far from idolatry in other things; in one thing only he cometh near it: his country is in some degree his idol. He doth not worship the sun because 'tis not peculiar to us; it rambleth about the world and is less kind to us than others. But for the earth of England, though perhaps inferior to that of many places abroad, to him there is a divinity in it; and he would rather die than see a spire of English grass trampled down by a foreign trespasser. He thinketh there are a great many of his mind, for all plants are apt to taste of the soil in which they grow; and we that grow here have a root that produceth in us a stock of English juice, which is not to be changed by grafting or foreign infusion; and I do not know whether anything less will prevail than the modern experiment by which the blood of one creature is transmitted into another,[24] according to which, before the French blood can be let into our bodies, every drop of our own must be drawn out of them.

Our Trimmer cannot but lament that by a sacrifice too great for one nation to make to another, we should be like a rich mine, made useless only for want of being wrought, and that the life and vigour which should move us against our enemies is miserably applied to tear our own bowels; that being made by our happy situation not only safer but, if we please, greater too than other countries which far exceed us in extent; that having courage by nature, learning by industry, and riches by trade, we should corrupt all these advantages so as to make them insignificant and, by a fatality which seemeth peculiar to us, misplace our active rage one against another, whilst we are turned into statues on that side where lieth our greatest danger; to be unconcerned not only at our neighbour's ruin but our own,[25] and let our island lie like a great

---

23. Evoking the doctrine of the Great Chain of Being, where the attempt to rise out of one's assigned place in the hierarchy causes one to fall to the lowest place of all, as Satan in his rebellion—when his great powers undergo corruption—becomes the worst of creatures; a theme reinforced below by the reference to the Titans, the giants who sought to storm Olympus and to recover the power won by Zeus.

24. Such experiments in transfusion were made possible when William Harvey (1578–1657), physician to Charles I, discovered the circulation of the blood and published his findings in 1628.

25. Halifax is alluding to both Charles II's continued dependence upon subsidies from Louis XIV and his readiness to withdraw from all alliances with the Dutch; as well as the internal conflicts that followed the Popish Plot, with the Duke of York (later James II) rallying forces to suppress the Whig leadership. Halifax was making an appeal to Charles

hulk in the sea, without rudder or sail, all men cast away in her, or as if we were all children in a great cradle and rocked asleep to a foreign tune.

I say when our Trimmer representeth to his mind our roses blasted and discoloured, whilst the lilies [26] triumph and grow insolent upon the comparison; when he considereth our once flourishing laurel, now withered and dying, and nothing left us but a remembrance of a better part in history than we shall make in the next age, which will be no more to us than an escutcheon [27] hung upon our door when we are dead; when he foreseeth from hence growing infamy from abroad, confusion at home, and all this without the possibility of a cure, in respect of the voluntary fetters good men put on themselves by their allegiance; without a good measure of preventing grace,[28] he would be tempted to go out of the world like a Roman philosopher [29] rather than endure the burthen of life under such a discouraging prospect. But mistakes, as all other things, have their periods, and many times the nearest cure is not to oppose them but stay till they are crushed with their own weight; for Nature will not allow anything to continue long that is violent. Violence is a wound, and as a wound must be curable in a little time; or else 'tis mortal, but a nation comes near to be immortal. Therefore the wound will one time or another be cured. . . .

[Conclusion]

To conclude, our Trimmer is so fully satisfied of the truth of those principles by which he is directed in reference to the public that he will neither be bawled, threatened, laughed, nor drunk out of them; and instead of being converted by the arguments of his adversaries to their opinions, he is very much confirmed in his own by them. He professeth solemnly that were it in his power to choose, he would rather have his ambition bounded by the commands of a great and wise master than let it range with a popular licence, though crowned with success. Yet he cannot commit such a sin against the glorious thing called liberty, nor let his soul stoop so much below itself as to be content without repining to have his reason wholly subdued, or the privilege of acting like a sensible creature torn from him by the imperious dictates of unlimited authority, in what hand soever it happens to be placed.

What is there in this that is so criminal as to deserve the penalty of that most singular apophthegm, a Trimmer is worse than a rebel? What do angry men ail to rail so against moderation? Doth it not look as if they were going to some very scurvy extreme that is too strong to be digested by the more considering part of mankind? These arbitrary methods, besides the injustice of them, are (God be thanked) very unskillful too, for they fright the birds, by talking so loud, from coming into the nets that are laid for them; and when men agree to rifle a house they seldom give warning, or blow a trumpet; but

II (as it happened, a month or so before the King's death) for a policy of greater independence abroad and toleration at home. For the so-called Popish Plot see Dryden's *Absalom and Achitophel* (and its Headnote).

26. The roses (white and red) of England versus the lilies of France.

27. The shield depicting the family coat-of-arms, displayed by proud descendants.

28. An allusion to "prevenient grace," that free gift of God's favor that is given before it is sought; here used more generally in the sense of good fortune or divine favor that anticipates the crime of despair and thus deters it.

29. That is, by suicide.

there are some small statesmen who are so full charged with their own expectations that they cannot contain. And kind heaven, by sending such a seasonable curse upon their undertakings, hath made their ignorance an antidote against their malice. Some of these cannot treat peaceably; yielding will not satisfy them, they will have men by storm. There are others that must have plots [30] to make their service more necessary and have an interest to keep them alive, since they are to live upon them; and persuade the king to retrench his own greatness so as to shrink into the head of a party, which is the betraying him into such an unprincely mistake, and to such a wilful diminution of himself, that they are the last enemies he ought to allow himself to forgive.

Such men, if they could, would prevail with the sun to shine only upon them and their friends, and to leave all the rest of the world in the dark. This is a very unusual monopoly and may come within the equity [31] of the law, which maketh it treason to imprison the king, when such unfitting bounds are put to his favour and he confined to the narrow limits of a particular set of men that would enclose him. These honest and only loyal gentlemen, if they may be allowed to bear witness for themselves, make a king their engine [32] and degrade him into a property at the very time that their flattery would make him believe they paid divine worship to him.

Besides these there is a flying squadron on both sides that are afraid the world should agree, small dabblers in conjuring that raise angry apparitions to keep men from being reconciled, like wasps that fly up and down, buzz and sting to keep men unquiet; but these insects are commonly short-lived creatures, and no doubt in a little time mankind will be rid of them. They were giants at least who fought once against heaven, but for such pigmies as these to contend against it is such a provoking folly that the insolent bunglers ought to be laughed and hissed out of the world for it. They should consider there is a soul in that great body of the people, which may for a time be drowsy and unactive, but when the leviathan [33] is roused it moveth like an angry creature, and will neither be convinced nor resisted. The people can never agree to show their united powers till they are extremely tempted and provoked to it, so that to apply cupping glasses [34] to a great beast naturally disposed to sleep, and to force the tame thing whether it will or no to be valiant, must be learnt out of some other book than Machiavel,[35] who would never have prescribed such a preposterous method.

30. Perhaps looking back to the Popish Plot (for which see Dryden, *Absalom and Achitophel*) but surely to the Rye House Plot of 1683, both involving the first Earl of Shaftesbury. The Rye House Plot, exposed by somewhat dubious evidence, was claimed to be a conspiracy to assassinate Charles II, and among those executed were Halifax's friends Lord Russell and Algernon Sidney (the latter also his wife's uncle). In both cases Halifax used his influence in vain to obtain a moderation of sentence.

31. Jurisdiction.

32. Instrument.

33. Whale; but with allusion to Hobbes's book of 1651 which represents (in its frontispiece) the multitude united in one great artificial person, the state or commonwealth, composed of the mass of individual men.

34. Used for drawing out blood.

35. Niccolo di Bernardo dei Machiavelli (1469–1527), the Florentine statesman and political theorist whose great work *The Prince* (1513) became a universal manual of political expediency.

It is to be remembered, that if princes have law and authority on their sides, the people on theirs may have Nature, which is a formidable adversary. Duty, justice, religion, nay, even human prudence, too, biddeth the people suffer anything rather than resist; but uncorrected Nature, where'er it feels the smart, will run to the nearest remedy. Men's passions in this case are to be considered as well as their duty, let it be never so strongly enforced; for if their passions are provoked, they being as much a part of us as our limbs, they lead men into a short way of arguing that admitteth no distinction, and from the foundation of self-defence they will draw inferences that will have miserable effects upon the quiet of a government.

Our Trimmer therefore dreads a general discontent, because he thinketh it differeth from a rebellion only as a spotted fever doth from the plague,[36] the same species under a lower degree of malignity. It worketh several ways, sometimes like a slow poison that hath its effects at a great distance from the time it was given, sometimes like dry flax prepared to catch at the first fire, or like seed in the ground ready to sprout upon the first shower. In every shape 'tis fatal, and our Trimmer thinketh no pains or precaution can be so great as to prevent it.

In short, he thinketh himself in the right, grounding his opinion upon that truth which equally hateth to be under the oppressions of wrangling sophistry on the one hand, or the short dictates of mistaken authority on the other.

Our Trimmer adoreth the goddess Truth, though in all ages she hath been scurvily used, as well as those that worshipped her. 'Tis of late become such a ruining virtue that mankind seemeth to be agreed to commend and avoid it; yet the want of practice which repealeth the other laws hath no influence upon the law of Truth, because it hath root in heaven, and an intrinsic value in itself, that can never be impaired. She showeth her greatness in this, that her enemies, even when they are successful, are ashamed to own it. Nothing but powerful Truth hath the prerogative of triumphing not only after victories but in spite of them, and to put conquest herself out of countenance; she may be kept under and suppressed, but her dignity still remaineth with her, even when she is in chains. Falsehood with all her impudence hath not enough to speak ill of her before her face; such majesty she carrieth about her that her most prosperous enemies are fain to whisper their treason. All the power upon earth can never extinguish her; she hath lived in all ages; and let the mistaken zeal of prevailing authority christen any opposition to it with what name they please, she maketh it not only an ugly and unmannerly, but a dangerous, thing to persist. She hath lived very retired indeed, nay sometimes so buried, that only some few of all the discerning part of mankind could have a glimpse of her. With all that, she hath eternity in her, she knoweth not how to die; and from the darkest clouds that shade and cover her she breaketh from time to time with triumph for her friends and terror to her enemies.

Our Trimmer, therefore, inspired by this divine virtue, thinketh fit to conclude with these assertions: that our climate is a Trimmer, between that part of the world where men are roasted and the other where they are frozen; that our Church is a Trimmer between the frenzy of platonic visions and the

---

36. The bubonic plague that had last ravaged London in 1665.

lethargic ignorance of popish dreams; that our laws are Trimmers between the excess of unbounded power and the extravagance of liberty not enough restrained; that true virtue hath ever been thought a Trimmer and to have its dwelling in the middle between the two extremes; that even God Almighty himself is divided between his two great attributes, his mercy and his justice.

In such company, our Trimmer is not ashamed of his name, and willingly leaveth to the bold champions of either extreme the honour of contending with no less adversaries than nature, religion, liberty, prudence, humanity, and common sense.

1684?   1688

JOHN WILMOT, EARL OF ROCHESTER
1647–1680

John Wilmot, Earl of Rochester, was the most brilliant wit and rake at the court of Charles II. He had studied Latin and some Greek at Oxford, and he was the author of the first free imitation of Horace's satires in English. During his years at court, which began when he was seventeen, he was feared for his satirical pen and his often savage practical jokes; "Mean in each action, lewd in every limb, / Manners themselves are mischievous in him," was the tribute of his enemy, Lord Mulgrave. To others his charm was irresistible: "There is not a woman who gives ear to him three times but she irretrievably loses her repuation." King Charles was said to have exclaimed, "Thou art the happiest fellow in my dominion. Let me perish if I do not envy thee thy impudence." But Rochester's notorious "sceptre lampoon" about Charles led to at least a brief exile. At the last, Rochester repented his way of life and took the Christian sacrament, dying "without a convulsion or so much as a groan," at the age of thirty-three.

Rochester's writings include some dabbling in drama, a number of fine lyric poems, and a few extended satires and epistles, of which the Satire Against Mankind is perhaps the most impressive. It reflects the skepticism of his age, going back to classical sources in Lucretius and the Epicureans, sometimes turning to modern versions of materialism, sometimes borrowing from those fideistic doctrines which sapped trust in man's reason in order to throw him upon faith. Perhaps the most influential immediate source was Thomas Hobbes, whose materialism was the ground for his view of man's restless, acquisitive, and competitive nature. This insatiable striving for security through power is built into the heroes and villains of many heroic plays of the Restoration, and it marks in some degree the naturalistic zest with which the rake avows and seeks to serve his appetites, disdaining meanwhile the hypocritical censure of no less acquisitive merchants, clergymen, and courtiers. In comedies like William Wycherley's The Country Wife or in Sir George Etherege's The Man of Mode (whose hero, Dorimant, was often taken as a portrait of Rochester), the frank libertinism of the heroes seems more honest than the pretended squeamishness of the women they easily seduce; their female counterparts are those clear-headed, self-commanding heroines who profess no shock but permit no exploitation. Rochester's Satire, notably in its "epilogue" (after l. 174), shows a double attitude: a yearning for authenticity as well as a scorn for hypocrisy, a belief in the possibilities of a generous goodness as well as a detestation of those crippling forms of timorous respectability Bernard Shaw was later to call the "seven deadly virtues." The speaker in the Satire shows this doubleness, too; if he seems a bitter Hobbist and disdainful hedonist in the first part, he reveals another aspect in the second—not devout but moral, an admirer not of institutions but of personal goodness, of freedom from both greed and cant.

A Satire Against Mankind

Were I (who to my cost already am
One of those strange, prodigious° creatures, man)
A spirit free to choose, for my own share,
What case° of flesh and blood I pleased to wear,
I'd be a dog, a monkey, or a bear,
Or anything but that vain animal
Who is so proud of being rational.
    The senses are too gross, and he'll contrive
A sixth to contradict the other five,
10 And before certain instinct° will prefer
Reason, which fifty times for one does err;
Reason, an *ignis fatuus*° in the mind,
Which, leaving light of nature, sense, behind,
Pathless and dangerous wandering ways it takes
Through error's fenny bogs and thorny brakes;°
Whilst the misguided follower climbs with pain
Mountains of whimseys, heaped in his own brain;
Stumbling from thought to thought falls headlong down
Into doubt's boundless sea, where, like to drown,
20 Books bear him up a while, and make him try
To swim with bladders of philosophy;
In hopes still to o'ertake the escaping light, —
The vapour dances in his dazzling° sight
Till, spent, it leaves him to eternal night.
Then old age and experience, hand in hand,
Lead him to death and make him understand,
After a search so painful and so long,
That all his life he has been in the wrong.
Huddled in dirt° the reasoning engine° lies,

prodigious monstrous
case cover, dress
certain instinct Although he does not invoke the orthodox view of instinct as the direct power of God acting in animals, Rochester makes similar claims for its superiority to reason. Pope in the *Essay on Man* III.79–98 presents the orthodox view: reason "but serves when pressed, / But honest Instinct comes a volunteer" (ll. 87 88); instinct "must go right, the other may go wrong" (l. 94); "in this 'tis God directs, in that 'tis Man" (l. 98).
ignis fatuus will-o'-the-wisp, the delusive light that can mislead one in a swamp or fen at night
brakes thickets

dazzling dazzled
dirt mud, mire; sordidness, filth
reasoning engine Rochester's point is not so much to reduce man to mechanism as to show him, in Johnson's definition, to be a "mechanical complication in which various movements and parts concur in one effect"—that is, to stress the sole end to which his being has been directed (an engine *for* reasoning) and to show it now in the mire which is the very opposite of elaborate contrivance. The adjectives of the following line emphasize the humanity of the "engine" but accord with the idea of man's misapplying his trust and skill (as in the contrast of "know" and "enjoy" in l. 34).

30 Who was so proud, so witty, and so wise.
        Pride drew him in, as cheats their bubbles° catch,
    And made him venture to be made a wretch.
    His wisdom did his happiness destroy,
    Aiming to know that world he should enjoy.
    And wit was his vain, frivolous pretence
    Of pleasing others at his own expense,
    For wits are treated just like common whores:
    First they're enjoyed, and then kicked out of doors.
    The pleasure past, a threatening doubt° remains
40 That frights the enjoyer with succeeding pains.
    Women and men of wit are dangerous tools,
    And ever fatal to admiring fools:
    Pleasure allures, and when the fops escape,
    'Tis not that they're beloved, but fortunate,
    And therefore what they fear at heart, they hate.
        But now, methinks, some formal band° and beard
    Takes me to task. Come on, sir; I'm prepared.
        'Then, by your favour, anything that's writ
    Against this gibing, jingling knack called wit
50 Likes° me abundantly; but° you take care
    Upon this point, not to be too severe.
    Perhaps my muse were fitter for this part,
    For I profess I can be very smart
    On wit, which I abhor with all my heart.
    I long to lash it in some sharp essay,
    But your grand indiscretion bids me stay
    And turns my tide of ink another way.
        'What rage ferments in your degenerate mind
    To make you rail at reason and mankind?
60 Blest, glorious man! to whom alone kind heaven
    An everlasting soul has freely given,
    Whom his great Maker took such care to make
    That from himself he did the image take
    And this fair frame in shining reason dressed
    To dignify his nature above beast;
    Reason, by whose aspiring influence
    We take a flight beyond material sense,
    Dive into mysteries, then soaring pierce
    The flaming limits of the universe,
70 Search heaven and hell, find out what's acted there,
    And give the world true grounds of hope and fear.'
        Hold, mighty man, I cry, all this we know
    From the pathetic pen of Ingelo,°

---

bubbles dupes
doubt as to possible infection in the case of
whores
formal band the wearer of a Geneva band, i.e.
a clergyman
Likes pleases

but so long as; if only
Ingelo Nathaniel Ingelo (1621?–83), the clerical
author of a long religious allegory in the form
of a romance, *Bentivolio and Urania* (1660),
popular in the period

From Patrick's *Pilgrim*,° Sibbes's soliloquies,°
And 'tis this very reason I despise:
This supernatural gift that makes a mite
Think he's the image of the infinite,
Comparing his short life, void of all rest,
To the eternal and the ever blest;
80 This busy, puzzling stirrer-up of doubt
That frames deep mysteries, then finds them out,°
Filling with frantic crowds of thinking fools
Those reverend bedlams,° colleges and schools;
Borne on whose wings, each heavy sot can pierce
The limits of the boundless universe;
So charming° ointments make an old witch fly
And bear a crippled carcass through the sky.
'Tis this exalted power, whose business lies
In nonsense and impossibilities,
90 This made a whimsical philosopher°
Before the spacious world, his tub prefer,
And we have modern cloistered coxcombs° who
Retire to think, 'cause they have nought to do.°
    But thoughts are given for action's government;
Where action ceases, thought's impertinent.°
Our sphere of action is life's happiness,
And he who thinks beyond thinks like an ass.
Thus, whilst against false reasoning I inveigh,
I own right reason,° which I would obey:
100 That reason which distinguishes by sense
And gives us rules of good and ill from thence,
That bounds desires with a reforming will°
To keep them more in vigour, not to kill.
Your reason hinders, mine helps to enjoy,
Renewing appetites yours would destroy.
My reason is my friend, yours is a cheat;
Hunger calls out, my reason bids me eat;
Perversely, yours your appetite does mock:
This asks for food, that answers, 'What's o'clock?'
110 This plain distinction, sir, your doubt secures:°
'Tis not true reason I despise, but yours.

Patrick's Pilgrim *The Parable of the Pilgrim*
(1664) by Simon Patrick, Bishop of Ely (1626–
1707), a work in the manner of Bunyan's later
allegory
Sibbes's soliloquies inspirational religious works
by the Puritan clergyman Richard Sibbes (1577–
1635)
finds them out claims to solve them easily
bedlams madhouses
charming magical
philosopher Diogenes (412?–323 B.C.), the
Greek Cynic, preached a life of extreme asceticism, living in a tub and teaching that virtue
consisted in the avoidance of all physical pleasure.
coxcombs fops (cf. l. 208), here applied to

empty pretenders
think . . . do recalling the contrast of "know"
and "enjoy" in l. 34
impertinent beside the point, of no use
right reason As Rochester defines it, this is preferable to *a priori* or deductive reason but is
hardly Right Reason as the term was generally
understood in the Renaissance. Rochester's
"right reason" is grounded in sense experience
(l. 100) and avoids asceticism (103), rather
serving as an instrument of pleasure or enjoyment by "renewing appetites" (105).
reforming will playing ironically upon the asceticism of some Reformation leaders, such as
John Calvin
secures resolves

Thus I think reason righted: but for man,
I'll ne'er recant; defend him if you can.
For all his pride and his philosophy,
'Tis evident beasts are, in their degree,
As wise at least and better far than he.
Those creatures are the wisest who attain
By surest means the ends at which they aim.
If therefore Jowler° finds and kills his hares
120   Better than Meres° supplies committee chairs,
Though one's a statesman, the other but a hound,
Jowler, in justice, would be wiser found.
　　You see how far man's wisdom here extends;
Look next if human nature makes amends:
Whose principles most generous are and just,
And to whose morals you would sooner trust.
Be judge yourself, I'll bring it to the test:
Which is the basest creature, man or beast?
Birds feed on birds, beasts on each other prey,
130   But savage man alone does man betray.
Pressed by necessity, they kill for food;
Man undoes man to do himself no good.
With teeth and claws by nature armed, they hunt
Nature's allowance, to supply their want.
But man, with smiles, embraces, friendship, praise,
Inhumanly his fellow's life betrays;
With voluntary pains works his distress,
Not through necessity, but wantonness.
　　For hunger or for love they fight and tear,
140   Whilst wretched man is still in arms for fear.°
For fear he arms, and is of arms afraid,
By fear to fear successively betrayed;
Base fear, the source whence his best passions came:
His boasted honour, and his dear-bought fame;
That lust of power, to which he's such a slave,
And for the which alone he dares be brave;
To which his various projects are designed;

Jowler a typical name for a hunting dog
Meres Sir Thomas Meres (1635–1715), a prominent Whig parliamentary leader, who served as chairman ("supplies . . . chairs") of many committees
wretched man . . . fear In this Rochester resembles Thomas Hobbes: "We see even in well-governed states, where there are laws and punishments appointed for offenders, yet particular men travel not without their sword by their sides, for their defences; neither sleep they without shutting not only their door against their fellow subjects, but also their trunks and coffers for fear of domestics. Can men give a clearer testimony of the distrust they have of each other, and all of all? How since they do this, and even countries as well as men, they

publicly profess their mutual fear and diffidence!" *De Cive,* or *The Citizen,* in Latin 1642, in English 1651. In various works, and most notably *Leviathan,* Hobbes showed the state arising from the intolerable condition of that state of nature that was a "war of every man against every man"; a war bred of distrust, self-seeking, the competition for necessities and for imaginary needs—most fundamentally of a fear of being overcome by others. Rochester plays upon the social restrictions to which man submits in the name of all those virtues that are merely rationalizations of his fear and desire for security, and he stresses more than Hobbes the ironic conversion of fear into more "respectable" passions.

Which makes him generous, affable, and kind;
For which he takes such pains to be thought wise,
50 And screws his actions in a forced disguise,
Leading a tedious life in misery
Under laborious, mean hypocrisy.
Look to the bottom of his vast design,
Wherein man's wisdom, power, and glory join:
The good he acts, the ill he does endure,
'Tis all from fear, to make himself secure.
Merely for safety, after fame we thirst,
For all men would be cowards if they durst.
    And honesty's against all common sense:
60 Men must be knaves, 'tis in their own defence.
Mankind's dishonest; if you think it fair
Amongst known cheats to play upon the square,
You'll be undone——
Nor can weak truth your reputation save:
The knaves will all agree to call you knave.
Wronged shall he live, insulted o'er, oppressed,
Who dares be less a villain than the rest.
    Thus, sir, you see what human nature craves:
Most men are cowards, all men should be knaves.
70 The difference lies, as far as I can see,
Not in the thing itself but the degree,
And all the subject matter of debate
Is only: Who's a knave of the first rate?

    All this with indignation have I hurled
At the pretending part of the proud world,
Who, swollen with selfish vanity, devise
False freedoms, holy cheats, and formal lies
Over their fellow slaves to tyrannize.
    But if in court so just a man there be
80 (In court a just man, yet unknown to me)
Who does his needful flattery direct
Not to oppress and ruin, but protect
(Since flattery, which way soever laid,
Is still a tax on that unhappy trade);
If so upright a statesman you can find,
Whose passions bend to his unbiased mind,
Who does his arts and policies apply
To raise his country, not his family,
Nor, while his pride owned° avarice withstands,
90 Receives close° bribes through friends' corrupted hands?
    Is there a churchman who on God relies;
Whose life his faith and doctrine justifies?

owned acknowledged, open   close secret

Not one blown up with vain prelatic pride,°
Who for reproof of sins does man deride;
Whose envious heart makes preaching a pretence,
With his obstreperous, saucy eloquence,
To chide at kings and rail at men of sense;
None of that sensual tribe whose talents lie
In avarice, pride, sloth, and gluttony;
200　Who hunt good livings° but abhor good lives;
Whose lust exalted to that height arrives
They act adultery with their own wives,
And ere a score of years completed be,
Can from the lofty pulpit proudly see
Half a large parish their own progeny;
Nor doting bishop who would be adored
For domineering at the council board,
A greater fop in business at fourscore,
Fonder of serious toys, affected more,
210　Than the gay, glittering fool at twenty proves
With all his noise, his tawdry clothes, and loves;
　　But a meek, humble man of honest sense,
Who, preaching peace, does practice continence;
Whose pious life's a proof he does believe
Mysterious truths, which no man can conceive.
If upon earth there dwell such God-like men,
I'll here recant my paradox to them,
Adore those shrines of virtue, homage pay,
And, with the rabble world, their laws obey.
220　　If such there are, yet grant me this at least:
Man differs more from man, than man from beast.
1675?   1680

JOHN DRYDEN ✓
1631–1700

Dryden's poetic career began with a schoolboy poem, an elegy to Lord Hastings, who had died of smallpox at nineteen. Dryden wrote with hectic extravagance in the fashionable late Metaphysical manner of John Cleveland, and he did remarkable things with poor Hastings's pustules: "Each little pimple had a tear in it, / To wail the fault its rising did commit / . . . Or were these gems sent to adorn his skin, / The cabinet of a richer soul within?" His first mature poem was the *Heroic Stanzas* on the death of Cromwell, and by 1660 he welcomed the restoration of Charles II with *Astraea Redux,* the first of a series of "public" poems in celebration or defense of that monarch. When the theaters reopened, Dryden wrote the first of his twenty-eight plays and collaborated briefly with Sir Robert Howard, whose sister he was to marry. Dryden did much to create the new heroic play, that frankly artificial, rather operatic form in which spectacle alternated

---

prelatic pride the self-importance of high church office

livings church appointments that carry an assured income

with the fierce and witty debates of fiery souls; the greatest of these was his double play, in ten acts, *The Conquest of Granada* (1670).

Dryden's literary reign, crowned by the wreath of the poet laureate in 1671, included several provinces: drama, criticism, both prose and verse translation, and a large body of poetry in all forms. "Perhaps no nation," Dr. Johnson wrote,

> ever produced a writer that enriched his language with such variety of models. To him we owe the improvement, perhaps the completion of our metre, the refinement of our language, and much of the correctness of our sentiments. . . . What was said of Rome adorned by Augustus may be applied by an easy metaphor to English poetry embellished by Dryden . . . he found it brick, and he left it marble.

In contrast to Johnson's splendid confidence—limited, it should be noted, to formal achievements—Dryden often expressed a double view (such as we see in the poems to Oldham and to Congreve), a sense that greater urbanity might have been gained only at the expense of vigor.

This double view is a constant element in Dryden's superb play of dialectic. As Johnson said, he taught men "to think naturally and to express forcibly"; he was "the first who joined argument with poetry." Of a skeptical turn of mind, Dryden could feel himself into any stance and imagine ideas with the intensity of one who gave them utter conviction. The splendid bravura debate between the languid courtly sensualist and the "natural" man, between the defiant atheist and the Christian saint, between the rationalistic pagan and the wily inquisitor—all these are conducted with such eloquence and cogency that they seem at once aria and argument. His comedies were not remarkable, and he felt some shame at having supplied the lubricity his times demanded; the greatest of his later plays, *All for Love* (1678) and *Don Sebastian* (1690), are tragedies, although the latter has a boldly satiric subplot.

This play of mind gave rise to a major critical essay in the form of a dialogue, *Of Dramatic Poesy: An Essay* (1668). A "sceptical" discourse, it is "sustained by persons of several opinions, all of them left doubtful." The "essay" (and the term is meant still to suggest the tentative and exploratory) is one of the first exercises of that typical Augustan effort to define issues by providing statement and counterstatement, thesis and antithesis, from which the tact of the reader must elicit the delicate and undefinable truth. Ancient and Modern, French and English, Jonson and Shakespeare are placed in an opposition that teases our judgment, just as in later critical prefaces Virgil and Ovid or Horace and Juvenal serve, through counterpoint, to suggest the true nature of metaphor or the full power of satire.

Dryden's politics show a similar dialectical movement. If he played with the ideas of Hobbes, it was usually through dubious spokesmen; if he celebrated royal authority (as in *Absalom and Achitophel*), he could strike a note of balance in a later poem to his kinsman John Driden (1700): "Betwixt the Prince and Parliament we stand; / The barriers of the state on either hand: / May neither overflow, for they drown the land!" If he scorned the fickle and restless mob, he scorned the egocentric tyrant no less; and some of his most brilliant dramatic moments are the explosion of the power-drive into madness, an insane rage to command those imaginary subjects that alone remain obedient to the tyrant's will.

Dryden's religious attitudes were the occasion for severe doubts of his sincerity. Born into a family of Puritan sympathies, he wrote one of the great defenses of the Anglican middle way in *Religio Laici* (1682). But the restless search for an authority that would resolve doubts and establish peace—both within the mind and among men—let him finally to Roman Catholicism. That he was led there just as the Catholic James II ascended the throne inevitably aroused suspicion of motives less honorable than sincere conviction; but, whatever their mixture, his motives surely included such conviction, and it is magnificently expressed in his defense of the persecuted Roman Catholic Church in _The Hind and the Panther_ (1687). There the Church of England appears as the Panther, "the lady of the spotted muff," weak and compromising in her alliance with more radical Protestant sects, ready to unsheathe her claws, for all her superficial gentility, in her use of the civil power.

In Dryden's translations we can see the full range of his power to assume different voices, styles, and visions, as he moves from superb Lucretian didacticism to Juvenalian ferocity, from Ovidian extravagance to Virgilian elegance. Not only did Dryden translate all the works of Virgil, he translated Plutarch's _Lives_ as well. The last may recall, finally, Dryden's great contribution to the emergence of an urbane and easy English prose; he had models in the age of Charles I, but his own example was one of the most effective in the age to come.

Of all the major writers in the period Dryden is the most thoroughly open to the energy that outruns moderation. His Cleopatra, in _All for Love,_ exclaims: "I have loved with such transcendent passion, / I soared at first quite out of reason's view, / And now am lost above it." The other side of that transcendence is the high folly or madness of Achitophel or of Alexander under the power of music. Dryden is always ready for excess, for the grand gesture or the bold metaphor; yet the excess often carries with it the levity of a holiday from restraint and the potential ironic recoil of a gesture extended an inch too far or held a moment too long. Behind all his achievements we can glimpse the self-conscious artist, fully abandoned only to art itself, and we can sense that presence in a remark that shows the amiable pride of a man nearly seventy: "Thoughts, such as they are, come crowding in so fast upon me that my only difficulty is to choose or to reject, to run them into verse or to give them the other harmony of prose."

Absalom and Achitophel

Dryden's great satire was written at a time when the crisis it presents was still unresolved. Charles II had been urged by Whig leaders, and particularly the first Earl of Shaftesbury, to exclude his Roman Catholic brother from succession to the throne. In efforts to arouse fear of Catholic power, the Whigs found explosive material in the apparent disclosures by Titus Oates, an ex-seminarian, that a Popish Plot existed to assassinate Charles (even his Catholic wife was accused of a conspiratorial role), to seize power by violent means, perhaps to burn London (the Great Fire of 1666 had been attributed by some to a Catholic plot). Oates's testimony was highly suspect, as was the man, and it showed a convenient power of expansion as his memory was stimulated by criticism. But enough shreds of confirming evidence (not least the indiscreet correspondence of the Duchess of York's secretary with Louis XIV's confessor, looking forward to the conversion of the English to the Catholic faith) could be gathered to give Oates's charges plausibility and to promote the Whig demands that

Charles legitimize his bastard son, the Duke of Monmouth, and make him his successor. As the Tory observer Roger L'Estrange later described events, the Whig

> faction had the ascendant of the government, and the multitude bore all before them like a torrent; the witnesses led the rabble; the plot-managers led the witnesses; and the Devil himself led the leaders; for they were to pass to their ends through subornation, perjury, hypocrisy, sacrilege, and treason.

By the time Dryden wrote, Charles had withstood Whig demands and achieved financial independence (through the French king) of a Parliament that tried to force his hand by withholding funds. He dissolved Parliament in March 1681, and Shaftesbury, charged with treason and arrested in July, was awaiting trial at the time Dryden's poem was published. (Shaftesbury was acquitted but never regained his earlier power.)

Dryden was not the first to adduce the biblical parallel of David and Absalom to Charles and his illegitimate son, Monmouth; but he was the first to exploit it so fully and adroitly, creating a constant interplay between biblical narrative and current history. He does more than that; to the story of Absalom's rebellion and his temptation by Achitophel, he brings a resonance not unlike that of Milton's treatment of the rebel angels in *Paradise Lost*. Dryden's figures are more obviously involved in duplicity or self-deception, and the splendid portraits of Whig leaders converge in a central pattern of destructive recklessness. Achitophel sponsors Monmouth precisely because his claim to the throne is unstable; his secret object is to undo monarchy itself, and in his obsessive and theory-ridden drive he is willing to run all the risks of anarchy.

In his treatment of David, Dryden opens with a tone of amused tolerance for the expansive energies of Charles and, somewhat in the manner of Halifax, sets David's easy love of pleasure against the more dangerous intensity of Achitophel; but once the rebellion gains its own reckless force, David emerges as a figure of severity and deep concern, surrounded by figures of dedication like Barzillai and his son. The movement of the poem can almost be seen as the earning of dignity for David by conflict and by trial.

Absalom and Achitophel

In pious times, ere priestcraft did begin,
Before polygamy was made a sin;
When man on many multiplied his kind,
Ere one to one was cursedly confined;
When nature prompted, and no law denied,
Promiscuous use of concubine and bride;
Then Israel's monarch after Heaven's own heart°
His vigorous warmth did variously impart
To wives and slaves; and, wide as his command,
10   Scattered his Maker's image through the land.
Michal,° of royal blood, the crown did wear;

after . . . heart See I Samuel 13:14, where Samuel warns Saul, "thy Kingdom shall not continue: the Lord hath sought him a man after his own heart."

Michal alluding to the childless Catherine of Braganza, who married Charles II in 1662

A soil ungrateful to the tiller's care:
Not so the rest; for several mothers° bore
To godlike David several sons before.
But since like slaves his bed they did ascend,
No true succession could their seed attend.
Of all this numerous progeny was none
So beautiful, so brave as Absalom:°
Whether, inspired by some diviner lust,
20   His father got him with a greater gust;°
Or that his conscious destiny made way,
By manly beauty, to imperial sway.
Early in foreign fields° he won renown,
With kings and states allied to Israel's crown:
In peace the thoughts of war he could remove,
And seemed as he were only born for love.
Whate'er he did was done with so much ease,
In him alone 'twas natural to please,
His motions all accompanied with grace;
30   And paradise was opened in his face.
With secret joy indulgent David viewed
His youthful image in his son renewed:
To all his wishes nothing he denied,
And made the charming Annabel° his bride.
What faults he had (for who from faults is free?)
His father could not or he would not see.
Some warm excesses which the law forbore,
Were construed youth that purged by boiling o'er,
And Amnon's murther,° by a specious name,
40   Was called a just revenge for injured fame.
Thus praised and loved the noble youth remained,
While David, undisturbed, in Sion° reigned.
But life can never be sincerely° blest;
Heaven punishes the bad, and proves° the best.
The Jews,° a headstrong, moody, murmuring race
As ever tried the extent and stretch of grace;
God's pampered people, whom, debauched with ease,
No king could govern nor no God could please;
(Gods they had tried° of every shape and size,

---

several mothers referring to Charles II's many
mistresses and his illegitimate children
Absalom James Scott (1649–85), created Duke
of Monmouth in 1663, born illegitimately to a
"Welsh woman of no good fame" (Clarendon);
"particularly beloved by the King; but the universal terror of husbands and lovers" (Gram-
mont); a brave commander of Charles's forces
in the Scottish campaign of 1679
gust appetite, relish
foreign fields with the French against the
Dutch (1672–73) and with the Dutch against
the French (1678)
Annabel Anne, Countess of Buccleuch (1651–

1732), of great beauty and "one of the wisest
and craftiest of her sex" (John Evelyn)
Amnon's murther Absalom arranged for the
death of his half-brother in revenge for the rape
of his sister, Tamar (II Samuel 13:28–29).
Monmouth did not murder but had his troopers
attack and disfigure a man who had insulted
Charles II.
Sion London
sincerely completely
proves tests
Jews English
Gods . . . tried referring to the numerous sects
that arose after the Reformation

50 That god-smiths could produce or priests devise:)
These Adam-wits, too fortunately free,
Began to dream they wanted° liberty;
And when no rule, no precedent was found
Of men by laws less circumscribed and bound,
They led their wild desires to woods and caves,
And thought that all but savages° were slaves.
They who, when Saul° was dead, without a blow,
Made foolish Ishbosheth° the crown forego;
Who banished David did from Hebron° bring,
60 And with a general shout proclaimed him king:
Those very Jews, who, at their very best,
Their humour° more than loyalty expressed,
Now wondered why so long they had obeyed
An idol monarch which their hands had made;
Thought they might ruin him they could create,
Or melt him to that golden calf,° a state.°
But these were random bolts; no formed design
Nor interest made the factious crowd to join:
The sober part of Israel, free from stain,
70 Well knew the value of a peaceful reign;
And, looking backward with a wise affright,
Saw seams of wounds, dishonest° to the sight:
In contemplation of whose ugly scars
They cursed the memory of civil wars.
The moderate sort of men, thus qualified,
Inclined the balance to the better side;
And David's mildness managed it so well,
The had found no occasion to rebel.
But when to sin our biased nature leans,
80 The careful Devil° is still at hand with means,
And providently pimps for ill desires.
The Good Old Cause° revived, a plot required
Plots, true or false, are necessary things
To raise up commonwealths and ruin kings.
     The inhabitants of old Jerusalem°
Were Jebusites;° the town so called from them;
And theirs the native right——
But when the chosen people° grew more strong,

wanted lacked
savages wild beasts
Saul Oliver Cromwell (1599–1658)
Ishbosheth Cromwell's son Richard (1626–1712)
Hebron Scotland, where Charles II was crowned king in 1651, long before he became King of England
humour mood
golden calf the idol worshiped by the Israelites while Moses was receiving the law on Mt. Sinai
state republic, which Dryden elsewhere scornfully describes as "that mock-appearance of a liberty, where all who have not part in the government are slaves"
dishonest shameful
careful Devil Cf. Dryden's remarks on the Devil's policy "to seduce mankind into the same rebellion with him, by telling him he might be yet freer than he was, more free than his nature would allow" (Epistle Dedicatory to All for Love, 1677).
Good Old Cause for the Commonwealth
Jerusalem London
Jebusites Roman Catholics
chosen people Protestants

The rightful cause at length became the wrong;
90 And every loss the men of Jebus bore,
They still were thought God's enemies the more.
Thus worn and weakened, well or ill content,
Submit they must to David's government:
Impoverished and deprived of all command,
Their taxes doubled as they lost their land;°
And, what was harder yet to flesh and blood,
Their gods disgraced and burnt like common wood.°
This set the heathen priesthood° in a flame,
For priests of all religions are the same:
100 Of whatsoe'er descent their godhead be,
Stock, stone, or other homely pedigree,
In his defence his servants are as bold
As if he had been born of beaten gold.
The Jewish rabbins,° though their enemies,
In this conclude them honest men and wise:
For 'twas their duty, all the learnèd think,
To espouse his cause by whom they eat and drink.
From hence began that Plot,° the nation's curse,
Bad in itself, but represented worse;
110 Raised in extremes, and in extremes decried;
With oaths affirmed, with dying vows denied;
Not weighed or winnowed° by the multitude;
But swallowed in the mass, unchewed and crude.
Some truth there was, but dashed and brewed with lies,
To please the fools and puzzle all the wise.
Succeeding times did equal folly call
Believing nothing or believing all.
The Egyptian° rites the Jebusites embraced,
Where gods were recommended by their taste.
120 Such savoury deities must needs be good
As served at once for worship and for food.°
By force they could not introduce these gods,
For ten to one in former days was odds;
So fraud was used (the sacrificer's° trade):
Fools are more hard to conquer than persuade.
Their busy teachers mingled with the Jews,
And raked for converts even the court and stews:°
Which Hebrew priests° the more unkindly took,

Impoverished . . . land as Roman Catholics were or might be by laws passed under Elizabeth I and still in force beyond Dryden's day
burnt . . . wood referring to the savage destruction of church images during the Commonwealth
heathen priesthood Roman Catholic priests
Jewish rabbins Church of England priests
Plot the Popish Plot (see Headnote)
winnowed sifted
Egyptian French and Roman Catholic; but also

referring to Egypt as the source of mysteries and superstition
worship . . . food referring to the doctrine of transubstantiation (the real presence of the body and blood of Christ in the bread and wine of Communion), a doctrine defended by Dryden after his conversion to Catholicism in 1685
sacrificer's priest's
stews brothels
Hebrew priests Church of England clergy

Because the fleece° accompanies the flock.
130 Some thought they God's anointed° meant to slay
By guns, invented since full many a day:
Our author swears it not; but who can know
How far the Devil and Jebusites may go?
This Plot, which failed for want of common sense,
Had yet a deep and dangerous consequence:
For, as when raging fevers boil the blood,
The standing lake soon floats into a flood,
And every hostile° humour, which before
Slept quiet in its channels, bubbles o'er;
140 So several factions from this first ferment
Work up to foam, and threat the government.
Some by their friends, more by themselves thought wise,
Opposed the power to which they could not rise.
Some had in courts been great and, thrown from thence,
Like fiends were hardened in impenitence.
Some by their monarch's fatal mercy grown
From pardoned rebels kinsmen to the throne,
Were raised in power and public office high;
Strong bands, if bands ungrateful men could tie.
150   Of these the false Achitophel° was first;
A name to all succeeding ages curst:
For close° designs and crooked counsels fit;
Sagacious, bold, and turbulent of wit;
Restless, unfixed in principles and place;
In power unpleased, impatient of disgrace:
A fiery soul, which, working out its way,
Fretted° the pigmy body° to decay,
And o'er-informed° the tenement of clay.
A daring pilot in extremity;
160 Pleased with the danger, when the waves went high,
He sought the storms; but, for a calm unfit,
Would steer too nigh the sands, to boast his wit.
Great wits are sure to madness near allied,
And thin partitions do their bounds° divide;
Else why should he, with wealth and honour blest,
Refuse his age the needful hours of rest?
Punish a body which he could not please;

fleece income from tithes
God's anointed the king
hostile contentious, excessive
Achitophel Anthony Ashley Cooper (1621–83), 1st Earl of Shaftesbury, who had been one of Cromwell's council of state but helped to arrange Charles II's return; as lord chancellor an excellent jurist and reformer of the Court of Chancery; after 1673 in opposition and by 1676 leader of those opposed to popery and arbitrary royal power; a man without equal "in

the art of governing parties and of making himself the head of them" (Dryden)
close secret
Fretted eroded
pigmy body in fact very small, and in any case too small for its "fiery soul"
o'er-informed filled to overflowing; that is, the soul, which should be the form of mind and body, is here too restless to serve that limited function. On the "informing soul," see Pope, *Essay on Criticism*, ll. 76–79.
bounds of genius (wit) and madness

Bankrupt of life, yet prodigal° of ease?
And all to leave what with his toil he won,
170   To that unfeathered two-legged thing,° a son;
Got° while his soul did huddled° notions try,
And born a shapeless lump, like anarchy.
In friendship false, implacable in hate;
Resolved to ruin or to rule the state.
To compass this the triple bond° he broke,
The pillars of the public safety shook,
And fitted Israel for a foreign yoke:°
Then seized with fear, yet still affecting fame,
Usurped a patriot's all-atoning name.
180   So easy still it proves in factious times
With public zeal to cancel private crimes.
How safe is treason and how sacred ill,
Where none can sin against the people's will;°
Where crowds can wink and no offence be known,
Since in another's guilt they find their own.
Yet fame deserved no enemy can grudge;
The statesman we abhor, but praise the judge.
In Israel's courts ne'er sat an Abbethdin°
With more discerning eyes or hands more clean;
190   Unbribed, unsought, the wretched to redress,
Swift of dispatch and easy of access.
O had he been content to serve the crown
With virtues only proper to the gown,°
Or had the rankness° of the soil been freed
From cockle° that oppressed the noble seed;
David for him his tuneful harp had strung,
And Heaven had wanted° one immortal song.
But wild ambition loves to slide, not stand,°
And fortune's ice prefers to virtue's land.
200   Achitophel, grown weary to possess
A lawful fame and lazy happiness,
Disdained the golden fruit to gather free,
And lent the crowd his arm to shake the tree.
Now, manifest of° crimes contrived long since,
He stood at bold defiance with his prince;
Held up the buckler of the people's cause

---

prodigal spendthrift
unfeathered . . . thing alluding to the famous
definition of man as a "featherless biped"
ascribed to Plato
Got in contrast to Absalom, ll. 17–22
huddled confused; concealed
triple bond the triple alliance of England, Holland, and Sweden against France (1668),
which Shaftesbury helped to break (not without
Charles's connivance, however)
foreign yoke that of France

Where none . . . will i.e. where popular approval can cancel all guilt
Abbethdin presiding judge of the Jewish civil
court
gown of the judge
rankness fertility
cockle weeds found in grain fields
wanted missed, in that David, the composer of
the Psalms, would have devoted one song to
Achitophel rather than to God
slide, not stand as in ll. 154, 161–62
manifest of showing openly

Against the crown, and skulked behind the laws.
The wished occasion of the Plot he takes,
Some circumstances finds, but more he makes.
210 By buzzing emissaries fills the ears
Of listening crowds with jealousies° and fears
Of arbitrary counsels brought to light,
And proves the king himself a Jebusite.
Weak arguments! which yet he knew full well
Were strong with people easy to rebel.
For, governed by the moon, the giddy Jews
Tread the same track when she the prime° renews;
And once in twenty years,° their scribes record,
By natural instinct they change their lord.
220 Achitophel still wants a chief, and none
Was found so fit as warlike Absalon:
Not that he wished his greatness to create,
(For politicians neither love nor hate,)
But, for he knew his title° not allowed
Would keep him still depending on the crowd:
That kingly power, thus ebbing out, might be
Drawn to the dregs of a democracy.°
Him he attempts with studied arts to please,
And sheds his venom° in such words as these:
230 'Auspicious° prince, at whose nativity
Some royal° planet ruled the southern sky,
Thy longing country's darling and desire,
Their cloudy pillar and their guardian fire,°
Their second Moses,° whose extended wand
Divides the seas, and shows the promised land,
Whose dawning day in every distant age
Has exercised the sacred prophets' rage:
The people's prayer, the glad diviners' theme,
The young men's vision, and the old men's dream!°
240 Thee, Saviour, thee, the nation's vows confess,
And, never satisfied with seeing, bless:
Swift unbespoken° pomps thy steps proclaim,

jealousies suspicion; see Butler, *Hudibras* I.i.3 and note

prime the beginning of a new cycle

twenty years as in Charles I's troubles with the Long Parliament about 1640, the restoration of Charles II in 1660, and the Popish Plot fever of 1678

his title to the throne (Charles II having made a formal denial in 1679 of his rumored marriage with Monmouth's mother)

democracy literally, rule of the people; regarded in classical thought as an unstable form of government, easily tending to tyranny or dictatorship

sheds his venom with suggestion of the serpent's temptation of Eve (cf. Milton, *Paradise Lost* IX)

Auspicious fortunate

royal promising kingship

cloudy pillar . . . fire In the flight of the Israelites from Egypt, the "Lord went before them by day in a pillar of cloud, to lead them the way; and by night in a pillar of fire, to give them light" (Exodus 13:21).

second Moses "And the Lord said unto Moses, wherefore criest thou unto me? . . . But lift up thy rod, and stretch out thy hand over the sea, and divide it: and the children of Israel shall go on dry ground through the midst of the sea" (Exodus 14:15–16)

The young . . . dream "Your old men shall dream dreams, your young men shall see visions" (Joel 2:28), a passage, like most of these, taken as a prophecy of Christ's reign (cf. l. 245)

unbespoken spontaneous

And stammering babes are taught to lisp thy name.
How long wilt thou the general joy detain,
Starve and defraud the people of thy reign?
Content ingloriously to pass thy days
Like one of virtue's fools that feeds on praise;
Till thy fresh glories, which now shine so bright,
Grow stale and tarnish with our daily sight.
250 Believe me, royal youth, thy fruit must be
Or gathered ripe or rot upon the tree.
Heaven has to all allotted, soon or late,
Some lucky revolution of their fate;
Whose motions, if we watch and guide with skill,
(For human good depends on human will,)
Our fortune rolls as from a smooth descent,
And from the first impression takes the bent;
But, if unseized, she glides away like wind
And leaves repenting folly far behind.
260 Now, now she meets you with a glorious prize,
And spreads her locks before her° as she flies.
Had thus old David, from whose loins you spring,
Not dared, when fortune called him, to be king,
At Gath° an exile he might still remain,
And Heaven's anointing oil had been in vain.
Let his successful youth your hopes engage;
But shun the example of declining age:
Behold him setting in his western skies,
The shadows lengthening as the vapours rise.
270 He is not now, as when on Jordan's sand°
The joyful people thronged to see him land,
Covering the beach and blackening all the strand;
But, like the Prince of Angels,° from his height
Comes tumbling downward with diminished light;
Betrayed by one poor plot to public scorn,
(Our only blessing since his curst return;)
Those heaps of people which one sheaf did bind,
Blown off and scattered by a puff of wind.
What strength can he to your designs oppose,
280 Naked of friends and round beset with foes?
If Pharaoh's° doubtful succour he should use,
A foreign aid would more incense the Jews:
Proud Egypt would dissembled friendship bring;
Foment the war, but not support the king:
Nor would the royal party e'er unite
With Pharaoh's arms to assist the Jebusite;

---

spreads . . . her to be seized by the forelock, like opportunity
Gath where David took refuge from Saul; Brussels, where Charles II was in exile
Jordan's sand as David crossed the river to resume his kingdom; Dover Beach, where Charles landed in 1660
Prince of Angels Satan; cf. *Paradise Lost* I. 84–87
Pharaoh's that of Louis XIV of France

Or if they should, their interest soon would break,
And with such odious aid make David weak.
All sorts of men by my successful arts,
290 Abhorring kings, estrange their altered hearts
From David's rule: and 'tis the general cry,
"Religion, commonwealth, and liberty."
If you, as champion of the public good,
Add to their arms a chief of royal blood,
What may not Israel hope, and what applause
Might such a general gain by such a cause?
Not barren praise alone, that gaudy flower
Fair only to the sight, but solid power;
And nobler is a limited command,
300 Given by the love of all your native land,
Than a successive title,° long and dark,
Drawn from the mouldy rolls of Noah's ark.'°
    What cannot praise effect in mighty minds,
When flattery soothes and when ambition blinds!
Desire of power, on earth a vicious weed,
Yet, sprung from high, is of celestial seed:
In God 'tis glory; and when men aspire,
'Tis but a spark too much of heavenly fire.
The ambitious youth, too covetous of fame,
310 Too full of angels' metal° in his frame,
Unwarily was led from virtue's ways,
Made drunk with honour, and debauched with praise.
Half loath and half consenting to the ill,
(For loyal blood within him struggled still,)
He thus replied: 'And what pretence have I
To take up arms for public liberty?
My father governs with unquestioned right;
The faith's defender and mankind's delight;
Good, gracious, just, observant of the laws;
320 And Heaven by wonders° has espoused his cause.
Whom has he wronged in all his peaceful reign?
Who sues for justice to his throne in vain?
What millions has he pardoned of his foes
Whom just revenge did to his wrath expose?
Mild, easy, humble, studious of our good;
Enclined to mercy and averse from blood.
If mildness ill with stubborn Israel suit,
His crime is God's belovèd attribute.
What could he gain, his people to betray,
330 Or change his right for arbitrary sway?

---

successive title a title based on legitimate succession
Noah's ark playing with the theory that kingship has its origin in the rule of the patriarchs

angels' metal the metal of angels (gold coins); the ambition (mettle) that led the angels to rebel
wonders signs of divine favor

Let haughty Pharaoh curse with such a reign
His fruitful Nile, and yoke a servile train.
If David's rule Jerusalem displease,
The dog-star° heats their brains to this disease.
Why then should I, encouraging the bad,
Turn rebel and run popularly mad?
Were he a tyrant who by lawless might
Oppressed the Jews and raised the Jebusite,
Well might I mourn; but nature's holy bands°
340   Would curb my spirits and restrain my hands:
The people might assert their liberty;
But what was right in them were crime in me.
His favour leaves me nothing to require,
Prevents° my wishes and outruns desire.
What more can I expect while David lives?
All but his kingly diadem he gives:
And that'—But there he paused; then sighing, said—
'Is justly destined for a worthier head.
For when my father from his toils shall rest,
350   And late augment the number of the blest,
His lawful issue shall the throne ascend,
Or the collateral line,° where that shall end.
His brother, though oppressed with vulgar spite,°
Yet dauntless, and secure of native right,
Of every royal virtue stands possessed;
Still dear to all the bravest and the best.
His courage foes, his friends his truth proclaim;
His loyalty the king, the world his fame.
His mercy even the offending crowd will find;
360   For sure he comes of a forgiving kind.°
Why should I then repine at Heaven's decree,
Which gives me no pretence to royalty?
Yet O that fate, propitiously inclined,
Had raised my birth or had debased my mind;°
To my large soul not all her treasure lent,
And then betrayed it to a mean descent!
I find, I find my mounting spirits bold,
And David's part disdains my mother's mould.
Why am I scanted by a niggard birth?
370   My soul disclaims the kindred of her earth,
And, made for empire, whispers me within,
"Desire of greatness is a godlike sin." '

dog-star Sirius (in Canis Major), thought to
cause heat and induce madness. See Pope,
Epistle to Dr. Arbuthnot, ll. 3–6, on the "dog-
days" of midsummer.
nature's . . . bands as son
Prevents anticipates
collateral line if not in direct descent, through

the nearest legitimate kin, in this case, his
brother James
vulgar spite popular opposition to his Roman
Catholicism
kind family, nature
Had raised . . . mind reminiscent of Satan's
great speech at the opening of *Paradise Lost,*
Book IV, especially ll. 58–61

Him staggering so when Hell's dire agent found,
While fainting Virtue scarce maintained her ground,
He pours fresh forces in, and thus replies: —
    'The eternal God, supremely good and wise,
Imparts not these prodigious gifts in vain:
What wonders are reserved to bless your reign!
Against your will, your arguments have shown,
380   Such virtue's only given to guide a throne.
Not that your father's mildness I contemn;
But manly force becomes the diadem.
'Tis true he grants the people all they crave,
And more, perhaps, then subjects ought to have:
For lavish grants suppose a monarch tame,
And more his goodness than his wit proclaim.
But when should people strive their bonds to break,
If not when kings are negligent or weak?
Let him give on till he can give no more,
390   The thrifty Sanhedrin° shall keep him poor;
And every shekel which he can receive
Shall cost a limb of his prerogative.°
To ply him with new plots shall be my care;
Or plunge him deep in some expensive war;
Which, when his treasure can no more supply,
He must with the remains of kingship buy.
His faithful friends, our jealousies and fears
Call Jebusites and Pharaoh's pensioners;
Whom when our fury from his aid has torn,
400   He shall be naked left to public scorn.
The next successor, whom I fear and hate,
My arts have made obnoxious to the state;
Turned all his virtues to his overthrow,
And gained our elders° to pronounce a foe.
His right,° for sums of necessary gold,
Shall first be pawned, and afterwards be sold;
Till time shall ever-wanting David draw
To pass your doubtful title into law:
If not, the people have a right supreme
410   To make their kings, for kings are made for them.
All empire is no more than power in trust,
Which, when resumed, can be no longer just.
Succession, for the general good designed,
In its own wrong a nation cannot bind;
If altering that the people can relieve,
Better one suffer than a nation grieve.

Sanhedrin the supreme council of the Jews; here
Parliament
prerogative those powers of the king uncircum-
scribed by law, which Parliament sought to
limit by its control of his finances

elders rulers; here Parliament, where a bill ex-
cluding James from the throne was supported
by Shaftesbury and passed Commons but was
rejected by Lords through the efforts of Halifax
right to succeed Charles

The Jews well know their power: ere Saul they chose,
God was their king,° and God they durst depose.
Urge now your piety, your filial name,
420   A father's right, and fear of future fame;
The public good, that universal call,
To which even Heaven submitted, answers all.
Nor let his love enchant your generous mind;
'Tis Nature's trick to propagate her kind.
Our fond begetters, who would never die,
Love but themselves in their posterity.
Or let his kindness by the effects be tried,
Or let him lay his vain pretence aside.
God said he loved your father; could he bring
430   A better proof than to anoint him king?
It surely showed he loved the shepherd well,
Who gave so fair a flock as Israel.
Would David have you thought his darling son?
What means he then, to alienate° the crown?
The name of godly he may blush to bear:
'Tis after God's own heart° to cheat his heir.
He to his brother gives supreme command;
To you a legacy of barren land,°
Perhaps the old harp, on which he thrums his lays,°
440   Or some dull Hebrew ballad in your praise.
Then the next heir, a prince severe and wise,
Already looks on you with jealous eyes;
Sees through the thin disguises of your arts,
And marks your progress in the people's hearts.
Though now his mighty soul its grief contains,
He meditates revenge who least complains;
And, like a lion, slumbering in the way,
Or sleep dissembling while he waits his prey,
His fearless foes within his distance draws,
450   Constrains his roaring, and contracts his paws;
Till at the last, his time for fury found,
He shoots with sudden vengeance from the ground;
The prostrate vulgar° passes o'er and spares,
But with a lordly rage his hunters tears.
Your case no tame expedients will afford:
Resolve on death, or conquest by the sword,
Which for no less a stake than life you draw;
And self-defence is nature's eldest law.

God . . . king the Commonwealth, established
in 1649, acknowledging only God as king (literally, a theocracy, as in l. 522), but followed
in 1653 by Cromwell's Protectorate
alienate convey the title to another person
God's . . . heart See l. 7 and note.

barren land the Border estate of Monmouth's
wife
lays the Psalms of David, with a reference to
Charles's love of music
vulgar common people

Leave the warm people no considering time;
For then rebellion may be thought a crime.
Prevail yourself of what occasion gives,
But try your title while your father lives;
And that your arms may have a fair pretence,
Proclaim you take them in the king's defence,
Whose sacred life each minute would expose
To plots from seeming friends and secret foes.
And who can sound the depth of David's soul?
Perhaps his fear his kindness may control.
He fears his brother, though he loves his son,
For plighted vows too late to be undone.
If so, by force he wishes to be gained;
Like women's lechery, to seem constrained.
Doubt not: but, when he most affects the frown,
Commit a pleasing rape upon the crown.
Secure his person to secure your cause:
They who possess the prince, possess the laws.'
    He said, and this advice above the rest
With Absalom's mild nature suited best:
Unblamed of life (ambition set aside,)
Not stained with cruelty nor puffed with pride;
How happy had he been if destiny
Had higher placed his birth, or not so high!
His kingly virtues might have claimed a throne
And blest all other countries but his own.
But charming greatness since so few refuse,
'Tis juster to lament him than accuse.
Strong were his hopes a rival to remove
With blandishments to gain the public love,
To head the faction while their zeal was hot,
And popularly prosecute the Plot.
To farther this, Achitophel unites
The malcontents of all the Israelites;
Whose differing parties he could wisely join,
For several ends, to serve the same design:
The best (and of the princes some were such)
Who thought the power of monarchy too much,
Mistaken men and patriots in their hearts,
Not wicked, but seduced by impious arts.
By these the springs of property were bent,
And wound so high they cracked the government.
The next for interest sought to embroil the state,
To sell their duty at a dearer rate,
And make their Jewish markets of the throne,
Pretending public good, to serve their own.
Others thought kings an useless heavy load,

Who cost too much and did too little good.
These were for laying honest David by,
On principles of pure good husbandry.°
With them joined all the haranguers of the throng
510 That thought to get preferment by the tongue.
Who follow next, a double danger bring,
Not only hating David, but the king:°
The Solymaean rout,° well-versed of old
In godly faction and in treason bold;
Cowering and quaking at a conqueror's sword,
But lofty to a lawful prince restored;
Saw with disdain an ethnic° plot begun
And scorned by Jebusites to be outdone.
Hot Levites° headed these; who, pulled before
520 From the ark, which in the Judges' days they bore,
Resumed their cant,° and with a zealous° cry
Pursued their old beloved Theocracy:
Where Sanhedrin and priest enslaved the nation
And justified their spoils by inspiration:
For who so fit for reign as Aaron's race,°
If once dominion they could found in grace.°
These led the pack; though not of surest scent,
Yet deepest mouthed° against the government.
A numerous host of dreaming saints° succeed
530 Of the true old enthusiastic° breed:
'Gainst form and order they their power employ,
Nothing to build and all things to destroy.
But far more numerous was the herd of such
Who think too little and who talk too much.
These, out of mere instinct, they knew not why,
Adored their fathers' God, and property;
And, by the same blind benefit of fate,
The Devil and the Jebusite did hate:
Born to be saved, even in their own despite,°
540 Because they could not help believing right.
Such were the tools; but a whole Hydra° more
Remains, of sprouting heads too long to score.
Some of their chiefs were princes of the land:

husbandry thrift
king monarchy
Solymaean rout London rabble (Solyma is Jerusalem)
ethnic Popish (or Gentile)
Levites the Presbyterian clergy, deprived of church livings by the Act of Uniformity (1662) and thus "pulled . . . from the ark" before the Plot; the "ark" being the established or state church, which in "the Judges' days" (the Commonwealth) they governed ("bore")
cant slogans, jargon
zealous fanatical
Aaron's race the priesthood

grace in purity of faith or God's election rather than natural or civil law. See Halifax, *The Character of a Trimmer:* "Our Trimmer approveth the principles of our church, that dominion is not founded in grace."
deepest mouthed baying most loudly in the pack of hunting dogs
dreaming saints radical Protestants and visionaries
enthusiastic with, as Henry More put it, "the misconceit of being inspired"
in . . . despite because predestined to the elect
Hydra the mythical monster that grew new heads as soon as the old were cut off

In the first rank of these did Zimri° stand;
A man so various, that he seemed to be
Not one, but all mankind's epitome:
Stiff in opinions, always in the wrong;
Was everything by starts, and nothing long;
But, in the course of one revolving moon,
550   Was chemist,° fiddler, statesman, and buffoon:
Then all for women, painting, rhyming, drinking.
Besides ten thousand freaks° that died in thinking.
Blest madman, who could every hour employ
With something new to wish or to enjoy!
Railing and praising were his usual themes;
And both (to show his judgment) in extremes:
So over-violent or over-civil
That every man, with him, was God or Devil.
In squandering wealth was his peculiar art:
560   Nothing went unrewarded but desert.
Beggared by fools, whom still he found° too late,
He had his jest, and they had his estate.
He laughed himself from court; then sought relief
By forming parties, but could ne'er be chief;
For, spite of him, the weight of business fell
On Absalom and wise Achitophel:
Thus, wicked but in will, of means bereft,
He left not faction, but of that was left.
    Titles and names 'twere tedious to rehearse
570   Of lords, below the dignity of verse.
Wits, warriors, Commonwealth's-men, were the best;
Kind husbands and mere nobles, all the rest.
And therefore, in the name of dulness, be
The well-hung Balaam° and cold Caleb,° free;
And canting Nadab° let oblivion damn,
Who made new porridge for the paschal lamb.°
Let friendship's holy band some names assure;
Some their own worth, and some let scorn secure.

Zimri George Villiers (1628–87), second Duke of Buckingham, chief minister to Charles, impeached in 1674 and active in opposition after that; a great wit, author of *The Rehearsal*, which mocked the heroic play and Dryden. "He was true to nothing, for he was not true to himself. He had no steadiness nor conduct. . . . He could never fix his thoughts, nor govern his estate" (Bishop Burnet). The biblical counterparts (there are two) are either lecherous (Numbers 25:6–15) or treacherous (I Kings 16:8–20).
chemist chemist and/or alchemist (according to Burnet, "for some years he thought he was very near finding the philosopher's stone")
freaks whims
found found out
well-hung Balaam probably Theophilus Hastings (1650–1701), 7th Earl of Huntingdon, who

left Shaftesbury and returned to support the king in 1681, and may therefore be based on the diviner who is called upon by Balak to curse the Israelites but blesses them instead (Numbers 22–24); "well-hung" a tribute either to verbal fluency or sexual vigor
cold Caleb probably Arthur Capel (1632–83), Earl of Essex (Numbers 13–14)
canting Nadab Lord Howard of Escrick (1626–94), formerly an Anabaptist preacher vehement against the king and clergy
Who . . . lamb i.e. who revised the Anglican service (called a "porridge" or "hodge-podge" by Dissenters) or worship ("the paschal lamb" is Christ) by taking Communion with lamb's wool (hot ale mixed with the pulp of apples) instead of wine; so Nadab "offered strange fare before the Lord" (Leviticus 10:1)

Nor shall the rascal rabble here have place,
580   Whom kings no titles gave, and God no grace:
Not bull-faced Jonas,° who could statutes draw
To mean rebellion, and make treason law.
But he, though bad, is followed by a worse,
The wretch who Heaven's anointed dared to curse:
Shimei,° whose youth did early promise bring
Of zeal to God and hatred to his king;
Did wisely from expensive sins refrain,
And never broke the Sabbath but for gain;°
Nor ever was he known an oath to vent,
590   Or curse, unless against the government.
Thus heaping wealth, by the most ready way
Among the Jews, which was to cheat and pray,
The city, to reward his pious hate
Against his master, chose him magistrate.
His hand a vare° of justice did uphold;
His neck was loaded with a chain of gold.
During his office, treason was no crime;
The sons of Belial° had a glorious time;
For Shimei, though not prodigal of pelf,
600   Yet loved his wicked neighbour° as himself.
When two or three were gathered° to declaim
Against the monarch of Jerusalem,
Shimei was always in the midst of them;
And if they cursed the king when he was by,
Would rather curse than break good company.
If any durst his factious friends accuse,
He packed a jury of dissenting Jews,
Whose fellow-feeling in the godly cause
Would free the suffering saint from human laws.
610   For laws are only made to punish those
Who serve the king, and to protect his foes.
If any leisure time he had from power,
(Because 'tis sin to misemploy an hour,)
His business was, by writing,° to persuade
That kings were useless and a clog to trade;
And, that his noble style he might refine,

---

bull-faced Jonas Sir William Jones (1631–82), attorney general and prosecutor in the Popish Plot trials until 1679, involved in drafting legislation to exclude James from the throne
Shimei Slingsby Bethel (1617–97), one of the two Whig sheriffs of London, a republican bitterly opposed to the king and able to pack juries with his enemies; based on the loyal supporter of Saul who curses and stones David (II Samuel 16:5–14)
gain alluding to Puritan thrift and middle-class enterprise, raised to new heights of hypocritical miserliness by Shimei
vare staff

sons of Belial i.e. sons of wickedness, as in *Paradise Lost* I.500–502 ("And when night / Darkens the streets, then wander forth the Sons / Of Belial, flown with insolence and wine"), where Restoration court rakes may be suggested; here turned by Dryden upon Puritan rebels
wicked neighbour converting Jesus' teaching in Matthew 22:39 from charity to complicity
gathered echoing the words of Jesus, "Where two or three are gathered together in my name, there am I in the midst of them" (Matthew 18:20)
by writing pamphlets such as *The Interest of Princes and States* (1680)

No Rechabite° more shunned the fumes of wine.
Chaste were his cellars, and his shrieval° board
The grossness of a city feast° abhorred:
620   His cooks, with long disuse, their trade forgot;
Cool was his kitchen, though his brains were hot.
Such frugal virtue malice may accuse,
But sure 'twas necessary to the Jews;
For towns once burnt° such magistrates require
As dare not tempt God's providence by fire.
With spiritual food° he fed his servants well,
But free from flesh that made the Jews rebel;
And Moses' laws he held in more account,
For forty days of fasting in the mount.°
630   To speak the rest, who better are forgot,
Would tire a well-breathed° witness of the Plot.
Yet, Corah,° thou shalt from oblivion pass:
Erect thyself, thou monumental brass,°
High as the serpent° of thy metal made,
While nations stand secure beneath thy shade.
What though his birth were base, yet comets rise
From earthy vapours, ere they shine in skies.
Prodigious actions may as well be done
By weaver's issue° as by prince's son.
640   This arch-attestor for the public good
By that one deed ennobles all his blood.
Who ever asked the witnesses' high race
Whose oath with martyrdom did Stephen° grace?
Ours was a Levite, and as times went then,
His tribe were God Almighty's gentlemen.
Sunk were his eyes, his voice was harsh and loud,
Sure signs he neither choleric was nor proud:
His long chin proved his wit; his saintlike grace
A church vermilion and a Moses' face.°
650   His memory, miraculously great,
Could plots, exceeding man's belief, repeat;
Which therefore cannot be accounted lies,

Rechabite one of the sect sworn "to drink no wine all our days" (Jeremiah 35:8)
shrieval sheriff's
city feast lavish hospitality, expected of the sheriff
towns . . . burnt referring to the great fire of London (1666), often interpreted as divine punishment
spiritual food a Prayer Book term for the Lord's Supper or Communion; here a thrifty substitute for home cooking ("fire")
mount Mt. Sinai, where Moses received the Ten Commandments (Exodus 34:28)
well-breathed long-winded
Corah Titus Oates (1649–1705), chief witness of the Plot. First an Anglican clergyman, he became a Roman Catholic in 1677 and studied abroad with the Jesuits, thus acquiring some credibility as a witness against them.
brass a metal known for impenetrability; hence insensibility or shamelessness
serpent "Moses made a serpent of brass, and put it on a pole" to cure his people of the bites of fiery serpents (Numbers 21:6–9)
weaver's issue Oates was the son of a weaver turned preacher.
Stephen the first martyr of the Christian church, stoned to death on the testimony of false witnesses (Acts 6–7)
church . . . face the ruddy, well-fed look of a clergyman, the ironic counterpart of the shining face with which Moses descended from Mt. Sinai

For human wit could never such devise.
Some future truths are mingled in his book;
But where the witness failed, the prophet° spoke:
Some things like visionary flights appear;
The spirit caught him up, the Lord knows where;
And gave him his rabbinical degree,
Unknown to foreign university.°
660　His judgment yet his memory did excel;
Which pieced his wondrous evidence so well,
And suited to the temper of the times,
Then groaning under Jebusitic crimes.
Let Israel's foes suspect his heavenly call,
And rashly judge his writ apocryphal;°
Our laws for such affronts have forfeits° made:
He takes his life, who takes away his trade.
Were I myself in witness Corah's place,
The wretch who did me such a dire disgrace
670　Should whet my memory, though once forgot,
To make him an appendix of my plot.
His zeal to Heaven made him his prince despise
And load his person with indignities;
But zeal peculiar privilege affords,
Indulging latitude to deeds and words;
And Corah might for Agag's murther° call,
In terms as coarse as Samuel used to Saul.
What others in his evidence did join,
(The best that could be had for love or coin)
680　In Corah's own predicament will fall;
For witness is a common name to all.
　　Surrounded thus with friends of every sort,
Deluded Absalom forsakes the court;
Impatient of high hopes, urged with renown,
And fired with near possession of a crown.
The admiring crowd are dazzled with surprise,
And on his goodly person feed their eyes.
His joy concealed, he sets himself to show,
On each side bowing popularly low;
690　His looks, his gestures, and his words he frames,
And with familiar ease repeats their names.
Thus formed by nature, furnished out with arts,
He glides unfelt into their secret hearts.
Then, with a kind compassionating look,
And sighs, bespeaking° pity ere he spoke,

---

prophet Oates kept recalling events he claimed
to have forgotten in earlier testimony
university e.g. the University of Salamanca,
which denied Oates's claim to have taken a
divinity degree there
apocryphal of doubtful authenticity
forfeits fines, compensations

Agag's murther i.e. the execution of Lord Staf-
ford, ordered on Oates's evidence in 1680. The
prophet Samuel harshly ordered Saul to execute
his captured enemy Agag, as the Lord had commanded (I Samuel 15).
bespeaking soliciting

Few words he said; but easy those and fit,
More slow than Hybla-drops,° and far more sweet.
    'I mourn, my countrymen, your lost estate;
Though far unable to prevent your fate:
700 Behold a banished man,° for your dear cause
Exposed a prey to arbitrary laws!
Yet O! that I alone could be undone,
Cut off from empire, and no more a son!
Now all your liberties a spoil are made;
Egypt and Tyrus° intercept your trade,
And Jebusites your sacred rites invade.
My father, whom with reverence yet I name,
Charmed into ease, is careless of his fame;
And, bribed with petty sums of foreign gold,
710 Is grown in Bathsheba's° embraces old;
Exalts his enemies, his friends destroys;
And all his power against himself employs.
He gives, and let him give, my right away;
But why should he his own and yours betray?
He, only he, can make the nation bleed,
And he alone from my revenge is freed.
Take then my tears' (with that he wiped his eyes)
''Tis all the aid my present power supplies:
No court-informer can these arms accuse;
720 These arms may sons against their fathers use:
And 'tis my wish the next successor's reign
May make no other Israelite complain.'
    Youth, beauty, graceful action seldom fail;
But common interest always will prevail,
And pity never ceases to be shown
To him who makes the people's wrongs his own.
The crowd, that still believe their kings oppress,
With lifted hands their young Messiah bless;
Who now begins his progress° to ordain
730 With chariots, horsemen, and a numerous train;
From east to west his glories he displays,
And, like the sun, the promised land surveys.
Fame runs before him as the morning star,°
And shouts of joy salute him from afar:

Hybla-drops drops of the honey for which Hybla
in Sicily was known
banished man Monmouth was banished in
September 1679, returned in November without
Charles's leave, and was greeted with popular
acclaim.
Tyrus Holland
Bathsheba's Louise de Kéroualle, the Duchess of
Portsmouth, Charles's mistress, suspected of
having a "powerful second" (Halifax) in the
French court. For David's adultery with Bath-
sheba, see II Samuel 11.

progress Monmouth's public journey in 1680
from London to the west of England, a bid for
popular support
morning star carrying on the messianic note of
l. 728 with other echoes: "the Lord God is a
sun and shield" (Psalms 84:11); "a land that
floweth with milk and honey, as the Lord . . .
hath promised thee" (Deuteronomy 27:3);
"And I will give him the morning star" (Revelation 2:28)

Each house receives him as a guardian god,
And consecrates the place of his abode.
But hospitable treats did most commend
Wise Issachar,° his wealthy western friend.
This moving court, that caught the people's eyes,
740   And seemed but pomp, did other ends disguise:
Achitophel had formed it, with intent
To sound the depths, and fathom, where it went,
The people's hearts; distinguish friends from foes,
And try their strength, before they came to blows.
Yet all was coloured with a smooth pretence
Of specious love, and duty to their prince.
Religion and redress of grievances,
Two names that always cheat and always please,
Are often urged; and good King David's life
750   Endangered by a brother and a wife.°
Thus in a pageant show a plot is made,
And peace itself is war in masquerade.
O foolish Israel! never warned by ill!
Still the same bait, and circumvented still!
Did ever men forsake their present ease,
In midst of health imagine a disease,
Take pains contingent° mischiefs to foresee,
Make heirs for monarchs, and for God decree?
What shall we think! Can people give away,
760   Both for themselves and sons their native sway?
Then they are left defenceless to the sword
Of each unbounded, arbitrary lord:°
And laws are vain by which we right enjoy,
If kings unquestioned can those laws destroy.
Yet if the crowd be judge of fit and just,
And kings are only officers in trust,°
Then this resuming covenant° was declared
When kings were made, or is for ever barred.
If those who gave the sceptre° could not tie
770   By their own deed their own posterity,
How then could Adam bind his future race?
How could his forfeit on mankind° take place?
Or how could heavenly justice damn us all,
Who ne'er consented to our father's fall?

Issachar Thomas Thynne (1648–82) of Long-leat (Wiltshire), the "Protestant Squire" and supporter of Monmouth
wife Oates accused the queen of high treason and of a plot to poison the king.
contingent possible
unbounded, arbitrary lord perhaps evoking the unlimited and indivisible power of the sovereign of Hobbes
in trust i.e. by contract which deputizes the sovereign power of the people to these officers
resuming covenant agreement that the people can resume their power at will in order to determine the succession to the throne
gave the sceptre the makers of the original covenant that established monarchy
forfeit on mankind alluding to the doctrine of Paul: "by one man's disobedience many were made sinners" (Romans 5:19), or "as in Adam all die, even so in Christ shall all be made alive" (I Corinthians 15:22)

Then° kings are slaves to those whom they command,
And tenants° to their people's pleasure stand.
Add, that the power for property allowed°
Is mischievously seated in the crowd;
For who can be secure of private right,
780   If sovereign sway may be dissolved by might?
Nor is the people's judgment always true:
The most may err as grossly as the few;
And faultless kings run down, by common cry,
For vice, oppression, and for tyranny.
What standard is there in a fickle rout,
Which, flowing to the mark, runs faster out?°
Nor only crowds, but Sanhedrins may be
Infected with this public lunacy,
And share the madness of rebellious times,
790   To murther monarchs for imagined crimes.
If they may give and take whene'er they please,
Not kings alone (the Godhead's images)
But government itself at length must fall
To nature's state,° where all have right to all.
Yet, grant our lords the people kings can make,
What prudent men a settled throne would shake?
For whatsoe'er their sufferings were before,
That change they covet makes them suffer more.
All other errors but disturb a state,
800   But innovation° is the blow of fate.
If ancient fabrics nod, and threat to fall,
To patch the flaws, and buttress up the wall,
Thus far 'tis duty: but here fix the mark;
For all beyond it is to touch our ark.°
To change foundations, cast the frame anew,
Is work for rebels, who base ends pursue,
At once divine and human laws control,°
And mend the parts by ruin of the whole.
The tampering world is subject to this curse,
810   To physic° their disease into a worse.
    Now what relief can righteous David bring?
How fatal 'tis to be too good a king!
Friends he has few, so high the madness grows;
Who dare be such, must be the people's foes.
Yet some there were, even in the worst of days;

Then if there is not this power to bind posterity
tenants i.e. on lease
for . . . allowed taken to be the people's property
flowing . . . out i.e. the higher the tide, the faster it runs out; an effect of the moon, literally the source of "lunacy" (l. 788 below)
nature's state Hobbes's view of the state of nature, a condition of "war of every man against

every man," in which "nothing can be unjust" and all property or power is "every man's . . . for so long as he can keep it" (*Leviathan* I.13)
innovation starting anew, revolution
ark to commit sacrilege, with reference to the Ark of the Covenant
control contradict, break
physic remedy

Some let me name, and naming is to praise.
    In this short file Barzillai° first appears;
Barzillai, crowned with honour and with years.
Long since, the rising rebels he withstood
820   In regions waste,° beyond the Jordan's flood:
Unfortunately brave to buoy the state;
But sinking underneath his master's fate:
In exile with his godlike prince he mourned;
For him he suffered, and with him returned.
The court he practised, not the courtier's art:
Large was his wealth, but larger was his heart,
Which well the noblest objects knew to choose,
The fighting warrior and recording Muse.
His bed could once a fruitful issue boast;
830   Now more than half a father's name is lost.°
His eldest hope,° with every grace adorned,
By me (so Heaven will have it) always mourned,
And always honoured, snatched in manhood's prime
By unequal fates, and Providence's crime;
Yet not before the goal of honour won,
All parts fulfilled of subject and of son:
Swift was the race, but short the time to run.
O narrow circle, but of power divine,
Scanted in space, but perfect in thy line!
840   By sea, by land, thy matchless worth was known,
Arms thy delight, and war was all thy own:
Thy force, infused, the fainting Tyrians propped;
And haughty Pharaoh found his fortune stopped.
O ancient honour! O unconquered hand,
Whom foes unpunished never could withstand!
But Israel was unworthy of thy name;
Short is the date of all immoderate fame.
It looks as Heaven our ruin had designed,
And durst not trust thy fortune and thy mind.
850   Now, free from earth, thy disencumbered soul
Mounts up and leaves behind the clouds and starry pole:
From thence thy kindred legions mayst thou bring,
To aid the guardian angel of thy king.
Here stop, my Muse, here cease thy painful flight;
No pinions can pursue immortal height:
Tell good Barzillai thou canst sing no more,
And tell thy soul she should have fled before.

Barzillai James Butler (1610–88), Duke of Ormonde and Lord Lieutenant of Ireland (to whom Dryden dedicated his translation of Plutarch's *Lives*); a generous supporter of the Royalist cause, based on the aged benefactor of David (II Samuel 19:31–39)
regions waste Ireland, where Ormonde fought for Charles I

more . . . lost six of his ten children having died
eldest hope Thomas, Earl of Ossory (1634–80), who distinguished himself at sea, and in support of the Dutch on land, against Louis XIV; victim of a fever; here seen in contrast with Achitophel's son (ll. 170–72)

Or fled she with his life, and left this verse
To hang on her departed patron's hearse?°
860　Now take thy steepy flight from Heaven, and see
If thou canst find on earth another *he:*
Another *he* would be too hard to find;
See then whom thou canst see not far behind.
Zadoc° the priest, whom, shunning power and place,
His lowly mind advanced to David's grace.
With him the Sagan of Jerusalem,°
Of hospitable soul and noble stem;
Him of the western dome,° whose weighty sense
Flows in fit words and heavenly eloquence.
870　The prophets' sons,° by such example led,
To learning and to loyalty were bred:
For colleges on bounteous kings depend,
And never rebel was to arts a friend.
To these succeed the pillars of the laws;
Who best could plead, and best can judge a cause.
Next them a train of loyal peers ascend;
Sharp-judging Adriel,° the Muses' friend;
Himself a Muse—in Sanhedrin's debate
True to his prince, but not a slave of state:
880　Whom David's love with honours did adorn,
That from his disobedient son° were torn.
Jotham° of piercing wit, and pregnant thought;
Endued by nature, and by learning taught
To move assemblies, who but only tried
The worse a while, then chose the better side:
Nor chose alone, but turned the balance too;
So much the weight of one brave man can do.
Hushai,° the friend of David in distress;
In public storms, of manly steadfastness:
890　By foreign treaties he informed his youth,
And joined experience to his native truth.
His frugal care supplied the wanting throne;
Frugal for that, but bounteous of his own:
'Tis easy conduct when exchequers flow,
But hard the task to manage well the low;
For sovereign power is too depressed or high,
When kings are forced to sell, or crowds to buy.

hearse the structure over a bier where verse
tributes were hung
Zadoc William Sancroft (1617–93), Archbishop
of Canterbury, subject of an early ode by Swift
Sagan of Jerusalem Henry Compton (1632–
1713), Bishop of London, of "noble stem" as
the son of the Earl of Southampton
western dome John Dolben (1625–86), Dean
of Westminster, a "most passionate and pathetic" preacher (John Evelyn)
prophets' sons boys of Westminster School

Adriel John Sheffield (1648–1721), Earl of
Mulgrave, patron of Dryden's poetry, author of
a well-known *Essay on Satire* (1680) and
Essay upon Poetry (1682)
son Monmouth
Jotham George Savile, Marquess of Halifax (see
Headnote to selection from his works)
Hushai Laurence Hyde (1642–1711), Claren-
don's son, who negotiated the Anglo-Dutch alli-
ance of 1678

Indulge one labour more, my weary Muse,
For Amiel:° who can Amiel's praise refuse?
900   Of ancient race by birth, but nobler yet
In his own worth, and without title great:
The Sanhedrin long time as chief he ruled,
Their reason guided, and their passion cooled:
So dextrous was he in the crown's defence,
So formed to speak a loyal nation's sense,
That, as their band was Israel's tribes in small,
So fit was he to represent them all.
Now rasher charioteers the seat ascend,
Whose loose careers his steady skill commend:
910   They, like the unequal ruler° of the day,
Misguide the seasons and mistake the way;
While he withdrawn at their mad labour smiles,
And safe enjoys the sabbath of his toils.
    These were the chief, a small but faithful band
Of worthies, in the breach who dared to stand,
And tempt the united fury of the land.
With grief they viewed such powerful engines bent,
To batter down the lawful government:
A numerous faction, with pretended frights,
920   In Sanhedrins to plume° the regal rights;
The true successor from the court removed;
The Plot, by hireling witnesses, improved.
These ills they saw, and, as their duty bound,
They showed the king the danger of the wound;
That no concessions from the throne would please,
But lenitives° fomented the disease;
That Absalom, ambitious of the crown,
Was made the lure to draw the people down;
That false Achitophel's pernicious hate
930   Had turned the Plot to ruin church and state;
The council violent, the rabble worse;
That Shimei taught Jerusalem to curse.
    With all these loads of injuries oppressed,
And long revolving in his careful° breast
The event of things, at last, his patience tired,
Thus from his royal throne, by Heaven inspired,
The godlike David spoke: with awful fear
His train their Maker in their master hear.
    'Thus long have I, by native mercy swayed,
940   My wrongs dissembled, my revenge delayed:
So willing to forgive the offending age;

Amiel Edward Seymour (1633–1708), Speaker
of the House of Commons, 1673–78
unequal ruler Phaeton, who attempted to drive
the sun chariot of his father, Apollo, across the
sky and lost control, upsetting the climate and

season
plume pluck away
lenitives pain killers
careful troubled

So much the father did the king assuage.
But now so far my clemency they slight,
The offenders question my forgiving right.
That one was made for many, they contend;
But 'tis to rule; for that's a monarch's end.
They call my tenderness of blood, my fear;
Though manly tempers can the longest bear.
Yet, since they will divert my native course,
950 'Tis time to show I am not good by force.
Those heaped affronts that haughty subjects bring,
Are burthens for a camel, not a king.
Kings are the public pillars of the state,
Born to sustain and prop the nation's weight;
If my young Samson° will pretend a call
To shake the column, let him share the fall:
But O that yet he would repent and live!
How easy 'tis for parents to forgive!
With how few tears a pardon might be won
960 From nature, pleading for a darling son!
Poor pitied youth, by my paternal care
Raised up to all the height his frame could bear!
Had God ordained his fate for empire born,
He would have given his soul another turn:
Gulled° with a patriot's° name, whose modern sense
Is one that would by law supplant his prince;
The people's brave,° the politician's tool;
Never was patriot yet, but was a fool.
Whence comes it that religion and the laws
970 Should more be Absalom's than David's cause?
His old instructor,° ere he lost his place,
Was never thought indued with so much grace.
Good heavens, how faction can a patriot paint!
My rebel ever proves my people's saint.
Would *they* impose an heir upon the throne?
Let Sanhedrins be taught to give their own.°
A king's at least a part of government,
And mine as requisite as their consent;
Without my leave a future king to choose,
980 Infers a right the present to depose.
True, they petition me to approve their choice;
But Esau's hands suit ill with Jacob's voice.°
My pious subjects for my safety pray;
Which to secure, they take my power away.

Samson who perished in the ruins of the temple he pulled down (Judges 16)
Gulled duped
patriot's as in l. 179 above
brave bully, champion
instructor Achitophel

their own what is in their power to give
Esau's . . . voice referring to Jacob's deception in winning his blind father's blessing: "The voice is Jacob's voice, but the hands are the hands of Esau" (Genesis 27:22)

From plots and treasons Heaven preserve my years,
But save me most from my petitioners!
Unsatiate as the barren womb or grave;
God cannot grant so much as they can crave.
What then is left but with a jealous eye
990   To guard the small remains of royalty?
The law shall still direct my peaceful sway,
And the same law teach rebels to obey:
Votes shall no more established power control°—
Such votes as make a part exceed the whole:
No groundless clamours shall my friends remove,
Nor crowds have power to punish ere they prove;°
For gods and godlike kings their care express,
Still to defend their servants in distress.
O that my power to saving were confined!
1000   Why am I forced, like Heaven, against my mind,
To make examples of another kind?
Must I at length the sword of justice draw?
O curst effects of necessary law!
How ill my fear they by my mercy scan!
Beware the fury of a patient man.
Law they require, let Law then show her face;
They could not be content to look on Grace,°
Her hinder parts, but with a daring eye
To tempt the terror of her front and die.°
1010   By their own arts, 'tis righteously decreed,
Those dire artificers of death shall bleed.
Against themselves their witnesses will swear,°
Till viper-like their mother Plot they tear,
And suck for nutriment that bloody gore,
Which was their principle of life before.°
Their Belial with their Belzebub° will fight;
Thus on my foes, my foes shall do me right.
Nor doubt the event;° for factious crowds engage,
In their first onset, all their brutal rage.
1020   Then let 'em take an unresisted course;
Retire, and traverse, and delude their force;
But, when they stand all breathless, urge the fight,
And rise upon 'em with redoubled might;
For lawful power is still superior found;
When long driven back, at length it stands the ground.'

control contravene
No groundless . . . prove instances of arbitrary power not in the king but the parliament
and the people
Grace the mercy expressed in ll. 939–44
Her hinder . . . die as God warns Moses that
no man can see His face (here "front" or brow)
and live: "thou shalt see my back parts; but
my face shall not be seen' (Exodus 33:23)

will swear as some already had, turning upon
the Whigs
Till viper-like . . . before like the offspring of
the dragon Error, who "suckèd up their dying
mothers blood, / Making her death their life,
and eke her hurt their good" (Spenser, The
Faerie Queene I.i.25)
Belial . . . Belzebub both among the debating
leaders of the fallen angels in Paradise Lost II
event outcome

He said. The Almighty, nodding, gave consent;
And peals of thunder shook the firmament.
Henceforth a series of new time° began,
The mighty years in long procession ran:
1030   Once more the godlike David was restored,
And willing nations knew their lawful lord.

                    1681

Mac Flecknoe

This superb mock-heroic satire, which looks ahead to Pope's achievement in *The Dunciad*, found its title in the death of a notoriously bad Irish poet, Richard Flecknoe (d. 1678). Dryden has Flecknoe choose a successor in Thomas Shadwell (1640–92), who liked to think of himself as the true heir of the great Ben Jonson (1572–1637). Shadwell, in fact, gave Jonson's plays unstinting praise and imitated them with more zeal than success; he added broader effects of bawdry and slapstick, as Dryden recalls in his satire (ll. 42, 181, 212). But, whatever his deviations from Jonson's art, Shadwell was impatient with Dryden's less than complete admiration of his master, and over ten years engaged Dryden in critical dispute on such matters as the true nature of wit. In 1673 Dryden wrote, "I know I honour Ben Jonson more than my little critics, because without vanity I may own I understand him better." In general the dispute had involved little animosity on either side, and the occasion for this poem is not altogether clear. The likeliest explanation is that Dryden resented Shadwell's praise of Buckingham's *The Rehearsal*, in which Dryden was ridiculed.

Mac Flecknoe

All human things are subject to decay,
And when fate summons, monarchs must obey.
This Flecknoe found, who, like Augustus,° young
Was called to empire, and had governed long;
In prose and verse, was owned, without dispute,
Through all the realms of *Nonsense*, absolute.
This agèd prince, now flourishing in peace,
And blest with issue of a large increase;
Worn out with business, did at length debate
10   To settle the succession of the state;
And, pondering which of all his sons was fit
To reign, and wage immortal war with wit,
Cried: ' 'Tis resolved; for nature pleads, that he
Should only rule, who most resembles me.

series of new time recalling the Virgilian prophecy in *Eclogue* IV: "Saturnian times / Roll round again, and mighty years, begun / From their first orb, in radiant circles run" (Dryden trans.)

like Augustus Octavius Caesar became first Roman emperor in 31 B.C. at the age of 32; he assumed the title of Augustus four years later and ruled for 45 years.

Sh—— alone my perfect image bears,
Mature in dulness from his tender years:
Sh—— alone, of all my sons, is he
Who stands confirmed in full stupidity.
The rest to some faint meaning make pretence,
20   But Sh—— never deviates into sense.
Some beams of wit on other souls may fall,
Strike through, and make a lucid interval;
But Sh——'s genuine night admits no ray,
His rising fogs prevail upon the day.
Besides, his goodly fabric° fills the eye,
And seems designed for thoughtless° majesty;
Thoughtless as monarch oaks that shade the plain,
And, spread in solemn state, supinely reign.
Heywood and Shirley° were but types° of thee,
30   Thou last great prophet of tautology.°
Even I, a dunce of more renown than they,
Was sent before but to prepare thy way;°
And, coarsely clad in Norwich drugget,° came
To teach the nations in thy greater name.
My warbling lute,° the lute I whilom° strung,
When to King John of Portugal° I sung,
Was but the prelude to that glorious day,
When thou on silver Thames° didst cut thy way,
With well-timed oars before the royal barge,
40   Swelled with the pride of thy celestial charge;
And big with hymn, commander of a host,
The like was ne'er in Epsom blankets tossed.°
Methinks I see the new Arion° sail,
The lute still trembling underneath thy nail.
At thy well-sharpened thumb from shore to shore
The treble squeaks for fear, the basses roar;
Echoes from Pissing Alley° Sh—— call,

---

fabric a term generally used for a building, as in l. 66 below; here a reference to Shadwell's corpulent body
thoughtless carefree; mindless
Heywood and Shirley Thomas Heywood (c. 1574–1641) and James Shirley (1596–1666), both popular and prolific dramatists (Heywood claiming a hand in 220 plays, Shirley the author of 36) before the closing of the theaters in 1642; held in low regard in Dryden's day
types prefigurations, as Old Testament patriarchs (Abraham, Noah), judges or kings (Samson, David, Solomon), and prophets were taken to prefigure Christ, who was their culmination (as he is the "last Adam")
tautology needless repetition in other words, here perhaps replacing "theology"
prepare thy way as John the Baptist does for Jesus (Matthew 3:3)
Norwich drugget a coarse fabric of wool and linen (like Shadwell, from Norfolk), the coun-

terpart of John's "raiment of camel's hair" (Matthew 3:4)
lute Shadwell was ridiculed, by Andrew Marvell among others, for his musical pretensions
whilom formerly
King John of Portugal Flecknoe had visited Portugal and claimed to have been patronized by the king.
silver Thames This phrase and many in succeeding lines, as well as the allusion to Arion, echo a celebration of King Charles by Edmund Waller (1606–87).
in . . . tossed as was Sir Samuel Hearty, the self-styled wit in Shadwell's play The Virtuoso (1676); with reference to Epsom Wells, an earlier Shadwell comedy (1672)
Arion the legendary Greek musician, saved from drowning by dolphins that were charmed by his music
Pissing Alley the actual name of five streets, one near the Thames

And Sh—— they resound from Aston Hall.°
About thy boat the little fishes throng,
50   As at the morning toast° that floats along.
Sometimes, as prince of thy harmonious band,
Thou wieldst thy papers in thy threshing hand.
St. André's° feet ne'er kept more equal time,
Not even the feet of thy own *Psyche's* rhyme;
Though they in number° as in sense excel:
So just, so like tautology, they fell,
That, pale with envy, Singleton° forswore
The lute and sword, which he in triumph bore,
And vowed he ne'er would act Villerius° more.'
60   Here stopped the good old sire, and wept for joy
In silent raptures of the hopeful boy.
All arguments, but most his plays, persuade,
That for anointed° dulness° he was made.
     Close to the walls which fair Augusta° bind,
(The fair Augusta much to fears° inclined),
An ancient fabric° raised to inform the sight,
There stood of yore, and Barbican° it hight:
A watchtower once; but now, so fate ordains,
Of all the pile° an empty name remains.
70   From its old ruins brothel-houses rise,
Scenes of lewd loves, and of polluted joys,
Where their vast courts the mother-strumpets keep,
And, undisturbed by watch,° in silence sleep.°
Near these a Nursery° erects its head,
Where queens are formed, and future heroes bred;
Where unfledged actors learn to laugh and cry,
Where infant punks° their tender voices try,
And little Maximins° the gods defy.
Great Fletcher° never treads in buskins here,

Aston Hall unidentified
morning toast sewage, feces
St. André's a French dancing master and chore-
ographer for Shadwell's opera *Psyche* (1675),
whose flat-footed verse is described in next line
number meter; quantity
Singleton John Singleton, one of the royal musicians
Villerius a character in Sir William Davenant's
Siege of Rhodes (1656), often ridiculed for presenting battles in recitative (requiring both "lute
and sword" of the actor) and thus sacrificing
sense to sound
anointed i.e. looking forward to the coronation
of a new king
dulness implying not simply the power to bore
but sluggishness of mind, a relapse from effort,
a substitution of the cheap and easy for the
excellent (cf. Pope's goddess Dulness, the
daughter of Chaos and Night, in *The Dunciad*)
Augusta London
fears aroused by the Popish Plot (cf. *Absalom
and Achitophel*)

fabric building
Barbican named for its former function as an
outer defense of the city
pile large building
watch constables
Where their . . . sleep a parody of two lines
from the epic *Davideis* (1656) by Abraham
Cowley: "Where their vast court the mother-
waters keep, / And undisturbed by moons in
silence sleep"; as are ll. 76–77, with "punks"
replacing "winds" in l. 77
Nursery a training school for actors
punks prostitutes
Maximins future performers of such heroic
figures as the Roman emperor in Dryden's
Tyrannic Love (1669), a cruel tyrant given to
self-exalting rant
Fletcher John Fletcher (1579–1625), collaborator of Francis Beaumont's (c. 1584–1616),
author of celebrated tragedies (hence "buskins," the thick-soled boots of Greek tragic
actors)

80 Nor greater Jonson° dares in socks appear;
But gentle Simkin° just reception finds
Amidst this monument of vanished minds:°
Pure clinches° the suburbian Muse affords,
And Panton° waging harmless war with words.
Here Flecknoe, as a place to fame well known,
Ambitiously designed his Sh——'s throne;
For ancient Dekker° prophesied long since,
That in this pile should reign a mighty prince,
Born for a scourge of wit and flail of sense;
90 To whom true dulness should some *Psyches* owe,
But worlds of *Misers* from his pen should flow;
Humorists and *Hypocrites* it should produce,°
Whole Raymond families and tribes of Bruce.°
    Now Empress Fame had published the renown
Of Sh——'s coronation through the town.
Roused by report of Fame, the nations meet,
From near Bunhill and distant Watling Street.°
No Persian carpets spread the imperial way,
But scattered limbs of mangled poets lay;
100 From dusty shops neglected authors come,
Martyrs of pies, and relics of the bum.°
Much Heywood, Shirley, Ogilby° there lay,
But loads of Sh—— almost choked the way.
Bilked stationers° for yeomen stood prepared,
And Herringman° was captain of the guard.
The hoary prince in majesty appeared,
High on a throne° of his own labours reared.
At his right hand our young Ascanius° sate,
Rome's other hope,° and pillar of the state.
110 His brows thick fogs, instead of glories, grace,
And lambent dulness played around his face.°
As Hannibal° did to the altars come,
Sworn by his sire a mortal foe to Rome;

Jonson Ben Jonson as writer of comedy ("socks," the light shoes of the Greek comic actors)
Simkin a typical clown in farces
monument . . . minds in Davenant's *Gondibert* a phrase for a library of dead authors; here transformed by play on the word "vanished"
clinches puns
Panton another farce character, perhaps a punster
Dekker Thomas Dekker (*c.* 1572–1632), an able but often "low" playwright, satirized by Ben Jonson, here taken as a counterpart of such Old Testament prophets as Isaiah
But worlds . . . produce referring to Shadwell's early plays: the unpublished *Hypocrite; The Humorists* (1671); and *The Miser* (1672), adapted from Molière
Raymond . . . Bruce witty characters in *The Humorists* and *The Virtuoso* (1676) respectively
near . . . Street a small area in the heart of the City, the commercial center of London and, as in Pope's *Dunciad,* the center of low taste
Martyrs . . . bum their unsold books providing paper for bakers' pans and for privies
Ogilby John Ogilby (1600–1676), feeble translator of Homer and Virgil and the copious author of original epics
bilked stationers cheated publishers
Herringman Henry Herringman, publisher of both Dryden and Shadwell until 1678
High . . . throne like Milton's Satan, "High on a throne of royal state," *Paradise Lost* II.1
Ascanius Shadwell as son to Flecknoe's Aeneas
Rome's other hope translating *Aeneid* XII.168
His brows . . . his face parodying *Aeneid* II. 680–84, later translated by Dryden: "from young Iülus' head / A lambent flame arose, which gently spread / Around his brows, and on his temples fed" (II.930–32)
Hannibal forced by his father at the age of nine to swear enmity to Rome, which he almost captured in 216 B.C.

So Sh—— swore, nor should his vow be vain,
That he till death true dulness would maintain;
And, in his father's right, and realm's defence,
Ne'er to have peace with wit, nor truce with sense.
The king himself the sacred unction° made,
As king by office, and as priest by trade.°
120   In his sinister° hand, instead of ball,
He placed a mighty mug of potent ale;
Love's Kingdom° to his right he did convey,
At once his sceptre, and his rule of sway;
Whose righteous lore the prince had practised young,
And from whose loins recorded *Psyche* sprung.
His temples, last, with poppies° were o'erspread,
That nodding seemed to consecrate his head.
Just at that point of time, if fame not lie,
On his left hand twelve reverend owls° did fly.
130   So Romulus, 'tis sung, by Tiber's brook,°
Presage of sway from twice six vultures took.
The admiring throng loud acclamations make,
And omens of his future empire take.
The sire then shook the honours of his head,°
And from his brows damps of oblivion shed
Full on the filial dulness: long he stood,
Repelling from his breast the raging god;°
At length burst out in this prophetic mood:
   'Heavens bless my son, from Ireland let him reign
140   To far Barbadoes° on the western main;
Of his dominion may no end be known,
And greater than his father's be his throne;
Beyond *Love's Kingdom* let him stretch his pen!'
He paused, and all the people cried, 'Amen.'
Then thus continued he: 'My son, advance
Still in new impudence, new ignorance.
Success let others teach, learn thou from me
Pangs without birth, and fruitless industry.
Let *Virtuosos* in five years be writ;
150   Yet not one thought accuse thy toil of wit.
Let gentle George° in triumph tread the stage,

---

unction oil for anointment
priest by trade Flecknoe was a Roman Catholic priest.
sinister left, the hand in which the British monarch holds an orb as emblem of the world, while he holds a scepter in his right
Love's Kingdom Flecknoe's "pastoral tragicomedy" of 1664
poppies as inducing sleep, but also with reference to Shadwell's use of opium
owls emblems of solemnity and gravity, either wise or stupid
Romulus . . . brook as related by Plutarch of the founder and first ruler of Rome
honours . . . head ornaments, thus locks or hair

Repelling . . . god like the Delphic priestess or the Cumaean Sibyl described in *Aeneid* VI. 46–51: "Her hair stood up; convulsive rage possessed / Her trembling limbs, and heaved her labouring breast. . . . / Her staring eyes with sparkling fury roll; / When all the god came rushing on her soul" (Dryden trans., VI.74–75, 78–79)
from Ireland . . . Barbadoes a vast empire largely of water
gentle George common nickname for Sir George Etherege (*c.* 1635–91), friend of Rochester and one of the most brilliant writers of Restoration comedies

Make Dorimant betray and Loveit rage;°
Let Cully, Cockwood, Fopling,° charm the pit,°
And in their folly show the writer's wit.
Yet still thy fools shall stand in thy defence,
And justify their author's want of sense.
Let 'em be all by thy own model made
Of dulness, and desire no foreign aid;
That they to future ages may be known,
160   Not copies drawn, but issue of thy own.
Nay, let thy men of wit too be the same,
All full of thee, and differing but in name.
But let no alien S-dl-y° interpose,
To lard with wit thy hungry *Epsom* prose.
And when false flowers of rhetoric thou wouldst cull,
Trust nature, do not labour to be dull;
But write thy best, and top; and, in each line,
Sir Formal's oratory° will be thine:
Sir Formal, though unsought, attends thy quill,
170   And does thy northern° dedications fill.
Nor let false friends seduce thy mind to fame,
By arrogating Jonson's hostile name.
Let father Flecknoe fire thy mind with praise,
And uncle Ogilby thy envy raise.
Thou art my blood, where Jonson has no part:
What share have we in nature, or in art?
Where did his wit on learning fix a brand,
And rail at arts he did not understand?
Where made he love in Prince Nicander's° vein,
180   Or swept the dust in *Psyche's* humble strain?
Where sold he bargains,° "whip-stitch, kiss my arse,"
Promised a play° and dwindled to a farce?
When did his Muse from Fletcher scenes purloin,
As thou whole Etherege dost transfuse to thine?
But so transfused, as oil on water's flow,
His always floats above, thine sinks below.
This is thy province, this thy wondrous way,
New humours to invent for each new play:
This is that boasted bias of thy mind,°

Make Dorimant . . . rage the rake-hero and his discarded mistress in *The Man of Mode* (1676), Etherege's finest play
Cully . . . Fopling comic fools in three of Etherege's plays
pit the floor of the theater, less fashionable than the box, more so than the gallery
S-dl-y Sir Charles Sedley (1638–1701), court wit and poet, who contributed a prologue (and many suspected more) to Shadwell's *Epsom Wells*
Sir Formal's oratory the rhetoric of that "most Ciceronian coxcomb," Sir Formal Trifle, in *The Virtuoso*
northern addressed to the Duke or Duchess of Newcastle; but also suggesting a climate where wit is scarce, what Laurence Sterne calls "Freezeland" or "Fogland" (*Tristram Shandy* VI.i)
Prince Nicander's a character in *Psyche*
sold he bargains induced a question that might be met with a coarse answer, here in the idiom of Sir Samuel Hearty of *The Virtuoso*
Promised a play as Shadwell had in the Dedication of *The Virtuoso*, where he professed to scorn "unnatural farce fools, which some intend for comical"
bias . . . mind terms from bowling (where weighting or shaping of the ball produces a curved path), recalling Shadwell's definition of humor (Epilogue, *The Humorists*): "A humour is the bias of the mind, / By which with violence

By which one way, to dulness, 'tis inclined;
Which makes thy writings lean on one side still,
And, in all changes, that way bends thy will.
Nor let thy mountain-belly make pretence
Of likeness;° thine's a tympany° of sense.
A tun° of man in thy large bulk is writ,
But sure thou art but a kilderkin° of wit.
Like mine, thy gentle numbers feebly creep;
Thy tragic Muse gives smiles, thy comic sleep.
With whate'er gall thou settest thyself to write,
Thy inoffensive satires never bite.
In thy felonious heart though venom lies,
It does but touch thy Irish° pen, and dies.
Thy genius calls thee not to purchase fame
In keen iambics,° but mild anagram.°
Leave writing plays, and choose for thy command
Some peaceful province in acrostic° land.
There thou mayst wings display and altars° raise,
And torture one poor word ten thousand ways.
Or, if thou wouldst thy different talents suit,
Set thy own songs, and sing them to thy lute.'
  He said: but his last words were scarcely heard;
For Bruce and Longvil° had a trap prepared,
And down they sent the yet declaiming bard.
Sinking he left his drugget robe behind,
Borne upwards by a subterranean wind.
The mantle fell to the young prophet's part,°
With double portion of his father's art.
1678?   1682

Religio Laici

This poem, cast in a form like that of the Horatian epistle, offers a defense of a moderate (layman's) Christianity against various enemies, particularly Deism in the part given below. Later in the poem Dryden goes on to consider the implications of Father Richard Simon's *Critical History of the Old Testament*, first published in 1678 and

'tis one way inclined; / It makes our actions lean on one side still, / And in all changes that way bends the will." But the invention of humors was Shadwell's own bias or humor: "I may say I ne'er produced a comedy that had not some natural humour in it not represented before, nor I hope never shall."
likeness to Jonson
tympany windiness that creates unnatural swelling; hence, vacuity
tun large wine cask
kilderkin a small cask, a quarter of a tun
Irish suggesting barbarity and want of skill, inherited from father Flecknoe
keen iambics sharp satiric verse
anagram rearrangement of letters to form a new word

acrostic a poem the first letters of whose lines spell a word or name
wings . . . altars in shaped poems like those of George Herbert ("Easter Wings" and "The Altar"). All these forms of "false wit" or verbal ingenuity without real function are summed up by Joseph Addison in *Spectator* Nos. 58–61 (1711).
Bruce and Longvil characters who perform this trapdoor trick on Sir Formal Trifle in *The Virtuoso*
prophet's part as with Elisha, who "took the mantle of Elijah that fell from him" so that the sons of the prophets say, "The spirit of Elijah does rest on Elisha" (II Kings 2:14–15); whereas Elijah ascends to heaven by a whirlwind, Flecknoe's descent produces a "subterranean" wind

four years later translated into English. That work cast doubt on the reliability of scriptural texts. Dryden defends the plain meaning of Scripture against those who impose their own forced interpretations upon it and against those who use its obscurities as a pretext for divisiveness. (In this he anticipates very clearly Swift's position in *A Tale of a Tub*.) In his attack upon Deism or natural religion, he asserts that reasoning from the evidence of nature to the existence and attributes of God is really less empirical than it claims. Deism, in his view, provides "only the faint remnants or dying flames of revealed religion" that have survived from earlier patriarchal times. "[W]e have not lifted up ourselves to God by the weak pinions of our reason, but he has been pleased to descend to us," and all natural religion is "no more than the twilight of revelation after the sun of it was set in the race of Noah." In the style of his poem, Dryden attempts to be "plain and natural and yet majestic," adopting the "legislative style" of the poet as "a kind of lawgiver." He concludes his preface: "A man is to be cheated into passion, but to be reasoned into truth."

From Religio Laici
or, a Layman's Faith

Dim as the borrowed beams of moon and stars°
To lonely, weary, wandering travelers,
Is Reason to the soul; and, as on high
Those rolling fires discover° but the sky,
Not light us here, so Reason's glimmering ray
Was lent, not to assure our doubtful way,
But guide us upward to a better day.
And as those nightly tapers disappear
When day's bright lord ascends our hemisphere;
10 So pale grows Reason at Religion's sight;
So dies, and so dissolves in supernatural light.°
Some few,° whose lamp shone brighter, have been led
From cause to cause, to nature's secret head;
And found that one first principle must be:
But what, or who, that universal He;
Whether some soul incompassing this ball,
Unmade, unmoved, yet making, moving all;°
Or various atoms' interfering dance°
Leapt into form (the noble work of chance);

stars planets
discover reveal
supernatural light The issue is whether man's reason is self-sufficient and needs no guide from revelation or whether it is totally fallible and can provide us with no guidance at all in matters of faith; the former position leads to Deism, the latter to Fideism. Dryden insists instead upon the continuity between the "borrowed beams" of reason and the "supernatural light" to which they lead us; the dissolution of reason's light is in a light of the same kind but of greater intensity, made available through Christian revelation.
few those ancient philosophers who were led by reason to the idea of a universal God, but could not agree about his nature
Unmade . . . moving all the Platonic conception of the World Soul, with echoes of Aristotle's "unmoved mover"
interfering dance colliding movement, as in Epicurean theory about the chance formation of a cosmic order

20 Or this great all was from eternity;°
Not even the Stagirite himself could see,
And Epicurus guessed as well as he:
As blindly groped they for a future state;
As rashly judged of providence and fate:
But least of all could their endeavours find
What most concerned the good of humankind;
For happiness° was never to be found,
But vanished from 'em like enchanted ground.
One thought content° the good to be enjoyed;
30 This every little accident destroyed:
The wiser madmen did for virtue° toil,
A thorny or at best a barren soil;
In pleasure° some their glutton souls would steep,
But found their line too short, the well too deep,
And leaky vessels which no bliss could keep.
Thus anxious thoughts in endless circles° roll,
Without a centre where to fix the soul;
In this wild maze their vain endeavours end:
How can the less the greater comprehend?
40 Or finite reason reach Infinity?
For what could fathom God were more than He.
The Deist thinks he stands on firmer ground;
Cries: 'Eúreka! the mighty secret's° found:
God is that spring of good, supreme and best;
We, made to serve, and in that service blest.
If so, some rules of worship must be given,
Distributed alike to all by Heaven:
Else God were partial, and to some denied
The means his justice should for all provide.
50 This general worship is to *praise* and *pray*,
One part to borrow blessings, one to pay;
And when frail nature slides into offence,
The sacrifice for crimes is penitence.
Yet, since the effects of providence, we find,
Are variously dispensed to humankind;
That vice triumphs and virtue suffers here
(A brand that sovereign justice cannot bear),
Our reason prompts us to a future state,

from eternity a hypothesis offered by Aristotle (the "Stagirite" of the next line)
happiness The conflict about the highest good (or *summum bonum*) of man was a counterpart of the conflict in cosmic theories.
content presumably a Stoic doctrine of serenity, which could be attained only by refusing to be unsettled by accident or chance
virtue as in Aristotelian ethics
pleasure as in Epicurean doctrines
endless circles recalling the orbital movements of "moon and stars" in the first line, as opposed to their center in the sun; seen as a "wild maze"

without the ordering principle that controls them (the failure of the great philosophers of antiquity to reach agreement was often used as a Christian argument against the "wisdom of this world")
mighty secret's as in Archimedes' discovery (with the exclamation, "I have found it!") of the way to determine the purity of gold by weighing its displacement of water. In what follows Dryden sums up the principal articles of Deist doctrine as set forth by Lord Herbert of Cherbury in *De Veritate* (1624) and later works by him and others.

The last appeal from fortune and from fate:
60   Where God's all-righteous ways will be declared,
The bad meet punishment, the good reward.'
    Thus man by his own strength to heaven would soar,
And would not be obliged to God for more.
Vain, wretched creature, how art thou misled
To think thy wit these godlike notions bred!
These truths are not the product of thy mind,
But dropped from heaven, and of a nobler kind.
Revealed Religion first informed thy sight,
And Reason saw not, till Faith sprung the light.
70   Hence all thy natural worship takes the source:
'Tis revelation what thou thinkest discourse.°
Else, how comest thou to see these truths so clear,
Which so obscure to heathens did appear?
Not Plato these, nor Aristotle found;
Nor he° whose wisdom oracles renowned.
Hast thou a wit so deep, or so sublime,
Or canst thou lower dive, or higher climb?°
Canst thou, by Reason, more of Godhead know
Than Plutarch, Seneca, or Cicero?°
80   Those giant wits, in happier ages born,
(When arms and arts did Greece and Rome adorn)
Knew no such system; no such piles° could raise
Of natural worship, built on prayer and praise,
To One Sole God:
Nor did remorse to expiate sin prescribe,
But slew their fellow creatures for a bribe:
The guiltless victim groaned for their offence,
And cruelty and blood was penitence.
If sheep and oxen could atone for men,
90   Ah! at how cheap a rate the rich might sin!
And great oppressors might Heaven's wrath beguile,
By offering his own creatures for a spoil!
    Darest thou, poor worm, offend Infinity?
And must the terms of peace be given by thee?
Then thou art Justice in the last appeal:
Thy easy God instructs thee to rebel;
And, like a king remote and weak, must take
What satisfaction thou art pleased to make.
    But if there be a power too just and strong
100 To wink at crimes and bear unpunished wrong;

---

discourse deliberative or discursive (as opposed
to intuitive) reason
Nor he Socrates
Hast thou . . . higher climb Cf. Job 11:7–8:
"Canst thou by searching find out God? canst
thou find out the Almighty unto perfection? It
is as high as heaven; what canst thou do?
deeper than hell; what canst thou know?"

Plutarch, Seneca, or Cicero moving from Greek
philosophers to those of Rome (where Plutarch,
although Greek, lectured on philosophy) and of
a later date (Plutarch, 46? A.D.–c. 120 A.D.;
Seneca, c. 3 B.C.–65 A.D.; Cicero, 106 B.C.–
43 B.C.)
piles structures

Look humbly upward, see his will disclose
The forfeit first and then the fine impose:
A mulct° thy poverty could never pay
Had not eternal wisdom found the way,
And with celestial wealth supplied thy store:
His justice makes the fine, his mercy quits the score.
See God descending in thy human frame;°
The offended suffering in the offender's name;
All thy misdeeds to him imputed see,
◀10 And all his righteousness devolved on thee.

    For granting we have sinned, and that the offence
Of man is made against Omnipotence,
Some price that bears proportion must be paid,
And infinite with infinite be weighed.
See then the Deist lost: remorse for vice,
Not paid; or paid, inadequate in price:
What farther means can Reason now direct,
Or what relief from human wit expect?
That shows us sick; and sadly are we sure
120 Still to be sick, till Heaven reveal the cure:
If then Heaven's will must needs be understood,
(Which must, if we want cure, and Heaven be good)
Let all records of will revealed be shown;
With Scripture all in equal balance thrown,
And our one sacred book will be that one.

            . . .

    What then remains, but, waiving each extreme,
The tides of ignorance and pride to stem?
Neither so rich a treasure° to forego;
430 Nor proudly seek beyond our power to know:
Faith is not built on disquisitions vain;
The things we must believe are few and plain:
But since men will believe more than they need,
And every man will make himself a creed,
In doubtful questions 'tis the safest way
To learn what unsuspected ancients say;
For 'tis not likely we should higher soar
In search of heaven than all the Church before;
Nor can we be deceived, unless we see
440 The Scripture and the Fathers° disagree.
If, after all, they stand suspected still,
(For no man's faith depends upon his will)
'Tis some relief that points not clearly known

---

mulct fine
in thy human frame the doctrine of the Incarnation as necessary to that of Atonement, a teaching that is distinctively Christian, as are the doctrines of imputed sin and righteousness in ll. 109–10

treasure the Bible
Fathers the early Church theologians who wrote within a few centuries of the Apostles and were therefore considered purest in doctrine

Without much hazard may be let alone:
And after hearing what our Church can say,
If still our Reason runs another way,
That private Reason 'tis more just to curb
Than by disputes the public peace disturb.
For points obscure are of small use to learn,
450   But common quiet° is mankind's concern.
    Thus have I made my own opinions clear;
Yet neither praise expect, nor censure fear:
And this unpolished, rugged verse I chose,
As fittest for discourse and nearest prose;
For while from sacred truth I do not swerve,
Tom Sternhold's° or Tom Sha - - - ll's° rhymes will serve.

1682

To the Memory of Mr. Oldham°

Farewell, too little, and too lately known,
Whom I began to think and call my own:
For sure our souls were near allied, and thine
Cast in the same poetic mould with mine.
One common note on either lyre did strike,
And knaves and fools we both abhorred alike.
To the same goal did both our studies drive;
The last set out the soonest did arrive.
Thus Nisus° fell upon the slippery place,
10   While his young friend performed and won the race.
O early ripe! to thy abundant store
What could advancing age have added more?
It might (what nature never gives the young)
Have taught the numbers° of thy native tongue.
But satire needs not those, and wit will shine
Through the harsh cadence of a rugged line:
A noble error, and but seldom made,
When poets are by too much force betrayed.
Thy generous fruits, though gathered ere their prime,
20   Still showed a quickness;° and maturing time

common quiet Cf. Richard Hooker, *Of the Laws of Ecclesiastical Polity* (1593–97), Preface, VI. 6: "So that of peace and quietness there is not any way possible unless the probable voice of every entire society or body politic overrule all private of like nature in the same body."
Tom Sternhold's with John Hopkins author of the metrical version of the Psalms completed in 1562
Tom Sha - - - ll's for Shadwell, see the Headnote to *Mac Flecknoe*
To the Memory of Mr. Oldham John Oldham (1652–83) first attracted Rochester's attention with his manuscript poems and after some years of teaching school came to London in 1681.

His *Satires upon the Jesuits* and other works had won him a reputation as a fiery writer of both odes and satires before he met Dryden, probably two years before his early death. By the time Dryden, who was twenty years older, wrote this poem, he had achieved his own reputation as a satirist with *Absalom and Achitophel.*
Nisus who with his young friend Euryalus took part in foot races at the funeral of Anchises; when Nisus slipped in the blood of a sacrifice, Euryalus won the race (*Aeneid* V.315 ff.)
numbers smoothness and control of verse
quickness vitality; playing upon the victory in the race as well

But mellows what we write to the dull sweets of rhyme.
Once more, hail and farewell; farewell, thou young,
But ah too short, Marcellus° of our tongue;
Thy brows with ivy, and with laurels° bound;
But fate and gloomy night encompass thee around.

1684

Lines on Milton°

Three poets, in three distant ages born,
Greece, Italy, and England did adorn.
The first in loftiness of thought surpassed,
The next in majesty, in both the last:
The force of Nature could no farther go;
To make a third, she joined the former two.

1688

To the Pious Memory of the Accomplished Young Lady, Mrs. Anne Killigrew

Excellent in the Two Sister-Arts
of Poesy and Painting, An Ode°

I

Thou youngest virgin-daughter° of the skies,
Made in the last promotion of the blest;
Whose palms,° new plucked from paradise,
In spreading branches more sublimely rise,
Rich with immortal green above the rest:
Whether,° adopted to some neighbouring star,
Thou rollest above us, in thy wandering race,
    Or, in procession fixed and regular,
    Moved with the heavens' majestic pace;

Marcellus the nephew and potential successor of the emperor Augustus; whose death at age twenty Virgil mourned in *Aeneid* VI.860 ff.
ivy . . . laurels the wreaths that crown the successful poet
fate and gloomy night Dryden retains a Roman idiom throughout, both in allusions and in tone; as a matter of fact, this line is a paraphrase of Virgil's line about Marcellus, VI.866
Lines on Milton first published in Tonson's illustrated edition of *Paradise Lost;* referring to Homer and Virgil as the great predecessors
Ode a free Pindaric ode, in the manner given currency by Abraham Cowley, a vehicle of sublime feeling such as could not be contained in regular forms and might be found not only in Pindar but also in the biblical prophets. This poem was praised by Dr. Johnson as "undoubtedly the noblest ode that our language ever has produced," the first part flowing "with a torrent of enthusiasm" (*Life of Dryden*).
virgin-daughter Anne Killigrew (1660–85), maid of honor to the Duchess of York, both poetess and painter, who died of smallpox at the age of 25; here she is seen promoted from her candidacy on earth (l. 21) to a place in heaven, in a way that fuses the elevation of the classical hero to the stars with that of the Christian hero to the company of saints
palms emblems of victory and rejoicing, as in Christ's entry into Jerusalem
Whether Dryden professes uncertainty (in the manner of Virgil) as to whether Anne has been placed among the nearer and lower stars (i.e. planets) as an angelic intelligence to guide their course; among the remoter fixed stars in their higher sphere; or, highest of all, among the seraphim about the throne of God.

10   Or, called to more superior bliss,
Thou treadest, with seraphims, the vast abyss:
Whatever happy region is thy place,
Cease thy celestial song a little space;
(Thou wilt have time enough for hymns divine,
    Since heaven's eternal year is thine.)
Here then a mortal Muse thy praise rehearse,°
        In no ignoble verse;
But such as thy own voice did practise here,
When thy first fruits of poesy were given,
20   To make thyself a welcome inmate there;
        While yet a young probationer,
        And candidate of heaven.

                II
If by traduction° came thy mind,
    Our wonder is the less to find
A soul so charming from a stock° so good;
Thy father was transfused into thy blood:
So wert thou born into the tuneful strain,
(An early, rich, and inexhausted vein.)
    But if thy preëxisting soul°
30   Was formed, at first, with myriads more,
It did through all the mighty poets roll
    Who Greek or Latin laurels wore
And was that Sappho last, which once it was before.
    If so, then cease thy flight, O heaven-born mind!
Thou hast no dross to purge° from thy rich ore;
Nor can thy soul a fairer mansion find,
Than was the beauteous frame she left behind:
Return, to fill or mend° the choir of thy celestial kind.

                III
    May we presume to say that at thy birth
40   New joy was sprung in heaven, as well as here on earth?
    For sure the milder planets did combine
    On thy auspicious horoscope° to shine,
    And even the most malicious were in trine.
    Thy brother-angels at thy birth
        Strung each his lyre and tuned it high,·

rehearse repeat
traduction begotten like her body by her father
(one possible origin of an immortal soul), and
thus inheriting his poetic gifts
stock Dr. Henry Killigrew, chaplain to Charles
I and a loyal supporter of his son, author of a
tragedy praised by Ben Jonson
preëxisting soul alluding to the Pythagorean
doctrine of metempsychosis, that souls go from
one body to another; in this case inhabiting first
the body of the splendid Greek poet Sappho
and at last returning to that form in the modern
Sappho, Anne Killigrew
dross to purge Plato, in the Timaeus, suggests
that the soul undergoes repeated incarnation as
a punishment until it is purged of evil or worldly
appetites.
mend improve, increase
auspicious horoscope favorable because of its
control by "milder" planets, with even the least
favorable planets "in trine" (120 degrees distant from each other) and therefore benign

That all the people of the sky
Might know a poetess was born on earth.
 And then, if ever, mortal ears
 Had heard the music of the spheres!°
And if no clustering swarm of bees°
On thy sweet mouth distilled their golden dew,
  'Twas that such vulgar miracles
  Heaven had no leisure to renew:
 For all the blest fraternity of love
Solemnized there thy birth and kept thy holiday above.

   IV
O gracious God! how far have we
Profaned thy heavenly gift of poesy!
Made prostitute and profligate the Muse,
Debased to each obscene and impious use,
Whose harmony was first ordained above
For tongues of angels, and for hymns of love!
O wretched we! why were we hurried down
 This lubric° and adulterate age,
(Nay, added fat° pollutions of our own,)
 To increase the steaming° ordures of the stage?
What can we say to excuse our *second fall?*
Let this thy *vestal,*° Heaven, atone for all:
Her Arethusian° stream remains unsoiled,
Unmixed with foreign filth, and undefiled;
Her wit was more than man, her innocence a child!

   v
Art° she had none, yet wanted° none;
 For nature did that want supply:
 So rich in treasures of her own,
 She might our boasted stores defy:
Such noble vigour did her verse adorn
That it seemed borrowed, where 'twas only born.
 Her morals too were in her bosom bred,
  By great examples daily fed,
What in the best of books, her father's life, she read.
And to be read herself she need not fear;
Each test, and every light, her Muse will bear,

---

music of the spheres The harmony produced by the movement of the heavenly bodies was thought to be inaudible to men since the Fall, except perhaps at the birth of Christ.
bees such as gathered on the lips of the infant Plato, according to legend, and prophesied his sweetness of speech
lubric lubricious, lewd
fat gross, indecent

steaming reeking
vestal virgin, like those who served the Roman goddess Vesta
Arethusian named for the nymph whom Diana changed to a fountain to save from violation by the river god Alpheus; cf. Milton, *Lycidas,* l. 85
Art "borrowed" (l. 76) as opposed to native "vigour"; "nurture" as opposed to "nature"
wanted needed

Though Epictetus with his lamp° were there.
Even love (for love sometimes her Muse expressed)
Was but a lambent° flame which played about her breast,
Light as the vapours of a morning dream:
So cold herself, whilst she such warmth expressed,
'Twas Cupid bathing in Diana's stream.

VI

Born to the spacious empire of the Nine,°
One would have thought she should have been content
90   To manage well that mighty government;
But what can young ambitious souls confine?
    To the next realm she stretched her sway,
    For *painture* near adjoining lay,
A plenteous province, and alluring prey.
    A chamber of dependences° was framed,
    (As conquerors will never want pretence,
        When armed, to justify the offence,)
And the whole fief in right of poetry she claimed.
The country open lay without defence;
100   For poets frequent inroads there had made,
        And perfectly could represent
        The shape, the face, with every lineament;
And all the large demains° which the *Dumb Sister*° swayed
    All bowed beneath her government;
    Received in triumph wheresoe'er she went.
Her pencil° drew whate'er her soul designed,
And oft the happy draught surpassed the image in her mind.
    The sylvan scenes° of herds and flocks,
    And fruitful plains and barren rocks,
110   Of shallow brooks that flowed so clear
    The bottom did the top appear;
    Of deeper too and ampler floods,
    Which, as in mirrors, showed the woods;
    Of lofty trees, with sacred shades,
    And perspectives of pleasant glades,
    Where nymphs of brightest form appear,
    And shaggy satyrs standing near,
    Which them at once admire and fear:
    The ruins too of some majestic piece,
120   Boasting the power of ancient Rome, or Greece,

Epictetus . . . lamp i.e. it underwent the severest moral scrutiny, such as that of the Stoic philosopher of the 1st century A.D.
lambent softly flickering, as opposed to "wanton" or passionate
Nine the Muses of writing, music, and dance
chamber of dependences a device used by Louis XIV to annex new territory, inducing (by threatened force) local authorities to set up "chambers" which might cede the lands to Louis through fictions drawn from feudal claims (thus "fief" in l. 98)
demains domains
Dumb Sister Painting
pencil painter's brush
sylvan scenes The following landscapes "conquered" by Anne were the typical subjects of 17th-century painters throughout Europe.

Whose statues, friezes, columns broken lie,
And, though defaced, the wonder of the eye:
What nature, art, bold fiction e'er durst frame,
Her forming hand gave feature to the name.
So strange a concourse ne'er was seen before,
But when the peopled ark the whole creation bore.

VII

The scene then changed: with bold erected look
Our martial king° the sight with reverence strook;
For, not content to express his outward part,
130 Her hand called out the image of his heart:
His warlike mind, his soul devoid of fear,
His high-designing thoughts were figured there,
As when, by magic, ghosts are made appear.
Our phoenix queen° was portrayed too so bright,
Beauty alone could beauty take so right:°
Her dress, her shape, her matchless grace,
Were all observed, as well as heavenly face.
With such a peerless majesty she stands,
As in that day she took the crown° from sacred hands;
140 Before a train of heroines was seen,
In beauty foremost, as in rank the queen.
Thus nothing to her genius was denied,
But like a ball of fire,° the further thrown,
Still with a greater blaze she shone,
And her bright soul broke out on every side.
What next she had designed, Heaven only knows;
To such immoderate growth her conquest rose
That fate alone its progress could oppose.

VIII

Now all those charms, that blooming grace,
150 The well-proportioned shape and beauteous face,
Shall never more be seen by mortal eyes:
In earth the much-lamented virgin lies!
Not wit nor piety could fate prevent;
Nor was the cruel destiny content
To finish all the murder at a blow,
To sweep at once her life and beauty too;
But, like a hardened felon, took a pride
To work more mischievously slow,
And plundered first, and then destroyed.
160 O double sacrilege on things divine,

---

martial king James II
queen Mary of Modena, wife of James II, to whose beauty Dryden had earlier paid tribute
take so right represent so well

crown Mary was crowned by the Archbishop of Canterbury on April 23, 1685.
ball of fire skyrocket

To rob the relic, and deface° the shrine!
　　But thus Orinda° died:
Heaven, by the same disease, did both translate;
As equal were their souls, so equal was their fate.

　　　　IX
　　Meantime her warlike brother° on the seas
　　His waving streamers to the winds displays,
And vows for his return, with vain devotion, pays.
　　　　Ah, generous youth, that wish forbear,
　　　　The winds too soon will waft thee here!
170　　Slack all thy sails, and fear to come,
Alas, thou knowst not, thou art wrecked at home!
No more shalt thou behold thy sister's face,
Thou hast already had her last embrace.
But look aloft, and if thou kennst from far
Among the Pleiads° a new kindled star;
If any sparkles than the rest more bright,
'Tis she that shines in that propitious light.

　　　　X
　　When in mid-air the golden trump° shall sound,
　　　　To raise the nations° under ground;
180　　　　When in the Valley of Jehoshaphat
The judging God° shall close the book of fate,
　　　　And there the last assizes° keep
　　　　For those who wake and those who sleep;
　　　　When rattling bones together fly
　　　　From the four corners of the sky;
When sinews o'er the skeletons are spread,
Those clothed with flesh, and life inspires the dead;
The sacred poets first shall hear the sound,
And foremost from the tomb shall bound,
190　　For they are covered with the lightest ground;
And straight, with inborn vigour, on the wing,
Like mounting larks, to the new morning sing.
There thou, sweet saint, before the choir shalt go,
As harbinger of heaven, the way to show,
The way which thou so well hast learned below.
　　　　　　　　1685

---

deface referring, as in lines above, to the disfigurement caused by smallpox
Orinda Katherine Philips (1631–64), the "Matchless Orinda," another latter-day Sappho
brother Henry Killigrew, naval captain and later admiral (d. 1712)
Pleiads the seven stars in Taurus, whose name was given to groups of poets, notably the French *Pléiade* of the 16th century, which included Ronsard and Du Bellay
trump "for the trumpet shall sound, and the

dead be raised incorruptible" (I Corinthians 15:52)
nations "I will also gather all nations, and will bring them down into the valley of Jehoshaphat" (Joel 3:2)
judging God "Jehoshaphat" means "Jehovah judges."
assizes court session, i.e. the Last Judgment, for both living and dead, the latter resurrected in body as well as soul to meet their judgment

A Song for St. Cecilia's Day,° 1687

I

From harmony, from heavenly harmony
   This universal frame° began:
   When Nature underneath a heap°
     Of jarring atoms lay,
     And could not heave her head,
The tuneful voice was heard from high:
     'Arise, ye more than dead.'
Then cold, and hot, and moist, and dry,
   In order to their stations° leap,
      And Music's power obey.
From harmony, from heavenly harmony
   This universal frame began:
   From harmony to harmony
Through all the compass of the notes it ran,
The diapason° closing full in Man.

II

What passion cannot Music raise and quell!°
   When Jubal° struck the corded shell,
   His listening brethren stood around,
   And, wondering, on their faces fell
   To worship that celestial sound.
Less than a god they thought there could not dwell
    Within the hollow of that shell
    That spoke so sweetly and so well.
What passion cannot Music raise and quell!

III

The Trumpet's loud clangour
    Excites us to arms,
With shrill notes of anger
    And mortal alarms.
The double double double beat
30   Of the thundering Drum
Cries: 'Hark! the foes come;
Charge, charge, 'tis too late to retreat.'

IV

The soft complaining Flute
    In dying notes discovers
The woes of hopeless lovers,
Whose dirge is whispered by the warbling Lute.

V

Sharp Violins° proclaim
Their jealous pangs, and desperation,
Fury, frantic indignation,
40 Depth of pains, and height of passion,
    For the fair, disdainful dame.

VI

But O! what art can teach,
    What human voice can reach,
The sacred Organ's praise?
    Notes inspiring holy love,
Notes that wing their heavenly ways
    To mend the choirs above.

VII

Orpheus could lead the savage race;
And trees unrooted left their place,
50   Sequacious of the lyre;°
But bright Cecilia raised the wonder higher:
When to her Organ vocal breath° was given,
An angel heard, and straight appeared,
    Mistaking earth for heaven.

GRAND CHORUS

As from the power of sacred lays°
The spheres began to move,

Sharp Violins Recently introduced into England, they seemed so in contrast to the duller viols. lyre Orpheus, who drew beasts and trees and stones after him, figured in traditional pagan myth as the power of music; here he is surpassed by Cecilia, who can draw men to heaven (as traditionally she converted her pagan lover Valerianus to love of God) or an angel down to earth.

vocal breath suggesting, apart from its use of pipes, the power of the organ to sustain notes like the human voice and therefore its superiority (as Cecilia's instrument) to Orpheus' lyre sacred lays the chorus of praise as both the initial ordering power of harmony and its achieved form, instituted in the music of the spheres

And sung the great Creator's praise
        To all the blest above;
So, when the last and dreadful hour
This crumbling pageant° shall devour,
The Trumpet shall be heard on high,
The dead shall live, the living die,
And Music shall untune° the sky.
                1687

Alexander's Feast

    or, The Power of Music;°
    An Ode in Honour of St. Cecilia's Day

        I

'Twas at the royal feast for Persia won°
        By Philip's warlike son:
    Aloft in awful state
    The godlike hero sate
        On his imperial throne:
His valiant peers were placed around;
Their brows with roses and with myrtles° bound:
(So should desert in arms be crowned.)
    The lovely Thais,° by his side,
Sat like a blooming Eastern bride
In flower of youth and beauty's pride.
        Happy, happy, happy pair!
    None but the brave,
    None but the brave,
    None but the brave deserves the fair.

    CHORUS
    Happy, happy, happy pair!
    None but the brave,
    None but the brave,
    None but the brave deserves the fair.

10

crumbling pageant the cosmos; with probably a reference to the performance itself, as in the masque or in Prospero's remarks on "this insubstantial pageant" (Shakespeare, *The Tempest* IV.i.155); with the trumpeter of the next line placed literally above the stage as he represents the "last trump" (cf. "Killigrew" ode, l. 178) and with the players about to "untune" (slacken the strings of) their instruments
Music . . . untune the trumpet, but also the power of harmony now seen as transcending the created world
Alexander's Feast . . . Music This ode, written ten years later than the earlier "St. Cecilia" ode, devotes itself to the theme of *musica humana* announced in the subtitle and embodies it in a dramatic action rather than a series of instrumental solos. Insofar as Timotheus, the mythical court musician of Alexander the Great, had the power to conjure roles and myths as well as pure emotions, the ode becomes a celebration of poetry as well as of music. The original musical setting (now lost) was composed by Jeremiah Clarke, but the ode was reset by Handel in 1736.
Persia won Alexander, son of Philip of Macedon, celebrating the fall of Persepolis and the defeat of Darius III (331 B.C.)
roses . . . myrtles symbols of love and sensuality
Thais the Athenian courtesan

II

20   Timotheus, placed on high
    Amid the tuneful choir,
    With flying fingers touched the lyre:
The trembling notes ascend the sky,
            And heavenly joys inspire.
The song began from Jove,
Who left his blissful seats above,
(Such is the power of mighty love.)
A dragon's fiery form belied the god:
Sublime on radiant spires° he rode,

30   When he to fair Olympia° pressed;
    And while he sought her snowy breast:
Then, round her slender waist he curled,
And stamped an image of himself, a sovereign of the world.°
The listening crowd admire° the lofty sound;
'A present deity,' they shout around;
'A present deity,' the vaulted roofs rebound:
    With ravished ears
    The monarch hears,
    Assumes the god,

40   Affects to nod,
And seems to shake the spheres.°

CHORUS

With ravished ears
The monarch hears,
Assumes the god,
Affects to nod,
And seems to shake the spheres.

III

The praise of Bacchus° then the sweet musician sung,
    Of Bacchus ever fair and ever young:
    'The jolly god in triumph comes;

50   Sound the trumpets; beat the drums;
      Flushed with a purple grace
      He shows his honest° face:
Now give the hautboys° breath; he comes, he comes.
    Bacchus, ever fair and young,
      Drinking joys did first ordain;

radiant spires shining coils; cf. Milton, *Paradise Lost* IX. 496–503 for the Serpent's motion "erect / Amidst his circling spires"
Olympia Olympias, the mother of Alexander, who claimed that her son was born not of Philip but of a supernatural serpent, here represented as Jove in a typical amorous disguise (that of a dragon), providing grounds for a belief in Alexander's divine origin to which Alexander readily succumbs

world as was Jove of the gods
admire wonder at, are awed by
seems . . . spheres Alexander is overcome by the fantasy of his own divinity and acts up to the role, convinced that his own nod, like Jove's, "shakes heavens's axles" (*Aeneid*, Dryden trans., X.154).
Bacchus god of wine and revelry
honest glorious
hautboys oboes

Bacchus' blessings are a treasure,
Drinking is the soldier's pleasure:
　　Rich the treasure,
　　Sweet the pleasure,
50 　Sweet is pleasure after pain.'

　　CHORUS
Bacchus' blessings are a treasure,
Drinking is the soldier's pleasure:
*　　Rich the treasure,*
*　　Sweet the pleasure,*
*　Sweet is pleasure after pain.*

　　IV
Soothed with the sound, the king grew vain;
　Fought all his battles o'er again;
And thrice he routed all his foes; and thrice he slew the slain.
The master° saw the madness rise;
70 His glowing cheeks, his ardent eyes;
And, while he heaven and earth defied,
Changed his hand and checked his pride.
　　He chose a mournful Muse,
　　　Soft pity to infuse:
He sung Darius great and good,
　　By too severe a fate,
Fallen, fallen, fallen, fallen,
　　Fallen from his high estate,
　　　And weltering in his blood;°
80 Deserted, at his utmost need,
By those his former bounty fed;
On the bare earth exposed he lies,
With not a friend to close his eyes.
With downcast looks the joyless victor sate,
　　Revolving in his altered soul
　　　The various turns of chance below;
　And, now and then, a sigh he stole;
　　And tears began to flow.

　　CHORUS
Revolving in his altered soul
90 *　The various turns of chance below;*
And, now and then, a sigh he stole;
*　And tears began to flow.*

---

master Timotheus, as master of the master of
the world, turning "his hand" (l. 72) to another
tune in order to subdue Alexander's mad "pride"
to "soft pity" (l. 74)
blood attacked by his own followers

V

The mighty master smiled, to see
That love was in the next degree:
'Twas but° a kindred sound to move,
For pity melts the mind to love.
   Softly sweet, in Lydian° measures,
   Soon he soothed his soul to pleasures.
   'War,' he sung, 'is toil and trouble;
100   Honour but an empty bubble.
     Never ending, still beginning,
   Fighting still, and still destroying,
     If the world be worth thy winning,
   Think, O think it worth enjoying.
     Lovely Thais sits beside thee,
     Take the good the gods provide thee.'
The many rend the skies with loud applause;
So Love was crowned, but Music won the cause.°
   The prince, unable to conceal his pain,
110   Gazed on the fair
     Who caused his care,
   And sighed and looked, sighed and looked,
   Sighed and looked, and sighed again:
At length, with love and wine at once oppressed,
The vanquished victor sunk upon her breast.

CHORUS

The prince, unable to conceal his pain,
   Gazed on the fair
   Who caused his care,
   And sighed and looked, sighed and looked,
120   *Sighed and looked, and sighed again:*
At length, with love and wine at once oppressed,
The vanquished victor sunk upon her breast.

VI

Now strike the golden lyre again:
A louder yet, and yet a louder strain.
Break his bands of sleep asunder,
And rouse him, like a rattling peal of thunder.
     Hark, hark, the horrid° sound
      Has raised up his head:
      As awaked from the dead,
130   And amazed, he stares around.
'Revenge, revenge!' Timotheus cries,

'Twas but i.e. it required only
Lydian one of the "soft or drinking modes,"
according to Plato; cf. Milton, *L'Allegro*, ll.
136–44

Music . . . cause insisting upon the power of
music to control the imagination through the
passions
horrid rough, terrible

'See the Furies° arise!
See the snakes that they rear,
How they hiss in their hair,
And the sparkles that flash from their eyes!
Behold a ghastly band,
Each a torch in his hand!
Those are Grecian ghosts that in battle were slain,
   And unburied remain
40   Inglorious on the plain:
   Give the vengeance due
   To the valiant crew.
Behold how they toss their torches on high,
  How they point to the Persian abodes,
And glittering temples of their hostile gods!'
The princes applaud with a furious joy;
And the king seized a flambeau° with zeal to destroy;
   Thais led the way,
   To light him to his prey,
50 And, like another Helen, fired another Troy.°

   CHORUS
And the king seized a flambeau with zeal to destroy;
   Thais led the way,
   To light him to his prey,
And, like another Helen, fired another Troy.

   VII
   Thus, long ago,
  Ere heaving bellows learned to blow,
   While organs yet were mute;
  Timotheus, to his breathing flute,
   And sounding lyre,
50 Could swell the soul to rage or kindle soft desire.
  At last, divine Cecilia came,
  Inventress of the vocal frame;°
The sweet enthusiast,° from her sacred store,
  Enlarged the former narrow bounds,
  And added length° to solemn sounds,
With nature's mother wit and arts unknown before.
  Let old Timotheus yield the prize,
  Or both divide the crown;

Furies the Erinyes, the three female spirits with snaky hair who punished those guilty of unavenged crimes, here demanding vengeance for Alexander's dead soldiers
flambeau torch
another Troy As Helen's passion for Paris led the Greeks to burn Troy, so Thais' zeal leads them to burn the palace of Persepolis.
vocal frame organ
enthusiast here used of one genuinely inspired by God rather than one suffering from that delusion
length through the organ's power to sustain notes

He raised a mortal to the skies;°
170   She drew an angel down.°

GRAND CHORUS

At last, divine Cecilia came,
Inventress of the vocal frame;
The sweet enthusiast, from her sacred store,
Enlarged the former narrow bounds,
And added length to solemn sounds,
With nature's mother wit and arts unknown before.
Let old Timotheus yield the prize,
Or both divide the crown;
He raised a mortal to the skies;
180   *She drew an angel down.*
1697

Translations

Dryden's translations indicate the variety of his uses of the heroic couplet, and they are often splendid poetry in their own right. His translation of a portion of Lucretius' *De Rerum Natura* as well as the opening of Juvenal's Sixth Satire is given here. For other translations by Dryden, see the passage from Juvenal in the section The Urban Scene and the tale of Baucis and Philemon from Ovid's *Metamorphoses* in the section The Mock Form.

The translation from Lucretius is interesting as an example of Epicurean thought, so widely revived in the seventeenth century and particularly in Restoration England. Lucretius' great didactic poem seeks to free man from superstitious fear by presenting a view of life grounded in the theory of atoms, i.e. accounting for all nature by the chance combinations of atoms. The third book, from which this passage is taken, insists upon the mortality of the soul and tries to free man of the idea that death is an experience rather than its absence. Lucretius is one of the chief transmitters of a naturalistic view of the world and of man, one which repudiates a view of divine creation and of supernatural ends and exalts pleasure—not necessarily a gross or merely physical one—as the only true end of man. Epicurean thought like that of Lucretius is constantly contrasted by eighteenth-century writers with Stoic thought, which seems much closer to Christianity because of its belief in a rational natural order that in turn reflects man's reason, a reason most fully expressed in its conquest of passion and its intuitive recognition of duty to others.

Dryden explains in a preface that he put aside his "natural diffidence and skepticism for a while, to take up that dogmatic way" of Lucretius; but he warns against Lucretius' doctrines and defends the immortality of the soul. More interesting is his discussion of the style and tone of Lucretius in the passage that follows.

The section from Juvenal's Sixth Satire is a wonderfully urbane and amused account of a primitivistic vision.

raised . . . skies caused Alexander to assume divine stature and rage, however delusively (thus music as a natural power)
drew . . . down as in the "St. Cecilia" ode, ll.

53–54, brought the full power of harmony, in the form of a guardian angel, to earth (thus music as a heavenly power)

[On Lucretius]

. . . If I am not mistaken, the distinguishing character of Lucretius (I mean of his soul and genius) is a certain kind of noble pride, and positive assertion of his opinions. He is everywhere confident of his own reason, and assuming an absolute command not only over his vulgar reader, but even his patron Memmius. For he is always bidding him attend, as if he had the rod over him; and using a magisterial authority, while he instructs him. From his time to ours, I know none so like him, as our poet and philosopher of Malmesbury. This is that perpetual dictatorship which is exercised by Lucretius; who though often in the wrong, yet seems to deal *bona fide* with his reader, and tells him nothing but what he thinks; in which plain sincerity, I believe he differs from our Hobbes, who could not but be convinced, or at least doubt of some eternal truths which he has opposed. But for Lucretius, he seems to disdain all manner of replies, and is so confident of his cause that he is beforehand with his antagonists; urging for them whatever he imagined they could say, and leaving them as he supposes, without an objection for the future. All this too, with so much scorn and indignation, as if he were assured of the triumph before he entered into the lists. From this sublime and daring genius of his, it must of necessity come to pass that his thoughts must be masculine, full of argumentation, and that sufficiently warm. From the same fiery temper proceeds the loftiness of his expressions, and the perpetual torrent of his verse, where the barrenness of his subject does not too much constrain the quickness of his fancy. For there is no doubt to be made, but that he could have been everywhere as poetical, as he is in his descriptions, and in the moral part of his philosophy, if he had not aimed more to instruct in his System of Nature, than to delight. But he was bent upon making Memmius a materialist, and teaching him to defy an invisible power. In short, he was so much an atheist that he forgot sometimes to be a poet. . . . [From Preface to *Sylvae*, 1685]

Lucretius: De Rerum Natura

From *The Latter Part of the Third Book*
Against the Fear of Death

What has this bugbear death to frighten man,
If souls can die, as well as bodies can?
For, as before our birth we felt no pain,
When Punic arms infested land and main,°
When heaven and earth were in confusion hurled,
For the debated empire of the world,
Which awed with dreadful expectation lay,
Sure to be slaves, uncertain who should sway:
So, when our mortal frame shall be disjoined,
10   The lifeless lump uncoupled from the mind,
From sense of grief and pain we shall be free;

Punic arms . . . main The three Punic wars   241 B.C., 218–201 B.C., and 149–146 B.C.
between Rome and Carthage took place in 264–   Lucretius lived from c. 94 to 55 B.C.

We shall not feel, because we shall not *be*.
Though earth in seas, and seas in heaven were lost,
We should not move, we only should be tossed.
Nay, even suppose when we have suffered fate,
The soul could feel in her divided state,
What's that to us? for we are only we
While souls and bodies in one frame agree.
Nay, though our atoms should revolve by chance,
20   And matter leap into the former dance;
Though time our life and motion could restore,
And make our bodies what they were before,
What gain to us would all this bustle bring?
The new-made man would be another thing.
When once an interrupting pause is made,
That individual being is decayed.
We, who are dead and gone, shall bear no part
In all the pleasures, nor shall feel the smart
Which to that other mortal shall accrue,
30   Whom of our matter time shall mould anew.

. . .

And therefore if a man bemoan his lot,
50   That after death his mouldering limbs shall rot,
Or flames or jaws of beasts devour his mass,
Know, he's an unsincere, unthinking ass.
A secret sting remains within his mind;
The fool is to his own cast offals° kind.
He boasts no sense can after death remain,
Yet makes himself a part of life again,
As if some other He could feel the pain.
If, while he live, this thought molest his head,
What wolf or vulture shall devour me dead?
60   He wastes his days in idle grief, nor can
Distinguish 'twixt the body and the man;
But thinks himself can still himself survive;
And, what when dead he feels not, feels alive.
Then he repines that he was born to die,
Nor knows in death there is no other He,
No living He remains his grief to vent,
And o'er his senseless carcass to lament.
If after death 'tis painful to be torn
By birds and beasts, then why not so to burn;
70   Or, drenched in floods of honey, to be soaked;
Embalmed, to be at once preserved and choked;
Or on an airy mountain's top to lie,
Exposed to cold and heaven's inclemency;
Or crowded in a tomb to be oppressed

offals carrion, waste

With monumental marble on thy breast?
  But to be snatched from all thy household joys,
From thy chaste wife, and thy dear prattling boys,
Whose little arms about thy legs are cast,
And climbing for a kiss prevent their mother's haste,
Inspiring secret pleasure through thy breast—
All these shall be no more: thy friends oppressed
Thy care and courage now no more shall free;
'Ah wretch!' thou criest, 'ah! miserable me!
One woeful day sweeps children, friends, and wife,
And all the brittle blessings of my life!'
Add one thing more, and all thou sayest is true;
Thy want and wish of them is vanished too:
Which, well considered, were a quick relief
To all thy vain imaginary grief.
For thou shalt sleep and never wake again,
And quitting life, shalt quit thy living pain.
But we, thy friends, shall all those sorrows find,
Which in forgetful death thou leavest behind;
No time shall dry our tears, nor drive thee from our mind.
The worst that can befall thee, measured right,
Is a sound slumber, and a long good-night.

                    .   .   .

What horror seest thou in that quiet state?
What bugbear dreams to fright thee after fate?
No ghost, no goblins, that still passage keep;
But all is there serene, in that eternal sleep.
For all the dismal tales that poets tell
Are verified on earth, and not in hell.
No Tantalus° looks up with fearful eye,
Or dreads the impending rock to crush him from on high;
But fear of chance on earth disturbs our easy hours,
Or vain imagined wrath of vain imagined powers.
No Tityus° torn by vultures lies in hell;
Nor could the lobes of his rank liver swell
To that prodigious mass for their eternal meal:
Not though his monstrous bulk had covered o'er
Nine spreading acres, or nine thousand more;
Not though the globe of earth had been the giant's floor:
Nor in eternal torments could he lie,
Nor could his corpse sufficient food supply.
But he's the Tityus, who by love oppressed,
Or tyrant passion preying on his breast,

Tantalus Punished for stealing the food of the
gods, he is usually pictured as immersed in
water up to his chin with fruit hanging over his
head, but both water and fruit receding as he
tries to assuage his thirst and hunger; Lucretius
follows Pindar in seeing his punishment as a
rock poised threateningly over his head but
never falling.
Tityus punished for assaulting Leto by having
two vultures forever tearing at his liver; as a
Titan he was supposed to cover nine acres of
ground

And ever-anxious thoughts, is robbed of rest.
200 The Sisyphus° is he, whom noise and strife
Seduce from all the soft retreats of life,
To vex the government, disturb the laws:
Drunk with the fumes of popular applause,
He courts the giddy crowd to make him great,°
And sweats and toils in vain to mount the sovereign seat.
For still to aim at power, and still to fail,
Ever to strive, and never to prevail,
What is it, but, in reason's true account,
To heave the stone against the rising mount?
210 Which urged, and laboured, and forced up with pain,
Recoils, and rolls impetuous down, and smokes along° the plain.
Then still to treat thy ever-craving mind
With every blessing and of every kind,
Yet never fill thy ravening appetite;
Though years and seasons vary thy delight,
Yet nothing to be seen of all the store,
But still the wolf within thee barks for more;
This is the fable's moral, which they tell
Of fifty foolish virgins° damned in hell
220 To leaky vessels, which the liquor spill;
To vessels of their sex, which none could ever fill.
As for the Dog,° the Furies, and their snakes,
The gloomy caverns, and the burning lakes,
And all the vain infernal trumpery,
They neither are, nor were, nor e'er can be.
But here on earth the guilty have in view
The mighty pains to mighty mischiefs due;
Racks, prisons, poisons, the Tarpeian rock,°
Stripes, hangmen, pitch, and suffocating smoke;
230 And last, and most, if these were cast behind,
The avenging horror of a conscious mind,
Whose deadly fear anticipates the blow,
And sees no end of punishment and woe;
But looks for more, at the last gasp of breath:
This makes a hell on earth, and life a death.

. . .

Why are we then so fond of mortal life,
Beset with dangers, and maintained with strife?
A life which all our care can never save;
One fate attends us, and one common grave.

Sisyphus punished by having always to roll a great stone uphill, only to have it roll down again before it reaches the top
He courts . . . great Dryden alters the original in ways that recall his account of Absalom.
smokes along drives at a great speed
fifty foolish virgins The Danaides, the daughters of Danaus, who at his order killed their hus-
bands on their wedding night; they were punished by having to draw water eternally in leaky vessels (a phrase also used of women who betray confidence, as the next lines indicate).
Dog Cerberus, the three-headed guardian of the gates of the underworld
Tarpeian rock the cliff from which murderers and traitors were thrown in Rome

Besides, we tread but a perpetual round;
We ne'er strike out, but beat the former ground,
And the same mawkish joys in the same track are found.
For still we think an absent blessing best,
Which cloys, and is no blessing when possessed;
310   A new arising wish expels it from the breast.
The feverish thirst of life increases still;
We call for more and more, and never have our fill,
Yet know not what tomorrow we shall try,
What dregs of life in the last draught may lie:
Nor, by the longest life we can attain,
One moment from the length of death we gain;
For all behind belongs to his eternal reign.
When once the Fates have cut the mortal thread,
The man as much to all intents is dead,
320   Who dies today, and will as long be so,
As he who died a thousand years ago.

                                1685

Juvenal

From *The Sixth Satire*°

In Saturn's reign,° at Nature's early birth,
There was that thing called chastity on earth;
When in a narrow cave, their common shade,°
The sheep, the shepherds, and their gods were laid:
When reeds, and leaves, and hides of beasts were spread
By mountain huswifes for their homely bed,
And mossy pillows raised, for the rude husband's head.
Unlike the niceness of our modern dames,
(Affected nymphs with new affected names,)
10   The Cynthias° and the Lesbias° of our years,
Who for a sparrow's death dissolve in tears;
Those first unpolished matrons, big and bold,
Gave suck to infants of gigantic mould;
Rough as their savage lords who ranged the wood,
And fat with acorns belched their windy food.
For when the world was buxom,° fresh, and young,

Juvenal . . . Sixth Satire This is the longest of
Juvenal's sixteen satires; written against immoral and affected women, it forms part of the
high rhetorical denunciation of corrupt Rome
that Dryden came so much to admire (see
below, Critical Prose). Juvenal was born c. 50
A.D. and wrote as late as 127; his attacks upon
the empire of Domitian constantly evoke an
earlier, more austere virtue, but in this instance
his golden age is ironically rendered as a boorish
and comic one. Dryden himself translated five of
Juvenal's satires, and Dr. Johnson was later to
write imitations of the third and tenth, the
former as *London* and the latter as *The Vanity
of Human Wishes*.
Saturn's reign the golden age of innocence
shade shelter
Cynthias Cynthia was celebrated by Propertius
(c. 54–c. 2 B.C.) in his account of their difficult
love.
Lesbias Lesbia was the subject of many poems
by Catullus (c. 84–c. 54 B.C.), including one on
the death of her sparrow.
buxom wanton, jolly

Her sons were undebauched and therefore strong;
And whether born in kindly° beds of earth,
Or struggling from the teeming oaks to birth,
20   Or from what other atoms they begun,
No sires they had, or, if a sire, the sun.

1693

Critical Prose

Dryden's criticism was unsystematic and for the most part occasional, arising from his wide-ranging undertakings as playwright, poet, and translator. There are often allusions to the systems of classical and Renaissance critics, and Dryden shows competence in Scholastic thought as well; but he is temperamentally opposed to system for himself, preferring what he calls a skeptical method. By this he does not mean a radical skepticism but rather a dialectical openness, a balancing of contraries and opposites, that saves him from rigorous folly and produces instead generosity and readiness to risk inconsistency.

The dialectical cast of Dryden's mind is nowhere more evident than here; if sometimes at the cost of firm argument, all the more revealing of the cross-currents of his age. Thus we can see him moving back and forth between the claims of rational order and of bold fancy, between justness and liveliness, between strictness and inclusiveness of form. This becomes most apparent in those great dialectical contrasts between representative authors—a device that was to survive as late as Dr. Johnson. In his discussion of Horace and Juvenal, we can see a gradual movement toward preference for the gravity of Juvenal, and the final paragraph on Juvenal (given below) is a fine statement of what satire was to become again in the age of Walpole.

The tributes to John Oldham (see above) and to William Congreve (see the Congreve section) are an important part of Dryden's criticism, as is, of course, *Mac Flecknoe*. In the first two poems, to younger men, there is a warm tribute to achievements Dryden is willing to measure favorably against his own; more than that, we can see his frank acknowledgment of losses inextricable from the gains which he promoted and in which he genuinely believed. Dryden always distinguishes nicely between the "glowing" and the "glaring," between the true vigor and the false, and *Mac Flecknoe* is a poem based upon such discriminations, a splendid anatomizing of the meretricious and maudlin.

The Poetic Process
[Wit and Fancy]

. . . The composition of all poems is or ought to be of wit, and wit in the poet, or wit writing (if you will give me leave to use a school distinction[1]), is no other than the faculty of imagination in the writer, which, like a nimble spaniel, beats over and ranges through the field of memory, till it springs the quarry it hunted after; or, without metaphor, which searches over all the memory for the species or ideas of those things which it designs to represent.

kindly congenial, kindred

1. That is, a distinction such as the Scholastics might make, on the analogy of *natura naturans* and *natura naturata*, the first a process and the second a product.

Wit written, is that which is well defined the happy result of thought, or product of that imagination. But to proceed from wit in the general notion of it to the proper wit of an heroic or historical poem, I judge it chiefly to consist in the delightful imaging of persons, actions, passions, or things. 'Tis not the jerk or sting of an epigram, nor the seeming contradiction of a poor antithesis (the delight of an ill-judging audience in a play of rhyme), nor the jingle of a more poor paranomasia:[2] neither is it so much the morality of a grave sentence,[3] affected by Lucan, but more sparingly used by Virgil; but it is some lively and apt description, dressed in such colours[4] of speech, that it sets before your eyes the absent object as perfectly and more delightfully than nature. So then, the first happiness of the poet's imagination is properly invention, or finding of the thought; the second is fancy, or the variation, driving[5] or moulding of that thought, as the judgement represents it proper to the subject; the third is elocution, or the art of clothing and adorning that thought so found and varied, in apt, significant, and sounding words: the quickness of the imagination is seen in the invention, the fertility in the fancy, and the accuracy in the expression. For the two first of these Ovid is famous amongst the poets, for the latter Virgil. Ovid images more often the movements and affections of the mind, either combating between two contrary passions, or extremely discomposed by one: his words therefore are the least part of his care, for he pictures nature in disorder, with which the study and choice of words is inconsistent. This is the proper wit of dialogue or discourse, and, consequently, of the drama, where all that is said is to be supposed the effect of sudden thought; which, though it excludes not the quickness of wit in repartees, yet admits not a too curious election of words, too frequent allusions, or use of tropes, or, in fine, anything that shows remoteness of thought, or labour in the writer. On the other side, Virgil speaks not so often to us in the person of another, like Ovid, but in his own; he relates almost all things as from himself, and thereby gains more liberty than the other to express his thoughts with all the graces of elocution, to write more figuratively, and to confess as well the labour as the force of his imagination. . . . [From "An Account of the Ensuing Poem . . .". Prefixed to *Annus Mirabilis*, 1666]

This worthless present was designed [for] you long before it was a play; when it was only a confused mass of thoughts, tumbling over one another in the dark; when the fancy was yet in its first work, moving the sleeping images of things towards the light, there to be distinguished, and then either chosen or rejected by the judgement: it was yours, my Lord, before I could call it mine. And, I confess, in that first tumult of my thoughts there appeared a disorderly kind of beauty in some of them, which gave me hope something worthy my Lord of Orrery might be drawn from them. . . . [From "To the Right Honorable Roger, Earl of Orrery." Prefixed to *The Rival Ladies*, 1664]

2. A pun or similar word play.
3. Moral axiom or maxim.
4. Figures.
5. The usual reading is "deriving," but George Watson points out that this has no authority in the editions Dryden supervised and is an unnecessary variant on "driving," which has the sense of carrying further or elaborating.

. . . Horace himself was cautious [6] to obtrude a new word on his readers, and makes custom and common use the best measure of receiving it into our writings. . . . The not observing this rule is that which the world has blamed in our satirist Cleveland;[7] to express a thing hard and unnaturally, is his new way of elocution. 'Tis true, no poet but may sometimes use a catachresis.[8]. . . But to do this always, and never be able to write a line without it, though it may be admired by some few pedants, will not pass upon those who know that wit is best conveyed to us in the most easy language and is most to be admired when a great thought comes dressed in words so commonly received that it is understood by the meanest apprehensions, as the best meat is the most easily digested: but we cannot read a verse of Cleveland's without making a face at it, as if every word were a pill to swallow. He gives us many times a hard nut to break our teeth, without a kernel for our pains.[9] So that there is this difference between his satires and Doctor Donne's, that the one gives us deep thoughts in common language, though rough cadence; the other gives us common thoughts in abstruse words: 'tis true, in some places his wit is independent of his words, as in that of the *Rebel Scot:*

> Had Cain been Scot God would have changed his doom;
> Not forced him wander, but confined him home.[10]

Si sic omnia dixisset! [11] This is wit in all languages: 'tis like mercury, never to be lost or killed;[12] and so that other:

> For beauty like white-powder makes no noise,
> And yet the silent hypocrite destroys.[13]

You see the last line is highly metaphorical, but it is so soft and gentle that it does not shock us as we read it. [From *Of Dramatic Poesy: An Essay,* 1668]

. . . Imagination in a man, or reasonable creature, is supposed to participate of reason, and when that governs, as it does in the belief of fiction, reason is not destroyed, but misled, or blinded: that can prescribe to the reason, during the time of the representation, somewhat like a weak belief of what it sees and hears; and reason suffers itself to be so hoodwinked, that it may better enjoy the pleasures of the fiction: but it is never so wholly made a captive as to be drawn headlong into a persuasion of those things which are most remote from

---

6. Slow or reluctant; cf. *Ars Poetica,* ll. 70–72: "Many terms will be revived which have fallen out of use, and many will fall in turn that now are current, if usage wills so, in whose power lies the judgment, the law, and the rule of speech."

7. John Cleveland (1613–58), the late Metaphysical poet and wit.

8. "The abuse of a trope, when the words are too far wrested from their native signification" (Johnson, *Dictionary*); cf. also Johnson's discussion of the Metaphysical poets.

9. In *A Tale of a Tub* Swift takes this further; he writes of wisdom as a nut "which, unless you choose with judgment, may cost you a tooth and pay you with nothing but a worm"; the figure of the rind and the kernel is a traditional means of exploring the relation of words to meaning.

10. *The Rebel Scot* (1644), ll. 63–64.

11. "If only he had always spoken this way—" (Juvenal, *Satires* X.123–24).

12. Stabilized, deprived of motion.

13. *Rupertismus,* ll. 39–40.

probability: 'tis in that case a free-born subject, not a slave; it will contribute willingly its assent, as far as it sees convenient, but will not be forced. . . . Fancy and reason go hand in hand; the first cannot leave the last behind; and though fancy, when it sees the wide gulf, would venture over, as the nimbler; yet it is withheld by reason, which will refuse to take the leap, when the distance over it appears too large. . . . [From *A Defense of an Essay of Dramatic Poesy*, 1668]

. . . Strong and glowing colours are the just resemblances [14] of bold metaphors, but both must be judiciously applied; for there is a difference betwixt daring and foolhardiness. Lucan and Statius [15] often ventured them too far; our Virgil never.

. . . 'Tis said of him that he read the second, fourth, and sixth books of his *Æneids* to Augustus Cæsar. In the sixth . . . the poet, speaking of Misenus the trumpeter, says:

> quo non præstantior alter
> ære ciere viros,

and broke off in the hemistich, or midst of the verse; but in the very reading, seized as it were with a divine fury, he made up the latter part of the hemistich with these following words:

> Martemque accendere cantu.[16]

How warm, nay, how glowing a colouring is this! In the beginning of his verse, the word *æs*, or brass, was taken for a trumpet, because the instrument was made of that metal, which of itself was fine; but in the latter end, which was made *ex tempore*, you see three metaphors, *Martemque . . . accendere . . . cantu*. Good Heavens! how the plain sense is raised by the beauty of the words! But this was happiness; the former might be only judgement: this was the *curiosa felicitas* [17] which Petronius attributes to Horace. . . . These hits of words a true poet often finds, as I may say, without seeking; but he knows their value when he finds them, and is infinitely pleased. A bad poet may sometimes light on them, but he discerns not a diamond from a Bristol-stone;[18] and would have been of the cock's mind in Aesop; a grain of barley would have pleased him better than the jewel.

. . . As the words, etc., are evidently shown to be the clothing of the thought in the same sense as colours are the clothing of the design, so the painter and the poet ought to judge exactly when the colouring and expressions are perfect

---

14. Counterparts; in this *Parallel,* which accompanied his translation of Charles Alphonse du Fresnoy's Latin poem *De arte graphica* (1688), Dryden pursues analogies between the "sister arts."

15. Lucan (39–65 A.D.), author of the epic *Bellum Civile,* better known as the *Pharsalia;* Statius (45–96 A.D.), best known for the epic *Thebaid.*

16. *Aeneid* VI.164–65: "Than whom none is superior in stirring men with brass [the trumpet], and in kindling Mars [war] with his song [playing]."

17. That is, cultivated felicity or planned good luck (*Satyricon,* l. 118); cf. Pope's play on *curiosa felicitas* in the *Essay on Criticism,* l. 142: "For there's a happiness as well as care."

18. Rock-crystal.

and then to think their work is truly finished. Apelles said of Protogenes [19] that he knew not when to give over. A work may be over-wrought as well as under-wrought: too much labour often takes away the spirit by adding to the polishing, so that there remains nothing but a dull correctness, a piece without any considerable faults, but with few beauties; for when the spirits are drawn off, there is nothing but a *caput mortuum*.[20] Statius never thought an expression could be bold enough; and if a bolder could be found, he rejected the first. Virgil had judgment enough to know daring was necessary; but he knew the difference betwixt a glowing colour and a glaring. . . . [From *A Parallel Betwixt Poetry and Painting*, 1695]

Critical Issues
[Subplots and Complex Structure]

And this leads me to wonder why Lisideius and many others should cry up the barrenness of the French plots above the variety and copiousness of the English. Their plots are single, they carry on one design which is pushed forward by all the actors, every scene in the play contributing and moving towards it. Our plays besides the main design, have under-plots or by-concernments, of less considerable persons and intrigues, which are carried on with the motion of the main plot: as they say the orb of the fixed stars and those of the planets, though they have motions of their own, are whirled about by the motion of the *primum mobile*, in which they are contained:[21] that similitude expresses much of the English stage, for if contrary motions may be found in nature to agree; if a planet can go east and west at the same time, one way by virtue of his own motion, the other by the force of the first mover, it will not be difficult to imagine how the under-plot, which is only different, not contrary to the great design, may naturally be conducted along with it. [From *Of Dramatic Poesy: An Essay*, 1668]

[Comedy and Farce]

. . . Comedy consists, though of low persons, yet of natural actions and characters; I mean such humours, adventures, and designs as are to be found and met with in the world. Farce, on the other side, consists of forced humours and unnatural events. Comedy presents us with the imperfections of human nature. Farce entertains us with what is monstrous and chimerical: the one causes laughter in those who can judge of men and manners, by the lively representation of their folly or corruption; the other produces the same effect in those who can judge of neither, and that only by its extravagances. The first works on the judgement and fancy; the latter on the fancy only: there is more of satisfaction in the former kind of laughter, and in the latter more of scorn. But how it happens that an impossible adventure should cause our mirth, I cannot so easily imagine. Something there may be in the oddness of it, because on the stage it is the common effect of things unexpected to surprise us into a

---

19. Apelles (4th century B.C.) was court painter to Philip and Alexander of Macedon; Protogenes was a contemporary of Apelles.
20. Literally, a death's head; hence the worthless residue of a distillation.
21. Cf. the opening lines of Dryden's "Anne Killigrew" ode.

delight: and that is to be ascribed to the strange appetite, as I may call it, of the fancy; which, like that of a longing woman,[22] often runs out into the most extravagant desires; and is better satisfied sometimes with loam, or with the rinds of trees, than with the wholesome nourishments of life. In short, there is the same difference betwixt farce and comedy as betwixt an empiric and a true physician: both of them may attain their ends; but what the one performs by hazard, the other does by skill. And as the artist is often unsuccessful, while the mountebank succeeds; so farces more commonly take the people than comedies. For to write unnatural things is the most probable way of pleasing them, who understand not nature. And a true poet often misses of applause because he cannot debase himself to write so ill as to please his audience. . . . [From Preface to *An Evening's Love,* 1671]

. . . There is yet a lower sort of poetry and painting, which is out of nature; for a farce is that in poetry which grotesque is in a picture. The persons and action of a farce are all unnatural, and the manners false, that is, inconsisting with the characters of mankind. Grotesque painting is the just resemblance of this; and Horace begins his *Art of Poetry* by describing such a figure, with a man's head, a horse's neck, the wings of a bird, and a fish's tail; parts of different species jumbled together, according to the mad imagination of the dauber; and the end of all this, as he tells you afterward, to cause laughter: a very monster in a Bartholomew Fair, for the mob to gape at for their twopence. Laughter is indeed the propriety [23] of a man, but just enough to distinguish him from his elder brother with four legs. 'Tis a kind of bastard-pleasure too, taken in at the eyes of the vulgar gazers, and at the ears of the beastly audience. Church-painters use it to divert the honest countryman at public prayers, and keep his eyes open at a heavy sermon. And farce-scribblers make use of the same noble invention to entertain citizens, country-gentlemen, and Covent Garden fops. If they are merry, all goes well on the poet's side. The better sort go thither too, but in despair of sense and the just images of nature, which are the adequate pleasures of the mind. But the author can give the stage no better than what was given him by nature; and the actors must represent such things as they are capable to perform, and by which both they and the scribbler may get their living. After all, 'tis a good thing to laugh at any rate, and if a straw can tickle a man, 'tis an instrument of happiness. Beasts can weep when they suffer, but they cannot laugh. . . . [From *A Parallel Betwixt Poetry and Painting,* 1695]

[Horace and Juvenal]
. . . Let the chastisements of Juvenal be never so necessary for his new kind of satire; let him declaim as wittily and sharply as he pleases: yet still the nicest and most delicate touches of satire consist in fine raillery. . . . How easy is it to call rogue and villain, and that wittily! But how hard to make a man appear a fool, a blockhead, or a knave, without using any of those opprobrious terms! To spare the grossness of the names, and to do the thing

22. That is, in her pregnancy.
23. Special property.

yet more severely, is to draw a full face, and to make the nose and cheeks stand out, and yet not to employ any depth of shadowing. This is the mystery of that noble trade, which yet no master can teach to his apprentice: he may give the rules, but the scholar is never the nearer in his practice. Neither is it true that this fineness of raillery is offensive. A witty man is tickled while he is hurt in this manner, and a fool feels it not. The occasion of an offence may possibly be given, but he cannot take it. If it be granted that in effect this way does more mischief; that a man is secretly wounded, and though he be not sensible himself, yet the malicious world will find it for him: yet there is still a vast difference betwixt the slovenly butchering of a man, and the fineness of a stroke that separates the head from the body, and leaves it standing in its place. . . .

. . . It must be granted by the favourers of Juvenal, that Horace is the more copious and profitable in his instructions of human life. But in my particular opinion, which I set not up for a standard to better judgements, Juvenal is the more delightful author. I am profited by both, I am pleased with both; but I owe more to Horace for my instruction, and more to Juvenal, for my pleasure. . . .

. . . I must confess, that the delight which Horace gives me is but languishing. Be pleased still to understand that I speak of my own taste only. He may ravish other men, but I am too stupid and insensible to be tickled. Where he barely grins himself, and, as Scaliger says, only shows his white teeth, he cannot provoke me to any laughter. His urbanity, that is, his good manners, are to be commended; but his wit is faint, and his salt,[24] if I may dare to say so, almost insipid. Juvenal is of a more vigorous and masculine wit; he gives me as much pleasure as I can bear. . . . Add to this, that his thoughts are as just as those of Horace, and much more elevated. His expressions are sonorous and more noble; his verse more numerous;[25] and his words are suitable to his thoughts, sublime and lofty. All these contribute to the pleasure of the reader, and the greater the soul of him who reads, his transports are the greater. Horace is always on the amble, Juvenal on the gallop, but his way is perpetually on carpet ground.[26] He goes with more impetuosity than Horace, but as securely; and the swiftness adds a more lively agitation to the spirits. . . .

The meat of Horace is more nourishing; but the cookery of Juvenal more exquisite; so that, granting Horace to be the more general philosopher, we cannot deny that Juvenal was the greater poet, I mean in satire. His thoughts are sharper, his indignation against vice is more vehement; his spirit has more of the commonwealth genius; he treats tyranny, and all the vices attending it, as they deserve, with the utmost rigour; and consequently, a noble soul is better pleased with a zealous vindicator of Roman liberty than with a temporizing poet, a well mannered court slave, and a man who is often afraid of laughing in the right place, who is ever decent because he is naturally servile. After all, Horace had the disadvantage of the times in which he lived; they were better for the man, but worse for the satirist. 'Tis generally said that those

24. Pungency.
25. Harmonious.
26. Even or smooth, as on soft turf.

enormous vices, which were practised under the reign of Domitian, were unknown in the time of Augustus Caesar, that therefore Juvenal had a larger field than Horace. Little follies were out of doors, when oppression was to be scourged instead of avarice. It was no longer time to turn into ridicule the false opinions of philosophers, when the Roman liberty was to be asserted. . . . [From *A Discourse Concerning the Original and Progress of Satire*, 1693]

Critical Judgments
[Shakespeare and Jonson]

To begin with Shakespeare; he was the man who of all modern, and perhaps ancient poets, had the largest and most comprehensive soul. All the images of nature were still present to him, and he drew them not laboriously, but luckily: when he describes anything, you more than see it, you feel it too. Those who accuse him to have wanted learning, give him the greater commendation: he was naturally learned; he needed not the spectacles of books to read nature; he looked inwards, and found her there. I cannot say he is everywhere alike; were he so, I should do him injury to compare him with the greatest of mankind. He is many times flat, insipid; his comic wit degenerating into clenches, his serious swelling into bombast. But he is always great when some great occasion is presented to him: no man can say he ever had a fit subject for his wit and did not then raise himself as high above the rest of poets,

Quantum lenta solent inter viburna cupressi.[27]

The consideration of this made Mr. Hales of Eton [28] say that there was no subject of which any poet ever writ, but he would produce it much better done in Shakespeare; and however others are now generally preferred before him, yet the age wherein he lived, which had contemporaries with him, Fletcher and Jonson, never equalled them to him in their esteem. And in the last king's Court,[29] when Ben's reputation was at highest, Sir John Suckling, and with him the greater part of the courtiers, set our Shakespeare far above him.

. . .

As for Jonson, to whose character I am now arrived, if we look upon him while he was himself (for his last plays were but his dotages), I think him the most learned and judicious writer which any theatre ever had. He was a most severe judge of himself as well as others. One cannot say he wanted wit, but rather that he was frugal of it. In his works you find little to retrench or alter. Wit and language, and humour also in some measure we had before him; but something of art was wanting to the drama till he came. He managed his strength to more advantage than any who preceded him. You seldom find him making love in any of his scenes, or endeavouring to move the passions; his genius was too sullen and saturnine to do it gracefully, especially when he knew he came after those who had performed both to such an height. Humour was his proper sphere, and in that he delighted most to represent mechanic

27. Virgil, *Eclogues* I.25: "as cypresses often do among bending osiers."
28. John Hales (1584–1656), a fellow of Eton College and a master of prose disputation; as in his *Golden Remains* (1659).
29. During the reign of Charles I (1625–49).

people. He was deeply conversant in the Ancients, both Greek and Latin, and he borrowed boldly from them. There is scarce a poet or historian among the Roman authors of those times whom he has not translated in *Sejanus* and *Catiline*. But he has done his robberies so openly, that one may see he fears not to be taxed by any law. He invades authors like a monarch, and what would be theft in other poets, is only victory in him. With the spoils of these writers he so represents old Rome to us, in its rites, ceremonies, and customs, that if one of their poets had written either of his tragedies, we had seen less of it than in him. If there was any fault in his language, 'twas that he weaved it too closely and laboriously, in his comedies especially: perhaps too, he did a little too much Romanize our tongue, leaving the words which he translated almost as much Latin as he found them: wherein though he learnedly followed their language, he did not enough comply with the idiom of ours. If I would compare him with Shakespeare, I must acknowledge him the more correct poet, but Shakespeare the greater wit. Shakespeare was the Homer, or father of our dramatic poets; Jonson was the Virgil, the pattern of elaborate writing. I admire him, but I love Shakespeare. . . . [From *Of Dramatic Poesy: An Essay*, 1668]

[Chaucer]

In the first place, as he is the father of English poetry, so I hold him in the same degree of veneration as the Grecians held Homer, or the Romans Virgil. He is a perpetual fountain of good sense; learned in all sciences; and therefore speaks properly on all subjects. As he knew what to say, so he knows also when to leave off; a continence which is practised by few writers, and scarcely by any of the Ancients, excepting Virgil and Horace. . . .

Chaucer followed nature everywhere; but was never so bold [as] to go beyond her. And there is a great difference of being *poeta* and *nimis poeta*,[30] if we may believe Catullus, as much as betwixt a modest behaviour and affectation. The verse of Chaucer, I confess, is not harmonious to us; but 'tis like the eloquence of one whom Tacitus[31] commends, it was *auribus istius temporis accommodata;* they who lived with him, and some time after him, thought it musical; and it continues so even in our judgement, if compared with the numbers of Lydgate and Gower his contemporaries. There is the rude sweetness of a Scotch tune in it, which is natural and pleasing, though not perfect. . . .

. . . He must have been a man of a most wonderful comprehensive nature, because, as it has been truly observed of him, he has taken into the compass of his *Canterbury Tales* the various manners and humours (as we now call them) of the whole English nation in his age. Not a single character has escaped him. All his pilgrims are severally distinguished from each other; and not only in their inclinations, but in their very physiognomies and persons. Baptista Porta[32] could not have described their natures better than by the marks which the poet gives them. The matter and manner of their tales and

30. Being a poet or being too much a poet; not from Catullus but from Martial, *Epigrams* III.xliv.4.
31. *De Oratoribus* XXI: "suited to the ears of another age."
32. Giambattista della Porta (1540–1615), Neapolitan physician and student of physiognomy, particularly of the influence of emotions on the face.

of their telling are so suited to their different educations, humours, and callings, that each of them would be improper in any other mouth. Even the grave and serious characters are distinguished by their several sorts of gravity. Their discourses are such as belong to their age, their calling, and their breeding; such as are becoming of them, and of them only. Some of his persons are vicious, and some virtuous; some are unlearned, or (as Chaucer calls them) lewd, and some are learned. Even the ribaldry of the low characters is different. The Reeve, the Miller, and the Cook, are several men, and distinguished from each other, as much as the mincing Lady Prioress and the broad-speaking gap-toothed Wife of Bath. But enough of this; there is such a variety of game springing up before me that I am distracted in my choice and know not which to follow. 'Tis sufficient to say according to the proverb that here is God's plenty. . . . [From Preface to *Fables, Ancient and Modern*, 1700]

WILLIAM CONGREVE
1670–1729

Congreve was born in Yorkshire but grew up in Ireland, where his father served as an army officer under the Duke of Ormonde. He was a fellow student of Swift both in school at Kilkenny and at Trinity College, Dublin, and one of Swift's earliest poems is an ode to Congreve. By 1691 Congreve had moved to London and become one of those young literary templars or law students who are familiar figures in the satire and comedy of the age; he frequented Will's coffeehouse and revised a short novel, *Incognita* (1692), for publication, then turned to songs and odes and to translations from Homer that won Dryden's praise. It was Dryden who sponsored his first comedy, *The Old Bachelor* (1693); feeling that it needed "only the fashionable cut of the town," Dryden tailored it to the proper length and helped it achieve a splendid success. In the course of its production Congreve fell in love with the beautiful young actress Anne Bracegirdle. "Would she could make of me a saint, / Or I of her a sinner," he wrote; but there is no evidence that either wish was fully granted. At any rate, he was to create the part of Millamant for her a few years later. By the time his third comedy, *Love for Love* (1695), had succeeded, Congreve was given a political sinecure through Whig patronage and responded with the usual celebratory odes. His tragedy *The Mourning Bride* (1697) was perhaps his greatest popular success, and the relative failure of *The Way of the World* (1700) ended his career as a playwright when he was only thirty. For almost thirty more years he remained a respected literary figure (to whom Pope dedicated his *Iliad*) and a witty and amiable companion, lionized by various ladies but captured by Henrietta, the younger Duchess of Marlborough, whose lover he remained until his death.

The Way of the World followed by two years Jeremy Collier's *A Short View of the Immorality and Profaneness of the English Stage* (1698), in which Congreve (with Dryden and Vanbrugh) bore the brunt of the attack. The play contains some ironic allusions to Collier's attack but shows as well the influence of Colley Cibber's success with *Love's Last Shift* (1698). In Cibber's play the rake hero is seduced into reformation by his wife in disguise. In Congreve's play the traditional rake becomes the villain, and Mirabell emerges as a new kind of hero. He cannot be claimed as saintly, for he has at least courted Lady Wishfort and had an affair with her widowed daughter; his command of intrigue is such as might serve baser ends than he pursues, and he shows a lively concern that Millamant not lose her fortune. He genuinely loves her, but, although her fortune is not at all the end of his marrying her, it is very much a necessary condition. Yet, for all Mirabell's prudence, he shows warmth, generosity, even recklessness in his love for Millamant and a cool sharp detachment from Fainall's more perverse and Machiavellian attitudes: "You have a taste extremely delicate," he tells him, "and are for refining on your pleasures."

In Fainall and Mrs. Marwood we can see the older libertinism of Restoration comedy, so openly avowed by Horner in Wycherley's *The Country Wife* (1675) and more problematically represented by Dorimant in Etherege's *The Man of Mode* (1676). The libertine has the virtues of honesty and self-awareness, a resistance to debilitating forms of hypocrisy and earnestness; he acts with almost a reformer's zeal in exposing appetites in others and fulfilling his own, achieving something like an intellectual demonstration in the very act of seduction. So long as this attitude is maintained with style and energy, it has both animal grace and cleansing liberation; when it becomes desperate, cruel, and rankly selfish, it seems more compulsive than free, more feverish than vigorous, and it readily falls victim to its own shortsightedness. In contrast we have a new hero and heroine, who have tact and grace, who can assume cunning where they must, who are deeply in love and yet playfully and warmly so rather than driven by passion. Their passion is real, but so is their desire for integrity and liberty, and their playfulness becomes a means of protecting themselves from each other as well as from those who threaten them from outside. They embody an ordering force, one that is critical and skeptical in the "proviso" scene but that leads toward marriage and even parenthood rather than a continuous dance of amours.

Mirabell and Millamant are given courtly names—he the adorer of beauty, she the woman of a thousand lovers—names that were originally the badges of platonic sublimation and later of cynical dissimulation, the mask worn by such a rake as Dorimant; their names distinguish them as well from such as Lady Wishfort or Witwoud, Fainall or Mincing. They reduce the rake and wronged virago to instances of false wit, to a level not so far above the fops and fools; for in their control and self-knowledge they define a true wit that makes all varieties of false wit seem akin. We can see this best in the brilliant dialogue, where the false note is not always easily distinguished from the true, and where true wit is often marked by its rueful acknowledgment of genuine feeling ("Well, if Mirabell should not make a good husband, I am a lost thing,—for I find I love him violently").

The Way of the World is in some ways the culmination of Restoration comedy and in others a turning point. It includes the wit—both in its satiric bite and its free extravagance—of earlier comedy, and like the best of it treats the most serious problems of personal integrity and social role beneath a surface of manners. But it celebrates as well a capacity for generous feeling and delicacy of sentiment that looks forward to a new sensibility. The play still holds the stage, in fact with more success today than when it was written; and its network of subterranean intrigue still puzzles the audience as it is gradually uncovered. That it was meant to do so seems clear; for "the way of the world" is one of feint and disguise, of plot and counterplot. And to master it requires a vigilance that Congreve never underestimates, even as he refuses to allow that it need cost us our hearts.

Dryden's poem to Congreve is given here in place of Congreve's own prologue and epilogue.

John Dryden: To My Dear Friend Mr. Congreve,°

On His Comedy Called *The Double-Dealer*

Well then, the promised hour is come at last;
The present age of wit obscures the past:
Strong were our sires, and as they fought they writ,
Conquering with force of arms, and dint of wit;
Theirs was the giant race before the flood;°
And thus, when Charles returned, our empire stood.
Like Janus° he the stubborn soil manured,
With rules of husbandry the rankness cured;
Tamed us to manners, when the stage was rude;
10   And boisterous English wit with art indued.
Our age was cultivated thus at length,
But what we gained in skill we lost in strength.
Our builders were with want of genius curst;
The second temple° was not like the first:
Till you, the best Vitruvius,° come at length;
Our beauties equal, but excel our strength.
Firm Doric pillars° found your solid base;
The fair Corinthian crowns the higher space:
Thus all below is strength, and all above is grace.
20   In easy dialogue is Fletcher's° praise;
He moved the mind, but had not power to raise.
Great Jonson° did by strength of judgment please;
Yet, doubling Fletcher's force, he wants his ease.
In differing talents both adorned their age;
One for the study, the other for the stage:
But both to Congreve justly shall submit,
One matched in judgment, both o'ermatched in wit.
In him all beauties of this age we see,
Etherege° his courtship, Southerne's° purity,

To . . . Mr. Congreve This tribute was published with Congreve's second comedy; Dryden had abandoned the stage and had (for political reasons) lost his posts as Poet Laureate and as Historiographer Royal. We see here, as everywhere in Dryden, a double view of the relation of present to past, a sense of loss as well as gain, a weighing of the claims of "strength" and "grace" (which only an exceptional writer, like Congreve, can reconcile).
the giant . . . flood the Elizabethans and Jacobeans who wrote and ruled before the Commonwealth, likened to the ancient patriarchs before the biblical deluge
Janus the god of beginnings. According to legend he reigned as a king in Italy and gave asylum to Saturn upon his flight from Jupiter; from Saturn he learned the arts of husbandry which here, in the guise of Charles II educated in France, he teaches.
second temple referring to the rebuilding of the temple in Jerusalem upon the return from exile

(Ezra 5, 6) in contrast with the original building by Solomon (Haggar 2:1–3)
Vitruvius the celebrated Roman architect and writer on architecture of the age of Augustus
Doric pillars As the simplest and most severe, these were placed at the lowest level of a building (such as the Colosseum), with Ionic and then Corinthian placed at higher levels, tapering from strength to grace.
Fletcher's John Fletcher (1579–1625), best known for his collaboration with Francis Beaumont, who (in Dryden's view) surpassed the French in comic repartee
Jonson Ben Jonson. See Dryden's discussion of him in the selections from his prose criticism.
Etherege Sir George Etherege (c. 1635–91), whose *The Man of Mode* (1676) raised Restoration love comedy to a new level of finesse
Southerne's Thomas Southerne (1660–1746), whose tragicomedies stressed pathos and "purity"

30   The satire, wit, and strength of Manly Wycherley.°
      All this in blooming youth you have achieved,
      Nor are your foiled contemporaries grieved.
      So much the sweetness of your manners move,
      We cannot envy you, because we love.
      Fabius° might joy in Scipio, when he saw
      A beardless consul made against the law;
      And join his suffrage to the votes of Rome,
      Though he with Hannibal was overcome.
      Thus old Romano° bowed to Raphael's fame,
40   And scholar to the youth he taught became.
         O that your brows my laurel had sustained;
      Well had I been deposed, if you had reigned!
      The father had descended for the son;
      For only you are lineal to the throne.
      Thus, when the state one Edward° did depose,
      A greater Edward in his room arose.
      But now, not I, but poetry is curst;
      For Tom the Second° reigns like Tom the First.
      But let 'em not mistake my patron's part,°
50   Nor call his charity their own desert.
      Yet this I prophesy: thou shalt be seen
      (Though with some short parenthesis between)
      High on the throne of wit; and, seated there,
      Not mine—that's little—but thy laurel wear.
      Thy first attempt an early promise made;
      That early promise this has more than paid.
      So bold, yet so judiciously you dare,
      That your least praise is to be regular.
      Time, place, and action, may with pains be wrought;
60   But genius must be born, and never can be taught.
      This is your portion; this your native store;
      Heaven, that but once was prodigal before,
      To Shakespeare gave as much; she could not give him more.
         Maintain your post: that's all the fame you need;
      For 'tis impossible you should proceed.
      Already I am worn with cares and age,
      And just abandoning the ungrateful stage;

Manly Wycherley William Wycherley (1641–1716), author of *The Country Wife* (1675) and here named for the hero of his *Plain Dealer* (1676)
Fabius (d. 203 B.C.) who opposed (in part out of jealousy) the young Scipio's policy for carrying war against Carthage into Africa; Scipio had been made consul (205 B.C.) before attaining the legal age; here Fabius is shown charmed by a Scipio who has Congreve's "sweetness"
Romano Giulio Romano (1492–1546) was in fact younger than Raphael (1483–1520) and was his pupil rather than his master; Dryden may have in mind Perugino (1446–1523?), in whose studio Raphael worked and whom he imitated and surpassed.

Edward Edward II was assassinated in 1327 and succeeded by Edward III, the conqueror of the French.
Tom the Second With the revolution of 1688 Dryden lost both the laureateship and his position as historiographer to Thomas Shadwell (see *Mac Flecknoe*); Shadwell was succeeded as laureate in 1692 by Nahum Tate, as historiographer by the critic Thomas Rymer ("Tom the Second").
my patron's part the Earl of Dorset, who, as Lord Chamberlain, held the power of appointing the laureate and historiographer but did not act on his own volition in removing Dryden

Unprofitably kept at Heaven's expense,
I live a rent-charge° on his providence:
70 But you, whom every Muse and Grace adorn,
Whom I foresee to better fortune born,
Be kind to my remains; and O defend,
Against your judgment, your departed friend!
Let not the insulting foe my fame pursue,
But shade those laurels which descend to you;
And take for tribute what these lines express:
You merit more; nor could my love do less.

1694

The Way of the World

> Audire est operae pretium, procedere recte
> Qui maechis non vultis—
> —Metuat doti deprensa.— [1]

CHARACTERS

FAINALL, *in love with Mrs. Marwood* [2]
MIRABELL, *in love with Mrs. Millamant*
WITWOUD ⎱ *followers of*
PETULANT ⎰ *Mrs. Millamant*
SIR WILFULL WITWOUD, *half brother to Witwoud and nephew to Lady Wishfort*
WAITWELL, *servant to Mirabell*
LADY WISHFORT, *enemy to Mirabell for having falsely pretended love to her*
MRS. MILLAMANT, *a fine lady, niece to Lady Wishfort, and loves Mirabell*
MRS. MARWOOD, *friend to Mr. Fainall, and likes Mirabell*
MRS. FAINALL, *daughter to Lady Wishfort and wife to Fainall, formerly friend
to Mirabell*
FOIBLE, *woman to Lady Wishfort*
MINCING, *woman to Mrs. Millamant*
DANCERS, FOOTMEN, *and* ATTENDANTS

SCENE: *London*

ACT I

A chocolate-house

[MIRABELL *and* FAINALL, *rising from cards.* BETTY *waiting.*[3]]

MIRABELL   You are a fortunate man, Mr. Fainall.

FAINALL   Have we done?

MIRABELL   What you please. I'll play on to entertain you.

FAINALL   No, I'll give you your revenge another time, when you are not so

---

rent-charge a rent forming a charge upon lands granted to one who is not the owner

1. "O you that do not wish well to the proceedings of adulterers, it is worth your while to hear how they are hampered on all sides.—Caught in the act, the woman fears for her dowry." Horace, *Satires* II.1.37–38, 131.
2. Unmarried ladies, as well as married ones, are called "Mrs."
3. That is, on them.

indifferent; you are thinking of something else now, and play too negligently. The coldness of a losing gamester lessens the pleasure of the winner. I'd no more play with a man that slighted his ill fortune, than I'd make love to a woman who undervalued the loss of her reputation.

MIRABELL   You have a taste extremely delicate, and are for refining on your pleasures.

FAINALL   Prithee, why so reserved? Something has put you out of humour.

MIRABELL   Not at all. I happen to be grave today, and you are gay; that's all.

FAINALL   Confess, Millamant and you quarrelled last night, after I left you; my fair cousin has some humours [4] that would tempt the patience of a Stoic. What! some coxcomb came in and was well received by her while you were by?

MIRABELL   Witwoud and Petulant; and what was worse, her aunt, your wife's mother, my evil genius; or to sum up all in her own name, my old Lady Wishfort came in.

FAINALL   Oh, there it is then! She has a lasting passion for you, and with reason. What, then my wife was there?

MIRABELL   Yes, and Mrs. Marwood and three or four more, whom I never saw before. Seeing me, they all put on their grave faces, whispered one another, then complained aloud of the vapours,[5] and after fell into a profound silence.

FAINALL   They had a mind to be rid of you.

MIRABELL   For which reason I resolved not to stir. At last the good old lady broke through her painful taciturnity with an invective against long visits. I would not have understood her, but Millamant joining in the argument, I rose and with a constrained smile told her I thought nothing was so easy as to know when a visit began to be troublesome. She reddened and I withdrew, without expecting [6] her reply.

FAINALL   You were to blame to resent what she spoke only in compliance with her aunt.

MIRABELL   She is more mistress of herself than to be under the necessity of such a resignation.

FAINALL   What? though half her fortune depends upon her marrying with my lady's approbation?

MIRABELL   I was then in such a humour that I should have been better pleased if she had been less discreet.

FAINALL   Now I remember, I wonder not they were weary of you; last night was one of their cabal-nights.[7] They have 'em three times a week and meet by turns at one another's apartments, where they come together like the coroner's inquest to sit upon the murdered reputations of the week. You and I are excluded; and it was once proposed that all the male sex should be excepted; [8] but somebody moved that to avoid scandal there might be one man of the community; upon which motion Witwoud and Petulant were enrolled members.

4. Moods, whims.
5. A fit of melancholy (a fashionable disease).
6. Waiting for.
7. Nights for secret meetings, devoted in politics to conspiracy, here to lesser intrigues.
8. Excluded.

MIRABELL   And who may have been the foundress of this sect? My Lady Wishfort, I warrant, who publishes her detestation of mankind; and full of the vigour of fifty-five, declares for a friend and ratafia; [9] and let posterity shift for itself, she'll breed no more.

FAINALL   The discovery of your sham addresses to her, to conceal your love to her niece, has provoked this separation. Had you dissembled better, things might have continued in the state of nature.[10]

MIRABELL   I did as much as man could with any reasonable conscience; I proceeded to the very last act of flattery with her, and was guilty of a song in her commendation. Nay, I got a friend to put her into a lampoon and compliment her with the imputation of an affair with a young fellow, which I carried so far that I told her the malicious town took notice that she was grown fat of a sudden; and when she lay in of a dropsy,[11] persuaded her she was reported to be in labour. The devil's in't if an old woman is to be flattered further, unless a man should endeavour downright personally to debauch her; and that my virtue forbade me. But for the discovery of that amour, I am indebted to your friend, or your wife's friend, Mrs. Marwood.

FAINALL   What should provoke her to be your enemy, without she has made you advances which you have slighted? Women do not easily forgive omissions of that nature.

MIRABELL   She was always civil to me till of late. I confess I am not one of those coxcombs who are apt to interpret a woman's good manners to her prejudice; and think that she who does not refuse 'em everything, can refuse 'em nothing.

FAINALL   You are a gallant man, Mirabell; and though you may have cruelty enough not to satisfy a lady's longing, you have too much generosity not to be tender of her honour. Yet you speak with an indifference which seems to be affected and confesses you are conscious of a negligence.

MIRABELL   You pursue the argument with a distrust that seems to be unaffected, and confesses you are conscious of a concern for which the lady is more indebted to you than your wife.

FAINALL   Fie, fie, friend, if you grow censorious I must leave you. I'll look upon the gamesters in the next room.

MIRABELL   Who are they?

FAINALL   Petulant and Witwoud. [To BETTY] Bring me some chocolate.
    [Exit]

MIRABELL   Betty, what says your clock?

BETTY   Turned of the last canonical hour,[12] sir. [Exit]

MIRABELL   How pertinently the jade answers me! Ha! almost one o'clock!
    [Looking on his watch] Oh, y'are come——
    [Enter a SERVANT]
    Well, is the grand affair over? You have been something tedious.

9. A fruit-flavored liqueur with a brandy base.
10. In their natural state; but with ironic reference to Eden before the fall or to the state Dryden describes in the opening lines of Absalom and Achitophel.
11. An illness that involves swelling with liquids.
12. That is, past the hours (from 8 A.M. to noon) when marriages could be performed in the Church of England.

SERVANT   Sir, there's such coupling at Pancras [13] that they stand behind one another, as 'twere in a country dance. Ours was the last couple to lead up; and no hopes appearing of dispatch,[14] besides, the parson growing hoarse, we were afraid his lungs would have failed before it came to our turn; so we drove round to Duke's Place; and there they were riveted in a trice.

MIRABELL   So, so, you are sure they are married.

SERVANT   Married and bedded, sir; I am witness.

MIRABELL   Have you the certificate?

SERVANT   Here it is, sir.

MIRABELL   Has the tailor brought Waitwell's clothes home, and the new liveries?

SERVANT   Yes, sir.

MIRABELL   That's well. Do you go home again, d'ye hear, and adjourn the consummation till farther order. Bid Waitwell shake his ears and Dame Partlet [15] rustle up her feathers, and meet me at one o'clock by Rosamond's Pond,[16] that I may see her before she returns to her lady; and as you tender [17] your ears, be secret.

[*Exit* SERVANT. *Re-enter* FAINALL (*and* BETTY)]

FAINALL   Joy of your success, Mirabell; you look pleased.

MIRABELL   Aye, I have been engaged in a matter of some sort of mirth, which is not yet ripe for discovery. I am glad this is not a cabal-night. I wonder, Fainall, that you who are married, and of consequence should be discreet, will suffer your wife to be of such a party.

FAINALL   Faith, I am not jealous. Besides, most who are engaged are women and relations; and for the men, they are of a kind too contemptible to give scandal.

MIRABELL   I am of another opinion. The greater the coxcomb, always the more the scandal; for a woman who is not a fool can have but one reason for associating with a man that is.

FAINALL   Are you jealous as often as you see Witwoud entertained by Millamant?

MIRABELL   Of her understanding I am, if not of her person.

FAINALL   You do her wrong; for to give her her due, she has wit.

MIRABELL   She has beauty enough to make any man think so, and complaisance enough not to contradict him who shall tell her so.

FAINALL   For a passionate lover, methinks you are a man somewhat too discerning in the failings of your mistress.

MIRABELL   And for a discerning man, somewhat too passionate a lover; for I like her with all her faults; nay, like her for her faults. Her follies are so natural, or so artful, that they become her; and those affections which

13. The churches of St. Pancras and St. James (in Duke's Place, mentioned below) permitted marriage without special license and were predictably busy.
14. Speed.
15. Chauntecleer's wife (Pertelote) in Chaucer's Nun's Priest's Tale, called Dame Partlet in Dryden's translation, *The Cock and the Fox* (1700).
16. A place of rendezvous in St. James's Park.
17. Value.

in another woman would be odious, serve but to make her more agreeable. I'll tell thee, Fainall, she once used me with that insolence, that in revenge I took her to pieces; sifted her and separated her failings; I studied 'em and got 'em by rote. The catalogue was so large that I was not without hopes, one day or other, to hate her heartily; to which end I so used myself to think of 'em that at length, contrary to my design and expectation, they gave me every hour less and less disturbance; till in a few days it became habitual to me to remember 'em without being displeased. They are now grown as familiar to me as my own frailties; and in all probability in a little time longer I shall like 'em as well.

FAINALL   Marry her, marry her; be half as well acquainted with her charms as you are with her defects, and my life on't, you are your own man again.

MIRABELL   Say you so?

FAINALL   Aye, aye; I have experience; I have a wife, and so forth.

[*Enter* MESSENGER]

MESSENGER   Is one Squire Witwoud here?

BETTY   Yes; what's your business?

MESSENGER   I have a letter for him, from his brother, Sir Wilfull, which I am charged to deliver into his own hands.

BETTY   He's in the next room, friend—that way.

[*Exit* MESSENGER]

MIRABELL   What, is the chief of that noble family in town, Sir Wilfull Witwoud?

FAINALL   He is expected today. Do you know him?

MIRABELL   I have seen him; he promises to be an extraordinary person; I think you have the honour to be related to him.

FAINALL   Yes; he is half-brother to this Witwoud by a former wife, who was sister to my Lady Wishfort, my wife's mother. If you marry Millamant, you must call cousins too.

MIRABELL   I had rather be his relation than his acquaintance.

FAINALL   He comes to town in order to equip himself for travel.

MIRABELL   For travel! Why the man that I mean is above forty.

FAINALL   No matter for that; 'tis for the honour of England, that all Europe should know we have blockheads of all ages.[18]

MIRABELL   I wonder there is not an Act of Parliament to save the credit of the nation and prohibit the exportation of fools.

FAINALL   By no means, 'tis better as 'tis; 'tis better to trade with a little loss, than to be quite eaten up with being overstocked.

MIRABELL   Pray, are the follies of this knight-errant,[19] and those of the squire his brother, anything related?

FAINALL   Not at all; Witwoud grows by the knight, like a medlar grafted on a crab.[20] One will melt in your mouth, and t'other set your teeth on edge; one is all pulp, and the other all core.

18. Europe usually saw them when they left the university, the customary occasion for a grand tour; for a younger "blockhead," see Pope, *Dunciad* IV.282–336.
19. Perhaps with reference to Hudibras and Ralpho in Butler's poem.
20. That is, Witwoud gains by the contrast, like a medlar (a soft fruit eaten only when it has begun to rot) grafted on a crabapple.

MIRABELL   So one will be rotten before he be ripe, and the other will be rotten without ever being ripe at all.

FAINALL   Sir Wilfull is an odd mixture of bashfulness and obstinacy. But when he's drunk, he's as loving as the monster in *The Tempest*,[21] and much after the same manner. To give the t'other his due, he has something of good nature and does not always want wit.

MIRABELL   Not always; but as often as his memory fails him, and his commonplace of comparisons.[22] He is a fool with a good memory and some few scraps of other folks' wit. He is one whose conversation can never be approved, yet it is now and then to be endured. He has indeed one good quality, he is not exceptious; [23] for he so passionately affects the reputation of understanding raillery [24] that he will construe an affront into a jest, and call downright rudeness and ill language, satire and fire.

FAINALL   If you have a mind to finish his picture, you have an opportunity to do it at full length. Behold the original.

[*Enter* WITWOUD]

WITWOUD   Afford me your compassion, my dears; pity me, Fainall, Mirabell, pity me.

MIRABELL   I do from my soul.

FAINALL   Why, what's the matter?

WITWOUD   No letters for me, Betty?

BETTY   Did not the messenger bring you one but now, sir?

WITWOUD   Aye, but no other?

BETTY   No, sir.

WITWOUD   That's hard, that's very hard;—a messenger, a mule, a beast of burden! He has brought me a letter from the fool my brother, as heavy as a panegyric in a funeral sermon, or a copy of commendatory verses from one poet to another.[25] And what's worse, 'tis as sure a forerunner of the author as an epistle dedicatory.

MIRABELL   A fool, and your brother, Witwoud!

WITWOUD   Aye, aye, my half-brother. My half-brother he is, no nearer upon honour.

MIRABELL   Then 'tis possible he may be but half a fool.

WITWOUD   Good, good, Mirabell, *le drôle!* [26] Good, good!—hang him, don't let's talk of him. Fainall, how does your lady? Gad, I say anything in the world to get this fellow out of my head. I beg pardon that I should ask a man of pleasure and the town, a question at once so foreign and domestic. But I talk like an old maid at a marriage, I don't know what I say. But she's the best woman in the world.

FAINALL   'Tis well you don't know what you say, or else your commendation would go near to make me either vain or jealous.

21. As Caliban is to Stephano and Trinculo when they make him drunk (II.ii).
22. That is, his memorandum book full of others' ingenious and far-fetched wit.
23. Peevish.
24. Banter or teasing; described by Swift in its ideal form as an apparent insult that turns out to be a compliment.
25. Both likely to run to great length.
26. The amusing fellow.

WITWOUD   No man in town lives well with a wife but Fainall. Your judgment, Mirabell?

MIRABELL   You had better step and ask his wife if you would be credibly informed.

WITWOUD   Mirabell.

MIRABELL   Aye.

WITWOUD   My dear, I ask ten thousand pardons.—Gad, I have forgot what I was going to say to you.

MIRABELL   I thank you heartily, heartily.

WITWOUD   No, but prithee excuse me—my memory is such a memory.

MIRABELL   Have a care of such apologies, Witwoud; for I never knew a fool but he affected to complain either of the spleen [27] or his memory.

FAINALL   What have you done with Petulant?

WITWOUD   He's reckoning his money—my money it was; I have no luck today.

FAINALL   You may allow him to win of you at play, for you are sure to be too hard for him at repartee. Since you monopolize the wit that is between you, the fortune must be his of course.

MIRABELL   I don't find that Petulant confesses the superiority of wit to be your talent, Witwoud.

WITWOUD   Come, come, you are malicious now, and would breed debates. Petulant's my friend, and a very honest fellow, and a very pretty fellow, and has a smattering—faith and troth, a pretty deal of an odd sort of a small wit. Nay, I'll do him justice. I'm his friend, I won't wrong him, neither.—And if he had but any judgment in the world, he would not be altogether contemptible. Come, come, don't detract from the merits of my friend.

FAINALL   You don't take your friend to be over-nicely bred.

WITWOUD   No, no, hang him, the rogue has no manners at all, that I must own—no more breeding than a bumbaily,[28] that I grant you.—'Tis pity, faith; the fellow has fire and life.

MIRABELL   What, courage?

WITWOUD   Hum, faith, I don't know as to that—I can't say as to that.—Yes, faith, in a controversy he'll contradict anybody.

MIRABELL   Though 'twere a man whom he feared or a woman whom he loved.

WITWOUD   Well, well, he does not always think before he speaks.—We have all our failings; you're too hard upon him, you are, faith. Let me excuse him—I can defend most of his faults, except one or two; one he has, that's the truth on't, if he were my brother, I could not acquit him.— That, indeed, I could wish were otherwise.

MIRABELL   Aye, marry, what's that, Witwoud?

WITWOUD   Oh, pardon me! Expose the infirmities of my friend?—No, my dear, excuse me there.

FAINALL   What! I warrant, he's unsincere, or 'tis some such trifle.

WITWOUD   No, no, what if he be? 'Tis no matter for that, his wit will excuse

---

27. Low spirits, the "vapors."
28. Sheriff's officer of the lowest rank.

that; a wit should no more be sincere than a woman constant; one argues a decay of parts as t'other of beauty.

MIRABELL   Maybe you think him too positive?

WITWOUD   No, no, his being positive is an incentive to argument and keeps up conversation.

FAINALL   Too illiterate.

WITWOUD   That! that's his happiness. His want of learning gives him the more opportunities to show his natural parts.

MIRABELL   He wants words.

WITWOUD   Aye; but I like him for that now; for his want of words gives me the pleasure very often to explain his meaning.

FAINALL   He's impudent.

WITWOUD   No, that's not it.

MIRABELL   Vain.

WITWOUD   No.

MIRABELL   What, he speaks unseasonable truths sometimes, because he has not wit enough to invent an evasion.

WITWOUD   Truths! Ha, ha, ha! No, no, since you will have it—I mean, he never speaks truth at all—that's all. He will lie like a chambermaid, or a woman of quality's porter. Now that is a fault.

[*Enter* COACHMAN]

COACHMAN   Is Master Petulant here, mistress?

BETTY   Yes.

COACHMAN   Three gentlewomen in the coach would speak with him.

FAINALL   O brave Petulant, three!

BETTY   I'll tell him.

COACHMAN   You must bring two dishes of chocolate and a glass of cinnamon-water.

[*Exeunt* BETTY *and* COACHMAN]

WITWOUD   That should be for two fasting strumpets and a bawd troubled with wind. Now you may know what the three are.

MIRABELL   You are very free with your friend's acquaintance.

WITWOUD   Aye, aye, friendship without freedom is as dull as love without enjoyment or wine without toasting; but to tell you a secret, these are trulls that he allows coach-hire, and something more by the week, to call on him once a day at public places.

MIRABELL   How!

WITWOUD   You shall see he won't go to 'em because there's no more company here to take notice of him.—Why, this is nothing to what he used to do—before he found out this way, I have known him call for himself——

FAINALL   Call for himself? What dost thou mean?

WITWOUD   Mean? why, he would slip you out of this chocolate-house, just when you had been talking to him.—As soon as your back was turned—whip he was gone; then trip to his lodging, clap on a hood and scarf, slap into a hackney-coach, and drive hither to the door again in a trice; where he would send in for himself—that I mean—call for himself, wait for himself, nay and what's more, not finding himself, sometimes leave a letter for himself.

MIRABELL   I confess this is something extraordinary—I believe he waits for himself now, he is so long a-coming. Oh, I ask his pardon!

[*Enter* PETULANT (*and* BETTY)]

BETTY   Sir, the coach stays.

PETULANT   Well, well; I come.—'Sbud,[29] a man had as good be a professed midwife as a professed whoremaster at this rate; to be knocked up and raised at all hours and in all places! Pox on 'em, I won't come.—D'ee hear, tell 'em I won't come. Let 'em snivel and cry their hearts out.

FAINALL   You are very cruel, Petulant.

PETULANT   All's one, let it pass—I have a humour to be cruel.

MIRABELL   I hope they are not persons of condition that you use at this rate.

PETULANT   Condition! condition's a dried fig, if I am not in humour. By this hand, if they were your—a—a—your what-d'ye-call-'ems themselves, they must wait or rub off [30] if I want appetite.

MIRABELL   What-d'ye-call-'ems! What are they, Witwoud?

WITWOUD   Empresses, my dear—by your what-d'ye-call-'ems he means sultana queens.[31]

PETULANT   Aye, Roxolanas.[32]

MIRABELL   Cry you mercy.

FAINALL   Witwoud says they are——

PETULANT   What does he say th'are?

WITWOUD   I—fine ladies, I say.

PETULANT   Pass on, Witwoud.—Hark 'ee, by this light, his relations—two co-heiresses his cousins, and an old aunt, that loves caterwauling better than a conventicle.[33]

WITWOUD   Ha, ha, ha! I had a mind to see how the rogue would come off.— Ha, ha, ha! Gad I can't be angry with him, if he said they were my mother and my sisters.

MIRABELL   No!

WITWOUD   No; the rogue's wit and readiness of invention charm me. Dear Petulant!

BETTY   They are gone, sir, in great anger.

PETULANT   Enough, let 'em trundle. Anger helps complexion, saves paint.

FAINALL   This continence is all dissembled; this is in order to have something to brag of the next time he makes court to Millamant, and swear he has abandoned the whole sex for her sake.

MIRABELL   Have you not left off your impudent pretensions there yet? I shall cut your throat, sometime or other, Petulant, about that business.

PETULANT   Aye, aye, let that pass—there are other throats to be cut—

MIRABELL   Meaning mine, sir?

PETULANT   Not I—I mean nobody—I know nothing—But there are uncles

---

29. 'Sbodikins, God's body.
30. Clear out.
31. Terms for prostitutes; perhaps based on their own practice, for, as Pope indicates, the brothel-keeper "By names of toasts retails each battered jade" (*Dunciad* II.134).
32. Roxolana is the wife of the sultan Solyman the Magnificent in Davenant's *Siege of Rhodes* (1656).
33. A Puritan church service.

and nephews in the world—and they may be rivals. What then? All's one for that——

MIRABELL   How! Hark 'ee, Petulant, come hither. Explain, or I shall call your interpreter.

PETULANT   Explain! I know nothing.—Why you have an uncle, have you not, lately come to town, and lodges by my Lady Wishfort's?

MIRABELL   True.

PETULANT   Why, that's enough.—You and he are not friends; and if he should marry and have a child, you may be disinherited, ha?

MIRABELL   Where hast thou stumbled upon all this truth?

PETULANT   All's one for that; why, then say I know something.

MIRABELL   Come, thou art an honest fellow, Petulant, and shalt make love to my mistress, thou sha't, faith. What hast thou heard of my uncle?

PETULANT   I? nothing, I. If throats are to be cut, let swords clash; snug's the word, I shrug and am silent.

MIRABELL   O raillery, raillery. Come, I know thou art in the women's secrets. —What, you're a cabalist. I know you stayed at Millamant's last night, after I went. Was there any mention made of my uncle or me? Tell me; if thou hadst but good nature equal to thy wit, Petulant, Tony Witwoud, who is now thy competitor in fame, would show as dim by thee as a dead whiting's eye by a pearl of Orient; [34] he would no more be seen by [35] thee than Mercury is by the sun. Come, I'm sure thou wo't tell me.

PETULANT   If I do, will you grant me common sense then, for the future?

MIRABELL   Faith, I'll do what I can for thee; and I'll pray that heaven may grant it thee in the meantime.

PETULANT   Well, hark'ee.

    [*They talk apart*]

FAINALL   Petulant and you both will find Mirabell as warm a rival as a lover.

WITWOUD   Pshaw, pshaw, that she laughs at Petulant is plain. And for my part —but that it is almost a fashion to admire her, I should—hark'ee—to tell you a secret, but let it go no further—between friends, I shall never break my heart for her.

FAINALL   How!

WITWOUD   She's handsome; but she's a sort of an uncertain woman.

FAINALL   I thought you had died for her.

WITWOUD   Umh—no——

FAINALL   She has wit.

WITWOUD   'Tis what she will hardly allow anybody else. Now, demme, I should hate that, if she were as handsome as Cleopatra. Mirabell is not so sure of her as he thinks for.

FAINALL   Why do you think so?

WITWOUD   We stayed pretty late there last night and heard something of an uncle to Mirabell who is lately come to town,—and is between him and the best part of his estate. Mirabell and he are at some distance, as my Lady Wishfort has been told; and you know she hates Mirabell worse

34. That is, of highest quality.
35. Beside.

than a Quaker hates a parrot, or than a fishmonger hates a hard frost. Whether this uncle has seen Mrs. Millamant or not, I cannot say; but there were items of such a treaty being in embryo; and if it should come to life, poor Mirabell would be in some sort unfortunately fobbed [36] i'faith.

FAINALL 'Tis impossible Millamant should hearken to it.

WITWOUD Faith, my dear, I can't tell; she's a woman and a kind of a humourist.[37]

MIRABELL [conversing with PETULANT] And this is the sum of what you could collect last night.

PETULANT The quintessence. Maybe Witwoud knows more; he stayed longer. Besides, they never mind him; they say anything before him.

MIRABELL I thought you had been the greatest favourite.

PETULANT Aye, tête-à-tête; but not in public, because I make remarks.

MIRABELL Do you?

PETULANT Aye, aye, pox, I'm malicious, man. Now, he's soft, you know; they are not in awe of him. The fellow's well bred; he's what you call a— what-d'ee-call-'em. A fine gentleman, but he's silly withal.

MIRABELL I thank you; I know as much as my curiosity requires.—Fainall, are you for the Mall? [38]

FAINALL Aye, I'll take a turn before dinner.

WITWOUD Aye, we'll all walk in the Park; the ladies talked of being there.

MIRABELL I thought you were obliged to watch for your brother Sir Wilfull's arrival.

WITWOUD No, no, he comes to his aunt's, my Lady Wishfort; pox on him, I shall be troubled with him too; what shall I do with the fool?

PETULANT Beg him for his estate, that I may beg you afterwards, and so have but one trouble with you both.

WITWOUD O rare Petulant! thou art as quick as a fire in a frosty morning; thou shalt to the Mall with us, and we'll be very severe.

PETULANT Enough! I'm in a humour to be severe.

MIRABELL Are you? Pray then walk by yourselves—let not us be accessory to your putting the ladies out of countenance with your senseless ribaldry, which you roar out aloud as often as they pass by you; and when you have made a handsome woman blush, then you think you have been severe.

PETULANT What, what? Then let 'em either show their innocence by not understanding what they hear, or else show their discretion by not hearing what they would not be thought to understand.

MIRABELL But hast not thou then sense enough to know that thou ought'st to to be most ashamed thyself, when thou has put another out of countenance?

PETULANT Not I, by this hand—I always take blushing either for a sign of guilt or ill breeding.

36. Done in.
37. One given to whim or caprice.
38. The promenade at St. James's Park.

MIRABELL   I confess you ought to think so. You are in the right, that you may plead the error of your judgment in defence of your practice.

Where modesty's ill manners, 'tis but fit
That impudence and malice pass for wit.
[*Exeunt*]

ACT II
St. James's Park

[*Enter* MRS. FAINALL *and* MRS. MARWOOD]

MRS. FAINALL   Aye, aye, dear Marwood, if we will be happy, we must find the means in ourselves, and among ourselves. Men are ever in extremes; either doting or averse. While they are lovers, if they have fire and sense, their jealousies are insupportable; and when they cease to love (we ought to think at least), they loathe; they look upon us with horror and distaste; they meet us like the ghosts of what we were, and as such, fly from us.

MRS. MARWOOD   True, 'tis an unhappy circumstance of life that love should ever die before us; and that the man so often should outlive the lover. But say what you will, 'tis better to be left than never to have been loved. To pass our youth in dull indifference, to refuse the sweets of life because they once must leave us, is as preposterous as to wish to have been born old because we one day must be old. For my part, my youth may wear and waste, but it shall never rust in my possession.

MRS. FAINALL   Then it seems you dissemble an aversion to mankind only in compliance with my mother's humour.

MRS. MARWOOD   Certainly. To be free, I have no taste of those insipid dry discourses with which our sex of force must entertain themselves apart from men. We may affect endearments to each other, profess eternal friendships, and seem to dote like lovers; but 'tis not in our natures long to persevere. Love will resume his empire in our breasts, and every heart, or soon or late, receive and readmit him as its lawful tyrant.

MRS. FAINALL   Bless me, how have I been deceived! Why, you profess a libertine.

MRS. MARWOOD   You see my friendship by my freedom. Come, be as sincere, acknowledge that your sentiments agree with mine.

MRS. FAINALL   Never.

MRS. MARWOOD   You hate mankind.

MRS. FAINALL   Heartily, inveterately.

MRS. MARWOOD   Your husband.

MRS. FAINALL   Most transcendently; aye, though I say it, meritoriously.

MRS. MARWOOD   Give me your hand upon it.

MRS. FAINALL   There.

MRS. MARWOOD   I join with you; what I have said has been to try you.

MRS. FAINALL   Is it possible? Dost thou hate those vipers, men?

MRS. MARWOOD   I have done hating 'em and am now come to despise 'em; the next thing I have to do is eternally to forget 'em.

MRS. FAINALL   There spoke the spirit of an Amazon, a Penthesilea.[1]

MRS. MARWOOD   And yet I am thinking sometimes to carry my aversion further.

MRS. FAINALL   How?

MRS. MARWOOD   Faith, by marrying; if I could but find one that loved me very well and would be thoroughly sensible of ill usage, I think I should do myself the violence of undergoing the ceremony.

MRS. FAINALL   You would not make him a cuckold?

MRS. MARWOOD   No; but I'd make him believe I did, and that's as bad.

MRS. FAINALL   Why, had not you as good do it?

MRS. MARWOOD   Oh, if he should ever discover it, he would then know the worst and be out of his pain; but I would have him ever to continue upon the rack of fear and jealousy.

MRS. FAINALL   Ingenious mischief! Would thou wert married to Mirabell.

MRS. MARWOOD   Would I were.

MRS. FAINALL   You change colour.

MRS. MARWOOD   Because I hate him.

MRS. FAINALL   So do I, but I can hear him named. But what reason have you to hate him in particular?

MRS. MARWOOD   I never loved him; he is, and always was, insufferably proud.

MRS. FAINALL   By the reason you give for your aversion, one would think it dissembled; for you have laid a fault to his charge of which his enemies must acquit him.

MRS. MARWOOD   Oh, then it seems you are one of his favourable enemies. Methinks you look a little pale, and now you flush again.

MRS. FAINALL   Do I? I think I am a little sick o' the sudden.

MRS. MARWOOD   What ails you?

MRS. FAINALL   My husband. Don't you see him? He turned short upon me unawares, and has almost overcome me.

[*Enter* FAINALL *and* MIRABELL]

MRS. MARWOOD   Ha, ha, ha! he comes opportunely for you.

MRS. FAINALL   For you, for he has brought Mirabell with him.

FAINALL   My dear.

MRS. FAINALL   My soul.

FAINALL   You don't look well today, child.

MRS. FAINALL   D'ee think so?

MIRABELL   He is the only man that does, madam.

MRS. FAINALL   The only man that would tell me so, at least; and the only man from whom I could hear it without mortification.

FAINALL   O my dear, I am satisfied of your tenderness; I know you cannot resent anything from me, especially what is an effect of my concern.

MRS. FAINALL   Mr. Mirabell, my mother interrupted you in a pleasant relation last night; I would fain hear it out.

MIRABELL   The persons concerned in that affair have yet a tolerable reputation.—I am afraid Mr. Fainall will be censorious.

MRS. FAINALL   He has a humour more prevailing than his curiosity, and will willingly dispense with the hearing of one scandalous story to avoid

---

1. Queen of the Amazons, the warlike tribe of women.

giving an occasion to make another by being seen to walk with his wife. This way, Mr. Mirabell, and I dare promise you will oblige us both. [*Exeunt* MRS. FAINALL *and* MIRABELL]

FAINALL   Excellent creature! Well, sure if I should live to be rid of my wife, I should be a miserable man.

MRS. MARWOOD   Aye!

FAINALL   For, having only that one hope, the accomplishment of it, of consequence, must put an end to all my hopes; and what a wretch is he who must survive his hopes! Nothing remains when that day comes but to sit down and weep like Alexander when he wanted other worlds to conquer.

MRS. MARWOOD   Will you not follow 'em?

FAINALL   Faith, I think not.

MRS. MARWOOD   Pray let us; I have a reason.

FAINALL   You are not jealous?

MRS. MARWOOD   Of whom?

FAINALL   Of Mirabell.

MRS. MARWOOD   If I am, is it inconsistent with my love to you that I am tender of your honour?

FAINALL   You would intimate, then, as if there were a fellow-feeling between my wife and him.

MRS. MARWOOD   I think she does not hate him to that degree she would be thought.

FAINALL   But he, I fear, is too insensible.

MRS. MARWOOD   It may be you are deceived.

FAINALL   It may be so. I do now begin to apprehend it.

MRS. MARWOOD   What?

FAINALL   That I have been deceived, madam, and you are false.

MRS. MARWOOD   That I am false! What mean you?

FAINALL   To let you know I see through all your little arts. Come, you both love him, and both have equally dissembled your aversion. Your mutual jealousies of one another have made you clash till you have both struck fire. I have seen the warm confession reddening on your cheeks and sparkling from your eyes.

MRS. MARWOOD   You do me wrong.

FAINALL   I do not. 'Twas for my ease to oversee [2] and wilfully neglect the gross advances made him by my wife, that by permitting her to be engaged I might continue unsuspected in my pleasures, and take you oftener to my arms in full security. But could you think, because the nodding husband would not wake, that e'er the watchful lover slept?

MRS. MARWOOD   And wherewithal can you reproach me?

FAINALL   With infidelity, with loving of another, with love of Mirabell.

MRS. MARWOOD   'Tis false. I challenge you to show an instance that can confirm your groundless accusation. I hate him.

FAINALL   And wherefore do you hate him? He is insensible, and your resentment follows his neglect. An instance? The injuries you have done him

2. Overlook.

are a proof: your interposing in his love. What cause had you to make discoveries of his pretended passion? To undeceive the credulous aunt and be the officious obstacle of his match with Millamant?

MRS. MARWOOD My obligations to my lady urged me. I had professed a friendship to her, and could not see her easy nature so abused by that dissembler.

FAINALL What, was it conscience then? Professed a friendship! Oh, the pious friendships of the female sex!

MRS. MARWOOD More tender, more sincere, and more enduring than all the vain and empty vows of men, whether professing love to us or mutual faith to one another.

FAINALL Ha, ha, ha! you are my wife's friend too.

MRS. MARWOOD Shame and ingratitude! Do you reproach me? You, you upbraid me! Have I been false to her through strict fidelity to you, and sacrificed my friendship to keep my love inviolate? And have you the baseness to charge me with the guilt, unmindful of the merit! To you it should be meritorious that I have been vicious. And do you reflect that guilt upon me, which should lie buried in your bosom?

FAINALL You misinterpret my reproof. I meant but to remind you of the slight account you once could make of strictest ties, when set in competition with your love to me.

MRS. MARWOOD 'Tis false; you urged it with deliberate malice—'twas spoke in scorn, and I never will forgive it.

FAINALL Your guilt, not your resentment, begets your rage. If yet you loved, you could forgive a jealousy; but you are stung to find you are discovered.

MRS. MARWOOD It shall be all discovered. You too shall be discovered; be sure you shall. I can but be exposed;—if I do it myself I shall prevent [3] your baseness.

FAINALL Why, what will you do?

MRS. MARWOOD Disclose it to your wife; own what has passed between us.

FAINALL Frenzy!

MRS. MARWOOD By all my wrongs I'll do't!—I'll publish to the world the injuries you have done me, both in my fame and fortune. With both I trusted you, you bankrupt in honour, as indigent of wealth!

FAINALL Your fame I have preserved. Your fortune has been bestowed as the prodigality of your love would have it, in pleasures which we both have shared. Yet, had not you been false, I had ere this repaid it. 'Tis true. Had you permitted Mirabell with Millamant to have stolen their marriage, my lady had been incensed beyond all means of reconcilement. Millamant had forfeited the moiety [4] of her fortune, which then would have descended to my wife. And wherefore did I marry, but to make lawful prize of a rich widow's wealth, and squander it on love and you?

MRS. MARWOOD Deceit and frivolous pretence!

FAINALL Death, am I not married? What's pretence? Am I not imprisoned,

3. Anticipate.
4. Half.

fettered? Have I not a wife? Nay, a wife that was a widow, a young widow, a handsome widow; and would be again a widow, but that I have a heart of proof,[5] and something of a constitution to bustle through the ways of wedlock and this world. Will you yet be reconciled to truth and me?

MRS. MARWOOD   Impossible. Truth and you are inconsistent. I hate you, and shall for ever.

FAINALL   For loving you?

MRS. MARWOOD   I loathe the name of love after such usage; and next to the guilt with which you would asperse me, I scorn you most. Farewell.

FAINALL   Nay, we must not part thus.

MRS. MARWOOD   Let me go.

FAINALL   Come, I'm sorry.

MRS. MARWOOD   I care not—let me go—break my hands, do—I'd leave 'em to get loose.

FAINALL   I would not hurt you for the world. Have I no other hold to keep you here?

MRS. MARWOOD   Well, I have deserved it all.

FAINALL   You know I love you.

MRS. MARWOOD   Poor dissembling!—Oh, that—well, it is not yet——

FAINALL   What? What is it not? What is it not yet? It is not yet too late——

MRS. MARWOOD   No, it is not yet too late—I have that comfort.

FAINALL   It is, to love another.

MRS. MARWOOD   But not to loathe, detest, abhor mankind, myself, and the whole treacherous world.

FAINALL   Nay, this is extravagance. Come, I ask your pardon—no tears—I was to blame, I could not love you and be easy in my doubts.—Pray forbear—I believe you; I'm convinced I've done you wrong; and any way, every way will make amends. I'll hate my wife yet more, damn her. I'll part with her, rob her of all she's worth, and will retire somewhere, anywhere, to another world. I'll marry thee—be pacified.— 'Sdeath, they come; hide your face, your tears. You have a mask; wear it a moment. This way, this way; be persuaded.
    [*Exeunt*]
    [*Enter* MIRABELL *and* MRS. FAINALL]

MRS. FAINALL   They are here yet.

MIRABELL   They are turning into the other walk.

MRS. FAINALL   While I only hated my husband, I could bear to see him; but since I have despised him, he's too offensive.

MIRABELL   Oh, you should hate with prudence.

MRS. FAINALL   Yes, for I have loved with indiscretion.

MIRABELL   You should have just so much disgust for your husband as may be sufficient to make you relish your lover.

MRS. FAINALL   You have been the cause that I have loved without bounds, and would you set limits to that aversion of which you have been the occasion? Why did you make me marry this man?

---

5. Proved strength, as of steel.

MIRABELL   Why do we daily commit disagreeable and dangerous actions? To save that idol, reputation. If the familiarities of our loves had produced that consequence of which you were apprehensive, where could you have fixed a father's name with credit, but on a husband? I knew Fainall to be a man lavish of his morals, an interested and professing friend,[6] a false and a designing lover; yet one whose wit and outward fair behaviour have gained a reputation with the town, enough to make that woman stand excused who has suffered herself to be won by his addresses. A better man ought not to have been sacrificed to the occasion; a worse had not answered to the purpose. When you are weary of him, you know your remedy.

MRS. FAINALL   I ought to stand in some degree of credit with you, Mirabell.

MIRABELL   In justice to you, I have made you privy to my whole design, and put it in your power to ruin or advance my fortune.

MRS. FAINALL   Whom have you instructed to represent your pretended uncle?

MIRABELL   Waitwell, my servant.

MRS. FAINALL   He is an humble servant to Foible, my mother's woman, and may win her to your interest.

MIRABELL   Care is taken for that. She is won and worn by this time. They were married this morning.

MRS. FAINALL   Who?

MIRABELL   Waitwell and Foible. I would not tempt my servant to betray me by trusting him too far. If your mother, in hopes to ruin me, should consent to marry my pretended uncle, he might, like Mosca in *The Fox*,[7] stand upon terms; so I made him sure beforehand.

MRS. FAINALL   So, if my poor mother is caught in a contract, you will discover [8] the imposture betimes, and release her by producing a certificate of her gallant's former marriage.

MIRABELL   Yes, upon condition she consent to my marriage with her niece, and surrender the moiety of her fortune in her possession.

MRS. FAINALL   She talked last night of endeavouring at a match between Millamant and your uncle.

MIRABELL   That was by Foible's direction and my instruction, that she might seem to carry it more privately.

MRS. FAINALL   Well, I have an opinion of your success, for I believe my lady will do anything to get a husband; and when she has this, which you have provided for her, I suppose she will submit to anything to get rid of him.

MIRABELL   Yes, I think the good lady would marry anything that resembled a man, though 'twere no more than what a butler could pinch out of a napkin.[9]

MRS. FAINALL   Female frailty! We must all come to it, if we live to be old, and feel the craving of a false appetite when the true is decayed.

6. Self-seeking and pretended friend.
7. Mosca, the clever servant who threatens to expose his master if his terms are not met, in Ben Johnson's *Volpone, or The Fox* (1606).
8. Uncover.
9. That is, as a decoration for the dinner table.

MIRABELL   An old woman's appetite is depraved like that of a girl. 'Tis the green-sickness [10] of a second childhood; and like the faint offer of a latter spring, serves but to usher in the fall, and withers in an affected bloom.

MRS. FAINALL   Here's your mistress.

[*Enter* MRS. MILLAMANT, WITWOUD, *and* MINCING]

MIRABELL   Here she comes, i'faith, full sail, with her fan spread and her streamers out, and a shoal of fools for tenders.[11]—Ha, no, I cry her mercy!

MRS. FAINALL   I see but one poor empty sculler; and he tows her woman after him.

MIRABELL   You seem to be unattended, madam. You used to have the *beau monde* [12] throng after you; and a flock of gay fine perukes [13] hovering round you.

WITWOUD   Like moths about a candle.—I had like to have lost my comparison for want of breath.

MILLAMANT   Oh, I have denied myself airs today. I have walked as fast through the crowd——

WITWOUD   As a favourite in disgrace, and with as few followers.

MILLAMANT   Dear Mr. Witwoud, truce with your similitudes; for I am as sick of 'em——

WITWOUD   As a physician of a good air.—I cannot help it, madam, though 'tis against myself.

MILLAMANT   Yet again! Mincing, stand between me and his wit.

WITWOUD   Do, Mrs. Mincing, like a screen before a great fire. I confess I do blaze today, I am too bright.

MRS. FAINALL   But, dear Millamant, why were you so long?

MILLAMANT   Long! Lord, have I not made violent haste? I have asked every living thing I met for you; I have enquired after you, as after a new fashion.

WITWOUD   Madam, truce with your similitudes. No, you met her husband, and did not ask him for her.

MIRABELL   By your leave, Witwoud, that were like enquiring after an old fashion, to ask a husband for his wife.

WITWOUD   Hum, a hit, a hit, a palpable hit! I confess it.

MRS. FAINALL   You were dressed before I came abroad.

MILLAMANT   Aye, that's true—oh, but then I had—Mincing, what had I? Why was I so long?

MINCING   O mem, your la'ship stayed to peruse a pecket [14] of letters.

MILLAMANT   Oh, aye, letters—I had letters—I am persecuted with letters—I hate letters. Nobody knows how to write letters; and yet one has 'em, one does not know why. They serve one to pin up one's hair.

---

10. An anemia of adolescent girls.
11. Perhaps a reminiscence of the description of Dalila in Milton's *Samson Agonistes* (1671): "Like a stately ship . . . / With all her bravery on, and tackle trim, / Sails filled, and streamers waving" (ll. 714–18).
12. Fashionable world.
13. Wigs, then fashionable dress for gentlemen.
14. Mincing affects genteel pronunciation, but not with uniform success.

WITWOUD   Is that the way? Pray, madam, do you pin up your hair with all your letters? I find I must keep copies.

MILLAMANT   Only with those in verse, Mr. Witwoud. I never pin up my hair with prose. I fancy one's hair would not curl if it were pinned up with prose. I think I tried once, Mincing.

MINCING   O mem, I shall never forget it.

MILLAMANT   Aye, poor Mincing tiffed [15] and tiffed all the morning.

MINCING   Till I had the cremp in my fingers, I'll vow, mem. And all to no purpose. But when your la'ship pins it up with poetry, it sits so pleasant the next day as anything, and is so pure and so crips.[16]

WITWOUD   Indeed, so 'crips'?

MINCING   You're such a critic, Mr. Witwoud.

MILLAMANT   Mirabell, did not you take exceptions last night? Oh, aye, and went away. Now I think on't I'm angry.—No, now I think on't I'm pleased—for I believe I gave you some pain.

MIRABELL   Does that please you?

MILLAMANT   Infinitely; I love to give pain.

MIRABELL   You would affect a cruelty which is not in your nature; your true vanity is in the power of pleasing.

MILLAMANT   Oh, I ask your pardon for that. One's cruelty is one's power, and when one parts with one's cruelty, one parts with one's power; and when one has parted with that, I fancy one's old and ugly.

MIRABELL   Aye, aye, suffer your cruelty to ruin the object of your power, to destroy your lover—and then how vain, how lost a thing you'll be! Nay, 'tis true: you are no longer handsome when you've lost your lover; your beauty dies upon the instant. For beauty is the lover's gift; 'tis he bestows your charms—your glass is all a cheat. The ugly and the old, whom the looking-glass mortifies, yet after commendation can be flattered by it, and discover beauties in it; for that reflects our praises, rather than your face.

MILLAMANT   Oh, the vanity of these men! Fainall, d'ee hear him? If they did not commend us, we were not handsome! Now you must know they could not commend one, if one was not handsome. Beauty the lover's gift—Lord, what is a lover, that it can give? Why, one makes lovers as fast as one pleases, and they live as long as one pleases, and they die as soon as one pleases; and then if one pleases, one makes more.

WITWOUD   Very pretty. Why you make no more of making of lovers, madam, than of making so many card-matches.[17]

MILLAMANT   One no more owes one's beauty to a lover than one's wit to an echo; they can but reflect what we look and say—vain empty things if we are silent or unseen, and want a being.

MIRABELL   Yet, to those two vain empty things you owe two the greatest pleasures of your life.

MILLAMANT   How so?

MIRABELL   To your lover you owe the pleasure of hearing yourselves praised; and to an echo the pleasure of hearing yourselves talk.

15. Arranged (Millamant's hair).
16. Crisp, i.e. curly.
17. Cards dipped in sulphur and used as matches.

WITWOUD   But I know a lady that loves talking so incessantly, she won't give an echo fair play; she has that everlasting rotation of tongue, that an echo must wait till she dies before it can catch her last words.

MILLAMANT   Oh, fiction! Fainall, let us leave these men.

MIRABELL [*aside to* MRS. FAINALL]   Draw off Witwoud.

MRS. FAINALL   Immediately.—I have a word or two for Mr. Witwoud.

MIRABELL   I would beg a little private audience too.

[*Exeunt* WITWOUD *and* MRS. FAINALL]

You had the tyranny to deny me last night, though you knew I came to impart a secret to you that concerned my love.

MILLAMANT   You saw I was engaged.

MIRABELL   Unkind! You had the leisure to entertain a herd of fools, things who visit you from their excessive idleness; bestowing on your easiness [18] that time which is the incumbrance of their lives. How can you find delight in such society? It is impossible they should admire you. They are not capable; or if they were, it should be to you as a mortification; for sure to please a fool is some degree of folly.

MILLAMANT   I please myself—besides, sometimes to converse with fools is for my health.

MIRABELL   Your health! Is there a worse disease than the conversation of fools?

MILLAMANT   Yes, the vapours; fools are physic for it, next to asafoetida.

MIRABELL   You are not in a course [19] of fools?

MILLAMANT   Mirabell, if you persist in this offensive freedom—you'll displease me. I think I must resolve, after all, not to have you.—We shan't agree.

MIRABELL   Not in our physic, it may be.

MILLAMANT   And yet our distemper in all likelihood will be the same; for we shall be sick of one another. I shan't endure to be reprimanded nor instructed; 'tis so dull to act always by advice and so tedious to be told of one's faults—I can't bear it. Well, I won't have you, Mirabell—I'm resolved—I think—you may go—ha, ha, ha! What would you give, that you could help loving me?

MIRABELL   I would give something that you did not know I could not help it.

MILLAMANT   Come, don't look grave then. Well, what do you say to me?

MIRABELL   I say that a man may as soon make a friend by his wit, or a fortune by his honesty, as win a woman with plain dealing and sincerity.

MILLAMANT   Sententious Mirabell! Prithee, don't look with that violent and inflexible wise face, like Solomon at the dividing of the child [20] in an old tapestry hanging.

MIRABELL   You are merry, madam, but I would persuade you for one moment to be serious.

MILLAMANT   What, with that face? No, if you keep your countenance, 'tis impossible I should hold mine. Well, after all, there is something very moving in a lovesick face. Ha, ha, ha!—well, I won't laugh; don't be peevish—heigho! Now I'll be melancholy, as melancholy as a watch-light.[21] Well, Mirabell, if ever you will win me, woo me now.—Nay, if

18. Indulgence.
19. That is, a course of "physic" or medicine.
20. That is, between the two mothers who claim it, I Kings 3:16–28.
21. Dim night-light.

you are so tedious, fare you well. I see they are walking away.

MIRABELL   Can you not find in the variety of your disposition one moment——

MILLAMANT   To hear you tell me that Foible's married and your plot like to speed? No.

MIRABELL   But how you came to know it——

MILLAMANT   Unless by the help of the devil, you can't imagine; unless she should tell me herself. Which of the two it may have been, I will leave you to consider; and when you have done thinking of that, think of me. [*Exit*]

MIRABELL   I have something more——. Gone!—Think of you! To think of a whirlwind, though 'twere in a whirlwind, were a case of more steady contemplation; a very tranquillity of mind and mansion. A fellow that lives in a windmill has not a more whimsical dwelling than the heart of a man that is lodged in a woman. There is no point of the compass to which they cannot turn, and by which they are not turned, and by one as well as another; for motion, not method, is their occupation. To know this, and yet continue to be in love, is to be made wise from the dictates of reason, and yet persevere to play the fool by the force of instinct.—Oh, here come my pair of turtles! [22]—What, billing so sweetly! Is not Valentine's Day over with you yet? [*Enter* WAITWELL *and* FOIBLE] Sirrah, Waitwell, why sure you think you were married for your own recreation, and not for my conveniency.

WAITWELL   Your pardon, sir. With submission, we have indeed been solacing in lawful delights; but still with an eye to business, sir. I have instructed her as well as I could. If she can take your directions as readily as my instructions, sir, your affairs are in a prosperous way.

MIRABELL   Give you joy, Mrs. Foible.

FOIBLE   O 'las, sir, I'm so ashamed—I'm afraid my lady has been in a thousand inquietudes for me. But I protest, sir, I made as much haste as I could.

WAITWELL   That she did indeed, sir. It was my fault that she did not make more.

MIRABELL   That I believe.

FOIBLE   But I told my lady as you instructed me, sir, that I had a prospect of seeing Sir Rowland, your uncle; and that I would put her ladyship's picture in my pocket to show him; which I'll be sure to say has made him so enamoured of her beauty that he burns with impatience to lie at her ladyship's feet and worship the original.

MIRABELL   Excellent Foible! Matrimony has made you eloquent in love.

WAITWELL   I think she has profited, sir. I think so.

FOIBLE   You have seen Madam Millamant, sir?

MIRABELL   Yes.

FOIBLE   I told her, sir, because I did not know that you might find an opportunity; she had so much company last night.

MIRABELL   Your diligence will merit more. In the meantime——[*Gives money*]

FOIBLE   O dear sir, your humble servant.

22. Turtledoves.

WAITWELL   Spouse!

MIRABELL   Stand off, sir, not a penny.—Go on and prosper, Foible. The lease
shall be made good and the farm stocked, if we succeed.

FOIBLE   I don't question your generosity, sir, and you need not doubt of
success. If you have no more commands, sir, I'll be gone; I'm sure my
lady is at her toilet and can't dress 'till I come.—Oh dear, I'm sure that
[*Looking out*] was Mrs. Marwood that went by in a mask; if she has
seen me with you I'm sure she'll tell my lady. I'll make haste home and
prevent her. Your servant, sir. B'w'y,[23] Waitwell.
[*Exit* FOIBLE]

WAITWELL   Sir Rowland, if you please.—The jade's so pert upon her preferment [24] she forgets herself.

MIRABELL   Come, sir, will you endeavour to forget yourself—and transform
into Sir Rowland.

WAITWELL   Why, sir, it will be impossible I should remember myself—married,
knighted, and attended all in one day! 'Tis enough to make any man
forget himself. The difficulty will be how to recover my acquaintance
and familiarity with my former self, and fall from my transformation to
a reformation into Waitwell. Nay, I shan't be quite the same Waitwell
neither—for now I remember me, I am married, and can't be my own
man again.

Aye, there's the grief; that's the sad change of life;
To lose my title, and yet keep my wife.   [*Exeunt*]

ACT III

A room in LADY WISHFORT's *house*
[LADY WISHFORT *at her toilet,* PEG *waiting*]

LADY WISHFORT   Merciful! no news of Foible yet?

PEG   No, madam.

LADY WISHFORT   I have no more patience. If I have not fretted myself till I
am pale again, there's no veracity in me. Fetch me the red—the red,
do you hear, sweetheart? An arrant [1] ash colour, as I'm a person. Look
you how this wench stirs! Why dost thou not fetch me a little red?
Didst thou not hear me, mopus? [2]

PEG   The red ratafia does your ladyship mean, or the cherry-brandy?

LADY WISHFORT   Ratafia, fool! No, fool. Not the ratafia, fool—grant me patience! I mean the Spanish paper,[3] idiot,—complexion, darling. Paint,
paint, paint, dost thou understand that, changeling, dangling thy hands
like bobbins before thee? Why dost thou not stir, puppet?—thou wooden
thing upon wires!

PEG   Lord, madam, your ladyship is so impatient. I cannot come at the paint,
madam; Mrs. Foible has locked it up, and carried the key with her.

23. Contraction of "God be with you" or "good-bye."
24. Advancement.

1. Thorough.
2. Dunce.
3. A cosmetic like rouge.

LADY WISHFORT   A pox take you both! Fetch me the cherry-brandy then. [*Exit* PEG] I'm as pale and as faint, I look like Mrs. Qualmsick the curate's wife, that's always breeding.—Wench, come, come, wench, what art thou doing, sipping? tasting? Save thee, dost thou not know the bottle? [*Enter* PEG *with a bottle and china cup*]

PEG   Madam, I was looking for a cup.

LADY WISHFORT   A cup, save thee! and what a cup hast thou brought! Dost thou take me for a fairy, to drink out of an acorn? Why didst thou not bring thy thimble? Hast thou ne'er a brass thimble clinking in thy pocket with a bit of nutmeg? [4] I warrant thee. Come, fill, fill.—So— again. [*One knocks*] See who that is.—Set down the bottle first. Here, under the table.—What, wouldst thou go with the bottle in thy hand like a tapster? As I'm a person, this wench has lived in an inn upon the road before she came to me, like Maritornes [5] the Asturian in *Don Quixote*. No Foible yet?

PEG   No, madam,—Mrs. Marwood.

LADY WISHFORT   Oh, Marwood! let her come in. Come in, good Marwood.
[*Enter* MRS. MARWOOD]

MRS. MARWOOD   I'm surprised to find your ladyship in dishabille at this time of day.

LADY WISHFORT   Foible's a lost thing; has been abroad since morning, and never heard of since.

MRS. MARWOOD   I saw her but now, as I came masked through the Park, in conference with Mirabell.

LADY WISHFORT   With Mirabell! You call my blood into my face with mentioning that traitor. She durst not have the confidence. I sent her to negotiate an affair in which if I'm detected I'm undone. If that wheedling villain has wrought upon Foible to detect me, I'm ruined. Oh, my dear friend, I'm a wretch of wretches if I'm detected.

MRS. MARWOOD   O madam, you cannot suspect Mrs. Foible's integrity.

LADY WISHFORT   Oh, he carries poison in his tongue that would corrupt integrity itself. If she has given him an opportunity, she has as good as put her integrity into his hands. Ah, dear Marwood, what's integrity to an opportunity?—Hark! I hear her. [*To* PEG] Go, you thing, and send her in!
[*Exit* PEG]
Dear friend, retire into my closet,[6] that I may examine her with more freedom.—You'll pardon me, dear friend, I can make bold with you. —There are books over the chimney—Quarles and Prynne, and *The Short View of the Stage*,[7] with Bunyan's works, to entertain you.
[*Exit* MARWOOD]

---

4. As good luck charms.
5. The ugly chambermaid in Cervantes's *Don Quixote*.
6. Small dressing room.
7. Francis Quarles, the emblem writer, was, like Bunyan, favorite moral reading of Puritans; William Prynne (1600–1669) was a Puritan critic of the stage (*Histriomastix,* 1632); Jeremy Collier (1650–1726), an Anglican clergyman, is consigned to this company for his *Short View of the Immorality and Profaneness of the English Stage* (1698), which included an attack on Congreve.

[*Enter* FOIBLE]

O Foible, where hast thou been? What hast thou been doing?

FOIBLE   Madam, I have seen the party.

LADY WISHFORT   But what has thou done?

FOIBLE   Nay, 'tis your ladyship has done, and are to do; I have only promised. But a man so enamoured—so transported! Well, here it is, all that is left; all that is not kissed away. Well, if worshipping of pictures be a sin—poor Sir Rowland, I say.

LADY WISHFORT   The miniature has been counted like [8]—but hast thou not betrayed me, Foible? Hast thou not detected me to that faithless Mirabell? What hadst thou to do with him in the Park? Answer me, has he got nothing out of thee?

FOIBLE [*aside*]   So, the devil has been beforehand with me; what shall I say? —Alas, madam, could I help it, if I met that confident thing? Was I in fault? If you had heard how he used me, and all upon your ladyship's account, I'm sure you would not suspect my fidelity. Nay, if that had been the worst, I could have borne; but he had a fling at your ladyship too, and then I could not hold, but, i'faith, I gave him his own.

LADY WISHFORT   Me? What did the filthy fellow say?

FOIBLE   O madam, 'tis a shame to say what he said—with his taunts and his fleers, tossing up his nose. 'Humh!' says he, 'what, you are a-hatching some plot,' says he, 'you are so early abroad, or catering,' [9] says he, 'ferreting for some disbanded officer, I warrant—half pay is but thin subsistence,' says he. 'Well, what pension does your lady propose? Let me see,' says he; 'what, she must come down pretty deep now, she's superannuated,' says he, 'and——'

LADY WISHFORT   Ods my life, I'll have him—I'll have him murdered. I'll have him poisoned. Where does he eat? I'll marry a drawer [10] to have him poisoned in his wine. I'll send for Robin from Locket's [11] immediately.

FOIBLE   Poison him? Poisoning's too good for him. Starve him, madam, starve him; marry Sir Rowland and get him disinherited. Oh, you would bless yourself, to hear what he said.

LADY WISHFORT   A villain! Superannuated!

FOIBLE   'Humh!' says he, 'I hear you are laying designs against me, too,' says he, 'and Mrs. Millamant is to marry my uncle' (he does not suspect a word of your ladyship); 'but,' says he, 'I'll fit you for that, I warrant you,' says he, 'I'll hamper you for that,' says he, 'you and your old frippery,[12] too,' says he, 'I'll handle you——'

LADY WISHFORT   Audacious villain! handle me! would he durst!—Frippery? old frippery! Was there ever such a foul-mouthed fellow? I'll be married tomorrow; I'll be contracted tonight.

FOIBLE   The sooner the better, madam.

LADY WISHFORT   Will Sir Rowland be here, say'st thou? When, Foible?

8. Considered a good likeness.
9. Providing for her needs, i.e. seeking out a former officer reduced to half-pay and willing to be bought.
10. Tapster or waiter.
11. A fashionable tavern.
12. Cast-off garments.

FOIBLE Incontinently,[13] madam. No new sheriff's wife expects the return of her husband after knighthood with that impatience in which Sir Rowland burns for the dear hour of kissing your ladyship's hands after dinner.

LADY WISHFORT Frippery? superannuated frippery! I'll frippery the villain; I'll reduce him to frippery and rags. A tatterdemalion!—I hope to see him hung with tatters, like a Long Lane pent-house,[14] or a gibbet-thief. A slander-mouthed railer! I warrant the spendthrift prodigal's in debt as much as the million lottery,[15] or the whole court upon a birthday.[16] I'll spoil his credit with his tailor. Yes, he shall have my niece with her fortune, he shall.

FOIBLE He! I hope to see him lodge in Ludgate first, and angle into Blackfriars for brass farthings, with an old mitten.[17]

LADY WISHFORT Aye, dear Foible; thank thee for that, dear Foible. He has put me out of all patience. I shall never recompose my features to receive Sir Rowland with any economy of face. This wretch has fretted me that I am absolutely decayed. Look, Foible.

FOIBLE Your ladyship has frowned a little too rashly, indeed, madam. There are some cracks discernible in the white varnish.

LADY WISHFORT Let me see the glass.—Cracks, say'st thou? Why, I am arrantly flayed. I look like an old peeled wall. Thou must repair me, Foible, before Sir Rowland comes; or I shall never keep up to my picture.

FOIBLE I warrant you, madam; a little art once made your picture like you; and now a little of the same art must make you like your picture. Your picture must sit for you, madam.

LADY WISHFORT But art thou sure Sir Rowland will not fail to come? Or will a' not fail when he does come? Will he be importunate, Foible, and push? For if he should not be importunate—I shall never break decorums—I shall die with confusion if I am forced to advance—oh no, I can never advance—I shall swoon if he should expect advances. No, I hope Sir Rowland is better bred than to put a lady to the necessity of breaking her forms. I won't be too coy neither. I won't give him despair—but a little disdain is not amiss; a little scorn is alluring.

FOIBLE A little scorn becomes your ladyship.

LADY WISHFORT Yes, but tenderness becomes me best—a sort of a dyingness. —You see that picture has a sort of a—ha, Foible? a swimmingness in the eyes. Yes, I'll look so. My niece affects it; but she wants features. Is Sir Rowland handsome? Let my toilet be removed—I'll dress above. I'll receive Sir Rowland here. Is he handsome? Don't answer me. I won't know; I'll be surprized. I'll be taken by surprize.

FOIBLE By storm, madam. Sir Rowland's a brisk man.

13. Immediately.
14. Stall for rags or old clothes.
15. A government lottery designed to raise a million pounds.
16. New clothes were expected of courtiers on the king's birthday; cf. the "birth-night beau" in Pope's *The Rape of the Lock* I.23.
17. Those in the debtors' prison (the Fleet) at Ludgate near Blackfriars would let down mittens or containers on a string in order to cadge money from passers-by.

LADY WISHFORT   Is he! Oh, then he'll importune, if he's a brisk man. I shall save decorums if Sir Rowland importunes. I have a mortal terror at the apprehension of offending against decorums. Nothing but importunity can surmount decorums. Oh, I'm glad he's a brisk man! Let my things be removed, good Foible.
[*Exit*]
[*Enter* MRS. FAINALL]

MRS. FAINALL   O Foible, I have been in a fright, lest I should come too late. That devil, Marwood, saw you in the Park with Mirabell, and I'm afraid will discover it to my lady.

FOIBLE   Discover what, madam?

MRS. FAINALL   Nay, nay, put not on that strange face. I am privy to the whole design, and know that Waitwell, to whom thou wert this morning married, is to personate Mirabell's uncle, and as such, winning my lady, to involve her in those difficulties from which Mirabell only must release her, by his making his conditions to have my cousin and her fortune left to her own disposal.

FOIBLE   O dear madam, I beg your pardon. It was not my confidence in your ladyship that was deficient; but I thought the former good correspondence between your ladyship and Mr. Mirabell might have hindered his communicating this secret.

MRS. FAINALL   Dear Foible, forget that.

FOIBLE   O dear madam, Mr. Mirabell is such a sweet winning gentleman—but your ladyship is the pattern of generosity. Sweet lady, to be so good! Mr. Mirabell cannot choose but be grateful. I find your ladyship has his heart still. Now, madam, I can safely tell your ladyship our success; Mrs. Marwood had told my lady, but I warrant I managed myself. I turned it all for the better. I told my lady that Mr. Mirabell railed at her. I laid horrid things to his charge, I'll vow; and my lady is so incensed, that she'll be contracted to Sir Rowland tonight, she says; I warrant I worked her up, that he may have her for asking for, as they say of a Welsh maidenhead.

MRS. FAINALL   O rare Foible!

FOIBLE   Madam, I beg your ladyship to acquaint Mr. Mirabell of his success. I would be seen as little as possible to speak to him; besides, I believe Madam Marwood watches me. She has a month's mind; [18] but I know Mr. Mirabell can't abide her.
[*Enter* FOOTMAN]
John, remove my lady's toilet. Madam, your servant. My lady is so impatient, I fear she'll come for me, if I stay.

MRS. FAINALL   I'll go with you up the back stairs, lest I should meet her.
[*Exeunt*]
[*Enter* MRS. MARWOOD]

MRS. MARWOOD   Indeed, Mrs. Engine,[19] is it thus with you? Are you become a go-between of this importance? Yes, I shall watch you. Why, this wench

18. Desire (for Mirabell).
19. Mrs. Instrument.

is the *passe-partout,* a very master-key to everybody's strong box. My friend Fainall,[20] have you carried it so swimmingly? I thought there was something in it; but it seems it's over with you. Your loathing is not from a want of appetite then, but from a surfeit. Else you could never be so cool to fall from a principal to be an assistant,—to procure for him! A pattern of generosity, that, I confess. Well, Mr. Fainall, you have met with your match.—O man, man! Woman, woman! The devil's an ass; if I were a painter, I would draw him like an idiot, a driveller with a bib and bells. Man should have his head and horns, and woman the rest of him. Poor simple fiend!—'Madam Marwood has a month's mind, but he can't abide her.'—'Twere better for him you had not been his confessor in that affair, without you could have kept his counsel closer. I shall not prove another pattern of generosity; he has not obliged me to that with those excesses of himself! And now I'll have none of him.—Here comes the good lady, panting ripe, with a heart full of hope, and a head full of care, like any chemist upon the day of projection.[21]

[*Enter* LADY WISHFORT]

LADY WISHFORT   Oh, dear Marwood, what shall I say for this rude forgetfulness?—but my dear friend is all goodness.

MRS. MARWOOD   No apologies, dear madam; I have been very well entertained.

LADY WISHFORT   As I'm a person, I am in a very chaos to think I should so forget myself: but I have such an olio [22] of affairs, really I know not what to do.—[*Calls*] Foible! I expect my nephew, Sir Wilfull, every moment, too. [*Calls again*] Why, Foible! He means to travel for improvement.

MRS. MARWOOD   Methinks Sir Wilfull should rather think of marrying than travelling, at his years. I hear he is turned of forty.

LADY WISHFORT   Oh, he's in less danger of being spoiled by his travels. I am against my nephew's marrying too young. It will be time enough when he comes back and has acquired discretion to choose for himself.

MRS. MARWOOD   Methinks Mrs. Millamant and he would make a very fit match. He may travel afterwards. 'Tis a thing very usual with young gentlemen.

LADY WISHFORT   I promise you I have thought on't—and since 'tis your judgment, I'll think on't again. I assure you I will. I value your judgment extremely. On my word, I'll propose it.

[*Enter* FOIBLE]

LADY WISHFORT   Come, come, Foible—I had forgot my nephew will be here before dinner. I must make haste.

FOIBLE   Mr. Witwoud and Mr. Petulant are come to dine with your ladyship.

LADY WISHFORT   Oh, dear, I can't appear till I'm dressed! Dear Marwood, shall I be free with you again, and beg you to entertain 'em? I'll make all imaginable haste. Dear friend, excuse me.

[*Exeunt* LADY WISHFORT *and* FOIBLE]

[*Enter* MRS. MILLAMANT *and* MINCING]

MILLAMANT   Sure never anything was so unbred as that odious man!—Marwood, your servant.

20. That is, Mrs. Fainall.
21. Like an alchemist on the day when he hopes finally to turn his metals into gold.
22. Hodgepodge.

MRS. MARWOOD   You have a colour; what's the matter?

MILLAMANT   That horrid fellow, Petulant, has provoked me into a flame. I have broken my fan. Mincing, lend me yours. Is not all the powder out of my hair?

MRS. MARWOOD   No. What has he done?

MILLAMANT   Nay, he has done nothing; he has only talked—nay, he has said nothing neither, but he has contradicted everything that has been said. For my part, I thought Witwoud and he would have quarrelled.

MINCING   I vow, mem, I thought once they would have fit.[23]

MILLAMANT   Well, 'tis a lamentable thing, I swear, that one has not the liberty of choosing one's acquaintance as one does one's clothes.

MRS. MARWOOD   If we had that liberty, we should be as weary of one set of acquaintance, though never so good, as we are of one suit, though never so fine. A fool and a doily stuff [24] would now and then find days of grace, and be worn for variety.

MILLAMANT   I could consent to wear 'em if they would wear alike; but fools never wear out—they are such *drap-de-Berry* [25] things. Without one could give 'em to one's chambermaid after a day or two!

MRS. MARWOOD   'Twere better so indeed. Or what think you of the playhouse? A fine, gay, glossy fool should be given there, like a new masking habit, after the masquerade is over and we have done with the disguise. For a fool's visit is always a disguise, and never admitted by a woman of wit but to blind her affair with a lover of sense. If you would but appear barefaced now and own Mirabell, you might as easily put off Petulant and Witwoud as your hood and scarf. And indeed 'tis time, for the town has found it, the secret is grown too big for the pretence. 'Tis like Mrs. Primly's great belly; she may lace it down before, but it burnishes [26] on her hips. Indeed, Millamant, you can no more conceal it, than my Lady Strammel can her face, that goodly face, which in defiance of her Rhenish-wine tea, will not be comprehended in a mask.[27]

MILLAMANT   I'll take my death, Marwood, you are more censorious than a decayed beauty, or a discarded toast.[28]—Mincing, tell the men they may come up. My aunt is not dressing here.—Their folly is less provoking than your malice. [*Exit* MINCING] The town has found it! What has it found? That Mirabell loves me is no more a secret than it is a secret that you discovered it to my aunt, or than the reason why you discovered it is a secret.

MRS. MARWOOD   You are nettled.

MILLAMANT   You're mistaken. Ridiculous!

MRS. MARWOOD   Indeed, my dear, you'll tear another fan if you don't mitigate those violent airs.

23. Fought.
24. Cheap woolen cloth.
25. Heavy, durable woolen.
26. Swells out.
27. Lady Strammel (the name implies an ugly woman), for all her efforts to reduce (with white Rhine wine), has an ample face that no mask can conceal.
28. One whose health is no longer drunk by lovers.

MILLAMANT   O silly! Ha, ha, ha! I could laugh immoderately. Poor Mirabell! His constancy to me has quite destroyed his complaisance for all the world beside. I swear, I never enjoined it him to be so coy. If I had the vanity to think he would obey me, I would command him to show more gallantry. 'Tis hardly well bred to be so particular on one hand, and so insensible on the other. But I despair to prevail and so let him follow his own way. Ha, ha, ha! Pardon me, dear creature, I must laugh, ha, ha, ha!—though I grant you 'tis a little barbarous, ha, ha, ha!

MRS. MARWOOD   What pity 'tis, so much fine raillery, and delivered with so significant gesture, should be so unhappily directed to miscarry.

MILLAMANT   Heh? Dear creature, I ask your pardon—I swear I did not mind [29] you.

MRS. MARWOOD   Mr. Mirabell and you both may think it a thing impossible, when I shall tell him by telling you——

MILLAMANT   O dear, what? for it is the same thing, if I hear it—ha, ha, ha!

MRS. MARWOOD   That I detest him, hate him, madam.

MILLAMANT   O madam, why so do I—and yet the creature loves me, ha, ha, ha! How can one forbear laughing to think of it. I am a sibyl [30] if I am not amazed to think what he can see in me. I'll take my death, I think you are handsomer—and within a year or two as young. If you could but stay for me, I should overtake you—but that cannot be. Well, that thought makes me melancholy. Now I'll be sad.

MRS. MARWOOD   Your merry note may be changed sooner than you think.

MILLAMANT   D'ye say so? Then I'm resolved I'll have a song to keep up my spirits.

[*Enter* MINCING]

MINCING   The gentlemen stay but to comb,[31] madam, and will wait on you.

MILLAMANT   Desire Mrs. —— that is in the next room to sing the song I would have learnt yesterday. You shall hear it, madam—not that there's any great matter in it—but 'tis agreeable to my humour.

SONG [32]

I

Love's but the frailty of the mind,
    When 'tis not with ambition joined;
A sickly flame, which if not fed expires;
And feeding, wastes in self-consuming fires.

II

'Tis not to wound a wanton boy
Or amorous youth, that gives the joy;

29. Pay attention to.
30. Seer, prophetess.
31. That is, their wigs.
32. The original text adds, "Set by Mr. John Eccles and sung by Mrs. Hodgson"; the former was Master of the King's Band and the latter a well-known singer and actress. The blank left in the dialogue allows Millamant to name whichever singer is available for the performance. The song, which seems designed to provoke Marwood, reflects her view of love more accurately than it does Millamant's.

But 'tis the glory to have pierced a swain,
For whom inferior beauties sighed in vain.

III
Then I alone the conquest prize,
    When I insult a rival's eyes:
If there's delight in love, 'tis when I see
That heart which others bleed for, bleed for me.

[*Enter* PETULANT *and* WITWOUD]

MILLAMANT   Is your animosity composed, gentlemen?

WITWOUD   Raillery, raillery, madam; we have no animosity—we hit off a little wit now and then, but no animosity. The falling out of wits is like the falling out of lovers.—We agree in the main,[33] like treble and base. Ha, Petulant?

PETULANT   Aye, in the main. But when I have a humour to contradict——

WITWOUD   Aye, when he has a humour to contradict, then I contradict too. What, I know my cue. Then we contradict one another like two battle-dores;[34] for contradictions beget one another like Jews.

PETULANT   If he says black's black—if I have a humour to say 'tis blue—let that pass—all's one for that. If I have a humour to prove it, it must be granted.

WITWOUD   Not positively must—but it may—it may.

PETULANT   Yes, it positively must, upon proof positive.

WITWOUD   Aye, upon proof positive it must; but upon proof presumptive it only may. That's a logical distinction now, madam.

MRS. MARWOOD   I perceive your debates are of importance and very learnedly handled.

PETULANT   Importance is one thing, and learning's another; but a debate's a debate, that I assert.

WITWOUD   Petulant's an enemy to learning; he relies altogether on his parts.[35]

PETULANT   No, I'm no enemy to learning; it hurts not me.

MRS. MARWOOD   That's a sign indeed it's no enemy to you.

PETULANT   No, no, it's no enemy to anybody, but them that have it.

MILLAMANT   Well, an illiterate man's my aversion. I wonder at the impudence of any illiterate man to offer to make love.

WITWOUD   That I confess I wonder at too.

MILLAMANT   Ah! to marry an ignorant that can hardly read or write!

PETULANT   Why should a man be ever the further from being married though he can't read, any more than he is from being hanged? The ordinary's [36] paid for setting the psalm, and the parish-priest for reading the ceremony. And for the rest which is to follow in both cases, a man may do it without book—so all's one for that.

---

33. Largely; but also in the mean, the middle part in which treble and bass harmonize.
34. Opponents in a game of badminton.
35. Natural powers.
36. The prison chaplain, who reads a Psalm before the hanging, as the parish priest presides at a wedding.

MILLAMANT   D'ye hear the creature? Lord, here's company, I'll be gone.

[*Exeunt* MILLAMANT *and* MINCING]

WITWOUD   In the name of Barthol'mew [37] and his fair, what have we here?

MRS. MARWOOD   'Tis your brother, I fancy. Don't you know him?

WITWOUD   Not I—yes, I think it is he—I've almost forgot him; I have not seen him since the Revolution.[38]

[*Enter* SIR WILFULL WITWOUD *in a country riding habit, and* SERVANT *to* LADY WISHFORT]

SERVANT   Sir, my lady's dressing. Here's company, if you please to walk in, in the meantime.

SIR WILFULL   Dressing! What, it's but morning here I warrant with you in London; we should count it towards afternoon in our parts down in Shropshire. Why then belike my aunt han't dined yet—ha, friend?

SERVANT   Your aunt, sir?

SIR WILFULL   My aunt, sir, yes, my aunt, sir, and your lady, sir; your lady is my aunt, sir. Why, what, dost thou not know me, friend? Why, then send somebody here that does. How long hast thou lived with thy lady, fellow, ha?

SERVANT   A week, sir; longer than anybody in the house, except my lady's woman.

SIR WILFULL   Why then belike thou dost not know thy lady if thou see'st her, ha, friend?

SERVANT   Why truly, sir, I cannot safely swear to her face in a morning, before she is dressed. 'Tis like I may give a shrewd guess at her by this time.

SIR WILFULL   Well, prithee try what thou canst do; if thou canst not guess, enquire her out, dost hear, fellow? And tell her, her nephew, Sir Wilfull Witwoud, is in the house.

SERVANT   I shall, sir.

SIR WILFULL   Hold ye, hear me, friend; a word with you in your ear; prithee who are these gallants?

SERVANT   Really, sir, I can't tell; there come so many here, 'tis hard to know 'em all.

[*Exit* SERVANT]

SIR WILFULL   Oons, this fellow knows less than a starling; [39] I don't think a' knows his own name.

MRS. MARWOOD   Mr. Witwoud, your brother is not behindhand in forgetfulness —I fancy he has forgot you too.

WITWOUD   I hope so—the devil take him that remembers first, I say.

SIR WILFULL   Save you, gentlemen and lady.

MRS. MARWOOD   For shame, Mr. Witwoud; why won't you speak to him?— And you, sir.

WITWOUD   Petulant, speak.

PETULANT   And you, sir.

---

37. St. Bartholomew gave his name to the fair held on his feast day (August 24) in the market at Smithfield; it was a scene of low entertainments, including exhibitions of monsters.
38. The Glorious Revolution of 1688.
39. Considered a stupid bird (part of Sir Wilfull's country lore).

SIR WILFULL   No offence, I hope. [*Salutes* [40] MARWOOD]

MRS. MARWOOD   No, sure, sir.

WITWOUD   This is a vile dog, I see that already. No offence! Ha, ha, ha! To him; to him, Petulant, smoke [41] him.

PETULANT   It seems as if you had come a journey, sir; hem, hem. [*Surveying him round*]

SIR WITWOUD   Very likely, sir, that it may seem so.

PETULANT   No offence, I hope, sir.

WITWOUD   Smoke the boots, the boots, Petulant, the boots; ha, ha, ha!

SIR WILFULL   Maybe not, sir; thereafter as [42] 'tis meant, sir.

PETULANT   Sir, I presume upon the information of your boots.

SIR WILFULL   Why, 'tis like you may, sir. If you are not satisfied with the information of my boots, sir, if you will step to the stable, you may enquire further of my horse, sir.

PETULANT   Your horse, sir! Your horse is an ass, sir!

SIR WILFULL   Do you speak by way of offence, sir?

MRS. MARWOOD   The gentleman's merry, that's all, sir.—[*Aside*] S'life, we shall have a quarrel betwixt an horse and an ass, before they find one another out.—You must not take anything amiss from your friends, sir. You are among your friends here, though it may be you don't know it. If I am not mistaken, you are Sir Wilfull Witwoud.

SIR WILFULL   Right, lady; I am Sir Wilfull Witwoud, so I write myself; no offence to anybody, I hope; and nephew to the Lady Wishfort of this mansion.

MRS. MARWOOD   Don't you know this gentleman, sir?

SIR WILFULL   Hum! What, sure 'tis not.—Yea, by'r Lady, but 'tis.—'Sheart, I know not whether 'tis or no.—Yea, but 'tis, by the Wrekin.[43] Brother Anthony! What, Tony, i'faith! What, dost thou not know me? By'r Lady, nor I thee, thou art so becravatted, and so beperiwigged.—'Sheart, why dost not speak? Art thou o'erjoyed?

WITWOUD   Odso, brother, is it you? Your servant, brother.

SIR WILFULL   Your servant! Why yours, sir. Your servant again.—'Sheart, and your friend and servant to that—and a—(*Puff*) and a flapdragon [44] for your service, sir, and a hare's foot, and a hare's scut [45] for your service, sir, an you be so cold and so courtly!

WITWOUD   No offence, I hope, brother.

SIR WILFULL   'Sheart, sir, but there is, and much offence. A pox, is this your Inns o' Court [46] breeding, not to know your friends and your relations, your elders, and your betters?

WITWOUD   Why, brother Wilfull of Salop,[47] you may be as short as a Shrews-

40. Kisses.
41. Smell him out.
42. Depending on how.
43. A high hill in Shropshire, the source of a local toast, "All friends round the Wrekin."
44. In a game, the raisins caught out of burning brandy.
45. Tail.
46. The four societies in London where lawyers had offices, and law students—such as Witwoud—lived during training.
47. Shropshire, of which Shrewsbury is a principal town; Witwoud puns on the crispness of a shortcake and the shortness of his half-brother's temper.

bury cake, if you please. But I tell you 'tis not modish to know relations in town. You think you're in the country, where great lubberly brothers slabber and kiss one another when they meet, like a call of sergeants.[48] 'Tis not the fashion here; 'tis not indeed, dear brother.

SIR WILFULL   The fashion's a fool; and you're a fop, dear brother. 'Sheart, I've suspected this. By'r Lady, I conjectured you were a fop since you began to change the style of your letters, and write in a scrap of paper gilt round the edges, no broader than a *subpoena*. I might expect this when you left off 'Honoured Brother,' and 'hoping you are in good health,' and so forth—to begin with a 'Rat me, knight, I'm so sick of a last night's debauch'—Od's heart, and then tell a familiar tale of a cock and a bull, and a whore and a bottle, and so conclude. You could write news before you were out of your time,[49] when you lived with honest Pumple Nose, the attorney of Furnival's Inn. You could intreat to be remembered then to your friends round the Wrekin. We could have gazettes then, and Dawks's Letter, and the weekly bill, 'till of late days.

PETULANT   'Slife, Witwoud, were you ever an attorney's [50] clerk? Of the family of the Furnivals? Ha, ha, ha!

WITWOUD   Aye, aye, but that was for a while. Not long, not long. Pshaw! I was not in my own power then. An orphan, and this fellow was my guardian; aye, aye, I was glad to consent to that man to come to London. He had the disposal of me then. If I had not agreed to that, I might have been bound prentice to a felt-maker in Shrewsbury; this fellow would have bound me to a maker of felts.

SIR WILFULL   'Sheart, and better than to be bound to a maker of fops, where, I suppose, you have served your time and now you may set up for yourself.

MRS. MARWOOD   You intend to travel, sir, as I'm informed.

SIR WILFULL   Belike I may, madam. I may chance to sail upon the salt seas, if my mind hold.

PETULANT   And the wind serve.

SIR WILFULL   Serve or not serve, I shan't ask license of you, sir; nor the weather-cock your companion. I direct my discourse to the lady, sir. 'Tis like my aunt may have told you, madam—yes, I have settled my concerns, I may say now, and am minded to see foreign parts. If an how that the peace holds, whereby, that is, taxes abate.[51]

MRS. MARWOOD   I thought you had designed for France at all adventures.

SIR WILFULL   I can't tell that; 'tis like I may, and 'tis like I may not. I am somewhat dainty in making a resolution,—because when I make it I keep it. I don't stand shill I, shall I, then; if I say't, I'll do't. But I have

48. Like a group of lawyers just admitted together to the rank of sergeant-at-law; here congratulating each other heartily on a unique occasion (unlike the more spontaneous warmth of country manners).

49. Before you had finished serving your term as apprentice, while Witwoud still provided news in his letters (such as might be found in Dawks's newsletter or in the weekly parish list of deaths).

50. An attorney was a legal agent without the rights of a barrister to plead cases and therefore had lower status (as did Furnival's among the Inns of Court).

51. The Peace of Ryswick (1697) ended the costly war against France, but for only a few years.

thoughts to tarry a small matter in town, to learn somewhat of your lingo first, before I cross the seas. I'd gladly have a spice of your French, as they say, whereby to hold discourse in foreign countries.

MRS. MARWOOD   Here is an academy in town for that use.

SIR WILFULL   There is? 'Tis like there may.

MRS. MARWOOD   No doubt you will return very much improved.

WITWOUD   Yes, refined, like a Dutch skipper from a whale-fishing.[52]

[*Enter* LADY WISHFORT *and* FAINALL]

LADY WISHFORT   Nephew, you are welcome.

SIR WILFULL   Aunt, your servant.

FAINALL   Sir Wilfull, your most faithful servant.

SIR WILFULL   Cousin Fainall, give me your hand.

LADY WISHFORT   Cousin Witwoud, your servant; Mr. Petulant, your servant. —Nephew, you are welcome again. Will you drink anything after your journey, nephew, before you eat? Dinner's almost ready.

SIR WILFULL   I'm very well, I thank you, aunt—however, I thank you for your courteous offer. 'Sheart, I was afraid you would have been in the fashion too, and have remembered to have forgot your relations. Here's your Cousin Tony, belike, I mayn't call him brother for fear of offence.

LADY WISHFORT   Oh, he's a rallier, nephew—my cousin's a wit; and your great wits always rally their best friends to choose.[53] When you have been abroad, nephew, you'll understand raillery better.

[FAINALL *and* MRS. MARWOOD *talk apart*]

SIR WILFULL   Why then let him hold his tongue in the meantime, and rail[54] when that day comes.

[*Enter* MINCING]

MINCING   Mem, I come to acquaint your la'ship that dinner is impatient.

SIR WILFULL   Impatient? Why then belike it won't stay till I pull off my boots. Sweetheart, can you help me to a pair of slippers? My man's with his horses, I warrant.

LADY WISHFORT   Fie, fie, nephew, you would not pull off your boots here. Go down into the hall—dinner shall stay for you.—My nephew's a little unbred, you'll pardon him, madam.—Gentlemen, will you walk?— Marwood——

MRS. MARWOOD   I'll follow you, madam, before Sir Wilfull is ready.

[*Manent*[55] MRS. MARWOOD *and* FAINALL]

FAINALL   Why then Foible's a bawd, an arrant, rank, match-making bawd. And I, it seems, am a husband, a rank husband; and my wife a very arrant, rank wife—all in the way of the world. 'Sdeath, to be an anticipated cuckold, a cuckold in embryo! Sure I was born with budding antlers like a young satyr, or a citizen's child.[56] 'Sdeath, to be outwitted,

52. That is, reeking of oil, as were all aboard whale-fishing ships.
53. As they like.
54. Sir Wilfull misses the crucial distinction between rallying or raillery and railing or scolding and denouncing (as well he might in this company).
55. "There remains."
56. That is, born to be cuckolded; for citizens (or "cits"), merchants in the City of London, were notoriously easy victims of the efforts of Westminster gallants to seduce their wives and thus to put horns on husbands' heads.

to be out-jilted—out-matrimonied! If I had kept my speed like a stag, 'twere somewhat—but to crawl after with my horns like a snail, and outstripped by my wife—'tis scurvy wedlock.

MRS. MARWOOD   Then shake it off. You have often wished for an opportunity to part, and now you have it. But first prevent their plot—the half of Millamant's fortune is too considerable to be parted with to a foe, to Mirabell.

FAINALL   Damn him, that had been mine had you not made that fond discovery[57]—that had been forfeited, had they been married. My wife had added lustre to my horns by that increase of fortune; I could have worn 'em tipped with gold, though my forehead had been furnished like a deputy-lieutenant's hall.[58]

MRS. MARWOOD   They may prove a cap of maintenance[59] to you still, if you can away with[60] your wife. And she's no worse than when you had her—I dare swear she had given up her game before she was married.

FAINALL   Hum! That may be.——She might throw up her cards; but I'll be hanged if she did not put Pam in her pocket.[61]

MRS. MARWOOD   You married her to keep you; and if you can contrive to have her keep you better than you expected, why should you not keep her longer than you intended?

FAINALL   The means, the means!

MRS. MARWOOD   Discover to my lady your wife's conduct; threaten to part with her. My lady loves her, and will come to any composition to save her reputation. Take the opportunity of breaking[62] it just upon the discovery of this imposture. My lady will be enraged beyond bounds, and sacrifice niece and fortune and all at that conjuncture. And let me alone to keep her warm; if she should flag in her part, I will not fail to prompt her.

FAINALL   Faith, this has an appearance.

MRS. MARWOOD   I'm sorry I hinted to my lady to endeavour a match between Millamant and Sir Wilfull; that may be an obstacle.

FAINALL   Oh, for that matter leave me to manage him; I'll disable him for that; he will drink like a Dane. After dinner, I'll set his hand in.

MRS. MARWOOD   Well, how do you stand affected towards your lady?

FAINALL   Why, faith, I'm thinking of it.—Let me see—I am married already, so that's over;—my wife has played the jade with me—well, that's over too;—I never loved her, or if I had, why that would have been over too by this time. Jealous of her I cannot be, for I am certain; so there's an end of jealousy. Weary of her, I am, and shall be—no, there's no end of that; no, no, that were too much to hope. Thus far concerning my repose. Now for my reputation.—As to my own, I married not for it; so that's out of the question.—And as to my part in my wife's—why,

57. Foolishly revealed it.
58. That is, full of antlers, like the hall of a country house.
59. A play upon the heraldic term for a two-pointed cap of high office.
60. Endure, put up with.
61. Keep an ace up her sleeve; actually Pam is jack of clubs but high card in loo.
62. Exposing.

she had parted with hers before; so bringing none to me, she can take none from me; 'tis against all rule of play, that I should lose to one who has not wherewithal to stake.

MRS. MARWOOD   Besides, you forget, marriage is honourable.

FAINALL   Hum! Faith, and that's well thought on; marriage is honourable, as you say, and if so, wherefore should cuckoldom be a discredit, being derived from so honourable a root?

MRS. MARWOOD   Nay, I know not; if the root be honourable, why not the branches? [63]

FAINALL   So, so, why this point's clear. Well, how do we proceed?

MRS. MARWOOD   I will contrive a letter which shall be delivered to my lady at the time when that rascal who is to act Sir Rowland is with her. It shall come as from an unknown hand—for the less I appear to know of the truth, the better I can play the incendiary. Besides, I would not have Foible provoked if I could help it,—because you know she knows some passages. Nay, I expect all will come out—but let the mine [64] be sprung first, and then I care not if I'm discovered.

FAINALL   If the worst come to the worst, I'll turn my wife to grass.—I have already a deed of settlement of the best part of her estate, which I wheedled out of her, and that you shall partake at least.

MRS. MARWOOD   I hope you are convinced that I hate Mirabell. Now you'll be no more jealous?

FAINALL   Jealous, no!—by this kiss—let husbands be jealous, but let the lover still believe. Or if he doubt, let it be only to endear his pleasure and prepare the joy that follows, when he proves his mistress true. But let husbands' doubts convert to endless jealousy; or if they have belief, let it corrupt to superstition and blind credulity. I am single and will herd no more with 'em. True, I wear the badge, but I'll disown the order. And since I take my leave of 'em, I care not if I leave 'em a common motto to their common crest:

All husbands must, or pain, or shame, endure;
The wise too jealous are, fools too secure.
[*Exeunt*]

ACT IV

A room in Lady Wishfort's house [1]

[*Enter* LADY WISHFORT *and* FOIBLE]

LADY WISHFORT   Is Sir Rowland coming, say'st thou, Foible? and are things in order?

FOIBLE   Yes, madam. I have put waxlights in the sconces, and placed the foot men in a row in the hall in their best liveries, with the coachman and postilion to fill up the equipage.

LADY WISHFORT   Have you pulvilled [2] the coachman and postilion that they may not stink of the stable when Sir Rowland comes by?

63. That is, with the image of branching horns or antlers.
64. A buried explosive charge.

1. The original text reads "Scene"—i.e. setting—"continues."
2. Powdered (and perfumed).

FOIBLE   Yes, madam.

LADY WISHFORT   And are the dancers and the music ready that he may be entertained in all points with correspondence to his passion?

FOIBLE   All is ready, madam.

LADY WISHFORT   And—well—and how do I look, Foible?

FOIBLE   Most killing well, madam.

LADY WISHFORT   Well, and how shall I receive him? In what figure shall I give his heart the first impression? There is a great deal in the first impression. Shall I sit?—No, I won't sit—I'll walk—aye, I'll walk from the door upon his entrance, and then turn full upon him.—No, that will be too sudden. I'll lie—aye, I'll lie down—I'll receive him in my little dressing-room; there's a couch—yes, yes, I'll give the first impression on a couch.—I won't lie neither, but loll and lean upon one elbow, with one foot a little dangling off, jogging in a thoughtful way—yes— and then as soon as he appears, start, aye, start and be surprized, and rise to meet him in a pretty disorder—yes—oh, nothing is more alluring than a levee [3] from a couch in some confusion.—It shows the foot to advantage, and furnishes with blushes and recomposing airs beyond comparison. Hark! There's a coach.

FOIBLE   'Tis he, madam.

LADY WISHFORT   Oh dear, has my nephew made his addresses to Millamant? I ordered him.

FOIBLE   Sir Wilfull is set in to drinking, madam, in the parlor.

LADY WISHFORT   Ods my life, I'll send him to her. Call her down, Foible; bring her hither. I'll send him as I go. When they are together, then come to me, Foible, that I may not be too long alone with Sir Rowland.

[Exit]

[Enter MRS. MILLAMANT and MRS. FAINALL]

FOIBLE   Madam, I stayed here, to tell your ladyship that Mr. Mirabell has waited this half-hour for an opportunity to talk with you, though my lady's orders were to leave you and Sir Wilfull together. Shall I tell Mr. Mirabell that you are at leisure?

MILLAMANT   No—what would the dear man have? I am thoughtful and would amuse myself,—bid him come another time.

[Repeating and walking about]

There never yet was woman made,
Nor shall, but to be curst.[4]

That's hard!

MRS. FAINALL   You are very fond of Sir John Suckling today, Millamant, and the poets.

MILLAMANT   Heh? [5] Aye, and filthy verses—so I am.

FOIBLE   Sir Wilfull is coming, madam. Shall I send Mr. Mirabell away?

MILLAMANT   Aye, if you please, Foible, send him away,—or send him hither,

---

3. Rising.

4. The opening lines of a poem by Sir John Suckling, through which—as in other quotations that follow—Millamant considers her plight: courted by Mirabell, whom she loves and believes to love her, but distrustful of the insincerity of lovers and of the "way of the world."

5. The original texts read "He," but this emendation has been proposed by A. E. Case.

—just as you will, dear Foible.—I think I'll see him—Shall I? Aye, let the wretch come. [*Repeating*]
Thyrsis, a youth of the inspired train.[6]
Dear Fainall, entertain Sir Wilfull—thou hast philosophy to undergo a fool; thou art married and hast patience.—I would confer with my own thoughts.

MRS. FAINALL   I am obliged to you that you would make me your proxy in this affair; but I have business of my own.
[*Enter* SIR WILFULL]
—O Sir Wilfull, you are come at the critical instant. There's your mistress up to the ears in love and contemplation; pursue your point now or never.

SIR WILFULL   Yes; my aunt would have it so,—I would gladly have been encouraged with a bottle or two, because I'm somewhat wary at first, before I am acquainted.—[*This while* MILLAMANT *walks about repeating to herself*] But I hope, after a time, I shall break my mind—that is, upon further acquaintance.—So for the present, cousin, I'll take my leave—if so be you'll be so kind to make my excuse, I'll return to my company——

MRS. FAINALL   Oh, fie, Sir Wilfull! What, you must not be daunted.

SIR WILFULL   Daunted! no, that's not it, it is not so much for that—for if so be that I set on't, I'll do't. But only for the present, 'tis sufficient till further acquaintance, that's all—your servant.

MRS. FAINALL   Nay, I'll swear you shall never lose so favourable an opportunity, if I can help it. I'll leave you together, and lock the door.
[*Exit*]

SIR WILFULL   Nay, nay, cousin,—I have forgot my gloves. What d'ye do?—'Sheart, a' has locked the door indeed, I think.—Nay, Cousin Fainall, open the door.—Pshaw, what a vixen trick is this?—Nay, now a' has seen me too.—Cousin, I made bold to pass through as it were—I think this door's enchanted——

MILLAMANT [*repeating*]
I prithee spare me, gentle boy,
Press me no more for that slight toy,—[7]

SIR WILFULL   Anan?[8] Cousin, your servant.

MILLAMANT [*repeating*]
That foolish trifle of a heart——
Sir Wilfull!

SIR WILFULL   Yes—your servant. No offence, I hope, cousin.

MILLAMANT [*repeating*]
I swear it will not do its part,
Though thou dost thine, employ'st thy power and art.
Natural, easy Suckling!

SIR WILFULL   Anan? Suckling? No such suckling neither, cousin, nor stripling. I thank heaven, I'm no minor.

6. The first line of *The Story of Phoebus and Daphne Applied,* by Edmund Waller.
7. From a song by Suckling, which ironically renders Sir Wilfull's awkward courtship in cavalier idiom.
8. What's that? (a rustic form).

MILLAMANT   Ah, rustic, ruder than Gothic! [9]

SIR WILFULL   Well, well, I shall understand your lingo one of these days, cousin; in the meanwhile I must answer in plain English.

MILLAMANT   Have you any business with me, Sir Wilfull?

SIR WILFULL   Not at present, cousin.—Yes, I made bold to see, to come and know if that how you were disposed to fetch a walk this evening, if so be that I might not be troublesome, I would have sought a walk with you.

MILLAMANT   A walk? What then?

SIR WILFULL   Nay, nothing—only for the walk's sake, that's all——

MILLAMANT   I nauseate walking; 'tis a country diversion; I loathe the country and everything that relates to it.

SIR WILFULL   Indeed! Hah! Look ye, look ye, you do? Nay, 'tis like you may.— Here are choice of pastimes here in town, as plays and the like; that must be confessed indeed.

MILLAMANT   Ah, l'étourdi! [10] I hate the town too.

SIR WILFULL   Dear heart, that's much.—Hah! that you should hate 'em both! Hah! 'tis like you may; there are some can't relish the town, and others can't away with the country,—'tis like you may be one of those, cousin.

MILLAMANT   Ha, ha, ha! Yes, 'tis like I may.—You have nothing further to say to me?

SIR WILFULL   Not at present, cousin.—'Tis like when I have an opportunity to be more private,—I may break my mind in some measure—I conjecture you partly guess.—However, that's as time shall try,—but spare to speak and spare to speed, [11] as they say.

MILLAMANT   If it is of no great importance, Sir Wilfull, you will oblige me to leave me; I have just now a little business——

SIR WILFULL   Enough, enough, cousin; yes, yes, all a case.—When you're disposed, when you're disposed. Now's as well as another time; and another time as well as now. All's one for that,—yes, yes, if your concerns call you, there's no haste; it will keep cold as they say.—Cousin, your servant.—I think this door's locked.

MILLAMANT   You may go this way, sir.

SIR WILFULL   Your servant! then with your leave I'll return to my company. [*Exit*]

MILLAMANT   Aye, aye; ha, ha, ha!
    Like Phoebus sung the no less amorous boy. [12]
    [*Enter* MIRABELL]

MIRABELL
    Like Daphne she, as lovely and as coy.
    Do you lock yourself up from me, to make my search more curious? [13]

9. That is, more rough and ill shaped even than barbarous Gothic (as opposed to classical grace and urbanity); perhaps suggestive of the rough Gothic parish churches to be found in most country villages.
10. Recalling the dolt who gives his name to Molière's comedy.
11. Succeed, thrive.
12. Returning to the Waller poem, which Mirabell immediately and aptly continues, playing in the succeeding lines on Apollo's pursuit of Daphne, who is changed to a laurel tree (the source of Apollo's crown).
13. Difficult.

Or is this pretty artifice contrived to signify that here the chase must
end, and my pursuit be crowned, for you can fly no further?

MILLAMANT   Vanity! No—I'll fly and be followed to the last moment. Though
I am upon the very verge of matrimony, I expect you should solicit me
as much as if I were wavering at the grate of a monastery,[14] with one
foot over the threshold. I'll be solicited to the very last, nay, and afterwards.

MIRABELL   What, after the last?

MILLAMANT   Oh, I should think I was poor and had nothing to bestow, if I
were reduced to an inglorious ease and freed from the agreeable fatigues
of solicitation.

MIRABELL   But do not you know, that when favours are conferred upon instant [15] and tedious solicitation, that they diminish in their value, and
that both the giver loses the grace and the receiver lessens his pleasure?

MILLAMANT   It may be in things of common application, but never sure in
love. Oh, I hate a lover that can dare to think he draws a moment's air
independent on the bounty of his mistress. There is not so impudent a
thing in nature as the saucy look of an assured man, confident of success.
The pedantic arrogance of a very husband has not so pragmatical [16] an
air. Ah! I'll never marry, unless I am first made sure of my will and
pleasure.

MIRABELL   Would you have 'em both before marriage? Or will you be contented with the first now and stay for the other till after grace?

MILLAMANT   Ah, don't be impertinent.—My dear liberty, shall I leave thee?
My faithful solitude, my darling contemplation, must I bid you then
adieu? Ay-h, adieu—my morning thoughts, agreeable wakings, indolent
slumbers, all ye *douceurs,* ye *sommeils du matin,*[17] adieu?—I can't do't,
'tis more than impossible. Positively, Mirabell, I'll lie abed in a morning
as long as I please.

MIRABELL   Then I'll get up in a morning as early as I please.

MILLAMANT   Ah! Idle creature, get up when you will.—And d'ye hear, I
won't be called names after I'm married; positively I won't be called
names.

MIRABELL   Names?

MILLAMANT   Aye, as wife, spouse, my dear, joy, jewel, love, sweetheart, and
the rest of that nauseous cant in which men and their wives are so ful-
somely familiar—I shall never bear that.—Good Mirabell, don't let us
be familiar or fond, nor kiss before folks, like my Lady Fadler [18] and
Sir Francis; nor go to Hyde Park together the first Sunday in a new
chariot to provoke eyes and whispers, and then never to be seen together
again, as if we were proud of one another the first week and ashamed
of one another for ever after. Let us never visit together nor go to a play
together, but let us be very strange [19] and well bred. Let us be as strange

14. Convent.
15. Urgent.
16. Conceited.
17. "Comforts and morning sleep."
18. Meaning Fondler.
19. Reserved.

as if we had been married a great while, and as well bred as if we were not married at all.

MIRABELL   Have you any more conditions to offer? Hitherto your demands are pretty reasonable.

MILLAMANT   Trifles,—as liberty to pay and receive visits to and from whom I please; to write and receive letters, without interrogatories or wry faces on your part. To wear what I please, and choose conversation with regard only to my own taste; to have no obligation upon me to converse with wits that I don't like, because they are your acquaintance; or to be intimate with fools because they may be your relations. Come to dinner when I please, dine in my dressing-room when I'm out of humour, without giving a reason. To have my closet inviolate; to be sole empress of my tea-table, which you must never presume to approach without first asking leave. And lastly, wherever I am, you shall always knock at the door before you come in. These articles subscribed, if I continue to endure you a little longer, I may by degrees dwindle into a wife.

MIRABELL   Your bill of fare is something advanced [20] in this latter account. Well, have I liberty to offer conditions—that when you are dwindled into a wife, I may not be beyond measure enlarged into a husband?

MILLAMANT   You have free leave. Propose your utmost; speak and spare not.

MIRABELL   I thank you. *Imprimis* [21] then, I covenant that your acquaintance be general; that you admit no sworn confidante or intimate of your own sex, no she-friend to screen her affairs under your countenance and tempt you to make trial of a mutual secrecy. No decoy-duck to wheedle you a fop-scrambling [22] to the play in a mask—then bring you home in a pretended fright, when you think you shall be found out—and rail at me for missing the play and disappointing the frolic which you had, to pick me up and prove my constancy.

MILLAMANT   Detestable *imprimis!* I go to the play in a mask!

MIRABELL   *Item,* I article,[23] that you continue to like your own face as long as I shall; and while it passes current with me, that you endeavour not to new-coin it. To which end, together with all vizards [24] for the day, I prohibit all masks for the night, made of oiled-skins and I know not what—hog's bones, hare's gall, pig-water, and the marrow of a roasted cat. In short, I forbid all commerce with the gentlewoman in What-d'ye-call-it Court. *Item,* I shut my doors against all bawds with baskets, and pennyworths of muslin, china, fans, atlases,[25] etc. *Item,* when you shall be breeding——

MILLAMANT   Ah! name it not.

MIRABELL   Which may be presumed, with a blessing on our endeavours——

MILLAMANT   Odious endeavours!

MIRABELL   I denounce against all strait lacing,[26] squeezing for a shape, till

---

20. Extended.
21. "First of all" (in the language of a legal contract).
22. Hoping to attract fops.
23. Stipulate.
24. Masks for dress, as opposed to cosmetic masks "for the night."
25. Oriental satins.
26. Tight lacing of corsets.

you mold my boy's head like a sugar-loaf, and instead of a man-child, make me the father to a crooked billet.[27] Lastly, to the dominion of the tea-table I submit,—but with proviso, that you exceed not in your province; but restrain yourself to native and simple tea-table drinks, as tea, chocolate, and coffee, as likewise to genuine and authorized tea-table talk—such as mending of fashions, spoiling reputations, railing at absent friends, and so forth—but that on no account you encroach upon the men's prerogative and presume to drink healths or toast fellows; for prevention of which I banish all foreign forces, all auxiliaries to the tea-table, as orange-brandy, all aniseed, cinnamon, citron, and Barbadoes waters, together with ratafia and the most noble spirit of clary,[28]—but for cowslip-wine, poppy water, and all dormitives,[29] those I allow. These provisos admitted, in other things I may prove a tractable and complying husband.

MILLAMANT   Oh, horrid provisos! filthy strong waters! I toast fellows, odious men! I hate your odious provisos.

MIRABELL   Then we're agreed. Shall I kiss your hand upon the contract? And here comes one to be a witness to the sealing of the deed.

[*Enter* MRS. FAINALL]

MILLAMANT   Fainall, what shall I do? Shall I have him? I think I must have him.

MRS. FAINALL   Aye, aye, take him, take him, what should you do?

MILLAMANT   Well then—I'll take my death, I'm in a horrid fright—Fainall, I shall never say it—well—I think—I'll endure you.

MRS. FAINALL   Fie, fie! have him, have him, and tell him so in plain terms; for I am sure you have a mind to him.

MILLAMANT   Are you? I think I have—and the horrid man looks as if he thought so too.—Well, you ridiculous thing you, I'll have you—I won't be kissed, nor I won't be thanked—here, kiss my hand though.—So, hold your tongue now, and don't say a word.

MRS. FAINALL   Mirabell, there's a necessity for your obedience;—you have neither time to talk nor stay. My mother is coming; and in my conscience, if she should see you, would fall into fits, and maybe not recover time enough to return to Sir Rowland, who as Foible tells me, is in a fair way to succeed. Therefore spare your ecstasies for another occasion, and slip down the back stairs, where Foible waits to consult you.

MILLAMANT   Aye, go, go. In the meantime I suppose you have said something to please me.

MIRABELL   I am all obedience.

[*Exit* MIRABELL]

MRS. FAINALL   Yonder Sir Wilfull's drunk; and so noisy that my mother has been forced to leave Sir Rowland to appease him; but he answers her only with singing and drinking.—What they have done by this time I know not; but Petulant and he were upon quarrelling as I came by.

27. Piece of firewood.
28. All of the alcoholic drinks ("strong waters").
29. Drinks that help one sleep.

MILLAMANT   Well, if Mirabell should not make a good husband, I am a lost thing—for I find I love him violently.

MRS. FAINALL   So it seems, when you mind not what's said to you.—If you doubt him, you had best take up with Sir Wilfull.

MILLAMANT   How can you name that superannuated lubber? foh!

[*Enter* WITWOUD *from drinking*]

MRS. FAINALL   So, is the fray made up, that you have left 'em?

WITWOUD   Left 'em? I could stay no longer—I have laughed like ten christ'-nings—I am tipsy with laughing.—If I had stayed any longer I should have burst,—I must have been let out and pieced in the sides like an unsized camlet.³⁰—Yes, yes, the fray is composed; my lady came in like a *nolle prosequi* ³¹ and stopped their proceedings.

MILLAMANT   What was the dispute?

WITWOUD   That's the jest; there was no dispute. They could neither of 'em speak for rage; and so fell a sputt'ring at one another like two roasting apples.

[*Enter* PETULANT *drunk*]

Now, Petulant, all's over, all's well. Gad, my head begins to whim it about.³²—Why dost thou not speak? Thou art both as drunk and as mute as a fish.

PETULANT   Look you, Mrs. Millamant—if you can love me, dear nymph—say it—and that's the conclusion—pass on, or pass off,—that's all.

WITWOUD   Thou hast uttered volumes, folios, in less than *decimo sexto*,³³ my dear Lacedemonian. Sirrah Petulant, thou art an epitomizer of words.

PETULANT   Witwoud—you are an annihilator of sense.

WITWOUD   Thou art a retailer of phrases, and dost deal in remnants of remnants, like a maker of pincushions—thou art in truth (metaphorically speaking) a speaker of shorthand.

PETULANT   Thou art (without a figure) just one half of an ass; and Baldwin ³⁴ yonder, thy half-brother, is the rest.—A gemini ³⁵ of asses split would make just four of you.

WITWOUD   Thou dost bite, my dear mustard seed; kiss me for that.

PETULANT   Stand off—I'll kiss no more males,—I have kissed your twin yonder in a humour of reconciliation, till he [*Hiccup*] rises upon my stomach like a radish.

MILLAMANT   Eh! filthy creature!—what was the quarrel?

PETULANT   There was no quarrel—there might have been a quarrel.

WITWOUD   If there had been words enow between 'em to have expressed provocation, they had gone together by the ears like a pair of castanets.

PETULANT   You were the quarrel.

MILLAMANT   Me!

---

30. Unstiffened cloth (of wool and silk).
31. A motion of the prosecution to withdraw its case.
32. Spin.
33. The smallest of books, in as few words as a Spartan ("Lacedemonian") or a summarizer could use.
34. The name of the ass in *Reynard the Fox*.
35. Pair of twins.

PETULANT   If I have a humour to quarrel, I can make less matters conclude premises. If you are not handsome, what then, if I have a humour to prove it?—If I shall have my reward, say so; if not, fight for your face the next time yourself.—I'll go sleep.

WITWOUD   Do, wrap thyself up like a woodlouse, and dream revenge—and hear me, if thou canst learn to write by tomorrow morning, pen me a challenge—I'll carry it for thee.

PETULANT   Carry your mistress's monkey a spider,[36]—go flea dogs and read romances!—I'll go to bed to my maid.

[*Exit*]

MRS. FAINALL   He's horridly drunk.—How came you all in this pickle?

WITWOUD   A plot, a plot, to get rid of the knight,—your husband's advice; but he sneaked off.

[*Enter* LADY WISHFORT, *and* SIR WILFULL, *drunk*]

LADY WISHFORT   Out upon't, out upon't, at years of discretion, and comport yourself at this rantipole [37] rate!

SIR WILFULL   No offence, aunt.

LADY WISHFORT   Offence? As I'm a person, I'm ashamed of you.—Fogh! how you stink of wine! D'ye think my niece will ever endure such a borachio! [38] you're an absolute borachio.

SIR WILFULL   Borachio!

LADY WISHFORT   At a time when you should commence an amour and put your best foot foremost——

SIR WILFULL   'Sheart, an you grutch me your liquor, make a bill. Give me more drink, and take my purse. [*Sings*]

> Prithee fill me the glass
> Till it laugh in my face,
> With ale that is potent and mellow;
> He that whines for a lass,
> Is an ignorant ass,
> For a bumper has not its fellow.

But if you would have me marry my cousin,—say the word, and I'll do't—Wilfull will do't, that's the word—Wilfull, will do't, that's my crest—my motto I have forgot.

LADY WISHFORT   My nephew's a little overtaken, cousin—but 'tis with drinking your health.—O' my word you are obliged to him——

SIR WILFULL   *In vino veritas,*[39] aunt.—If I drunk your health today, cousin, —I am a borachio. But if you have a mind to be married, say the word, and send for the piper; Wilfull will do't. If not, dust it away, and let's have t'other round.—Tony, 'odsheart, where's Tony.—Tony's an honest fellow, but he spits after a bumper, and that's a fault. [*Sings*]

> We'll drink and we'll never ha' done, boys,
> Put the glass then around with the sun, boys,

36. Monkeys were believed to eat insects; for lice, see Swift, *A Tale of a Tub,* II.
37. Ill-mannered.
38. Drunkard, from Spanish term for wine bag.
39. "In wine there is truth."

Let Apollo's example invite us;
  For he's drunk every night,
  And that makes him so bright,
And he's able next morning to light us.

The sun's a good pimple,[40] an honest soaker; he has a cellar at your Antipodes. If I travel, aunt, I touch at your Antipodes.—Your Antipodes are a good rascally sort of topsy-turvy fellows. If I had a bumper, I'd stand upon my head and drink a health to 'em.—A match or no match, cousin with the hard name?—Aunt, Wilfull will do't. If she has her maidenhead, let her look to't; if she has not, let her keep her own counsel in the meantime, and cry out at the nine months' end.

MILLAMANT Your pardon, madam, I can stay no longer—Sir Wilfull grows very powerful. Egh! how he smells! I shall be overcome if I stay. Come, cousin.

[*Exeunt* MILLAMANT *and* MRS. FAINALL]

LADY WISHFORT Smells! he would poison a tallow-chandler and his family.[41] Beastly creature, I know not what to do with him.—Travel, quoth a; aye travel, travel, get thee gone, get thee but far enough, to the Saracens, or the Tartars, or the Turks—for thou art not fit to live in a Christian commonwealth, thou beastly pagan.

SIR WILFULL Turks, no; no Turks, aunt. Your Turks are infidels, and believe not in the grape. Your Mahometan, your Mussulman, is a dry stinkard —no offence, aunt. My map says that your Turk is not so honest a man as your Christian— I cannot find by the map that your Mufti is orthodox —whereby it is a plain case, that orthodox is a hard word, aunt, and [*Hiccup*] Greek for claret. [*Sings*]

To drink is a Christian diversion,
Unknown to the Turk and the Persian:
  Let Mahometan fools
  Live by heathenish rules,
And be damned over tea-cups and coffee.
  But let British lads sing,
  Crown a health to the king,
And a fig for your sultan and sophy.[42]

Ah, Tony!

[*Enter* FOIBLE *and whispers* LADY WISHFORT]

LADY WISHFORT Sir Rowland impatient? Good lack! what shall I do with this beastly tumbril?[43]—Go lie down and sleep, you sot—or as I'm a person, I'll have you bastinadoed with broomsticks. Call up the wenches.

[*Exit* FOIBLE]

SIR WILFULL Ahey! Wenches, where are the wenches?

LADY WISHFORT Dear Cousin Witwoud, get him away, and you will bind me to

40. Companion.
41. Who are not very fragrant to begin with.
42. Shah.
43. Wagon, dung cart.

you inviolably. I have an affair of moment that invades me with some precipitation.—You will oblige me to all futurity.

WITWOUD   Come, knight.—Pox on him, I don't know what to say to him.—Will you go to a cock-match?

SIR WILFULL   With a wench, Tony? Is she a shake-bag,[44] sirrah? Let me bite your cheek for that.

WITWOUD   Horrible! He has a breath like a bagpipe.—Aye, aye; come, will you march, my Salopian?[45]

SIR WILFULL   Lead on, little Tony—I'll follow thee, my Anthony, my Tantony. Sirrah, thou sha't be my Tantony;[46] and I'll be thy pig.

—And a fig for your sultan and sophy.
[*Exit singing with* WITWOUD]

LADY WISHFORT   This will never do. It will never make a match.—At least before he has been abroad.
[*Enter* WAITWELL, *disguised as for* SIR ROWLAND]
Dear Sir Rowland, I am confounded with confusion at the retrospection of my own rudeness,—I have more pardons to ask than the pope distributes in the year of jubilee. But I hope where there is likely to be so near an alliance, we may unbend the severity of decorum and dispense with a little ceremony.

WAITWELL   My impatience, madam, is the effect of my transport;—and till I have the possession of your adorable person, I am tantalized on a rack; and do but hang, madam, on the tenter[47] of expectation.

LADY WISHFORT   You have excess of gallantry, Sir Rowland, and press things to a conclusion with a most prevailing vehemence.—But a day or two for decency of marriage——

WAITWELL   For decency of funeral, madam. The delay will break my heart—or if that should fail, I shall be poisoned. My nephew will get an inkling of my designs and poison me,—and I would willingly starve him before I die—I would gladly go out of the world with that satisfaction. That would be some comfort to me, if I could but live so long as to be revenged on that unnatural viper.

LADY WISHFORT   Is he so unnatural, say you? Truly I would contribute much both to the saving of your life and the accomplishment of your revenge. Not that I respect[48] myself, though he has been a perfidious wretch to me.

WAITWELL   Perfidious to you!

LADY WISHFORT   O Sir Rowland, the hours that he has died away at my feet, the tears that he has shed, the oaths that he has sworn, the palpitations that he has felt, the trances, and the tremblings, the ardours and the ecstasies, the kneelings and the risings, the heart-heavings, and the hand-grippings, the pangs and the pathetic regards of his protesting eyes! Oh, no memory can register!

44. Gamecock.
45. Shropshireman.
46. St. Anthony was usually shown with a pig, as the patron of swineherds.
47. Tenterhook.
48. Regard, think of.

WAITWELL   What, my rival! is the rebel my rival? a' dies!

LADY WISHFORT   No, don't kill him at once, Sir Rowland; starve him gradually inch by inch.

WAITWELL   I'll do't. In three weeks he shall be barefoot; in a month out at knees with begging an alms;—he shall starve upward and upward, till he has nothing living but his head, and then go out in a stink like a candle's end upon a save-all.[49]

LADY WISHFORT   Well, Sir Rowland, you have the way,—you are no novice in the labyrinth of love—you have the clue.—But as I am a person, Sir Rowland, you must not attribute my yielding to any sinister appetite, or indigestion of widowhood; nor impute my complacency to any lethargy of continence. I hope you do not think me prone to any iteration of nuptials.——

WAITWELL   Far be it from me——

LADY WISHFORT   If you do, I protest I must recede—or think that I have made a prostitution of decorums, but in the vehemence of compassion and to save the life of a person of so much importance——

WAITWELL   I esteem it so——

LADY WISHFORT   Or else you wrong my condescension——

WAITWELL   I do not, I do not——

LADY WISHFORT   Indeed you do.

WAITWELL   I do not, fair shrine of virtue.

LADY WISHFORT   If you think the least scruple of carnality was an ingredient——

WAITWELL   Dear madam, no. You are all camphire[50] and frankincense, all chastity and odour.

LADY WISHFORT   Or that——

[Enter FOIBLE]

FOIBLE   Madam, the dancers are ready, and there's one with a letter, who must deliver it into your own hands.

LADY WISHFORT   Sir Rowland, will you give me leave? Think favourably, judge candidly, and conclude you have found a person who would suffer racks in honour's cause, dear Sir Rowland, and will wait on you incessantly. [Exit]

WAITWELL   Fie, fie!—What a slavery have I undergone! Spouse, hast thou any cordial?—I want spirits.

FOIBLE   What a washy rogue art thou to pant thus for a quarter of an hour's lying and swearing to a fine lady!

WAITWELL   Oh, she is the antidote to desire. Spouse, thou wilt fare the worse for't—I shall have no appetite to iteration of nuptials—this eight and forty hours:—by this hand I'd rather be a chairman in the dog-days[51]— than act Sir Rowland till this time tomorrow.

[Enter LADY WISHFORT with a letter]

---

49. A small pan inserted under candlesticks to save the ends of candles.
50. Camphor, used to lessen sexual passion; here coupled with a fragrance used on sacred occasions (both "the antidote to desire").
51. One who carries a sedan-chair in hottest summer.

LADY WISHFORT   Call in the dancers.—Sir Rowland, we'll sit, if you please, and see the entertainment.

[*Dance*]

Now with your permission, Sir Rowland, I will peruse my letter—I would open it in your presence because I would not make you uneasy. If it should make you uneasy I would burn it—speak if it does—but you may see by the superscription it is like a woman's hand.

FOIBLE [*to him*]   By heaven! Mrs. Marwood's, I know it;—my heart aches—get it from her—

WAITWELL   A woman's hand? No, madam, that's no woman's hand, I see that already. That's somebody whose throat must be cut.

LADY WISHFORT   Nay, Sir Rowland, since you give me a proof of your passion by your jealousy, I promise you I'll make you a return, by a frank communication.—You shall see it—we'll open it together—look you here.

[*Reads*] 'Madam, though unknown to you,'—Look you there, 'tis from nobody that I know—'I have that honour for your character, that I think myself obliged to let you know you are abused. He who pretends to be Sir Rowland is a cheat and a rascal——' Oh heavens! what's this?

FOIBLE [*aside*]   Unfortunate, all's ruined.

WAITWELL   How, how, let me see, let me see! [*Reading*] 'A rascal, and disguised and suborned for that imposture,'—O villainy! O villainy!—'by the contrivance of——'

LADY WISHFORT   I shall faint, I shall die, I shall die, oh!

FOIBLE [*to him*]   Say 'tis your nephew's hand.—Quickly, his plot, swear, swear it.

WAITWELL   Here's a villain! Madam, don't you perceive it, don't you see it?

LADY WISHFORT   Too well, too well. I have seen too much.

WAITWELL   I told you at first I knew the hand. A woman's hand? The rascal writes a sort of a large hand, your Roman hand. I saw there was a throat to be cut presently. If he were my son, as he is my nephew, I'd pistol him——

FOIBLE   O treachery! But are you sure, Sir Rowland, it is his writing?

WAITWELL   Sure? am I here? do I live? do I love this pearl of India? I have twenty letters in my pocket from him, in the same character.

LADY WISHFORT   How!

FOIBLE   Oh, what luck it is, Sir Rowland, that you were present at this juncture! This was the business that brought Mr. Mirabell disguised to Madam Millamant this afternoon. I thought something was contriving when he stole by me and would have hid his face.

LADY WISHFORT   How, how!—I heard the villain was in the house indeed, and now I remember, my niece went away abruptly when Sir Wilfull was to have made his addresses.

FOIBLE   Then, then, madam, Mr. Mirabell waited for her in her chamber, but I would not tell your ladyship to discompose you when you were to receive Sir Rowland.

WAITWELL   Enough, his date is short.

FOIBLE   No, good Sir Rowland, don't incur the law.

WAITWELL   Law! I care not for law. I can but die, and 'tis in a good cause
—my lady shall be satisfied of my truth and innocence, though it cost
me my life.

LADY WISHFORT   No, dear Sir Rowland, don't fight; if you should be killed I
must never show my face; or hanged—oh, consider my reputation, Sir
Rowland! No, you shan't fight. I'll go in and examine my niece; I'll
make her confess. I conjure you, Sir Rowland, by all your love, not to
fight.

WAITWELL   I am charmed, madam, I obey. But some proof you must let me
give you;—I'll go for a black box, which contains the writings of my
whole estate, and deliver that into your hands.

LADY WISHFORT   Aye, dear Sir Rowland, that will be some comfort; bring the
black box.

WAITWELL   And may I presume to bring a contract to be signed this night?
May I hope so far?

LADY WISHFORT   Bring what you will; but come alive, pray come alive. Oh,
this is a happy discovery![52]

WAITWELL   Dead or alive I'll come—and married we will be in spite of
treachery; aye, and get an heir that shall defeat the last remaining
glimpse of hope in my abandoned nephew. Come, my buxom widow:

Ere long you shall substantial proof receive
That I'm an arrant [53] knight——

FOIBLE [aside]   Or arrant knave.
[Exeunt]

ACT V
A room in Lady Wishfort's house [1]
[LADY WISHFORT *and* FOIBLE]

LADY WISHFORT   Out of my house, out of my house, thou viper, thou serpent,
that I have fostered! thou bosom traitress, that I raised from nothing!—
begone, begone, begone, go, go!—that I took from washing of old
gauze and weaving of dead hair,[2] with a bleak blue nose, over a chafing-
dish of starved embers, and dining behind a traverse rag, in a shop no
bigger than a bird-cage,—go, go, starve again, do, do!

FOIBLE   Dear madam, I'll beg pardon on my knees.

LADY WISHFORT   Away, out, out, go set up for yourself again!—do, drive a
trade, do, with your threepenny worth of small ware, flaunting upon a
pack-thread, under a brandy-seller's bulk,[3] or against a dead wall by a
ballad-monger! Go, hang out an old Frisoneer gorget, with a yard of
yellow colberteen [4] again! do! an old gnawed mask, two rows of pins,

52. Fortunate disclosure.
53. Punning on (1) errant or wandering; (2) arrant or thoroughgoing; cf. Butler, *Hudibras*
I.i.21, 193.

1. Once more the original text reads "Scene continues."
2. That is, wig-making.
3. Displaying it on thick string, under a covered stall, or against a blank wall.
4. A woolen neckpiece with coarse yellow lace.

and a child's fiddle; a glass necklace with the beads broken, and a quilted nightcap with one ear! Go, go, drive a trade!—These were your commodities, you treacherous trull, this was your merchandise you dealt in, when I took you into my house, placed you next myself, and made you governante [5] of my whole family! You have forgot this, have you, now you have feathered your nest?

FOIBLE   No, no, dear madam. Do but hear me, have but a moment's patience —I'll confess all. Mr. Mirabell seduced me; I am not the first that he has wheedled with his dissembling tongue; your ladyship's own wisdom has been deluded by him,—then how should I, a poor ignorant, defend myself? O madam, if you knew but what he promised me, and how he assured me your ladyship should come to no damage!—Or else the wealth of the Indies should not have bribed me to conspire against so good, so sweet, so kind a lady as you have been to me.

LADY WISHFORT   No damage? What, to betray me, to marry me to a cast [6] servingman; to make me a receptacle, an hospital for a decayed pimp? No damage? O thou frontless [7] impudence, more than a big-bellied actress!

FOIBLE   Pray, do but hear me, madam; he could not marry your ladyship, madam.—No indeed, his marriage was to have been void in law; for he was married to me first, to secure your ladyship. He could not have bedded your ladyship; for if he had consummated with your ladyship, he must have run the risk of the law and been put upon his clergy.[8] —Yes indeed, I enquired of the law in that case before I would meddle or make.

LADY WISHFORT   What, then I have been your property, have I? I have been convenient to you, it seems—while you were catering for Mirabell, I have been broker for you? What, have you made a passive bawd of me?—This exceeds all precedent; I am brought to fine uses, to become a botcher [9] of second-hand marriages between Abigails and Andrews! [10] I'll couple you! Yes, I'll baste you together, you and your Philander! [11] I'll Duke's Place you, as I'm a person. Your turtle is in custody already; you shall coo in the same cage, if there be constable or warrant in the parish.
    [Exit]

FOIBLE   Oh, that ever I was born! Oh, that I was ever married!—A bride, aye, I shall be a Bridewell [12] bride. Oh!
    [Enter MRS. FAINALL]

MRS. FAINALL   Poor Foible, what's the matter?

5. Housekeeper.
6. Cast-off.
7. Shameless, as actresses were often regarded; cf. Dryden, *Mac Flecknoe,* ll. 74–77.
8. Obliged to plead "benefit of clergy," i.e. avoid the death penalty by proving he could read. (Clergy once could claim thereby the right to be tried in ecclesiastical rather than civil courts.)
9. Patcher.
10. Conventional names for maids and valets.
11. Lover.
12. Bridewell was the prison for women, where they were often required to beat hemp.

FOIBLE   O madam, my lady's gone for a constable; I shall be had to a justice, and put to Bridewell to beat hemp! Poor Waitwell's gone to prison already.

MRS. FAINALL   Have a good heart, Foible; Mirabell's gone to give security for him. This is all Marwood's and my husband's doing.

FOIBLE   Yes, yes; I know it, madam; she was in my lady's closet, and overheard all that you said to me before dinner. She sent the letter to my lady; and, that missing effect, Mr. Fainall laid this plot to arrest Waitwell when he pretended to go for the papers; and in the meantime Mrs. Marwood declared all to my lady.

MRS. FAINALL   Was there no mention made of me in the letter?—My mother does not suspect my being in the confederacy? I fancy Marwood has not told her, though she has told my husband.

FOIBLE   Yes, madam; but my lady did not see that part; we stifled the letter before she read so far. Has that mischievous devil told Mr. Fainall of your ladyship then?

MRS. FAINALL   Aye, all's out, my affair with Mirabell, everything discovered. This is the last day of our living together; that's my comfort.

FOIBLE   Indeed, madam, and so 'tis a comfort if you knew all;—he has been even with your ladyship, which I could have told you long enough since, but I love to keep peace and quietness, by my good will. I had rather bring friends together than set 'em at distance. But Mrs. Marwood and he are nearer related than ever their parents thought for.

MRS. FAINALL   Say'st thou so, Foible? Canst thou prove this?

FOIBLE   I can take my oath of it, madam, so can Mrs. Mincing; we have had many a fair word from Madam Marwood, to conceal something that passed in our chamber one evening when you were at Hyde Park;—and we were thought to have gone a-walking, but we went up unawares— though we were sworn to secrecy too. Madam Marwood took a book and swore us upon it; but it was but a book of verses and poems. So as long as it was not a Bible oath, we may break it with a safe conscience.

MRS. FAINALL   This discovery is the most opportune thing I could wish. Now, Mincing?

[*Enter* MINCING]

MINCING   My lady would speak with Mrs. Foible, mem. Mr. Mirabell is with her; he has set your spouse at liberty, Mrs. Foible, and would have you hide yourself in my lady's closet till my old lady's anger is abated. Oh, my old lady is in a perilous passion at something Mr. Fainall has said; he swears, and my old lady cries. There's a fearful hurricane, I vow. He says, mem, how that he'll have my lady's fortune made over to him or he'll be divorced.

MRS. FAINALL   Does your lady and Mirabell know that?

MINCING   Yes, mem, they have sent me to see if Sir Wilfull be sober, and to bring him to them. My lady is resolved to have him, I think, rather than lose such a vast sum as six thousand pound. Oh, come, Mrs. Foible, I hear my old lady.

MRS. FAINALL   Foible, you must tell Mincing that she must prepare to vouch when I call her.

FOIBLE   Yes, yes, madam.

MINCING   Oh, yes, mem, I'll vouch anything for your ladyship's service, be what it will.

[*Exeunt* MINCING *and* FOIBLE]

[*Enter* LADY WISHFORT *and* MRS. MARWOOD]

LADY WISHFORT   Oh, my dear friend, how can I enumerate the benefits that I have received from your goodness? To you I owe the timely discovery of the false vows of Mirabell, to you the detection of the impostor Sir Rowland. And now you are become an intercessor with my son-in-law, to save the honour of my house, and compound for the frailties of my daughter. Well, friend, you are enough to reconcile me to the bad world, or else I would retire to deserts and solitudes, and feed harmless sheep by groves and purling streams. Dear Marwood, let us leave the world, and retire by ourselves and be shepherdesses.

MRS. MARWOOD   Let us first dispatch the affair in hand, madam. We shall have leisure to think of retirement afterwards.—Here is one who is concerned in the treaty.

LADY WISHFORT   O daughter, daughter, is it possible thou shouldst be my child, bone of my bone, and flesh of my flesh, and as I may say, another me; and yet transgress the most minute particle of severe virtue? Is it possible you should lean aside to iniquity, who have been cast in the direct mold of virtue? I have not only been a mold but a pattern for you, and a model for you, after you were brought into the world.

MRS. FAINALL   I don't understand your ladyship.

LADY WISHFORT   Not understand? Why, have you not been naught? [13] Have you not been sophisticated? [14] Not understand? Here I am ruined to compound for your caprices and your cuckoldoms. I must pawn my plate and my jewels, and ruin my niece, and all little enough——

MRS. FAINALL   I am wronged and abused, and so are you. 'Tis a false accusation, as false as hell, as false as your friend there, aye, or your friend's friend, my false husband.

MRS. MARWOOD   My friend, Mrs. Fainall? Your husband my friend! what do you mean?

MRS. FAINALL   I know what I mean, madam, and so do you; and so shall the world at a time convenient.

MRS. MARWOOD   I am sorry to see you so passionate, madam. More temper [15] would look more like innocence. But I have done. I am sorry my zeal to serve your ladyship and family should admit of misconstruction or make me liable to affronts. You will pardon me, madam, if I meddle no more with an affair in which I am not personally concerned.

LADY WISHFORT   O dear friend, I am so ashamed that you should meet with such returns;—[*To* MRS. FAINALL] You ought to ask pardon on your knees, ungrateful creature! She deserves more from you, than all your life can accomplish.—[*To* MRS. MARWOOD] Oh, don't leave me destitute in this perplexity!—no, stick to me, my good genius.

13. Immoral.
14. Corrupted.
15. Composure.

MRS. FAINALL   I tell you, madam, you're abused.—Stick to you? aye, like a leech, to suck your best blood—she'll drop off when she's full. Madam, you sha' not pawn a bodkin,[16] nor part with a brass counter in composition for me. I defy 'em all. Let 'em prove their aspersions. I know my own innocence, and dare stand by a trial.
[*Exit*]

LADY WISHFORT   Why, if she should be innocent, if she should be wronged after all, ha? I don't know what to think,—and I promise you, her education has been unexceptionable—I may say it; for I chiefly made it my own care to initiate her very infancy in the rudiments of virtue, and to impress upon her tender years a young odium and aversion to the very sight of men;—aye, friend, she would ha' shrieked if she had but seen a man, till she was in her teens! As I'm a person, 'tis true. She was never suffered to play wih a male-child, though but in coats; nay, her very babies [17] were of the feminine gender. Oh, she never looked a man in the face but her own father or the chaplain, and him we made a shift to put upon her for a woman, by the help of his long garments and his sleek face, till she was going in her fifteen.

MRS. MARWOOD   'Twas much she should be deceived so long.

LADY WISHFORT   I warrant you, or she would never have borne to have been catechized by him; and have heard his long lectures against singing and dancing and such debaucheries; and going to filthy plays, and profane music-meetings, where the lewd trebles squeak nothing but bawdy, and the basses roar blasphemy. Oh, she would have swooned at the sight or name of an obscene play-book—and can I think, after all this, that my daughter can be naught? What, a whore? And thought it excommunication to set her foot within the door of a playhouse! [18] O my dear friend, I can't believe it. No, no! As she says, let him prove it, let him prove it!

MRS. MARWOOD   Prove it, madam? What, and have your name prostituted in a public court? Yours and your daughter's reputation worried at the bar by a pack of bawling lawyers? To be ushered in with an 'Oyez' of scandal; and have your case opened by an old fumbling lecher in a quoif [19] like a man midwife, to bring your daughter's infamy to light; to be a theme for legal punsters, and quibblers by the statute; and become a jest, against a rule of court, where there is no precedent for a jest in any record, not even in Doomsday Book; [20] to discompose the gravity of the bench, and provoke naughty interrogatories in more naughty law Latin; while the good judge, tickled with the proceeding, simpers under a grey beard, and fidges off and on his cushion as if he had swallowed cantharides, or sat upon cowitch! [21]

16. Hairpin.
17. Dolls.
18. Here, as in Lady Wishfort's mixture of Puritan works and Jeremy Collier's tract in her closet, Congreve is mocking Collier's denunciation of the immorality of the stage.
19. Lawyer's cap.
20. The oldest of legal records, a survey of lands made in 1085–86 by order of William the Conqueror.
21. Fidgets as if he had swallowed the aphrodisiac Spanish fly or sat upon cowhage, a plant covered with stinging hairs.

LADY WISHFORT   Oh, 'tis very hard!

MRS. MARWOOD   And then to have my young revellers of the Temple take notes, like 'prentices at a conventicle; [22] and after, talk it all over again in Commons, or before drawers in an eating-house.

LADY WISHFORT   Worse and worse!

MRS. MARWOOD   Nay, this is nothing; if it would end here, 'twere well. But it must after this be consigned by the shorthand writers to the public press; and from thence be transferred to the hands, nay, into the throats and lungs of hawkers, with voices more licentious than the loud flounderman's, or the woman that cries grey-pease; and this you must hear till you are stunned; nay, you must hear nothing else for some days.

LADY WISHFORT   Oh, 'tis insupportable. No, no, dear friend, make it up, make it up; aye, aye, I'll compound. I'll give up all, myself and my all, my niece and her all,—anything, everything for composition.

MRS. MARWOOD   Nay, madam, I advise nothing; I only lay before you, as a friend, the inconveniencies which perhaps you have overseen. Here comes Mr. Fainall. If he will be satisfied to huddle up all in silence, I shall be glad. You must think I would rather congratulate than condole with you.

[*Enter* FAINALL]

LADY WISHFORT   Aye, aye, I do not doubt it, dear Marwood; no, no, I do not doubt it.

FAINALL   Well, madam; I have suffered myself to be overcome by the importunity of this lady your friend; and am content you shall enjoy your own proper estate during life, on condition you oblige yourself never to marry, under such penalty as I think convenient.

LADY WISHFORT   Never to marry?

FAINALL   No more Sir Rowlands;—the next imposture may not be so timely detected.

MRS. MARWOOD   That condition, I dare answer, my lady will consent to without difficulty; she has already but·too much experienced the perfidiousness of men. Besides, madam, when we retire to our pastoral solitude we shall bid adieu to all other thoughts.

LADY WISHFORT   Aye, that's true; but in case of necessity, as of health, or some such emergency——

FAINALL   Oh, if you are prescribed marriage, you shall be considered; I will only reserve to myself the power to choose for you. If your physic be wholesome, it matters not who is your apothecary. Next, my wife shall settle on me the remainder of her fortune not made over already, and for her maintenance depend entirely on my discretion.

LADY WISHFORT   This is most inhumanly savage; exceeding the barbarity of a Muscovite husband.

FAINALL   I learned it from his Czarish majesty's retinue,[23] in a winter evening's conference over brandy and pepper, amongst other secrets of matrimony and policy as they are at present practised in the northern

22. Law students taking notes like apprentices sent by their Puritan masters to report on a sermon.
23. Peter the Great had visited London in 1698.

hemisphere. But this must be agreed unto, and that positively. Lastly, I will be endowed, in right of my wife, with that six thousand pound which is the moiety of Mrs. Millamant's fortune in your possession; and which she has forfeited (as will appear by the last will and testament of your deceased husband, Sir Jonathan Wishfort) by her disobedience in contracting herself against your consent or knowledge; and by refusing the offered match with Sir Wilfull Witwoud, which you, like a careful aunt, had provided for her.

LADY WISHFORT   My nephew was *non compos*,[24] and could not make his addresses.

FAINALL   I come to make demands,—I'll hear no objections.

LADY WISHFORT   You will grant me time to consider?

FAINALL   Yes, while the instrument is drawing, to which you must set your hand till more sufficient deeds can be perfected, which I will take care shall be done with all possible speed. In the meanwhile, I will go for the said instrument, and till my return you may balance this matter in your own discretion.

[*Exit* FAINALL]

LADY WISHFORT   This insolence is beyond all precedent, all parallel; must I be subject to this merciless villain?

MRS. MARWOOD   'Tis severe indeed, madam, that you should smart for your daughter's wantonness.

LADY WISHFORT   'Twas against my consent that she married this barbarian, but she would have him, though her year [25] was not out.—Ah! her first husband, my son Languish, would not have carried it thus. Well, that was my choice, this is hers; she is matched now with a witness.[26] I shall be mad! Dear friend, is there no comfort for me? Must I live to be confiscated at this rebel-rate? [27]—Here come two more of my Egyptian plagues,[28] too.

[*Enter* MILLAMANT *and* SIR WILFULL]

SIR WILFULL   Aunt, your servant.

LADY WISHFORT   Out, caterpillar, call not me aunt! I know thee not!

SIR WILFULL   I confess I have been a little in disguise,[29] as they say,—'sheart! and I'm sorry for't. What would you have? I hope I committed no offence, aunt—and if I did I am willing to make satisfaction; and what can a man say fairer? If I have broke anything, I'll pay for't, an it cost a pound. And so let that content for what's past, and make no more words. For what's to come, to pleasure you I'm willing to marry my cousin. So pray let's all be friends; she and I are agreed upon the matter before a witness.

LADY WISHFORT   How's this, dear niece? Have I any comfort? Can this be true?

24. "Not of sound mind."
25. Of mourning as a widow.
26. With a vengeance.
27. That is, as completely as if I were a rebel.
28. The plagues visited upon Pharaoh for holding the Israelites in bondage (Exodus 7–12).
29. That is, not myself (a euphemism for "drunk").

MILLAMANT   I am content to be a sacrifice to your repose, madam; and to convince you that I had no hand in the plot, as you were misinformed, I have laid my commands on Mirabell to come in person, and be a witness that I give my hand to this flower of knighthood; and for the contract that passed between Mirabell and me, I have obliged him to make a resignation of it in your ladyship's presence. He is without, and waits your leave for admittance.

LADY WISHFORT   Well, I'll swear I am something revived at this testimony of your obedience; but I cannot admit that traitor;—I fear I cannot fortify myself to support his appearance. He is as terrible to me as a Gorgon; if I see him, I fear I shall turn to stone, petrify incessantly.[30]

MILLAMANT   If you disoblige him, he may resent your refusal, and insist upon the contract still. Then, 'tis the last time he will be offensive to you.

LADY WISHFORT   Are you sure it will be the last time?—If I were sure of that —shall I never see him again?

MILLAMANT   Sir Wilfull, you and he are to travel together, are you not?

SIR WILFULL   'Sheart, the gentleman's a civil gentleman, aunt, let him come in; why, we are sworn brothers and fellow-travellers. We are to be Pylades [31] and Orestes, he and I. He is to be my interpreter in foreign parts. He has been overseas once already; and with proviso that I marry my cousin, will cross 'em once again, only to bear me company. —'Sheart, I'll call him in;—an I set on't once, he shall come in; and see who'll hinder him.
[Exit]

MRS. MARWOOD [aside]   This is precious fooling, if it would pass; but I'll know the bottom of it.

LADY WISHFORT   O dear Marwood, you are not going?

MRS. MARWOOD   Not far, madam; I'll return immediately.
[Exit]
[Re-enter SIR WILFULL and MIRABELL]

SIR WILFULL   Look up, man, I'll stand by you; 'sbud, an she do frown, she can't kill you;—besides—hark'ee, she dare not frown desperately, because her face is none of her own; 'sheart, an she should, her forehead would wrinkle like the coat of a cream-cheese; but mum for that, fellow-traveller.

MIRABELL   If a deep sense of the many injuries I have offered to so good a lady, with a sincere remorse and a hearty contrition, can but obtain the least glance of compassion, I am too happy.—Ah, madam, there was a time—but let it be forgotten—I confess I have deservedly forfeited the high place I once held, of sighing at your feet; nay, kill me not, by turning from me in disdain—I come not to plead for favour,—nay, not for pardon; I am a suppliant only for your pity—I am going where I never shall behold you more——

SIR WILFULL—How, fellow-traveller! You shall go by yourself then.

MIRABELL   Let me be pitied first; and afterwards forgotten—I ask no more.

---

30. That is, instantly; as did those who beheld the face of the snake-haired Gorgon.
31. The loyal friend of Agamemnon's son and avenger.

SIR WILFULL   By'r Lady, a very reasonable request, and will cost you nothing, aunt. Come, come, forgive and forget, aunt; why you must, an you are a Christian.

MIRABELL   Consider, madam, in reality you could not receive much prejudice; it was an innocent device, though I confess it had a face of guiltiness,— it was at most an artifice which love contrived—and errors which love produces have ever been accounted venial. At least think it is punishment enough, that I have lost what in my heart I hold most dear, that to your cruel indignation I have offered up this beauty, and with her my peace and quiet; nay, all my hopes of future comfort.

SIR WILFULL   An he does not move me, would I might never be o' the quorum! [32]—an it were not as good a deed as to drink, to give her to him again, I would I might never take shipping!—Aunt, if you don't forgive quickly, I shall melt, I can tell you that. My contract went no further than a little mouth glue,[33] and that's hardly dry;—one doleful sigh more from my fellow-traveller and 'tis dissolved.

LADY WISHFORT   Well, nephew, upon your account.—Ah, he has a false insinuating tongue!—Well, sir, I will stifle my just resentment at my nephew's request. I will endeavour what I can to forget—but on proviso that you resign the contract with my niece immediately.

MIRABELL   It is in writing and with papers of concern; but I have sent my servant for it, and will deliver it to you, with all acknowledgments for your transcendent goodness.

LADY WISHFORT [apart]   Oh, he has witchcraft in his eyes and tongue! When I did not see him, I could have bribed a villain to his assassination; but his appearance rakes the embers which have so long lain smothered in my breast.

[Enter FAINALL and MRS. MARWOOD]

FAINALL   Your date of deliberation, madam, is expired. Here is the instrument; are you prepared to sign?

LADY WISHFORT   If I were prepared, I am not impowered. My niece exerts a lawful claim, having matched herself by my direction to Sir Wilfull.

FAINALL   That sham is too gross to pass on me, though 'tis imposed on you, madam.

MILLAMANT   Sir, I have given my consent.

MIRABELL   And, sir, I have resigned my pretensions.

SIR WILFULL   And sir, I assert my right; and will maintain it in defiance of you, sir, and of your instrument. 'Sheart, an you talk of an instrument, sir, I have an old fox [34] by my thigh shall hack your instrument of ram vellum [35] to shreds, sir! It shall not be sufficient for a mittimus [36] or a tailor's measure; therefore, withdraw your instrument, sir, or by'r Lady I shall draw mine.

LADY WISHFORT   Hold, nephew, hold!

32. Group of Justices of the Peace who must be present to constitute a legal court session.
33. Oral promise.
34. Sword.
35. Legal sheepskin.
36. Warrant of arrest.

MILLAMANT   Good Sir Wilfull, respite your valour!

FAINALL   Indeed? Are you provided of a guard, with your single beefeater [37] there? But I'm prepared for you, and insist upon my first proposal. You shall submit your own estate to my management, and absolutely make over my wife's to my sole use, as pursuant to the purport and tenor of this other covenant.[38] [*To* MRS. MILLAMANT] I suppose, madam, your consent is not requisite in this case; nor, Mr. Mirabell, your resignation; nor, Sir Wilfull, your right. You may draw your fox if you please, sir, and make a bear-garden [39] flourish somewhere else; for here it will not avail. This, my Lady Wishfort, must be subscribed, or your darling daughter's turned adrift, like a leaky hulk to sink or swim, as she and the current of this lewd town can agree.

LADY WISHFORT   Is there no means, no remedy, to stop my ruin? Ungrateful wretch! dost thou not owe thy being, thy subsistence, to my daughter's fortune?

FAINALL   I'll answer you when I have the rest of it in my possession.

MIRABELL   But that you would not accept of a remedy from my hands—I own I have not deserved you should owe any obligation to me; or else perhaps I could advise——

LADY WISHFORT   Oh, what? what? to save me and my child from ruin, from want, I'll forgive all that's past; nay, I'll consent to anything to come, to be delivered from this tyranny.

MIRABELL   Aye, madam, but that is too late; my reward is intercepted. You have disposed of her who only could have made me a compensation for all my services;—but be it as it may, I am resolved I'll serve you—you shall not be wronged in this savage manner!

LADY WISHFORT   How! Dear Mr. Mirabell, can you be so generous at last! But it is not possible. Hark'ee, I'll break my nephew's match, you shall have my niece yet and all her fortune, if you can but save me from this imminent danger.

MIRABELL   Will you? I take you at your word. I ask no more. I must have leave for two criminals to appear.

LADY WISHFORT   Aye, aye, anybody, anybody!

MIRABELL   Foible is one, and a penitent.

[*Enter* MRS. FAINALL, FOIBLE, *and* MINCING]

MRS. MARWOOD [*to* FAINALL]   Oh, my shame! these corrupt things are bought and brought hither to expose me.

[MIRABELL *and* LADY WISHFORT *go to* MRS. FAINALL *and* FOIBLE]

FAINALL   If it must all come out, why let 'em know it; 'tis but *the way of the world*. That shall not urge me to relinquish or abate one tittle of my terms; no, I will insist the more.

FOIBLE   Yes, indeed, madam, I'll take my Bible oath of it.

MINCING   And so will I, mem.

37. Name for a guard at the Tower of London.
38. Fainall, dropping his claim to Millamant's money, returns to his original demands ("this other covenant"), the price of remaining married and creating no scandal; this does not involve Millamant, Mirabell, or Sir Wilfull.
39. A place where bear-baiting noisily took place.

LADY WISHFORT O Marwood, Marwood, art thou false? my friend deceive me? Hast thou been a wicked accomplice with that profligate man?

MRS. MARWOOD Have you so much ingratitude and injustice to give credit against your friend, to the aspersions of two such mercenary trulls?

MINCING Mercenary, mem? I scorn your words. 'Tis true we found you and Mr. Fainall in the blue garret; by the same token, you swore us to secrecy upon Messalinas's poems.[40] Mercenary? No, if we would have been mercenary, we should have held our tongues; you would have bribed us sufficiently.

FAINALL Go, you are an insignificant thing!—Well, what are you the better for this! Is this Mr. Mirabell's expedient? I'll be put off no longer.—You, thing that was a wife, shall smart for this! I will not leave thee wherewithal to hide thy shame; your body shall be naked as your reputation.

MRS. FAINALL I despise you, and defy your malice! You have aspersed me wrongfully—I have proved your falsehood. Go you and your treacherous—I will not name it—but starve together—perish!

FAINALL Not while you are worth a groat, indeed, my dear. Madam, I'll be fooled no longer.

LADY WISHFORT Ah, Mr. Mirabell, this is small comfort, the detection of this affair.

MIRABELL Oh, in good time. Your leave for the other offender and penitent to appear, madam.

[*Enter* WAITWELL *with a box of writings*]

LADY WISHFORT O Sir Rowland!—Well, rascal!

WAITWELL What your ladyship pleases. I have brought the black box at last, madam.

MIRABELL Give it me. Madam, you remember your promise.

LADY WISHFORT Aye, dear sir.

MIRABELL Where are the gentlemen?

WAITWELL At hand, sir, rubbing their eyes—just risen from sleep.

FAINALL 'Sdeath, what's this to me? I'll not wait your private concerns.

[*Enter* PETULANT *and* WITWOUD]

PETULANT How now? what's the matter? whose hand's out? [41]

WITWOUD Heyday! what, are you all got together, like players at the end of the last act?

MIRABELL You may remember, gentlemen, I once requested your hands as witnesses to a certain parchment.

WITWOUD Aye, I do, my hand I remember—Petulant set his mark.

MIRABELL You wrong him; his name is fairly written, as shall appear.—You do not remember, gentlemen, anything of what that parchment contained? [*Undoing the box*]

WITWOUD No.

PETULANT Not I. I writ, I read nothing.

MIRABELL Very well, now you shall know.—Madam, your promise.

LADY WISHFORT Aye, aye, sir, upon my honour.

40. Presumably Mincing's version of *Miscellaneous Poems;* Messalina was the licentious wife of the Roman emperor Claudius.
41. Who's making trouble?

MIRABELL.   Mr. Fainall, it is now time that you should know that your lady, while she was at her own disposal, and before you had by your insinuations wheedled her out of a pretended settlement of the greatest part of her fortune——

FAINALL   Sir! pretended!

MIRABELL   Yes, sir. I say that this lady while a widow, having, it seems, received some cautions respecting your inconstancy and tyranny of temper, which from her own partial opinion and fondness of you she could never have suspected—she did, I say, by the wholesome advice of friends and of sages learned in the laws of this land, deliver this same as her act and deed to me in trust, and to the uses within mentioned. You may read if you please [*Holding out the parchment*]— though perhaps what is inscribed on the back may serve your occasions.

FAINALL   Very likely, sir. What's here? Damnation! [*Reads*] 'A deed of conveyance of the whole estate real of Arabella Languish, widow, in trust to Edward Mirabell.'— Confusion!

MIRABELL   Even so, sir; 'tis *the way of the world*, sir—of the widows of the world. I suppose this deed may bear an elder date than what you have obtained from your lady.

FAINALL   Perfidious fiend! then thus I'll be revenged. [*Offers to run at* MRS. FAINALL]

SIR WILFULL   Hold, sir! now you may make your bear-garden flourish somewhere else, sir.

FAINALL   Mirabell, you shall hear of this, sir, be sure you shall.—Let me pass, oaf.

[*Exit*]

MRS. FAINALL [*to* MRS. MARWOOD]   Madam, you seem to stifle your resentment. You had better give it vent.

MRS. MARWOOD   Yes, it shall have vent—and to your confusion, or I'll perish in the attempt.

[*Exit*]

LADY WISHFORT   O daughter, daughter! 'tis plain thou hast inherited thy mother's prudence.

MRS. FAINALL   Thank Mr. Mirabell, a cautious friend, to whose advice all is owing.

LADY WISHFORT   Well, Mr. Mirabell, you have kept your promise—and I must perform mine.—First, I pardon for your sake Sir Rowland there and Foible;—the next thing is to break the matter to my nephew— and how to do that——

MIRABELL   For that, madam, give yourself no trouble; let me have your consent. Sir Wilfull is my friend; he has had compassion upon lovers, and generously engaged a volunteer in this action, for our service, and now designs to prosecute his travels.

SIR WILFULL   'Sheart, aunt, I have no mind to marry. My cousin's a fine lady, and the gentleman loves her and she loves him, and they deserve one another; my resolution is to see foreign parts—I have set on't—and when I'm set on't, I must do't. And if these two gentlemen would travel too, I think they may be spared.

PETULANT   For my part, I say little—I think things are best off or on.

WITWOUD   I'gad, I understand nothing of the matter; I'm in a maze yet, like a dog in a dancing-school.

LADY WISHFORT   Well, sir, take her, and with her all the joy I can give you.

MILLAMANT   Why does not the man take me? Would you have me give myself to you over again?

MIRABELL   Aye, and over and over again; for I would have you as often as possibly I can. [*Kisses her hand*] Well, heaven grant I love you not too well, that's all my fear.

SIR WILFULL   'Sheart, you'll have him time enough to toy after you're married; or if you will toy now, let us have a dance in the meantime, that we who are not lovers may have some other employment besides looking on.

MIRABELL   With all my heart, dear Sir Wilfull. What shall we do for music?

FOIBLE   O sir, some that were provided for Sir Rowland's entertainment are yet within call.

[*A dance*]

LADY WISHFORT   As I am a person, I can hold out no longer; I have wasted my spirits so today already, that I am ready to sink under the fatigue; and I cannot but have some fears upon me yet that my son Fainall will pursue some desperate course.

MIRABELL   Madam, disquiet not yourself on that account; to my knowledge his circumstances are such he must of force comply. For my part, I will contribute all that in me lies to a reunion; in the meantime, madam [*To* MRS. FAINALL], let me before these witnesses restore to you this deed of trust. It may be a means, well managed, to make you live easily together.

From hence let those be warned, who mean to wed;
Lest mutual falsehood stain the bridal-bed;
For each deceiver to his cost may find,
That marriage frauds too oft are paid in kind.

[*Exeunt omnes*]
1700

JONATHAN SWIFT
1667–1745

Swift is the greatest ironist in English literature, and he has as a result been accused of all the malevolence and blindness that resentment can invent. He does not allow man much comfort or dignity, and he cruelly reduces grand pretensions to systematic follies and mechanized brutality. In fact, Swift's characteristic device is to invent some rational basis for the behavior that men fall into unthinkingly or self-indulgently; by rationalizing folly, by finding eloquent arguments for the unspeakable, Swift divorces intention (usually noble) from achievement (somewhat shabbier) and shows what one would have to intend if one were to undertake deliberately what men in fact accomplish. If we live by exploiting others, we are only a short way (just enough to save our self-esteem) from cannibalism, and Swift shocks us with that possibility in

A Modest Proposal. If we have turned religion into an accommodation of our "schemes of wealth and power," always sure to secure a blessing for what is profitable or expedient, we are on the way to abolishing Christianity, and we need not go through the explicit motions, given our great skill at simply undermining the faith by which we might otherwise be judged. There is no wonder that Swift has aroused resentment; there are great temptations to misread him and make him a historical curiosity. The easiest way of all is to attribute his unaccommodating irony to the psychological aberrations of a disturbed or conflict-torn man.

Swift was born in Ireland of English parents and, after studying at Trinity College, Dublin, he entered the household of Sir William Temple, a retired diplomat, as a secretary. Temple lived in retirement outside of London, and he had a fine library, which Swift used well. It was in Temple's household that Swift first met Hester Johnson, with whose education he helped, and upon whose affection he depended greatly during their years together in Dublin. His relations with Temple were close but difficult, and Swift left at one point to become an Anglican parish priest in northern Ireland. Upon his return to England he remained with Temple until the latter's death, helping prepare Temple's works for publication and writing his own remarkable first volume of satire, which included *A Tale of a Tub* and *The Battle of the Books* (written in the 1690's and published in 1704). While the *Tale* had great success, its ironic treatment of the church probably hurt Swift's ecclessiastical career.

In 1707 Swift was sent by the Church of Ireland to seek financial benefits from Queen Anne; during his year's stay in London, he became accepted as a man of letters and was close to Addison's literary circle. When he returned to London in 1710, he left the Whigs and gave his support to the Tory ministry of Robert Harley, later Earl of Oxford, on the grounds that the Whigs might sell the church short in their encouragement of Dissenters. For most of the four years that followed, until the fall of the ministry with the death of the Queen, Swift became a principal spokesman and propagandist for the Tories, through such a periodical as *The Examiner* and through such political pamphlets as *The Conduct of the Allies* (1713). He became a leading spirit in the Scriblerus Club with Pope and Dr. Arbuthnot, and he was able to win patronage for friends in difficulty, Addison among them.

With the fall of the ministry, Swift (who had been appointed Dean of St. Patrick's Cathedral, Dublin, in 1713) began his long Irish exile, the hope of a bishopric in England vanishing and the visits to London growing infrequent. He became in some measure an Irish patriot, trying to stir the Irish to self-respect and to resistance against English exploitation; and he won a considerable battle against Sir Robert Walpole through his *Drapier's Letters* of 1724–25. *Gulliver's Travels* contained strong political satire, and Swift had a hand in encouraging both Gay's *Beggar's Opera* and Pope's *Dunciad* in the following years. Throughout his lifetime Swift created a body of distinctive poetry, and finally his irony turned to a compendium of "polite conversation" and a penetrating set of *Directions to Servants*. At the end Swift's mind and memory gave way after years of labyrinthine vertigo, a disease of the middle ear that disturbed his sense of balance; he was cared for by others until his death, which fell in the year after Pope's.

Swift's irony required that he write in many guises, and each of these guises (masks or *personae*, as they have been called) tends to become in some degree a fool among knaves, a man more obtuse and more innocent than the wilier and more clear-headedly vicious knaves. The fool gives them away without meaning to betray, for he guilelessly acknowledges what they know enough to conceal. This contributes to that style of cool understatement which exacts from the reader a moral judgment it does not explicitly provide; in *Gulliver's Travels* it produces a surface of meticulously realistic narration such as the novel might later use. But in Swift's hands this very precision of recorded detail is meant to strike us with its failure to judge or feel and to require us to do so instead.

The Battle of the Books

Swift carries on the wide-ranging quarrel of the Ancients and Moderns which divided scholars in seventeenth-century France. Involved in the quarrel was the whole idea of progress. Were the Moderns inferior to the great Ancients, or were they their equals or even superiors? The defenders of the Ancients could claim that writers of later ages had done little more than borrow from the greatness of Homer and Virgil, Horace and Terence. They traced a pattern of slow but steady degeneration in the history of man. The defenders of the Moderns could point to the dead hand of Aristotle upon history and science and the great achievements that arose among the Moderns with the overthrow of foolish reverence for ancient authorities.

In England the quarrel took a special turn when Sir William Temple, Swift's patron, praised the work of Aesop and Phalaris at the expense of the Moderns, only to bring down the learned criticism of Richard Bentley, the greatest classical scholar of his time, who proved that Temple's Ancients were not nearly so ancient as Temple had thought them. The conflict also represented a clash between literary humanism and philological science, and Swift entered it with an effort to show the arrogance and insensitivity of those Moderns who could date a poem accurately but could neither write nor read one well. He invented the fable of a battle (presented in mock-heroic vein) among the books in the royal library (where Bentley was keeper of books), but the finest episode in the work is an interlude in which a pompous and ill-tempered Modern, the Spider, finds his Gothic cobweb invaded by a Bee. It should be noted that Gothic architecture and scholastic disputation were cheerfully granted to the Moderns by Swift, and Horatian urbanity—so recently revived as a model of style— is a quality of his Ancients. The Ancients, for Swift, represent those who keep the past alive in the present, fostering the virtues of antiquity and not—like Cornelius Scriblerus, in another satire to which Swift contributed—revering its rust. The Moderns in their ambition to be self-sufficient risk parochial narrowness; their manners show a failure of humanity as well as of humanism.

From A Full and True Account of the Battle Fought Last Friday, Between the Ancient and Modern Books in St. James's Library

[Episode of the Spider and the Bee]

Things were at this crisis when a material accident fell out. For upon the highest corner of a large window there dwelt a certain Spider, swollen up to the first magnitude by the destruction of infinite numbers of flies, whose spoils lay scattered before the gates of his palace, like human bones before the cave of some giant.[1] The avenues to his castle were guarded with turnpikes and palisadoes, all after the modern way of fortification.[2] After you had passed several courts, you came to the centre, wherein you might behold the constable [3] himself in his own lodgings, which had windows fronting to each avenue and ports [4] to sally out upon all occasions of prey or defence. In this mansion he had for some time dwelt in peace and plenty, without danger to his person by swallows from above or to his palace by brooms from below; when it was the pleasure of Fortune to conduct thither a wandering Bee, to whose curiosity a broken pane in the glass had discovered itself, and in he went; where, expatiating a while, he at last happened to alight upon one of the outward walls of the Spider's citadel; which, yielding to the unequal weight, sunk down to the very foundation. Thrice he endeavoured to force his passage, and thrice the centre shook. The Spider within, feeling the terrible convulsion, supposed at first that Nature was approaching to her final dissolution; [5] or else that Beelzebub [6] with all his legions was come to revenge the death of many thousands of his subjects, whom his enemy had slain and devoured. However, he at length valiantly resolved to issue forth and meet his fate. Meanwhile the Bee had acquitted himself of his toils,[7] and, posted securely at some distance, was employed in cleansing his wings and disengaging them from the ragged remnants of the cobweb. By this time the Spider was adventured out, when, beholding the chasms and ruins and dilapidations of his fortress, he was very near at his wit's end; he stormed and swore like a madman and swelled till he was ready to burst. At length, casting his eye upon the Bee and wisely gathering causes from events (for they knew each other by sight): 'A plague split you,' said he, 'for a giddy son of a whore. Is it you, with a vengeance, that have made this litter here? Could not you look before you, and be d—ned? Do you think I have nothing else to do, in the devil's name, but to mend and repair after your arse?'

'Good words, friend,' said the Bee (having now pruned himself and being disposed to droll), 'I'll give you my hand and word to come near your kennel no more; I was never in such a confounded pickle since I was born.'

'Sirrah,' replied the Spider, 'if it were not for breaking an old custom in our family never to stir abroad against an enemy, I should come and teach you better manners.'

'I pray have patience,' said the Bee, 'or you will spend your substance, and, for aught I see, you may stand in need of it all towards the repair of your house.'

'Rogue, rogue,' replied the Spider, 'yet methinks you should have more respect to a person whom all the world allows to be so much your betters.'

1. With echoes of Romance literature, which was defended later in the 18th century on the analogy of Gothic architecture.
2. One of the fields in which the Moderns were generally granted eminence, as was mathematics.
3. The keeper of a royal fortress or castle.
4. Gateways.
5. Swift often satirizes the gullible and superstitious fears of scientists.
6. Literally, the god of flies.
7. Snares, nets.

'By my troth,' said the Bee, 'the comparison will amount to a very good jest, and you will do me a favour to let me know the reasons that all the world is pleased to use in so hopeful [8] a dispute.'

At this the Spider, having swelled himself into the size and posture of a disputant, began his argument in the true spirit of controversy, with a resolution to be heartily scurrilous and angry, to urge on his own reasons without the least regard to the answers or objections of his opposite, and fully predetermined in his mind against all conviction.

'Not to disparage myself,' said he, 'by the comparison with such a rascal, what art thou but a vagabond without house or home, without stock or inheritance, born to no possession of your own but a pair of wings and a drone-pipe? Your livelihood is an universal plunder upon nature, a freebooter over fields and gardens; and, for the sake of stealing, will rob a nettle as easily as a violet. Whereas I am a domestic animal, furnished with a native stock within myself. This large castle (to show my improvements in the mathematics) is all built with my own hands, and the materials extracted altogether out of my own person.'

'I am glad,' answered the Bee, 'to hear you grant at least that I am come honestly by my wings and my voice; for then, it seems, I am obliged to Heaven alone for my flights and my music; and Providence would never have bestowed on me two such gifts without designing them for the noblest ends. I visit indeed all the flowers and blossoms of the field and the garden; but whatever I collect from thence enriches myself, without the least injury to their beauty, their smell, or their taste. Now, for you and your skill in architecture and other mathematics, I have little to say. In that building of yours there might, for aught I know, have been labour and method enough; but, by woful experience for us both, 'tis too plain the materials are naught, and I hope you will henceforth take warning and consider duration and matter as well as method and art. You boast, indeed, of being obliged to no other creature but of drawing and spinning out all from yourself; that is to say, if we may judge of the liquor in the vessel by what issues out, you possess a good plentiful store of dirt and poison in your breast; and, though I would by no means lessen or disparage your genuine stock of either, yet I doubt you are somewhat obliged, for an increase of both, to a little foreign assistance. Your inherent portion of dirt does not fail of acquisitions by sweepings exhaled from below; and one insect furnishes you with a share of poison to destroy another. So that, in short, the question comes all to this: whether is the nobler being of the two that which, by a lazy contemplation of four inches round, by an overweening pride which, feeding and engendering on itself, turns all into excrement and venom, producing nothing at all but flybane and a cobweb; or that which, by an universal range, with long search, much study, true judgement, and distinction of things, brings home honey and wax.'

This dispute was managed with such eagerness, clamour, and warmth, that the two parties of Books, in arms below, stood silent a while, waiting in suspense what would be the issue, which was not long undetermined: for the Bee, grown impatient at so much loss of time, fled straight away to a bed of roses without

8. Promising.

looking for a reply, and left the Spider like an orator, collected in himself and just prepared to burst out.

It happened upon this emergency that Aesop broke silence first. He had been of late most barbarously treated by a strange effect of the regent's humanity, who had tore off his title-page, sorely defaced one half of his leaves, and chained him fast among a shelf of Moderns. Where, soon discovering how high the quarrel was like to proceed, he tried all his arts, and turned himself to a thousand forms.[9] At length, in the borrowed shape of an ass, the regent mistook him for a Modern; by which means he had time and opportunity to escape to the Ancients, just when the Spider and the Bee were entering into their contest, to which he gave his attention with a world of pleasure; and when it was ended, swore in the loudest key that in all his life he had never known two cases so parallel and adapt to each other as that in the window and this upon the shelves. 'The disputants,' said he, 'have admirably managed the dispute between them, have taken in the full strength of all that is to be said on both sides, and exhausted the substance of every argument *pro* and *con*. It is but to adjust the reasonings of both to the present quarrel, then to compare and apply the labours and fruits of each, as the Bee has learnedly deduced them, and we shall find the conclusion fall plain and close upon the Moderns and us. For, pray, gentlemen, was ever anything so modern as the Spider in his air, his turns,[10] and his paradoxes? He argues in the behalf of you his brethren and himself with many boastings of his native stock and great genius, that he spins and spits wholly from himself, and scorns to own any obligation or assistance from without. Then he displays to you his great skill in architecture and improvement in the mathematics. To all this the Bee, as an advocate retained by us the Ancients, thinks fit to answer that, if one may judge of the great genius or inventions of the Moderns by what they have produced, you will hardly have countenance to bear you out in boasting of either. Erect your schemes with as much method and skill as you please; yet, if the materials be nothing but dirt, spun out of your own entrails (the guts of modern brains), the edifice will conclude at last in a cobweb, the duration of which, like that of other spiders' webs, may be imputed to their being forgotten, or neglected, or hid in a corner. For anything else of genuine that the Moderns may pretend to, I cannot recollect, unless it be a large vein of wrangling and satire, much of a nature and substance with the Spider's poison; which, however they pretend to spit wholly out of themselves, is improved by the same arts, by feeding upon the insects and vermin of the age. As for us the Ancients, we are content with the Bee to pretend to nothing of our own beyond our wings and our voice, that is to say, our flights and our language. For the rest, whatever we have got, has been by infinite labour and search and ranging through every corner of nature; the difference is that, instead of dirt and poison, we have rather chosen to fill our hives with honey and wax, thus furnishing mankind with the two noblest of things, which are sweetness and light.' [11]

1704

9. Referring to the many animals Aesop had characterized in his fables.
10. Witty plays on words (used ironically of his spluttering abuse).
11. The terms later borrowed and extended by Matthew Arnold in *Culture and Anarchy* (1869).

A Tale of a Tub

A Tale of a Tub, originally published in one volume with *The Battle of the Books* and *The Mechanical Operation of the Spirit,* a satire on religious enthusiasm, marks a turning point in English literature. It looks back to the age of baroque and Metaphysical wit—in such prose as the sermons of John Donne or Lancelot Andrewes or the secular works of Robert Burton and Sir Thomas Browne; in such verse as that of Cowley, whom Swift imitated in his earliest poems—and in looking back, through parody, it sees false and ingenious verbal wit and self-flattering sophistry. Swift mocks the extravagant arguments through metaphor, the fanciful system-building, and the constant "wresting" of terms. Behind this last concern, which had been awakened by the preaching of witty Anglican and enthusiastic Puritan alike, lay the words of Peter (II Peter 3:16) on the epistles of Paul: "in which are some things hard to be understood, which they that are unlearned and unstable wrest, as they do also the other Scriptures, unto their own destruction."

But the *Tale* is a twofold attack: upon the corruption of religion and of learning. The counterpart of the extremes in religion—"the frenzy of Platonic visions and the lethargic ignorance of Popish dreams," as Halifax called them—is the false learning that cultivates the letter at the expense of spirit, words at the expense of meaning. Here Swift returns to the attack upon Bentley he undertook in *The Battle* but extends his attack to include the other extreme of learning as well—superficiality, gullibility, and laziness. His point is that extremes meet, that the pride in self which creates carping arrogance in some produces obtuse complacency in others. The Spider's "lazy contemplation of four inches round" is easier to maintain if the Modern is convinced of his own inherent greatness, and Swift mocks this by showing the Moderns finding "momentous truths" in their most trivial and ephemeral effusions. They do this by ingenious allegorizing, in the manner of Bunyan or his more learned scholarly counterparts, and allegory releases the will to believe, overriding all empirical evidence or restraint from outside. It becomes the vehicle of the private will and imagination, and Swift finally treats the uncontrolled fancy, as Locke and others had done before him, as a kind of madness.

The *Tale* is, in form, an ingeniously baroque structure. After many prefatory and dedicatory sections, it interweaves an allegorical tale with self-styled digressions that gradually overwhelm the tale. (As Hobbes says, in the eighth chapter of *Leviathan,* "A great fancy is one kind of madness such as they have that, entering into any discourse, are snatched from their purpose . . . into so many and so long digressions and parentheses that they utterly lose themselves.") Swift's "digressions" are, in fact, the heart of the work, and the greatest of them is given below. They embody the themes of fancy, wit, and reason in the secular world, while the allegory presents the career of the Christian church once it enters the world. It is embodied in three brothers: Peter (the Church of Rome), Martin (Luther's moderate reforming Protestantism and the Church of England in particular), and Jack (Calvinism and other forms of radical Protestantism). The brothers are meant to live together in peace, but, as they enter the world—as in Section II below—they become more and more at odds, until Peter kicks the others out of doors. Recovering his senses, Martin tries to restore the original form of his coat and realizes that he cannot achieve pristine purity without damaging the fabric. He leaves some of those accretions that cannot safely be removed; but Jack, in utter reaction, tears his to shreds rather than have it show any trace of Peter's influence. The result, ironically, is that Peter's elaborate finery and Jack's rags look—at any distance—indistinguishable, and the modest "trimmer" Martin is hated by both.

The Digression on Madness has sometimes been discussed as if it were wholly negative in implication, as if it prepared us to accept the surfaces of things, only to damn us for doing so. But one must ask whether the defense of surface is meant to be plausible, and this is best determined by asking to what surface is opposed. The speaker involves us in an impossible choice between carping and superficiality, between mangling and piercing on the one hand and skimming on the other. Between these extremes the ideal of true analysis and tactful perception is lost, just as Martin is crowded off the scene by the barbarous vigor of Peter and Jack. The same problem recurs in the fourth voyage of *Gulliver's Travels,* where we must find a norm somewhere between the undisturbed rationality of the Houyhnhnms and the savage passions of the Yahoos.

Section IX makes clear, as earlier sections of the *Tale* have revealed, that Swift is writing in the guise of a Modern hack, full of avowed respect for all forms of modernity and of scorn for old-fashioned "common forms." He writes of madness with special authority as a former inhabitant of Bedlam, and he has all the zeal of a "projector," a man with schemes for public improvements that will win him profit or praise. The guise is a transparent one, for it is clearly the vehicle of a savage irony; but it accounts for the imperturbable ease with which the author both contradicts himself and gives himself away. We see through the speaker; he is given the relative consistency of a type, both psychological and social, that is meant to be recognized and to be given only so much credit as his limitations merit. He is less obviously a *persona* (that is, a mask or assumed identity) than Lemuel Gulliver, who has a name and a fuller history, but we miss much of his meaning if we ignore the allusiveness to contemporary styles and attitudes that shapes his role.

The title of Swift's work comes from a proverbial phrase for a nonsensical *jeu d'esprit* or whimsy, but he mockingly allegorizes it as the tub seamen throw out to distract a threatening whale, the whale in this case being the dangerous doctrines of Thomas Hobbes's *Leviathan.* So influential has that work been in seducing the young wits that serious disturbances might arise if they were not kept busy with harmless tasks, Swift implies, and this book is offered as an absorbing puzzle. In fact, it mocks their modernity and seeks to recall them to sanity.

From A Tale of a Tub

Written for the Universal Improvement of Mankind

Section II

Once upon a time there was a man who had three sons by one wife, and all at a birth; neither could the midwife tell certainly which was the eldest. Their father died while they were young; and upon his deathbed, calling the lads to him, spoke thus:

'Sons, because I have purchased no estate, nor was born to any, I have long considered of some good legacies to bequeath you; and at last, with much care, as well as expense, have provided each of you (here they are) a new coat. Now, you are to understand, that these coats have two virtues contained in them: one is that with good wearing they will last you fresh and sound as long as you live; the other is that they will grow in the same proportion with your bodies, lengthening and widening of themselves, so as to be always fit. Here, let me see them on you before I die. So, very well; pray, children, wear them clean and brush them often. You will find in my will [1] (here it is) full instructions in every particular concerning the wearing and management of your coats; wherein you must be very exact, to avoid the penalties I have appointed for every transgression or neglect, upon which your future fortunes will entirely depend. I have also commanded in my will, that you should live together in one house like brethren and friends, for then you will be sure to thrive, and not otherwise.'

Here the story says this good father died, and the three sons went all together to seek their fortunes.

I shall not trouble you with recounting what adventures they met for the first seven years, any farther than by taking notice that they carefully observed their father's will and kept their coats in very good order: that they travelled through several countries, encountered a reasonable quantity of giants, and slew certain dragons.[2]

Being now arrived at the proper age for producing themselves, they came up to town and fell in love with the ladies, but especially three, who about that time were in chief reputation: the Duchess d'Argent, Madame de Grands Titres, and the Countess d'Orgueil.[3] On their first appearance our three adventurers met with a very bad reception; and soon with great sagacity guessing out the reason, they quickly began to improve in the good qualities of the town. They writ, and rallied, and rhymed, and sung, and said, and said nothing: they drank, and fought, and whored, and slept, and swore, and took snuff: they went to new plays on the first night, haunted the chocolate-houses, beat the watch, lay on bulks,[4] and got claps: they bilked [5] hackney-coachmen, ran in debt with shop keepers, and lay with their wives: they killed bailiffs, kicked fiddlers down stairs, eat at Locket's,[6] loitered at Will's: [7] they talked of the drawing-room and never came there: dined with lords they never saw: whispered a duchess, and spoke never a word: [8] exposed the scrawls of their laundress for billetdoux of quality: came ever just from court and were never seen in it: attended the levee *sub dio:* [9] got a list of peers by heart in one company, and with great familiarity retailed them in another. Above all, they

---

1. That is, the New Testament, which provides all that is necessary to know for the sake of salvation (and presumably also for the sake of morality or "decency" in its fullest sense, i.e. what is "fitting"); "by the coats are meant the doctrine and faith of Christianity, by the wisdom of the Divine Founder fitted to all times, places, and circumstances." (Swift)

2. The traditional Romance elements of Christian allegory (as in *The Faerie Queene* I or Bunyan's account of Apollyon) are rapidly disposed of, and the era of "primitive Christianity" gives way to the role of the church in the world (here the world is cut to the scale of the "grand monde" or world of fashionable society).

3. Covetousness (wealth), ambition (great titles), and pride.

4. Stalls outside shops, where impoverished poets sometimes slept.

5. Cheated.

6. A fashionable tavern.

7. The well-known literary coffeehouse.

8. That is, whispered about but never spoke a word to.

9. That is, attended the official reception ("levee") only in the open air ("*sub dio*").

constantly attended those Committees of Senators who are silent in the House and loud in the coffee-house; where they nightly adjourn to chew the cud of politics and are encompassed with a ring of disciples who lie in wait to catch up their droppings. The three brothers had acquired forty other qualifications of the like stamp, too tedious to recount, and by consequence were justly reckoned the most accomplished persons in the town. But all would not suffice, and the ladies aforesaid continued still inflexible. To clear up which difficulty I must, with the reader's good leave and patience, have recourse to some points of weight, which the authors of that age have not sufficiently illustrated.

For about this time it happened a sect arose, whose tenets obtained and spread very far, especially in the *grand monde* and among everybody of good fashion. They worshipped a sort of idol, who, as their doctrine delivered, did daily create men by a kind of manufactory operation. This idol they placed in the highest parts of the house on an altar erected about three foot: he was shown in the posture of a Persian emperor, sitting on a superficies, with his legs interwoven under him.[10] This god had a goose for his ensign, whence it is that some learned men pretend to deduce his original from Jupiter Capitolinus.[11] At his left hand, beneath the altar, Hell seemed to open, and catch at the animals the idol was creating; to prevent which, certain of his priests hourly flung in pieces of the uninformed mass, or substance, and sometimes whole limbs already enlivened, which that horrid gulf insatiably swallowed, terrible to behold. The goose was also held a subaltern divinity or *deus minorum gentium*,[12] before whose shrine was sacrificed that creature whose hourly food is human gore and who is in so great renown abroad for being the delight and favourite of the Egyptian Cercopithecus.[13] Millions of these animals were cruelly slaughtered every day to appease the hunger of that consuming deity. The chief idol was also worshipped as the inventor of the yard and the needle; [14] whether as the god of seamen or on account of certain other mystical attributes hath not been sufficiently cleared.

The worshippers of this deity had also a system of their belief which seemed to turn upon the following fundamental. They held the universe to be a large suit of clothes which invests everything: that the earth is invested by the air; the air is invested by the stars; and the stars are invested by the *primum mobile*.[15] Look on this globe of earth, you will find it to be a very complete and fashionable dress. What is that which some call land, but a fine coat faced with green? or the sea, but a waistcoat of water-tabby? [16] Proceed to the par-

10. The "idol" is a tailor, the "goose" his smoothing-iron (named for the shape of its handle), and "Hell" is his receptacle for scraps of cloth (cf. Butler, *Hudibras* I.i.238).
11. Jupiter had a temple on the Capitoline Hill, where the sacred geese of Rome were also kept.
12. Subordinate deity or "god of the lesser tribes."
13. "The Egyptians worshipped a monkey, which animal is very fond of eating lice, styled here creatures that feed on human gore." (Swift)
14. Punning on the tailor's yardstick and needle as the nautical spar to hold sails and the compass needle.
15. Since the spheres of the planets and stars were seen as concentric, each might be said to be "dressed" (i.e. "invested") with the next outer one; the *primum mobile* was the outermost sphere, beyond which was the empyrean or seat of God (cf. Dryden's "Anne Killigrew" and "St. Cecilia" odes).
16. Watered silk, taffeta.

ticular works of the creation, you will find how curious [17] Journeyman Nature hath been to trim up the vegetable [18] beaux; observe how sparkish a periwig [19] adorns the head of a beech and what a fine doublet of white satin is worn by the birch. To conclude from all, what is man himself but a micro-coat,[20] or rather a complete suit of clothes with all its trimmings? As to his body, there can be no dispute; but examine even the acquirements of his mind, you will find them all contribute in their order towards furnishing out an exact dress. To instance no more: is not religion a cloak; honesty a pair of shoes worn out in the dirt; self-love a surtout; [21] vanity a shirt; and conscience a pair of breeches, which, though a cover for lewdness as well as nastiness, is easily slipped down for the service of both?

These *postulata* [22] being admitted, it will follow in due course of reasoning that those beings which the world calls improperly suits of clothes are in reality the most refined species of animals; or to proceed higher, that they are rational creatures or men. For is it not manifest that they live, and move, and talk, and perform all other offices of human life? Are not beauty, and wit, and mien, and breeding their inseparable proprieties? [23] In short, we see nothing but them, hear nothing but them. Is it not they who walk the streets, fill up parliament , coffee-, play-, bawdy-houses? 'Tis true, indeed, that these animals, which are vulgarly called suits of clothes, or dresses, do, according to certain compositions, receive different appellations. If one of them be trimmed up with a gold chain and a red gown and a white rod and a great horse, it is called a Lord-Mayor; if certain ermines and furs be placed in a certain position, we style them a Judge; and so an apt conjunction of lawn [24] and black satin we entitle a Bishop.

Others of these professors, though agreeing in the main system, were yet more refined upon certain branches of it; and held that man was an animal compounded of two dresses, the natural and the celestial suit, which were the body and the soul: that the soul was the outward, and the body the inward clothing; that the latter was *ex traduce;* [25] but the former of daily creation and circumfusion. This last they proved by Scripture, because *in them we live, and move, and have our being;* [26] as likewise by philosophy, because they are *all in all, and all in every part.*[27] Besides, said they, separate these two, and you

17. Careful.
18. Vegetative.
19. A wig large and fashionable enough for a young fop (Swift writes of a "shrivelled beau . . . within the penthouse of a modern periwig" in *The Battle of the Books*).
20. "Alluding to the word *microcosm,* or a little world, as man hath been called by the philosophers." (Swift)
21. Loose overcoat or outer garment.
22. Assumptions, conditions (of an argument).
23. Standards.
24. Fine linen.
25. Transmitted at birth (cf. Dryden, "Anne Killigrew" ode, l. 23).
26. "In Him we live, and move, and have our being." (Acts 17:28)
27. Sir John Davies, *Nosce Teipsum* (1599), in using this phrase to describe the soul, follows Aristotelian theory. This dazzling reversal of inside and outside makes the soul (reduced to social manners and professional roles) the dress of the body and a welcome cover for its ugliness. The soul, in its traditional sense as the intellectual and moral power that resides within the body and controls it, simply disappears; for this world gives all its attention to worldly attainments or dress, and ceases, in a sense, to have a spiritual life.

will find the body to be only a senseless unsavoury carcass. By all which it is manifest that the outward dress must needs be the soul.

To this system of religion were tagged several subaltern doctrines which were entertained with great vogue; as particularly, the faculties of the mind were deduced by the learned among them in this manner: embroidery was sheer wit; [28] gold fringe was agreeable conversation; gold lace was repartee; a huge long periwig was humour; [29] and a coat full of powder was very good raillery: [30] all which required abundance of *finesse* and *delicatesse* to manage with advantage as well as a strict observance after times and fashions.[31]

I have, with much pains and reading, collected out of ancient authors, this short summary of a body of philosophy and divinity which seems to have been composed by a vein and race of thinking very different from any other systems, either ancient or modern. And it was not merely to entertain or satisfy the reader's curiosity but rather to give him light into several circumstances of the following story; that knowing the state of dispositions and opinions in an age so remote, he may better comprehend those great events which were the issue of them. I advise therefore the courteous reader to peruse with a world of application, again and again, whatever I have written upon this matter. And leaving these broken ends, I carefully gather up the chief thread of my story and proceed.

These opinions, therefore, were so universal, as well as the practices of them, among the refined part of court and town, that our three brother-adventurers, as their circumstances then stood, were strangely at a loss. For, on the one side, the three ladies they addressed themselves to (whom we have named already) were ever at the very top of the fashion and abhorred all that were below it but the breadth of a hair. On the other side, their father's will was very precise, and it was the main precept in it, with the greatest penalties annexed, not to add to, or diminish from, their coats one thread without a positive command in the will. Now, the coats their father had left them were, 'tis true, of very good cloth, and, besides, so neatly sewn, you would swear they were all of a piece; [32] but, at the same time, very plain, and with little or no ornament: and it happened that before they were a month in town, great shoulder-knots [33] came up. Straight all the world was shoulder-knots; no approaching the ladies' *ruelles* [34] without the quota of shoulder-knots. That fellow, cries one, has no soul; where is his shoulder-knot? Our three brethren soon discovered their want by sad experience, meeting in their walks with forty

28. Perhaps derived from "sheer" in the sense of "very fine" or "diaphanous" as applied to fabrics; probably implying mere verbal play without real point.
29. Probably implying mere whim or caprice.
30. Banter, good-humored teasing.
31. "Nothing is so very tender as a modern piece of wit, and which is apt to suffer so much in the carriage. Some things are extremely witty *today* or *fasting* or *in this place* or at *eight o'clock* . . . any of which, by the smallest transposal or misapplication, is utterly annihilate. . . . Such a jest there is that will not pass out of Covent Garden; and such a one that is nowhere intelligible but at Hyde Park Corner." (Preface, *A Tale of a Tub*)
32. Alluding to Christ's robe, often taken as a symbol of the Christian religion: "now the coat was without seam, woven from the top throughout" (John 19:23).
33. Knots of ribbon or lace, introduced from France about 1670; "By this is understood the first introducing of pageantry and unnecessary ornaments in the church." (Swift)
34. Bedrooms used as salons for morning receptions.

mortifications and indignities. If they went to the play-house, the doorkeeper showed them into the twelve-penny gallery. If they called a boat, says a waterman, 'I am first sculler.' [35] If they stepped to the Rose to take a bottle, the drawer would cry, 'Friend, we sell no ale.' If they went to visit a lady, a footman met them at the door with, 'Pray send up your message.' In this unhappy case, they went immediately to consult their father's will, read it over and over, but not a word of the shoulder-knot. What should they do? What temper should they find? Obedience was absolutely necessary, and yet shoulder-knots appeared extremely requisite. After much thought, one of the brothers, who happened to be more book-learned than the other two, said, he had found an expedient. ' 'Tis true,' said he, 'there is nothing here in this will, *totidem verbis*, making mention of shoulder-knots: but I dare conjecture we may find them *inclusivè*, or *totidem syllabis*.' [36] This distinction was immediately approved by all; and so they fell again to examine the will. But their evil star had so directed the matter that the first syllable was not to be found in the whole writing. Upon which disappointment he who found the former evasion took heart and said, 'Brothers, there is yet hopes; for though we cannot find them *totidem verbis*, nor *totidem syllabis*, I dare engage we shall make them out, *tertio modo*, or *totidem literis*.' [37] This discovery was also highly commended, upon which they fell once more to the scrutiny and picked out S,H,O,U,L,D,E,R; when the same planet,[38] enemy to their repose, had wonderfully contrived that a K was not to be found. Here was a weighty difficulty! But the distinguishing brother (for whom we shall hereafter find a name) now his hand was in, proved by a very good argument, that K was a modern illegitimate letter unknown to the learned ages, nor anywhere to be found in ancient manuscripts. 'Tis true, said he, the word *Calendæ* hath in Q.V.C.[39] been sometimes writ with a K, but erroneously; for in the best copies it has been ever spelt with a C. And by consequence it was a gross mistake in our language to spell Knot with a K; but that from henceforward he would take care it should be writ with a C. Upon this all farther difficulty vanished; shoulder-knots were made clearly out to be *jure paterno:* [40] and our three gentlemen swaggered with as large and as flaunting ones as the best.

But as human happiness is of a very short duration, so in those days were human fashions, upon which it entirely depends. Shoulder-knots had their time, and we must now imagine them in their decline; for a certain lord came just from Paris with fifty yards of gold lace upon his coat, exactly trimmed after the court fashion of that month. In two days all mankind appeared closed up in bars of gold lace: whoever durst peep abroad without his complement of gold lace was as scandalous as a ——, and as ill received among the women. What should our three knights do in this momentous affair? They had sufficiently strained a point already in the affair of shoulder-knots. Upon recourse to

35. That is, they are being offered the cheaper boat, a "sculler," rowed by one man rather than two; in the same way, they are offered cheap seats at the theater and ale instead of wine at the tavern, and are denied admission to the lady's salon.
36. That is, not in so many *words*, but included within them in so many *syllables*.
37. That is, by a third means, in so many *letters*.
38. That is, unfavorable destiny, the "evil star."
39. *Quibusdam veteribus codicibus* ("in some ancient manuscripts").
40. "According to paternal law," a parody of *jure divino*.

the will, nothing appeared there but *altum silentium*.[41] That of the shoulder-knots was a loose, flying, circumstantial point; but this of gold lace seemed too considerable an alteration without better warrant. It did *aliquo modo essentiæ adhærere*,[42] and therefore required a positive precept. But about this time it fell out that the learned brother aforesaid had read *Aristotelis Dialectica*,[43] and especially that wonderful piece *de Interpretatione*, which has the faculty of teaching its readers to find out a meaning in everything but itself, like commentators on the Revelations, who proceed prophets without understanding a syllable of the text. 'Brothers,' said he, 'you are to be informed that of wills *duo sunt genera*, nuncupatory and scriptory;[44] that in the scriptory will here before us, there is no precept or mention about gold lace, *conceditur:*[45] but, *si idem affirmetur de nuncupatorio, negatur*.[46] For, brothers, if you remember, we heard a fellow say, when we were boys, that he heard my father's man say that he heard my father say that he would advise his sons to get gold lace on their coats as soon as ever they could procure money to buy it.' 'By G—! that is very true,' cries the other. 'I remember it perfectly well,' said the third. And so without more ado they got the largest gold lace in the parish and walked about as fine as lords. . . .

Next winter a player, hired for the purpose by the corporation of fringe-makers, acted his part in a new comedy all covered with silver fringe and, according to the laudable custom, gave rise to that fashion. Upon which the brothers, consulting their father's will, to their great astonishment found these words; '*Item*, I charge and command my said three sons to wear no sort of silver fringe upon or about their said coats,' etc., with a penalty, in case of disobedience, too long here to insert. However, after some pause, the brother so often mentioned for his erudition, who was well skilled in criticisms, had found in a certain author, which he said should be nameless, that the same word, which in the will is called fringe, does also signify a broom-stick, and doubtless ought to have the same interpretation in this paragraph. This another of the brothers disliked, because of that epithet *silver*, which could not, he humbly conceived, in propriety of speech, be reasonably applied to a broom-stick; but it was replied upon him, that this epithet was understood in a mythological and allegorical sense. However, he objected again, why their father should forbid them to wear a broom-stick on their coats, a caution that seemed unnatural and impertinent;[47] upon which he was taken up short, as one that spoke irreverently of a mystery, which doubtless was very useful and significant, but ought not to be over-curiously pried into or nicely[48] reasoned upon. And, in short, their father's authority being now considerably sunk, this expedient was allowed to serve as a lawful dispensation for wearing their full proportion of silver fringe.

41. "Profound silence."
42. "In some manner belong to the essence."
43. A Latin compendium of Aristotle's logical treatises.
44. "There are two sorts," by word of mouth and written.
45. "It may be granted."
46. "If the same be affirmed of the oral will, it is denied." "By this is meant *tradition*, allowed to have equal authority with Scripture, or rather greater." (Swift)
47. Irrelevant.
48. Delicately, closely.

A while after was revived an old fashion, long antiquated, of embroidery with Indian figures of men, women, and children.[49] Here they had no occasion to examine the will. They remembered but too well how their father had always abhorred this fashion; that he made several paragraphs on purpose, importing his utter detestation of it and bestowing his everlasting curse to his sons whenever they should wear it. For all this, in a few days they appeared higher in the fashion than anybody else in the town. But they solved the matter by saying that these figures were not at all the same with those that were formerly worn and were meant in the will. Besides, they did not wear them in the sense as forbidden by their father; but as they were a commendable custom and of great use to the public. That these rigorous clauses in the will did therefore require some allowance and a favourable interpretation, and ought to be understood *cum grano salis*.[50]

But fashions perpetually altering in that age, the scholastic brother grew weary of searching farther evasions and solving everlasting contradictions; resolved, therefore, at all hazards to comply with the modes of the world, they concerted matters together and agreed unanimously to lock up their father's will in a strong box [51] brought out of Greece or Italy (I have forgot which), and trouble themselves no farther to examine it, but only refer to its authority whenever they thought fit. In consequence whereof, a while after, it grew a general mode to wear an infinite number of points,[52] most of them tagged with silver: upon which, the scholar pronounced *ex cathedra*,[53] that points were absolutely *jure paterno*, as they might very well remember. 'Tis true, indeed, the fashion prescribed somewhat more than were directly named in the will; however, that they, as heirs-general of their father, had power to make and add certain clauses for public emolument, though not deducible, *totidem verbis*, from the letter of the will, or else *multa absurda sequerentur*.[54] This was understood for canonical,[55] and therefore on the following Sunday they came to church all covered with points.

The learned brother, so often mentioned, was reckoned the best scholar in all that or the next street to it; insomuch as, having run something behind-hand [56] with the world, he obtained the favour from a certain lord,[57] to receive him into his house, and to teach his children. A while after the lord died, and he, by long practice upon his father's will, found the way of contriving a deed of conveyance of that house to himself and his heirs; upon which he took possession, turned the young squires out, and received his brothers in their stead.

49. "The images of saints, the Blessed Virgin, and our Savior an infant." (Swift)
50. "With a grain of salt."
51. That is, the forbidding of the use of Scripture in the vernacular, and requiring the Latin Vulgate translation or the original Greek of the New Testament.
52. Laces or ties with metal tips.
53. "From the (papal) throne."
54. "Many absurdities would follow."
55. According to church law.
56. In debt.
57. Referring to the Donation of Constantine, the alleged document by which the first Christian emperor, Constantine the Great, conferred all his rights, honors, and property as Emperor of the West on the Pope of Rome and his successors; a document "the Popes . . . have never been able to produce." (Swift)

Section IX

A Digression Concerning the Original, the Use, and
Improvement of Madness, in a Commonwealth

Nor shall it any ways detract from the just reputation of this famous sect [1]
that its rise and institution are owing to such an author as I have described
Jack to be—a person whose intellectuals were overturned and his brain shaken
out of its natural position; which we commonly suppose to be a distemper and
call by the name of madness or frenzy. For if we take a survey of the greatest
actions that have been performed in the world under the influence of single
men, which are the establishment of new empires by conquest, the advance
and progress of new schemes in philosophy, and the contriving, as well as the
propagating, of new religions; we shall find the authors of them all to have been
persons whose natural reason had admitted great revolutions from their diet,
their education, the prevalency of some certain temper, together with the
particular influence of air and climate. Besides, there is something individual in
human minds that easily kindles at the accidental approach and collision of
certain circumstances, which, though of paltry and mean appearance, do often
flame out into the greatest emergencies of life. For great turns are not always
given by strong hands but by lucky adaption and at proper seasons; and it is
of no import where the fire was kindled if the vapour has once got up into the
brain. For the upper region of man is furnished like the middle region of the
air; the materials are formed from causes of the widest difference, yet produce
at last the same substance and effect. Mists arise from the earth, steams from
dunghills, exhalations from the sea, and smoke from fire; yet all clouds are the
same in composition as well as consequences, and the fumes issuing from a
jakes [2] will furnish as comely and useful a vapour as incense from an altar.
Thus far, I suppose, will easily be granted me; and then it will follow, that,
as the face of nature never produces rain but when it is overcast and disturbed,
so human understanding, seated in the brain, must be troubled and overspread
by vapours ascending from the lower faculties to water the invention [3] and
render it fruitful. Now, although these vapours (as it hath been already said)
are of as various original as those of the skies, yet the crop they produce differs
both in kind and degree, merely according to the soil. I will produce two
instances to prove and explain what I am now advancing.

A certain great prince [4] raised a mighty army, filled his coffers with infinite
treasures, provided an invincible fleet, and all this without giving [5] the least

1. Aeolism, the worship of wind (named for the keeper of the winds in the *Odyssey*
and the *Aeneid*), a system that rationalizes Jack's religious enthusiasm much as the clothes
philosophy of Section II does Peter's manipulation of the words of the will.
2. Privy or cesspool.
3. The faculty for making discoveries; a term often applied in the age to poetic wit or
imagination (cf. Dryden's Critical Prose, above).
4. Henry IV of France (1553–1610) was obsessed with a late passion for the young
Princesse de Condé, who was taken by her husband (he was to have been only a convenient figurehead) to the Spanish Netherlands, out of Henry's reach. After a futile
effort to abduct her, Henry (enraged and perhaps somewhat mad) began military preparations against the Spanish province, but he was stabbed to death before he could proceed.
5. Revealing.

part of his design to his greatest ministers or his nearest favourites. Immediately the whole world was alarmed; the neighbouring crowns in trembling expectation towards what point the storm would burst, the small politicians everywhere forming profound conjectures. Some believed he had laid a scheme for universal monarchy; others, after much insight, determined the matter to be a project for pulling down the Pope and setting up the reformed religion, which had once been his own. Some, again, of a deeper sagacity, sent him into Asia to subdue the Turk and recover Palestine. In the midst of all these projects and preparations, a certain state-surgeon, gathering the nature of the disease by these symptoms, attempted the cure, at one blow performed the operation, broke the bag, and out flew the vapour; nor did anything want to render it a complete remedy, only that the prince unfortunately happened to die in the performance. Now, is the reader exceeding curious to learn from whence this vapour took its rise which had so long set the nations at a gaze? What secret wheel, what hidden spring, could put into motion so wonderful an engine? It was afterwards discovered that the movement of this whole machine had been directed by an absent female, whose eyes had raised a protuberancy, and, before emission, she was removed into an enemy's country. What should an unhappy prince do in such ticklish circumstances as these? He tried in vain the poet's never-failing receipt of *corpora quæque;* for

> Idque petit corpus mens unde est saucia amore:
> Unde feritur, eo tendit, gestitque coire. (LUCRETIUS) [6]

Having to no purpose used all peaceable endeavours, the collected part of the semen, raised and inflamed, became adust, converted to choler, turned head upon the spinal duct [7] and ascended to the brain. The very same principle that influences a bully to break the windows of a whore who has jilted him naturally stirs up a great prince to raise mighty armies and dream of nothing but sieges, battles, and victories.

> ———Teterrima belli
> Causa.———[8]

The other instance is what I have read somewhere in a very ancient author of a mighty king who, for the space of above thirty years, amused himself to take and lose towns, beat armies and be beaten, drive princes out of their dominions; fright children from their bread and butter; burn, lay waste, plunder, dragoon, massacre subject and stranger, friend and foe, male and female. 'Tis recorded that the philosophers of each country were in grave dispute upon causes natural, moral, and political, to find out where they should assign an original solution of this phenomenon. At last the vapour or spirit which animated the hero's brain, being in perpetual circulation, seized upon that region

---

6. "Indulging one's lust at once with any persons at hand ["in corpore quaeque" IV.1065] so as not to allow unendurable desire to develop"; the following lines describe "that body through which the mind is wounded by love" (IV.1048) and how "each strains towards the one from whom the blow has come and struggles to unite" (IV.1055).
7. That is, became burned or parched, turned to bile (the source of anger or rage), invaded the spinal duct.
8. "For a whore had been, before Helen, a terrible cause of war." Horace, *Satires* I.iii.107.

of the human body so renowned for furnishing the *zibeta occidentalis*,[9] and, gathering there into a tumour, left the rest of the world for that time in peace. Of such mighty consequence it is where those exhalations fix and of so little from whence they proceed. The same spirits, which, in their superior progress, would conquer a kingdom, descending upon the anus, conclude in a fistula.[10]

Let us next examine the great introducers of new schemes in philosophy, and search till we can find from what faculty of the soul the disposition arises in mortal man of taking it into his head to advance new systems with such an eager zeal, in things agreed on all hands impossible to be known; from what seeds this disposition springs, and to what quality of human nature these grand innovators have been indebted for their number of disciples. Because it is plain that several of the chief among them, both ancient and modern, were usually mistaken by their adversaries, and indeed by all except their own followers, to have been persons crazed or out of their wits; having generally proceeded, in the common course of their words and actions by a method very different from the vulgar dictates of unrefined reason; agreeing for the most part in their several models with their present undoubted successors in the academy of modern Bedlam [11] (whose merits and principles I shall farther examine in due place). Of this kind were *Epicurus, Diogenes, Apollonius, Lucretius, Paracelsus, Descartes*,[12] and others, who, if they were now in the world, tied fast, and separate from their followers, would, in this our undistinguishing age, incur manifest danger of phlebotomy and whips and chains and dark chambers and straw. For what man in the natural state or course of thinking did ever conceive it in his power to reduce the notions of all mankind exactly to the same length and breadth and height of his own? Yet this is the first humble and civil design of all innovators in the empire of reason. Epicurus modestly hoped that, one time or other, a certain fortuitous concourse of all men's opinions, after perpetual justlings, the sharp with the smooth, the light and the heavy, the round and the square, would, by certain clinamina,[13] unite in the notions of atoms and void, as these did in the originals of all things. Cartesius reckoned to

---

9. "Paracelsus, who was so famous for chemistry, tried an experiment upon human excrement to make perfume of it, which, when he had brought to perfection, he called *Ziberta Occidentalis*, or western-civet, the back parts of a man (according to his division . . .) being the west." (Swift)

10. A pipelike ulcer with a narrow opening.

11. The Hospital of St. Mary of Bethlehem, long a madhouse, regularly open to visitors and sightseers as a public show.

12. All these men were creators or defenders of systems. Epicurus (341?–270 B.C.), the Greek philosopher, and Lucretius (96?–55 B.C.), the Roman poet, were atomists, attributing all life to the "fortuitous concourse" of atoms. Diogenes (4th century B.C.), the Greek Cynic philosopher, defied conventional rules of conduct and lived in an earthenware tub to demonstrate the austere simplicity he preached. Apollonius of Tyana (c. 4th century B.C.) was a wandering Pythagorean philosopher and mystic and a precursor of the occult Hermetic philosophy. Paracelsus (1490?–1541) was an alchemist as well as a chemist, a neoplatonic visionary and mystic in his system of medicine. René Descartes (1596–1650), having separated mind from extended matter (except for their interaction through the pineal gland), erected a mechanical and mathematical system of the material universe.

13. The inherent "swerves" of the atoms, which led to their varying patterns of collision and rebound, thus forming bodies of greater or lesser density; here Epicurus' material explanation is ironically applied to the interaction of minds or opinions in order to account for proselytizing.

see, before he died, the sentiments of all philosophers like so many lesser stars in his romantic system, wrapped and drawn within.his own vortex.[14] Now, I would gladly be informed, how it is possible to account for such imaginations as these in particular men without recourse to my phenomenon of vapours ascending from the lower faculties to overshadow the brain, and there distilling into conceptions for which the narrowness of our mother-tongue has not yet assigned any other name besides that of madness or frenzy.

Let us therefore now conjecture how it comes to pass that none of these great prescribers do ever fail providing themselves and their notions with a number of implicit disciples. And, I think, the reason is easy to be assigned: for there is a peculiar string in the harmony of human understanding which, in several individuals, is exactly of the same tuning. This, if you can dexterously screw up to its right key and then strike gently upon it, whenever you have the good fortune to light among those of the same pitch, they will, by a secret necessary sympathy, strike exactly at the same time. And in this one circumstance lies all the skill or luck of the matter; for, if you chance to jar the string among those who are either above or below your own height, instead of subscribing to your doctrine, they will tie you fast, call you mad, and feed you with bread and water.

It is therefore a point of the nicest [15] conduct to distinguish and adapt this noble talent with respect to the differences of persons and of times. Cicero understood this very well, when writing to a friend in England, with a caution, among other matters, to beware of being cheated by our hackney-coachmen (who, it seems, in those days were as arrant [16] rascals as they are now), has these remarkable words: *Est quod gaudeas te in ista loca venisse, ubi aliquid sapere viderere.*[17] For, to speak a bold truth, it is a fatal miscarriage so ill to order affairs, as to pass for a fool in one company when in another you might be treated as a philosopher. Which I desire some certain gentlemen of my acquaintance to lay up in their hearts as a very seasonable *innuendo.*

This, indeed, was the fatal mistake of that worthy gentleman, my most ingenious friend, Mr. W-tt-n:[18] a person, in appearance, ordained for great designs as well as performances; whether you will consider his notions or his looks. Surely no man ever advanced into the public with fitter qualifications of body and mind for the propagation of a new religion. Oh, had those happy talents, misapplied to vain philosophy, been turned into their proper channels of dreams and visions, where distortion of mind and countenance are of such sovereign use, the base detracting world would not then have dared to report that something is amiss, that his brain hath undergone an unlucky shake; which

14. The *tourbillon* or whirlpool of material particles, creating a circular motion that is communicated from one body to another; it was applied to the heavenly bodies, as when one star is drawn into the stronger vortex of another's motion.
15. Subtlest.
16. Thorough.
17. "There is reason to rejoice that you have come to those places where you pass as a man of legal ability." Cicero, *Letters to Friends* VII.10 (to Trebatius). In VII.6 Cicero warns that Trebatius must look out in Britain that he is not cheated by the charioteers.
18. William Wotton had joined Bentley in the attack upon Temple; a clergyman, he also wrote what he intended as a damning explanation of Swift's meaning in *A Tale of a Tub,* but Swift used Wotton's remarks as explanatory notes in his 1710 edition.

even his brother modernists themselves, like ungrates, do whisper so loud, it reaches up to the very garret I am now writing in.

Lastly, whosoever pleases to look into the fountains of enthusiasm, from whence, in all ages, have eternally proceeded such fattening [19] streams, will find the spring-head to have been as troubled and muddy as the current. Of such great emolument is a tincture of this vapour which the world calls madness, that without its help, the world would not only be deprived of those two great blessings, conquests and systems, but even all mankind would unhappily be reduced to the same belief in things invisible. Now, the former *postulatum* being held, that it is of no import from what originals this vapour proceeds, but either in what angles it strikes and spreads over the understanding or upon what species of brain it ascends; it will be a very delicate point to cut the feather and divide the several reasons [20] to a nice and curious reader how this numerical difference in the brain can produce effects of so vast a difference from the same vapour, as to be the sole point of individuation between Alexander the Great, Jack of Leyden,[21] and Monsieur Des Cartes. The present argument is the most abstracted that ever I engaged in; it strains my faculties to their highest stretch; and I desire the reader to attend with utmost perpensity for I now proceed to unravel this knotty point.

There is in mankind a certain   .   .   .   .

.   .   .   .

Hic multa   .   .   .   .
desiderantur.[22]   .   .   .   .

.   .   .   .   .   And this I take to be a clear solution of the matter.

Having therefore so narrowly passed through this intricate difficulty, the reader will, I am sure, agree with me in the conclusion that if the moderns mean by madness only a disturbance or transposition of the brain, by force of certain vapours issuing up from the lower faculties, then has this madness been the parent of all those mighty revolutions that have happened in empire, in philosophy, and in religion. For the brain, in its natural position and state of serenity, disposeth its owner to pass his life in the common forms, without any thought of subduing multitudes to his own power, his reasons, or his visions; and the more he shapes his understanding by the pattern of human learning, the less he is inclined to form parties after his particular notions, because that instructs him in his private infirmities as well as in the stubborn ignorance of the people.

But when a man's fancy gets astride of his reason, when imagination is at cuffs with the senses, and common understanding as well as common sense is kicked out of doors; the first proselyte he makes is himself; and when that is once compassed, the difficulty is not so great in bringing over others; a

19. Nourishing.

20. That is, to split hairs or make subtle distinctions.

21. John of Leyden (1509–36), here forming a bridge between military conquest and intellectual system, was a Dutch Anabaptist who founded a short-lived communistic and polygamous "Kingdom of Zion" in the German city of Münster.

22. "Here many things are lacking," a conventional phrase in the editing of a damaged manuscript, a technique Swift parodies throughout the *Tale* and uses, as here, to create an effect of anticlimax.

strong delusion always operating from without as vigorously as from within. For cant and vision are to the ear and the eye the same that tickling is to the touch. Those entertainments and pleasures we most value in life are such as dupe and play the wag with the senses. For, if we take an examination of what is generally understood by happiness as it has respect either to the understanding or the senses, we shall find all its properties and adjuncts [23] will herd under this short definition, that it is a perpetual possession of being well deceived.

And, first, with relation to the mind or understanding, 'tis manifest what mighty advantages fiction has over truth; and the reason is just at our elbow, because imagination can build nobler scenes and produce more wonderful revolutions than fortune or nature will be at expense to furnish. Nor is mankind so much to blame in his choice thus determining him, if we consider that the debate merely lies between things past and things conceived; and so the question is only this:—whether things that have place in the imagination may not as properly be said to exist as those that are seated in the memory, which may be justly held in the affirmative, and very much to the advantage of the former, since this is acknowledged to be the womb of things and the other allowed to be no more than the grave.

Again, if we take this definition of happiness and examine it with reference to the senses, it will be acknowledged wonderfully adapt. How fading and insipid do all objects accost us that are not conveyed in the vehicle of delusion! How shrunk is everything as it appears in the glass of nature! So that if it were not for the assistance of artificial mediums, false lights, refracted angles, varnish, and tinsel, there would be a mighty level in the felicity and enjoyments of mortal men. If this were seriously considered by the world, as I have a certain reason to suspect it hardly will, men would no longer reckon among their high points of wisdom the art of exposing weak sides and publishing infirmities; an employment, in my opinion, neither better nor worse than that of unmasking, which, I think, has never been allowed [24] fair usage, either in the world or the play-house.

In the proportion that credulity is a more peaceful possession of the mind than curiosity, so far preferable is that wisdom which converses about the surface to that pretended philosophy which enters into the depth of things and then comes gravely back with information and discoveries, that in the inside they are good for nothing. The two senses to which all objects first address themselves are the sight and the touch; these never examine farther than the colour, the shape, the size, and whatever other qualities dwell or are drawn by art upon the outward of bodies; and then comes reason officiously with tools for cutting, and opening, and mangling, and piercing, offering to demonstrate that they are not of the same consistence quite through.

Now I take all this to be the last degree of perverting nature; one of whose eternal laws it is to put her best furniture forward. And therefore, in order to save the charges of all such expensive anatomy for the time to come, I do here think fit to inform the reader, that in such conclusions as these, reason

23. Essential and nonessential characteristics.
24. Judged to be.

is certainly in the right, and that in most corporeal beings which have fallen under my cognizance the outside hath been infinitely preferable to the in; whereof I have been farther convinced from some late experiments.

Last week I saw a woman flayed, and you will hardly believe how much it altered her person for the worse. Yesterday I ordered the carcass of a beau to be stripped in my presence, when we were all amazed to find so many unsuspected faults under one suit of clothes. Then I laid open his brain, his heart, and his spleen; but I plainly perceived at every operation that the farther we proceeded, we found the defects increase upon us in number and bulk; from all which I justly formed this conclusion to myself: that whatever philosopher or projector can find out an art to sodder and patch up the flaws and imperfections of nature will deserve much better of mankind, and teach us a more useful science, than that so much in present esteem of widening and exposing them (like him who held anatomy to be the ultimate end of physic [25]). And he whose fortunes and dispositions have placed him in a convenient station to enjoy the fruits of this noble art; he that can, with Epicurus,[26] content his ideas with the films and images that fly off upon his senses from the superficies of things; such a man, truly wise, creams off nature, leaving the sour and the dregs for philosophy and reason to lap up. This is the sublime and refined point of felicity, called the possession of being well deceived; the serene peaceful state of being a fool among knaves.

But to return to madness. It is certain that, according to the system I have above deduced, every species thereof proceeds from a redundancy of vapours; therefore, as some kinds of frenzy give double strength to the sinews, so there are of other species, which add vigour and life and spirit to the brain. Now, it usually happens that these active spirits, getting possession of the brain, resemble those that haunt other waste and empty dwellings, which, for want of business, either vanish and carry away a piece of the house, or else stay at home and fling it all out of the windows. By which, are mystically displayed the two principal branches of madness, and which some philosophers, not considering so well as I, have mistaken to be different in their causes, overhastily assigning the first to deficiency and the other to redundance.

I think it therefore manifest, from what I have here advanced, that the main point of skill and address is to furnish employment for this redundancy of vapour and prudently to adjust the season of it; by which means it may certainly become of cardinal and catholic emolument in a commonwealth. Thus one man, choosing a proper juncture, leaps into a gulf, from whence proceeds a hero, and is called the saver of his country; another achieves the same enterprise, but, unluckily timing it, has left the brand of madness fixed as a reproach upon his memory; upon so nice a distinction, are we taught to repeat the name of Curtius with reverence and love, that of Empedocles with hatred and contempt.[27] Thus also it is usually conceived that the elder

25. That is, reversing ends and means, making surgery the end for which therapy exists.
26. Who had a materialistic account of sense perception: the surfaces ("superficies") discharged fine films, which were replicas of the object and were able to penetrate the sense organs of the perceiver.
27. When a chasm suddenly opened in the Roman forum, with the prophecy that it would close only when the chief strength of Rome had been sacrificed, Marcus Curtius—

Brutus [28] only personated the fool and madman for the good of the public; but this was nothing else than a redundancy of the same vapour long misapplied, called by the Latins *ingenium par negotiis;* [29] or (to translate it as nearly as I can) a sort of frenzy, never in its right element, till you take it up in business of the state.

Upon all which, and many other reasons of equal weight though not equally curious, I do here gladly embrace an opportunity I have long sought for, of recommending it as a very noble undertaking to Sir Edward Seymour, Sir Christopher Musgrave, Sir John Bowls, John How, Esq., and other patriots [30] concerned, that they would move for leave to bring in a bill for appointing commissioners to inspect into Bedlam and the parts adjacent; who shall be empowered to send for persons, papers, and records, to examine into the merits and qualifications of every student and professor, to observe with utmost exactness their several dispositions and behaviour, by which means duly distinguishing and adapting their talents, they might produce admirable instruments for the several offices in a state, _____, [31] civil, and military, proceeding in such methods as I shall here humbly propose. And I hope the gentle reader will give some allowance to my great solicitudes in this important affair, upon account of the high esteem I have borne that honourable society, whereof I had some time the happiness to be an unworthy member.

Is any student tearing his straw in piece-meal, swearing and blaspheming, biting his grate, foaming at the mouth, and emptying his piss-pot in the spectators' faces? Let the right worshipful the commissioners of inspection give him a regiment of dragoons, and send him into Flanders among the rest. Is another eternally talking, sputtering, gaping, bawling, in a sound without period or article? What wonderful talents are here mislaid! Let him be furnished immediately with a green bag and papers, and threepence in his pocket, and away with him to Westminster Hall. [32] You will find a third gravely taking the dimensions of his kennel, a person of foresight and insight, though kept quite in the dark; for why, like Moses, *ecce cornuta erat ejus facies.* [33] He walks duly in one pace, entreats your penny with due gravity and ceremony, talks much of hard times, and taxes, and the whore of Babylon, bars up the wooden window of his cell constantly at eight o'clock, dreams of fire, and shoplifters, and court-customers, and privileged places. Now, what a figure would all these acquirements amount to, if the owner were sent into the City among his brethren! [34]

interpreting the strength to be arms and valor—leaped in, armed and on horseback. According to some accounts, Empedocles (fl. 450), the philosopher and statesman of Sicily, threw himself into the crater of Mt. Etna so that the manner of his death might not be known and that he might later pass for a god, but the secret was revealed by Etna's rejecting one of his sandals (or casting it out in an eruption).

28. Lucius Junius Brutus, the nephew of the tyrannous Roman king Tarquin the Proud, assumed the guise of madness to avoid being killed by his uncle, as his brother had been.

29. "A head for business." Tacitus, *Annals* VI.39 and XVI.18.

30. Leading members of the House of Commons, one of them (Bowls) himself mad by 1701.

31. "Ecclesiastical" is omitted.

32. A lawyer's coach fare from the Inns of Court to the law courts at Westminster.

33. "Behold his face was shining." Vulgate text of Exodus 34:30.

34. That is, as a shopkeeper in the City, the commercial part of London.

Behold a fourth, in much and deep conversation with himself, biting his thumbs at proper junctures, his countenance checkered with business and design, sometimes walking very fast, with his eyes nailed to a paper that he holds in his hands; a great saver of time, somewhat thick of hearing, very short of sight, but more of memory; a man ever in haste, a great hatcher and breeder of business, and excellent at the famous art of whispering nothing; a huge idolater of monosyllables and procrastination, so ready to give his word to everybody that he never keeps it; one that has forgot the common meaning of words but an admirable retainer of the sound; extremely subject to the looseness,[35] for his occasions are perpetually calling him away. If you approach his grate in his familiar intervals: 'Sir,' says he, 'give me a penny, and I'll sing you a song; but give me the penny first.' (Hence comes the common saying, and commoner practice, of parting with money for a song.) What a complete system of court skill is here described in every branch of it, and all utterly lost with wrong application!

Accost the hole of another kennel, first stopping your nose; you will behold a surly, gloomy, nasty, slovenly mortal, raking in his own dung and dabbling in his urine. The best part of his diet is the reversion [36] of his own ordure, which, expiring into steams, whirls perpetually about, and at last re-infunds.[37] His complexion is of a dirty yellow, with a thin scattered beard, exactly agreeable to that of his diet upon its first declination, like other insects, who, having their birth and education in an excrement, from thence borrow their colour and their smell. The student of this apartment is very sparing of his words, but somewhat over-liberal of his breath. He holds his hand out ready to receive your penny, and immediately upon receipt withdraws to his former occupations. Now, is it not amazing to think, the society of Warwick-lane [38] should have no more concern for the recovery of so useful a member; who, if one may judge from these appearances, would become the greatest ornament to that illustrious body?

Another student struts up fiercely to your teeth, puffing with his lips, half squeezing out his eyes, and very graciously holds you out his hand to kiss. The keeper desires you not to be afraid of this professor, for he will do you no hurt; to him alone is allowed the liberty of the antechamber, and the orator of the place gives you to understand that this solemn person is a tailor run mad with pride. This considerable student is adorned with many other qualities, upon which, at present, I shall not farther enlarge . . . Hark in your ear . . . I am strangely mistaken, if all his address, his motions, and his airs, would not then be very natural, and in their proper element.[39]

I shall not descend so minutely, as to insist upon the vast number of beaux, fiddlers, poets, and politicians that the world might recover by such a reformation; but what is more material, besides the clear gain redounding to the commonwealth, by so large an acquisition of persons to employ whose talents

35. Diarrhea.
36. Return to its original state.
37. Pours in again.
38. The Royal College of Physicians.
39. "I cannot conjecture what the author means here, or how the chasm could be filled, though it is capable of more than one interpretation" (Swift).

and acquirements, if I may be so bold as to affirm it, are now buried or at least misapplied; it would be a mighty advantage accruing to the public from this inquiry that all these would very much excel and arrive at great perfection in their several kinds; which, I think, is manifest from what I have already shown and shall enforce by this one plain instance, that even I myself, the author of these momentous truths, am a person whose imaginations are hard-mouthed [40] and exceedingly disposed to run away with his reason, which I have observed from long experience to be a very light rider and easily shook off; upon which account my friends will never trust me alone without a solemn promise to vent my speculations in this or the like manner, for the universal benefit of human kind; which perhaps the gentle, courteous, and candid reader, brimful of that modern charity and tenderness usually annexed to his office, will be very hardly persuaded to believe.

1697–1704?   1704

An Argument Against Abolishing Christianity in England

The Test Act of 1673 excluded from public office those who refused the sacrament of the Church of England, but dissenters held office by taking the Anglican sacrament only once. To prevent this evasion, Tories in Commons had three times introduced a Bill for Preventing Occasional Conformity, which was defeated in each case by the Whig lords. There were, in fact, strong Whig efforts to repeal the Test Act both in Ireland and in England. Swift saw this as a real threat to the established church, for an opening of power to an alliance of Whigs and dissenters could lead to disestablishment in time. The *Argument* is presented as the cool proposal of a man who takes for granted that only "nominal" Christianity can any longer survive and argues that it does not threaten, but can even serve, "schemes of wealth and power"—presumably the only ones his public takes seriously. This dismissal of discussion of real Christianity builds up tremendous pressure, as what are taken for granted as the only acceptable terms of discussion become more and more shabbily expedient, more grossly a matter of a power calculus and of cash accounting.

An Argument

> To Prove That the Abolishing of Christianity in England May, as Things Now Stand, Be Attended with Some Inconveniencies, and Perhaps, Not Produce Those Many Good Effects Proposed Thereby

I am very sensible what a weakness and presumption it is to reason against the general humour and disposition of the world. I remember it was with great justice, and a due regard to the freedom both of the public and the press, forbidden upon severe penalties to write, or discourse, or lay wagers against the Union [1] even before it was confirmed by Parliament, because that

---

40. Not easily controlled by bit or rein.

1. The Act of Union between England and Scotland (1707) uniting their two parliaments, opposed by Swift for its possible threat to the Sacramental Test, but also strongly opposed by the Jacobite supporters of the exiled Stuarts.

was looked upon as a design to oppose the current of the people, which besides the folly of it, is a manifest breach of the fundamental law that makes this majority of opinion the voice of God.[2] In like manner, and for the very same reasons, it may perhaps be neither safe nor prudent to argue against the abolishing of Christianity: at a juncture when all parties seem so unanimously determined upon the point, as we cannot but allow from their actions, their discourses, and their writings. However, I know not how, whether from the affectation of singularity or the perverseness of human nature, but so it unhappily falls out that I cannot be entirely of this opinion. Nay, although I were sure an order were issued out for my immediate prosecution by the Attorney-General, I should still confess that in the present posture of our affairs at home or abroad, I do not yet see the absolute necessity of extirpating the Christian religion from among us.

This perhaps may appear too great a paradox even for our wise and paradoxical age to endure; therefore I shall handle it with all tenderness, and with the utmost deference to that great and profound majority which is of another sentiment.

And yet the curious may please to observe, how much the genius of a nation is liable to alter in half an age. I have heard it affirmed for certain by some very old people that the contrary opinion was even in their memories as much in vogue as the other is now. And that a project for the abolishing of Christianity would then have appeared as singular, and been thought as absurd, as it would be at this time to write or discourse in its defence.

Therefore I freely own that all appearances are against me. The system of the gospel, after the fate of other systems, is generally antiquated and exploded; and the mass or body of the common people, among whom it seems to have had its latest credit, are now grown as much ashamed of it as their betters; opinions, like fashions, always descending from those of quality to the middle sort, and thence to the vulgar, where at length they are dropped and vanish.

But here I would not be mistaken, and must therefore be so bold as to borrow a distinction from the writers on the other side, when they make a difference between nominal and real Trinitarians. I hope no reader imagines me so weak to stand up in the defence of real Christianity, such as used, in primitive times (if we may believe the authors of those ages), to have an influence upon men's belief and actions: to offer at the restoring of that would indeed be a wild project; it would be to dig up foundations; to destroy, at one blow, all the wit, and half the learning, of the kingdom; to break the entire frame and constitution of things; to ruin trade, extinguish arts and sciences, with the professors of them; in short, to turn our courts, exchanges, and shops, into deserts; and would be full as absurd as the proposal of Horace,[3] where he advises the Romans, all in a body, to leave their city and seek a new seat in some remote part of the world, by way of cure for the corruption of their manners.

Therefore I think this caution was in itself altogether unnecessary (which I

2. Cf. Preface to *A Tale of a Tub*: "I am so entirely satisfied with the whole present procedure of human things that I have been for some years preparing materials towards *A Panegyric upon the World*, to which I intended to add a second part entitled *A Modest Defense of the Proceedings of the Rabble in All Ages*."
3. In *Epode* XVI.

have inserted only to prevent all possibility of cavilling) since every candid reader will easily understand my discourse to be intended only in defence of nominal Christianity; the other having been for some time wholly laid aside by general consent as utterly inconsistent with our present schemes of wealth and power.

But why we should therefore cast off the name and title of Christians, although the general opinion and resolution be so violent for it, I confess I cannot (with submission) apprehend the consequence necessary. However, since the undertakers propose such wonderful advantages to the nation by this project and advance many plausible objections against the system of Christianity, I shall briefly consider the strength of both, fairly allow them their greatest weight, and offer such answers as I think most reasonable. After which I will beg leave to show what inconveniencies may possibly happen by such an innovation in the present posture of our affairs.

First, one great advantage proposed by the abolishing of Christianity is that it would very much enlarge and establish liberty of conscience, that great bulwark of our nation and of the Protestant religion; which is still too much limited by priestcraft, notwithstanding all the good intentions of the legislature, as we have lately found by a severe instance. For it is confidently reported that two young gentlemen of great hopes, bright wit, and profound judgment, who, upon a thorough examination of causes and effects, and by the mere force of natural abilities, without the least tincture of learning, having made a discovery that there was no God, and generously communicating their thoughts for the good of the public, were some time ago, by an unparalleled severity, and upon I know not what obsolete law, broke [4] for blasphemy. And as it has been wisely observed, if persecution once begins, no man alive knows how far it may reach, or where it will end.

In answer to all which, with deference to wiser judgments, I think this rather shows the necessity of a nominal religion among us. Great wits love to be free with the highest objects; and if they cannot be allowed a God to revile or renounce, they will speak evil of dignities, abuse the government, and reflect upon the Ministry; which I am sure few will deny to be of much more pernicious consequence, according to the saying of Tiberius, *deorum offensa diis curae*.[5] As to the particular fact related, I think it is not fair to argue from one instance; perhaps another cannot be produced: yet (to the comfort of all those who may be apprehensive of persecution) blasphemy, we know, is freely spoke a million of times in every coffeehouse and tavern, or wherever else good company meet. It must be allowed, indeed, that to break an English freeborn officer only for blasphemy was, to speak the gentlest of such an action, a very high strain of absolute power. Little can be said in excuse for the general; perhaps he was afraid it might give offence to the allies,[6] among whom, for aught we know, it may be the custom of the country to believe a God. But if he argued, as some have done, upon a mistaken principle that an officer

4. Ruined.
5. Tacitus, *Annals* I.73, which reads *injurias* instead of *offensa;* when the emperor Tiberius was told that a witness had injured the divinity of Augustus by swearing a false oath in his name, the reply was, "It is for the gods to punish their own wrongs."
6. Holland, Austria, Savoy, Portugal, and many German states (in the War of the Spanish Succession, against France).

who is guilty of speaking blasphemy may some time or other proceed so far as to raise a mutiny, the consequence is by no means to be admitted; for surely the commander of an English army is likely to be but ill obeyed, whose soldiers fear and reverence him as little as they do a Deity.

It is further objected against the gospel system that it obliges men to the belief of things too difficult for freethinkers, and such who have shaken off the prejudices that usually cling to a confined education. To which I answer, that men should be cautious how they raise objections which reflect upon the wisdom of the nation. Is not everybody freely allowed to believe whatever he pleases and to publish his belief to the world whenever he thinks fit, especially if it serves to strengthen the party which is in the right? Would any indifferent foreigner who should read the trumpery lately written by Asgil, Tindal, Toland, Coward,[7] and forty more, imagine the gospel to be our rule of faith and confirmed by parliaments? Does any man either believe, or say he believes, or desire to have it thought that he says he believes, one syllable of the matter? And is any man worse received upon that score, or does he find his want of nominal faith a disadvantage to him in the pursuit of any civil or military employment? What if there be an old dormant statute or two against him, are they not now obsolete to a degree that Empson and Dudley [8] themselves, if they were now alive, would find it impossible to put them in execution?

It is likewise urged that there are, by computation, in this kingdom, above ten thousand parsons, whose revenues added to those of my lords the Bishops, would suffice to maintain at least two hundred young gentlemen of wit and pleasure and freethinking, enemies to priestcraft, narrow principles, pedantry, and prejudices; who might be an ornament to the court and town: and then again, so great a number of able [-bodied] divines might be a recruit to our fleet and armies. This indeed appears to be a consideration of some weight: but then, on the other side, several things deserve to be considered likewise: as first, whether it may not be thought necessary, that in certain tracts of country, like what we call parishes, there shall be one man at least of abilities to read and write. Then it seems a wrong computation that the revenues of the Church throughout this island, would be large enough to maintain two hundred young gentlemen, or even half that number, after the present refined way of living; that is, to allow each of them such a rent as, in the modern form of speech, would make them easy. But still there is in this project a greater mischief behind; and we ought to beware of the woman's folly who killed the hen that every morning laid her a golden egg. For, pray what would become of the race of men in the next age if we had nothing to trust to beside the scrofulous, consumptive productions furnished by our men of wit and pleasure, when,

7. John Asgil (1659–1738), an Irish lawyer, published in 1699 a work showing that man might achieve eternal life without undergoing death, a doctrine which he based on the Gospels but which caused his expulsion from Parliament. Matthew Tindal (1657–1733), earlier a Roman Catholic, later an Anglican, was the author of the extremely anticlerical *The Rights of the Christian Church Asserted,* a book burnt by order of Commons. James Junius Toland (1670–1722) carried Locke's views further toward Deism in *Christianity Not Mysterious.* William Coward (1657–1725) was a physician who held that the soul died with the body.

8. Richard Empson and Edmund Dudley were agents of Henry VII who revived obsolete statutes in order to raise new revenues.

having squandered away their vigour, health, and estates, they are forced, by some disagreeable marriage, to piece up their broken fortunes and entail[9] rottenness and politeness on their posterity? Now, here are ten thousand persons reduced, by the wise regulations of Henry the Eighth,[10] to the necessity of a low diet, and moderate exercise, who are the only great restorers of our breed, without which the nation would, in an age or two, become but one great hospital.

Another advantage proposed by the abolishing of Christianity is the clear gain of one day in seven, which is now entirely lost, and consequently the kingdom one seventh less considerable in trade, business, and pleasure; beside the loss to the public of so many stately structures, now in the hands of the clergy, which might be converted into play-houses, exchanges, market-houses, common dormitories, and other public edifices.

I hope I shall be forgiven a hard word, if I call this a perfect cavil. I readily own there has been an old custom, time out of mind, for people to assemble in the churches every Sunday, and that shops are still frequently shut in order, as it is conceived, to preserve the memory of that ancient practice; but how this can prove a hindrance to business or pleasure is hard to imagine. What if the men of pleasure are forced, one day in the week, to game at home instead of the chocolatehouse? Are not the taverns and coffeehouses open? Can there be a more convenient season for taking a dose of physic?[11] Are fewer claps[12] got upon Sundays than other days? Is not that the chief day for traders to sum up the accounts of the week, and for lawyers to prepare their briefs? But I would fain know, how it can be pretended that the churches are misapplied? Where are more appointments and rendezvouses of gallantry? Where more care to appear in the foremost box, with greater advantage of dress? Where more meetings for business? Where more bargains driven of all sorts? And where so many conveniences or enticements to sleep?

There is one advantage greater than any of the foregoing proposed by the abolishing of Christianity; that it will utterly extinguish parties among us, by removing those factious distinctions of High and Low Church, of Whig and Tory, Presbyterian and Church of England, which are now so many grievous clogs upon public proceedings, and are apt to dispose men to prefer the gratifying themselves, or depressing their adversaries, before the most important interest of the state.

I confess, if it were certain that so great an advantage would redound to the nation by this expedient, I would submit and be silent; but will any man say, that if the words *whoring, drinking, cheating, lying, stealing,* were, by act of Parliament, ejected out of the English tongue and dictionaries, we should all awake next morning chaste and temperate, honest and just, and lovers of truth? Is this a fair consequence? Or, if the physicians would forbid us to pronounce the words *pox, gout, rheumatism,* and *stone,* would that expedient serve, like so many talismans, to destroy the diseases themselves? Are party and faction rooted in men's hearts no deeper than phrases borrowed from religion, or founded upon no firmer principles? And is our language so poor

9. Impose through inheritance.
10. In plundering the monasteries and exacting from them payments to the crown; Swift loathed Henry VIII.
11. Medicine.
12. Gonorrhea.

that we cannot find other terms to express them? Are *envy, pride, avarice,* and *ambition* such ill nomenclators, that they cannot furnish appellations for their owners? Will not *heydukes* and *mamalukes, mandarins,* and *potshaws,*[13] or any other words formed at pleasure, serve to distinguish those who are in the Ministry from others who would be in it if they could? What, for instance, is easier than to vary the form of speech, and instead of the word *Church,* make it a question in politics, whether the *Monument* be in danger? [14] Because religion was nearest at hand to furnish a few convenient phrases, is our invention so barren we can find no other? Suppose, for argument sake, that the Tories favoured Margarita, the Whigs Mrs. Tofts,[15] and the Trimmers [16] Valentini; would not *Margaritians, Toftians,* and *Valentinians* be very tolerable marks of distinction? The *Prasini* and *Veniti,* two most virulent factions in Italy,[17] began (if I remember right) by a distinction of colours in ribbons; which we might do with as good a grace about the dignity of the blue and the green, and would serve as properly to divide the court, the Parliament, and the kingdom, between them, as any terms of art [18] whatsoever borrowed from religion. Therefore, I think, there is little force in this objection against Christianity, or prospect of so great an advantage as is proposed in the abolishing of it.

It is again objected, as a very absurd, ridiculous custom, that a set of men should be suffered, much less employed and hired, to bawl one day in seven against the lawfulness of those methods most in use towards the pursuit of greatness, riches, and pleasure, which are the constant practice of all men alive on the other six. But this objection is, I think, a little unworthy so refined an age as ours. Let us argue this matter calmly: I appeal to the breast of any polite freethinker whether, in the pursuit of gratifying a predominant passion, he hath not always felt a wonderful incitement by reflecting it was a thing forbidden: and, therefore, we see, in order to cultivate this taste, the wisdom of the nation hath taken special care that the ladies should be furnished with prohibited silks, and the men with prohibited wine.[19] And, indeed, it were to be wished that some other prohibitions were promoted in order to improve the pleasures of the town; which, for want of such expedients, begin already, as I am told, to flag and grow languid, giving way daily to cruel inroads from the spleen.[20]

---

13. Used as nonsense words, but in fact with meanings; respectively, Hungarian footsoldiers or Polish attendants on noblemen (originally robbers or brigands and properly *hajduka*); ruling military class in Egypt; Chinese officials; Persian emperor or sultan, perhaps confused with Turkish pashas or officers.
14. The Monument, built by Sir Christopher Wren in 1666 as a memorial of the Great Fire of London, carried an inscription blaming the Catholics for the fire.
15. Margaritá and Valentini were rival Italian opera singers, and Mrs. Catherine Tofts an English competitor who sang Italian opera.
16. For Trimmers, see the selection from Halifax above.
17. The Greens and Blues, rival factions in Roman chariot races, whose enmity was carried over to Constantinople, where it caused civil war in the reign of Justinian; also alluding to the blue ribbon of the English Order of the Garter and the green of the Scottish Order of the Thistle.
18. Technical terms, often used divisively by sectarians.
19. Prohibited by the war with France but often smuggled.
20. A melancholy affliction, ironically regarded by many as an affectation, but vaguely attributed to the mysterious secretions of the spleen.

It is likewise proposed as a great advantage to the public that if we once discard the system of the gospel, all religion will of course be banished for ever; and consequently, along with it, those grievous prejudices of education, which, under the names of *virtue, conscience, honour, justice,* and the like, are so apt to disturb the peace of human minds, and the notions whereof are so hard to be eradicated by right reason or freethinking, sometimes during the whole course of our lives.

Here first I observe how difficult it is to get rid of a phrase which the world is once grown fond of, though the occasion that first produced it be entirely taken away. For several years past, if a man had but an ill-favoured nose, the deep-thinkers of the age would, some way or other, contrive to impute the cause to the prejudice of his education. From this fountain were said to be derived all our foolish notions of justice, piety, love of our country; all our opinions of God or a future state, heaven, hell, and the like: and there might formerly perhaps have been some pretence for this charge. But so effectual care has been since taken to remove those prejudices by an entire change in the methods of education, that (with honour I mention it to our polite innovators) the young gentlemen who are now on the scene seem to have not the least tincture left of those infusions or string [21] of those weeds: and, by consequence, the reason for abolishing nominal Christianity upon that pretext is wholly ceased.

For the rest, it may perhaps admit a controversy whether the banishing all notions of religion whatsoever would be convenient for the vulgar.[22] Not that I am in the least of opinion with those who hold religion to have been the invention of politicians to keep the lower part of the world in awe by the fear of invisible powers; unless mankind were then very different from what it is now: for I look upon the mass or body of our people here in England to be as freethinkers, that is to say, as staunch unbelievers, as any of the highest rank. But I conceive some scattered notions about a superior power to be of singular use for the common people, as furnishing excellent materials to keep children quiet when they grow peevish, and providing topics of amusement in a tedious winter-night.

Lastly, it is proposed, as a singular advantage, that the abolishing of Christianity will very much contribute to the uniting of Protestants, by enlarging the terms of communion, so as to take in all sorts of dissenters, who are now shut out of the pale upon account of a few ceremonies, which all sides confess to be things indifferent;[23] that this alone will effectually answer the great ends of a scheme for comprehension, by opening a large noble gate at which all bodies may enter; whereas the chaffering with dissenters, and dodging about this or the other ceremony, is but like opening a few wickets,[24] and leaving them at jar,[25] by which no more than one can get in at a time, and that not without stooping, and sideling, and squeezing his body.

To all this I answer, that there is one darling inclination of mankind which

21. Shoots or root fibers.
22. The common people, the uneducated.
23. Matters of no importance and usually left undecided by church doctrine.
24. Small openings in large gates.
25. Ajar.

usually affects to be a retainer to religion, although she be neither its parent, its godmother, or its friend; I mean the spirit of opposition, that lived long before Christianity and can easily subsist without it. Let us, for instance, examine wherein the opposition of sectaries among us consists; we shall find Christianity to have no share in it at all. Does the gospel anywhere prescribe a starched, squeezed countenance, a stiff, formal gait, a singularity of manners and habit, or any affected modes of speech different from the reasonable part of mankind? [26] Yet, if Christianity did not lend its name to stand in the gap and to employ or divert these humours, they must of necessity be spent in contraventions to the laws of the land and disturbance of the public peace. There is a portion of enthusiasm assigned to every nation, which, if it hath not proper objects to work on, will burst out and set all in a flame. If the quiet of a state can be bought by only flinging men a few ceremonies to devour, it is a purchase no wise man would refuse. Let the mastiffs amuse themselves about a sheep's skin stuffed with hay, provided it will keep them from worrying the flock. The institution of convents abroad, seems, in one point, a strain of great wisdom; there being few irregularities in human passions that may not have recourse to vent themselves in some of those orders, which are so many retreats for the speculative, the melancholy, the proud, the silent, the politic, and the morose to spend themselves and evaporate the noxious particles; for each of whom, we, in this island, are forced to provide a several sect of religion to keep them quiet: and whenever Christianity shall be abolished, the legislature must find some other expedient to employ and entertain them. For what imports it how large a gate you open, if there will be always left a number who place a pride and a merit in refusing to enter?

Having thus considered the most important objections against Christianity and the chief advantages proposed by the abolishing thereof, I shall now, with equal deference and submission to wiser judgments as before, proceed to mention a few inconveniences that may happen, if the gospel should be repealed, which perhaps the projectors may not have sufficiently considered.

And first, I am very sensible how much the gentlemen of wit and pleasure are apt to murmur, and be choqued [27] at the sight of so many daggled-tail [28] parsons, who happen to fall in their way and offend their eyes; but, at the same time, these wise reformers do not consider what an advantage and felicity it is for great wits to be always provided with objects of scorn and contempt in order to exercise and improve their talents, and divert their spleen from falling on each other or on themselves; especially when all this may be done without the least imaginable danger to their persons.

And to urge another argument of a parallel nature: if Christianity were once abolished, how could the freethinkers, the strong reasoners, and the men of profound learning be able to find another subject so calculated in all points whereon to display their abilities? what wonderful productions of wit should we be deprived of from those whose genius, by continual practice, hath been wholly turned upon raillery and invectives against religion, and would there-

26. Typical manners of the Puritan sects; for this view of "affected modes of speech" see the criticism of Christian in Vanity Fair (Bunyan, *The Pilgrim's Progress*).
27. Shocked (taken from the French form).
28. Mud-bespattered.

fore never be able to shine or distinguish themselves upon any other subject! We are daily complaining of the great decline of wit among us, and would we take away the greatest, perhaps the only, topic we have left? Who would ever have suspected Asgil for a wit, or Toland for a philosopher, if the inexhaustible stock of Christianity had not been at hand to provide them with materials? What other subject, through all art or nature, could have produced Tindal for a profound author or furnished him with readers? It is the wise choice of the subject that alone adorns and distinguishes the writer. For, had an hundred such pens as these been employed on the side of religion, they would have immediately sunk into silence and oblivion.

Nor do I think it wholly groundless, or my fears altogether imaginary, that the abolishing Christianity may perhaps bring the Church in danger, or at least put the senate to the trouble of another securing vote.[29] I desire I may not be mistaken; I am far from presuming to affirm, or think, that the Church is in danger at present or as things now stand; but we know not how soon it may be so when the Christian religion is repealed. As plausible as this project seems, there may a dangerous design lurk under it. Nothing can be more notorious than that the Atheists, Deists, Socinians,[30] Anti-trinitarians, and other subdivisions of freethinkers are persons of little zeal for the present ecclesiastical establishment: their declared opinion is for repealing the Sacramental Test; they are very indifferent with regard to ceremonies; nor do they hold the *jus divinum* [31] of episcopacy; therefore this may be intended as one politic step towards altering the constitution of the Church established, and setting up Presbytery in the stead, which I leave to be further considered by those at the helm.

In the last place, I think nothing can be more plain than that, by this expedient, we shall run into the evil we chiefly pretend to avoid: and that the abolishment of the Christian religion will be the readiest course we can take to introduce Popery. And I am the more inclined to this opinion because we know it has been the constant practice of the Jesuits to send over emissaries with instructions to personate themselves members of the several prevailing sects among us. So it is recorded, that they have at sundry times appeared in the guise of Presbyterians, Anabaptists, Independents, and Quakers, according as any of these were most in credit; so, since the fashion hath been taken up of exploding religion, the popish missionaries have not been wanting [32] to mix with the freethinkers; among whom Toland, the great oracle of the Anti-christians, is an Irish priest, the son of an Irish priest; and the most learned and ingenious author of a book called *The Rights of the Christian Church* was in a proper juncture reconciled to the Romish faith, whose true son, as appears by an hundred passages in his treatise he still continues. Perhaps I could add some others to the number; but the fact is beyond dispute and the reasoning they proceed by is right: for, supposing Christianity to be extinguished, the

29. Such as the resolution Commons passed in 1701 for "the securing of the Protestant religion, by law established."

30. Followers of Laelius and Faustus Socinus, Italian theologians of the 16th century who denied the divinity of Christ and the supernatural status of the sacraments.

31. "Divine right" (claiming the example of the Apostles).

32. Lacking.

people will never be at ease till they find out some other method of worship; which will as infallibly produce superstition as this will end in Popery.

And therefore, if, notwithstanding all I have said, it shall still be thought necessary to have a bill brought in for repealing Christianity, I would humbly offer an amendment that instead of the word, Christianity, may be put religion in general; which, I conceive, will much better answer all the good ends proposed by the projectors of it. For, as long as we leave in being a God and his Providence, with all the necessary consequences which curious and inquisitive men will be apt to draw from such premises, we do not strike at the root of the evil, although we should ever so effectually annihilate the present scheme of the gospel: for, of what use is freedom of thought if it will not produce freedom of action, which is the sole end, how remote soever in appearance, of all objections against Christianity; and therefore, the freethinkers consider it as a sort of edifice wherein all the parts have such a mutual dependence on each other that if you happen to pull out one single nail, the whole fabric must fall to the ground. This was happily expressed by him who had heard of a text brought for proof of the Trinity, which in an ancient manuscript was differently read; he thereupon immediately took the hint, and by a sudden deduction of a long *sorites*,[33] most logically concluded; 'Why, if it be as you say, I may safely whore and drink on, and defy the parson.' From which, and many the like instances easy to be produced, I think nothing can be more manifest than that the quarrel is not against any particular points of hard digestion in the Christian system but against religion in general; which, by laying restraints on human nature, is supposed the great enemy to the freedom of thought and action.

Upon the whole, if it shall still be thought for the benefit of church and state that Christianity be abolished, I conceive, however, it may be more convenient to defer the execution to a time of peace; and not venture in this conjuncture to disoblige our allies, who, as it falls out, are all Christians, and many of them, by the prejudices of their education, so bigoted as to place a sort of pride in the appellation. If upon being rejected by them, we are to trust to an alliance with the Turk, we shall find ourselves much deceived: for, as he is too remote and generally engaged in war with the Persian emperor, so his people would be more scandalized at our infidelity than our Christian neighbours. Because the Turks are not only strict observers of religious worship but, what is worse, believe a God; which is more than is required of us even while we preserve the name of Christians.

To conclude: whatever some may think of the great advantages to trade by this favourite scheme, I do very much apprehend that in six months' time after the act is passed for the extirpation of the gospel, the Bank and East India stock may fall at least one *per cent*.[34] And since that is fifty times more than ever the wisdom of our age thought fit to venture for the preservation of Christianity, there is no reason we should be at so great a loss merely for the sake of destroying it.

1708   1711

33. A long and tenuous chain of reasoning.
34. The Bank of England (founded in 1695 by William III) and the East India Company, both largely Whig concerns.

A Modest Proposal

This concise and fiercely ironic tract is based upon England's exploitation of Ireland, which was forbidden to trade on its own with other countries but used as a source of raw materials and cheap food. Swift writes as an eager collaborator, an Irish projector who at last finds a scheme that will enrich Ireland without offending the English; it will, moreover, at last make Ireland's people "the riches of a nation," as a large working force was traditionally believed to be. The projector in whose guise Swift writes can sustain without conflict an idiom of humane tenderness, somewhat cloying in fact, with the zeal of a ruthlessly commercial breeder of beef. Clearly, the cannibalism that solves Ireland's problem is simply a metaphor for the exploitation that has created it, and "dressing them hot under the knife" shows insensibility only different in degree from counting on the poor to die "as fast as they reasonably can." The tract does not spare the Irish, either, for one of the worst evils of exploitation is that it degrades and brutalizes its victims; Swift is enraged by their passivity, and that too requires its terrible metaphors.

A Modest Proposal

for
Preventing the Children of Poor People in Ireland from Being a Burden to Their Parents or Country, and for Making Them Beneficial to the Public

It is a melancholy object to those who walk through this great town, or travel in the country, when they see the streets, the roads, and cabin-doors crowded with beggars of the female sex, followed by three, four, or six children, all in rags, and importuning every passenger for an alms. These mothers, instead of being able to work for their honest livelihood, are forced to employ all their time in strolling to beg sustenance for their helpless infants: who, as they grow up, either turn thieves for want of work, or leave their dear native country to fight for the Pretender in Spain, or sell themselves to the Barbadoes.[1]

I think it is agreed by all parties, that this prodigious number of children in the arms, or on the backs, or at the heels of their mothers, and frequently of their fathers, is, in the present deplorable state of the kingdom, a very great additional grievance; and, therefore, whoever could find out a fair, cheap, and easy method of making these children sound and useful members of the commonwealth, would deserve so well of the public, as to have his statue set up for a preserver of the nation.[2]

But my intention is very far from being confined to provide only for the children of professed beggars, it is of a much greater extent, and shall take in the

1. Many Irish Catholics enlisted in French and Spanish forces, the latter employed in the effort to restore the Stuart Pretender to the English throne in 1718; emigration to the West Indies from Ireland had reached the rate of almost fifteen hundred a year (and often led to desperate servitude).
2. The idiom of the "projector," the enthusiastic proponent of public remedies (often suspected of having an eye on his own glory).

whole number of infants at a certain age, who are born of parents in effect as little able to support them as those who demand our charity in the streets.

As to my own part, having turned my thoughts for many years upon this important subject, and maturely weighed the several schemes of other projectors, I have always found them grossly mistaken in their computation. It is true, a child, just dropped from its dam,[3] may be supported by her milk for a solar year with little other nourishment; at most, not above the value of two shillings, which the mother may certainly get, or the value in scraps, by her lawful occupation of begging; and it is exactly at one year old that I propose to provide for them in such a manner, as, instead of being a charge upon their parents or the parish, or wanting food and raiment for the rest of their lives, they shall, on the contrary, contribute to the feeding, and partly to the clothing, of many thousands.

There is likewise another great advantage in my scheme, that it will prevent those voluntary abortions, and that horrid practice of women murdering their bastard children, alas, too frequent among us, sacrificing the poor innocent babes, I doubt more to avoid the expense than the shame, which would move tears and pity in the most savage and inhuman breast.

The number of souls in this kingdom being usually reckoned one millon and a half, of these I calculate there may be about two hundred thousand couple whose wives are breeders; from which number I subtract thirty thousand couple, who are able to maintain their own children (although I apprehend there cannot be so many, under the present distresses of the kingdom); but this being granted, there will remain an hundred and seventy thousand breeders. I again subtract fifty thousand for those women who miscarry, or whose children die by accident or disease within the year. There only remain a hundred and twenty thousand children of poor parents annually born. The question therefore is how this number shall be reared and provided for? which, as I have already said, under the present situation of affairs, is utterly impossible by all the methods hitherto proposed. For we can neither employ them in handicraft or agriculture; we neither build houses (I mean in the country) nor cultivate land: they can very seldom pick up a livelihood by stealing until they arrive at six years old, except where they are of towardly parts; although I confess they learn the rudiments much earlier; during which time they can, however, be properly looked upon only as probationers; as I have been informed by a principal gentleman in the county of Cavan,[4] who protested to me, that he never knew above one or two instances under the age of six, even in a part of the kingdom so renowned for the quickest proficiency in that art.

I am assured by our merchants that a boy or a girl before twelve years old is no saleable commodity; and even when they come to this age they will not yield above three pounds or three pounds and half-a-crown at most, on the exchange; which cannot turn to account either to the parents or kingdom, the charge of nutriment and rags having been at least four times that value.

I shall now, therefore, humbly propose my own thoughts, which I hope will not be liable to the least objection.

3. The idiom now of the cattle breeder.
4. One of the poorest districts of Ireland.

I have been assured by a very knowing American [5] of my acquaintance in London, that a young healthy child, well nursed, is, at a year old, a most delicious, nourishing, and wholesome food, whether stewed, roasted, baked, or boiled; and I make no doubt that it will equally serve in a fricassee or a ragout.[6]

I do therefore humbly offer it to public consideration, that of the hundred and twenty thousand children already computed, twenty thousand may be reserved for breed, whereof only one-fourth part to be males; which is more than we allow to sheep, black cattle, or swine; and my reason is, that these children are seldom the fruits of marriage, a circumstance not much regarded by our savages, therefore one male will be sufficient to serve four females. That the remaining hundred thousand may, at a year old, be offered in sale to the persons of quality and fortune through the kingdom; always advising the mother to let them suck plentifully in the last month, so as to render them plump and fat for a good table. A child will make two dishes at an entertainment for friends; and when the family dines alone, the fore or hind quarter will make a reasonable dish, and, seasoned with a little pepper or salt, will be very good boiled on the fourth day, especially in winter.

I have reckoned, upon a medium, that a child just born will weigh twelve pounds, and in a solar year, if tolerably nursed, increaseth to twenty-eight pounds.

I grant this food will be somewhat dear, and therefore very proper for landlords, who, as they have already devoured most of the parents, seem to have the best title to the children.

Infants' flesh will be in season throughout the year, but more plentifully in March, and a little before and after: for we are told by a grave author, an eminent French physician,[7] that fish being a prolific [8] diet, there are more children born in Roman Catholic countries about nine months after Lent than at any other season; therefore, reckoning a year after Lent, the markets will be more glutted than usual, because the number of popish infants is at least three to one in this kingdom; and therefore it will have one other collateral advantage, by lessening the number of papists among us.

I have already computed the charge of nursing a beggar's child (in which list I reckon all cottagers, labourers, and four-fifths of the farmers) to be about two shillings per annum, rags included; and I believe no gentleman would repine to give ten shillings for the carcass of a good fat child, which, as I have said, will make four dishes of excellent nutritive meat, when he has only some particular friend, or his own family, to dine with him. Thus the squire will learn to be a good landlord, and grow popular among his tenants; the mother will have eight shillings net profit, and be fit for work till she produces another child.

Those who are more thrifty (as I must confess the times require) may flay

---

5. Presumably American Indian, many of whom were believed by the English to enjoy cannibalism.

6. A French stew, one of the foreign dishes ("olios and ragouts") Swift mocks elsewhere as affectations.

7. François Rabelais (c. 1494–1553), *Gargantua and Pantagruel* V.29.

8. Generative.

the carcass; the skin of which, artificially dressed, will make admirable gloves for ladies, and summer-boots for fine gentlemen.

As to our city of Dublin, shambles [9] may be appointed for this purpose in the most convenient parts of it, and butchers we may be assured will not be wanting; although I rather recommend buying the children alive, and dressing them hot from the knife, as we do roasting pigs.

A very worthy person, a true lover of his country, and whose virtues I highly esteem, was lately pleased, in discoursing on this matter, to offer a refinement upon my scheme. He said, that many gentlemen of this kingdom, having of late destroyed their deer, he conceived that the want of venison might be well supplied by the bodies of young lads and maidens, not exceeding fourteen years of age, nor under twelve; so great a number of both sexes in every country being now ready to starve for want of work and service; and these to be disposed of by their parents, if alive, or otherwise by their nearest relations. But, with due deference to so excellent a friend, and so deserving a patriot, I cannot be altogether in his sentiments; for as to the males, my American acquaintance assured me from frequent experience, that their flesh was generally tough and lean, like that of our schoolboys, by continual exercise, and their taste disagreeable; and to fatten them would not answer the charge. Then as to the females, it would, I think, with humble submission, be a loss to the public, because they soon would become breeders themselves: and besides, it is not improbable that some scrupulous people might be apt to censure such a practice (although indeed very unjustly) as a little bordering upon cruelty; which, I confess hath always been with me the strongest objection against any project, how well soever intended.

But in order to justify my friend, he confessed that this expedient was put into his head by the famous Psalmanazar,[10] a native of the island Formosa, who came from thence to London above twenty years ago; and in conversation told my friend, that in his country, when any young person happened to be put to death, the executioner sold the carcass to persons of quality as a prime dainty; and that in his time the body of a plump girl of fifteen, who was crucified for an attempt to poison the emperor, was sold to his Imperial Majesty's prime minister of state,[11] and other great mandarins of the court, in joints from the gibbet, at four hundred crowns. Neither indeed can I deny, that if the same use were made of several plump young girls in this town, who, without one single groat to their fortunes, cannot stir abroad without a chair, and appear at playhouse and assemblies [12] in foreign fineries which they never will pay for, the kingdom would not be the worse.

Some persons of a desponding spirit are in great concern about that vast number of poor people who are aged, diseased, or maimed; and I have been desired to employ my thoughts what course may be taken to ease the nation of so grievous an encumbrance. But I am not in the least pain upon that matter,

9. Slaughterhouses.
10. George Psalmanazar (1679-1763), a Frenchman who pretended to be a Formosan and wrote (in English) a fraudulent book about his "native" land.
11. Probably a reference to Walpole.
12. Social gatherings (Swift had sought an Irish boycott of all such foreign luxuries of dress or diet).

because it is very well known, that they are every day dying, and rotting, by cold and famine, and filth and vermin, as fast as can be reasonably expected. And as to the younger labourers, they are now in almost as hopeful a condition: they cannot get work, and consequently pine away for want of nourishment, to a degree, that if at any time they are accidentally hired to common labour, they have not strength to perform it; and thus the country and themselves are happily delivered from the evils to come.

I have too long digressed, and therefore shall return to my subject. I think the advantages by the proposal which I have made are obvious and many, as well as of the highest importance.

For first, as I have already observed, it would greatly lessen the number of papists, with whom we are yearly overrun, being the principal breeders of the nation as well as our most dangerous enemies; and who stay at home on purpose with a design to deliver the kingdom to the Pretender, hoping to take their advantage by the absence of so many good Protestants, who have chosen rather to leave their country than stay at home and pay tithes against their conscience to an idolatrous Episcopal curate.[13]

Secondly, the poorer tenants will have something valuable of their own, which by law may be made liable to distress, and help to pay their landlord's rent; their corn and cattle being already seized, and money a thing unknown.

Thirdly, whereas the maintenance of an hundred thousand children, from two years old and upwards, cannot be computed at less than ten shillings a piece per annum, the nation's stock will be thereby increased fifty thousand pounds per annum; besides the profit of a new dish introduced to the tables of all gentlemen of fortune in the kingdom who have any refinement in taste. And the money will circulate among ourselves, the goods being entirely of our own growth and manufacture.

Fourthly, the constant breeders, besides the gain of eight shillings sterling per annum by the sale of their children, will be rid of the charge of maintaining them after the first year.

Fifthly, this food would likewise bring great custom to taverns; where the vintners will certainly be so prudent as to procure the best receipts for dressing it to perfection, and, consequently, have their houses frequented by all the fine gentlemen, who justly value themselves upon their knowledge in good eating: and a skilful cook, who understands how to oblige his guests, will contrive to make it as expensive as they please.

Sixthly, this would be a great inducement to marriage, which all wise nations have either encouraged by rewards, or enforced by laws and penalties. It would increase the care and tenderness of mothers towards their children, when they were sure of a settlement for life to the poor babes, provided in some sort by the public, to their annual profit instead of expense. We should soon see an honest emulation among the married women, which of them could bring the

---

13. Swift is mocking the castigation of the Catholics, for he regarded it as a typical propaganda device of the Whigs and Protestants; his own experience as a clergyman in northern Ireland had given him reason to fear and distrust the energies of the dissenting Protestants, and he questions their motives (money or conscience) for leaving Ireland. The word "idolatrous" was added in 1735 after renewed agitation to remove the Sacramental Test, with the implication that Anglican forms and doctrines were intolerable to other Protestants.

fattest child to the market. Men would become as fond of their wives during the time of their pregnancy, as they are now of their mares in foal, their cows in calf, or sows when they are ready to farrow; nor offer to beat or kick them (as is too frequent a practice) for fear of a miscarriage.

Many other advantages might be enumerated. For instance, the addition of some thousand carcasses in our exportation of barrelled beef; the propagation of swine's flesh, and improvement in the art of making good bacon, so much wanted among us by the great destruction of pigs, too frequent at our tables, which are no way comparable in taste or magnificence to a well-grown, fat yearling child, which, roasted whole, will make a considerable figure at a Lord Mayor's feast, or any other public entertainment. But this, and many others, I omit, being studious of brevity.

Supposing that one thousand families in this city would be constant customers for infants' flesh, besides others who might have it at merry meetings, particularly weddings and christenings, I compute that Dublin would take off annually about twenty thousand carcasses; and the rest of the kingdom (where probably they will be sold somewhat cheaper) the remaining eighty thousand.

I can think of no one objection that will possibly be raised against this proposal, unless it should be urged, that the number of people will be thereby much lessened in the kingdom. This I freely own, and it was indeed one principal design in offering it to the world. I desire the reader will observe that I calculate my remedy for this one individual kingdom of Ireland, and for no other that ever was, is, or I think ever can be, upon earth. Therefore let no man talk to me of other expedients: [14] of taxing our absentees at five shillings a pound: of using neither clothes nor household-furniture except what is of our own growth and manufacture: of utterly rejecting the materials and instruments that promote foreign luxury: of curing the expensiveness of pride, vanity, idleness, and gaming in our women; of introducing a vein of parsimony, prudence, and temperance: of learning to love our country, wherein we differ even from Laplanders, and the inhabitants of Topinamboo: [15] of quitting our animosities and factions, nor act any longer like the Jews, who were murdering one another at the very moment their city was taken: [16] of being a little cautious not to sell our country and consciences for nothing: of teaching landlords to have at least one degree of mercy towards their tenants: lastly, of putting a spirit of honesty, industry, and skill into our shopkeepers; who, if a resolution could now be taken to buy only our native goods, would immediately unite to cheat and exact upon us in the price, the measure, and the goodness, nor could ever yet be brought to make one fair proposal of just dealing, though often and earnestly invited to it.

Therefore I repeat, let no man talk to me of these and the like expedients, till he hath at least some glimpse of hope that there will ever be some hearty and sincere attempt to put them in practice.

But, as to myself, having been wearied out for many years with offering vain, idle, visionary thoughts, and at length utterly despairing of success, I

14. The following are, of course, Swift's own genuine proposals for Ireland.
15. A region of Brazil known for wildness and barbarous stupidity.
16. When Jerusalem fell to Nebuchadnezzar (II Kings 24, 25; II Chronicles 36), with the suggestion that English domination is Ireland's Babylonian captivity.

fortunately fell upon this proposal; which, as it is wholly new, so it hath something solid and real, of no expense and little trouble, full in our own power, and whereby we can incur no danger in disobliging England. For this kind of commodity will not bear exportation, the flesh being of too tender a consistence to admit a long continuance in salt, although perhaps I could name a country which would be glad to eat up our whole nation without it.

After all, I am not so violently bent upon my own opinion as to reject any offer proposed by wise men which shall be found equally innocent, cheap, easy, and effectual. But before something of that kind shall be advanced in contradiction to my scheme, and offering a better, I desire the author, or authors, will be pleased maturely to consider two points. First, as things now stand, how they will be able to find food and raiment for a hundred thousand useless mouths and backs? And, secondly, there being a round million of creatures in human figure throughout this kingdom, whose whole subsistence put into a common stock would leave them in debt two millions of pounds sterling, adding those who are beggars by profession, to the bulk of farmers, cottagers, and labourers, with the wives and children who are beggars in effect; I desire those politicians who dislike my overture, and may perhaps be so bold as to attempt an answer, that they will first ask the parents of these mortals, whether they would not at this day think it a great happiness to have been sold for food at a year old, in the manner I prescribe, and thereby have avoided such a perpetual scene of misfortunes as they have since gone through, by the oppression of landlords, the impossibility of paying rent without money or trade, the want of common sustenance, with neither house nor clothes to cover them from the inclemencies of weather, and the most inevitable prospect of entailing the like, or greater miseries, upon their breed for ever.

I profess, in the sincerity of my heart, that I have not the least personal interest in endeavouring to promote this necessary work, having no other motive than the public good of my country, by advancing our trade, providing for infants, relieving the poor, and giving some pleasure to the rich. I have no children by which I can propose to get a single penny; the youngest being nine years old, and my wife past child-bearing.

1729

Swift's Poems

Swift began his poetic career with Pindaric odes in the manner of Abraham Cowley, but he soon found his characteristic idiom in the Hudibrastic tetrameter couplet. His poetry is a constant warfare against the false sublime and other forms of specious exaltation, and his dry, colloquial undercutting of pretension is to be seen alike in "Baucis and Philemon" (see The Mock Form), in the birthday poems to Stella (tender and warm as they are), and in caustic or scatological satires such as "The Day of Judgment" and "Cassinus and Peter." The two "city" poems (see The Urban Scene), written in pentameter to burlesque the current form of pastoral and georgic poetry, are further examples of Swift's reduction of unthinking celebration and of his opposition of the commonplace lowness of everyday life to the conventions of literary style.

Phyllis
Or, The Progress of Love

Desponding Phyllis was endued
With every talent of a prude:
She trembled when a man drew near;
Salute her, and she turned her ear:
If o'er against her you were placed,
She durst not look above your waist:
She'd rather take you to her bed,
Than let you see her dress her head;
In church you heard her, through the crowd,
10 Repeat the absolution loud:
In church, secure behind her fan,
She durst behold that monster, man:
There practised how to place her head,
And bit her lips to make them red;
Or, on the mat devoutly kneeling,
Would lift her eyes up to the ceiling.
And heave her bosom unaware,
For neighbouring beaux to see it bare.
    At length a lucky lover came,
20 And found admittance from the dame.
Suppose all parties now agreed,
The writings drawn, the lawyer fee'd,
The vicar and the ring bespoke:
Guess, how could such a match be broke?
See then what mortals place their bliss in!
Next morn betimes the bride was missing:
The mother screamed, the father chid;
Where can this idle wench be hid?
No news of Phyl! the bridegroom came,
30 And thought his bride had skulked for shame;
Because her father used to say
The girl had such a bashful way.
    Now John the butler must be sent
To learn the way that Phyllis went:
The groom was wished to saddle Crop;
For John must neither light nor stop,
But find her whereso'er she fled,
And bring her back alive or dead.
See here again the devil to do;
40 For truly John was missing too:
The horse and pillion° both were gone!
Phyllis, it seems, was fled with John.
Old Madam, who went up to find

pillion saddle for the person who rode behind
(usually a woman)

228

What papers Phyl had left behind,
A letter on the toilet° sees,
'To my much-honoured father—these—'
('Tis always done, romances tell us,
When daughters run away with fellows)
Filled with the choicest commonplaces,
50   By others used in the like cases.
'That long ago a fortune-teller
Exactly said what now befell her;
And in a glass had made her see
A serving-man of low degree.
It was her fate, must be forgiven;
For marriages are made in Heaven:
His pardon begged: but, to be plain,
She'd do't if 'twere to do again:
Thank God, 'twas neither shame nor sin,
60   For John was come of honest kin.
Love never thinks of rich and poor;
She'd beg with John from door to door.
Forgive her, if it be a crime;
She'll never do't another time.
She ne'er before in all her life
Once disobeyed him, maid nor wife.'
One argument she summed up all in,
'The thing was done and past recalling;
And therefore hoped she would recover
70   His favour, when his passion's over.
She valued not what others thought her,
And was—his most obedient daughter.'
    Fair maidens all, attend the Muse,
Who now the wandering pair pursues:
Away they rode in homely° sort,
Their journey long, their money short;
The loving couple well bemired;
The horse and both the riders tired:
Their victuals bad, their lodging worse;
80   Phyl cried, and John began to curse:
Phyl wished that she had strained a limb,
When first she ventured out with him;
John wished that he had broke a leg,
When first for her he quitted Peg.
    But what adventures more befell 'em,
The Muse has now no time to tell 'em;
How Johnny wheedled, threatened, fawned,
Till Phyllis all her trinkets pawned:
How oft she broke her marriage vows,

toilet dressing table   **homely** simple, plain

90   In kindness to maintain her spouse,
Till swains unwholesome° spoiled the trade;
For now the surgeon must be paid,
To whom those perquisites are gone,
In Christian justice due to John.
    When food and raiment now grew scarce,
Fate put a period° to the farce,
And with exact poetic justice;
For John is landlord, Phyllis hostess;
They keep, at Staines, the Old Blue Boar,
100   Are cat and dog, and rogue and whore.
1719   1727

On Stella's Birthday°

Stella this day is thirty-four,
(We won't dispute a year or more:)
However, Stella, be not troubled,
Although thy size and years are doubled
Since first I saw thee at sixteen,
The brightest virgin on the green;
So little is thy form declined,
Made up so largely in thy mind.
    O, would it please the gods to split
10   Thy beauty, size, and years, and wit,
No age could furnish out a pair
Of nymphs so graceful, wise, and fair;
With half the lustre of your eyes,
With half your wit, your years, and size.
And then, before it grew too late,
How should I beg of gentle fate,
(That either nymph might have her swain,)
To split my worship too in twain.
1719   1727

Stella's Birthday°

    March 13, 1727
This day, whate'er the fates decree,
Shall still° be kept with joy by me:
This day then let us not be told,

unwholesome diseased
period end
On Stella's Birthday This is the first of a series of birthday poems Swift wrote for Hester Johnson; it was written in fact for her thirty-eighth birthday on March 13, 1719. We can see here the tenderness and gentle mockery that characterize these poems as they do Swift's letters in the so-called *Journal to Stella.*
Stella's Birthday This is the last of the series; Stella died on January 28, 1728.
still always

That you are sick, and I grown old;
Nor think on our approaching ills,
And talk of spectacles and pills;
Tomorrow will be time enough
To hear such mortifying° stuff.
Yet, since from reason may be brought
10 A better and more pleasing thought,
Which can, in spite of all decays,
Support a few remaining days;
From not the gravest of divines
Accept for once some serious lines.
    Although we now can form no more
Long schemes of life, as heretofore;
Yet you, while time is running fast,
Can look with joy on what is past.
    Were future happiness and pain
20 A mere contrivance of the brain;
As atheists argue, to entice
And fit their proselytes for vice;
(The only comfort they propose,
To have companions in their woes)
Grant this the case; yet sure 'tis hard
That virtue, styled its own reward,
And by all sages understood
To be the chief of human good,
Should acting die, nor leave behind
30 Some lasting pleasure in the mind,
Which, by remembrance, will assuage
Grief, sickness, poverty, and age;
And strongly shoot a radiant dart
To shine through life's declining part.
    Say, Stella, feel you no content,
Reflecting on a life well spent?
Your skilful hand employed to save
Despairing wretches from the grave;
And then supporting with your store
40 Those whom you dragged from death before:°
So Providence on mortals waits,
Preserving what it first creates.
Your generous boldness to defend
An innocent and absent friend;
That courage which can make you just
To merit humbled in the dust;
The detestation you express
For vice in all its glittering dress;

mortifying humbling, but also destroying vital
or active powers
from death before Swift is eloquent in his tributes to Stella's charity, both in nursing the sick
and in supporting them from her limited income.

That patience under torturing pain,
50   Where stubborn Stoics would complain:
     Must these like empty shadows pass,
Or forms reflected from a glass?
Or mere chimeras in the mind,
That fly and leave no marks behind?
Does not the body thrive and grow
By food of twenty years ago?
And, had it not been still supplied,
It must a thousand times have died.
Then who with reason can maintain
60   That no effects of food remain?
And is not virtue in mankind
The nutriment that feeds the mind;
Upheld by each good action past,
And still continued by the last?
Then, who with reason can pretend
That all effects of virtue end?
     Believe me, Stella, when you show
That true contempt for things below,
Nor prize your life for other ends,
70   Than merely to oblige your friends;
Your former actions claim their part;
And join to fortify your heart.
For Virtue in her daily race,
Like Janus,° bears a double face;
Looks back with joy where she has gone,
And therefore goes with courage on:
She at your sickly couch will wait,
And guide you to a better state.
     O then, whatever Heaven intends,
80   Take pity on your pitying friends!
Nor let your ills affect your mind,
To fancy they can be unkind.
Me, surely me, you ought to spare,
Who gladly would your suffering share;
Or give my scrap of life to you,
And think it far beneath your due;
You, to whose care so oft I owe
That I'm alive to tell you so.
1727   1727

Janus the god of beginnings, his symbol a
double-faced head, looking both forward and
backward

The Day of Judgment

With a whirl of thought oppressed,
I sunk from reverie to rest.
A horrid vision seized my head,
I saw the graves give up their dead!
Jove, armed with terrors, bursts the skies,
And thunder roars and lightning flies!
Amazed, confused, its fate unknown,
The world stands trembling at his throne!
While each pale sinner hangs his head,
¹⁰ Jove, nodding, shook the heavens, and said:
'Offending race of human kind,
By nature, reason, learning, blind;
You who, through frailty, stepped aside;
And you who never fell—through pride:
You who in different sects have shammed,
And come to see each other damned;
(So some folk told you, but they knew
No more of Jove's designs than you)
The world's mad business now is o'er,
²⁰ And I resent these pranks no more.
I to such blockheads set my wit!
I damn such fools!—Go, go, you're bit.'
1731?   1774

Cassinus and Peter°

A Tragical Elegy
Two college sophs of Cambridge growth,
Both special wits and lovers both,
Conferring, as they used to meet,
On love and books, in rapture sweet;
(Muse find me names to fix my metre,
Cassinus this, and t'other Peter.)
Friend Peter to Cassinus goes,
To chat a while and warm his nose:
But such a sight was never seen,
¹⁰ The lad lay swallowed up in spleen.°
He seemed as just crept out of bed;
One greasy stocking round his head,
The t'other he sat down to darn,

Cassinus and Peter This poem deserves study rather than the curious notoriety it has received. The last line is often cited as evidence of Swift's horror of bodily functions, as if the poem were not a consistent mockery of the fatuously romantic idealist, down to his own slovenliness (only in part the result of distraction) and his visionary mad fit in ll. 79–88, similar to those of Dryden's heroic plays or of later 18th-century odes.
spleen melancholy, "vapors"; as the ensuing picture reveals, the image of a distracted lover

With threads of different coloured yarn;
His breeches torn, exposing wide
A ragged shirt and tawny hide.
Scorched were his shins, his legs were bare,
But well embrowned with dirt and hair.
A rug was o'er his shoulders thrown,
20   (A rug, for nightgown he had none,)
His jordan° stood in manner fitting
Between his legs, to spew° or spit in;
His ancient pipe, in sable dyed,
And half unsmoked, lay by his side.
　　Him thus accoutred Peter found,
With eyes in smoke and weeping drowned;
The leavings of his last night's pot°
On embers placed, to drink it hot.
　　'Why, Cassy, thou wilt doze thy pate:
30   What makes thee lie a-bed so late?
The finch, the linnet, and the thrush,
Their matins chant in every bush;
And I have heard thee oft salute
Aurora with thy early flute.
Heaven send thou hast not got the hyps!°
How! not a word come from thy lips?'
　　Then gave him some familiar thumps,
A college joke to cure the dumps.
　　The swain at last, with grief opprest,
40   Cried, 'Celia!' thrice, and sighed the rest.
　　'Dear Cassy, though to ask I dread,
Yet ask I must—is Celia dead?'
　　'How happy I, were that the worst!
But I was fated to be curst!'
　　'Come, tell us, has she played the whore?'
　　'O Peter, would it were no more!'
　　'Why, plague confound her sandy locks!
Say, has the small or greater pox°
Sunk down her nose, or seamed her face?
50   Be easy, 'tis a common case.'
　　'O Peter! beauty's but a varnish,
Which time and accidents will tarnish:
But Celia has contrived to blast
Those beauties that might ever last.
Nor can imagination guess,
Nor eloquence divine express,
How that ungrateful charming maid

jordan chamber pot
spew vomit
pot of wine
hyps hypochondria

small . . . pox smallpox or syphilis, the latter
causing collapse of the bridge of the nose in advanced stages

My purest passion has betrayed:
Conceive the most envenomed dart
60 To pierce an injured lover's heart.'
   'Why, hang her; though she seemed so coy,
I know, she loves the barber's boy.'
   'Friend Peter, this I could excuse,
For every nymph has leave to choose;
Nor have I reason to complain,
She loves a more deserving swain.
But oh! how ill hast thou divined
A crime that shocks all humankind;
A deed unknown to female race,
70 At which the sun should hide his face:
Advice in vain you would apply—
Then leave me to despair and die.
Yet, kind Arcadians,° on my urn
These elegies and sonnets burn;
And on the marble grave these rhymes,
A monument to after-times—
"Here Cassy lies, by Celia slain,
And dying, never told his pain."
Vain empty world, farewell. But hark,
80 The loud Cerberian triple bark;°
And there—behold Alecto° stand,
A whip of scorpions in her hand:
Lo, Charon° from his leaky wherry
Beckoning to waft me o'er the ferry:
I come! I come! Medusa° see,
Her serpents hiss direct at me.
Begone; unhand me, hellish fry:
Avaunt—ye cannot say 'twas I.'°
   'Dear Cassy, thou must purge and bleed;°
90 I fear thou wilt be mad indeed.
But now, by friendship's sacred laws,
I here conjure thee, tell the cause;
And Celia's horrid fact relate:
Thy friend would gladly share thy fate.'
   'To force it out, my heart must rend;
Yet when conjured by such a friend—
Think, Peter, how my soul is racked!
These eyes, these eyes, beheld the fact.

Arcadians the shepherds of pastoral Greece. A famous subject of paintings and prints is a group of shepherds peering at a gravestone that reads "Et in Arcadia ego," interpreted as Death's saying, "Even in Arcadia I am."
Cerberian . . . bark the bark of three-headed Cerberus at the gates of the underworld
Alecto one of the three Furies
Charon the ferryman of the dead across the Styx

Medusa the gorgon whose locks are snakes and whose gaze can turn anything to stone
Avaunt . . . 'twas I "See *Macbeth*" (Swift); a condensation of two outcries of Macbeth upon seeing Banquo's ghost: "Thou canst not say I did it" and "Avaunt! and quit my sight!" (III.iv.50, 93)
purge and bleed laxatives and blood-letting as cures for the spleen

Now bend thine ear, since out it must;
100   But, when thou seest me laid in dust,
The secret thou shalt ne'er impart,
Not to the nymph that keeps thy heart;
(How would her virgin soul bemoan
A crime to all her sex unknown!)
Nor whisper to the tattling reeds°
The blackest of all female deeds;
Nor blab it on the lonely rocks,
Where Echo sits, and listening mocks;°
Nor let the zephyr's treacherous gale
110   Through Cambridge waft the direful tale;
Nor to the chattering feathered race°
Discover° Celia's foul disgrace.
But, if you fail, my spectre dread,
Attending nightly round your bed—
And yet I dare confide in you;
So take my secret, and adieu:
    Nor wonder how I lost my wits;
Oh! Celia, Celia, Celia shits!'

1734

Gulliver's Travels

Gulliver's Travels (as the book has come to be known) was probably begun by 1720 and completed in the summer of 1725; the publisher received the manuscript "he knew not whence, nor from whom, dropped at his house in the dark, from a hackney-coach." The book had immediate success. "From the highest to the lowest it is universally read," Gay wrote to Swift in Ireland, "from the cabinet-council to the nursery." And Pope wrote, "The countenance with which it is received by some statesmen is delightful; I wish I could tell you how every single man looks upon it, to observe which has been my whole diversion this fortnight." In 1735, when Swift supervised a new edition, he added the letter from Gulliver to his cousin Sympson which is given here; and the lament of Mary Gulliver is one of a series of poems inspired by the *Travels* and written in all probability by Gay, perhaps with Pope's collaboration.

    Swift's great satire is recounted by a stolid, unimaginative, decent man who can, under the stress of pride, become arrogantly complacent or—once he has suffered disenchantment—arrogantly misanthropic. "I tell you after all that I do not hate mankind," Swift wrote to Pope in 1725; "it is *vous autres* who hate them because you would have them reasonable animals, and are angry for being disappointed." "You others" includes Gulliver himself, who seems blandly persuaded that man is a rational animal until he discovers what a truly rational animal is (in the form of a

the tattling reeds to which Midas' wife confided the terrible secret that he had ass's ears
listening mocks The nymph Echo was punished (for impeding Hera's investigation of Zeus' adul-teries) by being denied all speech except what she could repeat of others' words.
chattering . . . race e.g. parrots
Discover disclose

horse) and what kind of animal man can be at worst (in the form, unfortunately, of man). Swift's own definition of man is a creature *rationis capax*, that is, capable of reason, but not at all securely in possession of it. What he presents in the great fourth voyage is the image of man in a state of full degeneration, his bestiality only intensified by his vestigial powers of mind; the Yahoo is offered as a limiting case of what man can become, and he inevitably raises the question of how far man has moved toward that limit already.

The Houyhnhnm, in contrast, is a thoroughly rational animal. He is no more than an animal in that he has no intimations of immortality or of divinity; Nature is the First Mother to whom in death he returns, and he can boast of himself as "the Perfection of Nature" but cannot imagine that he might be something more. His life is mild and temperate, for his passions are thoroughly in the control of his reason; and his reason is an immediate, practical, intuitive power for discerning what is right as well as what is efficient. Houyhnhnm life, then, is neither spirited nor spiritual; it has the virtues of simplicity, honesty, and peacefulness. These are virtues man rarely attains and often wishes he could, but they are not the virtues he celebrates in his heroic, erotic, or visionary art. It is to be expected, then, that that life would not finally have great appeal to man's nature, and Swift teases us with the fact—that rational goodness is something we cannot long endure.

Is the alternative to be a Yahoo? Gulliver, once he awakens to disenchantment with men, cannot really imagine more than these two alternatives and ignores the extent to which he differs from either. Resolved to pass as a Houyhnhnm and affecting the outward mannerisms (of neigh and canter), he desperately seeks to dissociate himself from the Yahoos and is mortified by their attraction to him as one of their kind. By the time of his return, when he encounters a friendly and generous Portuguese captain, Gulliver can only see a Yahoo (as, with terror and disgust, he does in his mirror); even more, he retreats in disgust from his family and seeks solace with horses, if only because they look and smell like Houyhnhnms. Having come belatedly to see below the surfaces he once unquestioningly accepted, Gulliver has not achieved discrimination; instead, he becomes devoted to a new surface.

How does this come about? In the first voyage, Gulliver finds himself among the Lilliputians, one-twelfth his bulk, and gradually adjusts to their scale of vision; for, while he decently refuses to enslave their enemies in Blefuscu (the only other island in their world and therefore the object of conquest), he rather proudly accepts the court honor of being named a *nardac*. And when he is accused of adultery with a minister's wife, he does not laugh at the incongruity, but solemnly defends himself against the charges. In Lilliput he discovers a people who once lived by rational institutions but have learned to pervert their laws into instruments of domination and self-seeking. Words have become emptied of meaning even as they remain full of prestige; the Emperor's subjects have learned to scamper for safety when he speaks of his mercy or lenity, and Gulliver must finally flee to save his own life.

In his second voyage, to Brobdingnag, the proportions are reversed, and Gulliver finds himself a Lilliputian in a land of giants. They are a mixed lot, but the King is, in contrast to George I of England, the best of them—large-souled, generous, with intellectual curiosity and an acute sense of justice. When Gulliver describes to him the institutions of England, the King easily perceives what Gulliver does not mention— the way in which they are open to corruption and the travesty they readily become. As the King sums it up, "By what I have gathered from your own relation, and the answers I have with much pains wringed and extorted from you, I cannot but conclude the bulk of your natives to be the most pernicious race of little odious vermin that nature ever suffered to crawl upon the surface of the earth." Undeterred, in fact stirred to pride, Gulliver offers to give the King the secret of gunpowder so that he can maim and destroy his enemies and gain absolute power; he does this with no active evil intent, but with the single-minded obliviousness that Swift so brilliantly catches in his satires (notably in the speaker of A Modest Proposal). When the King refuses with horror, Gulliver describes with scorn the limited culture of Brobdingnag: short clear laws and no need for lawyers, no tolerance for metaphysics and (it is implied) religious mystery, a balanced ("mixed") state without internal factions or rivalries, a lucid prose and the refusal to write unnecessary books. It is hardly what a European would call "civilization," and it looks ahead (as a fallible but reformed society) to the devastating rationality of the Houyhnhnms.

The third voyage takes Gulliver to Laputa, the flying island, where everyone who counts is addicted to "pure" pursuits—astronomy and music—and utterly divorced from the practical life around him. With one telling exception: the island is a portable court and descends over any province that aspires to freedom, denying it light or rainfall, even ready to crush it to earth in order to maintain power. On the mainland Gulliver encounters Lord Munodi (who, as his name indicates, hates this world), a man of taste and judgment, who must bow to the fashions for experiment and innovation. Whatever is done must be done with the greatest possible show of ingenuity (if pincushions are needed, they must be made out of marble), and the Grand Academy of Lagado (a satire on the Royal Society of England) is devoted to elaborate pseudo-science, designed not for use but for show. Among his other adventures, Gulliver encounters the Struldbruggs, a special race blessed with immortality, or rather cursed with it, for they are not free of degeneration; instead of being oracles of wisdom, they soon descend into a bickering, avaricious, melancholy senility.

At every point Gulliver is confronted with the distinction between idea and execution, the rational possibility and the corrupt practice, the capacity for reason and the passionate degeneracy that overtakes it. His responses are never acute; he may resent an injury or an insult, sidestep a larcenous or murderous gesture, but he remains essentially uncritical and unreflective. In the fourth voyage all that he has seen is made inescapable, and he moves from an insensitive complacency to an unthinking misanthropy, simply redirecting his pride from identification with his kind to hatred of them and to a new and impossible effort at identification with the Houyhnhnms. What Swift means us to conclude has been much debated by scholars. Is he ridiculing a naïve trust in reason and presenting us with a horrible rationalistic utopia of horses, or is he rather showing us how little we really want to be reasonable and how easily we allow the glamour of our corruption to persuade us of its greatness (in contrast with its ugly enactment by the Yahoos)? However one resolves the questions, one can see why a modern critic (T. S. Eliot) refers to Swift's account of Gulliver's fourth voyage as one of the greatest triumphs of the human spirit.

From Travels into Several Remote Nations of the World

A Voyage to the Country of the Houyhnhnms

Chapter One: The author sets out as captain of a ship. His men conspire against him, confine him a long time to his cabin. Set him on shore in an unknown land. He travels up into the country. The Yahoos, a strange sort of animal, described. The author meets two Houyhnhnms.

I continued at home with my wife and children about five months in a very happy condition, if I could have learned the lesson of knowing when I was well. I left my poor wife big with child and accepted an advantageous offer made me to be captain of the *Adventure,* a stout merchantman of 350 tons: for I understood navigation well, and being grown weary of a surgeon's employment at sea, which however I could exercise upon occasion, I took a skilful young man of that calling, one Robert Purefoy, into my ship. We set sail for Portsmouth upon the 7th day of September, 1710; on the 14th, we met with Captain Pocock of Bristol, at Teneriffe,[1] who was going to the bay of Campechy, to cut logwood.[2] On the 16th, he was parted from us by a storm; I heard since my return that his ship foundered and none escaped but one cabin-boy. He was an honest man and a good sailor but a little too positive in his own opinions, which was the cause of his destruction, as it hath been of several others. For if he had followed my advice, he might at this time have been safe at home with his family as well as myself.

I had several men died in my ship of calentures,[3] so that I was forced to get recruits out of Barbadoes and the Leeward Islands,[4] where I touched by the direction of the merchants who employed me, which I had soon too much cause to repent; for I found afterwards that most of them had been buccaneers. I had fifty hands on board, and my orders were that I should trade with the Indians in the South Sea and make what discoveries I could. These rogues whom I had picked up debauched my other men, and they all formed a conspiracy to seize the ship and secure me; which they did one morning, rushing into my cabin and binding me hand and foot, threatening to throw me overboard if I offered to stir. I told them I was their prisoner and would submit. This they made me swear to do, and then unbound me, only fastening one of my legs with a chain near my bed, and placed a sentry at my door with his piece charged, who was commanded to shoot me dead if I attempted my liberty. They sent me down victuals and drink and took the government of the ship to themselves. Their design was to turn pirates and plunder the Spaniards, which they could not do till they got more men. But first they resolved to sell the goods in the ship and then go to Madagascar for recruits, several among them having died since my confinement. They sailed many weeks and traded with the Indians, but I knew not what course they took, being kept close prisoner

---

1. The largest of the Canary Islands.
2. On the Gulf of Mexico in Yucatán; a source of "campeachy wood," used for making dyes.
3. Tropical fevers.
4. In the West Indies.

in my cabin and expecting nothing less than to be murdered, as they often threatened me.

Upon the 9th day of May, 1711, one James Welch came down to my cabin and said he had orders from the captain to set me ashore. I expostulated with him, but in vain; neither would he so much as tell me who their new captain was. They forced me into the long-boat, letting me put on my best suit of clothes, which were as good as new, and a small bundle of linen, but no arms except my hanger; [5] and they were so civil as not to search my pockets, into which I conveyed what money I had, with some other little necessaries. They rowed about a league and then set me down on a strand. I desired them to tell me what country it was. They all swore they knew no more than myself, but said that the captain (as they called him) was resolved, after they had sold the lading,[6] to get rid of me in the first place where they discovered land. They pushed off immediately, advising me to make haste for fear of being overtaken by the tide, and bade me farewell.[7]

In this desolate condition I advanced forward and soon got upon firm ground, where I sat down on a bank to rest myself and consider what I had best to do. When I was a little refreshed I went up into the country, resolving to deliver myself to the first savages I should meet and purchase my life from them by some bracelets, glass rings, and other toys [8] which sailors usually provide themselves with in those voyages, and whereof I had some about me. The land was divided by long rows of trees, not regularly planted, but naturally growing; there was great plenty of grass, and several fields of oats. I walked very circumspectly for fear of being surprised or suddenly shot with an arrow from behind or on either side. I fell into a beaten road, where I saw many tracks of human feet, and some of cows, but most of horses.

At last I beheld several animals in a field, and one or two of the same kind sitting in trees. Their shape was very singular and deformed, which a little discomposed me, so that I lay down behind a thicket to observe them better. Some of them coming forward near the place where I lay, gave me an opportunity of distinctly marking their form. Their heads and breasts were covered with a thick hair, some frizzled and others lank; they had beards like goats, and a long ridge of hair down their backs and the foreparts of their legs and feet, but the rest of their bodies were bare, so that I might see their skins, which were of a brown buff colour. They had no tails, nor any hair at all on their buttocks, except about the anus; which, I presume, nature had placed there to defend them as they sat on the ground; for this posture they used, as well as lying down, and often stood on their hind feet. They climbed high trees as nimbly as a squirrel, for they had strong extended claws before and behind, terminating in sharp points, and hooked. They would often spring and bound and leap with prodigious agility. The females were not so large as the males; they had long lank hair on their heads, but none on their faces, nor

5. A short broad sword.
6. Cargo.
7. In his first voyage, Gulliver is shipwrecked in a storm; in his second, left behind by his shipmates; in the third, set adrift by pirates; in the fourth, abandoned by mutineers. There is clear progression from natural causes to deliberate evil.
8. Trinkets.

anything more than a sort of down on the rest of their bodies, except about the anus and pudenda. Their dugs hung between their fore-feet and often reached almost to the ground as they walked. The hair of both sexes was of several colours, brown, red, black, and yellow. Upon the whole, I never beheld in all my travels so disagreeable an animal or one against which I naturally conceived so strong an antipathy. So that thinking I had seen enough, full of contempt and aversion, I got up and pursued the beaten road, hoping it might direct me to the cabin of some Indian.

I had not gone far when I met one of these creatures full in my way and coming up directly to me. The ugly monster, when he saw me, distorted several ways every feature of his visage and stared as at an object he had never seen before; then approaching nearer, lifted up his forepaw, whether out of curiosity or mischief, I could not tell. But I drew my hanger and gave him a good blow with the flat side of it, for I durst not strike him with the edge, fearing the inhabitants might be provoked against me if they should come to know that I had killed or maimed any of their cattle. When the beast felt the smart, he drew back and roared so loud that a herd of at least forty came flocking about me from the next field, howling and making odious faces; but I ran to the body of a tree and, leaning my back against it, kept them off by waving my hanger. Several of this cursed brood, getting hold of the branches behind, leaped up into the tree, from whence they began to discharge their excrements on my head: however, I escaped pretty well by sticking close to the stem of the tree, but was almost stifled with the filth, which fell about me on every side.

In the midst of this distress, I observed them all to run away on a sudden as fast as they could, at which I ventured to leave the tree and pursue the road, wondering what it was that could put them into this fright. But looking on my left hand, I saw a horse walking softly in the field, which, my persecutors having sooner discovered, was the cause of their flight. The horse started a little when he came near me but, soon recovering himself, looked full in my face with manifest tokens of wonder: he viewed my hands and feet, walking round me several times. I would have pursued my journey, but he placed himself directly in the way, yet looking with a very mild aspect, never offering the least violence. We stood gazing at each other for some time; at last I took the boldness to reach my hand towards his neck with a design to stroke it, using the common style and whistle of jockeys when they are going to handle a strange horse. But this animal, seeming to receive my civilities with disdain, shook his head and bent his brows, softly raising up his left forefoot to remove my hand. Then he neighed three or four times, but in so different a cadence that I almost began to think he was speaking to himself in some language of his own.

While he and I were thus employed, another horse came up; who applying himself to [9] the first in a very formal manner, they gently struck each other's right hoof before, neighing several times by turns and varying the sound, which seemed to be almost articulate.[10] They went some paces off as if it were to confer together, walking side by side, backward and forward, like persons

9. Accosting, approaching.
10. Meaningful.

deliberating upon some affair of weight, but often turning their eyes towards me as it were to watch that I might not escape. I was amazed to see such actions and behaviour in brute beasts, and concluded with myself that, if the inhabitants of this country were endued with a proportionable degree of reason, they must needs be the wisest people upon earth. This thought gave me so much comfort that I resolved to go forward until I could discover some house or village or meet with any of the natives, leaving the two horses to discourse together as they pleased. But the first, who was a dapple grey, observing me to steal off, neighed after me in so expressive a tone that I fancied myself to understand what he meant; whereupon I turned back and came near him, to expect [11] his farther commands: but concealing my fear as much as I could, for I began to be in some pain how this adventure might terminate; and the reader will easily believe I did not much like my present situation.

The two horses came up close to me, looking with great earnestness upon my face and hands. The grey steed rubbed my hat all around with his right fore-hoof and discomposed it so much that I was forced to adjust it better by taking it off and settling it again; whereat both he and his companion (who was a brown bay) appeared to be much surprised. The latter felt the lappet [12] of my coat, and finding it to hang loose about me, they both looked with new signs of wonder. He stroked my right hand, seeming to admire [13] the softness and colour; but he squeezed it so hard between his hoof and his pastern [14] that I was forced to roar; after which they both touched me with all possible tenderness. They were under great perplexity about my shoes and stockings, which they felt very often, neighing to each other and using various gestures, not unlike those of a philosopher [15] when he would attempt to solve some new and difficult phenomenon.

Upon the whole, the behaviour of these animals was so orderly and rational, so acute and judicious, that I at last concluded they must needs be magicians who had thus metamorphosed themselves upon some design, and, seeing a stranger in the way, were resolved to divert themselves with him; or perhaps were really amazed at the sight of a man so very different in habit, feature, and complexion from those who might probably live in so remote a climate. Upon the strength of this reasoning, I ventured to address them in the following manner: 'Gentlemen, if you be conjurers, as I have good cause to believe, you can understand any language; therefore I make bold to let your Worships know that I am a poor distressed Englishman driven by his misfortunes upon your coast, and I entreat one of you to let me ride upon his back, as if he were a real horse, to some house or village where I can be relieved. In return of which favour, I will make you a present of this knife and bracelet' (taking them out of my pocket). The two creatures stood silent while I spoke, seeming to listen with great attention; and when I had ended they neighed frequently towards each other, as if they were engaged in serious conversation. I plainly observed that their language expressed the passions very well, and the words

11. Await.
12. Flap or lapel.
13. Wonder at.
14. The joint at the back of a horse's leg, just above the hoof.
15. That is, natural philosopher or scientist.

might with little pains be resolved into an alphabet more easily than the Chinese.

I could frequently distinguish the word *Yahoo*, which was repeated by each of them several times; and, although it was impossible for me to conjecture what it meant, yet while the two horses were busy in conversation I endeavoured to practice this word upon my tongue; and as soon as they were silent, I boldly pronounced *Yahoo* in a loud voice, imitating, at the same time, as near as I could, the neighing of a horse; at which they were both visibly surprised, and the grey repeated the same word twice, as if he meant to teach me the right accent, wherein I spoke after him as well as I could and found myself perceivably to improve every time, although very far from any degree of perfection. Then the bay tried me with a second word much harder to be pronounced; but reducing it to the English orthography, may be spelt thus, *Houyhnhnm*. I did not succeed in this so well as the former, but after two or three farther trials I had better fortune; and they both appeared amazed at my capacity.

After some farther discourse, which I then conjectured might relate to me, the two friends took their leaves, with the same compliment of striking each other's hoof; and the grey made me signs that I should walk before him, wherein I thought it prudent to comply till I could find a better director. When I offered to slacken my pace, he would cry *Hhuun, Hhuun;* I guessed his meaning and gave him to understand, as well as I could, that I was weary and not able to walk faster; upon which he would stand a while to let me rest.

Chapter Two: The author conducted by a Houyhnhnm to his house. The house described. The author's reception. The food of the Houyhnhnms. The author, in distress for want of meat, is at last relieved. His manner of feeding in that country.

Having travelled about three miles, we came to a long kind of building, made of timber stuck in the ground and wattled across;[1] the roof was low and covered with straw. I now began to be a little comforted and took out some toys which travellers usually carry for presents to the savage Indians of America and other parts, in hopes the people of the house would be thereby encouraged to receive me kindly. The horse made me a sign to go in first; it was a large room with a smooth clay floor and a rack and manger extending the whole length on one side. There were three nags and two mares, not eating, but some of them sitting down upon their hams, which I very much wondered at; but wondered more to see the rest employed in domestic business. The last seemed but ordinary cattle; however, this confirmed my first opinion, that a people who could so far civilize brute animals must needs excel in wisdom all the nations of the world. The grey came in just after and thereby prevented any ill treatment which the others might have given me. He neighed to them several times in a style of authority and received answers.

Beyond this room there were three others, reaching the length of the house, to which you passed through three doors, opposite to each other in the manner

---

1. Woven across with twigs or light branches.

of a vista.[2] We went through the second room towards the third; here the grey walked in first, beckoning me to attend. I waited in the second room and got ready my presents for the master and mistress of the house: they were two knives, three bracelets of false pearl, a small looking-glass, and a bead necklace. The horse neighed three or four times, and I waited to hear some answers in human voice; but I heard no other returns than in the same dialect, only one or two a little shriller than his. I began to think that this house must belong to some person of great note among them, because there appeared so much ceremony before I could gain admittance. But that a man of quality should be served all by horses was beyond my comprehension. I feared my brain was disturbed by my sufferings and misfortunes: I roused myself, and looked about me in the room where I was left alone; this was furnished as the first, only after a more elegant manner. I rubbed my eyes often, but the same objects still occurred. I pinched my arms and sides to awake myself, hoping I might be in a dream. I then absolutely concluded that all these appearances could be nothing else but necromancy [3] and magic. But I had no time to pursue these reflections; for the grey horse came to the door and made me a sign to follow him into the third room, where I saw a very comely mare, together with a colt and foal, sitting on their haunches, upon mats of straw not unartfully made and perfectly neat and clean.

The mare, soon after my entrance, rose from her mat, and coming up close, after having nicely [4] observed my hands and face, gave me a most contemptuous look; then turning to the horse, I heard the word *Yahoo* often repeated betwixt them; the meaning of which word I could not then comprehend, although it were the first I had learned to pronounce. But I was soon better informed, to my everlasting mortification: for the horse beckoning to me with his head, and repeating the word *Hhuun, Hhuun,* as he did upon the road, which I understood was to attend him, led me out into a kind of court, where was another building at some distance from the house. Here we entered, and I saw three of those detestable creatures which I first met after my landing, feeding upon roots and the flesh of some animals, which I afterwards found to be that of asses and dogs, and now and then a cow dead by accident or disease. They were all tied by the neck with strong withes [5] fastened to a beam; they held their food between the claws of their forefeet and tore it with their teeth.

The master horse ordered a sorrel nag, one of his servants, to untie the largest of these animals and take him into the yard. The beast and I were brought close together, and our countenances diligently compared both by master and servant, who thereupon repeated several times the word *Yahoo.* My horror and astonishment are not to be described when I observed, in this abominable animal, a perfect human figure. The face of it indeed was flat and broad, the nose depressed, the lips large, and the mouth wide. But these differences are common to all savage nations, where the lineaments of the countenance are distorted by the natives suffering their infants to lie grovelling on the earth, or by carrying them on their backs, nuzzling with their face

2. An opening that allows an extended view.
3. Enchantment.
4. Carefully.
5. Flexible willow branches.

against the mother's shoulders. The forefeet of the Yahoo differed from my hands in nothing else but the length of the nails, the coarseness and brownness of the palms, and the hairiness on the backs. There was the same resemblance between our feet, with the same differences, which I knew very well, although the horses did not, because of my shoes and stockings; the same in every part of our bodies, except as to hairiness and colour, which I have already described.

The great difficulty that seemed to stick with the two horses was to see the rest of my body so very different from that of a Yahoo; for which I was obliged to my clothes, whereof they had no conception. The sorrel nag offered me a root, which he held (after their manner, as we shall describe in its proper place) between his hoof and pastern.[6] I took it in my hand and, having smelt it, returned it to him as civilly as I could. He brought out of the Yahoo's kennel a piece of ass's flesh, but it smelt so offensively that I turned from it with loathing. He then threw it to the Yahoo, by whom it was greedily devoured. He afterwards showed me a wisp of hay and a fetlock full of oats; but I shook my head to signify that neither of these were food for me. And indeed, I now apprehended that I must absolutely starve if I did not get to some of my own species: for as to those filthy Yahoos, although there were few greater lovers of mankind, at that time, than myself, yet I confess I never saw any sensitive [7] being so detestable on all accounts; and the more I came near them, the more hateful they grew, while I stayed in that country. This the master horse observed by my behaviour, and therefore sent the Yahoo back to his kennel. He then put his fore-hoof to his mouth, at which I was much surprised, although he did it with ease and with a motion that appeared perfectly natural, and made other signs to know what I would eat; but I could not return him such an answer as he was able to apprehend; and if he had understood me, I did not see how it was possible to contrive any way for finding myself nourishment. While we were thus engaged, I observed a cow passing by, whereupon I pointed to her and expressed a desire to let me go and milk her. This had its effect; for he led me back into the house and ordered a mare-servant to open a room where a good store of milk lay in earthen and wooden vessels, after a very orderly and cleanly manner. She gave me a large bowl full, of which I drank very heartily, and found myself well refreshed.

About noon I saw coming towards the house a kind of vehicle drawn like a sledge by four Yahoos. There was in it an old steed, who seemed to be of quality; [8] he alighted with his hind feet forward, having by accident got a hurt in his left forefoot. He came to dine with our horse, who received him with great civility. They dined in the best room and had oats boiled in milk for the second course, which the old horse eat [9] warm, but the rest cold. Their mangers were placed circular in the middle of the room and divided into several partitions, round which they sat on their haunches upon bosses [10] of straw. In the middle was a large rack with angles answering to every partition of the manger. So that each horse and mare eat their own hay and their own mash of oats and milk, with much decency and regularity. The behaviour of the

6. The joint at the back of a horse's leg, just above the hoof.
7. With power of the senses.
8. High rank.
9. The normal past form, the counterpart of modern "ate" and pronounced "ett."
10. Hassocks.

young colt and foal appeared very modest, and that of the master and mistress extremely cheerful and complaisant [11] to their guest. The grey ordered me to stand by him, and much discourse passed between him and his friend concerning me, as I found by the stranger's often looking on me, and the frequent repetition of the word *Yahoo*.

I happened to wear my gloves, which the master grey observing, seemed perplexed, discovering signs of wonder what I had done to my forefeet. He put his hoof three or four times to them, as if he would signify that I should reduce them to their former shape, which I presently did, pulling off both my gloves and putting them into my pocket. This occasioned farther talk, and I saw the company was pleased with my behaviour, whereof I soon found the good effects. I was ordered to speak the few words I understood, and while they were at dinner, the master taught me the names for oats, milk, fire, water, and some others: which I could readily pronounce after him, having from my youth a great facility in learning languages.[12]

When dinner was done, the master horse took me aside, and by signs and words made me understand the concern he was in that I had nothing to eat. Oats in their tongue are called *hlunnh*. This word I pronounced two or three times; for although I had refused them at first, yet upon second thoughts, I considered that I could contrive to make of them a kind of bread, which might be sufficient with milk to keep me alive till I could make my escape to some other country and to creatures of my own species. The horse immediately ordered a white mare-servant of his family to bring me a good quantity of oats in a sort of wooden tray. These I heated before the fire as well as I could, and rubbed them till the husks came off, which I made a shift to winnow from the grain. I ground and beat them between two stones, then took water and made them into a paste or cake, which I toasted at the fire and eat warm with milk. It was at first a very insipid diet, although common enough in many parts of Europe, but grew tolerable by time; and having been often reduced to hard fare in my life, this was not the first experiment I had made how easily nature is satisfied. And I cannot but observe that I never had one hour's sickness while I stayed in this island. It is true, I sometimes made a shift to catch a rabbit or bird, by springes [13] made of Yahoos' hairs; and I often gathered wholesome herbs, which I boiled or eat as salads with my bread; and now and then, for a rarity, I made a little butter and drank the whey. I was at first at a great loss for salt; but custom soon reconciled the want of it; and I am confident that the frequent use of salt among us is an effect of luxury and was first introduced only as a provocative to drink; except where it is necessary for preserving of flesh in long voyages or in places remote from great markets. For we observe no animal to be fond of it but man: [14] and as to myself, when I left

11. Courteous.

12. Gulliver's facility with strange languages is part of his pattern of adaptability to external circumstances, but it is seldom accompanied by penetration into their moral implications.

13. Snares.

14. This error may be Swift's but is more likely a deliberate sign of Gulliver's unreliability in his enthusiasm for a simple "natural" life and a forecast of his soon-to-be-avowed adoration of the Houyhnhnms (Chapter 7).

this country, it was a great while before I could endure the taste of it in anything that I eat.

This is enough to say upon the subject of my diet, wherewith other travellers fill their books, as if the readers were personally concerned whether we fare well or ill.[15] However, it was necessary to mention this matter lest the world should think it impossible that I could find sustenance for three years in such a country and among such inhabitants.

When it grew towards evening, the master horse ordered a place for me to lodge in; it was but six yards from the house, and separated from the stable of the Yahoos. Here I got some straw and, covering myself with my own clothes, slept very sound. But I was in a short time better accommodated, as the reader shall know hereafter, when I come to treat more particularly about my way of living.

Chapter Three: The author studious to learn the language, the Houyhnhnm his master assists in teaching him. The language described. Several Houyhnhnms of quality come out of curiosity to see the author. He gives his master a short account of his voyage.

My principal endeavour was to learn the language, which my master (for so I shall henceforth call him) and his children, and every servant of his house, were desirous to teach me. For they looked upon it as a prodigy that a brute animal should discover such marks of a rational creature. I pointed to everything and inquired the name of it, which I wrote down in my journal-book when I was alone, and corrected my bad accent by desiring those of the family to pronounce it often. In this employment a sorrel nag, one of the under-servants, was very ready to assist me.

In speaking, they pronounce through the nose and throat; and their language approaches nearest to the High Dutch or German of any I know in Europe, but is much more graceful and significant. The Emperor Charles V made almost the same observation when he said that, if he were to speak to his horse, it should be in High Dutch.[1]

The curiosity and impatience of my master were so great that he spent many hours of his leisure to instruct me. He was convinced (as he afterwards told me) that I must be a Yahoo, but my teachableness, civility, and cleanliness astonished him, which were qualities altogether so opposite to those animals. He was most perplexed about my clothes, reasoning sometimes with himself whether they were a part of my body; for I never pulled them off till the family were asleep and got them on before they waked in the morning. My master was eager to learn from whence I came, how I acquired those appearances of reason which I discovered in all my actions, and to know my story from my own mouth, which he hoped he should soon do by the great proficiency I made in learning and pronouncing their words and sentences. To help

---

15. If there is a greater and more frequent fault than this self-importance in travel books, it is the needless putting down of other writers; Swift's book is, whatever else, in part a satire upon the form.

1. Charles V (1500–1558), King of Spain and ruler of the Holy Roman Empire, is reported to have said that he would address his God in Spanish, his mistress in Italian, and his horse in German.

my memory, I formed all I learned into the English alphabet and writ the words down with the translations. This last, after some time, I ventured to do in my master's presence. It cost me much trouble to explain to him what I was doing; for the inhabitants have not the least idea of books or literature.[2]

In about ten weeks time I was able to understand most of his questions, and in three months could give him some tolerable answers. He was extremely curious to know from what part of the country I came and how I was taught to imitate a rational creature, because the Yahoos (whom he saw I exactly resembled in my head, hands, and face, that were only visible), with some appearance of cunning and the strongest disposition to mischief, were observed to be the most unteachable of all brutes. I answered that I came over the sea from a far place, with many others of my own kind, in a great hollow vessel made of the bodies of trees; that my companions forced me to land on this coast and then left me to shift for myself. It was with some difficulty and by the help of many signs that I brought him to understand me. He replied that I must needs be mistaken, or that I 'said the thing which was not.' (For they have no words in their language to express lying or falsehood.) He knew it was impossible that there could be a country beyond the sea, or that a parcel of brutes could move a wooden vessel whither they pleased upon water. He was sure no Houyhnhnm alive could make such a vessel, or would trust Yahoos to manage it.

The word *Houyhnhnm,* in their tongue, signifies a *horse,* and in its etymology, *the Perfection of Nature.*[3] I told my master, that I was at a loss for expression but would improve as fast as I could; and hoped in a short time I should be able to tell him wonders. He was pleased to direct his own mare, his colt and foal, and the servants of the family to take all opportunities of instructing me, and every day for two or three hours he was at the same pains himself. Several horses and mares of quality in the neighbourhood came often to our house upon the report spread of a wonderful Yahoo that could speak like a Houyhnhnm and seemed in his words and actions to discover some glimmerings of reason. These delighted to converse with me; they put many questions and received such answers as I was able to return. By all which advantages I made so great a progress that in five months from my arrival I understood whatever was spoke and could express myself tolerably well.

The Houyhnhnms who came to visit my master out of a design of seeing and talking with me could hardly believe me to be a right[4] Yahoo, because my body had a different covering from others of my kind. They were astonished to observe me without the usual hair or skin except on my head, face, and hands; but I discovered that secret to my master, upon an accident which happened about a fortnight before.

I have already told the reader that every night, when the family were gone to bed, it was my custom to strip and cover myself with clothes. It happened

2. In the more limited sense of writing, for they have some poetic and rhetorical powers.
3. That is, as the culmination and master of all natural life, as man has traditionally regarded himself; unlike man, they have no conception of anything supernatural or of a deity other than Nature itself, nor do they have any experience of a "fallen" Nature (except in the Yahoos).
4. True, genuine.

one morning early that my master sent for me by the sorrel nag, who was his valet. When he came, I was fast asleep, my clothes fallen off on one side and my shirt above my waist. I awaked at the noise he made and observed him to deliver his message in some disorder; after which he went to my master and in a great fright gave him a very confused account of what he had seen. This I presently discovered; for going, as soon as I was dressed, to pay my attendance upon his Honour, he asked me the meaning of what his servant had reported, that I was not the same thing when I slept as I appeared to be at other times; that his valet assured him some part of me was white, some yellow, at least not so white, and some brown.

I had hitherto concealed the secret of my dress in order to distinguish myself as much as possible from that cursed race of Yahoos; but now I found it in vain to do so any longer. Besides, I considered that my clothes and shoes would soon wear out, which already were in a declining condition, and must be supplied by some contrivance from the hides of Yahoos or other brutes; whereby the whole secret would be known. I therefore told my master that, in the country from whence I came, those of my kind always covered their bodies with the hairs of certain animals prepared by art, as well for decency as to avoid inclemencies of air both hot and cold; of which, as to my own person, I would give him immediate conviction if he pleased to command me, only desiring his excuse if I did not expose those parts that nature taught us to conceal. He said my discourse was all very strange, but especially the last part; for he could not understand why nature should teach us to conceal what nature had given. That neither himself nor family were ashamed of any parts of their bodies; but however I might do as I pleased. Whereupon, I first unbuttoned my coat and pulled it off. I did the same with my waistcoat; I drew off my shoes, stockings, and breeches. I let my shirt down to my waist and drew up the bottom, fastening it like a girdle about my middle to hide my nakedness.

My master observed the whole performance with great signs of curiosity and admiration. He took up all my clothes in his pastern, one piece after another, and examined them diligently. He then stroked my body very gently and looked around me several times, after which he said it was plain I must be a perfect Yahoo; but that I differed very much from the rest of my species in the whiteness and smoothness of my skin, my want of hair in several parts of my body, the shape and shortness of my claws behind and before, and my affectation of walking continually on my two hinder feet. He desired to see no more and gave me leave to put on my clothes again, for I was shuddering with cold.

I expressed my uneasiness at his giving me so often the appellation of *Yahoo,* an odious animal for which I had so utter an hatred and contempt. I begged he would forbear applying that word to me and take the same order in his family and among his friends whom he suffered to see me. I requested likewise that the secret of my having a false covering to my body might be known to none but himself, at least as long as my present clothing should last; for as to what the sorrel nag his valet had observed, his Honour might command him to conceal it.

All this my master very graciously consented to, and thus the secret was kept till my clothes began to wear out, which I was forced to supply by several contrivances that shall hereafter be mentioned. In the meantime he desired I would go on with my utmost diligence to learn their language, because he was more astonished at my capacity for speech and reason than at the figure of my body, whether it were covered or no; adding that he waited with some impatience to hear the wonders which I promised to tell him.

From thenceforward he doubled the pains he had been at to instruct me. He brought me into all company and made them treat me with civility, because, as he told them privately, this would put me into good humour and make me more diverting.

Every day when I waited on him, beside the trouble he was at in teaching, he would ask me several questions concerning myself, which I answered as well as I could; and by those means he had already received some general ideas, although very imperfect. It would be tedious to relate the several steps by which I advanced to a more regular conversation: but the first account I gave of myself in any order and length was to this purpose:

That I came from a very far country, as I already had attempted to tell him, with about fifty more of my own species; that we travelled upon the seas in a great hollow vessel made of wood and larger than his Honour's house. I described the ship to him in the best terms I could and explained by the help of my handkerchief displayed how it was driven forward by the wind; that upon a quarrel among us, I was set on shore on this coast, where I walked forward without knowing whither, till he delivered me from the persecution of those execrable Yahoos. He asked me who made the ship, and how it was possible that the Houyhnhnms of my country would leave it to the management of brutes? My answer was that I durst proceed no farther in my relation unless he would give me his word and honour that he would not be offended, and then I would tell him the wonders I had so often promised. He agreed; and I went on by assuring him that the ship was made by creatures like myself, who in all the countries I had travelled, as well as in my own, were the only governing, rational animals; and that upon my arrival hither I was as much astonished to see the Houyhnhnms act like rational beings as he or his friends could be in finding some marks of reason in a creature he was pleased to call a Yahoo, to which I owned my resemblance in every part, but could not account for their degenerate and brutal nature. I said farther, that if good fortune ever restored me to my native country to relate my travels hither, as I resolved to do, everybody would believe that I 'said the thing which was not'; that I invented the story out of my own head; and with all possible respect to himself, his family, and friends, and under his promise of not being offended, our countrymen would hardly think it probable that a Houyhnhnm should be the presiding creature of a nation and a Yahoo the brute.

Chapter Four: The Houyhnhnms' notion of truth and falsehood. The author's discourse disapproved by his master. The author gives a more particular account of himself and the accidents of his voyage.

My master heard me with great appearances of uneasiness in his countenance, because *doubting* or *not believing* are so little known in this country that the inhabitants cannot tell how to behave themselves under such circumstances.

And I remember, in frequent discourses with my master concerning the nature of manhood in other parts of the world, having occasion to talk of *lying* and *false representation*, it was with much difficulty that he comprehended what I meant, although he had otherwise a most acute judgment. For he argued thus: that the use of speech was to make us understand one another and to receive information of facts; now if any one *said the thing which was not*, these ends were defeated; because I cannot properly be said to understand him, and I am so far from receiving information that he leaves me worse than in ignorance, for I am led to believe a thing *black* when it is *white* and *short* when it is *long*. And these were all the notions he had concerning that faculty of *lying*, so perfectly well understood and so universally practised among human creatures.

To return from this digression, when I asserted that the Yahoos were the only governing animals in my country, which my master said was altogether past his conception, he desired to know whether we had Houyhnhnms among us and what was their employment. I told him, we had great numbers, that in summer they grazed in the fields and in winter were kept in houses with hay and oats, where Yahoo servants were employed to rub their skins smooth, comb their manes, pick their feet, serve them with food, and make their beds. 'I understand you well,' said my master, 'it is now very plain from all you have spoken that, whatever share of reason the Yahoos pretend to, the Houyhnhnms are your masters. I heartily wish our Yahoos would be so tractable.' I begged his Honour would please to excuse me from proceeding any farther, because I was very certain that the account he expected from me would be highly displeasing. But he insisted in commanding me to let him know the best and the worst. I told him he should be obeyed. I owned that the Houyhnhnms among us, whom we called horses,[1] were the most generous [2] and comely animal we had, that they excelled in strength and swiftness; and when they belonged to persons of quality, employed in travelling, racing, and drawing chariots, they were treated with much kindness and care, till they fell into diseases or became foundered in the feet; but then they were sold and used to all kind of drudgery till they died; after which their skins were stripped and sold for what they were worth, and their bodies left to be devoured by dogs and birds of prey.[3] But the common race of horses had not so good fortune, being kept by farmers and carriers and other mean people, who put them to greater labour and feed them worse. I described, as well as I could, our way of riding, the shape and use of a bridle, a saddle, a spur, and a whip, of harness and wheels. I added, that we fastened plates of a certain hard substance called *iron* at the bottom of their feet, to preserve their hoofs from being broken by the stony ways on which we often travelled.

My master, after some expressions of great indignation, wondered how we dared to venture upon a Houyhnhnm's back, for he was sure that the weakest servant in his house would be able to shake off the strongest Yahoo, or by lying down and rolling upon his back squeeze the brute to death. I answered that

1. Gulliver collapses the distinction between horses and Houyhnhnms, as he has between men and Yahoos, placing external resemblances above the differences of inner capacity.
2. Noble.
3. Ironically echoing the phrase Homer applies to unburied warriors.

our horses were trained up from three or four years old to the several uses we intended them for; that if any of them proved intolerably vicious, they were employed for carriages; that they were severely beaten while they were young for any mischievous tricks; that the males, designed for the common use of riding or draught, were generally castrated about two years after their birth to take down their spirits and make them more tame and gentle; that they were indeed sensible of [4] rewards and punishments; but his Honour would please to consider that they had not the least tincture of reason any more than the Yahoos in this country.

It put me to the pains of many circumlocutions to give my master a right idea of what I spoke; for their language doth not abound in variety of words, because their wants and passions are fewer than among us. But it is impossible to express his noble resentment at our savage treatment of the Houyhnhnm race, particularly after I had explained the manner and use of castrating horses among us to hinder them from propagating their kind and to render them more servile. He said, if it were possible there could be any country where Yahoos alone were endued with reason, they certainly must be the governing animal, because reason will in time always prevail against brutal strength. But, considering the frame of our bodies, and especially of mine, he thought no creature of equal bulk was so ill contrived for employing that reason in the common offices of life; whereupon he desired to know whether those among whom I lived resembled me or the Yahoos of his country.

I assured him that I was as well shaped as most of my age: but the younger and the females were much more soft and tender, and the skins of the latter generally as white as milk. He said I differed indeed from other Yahoos, being much more cleanly and not altogether so deformed; but in point of real advantage he thought I differed for the worse. That my nails were of no use either to my fore or hinder feet; as to my forefeet, he could not properly call them by that name, for he never observed me to walk upon them; that they were too soft to bear the ground; that I generally went with them uncovered, neither was the covering I sometimes wore on them of the same shape or so strong as that on my feet behind. That I could not walk with any security, for if either of my hinder feet slipped, I must inevitably fall. He then began to find fault with other parts of my body, the flatness of my face, the prominence of my nose, my eyes placed directly in front, so that I could not look on either side without turning my head: that I was not able to feed myself without lifting one of my forefeet to my mouth: and therefore nature had placed those joints to answer that necessity. He knew not what could be the use of those several clefts and divisions in my feet behind; that these were too soft to bear the hardness and sharpness of stones without a covering made from the skin of some other brute; that my whole body wanted a fence against heat and cold, which I was forced to put on and off every day with tediousness and trouble. And lastly that he observed every animal in this country naturally to abhor the Yahoos, whom the weaker avoided and the stronger drove from them. So that supposing us to have the gift of reason, he could not see how it were possible to cure that natural antipathy which every creature discovered [5] against us; nor

4. Responsive to.
5. Revealed.

consequently how we could tame and render them serviceable. However, he would (as he said) debate the matter no farther, because he was more desirous to know my own story, the country where I was born, and the several actions and events of my life before I came hither.

I assured him how extremely desirous I was that he should be satisfied in every point; but I doubted much whether it would be possible for me to explain myself on several subjects whereof his Honour could have no conception, because I saw nothing in his country to which I could resemble [6] them. That, however, I would do my best and strive to express myself by similitudes, humbly, desiring his assistance when I wanted proper words, which he was pleased to promise me.

I said my birth was of honest parents, in an island called England, which was remote from this country as many days' journey as the strongest of his Honour's servants could travel in the annual course of the sun. That I was bred a surgeon, whose trade it is to cure wounds and hurts in the body got by accident or violence; that my country was governed by a female man, whom we called a *queen*.[7] That I left it to get riches, whereby I might maintain myself and family when I should return. That in my last voyage I was commander of the ship, and had about fifty Yahoos under me, many of which died at sea, and I was forced to supply them by others picked out from several nations. That our ship was twice in danger of being sunk; the first time by a great storm and the second by striking against a rock. Here my master interposed by asking me how I could persuade strangers out of different countries to venture with me after the losses I had sustained and the hazards I had run. I said they were fellows of desperate fortunes, forced to fly from the places of their birth on account of their poverty or their crimes. Some were undone by lawsuits; others spent all they had in drinking, whoring, and gaming; others fled for treason; many for murder, theft, poisoning, robbery, perjury, forgery, coining false money, for committing rapes or sodomy, for flying from their colours or deserting to the enemy, and most of them had broken prison. None of these durst return to their native countries for fear of being hanged or of starving in a jail; and therefore were under a necessity of seeking a livelihood in other places.

During this discourse, my master was pleased often to interrupt me; I had made use of many circumlocutions in describing to him the nature of the several crimes for which most of our crew had been forced to fly their country. This labour took up several days' conversation before he was able to comprehend me. He was wholly at a loss to know what could be the use or necessity of practising those vices. To clear up which I endeavoured to give him some ideas of the desire of power and riches; of the terrible effects of lust, intemperance, malice, and envy. All this I was forced to define and describe by putting of cases and making suppositions. After which, like one whose imagination was struck with something never seen or heard of before, he would lift up his eyes with amazement and indignation. Power, government, war, law, punishment, and a thousand other things had no terms wherein that language could express them, which made the difficulty almost insuperable to

6. Compare.
7. Queen Anne, who ruled from 1702 to 1714.

give my master any conception of what I meant. But being of an excellent understanding, much improved by contemplation and converse, he at last arrived at a competent knowledge of what human nature in our parts of the world is capable to perform, and desired I would give him some particular account of that land which we call Europe, especially of my own country.

Chapter Five: The author at his master's command informs him of the state of England. The causes of war among the princes of Europe. The author begins to explain the English constitution.

The reader may please to observe, that the following extract of many conversations I had with my master contains a summary of the most material points which were discoursed at several times for above two years; his Honour often desiring fuller satisfaction as I farther improved in the Houyhnhnm tongue. I laid before him, as well as I could, the whole state of Europe; I discoursed of trade and manufactures, of arts and sciences; and the answers I gave to all the questions he made, as they arose upon several subjects, were a fund of conversation not to be exhausted. But I shall here only set down the substance of what passed between us concerning my own country, reducing it into order as well as I can, without any regard to time or other circumstances, while I strictly adhere to truth. My only concern is that I shall hardly be able to do justice to my master's arguments and expressions, which must needs suffer by any want of capacity, as well as by a translation into our barbarous English.[1]

In obedience therefore to his Honour's commands, I related to him the Revolution under the Prince of Orange; the long war with France entered into by the said prince and renewed by his successor the present queen, wherein the greatest powers of Christendom were engaged, and which still continued.[2] I computed, at his request, that about a million of Yahoos might have been killed in the whole progress of it, and perhaps a hundred or more cities taken, and five times as many ships burnt or sunk.

He asked me what were the usual causes or motives that made one country go to war with another. I answered they were innumerable, but I should only mention a few of the chief: sometimes the ambition of princes, who never think they have land or people enough to govern: sometimes the corruption of ministers, who engage their master in a war in order to stifle or divert the clamour of the subjects against their evil administration. Difference in opinions[3] hath cost many millions of lives: for instance, whether *flesh* be

1. Gulliver's first overt revulsion from European culture.

2. William of Orange (1605–1702) succeeded James II as William III of England in the Glorious Revolution of 1688. He fought against France until 1697, when Louis XIV acknowledged his claim to the English throne, but resumed the war in 1701, when Louis gave his recognition to James's heir, the Stuart Pretender. Anne (1665–1714) carried on the War of the Spanish Succession, which ended in 1713, while Gulliver was still among the Houyhnhnms.

3. Alluding to such doctrinal quarrels among the churches as that of transubstantiation (whether the body and blood of Christ are really or only symbolically present in the Eucharistic bread and wine), the use of music in worship (offensive to some radical Protestants), the veneration of an image or crucifix (condemned by Calvinists), and the proper form of church vestments.

bread or *bread* be *flesh;* whether the juice of a certain *berry* be *blood* or *wine;* whether *whistling* be a vice or a virtue; whether it be better to *kiss a post* or throw it into the fire; what is the best colour for a *coat,* whether *black, white, red, or grey;* and whether it should be *long* or *short, narrow* or *wide, dirty* or *clean,* with many more. Neither are any wars so furious and bloody or of so long continuance as those occasioned by difference in opinion, especially if it be in things indifferent.[4]

Sometimes the quarrel between two princes is to decide which of them shall dispossess a third of his dominions, where neither of them pretend to any right. Sometimes one prince quarrelleth with another for fear the other should quarrel with him. Sometimes a war is entered upon because the enemy is too *strong,* and sometimes because he is too *weak.* Sometimes our neighbours *want* the things which we *have,* or *have* the things which we *want;* and we both fight till they take ours or give us theirs. It is a very justifiable cause of war to invade a country after the people have been wasted by famine, destroyed by pestilence, or embroiled by factions amongst themselves. It is justifiable to enter into a war against our nearest ally when one of his towns lies convenient for us, or a territory of land that would render our dominions round and compact. If a prince send forces into a nation where the people are poor and ignorant, he may lawfully put half of them to death and make slaves of the rest, in order to civilize and reduce them from their barbarous way of living. It is a very kingly, honourable, and frequent practice, when one prince desires the assistance of another to secure him against an invasion, that the assistant, when he hath driven out the invader, should seize on the dominions himself, and kill, imprison, or banish the prince he came to relieve. Alliance by blood or marriage is a sufficient cause of war between princes, and, the nearer the kindred is, the greater is their disposition to quarrel: *poor* nations are *hungry* and *rich* nations are *proud,* and pride and hunger will ever be at variance. For these reasons, the trade of a soldier is held the most honourable of all others: because a soldier is a Yahoo hired to kill in cold blood as many of his own species, who have never offended him, as possibly he can.

There is likewise a kind of beggarly princes in Europe, not able to make war by themselves, who hire out their troops to richer nations, for so much a day to each man; of which they keep three-fourths to themselves, and it is the best part of their maintenance; such are those in Germany and many northern parts of Europe.[5]

What you have told me (said my master) upon the subject of war does indeed discover most admirably the effects of that reason you pretend to: however, it is happy that the *shame* is greater than the *danger,* and that nature hath left you utterly uncapable of doing much mischief. For your mouths lying flat with your faces, you can hardly bite each other to any purpose unless by consent. Then as to the claws upon your feet before and behind, they are so short and tender that one of our Yahoos would drive a dozen of yours

---

4. Matters not essential to belief; technically, upon which the church has not chosen to give a decision.

5. George I of England, who ruled from 1714 to 1727, had supplied mercenaries to other nations while still Elector of Hanover.

before him. And therefore in recounting the numbers of those who have been killed in battle, I cannot but think that you have *said the thing which is not.*

I could not forbear shaking my head and smiling a little at his ignorance. And being no stranger to the art of war, I gave him a description of cannons, culverins,[6] muskets, carabines,[7] pistols, bullets, powder, swords, bayonets, battles, sieges, retreats, attacks, undermines, countermines,[8] bombardments, sea-fights; ships sunk with a thousand men; twenty thousand killed on each side; dying groans, limbs flying in the air, smoke, noise, confusion, trampling to death under horses' feet; flight, pursuit, victory; fields strewed with carcasses left for food to dogs and wolves and birds of prey; plundering, stripping, ravishing, burning, and destroying. And to set forth the valour of my own dear countrymen, I assured him, that I had seen them blow up a hundred enemies at once in a siege, and as many in a ship, and beheld the dead bodies drop down in pieces from the clouds, to the great diversion of all the spectators.

I was going on to more particulars when my master commanded me silence. He said whoever understood the nature of Yahoos might easily believe it possible for so vile an animal to be capable of every action I had named, if their strength and cunning equalled their malice. But as my discourse had increased his abhorrence of the whole species, so he found it gave him a disturbance in his mind to which he was wholly a stranger before. He thought his ears being used to such abominable words might by degrees admit them with less detestation. That although he hated the Yahoos of this country, yet he no more blamed them for their odious qualities than he did a *gnnayh* (a bird of prey) for its cruelty or a sharp stone for cutting his hoof. But when a creature pretending to reason could be capable of such enormities, he dreaded lest the corruption of that faculty might be worse than brutality [9] itself. He seemed therefore confident that, instead of reason, we were only possessed of some quality fitted to increase our natural vices; as the reflection from a troubled stream returns the image of an ill-shapen body not only *larger* but more *distorted.*

He added that he had heard too much upon the subject of war both in this and some former discourses. There was another point which a little perplexed him at present. I had said, that some of our crew left their country on account of being ruined by *law;* that I had already explained the meaning of the word; but he was at loss how it should come to pass that the *law,* which was intended for every man's preservation, should be any man's ruin. Therefore he desired to be farther satisfied what I meant by law, and the dispensers thereof according to the present practice in my own country; because he thought nature and reason were sufficient guides for a reasonable animal, as we pretended to be, in showing us what we ought to do and what to avoid.

I assured his Honour that law was a science wherein I had not much conversed further than by employing advocates, in vain, upon some injustices that had been done me. However, I would give him all the satisfaction I was able.

---

6. Very long cannons.
7. Carbines, firearms used by the cavalry.
8. Excavations made under the walls of a fortress and those made as a defensive countermeasure.
9. That is, brute insensibility.

I said there was a society of men among us bred up from their youth in the art of proving by words multiplied for the purpose, that white is black and black is white, according as they are paid. To this society all the rest of the people are slaves.

For example, if my neighbour hath a mind to my cow, he hires a lawyer to prove that he ought to have my cow from me. I must then hire another to defend my right, it being against all rules of law that any man should be allowed to speak for himself. Now in this case, I who am the true owner lie under two great disadvantages. First, my lawyer, being practised almost from his cradle in defending falsehood, is quite out of his element when he would be an advocate for justice, which as an office unnatural he always attempts with great awkwardness, if not with ill will. The second disadvantage is, that my lawyer must proceed with great caution, or else he will be reprimanded by the judges, and abhorred by his brethren, as one that would lessen the practice of the law. And therefore I have but two methods to preserve my cow. The first is to gain over my adversary's lawyer with a double fee, who will then betray his client by insinuating that he hath justice on his side. The second way is for my lawyer to make my cause appear as unjust as he can, by allowing the cow to belong to my adversary; and this if it be skilfully done will certainly bespeak the favour of the bench.

Now, your Honour is to know that these judges are persons appointed to decide all controversies of property as well as for the trial of criminals, and picked out from the most dextrous lawyers who are grown old or lazy and, having been biassed all their lives against truth and equity, lie under such a fatal necessity of favouring fraud, perjury, and oppression, that I have known some of them to have refused a large bribe from the side where justice lay, rather than injure the faculty [10] by doing anything unbecoming their nature or their office.

It is a maxim among these lawyers that whatever hath been done before may legally be done again: and therefore they take special care to record all the decisions formerly made against common justice and the general reason of mankind. These, under the name of *precedents*, they produce as authorities to justify the most iniquitous opinions; and the judges never fail of decreeing accordingly.

In pleading, they studiously avoid entering into the merits of the cause, but are loud, violent, and tedious in dwelling upon all circumstances which are not to the purpose. For instance, in the case already mentioned; they never desire to know what claim or title my adversary hath to my cow, but whether the said cow were red or black, her horns long or short; whether the field I graze her in be round or square, whether she were milked at home or abroad, what diseases she is subject to, and the like; after which they consult precedents, adjourn the cause from time to time, and in ten, twenty, or thirty years come to an issue. [11]

It is likewise to be observed that this society hath a peculiar cant and jargon of their own that no other mortal can understand and wherein all their laws are written, which they take special care to multiply; whereby they have

10. Profession.
11. Decision, result.

wholly confounded the very essence of truth and falsehood, of right and wrong; so that it will take thirty years to decide whether the field left me by my ancestors for six generations belongs to me or to a stranger three hundred miles off.

In the trial of persons accused for crimes against the state the method is much more short and commendable: the judge first sends to sound the disposition of those in power, after which he can easily hang or save the criminal, strictly preserving all due forms of law.

Here my master, interposing, said it was a pity that creatures endowed with such prodigious abilities of mind as these lawyers, by the description I gave of them, must certainly be, were not rather encouraged to be instructors of others in wisdom and knowledge. In answer to which I assured his Honour that in all points out of their own trade they were usually the most ignorant and stupid generation [12] among us, the most despicable in common conversation, avowed enemies to all knowledge and learning, and equally disposed to pervert the general reason of mankind in every other subject of discourse as in that of their own profession.

Chapter Six: A continuation of the state of England. The character of a first minister.

My master was yet wholly at a loss to understand what motives could incite this race of lawyers to perplex, disquiet, and weary themselves by engaging in a confederacy of injustice, merely for the sake of injuring their fellow-animals; neither could he comprehend what I meant in saying they did it for hire. Whereupon I was at much pains to describe to him the use of money, the materials it was made of, and the value of the metals; that when a Yahoo had got a great store of this precious substance, he was able to purchase whatever he had a mind to, the finest clothing, the noblest houses, great tracts of land, the most costly meats and drinks, and have his choice of the most beautiful females. Therefore since money alone was able to perform all these feats, our Yahoos thought they could never have enough of it to spend or to save, as they found themselves inclined from their natural bent either to profusion or avarice. That the rich man enjoyed the fruit of the poor man's labour, and the latter were a thousand to one in proportion to the former. That the bulk of our people was forced to live miserably, by labouring every day for small wages to make a few live plentifully.

I enlarged myself much on these and many other particulars to the same purpose: but his Honour was still to seek; [1] for he went upon a supposition that all animals had a title to their share in the productions of the earth, and especially those who presided over the rest. Therefore he desired I would let him know what these costly meats were, and how any of us happened to want [2] them. Whereupon I enumerated as many sorts as came into my head, with the various methods of dressing them, which could not be done without sending vessels by sea to every part of the world, as well for liquors to drink

12. Breed.

1. At a loss to understand.
2. Lack.

as for sauces and innumerable other conveniencies. I assured him that this whole globe of earth must be at least three times gone round before one of our better female Yahoos could get her breakfast or a cup to put it in. He said that must needs be a miserable country which cannot furnish food for its own inhabitants.

But what he chiefly wondered at was how such vast tracts of ground as I described should be wholly without fresh water, and the people put to the necessity of sending over the sea for drink. I replied that England (the dear place of my nativity) was computed to produce three times the quantity of food more than its inhabitants are able to consume, as well as liquors extracted from grain or pressed out of the fruit of certain trees, which made excellent drink, and the same proportion in every other convenience of life. But in order to feed the luxury and intemperance of the males and the vanity of the females, we sent away the greatest part of our necessary things to other countries, from whence in return we brought the materials of diseases, folly, and vice, to spend among ourselves. Hence it follows of necessity that vast numbers of our people are compelled to seek their livelihood by begging, robbing, stealing, cheating, pimping, forswearing, flattering, suborning, forging, gaming, lying, fawning, hectoring, voting, scribbling, star-gazing, poisoning, whoring, canting, libelling, free-thinking, and the like occupations: every one of which terms I was at much pains to make him understand.

That wine was not imported among us from foreign countries to supply the want of water or other drinks, but because it was a sort of liquid which made us merry by putting us out of our senses; diverted all melancholy thoughts, begat wild extravagant imaginations in the brain, raised our hopes, and banished our fears, suspended every office of reason for a time, and deprived us of the use of our limbs, until we fell into a profound sleep; although it must be confessed that we always awaked sick and dispirited, and that the use of this liquor filled us with diseases which made our lives uncomfortable and short.

But beside all this, the bulk of our people supported themselves by furnishing the necessities or conveniences of life to the rich and to each other. For instance, when I am at home and dressed as I ought to be, I carry on my body the workmanship of an hundred tradesmen; the building and furniture of my house employ as many more, and five times the number to adorn my wife.

I was going on to tell him of another sort of people who get their livelihood by attending the sick, having upon some occasions informed his Honour that many of my crew had died of diseases. But here it was with the utmost difficulty that I brought him to apprehend what I meant. He could easily conceive that a Houyhnhnm grew weak and heavy a few days before his death, or by some accident might hurt a limb. But that nature, who works all things to perfection, should suffer any pains to breed in our bodies, he thought impossible, and desired to know the reason of so unaccountable an evil. I told him we fed on a thousand things which operated contrary to each other; that we eat when we were not hungry and drank without the provocation of thirst; that we sat whole nights drinking strong liquors without eating a bit, which disposed us to sloth, enflamed our bodies, and precipitated or prevented digestion. That prostitute female Yahoos acquired a certain malady which bred rottenness in the bones of those who fell into their embraces; that this and many other diseases were propagated from father to son, so that great numbers come into the world with complicated maladies upon them. That it would be endless to give him a catalogue of all diseases incident to human bodies; for they could not be fewer than five or six hundred, spread over every limb and joint; in short, every part, external and intestine, having diseases appropriated to each. To remedy which, there was a sort of people bred up among us in the profession or pretence of curing the sick. And because I had some skill in the faculty, I would, in gratitude to his Honour, let him know the whole mystery [3] and method by which they proceed.

Their fundamental is that all diseases arise from repletion, from whence they conclude that a great evacuation of the body is necessary, either through the natural passage or upwards at the mouth. Their next business is, from herbs, minerals, gums, oils, shells, salts, juices, seaweed, excrements, barks of trees, serpents, toads, frogs, spiders, dead men's flesh and bones, birds, beasts, and fishes, to form a composition for smell and taste the most abominable, nauseous, and detestable that they can possibly contrive, which the stomach immediately rejects with loathing, and this they call a vomit; or else from the same storehouse, with some other poisonous additions, they command us to take in at the orifice above or below (just as the physician then happens to be disposed) a medicine equally annoying and disgustful to the bowels, which, relaxing the belly, drives down all before it, and this they call a purge or a clyster.[4] For nature (as the physicians allege) having intended the superior anterior orifice only for the intromission of solids and liquids and the inferior posterior for ejection, these artists, ingeniously considering that in all diseases nature is forced out of her seat, therefore to replace her in it, the body must be treated in a manner directly contrary, by interchanging the use of each orifice, forcing solids and liquids in at the anus and making evacuations at the mouth.

But besides real diseases we are subject to many that are only imaginary, for which the physicians have invented imaginary cures; these have their several names, and so have the drugs that are proper for them, and with these our female Yahoos are always infested.

One great excellency in this tribe is their skill at prognostics, wherein they seldom fail; their predictions in real diseases, when they rise to any degree of malignity, generally portending death, which is always in their power when recovery is not: and therefore, upon any unexpected signs of amendment, after they have pronounced their sentence, rather than be accused as false prophets, they know how to approve [5] their sagacity to the world by a seasonable dose.

They are likewise of special use to husbands and wives who are grown weary of their mates, to eldest sons, to great ministers of state, and often to princes.

I had formerly upon occasion discoursed with my master upon the nature of our government in general, and particularly of our own excellent constitution, deservedly the wonder and envy of the whole world. But having here acciden-

3. Trade secret.
4. Enema.
5. Demonstrate.

tally mentioned a *minister of state,* he commanded me some time after to inform him, what species of Yahoo I particularly meant by that appellation.

I told him that a *first* or *chief minister of state,*[6] whom I intended to describe, was a creature wholly exempt from joy and grief, love and hatred, pity and anger; at least makes use of no other passions but a violent desire of wealth, power, and titles; that he applies his words to all uses except to the indication of his mind; that he never tells a *truth* but with an intent that you should take it for a *lie,* nor a *lie* but with a design that you should take it for a *truth;* that those he speaks worst of behind their backs are in the surest way to preferment; and whenever he begins to praise you to others or to yourself, you are from that day forlorn.[7] The worst mark you can receive is a *promise,* especially when it is confirmed with an oath; after which every wise man retires and gives over all hopes.

There are three methods by which a man may rise to be chief minister: the first is by knowing how with prudence to dispose of a wife, a daughter, or a sister; the second, by betraying or undermining his predecessor; and the third is by a *furious zeal* in public assemblies against the corruptions of the court. But a wise prince would rather choose to employ those who practise the last of these methods; because such zealots prove always the most obsequious and subservient to the will and passions of their master. That these *ministers,* having all employments at their disposal, preserve themselves in power by bribing the majority of a senate or great council; and at last, by an expedient called an *act of indemnity* [8] (whereof I described the nature to him) they secure themselves from after reckonings, and retire from the public laden with the spoils of the nation.

The palace of a chief minister is a seminary to breed up others in his own trade: the pages, lackeys, and porter, by imitating their master, become ministers of state in their several districts, and learn to excel in the three principal ingredients, of *insolence, lying,* and *bribery.* Accordingly, they have a subaltern [9] court paid to them by persons of the best rank, and sometimes by the force of dexterity and impudence arrive through several gradations to be successors to their lord.

He is usually governed by a decayed wench or favourite footman, who are the tunnels through which all graces [10] are conveyed and may properly be called, in the last resort, the governors of the kingdom.

One day my master, having heard me mention the nobility of my country, was pleased to make me a compliment which I could not pretend to deserve:

6. Clearly a reference to Sir Robert Walpole (1676–1745), the first minister to be called "prime" (not an official title) because of his pre-eminence under the rule of George I and later, with the co-operation of Queen Caroline, of George II as well; the object of attacks by Swift, Pope, and Gay—on the score not only of his tyrannical political control but also of his use of writers as paid hacks of official policy.

7. Doomed, lost.

8. Such acts were often passed (with good reason) to free ministers from being prosecuted for actions in office by those who succeeded them to power; but they could become, as Swift pointed out in 1710, laws "enacted to take away the force of all laws whatsoever, by which a man may safely commit upon the last of June what he would be infallibly hanged for if he committed on the first of July" (*Examiner,* No. 18).

9. Subordinate.

10. Favors.

that he was sure I must have been born of some noble family, because I far exceeded in shape, colour, and cleanliness all the Yahoos of his nation, although I seemed to fail in strength and agility, which must be imputed to my different way of living from those other brutes; and, besides, I was not only endowed with the faculty of speech, but likewise with some rudiments of reason, to a degree that with all his acquaintance I passed for a prodigy.[11]

He made me observe, that among the Houyhnhnms, the *white*, the *sorrel*, and the *iron-grey*, were not so exactly shaped as the *bay*, the *dapple-grey*, and the *black*, nor born with equal talents of mind or a capacity to improve them; and therefore continued always in the condition of servants without ever aspiring to match out of their own race, which in that country would be reckoned monstrous and unnatural.

I made his Honour my most humble acknowledgments for the good opinion he was pleased to conceive of me; but assured him at the same time that my birth was of the lower sort, having been born of plain honest parents who were just able to give me a tolerable education: that *nobility* among us was altogether a different thing from the idea he had of it; that our young noblemen are bred from their childhood in idleness and luxury; that as soon as years will permit, they consume their vigour and contract odious diseases among lewd females; and when their fortunes are almost ruined, they marry some woman of mean birth, disagreeable person, and unsound constitution, merely for the sake of money, whom they hate and despise. That the productions of such marriages are generally scrofulous, rickety, or deformed children, by which means the family seldom continues above three generations, unless the wife take care to provide a healthy father among her neighbours or domestics, in order to improve and continue the breed. That a weak diseased body, a meagre countenance, and sallow complexion are the true marks of noble blood; and a healthy robust appearance is so disgraceful in a man of quality that the world concludes his real father to have been a groom or a coachman. The imperfections of his mind run parallel with those of his body, being a composition of spleen,[12] dullness, ignorance, caprice, sensuality, and pride.

Without the consent of this illustrious body [13] no law can be enacted, repealed, or altered, and these nobles have likewise the decision of all our possessions without appeal.

Chapter Seven: The author's great love of his native country. His master's observations upon the constitution and administration of England, as described by the author, with parallel cases and comparisons. His master's observations upon human nature.

The reader may be disposed to wonder how I could prevail on myself to give so free a representation of my own species among a race of mortals who were already too apt to conceive the vilest opinion of humankind from the entire

11. Wonder.
12. Temper or passion; the function of the spleen was not known in Swift's age, and to it was attributed a variety of psychosomatic symptoms—melancholy, gloom, ennui, hypochondria, the "vapors"—which were often fashionable, as is pointed out later in the chapter, among "the lazy, the luxurious, and the rich."
13. The House of Lords.

congruity betwixt me and their Yahoos. But I must freely confess that the many virtues of those excellent quadrupeds, placed in opposite view to human corruptions, had so far opened my eyes and enlarged my understanding that I began to view the actions and passions of man in a very different light, and to think the honour of my own kind not worth managing; [1] which, besides, it was impossible for me to do before a person of so acute a judgment as my master, who daily convinced me of a thousand faults in myself whereof I had not the least perception before, and which with us would never be numbered even among human infirmities. I had likewise learned from his example an utter detestation of all falsehood or disguise; and truth appeared so amiable to me that I determined upon sacrificing everything to it.

Let me deal so candidly with the reader as to confess that there was yet a much stronger motive for the freedom I took in my representation of things. I had not been a year in this country before I contracted such a love and veneration for the inhabitants that I entered on a firm resolution never to return to humankind, but to pass the rest of my life among these admirable Houyhnhnms in the contemplation and practice of every virtue; where I could have no example or incitement to vice. But it was decreed by Fortune, my perpetual enemy, that so great a felicity should not fall to my share. However, it is now some comfort to reflect that in what I said of my countrymen I extenuated their faults as much as I durst before so strict an examiner, and upon every article gave as favourable a turn as the matter would bear. For, indeed, who is there alive that will not be swayed by his bias and partiality to the place of his birth?

I have related the substance of several conversations I had with my master, during the greatest part of the time I had the honour to be in his service, but have indeed for brevity sake omitted much more than is here set down.

When I had answered all his questions, and his curiosity seemed to be fully satisfied, he sent for me one morning early and, commanding me to sit down at some distance (an honour which he had never before conferred upon me), he said he had been very seriously considering my whole story, as far as it related both to myself and my country: that he looked upon us as a sort of animals to whose share, by what accident he could not conjecture, some small pittance of reason had fallen, whereof we made no other use than by its assistance to aggravate our natural corruptions and to acquire new ones which nature had not given us. That we disarmed ourselves of the few abilities she had bestowed, had been very successful in multiplying our original wants, and seemed to spend our whole lives in vain endeavours to supply them by our own inventions. That as to myself, it was manifest I had neither the strength or agility of a common Yahoo, that I walked infirmly on my hinder feet, had found out a contrivance to make my claws of no use or defence and to remove the hair from my chin, which was intended as a shelter from the sun and the weather. Lastly, that I could neither run with speed nor climb trees like my brethren (as he called them), the Yahoos in this country.

That our institutions of government and law were plainly owing to our gross defects in reason and, by consequence, in virtue; because reason alone is sufficient to govern a rational creature; which was therefore a character we had

1. Protecting.

no pretence to challenge, even from the account I had given of my own people, although he manifestly perceived that in order to favour them I had concealed many particulars and often *said the thing which was not.*

He was the more confirmed in this opinion because he observed that, as I agreed in every feature of my body with other Yahoos, except where it was to my real disadvantage in point of strength, speed, and activity, the shortness of my claws, and some other particulars where nature had no part; so from the representation I had given him of our lives, our manners, and our actions, he found as near a resemblance in the disposition of our minds. He said the Yahoos were known to hate one another more than they did any different species of animals; and the reason usually assigned was the odiousness of their own shapes, which all could see in the rest but not in themselves. He had therefore begun to think it not unwise in us to cover our bodies and, by that invention, conceal many of our deformities from each other, which would else be hardly supportable. But he now found he had been mistaken and that the dissensions of those brutes in his country were owing to the same cause with ours, as I had described them. For if (said he) you throw among five Yahoos as much food as would be sufficient for fifty, they will, instead of eating peaceably, fall together by the ears, each single one impatient to have all to itself; and therefore a servant was usually employed to stand by while they were feeding abroad, and those kept at home were tied at a distance from each other. That if a cow died of age or accident before a Houyhnhnm could secure it for his own Yahoos, those in the neighbourhood would come in herds to seize it, and then would ensue such a battle as I had described, with terrible wounds made by their claws on both sides, although they seldom were able to kill one another for want of such convenient instruments of death as we had invented. At other times the like battles have been fought between the Yahoos of several neighbourhoods without any visible cause; those of one district watching all opportunities to surprise the next before they are prepared. But if they find their project hath miscarried, they return home, and, for want of enemies, engage in what I call a civil war among themselves.

That in some fields of this country there are certain shining stones of several colours, whereof the Yahoos are violently fond, and when part of these stones are fixed in the earth, as it sometimes happeneth, they will dig with their claws for whole days to get them out, and carry them away, and hide them by heaps in their kennels; but still looking round with great caution for fear their comrades should find out their treasure. My master said he could never discover the reason of this unnatural appetite or how these stones could be of any use to a Yahoo; but now he believed it might proceed from the same principle of avarice which I had ascribed to mankind; that he had once, by way of experiment, privately removed a heap of these stones from the place where one of his Yahoos had buried it: whereupon the sordid animal, missing his treasure, by his loud lamenting brought the whole herd to the place, there miserably howled, then fell to biting and tearing the rest, began to pine away, would neither eat, nor sleep, nor work, till he ordered a servant privately to convey the stones into the same hole and hide them as before; which when his Yahoo had found, he presently recovered his spirits and good humour, but took care to remove them to a better hiding-place, and hath ever since been a very serviceable brute.

My master farther assured me, which I also observed myself, that in the fields where these shining stones abound, the fiercest and most frequent battles are fought, occasioned by perpetual inroads of the neighbouring Yahoos.

He said it was common when two Yahoos discovered such a stone in a field and were contending which of them should be the proprietor, a third would take the advantage and carry it away from them both; which my master would needs contend to have some resemblance with our *suits at law;* wherein I thought it for our credit not to undeceive him; since the decision he mentioned was much more equitable than many decrees among us: because the plaintiff and defendant there lost nothing beside the stone they contended for, whereas our *courts of equity* would never have dismissed the cause while either of them had anything left.

My master, continuing his discourse, said, there was nothing that rendered the Yahoos more odious than their undistinguishing appetite to devour everything that came in their way, whether herbs, roots, berries, corrupted flesh of animals, or all mingled together: and it was peculiar in their temper that they were fonder of what they could get by rapine or stealth at a greater distance than much better food provided for them at home. If their prey held out, they would eat till they were ready to burst, after which nature had pointed out to them a certain root that gave them a general evacuation.

There was also another kind of root very juicy, but something rare and difficult to be found, which the Yahoos sought for with much eagerness and would suck it with great delight; and it produced in them the same effects that wine hath upon us. It would make them sometimes hug and sometimes tear one another; they would howl and grin, and chatter, and reel, and tumble, and then fall asleep in the mud.

I did indeed observe that the Yahoos were the only animals in this country subject to any diseases; which, however, were much fewer than horses have among us, and contracted not by any ill treatment they meet with but by the nastiness and greediness of that sordid brute. Neither has their language any more than a general appellation for those maladies, which is borrowed from the name of the beast, and called *Hnea Yahoo,* or the *Yahoo's Evil;* and the cure prescribed is a mixture of their own dung and urine forcibly put down the Yahoo's throat. This I have since often known to have been taken with success and do here freely recommend it to my countrymen for the public good, as an admirable specific against all diseases produced by repletion.

As to learning, government, arts, manufactures, and the like, my master confessed he could find little or no resemblance between the Yahoos of that country and those in ours. For he only meant to observe what parity there was in our natures. He had heard indeed some curious Houyhnhnms observe that in most herds there was a sort of ruling Yahoo (as among us there is generally some leading or principal stag in a park), who was always more deformed in body and mischievous in disposition than any of the rest. That this leader had usually a favourite as like himself as he could get, whose employment was to lick his master's feet and posteriors and drive the female Yahoos to his kennel; for which he was now and then rewarded with a piece of ass's flesh. This favourite is hated by the whole herd, and therefore to protect himself keeps always near the person of his leader. He usually continues in office till a worse can be found; but the very moment he is discarded, his successor, at the head of all the

Yahoos in that district, young and old, male and female, come in a body and discharge their excrements upon him from head to foot. But how far this might be applicable to our *courts* and *favourites,* and *ministers of state,* my master said I could best determine.

I durst make no return to this malicious insinuation, which debased human understanding below the sagacity of a common *hound,* who has judgment enough to distinguish and follow the cry of the ablest dog in the pack without being ever mistaken.

My master told me there were some qualities remarkable in the Yahoos which he had not observed me to mention, or at least very slightly, in the accounts I had given him of humankind. He said those animals, like other brutes, had their females in common; but in this they differed, that the she-Yahoo would admit the male while she was pregnant and that the hees would quarrel and fight with the females as fiercely as with each other. Both which practices were such degrees of infamous brutality that no other sensitive creature ever arrived at.

Another thing he wondered at in the Yahoos was their strange disposition to nastiness and dirt, whereas there appears to be a natural love of cleanliness in all other animals. As to the two former accusations, I was glad to let them pass without any reply because I had not a word to offer upon them in defence of my species, which otherwise I certainly had done from my own inclinations. But I could have easily vindicated humankind from the imputation of singularity upon the last article if there had been any *swine* in that country (as unluckily for me there were not), which, although it may be a sweeter quadruped than a Yahoo, cannot, I humbly conceive, in justice pretend to more cleanliness; and so his Honour himself must have owned, if he had seen their filthy way of feeding and their custom of wallowing and sleeping in the mud.

My master likewise mentioned another quality which his servants had discovered in several Yahoos and to him was wholly unaccountable. He said a fancy would sometimes take a Yahoo to retire into a corner, to lie down and howl, and groan, and spurn away all that came near him, although he were young and fat, and wanted neither food nor water; nor did the servants imagine what could possibly ail him. And the only remedy they found was to set him to hard work, after which he would infallibly come to himself. To this I was silent out of partiality to my own kind; yet here I could plainly discover the true seeds of *spleen,* which only seizeth on the *lazy,* the *luxurious,* and the *rich;* who, if they were forced to undergo the same regimen, I would undertake for the cure.

His Honour had farther observed that a female Yahoo would often stand behind a bank or a bush, to gaze on the young males passing by, and then appear and hide, using many antic gestures and grimaces, at which time it was observed that she had a most offensive smell; and when any of the males advanced, would slowly retire, looking often back, and with a counterfeit show of fear run off into some convenient place where she knew the male would follow her.

At other times if a female stranger came among them, three or four of her own sex would get about her and stare and chatter, and grin, and smell her all over, and then turn off with gestures that seemed to express contempt and disdain.

Perhaps my master might refine a little in these speculations, which he had drawn from what he observed himself or had been told him by others: however, I could not reflect without some amazement, and much sorrow, that the rudiments of *lewdness, coquetry, censure,* and *scandal* should have place by instinct in womankind.

I expected every moment that my master would accuse the Yahoos of those unnatural appetites in both sexes so common among us. But nature, it seems, hath not been so expert a schoolmistress; and these politer pleasures are entirely the productions of art and reason, on our side of the globe.

Chapter Eight: The author relateth several particulars of the Yahoos. The great virtues of the Houyhnhnms. The education and exercise of their youth. Their General Assembly.

As I ought to have understood human nature much better than I supposed it possible for my master to do, so it was easy to apply the character he gave of the Yahoos to myself and my countrymen, and I believed I could yet make farther discoveries from my own observation. I therefore often begged his Honour to let me go among the herds of Yahoos in the neighbourhood, to which he always very graciously consented, being perfectly convinced that the hatred I bore those brutes would never suffer me to be corrupted by them; and his Honour ordered one of his servants, a strong sorrel nag, very honest and good-natured, to be my guard, without whose protection I durst not undertake such adventures. For I have already told the reader how much I was pestered by those odious animals upon my first arrival. And I afterwards failed very narrowly three or four times of falling into their clutches, when I happened to stray at any distance without my hanger. And I have reason to believe they had some imagination that I was of their own species, which I often assisted myself by stripping up my sleeves and showing my naked arms and breast in their sight, when my protector was with me. At which times they would approach as near as they durst and imitate my actions after the manner of monkeys but ever with great signs of hatred, as a tame jackdaw, with cap and stockings, is always persecuted by the wild ones when he happens to be got among them.

They are prodigiously nimble from their infancy; however, I once caught a young male of three years old, and endeavoured by all marks of tenderness to make it quiet; but the little imp fell a-squalling, and scratching, and biting with such violence, that I was forced to let it go; and it was high time, for a whole troop of old ones came about us at the noise, but finding the cub was safe (for away it ran), and my sorrel nag being by, they durst not venture near us. I observed the young animal's flesh to smell very rank, and the stink was somewhat between a weasel and a fox, but much more disagreeable. I forgot another circumstance (and perhaps I might have the reader's pardon if it were wholly omitted) that while I held the odious vermin in my hands, it voided its filthy excrement of a yellow liquid substance all over my clothes; but by good fortune there was a small brook hard by where I washed myself as clean as I could, although I durst not come into my master's presence until I were sufficiently aired.

By what I could discover, the Yahoos appear to be the most unteachable of all animals, their capacities never reaching higher than to draw or carry burthens. Yet I am of opinion this defect ariseth chiefly from a perverse, restive disposition. For they are cunning, malicious, treacherous, and revengeful. They are strong and hardy, but of a cowardly spirit, and by consequence insolent, abject, and cruel. It is observed, that the red-haired of both sexes are more libidinous and mischievous than the rest, whom yet they much exceed in strength and activity.

The Houyhnhnms keep the Yahoos for present use in huts not far from the house; but the rest are sent abroad to certain fields where they dig up roots, eat several kinds of herbs, and search about for carrion, or sometimes catch weasels and *luhimuhs* (a sort of wild rat), which they greedily devour. Nature hath taught them to dig deep holes with their nails on the side of a rising ground, wherein they lie by themselves; only the kennels of the females are larger, sufficient to hold two or three cubs.

They swim from their infancy like frogs and are able to continue long under water, where they often take fish, which the females carry home to their young. And upon this occasion, I hope the reader will pardon my relating an odd adventure.

Being one day abroad with my protector the sorrel nag, and the weather exceeding hot, I entreated him to let me bathe in a river that was near. He consented, and I immediately stripped myself stark naked and went down softly into the stream. It happened that a young female Yahoo, standing behind a bank, saw the whole proceeding and, inflamed by desire, as the nag and I conjectured, came running with all speed and leaped into the water within five yards of the place where I bathed. I was never in my life so terribly frighted; the nag was grazing at some distance, not suspecting any harm. She embraced me after a most fulsome manner; I roared as loud as I could, and the nag came galloping towards me, whereupon she quitted her grasp, with the utmost reluctancy, and leaped upon the opposite bank, where she stood gazing and howling all the time I was putting on my clothes.

This was matter of diversion to my master and his family, as well as of mortification to myself. For now I could no longer deny that I was a real Yahoo in every limb and feature, since the females had a natural propensity to me as one of their own species: neither was the hair of this brute of a red colour (which might have been some excuse for an appetite a little irregular) but black as a sloe, and her countenance did not make an appearance altogether so hideous as the rest of the kind; for I think she could not be above eleven years old.

Having already lived three years in this country, the reader I suppose will expect that I should, like other travellers, give him some account of the manners and customs of its inhabitants, which it was indeed my principal study to learn.

As these noble Houyhnhnms are endowed by nature with a general disposition to all virtues and have no conceptions or ideas of what is evil in a rational creature, so their grand maxim is to cultivate reason and to be wholly governed by it. Neither is reason among them a point problematical as with us, where men can argue with plausibility on both sides of a question, but strikes you with immediate conviction, as it must needs do where it is not mingled, obscured, or discoloured by passion and interest. I remember it was with extreme difficulty that I could bring my master to understand the meaning of the word *opinion* or how a point could be disputable; because reason taught us to affirm or deny only where we are certain, and beyond our knowledge we cannot do either. So that controversies, wranglings, disputes, and positiveness in false or dubious propositions are evils unknown among the Houyhnhnms. In the like manner, when I used to explain to him our several systems of *natural philosophy*, he would laugh that a creature pretending to *reason* should value itself upon the knowledge of other people's conjectures and in things where that knowledge, if it were certain, could be of no use. Wherein he agreed entirely with the sentiments of Socrates, as Plato delivers them; [1] which I mention as the highest honour I can do that prince of philosophers. I have often since reflected what destruction such a doctrine would make in the libraries of Europe, and how many paths to fame would be then shut up in the learned world.

Friendship and *benevolence* are the two principal virtues among the Houyhnhnms, and these not confined to particular objects, but universal to the whole race. For a stranger from the remotest part is equally treated with the nearest neighbour, and wherever he goes looks upon himself as at home. They preserve *decency* and *civility* in the highest degrees, but are altogether ignorant of *ceremony*. They have no fondness [2] for their colts or foals, but the care they take in educating them proceeds entirely from the dictates of reason. And I observed my master to show the same affection to his neighbour's issue that he had for his own. They will have it that nature teaches them to love the whole species, and it is reason only that maketh a distinction of persons, where there is a superior degree of virtue.

When the matron Houyhnhnms have produced one of each sex, they no longer accompany with their consorts except they lose one of their issue by some casualty, which very seldom happens: but in such a case they meet again, or, when the like accident befalls a person whose wife is past bearing, some other couple bestows on him one of their own colts, and then go together a second time till the mother be pregnant. This caution is necessary to prevent the country from being overburthened with numbers. But the race of inferior Houyhnhnms bred up to be servants is not so strictly limited upon this article; these are allowed to produce three of each sex to be domestics in the noble families.

In their marriages they are exactly careful to choose such colours as will not make any disagreeable mixture in the breed. *Strength* is chiefly valued in the male, and *comeliness* in the female, not upon the account of *love*, but to preserve the race from degenerating; for where a female happens to excel in strength, a consort is chosen with regard to *comeliness*. Courtship, love, presents, jointures, settlements, have no place in their thoughts or terms whereby to express them in their language. The young couple meet and are joined merely because it is the determination of their parents and friends: it is what they see done every day, and they look upon it as one of the necessary actions in a reasonable being. But the violation of marriage, or any other unchastity,

1. Perhaps a reference to Plato's *Phaedo* 97–98, where Socrates describes his high hopes upon hearing of Anaxagoras' doctrines and his disappointment on learning more.
2. Doting or foolish affection.

was never heard of: and the married pair pass their lives with the same friendship and mutual benevolence that they bear to all others of the same species
who come in their way; without jealousy, fondness, quarrelling, or discontent.

In educating the youth of both sexes, their method is admirable and highly
deserves our imitation. These are not suffered to taste a grain of oats, except
upon certain days, till eighteen years old; nor milk but very rarely; and in
summer they graze two hours in the morning and as many in the evening,
which their parents likewise observe, but the servants are not allowed above
half that time, and a great part of their grass is brought home, which they
eat at the most convenient hours, when they can be best spared from work.

Temperance, industry, exercise and *cleanliness,* are the lessons equally
enjoined to the young ones of both sexes: and my master thought it monstrous
in us to give the females a different kind of education from the males except
in some articles of domestic management; whereby, as he truly observed, one
half of our natives were good for nothing but bringing children into the world:
and to trust the care of their children to such useless animals, he said, was yet
a greater instance of brutality.

But the Houyhnhnms train up their youth to strength, speed, and hardiness
by exercising them in running races up and down steep hills or over hard
stony grounds; and when they are all in a sweat, they are ordered to leap over
head and ears into a pond or a river. Four times a year the youth of certain
districts meet to show their proficiency in running and leaping and other feats
of strength or agility, where the victor is rewarded with a song made in his or
her praise. On this festival the servants drive a herd of Yahoos into the field,
laden with hay and oats and milk for a repast to the Houyhnhnms; after which
these brutes are immediately driven back again for fear of being noisome to the
assembly.

Every fourth year, at the vernal equinox, there is a representative council of
the whole nation, which meets in a plain about twenty miles from our house,
and continues about five or six days. Here they inquire into the state and condition of the several districts: whether they abound or be deficient in hay or
oats, or cows or Yahoos. And wherever there is any want (which is but seldom)
it is immediately supplied by unanimous consent and contribution. Here likewise the regulation of children is settled: as for instance, if a Houyhnhnm hath
two males, he changeth one of them with another who hath two females; and
when a child hath been lost by any casualty, where the mother is past breeding,
it is determind what family in the district shall breed another to supply the
loss.

*Chapter Nine: A grand debate at the General Assembly of the Houyhnhnms,
and how it was determined. The learning of the Houyhnhnms. Their buildings.
Their manner of burials. The defectiveness of their language.*

One of these grand assemblies was held in my time, about three months before
my departure, whither my master went as the representative of our district.
In this council was resumed their old debate, and indeed the only debate that
ever happened in their country; whereof my master after his return gave me a
very particular account.

The question to be debated was whether the Yahoos should be exterminated from the face of the earth. One of the members for the affirmative offered several arguments of great strength and weight, alleging that, as the Yahoos were the most filthy, noisome, and deformed animal which nature ever produced, so they were the most restive and indocible, mischievous and malicious: they would privately suck the teats of the Houyhnhnms' cows, kill and devour their cats, trample down their oats and grass, if they were not continually watched, and commit a thousand other extravagancies. He took notice of a general tradition that Yahoos had not been always in their country: but that many ages ago two of these brutes appeared together upon a mountain,[1] whether produced by the heat of the sun upon corrupted mud and slime or from the ooze and froth of the sea was never known. That these Yahoos engendered, and their brood in a short time grew so numerous as to overrun and infest the whole nation. That the Houyhnhnms, to get rid of this evil, made a general hunting, and at last enclosed the whole herd; and, destroying the elder, every Houyhnhnm kept two young ones in a kennel and brought them to such a degree of tameness as an animal so savage by nature can be capable of acquiring, using them for draft and carriage. That there seemed to be much truth in this tradition, and that those creatures could not be *ylnhniamshy* (or *aborigines* of the land) because of the violent hatred the Houyhnhnms, as well as all other animals, bore them; which although their evil disposition sufficiently deserved, could never have arrived at so high a degree if they had been aborigines, or else they would have long since been rooted out. That the inhabitants, taking a fancy to use the service of the Yahoos, had very imprudently neglected to cultivate the breed of asses, which were a comely animal, easily kept, more tame and orderly, without any offensive smell, strong enough for labour, although they yield to the other in agility of body; and if their braying be no agreeable sound, it is far preferable to the horrible howlings of the Yahoos.

Several others declared their sentiments to the same purpose, when my master proposed an expedient to the assembly, whereof he had indeed borrowed the hint from me. He approved of the tradition mentioned by the honourable member who spoke before, and affirmed that the two Yahoos said to be first seen among them had been driven thither over the sea; that coming to land and being forsaken by their companions, they retired to the mountains and, degenerating by degrees, became in process of time much more savage than those of their own species in the country from whence these two originals came. The reason of his assertion was that he had now in his possession a certain wonderful Yahoo (meaning myself) which most of them had heard of and many of them had seen. He then related to them how he first found me; that my body was all covered with an artificial composure [2] of the skins and hairs of other animals: that I spoke in a language of my own and had thoroughly learned theirs: that I had related to him the accidents which brought me thither: that when he saw me without my covering, I was an exact Yahoo in

1. Perhaps offered by Swift with some ironic suggestion of the fallen Adam and Eve descending from the "mountain" where Milton placed the Garden of Eden (*Paradise Lost* IV.226); but, of course, all nature falls with man in Milton's poem.
2. Composition.

every part, only of a whiter colour, less hairy, and with shorter claws. He added, how I had endeavoured to persuade him that in my own and other countries the Yahoos acted as the governing, rational animal, and held the Houyhnhnms in servitude: that he observed in me all the qualities of a Yahoo, only a little more civilized by some tincture of reason, which however was in a degree as far inferior to the Houyhnhnm race as the Yahoos of their country were to me: that, among other things, I mentioned a custom we had of castrating Houyhnhnms when they were young in order to render them tame; that the operation was easy and safe; that it was no shame to learn wisdom from brutes, as industry is taught by the ant and building by the swallow. (For so I translate the word *lyhannh*, although it be a much larger fowl.) That this invention might be practised upon the younger Yahoos here, which, besides rendering them tractable and fitter for use, would in an age put an end to the whole species without destroying life. That in the meantime the Houyhnhnms should be *exhorted* to cultivate the breed of asses, which, as they are in all respects more valuable brutes, so they have this advantage, to be fit for service at five years old, which the others are not till twelve.

This was all my master thought fit to tell me at that time of what passed in the grand council. But he was pleased to conceal one particular which related personally to myself, whereof I soon felt the unhappy effect, as the reader will know in its proper place, and from whence I date all the succeeding misfortunes of my life.

The Houyhnhnms have no letters, and consequently their knowledge is all traditional. But there happening few events of any moment among a people so well united, naturally disposed to every virtue, wholly governed by reason, and cut off from all commerce with other nations, the historical part is easily preserved without burthening their memories. I have already observed that they are subject to no diseases, and therefore can have no need of physicians. However, they have excellent medicines composed of herbs, to cure accidental bruises and cuts in the pastern or frog [3] of the foot by sharp stones, as well as other maims and hurts in the several parts of the body.

They calculate the year by the revolution of the sun and the moon, but use no subdivisions into weeks. They are well enough acquainted with the motions of those two luminaries and understand the nature of eclipses; and this is the utmost progress of their astronomy.

In poetry they must be allowed to excel all other mortals; wherein the justness of their similes and the minuteness as well as exactness of their descriptions are indeed inimitable. Their verses abound very much in both of these and usually contain either some exalted notions of friendship and benevolence, or the praises of those who were victors in races and other bodily exercises. Their buildings, although very rude and simple, are not inconvenient, but well contrived to defend them from all injuries of cold and heat. They have a kind of tree which at forty years old loosens in the root and falls with the first storm; it grows very straight and, being pointed like stakes with a sharp stone (for the Houyhnhnms know not the use of iron), they stick them erect in the ground about ten inches asunder, and then weave in oat-straw or sometimes

3. The horny sole.

wattles betwixt them. The roof is made after the same manner and so are the doors.

The Houyhnhnms use the hollow part between the pastern and the hoof of their forefeet as we do our hands, and this with greater dexterity than I could at first imagine. I have seen a white mare of our family thread a needle (which I lent her on purpose) with that joint. They milk their cows, reap their oats, and do all the work which requires hands, in the same manner. They have a kind of hard flints, which, by grinding against other stones, they form into instruments that serve instead of wedges, axes, and hammers. With tools made of these flints they likewise cut their hay and reap their oats, which there groweth naturally in several fields: the Yahoos draw home the sheaves in carriages, and the servants tread them in certain covered huts, to get out the grain, which is kept in stores. They make a rude kind of earthen and wooden vessels and bake the former in the sun.

If they can avoid casualties, they die only of old age, and are buried in the obscurest places that can be found, their friends and relations expressing neither joy nor grief at their departure; nor does the dying person discover the least regret that he is leaving the world, any more than if he were upon returning home from a visit to one of his neighbours. I remember my master having once made an appointment with a friend and his family to come to his house upon some affair of importance; on the day fixed, the mistress and her two children came very late. She made two excuses, first for her husband, who, as she said, happened that very morning to *lhnuwnh*. The word is strongly expressive in their language but not easily rendered into English; it signifies, *to retire to his first mother*. Her excuse for not coming sooner was that, her husband dying late in the morning, she was a good while consulting her servants about a convenient place where his body should be laid; and I observed she behaved herself at our house as cheerfully as the rest; she died about three months after.

They live generally to seventy or seventy-five years, very seldom to fourscore; some weeks before their death they feel a gradual decay, but without pain. During this time they are much visited by their friends because they cannot go abroad with their usual ease and satisfaction. However, about ten days before their death, which they seldom fail in computing, they return the visits that have been made them by those who are nearest in the neighbourhood, being carried in a convenient sledge drawn by Yahoos, which vehicle they use, not only upon this occasion but when they grow old, upon long journeys, or when they are lamed by any accident. And therefore when the dying Houyhnhnms return those visits, they take a solemn leave of their friends, as if they were going to some remote part of the country where they designed to pass the rest of their lives.

I know not whether it may be worth observing that the Houyhnhnms have no word in their language to express anything that is evil, except what they borrow from the deformities or ill qualities of the Yahoos. Thus they denote the folly of a servant, an omission of a child, a stone that cuts their feet, a continuance of foul or unseasonable weather, and the like, by adding to each the epithet of *yahoo*. For instance, *hhnm yahoo, whnaholm yahoo, ynlhmnawihlma yahoo*, and an ill-contrived house *ynholmhnmrohlnw yahoo*.

I could with great pleasure enlarge farther upon the manners and virtues of this excellent people; but, intending in a short time to publish a volume by itself expressly upon that subject, I refer the reader thither; and in the meantime, proceed to relate my own sad catastrophe.

Chapter Ten: The author's economy and happy life among the Houyhnhnms. His great improvement in virtue by conversing with them. Their conversations. The author hath notice given him by his master that he must depart from the country. He falls into a swoon for grief, but submits. He contrives and finishes a canoe, by the help of a fellow servant, and puts to sea at a venture.

I had settled my little economy to my own heart's content. My master had ordered a room to be made for me after their manner about six yards from the house, the sides and floors of which I plastered with clay and covered with rush mats of my own contriving; I had beaten hemp, which there grows wild, and made of it a sort of ticking: this I filled with the feathers of several birds I had taken with springes made of Yahoos' hairs, and were excellent food. I had worked two chairs with my knife, the sorrel nag helping me in the grosser and more laborious part. When my clothes were worn to rags, I made myself others with the skins of rabbits and of a certain beautiful animal about the same size, called *nnuhnoh*, the skin of which is covered with a fine down. Of these I likewise made very tolerable stockings. I soled my shoes with wood which I cut from a tree and fitted to the upper leather; and when this was worn out, I supplied it with the skins of Yahoos dried in the sun. I often got honey out of hollow trees, which I mingled with water, or eat it with my bread. No man could more verify the truth of these two maxims, *That nature is very easily satisfied* and *That necessity is the mother of invention.* I enjoyed perfect health of body and tranquillity of mind; I did not feel the treachery or inconstancy of a friend, nor the injuries of a secret or open enemy. I had no occasion of bribing, flattering, or pimping to procure the favour of any great man or of his minion. I wanted no fence against fraud or oppression; here was neither physician to destroy my body, nor lawyer to ruin my fortune; no informer to watch my words and actions or forge accusations against me for hire: here were no gibers, censurers, backbiters, pickpockets, highwaymen, housebreakers, attorneys, bawds, buffoons, gamesters, politicians, wits, splenetics, tedious talkers, controvertists, ravishers, murderers, robbers, virtuosos: [1] no leaders or followers of party and faction: no encouragers to vice by seducement or examples: no dungeon, axes, gibbets, whipping-posts, or pillories: no cheating shopkeepers or mechanics: no pride, vanity, or affectation: no fops, bullies, drunkards, strolling whores, or poxes: [2] no ranting, lewd, expensive wives: no stupid, proud pedants: no importunate, overbearing, quarrelsome, noisy, roaring, empty, conceited, swearing companions: no scoundrels raised from the dust upon the merit of their vices, or nobility thrown into it on account of their virtues: no lords, fiddlers, judges, or dancing-masters.

I had the favour of being admitted to several Houyhnhnms who came to visit or dine with my master; where his Honour graciously suffered me to wait in

1. Amateur scientists.
2. Venereal diseases.

the room and listen to their discourse. Both he and his company would often descend to ask me questions and receive my answers. I had also sometimes the honour of attending my master in his visits to others. I never presumed to speak except in answer to a question, and then I did it with inward regret, because it was a loss of so much time for improving myself: but I was infinitely delighted with the station of an humble auditor in such conversations, where nothing passed but what was useful, expressed in the fewest and most significant words: where (as I have already said) the greatest decency [3] was observed without the least degree of ceremony; where no person spoke without being pleased himself and pleasing his companions; where there was no interruptions, tediousness, heat, or difference of sentiments. They have a notion that, when people are met together, a short silence doth much improve conversation: this I found to be true; for during those little intermissions of talk, new ideas would arise in their minds, which very much enlivened the discourse. Their subjects are generally on friendship and benevolence, on order and economy, sometimes upon the visible operations of nature or ancient traditions, upon the bounds and limits of virtue, upon the unerring rules of reason, or upon some determinations to be taken at the next Great Assembly, and often upon the various excellencies of poetry. I may add without vanity that my presence often gave them sufficient matter for discourse, because it afforded my master an occasion of letting his friends into the history of me and my country, upon which they were all pleased to descant in a manner not very advantageous to humankind; and for that reason I shall not repeat what they said: only I may be allowed to observe, that his Honour, to my great admiration, appeared to understand the nature of Yahoos much better than myself. He went through all our vices and follies and discovered many which I had never mentioned to him, by only supposing what qualities a Yahoo of their country, with a small proportion of reason, might be capable of exerting; and concluded, with too much probability, how vile as well as miserable such a creature must be.

I freely confess that all the little knowledge I have of any value was acquired by the lectures I received from my master and from hearing the discourses of him and his friends; to which I should be prouder to listen than to dictate to the greatest and wisest assembly in Europe. I admired the strength, comeliness, and speed of the inhabitants; and such a constellation of virtues in such amiable persons produced in me the highest veneration. At first, indeed, I did not feel that natural awe which the Yahoos and all other animals bear towards them; but it grew upon me by degrees, much sooner than I imagined, and was mingled with a respectful love and gratitude, that they would condescend to distinguish me from the rest of my species.

When I thought of my family, my friends, my countrymen, or human race in general, I considered them as they really were, Yahoos in shape and disposition, perhaps a little more civilized and qualified with the gift of speech, but making no other use of reason than to improve and multiply those vices whereof their brethren in this country had only the share that nature allotted them. When I happened to behold the reflection of my own form in a lake or fountain, I turned away my face in horror and detestation of myself, and could better

3. Decorum, sense of form.

endure the sight of a common Yahoo than of my own person. By conversing with the Houyhnhnms and looking upon them with delight, I fell to imitate their gait and gesture, which is now grown into a habit, and my friends often tell me in a blunt way that I *trot like a horse;* which, however, I take for a great compliment: neither shall I disown that in speaking I am apt to fall into the voice and manner of the Houyhnhnms, and hear myself ridiculed on that account without the least mortification.

In the midst of this happiness, when I looked upon myself to be fully settled for life, my master sent for me one morning a little earlier than his usual hour. I observed by his countenance that he was in some perplexity and at a loss how to begin what he had to speak. After a short silence he told me he did not know how I would take what he was going to say; that in the last General Assembly, when the affair of the Yahoos was entered upon, the representatives had taken offence at his keeping a Yahoo (meaning myself) in his family more like a Houyhnhnm than a brute animal. That he was known frequently to converse with me, as if he could receive some advantage or pleasure in my company: that such a practice was not agreeable to reason or nature, or a thing ever heard of before among them. The assembly did therefore *exhort* him either to employ me like the rest of my species or command me to swim back to the place from whence I came. That the first of these expedients was utterly rejected by all the Houyhnhnms who had ever seen me at his house or their own: for they alleged that, because I had some rudiments of reason, added to the natural pravity [4] of those animals, it was to be feared I might be able to seduce them into the woody and mountainous parts of the country and bring them in troops by night to destroy the Houyhnhnms' cattle, as being naturally of the ravenous kind and averse from labour.

My master added that he was daily pressed by the Houyhnhnms of the neighbourhood to have the assembly's *exhortation* executed, which he could not put off much longer. He doubted it would be impossible for me to swim to another country, and therefore wished I would contrive some sort of vehicle, resembling those I had described to him, that might carry me on the sea, in which work I should have the assistance of his own servants, as well as those of his neighbours. He concluded that for his own part he could have been content to keep me in his service as long as I lived, because he found I had cured myself of some bad habits and dispositions by endeavouring, as far as my inferior nature was capable, to imitate the Houyhnhnms.

I should here observe to the reader that a decree of the General Assembly in this country is expressed by the word *hnhloayn,* which signifies an *exhortation,* as near as I can render it: for they have no conception how a rational creature can be *compelled,* but only advised or *exhorted,* because no person can disobey reason without giving up his claim to be a rational creature.

I was struck with the utmost grief and despair at my master's discourse, and, being unable to support the agonies I was under, I fell into a swoon at his feet. When I came to myself he told me that he concluded I had been dead. (For these people are subject to no such imbecilities [5] of nature.) I answered, in a faint voice, that death would have been too great an happiness; that

4. Viciousness.
5. Frailties, weaknesses.

although I could not blame the assembly's *exhortation* or the urgency of his friends, yet, in my weak and corrupt judgment, I thought it might consist with reason to have been less rigorous. That I could not swim a league, and probably the nearest land to theirs might be distant above an hundred; that many materials, necessary for making a small vessel to carry me off, were wholly wanting in this country, which, however, I would attempt in obedience and gratitude to his Honour, although I concluded the thing to be impossible, and therefore looked on myself as already devoted [6] to destruction. That the certain prospect of an unnatural death was the least of my evils: for, supposing I should escape with life by some strange adventure, how could I think with temper [7] of passing my days among Yahoos and relapsing into my old corruptions for want of examples to lead and keep me within the paths of virtue? That I knew too well upon what solid reasons all the determinations of the wise Houyhnhnms were founded not to be shaken by arguments of mine, a miserable Yahoo; and therefore, after presenting him with my humble thanks for the offer of his servants' assistance in making a vessel and desiring a reasonable time for so difficult a work, I told him I would endeavour to preserve a wretched being; and, if ever I returned to England, was not without hopes of being useful to my own species by celebrating the praises of the renowned Houyhnhnms and proposing their virtues to the imitation of mankind.

My master in a few words made me a very gracious reply, allowed me the space of two months to finish my boat, and ordered the sorrel nag, my fellow-servant (for so at this distance I may presume to call him) to follow my instructions, because I told my master that his help would be sufficient, and I knew he had a tenderness for me.

In his company my first business was to go to that part of the coast where my rebellious crew had ordered me to be set on shore. I got upon a height and, looking on every side into the sea, fancied I saw a small island towards the northeast. I took out my pocket-glass and could then clearly distinguish it about five leagues off, as I computed; but it appeared to the sorrel nag to be only a blue cloud: for, as he had no conception of any country beside his own, so he could not be as expert in distinguishing remote objects at sea as we who so much converse in that element.

After I had discovered this island, I considered no farther; but resolved it should, if possible, be the first place of my banishment, leaving the consequence to fortune.

I returned home and, consulting with the sorrel nag, we went into a copse at some distance, where I with my knife, and he with a sharp flint fastened very artificially,[8] after their manner, to a wooden handle, cut down several oak wattles about the thickness of a walking-staff, and some larger pieces. But I shall not trouble the reader with a particular description of my own mechanics; let it suffice to say that in six weeks' time, with the help of the sorrel nag, who performed the parts that required most labour, I finished a sort of Indian canoe, but much larger, covering it with the skins of Yahoos well

6. Doomed.
7. Equanimity.
8. Artfully.

stitched together with hempen threads of my own making. My sail was like-wise composed of the skins of the same animal; but I made use of the youngest I could get, the older being too tough and thick, and I likewise provided my-self with four paddles. I laid in a stock of boiled flesh of rabbits and fowls, and took with me two vessels, one filled with milk and the other with water.

I tried my canoe in a large pond near my master's house and then corrected in it what was amiss; stopping all the chinks with Yahoos' tallow till I found it staunch and able to bear me and my freight. And when it was as complete as I could possibly make it, I had it drawn on a carriage very gently by Yahoos to the seaside, under the conduct of the sorrel nag and another servant.

When all was ready and the day came for my departure, I took leave of my master and lady and the whole family, my eyes flowing with tears and my heart quite sunk with grief. But his Honour, out of curiosity, and perhaps (if I may speak it without vanity) partly out of kindness, was determined to see me in my canoe and got several of his neighbouring friends to accompany him. I was forced to wait above an hour for the tide, and then observing the wind very fortunately bearing towards the island to which I intended to steer my course, I took a second leave of my master: but as I was going to prostrate myself to kiss his hoof, he did me the honour to raise it gently to my mouth. I am not ignorant how much I have been censured for mentioning this last particular. Detractors are pleased to think it improbable that so illustrious a person should descend to give so great a mark of distinction to a creature so inferior as I. Neither have I forgot how apt some travellers are to boast of extraordinary favours they have received. But if these censurers were better acquainted with the noble and courteous disposition of the Houyhnhnms, they would soon change their opinion.

I paid my respects to the rest of the Houyhnhnms in his Honour's company; then getting into my canoe, I pushed off from shore.

Chapter Eleven: The author's dangerous voyage. He arrives at New Holland, hoping to settle there. Is wounded with an arrow by one of the natives. Is seized and carried by force into a Portuguese ship. The great civilities of the captain. The author arrives at England.

I began this desperate voyage on February 15, 1714-5; [1] at 9 o'clock in the morning. The wind was very favourable; however, I made use at first only of my paddles, but considering I should soon be weary and that the wind might probably chop about, I ventured to set up my little sail; and thus with the help of the tide I went at the rate of a league and a half an hour, as near as I could guess. My master and his friends continued on the shore till I was almost out of sight; and I often heard the sorrel nag (who always loved me) crying out, *Hnuy illa nyha maiah Yahoo*, Take care of thyself, gentle Yahoo.

My design was, if possible, to discover some small island uninhabited, yet sufficient by my labour to furnish me with necessaries of life; which I would have thought a greater happiness than to be first minister in the politest court of Europe, so horrible was the idea I conceived of returning to live in the society and under the government of Yahoos. For in such a solitude as I desired, I could at least enjoy my own thoughts and reflect with delight on the

1. That is, in 1715; in England, the legal year began on March 25 until 1753.

virtues of those inimitable Houyhnhnms, without any opportunity of degenerating into the vices and corruptions of my own species.

The reader may remember what I related when my crew conspired against
me and confined me to my cabin. How I continued there several weeks without knowing what course we took, and when I was put ashore in the long-boat
how the sailors told me with oaths, whether true or false, that they knew not
in what part of the world we were. However, I did then believe us to be about
ten degrees southward of the Cape of Good Hope, or about 45 degrees southern
latitude, as I gathered from some general words I overheard among them,
being, I supposed, to the southeast in their intended voyage to Madagascar.
And although this were but little better than conjecture, yet I resolved to steer
my course eastward, hoping to reach the southwest coast of New Holland,[2]
and perhaps some such island as I desired lying westward of it. The wind was
full west, and by six in the evening I computed I had gone eastward at least
eighteen leagues, when I spied a very small island about half a league off,
which I soon reached. It was nothing but a rock, with one creek, naturally
arched by the force of tempests. Here I put in my canoe and, climbing a part
of the rock, I could plainly discover land to the east, extending from south to
north. I lay all night in my canoe and, repeating my voyage early in the morning, I arrived in seven hours to the southeast point of New Holland. This
confirmed me in the opinion I have long entertained that the maps and charts
place this country at least three degrees more to the east than it really is; which
thought I communicated many years ago to my worthy friend Mr. Herman
Moll[3] and gave him my reasons for it, although he hath rather chosen to
follow other authors.

I saw no inhabitants in the place where I landed and, being unarmed, I was
afraid of venturing far into the country. I found some shellfish on the shore
and eat them raw, not daring to kindle a fire for fear of being discovered by
the natives. I continued three days feeding on oysters and limpets, to save
my own provisions, and I fortunately found a brook of excellent water, which
gave me great relief.

On the fourth day, venturing out early a little too far, I saw twenty or thirty
natives upon a height not above five hundred yards from me. They were stark
naked, men, women, and children, round a fire, as I could discover by the
smoke. One of them spied me and gave notice to the rest; five of them advanced towards me, leaving the women and children at the fire. I made what
haste I could to the shore and, getting into my canoe, shoved off: the savages,
observing me retreat, ran after me; and before I could get far enough into the
sea, discharged an arrow which wounded me deeply on the inside of my left
knee (I shall carry the mark to my grave). I apprehended the arrow might
be poisoned and, paddling out of the reach of their darts (being a calm day),
I made a shift to suck the wound and dress it as well as I could.

I was at a loss what to do, for I durst not return to the same landing-place,
but stood to the north, and was forced to paddle; for the wind, although very
gentle, was against me, blowing northwest. As I was looking about for a secure

2. Tasmania.

3. Herman Moll (d. 1732), a Dutch mapmaker who settled in England about 1698 and
whose maps became widely accepted there, providing the basis for the imaginary maps
that accompanied the original editions of *Gulliver's Travels*.

landing-place, I saw a sail to the north-northeast, which appearing every minute more visible, I was in some doubt whether I should wait for them or no; but at last my detestation of the Yahoo race prevailed and, turning my canoe, I sailed and paddled together to the south and got into the same creek from whence I set out in the morning, choosing rather to trust myself among these barbarians than live with European Yahoos. I drew up my canoe as close as I could to the shore and hid myself behind a stone by the little brook, which, as I have already said, was excellent water.

The ship came within a half a league of this creek, and sent out her long-boat with vessels to take in fresh water (for the place, it seems, was very well known), but I did not observe it until the boat was almost on shore and it was too late to seek another hiding-place. The seamen at their landing observed my canoe and, rummaging it all over, easily conjectured that the owner could not be far off. Four of them well armed searched every cranny and lurking-hole, till at last they found me flat on my face behind the stone. They gazed a while in admiration at my strange uncouth dress, my coat made of skins, my wooden-soled shoes, and my furred stockings; from whence, however, they concluded I was not a native of the place, who all go naked. One of the seamen in Portuguese bid me rise, and asked who I was. I understood that language very well and, getting upon my feet, said I was a poor Yahoo, banished from the Houyhnhnms, and desired they would please to let me depart. They admired to hear me answer them in their own tongue, and saw by my complexion I must be an European, but were at loss to know what I meant by Yahoos and Houyhnhnms; and at the same time fell a-laughing at my strange tone in speaking, which resembled the neighing of a horse. I trembled all the while betwixt fear and hatred: I again desired leave to depart and was gently moving to my canoe; but they laid hold on me, desiring to know what country I was of, whence I came, with many other questions. I told them I was born in England, from whence I came about five years ago, and then their country and ours were at peace. I therefore hoped they would not treat me as an enemy since I meant them no harm, but was a poor Yahoo seeking some desolate place where to pass the remainder of his unfortunate life.

When they began to talk, I thought I never heard or saw anything so un-natural; for it appeared to me as monstrous as if a dog or a cow should speak in England, or a Yahoo in Houyhnhnmland. The honest Portuguese were equally amazed at my strange dress and the odd manner of delivering my words, which however they understood very well. They spoke to me with great humanity and said they were sure their captain would carry me *gratis* to Lisbon, from whence I might return to my own country; that two of the seamen would go back to the ship, inform the captain of what they had seen, and receive his orders; in the meantime, unless I would give my solemn oath not to fly, they would secure me by force. I thought it best to comply with their proposal. They were very curious to know my story, but I gave them very little satisfaction; and they all conjectured that my misfortunes had impaired my reason. In two hours the boat, which went loaden with vessels of water, returned with the captain's commands to fetch me on board. I fell on my knees to preserve my liberty; but all was in vain, and the men, having tied me with cords, heaved me into the boat, from whence I was taken into the ship and from thence into the captain's cabin.

His name was Pedro de Mendez; he was a very courteous and generous person. He entreated me to give some account of myself, and desired to know what I would eat or drink; said I should be used as well as himself, and spoke so many obliging things that I wondered to find such civilities from a Yahoo. However, I remained silent and sullen; I was ready to faint at the very smell of him and his men. At last I desired something to eat out of my own canoe; but he ordered me a chicken and some excellent wine, and then directed that I should be put to bed in a very clean cabin. I would not undress myself but lay on the bed-clothes, and in half an hour stole out, when I thought the crew was at dinner, and getting to the side of the ship was going to leap into the sea and swim for my life rather than continue among Yahoos. But one of the seamen prevented me, and having informed the captain, I was chained to my cabin.

After dinner Don Pedro came to me and desired to know my reason for so desperate an attempt: assured me he only meant to do me all the service he was able, and spoke so very movingly that at last I descended to treat him like an animal which had some little portion of reason. I gave him a very short relation of my voyage, of the conspiracy against me by my own men, of the country where they set me on shore, and of my three years' residence there. All which he looked upon as if it were a dream or a vision; whereat I took great offence; for I had quite forgot the faculty of lying, so peculiar to Yahoos in all countries where they preside, and, consequently, the disposition of suspecting truth in others of their own species. I asked him whether it were the custom of his country to *say the thing that was not*. I assured him I had almost forgot what he meant by falsehood, and, if I had lived a thousand years in Houyhnhnmland, I should never have heard a lie from the meanest servant; that I was altogether indifferent whether he believed me or no; but however, in return for his favours, I would give so much allowance to the corruption of his nature as to answer any objection he would please to make, and he might easily discover the truth.

The captain, a wise man, after many endeavours to catch me tripping in some part of my story, at last began to have a better opinion of my veracity, and the rather because, he confessed, he met with a Dutch skipper, who pretended to have landed with five others of his crew upon a certain island or continent south of New Holland, where they went for fresh water, and observed a horse driving before him several animals exactly resembling those I described under the name of Yahoos, with some other particulars, which the captain said he had forgot, because he then concluded them all to be lies. But he added that since I professed so inviolable an attachment to truth, I must give him my word of honour to bear him company in this voyage without attempting anything against my life, or else he would continue me a prisoner till we arrived in Lisbon. I gave him the promise he required; but at the same time protested that I would suffer the greatest hardships rather than return to live among Yahoos.

Our voyage passed without any considerable accident. In gratitude to the captain I sometimes sat with him at his earnest request and strove to conceal my antipathy against humankind, although it often broke out, which he suffered to pass without observation. But the greatest part of the day I confined myself to my cabin to avoid seeing any of the crew. The captain had often entreated me to strip myself of my savage dress, and offered to lend me the best suit of clothes he had. This I would not be prevailed on to accept, abhorring to cover myself with anything that had been on the back of a Yahoo. I only desired he would lend me two clean shirts, which having been washed since he wore them, I believed would not so much defile me. These I changed every second day, and washed them myself.

We arrived at Lisbon, Nov. 5, 1715. At our landing the captain forced me to cover myself with his cloak, to prevent the rabble from crowding about me. I was conveyed to his own house, and, at my earnest request, he led me up to the highest room backwards.[4] I conjured him to conceal from all persons what I had told him of the Houyhnhnms, because the least hint of such a story would not only draw numbers of people to see me, but probably put me in danger of being imprisoned or burnt by the Inquisition. The captain persuaded me to accept a suit of clothes newly made, but I would not suffer the tailor to take my measure; however, Don Pedro being almost of my size, they fitted me well enough. He accoutred me with other necessaries all new, which I aired for twenty-four hours before I would use them.

The captain had no wife, nor above three servants, none of which were suffered to attend at meals, and his whole deportment was so obliging, added to very good *human* understanding, that I really began to tolerate his company. He gained so far upon me that I ventured to look out of the back window. By degrees I was brought into another room, from whence I peeped into the street, but drew my head back in a fright. In a week's time he seduced me down to the door. I found my terror gradually lessened, but my hatred and contempt seemed to increase. I was at last bold enough to walk the street in his company, but kept my nose well stopped with rue,[5] or sometimes with tobacco.

In ten days Don Pedro, to whom I had given some account of my domestic affairs, put it upon me as a point of honour and conscience that I ought to return to my native country and live at home with my wife and children. He told me there was an English ship in the port just ready to sail, and he would furnish me with all things necessary. It would be tedious to repeat his arguments and my contradictions. He said it was altogether impossible to find such a solitary island as I had desired to live in; but I might command in my own house and pass my time in a manner as recluse as I pleased.

I complied at last, finding I could not do better. I left Lisbon the 24th day of November in an English merchantman, but who was the master I never inquired. Don Pedro accompanied me to the ship and lent me twenty pounds. He took kind leave of me and embraced me at parting, which I bore as well as I could. During this last voyage I had no commerce with the master or any of his men, but pretending I was sick kept close in my cabin. On the fifth of December, 1715, we cast anchor in the Downs [6] about nine in the morning, and at three in the afternoon I got safe to my house at Redriff.[7]

4. At the back of the house.
5. A strong-scented herb.
6. An anchorage near Dover where ships might discharge passengers and take on pilots for the navigation of the Thames estuary.
7. Rotherhithe, the dock section of East London south of the Thames.

My wife and family received me with great surprise and joy, because they concluded me certainly dead; but I must freely confess the sight of them filled me only with hatred, disgust, and contempt, and the more by reflecting on the near alliance I had to them. For although, since my unfortunate exile from the Houyhnhnm country, I had compelled myself to tolerate the sight of Yahoos, and to converse with Don Pedro de Mendez, yet my memory and imaginations were perpetually filled with the virtues and ideas of those exalted Houyhnhnms. And when I began to consider that by copulating with one of the Yahoo species I had become a parent of more, it struck me with the utmost shame, confusion, and horror.

As soon as I entered the house, my wife took me in her arms and kissed me, at which, having not been used to the touch of that odious animal for so many years, I fell in a swoon for almost an hour. At the time I am writing it is five years since my last return to England: during the first year I could not endure my wife or children in my presence; the very smell of them was intolerable, much less could I suffer them to eat in the same room. To this hour they dare not presume to touch my bread or drink out of the same cup, neither was I ever able to let one of them take me by the hand. The first money I laid out was to buy two young stone-horses; [8] which I keep in a good stable, and next to them the groom is my greatest favourite; for I feel my spirits revived by the smell he contracts in the stable. My horses understand me tolerably well; I converse with them at least four hours every day. They are strangers to bridle or saddle; they live in great amity with me and friendship to each other.

Chapter Twelve: The author's veracity. His design in publishing this work. His censure of those travellers who swerve from the truth. The author clears himself from any sinister ends in writing. An objection answered. The method of planting colonies. His native country commended. The right of the Crown to those countries described by the author is justified. The difficulty of conquering them. The author takes his last leave of the reader, proposeth his manner of living for the future, gives good advice, and concludeth.

Thus, gentle reader, I have given thee a faithful history of my travels for sixteen years and above seven months, wherein I have not been so studious of ornament as of truth. I could perhaps like others have astonished thee with strange improbable tales; but I rather chose to relate plain matter of fact in the simplest manner and style, because my principal design was to inform and not to amuse thee.

It is easy for us who travel into remote countries, which are seldom visited by Englishmen or other Europeans, to form descriptions of wonderful animals both at sea and land; whereas a traveller's chief aim should be to make men wiser and better and to improve their minds by the bad as well as good example of what they deliver concerning foreign places.

I could heartily wish a law were enacted that every traveller, before he were permitted to publish his voyages, should be obliged to make oath before the Lord High Chancellor that all he intended to print was absolutely true

8. Stallions.

to the best of his knowledge; for then the world would no longer be deceived as it usually is while some writers, to make their works pass the better upon the public, impose the grossest falsities on the unwary reader. I have perused several books of travels with great delight in my younger days; but having since gone over most parts of the globe and been able to contradict many fabulous accounts from my own observation, it hath given me a great disgust against this part of reading, and some indignation to see the credulity of mankind so impudently abused. Therefore since my acquaintance were pleased to think my poor endeavours might not be unacceptable to my country, I imposed on myself as a maxim, never to be swerved from, that I would *strictly adhere to truth;* neither indeed can I be ever under the least temptation to vary from it, while I retain in my mind the lectures and example of my noble master and the other illustrious Houyhnhnms, of whom I had so long the honour to be an humble hearer.

—Nec si miserum Fortuna Sinonem
Finxit, vanum etiam mendacemque improba finget.[1]

I know very well how little reputation is to be got by writings which require neither genius nor learning, nor indeed any other talent, except a good memory or an exact journal. I know likewise that writers of travels, like dictionary-makers, are sunk into oblivion by the weight and bulk of those who come last and therefore lie uppermost. And it is highly probable that such travellers who shall hereafter visit the countries described in this work of mine, may, by detecting my errors (if there be any) and adding many new discoveries of their own, jostle me out of vogue and stand in my place, making the world forget that ever I was an author. This indeed would be too great a mortification if I wrote for fame: but, as my sole intention was the *public good,*[2] I cannot be altogether disappointed. For who can read of the virtues I have mentioned in the glorious Houyhnhnms without being ashamed of his own vices, when he considers himself as the reasoning, governing animal of his country? I shall say nothing of those remote nations where Yahoos preside, amongst which the least corrupted are the Brobdingnagians, whose wise maxims in morality and government it would be our happiness to observe. But I forbear descanting further and rather leave the judicious reader to his own remarks and applications.

I am not a little pleased that this work of mine can possibly meet with no censurers: for what objections can be made against a writer who relates only plain facts that happened in such distant countries, where we have not the least interest with respect either to trade or negotiations? I have carefully avoided every fault with which common writers of travels are often too justly charged. Besides, I meddle not the least with any *party,* but write without passion, prejudice, or ill-will against any man or number of men whatsoever.

1. "Nor, if false Fortune has made Sinon wretched, shall she make him empty and deceitful as well," Virgil, *Aeneid* II.79–80; but Sinon is the treacherous Greek who is about to persuade the Trojans to admit the wooden horse into their city.
2. Often a suspect claim (cf. the opening of *A Modest Proposal*) on the grounds of outright hypocrisy or zealous self-deception; Gulliver's pride is implied, however genuine his sincerity.

I write for the noblest end, to inform and instruct mankind, over whom I may, without breach of modesty, pretend to some superiority from the advantages I received by conversing so long among the most accomplished Houyhnhnms. I write without any view towards profit or praise. I never suffer a word to pass that may look like reflection or possibly give the least offence even to those who are most ready to take it. So that I hope I may with justice pronounce myself an author perfectly blameless, against whom the tribes of answerers, considerers, observers, reflecters, detecters, remarkers,[3] will never be able to find matter for exercising their talents.

I confess it was whispered to me that I was bound in duty, as a subject of England, to have given in a memorial to a secretary of state at my first coming over; because whatever lands are discovered by a subject belong to the Crown. But I doubt whether our conquests in the countries I treat of would be as easy as those of Ferdinando Cortez over the naked Americans.[4] The Lilliputians, I think, are hardly worth the charge of a fleet and army to reduce them, and I question whether it might be prudent or safe to attempt the Brobdingnagians. Or whether an English army would be much at their ease with the Flying Island over their heads. The Houyhnhnms, indeed, appear not to be so well prepared for war, a science to which they are perfect strangers, and especially against missive weapons.[5] However, supposing myself to be a minister of state, I could never give my advice for invading them. Their prudence, unanimity, unacquaintedness with fear, and their love of their country would amply supply all defects in the military art. Imagine twenty thousand of them breaking into the midst of an European army, confounding the ranks, overturning the carriages,[6] battering the warriors' faces into mummy[7] by terrible yerks[8] from their hinder hoofs. For they would well deserve the character given to Augustus: *Recalcitrat undique tutus.*[9] But instead of proposals for conquering that magnanimous[10] nation, I rather wish they were in a capacity or disposition to send a sufficient number of their inhabitants for civilizing Europe, by teaching us the first principles of honour, justice, truth, temperance, public spirit, fortitude, chastity, friendship, benevolence, and fidelity. The *names* of all which virtues are still retained among us in most languages and are to be met with in modern as well as ancient authors; which I am able to assert from my own small reading.

But I had another reason which made me less forward to enlarge his Majesty's dominions by my discoveries. To say the truth, I had conceived a few scruples with relation to the distributive justice of princes upon those occasions. For instance, a crew of pirates are driven by a storm they know not whither, at length a boy discovers land from the topmast, they go on

3. The usual terms by which authors of hostile replies were designated.
4. Cortez succeeded so easily in his conquest of Mexico (1519) because the Aztecs were awed by the ships and firearms of the Spaniards and by the fact that they were mounted on horses.
5. Those thrown or shot, rather than hand weapons.
6. Gun carriages.
7. Pulp.
8. Kicks.
9. "He kicks back with safety on every side." Horace, *Satires* II.i.20.
10. Large-souled, noble.

shore to rob and plunder, they see an harmless people, are entertained with kindness, they give the country a new name, they take formal possession of it for the king, they set up a rotten plank or a stone for a memorial, they murder two or three dozen of the natives, bring away a couple more by force for a sample, return home, and get their pardon. Here commences a new dominion acquired with a title by *divine right*.[11] Ships are sent with the first opportunity, the natives driven out or destroyed, their princes tortured to discover their gold, a free license given to all acts of inhumanity and lust, the earth reeking with the blood of its inhabitants: and this execrable crew of butchers employed in so pious an expedition is a *modern colony* sent to convert and civilize an idolatrous and barbarous people.

But this description, I confess, doth by no means affect the British nation, who may be an example to the whole world for their wisdom, care, and justice in planting colonies; their liberal endowments for the advancement of religion and learning; their choice of devout and able pastors to propagate Christianity; their caution in stocking their provinces with people of sober lives and conversations from this, the mother kingdom; [12] their strict regard to the distribution of justice in supplying the civil administration through all their colonies with officers of the greatest abilities, utter strangers to corruption; and to crown all, by sending the most vigilant and virtuous governors, who have no other views than the happiness of the people over whom they preside, and the honour of the king their master.

But as those countries which I have described do not appear to have any desire of being conquered and enslaved, murdered, or driven out by colonies, nor abound either in gold, silver, sugar, or tobacco; I did humbly conceive they were by no means proper objects of our zeal, our valour, or our interest. However, if those whom it more concerns think fit to be of another opinion, I am ready to depose, when I shall be lawfully called, that no European did ever visit these countries before me. I mean, if the inhabitants ought to be believed; unless a dispute may arise about the two Yahoos, said to have been seen many ages ago on a mountain in Houyhnhnmland, from whence, the opinion is, that the race of those brutes hath descended; and these, for anything I know, may have been English, which indeed I was apt to suspect from the lineaments of their posterity's countenances, although very much defaced. But how far that will go to make out a title, I leave to the learned in colony-law.

But as to the formality of taking possession in my sovereign's name, it never came once into my thoughts; and if it had, yet as my affairs then stood, I should perhaps, in point of prudence and self-preservation, have put it off to a better opportunity.

Having thus answered the *only* objection that can be raised against me as a traveller, I here take a final leave of my courteous readers, and return to enjoy my own speculations in my little garden at Redriff, to apply those excellent lessons of virtue which I learned among the Houyhnhnms, to instruct the

11. The doctrine of divine right of kings (discussed earlier by Halifax and Dryden) had been current in England since James I and was defended by many so long as the Stuarts held the throne; here it is applied to the specious justification of rule by conquest, as it had been by Spain in the New World.
12. Transportation to the colonies was an alternative to hanging for many serious crimes, and it was used to supply the colonists with a labor force.

Yahoos of my own family as far as I shall find them docible [13] animals, to behold my figure often in a glass, and thus if possible habituate myself by time to tolerate the sight of a human creature; to lament the brutality [14] of Houyhnhnms in my own country, but always treat their persons with respect for the sake of my noble master, his family, his friends, and the whole Houyhnhnm race, whom these of ours have the honour to resemble in all their lineaments, however their intellectuals came to degenerate.

I began last week to permit my wife to sit at dinner with me, at the farthest end of a long table, and to answer (but with the utmost brevity) the few questions I asked her. Yet the smell of a Yahoo continuing very offensive, I always keep my nose well stopped with rue, lavender, or tobacco leaves. And although it be hard for a man late in life to remove old habits, I am not altogether out of hopes in some time to suffer a neighbour Yahoo in my company without the apprehensions I am yet under of his teeth or his claws.

My reconcilement to the Yahoo-kind in general might not be so difficult if they would be content with those vices and follies only which nature hath entitled them to. I am not in the least provoked at the sight of a lawyer, a pickpocket, a colonel, a fool, a lord, a gamester, a politician, a whoremonger, a physician, an evidence,[15] a suborner, an attorney, a traitor, or the like; this is all according to the due course of things: but when I behold a lump of deformity and diseases both in body and mind, smitten with *pride,* it immediately breaks all the measures of my patience; neither shall I be ever able to comprehend how such an animal and such a vice could tally together. The wise and virtuous Houyhnhnms, who abound in all excellencies that can adorn a rational creature, have no name for this vice in their language, which hath no terms to express anything that is evil except those whereby they describe the detestable qualities of their Yahoos, among which they were not able to distinguish this of pride, for want of thoroughly understanding human nature as it showeth itself in other countries where that animal presides. But I, who had more experience, could plainly observe some rudiments of it among the wild Yahoos.

But the Houyhnhnms, who live under the government of reason, are no more proud of the good qualities they possess than I should be for not wanting a leg or an arm; which no man in his wits would boast of, although he must be miserable without them. I dwell the longer upon this subject from the desire I have to make the society of an English Yahoo by any means not insupportable, and therefore I here entreat those who have any tincture of this absurd vice that they will not presume to appear in my sight.

1726

A Letter from Capt. Gulliver to His Cousin Sympson [1]

I hope you will be ready to own publicly, whenever you shall be called to it, that by your great and frequent urgency you prevailed on me to publish a

---

13. Teachable.
14. That is, animality.
15. Paid informer.

1. This letter first appeared in Faulkner's edition of 1735 and was probably written close to that year rather than in 1727, as it was dated; Sympson was the fictitious name under which negotiations were first made to publish the book.

very loose and uncorrect account of my travels; with direction to hire some young gentlemen of either university to put them in order and correct the style, as my cousin Dampier did by my advice, in his book called *A Voyage Round the World*.[2] But I do not remember I gave you power to consent that anything should be omitted, and much less that anything should be inserted: [3] therefore, as to the latter, I do here renounce everything of that kind; particularly a paragraph about her Majesty, the late Queen Anne, of most pious and glorious memory; although I did reverence and esteem her more than any of human species. But you or your interpolator ought to have considered that, as it was not my inclination, so was it not decent to praise any animal of our composition [4] before my master Houyhnhnm: and besides, the fact was altogether false; for to my knowledge, being in England during some part of her Majesty's reign, she did govern by a chief minister; nay, even by two successively; the first whereof was the Lord of Godolphin, and the second the Lord of Oxford; [5] so that you have made me *say the thing that was not*. Likewise, in the account of the Academy of Projectors and several passages of my discourse to my master Houyhnhnm, you have either omitted some material circumstances, or minced or changed them in such a manner that I do hardly know mine own work. When I formerly hinted to you something of this in a letter, you were pleased to answer that you were afraid of giving offence; that people in power were very watchful over the press and apt not only to interpret but to punish everything which looked like an *innuendo* (as I think you called it). But pray, how could that which I spoke so many years ago and at above five thousand leagues distance, in another reign, be applied to any of the Yahoos who now are said to govern the herd,[6] especially at a time when I little thought on or feared the unhappiness of living under them? Have not I the most reason to complain when I see these very Yahoos carried by Houyhnhnms in a vehicle, as if these were brutes and those the rational creatures? And, indeed, to avoid so monstrous and detestable a sight was one principal motive of my retirement hither.

Thus much I thought proper to tell you in relation to your self and to the trust I reposed in you.

I do in the next place complain of my own great want of judgment in being prevailed upon by the intreaties and false reasonings of you and some others, very much against mine own opinion, to suffer my travels to be published. Pray bring to your mind how often I desired you to consider, when you insisted on the motive of public good, that the Yahoos were a species of animals utterly incapable of amendment by precepts or examples, and so it hath proved; for instead of seeing a full stop put to all abuses and corruptions, at least in this little island, as I had reason to expect: behold, after above six

2. William Dampier (1652–1715), whose very popular work *A New Voyage Round the World* appeared in 1697 and is often parodied in *Gulliver's Travels*.
3. As was done, to moderate the satire, by the first publisher, Benjamin Motte.
4. Kind.
5. The 1st Earl of Godolphin from 1702 until 1710; thereafter Robert Harley, 1st Earl of Oxford and the friend of Swift and Pope, until 1714.
6. An ironic reference to the highly topical satire against Walpole and the court of George I that runs through the book.

months' warning, I cannot learn that my book hath produced one single effect according to mine intentions. I desired you would let me know by a letter when party and faction were extinguished; judges learned and upright; pleaders honest and modest, with some tincture of common sense; and Smithfield [7] blazing with pyramids of law-books; the young nobility's education entirely changed; the physicians banished; the female Yahoos abounding in virtue, honour, truth and good sense; courts and levees of great ministers thoroughly weeded and swept; wit, merit and learning rewarded; all disgracers of the press in prose and verse condemned to eat nothing but their own cotton [8] and quench their thirst with their own ink. These and a thousand other reformations I firmly counted upon by your encouragement, as indeed they were plainly deducible from the precepts delivered in my book. And it must be owned that seven months were a sufficient time to correct every vice and folly to which Yahoos are subject, if their natures had been capable of the least disposition to virtue or wisdom; yet so far have you been from answering mine expectation in any of your letters, that on the contrary you are loading our carrier every week with libels, and keys, and reflections, and memoirs, and second parts; wherein I see myself accused of reflecting upon great statesfolk; of degrading human nature (for so they have still the confidence to style it), and of abusing the female sex. I find likewise that the writers of those bundles are not agreed among themselves; for some of them will not allow me to be author of mine own travels, and others make me author of books to which I am wholly a stranger.[9]

I find likewise that your printer hath been so careless as to confound the times and mistake the dates of my several voyages and returns, neither assigning the true year or the true month or day of the month; and I hear the original manuscript is all destroyed since the publication of my book. Neither have I any copy left; however, I have sent you some corrections, which you may insert if ever there should be a second edition: and yet I cannot stand to [10] them, but shall leave that matter to my judicious and candid readers to adjust it as they please.

I hear some of our sea-Yahoos find fault with my sea-language, as not proper in many parts nor now in use. I cannot help it. In my first voyages, while I was young, I was instructed by the oldest mariners and learned to speak as they did. But I have since found that the sea-Yahoos are apt, like the land ones, to become new-fangled in their words; which the latter change every year, insomuch as I remember upon each return to mine own country, their old dialect was so altered that I could hardly understand the new. And I observe, when any Yahoo comes from London out of curiosity to visit me at mine own house, we neither of us are able to deliver our conceptions in a manner intelligible to the other.

7. The London cattle market where heretics and murderers had been burned; Gulliver seems to call for a burning of false books such as Savonarola conducted in 15th-century Florence and the Inquisition did later.
8. Paper.
9. Referring to the numerous spurious "continuations" and imitations, as well as a "complete key."
10. Insist upon.

If the censure of Yahoos could any way affect me, I should have great reason to complain that some of them are so bold as to think my book of travels a mere fiction out of mine own brain; and have gone so far as to drop hints that the Houyhnhnms and Yahoos have no more existence than the inhabitants of Utopia.[11]

Indeed I must confess, that as to the people of Lilliput, Brobdingrag (for so the word should have been spelt, and not erroneously *Brobdingnag*), and Laputa, I have never yet heard of any Yahoo so presumptuous as to dispute their being or the facts I have related concerning them; because the truth immediately strikes every reader with conviction. And is there less probability in my account of the Houyhnhnms or Yahoos when it is manifest as to the latter, there are so many thousands even in this city who only differ from their brother brutes in Houyhnhnmland because they use a sort of a jabber and do not go naked? I wrote for their amendment and not their approbation. The united praise of the whole race would be of less consequence to me than the neighing of those two degenerate Houyhnhnms I keep in my stable; because from these, degenerate as they are, I still improve in some virtues, without any mixture of vice.

Do these miserable animals presume to think that I am so far degenerated as to defend my veracity? Yahoo as I am, it is well known through all Houyhnhnmland that, by the instructions and example of my illustrious master, I was able in the compass of two years (although I confess with the utmost difficulty) to remove that infernal habit of lying, shuffling, deceiving, and equivocating so deeply rooted in the very souls of all my species, especially the Europeans.

I have other complaints to make upon this vexatious occasion; but I forbear troubling myself or you any further. I must freely confess that since my last return some corruptions of my Yahoo nature have revived in me by conversing with a few of your species, and particularly those of mine own family, by an unavoidable necessity; else I should never have attempted so absurd a project as that of reforming the Yahoo race in this kingdom; but I have now done with all such visionary schemes forever.

1735

From John Gay and Alexander Pope: Mary Gulliver to Captain Lemuel Gulliver

Welcome, thrice welcome to thy native place!
—What, touch me not? what, shun a wife's embrace?
Have I for this thy tedious absence borne
And waked and wished whole nights for thy return?
In five long years I took no second spouse;
What Redriff wife so long hath kept her vows?
Your eyes, your nose, inconstancy betray;

11. Utopia (from the Greek for "nowhere") was the name Sir Thomas More gave to his "ideal" commonwealth, and his great ironic work (1516) immensely influenced Swift.

Your nose you stop, your eyes you turn away.
'Tis said, that thou shouldst cleave unto thy wife;
10 Once *thou* didst cleave, and *I* could cleave for life.
Hear and relent! hark, how thy children moan;
Be kind at least to these, they are thy own:
Behold, and count them all; secure to find
The honest number that you left behind.
See how they pat thee with their pretty paws:
Why start you? are they snakes? or have they claws?
Thy Christian seed, our mutual flesh and bone:
Be kind at least to these, they are thy own.

.   .   .

My bed (the scene of all our former joys,
40 Witness two lovely girls, two lovely boys)
Alone I press; in dreams I call my dear,
I stretch my hand, no Gulliver is there!
I wake, I rise, and shivering with the frost,
Search all the house; my Gulliver is lost!
Forth in the street I rush with frantic cries:
The windows open; all the neighbours rise:
Where sleeps my Gulliver? *O tell me where?*
The neighbours answer, *With the sorrel mare.*

At early morn, I to the market haste,
50 (Studious in everything to please thy taste)
A curious fowl and sparagrass I chose,
(For I remember you were fond of those),
Three shillings cost the first, the last seven groats;
Sullen you turn from both, and call for *oats.*

.   .   .

Nay, would kind *Jove* my organs so dispose,
To hymn harmonious *Houyhnhnm* through the nose,
I'd call thee *Houyhnhnm,* that high sounding name,
Thy children's noses all should twang the same,
So might I find my loving spouse of course
110 Endued with all the virtues of a horse.

1727

THE MOCK FORM

One of the opportunities the poet gains from a clearly formalized set of genres and from clearly articulated levels of style (we can see the two related to each other and to the levels of society as well by Thomas Hobbes in his *Answer to Davenant's Preface to Gondibert*) is that of playing upon or against the forms. We can see this most clearly in mock-heroic poetry, where the style is highest and achieves its elevation by exclusion; the grand style, especially in the eighteenth century, strives for generality and repudiates the time-bound particular. In his "ironical discourse," for example, Sir Joshua Reynolds scornfully proposes that the sculptor's model be carefully dressed in the latest fashion by his tailor; the next step, he adds, would be "to add colour to these statues, which will complete the deception. . . ." Pope, it is true, defends "small circumstances" (in the farewell of Hector) against the tyrannic view that "a poet ought only to collect the great and noble particulars," but he defends them insofar as they are significantly characteristic. "The question," as he puts it in the Postscript in the *Odyssey* (1726), "is how far a poet, in pursuing a description or image of an action, can attach himself to little circumstances without vulgarity or trifling."

In travesty the poet dresses (*trans-vestire*) a high subject in low costume; in mock heroic he dresses a low subject in high style. In both cases he creates a deliberate incongruity between subject and form and points up the artificiality of the form. This may work both ways: he may remind us how much of human complexity and sheer physical circumstance is excluded by high forms, how vacuous they may become as they move toward the academic and attain a rigid pomposity; or he may remind us how far our present world, caught in its up-to-the-minute modishness or all its embarrassment of particulars, falls below the heroic simplicity of the past or the persistent vision of human greatness. As Dr. Johnson says of John Philips's *The Splendid Shilling*, "to degrade the sounding words of Milton by an application to the lowest and most trivial things gratifies the mind with a momentary triumph over that grandeur which hitherto held its captives in admiration. . . ." Such a poem as Philips's is not an attack upon Milton any more than Pope's *Rape of the Lock* is an attack upon epic; each poem plays with the nature of our imagination and explores its capacity for creating myth, exposing its workings with affection as well as "triumph." In Butler's *Hudibras* the burlesque techniques work to degrade their subject, which is not given even playful dignity by the romance and heroic elements; these serve, instead, to define lunatic pretensions as they are fused with the grubbiest of physical detail.

In *The Shepherd's Week* Gay mocks Ambrose Philips's effort to make the pastoral realistic. Pope had described that form (with Virgil as his model) as "an image of what they call the Golden Age." We are "not to describe our shepherds as shepherds at this day really are"—for that would be to literalize myth—"but as they may be conceived then to have been when the best of men followed the employment." Philips (invoking Theocritus and Spenser) produced something closer to literal shepherds speaking their modern version of a Doric dialect, and Pope ironically commended his "simplicity." For "simplicity" remains throughout the age a key word. Both Swift and Pope are anxious to protect its meaning from mere lack of refinement or art; it must not be slovenliness or the merely "primitive" any more than it can be precious and too conspicuously artificial. It is art concealing art, like the "natural," neither gross nor infantile, but characteristic of man at his fullest and most mature. Gay's *Shepherd's Week* sets out to ridicule Philips's misplaced realism, and in that it succeeds admirably (creating a group of low rustics who undermine the mythical forms in which they are placed); but he also moves—as the satirist does—into a realism that begins to win our respect by displacing value from the mythical and literary to the actual and literal. As Dr. Johnson puts it,

> the effect of reality and truth became conspicuous, even when the intention was to show them grovelling and degraded. These Pastorals became popular and were read with delight as just representations of rural manners and occupations by those who had no interest in the rivalry of the poets nor knowledge of the critical dispute.

That is an overstatement, for no degree of ignorance of the critical dispute can blind us to the tellingly low aspect of Gay's figures, but the poems became an interesting case of the generation of a new vision from the conflict of older forms.

Something of the same sort may be seen in the two poems on Baucis and Philemon. Dryden's translation of Ovid somewhat intensifies the comic charm of the humble household, which is conceived in its very absence of grandeur (but is given equivalent nobility in its warmth of hospitality). But such tendencies as Dryden may have to sentimentalize the humble old couple and to elevate their good nature are undercut by Swift's brisker version, which lowers the characters and plays elaborately on the machinery of metamorphosis. His Baucis and Philemon are hardly allowed the dignity that their goodness warrants; they carry their commonplaceness into new guises, and even their death loses the tenderness of Dryden's duet.

One can take this further. The life of retirement is often set against the heroic and celebrated in the age in poems of country life, close in spirit to the pastorals or georgics of Virgil and often drawing their inspiration from them. Here again the temptation is great to sentimentalize, to claim for the absence of worldly greatness the implicit glories of a greater goodness. Matthew Prior's *An Epitaph* takes as its epigraph a famous chorus from Seneca's *Thyestes,* which became one of the key texts for the life of retirement (we can see it echoed at the close of Pope's *Epistle to Dr. Arbuthnot,* for example). It is given here in Andrew Marvell's translation, and it must be put beside the banal life of moral vacuity Prior offers in its place.

JOHN PHILIPS
1676–1709

From The Splendid Shilling

An Imitation of Milton°

Happy the man who, void of cares and strife,
In silken or in leathern purse retains
A Splendid Shilling: he nor hears with pain
New oysters cried, nor sighs for cheerful ale;
But with his friends, when nightly mists arise,
To Juniper's, Magpie, or Town Hall° repairs:
Where, mindful of the nymph whose wanton eye
Transfixed his soul and kindled amorous flames,
Chloe or Phyllis, he each circling glass
10   Wisheth her health and joy and equal love.
Meanwhile he smokes, and laughs at merry tale,
Or pun ambiguous, or conundrum quaint.

An Imitation of Milton Philips read Milton with great pleasure (according to legend, while his long hair was being combed) at Westminster and later at Oxford, and he finally abandoned the study of medicine for a literary career. *The Splendid Shilling* (which Addison regarded as the "finest burlesque poem in the English language") won him Tory patronage. In addition to political poems he wrote an imitation of Virgil's *Georgics* in Miltonic blank verse, the influential poem *Cyder.*
Juniper's . . . Town Hall The first may be the name of an innkeeper; the others were Oxford alehouses.

But I, whom griping penury surrounds,
And hunger, sure attendant upon want,
With scanty offals,° and small acid tiff°
(Wretched repast!) my meagre corpse sustain:
Then solitary walk, or doze at home
In garret vile, and with a warming puff
Regale chilled fingers; or from tube as black
20   As winter chimney or well polished jet
Exhale mundungus,° ill-perfuming scent:
Not blacker tube nor of a shorter size
Smokes Cambro-Briton° (versed in pedigree,
Sprung from Cadwalader and Arthur, kings
Full famous in romantic tale) when he
O'er many a craggy hill and barren cliff,
Upon a cargo of famed Cestrian° cheese
High over-shadowing rides, with a design
To vend his wares, or at the Arvonian° mart,
30   Or Maridunum,° or the ancient town
Yclept Brechinia,° or where Vaga's stream°
Encircles Ariconium,° fruitful soil,
Whence flow nectareous wines, that well may vie
With Massic, Setin, or renowned Falern.°

    Thus while my joyless minutes tedious flow
With looks demure and silent pace, a dun,°
Horrible monster! hated by gods and men,
To my aerial citadel ascends;
With vocal heel thrice thundering at my gates,
40   With hideous accent thrice he calls; I know
The voice ill-boding and the solemn sound.
What should I do? or whither turn? Amazed,
Confounded, to the dark recess I fly
Of woodhole; straight my bristling hairs erect
Through sudden fear; a chilly sweat bedews
My shuddering limbs, and, wonderful to tell,
My tongue forgets her faculty of speech,
So horrible he seems; his faded brow
Entrenched with many a frown and conic beard
50   And spreading band,° admired by modern saints,
Disastrous acts forebode; in his right hand
Long scrolls of paper solemnly he waves,
With characters and figures dire inscribed
Grievous to mortal eyes; (ye gods avert
Such plagues from righteous men!) behind him stalks

offals fragments
tiff poor or weak liquor
mundungus strong-smelling tobacco
Cambro-Briton Welshman
Cestrian Cheshire
Arvonian at Carnarvon
Maridunum Camarthen in Wales
Yclept Brechinia named Brecon

Vaga's stream the river Wye
Ariconium Kenchester
Massic . . . Falern old Italian wines from
Monte Massico, Satia, or the Falernian Field in
Campania
dun bill collector
band strips hanging from the collar, associated
with clerical dress (as in Geneva bands)

Another monster, not unlike himself,
Sullen of aspect, by the vulgar called
A catchpole,° whose polluted hands the gods
With force incredible and magic charms
60   Erst have indued; if he his ample palm
Should haply on ill-fated shoulder lay
Of debtor, straight his body to the touch
Obsequious,° as whilom° knights were wont,
To some enchanted castle is conveyed,
Where gates impregnable and coercive chains
In durance strict detain him, till in form
Of money Pallas sets the captive free.

.   .   .

Thus do I live from pleasure quite debarred,
Nor taste the fruits that the sun's genial rays
Mature, John-apple,° nor the downy peach,
Nor walnut in rough-furrowed coat secure,
Nor medlar,° fruit delicious in decay.
120 Afflictions great! yet greater still remain:
My galligaskins° that have long withstood
The winter's fury and encroaching frosts,
By time subdued, (what will not time subdue!)
An horrid chasm disclose, with orifice
Wide, discontinuous; at which the winds
Eurus and Auster,° and the dreadful force
Of Boreas,° that congeals the Cronian° waves,
Tumultuous enter with dire chilling blasts
Portending agues. Thus a well-fraught ship
130 Long sailed secure, or through the Aegean deep,
Or the Ionian, till cruising near
The Lilybean° shore, with hideous crush
On Scylla or Charybdis,° dangerous rocks,
She strikes rebounding, whence the shattered oak,
So fierce a shock unable to withstand,
Admits the sea; in at the gaping side
The crowding waves gush with impetuous rage,
Resistless, overwhelming; horrors seize
The mariners, death in their eyes appears,
140 They stare, they lave, they pump, they swear, they pray:
Vain efforts! still the battering waves rush in
Implacable, till deluged by the foam,
The ship sinks foundering in the vast abyss.

1701

---

catchpole officer who arrests for debt; bum-
bailiff
Obsequious fully yielding, freely following
whilom formerly
John-apple a "keeping apple" that lasts two
years and is at its best when shriveled
medlar eaten only when overripe
galligaskins breeches

Eurus and Auster east and south winds
Boreas north wind
Cronian Arctic, as in *Paradise Lost* X.290
Lilybean Sicilian
Scylla or Charybdis the mythical monsters here
identified with the rocks on the east coast of
Sicily and the west of Italy

JOHN GAY

From The Shepherd's Week°

Wednesday; or, The Dumps°

The wailings of a maiden I recite,
A maiden fair that Sparabella° hight.
Such strains ne'er warble in the linnet's throat,
Nor the gay goldfinch chaunts so sweet a note.
No magpie chattered, nor the painted jay,
No ox was heard to low, nor ass to bray.
No rustling breezes played the leaves among,
While thus her madrigal° the damsel sung.
   A while, O D'Urfey,° lend an ear or twain,
10 Nor, though in homely guise, my verse disdain;
Whether thou seekest new kingdoms in the sun,°
Whether thy muse does at Newmarket° run,
Or does with gossips at a feast regale,
And heighten her conceits with sack° and ale,
Or else at wakes with Joan and Hodge° rejoice,
Where D'Urfey's lyrics swell in every voice;
Yet suffer me, thou bard of wondrous meed,°
Amid thy bays to weave this rural weed.
   Now the sun drove adown the western road,
20 And oxen laid at rest forget the goad,
The clown° fatigued trudged homeward with his spade,
Across the meadows stretched the lengthened shade;
When Sparabella pensive and forlorn,
Alike with yearning love and labour worn,
Leaned on her rake, and straight with doleful guise
Did this sad plaint in moanful notes devise.
   'Come night as dark as pitch, surround my head,
From Sparabella Bumkinet is fled;
The ribbon that his valorous cudgel won,
30 'Last Sunday happier Clumsilis put on.
Sure if he'd eyes (but Love, they say, has none)
I whilom by that ribbon had been known.
Ah, well-a-day! I'm shent° with baneful smart,

Th Shepherd's Week See the Headnote on John Gay for his career; for selections from *Trivia* (1716), see The Urban Scene.
Dumps "Dumps, or Dumbs, made use of to express a fit of the sullens" (Gay, who goes on to provide an elaborate piece of mock-pedantic etymology in the manner of E.K.'s notes to Spenser's *The Shepherd's Calendar*, Ambrose Philips's chief model)
Sparabella the first of Gay's distortions of conventional rustic or pastoral names, here Clarabella given a note of sexual license from the notoriously lecherous sparrow
madrigal love lyric

D'Urfey the popular song writer Thomas D'Urfey (1653–1723), from whom Gay draws in *The Beggar's Opera*
new . . . sun referring to D'Urfey's "opera" *Wonders in the Sun* (1706)
Newmarket the scene of horse races celebrated by D'Urfey in a well-known song
sack dry white wine
Joan and Hodge stock names for rural figures
meed "an old word for fame or renown" (Gay)
clown peasant, bumpkin
shent "an old word signifying *hurt* or harmed" (Gay)

For with the ribbon he bestowed his heart.
   'My plaint, ye lasses, with this burthen aid,
'Tis hard so true a damsel dies a maid.
   'Shall heavy Clumsilis with me compare?
View this, ye lovers, and like me despair.
Her blubbered lip by smutty pipes is worn,
40   And in her breath tobacco whiffs are borne;
The cleanly cheese-press she could never turn,
Her awkward fist did ne'er employ the churn;
If e'er she brewed, the drink would straight go sour,
Before it ever felt the thunder's power:°
No huswifry the dowdy creature knew;
To sum up all, her tongue confessed the shrew.
   'My plaint, ye lasses, with this burthen aid,
'Tis hard so true a damsel dies a maid.
   'I've often seen my visage in yon lake,
50   Nor are my features of the homeliest make.
Though Clumsilis may boast a whiter dye,
Yet the black sloe turns in my rolling eye;
And fairest blossoms drop with every blast,
But the brown beauty will like hollies last.
Her wan complexion's like the withered leek,
While Katherine pears adorn my ruddy cheek.
Yet she, alas! the witless lout hath won,
And by her gain, poor Sparabell's undone!
Let hares and hounds in coupling straps unite,
60   The clucking hen make friendship with the kite,
Let the fox simply wear the nuptial noose,
And join in wedlock with the waddling goose,
For love hath brought a stranger thing to pass,
The fairest shepherd weds the foulest lass.
   'My plaint, ye lasses, with this burthen aid,
'Tis hard so true a damsel dies a maid.
   'Sooner shall cats disport in waters clear,
And speckled mackerels graze the meadows fair,
Sooner shall screech-owls bask in sunny day,
70   And the slow ass on trees, like squirrels, play,
Sooner shall snails on insect pinions rove,
Then I forget my shepherd's wonted love.
   'My plaint, ye lasses, with this burthen aid,
'Tis hard so true a damsel dies a maid.
   'Ah! didst thou know what proffers I withstood,
When late I met the Squire in yonder wood!
To me he sped, regardless of his game,
While all my cheek was glowing red with shame;
My lip he kissed, and praised my healthful look,

thunder's power to sour liquids

80 Then from his purse of silk a guinea took,
    Into my hand he forced the tempting gold,
    While I with modest struggling broke his hold.
    He swore that Dick in livery striped with lace,
    Should wed me soon to keep me from disgrace;
    But I nor footman prized nor golden fee,
    For what is lace or gold compared to thee?
        'My plaint, ye lasses, with this burthen aid,
    'Tis hard so true a damsel dies a maid.
        'Now plain I ken whence Love his rise begun.
90 Sure he was born some bloody butcher's son,
    Bred up in shambles,° where our younglings° slain,
    Erst taught him mischief and to sport with pain.
    The father only silly sheep annoys,
    The son the sillier shepherdess destroys.
    Does son or father greater mischief do?
    The sire is cruel, so the son is too.
        'My plaint, ye lasses, with this burthen aid,
    'Tis hard so true a damsel dies a maid.
        'Farewell, ye woods, ye meads, ye streams that flow;
100 A sudden death shall rid me of my woe.
    This penknife keen my windpipe shall divide.
    What, shall I fall as squeaking pigs have died!
    No—To some tree this carcass I'll suspend.
    But worrying curs find such untimely end!
    I'll speed me to the pond, where the high stool
    On the long plank hangs o'er the muddy pool,
    That stool,° the dread of every scolding quean;°
    Yet, sure a lover should not die so mean!
    There placed aloft, I'll rave and rail by fits,
110 Though all the parish say I've lost my wits;
    And thence, if courage holds, my self I'll throw,
    And quench my passion in the lake below.
        'Ye lasses, cease your burthen, cease to moan,
    And, by my case forewarned, go mind your own.'
        The sun was set; the night came on a-pace,
    And falling dews bewet around the place,
    The bat takes airy rounds on leathern wings,
    And the hoarse owl his woeful dirges sings;
    The prudent maiden deems it now too late,
120 And till tomorrow comes defers her fate.

1714

shambles slaughterhouses
younglings young animals
stool the ducking stool, into which scolds were
fastened in order to be ducked in the pond
quean slut

JOHN DRYDEN

From Baucis and Philemon

Out of the Eighth Book of Ovid's Metamorphoses

Heaven's power is infinite; earth, air, and sea,
The manufactured mass, the making power obey.
By proof to clear your doubt: in Phrygian ground
Two neighbouring trees, with walls encompassed round,
Stand on a moderate rise, with wonder shown,
One a hard oak, a softer linden one. . . .
21 Not far from thence is seen a lake, the haunt
Of coots and of the fishing cormorant:
Here Jove with Hermes came; but in disguise
Of mortal men concealed their deities:
One laid aside his thunder, one his rod;
And many toilsome steps together trod;
For harbour at a thousand doors they knocked—
Not one of all the thousand but was locked.
At last an hospitable house they found,
30 A homely° shed; the roof, not far from ground,
Was thatched with reeds, and straw together bound.
There Baucis and Philemon lived, and there
Had lived long married, and a happy pair:
Now old in love, though little was their store,
Inured to want, their poverty they bore,
Nor aimed at wealth, professing° to be poor.
For master or for servant here to call,
Was all alike, where only two were all.
Command was none, where equal love was paid,
40 Or rather both commanded, both obeyed.
   From lofty roofs the gods repulsed before,
Now, stooping, entered through the little door;
The man (their hearty welcome first expressed)
A common settle drew for either guest,
Inviting each his weary limbs to rest.
But e'er they sat, officious° Baucis lays
Two cushions stuffed with straw, the seat to raise;
Coarse, but the best she had; then rakes the load
Of ashes from the hearth, and spreads abroad
50 The living coals, and, lest they should expire,
With leaves and barks she feeds her infant fire:
It smokes, and then with trembling breath she blows,
Till in a cheerful blaze the flames arose.
With brushwood and with chips she strengthens these,
And adds at last the boughs of rotten trees.

homely humble   **officious** full of good offices, solicitous
professing openly declaring themselves

The fire thus formed, she sets the kettle on—
Like burnished gold the little seether shone—
Next took the coleworts° which her husband got
From his own ground (a small well-watered spot);
60   She stripped the stalks of all their leaves; the best
She culled, and then with handy care she dressed.
High o'er the hearth a chine of bacon hung:
Good old Philemon seized it with a prong,
And from the sooty rafter drew it down;
Then cut a slice, but scarce enough for one;
Yet a large portion of a little store,
Which for their sakes alone he wished were more.
This in the pot he plunged without delay,
To tame the flesh and drain the salt away.
70   The time between, before the fire they sat,
And shortened the delay by pleasing chat.
    A beam there was, on which a beechen pail
Hung by the handle, on a driven nail:
This filled with water, gently warmed, they set
Before their guests; in this they bathed their feet,
And after with clean towels dried their sweat.
This done, the host produced the genial bed,
Sallow° the feet, the borders, and the stead
Which with no costly coverlet they spread,
80   But coarse old garments; yet such robes as these
They laid alone° at feasts, on holidays.
The good old housewife tucking up her gown,
The table sets; the invited gods lie down.
The trivet table of a foot was lame°—
A blot which prudent Baucis overcame,
Who thrusts beneath the limping leg, a sherd;°
So was the mended board exactly reared:
Then rubbed it o'er with newly gathered mint,
A wholesome herb, that breathed a grateful scent.
90   Pallas° began the feast, where first was seen
The party-coloured° olive, black and green;
Autumnal cornels° next in order served,
In lees of wine° well pickled, and preserved;
A garden salad was the third supply,
Of endive, radishes, and succory;°
Then curds and cream, the flower of country fare,
And new-laid eggs, which Baucis' busy care
Turned by a gentle fire, and roasted rare.

---

coleworts cabbages
Sallow dingy
alone only
trivet . . . lame the three-legged table was short in one leg
sherd bit of earthenware

Pallas to whom the olive was sacred
party-coloured of mixed colors
cornels the red fruit of the cornelian cherry tree
lees of wine vinegary dregs of wine
succory chicory

All these in earthen ware were served to board;
And, next in place, an earthen pitcher, stored
With liquor of the best the cottage could afford.
This was the table's ornament and pride,
With figures wrought: like pages at his side
Stood beechen bowls; and these were shining clean,
Varnished with wax without, and lined within.
By this the boiling kettle had prepared,
And to the table sent the smoking lard,°
On which with eager appetite they dine,
A savoury bit that served to relish wine;
The wine itself was suiting to the rest,
Still working in the must,° and lately pressed.
The second course succeeds like that before;
Plums, apples, nuts, and, of their wintry store,
Dry figs and grapes, and wrinkled dates were set
In canisters, to enlarge the little treat.
All these a milk-white honeycomb surround,
Which in the midst the country banquet crowned.
But the kind hosts their entertainment grace
With hearty welcome and an open face:
In all they did you might discern with ease
A willing mind and a desire to please.
　　Meantime the beechen bowls went round and still,
Though often emptied, were observed to fill;
Filled without hands, and of their own accord
Ran without feet, and danced about the board.
Devotion seized the pair, to see the feast
With wine, and of no common grape, increased;
And up they held their hands, and fell to prayer,
Excusing, as they could, their country fare.
　　One goose they had ('twas all they could allow),
A wakeful sentry, and on duty now,
Whom to the gods for sacrifice they vow:
Her, with malicious zeal, the couple viewed;
She ran for life, and, limping, they pursued.
Full well the fowl perceived their bad intent,
And would not make her masters' compliment;
But, persecuted, to the powers she flies,
And close between the legs of Jove she lies.
He, with a gracious ear, the suppliant heard,
And saved her life; then what he was declared,
And owned° the god. 'The neighbourhood,' said he,
'Shall justly perish for impiety:
You stand alone exempted; but obey
With speed, and follow where we lead the way;

lard bacon　　　　　　　　　　　　　**owned** acknowledged himself
working in the must fermenting

Leave these accurst, and to the mountain's height
Ascend, nor once look backward in your flight.'
   They haste, and what their tardy feet denied,
The trusty staff (their better leg) supplied.
An arrow's flight they wanted° to the top,
150   And there secure, but spent with travel, stop;
Then turn their now no more forbidden eyes:
Lost in a lake the floated level° lies;
A watery desert covers all the plains;
Their cot° alone, as in an isle, remains;
Wondering with weeping eyes, while they deplore
Their neighbours' fate and country now no more,
Their little shed, scarce large enough for two,
Seems, from the ground increased, in height and bulk to grow.
A stately temple shoots within the skies;
160   The crotches of their cot in columns rise;
The pavement polished marble they behold,
The gates with sculpture graced, the spires and tiles of gold.
   Then thus the Sire of Gods, with look serene:
'Speak thy desire, thou only just of men;
And thou, O woman, only worthy found
To be with such a man in marriage bound.'
   A while they whisper; then, to Jove addressed,
Philemon thus prefers° their joint request:
'We crave to serve before your sacred shrine,
170   And offer at your altars rites divine;
And since not any action of our life
Has been polluted with domestic strife,
We beg one hour of death; that neither she
With widow's tears may live to bury me,
Nor weeping I, with withered arms, may bear
My breathless Baucis to the sepulchre.'
   The godheads sign their suit. They run their race
In the same tenor all the appointed space;
Then, when their hour was come, while they relate
180   These past adventures at the temple gate,
Old Baucis is by old Philemon seen
Sprouting with sudden leaves of sprightly green;
Old Baucis looked where old Philemon stood,
And saw his lengthened arms a sprouting wood.
New roots their fastened feet begin to bind,
Their bodies stiffen in a rising rind:
Then, ere the bark above their shoulders grew,
They give and take at once their last adieu;
At once: 'Farewell, O faithful spouse,' they said;
190   At once the incroaching rinds their closing lips invade.

wanted had to travel   cot dwelling
floated level flooded surface   prefers offers

Even yet, an ancient Tyanaean° shows
A spreading oak, that near a linden grows;
The neighbourhood confirm the prodigy,
Grave men, not vain of tongue, or like to lie.
I saw myself the garlands on their boughs,
And tablets hung for gifts of granted vows;
And offering fresher up, with pious prayer,
'The good,' said I, 'are God's peculiar care,
And such as honour Heaven, shall heavenly honour share.'

1700

JONATHAN SWIFT

Baucis and Philemon

Imitated from the Eighth Book of Ovid

In ancient times, as story tells,
The saints would often leave their cells,
And stroll about, but hide their quality,
To try good people's hospitality.
   It happened on a winter night,
As authors of the legend write,
Two brother hermits, saints by trade,
Taking their tour in masquerade,
Disguised in tattered habits, went
To a small village down in Kent;
Where, in the strollers' canting strain,
They begged from door to door in vain,
Tried every tone might pity win;
But not a soul would let them in.
   Our wandering saints, in woeful state,
Treated at this ungodly rate,
Having through all the village passed,
To a small cottage came at last
Where dwelt a good old honest yeoman,
Called in the neighbourhood Philemon;
Who kindly did these saints invite
In his poor hut to pass the night;
And then the hospitable sire
Bid Goody° Baucis mend the fire
While he from out the chimney took
A flitch of bacon off the hook,
And freely from the fattest side
Cut out large slices to be fried;
Then stepped aside to fetch 'em drink,

10

20

Tyanaean a native of Tyana (in Asia Minor)   Goody a contracted form of goodwife

30   Filled a large jug up to the brink,
   And saw it fairly twice go round;
   Yet (what was wonderful) they found
   'Twas still replenished to the top,
   As if they ne'er had touched a drop.
   The good old couple were amazed,
   And often on each other gazed;
   For both were frightened to the heart,
   And just began to cry, 'What ar't!'
   Then softly turned aside, to view
40   Whether the lights were burning blue.°
   The gentle pilgrims, soon aware on't,
   Told 'em their calling and their errand:
   'Good folks, you need not be afraid,
   We are but saints,' the hermits said;
   'No hurt shall come to you or yours:
   But, for that pack of churlish boors,
   Not fit to live on Christian ground,
   They and their houses shall be drowned:
   While you shall see your cottage rise,
50   And grow a church before your eyes.'
     They scarce had spoke, when fair and soft,
   The roof began to mount aloft;
   Aloft rose every beam and rafter;
   The heavy wall climbed slowly after.
     The chimney widened, and grew higher,
   Became a steeple with a spire.
     The kettle to the top was hoist,
   And there stood fastened to a joist,
   But with the upside down, to show
60   Its inclinations for below:
   In vain; for a superior force
   Applied at bottom stops its course:
   Doomed ever in suspense to dwell,
   'Tis now no kettle, but a bell.
     A wooden jack,° which had almost
   Lost by disuse the art to roast,
   A sudden alteration feels,
   Increased by new intestine wheels;
   And, what exalts the wonder more,
70   The number made the motion slower.
   The flier, though it had leaden feet,
   Turned round so quick you scarce could see't;
   But, slackened by some secret power,
   Now hardly moves an inch an hour.
   The jack and chimney, near allied,

burning blue as candles were believed to do   **jack** a device for turning the roasting spit
in the presence of evil spirits

Had never left each other's side;
The chimney to a steeple grown,
The jack would not be left alone;
But, up against the steeple reared,
Became a clock, and still adhered;
And still its love to household cares
By a shrill voice at noon declares,
Warning the cookmaid not to burn
That roast meat which it cannot turn.

The groaning chair began to crawl
Like an huge snail along the wall;
There stuck aloft in public view,
And with small change, a pulpit grew.

The porringers, that in a row
Hung high, and made a glittering show,
To a less noble substance changed,
Were now but leathern buckets° ranged.

The ballads, pasted on the wall,
Of Joan of France, and English Moll,°
Fair Rosamond,° and Robin Hood,
The little Children in the Wood,
Now seemed to look abundance better,
Improved in picture, size and letter:
And, high in order placed, describe
The heraldry of every tribe.°

A bedstead of the antique mode,
Compact of timber many a load,
Such as our ancestors did use,
Was metamorphosed into pews;
Which still their ancient nature keep
By lodging folks disposed to sleep.

The cottage, by such feats as these,
Grown to a church by just degrees,
The hermits then desired their host
To ask for what he fancied most.
Philemon, having paused a while,
Returned 'em thanks in homely style;
Then said, 'My house is grown so fine,
Methinks, I still would call it mine.
I'm old, and fain would live at ease;
Make me the parson, if you please.'

He spoke, and presently he feels
His grazier's° coat fall down his heels:
He sees, yet hardly can believe,

120   About each arm a pudding sleeve;°
    His waistcoat to a cassock grew,
    And both assumed a sable hue;
    But, being old, continued just
    As threadbare and as full of dust.
    His talk was now of tithes and dues:
    He smoked his pipe and read the news;
    Knew how to preach old sermons next,
    Vamped° in the preface and the text;
    At christenings well could act his part,
130   And had the service all by heart:
    Wished women might have children fast,
    And thought whose sow had farrowed last;
    Against dissenters would repine,
    And stood up firm for right divine;°
    Found his head filled with many a system;
    But classic authors,—he ne'er missed 'em.
      Thus having furbished up a parson,
    Dame Baucis next they played their farce on.
    Instead of homespun coifs,° were seen
140   Good pinners edged with colberteen;°
    Her petticoat transformed apace,
    Became black satin, flounced° with lace.
    Plain 'Goody' would no longer down,
    'Twas 'Madam,' in her grogram° gown.
    Philemon was in great surprise,
    And hardly could believe his eyes.
    Amazed to see her look so prim,°
    And she admired as much at him.
      Thus happy in their change of life,
150   Were several years this man and wife:
    When on a day, which proved their last,
    Discoursing on old stories past,
    They went by chance, amidst their talk,
    To the churchyard to take a walk;
    When Baucis hastily cried out,
    'My dear, I see your forehead sprout!'
    'Sprout,' quoth the man; 'what's this you tell us?
    I hope you don't believe me jealous!°
    But yet, methinks I feel it true,
160   And really yours is budding too—
    Nay,—now I cannot stir my foot;

pudding sleeve a full, bulging (perhaps padded) sleeve
Vamped reworked (the "text" here being the scriptural topic)
right divine i.e. the church structure as derived from the Apostles; perhaps also showing the Tory political cast of the lower clergy, as opposed to many Whig bishops

coifs close-fitting caps
pinners . . . colberteen caps with flaps edged with lace
flounced covered with a second tier
grogram grosgrain, a fabric all or partly of silk
prim smart
jealous referring to cuckold's horns, often called "branches" for antlers

It feels as if 'twere taking root.'
 Description would but tire my Muse,
In short, they both were turned to yews.
Old Goodman Dobson of the green
Remembers he the trees has seen;
He'll talk of them from noon till night,
And goes with folks to show the sight;
On Sundays, after evening prayer,
He gathers all the parish there;
Points out the place of either yew,
Here Baucis, there Philemon, grew:
Till once a parson of our town,
To mend his barn, cut Baucis down;
At which, 'tis hard to be believed
How much the other tree was grieved,
Grew scrubby, died a-top, was stunted;
So the next parson stubbed and burnt it.
        1708

MATTHEW PRIOR
1664–1721

An Epitaph°

  Climb at court for me that will
  Tottering favour's pinnacle;
  All I seek is to lie still.
  Settled in some secret nest
  In calm leisure let me rest,
  And far off the public stage
  Pass away my silent age.
  Thus when without noise, unknown,
  I have lived out all my span,
  I shall die without a groan
  An old honest country man.
  Who exposed to others' eyes
  Into his own heart ne'er pries,
  Death to him's a strange surprise.
  SENECA, *Thyestes*, Chorus, Act II
  (ANDREW MARVELL trans.)

 Interred beneath this marble stone
Lie sauntering Jack and idle Joan.
While rolling threescore years and one

An Epitaph Matthew Prior (1664–1721) had a long diplomatic career and took an important role in negotiating the Peace of Utrecht in 1713. His poetry ranges from philosophical works like *Solomon on the Vanity of the World* to brilliant love lyrics, and among his finest poems is the Hudibrastic *Alma*, a dialogue on the nature of the soul and its faculties. An admirer of Butler, Prior praised his art in *Alma*: "His noble negligences teach / What others' toils despair to reach. / He, perfect dancer, climbs the rope, / And balances your fear and hope / . . . With wonder you approve his sleight, / And owe your pleasure to your fright."

Did round this globe their courses run;
If human things went ill or well;
If changing empires rose or fell;
The morning past, the evening came,
And found this couple still the same.
They walked and eat, good folks: What then?
10 Why then they walked and eat again:
They soundly slept the night away:
They did just nothing all the day:
And having buried children four,
Would not take pains to try for more.
Nor sister either had, nor brother:
They seemed just tallied for each other.

   Their moral and economy
Most perfectly they made agree:
Each virtue kept its proper bound,
20 Nor trespassed on the other's ground.
Nor fame, nor censure they regarded:
They neither punished, nor rewarded.
He cared not what the footmen did:
Her maids she neither praised, nor chid:
So every servant took his course;
And bad at first, they all grew worse.
Slothful disorder filled his stable;
And sluttish plenty decked her table.
Their beer was strong; their wine was port;
30 Their meal was large; their grace was short.
They gave the poor the remnant-meat,
Just when it grew not fit to eat.

   They paid the church and parish rate;°
And took, but read not the receipt:
For which they claimed their Sunday's due
Of slumbering in an upper pew.

   No man's defects sought they to know;
So never made themselves a foe.
No man's good deeds did they commend;
40 So never raised themselves a friend.
Nor cherished they relations poor:
That might decrease their present store:
Nor barn nor house did they repair:
That might oblige their future heir.

   They neither added, nor confounded;°
They neither wanted, nor abounded.
Each Christmas they accompts did clear;

rate tax   confounded wasted

And wound their bottom° round the year.
Nor tear, nor smile did they employ
50   At news of public grief, or joy.
When bells were rung, and bonfires made,
If asked, they ne'er denied their aid:
Their jug was to the ringers° carried,
Who ever either died, or married.
Their billet° at the fire was found,
Who ever was deposed, or crowned.

Nor good, nor bad, nor fools, nor wise;
They would not learn, nor could advise:
Without love, hatred, joy, or fear,
60   They led—a kind of—as it were:
Nor wished, nor cared, nor laughed, nor cried:
And so they lived; and so they died.

1718

ALEXANDER POPE
1688–1744

Pope was the great poet of his age, and he made that role a more exacting and influential one than it had ever been before in England. Chaucer had been a court poet and had served as a diplomat; Milton had been virtually foreign minister under Cromwell. But Pope commanded hatred and admiration, both as poet and as man, throughout his career of private citizen and public conscience. He could boast in a late poem, "I must be proud to see / Men not afraid of God, afraid of me." And while he fully earned the right to make the boast, he often doubted the wisdom of his engagement. We can see in his career a constant division between the attraction of a retired life and the claims, early, of literary ambition and, late, of active political concern—a political life such as only a man too independent to be bought and too gifted to be suppressed could maintain in Walpole's England.

Those who wish to find disabilities for which ambition compensates can find more than his share in Pope. Born to Catholic parents and, however heterodox at moments, loyal to their faith, he suffered first of all the penalties of being a Catholic in a country easily alarmed by the threat of intrigue and invasion. Catholics were forbidden by law to own land or to live within ten miles of London, and, if the laws were rarely enforced, they could be invoked in times of panic. Pope's parents moved near the time of his birth to Binfield in Windsor Forest, and later Pope rented a villa at Twickenham, near London but outside the ten-mile limit. As a Catholic he was denied admission to a university or the right to hold public office, and he was subject as well to double taxation. Nor did his enemies ever allow him to forget his status as a Catholic; but they made even more of his dwarf-like stature and of his crooked body, misshapen from adolescence by a tubercular ailment ("little Alexander," he described himself to a friend, whom "the women laugh at")

bottom a skein or ball of thread   billet gift of firewood
ringers bell-ringers, on whatever occasion

The compensations took various forms, occasionally the unconvincing posture of a rake, more often precocious literary skill and application and a great talent for friendship. His early friendships with distinguished elderly writers and retired statesmen (which combined charming deference with intellectual equality) were the first of a long series that took the place of more intimate ties. There was a rather romantic, somewhat histrionic attachment to the witty and ultimately spiteful Lady Mary Wortley Montagu (once a candidate for Congreve's affection), and there was something like real intimacy with Martha Blount; but the friendships seem, at this remove, the more essential attachments.

Pope divided his works at one point into "pure description" and "sense"; and, if those terms mean anything, they mark a movement in the late 1720's from a career of intense literary concerns to one of deeper moral engagement. There is no very sharp distinction, for such early works as the *Essay on Criticism* and *Windsor Forest* show moral and even political concern. The earlier career reached its culmination in the great labor of translating Homer, an undertaking that demanded all of Pope's energies and that rewarded him with financial independence. In the course of his earlier career, Pope had become deeply involved in the literary politics of the day, which were neither distinct from nor less vicious than those of the larger public sphere. His very talent was taken as arrogance by some; and Pope, through eagerness for fame and a certain bravado of manner, did little to make his superiority easy to ignore, or even to endure. In his difficult relations with Joseph Addison, who received literary adulation at Button's coffeehouse and could reward it with Whig patronage, Pope may have seemed a self-seeking outsider or even the instrument of his Tory friends. At any rate, Addison condoned strong efforts by his followers to smother Pope's reputation and to kill the prospects of his Homer.

In 1728 Pope paid off scores with *The Dunciad*. He created a brilliant mock-epic framework within which to gather and display—like a collection of butterflies, wasps, and spiders—all those who had maligned him without cause. Thereafter, each gesture he made could be read as defense or attack, and it was only by concealing his authorship that he could get a fair (and favorable) reception for so impersonal a work as the *Essay on Man* (1733–34). The *Essay* marks the last full effort of the contemplative poet: it is a work in a Socratic spirit, seeking to undo the quarrels men make with themselves and their world. This was to have been the first part of a large philosophical work, but the rest finally emerged as a series of "moral essays" or "ethic epistles" (of which *To Burlington* and *To a Lady* are two) and in the satire on false learning in the *New Dunciad* (1743).

The themes of *The Dunciad* looked back to Swift's great early satire, *A Tale of a Tub;* Pope's poem was written in part during a visit from Swift and, when completed, dedicated to him. The two men had met by 1712; and in the next few years, with Dr. John Arbuthnot (who had created the character of John Bull in a series of political satires) and with others—John Gay among them—they undertook the project of ridiculing false learning in a series of papers purportedly written by Martinus Scriblerus, a leaden-witted, pedantic, and indefatigable searcher after natural curiosities and verbal subtleties. The Scriblerus papers, begun about 1714, were not published till years later, but the project was important for providing an imaginative form which could yield Pope's "variorum" edition of *The Dunciad* with Scriblerian commentary, or perhaps even that more modest and less sedentary kin to Scriblerus, Lemuel Gulliver.

Pope's loyalty to these Tory friends—as well as to Queen Anne's chief ministers, Oxford and Bolingbroke—moved him more and more toward a political role. He had been on good personal terms with Sir Robert Walpole, but increasingly he became offended by the ways in which Walpole promoted and embodied the corruptions of the time: the systematic control of power through bribery, the use of hirelings and hacks to malign or silence the opposition, the awarding of honors for serviceable mediocrity, the insatiable appetite for ostentatious grandeur. Pope may well have exaggerated the threat that Walpole represented and have been somewhat eager to see apocalypse where there was only muddle. As Gibbon put it, "The fall of an unpopular Minister was not succeeded, according to general expectation, by a millennium of happiness and virtue." But Pope erected an image of Walpole and his England to stand beside Juvenal's vision of Rome under the rule of Domitian or Byron's and Stendhal's vision of the reaction that followed the French Revolution and Napoleon. The historicity of Pope's world is not our primary concern today, but rather the powerful and all-embracing imaginative form into which he built the details of his time as he did shells and minerals into the arches of his grotto at Twickenham. If the grotto was the retreat of the contemplative private man, and its natural beauties framed the life of retirement, so the greater poetic structure of the satires served no less to exercise the public conscience and to voice an outrage too strong to condone either pretext or pretension.

Pope gained a reputation for deviousness from which his reputation as a poet has often suffered. It arose in part because, like Halifax, he respected men more than parties; in part because he would damn in one withering line a fool who felt he had a claim to two; in part because he was attentive to his own image, editing and revising his letters before he published them, claiming the advantage of second thoughts and of nobler impulses than were spontaneously given. Yet the self-defense was a proportionate reaction to the abuse; and if Pope may be said to have created himself anew for posterity, the creation was still his. John Ruskin, the Victorian critic, pays tribute to his concise and forceful expression of a "benevolence, humble, rational, and resigned"; it is not all of Pope nor even his greatest achievement, but it is a part of all the rest.

An Essay on Criticism

This Horatian essay, Pope's first major poem, is the culmination of those years of literary study and discussion that Pope conducted at Binfield. His choice of criticism as its subject reflects the concern with self-definition of an age that had reacted against baroque wit and sought to cultivate the urbanity of Roman (as well as modern French) models. But a more immediate concern was the social one of how writers and critics were to behave in the new open forum that replaced gentlemanly amateurism and patronage. Critics were more numerous than ever before. As one of the least amiable of them, Thomas Rymer, complained, "till of late years England was as free from critics as it is from wolves," but now "they who are least acquainted with the game are aptest to bark at everything that comes in their way." Swift complained of those critics who read only to damn: "as barbarous as a judge who should take up a resolution to hang all men that came before him upon trial." And Dryden had traced the most malevolent criticism to failed writers: "the corruption of a poet is the generation of a critic."

Pope writes in a spirit of moderation, trying to free criticism of its partiality and its animosity. He offers a generous account of the value and limits of rules and a warning above all against the pride that sets self against nature, the fashionable against the universal. The theme of pride, whether of the individual or the coterie, creates a pattern of imagery that underlies the poem at every point and gives it more strength than its casual surface might suggest. We see the light of heaven descending into the "glimmering light" of the individual mind, as it once did more strikingly in the "celestial fire" of ancient genius. We see the light of nature as "clear, unchanged, and universal," opposed to the glaring, refracted light of false wit. The light of nature, like that of true expression, "clears and improves"—that is, dresses to advantage— "whate'er it shines upon," self-effacing in order to bring each object to its full realization. In contrast, the glitter of false wit conceals the "naked nature" (or rather hopes to conceal its absence) and buries what might have been "living grace" in a tawdry display of verbal wit. Behind these images there may be traces of an implicit scheme familiar in neoplatonic thought: the light of the One descends through emanation, forming and beautifying the Many. As it informs the individual soul and awakens it to the radiance of beauty in the world, it stirs the soul to reascend toward the One. Such a system is explicit in Shaftesbury's *The Moralists;* in Pope's less rhapsodic "essay" there are only glimpses and vestiges, just as in Dryden's urbane and "skeptical" criticism there are only occasional evocations of neoplatonism (except for the extended quotation from Giovanni Bellori in *The Parallel Betwixt Painting and Poetry*) or as in Reynolds's *Discourses* we see the translation of a neoplatonic scheme into empirical terms.

From An Essay on Criticism

'Tis hard to say, if greater want of skill
Appear in writing or in judging ill;
But, of the two, less dangerous is the offence
To tire our patience, than mislead our sense.
Some few in that, but numbers err in this,
Ten censure wrong for one who writes amiss;
A fool might once himself alone expose,
Now one in verse makes many more in prose.
    'Tis with our judgments as our watches; none
10 Go just alike, yet each believes his own.
In poets as true genius is but rare,
True taste as seldom is the critic's share;
Both must alike from Heaven derive their light,
These born to judge, as well as those to write.
Let such teach others who themselves excel,
And censure freely who have written well.
Authors are partial to their wit, 'tis true,

But are not critics to their judgment too?
     Yet if we look more closely, we shall find
20 Most have the seeds of judgment in their mind;
     Nature affords at least a glimmering light;°
     The lines, though touched but faintly, are drawn right.
     But as the slightest sketch, if justly traced,
     Is by ill colouring but the more disgraced,
     So by false learning is good sense° defaced;
     Some are bewildered in the maze of schools,°
     And some made coxcombs° Nature meant but fools.
     In search of wit these lose their common sense,
     And then turn critics in their own defence.
30 Each burns alike, who can, or cannot write,
     Or with a rival's or an eunuch's spite.
     All fools have still an itching to deride,
     And fain would be upon the laughing side;
     If Maevius° scribble in Apollo's° spite,
     There are who judge still worse than he can write.
     Some have at first for wits, then poets past,
     Turned critics next, and proved plain fools at last;
     Some neither can for wits nor critics pass,
     As heavy mules are neither horse nor ass.
40 Those half-learned witlings, numerous in our isle,
     As half-formed insects on the banks of Nile;
     Unfinished things, one knows not what to call,
     Their generation's so equivocal:°
     To tell° 'em, would a hundred tongues require,
     Or one vain wit's, that might a hundred tire.
     But you who seek to give and merit fame,
     And justly bear a critic's noble name,
     Be sure yourself and your own reach to know,
     How far your genius, taste, and learning go;
50 Launch not beyond your depth, but be discreet,
     And mark that point where sense and dulness meet.
     Nature to all things fixed the limits fit,
     And wisely curbed proud man's pretending wit:

glimmering light Sir William Temple (*Of Poetry*) describes poetic inspiration as "the pure and free gift of Heaven or of Nature . . . a fire kindled out of some hidden spark of the very first conception." So, too, Shaftesbury in *The Moralists* III.ii speaks of the "conceptions" of the mind and its "mental children": "Nor could it ever have been thus impregnated by any other mind than that which formed it at the beginning; and which . . . is original to all mental as well as other beauty." For a further development of this theme, which insists upon the divine source of man's powers of creation (or, in Pope, judgment), see also William Collins, *Ode on the Poetical Character*.
good sense related to the "glimmering light" and "seeds of judgment" (ll. 20–21) which may be fulfilled through true learning (as the sketch may be realized by proper coloring) or may be destroyed through false
schools of thought or criticism, the very existence of "schools" implying a diffraction of the light of heaven into self-limiting partisanship
coxcombs fops, superficial pretenders
Maevius a bad poet of Virgil's age
Apollo's as god and inspirer of true poetry
Those . . . equivocal referring to the belief that insects and vermin were spontaneously generated by the mud of the Nile; they are described by Dryden as "part kindled into life, and part a lump of unformed unanimated matter" (Dedication, *Aeneid*)
tell count

As on the land while here the ocean gains,
In other parts it leaves wide sandy plains;
Thus in the soul while memory prevails,
The solid power of understanding fails;
Where beams of warm imagination play,
The memory's soft figures melt away.
60   One science° only will one genius fit,
So vast is art, so narrow human wit;°
Not only bounded to peculiar arts,
But oft in those confined to single parts.
Like kings we lose the conquests gained before,
By vain ambition still to make them more;
Each might his several province well command,
Would all but stoop to what they understand.
   First follow Nature, and your judgment frame
By her just standard, which is still° the same:
70   Unerring NATURE, still divinely bright,
One clear, unchanged, and universal light,
Life, force, and beauty, must to all impart,
At once the source, and end, and test of art.
Art from that fund each just supply provides,
Works without show, and without pomp presides:
In some fair body thus the informing soul°
With spirits feeds, with vigour fills the whole,
Each motion guides, and every nerve sustains;
Itself unseen, but in the effects, remains.
80   Some to whom Heaven in wit has been profuse,
Want as much more,° to turn it to its use;
For wit and judgment often are at strife,
Though meant each other's aid, like man and wife.
'Tis more to guide than spur the Muse's steed;°
Restrain his fury, than provoke his speed;
The wingèd courser, like a generous° horse,
Shows most true mettle when you check his course.
   Those RULES of old discovered, not devised,
Are Nature still, but Nature methodized;
90   Nature, like liberty,° is but restrained

---

science form of learning or knowledge
So vast . . . wit recalling the maxim of Hippocrates, "Life is short, but art is long" or, in the Latin version, "Ars longa, vita brevis est" (*Aphorisms* I.i)
still always; cf. Dryden, "For Nature is still the same in all ages, and can never be contrary to herself" (*Parallel Betwixt Poetry and Painting*, 1695)
informing soul the animating power and governing structure; cf. Dryden, *Absalom and Achitophel*, ll. 157–59, for ironic account of the "fiery soul" that "o'er-informs"
as much more distinguishing implicitly between wit as invention and fancy ("quickness" and "fertility") and wit as elocution or expression

("accuracy") as in Dryden's preface to *Annus Mirabilis* (see above, his Critical Prose); or, to put it another way, insisting upon the interdependence of wit and judgment, for if like man and wife they become one, each implies the other and may be called by the same name
Muse's steed Pegasus, the winged horse
generous spirited
liberty in early editions "monarchy"; in both cases implying that the sovereign power, whether the king or the people, limits itself willingly as the condition of its rule, just as God is often conceived as limiting himself to rational rather than merely arbitrary exercise of power (for the exception, see l. 162)

By the same laws which first herself ordained.
Hear how learnèd Greece her useful rules indites,
When to repress, and when indulge our flights:
High on Parnassus'° top her sons she showed,
And pointed out those arduous paths they trod,
Held from afar, aloft, the immortal prize,
And urged the rest by equal steps to rise;
Just precepts thus from great examples given,
She drew from them what they derived from Heaven.
100 The generous critic fanned the poet's fire,
And taught the world with reason to admire.
Then criticism the Muses' handmaid proved,
To dress her charms,° and make her more beloved;
But following wits from that intention strayed,
Who could not win the mistress, wooed the maid;
Against the poets their own arms they turned,
Sure to hate most the men from whom they learned.
So modern 'pothecaries, taught the art
By doctor's bills° to play the doctor's part,
110 Bold in the practice of mistaken° rules,
Prescribed, apply, and call their masters fools.
Some on the leaves° of ancient authors prey,
Nor time nor moths e'er spoiled so much as they:
Some drily plain, without invention's° aid,
Write dull receipts° how poems may be made:
These leave the sense, their learning to display,
And those explain the meaning quite away.
You then whose judgment the right course would steer,
Know well each ancient's proper character;
120 His fable,° subject, scope° in every page;
Religion, country, genius of his age:
Without all these at once before your eyes,
Cavil you may, but never criticize.
Be Homer's works your study and delight,
Read them by day, and meditate by night;
Thence form your judgment, thence your maxims bring,
And trace the Muses upward to their spring;
Still with itself compared, his text peruse;
And let your comment be the Mantuan Muse.°
130 When first young Maro° in his boundless mind

Parnassus' the sacred mountain of the Muses
dress her charms implying both to clothe or interpret and to rectify or adjust; the former action making them more apparent, the latter bringing them to fuller realization; cf. *The Rape of the Lock* I.139–44
bills prescriptions
mistaken misunderstood
leaves textual emendators and commentators seen as devouring grubs

invention's imagination, wit
receipts formulae, recipes. Pope later wrote a mocking "receipt" for cooking up an epic poem.
fable plot
scope "aim, final end" (Johnson)
Mantuan Muse Virgil's *Aeneid*, the best commentary on Homer
Maro Virgil

A work to outlast immortal Rome designed,
Perhaps he seemed° above the critic's law,
And but from Nature's fountains scorned to draw:
But when to examine every part he came,
Nature and Homer were, he found, the same:
Convinced, amazed, he checks the bold design,
And rules as strict his laboured work confine,
As if the Stagirite° o'erlooked each line.
Learn hence for ancient rules a just esteem;
140 To copy nature is to copy them.
    Some beauties yet no precepts can declare,
For there's a happiness° as well as care.
Music resembles poetry, in each
Are nameless graces° which no methods teach,
And which a master hand alone can reach.
If, where the rules not far enough extend,
(Since rules were made but to promote their end)
Some lucky licence answer to the full
The intent proposed, that licence is a rule.
150 Thus Pegasus, a nearer way to take,
May boldly deviate from the common track;
From vulgar bounds with brave° disorder part,
And snatch a grace beyond the reach of art,
Which, without passing through the judgment, gains
The heart, and all its end at once attains.
In prospects, thus, some objects please our eyes,
Which out of nature's common order rise,
The shapeless rock, or hanging precipice.°
Great wits sometimes may gloriously offend,
160 And rise to faults true critics dare not mend.
But though the ancients thus their rules invade,
(As kings dispense with laws themselves have made)
Moderns, beware! or if you must offend
Against the precept, ne'er transgress its end;
Let it be seldom, and compelled by need,
And have, at least, their precedent to plead.
The critic else proceeds without remorse,
Seizes your fame, and puts his laws in force.
    I know there are, to whose presumptuous thoughts
170 Those freer beauties, even in them, seem faults:
Some figures monstrous and misshaped appear,
Considered singly, or beheld too near,

seemed i.e. to himself
Stagirite Aristotle, whose *Poetics* analyzed the forms of epic and tragedy
happiness felicity, good fortune (as opposed to "care"), as in "lucky license," l. 148
nameless graces alluding to the expression "je ne sais quoi," which had gained currency in French criticism as a tribute to the value which

eludes categorizing; thus René Rapin speaks of "mysteries" which there is "no method to teach" —"the hidden graces, the insensible charms, and all that secret power of poetry which passes to the heart" (1674)
brave daring; but also magnificent, brilliant
rock . . . precipice See below, The Garden and the Wild, for discussion of the "sublime."

Which, but proportioned to their light or place,
Due distance reconciles to form and grace.
A prudent chief not always must display
His powers in equal ranks, and fair array,
But with the occasion and the place comply,
Conceal his force, nay seem sometimes to fly.
Those oft are stratagems which error seem,
180 Nor is it Homer nods, but we that dream.
    Still green with bays° each ancient altar° stands,
Above the reach of sacrilegious hands,
Secure from flames, from envy's fiercer rage,
Destructive war, and all-involving age.
See, from each clime the learned their incense bring!
Hear, in all tongues consenting° paeans ring!
In praise so just, let every voice be joined,
And fill the general chorus of mankind!
Hail Bards triumphant! born in happier days;
190 Immortal heirs of universal praise!
Whose honours with increase of ages grow,
As streams roll down, enlarging as they flow!
Nations unborn your mighty names shall sound,
And worlds applaud that must not yet be found!
Oh may some spark of your celestial fire,
The last, the meanest of your sons inspire,
(That on weak wings, from far, pursues your flights;
Glows while he reads, but trembles as he writes)
To teach vain wits a science little known,
200 To admire superior sense, and doubt their own!
    Of all the causes which conspire to blind
Man's erring judgment, and misguide the mind,
What the weak head with strongest bias rules,
Is *pride*, the never-failing vice of fools.
Whatever Nature has in worth denied,
She gives in large recruits° of needful° pride;
For as in bodies, thus in souls, we find
What wants° in blood and spirits, swelled with wind;
Pride, where wit fails, steps in to our defence,
210 And fills up all the mighty void of sense.
If once right reason drives that cloud away,
Truth breaks upon us with resistless day;
Trust not yourself; but your defects to know,
Make use of every friend—and every foe.
    A *little learning* is a dangerous thing;
Drink deep, or taste not the Pierian spring:°

bays the laurel that crowns the poet
altar the works of the ancients
consenting harmonious, unanimous
recruits additional supplies

needful needed (in the absence of "worth");
but also demanding, or arrogant
wants is lacking
Pierian spring a spring sacred to the Muses

There shallow draughts intoxicate the brain,
And drinking largely° sobers us again.
Fired at first sight with what the Muse imparts,
220   In fearless youth we tempt the heights of arts,
While from the bounded level of our mind,
Short views we take, nor see the lengths behind,
But more advanced, behold with strange surprise
New, distant scenes of endless science° rise!
So pleased at first, the towering Alps we try,
Mount o'er the vales, and seem to tread the sky;
The eternal snows appear already past,
And the first clouds and mountains seem the last:
But those attained, we tremble to survey
230   The growing labours of the lengthened way,
The increasing prospect tires our wandering eyes,
Hills peep o'er hills, and Alps on Alps arise!
    A perfect judge will read each work of wit
With the same spirit that its author writ:
Survey the WHOLE, nor seek slight faults to find,
Where nature moves, and rapture warms the mind;
Nor lose, for that malignant dull delight,
The generous pleasure to be charmed with wit.
But in such lays as neither ebb, nor flow,
240   Correctly cold, and regularly° low,
That shunning faults, one quiet tenor keep;
We cannot blame indeed—but we may sleep.
In wit, as nature, what affects our hearts
Is not the exactness° of peculiar° parts;
'Tis not a lip, or eye, we beauty call,
But the joint force and full result of all.
Thus when we view some well-proportioned dome,°
(The world's just wonder, and even thine O Rome!)
No single parts unequally surprise;
250   All comes united to the admiring° eyes;
No monstrous height, or breadth, or length appear;
The whole at once is bold, and regular.
    Whoever thinks a faultless piece to see,
Thinks what ne'er was, nor is, nor e'er shall be.
In every work regard the writer's end,
Since none can compass more than they intend;
And if the means be just, the conduct° true,
Applause, in spite of trivial faults, is due.

---

largely deeply
science knowledge
Correctly . . . regularly obedient to the rules
but without the vigor of imagination
exactness correctness, strict conformity to rule
peculiar particular, or separate
dome building, whether domed or not; but the
dome of such a cathedral as St. Peter's in Rome
or St. Paul's in London provides a fine instance
of unifying design
admiring wondering or awe-struck as well as
approving
conduct execution

As men of breeding, sometimes men of wit,°
260   To avoid great errors, must the less commit,
Neglect the rules each verbal critic° lays,
For not to know some trifles, is a praise.
Most critics, fond of some subservient art,
Still make the whole depend upon a part,
They talk of principles, but notions° prize,
And all to one loved folly sacrifice.

                . . .

Thus critics, of less judgment than caprice,
Curious,° not knowing, not exact, but nice,°
Form short ideas; and offend in arts
(As most in manners) by a love to parts.°
Some to *conceit*° alone their taste confine,
290   And glittering thoughts struck out at every line;
Pleased with a work where nothing's just or fit;
One glaring chaos and wild heap of wit:
Poets like painters, thus, unskilled to trace
The naked nature and the living grace,
With gold and jewels cover every part,
And hide with ornaments their want of art.
True wit is nature to advantage dressed,
What oft was thought, but ne'er so well expressed,
Something, whose truth convinced at sight we find,
300   That gives us back the image of our mind.
As shades° more sweetly recommend the light,
So modest plainness sets off sprightly wit:
For works may have more wit than does 'em good,
As bodies perish through excess of blood.°
Others for *language* all their care express,
And value books, as women men, for dress:
Their praise is still—the style is excellent:
The sense, they humbly take upon content.°
Words are like leaves; and where they most abound,
310   Much fruit of sense beneath is rarely found.
False eloquence, like the prismatic glass,
Its gaudy colours spreads on every place;
The face of nature we no more survey,
All glares alike, without distinction gay:

---

breeding . . . wit playing on the analogy between the tact of good manners and that of art
verbal critic those concerned with details of
language to the neglect of larger function
notions prejudices, unexamined ideas
Curious difficult to please
nice squeamish, overly fastidious
parts isolated gifts; in criticism, the "one
loved folly"; in manners, one's pleasure in one's
own talents (as in "a man of parts")

conceit farfetched comparison or metaphor,
such as had been favored by the Metaphysical
poets; see Dryden's Critical Prose and Johnson
on the Metaphysical poets
shades Cf. *Windsor Forest,* ll. 17–18 (below,
The Garden and the Wild), and *Epistle to Burlington,* ll. 53–56.
excess of blood as, it was believed, in apoplexy
upon content on trust

But true expression, like the unchanging sun,
Clears and improves whate'er it shines upon,
It gilds all objects, but it alters none.
Expression is the dress of thought, and still
Appears more decent° as more suitable;
320   A vile° conceit in pompous words expressed,
Is like a clown° in regal purple dressed;
For different styles with different subjects sort,
As several garbs with country, town, and court.
Some by old words° to fame have made pretence;
Ancients in phrase, mere moderns in their sense!
Such laboured nothings, in so strange a style,
Amaze the unlearned, and make the learnèd smile.
Unlucky, as Fungoso in the play,°
These sparks° with awkward vanity display
330   What the fine gentleman wore yesterday;
And but so mimic ancient wits at best,
As apes° our grandsires in their doublets drest.
In words, as fashions, the same rule will hold;
Alike fantastic, if too new, or old;
Be not the first by whom the new are tried,
Nor yet the last to lay the old aside.
          But most by *numbers°* judge a poet's song,
And smooth or rough, with them, is right or wrong;
In the bright Muse though thousand charms conspire,
340   Her voice is all these tuneful fools admire,
Who haunt Parnassus but to please their ear,
Not mend their minds; as some to church repair,
Not for the doctrine but the music there.
These equal syllables alone require,
Though oft the ear the open vowels tire,°
While expletives their feeble aid do join,
And ten low words oft creep in one dull line,
While they ring round the same unvaried chimes,
With sure returns of still expected rhymes.
350   Where'er you find 'the cooling western breeze,'
In the next line, it 'whispers through the trees';
If crystal streams 'with pleasing murmurs creep,'
The reader's threatened (not in vain) with 'sleep.'
Then, at the last and only couplet fraught

---

decent appropriate, becoming. In a letter to
Pope in 1706 William Walsh had written that
expression is "indeed the same thing to wit, as
dress is to beauty."
vile low or inept
clown rustic, peasant
old words archaic diction such as Spenser uses
at times, clumsily imitated by Ambrose Philips
in his pastorals and parodied by John Gay in
The Shepherd's Week (see above, The Mock
Form)

play Ben Jonson's *Every Man out of His Humour* (1599); Fungoso cannot keep up with
current fashions
sparks fops, beaux
apes monkeys dressed elaborately to provide
amusement
numbers versification, sound patterns
Though . . . tire This is the first of a series of
parodies wherein Pope illustrates the excesses
each critical prejudice encourages; here "equal
syllables" are rendered.

With some unmeaning thing they call a thought,
A needless Alexandrine° ends the song,
That, like a wounded snake, drags its slow length along.
Leave such to tune their own dull rhymes, and know
What's roundly smooth, or languishingly slow;
360 And praise the easy vigour of a line
Where Denham's strength, and Waller's sweetness° join.
True ease in writing comes from art, not chance,
As those move easiest who have learned to dance.
'Tis not enough no harshness gives offence,
The sound must seem an echo to the sense.
Soft is the strain° when Zephyr° gently blows,
And the smooth stream in smoother numbers flows;
But when loud surges lash the sounding shore,
The hoarse, rough verse should like the torrent roar.
370 When Ajax° strives, some rock's vast weight to throw,
The line too labours, and the words move slow;
Not so, when swift Camilla° scours the plain,
Flies o'er the unbending corn, and skims along the main.
Hear how Timotheus'° varied lays surprise,
And bid alternate passions fall and rise!
While, at each change, the son of Libyan Jove°
Now burns with glory, and then melts with love;
Now his fierce eyes with sparkling fury glow;
Now sighs steal out, and tears begin to flow:
380 Persians and Greeks like turns° of nature found,
And the world's victor stood subdued by sound!
The power of music all our hearts allow,
And what Timotheus was, is DRYDEN now.

. . .

1711

The Rape of the Lock

Pope's friend John Caryll was concerned about the estrangement between two prominent Roman Catholic families caused when Robert, Lord Petre, cut off a lock of hair
from the head of Arabella Fermor (known as "Belle"). As Pope explained it, Caryll,
"a common acquaintance and well-wisher to both, desired me to write a poem and
make a jest of it, and laugh them together again." Pope's poem failed to persuade
Arabella to resume her engagement to Lord Petre, and it soon outgrew its occasion.

Alexandrine a line of twelve syllables and six
stresses, illustrated in the following line
Denham's . . . sweetness These two 17th-
century poets were often praised for complementary virtues (conciseness to the point of
harshness, "strong lines" as opposed to harmonious musicality) which the Augustans
sought to fuse.
Soft is the strain illustrating, as do the next
eight lines, the maxim of l. 365

Zephyr the west wind
Ajax the rough hero in Homer's *Iliad* XII.378–86
Camilla the female warrior in Virgil's *Aeneid*
VII.808 ff.
Timotheus' the bard as shown in Dryden's *Alex-
ander's Feast*
son . . . Jove Alexander the Great
like turns similar alternations

Originally written in two cantos in 1712, it was amplified with mock-epic "machinery" and new incidents and appeared in five cantos in 1714 (Clarissa's speech in Canto V was not added until 1717).

The poem exults in the very triviality of its action, stressing the charm of a light, gay, and thoughtless world, upon which it lavishes all the gravity of tone and diction that might be allowed Achilles or Aeneas. Pope constantly plays games with scale. The sylphs—drawn from the occult and fantastic Rosicrucian mythology—are diminutive counterparts of classical deities or Miltonic angels, and they bring all the solicitude of solemn guardians to Belinda's petticoat and her hair. So, too, the full intensity of epic combat takes place not on the windy plains of Troy but on the "velvet plain" of the card table, where heroic battles are tricks in the game of ombre, and regal warriors defend the honor of their suits. The charm of this world deflects the contempt that Butler confers upon the manikins of *Hudibras,* misshapen as they are in mind and body; it exacts an attitude more subtle than moral superiority, more complicated than moral censure. Part of that attitude involves the recognition that the sylphs and gnomes are not so much external guardians as projections outward of states of mind, from coquettish concern with one's appearance to the self-pitying rancor of the spoilsport; and the ideal of good humor, explicity introduced by Clarissa but in fact everywhere present, has its own seriousness as a call to candor, warmth, and tolerance. There is a sense in which the poem is mocking neither its own world nor the imaginative world of the epic but simply putting them side by side, small and great, with a quizzical sense of their parallelism as well as their conflict.

The Rape of the Lock

An Heroi-Comical Poem

Canto I

What dire offence from amorous causes springs,
What mighty contests rise from trivial things,
I sing—This verse to CARYLL, Muse! is due;
This, even Belinda may vouchsafe to view:
Slight is the subject, but not so the praise,
If she inspire, and he approve my lays.
    Say what strange motive, Goddess! could compel
A well-bred Lord to assault a gentle Belle?
O say what stranger cause, yet unexplored,
10   Could make a gentle Belle reject a Lord?
In tasks so bold, can little men engage,
And in soft bosoms dwells such mighty rage?°
    Sol through white curtains shot a timorous ray,
And oped those eyes that must eclipse the day:
Now lapdogs give themselves the rousing shake,

---

in soft . . . rage Having opened with traditional epic "proposition" and invocation, Pope imitates as well the epic questions, here parodying Virgil's *Aeneid* I.ii, "Can heavenly minds such high resentment show?" (Dryden trans.). So in the following lines (13–14) he plays upon Petrarchan conventions to elevate Belinda.

And sleepless lovers, just at twelve, awake:
Thrice rung the bell, the slipper knocked the ground,
And the pressed watch° returned a silver sound.
Belinda still her downy pillow prest,
20 Her guardian Sylph° prolonged the balmy rest.
'Twas he had summoned to her silent bed
The morning dream that hovered o'er her head.
A youth more glittering than a birth-night beau°
(That even in slumber caused her cheek to glow)
Seemed to her ear his winning lips to lay,
And thus in whispers said, or seemed to say:
   'Fairest of mortals, thou distinguished care
Of thousand bright inhabitants of air!
If e'er one vision touched thy infant thought,
30 Of all the nurse and all the priest° have taught,
Of airy elves by moonlight shadows seen,
The silver token, and the circled green,°
Or virgins visited by angel powers,°
With golden crowns and wreaths of heavenly flowers,
Hear and believe! thy own importance know,
Nor bound thy narrow views to things below.
Some secret truths, from learnèd pride concealed,
To maids alone and children are revealed:
What though no credit doubting wits may give?
40 The fair and innocent shall still believe.
Know, then, unnumbered spirits round thee fly,
The light militia of the lower sky;
These, though unseen, are ever on the wing,
Hang o'er the box, and hover round the Ring.°
Think what an equipage° thou hast in air,
And view with scorn two pages and a chair.°
As now your own, our beings were of old,
And once enclosed in woman's beauteous mould;
Thence, by a soft transition, we repair
50 From earthly vehicles° to these of air.

---

pressed watch It responds with chimes for the nearest hour and quarter-hour.
Sylph One of the spirits inhabiting the four elements (sylphs the air, gnomes the earth, nymphs water, and salamanders fire); the Sylphs "are the best-conditioned creatures imaginable," serving faithfully "upon a condition very easy to all true adepts, an inviolate preservation of chastity" (Pope). While the Sylph appears as a guardian angel, his whisper (ll. 25–26) may recall Satan's early temptation of Eve in *Paradise Lost* IV and his later successful appeal to her pride in Book IX.
birth-night beau courtier splendidly dressed for the king's birthday. For this guise, one may compare the dream used by Archimago to tempt the Red Cross Knight in *The Faerie Queene* I.i.
nurse . . . priest considered as sources of su-
perstition, the nurse contributing the elves, the priest the angels
circled green referring to the phosphoric light ("fairy sparks") and the withered circles in the grass ("fairy rings") that were taken as signs of the fairies' presence
virgins . . . powers invoking the Annunciation to the Virgin but also the mystical experience of many saints, such as Teresa of Avila; clearly a romantic dream of glory for a young girl
Ring a circular drive in Hyde Park; like the theater box, a common scene of flirtation
equipage carriage with horses and footmen
chair a sedan chair, in which passengers were carried
vehicles both the "equipage" and the terrestrial form in which the soul was embodied

Think not, when woman's transient breath is fled,
That all her vanities at once are dead:
Succeeding vanities she still regards,
And though she plays no more, o'erlooks the cards.
Her joy in gilded chariots, when alive,
And love of ombre,° after death survive.
For when the fair in all their pride expire,
To their first elements° their souls retire:
The sprites of fiery termagants in flame
60 Mount up, and take a Salamander's° name.
Soft yielding minds to water glide away,
And sip, with Nymphs, their elemental tea.°
The graver prude sinks downward to a Gnome,°
In search of mischief still on earth to roam.
The light coquettes in Sylphs aloft repair,
And sport and flutter in the fields of air.
    'Know farther yet; whoever fair and chaste
Rejects mankind, is by some Sylph embraced:
For spirits, freed from mortal laws, with ease
70 Assume what sexes and what shapes they please.°
What guards the purity of melting maids,
In courtly balls and midnight masquerades,
Safe from the treacherous friend, the daring spark,
The glance by day, the whisper in the dark;
When kind occasion prompts their warm desires,
When music softens, and when dancing fires?
'Tis but their Sylph, the wise celestials know,
Though *honour* is the word with men below.
    'Some nymphs there are, too conscious of their face,
80 For life predestined to the Gnomes' embrace.
These swell their prospects and exalt their pride,
When offers are disdained, and love denied.
Then gay ideas crowd the vacant brain,
While peers and dukes, and all their sweeping train,
And garters, stars, and coronets° appear,
And in soft sounds, *Your Grace*° salutes their ear.
'Tis these that early taint the female soul,
Instruct the eyes of young coquettes to roll,
Teach infant cheeks a bidden blush to know,
90 And little hearts to flutter at a beau.
    'Oft when the world imagine women stray,

---

ombre a popular card game similar to whist or
bridge; see note to III.27 below. Another Virgilian echo: "The love of horses which they had
alive, / And care of chariots after death survive"
(Dryden trans. VI.890 ff.).
first elements the four (earth, air, fire, water)
of which all material things are composed
Salamander's named for the animal which was
believed to live unharmed in the midst of fire
tea pronounced "tay"
Gnome one of the "demons of earth" which
"delight in mischief" (Pope)
what sexes . . . please as can the angels in
Paradise Lost I.427–31
garters . . . coronets emblems of high court
honors
Your Grace the address to a peeress

The Sylphs through mystic mazes guide their way,
Through all the giddy circle they pursue,
And old impertinence° expel by new.
What tender maid but must a victim fall
To one man's treat, but for another's ball?
When Florio speaks, what virgin could withstand,
If gentle Damon did not squeeze her hand?
With varying vanities, from every part,
100 They shift the moving toyshop° of their heart;
Where wigs with wigs, with sword-knots sword-knots
    strive,
Beaux banish beaux, and coaches coaches drive.°
This erring mortals levity may call,
Oh blind to truth! the Sylphs contrive it all.
    'Of these am I, who thy protection claim,
A watchful sprite, and Ariel is my name.
Late, as I ranged the crystal wilds of air,
In the clear mirror of thy ruling star
I saw, alas! some dread event impend,
110 Ere to the main this morning sun descend.
But heaven reveals not what, or how, or where:
Warned by the Sylph, oh pious maid, beware!
This to disclose is all thy guardian can:
Beware of all, but most beware of man!'
    He said; when Shock,° who thought she slept too long,
Leaped up, and waked his mistress with his tongue.
'Twas then, Belinda, if report say true,
Thy eyes first opened on a billet-doux;
Wounds, charms and ardours were no sooner read,
120 But all the vision vanished from thy head.
    And now, unveiled, the toilet° stands displayed,
Each silver vase in mystic order laid.
First, robed in white, the nymph intent adores,
With head uncovered, the cosmetic powers.
A heavenly image in the glass appears,
To that she bends, to that her eyes she rears;
The inferior priestess,° at her altar's side,
Trembling, begins the sacred rites of pride.
Unnumbered treasures ope at once, and here
130 The various offerings of the world appear;
From each she nicely culls with curious° toil,

---

impertinence trifle, frivolity
toyshop "where playthings and little nice manufactures are sold" (Johnson)
Where wigs . . . drive Cf. Homer, *Iliad* IV.
508–9: "Now shield with shield, with helmet
helmet closed, / To armor armor, lance to lance
opposed" (Pope trans.). "Sword knots" were
ribbons tied to hilts; they help reduce the scale
qualitatively from use to decoration.

Shock name for a lapdog with very long hair
toilet The dressing-table is ironically presented
as an altar, where "cosmetic powers" (l. 124)
displace "cosmic."
inferior priestess the maid Betty; Belinda is
the high priestess as well as the source of the
"heavenly image" (l. 125)
curious careful, full of nicety

And decks the goddess with the glittering spoil.
This casket India's glowing gems unlocks,
And all Arabia° breathes from yonder box.
The tortoise here and elephant unite,
Transformed to combs, the speckled and the white.°
Here files° of pins extend their shining rows,
Puffs, powder, patches,° bibles, billet-doux.
Now awful° beauty puts on all its arms;
140   The fair each moment rises in her charms,
Repairs her smiles, awakens every grace,
And calls forth all the wonders of her face;
Sees by degrees a purer blush° arise,
And keener lightnings° quicken in her eyes.
The busy Sylphs surround their darling care;
These set the head, and those divide the hair,
Some fold the sleeve, whilst others plait the gown;
And Betty's praised for labours not her own.

     Canto II
Not with more glories, in the ethereal plain,°
The sun first rises o'er the purpled main,°
Than issuing forth, the rival of his beams
Launched on the bosom of the silver Thames.°
Fair nymphs and well-dressed youths around her shone,
But every eye was fixed on her alone.
On her white breast a sparkling cross she wore,
Which Jews might kiss, and infidels adore.°
Her lively looks a sprightly mind disclose,
10   Quick as her eyes, and as unfixed as those:
Favours to none, to all she smiles extends,
Oft she rejects, but never once offends.
Bright as the sun, her eyes the gazers strike,
And, like the sun, they shine on all alike.
Yet graceful ease, and sweetness void of pride,
Might hide her faults, if belles had faults to hide:
If to her share some female errors fall,
Look on her face, and you'll forget 'em all.
    This nymph, to the destruction of mankind,
20   Nourished two locks, which graceful hung behind
In equal curls, and well conspired to deck
With shining ringlets the smooth ivory neck.
Love in these labyrinths his slaves detains,

Arabia the source of perfumes
speckled . . . white tortoise-shell and ivory
files as of soldiers on parade
patches tiny pieces of black silk pasted on the
face to enhance the skin's whiteness
awful awe-inspiring, like the epic hero arming
himself
purer blush a more even redness, the result of
rouge

lightnings induced by drops of belladonna
ethereal plain the sky
purpled main the sea reddened by dawn to a
"royal purple"
silver Thames Belinda is taking a boat from
London to Hampton Court.
Jews . . . adore the kissing or adoration of the
cross marking conversion to a new faith

And mighty hearts are held in slender chains.
With hairy springes° we the birds betray,
Slight lines of hair surprise the finny prey,
Fair tresses man's imperial race ensnare,
And beauty draws us with a single hair.
    The adventurous Baron the bright locks admired,
He saw, he wished, and to the prize aspired:
Resolved to win, he meditates the way,
By force to ravish, or by fraud betray;
For when success a lover's toil attends,
Few ask, if fraud or force attained his ends.
    For this, ere Phoebus rose,° he had implored
Propitious heaven, and every power adored,
But chiefly Love—to Love an altar built,
Of twelve vast French romances,° neatly gilt.
There lay three garters, half a pair of gloves;
And all the trophies of his former loves.
With tender billets-doux he lights the pyre,
And breathes three amorous sighs to raise the fire;
Then prostrate falls, and begs with ardent eyes
Soon to obtain, and long possess, the prize:
The powers gave ear, and granted half his prayer;
The rest, the winds dispersed in empty air.°
    But now secure the painted vessel glides,
The sunbeams trembling on the floating tides,
While melting music steals upon the sky,
And softened sounds along the waters die.
Smooth flow the waves, the zephyrs gently play,
Belinda smiled, and all the world was gay.
All but the Sylph—with careful thoughts opprest,
The impending woe sat heavy on his breast.
He summons strait his denizens° of air;
The lucid squadrons round the sails repair:
Soft o'er the shrouds° aërial whispers breathe,
That seemed but zephrys to the train beneath.
Some to the sun their insect wings unfold,
Waft on the breeze, or sink in clouds of gold;
Transparent forms, too fine for mortal sight,
Their fluid bodies half dissolved in light.
Loose to the wind their airy garments flew,
Thin glittering textures of the filmy dew;
Dipped in the richest tincture of the skies,
Where light disports in ever-mingling dyes,

30 (line marker)
40 (line marker)
50 (line marker)
60 (line marker)

---

springes snares
ere . . . rose before sunrise
French romances notoriously long and highly
conventionalized love stories, here handsomely
bound in leather with gold titles and ornaments
The powers . . . air Cf. Virgil, Aeneid II.794–

95: "Apollo heard, and granting half his prayer,
/ Shuffled in winds the rest, and tossed in empty
air" (Dryden trans.).
denizens inhabitants
shrouds ropes (appropriate to a greater vessel
than the river boat)

While every beam new transient colours flings,
Colours that change whene'er they wave their wings.
Amid the circle, on the gilded mast,
70   Superior by the head,° was Ariel placed;
His purple pinions opening to the sun,
He raised his azure wand, and thus begun.
    'Ye Sylphs and Sylphids, to your chief give ear,
Fays, Fairies, Genii, Elves, and Daemons, hear!°
Ye know the spheres and various tasks assigned
By laws eternal to the aërial kind.
Some in the fields of purest aether° play,
And bask and whiten in the blaze of day.
Some guide the course of wandering orbs° on high,
80   Or roll the planets through the boundless sky.
Some less refined, beneath the moon's pale light
Pursue the stars that shoot athwart the night,
Or suck the mists in grosser air below,
Or dip their pinions in the painted bow,°
Or brew fierce tempests on the wintry main,
Or o'er the glebe° distil the kindly rain.
Others on earth o'er human race preside,
Watch all their ways, and all their actions guide:
Of these the chief the care of nations own,
90   And guard with arms divine the British throne.
    'Our humbler province is to tend the fair,
Not a less pleasing, though less glorious care.
To save the powder from too rude a gale,°
Nor let the imprisoned essences° exhale,
To draw fresh colours from the vernal flowers,
To steal from rainbows e'er they drop in showers
A brighter wash;° to curl their waving hairs,
Assist their blushes, and inspire their airs;
Nay oft, in dreams, invention we bestow,
100   To change a flounce, or add a furbelow.°
    'This day, black omens threat the brightest fair
That e'er deserved a watchful spirit's care;
Some dire disaster, or by force, or sleight,
But what, or where, the fates have wrapped in night:
Whether the nymph shall break Diana's law,°
Or some frail China jar receive a flaw,
Or stain her honour, or her new brocade,

Superior . . . head taller, like the typical epic
hero
Ye Sylphs . . . hear Cf. *Paradise Lost* V.600–
602: "Hear all ye Angels, progeny of light, /
Thrones, Dominations, Princedoms, Virtues,
Powers, / Hear my decree. . . ."
purest aether the air above the moon
wandering orbs comets, sometimes regarded as
wandering planets

painted bow rainbow
glebe farmland
too rude a gale too rough a breeze
essences bottled perfumes
wash tinting rinse
furbelow ruffle
Diana's law virginity

Forget her prayers, or miss a masquerade,
Or lose her heart, or necklace, at a ball;
10 Or whether Heaven has doomed that Shock must fall.
Haste then, ye spirits! to your charge repair:
The fluttering fan be Zephyretta's care;
The drops° to thee, Brillante, we consign;
And, Momentilla, let the watch be thine;
Do thou, Crispissa,° tend her favourite lock;
Ariel himself shall be the guard of Shock.
     'To fifty chosen Sylphs, of special note,
We trust the important charge, the petticoat:
Oft have we known that sevenfold fence to fail,
20 Though stiff with hoops, and armed with ribs of whale.°
Form a strong line° about the silver bound,
And guard the wide circumference around.
     'Whatever spirit, careless of his charge,
His post neglects, or leaves the fair at large,
Shall feel sharp vengeance soon o'ertake his sins,
Be stopped in vials, or transfixed with pins;
Or plunged in lakes of bitter washes lie,
Or wedged whole ages in a bodkin's° eye:
Gums and pomatums° shall his flight restrain,
30 While clogged he beats his silken wings in vain;
Or alum styptics with contracting power
Shrink his thin essence like a rivelled flower.
Or as Ixion° fixed, the wretch shall feel
The giddy motion of the whirling mill,°
In fumes of burning chocolate shall glow,
And tremble at the sea that froths below!'
     He spoke; the spirits from the sails descend;
Some, orb in orb, around the nymph extend,
Some thrid the mazy ringlets of her hair,
40 Some hang upon the pendants of her ear;
With beating hearts the dire event they wait,
Anxious, and trembling for the birth of fate.°

Canto III

Close by those meads, for ever crowned with flowers,
Where Thames with pride surveys his rising towers,
There stands a structure° of majestic frame,
Which from the neighbouring Hampton takes its name.
Here Britain's statesmen oft the fall foredoom

drops diamond earrings
Crispissa from "crisp," in its old sense of "curl"
whale whalebone
line i.e. of defense; the petticoat is described in terms used for an epic shield
bodkin's needle's
Gums and pomatums cosmetic ointments
Ixion the King of Thessaly who sought to seduce the goddess Hera and was bound by Zeus in hell to an eternally revolving wheel
mill for beating chocolate
birth of fate Cf. Homer, Iliad IV.112: "And fate now labours with some vast event" (Pope trans.).
structure Hampton Court, the largest of the royal palaces

Of foreign tyrants, and of nymphs at home;
Here thou, great Anna!° whom three realms obey,
Dost sometimes counsel take—and sometimes tea.
   Hither the heroes and the nymphs resort,
To taste awhile the pleasures of a court;
In various talk the instructive hours they past,
Who gave the ball, or paid the visit last;
One speaks the glory of the British queen,
And one describes a charming Indian screen;
A third interprets motions, looks, and eyes;
At every word a reputation dies.
Snuff, or the fan, supply each pause of chat,
With singing, laughing, ogling, *and all that.*
   Meanwhile, declining from the noon of day,
The sun obliquely shoots his burning ray;
The hungry judges soon the sentence sign,
And wretches hang that jurymen may dine;
The merchant from the Exchange returns in peace,
And the long labours of the toilet cease—
Belinda now, whom thirst of fame invites,
Burns to encounter two adventurous knights,
At ombre° singly to decide their doom;
And swells her breast with conquests yet to come.
Straight the three bands prepare in arms to join,
Each band the number of the sacred nine.
Soon as she spread her hand, the aërial guard
Descend, and sit on each important card:
First Ariel perched upon a Matadore,°
Then each, according to the rank they bore;
For Sylphs, yet mindful of their ancient race,
Are, as when women, wondrous fond of place.°
   Behold, four Kings in majesty revered,°
With hoary whiskers and a forky beard;
And four fair Queens whose hands sustain a flower,
The expressive emblem of their softer power;
Four Knaves in garbs succinct,° a trusty band,
Caps on their heads, and halberts° in their hand;
And particoloured troops, a shining train,
Draw forth to combat on the velvet plain.°
   The skilful nymph reviews her force with care;

10

20

30

40

Anna Queen Anne, ruler of Great Britain and Ireland as well as claimant to France
ombre a card game related to whist or modern bridge, played with forty cards—the 10's, 9's, and 8's being removed from the deck; there are three players, each holding nine cards, and the one who contracts to take most tricks is called the "ombre" (from Spanish for "man") and chooses the trumps
Matadore one of the three cards of highest value
place rank

revered There follows a parody of the traditional epic review of forces, in which the royal figures are given the appearance they bear on playing cards.
succinct tucked up
halberts battle axes fixed to long poles
velvet plain typical poetic diction for a smooth grassy field, here applied to the card table covered with green velvet; cf. also "verdant field" (l. 52) and "level green" (l. 80)

'Let spades be trumps!' she said, and trumps they were.°
   Now move to war her sable Matadores,°
In show like leaders of the swarthy Moors.
Spadillio first, unconquerable lord!
50 Led off two captive trumps, and swept the board.
As many more Manillio forced to yield,
And marched a victor from the verdant field.
Him Basto followed, but his fate more hard
Gained but one trump and one plebeian card.
With his broad sabre next, a chief in years,
The hoary Majesty of Spades appears,
Puts forth one manly leg,° to sight revealed;
The rest, his many-coloured robe concealed.
The rebel Knave, who dares his prince engage,
60 Proves the just victim of his royal rage.
Even mighty Pam,° that kings and queens o'erthrew,
And mowed down armies in the fights of Lu,
Sad chance of war! now, destitute of aid,
Falls undistinguished by the victor spade!
   Thus far both armies to Belinda yield;
Now to the Baron fate inclines the field.
His warlike Amazon° her host invades,
The imperial consort of the crown of spades.
The club's black tyrant first her victim died,
70 Spite of his haughty mien and barbarous pride:
What boots° the regal circle on his head,
His giant limbs in state unwieldy spread?
That long behind he trails his pompous robe,
And of all monarchs only grasps the globe?'
   The Baron now his diamonds pours apace;
The embroidered King who shows but half his face,
And his refulgent Queen, with powers combined,
Of broken troops an easy conquest find.
Clubs, diamonds, hearts, in wild disorder seen,
80 With throngs promiscuous strew the level green.
Thus when dispersed a routed army runs,
Of Asia's troops, and Afric's sable sons,
With like confusion different nations fly,
Of various habit and of various dye,
The pierced battalions disunited fall,

Let spades . . . were Cf. Genesis 1:3: "And
God said, Let there be light; and there was
light."
Matadores The highest cards (determined by
choice of trumps) are seen as epic heroes taking
the field; they are the ace of spades (Spadillio),
the two of spades (Manillio), and the ace of
clubs (Basto).
Puts forth . . . leg as pictured on the playing
card

Pam knave of clubs, strongest card in the game
of loo
Amazon the queen of spades seen as a female
warrior; giving the Baron the first of four
successive tricks
What boots introducing a typical epic lament
for the decline of greatness (here symbolized
in the "globe" the monarch holds as an emblem of his realm)

In heaps on heaps; one fate o'erwhelms them all.
   The Knave of Diamonds tries his wily arts,
And wins (oh shameful chance!) the Queen of Hearts.
At this, the blood the virgin's cheek forsook,
90   A livid paleness spreads o'er all her look;
She sees, and trembles at the approaching ill,
Just in the jaws of ruin, and Codille.°
And now (as oft in some distempered state)
On one nice trick° depends the general fate.
An Ace of Hearts steps forth: the King unseen
Lurked in her hand, and mourned his captive Queen.
He springs to vengeance with an eager pace,
And falls like thunder on the prostrate Ace.°
The nymph exulting fills with shouts the sky,
100   The walls, the woods, and long canals reply.
   Oh thoughtless mortals! ever blind to fate,°
Too soon dejected, and too soon elate!
Sudden these honours shall be snatched away,
And cursed for ever this victorious day.
   For lo! the board with cups and spoons is crowned,
The berries° crackle, and the mill turns round.
On shining altars of Japan° they raise
The silver lamp; the fiery spirits° blaze.
From silver spouts the grateful° liquors glide,
110   While China's earth° receives the smoking tide.
At once they gratify their scent and taste,
And frequent cups prolong the rich repast.
Straight hover round the fair her airy band;
Some, as she sipped, the fuming liquor fanned,
Some o'er her lap their careful plumes displayed,
Trembling, and conscious of the rich brocade.
Coffee (which makes the politician wise,
And see through all things with his half-shut eyes)
Sent up in vapours to the Baron's brain
120   New stratagems, the radiant lock to gain.
Ah cease, rash youth! desist ere 'tis too late,
Fear the just gods, and think of Scylla's fate!°
Changed to a bird, and sent to flit in air,
She dearly pays for Nisus' injured hair!
   But when to mischief mortals bend their will,

Codille literally "elbow"; defeat, if the Baron wins a fifth trick
nice trick precise or careful play, with suggestion of political intrigue in "some distempered state" (l. 93)
Ace outranked by the king in the red suits; Belinda takes the trick and the game
blind to fate part of the typical epic warning in the moment of pride
berries coffee beans being ground

Japan japanned or lacquered tables
spirits in the spirit lamps that heat the coffee
grateful pleasing
China's earth the cups of earthenware or China
Scylla's fate Scylla plucked the purple hair (which was the source of his power) from the head of her royal father, Nisus, in order to give it to her lover, Minos. Her lover was shocked and refused it, and she was changed into a sea bird (see Ovid, *Metamorphoses* VIII).

How soon they find fit instruments of ill!
Just then, Clarissa drew with tempting grace
A two-edged weapon from her shining case;
So ladies in romance assist their knight,
130   Present the spear, and arm him for the fight.
He takes the gift with reverence, and extends
The little engine on his fingers' ends;
This just behind Belinda's neck he spread,
As o'er the fragrant steams she bends her head.
Swift to the lock a thousand sprites repair,
A thousand wings, by turns, blow back the hair,
And thrice they twitched the diamond in her ear;
Thrice she looked back, and thrice the foe drew near.
Just in that instant, anxious Ariel sought
140   The close recesses of the virgin's thought;
As, on the nosegay° in her breast reclined,
He watched the ideas rising in her mind,
Sudden he viewed, in spite of all her art,
An earthly lover lurking at her heart.
Amazed, confused, he found his power expired,
Resigned to fate, and with a sigh retired.
   The peer now spreads the glittering forfex° wide,
To enclose the lock; now joins it, to divide.
Even then, before the fatal engine closed,
150   A wretched Sylph too fondly interposed;
Fate urged the shears, and cut the Sylph in twain
(But airy substance soon unites° again),
The meeting points the sacred hair dissever
From the fair head, for ever and for ever!
   Then flashed the living lightning from her eyes,
And screams of horror rend the affrighted skies.
Not louder shrieks to pitying heaven are cast,
When husbands or when lapdogs breathe their last,
Or when rich China vessels, fallen from high,
160   In glittering dust and painted fragments lie!
   'Let wreaths of triumph now my temples twine,'
(The victor cried) 'the glorious prize is mine!
While fish in streams, or birds delight in air,
Or in a coach and six the British fair,
As long as Atalantis° shall be read,
Or the small pillow grace a lady's bed,
While visits shall be paid on solemn days,
When numerous wax-lights in bright order blaze,
While nymphs take treats, or assignations give,

---

nosegay corsage of flowers
forfex Latinate diction for the pair of scissors
soon unites Cf. Milton's account of Satan pierced
by Michael's sword: "but the ethereal substance

closed / Not long divisible" (*Paradise Lost* VI.
330–31).
Atalantis a popular book of the day, full of
court scandal

170   So long my honour, name, and praise shall live!'
 What time would spare, from steel° receives its date,
And monuments, like men, submit to fate!
Steel could the labour of the gods destroy,
And strike to dust the imperial towers of Troy;
Steel could the works of mortal pride confound,
And hew triumphal arches to the ground.
What wonder then, fair nymph! thy hairs should feel
The conquering force of unresisted steel?

 Canto IV
But anxious cares the pensive nymph oppressed,°
And secret passions laboured in her breast.
Not youthful kings in battle seized alive,
Not scornful virgins who their charms survive,
Not ardent lovers robbed of all their bliss,
Not ancient ladies when refused a kiss,
Not tyrants fierce that unrepenting die,
Not Cynthia when her manteau's° pinned awry,
E'er felt such rage, resentment, and despair,
10   As thou, sad virgin! for thy ravished hair.
 For, that sad moment, when the Sylphs withdrew,
And Ariel weeping from Belinda flew,
Umbriel,° a dusky melancholy sprite
As ever sullied the fair face of light,
Down to the central earth, his proper scene,
Repaired to search the gloomy Cave of Spleen.°
 Swift on his sooty pinions flits the Gnome,
And in a vapour reached the dismal dome.°
No cheerful breeze this sullen region knows,
20   The dreaded East° is all the wind that blows.
Here, in a grotto, sheltered close from air,
And screened in shades from day's detested glare,
She sighs for ever on her pensive bed,
Pain at her side, and Megrim° at her head.
 Two handmaids wait the throne: alike in place,
But differing far in figure and in face.
Here stood Ill Nature like an ancient maid,
Her wrinkled form in black and white arrayed;
With store of prayers, for mornings, nights, and noons,
30   Her hand is filled; her bosom with lampoons.°

---

steel the fatal power of arms, which destroys even the Troy built by Apollo and Poseidon
But anxious . . . oppressed Cf. *Aeneid* IV.1 "But anxious cares already seized the Queen" (Dryden trans.).
manteau's mantua, loose robe or hood
Umbriel a gnome and former prude, named for "umbra," Latin for "shadow"
Cave of Spleen an epic visit to the underworld; suggestive of Spenser's caves of Mammon, Despair, and Night. Spleen was the name

(drawn from the bodily organ, whose function was not clearly understood) for the fashionable psychosomatic ailment of the day, involving melancholy, self-pity, and hypochondria; particularly rife among those who could afford it.
dome dwelling
East The east wind was taken as a cause of spleen.
Megrim migraine headache
lampoons ill-tempered satires or caricatures

There Affection, with a sickly mien
Shows in her cheek the roses of eighteen,
Practiced to lisp, and hang the head aside,
Faints into airs, and languishes with pride;
On the rich quilt sinks with becoming woe,
Wrapped in a gown for sickness, and for show.
The fair ones feel such maladies as these,
When each new nightdress gives a new disease.
    A constant vapour o'er the palace flies;
40 Strange phantoms° rising as the mists arise;
Dreadful, as hermit's dreams in haunted shades,
Or bright as visions of expiring° maids.
Now glaring fiends, and snakes on rolling spires,°
Pale spectres, gaping tombs, and purple fires:
Now lakes of liquid gold, Elysian scenes,°
And crystal domes, and angels in machines.
    Unnumbered throngs on every side are seen
Of bodies changed° to various forms by Spleen.
Here living teapots stand, one arm held out,
50 One bent; the handle this, and that the spout:
A pipkin° there like Homer's tripod walks;
Here sighs a jar, and there a goose-pie° talks;
Men prove with child, as powerful fancy works,
And maids, turned bottles, call aloud for corks.
    Safe passed the Gnome through this fantastic band,
A branch of healing spleenwort° in his hand.
Then thus addressed the power: 'Hail, wayward Queen!
Who rule the sex to fifty from fifteen,
Parent of vapours° and of female wit,
60 Who give the hysteric, or poetic fit,
On various tempers act by various ways,
Make some take physic,° others scribble plays;
Who cause the proud their visits to delay,
And send the godly in a pet to pray.
A nymph there is, that all thy power disdains,
And thousands more in equal mirth maintains.
But oh! if e'er thy Gnome could spoil a grace,
Or raise a pimple on a beauteous face,
Like citron-waters° matrons' cheeks inflame,

---

phantoms fantasies
expiring literally, dying; in the traditionally punning sense, coming to sexual climax (as might be suggested in the erotic intensity with which saints' raptures were sometimes presented)
spires coils
Elysian scenes not only fantasies of bliss but scenes such as contemporary opera and pantomime lavishly presented ("angels in machines")
bodies changed in fantasies that seem psychotic and clearly sexual in some cases, such as the repressed lives of prudes might have engendered
pipkin small earthenware boiler on a tripod;

for Hephaistos' "walking" tripods, see Homer, *Iliad* XVIII.439 ff.
goose-pie "alludes to a real fact; a lady of distinction imagined herself in this condition" (Pope)
spleenwort a fern that protected one against the excesses of the spleen
vapours roughly the same ailment as spleen, melancholy moodiness, here identified with hysteria
physic medicine
citron-waters brandy flavored with lemon

70   Or change complexions at a losing game;
  If e'er with airy horns° I planted heads,
  Or rumpled petticoats, or tumbled beds,
  Or caused suspicion when no soul was rude,
  Or discomposed the headdress of a prude,
  Or e'er to costive° lapdog gave disease,
  Which not the tears of brightest eyes could ease:
  Hear me, and touch Belinda with chagrin;
  That single act gives half the world the spleen.'
   The goddess with a discontented air
80   Seems to reject him, though she grants his prayer.
  A wondrous bag with both her hands she binds,
  Like that where once Ulysses° held the winds;
  There she collects the force of female lungs,
  Sighs, sobs, and passions, and the war of tongues.
  A vial next she fills with fainting fears,
  Soft sorrows, melting griefs, and flowing tears.
  The Gnome rejoicing bears her gifts away,
  Spreads his black wings, and slowly mounts to day.
   Sunk in Thalestris'° arms the nymph he found,
90   Her eyes dejected and her hair unbound.
  Full o'er their heads the swelling bag he rent,
  And all the furies issued at the vent.
  Belinda burns with more than mortal ire,
  And fierce Thalestris fans the rising fire.
  'O wretched maid!' she spread her hands, and cried,
  (While Hampton's echoes, 'Wretched maid!' replied)
  'Was it for this you took such constant care
  The bodkin,° comb, and essence to prepare;
  For this your locks in paper durance° bound,
100   For this with torturing irons wreathed around?
  For this with fillets° strained your tender head,
  And bravely bore the double loads of lead?
  Gods! shall the ravisher display your hair,
  While the fops envy, and the ladies stare!
  Honour forbid! at whose unrivalled shrine
  Ease, pleasure, virtue, all, our sex resign.
  Methinks already I your tears survey,
  Already hear the horrid things they say,
  Already see you a degraded toast,°
110   And all your honour in a whisper lost!

airy horns the sign of the cuckold
costive constipated
Ulysses when given a bag filled with the winds by Aeolus (*Odyssey* X.19 ff.)
Thalestris' named for a queen of the Amazons, thus fiercely militant
bodkin hairpin
paper durance heroic diction for curling papers

as for curling ("torturing") irons in the next line
fillets headbands, worn by priestesses in the *Aeneid*, but here part of the machinery of hair-dressing, as are the "loads of lead" in the next line
toast "a celebrated woman whose health is often drunk" (Johnson); the "degraded" implies some boastfulness in the toaster

How shall I, then, your helpless fame defend?
'Twill then be infamy to seem your friend!
And shall this prize,° the inestimable prize,
Exposed through crystal to the gazing eyes,
And heightened by the diamond's circling rays,
On that rapacious hand for ever blaze?
Sooner shall grass in Hyde Park Circus° grow,
And wits take lodgings in the sound of Bow;°
Sooner let earth, air, sea, to chaos fall,
20   Men, monkeys, lapdogs, parrots, perish all!'
      She said; then raging to Sir Plume repairs,
And bids her beau demand the precious hairs:
(Sir Plume, of amber snuffbox justly vain,
And the nice conduct of a clouded° cane)
With earnest eyes, and round unthinking face,
He first the snuffbox opened, then the case,
And thus broke out—'My Lord, why, what the devil?
Z—ds! damn the lock! 'fore Gad, you must be civil!
Plague on't! 'tis past a jest—nay prithee, pox!
30   Give her the hair'—he spoke, and rapped his box.
      'It grieves me much' (replied the peer again)
'Who speaks so well should ever speak in vain.
But by this lock, this sacred lock I swear,°
(Which never more shall join its parted hair,
Which never more its honours shall renew,
Clipped from the lovely head where late it grew)
That while my nostrils draw the vital air,
This hand, which won it, shall for ever wear.'
He spoke, and speaking, in proud triumph spread
40   The long-contended honours° of her head.
      But Umbriel, hateful Gnome! forbears not so;
He breaks the vial whence the sorrows flow.
Then see! the nymph in beauteous grief appears,
Her eyes half languishing, half drowned in tears;
On her heaved bosom hung her drooping head,
Which, with a sigh, she raised; and thus she said:
      'For ever cursed be this detested day,°
Which snatched my best, my favourite curl away!
Happy! ah ten times happy had I been,
50   If Hampton Court these eyes had never seen!
Yet am not I the first mistaken maid,
By love of courts to numerous ills betrayed.

---

prize the lock of her hair encased in a ring
Hyde Park Circus the Ring (see I.44), where
carriages kept the grass from growing
Bow near St. Mary-le-Bow, in the unfashionable
merchants' quarter of London as opposed to the
polite (west) end
clouded fashionably mottled or veined
this lock . . . swear Cf. Achilles' oath: "Now

by this sacred sceptre, hear me swear, / Which
never more shall leaves or blossoms bear . . ."
(Pope trans., *Iliad* I.309–10).
honours beauties
For ever . . . day This speech is based on
Achilles' lament for Patroclus (*Iliad* XVIII.
107 ff.).

Oh had I rather unadmired remained
In some lone isle, or distant northern land;
Where the gilt chariot never marks the way,
Where none learn ombre; none e'er taste bohea!°
There kept my charms concealed from mortal eye,
Like roses that in deserts bloom and die.
What moved my mind with youthful lords to roam?
160   O had I stayed, and said my prayers at home!
'Twas this, the morning omens seemed to tell;
Thrice from my trembling hand the patch box fell;
The tottering china shook without a wind,
Nay, Poll sat mute, and Shock was most unkind!
A Sylph too warned me of the threats of fate,
In mystic visions, now believed too late!
See the poor remnants of these slighted hairs!
My hands shall rend what even thy rapine spares:
These, in two sable ringlets taught to break,
170   Once gave new beauties to the snowy neck;
The sister lock now sits uncouth, alone,
And in its fellow's fate foresees its own;
Uncurled it hangs, the fatal shears demands;
And tempts once more thy sacrilegious hands.
Oh hadst thou, cruel! been content to seize
Hairs less in sight, or any hairs but these!'°

     Canto V
She said: the pitying audience melt in tears,
But fate and Jove had stopped the Baron's ears.
In vain Thalestris with reproach assails,
For who can move when fair Belinda fails?
Not half so fixed the Trojan could remain,
While Anna° begged and Dido raged in vain.
Then grave Clarissa° graceful waved her fan;
Silence ensued, and thus the nymph began.
     'Say why are beauties praised and honoured most,
10   The wise man's passion, and the vain° man's toast?
Why decked with all that land and sea afford,
Why angels called, and angel-like adored?
Why round our coaches crowd the white-gloved beaux,

bohea a kind of tea
any . . . these The joke here is that while Belinda doesn't mean her pubic hair, her whole rhetoric of honor (exteriors and reputations matter more than interior truths) leads her to invoke it inadvertently; the poet's wit traps her, much as Malvolio, in *Twelfth Night* (III.iv) is trapped into saying a bit of bawdry his Puritanism would never allow him consciously to utter.
Anna who failed to persuade Aeneas to remain faithful to her sister Dido (*Aeneid* IV)
Clarissa "A new character introduced in the subsequent editions, to open more clearly the moral of the poem, in a parody of the speech of Sarpedon to Glaucus in Homer" (Pope); cf. especially the final lines of the speech: "But since, alas! ignoble age must come, / Disease, and death's inexorable doom; / The life which others pay, let us bestow, / And give to Fame what we to Nature owe; / Brave though we fall, and honoured if we live, / Or let us glory gain, or glory give!" (Pope trans., *Iliad* XII. 391–96). The transposition of scale moves from "valour" as a source of merit to "good humour." **vain** both foolish and boastful

Why bows the side-box from its inmost rows?
How vain are all these glories, all our pains,
Unless good sense preserve what beauty gains:
That men may say, when we the front-box grace,
"Behold the first in virtue, as in face!"
Oh! if to dance all night, and dress all day,
20   Charmed the smallpox,° or chased old age away,
Who would not scorn what housewife's cares produce,
Or who would learn one earthly thing of use?
To patch, nay ogle, might become a saint,
Nor could it sure be such a sin to paint.
But since, alas! frail beauty must decay,
Curled or uncurled, since locks will turn to grey;
Since painted or not painted, all shall fade,
And she who scorns a man, must die a maid;
What then remains, but well our power to use,
30   And keep good humour still whate'er we lose?
And trust me, dear! good humour can prevail,
When airs, and flights, and screams, and scolding fail.
Beauties in vain their pretty eyes may roll;
Charms strike the sight, but merit wins the soul.'
  So spoke the dame, but no applause ensued;
Belinda frowned, Thalestris called her prude.
'To arms, to arms!' the fierce virago° cries,
And swift as lightning to the combat flies.
All side in parties, and begin the attack;
40   Fans clap, silks rustle, and tough whalebones crack;
Heroes' and heroines' shouts confusedly rise,
And bass and treble voices strike the skies.
No common weapons in their hands are found;
Like gods they fight, nor dread a mortal wound.
  So when bold Homer makes the gods engage,
And heavenly breasts with human passions rage;
'Gainst Pallas,° Mars; Latona,° Hermes arms;
And all Olympus rings with loud alarms.
Jove's thunder roars, heaven trembles all around;
50   Blue Neptune storms, the bellowing deeps resound;
Earth shakes her nodding towers, the ground gives way;
And the pale ghosts start at the flash of day!
  Triumphant Umbriel on a sconce's height
Clapped his glad wings, and sat to view the fight:
Propped on their bodkin spears, the sprites survey
The growing combat, or assist the fray.
  While through the press enraged Thalestris flies,
And scatters death around from both her eyes,

smallpox common and disfiguring disease at the
time
virago man-like woman

Pallas Athena
Latona the mother of Apollo and Diana (Pope
latinized Greek names in his translations)

A beau and witling perished in the throng;
60 One died in metaphor, and one in song.
'O cruel nymph! a living death I bear,'
Cried Dapperwit,° and sunk beside his chair.
A mournful glance Sir Fopling upwards cast,
'Those eyes are made so killing'—was his last.
Thus on Maeander's flowery margin lies
The expiring swan,° and as he sings he dies.
    When bold Sir Plume had drawn Clarissa down,
Chloe stepped in, and killed him with a frown;
She smiled to see the doughty hero slain,
70 But at her smile, the beau revived again.
    Now Jove suspends his golden scales° in air,
Weighs the men's wits against the lady's hair;
The doubtful beam long nods from side to side;
At length the wits mount up, the hairs subside.
    See, fierce Belinda on the Baron flies,
With more than usual lightning in her eyes;
Nor feared the Chief the unequal fight to try,
Who sought no more than on his foe to die.°
But this bold lord, with manly strength endued,
80 She with one finger and a thumb subdued:
Just where the breath of life his nostrils drew,
A charge of snuff the wily virgin threw;
The Gnomes direct, to every atom just,
The pungent grains of titillating dust.
Sudden, with starting tears each eye o'erflows,
And the high dome re-echoes to his nose.
    'Now meet thy fate,' incensed Belinda cried,
And drew a deadly bodkin from her side.
(The same,° his ancient personage to deck,
90 Her great great grandsire wore about his neck
In three seal rings; which after, melted down,
Formed a vast buckle for his widow's gown:
Her infant grandame's° whistle next it grew,
The bells she jingled, and the whistle blew;
Then in a bodkin graced her mother's hairs,
Which long she wore, and now Belinda wears.)
    'Boast not my fall' (he cried) 'insulting foe!
Thou by some other shalt be laid as low.
Nor think, to die dejects my lofty mind;
100 All that I dread is leaving you behind!

Dapperwit like "Sir Fopling" below, the typical name of a false wit or fop in Restoration comedy
expiring swan The swan, on the banks of the wandering river Maeander, sings most sweetly as he dies.
golden scales an epic convention in both Homer and Virgil

to die in the double sense of "expiring" (IV.42), as elsewhere in this section, e.g. "laid as low" (l. 98)
The same a parody of epic accounts of the descent of armor or of Agamemnon's scepter
grandame's grandmother's

Rather than so, ah let me still survive,
And burn in Cupid's flames—but burn alive.'
    'Restore the lock!' she cries; and all around
'Restore the lock!' the vaulted roofs rebound.
Not fierce Othello in so loud a strain
Roared for the handkerchief° that caused his pain.
But see how oft ambitious aims are crossed,
And chiefs contend till all the prize is lost!
The lock, obtained with guilt, and kept with pain,
In every place is sought, but sought in vain:
With such a prize no mortal must be blest,
So heaven decrees! with heaven who can contest?
    Some thought it mounted to the lunar sphere,°
Since all things lost on earth are treasured there.
There heroes' wits are kept in ponderous vases,
And beaus' in snuffboxes and tweezer cases.
There broken vows, and deathbed alms are found,
And lovers' hearts with ends of riband bound;
The courtier's promises, and sick man's prayers,
The smiles of harlots, and the tears of heirs,
Cages for gnats, and chains to yoke a flea,
Dried butterflies, and tomes of casuistry.°
    But trust the Muse—she saw it upward rise,
Though marked by none but quick, poetic eyes:
(So Rome's great founder° to the heavens withdrew,
To Proculus alone confessed in view.)
A sudden star, it shot through liquid° air,
And drew behind a radiant trail of hair.°
Not Berenice's locks° first rose so bright,
The heavens bespangling with dishevelled light.
The Sylphs behold it kindling as it flies,
And pleased pursue its progress through the skies.
    This the beau monde° shall from the Mall° survey,
And hail with music its propitious ray.
This, the blest lover shall for Venus take,
And send up vows from Rosamonda's lake.°

10
20
30

Roared . . . handkerchief   perhaps   evoking
Thomas Rymer's famous objections to the triviality of the occasion in Shakespeare's play: "So
much ado, so much stress, so much passion and
repetition about an handkerchief!" (*A Short
View of Tragedy*, 1693)
lunar sphere reminiscent of Milton's Limbo of
Vanity in *Paradise Lost* III.445–46, "Up hither
like aerial vapours flew / All things transitory
and vain," but even more of Milton's source
in Ariosto, *Orlando Furioso* XXXIV.lxviii ff.,
where the moral tone is lighter and the objects
more trivial and minutely specified
casuistry Pope wrote in a letter of 1708 about
"deep divines, profound casuists, grave philosophers who have written . . . whole tomes and
voluminous treatises about nothing"; casuistry

was the difficult (and sometimes hair-splitting)
application of general ethical rules to individual
cases.
founder Romulus, who disappeared in a storm
and whose ascent to the heavens was attested
only by the senator Proculus
liquid clear
trail of hair like the tail of a comet, whose
name means "hairy star"
Berenice's locks The queen's hair, offered to
Aphrodite to ensure her husband's safe return
from battle, disappeared from the temple and
was transformed into a constellation.
beau monde fashionable world
Mall the promenade in St. James's Park
Rosamonda's lake a pond in the same park,
associated with unhappy lovers

This Partridge° soon shall view in cloudless skies,
When next he looks through Galileo's eyes;°
And hence the egregious wizard shall foredoom
140   The fate of Louis, and the fall of Rome.
    Then cease, bright nymph! to mourn thy ravished hair
Which adds new glory to the shining sphere!
Not all the tresses that fair head can boast
Shall draw such envy as the lock you lost.
For, after all the murders of your eye,
When, after millions slain, yourself shall die;
When those fair suns shall set, as set they must,
And all those tresses shall be laid in dust;
This lock, the Muse shall consecrate to fame,
150   And midst the stars inscribe Belinda's name!
                    1712–14

Elegy to the Memory of an Unfortunate Lady

With *Eloisa to Abelard,* also published in 1717, this represents the most romantic strain in Pope's poetry, and the defense of a "brave disorder" is more thoroughgoing here than in *Eloisa.* (These poems, it should be said, were chosen for highest, and at times for exclusive, praise among Pope's works by some later eighteenth-century critics who reacted against Pope's involvement in the daily life of his time.) The poem draws upon the pattern of Roman elegy, notably in Ovid, Tibullus, and Propertius; and it creates a situation comparable to those presented in Ovid's *Heroides,* where women spoke with deep feeling of the wrongs done them, or in Nicholas Rowe's "she-tragedies" (such as *The Fair Penitent* of 1703, *Jane Shore* of 1714, or *Lady Jane Grey* of 1715), which turned from the more heroic vein to the pathetic and drew upon such sources as Thomas Otway and Racine.

    The identity of the lady has aroused much futile speculation. All we need to know about her can be surmised from the poet's lament. That opens with the vision of a ghost who still bears the wound and the weapon of her suicide, as if she had been rejected by heaven as she had by her guardian before. Her wandering the earth after death seems the counterpart of her burial abroad in unhallowed ground. Tellingly, as the poet asserts her dignity and even her sanctity, he laments as well her mortality and his own, stressing both the threats that beset human feeling and the grandeur of its intensity, moving from heroic passion to tender compassion.

Elegy to the Memory of an Unfortunate Lady

What beckoning ghost, along the moonlight shade
Invites my steps, and points to yonder glade?
'Tis she!—but why that bleeding bosom gored,

Partridge a notorious astrologer (ridiculed by Swift) who predicted public events, such as those in l. 140   **Galileo's eyes** telescope

Why dimly gleams the visionary sword?
Oh ever beauteous, ever friendly! tell,
Is it, in heaven, a crime to love too well?
To bear too tender, or too firm a heart,
To act a lover's or a Roman's part?°
Is there no bright reversion° in the sky,
10   For those who greatly think, or bravely die?
      Why bade ye else, ye Powers! her soul aspire
Above the vulgar flight of low desire?
Ambition first sprung from your blest abodes;
The glorious fault of angels and of gods:°
Thence to their images on earth it flows,
And in the breasts of kings and heroes glows.
Most souls, 'tis true, but peep out once an age,
Dull sullen prisoners in the body's cage:
Dim lights of life, that burn a length of years
20   Useless, unseen, as lamps in sepulchres;
Like eastern kings° a lazy state they keep,
And close confined to their own palace, sleep.
      From these perhaps (ere nature bade her die)
Fate snatched her early to the pitying sky.
As into air the purer spirits flow,
And separate from their kindred dregs below;°
So flew the soul to its congenial place,
Nor left one virtue to redeem her race.
      But thou, false guardian of a charge too good,
30   Thou, mean deserter of thy brother's blood!
See on these ruby lips the trembling breath,
These cheeks, now fading at the blast of death;
Cold is that breast which warmed the world before,
And those love-darting eyes must roll no more.
Thus, if eternal justice rules the ball,
Thus shall your wives, and thus your children fall:
On all the line a sudden vengeance waits,
And frequent hearses shall besiege your gates.
There passengers shall stand, and pointing say,
40   (While the long funerals blacken all the way)
Lo these were they, whose souls the Furies° steeled,
And cursed with hearts unknowing how to yield.
Thus unlamented pass the proud away,
The gaze of fools, and pageant of a day!
So perish all, whose breast ne'er learned to glow

Roman's part commit suicide
reversion literally, a property one expects to obtain; something restored after a period to its true owner
glorious fault . . . gods referring to the rebellion of heavenly angels (as in *Paradise Lost*) or of the Titans against Zeus, but also recalling the discussion of ambition as a "spark too much of heavenly fire" in Dryden, *Absalom and Achitophel*, l. 307, or those "great wits" who

"gloriously offend" in Pope, *Essay on Criticism*, l. 152
Like eastern kings Cf. *Epistle to Dr. Arbuthnot*, l. 220.
separate . . . below the purification process of chemical distillation
Furies the avenging goddesses, here punishing the guardian's family for cruelty by cursing them with unremitting obduracy

For others' good, or melt at others' woe.
   What can atone (oh ever-injured shade!)
Thy fate unpitied, and thy rites unpaid?
No friend's complaint, no kind domestic tear
50 Pleased thy pale ghost, or graced thy mournful bier.
By foreign hands thy dying eyes were closed,
By foreign hands thy decent limbs composed,
By foreign hands thy humble grave adorned,
By strangers honoured, and by strangers mourned!
What though no friends in sable weeds appear,
Grieve for an hour, perhaps, then mourn a year,
And bear about the mockery of woe
To midnight dances, and the public show?
What though no weeping Loves° thy ashes grace,
60 Nor polished marble emulate° thy face?
What though no sacred earth° allow thee room,
Nor hallowed dirge be muttered o'er thy tomb?
Yet shall thy grave with rising flowers be drest,
And the green turf lie lightly on thy breast:
There shall the morn her earliest tears bestow,
There the first roses of the year shall blow;°
While angels with their silver wings o'ershade
The ground, now sacred by thy reliques° made.
   So peaceful rests, without a stone, a name,
70 What once had beauty, titles, wealth, and fame.
How loved, how honoured once, avails thee not,
To whom related, or by whom begot;
A heap of dust alone remains of thee,
'Tis all thou art, and all the proud shall be!
   Poets themselves must fall, like those they sung,
Deaf the praised ear, and mute the tuneful tongue.
Even he, whose soul now melts in mournful lays,
Shall shortly want the generous tear he pays;
Then from his closing eyes thy form shall part,
80 And the last pang shall tear thee from his heart,
Life's idle business at one gasp be o'er,
The Muse forgot, and thou beloved no more!

                1717

Loves funerary monuments in the form of mourning cupids
emulate rival, reproduce
sacred earth Presumably because of her suicide, the lady is denied burial in consecrated ground and the performance of Christian rites ("hallowed dirge"); in contrast, Nature pays her honors in flowers, turf, and the "tears" of morning dew.
blow blossom
reliques remains, often used of a saint's remains; here making sacred the ground in which they lie

An Essay on Man

This is Pope's effort to recall man to those truths he professes to believe but finds hard to live by. The essay deals with the complaints that man raises against his nature and his fate, complaints that grow out of the false expectations of pride: that man is the sole end of the universe and that he can enjoy stable self-mastery. The lesson he must relearn is that of God's impartial order—the Great Chain of Being, linking every kind of creature from lowest to highest—and of his place within it. Man is the most dangerous link, neither securely rational nor governed by sure instinct, a volatile mixture (as the opening passage of the second epistle of the *Essay* reveals) and therefore an unstable one. The *Essay* insists upon man's incompleteness, upon his dependent existence within a vast harmony in which nothing can quite subsist without the support of all other creatures. In the final epistle man is taught to find his happiness not in externals but in humility, not in expansion and conquest but in the contraction that opens out in turn as love rather than possession, admitting all creatures into the spreading circle of one's love. Man finds himself, as in traditional Christianity, by losing himself; as he takes "every creature in, of every kind," he finds his earth a new Eden and becomes once more a creature in God's image: "Earth smiles around, with boundless bounty blest, / And Heaven beholds its image in his breast."

In the third epistle Pope treats man's political and social order, and in the passage given below he traces man's career from the state of nature, through the fall into superstition and tyranny, to the ultimate recovery of order through human institutions. Pope differs from the Epicureans, and from Hobbes and Mandeville, in seeing the state of nature as one of society rather than of chaotic individual impulse and appetite. The recovery of political order is for Pope, as for Hobbes and Mandeville, forced upon man by the intolerable insecurity of that state that they call natural but Pope regards as a fallen one; in the process, as Pope presents it, man rediscovers what is inherently natural. The political state is not, therefore, a mere work of artifice, nor is its authority the merely arbitrary one of established power. It is an embodiment, however imperfect, of a natural order and can claim legitimacy by an appeal to natural law.

An Essay on Man

From *Epistle II*

I. Know then thyself, presume not God to scan;°
The proper study of mankind is Man.
Placed on this isthmus of a middle state,
A being darkly wise, and rudely° great:
With too much knowledge for the Sceptic side,°
With too much weakness for the Stoic's pride,°
He hangs between; in doubt to act, or rest,
In doubt to deem himself a god, or beast;

scan criticize, judge
rudely turbulently, roughly

Sceptic side the distrust of the possibility of certain knowledge
Stoic's pride the mastery of all passions

In doubt his mind or body to prefer,
10   Born but to die, and reasoning but to err;
Alike in ignorance, his reason such,
Whether he thinks too little, or too much:
Chaos of thought and passion, all confused;
Still by himself abused, or disabused;
Created half to rise, and half to fall;
Great lord of all things, yet a prey to all;
Sole judge of truth, in endless error hurled:
The glory, jest, and riddle of the world! . . .

From *Epistle III*

IV. Nor think, in NATURE's STATE they blindly trod;
The state of nature° was the reign of God:
Self-love and social at her birth began,
150   Union the bond of all things, and of man.
Pride then was not; nor arts, that pride to aid;
Man walked with beast, joint tenant of the shade;
The same his table, and the same his bed;
No murder clothed him, and no murder fed.
In the same temple, the resounding wood,
All vocal beings hymned their equal° God:
The shrine with gore unstained, with gold undressed,
Unbribed, unbloody,° stood the blameless priest:
Heaven's attribute was universal care,
160   And man's prerogative to rule, but spare.
Ah! how unlike the man of times to come!
Of half that live the butcher and the tomb;°
Who, foe to nature, hears the general groan,
Murders their species and betrays his own.
But just disease to luxury succeeds,
And every death its own avenger breeds;
The fury-passions from that blood began,
And turned on man a fiercer savage,° man.
See him from nature rising slow to art!
170   To copy instinct then was reason's part;
Thus then to man the voice of Nature spake—
'Go, from the creatures thy instructions take:
Learn from the birds what food the thickets yield;
Learn from the beasts the physic° of the field;
Thy arts of building from the bee° receive;
Learn of the mole to plough, the worm° to weave;

---

state of nature rejecting Hobbes's view of it as a state of war in which man was a "wolf to man" and human life was "nasty, brutish, and short"; social love is not artificial but natural, and order or union is part of the frame of nature
equal common, impartial

unbloody not yet sacrificing animals or fellow men
butcher . . . tomb slayer and devourer
savage wild animal
physic medicinal herbs
bee as architect of honeycombed hives
worm silkworm

Learn of the little nautilus° to sail,
Spread the thin oar, and catch the driving gale.
Here too all forms of social union find,
180 And hence let reason, late, instruct mankind:
Here subterranean works° and cities see;
There towns aerial° on the waving tree.
Learn each small people's genius, policies,
The ant's republic, and the realm of bees;°
How those in common all their wealth bestow,
And anarchy without confusion know;
And these for ever, though a monarch reign,
Their separate cells and properties maintain.
Mark what unvaried laws preserve each state,
190 Laws wise as nature, and as fixed as fate.
In vain thy reason finer webs shall draw,
Entangle justice in her net of law,
And right, too rigid, harden into wrong;
Still for the strong too weak, the weak too strong.
Yet go! and thus o'er all the creatures sway,
Thus let the wiser make the rest obey,
And, for those arts mere instinct could afford,
Be crowned as monarchs, or as gods adored.'

    V. Great Nature spoke; observant men obeyed;
200 Cities were built, societies were made:
Here rose one little state; another near
Grew by like means, and joined, through love or fear.
Did here the trees with ruddier burdens bend,
And there the streams in purer rills descend?
What war could ravish, commerce could bestow,
And he returned a friend, who came a foe.
Converse and love mankind might strongly draw,
When love was liberty, and nature law.
Thus states were formed; the name of king unknown,
210 Till common interest placed the sway in one.
'Twas virtue only (or in arts or arms,
Diffusing blessings, or averting harms)
The same which in a sire the sons obeyed,
A prince the father of a people made.

    VI. Till then, by nature crowned, each patriarch sate,
King, priest, and parent of his growing state;
On him, their second providence, they hung,
Their law his eye, their oracle his tongue.

---

nautilus "They swim on the surface of the sea, on the back of their shells, which exactly resemble the hulk of a ship; they raise two feet like masts and extend a membrane between them which serves as a sail; the other two feet they employ as oars at the side" (Pope).

subterranean works anthills
towns aerial beehives
ant's republic . . . bees representing egalitarian and monarchical states, respectively, in the next four lines

He from the wondering° furrow called the food,
220   Taught to command the fire, control the flood,
Draw forth the monsters of the abyss profound,
Or fetch the aërial eagle to the ground.
Till drooping, sickening, dying they began
Whom they revered as god to mourn as man:
Then, looking up from sire to sire, explored°
One great first father, and that first adored.
Or plain tradition that this All begun,°
Conveyed unbroken faith from sire to son,
The worker from the work distinct was known,
230   And simple reason never sought but one:
Ere wit oblique° had broke that steady light,
Man, like his Maker, saw that all was right,°
To virtue, in the paths of pleasure, trod,
And owned a Father when he owned a God.
LOVE all the faith, and all the allegiance then;
For nature knew no right divine° in men,
No ill could fear in God; and understood
A sovereign being but a sovereign good.
True faith, true policy,° united ran,
240   This was but love of God, and this of man.
     Who first taught souls enslaved, and realms undone,
The enormous° faith of many made for one;°
That proud exception to all nature's laws,
To invert the world, and counterwork its Cause?°
Force first made conquest, and that conquest, law;
Till superstition taught the tyrant awe,
Then shared the tyranny, then lent it aid,
And gods of conquerors, slaves of subjects made:
She,° midst the lightning's blaze, and thunder's sound,
250   When rocked the mountains, and when groaned the ground,
She taught the weak to bend, the proud to pray,
To power unseen, and mightier far than they:
She, from the rending earth and bursting skies,
Saw gods descend and fiends infernal rise:
Here fixed the dreadful, there the blest abodes;
Fear made her devils, and weak hope her gods;
Gods partial, changeful, passionate, unjust,

---

wondering sharing the amazement of the people
explored discovered by inference
this All begun the world as created rather than eternal and self-subsistent, a theistic rather than a pantheistic view, which leads man to distinguish the creature from the Creator (l. 229)
wit oblique prismatically breaking the "steady light," as in the *Essay on Criticism*, ll. 311–12
all was right Cf. Genesis 1:31: "And God saw every thing that he had made, and, behold, it was very good."
right divine arbitrary power conferred upon specific men by God, as was claimed by the divine right of kings
policy government
enormous monstrous
many made for one "In this Aristotle placeth the difference between a king and a tyrant, that the first supposeth himself made for the people, the other that the people are made for him" (William Warburton, citing *Politics* V.10).
To invert . . . Cause repudiating God's design that all creatures serve each other
She superstition

Whose attributes were rage, revenge, or lust;
Such as the souls of cowards might conceive,
And, formed like tyrants, tyrants would believe.°
Zeal° then, not charity, became the guide,
And hell was built on spite, and heaven on pride.
Then sacred seemed the ethereal vault no more;
Altars grew marble then, and reeked with gore:
Then first the flamen° tasted living food;
Next his grim idol smeared with human blood;°
With heaven's own thunders shook the world below,
And played the god an engine on his foe.°
    So drives self-love, through just and through unjust,
To one man's power, ambition, lucre, lust:
The same self-love, in all, becomes the cause
Of what restrains him, government and laws.
For, what one likes if others like as well,
What serves one will,° when many wills rebel?
How shall he keep, what, sleeping or awake,
A weaker may surprise, a stronger take?
His safety must his liberty restrain:
All join to guard what each desires to gain.
Forced into virtue thus by self-defence,
Even kings learned justice and benevolence:
Self-love forsook the path it first pursued,
And found the private in the public good.
    'Twas then, the studious head or generous mind,
Follower of God or friend of humankind,
Poet or patriot, rose but to restore
The faith and moral,° Nature gave before;
Relumed her ancient light, not kindled new;°
If not God's image, yet his shadow drew:
Taught power's due use to people and to kings,
Taught nor to slack, nor strain its tender strings,°
The less, or greater, set so justly true,
That touching one must strike° the other too;
Till jarring° interests of themselves create
The according music of a well-mixed state.°

60
270
280
290

formed . . . believe A worship "grounded not on love but fear," for "the superstitious man looks on the Great Father of all as a tyrant. . . . Accordingly he serves his Maker but as slaves do their tyrants, with a gloomy savage zeal against his fellow-creatures . . . though at the same time he trembles with the dread of being ill-used himself." (Pope)
Zeal fanaticism
flamen priest
smeared . . . blood Cf. Milton, Paradise Lost I.392–93: "First Moloch, horrid king, besmeared with blood / Of human sacrifice . . .".
played . . . foe i.e. turned God into a piece of artillery, an instrument of man's own will and vengeance

What . . . will of what force is one will?
moral moral principles, as above in ll. 235–40
Relumed . . . new revived the natural order rather than invented society for the first time
tender strings as in musical instruments, whose harmony was a common analogy for political order
strike cause to reverberate
jarring conflicting, discordant
well-mixed state The mixed state was a balance of the power of the One, the Few, and the Many; such a balance was believed to give the state the stability to endure, and to withstand the claims of rival factions within it.

Such is the world's great harmony, that springs
From order, union, full consent of things!
Where small and great, where weak and mighty, made
To serve, not suffer, strengthen, not invade,
More powerful each as needful to the rest,
300   And, in proportion as it blesses, blest,
Draw to one point, and to one centre bring
Beast, man, or angel, servant, lord, or king,
    For forms of government let fools contest;
Whate'er is best administered is best:°
For modes of faith, let graceless° zealots fight;
His can't be wrong whose life is in the right:
In faith and hope the world will disagree,
But all mankind's concern is charity:
All must be false that thwart this one great end,
310   And all of God, that bless mankind or mend.
    Man, like the generous vine,° supported lives;
The strength he gains is from the embrace he gives.
On their own axis as the planets run,°
Yet make at once their circle round the sun:
So two consistent motions act the soul;
And one regards itself, and one the Whole.
    Thus God and Nature linked the general frame,
And bade self-love and social be the same.
1731?   1733

To Richard Boyle, Earl of Burlington

Richard Boyle, third Earl of Burlington (1695–1753), studied architecture in Italy,
designed buildings himself and commissioned works by others, and sponsored publication of the designs of Andrea Palladio and Inigo Jones. In opposition to the
baroque of Sir Christopher Wren and Sir John Vanbrugh, he promoted a more severe
classicism and spent great sums on public buildings in that spirit. This epistle is
an important document of eighteenth-century taste. It sets forth a theory of landscape gardening that Pope had already begun to apply in his own estate and, even
more, in his advice to affluent landowners. What he recommends is a "natural"
garden, which came to be known through Europe as an "English garden"; that is,
one which does not disdain artifice (as no garden can) but seeks to adjust its improvements to the tendencies of the landscape and to bring to fulfillment what is latently
there rather than impose a formal design upon it. It is a garden of concealed bound-
aries, of variety of light and shade, and with the power to evoke the landscapes

---

Whate'er . . . best Pope later explained that
he did not mean "that no one form of government is, in itself, better than another . . . but
that no form of government, however excellent
or preferable in itself, can be sufficient to make
a people happy, unless it be administered with
integrity."

graceless crude; but also, without divine grace
generous vine as in traditional fables of the
love of the vine and the elm, "generous" in giving of oneself to another
run rotate

painted by the great masters of the seventeenth century—Nicolas Poussin, Claude Lorrain, and others (see below, The Garden and the Wild).

The poem is also an interesting discussion of architectural form and function, and, most generally, of the relationship between taste and morality—a problem first raised in the *Essay on Criticism*. Pride is once more a central theme; here, too, it creates objects that are meant to stun, to astonish, to captivate by size or cost, and it neglects the function of part in a whole. The whole is hospitality in Timon's villa; but, more than that, it is generosity and concern for others, even concern for a reality that bounds, limits, and—in the good man—extends and fulfills the self. We can see that whole restored when "laughing Ceres" reassumes Timon's land or when Burlington sponsors, in contrast to the ornamental projects of "imitating fools," public works that gain their dignity, and even their beauty, from solid public use.

The identity of Timon caused Pope much pain; Timon was claimed by the malice of others to refer to Lord Chandos, who had befriended Pope and who, it should be said, dismissed the rumors himself. There now seems reason to see behind Timon, or at least some aspects of him, the figure of Walpole—at his huge house at Houghton —imposing his will in displays of magnificence (which Pope treats as unwitting self-exposure) and turning away Pope's satire by having his supporters direct it to Chandos. If Timon be taken as Walpole, he is only one aspect of that "great man" and a contemptibly trivialized version at that; but he serves to relate the realms of art and politics, and to show the opposition of the tyrannous private will to the generous harmony of a natural order.

The essay was first called *Of Taste* and later *Of False Taste*.

To Richard Boyle, Earl of Burlington

Of the Use of Riches

'Tis strange, the miser should his cares employ
To gain those riches he can ne'er enjoy:
Is it less strange, the prodigal should waste
His wealth, to purchase what he ne'er can taste?
Not for himself he sees, or hears, or eats;
Artists must choose his pictures, music, meats:
He buys for Topham,° drawings and designs,
For Pembroke,° statues, dirty gods, and coins;
Rare monkish manuscripts for Hearne° alone,
10   And books for Mead,° and butterflies for Sloane.°
Think we all these are for himself! no more
Than his fine wife, alas! or finer whore.

Topham Richard Topham (d. 1735), a "gentleman famous for a judicious collection of drawings" (Pope)
Pembroke Thomas Herbert, 8th Earl of Pembroke (1656–1733), had large collections of statues, pictures, and coins at Wilton House.
Hearne Thomas Hearne (1678–1735), eminent medievalist and editor of early English chronicles
Mead Richard Mead (1673–1754), royal physician and friend of Pope, collector of some 30,000 books
Sloane Sir Hans Sloane (1660–1753), also royal physician and master of "the finest collection in Europe of natural curiosities" (Pope)

For what has Virro° painted, built, and planted?
Only to show, how many tastes he wanted.°
What brought Sir Visto's° ill got wealth to waste?
Some demon whispered, 'Visto! have a taste.'
Heaven visits with a taste the wealthy fool,
And needs no rod° but Ripley° with a rule.°
See! sportive fate, to punish awkward pride,
20 Bids Bubo° build, and sends him such a guide:
A standing sermon, at each year's expense,
That never coxcomb° reached magnificence!°
     You° show us, Rome was glorious, not profuse,
And pompous buildings once were things of use.
Yet shall (my Lord) your just, your noble rules
Fill half the land with imitating fools;
Who random drawings from your sheets shall take,
And of one beauty many blunders make;
Load some vain church with old theatric state,°
30 Turn arcs of triumph° to a garden gate;
Reverse your ornaments, and hang them all
On some patched dog-hole eked with ends of wall;
Then clap four slices of pilaster° on't,
That, laced with bits of rustic,° makes a front;°
Shall call the winds through long arcades to roar,
Proud to catch cold at a Venetian door;°
Conscious they act a true Palladian part,
And, if they starve,° they starve by rules of art.
     Oft have you hinted to your brother peer,
40 A certain truth, which many buy too dear:
Something there is more needful than expense,
And something previous even to taste—'tis sense:
Good sense, which only is the gift of Heaven,°
And though no science, fairly worth the seven:

Virro named for the contemptible rich patron in Juvenal's Fifth Satire
wanted lacked
Visto's named for a vista, a long view through an avenue of trees
rod punishment
Ripley Thomas Ripley (d. 1758), a mediocre but politically favored architect, a protégé of Walpole, hired to execute others' plans for Walpole's hall at Houghton; as Pope put it, "a carpenter employed by a First Minister, who raised him into an architect without any genius in the art"
rule carpenter's rule, as a form of "rod"; also a misapplied principle, as in ll. 25–26
Bubo Latin for owl; a reference to Bubb Dodington, a Whig politician who spent £140,000 completing a country house designed by Sir John Vanbrugh
coxcomb fop, pretender
magnificence not merely splendor but, according to Aristotle (*Nicomachean Ethics* IV.2), spending generously on public works rather than on one's own
You Burlington, then publishing the *Antiquities*

of *Rome* by the great Italian architect Andrea Palladio (1518–80), and other architectural drawings whose "sheets" (l. 27) might be searched for ornamental details by those without a true sense of their "use" (l. 24)
theatric state the misapplied details of a Roman amphitheater; the use of classical detail to achieve baroque theatricality
arcs of triumph Roman triumphal arches reduced in scale and used as models for ornamental gateways
pilaster a column attached to a wall
laced . . . rustic embellished with rustication, the imitation of naturally rough stones
front "frontispiece," the formal entrance to a building
Venetian door Palladio invented the Venetian door and window, consisting of an opening with an arched top set between two smaller rectangular openings; these, originally essential to the structural design of Palladio's buildings, became isolated decorative elements.
starve because of cost and the great distances that food had to be brought
gift of Heaven Cf. *Essay on Criticism*, l. 13.

A light, which in yourself you must perceive;
Jones° and Le Nôtre° have it not to give.
  To build, to plant, whatever you intend,
To rear the column, or the arch to bend,
To swell the terrace, or to sink the grot;°
50 In all, let Nature never be forgot.
But treat the goddess like a modest fair,
Nor overdress, nor leave her wholly bare;
Let not each beauty everywhere be spied,
Where half the skill is decently° to hide.
He gains all points, who pleasingly confounds,
Surprises, varies, and conceals the bounds.
  Consult the genius of the place° in all;
That tells the waters or to rise, or fall;
Or helps the ambitious hill the heavens to scale,
60 Or scoops in circling theatres° the vale;
Calls in the country, catches opening glades,
Joins willing woods, and varies shades from shades;
Now breaks, or now directs, the intending lines;°
Paints° as you plant, and, as you work, designs.
  Still follow sense, of every art the soul,
Parts answering parts shall slide into a whole,
Spontaneous beauties all around advance,
Start even from difficulty, strike from chance;
Nature shall join you; time shall make it grow
70 A work to wonder at—perhaps a Stowe.°
  Without it, proud Versailles!° thy glory falls;
And Nero's terraces° desert their walls:
The vast parterres° a thousand hands shall make,
Lo! Cobham comes, and floats° them with a lake:
Or cut wide views° through mountains to the plains,
You'll wish your hill or sheltered seat° again.
Even in an ornament its place remark,
Nor in an Hermitage set Dr. Clarke.°
  Behold Villario's ten years' toil complete;

Jones Inigo Jones (1573–1652), the distinguished architect and scene designer
Le Nôtre André Le Nôtre (1613–1700), the great French designer of formal gardens, notably those at Versailles
grot grotto, artificial cave
decently modestly, appropriately
genius of the place the character of the natural landscape; also the tutelary deity or *genius loci* who inhabited each place and guarded it
theatres the curving slopes of classical amphitheaters
intending lines which lead the eye forward
Paints with color, and perhaps composes in such designs as landscape painters had used
Stowe the house and gardens of Richard Temple, Lord Cobham (1675–1749), of which Pope wrote at the time, "if anything under Paradise could set me beyond all earthly cogitations, Stowe might do it"

Versailles the formal gardens of Louis XIV's palace
Nero's terraces the elaborate works of the Golden House of Nero, in Rome
parterres formal terraces
floats floods
cut wide views "This was done . . . by a wealthy citizen . . . by which means (merely to overlook a dead plain) he let in the north wind upon his house and parterre, which were before adorned and defended by beautiful woods" (Pope).
seat country house
Hermitage . . . Dr. Clarke Samuel Clarke (1675–1729) was a liberal theologian and student of science, rationalistic and unorthodox, hardly the man for a "hermitage." That is the name of an ornamental building in Richmond Park where Queen Caroline placed busts of Clarke, her favorite, as well as of Locke, Newton, and others.

80 His quincunx° darkens, his espaliers° meet;
The wood supports the plain, the parts unite,
And strength of shade contends with strength of light;
A waving glow the bloomy beds display,
Blushing in bright diversities of day,
With silver-quivering rills meandered o'er—
Enjoy them, you! Villario can no more;
Tired of the scene parterres and fountains yield,
He finds at last he better likes a field.
Through his young woods how pleased Sabinus strayed,
90 Or sat delighted in the thickening shade,
With annual joy the reddening shoots to greet,
Or see the stretching branches long to meet!
His son's fine taste an opener vista loves,
Foe to the dryads° of his father's groves;
One boundless green, or flourished carpet° views,
With all the mournful family of yews;°
The thriving plants ignoble broomsticks made,
Now sweep those alleys they were born to shade.
At Timon's Villa let us pass a day,
100 Where all cry out, 'What sums are thrown away!'
So proud, so grand; of that stupendous air,
Soft and agreeable come never there.
Greatness, with Timon, dwells in such a draught
As brings all Brobdingnag° before your thought.
To compass this, his building is a town,
His pond an ocean, his parterre a down:
Who but must laugh, the master when he sees,
A puny insect, shivering at a breeze!
Lo, what huge heaps of littleness around!
110 The whole, a laboured quarry above ground.
Two cupids squirt before: a lake behind
Improves the keenness of the northern wind.°
His gardens next your admiration call,
On every side you look, behold the wall!
No pleasing intricacies intervene,
No artful wildness to perplex the scene;
Grove nods at grove, each alley has a brother,
And half the platform just reflects the other.
The suffering eye inverted Nature sees,
120 Trees cut to statues,° statues thick as trees;

quincunx a planting of five trees, four at the corners and one in the center
espaliers trees fastened to a wall
dryads tree nymphs
flourished carpet a terrace with elaborate scrolled beds, here opposed to the contrary vice, the nakedness of a "boundless green"
yews typical planting in cemeteries; here simply forming "pyramids of dark green continually repeated, not unlike a funeral procession" (Pope)
Brobdingnag the land of giants (in the proportion of 12:1 to man) in the second voyage of Swift's *Gulliver's Travels;* all this emphasizing the irony of calling Timon's sprawling palace a "villa"
northern wind an instance of the neglect of function in the "improvement" of landscape; cf. l. 75
Trees . . . statues referring to the topiary art of trimming trees or hedges into sculpturesque shapes

With here a fountain, never to be played;
And there a summerhouse, that knows no shade;
Here Amphitrite° sails through myrtle bowers;
There gladiators fight, or die in flowers;
Unwatered see the drooping sea-horse mourn,
And swallows roost in Nilus' dusty urn.°
   My Lord advances with majestic mien,
Smit with the mighty pleasure, to be seen:
But soft—by regular approach—not yet—
130 First through the length of yon hot terrace sweat;
And when up ten steep slopes you've dragged your thighs,
Just at his study door he'll bless your eyes.
   His study! with what authors is it stored?
In books, not authors, curious is my Lord;
To all their dated backs° he turns you round:
These Aldus° printed, those Du Sueil° has bound.
Lo, some are vellum, and the rest as good
For all his Lordship knows, but they are wood.
For Locke or Milton 'tis in vain to look,
140 These shelves admit not any modern book.
   And now the chapel's silver bell you hear,
That summons you to all the pride of prayer:
Light quirks of music, broken and uneven,
Make the soul dance upon a jig to Heaven.
On painted ceilings you devoutly stare,
Where sprawl the saints of Verrio or Laguerre,°
On gilded clouds in fair expansion lie,
And bring all Paradise before your eye.
To rest, the cushion and soft dean° invite,
150 Who never mentions Hell to ears polite.
   But hark! the chiming clocks to dinner call;
A hundred footsteps scrape the marble hall:
The rich buffet well-coloured serpents grace,
And gaping tritons° spew to wash your face.
Is this a dinner? this a genial room?
No, 'tis a temple, and a hecatomb.°
A solemn sacrifice, performed in state,

Amphitrite a sea nymph, wife of Poseidon and
mother of Triton
Nilus' . . . urn the urn that accompanies the
statue of the reclining river god and from
which the waters of the river should pour forth
dated backs early or rare editions with the
date stamped in gold on the spine of the binding. "Many delight chiefly in the elegance of the
print or the binding; some have carried it so far
as to cause the upper shelves to be filled with
painted books of wood" (Pope).
Aldus Aldus Manutius (1450–1515), the great
Venetian printer
Du Sueil Augustin Desueil (1673–1746), a
Parisian bookbinder of note
Verrio or Laguerre Antonio Verrio (1639–

1707) and Louis Laguerre (1663–1721) were
fashionable court artists, here creators of baroque
ceiling paintings.
soft dean "This is a fact; a reverend Dean
preaching at Court, threatened the sinner with
punishment in 'a place which he thought it not
decent to name in so polite an assembly'"
(Pope).
gaping tritons "Taxes the incongruity of ornaments . . . where an open mouth ejects the
water into a fountain or where shocking images
of serpents, etc. are introduced in grottos or
buffets" (Pope). "Tritons" have an upper human
form and a lower fishy one, like mermaids.
hecatomb sacrificial slaughter of a hundred oxen

You drink by measure, and to minutes eat.
So quick retires each flying course, you'd swear
160 Sancho's dread Doctor and his wand° were there.
Between each act the trembling salvers ring,
From soup to sweet wine, and God bless the King.°
In plenty starving, tantalized in state,
And complaisantly helped to all I hate,
Treated, caressed, and tired, I take my leave,
Sick of his civil pride from morn to eve;
I curse such lavish cost, and little skill,
And swear no day was ever passed so ill.
      Yet hence the poor are clothed, the hungry fed;
170 Health to himself, and to his infants bread
The labourer bears: what his hard heart denies,
His charitable vanity supplies.°
      Another age shall see the golden ear°
Embrown the slope, and nod on the parterre,
Deep harvests bury all his pride has planned,
And laughing Ceres° reassume° the land.
      Who then shall grace, or who improve the soil?
Who plants like Bathurst,° or who builds like Boyle.°
'Tis use alone that sanctifies expense,
180 And splendour borrows all her rays from sense.
      His father's acres who enjoys in peace,
Or makes his neighbours glad, if he increase:
Whose cheerful tenants bless their yearly toil,
Yet to their Lord owe more than to the soil;
Whose ample lawns are not ashamed to feed
The milky heifer and deserving steed;
Whose rising forests, not for pride or show,
But future buildings, future navies, grow:
Let his plantations stretch from down to down,
190 First shade a country, and then raise a town.
      You too proceed! make falling arts your care,
Erect new wonders, and the old repair;
Jones and Palladio to themselves restore,
And be whate'er Vitruvius° was before:
Till kings call forth the ideas of your mind,
Proud to accomplish what such hands designed,
Bid harbours open, public ways extend,

Sancho's . . . wand Cf. Cervantes, *Don Quixote*
II.xlvii, where the doctor has the food Sancho
yearns for whisked away before he can eat it.
From soup . . . King from the beginning of the
meal to the concluding toast in port
charitable . . . supplies Cf. Atossa in *To a
Lady,* ll. 149–50.
golden ear of wheat
laughing Ceres the Roman goddess of agriculture, cheerfully bounteous and/or scornfully
amused by Timon's unnatural art

reassume regain possession, as a monarch does
a kingdom
Bathurst Allen, Lord Bathurst, (1685–1775),
friend of Congreve, Swift, Pope, and (years
later) of Laurence Sterne; an enthusiastic landscape gardener
Boyle Lord Burlington
Vitruvius Marcus Vitruvius Pollio (1st century
B.C.), the author of the most influential classical
work on architecture

Bid temples,° worthier of the God, ascend;
Bid the broad arch° the dangerous flood contain,
200　The mole projected break the roaring main;
Back to his bounds their subject sea command,
And roll obedient rivers through the land:
These honours, peace to happy Britain brings,
These are imperial works, and worthy kings.°

1731

To a Lady

Of the Characters of Women

Nothing so true as what you once let fall,
'Most women have no characters at all.'
Matter too soft a lasting mark to bear,
And best distinguished by black, brown, or fair.
　How many pictures° of one nymph we view,
All how unlike each other, all how true!
Arcadia's countess,° here, in ermined pride,
Is, there, Pastora° by a fountain side:
Here Fannia,° leering on her own good man,
10　And there, a naked Leda° with a swan.
Let then the fair one beautifully cry,
In Magdalen's loose hair and lifted eye,°
Or dressed in smiles of sweet Cecilia° shine,
With simpering angels, palms, and harps divine;
Whether the charmer sinner it, or saint it,
If folly grow romantic,° I must paint it.
　Come then, the colours and the ground° prepare!
Dip in the rainbow, trick her off° in air,

temples churches. Pope explains that because of graft and misuse of funds "some new-built churches . . . were ready to fall, being founded in boggy land . . . others were vilely executed."
broad arch A proposal to build a new Westminster Bridge was rejected, then its execution entrusted to Ripley, "the carpenter . . . who would have made it a wooden one," but finally built of stone with Burlington as a commissioner (Pope).
imperial . . . kings recalling *Aeneid* VI.852, where Anchises sums up his prophecy to Aeneas of the future of Rome: let others pursue sculpture, rhetoric, or astronomy; Rome has as its task "to tame the proud, the fettered slave to free; / These are imperial arts, and worthy thee"
pictures "Attitudes in which several ladies affected to be drawn, and sometimes one lady in them all" (Pope)
Arcadia's countess suggested by Sir Philip Sidney's romance, *The Countess of Pembroke's*

Arcadia (1590), and perhaps referring to the wife of Thomas, Earl of Pembroke (1656–1733), a great collector and patron of art
Pastora a shepherdess, in contrast with "ermined pride"
Fannia the name of a Roman adulteress
Leda a popular Renaissance subject, as in the painting (now lost) by Leonardo da Vinci, a copy of which hung at Wilton House, the Pembroke seat
loose hair . . . eye typical attributes of the Magdalene in Renaissance painting; the loose hair recalling her drying of Christ's feet with it but also (as in Titian's version) only partially concealing her bare bosom
Cecilia the patron saint of music (celebrated in an ode by Dryden; see above), often shown in her ascent to heaven
romantic extravagant
ground the prepared surface to which paints will be applied
trick her off sketch her

Choose a firm cloud, before it fall, and in it
20   Catch, ere she change, the Cynthia° of this minute.
      Rufa,° whose eye quick-glancing o'er the park,
Attracts each light gay meteor of a spark,°
Agrees as ill with Rufa studying Locke,°
As Sappho's diamonds with her dirty smock,
Or Sappho° at her toilet's greasy task,
With Sappho fragrant at an evening mask:°
So morning insects that in muck° begun,
Shine, buzz, and flyblow° in the setting sun.
      How soft is Silia! fearful to offend,
30   The frail one's advocate, the weak one's friend:
To her, Calista proved her conduct nice,°
And good Simplicius asks of her advice.
Sudden, she storms! she raves! You tip the wink,°
But spare your censure; Silia does not drink.
All eyes may see from what the change arose,
All eyes may see—a pimple on her nose.
      Papillia,° wedded to her amorous spark,
Sighs for the shades—'How charming is a park!'
A park is purchased, but the fair he sees
40   All bathed in tears—'Oh, odious, odious trees!'
      Ladies, like variegated° tulips, show;
'Tis to their changes half their charms we owe;
Fine by defect, and delicately weak,
Their happy spots the nice° admirer take,
'Twas thus Calypso° once each heart alarmed,
Awed without virtue, without beauty charmed;
Her tongue bewitched as oddly as her eyes,
Less wit than mimic, more a wit than wise;
Strange graces still, and stranger flights she had,
50   Was just not ugly, and was just not mad;
Yet ne'er so sure our passion to create,
As when she touched the brink of all we hate.
      Narcissa's° nature, tolerably mild,
To make a wash,° would hardly stew a child;
Has even been proved to grant a lover's prayer,
And paid a tradesman once to make him stare;
Gave alms at Easter, in a Christian trim,°

Cynthia Diana, here the fickle goddess of the constantly changing moon
Rufa so named for her red hair, regarded as a sign of wantonness
spark beau
Locke The philosophy of John Locke (1632–1704) was made a fashionable study by Addison and Steele in the *Spectator* papers.
Sappho a woman poet (cf. Dryden's "Anne Killigrew" ode for this usage), probably Lady Mary Wortley Montagu, notorious for slovenliness
mask masked ball
muck referring to the belief that insects were generated by corruption; cf. *Essay on Criticism*, ll. 41–43
flyblow generate
nice proper, punctilious
tip the wink make a surmise
Papillia Latin for butterfly
variegated streaked, varied in color
nice discriminating
Calypso named for the nymph who detained Odysseus for seven years
Narcissa's whose name suggests vanity
wash for complexion or hair
trim dress, manner

And made a widow happy, for a whim.
Why then declare good-nature is her scorn,
60   When 'tis by that alone she can be borne?
Why pique all mortals, yet affect a name?
A fool to pleasure, yet a slave to fame:
Now deep in Taylor° and the Book of Martyrs,°
Now drinking citron° with his Grace° and Chartres:°
Now conscience chills her, and now passion burns;
And atheism and religion take their turns;
A very heathen in the carnal part,
Yet still a sad,° good Christian at her heart.
    See Sin in state, majestically drunk;
70   Proud as a peeress, prouder as a punk;°
Chaste to her husband, frank° to all beside,
A teeming mistress, but a barren bride.
What then? let blood and body bear the fault,
Her head's untouched, that noble seat of thought:
Such this day's doctrine—in another fit
She sins with poets through pure love of wit.
What has not fired her bosom or her brain?
Caesar and Tallboy,° Charles° and Charlemagne.
As Helluo,° late dictator of the feast,
80   The nose of hautgout,° and the tip of taste,
Critiqued your wine, and analyzed your meat,
Yet on plain pudding deigned at home to eat;
So Philomedé, lecturing all mankind
On the soft passion, and the taste refined,
The address, the delicacy—stoops at once,
And makes her hearty meal upon a dunce.
    Flavia's° a wit, has too much sense to pray;
To toast our wants and wishes, is her way;
Nor asks of God, but of her stars, to give
90   The mighty blessing, 'while we live, to live.'
Then all for death, that opiate of the soul!
Lucretia's° dagger, Rosamonda's° bowl.
Say, what can cause such impotence of mind?
A spark too fickle, or a spouse too kind.
Wise wretch! with pleasures too refined to please;
With too much spirit to be e'er at ease;
With too much quickness ever to be taught;

Taylor Jeremy Taylor (1613–67), whose *Holy
Living* and *Holy Dying* were extremely popular devotional works
Book of Martyrs the popular title of the work
by John Foxe (1516–87)
citron brandy flavored with lemon peel
his Grace a duke, perhaps her lover
Chartres usurer and libertine (cf. *Satires* II.i)
sad sober
punk whore
frank free

Tallboy a booby lover in Richard Brome's *The
Jovial Crew* (1641)
Charles a common name for a footman
Helluo Latin for glutton
hautgout anything with a strong scent or flavor
Flavia's named for blond hair
Lucretia's the Roman matron who committed
suicide when she was raped by Tarquin
Rosamonda's Rosamond Clifford (d. 1177),
mistress of Henry II, forced by his queen to
drink poison

With too much thinking to have common thought:
You purchase pain with all that joy can give,
100   And die of nothing but a rage to live.
    Turn then from wits; and look on Simo's mate,
No ass so meek, no ass so obstinate.
Or her, that owns her faults, but never mends,
Because she's honest, and the best of friends.
Or her, whose life the Church and scandal share,
For ever in a passion, or a prayer.
Or her, who laughs at Hell, but (like her Grace)
Cries, 'Ah! how charming, if there's no such place!'
Or who in sweet vicissitude appears
110   Of mirth and opium, ratafie° and tears,
The daily anodyne, and nightly draught,
To kill those foes to fair ones, time and thought.
Woman and fool are two hard things to hit;
For true no-meaning puzzles more than wit.
    But what are these to great Atossa's° mind?
Scarce once herself, by turns all womankind!
Who, with herself, or others, from her birth
Finds all her life one warfare upon earth:
Shines in exposing knaves and painting fools,
120   Yet is whate'er she hates and ridicules.
No thought advances, but her eddy brain
Whisks it about, and down it goes again.
Full sixty years the world has been her trade,
The wisest fool much time has ever made.
From loveless youth to unrespected age,
No passion gratified except her rage.
So much the fury still outran the wit,
The pleasure missed her, and the scandal hit.
Who breaks with her provokes revenge from hell,
130   But he's a bolder man who dares be well.
Her every turn with violence pursued,
Nor more a storm her hate than gratitude:
To that each passion turns, or soon or late;
Love, if it makes her yield, must make her hate:
Superiors? death! and equals? what a curse!
But an inferior not dependent? worse.
Offend her, and she knows not to forgive;
Oblige her, and she'll hate you while you live:
But die, and she'll adore you—Then the bust°
140   And temple° rise—then fall again to dust.
Last night, her Lord was all that's good and great;

ratafie fruit-flavored liqueur with a brandy base
Atossa's named for the daughter of the Persian
emperor Cyrus the Great and the mother of
Xerxes; probably based upon Katharine Darnley,
Duchess of Buckinghamshire (1682?–1743) and

daughter of James II (although long believed to
be Sarah, Duchess of Marlborough)
bust funerary monument
temple sepulcher

A knave this morning, and his will a cheat.
Strange! by the means defeated of the ends,
By spirit robbed of power, by warmth of friends,
By wealth of followers! without one distress,
Sick of herself through very selfishness!
Atossa, cursed with every granted prayer,
Childless with all her children, wants an heir.
To heirs unknown descends the unguarded store,
150 Or wanders, Heaven-directed, to the poor.
     Pictures like these, dear Madam, to design,
Asks no firm hand, and no unerring line;
Some wandering touches, some reflected light,
Some flying stroke alone can hit 'em right:
For how should equal° colours do the knack?
Chameleons who can paint in white and black?
     'Yet Chloe sure was formed without a spot'—
Nature in her then erred not, but forgot.
'With every pleasing, every prudent part,
160 Say, what can Chloe want?'—She wants a heart.
She speaks, behaves, and acts just as she ought;
But never, never, reached one generous thought.
Virtue she finds too painful an endeavour,
Content to dwell in decencies° for ever.
So very reasonable, so unmoved,
As never yet to love, or to be loved.
She, while her lover pants upon her breast,
Can mark the figures on an Indian chest;
And when she sees her friend in deep despair,
170 Observes how much a chintz exceeds mohair.
Forbid it Heaven, a favour or a debt
She e'er should cancel—but she may forget.
Safe is your secret still in Chloe's ear;
But none of Chloe's shall you ever hear.
Of all her dears she never slandered one,
But cares not if a thousand are undone.
Would Chloe know if you're alive or dead?
She bids her footman put it in her head.
Chloe is prudent—Would you too be wise?
180 Then never break your heart when Chloe dies.
     One certain portrait may (I grant) be seen,
Which Heaven has varnished out, and made a *Queen:*°
The same for ever! and described by all
With truth and goodness, as with crown and ball.°
Poets heap virtues, painters gems at will,

---

equal solid, unvaried
decencies proprieties
Queen Caroline, who exercised her influence over George II in alliance with Sir Robert Wal-

pole and favored Lord Hervey, the Sporus of Pope's *Epistle to Dr. Arbuthnot*
ball one of the symbols of rule

And show their zeal, and hide their want of skill.°
'Tis well—but, artists! who can paint or write,
To draw the naked is your true delight.
That robe of quality so struts and swells,
190 None see what parts of nature it conceals:
The exactest traits of body or of mind,
We owe to models of an humble kind.
If Queensberry° to strip there's no compelling,
'Tis from a handmaid we must take a Helen.°
From peer or bishop 'tis no easy thing
To draw the man who loves his God, or king:
Alas! I copy (or my draught° would fail)
From honest Mah'met,° or plain Parson Hale.°
But grant, in public men sometimes are shown,
200 A woman's seen in private life alone:
Our bolder talents in full light displayed;
Your virtues open fairest in the shade.
Bred to disguise, in public 'tis you hide;
There, none distinguish twixt your shame or pride,
Weakness or delicacy; all so nice,
That each may seem a virtue, or a vice.
In men, we various ruling passions° find;
In women, two almost divide the kind;
Those, only fixed, they first or last obey,
210 The love of pleasure, and the love of sway.
That, Nature gives; and where the lesson taught
Is but to please, can pleasure seem a fault?
Experience, this; by man's oppression curst,
They seek the second not to lose the first.
Men, some to business, some to pleasure take;
But every woman is at heart a rake:
Men, some to quiet, some to public strife;
But every lady would be queen for life.
Yet mark the fate of a whole sex of queens!
220 Power all their end, but beauty all the means:
In youth they conquer, with so wild a rage,
As leaves them scarce a subject in their age:
For foreign glory, foreign joy, they roam;
No thought of peace or happiness at home.
But wisdom's triumph is well-timed retreat,
As hard a science to the fair as great!

---

hide . . . skill Cf. *Essay on Criticism*, ll. 293–96.
Queensberry Catherine Hyde, Duchess of Queensberry (1700–1777), friend and protectress of John Gay, and one of the most beautiful women of her day
Helen of Troy
draught sketch
Mah'met "Servant to the late King, said to be the son of a Turkish Bassa, whom he took at the siege of Buda, and constantly kept about his person" (Pope)
Parson Hale Dr. Stephen Hales (1677–1761), physiologist and admirable parish priest, a friend of Pope
ruling passions The ruling passions, for Pope, were ineradicable drives which might take disguised forms as they bent other passions to their control and which proved, upon scrutiny, to underlie all other motives. See *Essay on Man* II.123 ff.

Beauties, like tyrants, old and friendless grown,
Yet hate repose, and dread to be alone,
Worn out in public, weary every eye,
Nor leave one sigh behind them when they die.
     Pleasures the sex, as children birds, pursue,
Still out of reach, yet never out of view;
Sure, if they catch, to spoil the toy° at most,
To covet flying, and regret when lost:
At last, to follies youth could scarce defend,
It grows their age's prudence to pretend;
Ashamed to own they gave delight before,
Reduced to feign it, when they give no more:
As hags° hold sabbaths, less for joy than spite,
So these their merry, miserable night;°
Still round and round the ghosts of beauty glide,
And haunt the places where their honour died.
     See how the world its veterans rewards!
A youth of frolics, an old age of cards;
Fair to no purpose, artful to no end,
Young without lovers, old without a friend;
A fop their passion, but their prize a sot;
Alive, ridiculous, and dead, forgot!
     Ah! Friend!° to dazzle let the vain design;
To raise the thought, and touch the heart be thine!
That charm shall grow, while what fatigues the Ring°
Flaunts and goes down, an unregarded thing:
So when the sun's broad beam has tired the sight,
All mild ascends the moon's more sober light,
Serene in virgin modesty° she shines,
And unobserved the glaring orb declines.
     Oh! blest with temper whose unclouded ray
Can make tomorrow cheerful as today;
She, who can love a sister's charms, or hear
Sighs for a daughter with unwounded ear;
She, who ne'er answers till a husband cools,
Or, if she rules him, never shows she rules;
Charms by accepting, by submitting sways,
Yet has her humour most when she obeys;
Let fops or fortune fly which way they will;
Disdains all loss of tickets,° or Codille;°
Spleen, vapours,° or smallpox,° above them all,
And mistress of herself, though China° fall.

230

240

250

260

---

toy plaything
hags witches, whose sabbaths (held at midnight) were orgies with demons and sorcerers
night visiting night
Friend Martha Blount (1690–1763), whom Pope knew all his mature life and honored in his will; they were close friends and were believed by some to be lovers
Ring the fashionable drive in Hyde Park
virgin modesty alluding to Diana as the virgin

goddess of the moon as well as to its silver light
tickets in lotteries
Codille a lost game of ombre (cf. *The Rape of the Lock* III.92)
Spleen, vapours fashionable forms of melancholy or moodiness
smallpox whose scars had disfigured Martha Blount's face
China For its double sense, see *The Rape of the Lock* III.110.

And yet, believe me, good as well as ill,
270   Woman's at best a contradiction still.
Heaven, when it strives to polish all it can
Its last best work, but forms a softer man;
Picks from each sex, to make the favourite blest,
Your love of pleasure, our desire of rest:
Blends, in exception to all general rules,
Your taste of follies, with our scorn of fools:
Reserve with frankness, art with truth allied,
Courage with softness, modesty with pride;
Fixed principles, with fancy ever new;
280   Shakes all together, and produces—You.
     Be this a woman's fame: with this unblest,
Toasts live a scorn, and queens may die a jest.
This Phoebus° promised (I forget the year)
When those blue eyes first opened on the sphere;
Ascendant Phoebus watched that hour with care,
Averted half your parents' simple prayer;
And gave you beauty, but denied the pelf°
That buys your sex a tyrant o'er itself.
The generous god,° who wit and gold refines,
290   And ripens spirits as he ripens mines,
Kept dross for duchesses, the world shall know it,
To you gave sense, good humour,° and a poet.

                                        1735

Imitations of Horace

Pope's "imitations of Horace" are among his finest works. Some of the poems are direct imitations and were published with the text of Horace beside them (or the text of Donne for the two satires of his that Pope "versified" in more regular couplets). Others are written in the manner of Horace but without precise models. One of these, originally described as "a Dialogue Something like Horace," became, with its companion poem, the Epilogue to the Satires in 1740; the *Epistle to Dr. Arbuthnot* has also been printed as a Prologue to the Satires.

The term "imitation" was first given currency by Dryden, when he distinguished among three kinds of translation: metaphrase, or word-by-word literal translation; paraphrase, or a translation that retains the meaning of the original but does so by departing from strict literalness; and finally imitation (of which Dryden was suspicious), which departs freely from the original text to create a new poem in its spirit, using the experience of a new age to take the place of earlier material. (One may compare "paraphrase" and "imitation" in two instances given here: Dryden's and Swift's versions of Ovid's tale of Baucis and Philemon appearing in the section The Mock Form, and Dryden's and Johnson's versions of Juvenal's Third Satire, in The Urban Scene.)

Phoebus as god of prophecy
pelf wealth
generous god Phoebus as god of poetry, which fosters true wit, and as god of the sun, by which gold is generated and "ripens" in the earth
good humour Cf. *The Rape of the Lock* V.29–34.

The imitation emerged in England (perhaps furthered through Boileau's example) in the work of Abraham Cowley and Sir John Denham, as Dryden recognized, and one can perhaps read Rochester's *Satire Against Mankind* as an "imitation" of Boileau's Eighth Satire. At any rate, it is part of the effect of an imitation that the reader be potentially aware of the text from which the poet departs and recognize the variation upon the original, as one does in a parody. Pope, in fact, applied the phrase "a parody from Horace" to *Satire* II.i given here; and he used the term all but interchangeably with imitation. Yet the imitation, while it cannot be fully grasped without some knowledge of the original, can in considerable measure stand on its own, and it is not a great leap from those imitations which have a specific model in Horace to those which have only the generalized one of Horace's satires and epistles.

Finally, one must ask what that generalized example implied. In Dryden's *Discourse on satire* (passages from which are given above in his Critical Prose section) Juvenal is exalted over Horace: "a noble soul is better pleased with a zealous vindication of Roman liberty than with a temporizing poet, a well mannered court slave, and a man . . . who is ever decent, because he is naturally servile." These charges against Horace haunt the age, but Shaftesbury distinguishes between Horace's "debauched, slavish, courtly state" and his "returning, recovering state." In the latter he returned to a "Socratic" philosophy and left Epicureanism behind him, and in his revived moral severity (with its elements of Stoicism) he put the appeal of the court behind him. It is in this later state that the conversational poems—the *sermones*—were written, and they can be seen as an expression of it. Pope tends to carry Horace's Socratic morality to a stage of deeper intensity, perhaps more readily comparable to that of Juvenal; and he dramatizes the poet's rising to superb indignation, even prophetic rage, as he creates his vision of triumphant Vice (in *Epilogue* I) or defends himself against resentful libels. The modulation of tone is remarkable in all these poems, from the seemingly timid and naïve victim to the morally outraged patriot, from the public wrath of satiric engagement to the personal warmth of friendship in retirement.

Epistle to Dr. Arbuthnot

Being the Prologue to the Satires

P. Shut, shut the door, good John!° fatigued, I said,
Tie up the knocker, say I'm sick, I'm dead.
The Dog-star° rages! nay 'tis past a doubt,
All Bedlam, or Parnassus,° is let out:
Fire in each eye, and papers in each hand,
They rave, recite, and madden round the land.
    What walls can guard me, or what shades can hide?
They pierce my thickets, through my grot° they glide;

good John Pope's servant John Serle
Dog-star Sirius, which reappears at the time of late summer heat; for Juvenal the season for the reading of new poems, whose pomposity and incompetence stung him to rage (see "Parnassus," l. 4)

Bedlam, or Parnassus inhabitants of the madhouse or (as they imagine) the mountain of the Muses
grot Pope's grotto at Twickenham was an underground retreat, an artificial cave encrusted with shells and minerals.

By land, by water,° they renew the charge;
10   They stop the chariot, and they board the barge.
No place is sacred, not the church is free;
Even Sunday shines no sabbath-day to me:
Then from the Mint° walks forth the man of rhyme,
Happy! to catch me just at dinner time.
    Is there a parson, much bemused in° beer,
A maudlin poetess, a rhyming peer,
A clerk, foredoomed his father's soul to cross,
Who pens a stanza, when he should *engross*.°
Is there, who, locked from ink and paper, scrawls
20   With desperate charcoal round his darkened walls?°
All fly to TWIT'NAM,° and in humble strain
Apply to me, to keep them mad or vain.
Arthur,° whose giddy son neglects the Laws,
Imputes to me and my damned works the cause:
Poor Cornus° sees his frantic wife elope,
And curses wit, and poetry, and Pope.°
    Friend to my life! (which did not you prolong,
The world had wanted many an idle song)
What drop or nostrum° can this plague remove?
30   Or which must end me, a fool's wrath or love?
A dire dilemma! either way I'm sped;°
If foes, they write, if friends, they read me dead.
Seized and tied down to judge, how wretched I!
Who can't be silent, and who will not lie;
To laugh were want of goodness and of grace,
And to be grave exceeds all power of face.
I sit with sad civility, I read
With honest anguish, and an aching head;
And drop at last, but in unwilling ears,
40   This saving counsel, 'Keep your piece nine years.'°
    'Nine years!' cries he, who high in Drury Lane,°
Lulled by soft zephyrs through the broken pane,
Rhymes ere he wakes, and prints before Term° ends,
Obliged by hunger, and request of friends:°
'The piece, you think, is incorrect? why, take it,

---

water Pope's house was on the Thames, and one could be rowed from London by scullers; "chariot" and "barge" suggest land and sea battles.
Mint a section of Southwark where debtors could stay without fear of arrest; on Sundays, however, there were no arrests anywhere
bemused in rhyming with the name of Laurence Eusden (1688–1730), a parson and poet laureate notoriously fond of drink
engross copy a legal document
darkened walls i.e. in confinement, probably in Bedlam
Twit'nam i.e. Twickenham, Pope's home
Arthur perhaps Arthur Moore, whose son (eager to shine as a wit) had plagiarized from Pope;

but the name is generic, like "Cornus" below
Cornus from Latin for a horn; hence a cuckold
Pope As a Roman Catholic, Pope could enjoy parodying the hysterical charges against all forms of popery.
drop or nostrum cures
sped i.e. to my grave
nine years the advice of Horace to the poet, *Ars Poetica*, ll. 386–89
Drury Lane street of theaters, prostitutes, and— here—writers in garrets
Term law court term, also the publishing season
Obliged . . . friends offering the second reason to conceal the first, a common procedure in prefaces

I'm all submission; what you'd have it, make it.'
   Three things another's modest wishes bound:
My friendship, and a prologue,° and ten pound.
   Pitholeon° sends to me: 'You know his Grace;
50   I want a patron; ask him for a place.'°
Pitholeon libelled me—'but here's a letter
Informs you, sir, 'twas when he knew no better.
Dare you refuse him? Curll° invites to dine;
He'll write a Journal, or he'll turn divine.'°
   Bless me! a packet.—' 'Tis a stranger sues,
A virgin tragedy, an orphan Muse.'
If I dislike it, 'Furies, death and rage!'
If I approve, 'Commend it to the stage.'
There (thank my stars) my whole commission ends,
60   The players and I are, luckily, no friends.
Fired that the house° reject him, ' 'Sdeath I'll print it,
And shame the fools—Your Interest, sir, with Lintot.'°
Lintot, dull rogue! will think your price too much:
'Not, sir, if you revise it, and retouch.'
All my demurs but double his attacks;
At last he whispers, 'Do; and we go snacks.'°
Glad of a quarrel, straight I clap the door,
'Sir, let me see your works and you no more.'
'Tis sung, when Midas' ears° began to spring,
70   (Midas, a sacred person and a King)
His very Minister who spied them first,
(Some say his Queen) was forced to speak, or burst.
And is not mine, my friend, a sorer case,
When every coxcomb perks them in my face?
   'Good friend, forbear! you deal in dangerous things.
I'd never name Queens, Ministers, or Kings;
Keep close to ears, and those let asses prick;
'Tis nothing   ' Nothing? if they bite and kick?
Out with it, DUNCIAD! let the secret pass,
80   That secret to each fool, that he's an ass:
The truth once told (and wherefore should we lie?)
The Queen of Midas slept, and so may I.
     You think this cruel? take it for a rule,
No creature smarts so little as a fool.

---

prologue often sought from well-known writers to help a play succeed
Pitholeon a foolish and pretentious poet mentioned by Horace, here a modern counterpart seeking influence with a nobleman
place position or sinecure
Curll Edmund Curll, notorious publisher of hacks, might commission him to write new libels or forge works in your name
Journal . . . divine sell his talents in party politics or religious controversy
house theater

Lintot Bernard Lintot, who published many of Pope's works
snacks shares
Midas' ears the ass's ears given him by Apollo for preferring Pan's music. Midas' wife (in some versions, his chief minister or barber) could not keep the secret entirely and whispered it into a hole in the earth, but the reeds that grew there repeated the message in the wind. (Since Walpole as chief minister and Caroline as queen virtually ruled in George II's place, they would have most reason to conceal the full extent of that King's stupidity.)

Let peals of laughter, Codrus!° round thee break,
Thou unconcerned canst hear the mighty crack:°
Pit, box, and gallery in convulsions hurled,
Thou standst unshook amidst a bursting world.
Who shames a scribbler? break one cobweb through,
He spins the slight, self-pleasing thread anew:
Destroy his fib or sophistry; in vain,
The creature's at his dirty work° again,
Throned in the centre of his thin designs,
Proud of a vast extent of flimsy lines!
Whom have I hurt? has poet yet or peer
Lost the arched eyebrow or Parnassian sneer?°
And has not Colley still his Lord and whore?
His butchers Henley,° his Freemasons Moore?°
Does not one table Bavius° still admit?
Still to one bishop Philips° seem a wit?
Still Sappho°—'Hold! for God's sake—you'll offend,
No names—be calm—learn prudence of a friend:
I too could write, and I am twice as tall;
But foes like these—' One flatterer's worse than all.
Of all mad creatures, if the learned are right,
It is the slaver kills, and not the bite.
A fool quite angry is quite innocent:
Alas! 'tis ten times worse when they *repent*.
    One dedicates in high heroic prose,
And ridicules beyond a hundred foes:
One from all Grubstreet° will my fame defend,
And, more abusive, calls himself my friend.
This prints my *Letters*,° that expects a bribe,
And others roar aloud, 'Subscribe, subscribe.'°
    There are, who to my person pay their court:
I cough like Horace, and, though lean, am short,
Ammon's great son° one shoulder had too high,
Such Ovid's nose, and 'Sir! you have an eye'—
Go on, obliging creatures, make me see
All that disgraced my betters, met in me.

90

100

110

120

Codrus a poet ridiculed by Virgil and Juvenal
mighty crack This phrase of Joseph Addison's
amused Pope by its total inadequacy to the idea
of cosmic catastrophe, and here Pope applies it
to stage thunder as Codrus's play is produced
and proves a catastrophe of a lesser sort.
dirty work since, like Swift's Spider in *The
Battle of the Books,* he spins a structure out of
his own excrement
Parnassian sneer referring to the current poet
laureate, Colley Cibber (as the phrase once had
to Lewis Theobald, *The Dunciad* II.5)
Henley See *Epilogue to the Satires* I.66 and note.
Moore James Moore-Smythe whom Pope regarded as a plagiarist, here cited as a leader
of Freemasons' processions
Bavius the bad poet of Virgil's and Horace's
day

Philips Ambrose Philips (1674–1749), notorious
for his rustic pastoral and his mock-naïve chil-
dren's verse (which won him the name of
Namby-Pamby), was secretary to Hugh Boulter,
Bishop of Armagh.
Sappho immediately invoking Pope's enemy,
Lady Mary Wortley Montagu, and implying her
support (like Philips's by the bishop) by Wal-
pole
Grubstreet the center and symbol of hack writers
Letters pirated (as some of Pope's were by
Curll) or forged
subscribe Books were often published with the
financial support of advance subscriptions.
Ammon's . . . son Alexander the Great, claim-
ing descent from Jupiter Ammon

Say for my comfort, languishing in bed,
'Just so immortal Maro° held his head':
And when I die, be sure you let me know
Great Homer died three thousand years ago.
      Why did I write? what sin to me unknown
Dipped me in ink, my parents' or my own?
As yet a child, nor yet a fool to fame,
I lisped in numbers,° for the numbers came.
I left no calling for this idle trade,
30 No duty broke, no father disobeyed.
The Muse but served to ease some friend, not wife,
To help me through this long disease, my life,
To second, ARBUTHNOT! thy art and care,
And teach the being you preserved, to bear.
      But why then publish? Granville° the polite,
And knowing Walsh, would tell me I could write;
Well-natured Garth inflamed with early praise;
And Congreve loved, and Swift endured my lays;
The courtly Talbot, Somers, Sheffield read,
40 Even mitred Rochester would nod the head,
And St. John's self (great Dryden's friends before)
With open arms received one poet more.
Happy my studies, when by these approved!
Happier their author, when by these beloved!
From these the world will judge of men and books,
Not from the Burnets, Oldmixons, and Cookes.°
      Soft were my numbers; who could take offence
While pure description held the place of sense?
Like gentle Fanny's° was my flowery theme,
50 A painted mistress, or a purling stream.
Yet then did Gildon° draw his venal quill;
I wished the man a dinner, and sat still.
Yet then did Dennis° rave in furious fret;
I never answered—I was not in debt.

Maro Virgil
numbers meter, verses
Granville The first of a series of statesmen, poets, critics, and patrons—all of high reputation—with whom Pope associates Dryden and himself (and thus himself with Dryden) in opposition to the hacks mentioned above; they are George Granville, Baron Lansdowne (1666–1735), to whom Pope dedicated *Windsor Forest*; William Walsh (1663–1708), his early literary adviser; Sir Samuel Garth (1661–1719), physician and poet; William Congreve; Jonathan Swift; Charles Talbot, Duke of Shrewsbury (1660–1718), statesman and sponsor of Pope's "versification" of Donne's satires; John Lord Somers (1651–1716), the Whig leader to whom Swift dedicated *A Tale of a Tub*; John Sheffield, Duke of Buckinghamshire and Normanby (1648–1721), whose poems Pope edited and to whom Dryden dedicated important work; Francis Atterbury, Bishop of Rochester (1662–1732), friend of Swift and Pope and himself a distinguished writer; and Henry St. John, Viscount Bolingbroke (1678–1751), chief minister under Anne, political theorist, close friend of Swift and Pope for many years.
Burnets . . . Cookes Thomas Burnet, John Oldmixon, and Thomas Cooke; "authors of secret and scandalous history" (Pope)
gentle Fanny's any conventional poet's, but also with special reference to John, Lord Hervey, who appears below as Sporus, ll. 305–33
Gildon Charles Gildon (1665–1724), a critic who had attacked Pope personally, perhaps (as Pope believed) at the instigation of Joseph Addison (the "Atticus" of ll. 193–214); hence a hireling or "venal" writer
Dennis John Dennis (1657–1734), critic and dramatist, abusively personal in his attacks on Pope; also suspected by Pope of selling his services to Addison

If want provoked, or madness made them print,
I waged no war with Bedlam or the Mint.
　　Did some more sober critic come abroad;
If wrong, I smiled; if right, I kissed the rod.
Pains, reading, study, are their just pretence,
160　　And all they want is spirit, taste, and sense.
Commas and points° they set exactly right,
And 'twere a sin to rob them of their mite.
Yet ne'er one sprig of laurel° graced these ribalds,°
From slashing Bentley down to piddling Tibalds:°
Each wight, who reads not, and but scans and spells,
Each word-catcher, that lives on syllables,
Even such small critics some regard may claim,
Preserved in Milton's or in Shakespeare's name.
Pretty! in amber° to observe the forms
170　　Of hairs, or straws, or dirt, or grubs, or worms!
The things, we know, are neither rich nor rare,
But wonder how the devil they got there.
　　Were others angry? I excused them too;
Well might they rage; I gave them but their due.
A man's true merit 'tis not hard to find;
But each man's secret standard in his mind,
That casting-weight° pride adds to emptiness,
This, who can gratify? for who can guess?
The bard° whom pilfered pastorals renown,
180　　Who turns a Persian tale for half a crown,°
Just writes to make his barrenness appear,
And strains, from hard-bound brains, eight lines a year;
He, who still wanting, though he lives on theft,
Steals much, spends little, yet has nothing left:
And he, who now to sense, now nonsense leaning,
Means not, but blunders round about a meaning:
And he, whose fustian's so sublimely bad,
It is not poetry, but prose run mad:
All these, my modest satire bade translate,
190　　And owned that nine such poets made a Tate.°

points periods, the concern of these "more sober" verbal critics
laurel the bay with which the true poet was crowned
ribalds buffoons
slashing Bentley . . . piddling Tibalds Richard Bentley (the subject of Swift's earlier attack in *The Battle of the Books* and *A Tale of a Tub*) and Lewis Theobald (1688–1744) were, among other things, textual scholars. Bentley's great learning was accompanied by ill temper toward his colleagues and arrogance toward the authors he edited. Theobald had properly exposed Pope's weaknesses as an editor of Shakespeare, but his own emendations of the text are a mixture of brilliant intuition and heavy self-display; like Bentley's, his literary sense is much less secure than his historical information. Theobald was the king of the dunces in the first version of *The Dunciad* (1728), but he was supplanted by Colley Cibber in the revision of 1743; Bentley preserved his place through all editions.
in amber as flies and other insects have been decoratively preserved
casting-weight that turns the balance
bard Ambrose Philips, whose pastoral poems were clumsily based on Spenser's and who also translated a book of *Persian Tales*
half a crown a prostitute's customary fee
Tate Nahum Tate (1652–1715), former poet laureate, "a cold writer of no invention" (Pope); the line is based on the saying that it takes nine tailors to make a man.

How did they fume, and stamp, and roar, and chafe!
And swear, not *Addison* himself was safe.
    Peace to all such! but were there one° whose fires
True genius kindles, and fair fame inspires;
Blest with each talent and each art to please,
And born to write, converse, and live with ease:
Should such a man, too fond to rule alone,
Bear, like the Turk,° no brother near the throne,
View him with scornful, yet with jealous eyes,
And hate for arts that caused himself to rise;   00
Damn with faint praise, assent with civil leer,
And without sneering, teach the rest to sneer;
Willing to wound, and yet afraid to strike,
Just hint a fault, and hesitate dislike;
Alike reserved to blame, or to commend,
A timorous foe, and a suspicious friend;
Dreading even fools, by flatterers besieged,
And so obliging, that he ne'er obliged;
Like Cato,° give his little Senate laws,
And sit attentive to his own applause;   10
While wits and templars° every sentence raise,
And wonder with a foolish face of praise—
Who but must laugh, if such a man there be?
Who would not weep, if Atticus were he?
    What though my name stood rubric° on the walls,
Or plastered posts, with claps,° in capitals?
Or smoking forth, a hundred hawkers' load,
On wings of wind came flying all abroad?
I sought no homage from the race that write;
I kept, like Asian monarchs,° from their sight: 20
Poems I heeded (now berhymed so long)
No more than thou, great GEORGE! a birthday song.°
I ne'er with wits or witlings passed my days,
To spread about the itch of verse and praise;
Nor like a puppy, daggled° through the town,

---

one In this portrait of Atticus, which had appeared earlier by itself, Pope is clearly suggesting Joseph Addison (1672–1719), the author of the tragedy *Cato* as well as of the *Tatler* and *Spectator*. Addison and Pope had considerable respect for each other's powers, but Pope had some reason to feel Addison's jealousy or at least lack of generosity toward a young writer who stood outside his circle and failed to do homage to him. The original Atticus was a man of letters and friend of Cicero.
like the Turk the Turkish rulers, who in fact had often executed close kinsmen to avoid the threat of rivalry
Cato In his prologue to Addison's play (1713), Pope had written "While Cato gives his little senate laws, / What bosom beats not in his country's cause? / Who sees him act, but envies

every deed? / Who hears him groan, and does not wish to bleed?" (ll. 23–26) Here those questions are echoed with a difference, and the august Roman senate is replaced by the coffee-house hangers-on whom Addison rules as a literary dictator.
templars law students, who often cultivated literary ambitions
stood rubric was posted in red letters in book-sellers' advertisements
with claps on posters; also with advertisements for cures for gonorrhea
like . . . monarchs in their withdrawal; cf. *Elegy to the Memory of an Unfortunate Lady*, ll. 21–22
birthday song the official ode of the laureate
daggled splashed in mud

To fetch and carry singsong up and down;
Nor at rehearsals sweat, and mouthed, and cried,
With handkerchief and orange° at my side;
But sick of fops, and poetry, and prate,
230   To *Bufo*° left the whole Castalian state.°
    Proud as Apollo on his forkèd hill,
Sat full-blown Bufo, puffed by every quill;
Fed with soft dedication all day long,
Horace and he° went hand in hand in song.
His library (where busts of poets dead
And a true Pindar stood without a head)
Received of wits an undistinguished race,
Who first his judgment asked, and then a place:
Much they extolled his pictures, much his seat,°
240   And flattered every day, and some days eat:
Till grown more frugal in his riper days,
He paid some bards with port, and some with praise;
To some a dry rehearsal was assigned,
And others (harder still) he paid in kind.°
Dryden alone (what wonder?) came not nigh,
Dryden alone escaped this judging eye:
But still the Great have kindness in reserve,
He helped to bury° whom he helped to starve.
    May some choice patron bless each gray goose quill!
250   May every Bavius have his Bufo still!
So, when a statesman wants a day's defence,
Or envy holds a whole week's war with sense,
Or simple pride for flattery makes demands,
May dunce by dunce be whistled off my hands!
Blest be the Great! for those they take away,°
And those they left me; for they left me GAY,°
Left me to see neglected genius bloom,
Neglected die, and tell it on his tomb:°
Of all thy blameless life the sole return
260   My Verse, and QUEENSBERRY° weeping o'er thy urn!
    Oh let me live my own, and die so too!
(To live and die is all I have to do:)°

---

orange sold in the theater as refreshment
Bufo a patron, his name taken from the Latin word for a toad, a creature that swells up with air
Castalian state poetry; named for the Muses' sacred spring on the "forkèd hill," Parnassus
Horace and he i.e. with Bufo as a modern Maecenas, replacing Horace's patron
seat estate
in kind with his own poems
helped to bury Dryden, who was poor most of his life, was given a lavish funeral; Bufo feels more secure with "poets dead" or with assured reputations.

take away "The Lord gave and the Lord hath taken away; blessed be the name of the Lord" (Job 1:21)
Gay John Gay, author of *The Beggar's Opera* and many poems, a close friend of Pope, Swift, and Arbuthnot
on his tomb Pope wrote Gay's epitaph.
Queensberry Charles Douglas, 3rd Duke of Queensberry (1698–1778), was, with his beautiful and witty wife, Gay's patron and friend.
To live . . . do a line adapted from Sir John Denham's poem *Of Prudence*

Maintain a poet's dignity and ease,
And see what friends, and read what books I please:
Above a patron, though I condescend
Some times to call a Minister my friend.
I was not born for courts or great affairs;
I pay my debts, believe, and say my prayers;
Can sleep without a poem in my head,
Nor know, if Dennis be alive or dead.
    Why am I asked what next shall see the light?
Heavens! was I born for nothing but to write?
Has life no joys for me? or (to be grave)
Have I no friend to serve, no soul to save?
'I found him close with Swift'—'Indeed? no doubt,'
(Cries prating Balbus) 'something will come out.'
'Tis all in vain, deny it as I will.
'No, such a Genius never can lie still';
And then for mine obligingly mistakes
The first Lampoon Sir *Will.* or *Bubo*° makes.
Poor guiltless I! and can I choose but smile,
When every coxcomb knows me by my *style?*
    Cursed be the verse, how well soe'er it flow,
That tends to make one worthy man my foe,
Give Virtue scandal, Innocence a fear,
Or from the soft-eyed virgin steal a tear!
But he who hurts a harmless neighbour's peace,
Insults fallen worth, or beauty in distress,
Who loves a lie, lame slander helps about,
Who writes a libel, or who copies out:
That fop, whose pride affects a patron's name,
Yet absent, wounds an author's honest fame:
Who can your merit selfishly approve,
And show the sense of it without the love;°
Who has the vanity to call you friend,
Yet wants the honour, injured, to defend;°
Who tells whate'er you think, whate'er you say,
And, if he lie not, must at least betray:
Who to the *Dean,* and *silver bell* can swear,
And sees at *Cannons* what was never there;°
Who reads, but with a lust to misapply,
Make satire a lampoon, and fiction, lie.
A lash like mine no honest man shall dread,

But all such babbling blockheads in his stead.
   Let *Sporus*° tremble—'What? that thing of silk,
Sporus, that mere white curd of ass's milk?
Satire or sense, alas! can Sporus feel?
Who breaks a butterfly upon a wheel?'°
Yet let me flap this bug with gilded wings,

310 This painted child of dirt that stinks and stings;
Whose buzz the witty and the fair annoys,
Yet wit ne'er tastes, and beauty ne'er enjoys:
So well-bred spaniels civilly delight
In mumbling of the game they dare not bite.
Eternal smiles his emptiness betray,
As shallow streams run dimpling all the way.
Whether in florid impotence he speaks,
And, as the prompter breathes, the puppet squeaks;
Or at the ear of Eve,° familiar toad,

320 Half froth, half venom, spits himself abroad,
In puns, or politics, or tales, or lies,
Or spite, or smut, or rhymes, or blasphemies.
His wit all seesaw, between *that* and *this,*
Now high, now low, now master up, now miss,
And he himself one vile antithesis.
Amphibious thing! that acting either part,
The trifling head, or the corrupted heart,
Fop at the toilet, flatterer at the board,
Now trips a Lady, and now struts a Lord.

330 Eve's tempter thus the Rabbins° have exprest,
A cherub's face, a reptile all the rest;
Beauty that shocks you, parts that none will trust,
Wit that can creep, and pride that licks the dust.
   Not Fortune's worshipper, nor fashion's fool,
Not lucre's madman, nor ambition's tool,
Not proud, nor servile; be one poet's praise,
That, if he pleased, he pleased by manly ways:
That flattery, even to kings, he held a shame,
And thought a lie in verse or prose the same.

340 That not in fancy's maze he wandered long,
But stooped° to truth and moralized his song:
That not for fame, but virtue's better end,
He stood° the furious foe, the timid friend,

Sporus Nero's homosexual favorite, a boy to whom he was married in public; appropriately used for Lord Hervey (1696–1743), prominent in the court of George II and especially close to Queen Caroline; a long-time confederate of Lady Mary Wortley Montagu in attacks upon Pope (Hervey's brilliant *Memoirs of the Reign of King George II* were not published until 1848)
wheel the rack or instrument of torture on which men were disjointed

Eve alluding to the early temptation, with Satan "squat like a toad, close at the ear of Eve" (*Paradise Lost* IV.800)
Rabbins rabbis, scholars of the Old Testament, whose image of Satan has often been represented in paintings of the temptation of Eve
stooped as a falcon is said to "stoop" to its prey
stood withstood, endured

The damning critic, half-approving wit,
The coxcomb hit, or fearing to be hit;
Laughed at the loss of friends he never had,
The dull, the proud, the wicked, and the mad;
The distant threats of vengeance on his head,
The blow unfelt, the tear he never shed;°
The tale revived, the lie so oft o'erthrown,   350
The imputed trash,° and dulness not his own;
The morals blackened when the writings 'scape,
The libeled person, and the pictured shape;°
Abuse, on all he loved, or loved him, spread,
A friend in exile, or a father, dead;
The whisper,° that to greatness still too near,
Perhaps, yet vibrates on his Sovereign's ear—
Welcome for thee, fair Virtue! all the past:
For thee, fair Virtue! welcome even the *last!*
    'But why insult the poor, affront the great?'   360
A knave's a knave, to me, in every state:
Alike my scorn, if he succeed or fail,
Sporus at court, or Japhet° in a jail,
A hireling scribbler, or a hireling peer,
Knight of the post° corrupt, or of the shire;
If on a pillory, or near a throne,
He gain his Prince's ear, or lose his own.°
Yet soft by nature, more a dupe than wit,
Sappho° can tell you how this man was bit:°
This dreaded satirist Dennis will confess   370
Foe to his pride, but friend to his distress,°
So humble, he has knocked at Tibbald's door,
Has drunk with Cibber, nay, has rhymed for Moore.°
Full ten years slandered, did he once reply?
Three thousand suns went down on Welsted's lie.
To please a mistress one aspersed his life;
He lashed him not, but let her be his wife:
Let Budgell charge low Grubstreet° on his quill,
And write whate'er he pleased, except his will;
Let the two Curlls° of town and court, abuse   380

blow . . . shed the false report, circulated in the pamphlet *A Pop upon Pope* (1728), that Pope had been subjected to a whipping
trash scandalous works published as his by Curll
pictured shape as when he was shown as a hunchbacked ape in the pamphlet *Pope Alexander's Supremacy and Infallibility Examined* (1729)
whisper by Lord Hervey
Japhet Japhet Crook, a forger
Knight . . . post a term for one who made his living by giving false evidence, as opposed to a legitimate knight (of the shire or county), who might also be corrupt
lose his own as Japhet Crook did by way of

punishment before he was exposed in the pillory or stocks
Sappho Lady Mary Wortley Montagu, to whom Pope once had been very close, after their estrangement joined Lord Hervey in attacking him.
bit deceived, fooled
his distress Pope had been helpful in Dennis's last years.
Moore unintentionally, for Moore-Smythe plagiarized from Pope
low Grubstreet contributions to the *Grub Street Journal* that accused Budgell of forging a will and making himself heir
two Curlls the publisher (l. 53), and Lord Hervey, his counterpart at court

His father, mother, body, soul, and Muse.
Yet why? that father held it for a rule,
It was a sin to call our neighbour fool:
That harmless mother thought no wife a whore:
Hear this, and spare his family, *James Moore!*
Unspotted names, and memorable long!
If there be force in virtue or in song.
    Of gentle blood (part shed in honour's cause,
While yet in *Britain* honour had applause)
390   Each parent sprung—'What fortune, pray?'—Their own,
And better got, than Bestia's° from the throne.
Born to no pride, inheriting no Strife,
Nor marrying discord in a noble wife,
Stranger to civil and religious rage,
The good man walked innoxious through his age.
No courts he saw, no suits would ever try,
Nor dared an oath, nor hazarded a lie.
Unlearned, he knew no schoolman's subtle art,°
No language, but the language of the heart.
400   By nature honest, by experience wise,
Healthy by temperance and by exercise;
His life, though long, to sickness passed unknown,
His death was instant, and without a groan.
O grant me, thus to live, and thus to die!
Who sprung from kings shall know less joy than I.
    O Friend!° may each domestic bliss be thine!
Be no unpleasing melancholy mine:
Me, let the tender office long engage,
To rock the cradle of reposing age,
410   With lenient° arts extend a mother's breath,°
Make Languor smile, and smooth the bed of Death,
Explore the thought, explain the asking eye,
And keep a while one parent from the sky!
On cares like these if length of days attend,
May Heaven, to bless those days, preserve my friend,
Preserve him social, cheerful, and serene,
And just as rich as when he served a Queen.°
Whether that blessing be denied or given,
Thus far was right, the rest belongs to Heaven.

1735

Bestia's a Roman consul bribed into a dishonorable peace; perhaps referring to the enormous grants made by Queen Anne to the victorious Duke of Marlborough
art i.e. casuistry, which might find ingenious reasons for condoning false actions. Pope's father refused to gain relief from anti-Catholic measures by taking an oath against the pope.
Friend Arbuthnot

lenient relieving
mother's breath Pope's mother died at an advanced age before this poem was published, but these lines had been written some years earlier; Pope's account of his solicitude and devotion seems to be an accurate one.
Queen Anne, to whom Arbuthnot had been court physician

The First Satire of the Second Book of Horace

To Mr. Fortescue°

P. There are (I scarce can think it, but am told),
There are, to whom my satire seems too bold:
Scarce to wise Peter° complaisant enough,
And something said of Chartres° much too rough.
The lines are weak, another's pleased to say,
Lord Fanny° spins a thousand such a day.
Timorous by nature, of the rich in awe,
I come to counsel learned in the law:
You'll give me, like a friend, both sage and free,°
Advice; and (as you use) without a fee.
F. I'd write no more.
P. Not write? but then I *think*,
And for my soul I cannot sleep a wink.
I nod in company, I wake at night,
Fools rush into my head, and so I write.
F. You could not do a worse thing for your life.
Why, if the nights seem tedious, take a wife;
Or rather truly, if your point be rest,
Lettuce and cowslip wine;° *Probatum est.*°
But talk with Celsus,° Celsus will advise
Hartshorn,° or something that shall close your eyes.
Or, if you needs must write, write CAESAR'S° praise,
You'll gain at least a *knighthood,* or the *bays.*°
P. What? like Sir Richard,° rumbling, rough, and fierce,
With ARMS, and GEORGE, and BRUNSWICK° crowd the verse,
Rend with tremendous sound your ears asunder,
With gun, drum, trumpet, blunderbuss, and thunder?
Or nobly wild, with Budgell's° fire and force,
Paint angels trembling round his falling horse?
F. Then all your Muse's softer art display,
Let CAROLINA° smooth the tuneful lay,

To Mr. Fortescue William Fortescue, a friend and legal adviser of Pope (as well as a friend and supporter of Sir Robert Walpole), replaces the celebrated Roman lawyer Trebatius of Horace's poem.
Peter Peter Walter (1664?–1746) was notorious as a moneylender to the aristocracy and was said to be worth £300,000 at his death; as Swift describes him, "That rogue, of genuine ministerial kind, / Can half the peerage by his arts bewitch" (*Epistle to Mr. Gay,* 1731); and Pope cites him often as the crassest commercial spirit of the age (cf. *Epilogue to the Satires* I.121; II.57).
Chartres Francis Charteris (1675–1732), gambler, usurer, debauchee
Lord Fanny Fannius was a foolish critic and enemy of Horace, and Pope regularly applied his version of the name to John, Lord Hervey, the Sporus of the *Epistle to Dr. Arbuthnot.*
free generous, open
Lettuce . . . wine Both were believed to induce sleep, and lettuce to counteract sexual desire.
Probatum est "it is proved" (to work)
Celsus a physician, named for the chief Roman writer on medicine
Hartshorn ammonia, used in sleeping potions
Caesar's King George II
bays poet laureateship
Sir Richard Blackmore, poet and physician (1655–1729), author of several wretched epics
Brunswick George II's inherited title, from the German duchy his family had ruled
Budgell's Eustace Budgell (1686–1737), cousin and protégé of Addison, who wrote a ludicrous celebration of George and of the horse shot out from under him in battle
Carolina Queen Caroline

Lull with AMELIA's° liquid name the Nine,°
And sweetly flow through all the royal line.
    P.   Alas! few verses touch their nicer° ear;
They scarce can bear their *laureate* twice a year;°
And justly CAESAR scorns the poet's lays,°
It is to *history* he trusts for praise.
    F.   Better be Cibber, I'll maintain it still,
Than ridicule all taste, blaspheme quadrille,°
Abuse the City's best good men° in metre,
40   And laugh at peers that put their trust in Peter.
Even those you touch not, hate you.
    P.   What should ail them?
    F.   A hundred smart in Timon and in Balaam.°
The fewer still you name, you wound the more;
Bond° is but one, but Harpax° is a score.
    P.   Each mortal has his pleasure: none deny
Scarsdale° his bottle, Darty° his ham-pie;
Ridotta° sips and dances, till she see
The doubling lustres° dance as fast as she;
Fox° loves the Senate, Hockley Hole° his brother,
50   Like in all else, as one egg to another.
I love to pour out all my self, as plain
As downright SHIPPEN° or as old MONTAIGNE:°
In them, as certain to be loved as seen,
The soul stood forth, nor kept a thought within;
In me what spots (for spots I have) appear,
Will prove at least the medium must be clear.
In this impartial glass, my Muse intends
Fair to expose myself, my foes, my friends;
Publish the present age; but where my text
60   Is vice too high,° reserve it for the next:
My foes shall wish my life a longer date,
And every friend the less lament my fate.
My head and heart thus flowing through my quill,

Amelia's the third of the royal children
Nine the Muses
nicer more delicate
twice a year at the New Year and the king's birthday, occasions for obligatory odes
poet's lays George II had a well-known dislike of poetry and was supposed to have complained of Pope, "Why will not my subjects write in prose?" With Colley Cibber as laureate, he had better grounds than usual.
quadrille a fashionable card game
City's . . . men prosperous merchants or financiers (cf. ll. 3 and 4 above)
Timon . . . Balaam fictitious characters in the *Epistle to Burlington*, ll. 99 ff., and another satire, the *Epistle to Bathurst*
Bond Denis Bond (d. 1747), expelled from Parliament for a breach of trust and convicted of embezzlement as well

Harpax from Greek for "robber," a name that could be widely applied
Scarsdale the Earl of Scarsdale, well known for his love of drink
Darty Charles Dartineuf, a celebrated epicure
Ridotta a type of society woman
lustres crystals in chandeliers
Fox Stephen Fox, friend of Lord Hervey and loyal supporter of Walpole
Hockley Hole where bear-baiting took place, a resort of Henry Fox, also a Walpole supporter
Shippen William Shippen, a leading Jacobite and opponent of Walpole, outspoken and incorruptible
Montaigne whose essays are candidly self-revealing, open, and free
high in rank or power

Verse-man or prose-man, term me which you will,
Papist or Protestant, or both between,
Like good Erasmus° in an honest mean,
In moderation placing all my glory,
While Tories call me Whig, and Whigs a Tory.
Satire's my weapon, but I'm too discreet
70   To run amuck and tilt at all I meet;
I only wear it in a land of hectors,°
Thieves, supercargoes,° sharpers, and directors.°
Save but our army! and let Jove encrust
Swords, pikes, and guns, with everlasting rust!
Peace is my dear delight—not Fleury's° more:
But touch me, and no Minister so sore.
Whoe'er offends, at some unlucky time
Slides into verse, and hitches in a rhyme,
Sacred to ridicule his whole life long,
80   And the sad burden° of some merry song.
　　　Slander or poison dread from Delia's rage,
Hard words or hanging, if your judge be Page.°
From furious Sappho° scarce a milder fate,
Poxed° by her love, or libelled by her hate.
Its proper power to hurt, each creature feels;
Bulls aim their horns, and asses lift their heels;
'Tis a bear's talent not to kick but hug;
And no man wonders he's not stung by Pug.°
So drink with Walters or with Chartres eat,
90   They'll never poison you, they'll only cheat.
　　　Then, learnèd sir! (to cut the matter short)
Whate'er my fate, or well or ill at Court,
Whether old age, with faint but cheerful ray,
Attends to gild the evening of my day,
Or death's black wing already be displayed,
To wrap me in the universal shade;
Whether the darkened room to muse invite,
Or whitened wall provoke the skewer to write:°
In durance, exile, Bedlam, or the Mint,°
00   Like Lee or Budgell,° I will rhyme and print.
　　F.   Alas, young man! your days can ne'er be long,

Erasmus the detached scholar and humanist, who refused to involve himself in the controversies of the Reformation
hectors bullies
supercargoes officers aboard ship who were concerned only with the cargo and were proverbial for their wealth
directors Those of the South Sea Company had been notorious for fraud.
Fleury's the French cardinal (1653–1743) who pursued, under Louis XV, a policy of peace
burden refrain

Page Sir Francis Page, a judge quick to see guilt and to punish severely
Sappho probably referring to Lady Mary Wortley Montagu, but no doubt to others as well
Poxed infected with syphilis
Pug a common name for a pet dog
provoke . . . write with whatever instruments are available in a madhouse or prison
Mint the sanctuary for debtors
Lee or Budgell The playwright Nathanael Lee (1653–92) and Budgell (l. 27) were both insane for a time.

In flower of age you perish for a song!
Plums° and directors, Shylock° and his wife,
Will club their testers,° now, to take your life!
   P. What? armed for virtue when I point the pen,
Brand the bold front° of shameless guilty men;
Dash the proud gamester in his gilded car;
Bare the mean heart that lurks beneath a star;°
Can there be wanting, to defend her cause,
110   Lights of the Church, or guardians of the laws?
Could pensioned Boileau° lash in honest strain
Flatterers and bigots even in Louis' reign?
Could laureate Dryden pimp and friar° engage,
Yet neither Charles nor James° be in a rage?
And I not strip the gilding off a knave,
Unplaced, unpensioned, no man's heir or slave?
I will, or perish in the generous cause:
Hear this, and tremble! you who 'scape the laws.
Yes, while I live, no rich or noble knave
120   Shall walk the world, in credit, to his grave.
To Virtue only and her friends a friend,
The world beside may murmur or commend.
Know, all the distant din that world can keep,
Rolls o'er my grotto,° and but soothes my sleep.
There, my retreat the best companions grace,
Chiefs out of war and statesmen out of place.°
There St. John° mingles with my friendly bowl,
The feast of reason and the flow of soul:
And he, whose lightning pierced the Iberian lines,°
130   Now forms my quincunx,° and now ranks my vines,
Or tames the genius of the stubborn plain,
Almost as quickly as he conquered Spain.
   Envy must own, I live among the great,
No pimp of pleasure, and no spy of state,
With eyes that pry not, tongue that ne'er repeats,
Fond to spread friendships, but to cover heats;
To help who want, to forward who excel;
This, all who know me, know; who love me, tell;

Plums those who had acquired the sum of £100,000
Shylock any usurer, but also an adaptation of the name of the Earl of Selkirk, a widely unloved Scottish peer
club their testers pool their wealth
front brow, where criminals were branded
star the decoration for Knight of the Garter
Boileau Nicolas Boileau-Despréaux (1636–1711), eminent poet and critic, a fierce satirist even in the royal post of historiographer and in the absolute monarchy of Louis XIV
pimp and friar combined in Friar Dominick, in Dryden's comedy *The Spanish Friar* (1680)
Charles nor James Charles had made Dryden laureate in 1670 and James II retained him in that post, although the Catholic monarch banned the play for its satire on the Roman clergy.
grotto the artificial cave on Pope's estate at Twickenham
place office
St. John Bolingbroke, formerly with Harley at the head of Queen Anne's government, for a long time in self-imposed exile abroad
he . . . Iberian lines Charles Mordaunt (1658–1735), Earl of Peterborough, who captured Barcelona and Valencia in 1705–6
quincunx a planting of five trees, one at the center of the square formed by the rest

And who unknown defame me, let them be
40 Scribblers or peers, alike are *mob* to me.
This is my plea, on this I rest my cause—
What saith my counsel, learnèd in the laws?
    F.   Your plea is good; but still I say, beware!
Laws are explained by men—so have a care.
It stands on record, that in Richard's° times
A man was hanged for very honest rhymes.
Consult the statute: *quart.* I think, it is,
Edwardi sext. or *prim. et quint. Eliz.*
See *Libels, Satires*—here you have it—read.
50   P.   *Libels* and *satires!* lawless things indeed!
But grave *epistles,* bringing vice to light,
Such as a King might read, a Bishop write,
Such as Sir Robert° would approve—
    F.   Indeed?
The case is altered—you may then proceed;
In such a cause the plaintiff will be hissed,
My Lords the Judges laugh, and you're dismissed.

                                              1733

Epilogue to the Satires

In Two Dialogues

Dialogue I

Fr[iend]. Not twice a twelvemonth you appear in print,
And when it comes, the court see nothing in't.
You grow correct, that once with rapture writ,
And are, besides, too *moral* for a wit.
Decay of parts, alas! we all must feel—
Why now, this moment, don't I see you steal?
'Tis all from Horace; Horace long before ye
Said, 'Tories called him Whig, and Whigs a Tory;'°
And taught his Romans, in much better metre,
10 'To laugh at fools who put their trust in Peter.'°
    But Horace, sir, was delicate, was nice;
Bubo° observes, he lashed no sort of *vice:*
Horace would say, Sir Billy° *served the crown,*
Blunt° could *do business,* Huggins° *knew the town;*

Richard's Richard III
Sir Robert Walpole
Tories called . . . Tory Cf. *Satire* II.i.68.
To laugh . . . Peter Peter Walter, the money-lender; see l. 121 below; Epilogue II. 57–58 and note; and, above, Satire II.i.3 and note, and II.i.40.
Bubo "Some guilty person very fond of making such an observation" (Pope); cf. *Epistle to Dr. Arbuthnot,* l. 280
Sir Billy Sir William Yonge (d. 1755), a prominent Whig of whom Lord Hervey wrote, "His

name was proverbially used to express everything pitiful, corrupt, and contemptible"
Blunt Sir John Blunt (1665–1733), director of the South Sea Company, upon whose collapse he was forced to render his estate of almost £200,000
Huggins John Huggins (d. 1745), warden of Fleet Prison. Found guilty of extortion and cruelty and tried for the murder of a prisoner, he was acquitted because of the testimony of prominent character witnesses.

In Sappho° touch the *failings of the sex,*
In reverend bishops note some *small neglects,*
And own, the Spaniard° did a *waggish thing,*
Who cropped our ears, and sent them to the king.
His sly, polite, insinuating style
20   Could please at court, and make Augustus smile:
An artful manager, that crept between
His friend and shame, and was a kind of *screen.*°
But 'faith your very friends will soon be sore;
Patriots° there are, who wish you'd jest no more—
And where's the glory? 'twill be only thought
The Great Man° never offered you a groat.
Go see Sir Robert——

P.   See Sir Robert!—hum—
And never laugh—for all my life to come?
Seen him I have, but in his happier hour
30   Of social pleasure, ill-exchanged for power;
Seen him, uncumbered with the venal tribe,
Smile without art, and win without a bribe.
Would he oblige me? let me only find,
He does not think me what he thinks mankind.°
Come, come, at all I laugh he laughs, no doubt;
The only difference is, I dare laugh out.

F. Why yes: with *Scripture* still you may be free;
A horselaugh, if you please, at *honesty;*
A joke on Jekyl,° or some odd *Old Whig*
40   Who never changed his principles, or wig:°
A patriot is a fool in every age,
Whom all Lord Chamberlains° allow the stage:
These nothing hurts; they keep their fashion still,
And wear their strange old virtue, as they will.

If any ask you, 'Who's the man, so near
His prince, that writes in verse, and has his ear?'
Why, answer Lyttleton,° and I'll engage

Sappho Cf. *Satire* II.i.83.
Spaniard The captain of a Spanish ship cut off the ear of an English ship captain, Jenkins, and told him to carry it to his master, the king. While this eventually helped bring on war with Spain, it was still being investigated at the time the poem appeared, and Pope's irony is directed in part at Walpole's extreme reluctance to risk war.
screen a "metaphor peculiarly appropriated to a certain person in power" (Pope); i.e. Walpole, who opposed parliamentary inquiries into public frauds and was accused of being a "corrupt and all-screening minister"
Patriots a term applied to those in opposition to Walpole "though some of them . . . had views too mean and interested to deserve that name" (Pope)
Great Man a common phrase for Walpole as first minister

what . . . mankind alluding to Walpole's reported maxim, "All men have their price"
Jekyl Sir Joseph Jekyl (1663–1738), "a true Whig in his principles, and a man of the utmost probity. He sometimes voted against the Court, which drew upon him the laugh here described of *one* who bestowed it equally upon religion and honesty." (Pope)
wig still wearing the full-bottomed wig, at that time out of fashion with younger men
Lord Chamberlains given authority by Walpole's Licensing Act (1737) to forbid performances of politically dangerous plays
Lyttleton George, Baron Lyttleton (1709–73), secretary to the Prince of Wales and a strong opponent of Walpole, "distinguished for both his writings and speeches in the spirit of liberty" (Pope)

The worthy youth shall ne'er be in a rage:
But were his verses vile, his whisper base,
50   You'd quickly find him in Lord Fanny's° case.
Sejanus, Wolsey,° hurt not honest Fleury,°
But well may put some statesmen in a fury.

Laugh then at any, but at fools or foes;
These you but anger, and you mend not those.
Laugh at your friends, and, if your friends are sore,
So much the better, you may laugh the more;
To vice and folly to confine the jest,
Sets half the world, God knows, against the rest,
Did not the sneer of more impartial men
60   At sense and virtue, balance all again.
Judicious wits spread wide the ridicule,
And charitably comfort knave and fool.

P. Dear sir, forgive the prejudice of youth:
Adieu distinction, satire, warmth, and truth!
Come, harmless characters that no one hit;
Come, Henley's oratory,° Osborn's wit!°
The honey dropping from Favonio's° tongue,
The flowers of Bubo, and the flow of Young!°
The gracious dew of pulpit eloquence,°
70   And all the well-whipped cream of courtly sense,
That first was Hervey's, Fox's next, and then
The Senate's, and then Hervey's once again.
O come, that easy Ciceronian style,
So Latin, yet so English all the while,
As, though the pride of Middleton and Bland,°
All boys may read, and girls may understand!
Then might I sing without the least offence,
And all I sung should be the *Nation's Sense;*°

Lord Fanny's John, Lord Hervey; cf. *Epistle to Dr. Arbuthnot*, ll.305–33

Sejanus, Wolsey "The one the wicked minister of Tiberius; the other, of Henry VIII. The writers against the Court usually bestowed these and other odious names on the Minister" (Pope). For such names applied to Walpole, see *Epilogue* II.137.

Fleury cardinal and minister to Louis XV of France, praised by the Patriots for his wisdom and honesty; cf. *Satire* II.i.75.

Henley's oratory John Henley, a popular preacher who called himself the "restorer of ancient eloquence," charged a shilling for admission, and trained gentlemen in elocution

Osborn's wit James Pitt, a journalist and political hireling, wrote in defense of Walpole under many names, among them Socrates and Francis Osborne; known for the "heaviness of his style" as Mother Osborne.

Favonio's from Favonius, the gentle west wind
The flowers . . . Young so coupled in the *Epistle to Dr. Arbuthnot*, l. 280. Dodington was not only dishonest but pretentious; Yonge (Young) was described by Lord Hervey as

"talking eloquently without a meaning and expatiating agreeably upon nothing."

pulpit eloquence In this and the following lines Pope refers to some florid flattery that he believed Lord Hervey had composed. It was delivered by Henry Fox as a parliamentary address on the occasion of Queen Caroline's death and became "The Senate's" (l. 72) when Commons approved it and sent it to the king. It later reappeared in Hervey's Latin epitaph for the Queen. Cf. *Epilogue* II.164–80.

Middleton and Bland Conyers Middleton, theologian and librarian at Cambridge, was writing a life of Cicero, dedicated to Hervey in 1741. He helped correct the Latin of Hervey's epitaph, described by Pope as "between Latin and English." Henry Bland, Provost of Eton, translated the last act of Addison's *Cato* into Latin and published it through Walpole's help. He may have helped with the epitaph, too; both men would represent learning used (even hired) to give pretentious form to court flattery.

Nation's Sense the official view, Walpole's word for "consensus"

Or teach the melancholy Muse to mourn,
80   Hang the sad verse on Carolina's urn,
And hail her passage to the realms of rest,
All parts performed, and *all* her children blest!°
So—satire is no more—I feel it die—
No *gazetteer*° more innocent than I—
And let, a-God's name, every fool and knave
Be graced through life, and flattered in his grave.
        F. Why so? If satire knows its time and place,
You still may lash the greatest—in disgrace:
For merit will by turns forsake them all.
90   Would you know when? exactly when they fall.
But let all satire in all changes spare
Immortal Selkirk,° and grave De la Ware.°
Silent and soft, as saints remove to Heaven,
All ties dissolved, and every sin forgiven,
These may some gentle ministerial wing
Receive, and place forever near a king!
There, where no passion, pride, or shame transport,
Lulled with the sweet nepenthe° of a court;
There, where no father's, brother's, friend's disgrace
100   Once break their rest, or stir them from their place:°
But past the sense of human miseries,
All tears are wiped for ever from all eyes;°
No cheek is known to blush, no heart to throb,
Save when they lose a question,° or a job.°
        P. Good Heaven forbid, that I should blast their
            glory,
Who know how like Whig ministers to Tory,
And when three sovereigns died, could scarce be vext,
Considering what a *gracious Prince* was next.
Have I, in silent wonder, seen such things
110   As pride in slaves, and avarice in kings;
And at a peer or peeress shall I fret
Who starves a sister, or forswears a debt?
Virtue, I grant you, is an empty boast;
But shall the dignity of *vice* be lost?
Ye Gods! shall Cibber's son° without rebuke,

All parts . . . blest Queen Caroline was reported to have died without taking the last sacrament and without being reconciled with her son, the Prince of Wales.
gazetteer a journalist hired by the government to present its view
Immortal Selkirk Charles Douglas, Earl of Selkirk (1663–1739). "He was of the Bedchamber to King William; he was so to King George I; he was so to King George II" (Pope).
grave De la Ware John West, 1st Earl De la Ware (1693–1766), an indefatigable supporter of Walpole, "very skillful in all the forms of the House, in which he discharged himself with great gravity" (Pope)
nepenthe a potion that brings forgetfulness of grief or suffering
place with a punning reference to political appointment
All tears . . . eyes Cf. "and the Lord God will wipe away tears from off all faces" (Isaiah 25:8).
question parliamentary motion
job opportunity for bribery or profit
Cibber's son Colley Cibber's son Theophilus, the actor

Swear like a lord, or Rich° outwhore a duke?
A favourite's porter with his master vie,
Be bribed as often, and as often lie?
Shall Ward° draw contracts with a statesman's skill?
120   Or Japhet° pocket, like his Grace,° a Will?
Is it for Bond,° or Peter,° (paltry things)
To pay their debts, or keep their faith, like kings?
If Blount° dispatched himself, he played the man,
And so mayst thou, illustrious Passeran!°
But shall a printer,° weary of his life,
Learn from their books, to hang himself and wife?
This, this, my friend, I cannot, must not bear;
Vice thus abused, demands a nation's care:
This calls the Church to deprecate our sin,
130   And hurls the thunder of the laws on *gin*.°

Let modest Foster,° if he will, excel
Ten metropolitans° in preaching well;
A simple Quaker, or a Quaker's wife,
Outdo Landaffe° in doctrine,—yea in life:
Let humble Allen,° with an awkward shame,
Do good by stealth, and blush to find it fame.
Virtue may choose the high or low degree,
'Tis just alike to Virtue, and to me;
Dwell in a monk, or light upon a king,
140   She's still the same, beloved, contented thing.
Vice is undone, if she forgets her birth,
And stoops from angels to the dregs of earth:
But 'tis the *fall* degrades her to a whore;
Let *greatness* own her, and she's mean no more:
Her birth, her beauty, crowds and courts confess,
Chaste matrons praise her, and grave bishops bless;°
In golden chains the willing world she draws,

Rich John Rich, theatrical manager; producer of pantomimes and of Gay's *The Beggar's Opera* (1728)
Ward John Ward (d. 1755), convicted of forgery and expelled from Commons in 1726
Japhet Japhet Crook, convicted in 1731 of forgery and of fraud in obtaining a will; condemned to stand in the pillory, have his ears cut off and his nose slit, forfeit his goods, and be imprisoned for life
his Grace Archbishop Wake handed the will of George I to his son, who suppressed it.
Bond Denis Bond, who embezzled the funds of the Charitable Corporation
Peter Peter Walter. See l. 10 above and Note; Epilogue II.57-58 and Note.
Blount Charles Blount (1654–93), deistic or freethinking writer who stabbed himself out of disappointed love and died of the wound
Passeran Alberto Radicati, Count of Passerano, a Piedmontese freethinker who fled to England, where he wrote a notorious defense of suicide

printer as in fact happened in 1732
gin whose excessive use was not successfully restrained by an Act of 1736
Foster James Foster, an Anabaptist minister and brilliant preacher whom Pope, it was reported, went to hear
metropolitans bishops
Landaffe the holder of a "poor bishopric in Wales, as poorly supplied" (Pope); i.e. both poor and poorly filled
humble Allen Ralph Allen of Bath (1694–1764), friend of Pope and Henry Fielding, reformer of the postal service, famous for his philanthropy
Chaste matrons . . . bless alluding to: (1) Justinian's elevation of the prostitute and entertainer Theodora as his empress; (2) Walpole's belated but scandalous marriage in 1738 to Molly Skerrett, his mistress of many years and the mother of two of his children; (3) in the following lines, the Scarlet Whore of Revelation 17

And hers the gospel is, and hers the laws,
Mounts the tribunal, lifts her scarlet head,
150 And sees pale Virtue carted° in her stead.
Lo! at the wheels of her triumphal car,°
Old England's Genius, rough with many a scar,
Dragged in the dust! his arms hang idly round,
His flag inverted° trails along the ground!
Our youth, all liveried° o'er with foreign gold,
Before her dance: behind her, crawl the old!
See thronging millions to the pagod° run,
And offer country, parent, wife, or son!
Hear her black trumpet through the land proclaim,
160 That 'Not to be corrupted is the shame.'
In soldier, churchman, patriot, man in power,
'Tis avarice all, ambition is no more!
See, all our nobles begging to be slaves!
See, all our fools aspiring to be knaves!
The wit of cheats, the courage of a whore,
Are what ten thousand envy and adore.
All, all look up, with reverential awe,
On crimes that scape, or triumph o'er the law:
While truth, worth, wisdom, daily they decry—
170 'Nothing is sacred now but villainy.'
        Yet may this verse (if such a verse remain)
Show there was one who held it in disdain.

Dialogue II
        Fr[iend], 'Tis all a libel—Paxton° (sir) will say.
P. Not yet, my friend! tomorrow faith it may;
And for that very cause I print today.
How should I fret to mangle every line,
In reverence to the sins of *Thirty-nine!*°
Vice with such giant strides comes on amain,
Invention strives to be before in vain;
Feign what I will, and paint it e'er so strong,
Some rising genius sins up to my song.
10   F. Yet none but you by name the guilty lash;
Even Guthry° saves half Newgate by a dash.
Spare then the person, and expose the vice.
P.   How, sir! not damn the sharper, but the dice?
Come on then, satire! general, unconfined,

carted exhibited as prostitutes were, or carried to execution
triumphal car the conqueror's chariot
flag inverted another reference (cf. ll. 17–18) to Walpole's foreign policy of peace at any price
liveried wearing the uniforms of service
pagod shrine or pagoda
Paxton Nicholas Paxton (d. 1744), an official appointed to scan new publications for slurs or libels upon Walpole's government
Thirty-nine The poem was originally published under the title *One Thousand Seven Hundred and Thirty-Eight*.
Guthry the ordinary or chaplain of Newgate Prison, who published the memoirs or confessions of criminals, "often prevailed upon to be so tender of their reputation as to set down no more than the initials of their name" (Pope)

Spread thy broad wing, and souse° on all the kind.
Ye statesmen, priests, of one religion all!
Ye tradesmen, vile, in army, court, or hall!°
Ye reverend atheists. F. Scandal! name them, who?
　　P. Why that's the thing you bid me not to do.
20　Who starved a sister, who forswore a debt,
I never named; the town's inquiring yet.
The poisoning dame— F. You mean—
　　P. I don't.—　　　　F. You do.
P. See, now I keep the secret, and not you!
The bribing statesmen— F. Hold! too high you go.
P. The bribed elector— F. There you stoop too low.
P. I fain would please you, if I knew with what:
Tell me, which knave is lawful game, which not?
Must great offenders, once escaped the crown,
Like royal harts, be never more run down?
30　Admit your law to spare the knight requires,
As beasts of nature may we hunt the squires?
Suppose I censure—you know what I mean—
To save a bishop, may I name a dean?°
　　F. A dean, sir? no: his fortune is not made;
You hurt a man that's rising in the trade.
　　P. If not the tradesman who set up today,
Much less the prentice who tomorrow may.
Down, down, proud satire! though a realm be spoiled,°
Arraign no mightier thief than wretched Wild;°
40　Or, if a court or country's made a job,°
Go drench° a pickpocket, and join the mob.
　　But, sir, I beg you (for the love of vice!)
The matter's weighty, pray consider twice;
Have you less pity for the needy cheat,
The poor and friendless villain, than the great?
Alas! the small discredit of a bribe
Scarce hurts the lawyer, but undoes the scribe.°
Then better sure it charity becomes
To tax directors, who (thank God) have plums;°
50　Still better, ministers; or, if the thing
May pinch even there—why, lay it on a king.
　　F. Stop! stop!
　　P.　　　　Must satire, then, nor rise nor fall?
Speak out, and bid me blame no rogues at all.
　　F. Yes, strike that Wild, I'll justify the blow.

souse swoop like a hawk on its prey
hall Westminster Hall, the chief law court of England
dean chief officer of a cathedral chapter, of lower rank than a bishop
spoiled despoiled
Wild Jonathan Wild, thief, fence, and informer, hanged in 1725 (see l. 55); cf. Gay, The Beg-

gar's Opera (whose character of Peachum is based on Wild) and accompanying selections from Defoe and Fielding
made a job turned to personal gain
drench a common punishment, by ducking or under the public pump
scribe the scrivener or copyist, law clerk
plums large sums, usually £ 100,000

P. Strike? why, the man was hanged ten years ago:
Who now that obsolete example fears?
Even Peter° trembles only for his ears.
    F. What, always Peter? Peter thinks you mad,
You make men desperate, if they once are bad:
60   Else might he take to virtue some years hence—
    P. As Selkirk, if he lives, will love the Prince.°
    F. Strange spleen to Selkirk!
    P.   Do I wrong the man?
God knows, I praise a courtier where I can.
When I confess, there is who feels for fame
And melts to goodness, need I Scarborough° name?
Pleased let me own, in Esher's peaceful grove°
(Where Kent° and Nature vie for Pelham's love)
The scene, the master, opening to my view,
I sit and dream I see my Craggs° anew!
70   Even in a bishop I can spy desert;
Secker° is decent, Rundle° has a heart,
Manners with candour are to Benson° given,
To Berkeley,° every virtue under heaven.
    But does the court a worthy man remove?
That instant, I declare, he has my love:
I shun his zenith, court his mild decline;
Thus Somers° once, and Halifax,° were mine.
Oft, in the clear, still mirror of retreat,
I studied Shrewsbury,° the wise and great:
80   Carleton's° calm sense, and Stanhope's° noble flame,
Compared, and knew their generous end the same:
How pleasing Atterbury's° softer hour!

Peter Peter Walter (*Epilogue* I.10, 121), who had just escaped the pillory the year before
As Selkirk . . . Prince Cf. "immortal Selkirk," *Epilogue* I.92 ff. Because of the hostility between the king and his son, Selkirk (always true to the man in power) cannot love the prince, but he will do so as soon as the prince in turn becomes king.
Scarborough an earl who was a steady adherent to the royal interest but "whose known honour and virtue made him esteemed by all parties" (Pope)
Esher's . . . Grove the estate in Surrey of Henry Pelham, a loyal Whig who succeeded Walpole to power in 1746
Kent William Kent (1685–1748), the architect, painter, and landscape gardener, a friend of Pope and protégé of Burlington. With Pope's advice he did much to promote the "natural" garden, and Esher was one of his finest works of "improvement"; see Headnote to *To . . . Burlington.*
Craggs "There never lived a more worthy nature, a more disinterested mind, a more open and friendly temper" (Pope)
Secker Thomas Secker, Bishop of Oxford and later Archbishop of Canterbury, famous for moderation, tolerance, and discretion
Rundle Thomas Rundle, Bishop of Derry, of

whom Pope wrote, "I never saw a man so seldom whom I like so much"
Benson Martin Benson, Bishop of Gloucester
Berkeley George Berkeley (1685–1753), Bishop of Cloyne, philosopher, friend of Swift and Pope
Somers John, Lord Somers, Lord Keeper under William III. Pope, who knew him after his retirement, found Somers both "a consummate politician" and "a man of learning and politeness"; cf. the *Epistle to Dr. Arbuthnot,* l. 139 and note.
Halifax Charles Montagu, 1st Earl of Halifax (1661–1715), statesman, poet, and patron; a supporter of Pope's translation of Homer
Shrewsbury minister in three reigns and Lord Lieutenant of Ireland; cf. "Courtly Talbot" in the *Epistle to Dr. Arbuthnot,* l. 139 and note
Carleton's Henry Boyle, Baron Carleton, held many offices, including President of the Council, under William III and Anne.
Stanhope's James, Earl Stanhope, commander of the British forces in Spain in 1708; "a nobleman of equal courage, spirit, and learning" (Pope)
Atterbury's Bishop of Rochester, imprisoned in 1722 for his correspondence with the Pretender, convicted of treason and banished. Pope testified in his behalf at the trial.

How shined the soul, unconquered in the Tower!
How can I Pulteney,° Chesterfield° forget,
While Roman spirit charms, and Attic wit:
Argyle,° the state's whole thunder born to wield,
And shake alike the senate and the field:
Or Wyndham,° just to freedom and the throne,
The master of our passions, and his own.
90   Names, which I long have loved, nor loved in vain,
Ranked with their friends, not numbered with their train;
And if yet higher° the proud list should end,
Still let me say! No follower, but a friend.
    Yet think not, friendship only prompts my lays;
I follow *virtue;* where she shines, I praise:
Point she to priest or elder, Whig or Tory,
Or round a Quaker's beaver cast a glory.
I never (to my sorrow I declare)
Dined with the Man of Ross,° or my Lord Mayor.°
100 Some, in their choice of friends (nay, look not grave)
Have still a secret bias to a knave:
To find an honest man I beat about,
And love him, court him, praise him, in or out.
    F. Then why so few commended?
    P.   Not so fierce;
Find you the virtue, and I'll find the verse.
But random praise—the task can ne'er be done;
Each mother asks it for her booby son,
Each widow asks it for *the best of men,*
For him she weeps, and him she weds again.
110 Praise cannot stoop, like satire, to the ground,
The number° may be hanged, but not be crowned.
Enough for half the greatest of these days,
To scape my censure, not expect my praise.
Are they not rich? what more can they pretend?
Dare they to hope a poet for their friend?
What Richelieu° wanted, Louis° scarce could gain,
And what young Ammon° wished, but wished in vain.
No power the muse's friendship can command;
No power, when virtue claims it, can withstand:

Pulteney William Pulteney (1686–1764), a leading opponent of Walpole and brilliant orator in Commons
Chesterfield Philip Dormer Stanhope, 4th Earl of Chesterfield (1694–1773) and grandson of Halifax, the Trimmer; another opponent of Walpole and friend of Pope; later author of famous letters to his son
Argyle John Campbell, 2nd Duke of Argyle, earlier a general, later an influential convert to the opposition to Walpole
Wyndham Sir William, a leader of the Tory opposition, a man of "the utmost judgment and temper" (Pope)
yet higher perhaps referring to Pope's friendship with the Prince of Wales

Man of Ross John Kyrle, celebrated by Pope in an earlier poem for the great public benefits he performed on an income of only £500 a year
my Lord Mayor Sir John Barnard, religious, modest, an example of both private and public virtue
number multitude, the many
Richelieu (1585–1642) French cardinal and statesman; principal minister of Louis XIII
Louis Louis XIV, patron of such poets as Boileau (cf. l. 231)
Ammon Alexander the Great, who envied Achilles the fame that Homer had bestowed

120   To Cato, Virgil paid one honest line;°
    O let my country's friends illumine mine!
    —What are you thinking? F. Faith, the thought's
              no sin,
    I think your friends are out, and would be in.
      P. If merely to come in, sir, they go out,
    The way they take is strangely round about.
      F. They too may be corrupted, you'll allow?
      P. I only call those knaves who are so now.
    Is that too little? Come then, I'll comply—
    Spirit of Arnall!° aid me while I lie.
130   Cobham's° a coward, Polwarth° is a slave,
    And Lyttleton° a dark, designing knave,
    St. John° has ever been a wealthy fool—
    But let me add, Sir Robert's° mighty dull,
    Has never made a friend in private life,
    And was, besides, a tyrant to his wife.
      But, pray, when others praise him, do I blame?
    Call Verres, Wolsey,° any odious name?
    Why rail they then, if but a wreath of mine,
    Oh all-accomplished° St. John! deck thy shrine?
140   What! shall each spur-galled hackney° of the day,
    When Paxton° gives him double pots° and pay,
    Or each new-pensioned sycophant, pretend°
    To break my windows if I treat a friend?°
    Then wisely plead, to me they meant no hurt,
    But 'twas my guest at whom they threw the dirt?
    Sure, if I spare the minister, no rules
    Of honour bind me, not to maul his tools;
    Sure, if they cannot cut, it may be said
    His saws are toothless, and his hatchet's lead.
150   It angered Turenne,° once upon a day,
    To see a footman kicked that took his pay:

line *Aeneid* VIII.670, "And far apart the good, and Cato giving them laws," perhaps in praise of Cato Uticensis, who upheld republican ideals; cf. Pope's adaptation of that line in an ironic vein (*Epistle to Dr. Arbuthnot,* l. 209 and note)
Arnall William Arnall, a hireling political journalist
Cobham's friend of Pope and the builder of Stowe (*Epistle to Burlington,* l. 70), a distinguished general discharged for opposing Walpole's screening of the South Sea Company directors; thereupon a leading opposition Whig
Polwarth Hugh Hume, 3rd Earl of Marchmont (1708–94), one of the "boy patriots" in the Whig opposition. Walpole respected his abilities and regretted his intransigent probity.
Lyttleton Cf. *Epilogue* I.29 and note; a patron of Fielding, who was to dedicate *Tom Jones* to him in 1749.
St. John Henry, Viscount Bolingbroke (1678–1751), friend of Pope, Swift, and Gay; leader with Harley of the Tory government under Anne

and of the opposition to Walpole later; a brilliant orator and man of learning, to whom Pope addressed the *Essay on Man*
Sir Robert's Walpole, ironically denied his real attributes. He was personally attractive and totally indifferent to his first wife's infidelities.
Verres, Wolsey Cf. *Epilogue* I.51 and note; both "names" were derived from men who had used their office to gain great personal wealth.
all-accomplished "Lord Bolingbroke is something superior to anything I have seen in human nature" (Pope).
hackney hack writer, hireling
Paxton The censor of l. 1 was also in charge of Walpole's patronage to hired journalists.
pots of ale
pretend attempt
treat a friend as happened at Twickenham when Pope was entertaining Bolingbroke and Lord Bathurst
Turenne (1611–75), Henri, vicomte de, Marshal of France

But when he heard the affront the fellow gave,
Knew one a man of honour, one a knave;
The prudent general turned it to a jest,
And begged, he'd take the pains to kick the rest.
Which not at present having time to do—
    F. Hold, sir! for God's sake, where's the affront to you?
Against your worship when had Selkirk writ?
Or Page° poured forth the torrent of his wit?
160 Or grant the bard whose distich all commend
[*In power a servant, out of power a friend*]°
To Walpole guilty of some venial sin,
What's that to you who ne'er was out nor in?
    The priest whose flattery bedropped the crown,
How hurt he you? he only stained the gown.
And how did, pray, the florid youth° offend,
Whose speech you took, and gave it to a friend?
P. Faith, it imports not much from whom it came;
Whoever borrowed, could not be to blame,
170 Since the whole House did afterwards the same.
Let courtly wits to wits afford supply,
As hog to hog in huts of Westphaly;
If one, through nature's bounty or his lord's,
Has what the frugal, dirty soil affords,
From him the next receives it, thick or thin,°
As pure a mess almost as it came in;
The blessed benefit, not there confined,
Drops to the third, who nuzzles close behind;
From tail to mouth, they feed and they carouse:
180 The last full fairly gives it to the *House.*
    F. This filthy simile, this beastly line,
Quite turns my stomach—
    P.   So does flattery mine;
And all your courtly civet cats can vent,
Perfume° to you, to me is excrement.
But hear me further—Japhet,° 'tis agreed,
Writ not, and Chartres° scarce could write or read,
In all the courts of Pindus° guiltless quite;
But pens can forge, my friend, that cannot write.
And must no egg in Japhet's face be thrown,
190 Because the deed he forged was not my own?
Must never patriot then declaim at gin,

Page Cf. *Satire* II.i.82.
In power . . . friend a line from Bubb Dodington's flattering verse epistle to Walpole, 1726.
Dodington had for a time become adviser to the
Prince of Wales, who was opposed to Walpole.
florid youth Cf. *Epilogue* I.71–72.
From him . . . thin Pope had earlier (1715)
used the simile elsewhere: "Now will gain praise
by copying other wits / As one hog lives on
what another shits."

Perfume made from a substance with a musky
odor secreted by the anal scent glands of the
civet cat
Japhet Japhet Crook the forger; cf. *Epilogue* I.
120 and *Epistle to Dr. Arbuthnot*, l. 363
Chartres Francis Charteris, gambler, usurer, debauchee; cf. *Satire* II.i.4
Pindus mountain in Thessaly, a seat of the
Muses; thus, in any literary judgment

Unless, good man! he has been fairly in?
No zealous pastor blame a failing spouse,
Without a staring reason° on his brows?
And each blasphemer quite escape the rod,
Because the insult's not on man, but God?
    Ask you what provocation I have had?
The strong antipathy of good to bad.
When truth or virtue an affront endures,
200   The affront is mine, my friend, and should be yours.
Mine, as a foe professed to false pretence,
Who think a coxcomb's honour like his sense;
Mine, as a friend to every worthy mind;
And mine as man, who feel for all mankind.°
    F. You're strangely proud.
    P.   So proud, I am no slave:
So impudent, I own myself no knave:
So odd, my country's ruin makes me grave.
Yes, I am proud; I must be proud to see
Men not afraid of God, afraid of me:
210   Safe from the bar, the pulpit, and the throne,
Yet touched and shamed by ridicule alone.
    O sacred weapon! left for truth's defence,
Sole dread of folly, vice, and insolence!
To all but heaven-directed hands denied,
The muse may give thee, but the gods must guide.
Reverent I touch thee! but with honest zeal;
To rouse the watchmen of the public weal,
To virtue's work provoke the tardy Hall,°
And goad the prelate slumbering in his stall.
220   Ye tinsel insects! whom a court maintains,
That counts your beauties only by your stains,
Spin all your cobwebs o'er the eye of day!
The muse's wing shall brush you all away:
All his Grace preaches, all his Lordship° sings,
All that makes saints of queens, and gods of kings,
All, all but truth, drops deadborn from the press,
Like the last gazette,° or the last address.°
    When black ambition stains a public cause,
A monarch's sword when mad vainglory draws,
230   Not Waller's wreath° can hide the nation's scar,
Nor Boileau° turn the feather to a star.
Not so, when diademed with rays divine,

---

staring reason cuckold's horns
And mine . . . mankind an adaptation of Terence: "I am a man, and I think nothing human
indifferent to me"
Hall Westminster Hall, as the seat of justice
Grace . . . Lordship bishop and peer
gazette official government journal

address the formal reply of Parliament to the
king's opening speech
Waller's wreath Edmund Waller's panegyrics to
Oliver Cromwell
Boileau who, in celebration of Louis XIV's conquest of the Lowlands, suggested that the
feather in Louis's hat would be a comet or star
portending disaster to his enemies

Touched with the flame that breaks from virtue's shrine,
Her priestess Muse forbids the good to die,
And opes the Temple of Eternity.
There, other trophies deck the truly brave,
Than such as Anstis° casts into the grave;
Far other stars° than * and * * wear,
And may descend to Mordington from Stair:°
(Such as on Hough's unsullied mitre shine,
Or beam, good Digby, from a heart like thine).°
Let Envy howl, while Heaven's whole chorus sings,
And bark at honour not conferred by kings;
Let Flattery sickening see the incense rise,
Sweet to the world, and grateful to the skies:
Truth guards the poet, sanctifies the line,
And makes immortal, verse as mean as mine.
    Yes, the last pen for freedom let me draw,
When truth stands trembling on the edge of law;
Here, last of Britons! let your names be read;
Are none, none living? let me praise the dead,
And for that cause which made your fathers shine,
Fall by the votes of their degenerate line.
    F. Alas! alas! pray end what you began,
And write next winter° more *Essays on Man.*

                    1738

The Dunciad

The poem was first published in three books in 1728, shortly after *Gulliver's Travels* and *The Beggar's Opera;* it was written in part during Swift's visit to England, and it was dedicated to Swift. In 1729 Pope amplified it as *The Dunciad Variorum* with prefaces and notes of an elaborate pseudo-scholarly sort, incorporating the forms of Dulness into the work, and he included an anthology of the scurrilous comments published about him by the dunces. Twelve years later Pope wrote a new fourth book and revised the poem, replacing the poet-critic Lewis Theobald with the playwright-actor-laureate Colley Cibber as the chief of the dunces. The dunces are, in fact, all those forces making for the debasement of English culture, and the action of the poem shows them moving westward, leaving the low scenes of the Smithfield Fair to take over the court (where George II presides in sublime indifference to questions

Anstis John Anstis, chief herald at arms, who devised symbols of honors that were often cast into the graves of great peers
stars symbols of the Order of the Garter; supply the names of (King) George and (Prince) Frederick
descend to . . . Stair from the Earl of Stair, a distinguished soldier and envoy, to Lord Mordington, whose wife kept a gambling house
Such as . . . thine "The one [John Hough, Bishop of Worcester] an assertor of the Church of England in opposition to the false measures

of King James II; the other [William, Lord Digby] as firmly attached to the cause of that king; both acting out of principle, and equally men of honour and virtue" (Pope)
write next winter "This was the last poem of the kind printed by our author, with a resolution to publish no more, but to enter thus, in the most plain and solemn manner he could, a sort of *protest* against that insuperable corruption and depravity of manners which he had been so unhappy as to live to see" (Pope).

of value). This westward movement from the City to Westminster is the ironic counter-part of Aeneas' bearing the culture of fallen Troy to Latium, to found a new empire which would culminate in the Augustan Age of Virgil.

The mythic action of the poem is the subversion of high by low, as the Titan daughter Dulness reclaims the ordered realms of the Olympian deities for original darkness. She is a vast bloated deity swathed in fogs, pent up in her own world like Swift's Spider; but she is also a projection into the form of divinity of those forces of sluggish inertia, relaxation of effort and thought, and selfish indolence that inhabit every man. To worship her is to choose something easier than excellence and some-thing less than full humanity. In the first three books Pope shows the archetypal dunce, the poet laureate Cibber; the epic games involving authors, publishers, and patrons (the games are debased and excremental, the physical index of moral and intellectual corruption); and the prophetic vision of Dulness's gradual movement from China to the West, marked by the fall of cultures in Greece and Rome and now England.

In the new fourth book Pope moves into the intellectual pursuits of man, reviving an earlier plan to deal with education and extending it to include politics and religion as well. At every point he shows the substitution of triviality for substance, of verbalism for wisdom, of relaxation for vigilance. The poem ends in a great yawn and a nation reduced to sleep, with only the poet himself awake to behold the eclipse of light and the triumph of the "uncreating word." This tragic close achieves a peculiar force: suddenly we see in all the minutiae of pedantry and frivolity a larger pattern, of mind surrendering its powers and of man subsiding—for all his refinements of pleasure—into barbarism.

From The Dunciad°

Book the Fourth

Yet, yet a moment, one dim ray of light
Indulge, dread Chaos, and eternal Night!°
Of darkness visible° so much be lent,
As half to show, half veil, the deep intent.
Ye Powers! whose mysteries restored I sing,
To whom Time bears me on his rapid wing,
Suspend a while your force inertly strong,
Then take at once the poet and the song.
      Now flamed the Dog-star's° unpropitious ray,
10   Smote every brain and withered every bay;

Dunciad The title is formed on the analogy of *Iliad* or *Aeneid;* its great subject is the dunce (whose name derived from that of the scholastic philosopher Duns Scotus) in all his manifesta-tions, from the simple blockhead to the vast force of Dulness itself.
dread Chaos . . . Night Chaos was, according to Hesiod, the progenitor of all the gods. In *Paradise Lost* II, Chaos and Night rule that portion of the universe that God has not yet ordered; so here they are the rulers "of ancient night," seeking to reclaim (through their daughter Dulness) the realms that have been seized from them for light and order. The "restoration of this empire is the action of the poem" (Pope-Warburton); hereafter P-W will be used for those notes that Warburton pro-vided on his own or from Pope's manuscripts.
darkness visible used of hell in *Paradise Lost* 1.63
Dog-star's of Sirius, visible in the hot late sum-mer; cf. *Epistle to Dr. Arbuthnot,* l. 3

Sick was the sun, the owl forsook his bower,
The moon-struck prophet felt the madding hour:
Then rose the seed of Chaos, and of Night,
To blot out order and extinguish light,
Of dull and venal a new world to mould,
And bring Saturnian days of lead and gold.°
　　She mounts the throne: her head a cloud concealed,
In broad effulgence all below revealed;°
('Tis thus aspiring Dulness ever shines)
20　Soft on her lap her laureate son reclines.
　　Beneath her footstool, *Science* groans in chains,
And *Wit* dreads exile, penalties, and pains.
There foamed rebellious *Logic*, gagged and bound,
There, stripped, fair *Rhetoric* languished on the ground;
His blunted arms by *Sophistry*° are borne,
And shameless *Billingsgate* her robes adorn.
Morality, by her false guardians drawn,
Chicane in furs, and *Casuistry* in lawn,°
Gasps, as they straiten° at each end the cord,
30　And dies, when Dulness gives her Page° the word.
Mad *Máthesis*° alone was unconfined,
Too mad for mere material chains to bind,
Now to pure space lifts her ecstatic stare,
Now running round the circle, finds it square.
But held in tenfold bonds the *Muses* lie,
Watched both by Envy's and by Flattery's eye:
There to her heart sad Tragedy addrest
The dagger wont to pierce the tyrant's breast;
But sober History restrained her rage,
40　And promised vengeance on a barbarous age.
There sunk Thalia,° nerveless, cold, and dead,
Had not her sister Satire held her head:
Nor couldst thou, Chesterfield!° a tear refuse,
Thou weptst, and with thee wept each gentle° Muse.
　　When lo! a harlot form° soft sliding by,

lead and gold The age of Saturn was tradition-ally the Golden Age, but Saturn was also an alchemical symbol for lead; here lead represents the "dull," and gold, as in the Satires, the "venal" or corrupted.
all below revealed recalling the old adage, cited by P-W, "The higher you climb, the more you show your arse"
Sophistry Dulness "admits something like each science" (P-W); thus Sophistry for Logic, Billingsgate (the shrill abuse of fishwives) for Rhetoric, etc.
furs . . . lawn law (the ermine robes of the judge) and church (the fine linen sleeves of a bishop), each corrupted into its characteristic substitute for morality; for "Casuistry," cf. *The Rape of the Lock* V.122
straiten tighten

Page punning on Sir Francis Page, the famous "hanging judge"; cf. *Satire* II.i.82
Máthesis pure mathematics, unlimited by appli-cation; suggestive of its mystical Pythagorean uses, here madly ambitious and deluded
Thalia Muse of comedy, all but killed by the censorship of Walpole's Licensing Act of 1737
Chesterfield who spoke eloquently against the Act; cf. *Epilogue* II.84
gentle as opposed to the low substitutes, e.g. Billingsgate
harlot form opera, which had gained new favor with the importation of Italian singers; resented for its spectacle and other excesses but chiefly for destroying the fusion of sound and sense that had been achieved in the English song tradition of the Renaissance; here presented with "affected airs"

With mincing step, small voice, and languid eye;
Foreign her air, her robe's discordant pride
In patchwork fluttering, and her head aside.
By singing peers upheld on either hand,
50   She tripped and laughed, too pretty much to stand;
Cast on the prostrate Nine a scornful look,
Then thus in quaint recitativo° spoke:
     'O *Cara! Cara!* silence all that train:
Joy to great Chaos! let Division° reign:
Chromatic tortures° soon shall drive them hence,
Break all their nerves, and fritter all their sense:
One trill shall harmonize joy, grief, and rage,
Wake the dull Church, and lull the ranting stage;
To the same notes thy sons shall hum, or snore,
60   And all thy yawning daughters cry, *encore.*
Another Phoebus, thy own Phoebus,° reigns,
Joys in my jigs, and dances in my chains.
But soon, ah soon, rebellion will commence,
If music meanly borrows aid from sense:
Strong in new arms, lo! giant Handel° stands,
Like bold Briareus,° with a hundred hands;
To stir, to rouse, to shake the soul he comes,
And Jove's own thunders follow Mars's drums.
Arrest him, Empress; or you sleep no more—'
70   She heard, and drove him to the Hibernian shore.
     And now had Fame's posterior trumpet° blown,
And all the nations summoned to the throne.
The young, the old, who feel her inward sway,
One instinct seizes, and transports away.
None need a guide, by sure attraction led,
And strong impulsive gravity° of head:
None want° a place, for all their centre found,
Hung to the goddess, and cohered around.
Not closer, orb in orb,° conglobed are seen
80   The buzzing bees about their dusky queen.
     The gathering number, as it moves along,

recitativo musical declamation, neither quite spoken nor quite sung
Division i.e. breaking up long notes into a succession of short ones and so dwelling on a single syllable of the word being sung; parodied by Swift in a mock-cantata
Chromatic tortures elaborate variations introducing notes that do not belong to the diatonic scale; "the Spartans forbade the use of it as languid and effeminate" (P-W)
thy own Phoebus i.e. the Apollo of *this* pseudo-art, but also referring to the French term *phébus,* "an appearance of light glimmering over the obscurity, a semblance of meaning without any real sense" (P-W, citing Bouhours)
Handel whose increase in "hands" in orchestra and chorus (see next line) "proved so much too manly for the fine gentlemen of his age that he

was obliged to remove his music into Ireland" (P-W), on whose "Hibernian shore" (Dublin) *The Messiah* was first performed in 1741. The power of Handel, as opposed to precious and feminine opera, is made clear in l. 67.
Briareus the giant of a hundred hands who fought for Zeus and the Olympians against the Titans
posterior trumpet "her second or more certain report" (P-W), but cf. also l.18 and note above
gravity solemnity; but also gravitational attraction or impulsion, as in ll.81–84
want lack
orb in orb Cf. Milton's account of the angels in Heaven: "Thus when in orbs / Of circuit inexpressible they stood, / Orb within orb" (*Paradise Lost* V.594–96).

Involves a vast involuntary throng,
Who gently drawn, and struggling less and less,
Roll in her vortex,° and her power confess.
Not those alone who passive own her laws,
But who, weak rebels,° more advance her cause:
Whate'er of dunce in college or in town
Sneers at another, in toupee or gown;°
Whate'er of mongrel no one class admits,
90   A wit with dunces, and a dunce with wits.
    Nor absent they, no members of her state,
Who pay her homage in her sons, the Great;°
Who, false to Phoebus, bow the knee to Baal;°
Or, impious, preach his word without a call.
Patrons, who sneak from living worth to dead,
Withhold the pension, and set up the head;°
Or vest dull Flattery in the sacred gown;°
Or give from fool to fool the laurel crown.
And (last and worst) with all the cant of wit,
100 Without the soul, the Muse's hypocrite.°
    There marched the bard and blockhead, side by side,
Who rhymed for hire, and patronized for pride.
Narcissus,° praised with all a parson's power,
Looked a white lily sunk beneath a shower.
There moved Montalto° with superior air;
His stretched-out arm displayed a volume fair;
Courtiers and patriots in two ranks divide,
Through both he passed, and bowed from side to side:
But as in graceful act, with awful eye
110 Composed he stood, bold Benson° thrust him by:
On two unequal crutches propped he came,
Milton's on this, on that one Johnston's name.
The decent knight retired with sober rage,
Withdrew his hand, and closed the pompous page.
But (happy for him as the times went then)
Appeared Apollo's mayor and aldermen,°
On whom three hundred gold-capped youths° await,

Roll . . . **vortex** eddy around her
weak rebels those petty critics who do little to
suppress Dulness but in fact only increase her
power
toupee or gown in curled periwig (fops) or in
academic gown (scholars)
Great the king and nobility
Baal any false god, presumably wealth or power
Withhold . . . head i.e. fail to support while
alive and parasitically honor after death
vest . . . gown confer an ecclesiastical gown
(with its income) upon a flatterer
Muse's hypocrite "He who thinks the only end
of poetry is to be witty . . . who cultivates only
such trifling talents in himself and encourages
only such in others" (P-W)
Narcissus Lord Hervey, an epileptic, had a very
white face; he was heavily flattered in the dedi-

cation of Dr. Middleton's *Life of Cicero* (1741);
cf. *Epilogue* I.69–76.
Montalto Sir Thomas Hanmer, pompous and
portly, published a lavish edition of Shakespeare
at his own expense and for his own glory.
Benson William Benson, for political reasons and
in spite of incompetence, succeeded Sir Christopher Wren as royal architect. He built a lavish
monument to Milton in Westminster Abbey and
commissioned a Latin translation of *Paradise
Lost;* he also published several editions of
Arthur Johnston's Latin version of the Psalms.
Apollo's . . . aldermen dignitaries of Oxford,
whose press agreed to publish Hanmer's Shakespeare
gold-capped youths with the gold tassel of
gentlemen-commoners, students who paid higher
fees in return for special privileges and dress

To lug the ponderous volume off in state.
When Dulness, smiling—'Thus revive the wits!
120   But murder first, and mince them all to bits;
As erst Medea° (cruel, so to save!)
A new edition of old Aeson gave;
Let standard authors, thus, like trophies born,
Appear more glorious as more hacked and torn,
And you, my critics! in the chequered shade,
Admire new light through holes yourselves have made.
'Leave not a foot of verse, a foot of stone,
A page, a grave, that they can call their own;
But spread, my sons, your glory thin or thick,
130   On passive paper, or on solid brick.
So by each bard an alderman° shall sit,
A heavy lord shall hang at every wit,
And while on Fame's triumphal car they ride,
Some slave of mine° be pinioned to their side.'
Now crowds on crowds around the goddess press,
Each eager to present their first address.
Dunce scorning dunce beholds the next advance,
But fop shows fop superior complaisance.°
When lo! a spectre° rose, whose index hand
140   Held forth the virtue of the dreadful wand;
His beavered brow a birchen garland wears,
Dropping with infant's blood, and mother's tears.
O'er every vein a shuddering horror runs;
Eton and Winton° shake through all their sons.
All flesh is humbled, Westminster's bold race
Shrink, and confess the genius° of the place:
The pale boy senator yet tingling stands,
And holds his breeches close with both his hands.
Then thus: 'Since man from beast by words is known,
150   Words are man's province, words we teach alone.°
When reason doubtful, like the Samian letter,°
Points him two ways, the narrower is the better.
Placed at the door of learning, youth to guide,
We never suffer it to stand too wide.
To ask, to guess, to know, as they commence,
As fancy opens the quick spring of sense,

Medea who, in one version of the legend, had Aeson's daughters cut their father into pieces and cast them into a cauldron, whence, with Medea's magic, he emerged restored to youth
alderman such as Alderman Barber, who proudly placed his own name on the monument he erected to Samuel Butler
slave of mine as in Rome, where a slave was chained beside the triumphant victor (to remind him of the mutability of fortune) while he rode through the city
complaisance tolerance
spectre Dr. Richard Busby (1605–95), the

famous headmaster of Westminster School, carrying his birch cane ("dreadful wand") for discipline (whence the "infant's blood"); cf. *Paradise Lost* I.392–93 for Moloch
Eton and Winton the latter Winchester; schools where Busby's influence still prevails
genius presiding deity
Since man . . . alone The humanist doctrine that eloquence is wisdom expressed now becomes a concern with words to the neglect of thought.
the Samian letter the letter Y, emblem of the crossroads of choice

We ply the memory, we load the brain,
Bind rebel wit, and double chain on chain,
Confine the thought to exercise the breath;
And keep them in the pale of words till death.
Whate'er the talents or howe'er designed,
We hang one jingling padlock° on the mind:
A poet the first day he dips his quill;
And what the last? a very poet still.
Pity! the charm works only in our wall,
Lost, lost too soon in yonder House or Hall.°
There truant Wyndham every Muse gave o'er,
There Talbot° sunk, and was a wit no more!
How sweet an Ovid, Murray° was our boast!
How many Martials were in Pulteney° lost!
Else sure some bard, to our eternal praise,
In twice ten thousand rhyming nights and days,
Had reached the work, the all that mortal can;
And South° beheld that masterpiece of man.'
       'Oh' (cried the goddess) 'for some pedant reign!
Some gentle James,° to bless the land again;
To stick the doctor's° chair into the throne,
Give law to words, or war with words alone,
Senates and courts with Greek and Latin rule,
And turn the Council to a grammar school!
For sure, if Dulness sees a grateful day,
'Tis in the shade of arbitrary sway.°
O! if my sons may learn one earthly thing,
Teach but that one, sufficient for a king:
That which my priests, and mine alone, maintain,
Which as it dies, or lives, we fall, or reign:
May you, may Cam and Isis,° preach it long!
The RIGHT DIVINE of kings to govern wrong.'
       Prompt at the call, around the goddess roll
Broad hats, and hoods, and caps, a sable shoal:
Thick and more thick the black blockade extends,

60
70
80
90

---

jingling padlock exercises in composing Greek and Latin verses
House or Hall Westminster Hall (the courts) or Parliament
Wyndham . . . Talbot two brilliant members of Parliament; cf. *Epilogue* II.79, 88
Murray William Murray (1705–93), later Lord Chief Justice and Earl of Mansfield; awarded a prize for a Latin poem by Busby ("our boast"), he became a distinguished statesman, jurist, and orator
Pulteney gifted in epigram like the Roman Martial, he became instead a political writer and leader in opposition to Walpole
South Dr. Robert South "declared a perfect epigram as difficult a performance as an epic poem, and the critics"—particularly Dryden—"say, 'an epic poem is the greatest work human

nature is capable of," (P-W). The epigram becomes the culmination of Busby's and Dulness's verbalism.
James James I was both a famous pedant and the first English monarch to claim the divine right of kings
doctor's teacher's
For sure . . . sway "no branch of learning thrives well under arbitrary government but verbal" (P-W). Timeliness is given by the charges of the opposition that Walpole's monarch was seeking to subject Parliament to "dependence on the Crown"; thus the pedant Stuart heavy and dull—becomes the counterpart of the heavier Hanoverian (manipulated as he is by Walpole).
Cam and Isis the universities of Cambridge and Oxford, named here for their rivers

A hundred head° of Aristotle's friends.°
Nor wert thou, Isis! wanting to the day,
Though Christ Church° long kept prudishly away.
Each staunch polemic,° stubborn as a rock,
Each fierce logician, still expelling Locke,°
Came whip and spur, and dashed through thin and thick
On German Crousaz, and Dutch Burgersdyck.°
As many quit the streams that murmuring fall
To lull the sons of Margaret and Clare Hall,°
Where Bentley° late tempestuous wont to sport
In troubled waters, but now sleeps in port.
Before them marched that awful Aristarch;°
Ploughed was his front with many a deep remark:°
His hat, which never vailed° to human pride,
Walker° with reverence took, and laid aside.
Low bowed the rest: he, kingly, did but nod;
So upright° Quakers please both man and God.
'Mistress! dismiss that rabble from your throne:
Avaunt——is Aristarchus yet unknown?
Thy mighty scholiast,° whose unwearied pains
Made Horace dull, and humbled Milton's strains.°
Turn what they will to verse, their toil is vain,
Critics like me shall make it prose again.
Roman and Greek grammarians! know your better:
Author of something yet more great than letter;
While towering o'er your alphabet, like Saul,
Stands our Digamma,° and o'ertops them all.
'Tis true, on words is still our whole debate,
Disputes of *Me* or *Te*, of *aut* or *at*,
To sound° or sink in *cano*, O or A,
Or give up Cicero° to C or K.
Let Freind affect to speak as Terence spoke,

200

210

220

---

head a term suggestive of cattle
Aristotle's friends those "faithful followers"
who, in spite of Cartesian and Newtonian
science, "never bowed the knee to Baal nor
acknowledged any strange god in philosophy"
(P-W)
Christ Church the one college at Oxford whose
dons were least under the spell of Dulness
polemic controversialist
still expelling Locke whose work was censured
in 1703 by the heads of Oxford
German . . . Burgersdyck cited as two instances of Aristotelian logicians
Margaret and Clare Hall St. John's and Clare
colleges in Cambridge, "particularly famous for
their skill in disputation" (P-W)
Bentley As master of Trinity College, Cambridge, Richard Bentley, the classical scholar so
long a target of Swift and Pope, had been at
odds with his fellows but was now at rest; with
a pun on "port," the wine plentifully drunk
after dinner.
Aristarch Bentley in the guise of Aristarchus,

the Homeric commentator and corrector (d.
150 B.C.)
remark a term used for a note or commentary in
Bentley's work
vailed yielded, was lowered
Walker the vice-master of Trinity
upright honest; also not bowing in prayer, as
Bentley will not bow before Dulness
scholiast commentator
humbled Milton's strains Bentley, as editor of
Milton, boldly "corrected" the text (and "humbled" its greatness) on the assumption that Milton's blindness allowed numerous errors to appear; he edited Horace also with arrogance and
insensitivity.
Digamma a letter restored by Bentley in his
projected edition of Homer. Since it was one
gamma set upon another, it was like Saul, who
was "higher than any of the people" (I Samuel
9:2).
sound stress
Cicero the pronunciation of whose name was
disputed (as was that of Latin generally)

1. John Dryden, 1693,
by Sir Godfrey Kneller (1649?–1723).
National Portrait Gallery, London.

2. Charles II, c. 1660-65,
?studio of John Michael Wright (1617–1700).
National Portrait Gallery.

3. William Congreve, 1709,
by Sir Godfrey Kneller.
National Portrait Gallery.

4. John Bunyan, 1684, by T. Sadler.
National Portrait Gallery.

5. Alexander Pope, ?1741, by L. F. Roubiliac (c. 1705–62).
Leeds City Art Galleries.

6. Sir Robert Walpole, 1738,
by J. M. Rysbrack (1694–1770).
National Portrait Gallery.

7. Jonathan Swift, by L. F. Roubiliac.
Trinity College, Dublin.

8. St. Paul's from the northwest.
A. F. Kersting.

9. The West Towers.

ENGLISH BAROQUE ARCHITECTURE

Sir Christopher Wren (1632–1723) came to architecture, at the prompting of Charles II, from a distinguished career in mathematics and astronomy. During a visit to Paris in 1665–66 he met the great Italian baroque architect Gianlorenzo Bernini (1598–1680), and brought back with him "almost all France in paper," i.e. in prints and architectural books. His designs included Hampton Court and the royal hospitals at Chelsea and Greenwich, university buildings at Oxford and Cambridge, and nearly fifty churches in London to replace or restore those damaged in the Great Fire of 1666. Of the last the most ambitious was St. Paul's Cathedral, begun in 1675 and completed in 1710. The bold and intricate west towers engage in constantly changing interplay with the massive dome as the viewer's perspective shifts. They are among the finest of the numerous and remarkably varied spires that were to dominate the London skyline for more than two centuries.

10. St. Bride, c. 1700.
A. F. Kersting.

11. St. Magnus-the-Martyr,
1705

12. St. Mary-le-Bow,
completed 1680.

13. St. Vedast, 1694–97.

14. Christ Church, Spitalfields.

15. St. Anne, Limehouse.
A. F. Kersting.

Nicholas Hawksmoor (1661–1736), Wren's chief assistant, later worked closely with Sir John Vanbrugh (1664–1726) on such buildings as Blenheim Palace and Castle Howard (see Fig. 16). The two East London churches shown here were begun in 1714 and completed in the late 1720's. Hawksmoor's intense and often somber art turned conventional forms to strikingly novel uses. In Christ Church he used the Palladian form, an arch flanked by two rectangular openings (as in the so-called Venetian window), first magnifying it to the scale of a triumphal arch in the lower storeys, then varying the pattern in shallower and more attenuated forms above. St. Anne, Limehouse, plays with concave and convex forms and concludes in a tower whose angularity suggests Gothic steeples without in fact using any Gothic forms.

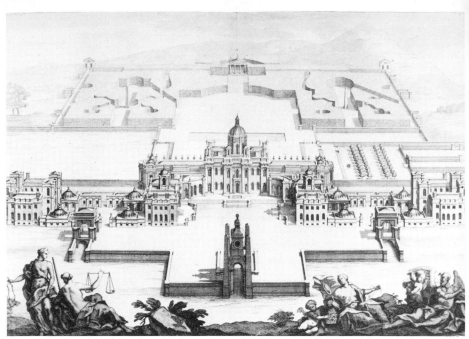

16. Vanbrugh and Hawksmoor, Castle Howard (begun c. 1699). From Colin Campbell, *Vitruvius Britannicus,* 1715. *The New York Public Library.*

Castle Howard, Yorkshire, is one of the most lavish and brilliant of baroque country houses, and its grounds are varied with ornamental buildings in bold shapes. Sir John Vanbrugh's Temple of the Winds was a belvedere; the porticos were designed to prevent direct sunlight but to admit "light of the most pleasing kind." Nicholas Hawksmoor's Mausoleum is set on a rise a mile from the house, its silhouette visible from great distances. Its exterior has twenty Doric columns whose spacing was criticized by Lord Burlington as unclassical in its closeness (see in contrast William Kent's Temple of Ancient Virtue, Fig. 20); and it was one of Burlington's protégés who added later the steps modeled on those at Chiswick House. Hawksmoor's building has survived Palladian criticism and improvement; it remains as he intended: self-enclosed, unaccommodating, formidably severe.

17. Vanbrugh, Temple of the Winds, built in the 1720's. *Country Life*, London.

18. Hawksmoor, Mausoleum, begun in 1729. *Country Life*.

19. Chiswick House, designed before 1727. A. F. Kersting.

PALLADIANISM

Lord Burlington (Richard Boyle, 1694–1753; see Pope's *Essay* to him), like the third Earl of Shaftesbury, reacted against Wren and English baroque architecture. Upon his return from Italy, Burlington undertook, with the assistance of William Kent (1685–1748), to work toward a more chaste, more authentic classicism than England had achieved before. He found his models in the Italian Renaissance architect Andrea Palladio (1508–80) and in Palladio's chief English follower, Inigo Jones (1573–1652); Burlington sponsored the publication of their designs and imitated their work, at times moving even closer to their Roman sources. Chiswick House, a country villa at Twickenham, derives in part from Palladio's Villa Rotonda at Vicenza. The austerity of the building itself is offset by the opulent decoration within and the natural, irregular gardens that surround it.

20. William Kent, Temple of Ancient Virtue in the gardens at Stowe.
Courtauld Institute of Art, London.

21. Henry Flitcroft (1697–1769), The Temple of Flora, c. 1745–50. *Country Life.*

22. The approach to the Pantheon (Flitcroft, c. 1752–56). *Country Life.*

THE GARDENS AT STOURHEAD

Stourhead, near the Wiltshire-Dorset border, was cultivated by banker Henry Hoare, from 1741. By 1765 Horace Walpole could declare it "one of the most picturesque scenes in the world." It was in part a Claude landscape realized in what had been originally barren downs; in fact, Claude's *Coast View of Delos with Aeneas* provided the elements of the design and perhaps the implicit theme of the founding of Rome.

23. Claude Lorrain, *Coast View of Delos with Aeneas*, c. 1672. *The National Gallery*, London.

24. *The Marriage Contract*

The groom's father, Earl Squander, relieves his gout while he negotiates a dowry for his son's marriage to a City merchant's daughter. Visible through the window is a half-finished Palladian building (Hogarth loathed William Kent and his sponsor, Lord Burlington) which has helped to impoverish him, but he ignores the mortgage debts the clerk holds out before him. The groom gazes at his true love in a mirror, while the bride flirts with the lawyer Silvertongue. The chains on the dogs suggest their bondage.

HOGARTH ON HIGH LIFE

William Hogarth (1697–1764) invented the narrative sequence of paintings that could in turn be engraved and sold widely as sets of prints. Although he attempted more solemn and ambitious "history" painting (that is, historical, biblical, or mythological subjects in the grand style), it was in "comic history" (as Henry Fielding named it in *Joseph Andrews*, 1742) that he achieved his greatest and most characteristic work. Earlier sequences like *The Harlot's Progress* and *The Rake's Progress* had enormous success; in *Marriage à la Mode*, 1743–45, Hogarth attempted to present a more refined, if scarcely more creditable, society. (See Figs. 24–30.) *The National Gallery.*

25. *Shortly after the Marriage*

The wife lazily, but seductively, stretches at breakfast after her late card party (it is now just past noon), but the exhausted young Viscount has just come in from a night on the town. His pursuits are indicated by the woman's cap the dog is pulling from his pocket. The pious steward indicates despair at the neglected household and the unpaid bills, both reflections of the marriage itself.

26. *The Visit to the Quack Doctor*

The Viscount cheerfully brings his childlike mistress for a cure of the venereal disease he has presumably given her. The cabinets of curiosities and the monstrous machines are only less sinister than the woman with the clasp-knife (the quack's assistant or possibly the brothel-keeper).

27. The Countess's Morning Levée

Since Earl Squander has died and her husband has inherited the title, the wife can now adorn her dressing-table with an Earl's coronet. She is receiving morning guests while her hair is dressed. The most intimate is lawyer Silvertongue, sprawling on the sofa beside Crébillon's notorious erotic novel *Le Sopha*. The page unpacks a statue of Actaeon, given a stag's head for seeing Diana naked but here suggesting the cuckold's horns. Among other guests are a fop in curling papers and a melodious *castrato*. Over their heads hangs a painting of Jupiter snatching up Ganymede; over the Countess's, one of Jupiter descending as a cloud to embrace Io.

28. *The Killing of the Earl*

The Earl has surprised his wife with Silvertongue in a hired room after the masquerade, and has been fatally wounded by the fleeing lawyer. The owner rushes in with the guard of the watch. Emblems of disguise are everywhere on floors and walls.

29. *The Suicide of the Countess*

The lawyer has been captured, tried, and executed; a printed copy of his dying speech lies beside the poison bottle of the Countess. As she dies the nurse brings her crippled child, and her thrifty merchant father removes her ring (since a suicide's property was forfeit to the state). The apothecary upbraids the foolish servant who bought the poison; the dog enjoys the meal; and the open window discloses the City of London, where buying and selling continue.

30. *Gin Lane,* 1751. Hogarth's attack on the ravages of gin drinking was paired with a print showing the decent and moderate life of Beer Street. Physical corruption and moral insensibility are reflected in decaying streets and in the ascendancy of the pawnbroker's sign over the steeple (topped with the grandiose figure of George I) of Hawksmoor's parish church of St. George, Bloomsbury. *Courtauld Institute of Art.*

31. *Chairing the Member*. The fourth picture of Hogarth's *Election* series, *c.* 1754, shows the bloated victor carried in triumph while battles still rage, and the pigs rush to perdition like the Gadarene swine of the biblical parable. *Sir John Soane Museum*, London.

32. *The Beggar's Opera*, Act III, Scene xi, 1729, with Macheath between Lucy Lockit and Polly Peachum. With an ironic use of allusion that anticipates Reynolds (see Fig. 39), Hogarth sets Peachum in the stance with which Christ confronts Mary Magdalene in traditional versions of the *Noli me tangere* motif. *Collection Mr. and Mrs. Paul Mellon*.

33. Samuel Johnson,
after Sir Joshua Reynolds.
National Portrait Gallery.

34. James Boswell, 1765,
in the costume of his visit to Rousseau,
by George Willison (1741–97).
National Galleries of Scotland, Edinburgh.

35. Thomas Gray, 1748,
by J. G. Eccardt (d. 1779).
National Portrait Gallery.

36. William Cowper, 1792,
by George Romney (1734–1802).
National Portrait Gallery.

37. Oliver Goldsmith, *c.* 1770,
studio of Sir Joshua Reynolds.
National Portrait Gallery.

38. Edward Gibbon, 1773,
by Sir Joshua Reynolds.
Collection Lord Rosebery, Dalmeny.

39. Sir Joshua Reynolds (1723–92), *Garrick between Tragedy and Comedy*, 1762. *Rothschild Collection.*

When Reynolds painted a boy in the costume and stance of Henry VIII, Horace Walpole remarked, "Is not there humour and satire in Sir Joshua's reducing Holbein's swaggering and colossal haughtiness of Henry VIII to the boyish jollity of Master Crewe?" Here Reynolds's treatment of Garrick is based on the traditional choice of Hercules. Just as Pleasure is usually represented by an erotic Venus, and Virtue by a martial Athena, so Comedy is painted in the manner of Correggio, and Tragedy in the manner of Guido Reni. Benjamin West based much of his heroic painting on a work of Poussin; but he borrowed the gesture of Tragedy from Reynolds's ironic pastiche of Guido.

40. Benjamin West (1738–1820), *The Choice of Hercules between Virtue and Pleasure*, 1764. *Victoria and Albert Museum*, London.

41. Admiral Viscount Keppel, 1780.
The Tate Gallery, London.

The extremes of Reynolds's vision: the heroic portrait and the pathetic but amusing image of a terrified child.

42. *The Strawberry Girl*, 1773.
The Wallace Collection, London
(Crown Copyright).

43. *Circa* 1773. *Royal Academy of Arts*, London.

44. Study for a Self Portrait, c. 1780. *Collection Mr. and Mrs. Paul Mellon.*

First we see the artist as hero, Reynolds as he might aspire to be, a painter in the costume of Rembrandt, with a head of Michelangelo beside him. Below is a self-portrait of the young artist, and above right is a self-portrait of the man whom the artist inhabits.

45. Age 25, 1748. *National Portrait Gallery.*

Thomas Gainsborough (1727–88) became a fashionable portrait painter, but he complained, "I'm sick of portraits and wish very much to take my viol da gamba and walk off to some sweet village where I can paint landscapes and enjoy the fag end of life in quietness and ease." He resisted even more the program of the "history" painter, for whom "there is no call in this country." Gainsborough's treatment of texture and surface made his portraits brilliant and flattering. At the same time he could cultivate a simplicity that was unheroic and singularly delicate.

46. The Honourable Mrs. Graham, 1777. *National Galleries of Scotland.*

47. *The Housemaid* (unfinished), c. 1786. *The Tate Gallery.*

48. William Blake, illustration for Gray's *The Bard*.

THE BARD

Thomas Gray's poem of 1757 inspired many painters and illustrators. Typically, William Blake was less concerned with natural setting than with the human form of the prophet-poet. John Martin (1789–1854) transcended the natural scene in his customary pursuit of colossal dimension and sublime intensity. What is striking in Martin's picture is that the landscape is at least as expressive as the human figure and becomes the symbol of human passion and energy at their utmost.

49. John Martin, *The Bard*. Collection Mr. and Mrs. Paul Mellon.

50. Wren, Tom Tower, 1681–82, Christ Church College, Oxford. *A. F. Kersting.*

GOTHIC TO GOTHICK

When Sir Christopher Wren was asked to complete Tom Tower at Christ Church College, Oxford, he "resolved it ought to be Gothic to agree with the founder's work; yet I have not continued so busy as he began." Hawksmoor, who completed the towers of Westminster Abbey as well as the court of All Souls College, Oxford (1715–40), used Gothic with a similar mixture of respect and freedom. The brilliant staccato style of the All Souls towers uses Gothic elements for effects that are typical of Hawksmoor, such as the light-holding angular surface of sharp recession and projection. In his Gothic garden temple, James Gibbs (1682–1754), trained in the Italian baroque and proficient as well in Palladian works (exemplified by St. Mary-le-Strand and St. Martin-in-the-Fields in London, the Radcliffe Camera at Oxford, and the Senate House at Cambridge), creates a work appropriately evocative: more a theater set than a true building. By the time Horace Walpole rebuilt his Twickenham house, Strawberry Hill (1750), in a Gothic idiom, the details—however authentic in many cases, such as the fan vaulting of the gallery—became decorative surface, akin to the irregular low-relief ornament of rococo vegetable forms.

51. Hawksmoor, Fellows' Buildings,
All Souls College, Oxford.
Courtauld Institute of Art.

52. James Gibbs, Gothic Temple, c. 1740,
in the gardens of Stowe.
Courtauld Institute of Art.

53. The Gallery, Strawberry Hill.
Country Life.

54. Henry Fuseli, *The Artist Moved by the Magnitude of Antique Fragments*, 1778–80. *Kunsthaus,* Zürich.

RUINS

As the art historian Nikolaus Pevsner puts it, for "a generalizing view of the style of 1750 a Chinese bridge, a miniature Pantheon, and a Gothic ruin all belong together. In fact . . . even Robert Adam enjoyed drawing ruins . . . and occasionally designed domestic work in a mildly medieval taste." Increasingly, archeological explorations of classical ruins were recorded in excellent prints. Robert Adam had explored Diocletian's Palace at Split in Yugoslavia; James ("Athenian") Stuart with his fellow architect Nicholas Revett spent five years in Greece and brought back careful studies of the Acropolis. As Fuseli's drawing shows, the interest was as romantic as it was scholarly; moreover, picturesque ruins were frequently constructed—as we see in the designs of Adam and Chambers. In Chambers's design, "There is a great quantity of cornices, and other fragments, spread over the ground, seemingly fallen from the buildings."

55. Robert Adam (1728–92), Design for a ruin to be built at Mistley Hall, 1761.
Victoria and Albert Museum.

56. Sir William Chambers (1723–96), Roman ruins at Kew Gardens, 1763.
Engraving by Woolett in Chambers's *Plans . . . of Gardens and Buildings at Kew,* 1763.

57. *The Green Monkey,* 1799.
Walker Art Gallery, Liverpool.

George Stubbs (1724–1806) resolved "to look into nature for himself, and consult and study *her only.*" In Italy he made no studies from the antique, and "differed always in opinion from his companions." He became a brilliant student of anatomy, performing elaborate dissections, on which he based his *Anatomy of the Horse* (1759). Noted as a portrait painter of race horses as well as of their owners, Stubbs also made remarkable studies of tigers, monkeys, and even a kangaroo.

58. *A Lion Attacking a Horse. Collection Mr. and Mrs. Paul Mellon.*

Joseph Wright of Derby (1734–94) was the first painter of distinction to celebrate the new industrial leaders, their buildings, and their technological concerns. The experiment with the air pump involves withdrawing air from the glass bell that holds the bird and then replenishing it just in time to save the bird's life; the children betray their fears, but the boy on the right is lowering a cage to hold the revived bird.

59. *An Experiment on a Bird in the Air Pump* (c. 1767–68). The Tate Gallery.

60. Joseph Wright of Derby, *The Old Man and Death*, 1773.
Wadsworth Atheneum, Hartford.

DEATH IN THE EIGHTEENTH CENTURY

Wright's picture draws on Aesop's fable of the old woodgatherer who calls for death to free him of his burdens but is appalled and reluctant to receive what he asks for. The engraving by Thomas Patch (1725–82) catches the appearance of Sterne in the spirit of *Tristram Shandy* and Yorick.

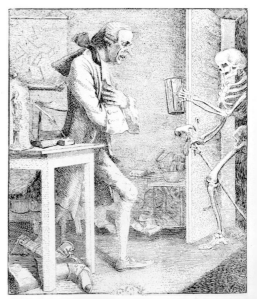

61. Thomas Patch, *Sterne and Death*, 1768.
Courtauld Institute of Art.

And Alsop° never but like Horace joke:
For me, what Virgil, Pliny may deny,
Manilius or Solinus° shall supply:
For Attic phrase in Plato let them seek,
I poach in Suidas° for unlicensed Greek.
In ancient sense if any needs will deal,
Be sure I give them fragments, not a meal:
What Gellius or Stobaeus° hashed before,
Or chewed by blind old scholiasts o'er and o'er.
The critic eye, that microscope of wit,
Sees hairs and pores, examines bit by bit;
How parts relate to parts, or they to whole,
The body's harmony, the beaming soul,°
Are things which Kuster, Burman, Wasse° shall see,
When man's whole frame is obvious to a *flea*.
     'Ah, think not, Mistress! more true Dulness lies
In folly's cap, than wisdom's grave disguise.
Like buoys that never sink into the flood,
On learning's surface we but lie and nod.
Thine is the genuine head of many a house,
And much divinity without a Noῦς.°
Nor could a Barrow work on every block,
Nor has one Atterbury° spoiled the flock.
See! still thy own, the heavy canon° roll,
And metaphysic smokes involve the pole.°
For thee we dim the eyes, and stuff the head
With all such reading as was never read:
For thee explain a thing till all men doubt it,
And write about it, Goddess, and about it:
So spins the silkworm small its slender store,
And labours till it clouds itself all o'er.
     'What though we let some better sort of fool
Thrid° every science, run through every school?
Never by tumbler through the hoops was shown
Such skill in passing all, and touching none.
He may indeed (if sober all this time)
Plague with dispute, or persecute with rhyme.

Freind . . . Alsop Robert Freind and Anthony Alsop, two scholars who grasped the true spirit of classical literature rather than its letter
Manilius or Solinus As a philologist, Bentley is interested not in literature but in words; for his purposes minor authors are as useful as major and as important.
Suidas (*c.* 1100 A.D.) a "dictionary writer, a collector of impertinent facts and barbarous words" (P-W)
Gellius or Stobaeus the former a Roman grammarian (d. 165 A.D.), the latter a Greek compiler of extracts from ancient authors (*c.* 400 A.D.)
the beaming soul i.e. irradiating the body with form

Kuster . . . Wasse classical scholars and editors of lesser writers
without a Noῦς Noῦς was the Platonic word for mind, or the first cause, and that system of divinity is here hinted at which terminates in blind nature without a νοῦς (P-W); cf. ll. 487–92 below.
Barrow . . . Atterbury Isaac Barrow (1630–77) and Atterbury were brilliant scholars and eloquent preachers, the former a fine mathematician, the latter a classical scholar; for the "block," cf. l. 270 below.
canon churchman, but also artillery (cannon)
pole sky, heavens
Thrid thread, trace

We only furnish what he cannot use,
Or wed to what he must divorce, a Muse:
Full in the midst of Euclid dip at once,
And petrify a genius to a dunce:
Or set on metaphysic ground to prance,
Show all his paces, not a step advance.
With the same cement, ever sure to bind,
We bring to one dead level every mind.
Then take him to develop, if you can,
270 And hew the block off, and get out the man.°
But wherefore waste I words? I see advance
Whore, pupil, and laced governor° from France.
Walker! our hat'——nor more he deigned to say,
But, stern as Ajax' spectre,° strode away.

In flowed at once a gay embroidered race,
And tittering pushed the pedants off the place:
Some would have spoken, but the voice was drowned
By the French horn, or by the opening° hound.
The first came forwards, with as easy mien,
280 As if he saw St. James's° and the Queen.
When thus the attendant orator° begun:
'Receive, great Empress! thy accomplished son,
Thine from the birth, and sacred° from the rod,
A dauntless infant! never scared with God.
The sire saw, one by one, his virtues wake:
The mother begged the blessing of a rake.
Thou gavest that ripeness, which so soon began,
And ceased so soon, he ne'er was boy, nor man.
Through school and college, thy kind cloud o'ercast,
290 Safe and unseen° the young Aeneas past:
Thence bursting glorious, all at once let down,°
Stunned with his giddy larum° half the town.
Intrepid then, o'er seas and lands he flew:°
Europe he saw, and Europe saw him too.
There all thy gifts and graces we display,
Thou, only thou, directing all our way!
To where the Seine, obsequious as she runs,
Pours at great Bourbon's feet her silken sons;°
Or Tiber, now no longer Roman, rolls,
300 Vain of Italian arts, Italian° souls:
To happy convents, bosomed deep in vines,

---

get out the man referring to the belief that in
every block of stone there is a statue waiting to
be freed
governor tutor
Ajax' spectre which turns sullenly from Odysseus in the underworld
opening baying, giving tongue
St. James's the royal palace
orator the tutor or governor of l. 272

sacred exempt
unseen veiled in a cloud as was Aeneas by
Venus when he entered Carthage (*Aeneid* I)
let down freed, released
larum commotion
flew on the Grand Tour
her silken sons France is seen as an absolute
monarchy encouraging luxury or effeminacy.
Italian as opposed to Roman

Where slumber abbots, purple as their wines:
To isles of fragrance, lily-silvered vales,
Diffusing languor in the panting gales:
To lands of singing, or of dancing slaves,
Love-whispering woods, and lute-resounding waves.
But chief her shrine where naked Venus keeps,
And Cupids ride the Lion of the Deeps;°
Where, eased of fleets, the Adriatic main
310 Wafts the smooth eunuch and enamoured swain.
Led by my hand, he sauntered Europe round,
And gathered every vice on Christian ground;
Saw every court, heard every king declare
His royal sense of operas or the fair;°
The stews° and palace equally explored,
Intrigued with glory, and with spirit whored;
Tried all *hors d'oeuvres*, all *liqueurs* defined,
Judicious drank, and greatly daring dined;
Dropped the dull lumber of the Latin store,°
320 Spoiled his own language, and acquired no more;
All classic learning lost on classic ground;
And last turned *air*, the echo of a sound!
See now, half-cured and perfectly well-bred,
With nothing but a solo in his head;
As much estate, and principle, and wit,
As Jansen, Fleetwood, Cibber° shall think fit;
Stolen° from a duel, followed by a nun,
And, if a borough choose him,° not undone;
See, to my country happy I restore
330 This glorious youth, and add one Venus more.
Her too receive (for her my soul adores)°
So may the sons of sons of sons of whores,
Prop thine, O Empress! like each neighbour throne,
And make a long posterity thy own.'
Pleased, she accepts the hero, and the dame,
Wraps in her veil, and frees from sense of shame.
     Then looked, and saw a lazy, lolling sort,
Unseen at church, at senate, or at court,
Of ever-listless loiterers, that attend
340 No cause, no trust, no duty, and no friend.
Thee too, my Paridel!° she marked thee there,
Stretched on the rack of a too easy chair,

Lion of the Deeps the winged lion, emblem of
Venice as a great mercantile and naval power;
famous at this time as the "brothel of Europe"
operas . . . fair typical conversational topics
of George II of England
stews brothels
Latin store classical learning
Jansen . . . Cibber all gamblers and the last

two theater managers, hence stewards and
tutors to youth
Stolen escaped
borough choose him because members of Parliament could not be arrested for debt
my soul adores Both pupil and tutor seem attached to the former nun and new Venus.
Paridel Spenser's name for an amorous wandering squire (*The Faerie Queene* III.ix–x)

And heard thy everlasting yawn confess
The pains and penalties of idleness.
She pitied! but her pity only shed
Benigner influence on thy nodding head.
   But Annius,° crafty seer, with ebon wand,
And well-dissembled emerald on his hand,
False as his gems, and cankered° as his coins,
350 Came, crammed with capon, from where Pollio° dines.
Soft, as the wily fox is seen to creep,
Where bask on sunny banks the simple sheep,
Walk round and round, now prying here, now there;
So he; but pious, whispered first his prayer:
   'Grant, gracious Goddess! grant me still to cheat,
O may thy cloud still cover the deceit!
Thy choicer mists on this assembly shed,
But pour them thickest on the noble head.
So shall each youth, assisted by our eyes,
360 See other Caesars, other Homers° rise;
Through twilight ages hunt the Athenian fowl,°
Which chalcis gods, and mortals call an owl,°
Now see an Attys, now a Cecrops° clear,
Nay, Mahomet!° the pigeon at thine ear;
Be rich in ancient brass, though not in gold,
And keep his Lares,° though his house be sold;
To headless Phoebe° his fair bride postpone,
Honour a Syrian prince° above his own;
Lord of an Otho,° if I vouch it true;
370 Blest in one Niger,° till he knows of two.'
Mummius° o'erheard him; Mummius, fool-renowned,°
Who like his Cheops stinks above the ground,
Fierce as a startled adder, swelled, and said,
Rattling an ancient sistrum° at his head:
   'Speakst thou of Syrian princes? Traitor base!
Mine, Goddess! mine is all the hornèd race.°

Annius named for a monk of Viterbo (1432–1502) famous for many forgeries of ancient manuscripts and inscriptions, committed out of vanity. His modern counterpart is more mercenary.
cankered corrupt
Pollio named for the Roman patron
other Caesars . . . Homers forged coins; here also a substitute form of greatness, such as the heroics of collecting and the artistry of acquisition
Athenian fowl the owl stamped on the coins of ancient Athens
Which chalcis . . . owl a line from Hobbes's flat-footed rendering of Homer, "chalcis" being Greek for a bird of prey
Attys . . . Cecrops forgeries of coins professedly issued by mythical kings of Athens
Mahomet Mohammed, who forbade all images, is here represented with the white pigeon that

brought him divine messages and which he claimed to be the angel Gabriel.
Lares Roman statues of household gods
headless Phoebe a mutilated statue of Diana, which pre-empts the place and affection due a living bride
Syrian prince presumably as represented on a medal
Otho coin of a Roman emperor who ruled very briefly
Niger another emperor of short reign, whose coins would be very rare
Mummius a dealer in Egyptian antiquities
fool-renowned "a compound epithet in the Greek manner, *renowned by fools* or *renowned for making fools*" (P-W)
sistrum a percussion instrument used in Egyptian religious rites
hornèd race the successors of Alexander, supposedly born of the gods, represented with horns

True, he had wit, to make their value rise;
From foolish Greeks to steal them, was as wise;
More glorious yet, from barbarous hands to keep,
When Sallee rovers° chased him on the deep.
Then taught by Hermes,° and divinely bold,
Down his own throat he risked the Grecian gold;
Received each demigod,° with pious care,
Deep in his entrails—I revered them there,
I bought them, shrouded in that living shrine,
And, at their second birth, they issue mine.'
    'Witness, great Ammon!° by whose horns I swore,'
(Replied soft Annius) 'this our paunch before
Still bears them, faithful; and that thus I eat,
Is to refund the medals with the meat.
To prove me, Goddess! clear of all design,
Bid me with Pollio sup, as well as dine:
There all the learned shall at the labour stand,
And Douglas° lend his soft, obstetric hand.'
    The goddess smiling seemed to give consent;
So back to Pollio, hand in hand, they went.
    Then thick as locusts blackening all the ground,
A tribe, with weeds and shells fantastic crowned,
Each with some wondrous gift approached the Power,
A nest, a toad, a fungus, or a flower.
But far the foremost, two, with earnest zeal,
And aspect ardent to the throne appeal.
    The first thus opened: 'Hear thy suppliant's call,
Great Queen, and common Mother of us all!
Fair from its humble bed I reared this flower,°
Suckled and cheered, with air, and sun, and shower,
Soft on the paper ruff its leaves° I spread,
Bright with the gilded button tipped its head,
Then throned in glass, and named it Caroline:°
Each maid cried, charming! and each youth, divine!
Did nature's pencil° ever blend such rays,
Such varied light in one promiscuous blaze?
Now prostrate! dead! behold that Caroline:
No maid cries, charming! and no youth, divine!
And lo the wretch! whose vile, whose insect lust
Laid this gay daughter of the spring in dust.
Oh punish him, or to the Elysian shades

Sallee rovers pirates from Morocco
Hermes as god of commerce but also patron of thieves
demigod coins of emperors who claimed that status; with suggestions of the Eucharist that are sustained by "pious care" and culminate in the Second Coming of l. 386
Ammon Jupiter Ammon, from whom Alexander and his heirs claimed descent
Douglas James Douglas, a famous obstetrician

and himself a collector of editions of Horace
flower a reference to the efforts in the age to produce a perfect carnation
leaves petals
Caroline for the queen, an ardent gardener; P-W pursue the theme of idolatry set forth in ll. 359–86 by citing a gardener who advertised his favorite flower as "*my* Queen Caroline"
pencil paintbrush

Dismiss my soul, where no carnation fades!'°
He ceased, and wept. With innocence of mien,
420   The accused stood forth, and thus addressed the queen:
'Of all the enamelled race,° whose silvery wing
Waves to the tepid zephyrs of the spring,
Or swims along the fluid atmosphere,
Once brightest shined this child of heat and air.
I saw, and started from its vernal bower
The rising game,° and chased from flower to flower.
It fled, I followed; now in hope, now pain;
It stopped, I stopped; it moved, I moved again.°
At last it fixed, 'twas on what plant it pleased,
430   And where it fixed, the beauteous bird° I seized:
Rose or carnation was below my care;
I meddle, Goddess! only in my sphere.
I tell the naked fact without disguise,
And, to excuse it, need but show the prize;
Whose spoils this paper° offers to your eye,
Fair even in death! this peerless *butterfly*.'
'My sons!' (she answered) 'both have done your parts:
Live happy both, and long promote our arts!
But hear a mother, when she recommends
440   To your fraternal care, our sleeping friends.°
The common soul, of Heaven's more frugal make,
Serves but to keep fools pert, and knaves awake:
A drowsy watchman, that just gives a knock,
And breaks our rest, to tell us what's a-clock.
Yet by some object every brain is stirred;
The dull may waken to a hummingbird;
The most recluse, discreetly opened find
Congenial matter in the cockle kind;°
The mind, in metaphysics at a loss,
450   May wander in a wilderness of moss;°
The head that turns at superlunar things,
Poised with a tail, may steer on Wilkins' wings.°
'O! would the sons of men once think their eyes
And reason given them but to study *flies*!
See nature in some partial narrow shape,
And let the author of the whole escape:
Learn but to trifle; or, who most observe,

no . . . fades Cf. I Peter 1:4 "To an inheritance incorruptible, and undefiled, and that
fadeth not away, reserved in heaven for you."
enamelled race colorful butterflies
started . . . game idiom of the huntsman
It fled . . . again Cf. Eve's words (*Paradise
Lost* IV.462–63) on first seeing her reflection in
the water, failing, like Narcissus, to recognize
what it is, and adoring it: "I started back, /
It started back; but pleased I soon returned, /
Pleased it returned as soon."

bird any winged creature; here the butterfly
this paper i.e. on which the butterfly is mounted
sleeping friends Cf. ll. 337–46 above.
cockle kind collections of scallop shells
moss of which three hundred species had been
identified
Wilkins' wings John Wilkins (1614–72), bishop
and first secretary of the Royal Society, proposed flights to the moon and started "some
volatile geniuses upon making wings for that
purpose" (P-W).

To wonder at their maker, not to serve!'°
'Be that my task' (replies a gloomy clerk,
60 Sworn foe to mystery,° yet divinely dark;
Whose pious hope aspires to see the day
When moral evidence° shall quite decay,
And damns implicit faith,° and holy lies,
Prompt to impose, and fond to dogmatize:)°
'Let others creep by timid steps, and slow,
On plain experience lay foundations low,
By common sense to common knowledge bred,
And last, to Nature's Cause through Nature led.°
All-seeing in thy mists, we want no guide,
70 Mother of arrogance, and source of pride!
We nobly take the high priori road,°
And reason downward, till we doubt of God:
Make Nature still encroach° upon his plan;
And shove him off as far as e'er we can:
Thrust some mechanic cause into his place,
Or bind in matter, or diffuse in space.°
Or, at one bound o'erleaping° all his laws,
Make God man's image, man the final cause,°
Find virtue local, all relation scorn,°
80 See all in self,° and but for self be born:
Of naught so certain as our *reason* still,
Of naught so doubtful as of *soul* and *will*.°

wonder . . . serve to lose themselves in the wonders of God's creation and to neglect his moral teaching
mystery religious mystery, doctrine that defies clear rational explanation, such as the Trinity
moral evidence the probability of the historical facts of the Bible, believed by some to decay as the events became more remote in time
implicit faith belief upon authority, unquestioning adherence without comprehension
Prompt . . . dogmatize the freethinker seen as dogmatically rejecting dogma, self-deceiving and complacently deductive even as he attacks "holy lies"
Nature's Cause . . . led Cf. *Essay on Man* IV. 331–32: "Slave to no sect, who takes no private road, / But looks through Nature, up to Nature's God."
high priori road the deductive or *a priori* method taken by Descartes in his *Meditations*, Spinoza in his *Ethics*, and Hobbes in his *Leviathan*
Nature . . . encroach explain away Providence by natural ("mechanic") causes, or create a metaphysical principle (such as Ralph Cudworth's "plastic nature") to displace or delimit a theistic God. God's "second causes" (those explicable in mechanical terms) assume more and more of the role once given to his "plan" or active ordering.
Thrust . . . space "The first of these follies is that of Descartes; the second of Hobbes; the third of some succeeding philosophers" (P-W). The last may include such as Henry More (1614–87), the Cambridge Platonist, who sepa-

rated extension from matter in order to attribute extension or pure space to spirit; space for More is "an obscure representation of the essential presence of the divine being." More in turn influenced Sir Isaac Newton's conception of absolute space, and it may be to the consequence of the Newtonian mechanical view (rather than its intention) that Pope is alluding so discreetly.
o'erleaping like Satan overleaping the walls of Eden (*Paradise Lost* IV.181)
man the final cause i.e. see human happiness as the sole end of the universe and see God and his varied creation as a means to that end
Find virtue . . . scorn Here the process of contraction continues; given man as the sole end of creation, the idea of "man" gives way to "men" and morality becomes relative to local customs rather than universal, absolute, or dependent on God's will.
self the final contraction of scale, in contrast to the movement of the *Essay on Man* IV.361–72 where the soul rises "from individual to the whole," from self to "friend, parent, neighbour," thence to "country" and "next all human race," until "every creature . . . of every kind" is loved. At that point instead of God's being made in man's image (l. 478 above)—"Heaven beholds its image in his breast"—man has absorbed the capacity for divine love.
soul and will The metaphysical and moral principles of human nature are neglected by the dogmatic rationalism of the freethinkers or deists.

Oh hide the God still more! and make us see
Such as Lucretius° drew, a God like Thee:
Wrapped up in self, a God without a thought,
Regardless of our merit or default.
Or that bright image to our fancy draw,
Which Theocles° in raptured vision saw,
While through poetic scenes the Genius roves,
490   Or wanders wild in academic groves;
That NATURE our society° adores,
Where Tindal° dictates, and Silenus° snores.'
    Roused at his name, up rose the bousy sire,
And shook from out his pipe the seeds of fire;°
Then snapped his box,° and stroked his belly down:
Rosy and reverend, though without a gown.°
Bland and familiar to the throne he came,
Led up the Youth, and called the goddess *Dame*.
Then thus: 'From priestcraft happily set free,
500   Lo! every finished son returns to thee:
First slave to words, then vassal to a name,°
Then dupe to party; child and man the same;
Bounded by nature, narrowed still by art,
A trifling head, and a contracted heart.
Thus bred, thus taught, how many have I seen,
Smiling on all, and smiled on by a queen.
Marked out for honours, honoured for their birth,
To thee the most rebellious things on earth:
Now to thy gentle shadow all are shrunk,
510   All melted down, in pension, or in punk!°
So Kent, so Berkeley° sneaked into the grave,
A monarch's half, and half a harlot's slave.
Poor W——° nipped in folly's broadest bloom,

Lucretius (*c.* 94 B.C.–55 B.C.) whose philosophical poem *De Rerum Natura* (following Epicurean thought) seeks to free man of his fears of anthropomorphic gods and presents nature as an impartial force, free of the concerns that vex man (therefore, like Dulness, sublimely indifferent to all distinctions of value)
Theocles the philosophical visionary in the Earl of Shaftesbury's *The Moralists* (1709), here made into a simple worshiper of Nature (his "Genius"), cultivating Platonic ecstasy in the wild landscape (see below, The Garden and the Wild)
our society the association of freethinkers
Tindal Matthew Tindal (1657–1733), a leading deist
Silenus the fat, drunken, and debauched companion of Dionysus who appears in Virgil's Sixth Eclogue, where he is made a spokesman of the Epicurean philosophy; here also associated with Thomas Gordon, a political writer whom Walpole made Commissioner of the Wine Licenses
seeds of fire parodying Epicurean language for atoms

box snuffbox
without a gown not a priest; Silenus is usually pictured naked
First slave . . . name There follows a "recapitulation of the whole course of modern education . . . which confines youth to the study of *words* only in schools, subjects them to the authority of *systems* in the universities, and deludes them with the names of *party-distinctions* in the world; all equally concurring to narrow the understanding and establish slavery and error in literature, philosophy, and politics. The whole finished in modern free-thinking; the completion of whatever is vain, wrong, and destructive to the happiness of mankind, as it establishes *self-love* for the sole principle of action" (P-W).
punk whore
So Kent, so Berkeley the Duke of Kent and Earl of Berkeley, both holders of the highest royal honor, Knight of the Garter; possibly indebted to one of George I's mistresses ("harlot's slave")
W—— perhaps the dissipated young Earl of Warwick

Who praises now? his chaplain on his tomb.
Then take them all, oh take them to thy breast!
Thy *Magus*,° Goddess! shall perform the rest.'
   With that, a WIZARD OLD his *Cup* extends;
Which whoso tastes, forgets his former friends,
Sire, ancestors, himself. One casts his eyes

20 Up to a *star*,° and like Endymion° dies:
A *feather*,° shooting from another's head,
Extracts his brain; and principle is fled;
Lost is his God, his country, everything;
And nothing left but homage to a king!
The vulgar herd turn off to roll with hogs,°
To run with horses, or to hunt with dogs;
But, sad example! never to escape
Their infamy, still keep the human shape.
But she, good goddess, sent to every child

30 Firm impudence, or stupefaction mild;
And straight succeeded, leaving shame no room,
Cibberian forehead,° or Cimmerian gloom.°
   Kind self-conceit to some her glass° applies,
Which no one looks in with another's eyes,
But, as the flatterer or dependent paint,
Beholds himself a patriot, chief, or saint.
   On others Interest her gay livery° flings,
Interest that waves on party-coloured° wings:
Turned to the sun, she casts a thousand dyes,

40 And, as she turns, the colours fall or rise.
   Others the Siren Sisters° warble round,
And empty heads console with empty sound.
No more, alas! the voice of fame they hear,
The balm of Dulness trickling in their ear.
Great C_____, H_____, P_____, R_____ , K _____,°
Why all your toils? your sons have learned to sing.
How quick ambition hastes to ridicule!
The sire is made a peer, the son a fool.
   On some, a priest succinct in amice white°

Magus adept in occult arts, high priest, "wizard"; Walpole is suggested, his use of bribery embodied in the "Cup of Self-love," as P-W call it, of the next line
star worn by Knights of the Garter or of the Bath
Endymion loved by the Moon, thrown into perpetual sleep and visited by her each night
feather worn in the cap of Knights of the Garter
roll with hogs like the Prodigal Son (Luke 15:11) or like those transformed by Circe; but her enchantment "took away the shape and left the human mind," whereas the Magus's cup "takes away the mind and leaves the human shape" (P-W)
Cibberian forehead the brazenness of Colley Cibber (1671–1757), the poet laureate of George II and King of the Dunces in the re-

vised *Dunciad*, particularly as shown in his autobiographical *Apology* (1740)
Cimmerian gloom referring to Homer's mythical land of constant mists and darkness, the appropriate habitat of the followers of Dulness
glass mirror
livery costume worn by retainers, whether courtiers or servants or both
party-coloured a pun on "parti-colored"; i.e. vari-colored
Siren Sisters the devotees of opera; cf. ll. 45 ff. and 324
Great . . . K—— noblemen ambitious for their families
priest . . . white a chef dressed in a white apron and cap, the counterpart of the priest's "amice" worn over head and shoulders with white vestments

550   Attends; all flesh is nothing in his sight!
Beeves, at his touch, at once to jelly turn,
And the huge boar is shrunk into an urn:°
The board with specious° miracles he loads,
Turns hares to larks, and pigeons into toads.
Another (for in all what one can shine?)
Explains the *sève* and *verdeur*° of the vine.
What cannot copious sacrifice atone?°
Thy truffles, Perigord! thy hams, Bayonne!
With French libation, and Italian strain,
560   Wash Bladen white, and expiate Hays's° stain.
Knight° lifts the head, for what are crowds undone
To three essential partridges in one?°
Gone every blush, and silent all reproach,
Contending princes mount them in their coach.

    Next bidding all draw near on bended knees,
The Queen confers her *titles* and *degrees.*
Her children first of more distinguished sort,
Who study Shakespeare at the Inns of Court,°
Impale a glowworm, or virtú° profess,
570   Shine in the dignity of F.R.S.°
Some, deep Freemasons,° join the silent race
Worthy to fill Pythagoras's place:°
Some botanists, or florists at the least;
Or issue members of an annual feast.°
Nor passed the meanest unregarded; one
Rose a Gregorian, one a Gormogon.°
The last, not least in honour or applause,
Isis and Cam made Doctors of her Laws.°

    Then, blessing all, 'Go, children of my care!
580   To practice now from theory repair.
All my commands are easy, short, and full:

Beeves . . . urn culinary miracles, where beef is reduced (by a form of mock-transubstantiation) to jelly, or boned meats are given decorative and amusing shapes by ingenious transformations as in l. 554
specious "showy; superficially, not solidly right" (Johnson)
sève . . . verdeur fineness of flavor and briskness of sparkling wines
sacrifice atone the yield of luxuries by famous French regions (Perigord, Bayonne) seen as religious offerings, with libations accompanied by operatic music in l. 559
Bladen . . . Hays's two notorious gamblers who "lived with utmost magnificence after its collapse in 1720, causing many to be "undone" first quality of England and even by princes of the blood of France" (P-W)
Knight Robert Knight, cashier of the South Sea Company, who fled England after its collapse in 1720, causing many to be "undone"
three . . . one two partridges dissolved into sauce for a third, with clear reference to the

mystery of the Trinity ("the incomprehensible union of the three persons in the Godhead," as Dr. Johnson defines it)
Shakespeare . . . Court lawyers who neglect their duties or studies to dabble in Shakespeare criticism
virtú amateur pursuit of arts or sciences; hence *virtuoso*
F.R.S. Fellow of the Royal Society, a title often granted at the time to untrained noblemen
Freemasons "where taciturnity is the *only* essential qualification, as it was the *chief* of the disciples of Pythagoras" (P-W)
Pythagoras's place referring to the ascetic brotherhood which pursued mathematical and religious mysteries at Croton in southern Italy, c. 600–450 B.C.; cf. l. 31 above
annual feast yearly banquet such as was held by the Freemasons or the Royal Society
Gregorian . . . Gormogon members of societies founded in ridicule of Freemasons
Isis and Cam . . . Laws Oxford and Cambridge bestowed honorary degrees.

My sons! be proud, be selfish, and be dull.
Guard my prerogative, assert my throne:
This nod confirms each privilege your own.
The cap and switch° be sacred to his Grace;
With staff and pumps° the Marquis lead the race;
From stage to stage° the licensed° Earl may run,
Paired with his fellow charioteer the sun;
The learnèd Baron butterflies design,°
590   Or draw to silk Arachne's subtile line,°
The Judge to dance his brother Sergeant° call;
The Senator at cricket urge the ball;
The Bishop stow (pontific luxury!)°
An hundred souls of turkeys in a pie;
The sturdy Squire to Gallic masters° stoop,
And drown his lands and manors in a soup.
Others import yet nobler arts from France,
Teach kings to fiddle, and make senates dance.°
Perhaps more high some daring son may soar,°
600   Proud to my list to add one monarch more;
And nobly conscious, princes are but things
Born for first ministers, as slaves for kings,
Tyrant supreme! shall three estates° command,
And MAKE ONE MIGHTY DUNCIAD OF THE LAND!'
    More she had spoke, but yawned—all nature nods:
What mortal can resist the yawn of gods?°
Churches and chapels° instantly it reached;
(St. James's first, for leaden Gilbert° preached)
Then catched the schools;° the Hall scarce kept awake;
610   The convocation gaped, but could not speak:
Lost was the nation's sense, nor could be found,

cap and switch of a jockey, here awarded to a lord devoted to horse racing
staff and pumps equipment of footmen or grooms, at the time a fashion among young gentlemen
stage to stage driving a stagecoach, as the Earl of Salisbury did
licensed as coach owners were; also "privileged"
design study and draw
draw . . . line try to obtain silken thread from spiders' webs (as Swift has the experimenters do in the Grand Academy of Lagado, *Gulliver's Travels* III.v)
Sergeant barrister; the "call of sergeants" involved ceremonies much like a dance
pontific luxury such as was in fact enjoyed at the time by the Bishop of Durham
Gallic masters who will introduce fashionable foreign tastes (here a costly "soup") to traditionally conservative country squires
dance perhaps "after their Prince" (P-W); in *Gulliver's Travels* I.iii Lilliputian courtiers are chosen for office by their agility in dancing on a tightrope
more high . . . soar referring to Walpole's virtual rule of England as first minister from

1721 until his fall in 1742, shortly before this was published
three estates Dulness subdues (as Walpole controlled through appointment, bribery, and appeal to interest) the three estates of nobility, clergy, and commoners.
yawn of gods "The Great Mother composes all, in the same manner as Minerva at the period of the *Odyssey*" (P-W)
chapels places of Dissenters' worship
leaden Gilbert Dr. John Gilbert, Dean of Exeter, was eloquent enough in manner; "leaden" is "an epithet from the age" Dulness "had just then restored" (P-W)
Then . . . schools "The progress of this yawn is judicious, natural, and worthy to be noted. First it seizeth the churches and chapels; then catcheth the schools, where, though the boys be unwilling to sleep, the masters are not; next Westminster Hall [the chief law courts], much more hard indeed to subdue, and not put totally to silence even by the Goddess; then the Convocation [of the clergy], which though extremely desirous to speak yet cannot; even the House of Commons, justly called the Sense of the Nation, is *lost* (that is to say *suspended*) during the yawn" (P-W).

While the long solemn unison went round:
Wide, and more wide, it spread o'er all the realm;
Even Palinurus° nodded at the helm:
The vapour mild o'er each committee crept;
Unfinished treaties in each office slept;
And chiefless armies dozed out the campaign;
And navies yawned for orders on the main.
　　O Muse! relate (for you can tell alone,
620　Wits have short memories, and dunces none)
Relate, who first, who last resigned to rest;
Whose heads she partly, whose completely blessed;
What charms could faction, what ambition lull,
The venal quiet, and entrance the dull;
Till drowned was sense, and shame, and right, and wrong—
O sing, and hush the nations with thy song!

　　　　❀　　　❀　　　❀

　　In vain, in vain—the all-composing hour
Resistless falls: the Muse obeys the power.
She comes! she comes! the sable throne behold
630　Of *Night* primeval, and of *Chaos* old!
Before her, *Fancy's* gilded clouds decay,
And all its varying rainbows die away.
Wit shoots in vain its momentary fires,
The meteor drops, and in a flash expires.
As one by one, at dread Medea's strain,°
The sickening stars fade off the ethereal plain;
As Argus' eyes° by Hermes' wand opprest,
Closed one by one to everlasting rest;
Thus at her felt approach, and secret might,
640　*Art* after *Art* goes out, and all is night.
See skulking *Truth* to her old cavern° fled,
Mountains of casuistry heaped o'er her head!
Philosophy, that leaned on Heaven before,
Shrinks to her second cause,° and is no more.
Physic of *Metaphysic*° begs defence,
And *Metaphysic* calls for aid on *Sense!*°
See *Mystery* to *Mathematics*° fly!

Palinurus the pilot of Aeneas' ship; here Walpole, pilot of the ship of state and, in the following lines, exhibiting passivity in foreign policy
dread Medea's strain In Seneca's *Medea* the enchantress, seeking revenge for Jason's desertion, calls back to life all the monstrous serpents and sings an incantation that causes the sun to halt and the stars to fall.
Argus' eyes placed all over his body so that some might always remain open; but he was slain by Hermes
Truth . . . cavern "alludes to the saying of Democritus, that truth lay at the bottom of a deep well" (P-W)

Shrinks . . . cause explains away divinity by natural causes; cf. ll. 471–82 above
Physic of Metaphysic natural science turning to traditional speculative metaphysics for its ground. Pope had originally written "the Stagirite's defense," suggesting the clinging to Aristotle he ridiculed in the universities.
Metaphysic . . . Sense metaphysics in turn depending upon sense data or empirical findings, completing, with the previous line, a vicious circle
Mystery to Mathematics religious mystery seeking deductive mathematical demonstration, perhaps infecting mathematics with an occult and mystical strain such as that of the Pythagoreans

In vain! they gaze, turn giddy, rave, and die.
Religion blushing veils her sacred fires,
50   And unawares *Morality* expires.
Nor public flame, nor private, dares to shine;
Nor human spark is left, nor glimpse divine!
Lo! thy dread empire, CHAOS! is restored;
Light dies before thy uncreating word:°
Thy hand, great anarch! lets the curtain fall;
And universal darkness buries all.

1741   1743

JOHN GAY
1685–1732

John Gay was perhaps too indolent and amiable to become a major writer, but he might have seemed one in an age that had no Swift or Pope. Gay moved from Devon to London as apprentice to a silk merchant, but he became secretary to Aaron Hill, an old schoolmate who had achieved some literary reputation. Gay supplemented his earnings from writing by gifts and sinecures, gained in part through the help of his more illustrious friends; and in later years the Duke and Duchess of Queensberry were his warm personal friends as well as patrons. He had a special gift for parody and burlesque. His career began with *Wine* (1708), an imitation of Milton in the manner of John Philips. Later, when Ambrose Philips's rustic pastorals were favored by the Addison group at the expense of Pope's more Virgilian work, Pope himself wrote an ironic attack upon Philips; but Gay followed up with *The Shepherd's Week* (1714), in which the parody of Philips turns into a fine, often tender, evocation of country life. Again in *Trivia* (1716) Gay broke new ground in his mock-georgic on "walking the streets of London." While he broke new ground, he was following the hint offered in Swift's *Description of a City Shower* (1710); and it was reportedly to Swift's suggestion that he write a "Newgate pastoral" that we owe *The Beggar's Opera*.

In writing his Newgate pastoral, Gay could draw upon the legend of the recently hanged Jonathan Wild. That devious criminal introduced thieves into their trade, acted as a fence for their loot, and preserved an air of bold respectability as he bargained with those who came to recover their property. (Defoe's narrative, given below, describes this beautifully.) But as soon as Wild gained the ultimate notoriety of execution, he was turned into the material of political satire. The opposition seized upon his likeness to Sir Robert Walpole: "As to party, he was both in principle and practice a right modern Whig, according to the definition of those gentlemen, which is expressed in their motto—*Keep what you get, and get what you can*" (*Mist's Weekly Journal*, May 12, 1725). So too Swift defended Gay's work by pointing to his "comparing those common robbers to robbers of the public; and their several stratagems of betraying, condemning, and hanging each other to the severals arts of politicians in times of corruption"—not at all the present time, Swift ironically observes (*The Intelligencer*, May 25, 1729). Henry Fielding was to pursue this parallel further in his

---

uncreating word referring to the terms "wisdom" and "word" (based on the Greek *logos*) for Christ as creator and orderer; here Dulness represents "uncreation," the restoration of Chaos

brilliantly ironic *Jonathan Wild,* of which a chapter is given below; in fact, he and (more plausibly) Swift have sometimes been suggested as the authors of the piece in *Mist's Weekly Journal.*

Gay is not content to use Peachum (named for "peaching" upon his hirelings in order to get a reward) to recall both Wild and Walpole. He creates other rogues, like Lockit, the corrupt official, and Macheath, the highwayman with a swaggering aristocratic air, to produce a spectrum of "greatness" such as Walpole and his colleagues embodied. Swift wrote to Gay with pleasure about the story that at the opening performance "two great Ministers were in a box together and all the world staring at them." Walpole, in fact, seems to have risen to the occasion by encoring the most damaging song, "When you censure the age" (II, x), and winning applause for his good humor. But we are also told that he avoided any further performances.

Gay had another satiric target, that of Italian opera, which had become the rage in England (as Pope's *Dunciad* IV.45 ff. testifies). As an instance of false taste, of aristocratic pretension, of corruption of manners akin to those of politics, Italian opera provides another of the specious forms of respectability that Gay everywhere attacks. Gay mocks the jealousy of rival Italian singers in Polly and Lucy, and he preserves the requisite artificial happy ending by having the Beggar sell out to the taste of his time. Most of all, however, in creating the "ballad opera" he reinstates the native English tradition of song (not, however, disdaining a borrowing from Handel) and the engaging informality of a mock-heroic of music itself. In fact, he can often count on the full resonance of the original popular song, well known to the audience, to give deeper irony to his adaptation of it to new words. Dr. Arbuthnot took Gay's own opera as a "touchstone to try the British taste on," as a way of recovering "our true inclinations . . . however artfully they may be disguised by a childish fondness for Italian poetry and music in preference to our own."

Yet here, as in other works, Gay's achievement outruns his satiric intentions. He creates, by the very mixture of the raffish and the heroic, by the sense of a life in which betrayal is taken for granted and where each may live only "some months longer," a distinctive world as compelling as any outside itself. Gay sees it with such ironic flexibility and detachment (one might almost say with such anticipation of the "alienation effect" that Bertolt Brecht was to claim for his adaptation, *The Three-Penny Opera,* and for other works) that we are never allowed the simple comforts of either sympathy or disgust. Polly is more innocent than the rest, her head addled by reading play-books and romances, but she imitates the fine ladies with a certain vanity, and she shows a degree of ruthlessness in her desire for romance. Macheath is a kind of Robin Hood, risking danger as Peachum never does, redistributing the "superfluities of mankind"; but he regards any woman as fair game and fills the brothels with the girls he seduces. Like the rest, the Peachums show a mincing elegance of language as they assert the most barbarous maxims; they defend crime in the devout idiom of middle-class mercantile thrift and of Puritan earnestness. Yet they seem thoroughly untroubled and sincere in their inverted morality; they need not adopt the hypocrisy of those who know better, like the "Screenmaster General," Walpole, or any of those in high life or low who nominally subscribe to virtue. To that extent Gay creates a wonderfully absurd world with its own logic; yet it is never so self-contained as to keep out those intimations of savage competition and self-interest that characterize high and low alike.

THE AIRS AND THEIR MUSIC

Like all ballad-operas which employ old and well-known tunes, *The Beggar's Opera* uses the device known in the Renaissance as *contrafactum,* the writing of new words to an old melody, for a wide range of effects. A whole satiric dimension can be invoked by playing the new words off against the audience's sense of the traditional ones. Amateur theatricals and school musical shows frequently use *contrafactum* to popular songs, but the joke is usually confined merely to the displacement of the original words itself, rather than being allowed to play with the exact quality of that displacement. For example, the stirring "Let us take the road" (Air XX) was sung to a march from Handel's opera *Rinaldo* (1711), whose heroic plot and grand Italianate operatic manner were the antithesis of Gay's underworld and simple song style. Air XLIV ("The modes of the court so common are grown") is sung to the tune of "Lillibullero," a famous late seventeenth-century political song, anti-Irish and anti-Catholic, used by the political enemies of James II. The song immediately preceding it, however, uses "Packington's Pound," a melody in constant use from the time of Henry VII both as a melody for newly composed lyrics and as the basis of purely instrumental variations; the audience would have had a sense of its being a familiar tune, and with a particular character perhaps given by words from a 1661 collection beginning "My masters and friends, and good people draw near."

In many cases, however, the specific echoes of the older words are underlined in Gay's lyric. In Air XXI ("If the heart of a man is depressed with cares") is sung to a lilting, *Siciliana*-like, 6/4 melody: Act II, Air III. But the original words written by

Thomas Durfey would have grated against the more tender lustiness of the lyric sung by Macheath, both for their cynical bawdry and for the reversed point of view (charm the girl to get her into bed, as opposed to the charming quality of women themselves):

> Would ye have a young virgin of fifteen years,
> You must tickle her fancy with "sweet" 's and "dear" 's.
> Ever toying, and playing, and sweetly, sweetly,
> Sing a love sonnet, and charm her ears.
> Wittily, prettily talk her down,

Chase her, and praise her, if fair or brown,
　Soothe her, and smooth her,
　And tease her, and please her,
And touch but her smicket, and all's your own.

A "smicket" was an under-smock, or chemise, the undermost women's garment in a day when women wore no underpants. Gay's third and fourth lines are a calculated parody of those of the older version, with the additional irony that the parody is sweeter and more generous than the cynical original.

The beautiful love duet in Act I, "Over the hills and far away" (Air XVI), uses the tune of a song a version of whose words survives even in Mother Goose nursery rhymes: the chorus has the haunting line "Over the hills and far away," which is repeated three times, but Gay saves the quotation of it for the last line of his text, making the audience's familiarity with it (they might have been half-humming along, half-mouthing the famous refrain words) contribute to its own poignancy.

Polly Peachum's marvelous aria in Act I ("Virgins are like the fair flower in its lustre," Air VI) gains additional ironic power from the very genre of song which is represented by its melody. The original words are empty and conventional operatic filler, ending with a mild paradox to give a slight turn of wit:

What shall I do to show how much I love her,
　How many millions of sighs can suffice?
That which wins other hearts ne'er can move her,
　Those common methods of love she'll despise:
I will love more than man e'er loved before me,
　Gaze on her all day and melt all the night,
Till for her own sake at last she'll implore me,
　To love her less to preserve her delight.

In Polly's aria, the "gaudy butterflies" who frolic around the girl-flower are of just the type of amorous town gentleman who might be singing Purcell's song, or writing the type of verse represented by its text. The additional irony that Covent Garden was a flower market as well as a theater, and that the very actresses and flower girls who plied their trade there may well have been country girls who ended up as London prostitutes, must have helped make this "the favourite tune in the *Beggar's Opera*" throughout the eighteenth century, as Dr. Burney writes of it in his *History of Music* (1770).

The Beggar's Opera

DRAMATIS PERSONAE [1]

MEN		WOMEN	
PEACHUM		MRS. PEACHUM	
LOCKIT		POLLY PEACHUM	
MACHEATH		LUCY LOCKIT	
FILCH		DIANA TRAPES	
JEREMY TWITCHER		MRS. COAXER	
CROOK-FINGERED JACK		DOLLY TRULL	
WAT DREARY		MRS. VIXEN	
ROBIN OF BAGSHOT	*Macheath's*	BETTY DOXY	*Women of*
NIMMING NED	*gang*	JENNY DIVER	*the town*
HARRY PADINGTON		MRS. SLAMMEKIN	
MATT OF THE MINT		SUKY TAWDRY	
BEN BUDGE		MOLLY BRAZEN	
BEGGAR			
PLAYER			

Constables, drawers, turnkey, etc.

INTRODUCTION

[BEGGAR, PLAYER]

BEGGAR   If poverty be a title to poetry, I am sure nobody can dispute mine. I own myself of the company of beggars, and I make one at their weekly festivals at St. Giles's.[2] I have a small yearly salary for my catches [3] and am welcome to a dinner there whenever I please, which is more than most poets can say.

PLAYER   As we live by the Muses, 'tis but gratitude in us to encourage poetical merit wherever we find it. The Muses, contrary to all other ladies, pay no distinction to dress, and never partially [4] mistake the pertness of embroidery for wit, nor the modesty of want for dullness. Be the

1. Many of the characters' names are derived from slang expressions of the time: a "twitcher" was a pickpocket; a "budge" was a sneak-thief; "nimming" was stealing; "trull" and "doxy" were names for prostitutes; "diver" for a pickpocket.
2. A section of London, named for the patron saint of beggars and lepers, and known for filth and squalor.
3. Songs, rounds.
4. With partiality or bias.

author who he will, we push his play as far as it will go. So (though you are in want) I wish you success heartily.

BEGGAR   This piece, I own, was originally writ for the celebrating the marriage of James Chanter and Moll Lay, two most excellent ballad-singers. I have introduced the similes that are in your celebrated operas: the swallow, the moth, the bee, the ship, the flower, etc. Besides, I have a prison-scene, which the ladies always reckon charmingly pathetic. As to the parts, I have observed such a nice impartiality to our two ladies that it is impossible for either of them to take offence.[5] I hope I may be forgiven that I have not made my opera throughout unnatural, like those in vogue; for I have no recitative: [6] excepting this, as I have consented to have neither prologue nor epilogue, it must be allowed an opera in all its forms. The piece indeed hath been heretofore frequently represented by ourselves in our great room at St. Giles's, so that I cannot too often acknowledge your charity in bringing it now on the stage.

PLAYER   But I see 'tis time for us to withdraw; the actors are preparing to begin. Play away the overture.   [*Exeunt*]

ACT I

SCENE I. PEACHUM's *house*

[PEACHUM *sitting at a table with a large book of accounts before him*]

AIR I—*An old woman clothed in gray, etc.*

Through all the employments of life,
    Each neighbour abuses his brother;
Whore and rogue they call husband and wife:
    All professions be-rogue one another.
The priest calls the lawyer a cheat,
    The lawyer be-knaves the divine;
And the statesman, because he's so great,
    Thinks his trade as honest as mine.

A lawyer is an honest employment; so is mine. Like me, too, he acts in a double capacity, both against rogues and for 'em; for 'tis but fitting that we should protect and encourage cheats, since we live by 'em.

SCENE II

[PEACHUM, FILCH]

FILCH   Sir, Black Moll hath sent word her trial comes on in the afternoon, and she hopes you will order matters so as to bring her off.

_____

5. Alluding to the public quarrels and rivalry of the two leading singers of Italian opera, Faustina and Cuzzoni, mocked in the quarrel of Polly and Lucy in II.xiii.
6. No portions half-sung, half-spoken.

PEACHUM   Why, she may plead her belly [7] at worst; to my knowledge she hath taken care of that security. But as the wench is very active and industrious, you may satisfy her that I'll soften the evidence.

FILCH   Tom Gagg, sir, is found guilty.

PEACHUM   A lazy dog! When I took him the time before, I told him what he would come to if he did not mend his hand. This is death without reprieve. I may venture to book him.   [Writes]

For Tom Gagg, forty pounds. Let Betty Sly know that I'll save her from transportation,[8] for I can get more by her staying in England.

FILCH   Betty hath brought more goods into our lock [9] to-year, than any five of the gang; and in truth, 'tis a pity to lose so good a customer.

PEACHUM   If none of the gang take her off, she may, in the common course of business, live a twelve-month longer. I love to let women 'scape. A good sportsman always lets the hen partridges fly, because the breed of the game depends upon them. Besides, here the law allows us no reward; there is nothing to be got by the death of women—except our wives.

FILCH   Without dispute, she is a fine woman! 'Twas to her I was obliged for my education, and (to say a bold word) she hath trained up more young fellows to the business than the gaming-table.

PEACHUM   Truly, Filch, thy observation is right. We and the surgeons are more beholden to women than all the professions besides.

FILCH

AIR II—*The bonny gray-eyed morn, etc.*

'Tis woman that seduces all mankind,
     By her we first were taught the wheedling arts;
Her very eyes can cheat; when most she's kind,
     She tricks us of our money with our hearts.
For her, like wolves by night we roam for prey,
     And practise every fraud to bribe her charms;
For suits of love, like law, are won by pay,
     And beauty must be fee'd into our arms.

PEACHUM   But make haste to Newgate,[10] boy, and let my friends know what I intend; for I love to make them easy one way or other.

FILCH   When a gentleman is long kept in suspense, penitence may break his spirit ever after. Besides, certainty gives a man a good air upon his trial, and makes him risk another without fear or scruple. But I'll away, for 'tis a pleasure to be the messenger of comfort to friends in affliction. [Exit]

7. Pregnancy, which could delay or prevent execution.
8. Tom Gagg is turned in for a reward, and Betty Sly saved (temporarily) from exile to American plantations for a seven- or fourteen-year period.
9. "A warehouse where stolen goods are deposited" (Gay).
10. The chief prison of London.

SCENE III

[PEACHUM]

PEACHUM   But 'tis now high time to look about me for a decent execution against next sessions.[11] I hate a lazy rogue, by whom one can get nothing till he is hanged. A register of the gang: [*Reading*] 'Crook-fingered Jack. A year and a half in the service.' Let me see how much the stock owes to his industry; one, two, three, four, five gold watches, and seven silver ones.—A mighty clean-handed fellow!—Sixteen snuff-boxes, five of them of true gold. Six dozen of handkerchiefs, four silver-hilted swords, half a dozen of shirts, three tie-periwigs, and a piece of broadcloth.—Considering these are only the fruits of his leisure hours, I don't know a prettier fellow, for no man alive hath a more engaging presence of mind upon the road.[12] 'Wat Dreary, alias Brown Will'—an irregular dog, who hath an underhand way of disposing of his goods. I'll try him only for a sessions or two longer upon his good behaviour. 'Harry Padington'—a poor petty-larceny rascal, without the least genius; that fellow, though he were to live these six months, will never come to the gallows with any credit. 'Slippery Sam'—he goes off the next sessions, for the villain hath the impudence to have views of following his trade as a tailor, which he calls an honest employment. 'Matt of the Mint'—listed not above a month ago, a promising sturdy fellow, and diligent in his way: somewhat too bold and hasty, and may raise good contributions on the public, if he does not cut himself short by murder. 'Tom Tipple'—a guzzling, soaking sot, who is always too drunk to stand himself, or to make others stand.[13] A cart[14] is abso-lutely necessary for him. 'Robin of Bagshot, alias Gorgon, alias Bluff Bob, alias Carbuncle, alias Bob Booty!—'[15]

SCENE IV

[PEACHUM, MRS. PEACHUM]

MRS. PEACHUM   What of Bob Booty, husband? I hope nothing bad hath be-tided him. You know, my dear, he's a favourite customer of mine. 'Twas he made me a present of this ring.

PEACHUM   I have set his name down in the black list, that's all, my dear; he spends his life among women, and as soon as his money is gone, one or other of the ladies will hang him for the reward, and there's forty pound lost to us forever.

MRS. PEACHUM   You know, my dear, I never meddle in matters of death; I always leave those affairs to you. Women indeed are bitter bad judges

11. The criminal court, held eight times a year; Peachum hopes to produce a felon for hanging at the next session.
12. As a highwayman.
13. Pay up; "stand and deliver" was the highwayman's cry.
14. That is, on which he is taken to the gallows.
15. Adaptations of popular nicknames for Sir Robert Walpole; Bagshot Heath was a place known for robberies.

in these cases, for they are so partial to the brave that they think every man handsome who is going to the camp [16] or the gallows.

AIR III—*Cold and raw, etc.*

If any wench Venus's girdle wear,
    Though she be never so ugly,
Lilies and roses will quickly appear,
    And her face look wondrous smugly.
Beneath the left ear so fit but a cord,
    (A rope so charming a zone is!)
The youth in his cart hath the air of a lord,
    And we cry, There dies an Adonis! [17]

But really, husband, you should not be too hard-hearted, for you never had a finer, braver set of men than at present. We have not had a murder among them all, these seven months. And truly, my dear, that is a great blessing.

PEACHUM   What a dickens is the woman always a-whimpering about murder for? No gentleman is ever looked upon the worse for killing a man in his own defence; and if business cannot be carried on without it, what would you have a gentleman do?

MRS. PEACHUM   If I am in the wrong, my dear, you must excuse me, for nobody can help the frailty of an over-scrupulous conscience.

PEACHUM   Murder is as fashionable a crime as a man can be guilty of. How many fine gentlemen have we in Newgate every year, purely upon that article! If they have wherewithal to persuade the jury to bring it in manslaughter, what are they the worse for it? So my dear, have done upon this subject. Was Captain Macheath here this morning, for the bank-notes [18] he left with you last week?

MRS. PEACHUM   Yes, my dear; and though the bank has stopped payment, he was so cheerful and so agreeable! Sure there is not a finer gentleman upon the road than the captain! If he comes from Bagshot at any reasonable hour he hath promised to make one this evening with Polly and me and Bob Booty, at a party of quadrille.[19] Pray, my dear, is the captain rich?

PEACHUM   The captain keeps too good company ever to grow rich. Marybone [20] and the chocolate-houses are his undoing. The man that proposes to get money by play should have the education of a fine gentleman, and be trained up to it from his youth.

MRS. PEACHUM   Really, I am sorry upon Polly's account the captain hath not

16. Army service.
17. Adonis, the beautiful youth loved by Aphrodite, when killed by a wild boar, was changed by the goddess into a purple flower; he was worshiped as a vegetation god in Cyprus and Greece.
18. Receipts for money deposited, i.e. promissory notes from a banker, like cashier's checks today.
19. A fashionable card game (like ombre).
20. Marylebone, a resort for gambling ("play"), as were chocolate houses.

more discretion. What business hath he to keep company with lords and gentlemen? He should leave them to prey upon one another.

PEACHUM   Upon Polly's account! What a plague does the woman mean? Upon Polly's account!

MRS. PEACHUM   Captain Macheath is very fond of the girl.

PEACHUM   And what then?

MRS. PEACHUM   If I have any skill in the ways of women, I am sure Polly thinks him a very pretty man.

PEACHUM   And what then? You would not be so mad to have the wench marry him! Gamesters and highwaymen are generally very good to their whores, but they are very devils to their wives.

MRS. PEACHUM   But if Polly should be in love, how should we help her, or how can she help herself? Poor girl, I am in the utmost concern about her.

AIR IV—*Why is your faithful slave disdained? etc.*

If love the virgin's heart invade,
How, like a moth, the simple maid
　　Still plays about the flame!
If soon she be not made a wife,
Her honour's singed, and then, for life,
She's—what I dare not name.

PEACHUM   Look ye, wife. A handsome wench in our way of business is as profitable as at the bar of a Temple [21] coffee-house, who looks upon it as her livelihood to grant every liberty but one. You see I would indulge the girl as far as prudently we can,—in anything but marriage! After that, my dear, how shall we be safe? Are we not then in her husband's power? For a husband hath the absolute power over all a wife's secrets but her own. If the girl had the discretion of a court lady, who can have a dozen young fellows at her ear without complying with one, I should not matter it; but Polly is tinder, and a spark will at once set her on a flame. Married! If the wench does not know her own profit, sure she knows her own pleasure better than to make herself a property! My daughter to me should be like a court lady to a minister of state, a key to the whole gang. Married! if the affair is not already done, I'll terrify her from it, by the example of our neighbours.

MRS. PEACHUM   Mayhap, my dear, you may injure the girl. She loves to imitate the fine ladies, and she may only allow the captain liberties in the view of interest.

PEACHUM   But 'tis your duty, my dear, to warn the girl against her ruin, and to instruct her how to make the most of her beauty. I'll go to her this moment, and sift her. [22] In the meantime, wife, rip out the coronets

---

21. At the Inns of Court, the center for lawyers and law students.
22. Question her, sound her out.

and marks of these dozen of cambric handkerchiefs, for I can dispose of them this afternoon to a chap [23] in the City.   [*Exit*]

SCENE V

[MRS. PEACHUM]

MRS. PEACHUM   Never was a man more out of the way in an argument than my husband! Why must our Polly, forsooth, differ from her sex and love only her husband? And why must Polly's marriage, contrary to all observation, make her the less followed by other men? All men are thieves in love, and like a woman the better for being another's property.

AIR V—*Of all the simple things we do, etc.*

A maid is like the golden ore,
    Which hath guineas intrinsical in't;
Whose worth is never known, before
    It is tried and impressed in the mint.
A wife's like a guinea in gold,
    Stamped with the name of her spouse;
Now here, now there; is bought, or is sold;
    And is current in every house.

SCENE VI

[MRS. PEACHUM, FILCH]

MRS. PEACHUM   Come hither, Filch. I am as fond of this child as though my mind misgave me he were my own. He hath as fine a hand at picking a pocket as a woman, and is as nimble-fingered as a juggler. If an unlucky session does not cut the rope of thy life, I pronounce, boy, thou wilt be a great man in history. Where was your post last night, my boy?

FILCH   I plied at the opera, madam; and considering 'twas neither dark nor rainy, so that there was no great hurry in getting chairs [24] and coaches, made a tolerable hand on't. These seven handkerchiefs, madam.

MRS. PEACHUM   Coloured ones, I see. They are of sure sale from our warehouse at Redriff [25] among the seamen.

FILCH   And this snuff-box.

MRS. PEACHUM   Set in gold! A pretty encouragement this to a young beginner.

FILCH   I had a fair tug at a charming gold watch. Pox take the tailors for making the fobs so deep and narrow. It stuck by the way, and I was forced to make my escape under a coach. Really, madam, I fear, I shall be cut off in the flower of my youth, so that every now and then (since I was pumped [26]) I have thoughts of taking up and going to sea.

23. Chapman, i.e. customer.
24. Sedan-chairs.
25. Rotherhithe, the dock district of south London.
26. Punished as a pickpocket by being held under a public water-pump.

MRS. PEACHUM   You should go to Hockley-in-the-Hole [27] and to Marybone, child, to learn valour. These are the schools that have bred so many brave men. I thought, boy, by this time, thou hadst lost fear as well as shame.—Poor lad! how little does he know as yet of the Old Bailey! [28] For the first fact I'll insure thee from being hanged; and going to sea, Filch, will come time enough upon a sentence of transportation. But now, since you have nothing better to do, even go to your book and learn your catechism; for really a man makes but an ill figure in the ordinary's [29] paper, who cannot give a satisfactory answer to his questions. But, hark you, my lad. Don't tell me a lie; for you know I hate a liar. Do you know of anything that hath passed between Captain Macheath and our Polly?

FILCH   I beg you, madam, don't ask me; for I must either tell a lie to you or to Miss Polly; for I promised her I would not tell.

MRS. PEACHUM   But when the honour of our family is concerned—

FILCH   I shall lead a sad life with Miss Polly if ever she come to know that I told you. Besides, I would not willingly forfeit my own honour by betraying anybody.

MRS. PEACHUM   Yonder comes my husband and Polly. Come, Filch, you shall go with me into my own room, and tell me the whole story. I'll give thee a glass of a most delicious cordial that I keep for my own drinking. [*Exeunt*]

SCENE VII

[PEACHUM, POLLY]

POLLY   I know as well as any of the fine ladies how to make the most of myself and of my man too. A woman knows how to be mercenary, though she hath never been in a court or at an assembly. We have it in our natures, papa. If I allow Captain Macheath some trifling liberties, I have this watch and other visible marks of his favour to show for it. A girl who cannot grant some things and refuse what is most material, will make but a poor hand of her beauty, and soon be thrown upon the common.[30]

AIR VI—*What shall I do to show how much I love her, etc.*

Virgins are like the fair flower in its lustre,
    Which in the garden enamels the ground;
Near it the bees in play flutter and cluster,
    And gaudy butterflies frolic around.
But, when once plucked, 'tis no longer alluring;
    To Covent Garden [31] 'tis sent (as yet sweet),

27. Scene of bear-baiting, sword-fighting, and wrestling.
28. The criminal court of London, attached to Newgate.
29. The chaplain of Newgate, who could recommend that a criminal be given a light sentence if he were able to show an ability to read; the ordinary also published the confessions of criminals in his reports, and these were often repentant and full of pious warning.
30. The common law or the common land, as a criminal or a vagrant.
31. The flower market.

There fades, and shrinks, and grows past all enduring,
　　Rots, stinks, and dies, and is trod under feet.

PEACHUM   You know, Polly, I am not against your toying and trifling with a
customer in the way of business, or to get out a secret or so. But if I
find out that you have played the fool and are married, you jade you,
I'll cut your throat, hussy! Now you know my mind.

SCENE VIII

[PEACHUM, POLLY, MRS. PEACHUM. MRS. PEACHUM
in a very great passion]

AIR VII—*Oh London is a fine town*

Our Polly is a sad slut! nor heeds what we have taught her.
I wonder any man alive will ever rear a daughter!
For she must have both hoods and gowns, and hoops to swell her pride,
With scarfs and stays, and gloves and lace; and she will have men
　　beside;
And when she's dressed with care and cost, all-tempting fine and gay,
As men should serve a cowcumber,[32] she flings herself away.

You baggage, you hussy! you inconsiderate jade! Had you been hanged,
it would not have vexed me, for that might have been your misfortune;
but to do such a mad thing by choice! The wench is married, husband.

PEACHUM   Married! The captain is a bold man and will risk anything for
money; to be sure, he believes her a fortune!—Do you think your
mother and I should have lived comfortably so long together, if ever
we had been married? Baggage!

MRS. PEACHUM   I knew she was always a proud slut; and now the wench hath
played the fool and married because, forsooth, she would do like the
gentry. Can you support the expense of a husband, hussy, in gaming,
drinking, and whoring? Have you money enough to carry on the daily
quarrels of man and wife about who shall squander most? There are not
many husbands and wives who can bear the charges of plaguing one
another in a handsome way. If you must be married, could you introduce nobody into our family but a highwayman? Why, thou foolish
jade, thou wilt be as ill used, and as much neglected, as if thou hadst
married a lord!

PEACHUM   Let not your anger, my dear, break through the rules of decency,
for the captain looks upon himself in the military capacity, as a gentleman by his profession. Besides what he hath already, I know he is in
a fair way of getting, or of dying; and both these ways, let me tell you,
are most excellent chances for a wife.—Tell me, hussy, are you ruined
or no?

MRS. PEACHUM   With Polly's fortune, she might very well have gone off to a
person of distinction. Yes, that you might, you pouting slut!

PEACHUM   What, is the wench dumb? Speak, or I'll make you plead by

32. Cucumber; something of no value.

squeezing out an answer from you. Are you really bound wife to him, or are you only upon liking?

[*Pinches her*]

POLLY   [*Screaming*] Oh!

MRS. PEACHUM   How the mother is to be pitied who hath handsome daughters! Locks, bolts, bars, and lectures of morality are nothing to them; they break through them all. They have as much pleasure in cheating a father and mother as in cheating at cards.

PEACHUM   Why, Polly, I shall soon know if you are married, by Macheath's keeping from our house.

POLLY

AIR VIII—*Grim king of the ghosts, etc.*

Can love be controlled by advice?
  Will Cupid our mothers obey?
Though my heart were as frozen as ice,
  At his flame 'twould have melted away.

When he kissed me, so closely he pressed,
  'Twas so sweet that I must have complied,
So I thought it both safest and best
  To marry, for fear you should chide.

MRS. PEACHUM   Then all the hopes of our family are gone for ever and ever!

PEACHUM   And Macheath may hang his father- and mother-in-law, in hope to get into their daughter's fortune!

POLLY   I did not marry him (as 'tis the fashion) coolly and deliberately for honour or money—but I love him.

MRS. PEACHUM   Love him! Worse and worse! I thought the girl had been better bred. O husband, husband! her folly makes me mad! my head swims! I'm distracted! I can't support myself—Oh!   [*Faints*]

PEACHUM   See, wench, to what a condition you have reduced your poor mother! A glass of cordial, this instant. How the poor woman takes it to heart! [*Polly goes out and returns with it*] Ah, hussy, now this is the only comfort your mother has left!

POLLY   Give her another glass, sir; my mama drinks double the quantity whenever she is out of order. This, you see, fetches her.

MRS. PEACHUM   The girl shows such a readiness, and so much concern, that I could almost find in my heart to forgive her.

AIR IX—*O Jenny, O Jenny, where hast thou been, etc.*

O Polly, you might have toyed and kissed;
  By keeping men off, you keep them on.

POLLY

But he so teased me,
  And he so pleased me,
What I did, you must have done—

MRS. PEACHUM   Not with a highwayman.—You sorry slut!

PEACHUM   A word with you, wife. 'Tis no new thing for a wench to take man without consent of parents. You know 'tis the frailty of woman, my dear.

MRS. PEACHUM   Yes, indeed, the sex is frail. But the first time a woman is frail, she should be somewhat nice,[33] methinks, for then or never is the time to make her fortune. After that, she hath nothing to do but to guard herself from being found out, and she may do what she pleases.

PEACHUM   Make yourself a little easy; I have a thought shall soon set all matters again to rights. Why so melancholy, Polly? Since what is done cannot be undone, we must all endeavour to make the best of it.

MRS. PEACHUM   Well, Polly, as far as one woman can forgive another, I forgive thee. Your father is too fond of you, hussy.

POLLY   Then all my sorrows are at an end.

MRS. PEACHUM   A mighty likely speech in troth, for a wench who is just married.

POLLY

AIR X—*Thomas, I cannot, etc.*

I, like a ship in storms, was tossed,
    Yet afraid to put into land;
For seized in the port, the vessel's lost,
    Whose treasure is contraband.
        The waves are laid,
        My duty's paid,
Oh, joy beyond expression!
        Thus, safe ashore,
        I ask no more,
My all is in my possession.

PEACHUM   I hear customers in t'other room. Go, talk with 'em, Polly; but come to us again as soon as they are gone.—But, hark ye, child, if 'tis the gentleman who was here yesterday about the repeating watch,[34] say, you believe we can't get intelligence of it till tomorrow—for I lent it to Suky Straddle, to make a figure with to-night at a tavern in Drury Lane. If t'other gentleman calls for the silver-hilted sword, you know beetle-browed Jemmy hath it on, and he doth not come from Tunbridge till Tuesday night; so that it cannot be had till then.   [*Exit* POLLY]

SCENE IX

[PEACHUM, MRS. PEACHUM]

PEACHUM   Dear wife, be a little pacified. Don't let your passion run away with your senses. Polly, I grant you, hath done a rash thing.

MRS. PEACHUM   If she had had only an intrigue with the fellow, why, the very best families have excused and huddled up a frailty of that sort. 'Tis marriage, husband, that makes it a blemish.

33. Fastidious, squeamish.
34. A watch that "repeats" or sounds the hour and quarter hour when pressed; cf. Pope, *Rape of the Lock* I.18.

PEACHUM   But money, wife, is the true fuller's earth for reputations; there is not a spot or a stain but what it can take out. A rich rogue nowadays is fit company for any gentleman, and the world, my dear, hath not such a contempt for roguery as you imagine. I tell you, wife, I can make this match turn to our advantage.

MRS. PEACHUM   I am very sensible, husband, that Captain Macheath is worth money, but I am in doubt whether he hath not two or three wives already, and then if he should die in a session or two, Polly's dower would come into dispute.

PEACHUM   That, indeed, is a point which ought to be considered.

AIR XI—*A soldier and a sailor*

A fox may steal your hens, sir,
A whore your health and pence, sir,
Your daughter rob your chest, sir,
Your wife may steal your rest, sir,
    A thief your goods and plate.
But this is all but picking,
With rest, pence, chest, and chicken;
It ever was decreed, sir,
If lawyer's hand is fee'd, sir,
    He steals your whole estate.

The lawyers are bitter enemies to those in our way. They don't care that anybody should get a clandestine livelihood but themselves.

SCENE X

[MRS. PEACHUM, PEACHUM, POLLY]

POLLY   'Twas only Nimming [35] Ned. He brought in a damask window-curtain, a hoop petticoat, a pair of silver candlesticks, a periwig, and one silk stocking, from the fire that happened last night.

PEACHUM   There is not a fellow that is cleverer in his way and saves more goods out of the fire, than Ned. But now, Polly, to your affair; for matters must not be left as they are. You are married then, it seems?

POLLY   Yes, sir.

PEACHUM   And how do you propose to live, child?

POLLY   Like other women, sir, upon the industry of my husband.

MRS. PEACHUM   What, is the wench turned fool? A highwayman's wife, like a soldier's, hath as little of his pay as of his company.

PEACHUM   And had not you the common views of a gentlewoman in your marriage, Polly?

POLLY   I don't know what you mean, sir.

PEACHUM   Of a jointure,[36] and of being a widow.

POLLY   But I love him, sir; how then could I have thoughts of parting with him?

35. That is, stealing, pilfering.
36. Property settled on a wife by her husband for her support after his death.

PEACHUM   Parting with him! Why, that is the whole scheme and intention of all marriage articles. The comfortable estate of widowhood is the only hope that keeps up a wife's spirits. Where is the woman who would scruple to be a wife, if she had it in her power to be a widow whenever she pleased? If you have any views of this sort, Polly, I shall think the match not so very unreasonable.

POLLY   How I dread to hear your advice! Yet I must beg you to explain yourself.

PEACHUM   Secure what he hath got, have him peached the next sessions, and then at once you are made a rich widow.

POLLY   What, murder the man I love! The blood runs cold at my heart with the very thought of it.

PEACHUM   Fie, Polly! What hath murder to do in the affair? Since the thing sooner or later must happen, I dare say the captain himself would like that we should get the reward for his death sooner than a stranger. Why, Polly, the captain knows that as 'tis his employment to rob, so 'tis ours to take robbers; every man in his business. So that there is no malice in the case.

MRS. PEACHUM   Aye, husband, now you have nicked the matter.[37] To have him peached is the only thing could ever make me forgive her.

POLLY

> AIR XII—*Now ponder well, ye parents dear*
>
> Oh, ponder well! be not severe;
>   So save a wretched wife!
> For on the rope that hangs my dear
>   Depends poor Polly's life.

MRS. PEACHUM   But your duty to your parents, hussy, obliges you to hang him. What would many a wife give for such an opportunity!

POLLY   What is a jointure, what is widowhood to me? I know my heart. I cannot survive him.

> AIR XIII—*Le printemps rappelle aux armes*
>
> The turtle [38] thus with plaintive crying,
>   Her lover dying,
> The turtle thus with plaintive crying,
>   Laments her dove.
> Down she drops, quite spent with sighing;
> Paired in death, as paired in love.

Thus, sir, it will happen to your poor Polly.

MRS. PEACHUM   What, is the fool in love in earnest then? I hate thee for being particular.[39] Why, wench, thou art a shame to thy very sex.

POLLY   But hear me, mother,—if you ever loved—

37. Hit the nail on the head.
38. Turtledove (The air: "Spring calls to arms").
39. Odd, peculiar.

MRS. PEACHUM   Those cursed play-books she reads have been her ruin. One word more, hussy, and I shall knock your brains out, if you have any.

PEACHUM   Keep out of the way, Polly, for fear of mischief, and consider what is proposed to you.

MRS. PEACHUM.   Away, hussy! Hang your husband, and be dutiful.

SCENE XI

[MRS. PEACHUM, PEACHUM, POLLY *listening*]

MRS. PEACHUM   The thing, husband, must and shall be done. For the sake of intelligence, we must take other measures and have him peached the next session without her consent. If she will not know her duty, we know ours.

PEACHUM   But really, my dear, it grieves one's heart to take off a great man. When I consider his personal bravery, his fine stratagem,[40] how much we have already got by him, and how much more we may get, methinks I can't find in my heart to have a hand in his death. I wish you could have made Polly undertake it.

MRS. PEACHUM   But in a case of necessity—our own lives are in danger.

PEACHUM   Then, indeed, we must comply with the customs of the world and make gratitude give way to interest. He shall be taken off.

MRS. PEACHUM   I'll undertake to manage Polly.

PEACHUM   And I'll prepare matters for the Old Bailey.   [*Exeunt*]

SCENE XII

[POLLY]

POLLY   Now I'm a wretch, indeed—methinks I see him already in the cart, sweeter and more lovely than the nosegay in his hand!—I hear the crowd extolling his resolution and intrepidity!—What volleys of sighs are sent from the windows of Holborn,[41] that so comely a youth should be brought to disgrace!—I see him at the tree! The whole circle are in tears!—even butchers weep!—Jack Ketch [42] himself hesitates to perform his duty, and would be glad to lose his fee by a reprieve. What then will become of Polly? As yet I may inform him of their design and aid him in his escape. It shall be so!—But then he flies, absents himself, and I bar myself from his dear, dear conversation! That too will distract me. If he keep out of the way, my papa and mama may in time relent, and we may be happy. If he stays, he is hanged, and then he is lost forever! He intended to lie concealed in my room till the dusk of evening. If they are abroad, I'll this instant let him out, lest some accident should prevent him.   [*Exit, and returns*]

---

40. Cunning (a term adapted from warfare to politics and robbery).
41. Along the way from Newgate Prison to the gallows ("tree") at Tyburn.
42. Traditional name for a hangman.

SCENE XIII

[POLLY, MACHEATH]

AIR XIV—*Pretty Parrot, say, etc.*

MACHEATH

> Pretty Polly, say,
> When I was away,
> Did your fancy never stray
> To some newer lover?

POLLY

> Without disguise,
> Heaving sighs,
> Doating eyes,
> My constant heart discover.
> Fondly let me loll!

MACHEATH

> O pretty, pretty Poll.

POLLY   And are you as fond as ever, my dear?

MACHEATH   Suspect my honour, my courage—suspect anything but my love. May my pistols miss fire, and my mare slip her shoulder while I am pursued, if I ever forsake thee!

POLLY   Nay, my dear, I have no reason to doubt you, for I find in the romance you lent me, none of the great heroes were ever false in love.

MACHEATH

AIR XV—*Pray, fair one, be kind*

> My heart was so free,
> It roved like the bee,
> Till Polly my passion requited;
> I sipped each flower,
> I changed every hour,
> But here every flower is united.

POLLY   Were you sentenced to transportation, sure, my dear, you could not leave me behind you, could you?

MACHEATH   Is there any power, any force that could tear me from thee? You might sooner tear a pension out of the hands of a courtier, a fee from a lawyer, a pretty woman from a looking glass, or any woman from quadrille. But to tear me from thee is impossible!

AIR XVI—*Over the hills and far away*

> Were I laid on Greenland's coast,
> And in my arms embraced my lass;
> Warm amidst eternal frost,
> Too soon the half year's night would pass.

POLLY

> Were I sold on Indian soil,
> Soon as the burning day was closed,

I could mock the sultry toil,
When on my charmer's breast reposed.
MACHEATH   And I would love you all the day,
POLLY   Every night would kiss and play,
MACHEATH   If with me you'd fondly stray
POLLY   Over the hills and far away.

POLLY   Yes, I would go with thee. But oh!—how shall I speak it? I must be torn from thee. We must part.
MACHEATH   How! Part!
POLLY   We must, we must. My papa and mama are set against thy life. They now, even now, are in search after thee. They are preparing evidence against thee. Thy life depends upon a moment.

AIR XVII—*'Gin thou wert mine awn thing*

Oh, what pain it is to part!
Can I leave thee, can I leave thee?
Oh, what pain it is to part!
Can thy Polly ever leave thee?
But lest death my love should thwart
And bring thee to the fatal cart,
Thus I tear thee from my bleeding heart!
Fly hence, and let me leave thee.

One kiss and then,—one kiss—begone—farewell.
MACHEATH   My hand, my heart, my dear, is so riveted to thine that I cannot unloose my hold.
POLLY   But my papa may intercept thee, and then I should lose the very glimmering of hope. A few weeks, perhaps, may reconcile us all. Shall thy Polly hear from thee?
MACHEATH   Must I then go?
POLLY   And will not absence change your love?
MACHEATH   If you doubt it, let me stay—and be hanged.
POLLY   Oh, I feâr! how I tremble! Go—but when safety will give you leave, you will be sure to see me again; for till then Polly is wretched.

> [*Parting, and looking back at each other with fondness;*
> *he at one door, she at the other.*]

MACHEATH
AIR XVIII—*Oh the broom, etc.*

The miser thus a shilling sees,
    Which he's obliged to pay,
With sighs resigns it by degrees,
    And fears 'tis gone for aye.

POLLY

The boy, thus, when his sparrow's flown,
    The bird in silence eyes;
But soon as out of sight 'tis gone,
    Whines, whimpers, sobs, and cries.

ACT II

SCENE I. *A tavern near Newgate*

[JEMMY TWITCHER,[1] CROOK-FINGERED JACK, WAT DREARY, ROBIN OF BAG-SHOT, NIMMING NED, HARRY PADINGTON, MATT OF THE MINT, BEN BUDGE,[2] *and the rest of the gang, at the table, with wine, brandy, and tobacco*]

BEN   But prithee, Matt, what is become of thy brother Tom? I have not seen him since my return from transportation.

MATT   Poor brother Tom had an accident this time twelve-month, and so clever a made fellow he was, that I could not save him from those flaying rascals the surgeons; and now, poor man, he is among the anatomics [3] at Surgeons' Hall.

BEN   So, it seems, his time was come.

JEM   But the present time is ours, and nobody alive hath more. Why are the laws levelled at us? Are we more dishonest than the rest of mankind? What we win, gentlemen, is our own by the law of arms and the right of conquest.

JACK   Where shall we find such another set of practical philosophers, who to a man are above the fear of death?

WAT   Sound men, and true!

ROBIN   Of tried courage, and indefatigable industry!

NED   Who is there here that would not die for his friend?

HARRY   Who is there here that would betray him for his interest?

MATT   Show me a gang of courtiers that can say as much.

BEN   We are for a just partition of the world, for every man hath a right to enjoy life.

MATT   We retrench the superfluities of mankind. The world is avaricious, and I hate avarice. A covetous fellow, like a jackdaw, steals what he was never made to enjoy, for the sake of hiding it. These are the robbers of mankind, for money was made for the free-hearted and generous; and where is the injury of taking from another what he hath not the heart to make use of?

JEM   Our several stations for the day are fixed. Good luck attend us! Fill the glasses.

MATT

AIR XIX—*Fill every glass, etc.*

Fill every glass, for wine inspires us,
    And fires us,
With courage, love, and joy.
Women and wine should life employ.
Is there aught else on earth desirous?

CHORUS
    Fill every glass, etc.

1. A name for a pickpocket or shoplifter.
2. A term for sneak-thief.
3. Skeletons.

SCENE II

[*To them enter* MACHEATH]

MACHEATH   Gentlemen, well met. My heart hath been with you this hour, but an unexpected affair hath detained me. No ceremony, I beg you.

MATT   We were just breaking up to go upon duty. Am I to have the honour of taking the air with you, sir, this evening upon the heath? I drink a dram now and then with the stage-coachmen in the way of friendship and intelligence, and I know that about this time there will be passengers upon the Western Road who are worth speaking with.

MACHEATH   I was to have been of that party—but—

MATT   But what, sir?

MACHEATH   Is there any man who suspects my courage?

MATT   We have all been witnesses of it.

MACHEATH   My honour and truth to the gang?

MATT   I'll be answerable for it.

MACHEATH   In the division of our booty, have I ever shown the least marks of avarice or injustice?

MATT   By these questions something seems to have ruffled you. Are any of us suspected?

MACHEATH   I have a fixed confidence, gentlemen, in you all, as men of honour, and as such I value and respect you. Peachum is a man that is useful to us.

MATT   Is he about to play us any foul play? I'll shoot him through the head.

MACHEATH   I beg you, gentlemen, act with conduct and discretion. A pistol is your last resort.

MATT   He knows nothing of this meeting.

MACHEATH   Business cannot go on without him. He is a man who knows the world and is a necessary agent to us. We have had a slight difference, and till it is accommodated I shall be obliged to keep out of his way. Any private dispute of mine shall be of no ill consequence to my friends. You must continue to act under his direction, for the moment we break loose from him, our gang is ruined.

MATT   As a bawd [4] to a whore, I grant you, he is to us of great convenience.

MACHEATH   Make him believe I have quitted the gang, which I can never do but with life. At our private quarters I will continue to meet you. A week or so will probably reconcile us.

MATT   Your instructions shall be observed. 'Tis now high time for us to repair to our several duties; so till the evening at our quarters in Moorfields we bid you farewell.

MACHEATH   I shall wish myself with you. Success attend you.

[*Sits down melancholy at the table*]

MATT

AIR XX—*March in Rinaldo,*[5] *with drums and trumpets*

Let us take the road.
    Hark! I hear the sound of coaches!

4. Pimp.
5. One of Handel's operas (1711).

The hour of attack approaches,
To your arms, brave boys, and load.

See the ball I hold!
Let the chymists [6] toil like asses,
Our fire their fire surpasses,
    And turns all our lead to gold.

[*The gang, ranged in the front of the stage, load their pistols, and stick them under their girdles, then go off singing the first part in chorus*]

SCENE III

[MACHEATH, DRAWER]

MACHEATH   What a fool is a fond wench; Polly is most confoundedly bit [7]—I love the sex. And a man who loves money might be as well contented with one guinea as I with one woman. The town perhaps hath been as much obliged to me, for recruiting it with free-hearted ladies, as to any recruiting officer in the army. If it were not for us, and the other gentlemen of the sword, Drury Lane [8] would be uninhabited.

AIR XXI—*Would you have a young virgin, etc.*

If the heart of a man is depressed with cares,
The mist is dispelled when a woman appears;
Like the notes of a fiddle, she sweetly, sweetly
Raises the spirits, and charms our ears.
    Roses and lilies her cheeks disclose,
    But her ripe lips are more sweet than those.
                    Press her,
                    Caress her
                    With blisses,
                    Her kisses
Dissolve us in pleasure and soft repose.

I must have women. There is nothing unbends the mind like them. Money is not so strong a cordial for the time. Drawer!—

[*Enter* DRAWER]

Is the porter gone for all the ladies, according to my directions?
DRAWER   I expect him back every minute. But you know, sir, you sent him as far as Hockley-in-the-Hole for three of the ladies, for one in Vinegar Yard, and for the rest of them somewhere about Lewkner's Lane.[9] Sure some of them are below, for I hear the bar bell. As they come I will show them up. Coming! coming!   [*Exit*]

---

6. Alchemists, who like thieves turn lead (as in the bullet or "ball") into gold by the use of fire or firing.
7. Deceived.
8. The center of prostitution.
9. Places of low reputation near Drury Lane.

SCENE IV

[MACHEATH, MRS. COAXER, DOLLY TRULL, MRS. VIXEN, BETTY DOXY, JENNY DIVER, MRS. SLAMMEKIN, SUKY TAWDRY, and MOLLY BRAZEN [10]]

MACHEATH   Dear Mrs. Coaxer, you are welcome. You look charmingly to-day. I hope you don't want the repairs of quality, and lay on paint.—Dolly Trull! kiss me, you slut; are you as amorous as ever, hussy? You are always so taken up with stealing hearts, that you don't allow yourself time to steal anything else. Ah Dolly, thou wilt ever be a coquette.— Mrs. Vixen, I'm yours! I always loved a woman of wit and spirit; they make charming mistresses, but plaguy wives.—Betty Doxy! come hither, hussy. Do you drink as hard as ever? You had better stick to good, wholesome beer; for in troth, Betty, strong waters will, in time, ruin your constitution. You should leave those to your betters.—What! and my pretty Jenny Diver too! As prim and demure as ever! There is not any prude, though ever so high bred, hath a more sanctified look, with a more mischievous heart. Ah! thou art a dear artful hypocrite!—Mrs. Slammekin! as careless and genteel as ever! all you fine ladies, who know your own beauty, affect an undress.—But see, here's Suky Tawdry come to contradict what I was saying. Everything she gets one way, she lays out upon her back. Why, Suky, you must keep at least a dozen tally-men. [11]—Molly Brazen! [*She kisses him*] That's well done. I love a free-hearted wench. Thou hast a most agreeable assurance, girl, and art as willing as a turtle.—But hark! I hear music. The harper is at the door. 'If music be the food of love, play on.' [12] Ere you seat yourselves, ladies, what think you of a dance? Come in.

[*Enter* HARPER]

Play the French tune that Mrs. Slammekin was so fond of.

[*A dance* à la ronde *in the French manner; near the end of it this song and chorus*]

AIR XXII—*Cotillion*

Youth's the season made for joys,
    Love is then our duty;
She alone who that employs,
    Well deserves her beauty.
      Let's be gay,
      While we may,
Beauty's a flower despised in decay.

CHORUS

    Youth's the season, etc.

    Let us drink and sport today,
      Ours is not to-morrow.

10. The names imply slattern (Trapes, Slammekin), prostitute (Trull, Doxy), pickpocket (Diver), etc.
11. Those who rent clothes or sell on credit.
12. The words of Duke Orsino at the opening of Shakespeare's *Twelfth Night*.

Love with youth flies swift away,
    Age is nought but sorrow.
      Dance and sing,
      Time's on the wing,
Life never knows the return of spring.

CHORUS

    Let us drink, etc.

MACHEATH   Now pray, ladies, take your places. Here, fellow. [*Pays the* HARPER] Bid the drawer bring us more wine.   [*Exit* HARPER] If any of the ladies choose gin, I hope they will be so free to call for it.

JENNY   You look as if you meant me. Wine is strong enough for me. Indeed, sir, I never drink strong waters but when I have the colic.

MACHEATH   Just the excuse of the fine ladies! Why, a lady of quality is never without the colic. I hope, Mrs. Coaxer, you have had good success of late in your visits among the mercers.[13]

MRS. COAXER   We have so many interlopers. Yet, with industry, one may still have a little picking. I carried a silver-flowered lute-string and a piece of black padesoy [14] to Mr. Peachum's lock but last week.

MRS. VIXEN   There's Molly Brazen hath the ogle of a rattlesnake. She riveted a linen-draper's eye so fast upon her, that he was nicked of three pieces of cambric before he could look off.

MOLLY BRAZEN   Oh, dear madam! But sure nothing can come up to your handling of laces! And then you have such a sweet deluding tongue! To cheat a man is nothing; but the woman must have fine parts indeed who cheats a woman!

MRS. VIXEN   Lace, madam, lies in a small compass, and is of easy conveyance. But you are apt, madam, to think too well of your friends.

MRS. COAXER   If any woman hath more art than another, to be sure, 'tis Jenny Diver. Though her fellow be never so agreeable, she can pick his pocket as coolly as if money were her only pleasure. Now, that is a command of the passions uncommon in a woman!

JENNY   I never go to the tavern with a man but in the view of business. I have other hours and other sort of men for my pleasure. But had I your address,[15] madam—

MACHEATH   Have done with your compliments, ladies, and drink about. You are not so fond of me, Jenny, as you use to be.

JENNY   'Tis not convenient, sir, to show my kindness among so many rivals. 'Tis your own choice, and not the warmth of my inclination, that will determine you.

    AIR XXIII—*All in a misty morning, etc.*

Before the barn-door crowing,
    The cock by hens attended,
His eyes around him throwing,
    Stands for a while suspended.

13. Silk merchants.
14. Expensive silks from France and Holland.
15. Skill, dexterity.

> Then one he singles from the crew,
>   And cheers the happy hen;
> With 'How do you do,' and 'How do you do,'
>   And 'How do you do' again.

MACHEATH   Ah Jenny! thou art a dear slut.

TRULL   Pray, madam, were you ever in keeping?

TAWDRY   I hope, madam, I han't been so long upon the town but I have met with some good fortune as well as my neighbours.

TRULL   Pardon me, madam, I meant no harm by the question; 'twas only in the way of conversation.

TAWDRY   Indeed, madam, if I had not been a fool, I might have lived very handsomely with my last friend. But upon his missing five guineas, he turned me off. Now, I never suspected he had counted them.

SLAMMEKIN   Who do you look upon, madam, as your best sort of keepers?

TRULL   That, madam, is thereafter as they be.

SLAMMEKIN   I, madam, was once kept by a Jew; and bating their religion, to women they are a good sort of people.

TAWDRY   Now for my part, I own I like an old fellow; for we always make them pay for what they can't do.

VIXEN   A spruce prentice, let me tell you, ladies, is no ill thing; they bleed freely.[16] I have sent at least two or three dozen of them in my time to the plantations.

JENNY   But to be sure, sir, with so much good fortune as you have had upon the road, you must be grown immensely rich.

MACHEATH   The road, indeed, hath done me justice, but the gaming-table hath been my ruin.

JENNY

AIR XXIV—*When once I lay with another man's wife, etc.*

> The gamesters and lawyers are jugglers [17] alike,
>   If they meddle, your all is in danger:
> Like gypsies, if once they can finger a souse,[18]
>   Your pockets they pick, and they pilfer your house,
> And give your estate to a stranger.

A man of courage should never put anything to the risk, but his life. These are the tools of a man of honour. Cards and dice are only fit for cowardly cheats, who prey upon their friends.

[*She takes up his pistol.* TAWDRY *takes up the other.*]

TAWDRY   This, sir, is fitter for your hand. Besides your loss of money, 'tis a loss to the ladies. Gaming takes you off from women. How fond could I be of you!—but before company, 'tis ill-bred.

MACHEATH   Wanton hussies!

JENNY   I must and will have a kiss, to give my wine a zest.

[*They take him about the neck, and make signs to Peachum and Constables, who rush in upon him*]

16. Pay well; and are later transported for robbing their masters.
17. Cunning cheats.
18. Small amount of money.

SCENE V

[*To them* PEACHUM *and* CONSTABLES]

PEACHUM   I seize you, sir, as my prisoner.

MACHEATH   Was this well done, Jenny? Women are decoy ducks: who can trust them? Beasts, jades, jilts, harpies, furies, whores!

PEACHUM   Your case, Mr. Macheath, is not particular. The greatest heroes have been ruined by women. But, do them justice, I must own they are a pretty sort of creatures, if we could trust them. You must now, sir, take your leave of the ladies, and if they have a mind to make you a visit, they will be sure to find you at home. This gentleman, ladies, lodges in Newgate. Constables, wait upon the captain to his lodgings.

MACHEATH

AIR XXV—*When first I laid siege to my Chloris, etc.*

At the tree I shall suffer with pleasure,
At the tree I shall suffer with pleasure;
    Let me go where I will,
    In all kinds of ill,
I shall find no such furies as these are.

PEACHUM   Ladies, I'll take care the reckoning [19] shall be discharged.

[*Exit* MACHEATH, *guarded, with* PEACHUM *and* CONSTABLES]

SCENE VI

[*The* WOMEN *remain*]

VIXEN   Look ye, Mrs. Jenny; though Mr. Peachum may have made a private bargain with you and Suky Tawdry for betraying the captain, as we were all assisting, we ought all to share alike.

COAXER   I think Mr. Peachum, after so long an acquaintance, might have trusted me as well as Jenny Diver.

SLAMMEKIN   I am sure at least three men of his hanging, and in a year's time too (if he did me justice), should be set down to my account.

TRULL   Mrs. Slammekin, that is not fair. For you know one of them was taken in bed with me.

JENNY   As far as a bowl of punch or a treat, I believe Mrs. Suky will join with me. As for anything else, ladies, you cannot in conscience expect it.

SLAMMEKIN   Dear madam—

TRULL   I would not for the world—[20]

SLAMMEKIN   'Tis impossible for me—

TRULL   As I hope to be saved, madam—

SLAMMEKIN   Nay, then I must stay here all night—

TRULL   Since you command me.   [*Exeunt with great ceremony*]

SCENE VII.   *Newgate*

[LOCKIT, TURNKEYS, MACHEATH, CONSTABLES]

LOCKIT   Noble captain, you are welcome. You have not been a lodger of mine this year and half. You know the custom, sir. Garnish,[21] captain, garnish! Hand me down those fetters there.

19. The bill (for drinks or their services).
20. The ladies debate, in a style of high courtesy, who shall go through the door first.
21. A demand for a fee.

MACHEATH   Those, Mr. Lockit, seem to be the heaviest of the whole set! With your leave, I should like the further pair better.

LOCKIT   Look ye, captain, we know what is fittest for our prisoners. When a gentleman uses me with civility, I always do the best I can to please him.—Hand them down, I say.—We have them of all prices, from one guinea to ten, and 'tis fitting every gentleman should please himself.

MACHEATH   I understand you, sir. [*Gives money*] The fees here are so many and so exorbitant, that few fortunes can bear the expence of getting off handsomely or of dying like a gentleman.

LOCKIT   Those, I see, will fit the captain better. Take down the further pair. Do but examine them, sir,—never was better work. How genteelly they are made! They will fit as easy as a glove, and the nicest man in England might not be ashamed to wear them. [*He puts on the chains*] If I had the best gentleman in the land in my custody, I could not equip him more handsomely. And so, sir—I now leave you to your private meditations.

SCENE VIII

[MACHEATH]

AIR XXVI—*Courtiers, courtiers, think it no harm, etc.*

Man may escape from rope and gun;
Nay, some have outlived the doctor's pill;
Who takes a woman must be undone,
    That basilisk [22] is sure to kill.
The fly that sips treacle is lost in the sweets,
So he that tastes woman, woman, woman,
    He that tastes woman, ruin meets.

To what a woeful plight have I brought myself! Here must I (all day long, till I am hanged) be confined to hear the reproaches of a wench who lays her ruin at my door. I am in the custody of her father, and to be sure if he knows of the matter, I shall have a fine time on't betwixt this and my execution. But I promised the wench marriage. What signifies a promise to a woman? Does not a man in marriage itself promise a hundred things that he never means to perform? Do all we can, women will believe us; for they look upon a promise as an excuse for following their own inclinations.—But here comes Lucy, and I cannot get from her. Would I were deaf!

SCENE IX

[MACHEATH, LUCY]

LUCY   You base man, you, how can you look me in the face after what hath passed between us? See here, perfidious wretch, how I am forced to bear about the load of infamy you have laid upon me—O Macheath!

22. A mythical reptile that can kill by its look.

thou hast robbed me of my quiet—to see thee tortured would give me pleasure.

AIR XXVII—*A lovely lass to a friar came, etc.*

Thus when a good housewife sees a rat
  In a trap in the morning taken,
With pleasure her heart goes pit-a-pat
  In revenge for her loss of bacon.
     Then she throws him
     To the dog or cat,
To be worried, crushed, and shaken.

MACHEATH   Have you no bowels,[23] no tenderness, my dear Lucy, to see a husband in these circumstances?

LUCY   A husband!

MACHEATH   In every respect but the form, and that, my dear, may be said over us at any time. Friends should not insist upon ceremonies. From a man of honour, his word is as good as his bond.

LUCY   'Tis the pleasure of all you fine men to insult the women you have ruined.

AIR XXVIII—*'Twas when the sea was roaring, etc.*

How cruel are the traitors
  Who lie and swear in jest,
To cheat unguarded creatures
  Of virtue, fame, and rest!

Whoever steals a shilling
  Through shame the guilt conceals;
In love, the perjured villain
  With boasts the theft reveals.

MACHEATH   The very first opportunity my dear (have but patience), you shall be my wife in whatever manner you please.

LUCY   Insinuating monster! And so you think I know nothing of the affair of Miss Polly Peachum. I could tear thy eyes out!

MACHEATH   Sure, Lucy, you can't be such a fool as to be jealous of Polly!

LUCY   Are you not married to her, you brute, you?

MACHEATH   Married! Very good. The wench gives it out only to vex thee, and to ruin me in thy good opinion. 'Tis true I go to the house; I chat with the girl, I kiss her, I say a thousand things to her (as all gentlemen do) that mean nothing, to divert myself; and now the silly jade hath set it about that I am married to her, to let me know what she would be at. Indeed, my dear Lucy, these violent passions may be of ill consequence to a woman in your condition.

LUCY   Come, come, captain, for all your assurance, you know that Miss Polly hath put it out of your power to do me the justice you promised me.

23. Compassion.

MACHEATH   A jealous woman believes everything her passion suggests. To convince you of my sincerity, if we can find the ordinary, I shall have no scruples of making you my wife—and I know the consequence of having two at a time.

LUCY   That you are only to be hanged, and so get rid of them both.

MACHEATH   I am ready, my dear Lucy, to give you satisfaction—if you think there is any in marriage. What can a man of honour say more?

LUCY   So then it seems you are not married to Miss Polly.

MACHEATH   You know, Lucy, the girl is prodigiously conceited. No man can say a civil thing to her, but (like other fine ladies) her vanity makes her think he's her own for ever and ever.

AIR XXIX—*The sun had loosed his weary teams, etc.*

The first time at the looking-glass
    The mother sets her daughter,
The image strikes the smiling lass
    With self-love ever after.
Each time she looks, she, fonder grown,
    Thinks every charm grows stronger.
But alas, vain maid, all eyes but your own
    Can see you are not younger.

When women consider their own beauties, they are all alike unreasonable in their demands; for they expect their lovers should like them as long as they like themselves.

LUCY   Yonder is my father. Perhaps this way we may light upon the ordinary, who shall try if you will be as good as your word; for I long to be made an honest woman.   [*Exeunt*]

SCENE X. *Lockit's room in Newgate*

[PEACHUM, LOCKIT *with an account-book*]

LOCKIT   In this last affair, brother Peachum, we are agreed. You have consented to go halves in Macheath.

PEACHUM   We shall never fall out about an execution. But as to that article, pray how stands our last year's account?

LOCKIT   If you will run your eye over it, you'll find 'tis fair and clearly stated.

PEACHUM   This long arrear of the government [24] is very hard upon us! Can it be expected that we should hang our acquaintance for nothing, when our betters will hardly save theirs without being paid for it? Unless the people in employment [25] pay better, I promise them for the future, I shall let other rogues live besides their own.

LOCKIT   Perhaps, brother, they are afraid these matters may be carried too far. We are treated, too, by them with contempt, as if our profession were not reputable.

24. In payment of rewards for capture and conviction of criminals.
25. Official posts.

PEACHUM   In one respect, indeed, our employment may be reckoned dishonest, because, like great statesmen, we encourage those who betray their friends.

LOCKIT   Such language, brother, anywhere else might turn to your prejudice. Learn to be more guarded, I beg you.

AIR XXX—*How happy are we, etc.*

> When you censure the age,
> Be cautious and sage,
> Lest the courtiers offended should be.
> If you mention vice or bribe,
> 'Tis so pat to all the tribe
> Each cries—That was levelled at me.

PEACHUM   Here's poor Ned Clincher's name, I see. Sure, brother Lockit, there was a little unfair proceeding in Ned's case; for he told me in the condemned hold, that for value received, you had promised him a session or two longer without molestation.

LOCKIT   Mr. Peachum, this is the first time my honour was ever called in question.

PEACHUM   Business is at an end if once we act dishonourably.

LOCKIT   Who accuses me?

PEACHUM   You are warm, brother.[26]

LOCKIT   He that attacks my honour, attacks my livelihood. And this usage, sir, is not to be borne.

PEACHUM   Since you provoke me to speak, I must tell you too, that Mrs. Coaxer charges you with defrauding her of her information-money for the apprehending of curl-pated Hugh. Indeed, indeed, brother, we must punctually pay our spies, or we shall have no information.

LOCKIT   Is this language to me, sirrah? Who have saved you from the gallows, sirrah!   [*Collaring each other*]

PEACHUM   If I am hanged, it shall be for ridding the world of an arrant rascal.

LOCKIT   This hand shall do the office of the halter [27] you deserve, and throttle you, you dog!   [*They break apart*]

PEACHUM   —Brother, brother,—we are both losers in the dispute—for you know we have it in our power to hang each other. You should not be so passionate.

LOCKIT   Nor you so provoking.

PEACHUM   'Tis our mutual interest, 'tis for the interest of the world, we should agree. If I said anything, brother, to the prejudice of your character, I ask pardon.

LOCKIT   Brother Peachum, I can forgive as well as resent.—Give me your hand. Suspicion does not become a friend.

PEACHUM   I only meant to give you occasion to justify yourself. But I must

---

26. Suggesting the growing quarrel between Walpole and his brother-in-law Lord Townshend, who was to leave office in 1730; with a possible imitation of the quarrel of Brutus and Cassius in Shakespeare's *Julius Caesar*.

27. Hangman's noose.

now step home, for I expect the gentleman about this snuff-box that Filch nimmed two nights ago in the park. I appointed him at this hour. [*Exit*]

[LOCKIT, LUCY]

LOCKIT   Whence come you, hussy?

LUCY   My tears might answer that question.

LOCKIT   You have then been whimpering and fondling, like a spaniel, over the fellow that hath abused you.

LUCY   One can't help love; one can't cure it. 'Tis not in my power to obey you, and hate him.

LOCKIT   Learn to bear your husband's death like a reasonable woman. 'Tis not the fashion, nowadays, so much as to affect sorrow upon these occasions. No woman would ever marry if she had not the chance of mortality for a release. Act like a woman of spirit, hussy, and thank your father for what he is doing.

LUCY

AIR XXXI—*Of a noble race was Shenkin, etc.*

Is then his fate decreed, sir?
    Such a man can I think of quitting?
When first we met, so moves me yet,
    Oh, see how my heart is splitting!

LOCKIT   Look ye, Lucy, there is no saving him. So, I think, you must even do like other widows,—buy yourself weeds and be cheerful.

AIR XXXII

You'll think, ere many days ensue,
    This sentence not severe;
I hang your husband, child, 'tis true,
    But with him hang your care.
        Twang dang dillo dee.

Like a good wife, go moan over your dying husband; that, child, is your duty.—Consider, girl, you can't have the man and the money too—so make yourself as easy as you can by getting all you can from him.
                                                            [*Exeunt*]

SCENE XII. *Another part of the prison*

[LUCY, MACHEATH]

LUCY   Though the ordinary was out of the way today, I hope, my dear, you will, upon the first opportunity, quiet my scruples.—Oh, sir!—my father's hard heart is not to be softened, and I am in the utmost despair.

MACHEATH   But if I could raise a small sum—would not twenty guineas, think you, move him?—Of all the arguments in the way of business, the perquisite [28] is the most prevailing.—Your father's perquisites for the escape of prisoners must amount to a considerable sum in the year. Money well timed and properly applied will do anything.

AIR XXXIII—*London ladies*

If you at an office solicit your due,
    And would not have matters neglected;
You must quicken the clerk with the perquisite too,
    To do what his duty directed.
Or would you the frowns of a lady prevent,
    She too has this palpable failing,
The perquisite softens her into consent;
    That reason with all is prevailing.

LUCY   What love or money can do shall be done, for all my comfort depends upon your safety.

SCENE XIII

[LUCY, MACHEATH, POLLY]

POLLY   Where is my dear husband?—Was a rope ever intended for this neck? —Oh, let me throw my arms about it, and throttle thee with love!— Why dost thou turn away from me?—'Tis thy Polly—'tis thy wife.

MACHEATH   Was there ever such an unfortunate rascal as I am!

LUCY   Was there ever such another villain!

POLLY   O Macheath! was it for this we parted? Taken! imprisoned! tried! hanged!—cruel reflection! I'll stay with thee till death—no force shall tear thy dear wife from thee now.—What means my love?   not one kind word!—not one kind look! Think what thy Polly suffers to see thee in this condition.

AIR XXXIV—*All in the downs, etc.*

Thus when the swallow, seeking prey,
    Within the sash is closely pent,
His consort, with bemoaning lay,
    Without, sits pining for the event.
Her chattering lovers all around her skim;
She heeds them not (poor bird)—her soul's with him.

MACHEATH   [*Aside*] I must disown her. The wench is distracted.

LUCY   Am I then bilked of my virtue? Can I have no reparation? Sure, men were born to lie, and women to believe them. O villain! villain!

POLLY   Am I not thy wife? Thy neglect of me, thy aversion to me, too severely proves it. Look on me. Tell me; am I not thy wife?

LUCY   Perfidious wretch!

POLLY   Barbarous husband!

LUCY   Hadst thou been hanged five months ago, I had been happy.

POLLY   And I too. If you had been kind to me till death, it would not have

28. "Something gained by a place or office over and above the settled wages" (Johnson).

vexed me—and that's no very unreasonable request (though from a wife) to a man who hath not above seven or eight days to live.

LUCY   Art thou then married to another? Hast thou two wives, monster?

MACHEATH   If women's tongues can cease for an answer—hear me.

LUCY   I won't! Flesh and blood can't bear my usage.

POLLY   Shall I not claim my own? Justice bids me speak.

MACHEATH

AIR XXXV—*Have you heard of a frolicsome ditty, etc.*

How happy I could be with either,
    Were t'other dear charmer away!
But while you thus tease me together,
To neither a word will I say;
    But tol de rol, etc.

POLLY   Sure, my dear, there ought to be some preference shown to a wife! At least she may claim the appearance of it. [*Aside*] He must be distracted with his misfortunes, or he could not use me thus!

LUCY   O villain, villain! thou hast deceived me—I could even inform against thee with pleasure. Not a prude wishes more heartily to have facts against her intimate acquaintance, than I now wish to have facts against thee. I would have her satisfaction, and they should all out.

AIR XXXVI—*Irish Trot*

POLLY   I'm bubbled.[29]
LUCY   I'm bubbled!
POLLY   Oh how I am troubled!
LUCY   Bamboozled, and bit!
POLLY   My distresses are doubled.
LUCY
When you come to the tree, should the hangman refuse,
These fingers, with pleasure, could fasten the noose.
    POLLY   I'm bubbled, etc.

MACHEATH   Be pacified, my dear Lucy! This is all a fetch of Polly's to make me desperate with you in case I get off. If I am hanged, she would fain have the credit of being thought my widow.—Really, Polly, this is no time for a dispute of this sort; for whenever you are talking of marriage, I am thinking of hanging.

POLLY   And hast thou the heart to persist in disowning me?

MACHEATH   And hast thou the heart to persist in persuading me that I am married? Why, Polly, dost thou seek to aggravate my misfortunes?

LUCY   Really, Miss Peachum, you but expose yourself. Besides, 'tis barbarous in you to worry a gentleman in his circumstances.

POLLY

AIR XXXVII

Cease your funning,
    Force or cunning

29. Cheated.

Never shall my heart trepan.[30]
>   All these sallies
>   Are but malice
> To seduce my constant man.
>   'Tis most certain,
>   By their flirting,
> Women oft have envy shown;
>   Pleased to ruin
>   Other's wooing;
> Never happy in their own!

LUCY   Decency, madam, methinks, might teach you to behave yourself with some reserve with the husband while his wife is present.

MACHEATH   But, seriously, Polly, this is carrying the joke a little too far.

LUCY   If you are determined, madam, to raise a disturbance in the prison, I shall be obliged to send for the turnkey to show you the door. I am sorry, madam, you force me to be so ill-bred.

POLLY   Give me leave to tell you, madam; these forward airs don't become you in the least, madam. And my duty, madam, obliges me to stay with my husband, madam.

LUCY

AIR XXXVIII—*Good-morrow, gossip Joan, etc.*

> Why, how now, Madam Flirt?
>   If you thus must chatter;
> And are for flinging dirt,
>   Let's try who best can spatter!
>   Madam Flirt!

POLLY

> Why, how now, saucy jade;
>   Sure the wench is tipsy!
> How can you see me made [*To him*]
>   The scoff of such a gipsy?
>   Saucy jade! [*To her*]

SCENE XIV

[LUCY, MACHEATH, POLLY, PEACHUM]

PEACHUM   Where's my wench? Ah hussy! hussy! Come you home, you slut; and when your fellow is hanged, hang yourself, to make your family some amends.

POLLY   Dear, dear father, do not tear me from him! I must speak; I have more to say to him. [*To* MACHEATH] Oh! twist thy fetters about me, that he may not haul me from thee!

PEACHUM   Sure, all women are alike! If ever they commit the folly, they are sure to commit another by exposing themselves. Away—not a word more—you are my prisoner now, hussy!

POLLY   [*Holding* MACHEATH, PEACHUM *pulling her*]

30. Deceive, beguile.

AIR XXXIX—*Irish howl*

No power on earth can e'er divide
The knot that sacred love hath tied.
When parents draw against our mind,
The true-love's knot they faster bind.
  Oh, oh ray, oh amborah—Oh, oh, etc.

[*Exeunt* POLLY *and* PEACHUM]

SCENE XV

[LUCY, MACHEATH]

MACHEATH   I am naturally compassionate, wife, so that I could not use the wench as she deserved, which made you at first suspect there was something in what she said.

LUCY   Indeed, my dear, I was strangely puzzled.

MACHEATH   If that had been the case, her father would never have brought me into this circumstance. No, Lucy, I had rather die than be false to thee.

LUCY   How happy am I if you say this from your heart! For I love thee so, that I could sooner bear to see thee hanged than in the arms of another.

MACHEATH   But couldst thou bear to see me hanged?

LUCY   O Macheath, I can never live to see that day.

MACHEATH   You see, Lucy; in the account of love you are in my debt, and you must now be convinced that I rather choose to die than to be another's. Make me, if possible, love thee more, and let me owe my life to thee. If you refuse to assist me, Peachum and your father will immediately put me beyond all means of escape.

LUCY   My father, I know, hath been drinking hard with the prisoners, and I fancy he is now taking his nap in his own room. If I can procure the keys, shall I go off with thee, my dear?

MACHEATH   If we are together, 'twill be impossible to lie concealed. As soon as the search begins to be a little cool, I will send to thee. Till then, my heart is thy prisoner.

LUCY   Come then, my dear husband, owe thy life to me—and though you love me not—be grateful. But that Polly runs in my head strangely.

MACHEATH   A moment of time may make us unhappy forever.

LUCY

AIR XL—*The lass of Patie's mill, etc.*

I like the fox shall grieve,
  Whose mate hath left her side,
Whom hounds, from morn till eve,
  Chase o'er the country wide,
Where can my lover hide?
  Where cheat the wary pack?
If love be not his guide,
  He never will come back!

ACT III

scene i. *Newgate*

[LOCKIT, LUCY]

LOCKIT   To be sure, wench, you must have been aiding and abetting to help him to this escape.

LUCY   Sir, here hath been Peachum and his daughter Polly, and to be sure they know the ways of Newgate as well as if they had been born and bred in the place all their lives. Why must all your suspicion light upon me?

LOCKIT   Lucy, Lucy, I will have none of these shuffling answers.

LUCY   Well then, if I know anything of him, I wish I may be burnt!

LOCKIT   Keep your temper, Lucy, or I shall pronounce you guilty.

LUCY   Keep yours, sir. I do wish I may be burnt, I do. And what can I say more to convince you.

LOCKIT   Did he tip handsomely? How much did he come down with? Come, hussy, don't cheat your father, and I shall not be angry with you. Perhaps you have made a better bargain with him than I could have done. How much, my good girl?

LUCY   You know, sir, I am fond of him, and would have given money to have kept him with me.

LOCKIT   Ah, Lucy! thy education might have put thee more upon thy guard; for a girl in the bar of an alehouse is always besieged.

LUCY   Dear sir, mention not my education, for 'twas to that I owe my ruin.

AIR XLI—*If love's a sweet passion, etc.*

When young, at the bar you first taught me to score,
And bid me be free of my lips, and no more.
I was kissed by the parson, the squire, and the sot;
When the guest was departed, the kiss was forgot.
But his kiss was so sweet, and so closely he prest,
That I languished and pined till I granted the rest.

If you can forgive me, sir, I will make a fair [1] confession, for to be sure he hath been a most barbarous villain to me.

LOCKIT   And so you have let him escape, hussy, have you?

LUCY   When a woman loves, a kind look, a tender word can persuade her to anything,—and I could ask no other bribe.

LOCKIT   Thou wilt always be a vulgar slut, Lucy. If you would not be looked upon as a fool, you should never do anything but upon the foot of interest. Those that act otherwise are their own bubbles.

LUCY   But love, sir, is a misfortune that may happen to the most discreet woman, and in love we are all fools alike. Notwithstanding all he swore, I am now fully convinced that Polly Peachum is actually his wife. Did I let him escape (fool that I was) to go to her? Polly will wheedle herself into his money, and then Peachum will hang him, and cheat us both.

1. Open.

LOCKIT   So I am to be ruined, because, forsooth, you must be in love!—a very pretty excuse!

LUCY   I could murder that impudent happy strumpet! I gave him his life, and that creature enjoys the sweets of it. Ungrateful Macheath!

AIR XLII—*South-sea Ballad*

My love is all madness and folly,
      Alone I lie,
      Toss, tumble, and cry;
What a happy creature is Polly!
Was e'er such a wretch as I!
With rage I redden like scarlet,
That my dear, inconstant varlet,
      Stark blind to my charms,
      Is lost in the arms
Of that jilt, that inveigling harlot!
This, this my resentment alarms.
      Stark blind to my charms,
      Is lost in the arms
Of that jilt, that inveigling harlot!

LOCKIT   And so, after all this michief, I must stay here to be entertained with your caterwauling, Mistress Puss! Out of my sight, wanton strumpet! You shall fast and fortify yourself into reason, with now and then a little handsome discipline to bring you to your senses. Go! [*Exit* LUCY]

SCENE II

[LOCKIT]

—Peachum then intends to outwit me in this affair, but I'll be even with him. The dog is leaky in his liquor; so I'll ply him that way, get the secret from him, and turn this affair to my own advantage. Lions, wolves, and vultures don't live together in herds, droves, or flocks. Of all animals of prey, man is the only sociable one. Every one of us preys upon his neighbour, and yet we herd together. Peachum is my companion, my friend. According to the custom of the world, indeed, he may quote thousands of precedents for cheating me. And shall not I make use of the privilege of friendship to make him a return?

AIR XLIII—*Packington's Pound*

Thus gamesters united in friendship are found,
Though they know that their industry all is a cheat;
They flock to their prey at the dice-box's sound,
And join to promote one another's deceit.
      But if by mishap
      They fail of a chap,[2]

2. Customer, victim.

To keep in their hands they each other entrap.
Like pikes,[3] lank with hunger, who miss of their ends,
They bite their companions, and prey on their friends.

Now, Peachum, you and I, like honest tradesmen, are to have a fair
trial which of us two can over-reach the other. [*Calls*] Lucy!

[*Enter* LUCY]

Are there any of Peachum's people now in the house?
LUCY   Filch, sir, is drinking a quartern [4] of strong waters in the next room
with Black Moll.
LOCKIT   Bid him come to me.   [*Exit* LUCY]

SCENE III

[LOCKIT, FILCH]

LOCKIT   Why, boy, thou lookest as if thou wert half starved—like a shotten
herring.[5]
FILCH   One had need have the constitution of a horse to go through the
business. Since the favourite child-getter was disabled by mishap, I
have picked up a little money by helping the ladies to a pregnancy
against their being called down to sentence. But if a man cannot get
an honest livelihood any easier way, I am sure 'tis what I can't undertake for another session.
LOCKIT   Truly, if that great man should tip off,[6] 'twould be an irreparable
loss. The vigour and prowess of a knight-errant never saved half of the
ladies in distress that he hath done.—But, boy, canst thou tell me
where thy master is to be found?
FILCH   At his lock, sir, at the Crooked Billet.
LOCKIT   Very well. I have nothing more with you. [*Exit* FILCH] I'll go to
him there, for I have many important affairs to settle with him; and
in the way of those transactions, I'll artfully get into his secret, so that
Macheath shall not remain a day longer out of my clutches.

SCENE IV. *A gaming-house*

[MACHEATH *in a fine tarnished coat,* BEN BUDGE, MATT OF THE MINT]

MACHEATH   I am sorry, gentlemen, the road was so barren of money. When
my friends are in difficulties, I am always glad that my fortune can
be serviceable to them. [*Gives them money*] You see, gentlemen, I am
not a mere court friend, who professes everything and will do nothing.

---

3. The pike was considered the most voracious of fish, and the pike pond is a frequent
eighteenth-century symbol of a scene of ruthless competition. The pike, moreover, is one
of the few creatures besides man that preys upon his own kind; cf. Rochester's *Satire upon
Mankind* for the theme.
4. Quarter-pint.
5. A herring that has spawned and shows signs of depletion.
6. That is, if Macheath (the "favourite child-getter") should die.

AIR XLIV—*Lillibullero*

The modes of the court so common are grown,
  That a true friend can hardly be met;
Friendship for interest is but a loan,
  Which they let out for what they can get.
    'Tis true, you find
    Some friends so kind,
Who will give you good counsel themselves to defend.
    In sorrowful ditty,
    They promise, they pity,
But shift you, for money, from friend to friend.

But we, gentlemen, have still honour enough to break through the corruptions of the world. And while I can serve you, you may command me.

BEN   It grieves my heart that so generous a man should be involved in such difficulties as oblige him to live with such ill company, and herd with gamesters.

MATT   See the partiality of mankind! One man may steal a horse, better than another look over a hedge.[7] Of all mechanics, of all servile handicraftsmen, a gamester is the vilest. But yet, as many of the quality are of the profession, he is admitted amongst the politest company. I wonder we are not more respected.

MACHEATH   There will be deep play tonight at Marybone and consequently money may be picked up upon the road. Meet me there, and I'll give you the hint who is worth setting.[8]

MATT   The fellow with a brown coat with a narrow gold binding, I am told, is never without money.

MACHEATH   What do you mean, Matt? Sure you will not think of meddling with him! He's a good honest kind of a fellow, and one of us.

BEN   To be sure, sir, we will put ourselves under your direction.

MACHEATH   Have an eye upon the money-lenders. A rouleau[9] or two would prove a pretty sort of an expedition. I hate extortion.[10]

MATT   These rouleaus are very pretty things. I hate your bank bills. There is such a hazard in putting them off.

MACHEATH   There is a certain man of distinction who in his time hath nicked me out of a great deal of the ready. He is in my cash,[11] Ben. I'll point him out to you this evening, and you shall draw upon him for the debt. —The company are met; I hear the dice-box in the other room. So, gentlemen, your servant! You'll meet me at Marybone.   [*Exeunt*]

7. That is, more safely than another man can merely look at one.
8. Setting upon to rob.
9. A roll of gold coins.
10. That is, the extortion of moneylenders (or usurers).
11. That is, he is in debt for the cash ("ready") of which he has cheated ("nicked") me; probably an allusion, as in the scene immediately following, to that "man of distinction" Walpole.

SCENE V. PEACHUM's *lock. A table with wine, brandy, pipes and tobacco*

[PEACHUM, LOCKIT]

LOCKIT   The Coronation account,[12] brother Peachum, is of so intricate a nature, that I believe it will never be settled.

PEACHUM   It consists, indeed, of a great variety of articles. It was worth to our people, in fees of different kinds, above ten installments.[13] This is part of the account, brother, that lies open before us.

LOCKIT   A lady's tail [14] of rich brocade—that, I see, is disposed of—

PEACHUM   To Mrs. Diana Trapes, the tallywoman, and she will make a good hand on't in shoes and slippers, to trick out young ladies upon their going into keeping.

LOCKIT   But I don't see any article of the jewels.

PEACHUM   Those are so well known that they must be sent abroad. You'll find them entered under the article of exportation. As for the snuff-boxes, watches, swords, etc., I thought it best to enter them under their several heads.

LOCKIT   Seven and twenty women's pockets [15] complete, with the several things therein contained—all sealed, numbered, and entered.

PEACHUM   But, brother, it is impossible for us now to enter upon this affair.— We should have the whole day before us.—Besides, the account of the last half-year's plate is in a book by itself, which lies at the other office.

LOCKIT   Bring us then more liquor.—Today shall be for pleasure—tomorrow for business.—Ah, brother, those daughters of ours are two slippery hussies. Keep a watchful eye upon Polly, and Macheath in a day or two shall be our own again.

AIR XLV.—*Down in the North Country, etc.*

What gudgeons [16] are we men!
　Every woman's easy prey;
Though we have felt the hook, again
　We bite and they betray.
The bird that hath been trapped,
　When he hears his calling mate,
To her he flies, again he's clapped
　Within the wiry grate.

PEACHUM   But what signifies catching the bird if your daughter Lucy will set open the door of the cage?

LOCKIT   If men were answerable for the follies and frailities of their wives

---

12. The goods stolen from the crowd at the coronation of George II (October 11, 1727); perhaps "the large civil list secured by Walpole for George II, whereby Walpole kept control over the government" (Edgar V. Roberts).
13. Annual installations of the Lord Mayor, another occasion for theft.
14. Train.
15. Small purses.
16. Fish easily caught; dupes.

and daughters, no friends could keep a good correspondence together for two days.—This is unkind of you, brother; for among good friends, what they say or do goes for nothing.

[*Enter* A SERVANT]

SERVANT   Sir, here's Mrs. Diana Trapes wants to speak with you.

PEACHUM   Shall we admit her, brother Lockit?

LOCKIT   By all means—she's a good customer, and a fine-spoken woman—and a woman who drinks and talks so freely will enliven the conversation.

PEACHUM   Desire her to walk in.   [*Exit* SERVANT]

SCENE VI

[PEACHUM, LOCKIT, MRS. TRAPES]

PEACHUM   Dear Mrs. Dye, your servant—one may know by your kiss that your gin is excellent.

TRAPES   I was always very curious [17] in my liquors.

LOCKIT   There is no perfumed breath like it. I have been long acquainted with the flavour of those lips—han't I, Mrs. Dye?

TRAPES   Fill it up.—I take as large draughts of liquor as I did of love.—I hate a flincher in either.

AIR XLVI—*A shepherd kept sheep, etc.*

In the days of my youth I could bill like a dove, fa, la, la, etc.
Like a sparrow at all times was ready for love, fa, la, la, etc.
The life of all mortals in kissing should pass,
Lip to lip while we're young—then lip to the glass, fa, la, etc.

But now, Mr. Peachum, to our business.—If you have blacks of any kind brought in of late—manteaus, velvet scarves, petticoats—let it be what it will, I am your chap; for all my ladies are very fond of mourning.

PEACHUM   Why, look ye, Mrs. Dye—you deal so hard with us, that we can afford to give the gentlemen who venture their lives for the goods little or nothing.

TRAPES   The hard times oblige me to go very near in my dealing. To be sure, of late years I have been a great sufferer by the Parliament.—Three thousand pounds would hardly make me amends.—The act for destroying the Mint [18] was a severe cut upon our business—till then, if a customer stepped out of the way—we knew where to have her. No doubt you know Mrs. Coaxer—there's a wench now (till to-day) with a good suit of clothes of mine upon her back, and I could never set eyes upon her for three months together. Since the act, too, against

---

17. "Choosy," discriminating.
18. Passed in 1723 to end the Mint's status as a sanctuary for debtors on the ground that the Southwark area had become a center for criminals.

imprisonment for small sums, my loss there too hath been very considerable; and it must be so, when a lady can borrow a handsome petticoat or a clean gown, and I not have the least hank [19] upon her! And, o' my conscience, nowadays most ladies take a delight in cheating when they can do it with safety!

PEACHUM   Madam, you had a handsome gold watch of us t'other day for seven guineas. Considering we must have our profit—to a gentleman upon the road, a gold watch will be scarce worth the taking.

TRAPES   Consider, Mr. Peachum, that watch was remarkable [20] and not of very safe sale. If you have any black velvet scarfs—they are handsome winter wear, and take with most gentlemen who deal with my customers. 'Tis I that put the ladies upon a good foot. 'Tis not youth or beauty that fixes their price. The gentlemen always pay according to their dress, from half a crown to two guineas; and yet those hussies make nothing of bilking me. Then, too, allowing for accidents.—I have eleven fine customers now down under the surgeon's hands; what with fees and other expenses, there are great goings-out, and no comings-in, and not a farthing to pay for at least a month's clothing. We run great risks—great risks indeed.

PEACHUM   As I remember, you said something just now of a Mrs. Coaxer.

TRAPES   Yes, sir. To be sure, I stripped her of a suit of my own clothes about two hours ago, and have left her as she should be, in her shift, with a lover of hers, at my house. She called him upstairs as he was going to Marybone in a hackney coach. And I hope, for her sake and mine, she will persuade the captain to redeem her, for the captain is very generous to the ladies.

LOCKIT   What captain?

TRAPES   He thought I did not know him—an intimate acquaintance of yours, Mr. Peachum—only Captain Macheath—as fine as a lord.

PEACHUM   To-morrow, dear Mrs. Dye, you shall set your own price upon any of the goods you like. We have at least half a dozen velvet scarfs, and all at your service. Will you give me leave to make you a present of this suit of nightclothes for your own wearing?—But are you sure it is Captain Macheath?

TRAPES   Though he thinks I have forgot him, nobody knows him better. I have taken a great deal of the captain's money in my time at second-hand, for he always loved to have his ladies well-dressed.

PEACHUM   Mr. Lockit and I have a little business with the captain—you understand me—and we will satisfy you for Mrs. Coaxer's debt.

LOCKIT   Depend upon it—we will deal like men of honour.

TRAPES   I don't enquire after your affairs—so whatever happens, I wash my hands on't. It hath always been my maxim, that one friend should assist another.—But if you please, I'll take one of the scarfs home with me. 'Tis always good to have something in hand.

19. Hold, claim.
20. Identifiable.

SCENE VII. *Newgate*

[LUCY]

LUCY   Jealousy, rage, love, and fear are at once tearing me to pieces. How I am weatherbeaten and shattered with distresses!

AIR XLVII—*One evening, having lost my way, etc.*

I'm like a skiff on the ocean tossed,
Now high, now low, with each billow borne;
With her rudder broke, and her anchor lost,
    Deserted and all forlorn.
While thus I lie rolling and tossing all night,
That Polly lies sporting on seas of delight!
    Revenge, revenge, revenge,
Shall appease my restless sprite.

—I have the ratsbane ready. I run no risk; for I can lay her death upon the gin, and so many die of that naturally that I shall never be called in question. But say I were to be hanged—I never could be hanged for anything that would give me greater comfort than the poisoning that slut.

[*Enter* FILCH]

FILCH   Madam, here's our Miss Polly come to wait upon you.

LUCY   Show her in.

SCENE VIII

[LUCY, POLLY]

LUCY   Dear madam, your servant. I hope you will pardon my passion when I was so happy to see you last. I was so overrun with the spleen, that I was perfectly out of myself. And really when one hath the spleen, everything is to be excused by a friend.

AIR XLVIII—*Now Roger, I'll tell thee, because thou'rt my son, etc.*

When a wife's in her pout,
  (As she's sometimes, no doubt);
The good husband, as meek as a lamb,
    Her vapours to still,
    First grants her her will,
And the quieting draught is a dram.
Poor man! And the quieting draught is a dram.

—I wish all our quarrels might have so comfortable a reconciliation.

POLLY   I have no excuse for my own behaviour, madam, but my misfortunes. And really, madam, I suffer too upon your account.

LUCY   But, Miss Polly—in the way of friendship, will you give me leave to propose a glass of cordial to you?

POLLY   Strong waters are apt to give me the headache; I hope, madam, you will excuse me.

LUCY   Not the greatest lady in the land could have better in her closet, for her own private drinking. You seem mighty low in spirits, my dear.

POLLY   I am sorry, madam, my health will not allow me to accept of your offer. I should not have left you in the rude manner I did when we met last, madam, had not my papa hauled me away so unexpectedly. I was indeed somewhat provoked, and perhaps might use some expressions that were disrespectful. But really, madam, the captain treated me with so much contempt and cruelty, that I deserved your pity rather than your resentment.

LUCY   But since his escape, no doubt, all matters are made up again.—Ah Polly! Polly! 'tis I am the unhappy wife, and he loves you as if you were only his mistress.

POLLY   Sure, madam, you cannot think me so happy as to be the object of your jealousy! A man is always afraid of a woman who loves him too well—so that I must expect to be neglected and avoided.

LUCY   Then our cases, my dear Polly, are exactly alike. Both of us, indeed, have been too fond.

AIR XLIX—*O Bessy Bell*

POLLY   A curse attends that woman's love,
  Who always would be pleasing.
LUCY   The pertness of the billing dove,
  Like tickling, is but teasing.
POLLY   What then in love can woman do?
LUCY   If we grow fond they shun us.
POLLY   And when we fly them, they pursue.
LUCY   But leave us when they've won us.

LUCY   Love is so very whimsical in both sexes that it is impossible to be lasting. But my heart is particular,[21] and contradicts my own observation.

POLLY   But really, mistress Lucy, by his last behaviour, I think I ought to envy you. When I was forced from him, he did not show the least tenderness. But perhaps he hath a heart not capable of it.

AIR L—*Would fate to me Belinda give, etc.*

Among the men, coquets we find,
Who court by turns all womankind;
And we grant all their hearts desired,
When they are flattered and admired.

The coquets of both sexes are self-lovers, and that is a love no other whatever can dispossess. I fear, my dear Lucy, our husband is one of those.

LUCY   Away with these melancholy reflections!—indeed, my dear Polly, we are both of us a cup too low. [*Going*] Let me prevail upon you to accept of my offer.

21. Peculiar, eccentric.

AIR LI—*Come, sweet lass, etc.*

> Come, sweet lass,
> Let's banish sorrow
> 'Till to-morrow;
> Come, sweet lass,
> Let's take a chirping [22] glass.
>   Wine can clear
>   The vapours of despair;
>   And make us light as air;
>   Then drink, and banish care.

I can't bear, child, to see you in such low spirits. And I must persuade you to what I know will do you good. [*Aside*] I shall now soon be even with the hypocritical strumpet.   [*Exit* LUCY]

SCENE IX

[POLLY]

POLLY   All this wheedling of Lucy cannot be for nothing—at this time too, when I know she hates me!—The dissembling of a woman is always the forerunner of mischief.—By pouring strong waters down my throat, she thinks to pump some secret out of me. I'll be upon my guard and won't taste a drop of her liquor, I'm resolved.

SCENE X

[LUCY, *with strong waters;* POLLY]

LUCY   Come, Miss Polly.

POLLY   Indeed, child, you have given yourself trouble to no purpose.—You must, my dear, excuse me.

LUCY   Really, Miss Polly, you are so squeamishly affected about taking a cup of strong waters as a lady before company. I vow, Polly, I shall take it monstrously ill if you refuse me.—Brandy and men (though women love them never so well) are always taken by us with some reluctance —unless 'tis in private.

POLLY   I protest, madam, it goes against me. What do I see! Macheath again in custody!—Now every glimmering of happiness is lost.

                         [*Drops the glass of liquor on the ground*]

LUCY   [*Aside*] Since things are thus, I am glad the wench hath escaped: for by this event 'tis plain she was not happy enough to deserve to be poisoned.

SCENE XI

[LOCKIT, MACHEATH, PEACHUM, LUCY, POLLY]

LOCKIT   Set your heart to rest, captain.—You have neither the chance of love or money for another escape; for you are ordered to be called down upon your trial immediately.

22. Cheerful.

PEACHUM   Away, hussies!—This is not a time for a man to be hampered with his wives. You see, the gentleman is in chains already.

LUCY   O husband, husband, my heart longed to see thee; but to see thee thus distracts me!

POLLY   Will not my dear husband look upon his Polly? Why hadst thou not flown to me for protection? With me thou hadst been safe.

AIR LII—*The last time I went o'er the moor, etc.*

POLLY   Hither, dear husband, turn your eyes.
LUCY   Bestow one glance to cheer me.
POLLY   Think, with that look, thy Polly dies.
LUCY   Oh shun me not—but hear me.
POLLY   'Tis Polly sues.
LUCY   —'Tis Lucy speaks.
POLLY   Is thus true love requited?
LUCY   My heart is bursting.
POLLY   —Mine too breaks.
LUCY   Must I?
POLLY   —Must I be slighted?

MACHEATH   What would you have me say, ladies?—You see, this affair will soon be at an end without my disobliging either of you.

PEACHUM   But the settling this point, captain, might prevent a lawsuit between your two widows.

MACHEATH

AIR LIII—*Tom Tinker's my true love, etc.*

Which way shall I turn me? How can I decide?
Wives, the day of our death, are as fond as a bride.
One wife is too much for most husbands to hear,
But two at a time there's no mortal can bear.
This way, and that way, and which way I will,
What would comfort the one, t'other wife would take ill.

POLLY   [*Aside*] But if his own misfortunes have made him insensible to mine, a father sure will be more compassionate. [*To* PEACHUM] Dear, dear sir, sink [23] the material evidence, and bring him off at his trial! Polly upon her knees begs it of you.

AIR LIV—*I am a poor shepherd undone*

When my hero in court appears,
    And stands arraigned for his life;
Then think of poor Polly's tears;
    For ah! poor Polly's his wife.
Like the sailor he holds up his hand,
    Distressed on the dashing wave.

23. Conceal.

To die a dry death at land,
   Is as bad as a watery grave.
    And alas, poor Polly;
    Alack, and well-a-day!
    Before I was in love,
    Oh, every month was May!

LUCY   [*To* LOCKIT] If Peachum's heart is hardened, sure you, sir, will have more compassion on a daughter. I know the evidence is in your power. How can you be a tyrant to me?   [*Kneeling*]

AIR LV—*Ianthe the lovely, etc.*

When he holds up his hand arraigned for his life,
Oh, think of your daughter, and think I'm his wife!
What are cannons, or bombs, or clashing of swords?
For death is more certain by witnesses' words.
Then nail up their lips; that dread thunder allay;
And each month of my life will hereafter be May.

LOCKIT   Macheath's time is come, Lucy. We know our own affairs; therefore let us have no more whimpering or whining.

AIR LVI—*A cobbler there was, etc.*

Ourselves, like the great, to secure a retreat,
When matters require it, must give up our gang.
    And good reason why,
    Or instead of the fry,[24]
    Even Peachum and I,
Like poor petty rascals, might hang, hang;
Like poor petty rascals might hang.

PEACHUM   Set your heart at rest, Polly. Your husband is to die to-day! therefore, if you are not already provided, 'tis high time to look about for another. There's comfort for you, you slut.

LOCKIT   We are ready, sir, to conduct you to the Old Bailey.

MACHEATH

AIR LVII—*Bonny Dundee*

The charge is prepared; the lawyers are met,
The judges all ranged (a terrible show!).
I go, undismayed—for death is a debt,
A debt on demand. So, take what I owe.
Then farewell, my love—dear charmers, adieu.
Contented I die—'tis the better for you.
Here ends all dispute the rest of our lives,
    For this way at once I please all my wives.

24. Small fish, lesser men.

Now, gentlemen, I am ready to attend you.

[*Exeunt* MACHEATH, LOCKIT *and* PEACHUM]

SCENE XII

[LUCY, POLLY, FILCH]

POLLY   Follow them, Filch, to the court; and when the trial is over, bring me a particular account of his behaviour, and of everything that happened. You'll find me here with Miss Lucy. [*Exit* FILCH] But why is all this music?

LUCY   The prisoners whose trials are put off till next sessions are diverting themselves.

POLLY   Sure there is nothing so charming as music! I'm fond of it to distraction! But alas! now, all mirth seems an insult upon my affliction. Let us retire, my dear Lucy, and indulge our sorrows. The noisy crew, you see, are coming upon us.   [*Exeunt*]

[A *dance of prisoners in chains, etc.*]

SCENE XIII. *The condemned hold*

[MACHEATH *in a melancholy posture*]

AIR LVIII—*Happy groves*

O cruel, cruel, cruel case!
Must I suffer this disgrace?

AIR LIX—*Of all the girls that are so smart*

Of all the friends in time of grief,
    When threatening death looks grimmer,
Not one so sure can bring relief,
    As this best friend, a brimmer.   [*Drinks*]

AIR LX—*Britons, strike home*

Since I must swing,—I scorn, I scorn to wince or whine.   [*Rises*]

AIR LXI—*Chevy Chase*

But now again my spirits sink;
I'll raise them high with wine.

                                          [*Drinks a glass of wine*]

AIR LXII—*To old Sir Simon the king*

But valour the stronger grows,
The stronger liquor we're drinking.
And how can we feel our woes,
When we've left the trouble of thinking?

                                                            [*Drinks*]

AIR LXIII—*Joy to great Cæsar*

If thus—a man can die.
Much bolder with brandy.

                            [*Pours out a bumper of brandy*]

AIR LXIV—*There was an old woman, etc.*

So I drink off this bumper.—And now I can stand the test.
And my comrades shall see that I die as brave as the best.

[Drinks]

AIR LXV—*Did you ever hear of a gallant sailor, etc.*

But can I leave my pretty hussies,
Without one tear or tender sigh?

AIR LXVI—*Why are mine eyes still flowing, etc.*

Their eyes, their lips, their busses,[25]
Recall my love.—Ah, must I die?

AIR LXVII—*Green sleeves*

Since laws were made for every degree,
To curb vice in others as well as me,
I wonder we han't better company,
            Upon Tyburn tree!
But gold from law can take out the sting;
And if rich men like us were to swing,
'Twould thin the land, such numbers to string
            Upon Tyburn tree!

[Enter a JAILOR*]*

JAILOR   Some friends of yours, captain, desire to be admitted. I leave you together.   *[Exit]*

SCENE XIV

[MACHEATH, BEN BUDGE, MATT OF THE MINT]

MACHEATH   For my having broke prison, you see, gentlemen, I am ordered immediate execution. The sheriff's officers, I believe, are now at the door. That Jemmy Twitcher should peach me, I own, surprised me! 'Tis a plain proof that the world is all alike, and that even our gang can no more trust one another than other people. Therefore, I beg you, gentlemen, look well to yourselves, for in all probability you may live some months longer.

MATT   We are heartily sorry, captain, for your misfortune. But 'tis what we must all come to.

MACHEATH   Peachum and Lockit, you know, are infamous scoundrels. Their lives are as much in your power as yours are in theirs. Remember your dying friend!—'Tis my last request. Bring those villains to the gallows before you, and I am satisfied.

MATT   We'll do't.

[Re-enter JAILOR*]*

25. Kisses.

JAILOR   Miss Polly and Miss Lucy entreat a word with you.

MACHEATH   Gentlemen, adieu.   [*Exeunt* BEN, MATT, *and* JAILOR]

SCENE XV

[LUCY, MACHEATH, POLLY]

MACHEATH   My dear Lucy—my dear Polly! Whatsoever hath passed between us is now at an end. If you are fond of marrying again, the best advice I can give you is to ship yourselves off for the West Indies, where you'll have a fair chance of getting a husband apiece—or by good luck, two or three, as you like best.

POLLY   How can I support this sight!

LUCY   [*Aside*] There is nothing moves one so much as a great man in distress.

AIR LXVIII—*All you that must take a leap, etc.*

LUCY   Would I might be hanged!

POLLY   —And I would so too!

LUCY   To be hanged with you.

POLLY   —My dear, with you.

MACHEATH   Oh, leave me to thought! I fear! I doubt! I tremble! I droop!—See, my courage is out.

[*Turns up the empty bottle*]

POLLY   No token of love?

MACHEATH   —See, my courage is out.

[*Turns up the empty pot*]

LUCY   No token of love?

POLLY   Adieu.

LUCY   Farewell!

MACHEATH   But hark! I hear the toll of the bell!

CHORUS   Tol de rol lol, etc.

[*Enter* JAILOR]

JAILOR   Four women more, captain, with a child apiece! See, here they come.

[*Enter* WOMEN *and* CHILDREN]

MACHEATH   What—four wives more!—This is too much.—Here, tell the sheriff's officers I am ready.   [*Exit* MACHEATH *guarded*]

SCENE XVI

[*To them enter* PLAYER *and* BEGGAR]

PLAYER   But, honest friend, I hope you don't intend that Macheath shall be really executed.

BEGGAR   Most certainly, sir. To make the piece perfect, I was for doing strict poetical justice. Macheath is to be hanged; and for the other personages of the drama, the audience must have supposed they were all either hanged or transported.

PLAYER   Why then, friend, this is a downright deep tragedy. The catastrophe is manifestly wrong, for an opera must end happily.

BEGGAR   Your objection, sir, is very just, and is easily removed; for you must allow that in this kind of drama, 'tis no matter how absurdly things are brought about. So—you rabble there! run and cry a reprieve!—let the prisoner be brought back to his wives in triumph.

PLAYER   All this we must do, to comply with the taste of the town.

BEGGAR   Through the whole piece you may observe such a similitude of manners in high and low life, that it is difficult to determine whether (in the fashionable vices) the fine gentlemen imitate the gentlemen of the road, or the gentlemen of the road the fine gentlemen. Had the play remained as I at first intended, it would have carried a most excellent moral. 'Twould have shown that the lower sort of people have their vices in a degree as well as the rich, and that they are punished for them.

SCENE XVII

[*To them* MACHEATH, *with rabble, etc.*]

MACHEATH   So it seems I am not left to my choice, but must have a wife at last.—Look ye, my dears, we will have no controversy now. Let us give this day to mirth, and I am sure she who thinks herself my wife will testify her joy by a dance.

ALL   Come, a dance—a dance!

MACHEATH   Ladies, I hope you will give me leave to present a partner to each of you. And (if I may without offence) for this time, I take Polly for mine. [*To* POLLY] And for life, you slut, for we were really married. As for the rest—but at present keep your own secret.

A Dance

AIR LXIX—*Lumps of pudding, etc.*

Thus I stand like the Turk, with his doxies around;
From all sides their glances his passion confound:
For black, brown, and fair, his inconstancy burns,
And the different beauties subdue him by turns.
Each calls forth her charms, to provoke his desires;
Though willing to all, with but one he retires.
But think of this maxim, and put off your sorrow,
The wretch of today may be happy tomorrow.

CHORUS   But think of this maxim, etc.

1728

DANIEL DEFOE
1660–1731

From The True and Genuine Accounts of the Life and Actions of the Late Jonathan Wild [1]

He was now master of his trade; poor and rich flocked to him. If anything was lost (whether by negligence in the owner, or vigilance and dexterity in the thief), away we went to Jonathan Wild; nay, advertisements were published, directing the finder of almost everything to bring it to Jonathan Wild, who was eminently empowered to take it and give the reward.

How infatuate were the people of this nation all this while! Did they consider, that at the very time that they treated this person with such a confidence, as if he had been appointed to the trade, he had, perhaps, the very goods in his keeping, waiting the advertisement for the reward, and that, perhaps, they had been stolen with that very intention?

It was not a little difficult to give his eminence his true title; he was, indeed, called a thief-catcher, and on some extraordinary occasions he was so. . . . But this was no explanation of his business at all, for his profits came in another way, not in catching the thief, but, more properly, in catching (that is, biting) the persons robbed. As for the thief, it was not his business to catch him as long as he would be subjected to his rules—that is to say, as often as he had committed any robberies, to bring it to him to be restored to the owner.

If the correspondence he kept was large, if the number of his instruments was very great, his dexterity in managing them was indeed wonderful; and how cleverly he kept himself out of the reach of the Act for receiving stolen goods . . . is hardly to be imagined; and yet we find he was never charged home till now, notwithstanding so many felons who he exasperated to the last degree, and made desperate by falling upon them to their destruction.

It is true, the young generation of thieves, who, as we may say, lived under him, were always kept low and poor, and could not subsist but by the bounty of their governor; and when they had a booty of any bulk or value, they knew not what to do with it but to deposit it, and get some money for the present use, and then have a little more upon its being disposed the right way.

For the managing this part he had his particular servants to take and receive, so that Jonathan received nothing, delivered nothing, nor could anything be fastened on him to his hurt, I mean for receiving stolen goods, and yet, as things stood, almost all the stolen goods were brought to him and put into his hands.

1. The full title goes on: *not Made up out of Fiction & Fable, but taken from his own Mouth, and Collected from Papers of his own Writing.* Unlike other journalists, Defoe did not prepare his tract for the day of Wild's execution, and he attacked those "absurd and ridiculous accounts" which preceded his. As always, Defoe is divided between moral outrage and an admiration for commercial resourcefulness and boldness; one can see this as well in *Moll Flanders* (1722), *Colonel Jacque* (1722), and *Roxana* (1724), the great novels about criminal life (and its reformation) that followed *Robinson Crusoe* (1719). Although Defoe's information was largely based on the other accounts he derided, he produces in his seemingly breathless flow of circumstantial detail the illusion of unedited reality; the very lack of syntactic ordering and emphasis seems a warrant of authenticity.

He openly kept his counting-house, or office, like a man of business, and had his books to enter everything in with the utmost exactness and regularity. When you first came to him to give him an account of anything lost, it was hinted to you that you must first deposit a crown; this was his retaining fee. Then you were asked some needful questions—that is to say, needful, not for his information, but for your amusement—as where you live, where the goods were lost, whether out of your house or out of your pocket, or whether on the highway, and the like; and your answers to them all were minuted down, as if in order to make a proper search and inquiry; whereas, perhaps, the very thing you came to inquire after was in the very room where you were, or not far off. After all this grimace [2] was at an end, you were desired to call again or send in a day or two, and then you should know whether he was able to do you any service or no, and so you were dismissed.

At your second coming you had some encouragement given you, that you would be served, but, perhaps, the terms were a little raised upon you, and you were told the rogue that had it was impudent, and that he insisted it was worth so much, and he could sell it when he would for double the money you offered; and that if you would not give him such a sum, he would not treat with you. 'However,' says Jonathan, 'if I can but come to the speech of him, I'll make him to be more reasonable.'

The next time he tells you that all he can bring the rogue to is, that—guineas being paid to the porter who shall bring the goods, and a promise upon honour that nothing shall be said to him, but just take and give, the gold watch, or the snuff-box, or whatever it is, shall be brought to you by such a time exactly; and thus, upon mutual assurances, the bargain is made for restoring the goods.

But then it remains to be asked, what Mr. Wild expects for his pains in managing this nice part; who answers, with an air of greatness, he leaves it to you; that he gets nothing by what is to be given the porter, that he is satisfied in being able to serve gentlemen in such a manner; so that it is in your breast to do what you think is handsome by Mr. Wild, who has taken a great deal of pains in it to do you a service.

It must be confessed that in all this, if there was no more than is mentioned, such a part might be acted on all sides without any guilt fastened anywhere but on the thief. For example, a house is robbed, or a lady has lost her gold watch. Jonathan, by his intelligence among the gang, finds out who has done it—that is to say, he is told 'tis such a one; 'tis no matter how he hears it, he is not bound to the discovery upon a hearsay; nor is he obliged to prosecute a felony committed on he does not know who, by he knows not who—that's none of his business.

However, having a kind of knowledge of the person, he sends to him, to let him know that if he is his own friend, he will carry, that is, send, the watch, or the cane, or the snuff-box, so and so, to such a place; and that if he does so, and the porter receives ten guineas or more, or less, whatever it is that is offered, all will be well; if not, he adds a threatening that he will be prosecuted with the utmost severity.

2. Masquerade, pretense.

Upon this, the thief sends the goods, has the money, and never sees Jonathan, nor any person else. What can Jonathan be charged with in such an affair as this? I must confess I do not see it; no, nor if the thief sends him a present of four or five guineas out of the money, provided, as he said, it is without any conditions made beforehand, or being present at the time 'tis done.

Nor, on the other hand, does the treating for delivering the goods, as above, with a second or third person give any room to fix anything on Jonathan; so that, in short, he treats both with the thief and with the person robbed, with the utmost safety and security. Indeed, I do not see why he might not have carried on such a commerce as this with the greatest ease, I do not say honesty, in the world, if he had gone no farther; for he took none of your money for restoring your goods, neither did he restore you any goods; you gave him money, indeed, for his trouble in inquiring out the thief, and for using his interest by awing or persuading to get your stolen goods sent you back, telling you what you must give to the porter that brings them, if you please, for he does not oblige you to give it.

But the danger lay on the other side of the question, namely, not being contented with what the person robbed gave upon the foot of a grateful acknowledgment for trouble; but impudently taking the goods of the thief, sending the porter himself, taking the money, and then capitulating with the thief for such a part of the reward, and then this thief coming in against him as a witness. This was the very case, in the fact, upon which Jonathan miscarried.

So that, in a word, Jonathan's avarice hanged him. It is true, in the case he was tried for, it was apparent that he set the robbery, as they express it; that is, he directed the persons to the place—nay, went with them to show them the shop, described the woman and the business; and after all, received the goods, and gave them the money for returning them, reserving it in his own power to take what more he pleased for himself; and at last all this was testified by the thieves themselves. . . .

1725

HENRY FIELDING
1707–1754

From The History of the Life of the Late
Mr. Jonathan Wild the Great [1]

Chapter XIV

Wild proceeds to the highest consummation of human GREATNESS

The day now drew nigh when our great man was to exemplify the last and noblest act of greatness by which any hero can signalize himself. This was the day of execution, or consummation, or apotheosis (for it is called by different names), which was to give our hero an opportunity of facing death and damnation, without any fear in his heart, or, at least without betraying any symptoms of it in his countenance. A completion of greatness which is heartily to be wished to every great man; nothing being more worthy of lamentation than when Fortune, like a lazy poet, winds up her catastrophe awkwardly, and, bestowing too little care on her fifth act, dismisses the hero with a sneaking and private exit, who had in the former part of the drama performed such notable exploits as must promise to every good judge among the spectators a noble, public, and exalted end.

But she was resolved to commit no such error in this instance. Our hero was too much and too deservedly her favourite to be neglected by her in his last moments; accordingly all efforts for a reprieve were vain, and the name of Wild stood at the head of those who were ordered for execution.

From the time he gave over all hopes of life, his conduct was truly great and admirable. Instead of showing any marks of dejection or contrition, he rather infused more confidence and assurance into his looks. He spent most of his hours in drinking with his friends. . . . In one of these compotations, being asked whether he was afraid to die, he answered, 'D—n me, it is only a dance without music.' Another time, when one expressed some sorrow for his misfortune, as he termed it, he said with great fierceness—'A man can die but once.' Again, when one of his intimate acquaintance hinted his hopes, that he would die like a man, he cocked his hat in defiance, and cried out greatly—'Zounds! who's afraid?'

. . .

On the eve of his apotheosis, Wild's lady desired to see him, to which he consented. This meeting was at first very tender on both sides; but it could

---

1. Henry Fielding began his literary career as a playwright, but his attacks upon political corruption provoked the Licensing Act of 1737, which submitted all plays to the censorship of the Lord Chamberlain. His satire found its outlet in the prose *Miscellanies* (1743) and particularly in the studied irony of *Jonathan Wild*. Here Fielding plays "goodness" (embodied in the Heartfree family) against "greatness," and he finds the counterparts of Wild's greatness (in a manner reminiscent of Swift) in such heroes as Caesar and Alexander and such contemporaries as Walpole. Following Gay's example, he presents Wild as a low parallel to "high life" and gives him the almost unwavering posture and rhetoric of greatness. This technique served as well to create such figures of high life as Lady Booby in *Joseph Andrews* (1742) or Lady Bellaston in *Tom Jones* (1749) and the innumerable rogues and hypocrites, lower in status but hardly in pretension, that populate those novels and *Amelia* (1751).

not continue so, for unluckily, some hints of former miscarriages intervening, as particularly when she asked him how he could have used her so barbarously once as calling her b——, and whether such language became a man, much less a gentleman, Wild flew into a violent passion, and swore she was the vilest of b——s to upbraid him at such a season with an unguarded word spoke long ago. She replied, with many tears, she was well enough served for her folly in visiting such a brute; but she had one comfort, however, that it would be the last time he could ever treat her so; that indeed she had some obligation to him, for that his cruelty to her would reconcile her to the fate he was to-morrow to suffer; and, indeed, nothing but such brutality could have made the consideration of his shameful death (so this weak woman called hanging), which was now inevitable, to be borne even without madness. She then proceeded to a recapitulation of his faults in an exacter order, and with more perfect memory, than one would have imagined her capable of; and it is probable would have rehearsed a complete catalogue had not our hero's patience failed him, so that with the utmost fury and violence he caught her by the hair and kicked her, as heartily as his chains would suffer him, out of the room.

At length the morning came which Fortune at his birth had resolutely ordained for the consummation of our hero's GREATNESS: he had himself indeed modestly declined the public honour she intended him, and had taken a quantity of laudanum in order to retire quietly off the stage; but we have already observed, in the course of our wonderful history, that to struggle against this lady's decrees is vain and impotent; and whether she hath determined you shall be hanged or be a prime minister, it is in either case lost labour to resist. Laudanum, therefore, being unable to stop the breath of our hero, which the fruit of hemp-seed,[2] and not the spirit of poppy seed, was to overcome, he was at the usual hour attended by the proper gentleman appointed for that purpose, and acquainted that the cart was ready. On this occasion he exerted that greatness of courage which hath been so much celebrated in other heroes; and, knowing it was impossible to resist, he gravely declared he would attend them. He then descended to that room where the fetters of great men are knocked off in a most solemn and ceremonious manner. Then shaking hands with his friends (to wit, those who were conducting him to the tree), and drinking their healths in a bumper of brandy, he ascended the cart, where he was no sooner seated than he received the acclamations of the multitude, who were highly ravished with his GREATNESS.

The cart now moved slowly on, being preceded by a troop of horse-guards bearing javelins in their hands, through streets lined with crowds all admiring the great behaviour of our hero, who rode on, sometimes sighing, sometimes swearing, sometimes singing or whistling, as his humour varied.

When he came to the tree of glory,[3] he was welcomed with an universal shout of the people, who were there assembled in prodigious numbers to behold a sight much more rare in populous cities than one would reasonably imagine it should be, viz., the proper catastrophe of a great man.

2. I.e. the rope.
3. The gallows, Tyburn Tree.

But though envy was, through fear, obliged to join the general voice in applause on this occasion, there were not wanting some who maligned this completion of glory, which was now about to be fulfilled to our hero, and endeavoured to prevent it by knocking him on the head as he stood under the tree while the ordinary [4] was performing his last office. They therefore began to batter the cart with stones, brick-bats, dirt, and all manner of mischievous weapons, some of which, erroneously playing on the robes of the ecclesiastic, made him so expeditious in his repetition that with wonderful alacrity he had ended almost in an instant, and conveyed himself into a place of safety in a hackney-coach, where he waited the conclusion with a temper of mind described in these verses:

Suave mari magno, turbantibus æquora ventis,
E terra alterius magnum spectare laborem.[5]

We must not, however, omit one circumstance, as it serves to show the most admirable conservation of character in our hero to his last moment, which was, that, whilst the ordinary was busy in his ejaculations, Wild, in the midst of the shower of stones, &c., which played upon him, applied his hands to the parson's pocket, and emptied it of his bottle-screw, which he carried out of the world in his hand.

The ordinary being now descended from the cart, Wild had just opportunity to cast his eyes around the crowd and to give them a hearty curse, when immediately the horses moved on, and with universal applause our hero swung out of this world.

Thus fell Jonathan Wild the GREAT, by a death as glorious as his life had been, and which was so truly agreeable to it that the latter must have been deplorably maimed and imperfect without the former; a death which hath been alone wanting to complete the characters of several ancient and modern heroes, whose histories would then have been read with much greater pleasure by the wisest in all ages. Indeed we could almost wish that whenever Fortune seems wantonly to deviate from her purpose and leaves her work imperfect in this particular, the historian would indulge himself in the license of poetry and romance and even do a violence to truth, to oblige his reader with a page which must be the most delightful in all his history and which could never fail of producing an instructive moral.

Narrow minds may possibly have some reason to be ashamed of going this way out of the world if their consciences can fly in their faces and assure them they have not merited such an honour; but he must be a fool who is ashamed of being hanged, who is not weak enough to be ashamed of having deserved it.

1743

---

4. The prison chaplain.
5. Lucretius, *De Rerum Natura* II.1–2: "Sweet it is, when the mighty sea is lashed by furious winds, to look from shore at the struggles of another."

THE URBAN SCENE

"Why, Sir, you find no man, at all intellectual, who is willing to leave London. No, Sir, when a man is tired of London, he is tired of life; for there is in London all that life can afford." Beside those famous words of Dr. Johnson's, spoken in 1777, one can place his observation in a letter fifteen years earlier, when, depressed during a visit to Lichfield, he "took the first opportunity of returning to a place, where, if there is not much happiness, there is, at least, such a diversity of good and evil that slight vexations do not fix upon the heart." For Boswell, on at least one occasion (and in fact many more, if not most, occasions) London was "the great scene of ambition, instruction, and amusement . . . comparatively speaking, a heaven upon earth."

By the beginning of the eighteenth century London was the largest city in Europe, having reached something more than a half-million people. The Great Fire of 1666 had destroyed more than 13,000 homes and four-fifths of all the buildings in the City proper, that is, the older and more heavily commercial area. Rebuilding created a more open city, expanding into surrounding fields, replacing overhanging half-timbered houses with rows of brick terraces, in many cases enclosing small green squares. Sir Christopher Wren's baroque city plan was not put into effect, but his designs were used for new churches that replaced the eighty-seven destroyed in the Fire; and in the last thirty years of the seventeenth century his great plan for St. Paul's Cathedral was executed, reaching completion in 1709. (See Figs. 8–13.)

Yet there remained much squalor, crowding, and crime, and among the poor a new addiction to gin. It is hard to estimate the quality of life in another age, for we tend to bring some of our own expectations and to neglect the more commonplace elements of stability that fail to win critical attention or pious celebration. If one were to consult only the prints of Hogarth, such as *Gin Lane* (Fig. 30), one would have the impression of a squalor and brutishness almost unendurable; but Hogarth was a satirist, whatever else, and he intensified what he saw. Such poems as Swift's and Gay's stress the impersonality of city life (which was also a source of its freedom), and essays like those of Addison and Steele present the opulence and diversity of its commercial life.

Addison at the Royal Exchange (handsomely rebuilt after the Great Fire) sees the glory of the merchant, and in his account of the color and richness trade has conferred upon England there is something very close to the treatment of man's perception giving sensuous beauty to the characterless substance of his material world. Defoe can share this enthusiasm for the tradesman: "He understands languages without books, geography without maps; his journals and trading voyages delineate the world . . . he sits in his counting house and converses with all nations and keeps up the most exquisite and extensive part of human society in a universal correspondence." But John Gay, in *The Beggar's Opera*, shows Peachum in his counting house deciding which of the thieves he has trained he shall turn in for a fee. His ledgers become a frightening symbol of the ruthlessness that Defoe, for all his praise of the tradesman, could understand as well. Gain is the "essence of his being," and there are, as a result, "more snares . . . and more allurements to him to turn knave than in any employment."

At times Defoe comes to the view that Mandeville exploits in paradox and satire: "It must be confessed, trade is almost universally founded on crime." In a figure like Moll Flanders we can see the enterprise of a tradeswoman who turns to theft and is unable to relinquish its excitement even when it is no longer required by necessity. "What a poor nation must we have been," Defoe writes, "if we had been a sober, religious, temperate nation?" And like Mandeville, he can add that the "wealth of the country is raised by its wickedness, and if it should be reformed it would be undone." We can see an earlier recognition of this, with its own ironic edge, in Swift's *Argument Against Abolishing Christianity* (and implicitly later in *Gulliver's Travels*). What all these observers recognize is the incompatibility of the Gospels or of Stoic virtue with the opulence and vigor of a city like London; so much the worse for the doctrine "which can only be learned from the New Testament, where it will ever remain," Mandeville concludes ironically, "in its purity and lustre."

If London, then, embodies what Swift calls our "schemes of wealth and power," it accommodates other kinds of vigor as well. "I own, Sir," Boswell remarks, "the spirits which I have in London make me do everything with more readiness and vigour. I can talk twice as much in London as anywhere else." One can set this against Pope's images of retirement, of "the feast of reason and the flow of soul," and one can, in fact, set the urban scene against the country house, the villa where man constantly dreams of recovering himself, freed of the pressures of external compulsion or of the temptations to compete in whatever race is being run. Each scene has its deceptions (as Timon's villa reminds us) and each its rewards; if the villa frames a vision of the serene individual in his stability (but in implicit opposition to court or city), so the city gives us the vitality of a social existence with its stress upon man's collective greatness rather than his individual integrity.

JOHN DRYDEN

From The Third Satire of Juvenal°

Return we to the dangers of the night:
430 And, first, behold our houses' dreadful height;
From whence come broken potsherds tumbling down;
And leaky ware, from garret windows thrown:
Well may they break our heads, that mark the flinty stone.
'Tis want of sense to sup abroad too late,
Unless thou first hast settled thy estate.
As many fates attend, thy steps to meet,
As there are waking windows in the street.
Bless the good gods, and think thy chance is rare,
To have a pisspot only for thy share.
440   The scouring° drunkard, if he does not fight
Before his bedtime, takes no rest that night;
Passing the tedious hours in greater pain
Than stern Achilles,° when his friend was slain:
'Tis so ridiculous, but so true withal,

The Third Satire of Juvenal Umbricius, at the point of leaving Rome for Cumae, "reckons up the several inconveniencies which arise from a city life and the many dangers which attend it" (Dryden).

scouring given to bullying or to cruel practical jokes
Achilles mourning for the death of Patroclus

A bully cannot sleep without a brawl:
Yet though his youthful blood be fired with wine,
He wants not wit the danger to decline;
Is cautious to avoid the coach and six,
And on the lackeys will no quarrel fix.
450 His train of flambeaux, and embroidered coat,
May privilege my lord to walk secure on foot.
But me, who must by moonlight homeward bend,
Or lighted only with a candle's end,
Poor me he fights, if that he fighting, where
He only cudgels, and I only bear.
He stands, and bids me stand; I must abide;
For he's the stronger, and is drunk beside.
    'Where did you whet your knife tonight?' he cries,
'And shred the leeks that in your stomach rise?
460 Whose windy beans have stuffed your guts, and where
Have your black thumbs been dipped in vinegar?
With what companion cobbler have you fed,
On old ox-cheeks, or he-goat's tougher head?
What, are you dumb? Quick, with your answer, quick,
Before my foot salutes you with a kick.
Say, in what nasty cellar, under ground,
Or what church porch, your rogueship may be found?'
Answer, or answer not, 'tis all the same:
He lays me on, and makes me bear the blame.
470 Before the bar, for beating him, you come;
This is a poor man's liberty in Rome.
You beg his pardon; happy to retreat
With some remaining teeth, to chew your meat.
    Nor is this all; for, when retired, you think
To sleep securely; when the candles wink,
When every door with iron chains is barred,
And roaring taverns are no longer heard;
The ruffian robbers, by no justice awed,
And unpaid cutthroat soldiers are abroad,
480 Those venal souls, who, hardened in each ill,
To save complaints and prosecution, kill.
Chased from their woods and bogs, the padders come
To this vast city as their native home;
To live at ease, and safely skulk in Rome.
    The forge in fetters only is employed;
Our iron mines exhausted and destroyed
In shackles; for these villains scarce allow
Goads for the teams, and plowshares for the plow.
O happy ages of our ancestors,
490 Beneath the kings and tribunitial powers!°

Beneath . . . powers in the days, long before
the empire, when Rome was governed by kings,
or later by consuls and tribunes of the people

One jail did all their criminals restrain,
Which, now, the walls of Rome can scarce contain.

1692

SAMUEL JOHNSON

From London: A Poem

In Imitation of the Third Satire of Juvenal°

Prepare for death, if here at night you roam,
And sign your will before you sup from home.
Some fiery fop, with new commission vain,
Who sleeps on brambles till he kills his man;
Some frolic drunkard, reeling from a feast,
Provokes a broil, and stabs you for a jest.
230   Yet even these heroes, mischievously gay,
Lords of the street, and terrors of the way;
Flushed as they are with folly, youth, and wine,
Their prudent insults to the poor confine;
Afar they mark the flambeau's bright approach,
And shun the shining train, and golden coach:
  In vain, these dangers past, your doors you close,
And hope the balmy blessings of repose:
Cruel with guilt, and daring with despair,
The midnight murderer bursts the faithless bar;
240   Invades the sacred hour of silent rest,
And leaves, unseen, a dagger in your breast.
  Scarce can our fields, such crowds at Tyburn die,
With hemp° the gallows and the fleet supply.
Propose your schemes, ye Senatorian band,
Whose Ways and Means support the sinking land;
Lest ropes be wanting in the tempting spring,
To rig another convoy for the k—g.
  A single jail, in ALFRED's golden reign,
Could half the nation's criminals contain;
250   Fair Justice then, without constraint adored,
Held high the steady scale, but deeped° the sword;
No spies were paid, no special juries known,
Blest age! but ah! how different from our own!

. . . .

1738

Imitation . . . Juvenal For the meaning of
"imitation" see the Headnote on Pope, Imitations of Horace. This passage in Johnson's version corresponds to the closer translation by
Dryden; Johnson adapts Juvenal's satire more
fully to a London setting.
hemp the material for the hangman's rope (used
in the gallows at Tyburn) or for the ship's ropes
necessary for the frequent journeys of George
II to Hanover and his mistress there (ll. 246–
47), an expense supported by the House of
Commons, whose "Ways and Means" are methods of raising money
deeped turned down

JONATHAN SWIFT

A Description of the Morning

Now hardly here and there a hackney-coach
Appearing, showed the ruddy morn's approach.
Now Betty° from her master's bed had flown,
And softly stole to discompose her own;
The slip-shod 'prentice from his master's door
Had pared the dirt and sprinkled° round the floor.
Now Moll had whirled her mop with dext'rous airs,
Prepared to scrub the entry and the stairs.
The youth with broomy stumps began to trace
10 The kennel-edge,° where wheels had worn the place.
The small-coal man° was heard with cadence deep,
Till drowned in shriller notes of chimney-sweep:
Duns° at his lordship's gate began to meet;
And brickdust Moll° had screamed through half the street.
The turnkey° now his flock returning sees,
Duly let out a-nights to steal for fees:
The watchful bailiffs take their silent stands,
And schoolboys lag with satchels in their hands.

1709

A Description of a City Shower

In Imitation of Virgil's Georgics

Careful observers may foretell the hour
(By sure prognostics) when to dread a shower.
While rain depends,° the pensive cat gives o'er
Her frolics and pursues her tail no more.
Returning home at night, you'll find the sink°
Strike your offended sense with double stink.
If you be wise, then go not far to dine:
You'll spend in coach-hire more than save in wine.
A coming shower your shooting corns presage,
10 Old aches° throb, your hollow tooth will rage;
Sauntering in coffeehouse is Dulman seen;
He damns the climate, and complains of spleen.°

Betty like Aurora, the goddess of the dawn, who must leave each morning the bed of her lover Tithonus
sprinkled suggesting the conventional morning shower, as Moll's mop does the gentle breeze
kennel-edge the curb of the road, where he is looking for old nails
small-coal man vendor of charcoal, beginning the sequence of urban counterparts to braying animals and singing birds

Duns bill collectors
brickdust Moll a woman selling powdered brick for cleaning knives
turnkey the jailer who lets his prisoners steal to earn the fees he exacts
depends impends
sink sewer
aches pronounced "aitches"
spleen melancholy, "vapours"

475

Meanwhile the South,° rising with dabbled° wings,
A sable cloud athwart the welkin° flings,
That swilled more liquor than it could contain,
And like a drunkard gives it up again.
Brisk Susan whips her linen from the rope,
While the first drizzling shower is borne aslope;
Such is that sprinkling which some careless quean°
20   Flirts on you from her mop, but not so clean:
You fly, invoke the gods; then, turning, stop
To rail; she singing, still whirls on her mop.
Not yet the dust had shunned the unequal strife,
But, aided by the wind, fought still for life,
And wafted with its foe by violent gust,
'Twas doubtful which was rain and which was dust.
Ah! where must needy poet seek for aid,
When dust and rain at once his coat invade?
His only coat, where dust confused with rain
30   Roughen the nap, and leave a mingled stain.
    Now in contiguous drops° the flood comes down,
Threatening with deluge this *devoted°* town.
To shops in crowds the daggled° females fly,
Pretend to cheapen° goods, but nothing buy.
The templar° spruce, while every spout's abroach,°
Stays till 'tis fair, yet seems to call a coach.
The tucked-up sempstress walks with hasty strides,
While streams run down her oiled umbrella's sides.
Here various kinds by various fortunes led,
40   Commence acquaintance underneath a shed.
Triumphant Tories and desponding Whigs
Forget their feuds, and join to save their wigs.
Boxed in a chair° the beau impatient sits,
While spouts run clattering o'er the roof by fits,
And ever and anon with frightful din
The leather° sounds; he trembles from within.
So when Troy chairmen bore the wooden steed,
Pregnant with Greeks impatient to be freed,
(Those bully Greeks, who, as the moderns do,
50   Instead of paying chairmen, ran them through),
Laocoon° struck the outside with his spear,
And each imprisoned hero quaked for fear.
    Now from all parts the swelling kennels° flow,

South south wind
dabbled splashed, soiled with mud
athwart the welkin across the sky (deliberate use of archaic-pastoral diction.)
quean wench
contiguous drops a deliberate latinate elevation of diction
devoted doomed (again heroic diction)
daggled mud-splashed

cheapen bargain for
templar law student
abroach gushing
chair closed sedan chair
leather the roof of the chair
Laocoon who questioned the value of the Trojan Horse and tested it (*Aeneid* II)
kennels gutters

And bear their trophies with them as they go:
Filth of all hues and odour seem to tell
What street they sailed from by their sight and smell.
They, as each torrent drives with rapid force,
From Smithfield° or St. Pulchre's° shape their course,
And in huge confluent join at Snow Hill Ridge,
60   Fall from the conduit prone to Holborn bridge.
Sweepings from butchers' stalls, dung, guts, and blood,
Drowned puppies, stinking sprats,° all drenched in mud,
Dead cats, and turnip-tops, come tumbling down the flood.°

                    1710

JOHN GAY

Trivia, or the Art of Walking the Streets of London°

From *Book II*

    Let due civilities be strictly paid.
The wall surrender to the hooded maid;
Nor let thy sturdy elbow's hasty rage
Jostle the feeble steps of trembling age:
And when the porter bends beneath his load,
50   And pants for breath, clear thou the crowded road:
But, above all, the groping blind direct,
And from the pressing throng the lame protect.
    You'll sometimes meet a fop, of nicest tread,
Whose mantling peruke° veils his empty head:
At every step he dreads the wall to lose,
And risks, to save a coach, his red-heeled shoes;
Him, like the miller, pass with caution by,
Lest from his shoulder clouds of powder fly:
But when the bully, with assuming pace,
60   Cocks his broad hat, edged round with tarnished lace,
Yield not the way; defy his strutting pride,
And thrust him to the muddy kennel's° side:
He never turns again, nor dares oppose,
But mutters coward curses as he goes.
    If drawn by business to a street unknown,
Let the sworn porter point thee through the town.
Be sure observe the signs, for signs remain

Smithfield the cattle market
St. Pulchre's the church of St. Sepulchre on Snow Hill
sprats small fish
Dead cats . . . flood The last three lines are Swift's parody of the triplet (which Dryden and others favored, especially in poetry of a high style) and the last line a parody of the extended (twelve-syllable) Alexandrine, with which the triplet often concluded.
Trivia . . . London Gay's poem, in three books, is a mock-georgic, applying the heroic celebration of rural labor to the urban task of getting through the traffic of the city.
mantling peruke enveloping wig
kennel's gutter's

Like faithful landmarks to the walking train.
Seek not from 'prentices to learn the way;
70   Those fabling boys will turn thy steps astray:
Ask the grave tradesman to direct thee right;
He ne'er deceives but when he profits by't.

. . .

Experienced men, inured to city ways,
Need not the calendar to count their days.
When through the town, with slow and solemn air,
Led by the nostril, walks the muzzled bear,
Behind him moves majestically dull,
410   The pride of Hockley-hole,° the surly bull;
Learn hence the periods of the week to name:
Mondays and Thursdays are the days of game.
When fishy stalls with doubled store are laid,
The golden-bellied carp, the broad-finned maid,°
Red-speckled trouts, the salmon's silver jowl,
The jointed lobster, and unscaly sole,
And luscious scallops to allure the tastes
Of rigid zealots to delicious fasts;
Wednesdays and Fridays, you'll observe from hence
420   Days when our sires were doomed to abstinence.
When dirty waters from balconies drop,
And dextrous damsels twirl the sprinkling mop,
And cleanse the spattered sash, and scrub the stairs,
Know Saturday's conclusive morn appears.
Successive cries the seasons' change declare,
And mark the monthly progress of the year.
Hark! how the streets with treble voices ring,
To sell the bounteous product of the spring:
Sweet-smelling flowers, and elder's early bud,
430   With nettle's tender shoots,° to cleanse the blood:
And when June's thunder cools the sultry skies,
Even Sundays are profaned by mack'rel cries.
Walnuts the fruiterer's hand, in autumn, stain,
Blue plums and juicy pears augment his gain;
Next oranges the longing boys entice
To trust their copper fortunes to the dice.
When rosemary, and bays, the poet's crown,
Are bawled in frequent cries through all the town,
Then judge the festival of Christmas near,
440   Christmas! the joyous period of the year.
Now with bright holly all your temples strow,
With laurel green, and sacred mistletoe.

. . .

Hockley-hole Hockley-in-the-Hold, the scene of
bear- and bull-baiting
maid a species of shad

nettle's . . . shoots to be eaten as a spring
remedy

From *Book III*

Where the mob gathers, swiftly shoot along,
Nor idly mingle in the noisy throng.
Lured by the silver hilt, amid the swarm
The subtle artist will thy side disarm:
Nor is thy flaxen wig with safety worn;
High on the shoulder in a basket borne
Lurks the sly boy, whose hand, to rapine bred,
Plucks off the curling honours of thy head.°
Here dives the skulking thief, with practised sleight
60   And unfelt fingers makes thy pocket light.
Where's now thy watch? with all its trinkets, flow;
And thy late snuff-box is no more thy own.
But, lo! his bolder thefts some tradesman spies,
Swift from his prey the scudding lurcher° flies:
Dextrous he 'scapes the coach with nimble bounds,
Whilst every honest tongue 'Stop thief' resounds.
So speeds the wily fox, alarmed by fear,
Who lately filched the turkey's callow care;°
Hounds following hounds, grow louder as he flies,
70   And injured tenants join the hunter's cries:
Breathless he stumbling falls. Ill-fated boy!
Why did not honest work thy youth employ?
Seized by rough hands, he's dragged amid the rout,
And stretched beneath the pump's incessant spout;°
Or plunged in miry pounds he gasping lies,
Mud chokes his mouth, and plasters o'er his eyes.
    Let not the ballad-singer's shrilling strain
Amid the swarm thy listening ear detain;
Guard well thy pocket; for these sirens stand
80   To aid the labours of the diving hand:
Confederate in the cheat, they draw the throng,
And cambric handkerchiefs reward the song.
But soon as coach or cart drives rattling on,
The rabble part, in shoals they backward run:
So Jove's loud bolts the mingled war divide,
And Greece and Troy retreat on either side.

. . .

Who can the various city frauds recite,
With all the petty rapines of the night?
Who now the guinea-dropper's bait° regards,
250   Tricked by the sharper's dice or juggler's cards?
Why should I warn thee ne'er to join the fray

---

honours . . . head a Virgilian phrase for ornaments, hence hair
lurcher petty thief
callow care young
beneath . . . spout a common punishment for
petty thieves

guinea-dropper's bait the apparently lost guinea
used as bait in a confidence game, which may
also involve a "sham-quarrel" (l. 252)

Where the sham-quarrel interrupts the way?
Lives there in these our days so soft a clown,
Braved° by the bully's oaths or threatening frown?
I need not strict enjoin the pockets' care,
When from the crowded play thou leadest the fair;
Who has not here or watch or snuff-box lost,
Or hankerchiefs that India's shuttle boast;
O! may thy virtue guard thee through the roads
260   Of Drury's mazy courts and dark abodes,
The harlots' guileful paths, who nightly stand
Where Catherine Street° descends into the Strand.
Say, vagrant Muse! their wiles and subtle arts,
To lure the strangers' unsuspecting hearts;
So shall our youth on healthful sinews tread,
And city cheeks grow warm with rural red.
    'Tis she who nightly strolls with sauntering pace,
No stubborn stays her yielding shape embrace;
Beneath the lamp her tawdry ribbons glare,
270   The new-scoured mantua° and the slattern air;
High-draggled° petticoats her travels show,
And hollow cheeks with artful blushes glow;
With flattering sounds she soothes the credulous ear,
My noble captain! charmer! love! my dear!
In ridinghood near tavern-doors she plies,
Or muffled pinners° hide her livid eyes;
With empty bandbox she delights to range,
And feigns a distant errand from the 'Change;
Nay, she will oft the Quaker's hood profane,
280   And trudge demure the rounds of Drury Lane:
She darts from sarcenet° ambush wily leers;
Twitches thy sleeve, or with familiar airs
Her fan will pat thy cheek: these snares disdain,
Nor gaze behind thee when she turns again.

· · ·

1716

Braved cowed
Catherine Street a block away from Drury
Lane, both the resort of prostitutes
mantua a loose cloak-like gown
High-draggled mud-spattered well above the
hem

pinners long flaps pinned to the cap and hanging
to the breast; here, perhaps a full headdress
sarcenet a soft silk, here used to modify "ambush"

JOSEPH ADDISON [1]

[The Royal Exchange]

There is no place in the town which I so much love to frequent as the Royal Exchange.[2] It gives me a secret satisfaction, and, in some measure, gratifies my vanity, as I am an Englishman, to see so rich an assembly of countrymen and foreigners consulting together upon the private business of mankind, and making this metropolis a kind of emporium for the whole earth. I must confess I look upon high-change [3] to be a great council, in which all considerable nations have their representatives. Factors in the trading world are what ambassadors are in the politic world; they negotiate affairs, conclude treaties, and maintain a good correspondence between those wealthy societies of men that are divided from one another by seas and oceans, or live on the different extremities of a continent. I have often been pleased to hear disputes adjusted between an inhabitant of Japan and an alderman of London, or to see a subject of the Great Mogul entering into a league with one of the Czar of Muscovy. I am infinitely delighted in mixing with these several ministers of commerce, as they are distinguished by their different walks and different languages: sometimes I am justled among a body of Armenians: sometimes I am lost in a crowd of Jews; and sometimes make one in a group of Dutchmen. I am a Dane, Swede, or Frenchman at different times, or rather fancy myself like the old philosopher,[4] who upon being asked what country-man he was, replied, that he was a citizen of the world.

Though I very frequently visit this busy multitude of people, I am known to nobody there but my friend Sir Andrew,[5] who often smiles upon me as he sees me bustling in the crowd, but at the same time connives at my presence without taking any further notice of me. There is indeed a merchant of Egypt, who just knows me by sight, having formerly remitted me some money to Grand Cairo; but as I am not versed in the modern Coptic, our conferences go no further than a bow and a grimace.[6]

This grand scene of business gives me an infinite variety of solid and substantial entertainments. As I am a great lover of mankind, my heart naturally overflows with pleasure at the sight of a prosperous and happy multitude, insomuch that at many public solemnities I cannot forbear expressing my joy with tears that have stolen down my cheeks. For this reason I am wonderfully delighted to see such a body of men thriving in their own private fortunes, and at the same time promoting the public stock; or in other words, raising estates

---

1. For Addison's career, see the Headnote to The Pleasures of the Imagination in the section entitled The Garden and the Wild.
2. Rebuilt in 1669 after the Great Fire as a large quadrangle of two stories surrounding a paved court; the interior of the court was lined with arched galleries and niches containing statues of the English monarchs, and in the center was a statue of Charles II as a Roman emperor.
3. The time of greatest activity.
4. Either Socrates or Diogenes the Cynic, to both of whom the remark has been attributed.
5. Sir Andrew Freeport, the merchant-hero of the *Spectator* (see note 1 to the Steele essay that follows).
6. Simply a nod or expression of cordiality.

for their own families, by bringing into their country whatever is wanting, and carrying out of it whatever is superfluous.

Nature seems to have taken a particular care to disseminate her blessings among the different regions of the world, with an eye to this mutual intercourse and traffic among mankind, that the natives of the several parts of the globe might have a kind of dependence upon one another, and be united together by their common interest. Almost every degree produces something peculiar to it. The food often grows in one country, and the sauce in another. The fruits of Portugal are corrected by the products of Barbadoes: the infusion of a China plant sweetened with the pith of an Indian cane. The Philippick [7] Islands give a flavour to our European bowls. The single dress of a woman of quality is often the product of an hundred climates. The muff and the fan come together from the different ends of the earth. The scarf is sent from the torrid zone, and the tippet [8] from beneath the Pole. The brocade petticoat rises out of the mines of Peru, and the diamond necklace out of the bowels of Indostan.

If we consider our own country in its natural prospect, without any of the benefits and advantages of commerce, what a barren uncomfortable spot of earth falls to our share! Natural historians tell us that no fruit grows originally among us, besides hips and haws, acorns and pig-nuts, with other delicacies of the like nature; that our climate of itself, and without the assistances of art, can make no further advances towards a plum than to a sloe, and carries an apple to no greater a perfection than a crab: that our melons, our peaches, our figs, our apricots, and cherries, are strangers among us, imported in different ages, and naturalized in our English gardens; and that they would all degenerate and fall away into the trash of our own country, if they were wholly neglected by the planter, and left to the mercy of our sun and soil.

Nor has traffic more enriched our vegetable world than it has improved the whole face of nature among us. Our ships are laden with the harvest of every climate: our tables are stored with spices, and oils, and wines: our rooms are filled with pyramids of China, and adorned with the workmanship of Japan: our morning's-draught comes to us from the remotest corners of the earth: we repair our bodies by the drugs of America, and repose ourselves under Indian canopies. My friend Sir Andrew calls the vineyards of France our gardens; the spice-islands our hot-beds; the Persians our silk-weavers, and the Chinese our potters. Nature indeed furnishes us with the bare necessaries of life, but traffic gives us a great variety of what is useful, and at the same time supplies us with every thing that is convenient and ornamental. Nor is it the least part of this our happiness, that whilst we enjoy the remotest products of the north and south, we are free from those extremities of weather which give them birth; that our eyes are refreshed with the green fields of Britain, at the same time that our palates are feasted with fruits that rise between the tropics.[9]

For these reasons there are not more useful members in a commonwealth

7. Philippine.
8. A fur garment for the neck and shoulders.
9. It is precisely this dependence upon worldwide commerce that such writers as Swift (in *A Modest Proposal*) and Goldsmith (in *The Deserted Village*) deplore as unnecessary luxury which the poor must be sacrificed to support.

than merchants. They knit mankind together in a mutual intercourse of good offices, distribute the gifts of nature, find work for the poor, add wealth to the rich, and magnificence to the great. Our English merchant converts the tin of his own country into gold, and exchanges his wool for rubies. The Mahometans are clothed in our British manufacture, and the inhabitants of the frozen zone warmed with the fleeces of our sheep.

When I have been upon the 'Change, I have often fancied one of our old kings standing in person, where he is represented in effigy, and looking down upon the wealthy concourse of people with which that place is every day filled. In this case, how would he be surprized to hear all the languages of Europe spoken in this little spot of his former dominions, and to see so many private men, who in his time would have been the vassals of some powerful baron, negotiating like princes for greater sums of money than were formerly to be met with in the royal treasury! Trade, without enlarging the British territories, has given us a kind of additional empire: it has multiplied the number of the rich, made our landed estates infinitely more valuable than they were formerly, and added to them an accession of other estates as valuable as the lands themselves.

[From *Spectator* No. 69, May 19, 1711]

RICHARD STEELE [1]

[The Hours of London]

It is an inexpressible pleasure to know a little of the world, and be of no character or significancy in it. To be ever unconcerned, and ever looking on new objects with an endless curiosity, is a delight known only to those who are turned for speculation: nay, they who enjoy it must value things only as they are the objects of speculation, without drawing any worldly advantage to themselves from them, but just as they are what contribute to their amusement, or the improvement of the mind. I lay one night last week at Richmond; and being restless, not out of dissatisfaction, but a certain busy inclination one sometimes has, I arose at four in the morning, and took boat for London, with a resolution to rove by boat and coach for the next four and twenty hours, till the many different objects I must needs meet with should tire my imagination, and give me an inclination to a repose more profound than I was at that time capable of. I beg people's pardon for an odd humour I am guilty of, and was often that day, which is saluting any person whom I like, whether I know him or not. This is a particularity would be tolerated in me, if they considered that the greatest pleasure I know I receive at my eyes, and that I am obliged to

1. Sir Richard Steele (1672–1729) was born in Dublin and studied at Oxford before entering army service. His literary career began with an early series (1701–5) of successful comedies, and in 1709 he began to edit a thrice-weekly paper, the *Tatler*, with the help of his school friend Joseph Addison. Both men edited the *Spectator* in 1711–12, and Steele moved increasingly into political journalism thereafter, defending Whig policies against such opponents as Jonathan Swift, winning the rewards of political office and (in 1715) a knighthood. Steele was a somewhat sentimental moralist and student of manners, and his attitudes find their best expression in his later comedy, *The Conscious Lovers* (1722).

an agreeable person for coming abroad into my view, as another is for the visit of conversation at their own houses.

The hours of the day and night are taken up, in the cities of London and Westminster, by people as different from each other as those who are born in different centuries. Men of six o'clock give way to those of nine, they of nine to the generation of twelve; and they of twelve disappear, and make room for the fashionable world, who have made two o'clock the noon of the day.

When we first put off from shore,[2] we soon fell in with a fleet of gardeners bound for the several market-ports of London; and it was the most pleasing scene imaginable to see the cheerfulness with which those industrious people plied their way to a certain sale of their goods. The banks on each side are as well peopled, and beautified with as agreeable plantations, as any spot on the earth; but the Thames itself, loaded with the product of each shore, added very much to the landscape. It was very easy to observe by their sailing, and the countenances of the ruddy virgins who were supercargoes,[3] the parts of the town to which they were bound. There was an air in the purveyors for Covent Garden, who frequently converse with morning rakes, very unlike the seemly sobriety of those bound for Stocks Market.[4]

Nothing remarkable happened in our voyage; but I landed with ten sail of apricot boats at Strand Bridge,[5] after having put in at Nine Elms, and taken in melons, consigned by Mr. Cuffe of that place, to Sarah Sewell and company, at their stall in Covent Garden. We arrived at Strand Bridge at six of the clock, and were unloading; when the hackney-coachmen of the foregoing night took their leave of each other at the Dark House,[6] to go to bed before the day was too far spent. Chimney-sweepers passed by us as we made [7] up to the market, and some raillery happened between one of the fruit-wenches and those black men, about the devil and Eve, with allusion to their several professions. I could not believe any place more entertaining than Covent Garden, where I strolled from one fruit-shop to another, with crowds of agreeable young women around me, who were purchasing fruit for their respective families. It was almost eight of the clock before I could leave that variety of objects. . . .

The day of people of fashion began now to break, and carts and hacks were mingled with equipages of show and vanity; when I resolved to walk it out of cheapness; but my unhappy curiosity is such that I find it always my interest to take coach, for some odd adventure among beggars, ballad-singers, or the like, detains and throws me into expense. It happened so immediately; for at the corner of Warwick Street, as I was listening to a new ballad, a ragged rascal, a beggar who knew me, came up to me, and began to turn the eyes of the good company upon me by telling me he was extreme poor, and should die in the streets for want of drink, except I immediately would have the charity to give him sixpence to go into the next alehouse and save his life. He urged, with a

2. Steele has spent the night at Richmond and boards a boat for London.
3. That is, carried as passengers.
4. A market for fish and meat on the site of the present Mansion House in the City of London, named for a pair of stocks once placed there for the punishment of criminals.
5. A landing place at the foot of Strand Lane.
6. The name derived from a one-time place of confinement for a madman.
7. Made our way.

melancholy face, that all his family had died of thirst. All the mob have humour, and two or three began to take the jest; by which Mr. Sturdy carried his point, and let me sneak off to a coach. As I drove along, it was a pleasing reflection to see the world so prettily chequered since I left Richmond, and the scene still filling with children of a new hour. This satisfaction increased as I moved towards the City; and gay signs, well-disposed streets, magnificent public structures, and wealthy shops, adorned with contented faces, made the joy still rising till we came into the centre of the City, and centre of the world of trade, the Exchange of London. As other men in the crowds about me were pleased with their hopes and bargains, I found my account in observing them in attention to their several interests. I, indeed, looked upon myself as the richest man that walked the Exchange that day; for my benevolence made me share the gains of every bargain that was made. It was not the least of the satisfactions in my survey to go upstairs, and pass the shops of agreeable females; to observe so many pretty hands busy in the foldings of ribands, and the utmost eagerness of agreeable faces in the sale of patches, pins, and wires, on each side the counters, was an amusement in which I should longer have indulged myself, had not the dear creatures called to me to ask what I wanted, when I could not answer only 'To look at you.' I went to one of the windows which opened to the area below, where all the several voices lost their distinction, and rose up in a confused humming; which created in me a reflection that could not come into the mind of any but of one a little too studious; for I said to myself, with a kind of pun in thought, 'What nonsense is all the hurry of this world to those who are above it?' In these or not much wiser thoughts I had like to have lost my place at the chop-house, where every man, according to the natural bashfulness or sullenness of our nation, eats in a public room a mess of broth, or chop of meat, in dumb silence, as if they had no pretence to speak to each other on the foot of being men, except they were of each other's acquaintance.

I went afterwards to Robin's,[8] and saw people who had dined with me at the fivepenny ordinary just before, give bills for the value of large estates; and could not but behold with great pleasure, property lodged in and transferred in a moment from such as would never be masters of half as much as is seemingly in them, and given from them every day they live. But before five in the afternoon I left the City, came to my common scene of Covent Garden, and passed the evening at Will's in attending the discourses of several sets of people, who relieved each other within my hearing on the subjects of cards, dice, love, learning, and politics. The last subject kept me till I heard the streets in the possession of the bellman, who had now the world to himself, and cried, 'Past two of clock.' This roused me from my seat, and I went to my lodging, led by a light,[9] whom I put into the discourse of his private economy, and made him give me an account of the charge, hazard, profit, and loss of a family that depended upon a link, with a design to end my trivial day with the generosity of sixpence, instead of a third part of that sum. When I came to my chamber I writ down these minutes; but was at a loss what instruction I should propose to my reader from the enumeration of so many insignificant

8. A coffeehouse in Exchange Alley.
9. A link man or hired torch-bearer.

matters and occurrences; and I thought it of great use, if they could learn with me to keep their minds open to gratification, and ready to receive it from anything it meets with. This one circumstance will make every face you see give you the satisfaction you now take in beholding that of a friend; will make every object a pleasing one; will make all the good which arrives to any man, an increase of happiness to yourself.

[From *Spectator* No. 454, August 11, 1712]

BERNARD MANDEVILLE
1670–1733

From The Fable of the Bees [1]

[Private Vices, Public Benefits]

. . . the merchant, that sends corn or cloth into foreign parts to purchase wines and brandies, encourages the growth or manufactory of his own country; he is a benefactor to navigation, increases the customs, and is many ways beneficial to the public; yet it is not to be denied, but that his greatest dependence is lavishness and drunkenness: For, if none were to drink wine but such only as stand in need of it, nor anybody more than his health required, that multitude of wine-merchants, vintners, coopers,[2] &c. that make such a considerable show in this flourishing city would be in a miserable condition. The same may be said not only of card and dice-makers that are the immediate ministers to a legion of vices, but of mercers,[3] upholsterers, tailors,

---

1. Bernard Mandeville, a Dutch physician, settled in London by 1699 and married an Englishwoman. In 1703 and 1704 he published fables in English verse, a burlesque poem *Typhon* in 1704, and in 1705 *The Grumbling Hive, or Knaves Turned Honest*. The last was a fable about a hive of bees that live in "luxury and ease" until a restless and quixotic desire for honesty destroys their society. "Then leave complaints," runs the moral; "fools only strive / To make a great and honest hive." In 1714 Mandeville reprinted this with a prose commentary under the title *The Fable of the Bees; or, Private Vices, Public Benefits*, and in subsequent years continued to amplify the prose. In 1723 the Grand Jury of Middlesex declared the book a public nuisance, but *The Fable* continued to appear and to grow in spite of much denunciation. Dr. Johnson declared that Mandeville "opened my views into real life very much," that his influence was great, if only in forcing men to modify their positions in both ethical and economic theory. For Mandeville pressed home the conflict between estimating motives and estimating consequences. Of his hive, he could write, "Thus every part was full of vice, / Yet the whole mass a paradise." So he could claim that a healthy society may require a measure of private selfishness (for he defines vice as meaning anything less than rigorous selflessness and adherence to virtue for its own sake), and he draws from this an attack upon those moral aspirations that underestimate or ignore the cost they exact. While he can be seen to support the mercantile spirit hailed by Addison and Steele, he does it without illusions of nobility and with a teasing awareness of the moral discomfort his paradox creates. In a sense, he recognizes the same conflicts that Swift explores, but his solution is simpler because he is ready to jettison more (although not without insisting upon the fact).
2. Barrel-makers.
3. Silk merchants.

and many others, that would be starved in half a year's time if pride and luxury were at once to be banished the nation. . . .

I shall be asked what benefit the public receives from thieves and house-breakers. They are, I own, very pernicious to human society, and every government ought to take all imaginable care to root out and destroy them; yet if all people were strictly honest, and nobody would meddle with or pry into anything but his own, half the smiths of the nation would want employment; and abundance of workmanship (which now serves for ornaments as well as defence) is to be seen everywhere both in town and country that would never have been thought of, but to secure us against the attempts of pilferers and robbers.

If what I have said be thought far-fetched, and my assertion seems still a paradox, I desire the reader to look upon the consumption of things, and he will find that the laziest and most unactive, the profligate and most mischievous, are all forced to do something for the common good; and whilst their mouths are not sewed up and they continue to wear and otherwise destroy what the industrious are daily employed about to make, fetch and procure, in spite of their teeth, obliged to help maintain the poor and the public charges. The labour of millions would soon be at an end, if there were not other millions, as I say, in the fable,

> . . . Employed,
> To see their handy-works destroyed.

But men are not to be judged by the consequences that may succeed their actions, but the facts themselves and the motives which it shall appear they acted from. If an ill-natured miser, who is almost a plum [4] and spends but fifty pounds a year, though he has no relation to inherit his wealth, should be robbed of five hundred or a thousand guineas, it is certain that as soon as this money should come to circulate, the nation would be the better for the robbery and receive the same and as real a benefit from it as if an archbishop had left the same sum to the public; yet justice and the peace of society require that he or they who robbed the miser should be hanged, though there were half a dozen of them concerned.

Thieves and pickpockets steal for a livelihood, and either what they can get honestly is not sufficient to keep them, or else they have an aversion to constant working: they want to gratify their senses, have victuals, strong drink, lewd women, and to be idle when they please. The victualler, who entertains them and takes their money, knowing which way they come at it, is very near as great a villain as his guests. But if he fleeces them well, minds his business, and is a prudent man, he may get money and be punctual with them he deals with. The trusty out-clerk, whose chief aim is his master's profit, sends him in what beer he wants and takes care not to lose his custom; while the man's money is good, he thinks it no business of his to examine whom he gets it by. In the meantime, the wealthy brewer, who leaves all the management to his servants, knows nothing of the matter, but keeps his coach, treats

4. A man worth £ 100,000.

his friends, and enjoys his pleasure with ease and a good conscience; he gets an estate, builds houses, and educates his children in plenty, without ever thinking on the labour which wretches perform, the shifts fools make, and the tricks knaves play to come at the commodity by the vast sale of which he amasses his great riches.

A highwayman having met with a considerable booty, gives a poor common harlot he fancies ten pounds to new-rig her from top to toe; is there a spruce mercer so conscientious that he will refuse to sell her a thread satin though he knew who she was? She must have shoes and stockings, gloves; the stay and mantua-maker,[5] the sempstress, the linen-draper,[6] all must get something by her, and a hundred different tradesmen dependent on those she laid her money out with may touch part of it before a month is at an end.

The generous gentleman, in the meantime, his money being near spent, ventured again on the road, but the second day having committed a robbery near Highgate, he was taken with one of his accomplices, and at the next sessions both were condemned and suffered the law. The money due on their conviction fell to three country fellows, on whom it was admirably well bestowed. One was an honest farmer, a sober painstaking man, but reduced by misfortunes; the summer before, by the mortality among the cattle, he had lost six cows out of ten, and now his landlord, to whom he owed thirty pounds, had seized on all his stock. The other was a day-labourer, who struggled hard with the world, had a sick wife at home, and several small children to provide for. The third was a gentleman's gardener, who maintained his father in prison, where, being bound [7] for a neighbour, he had lain for twelve pounds almost a year and a half; this act of filial duty was the more meritorious, because he had for some time been engaged to a young woman, whose parents lived in good circumstances, but would not give their consent before our gardener had fifty guineas of his own to show. They received above fourscore pounds each, which extricated every one of them out of the difficulties they laboured under, and made them, in their opinion, the happiest people in the world.

Nothing is more destructive, either in regard to the health or the vigilance and industry of the poor, than the infamous liquor, the name of which, derived from Juniper in Dutch, is now by frequent use and the laconic spirit of the nation from a word of middling length shrunk into a monosyllable, intoxicating Gin, that charms the unactive, the desperate and crazy of either sex, and makes the starving sot behold his rags and nakedness with stupid indolence, or banter both in senseless laughter and more insipid jests! It is a fiery lake that sets the brain in flame, burns up the entrails, and scorches every part within; and, at the same time, a Lethe [8] of oblivion, in which the wretch immersed drowns his most pinching cares and, with his reason, all anxious reflection on brats that cry for food, hard winter-frosts, and horrid empty home. . . .

Among the doting admirers of this liquid poison, many of the meanest rank, from a sincere affection to the commodity itself, become dealers in it, and

5. Dressmaker.
6. Merchant of linen goods.
7. Responsible for the debts of.
8. The river of Hades whose water produced loss of memory.

take delight to help others to what they love themselves, as whores commence bawds [9] to make the profits of one trade subservient to the pleasures of
the other. But as these starvelings commonly drink more than their gains, they
seldom, by selling, mend the wretchedness of condition they laboured under
while they were only buyers. In the fag-end [10] and outskirts of the town and
all places of the vilest resort, it is sold in some part or other of almost every
house, frequently in cellars, and sometimes in the garret. . . .

The vast number of the shops I speak of throughout the city and suburbs
are an astonishing evidence of the many seducers that, in a lawful occupation,
are accessory to the introduction and increase of all the sloth, sottishness, want,
and misery which the abuse of strong waters is the immediate cause of, to lift
above mediocrity perhaps half a score men that deal in the same commodity
by wholesale, while, among the retailers, though qualified as I required, a
much greater number are broke and ruined for not abstaining from the
Circean cup [11] they hold out to others, and the more fortunate are their whole
lifetime obliged to take the uncommon pains, endure the hardships, and
swallow all the ungrateful and shocking things I named, for little or nothing
beyond a bare sustenance and their daily bread.

The short-sighted vulgar [12] in the chain of-causes seldom can see further
than one link; but those who can enlarge their view and will give themselves
the leisure of gazing on the prospect of concatenated events may, in a hundred
places, see good spring up and pullulate from evil, as naturally as chickens do
from eggs. The money that arises from the duties upon malt is a considerable
part of the national revenue, and should no spirits be distilled from it, the
public treasure would prodigiously suffer on that head. But if we would set
in a true light the many advantages and large catalogue of solid blessings that
accrue from, and are owing to, the evil I treat of, we are to consider the rents
that are received, the ground that is tilled, the tools that are made, the cattle
that are employed, and above all, the multitude of poor that are maintained,
by the variety of labour required in husbandry, in malting, in carriage and
distillation, before we can have the product of malt which we call low wines,
and is but the beginning from which the various spirits are afterwards to be
made.

Besides this, a sharp-sighted good-humoured man might pick up abundance
of good from the rubbish, which I have all flung away for evil. He would tell
me, that whatever sloth and sottishness might be occasioned by the abuse of
malt-spirits, the moderate use of it was of inestimable benefit to the poor, who
could purchase no cordials of higher prices; that it was an universal comfort,
not only in cold and weariness, but most of the afflctions that are peculiar to
the necessitous, and had often to the most destitute supplied the places of
meat, drink, clothes, and lodging. That the stupid indolence in the most
wretched condition occasioned by those composing draughts, which I complained of, was a blessing to thousands, for that certainly those were the
happiest, who felt the least pain. As to diseases, he would say, that, as it

9. Keepers of brothels.
10. Shabby quarters.
11. Whose contents turned men to swine.
12. Mob, common people.

caused some, so it cured others, and that if the excess in those liquors had been sudden death to some few, the habit of drinking them daily prolonged the lives of many, whom once it agreed with; that for the loss sustained from the insignificant quarrels it created at home, we were overpaid in the advantage we received from it abroad, by upholding the courage of soldiers, and animating the sailors to the combat. . . .

If I should ever urge to him that to have here and there one great and eminent distiller was a poor equivalent for the vile means, the certain want, and lasting misery of so many thousand wretches as were necessary to raise them, he would answer that of this I could be no judge, because I do not know what vast benefit they might afterwards be of to the commonwealth. Perhaps, would he say, the man thus raised will exert himself in the commission of the peace or other station with vigilance and zeal against the dissolute and disaffected, and, retaining his stirring temper, be as industrious in spreading loyalty and the reformation of manners throughout every cranny of the wide populous town as once he was in filling it with spirits; till he becomes at last the scourge of whores, of vagabonds and beggars, the terror of rioters and discontented rabbles, and constant plague to sabbath-breaking butchers. Here my good-humoured antagonist would exult and triumph over me, especially if he could instance to me such a bright example; what an uncommon blessing, would he cry out, is this man to his country! how shining and illustrious his virtue!

To justify his exclamation, he would demonstrate to me that it was impossible to give a fuller evidence of self-denial in a grateful mind than to see him, at the expence of his quiet and hazard of his life and limbs, be always harassing, and even for trifles persecuting, that very class of men to whom he owes his fortune, from no other motive than his aversion to idleness and great concern for religion and the public welfare. . . .

Who would imagine that virtuous women, unknowingly, should be instrumental in promoting the advantage of prostitutes? Or (what still seems the greater paradox) that incontinence should be made serviceable to the preservation of chastity? and yet nothing is more true. A vicious young fellow, after having been an hour or two at church, a ball, or any other assembly, where there is a great parcel of handsome women dressed to the best advantage, will have his imagination more fired than if he had the same time been polling at Guildhall [13] or walking in the country among a flock of sheep. The consequence of this is that he will strive to satisfy the appetite that is raised in him; and when he find honest women obstinate and uncomatable,[14] it is very natural to think that he will hasten to others that are more compliable. Who would so much as surmise that this is the fault of the virtuous women? They have no thoughts of men in dressing themselves, poor souls, and endeavour only to appear clean and decent, every one according to her quality. . . .

[The Theory of Virtue]
I expect to be asked why in the fable I have called those pleasures real that are directly opposite to those which I own the wise men of all ages have

13. Voting for Parliament.
14. That is, un-come-at-able.

extolled as the most valuable? My answer is, because I do not call things pleasures which men say are best, but such as they seem to be most pleased with; how can I believe that a man's chief delight is in the embellishments of the mind when I see him ever employed about and daily pursue the pleasures that are contrary to them? John never cuts any pudding, but just enough that you can't say he took none; this little bit, after much chomping and chewing, you see goes down with him like chopped hay; after that he falls upon the beef with a voracious appetite and crams himself up to his throat. Is it not provoking to hear John cry every day that pudding is all his delight and that he don't value the beef of a farthing?

I could swagger about fortitude and the contempt of riches as much as Seneca [15] himself and would undertake to write twice as much in behalf of poverty as ever he did; for the tenth part of his estate, I could teach the way to his *summum bonum* [16] as exactly as I know my way home. I could tell people to extricate themselves from all worldly engagements; and to purify the mind they must divest themselves of their passions, as men take out the furniture when they would clean a room thoroughly; and I am clearly of the opinion that the malice and most severe strokes of fortune can do no more injury to a mind thus stripped of all fears, wishes, and inclinations, than a blind horse can do in an empty barn. In the theory of all this I am very perfect, but the practice is very difficult; and if you went about picking my pocket, offered to take the victuals from before me when I am hungry, or made but the least motion of spitting in my face, I dare not promise how philosophically I should behave myself. But that I am forced to submit to every caprice of my unruly nature, you will say, is no argument that others are as little masters of theirs, and therefore I am willing to pay adoration to virtue whenever I can meet with it, with a proviso that I shall not be obliged to admit any as such where I can see no self-denial, or to judge of men's sentiments from their words where I have their lives before me. . . .

What must we do in this dilemma? Shall we be so uncharitable as, judging from men's actions, to say that all the world prevaricates and that this is not their opinion, let them talk what they will? Or shall we be so silly as, relying on what they say, to think them sincere in their sentiments and so not believe our own eyes? Or shall we rather endeavour to believe ourselves and them too, and say with Montaigne that they imagine and are fully persuaded that they believe what they do not believe? These are his words: 'Some impose on the world and would be thought to believe what they really do not: but much the greater number impose upon themselves, not considering, nor thoroughly apprehending what it is to believe.' But this is making all mankind either fools or imposters, which, to avoid, there is nothing left us but to say what Mr. Bayle [17] has endeavoured to prove at large in his Reflections on Comets: 'that man is so unaccountable a creature as to act most commonly against his principle'; and this is so far from being injurious that it is a compliment to human nature, for we must say either this or worse.

15. Lucius Annaeus Seneca (3. b.c.–65 a.d.) the Roman Stoic philosopher, who wrote eloquently on poverty although he amassed a huge fortune.
16. "Highest good" (the moral end of man).
17. Pierre Bayle (1647–1706), French skeptical philosopher, who had a great influence on Mandeville.

This contradiction in the frame of man is the reason that the theory of virtue is so well understood and the practice of it so rarely to be met with. If you ask me where to look for those beautiful shining qualities of prime ministers and the great favourites of princes that are so finely painted in dedications, addresses, epitaphs, funeral sermons, and inscriptions, I answer, there, and nowhere else. Where would you look for the excellency of a statue but in that part which you see of it? It is the polished outside only that has the skill and labour of the sculptor to boast of; what is out of sight is untouched. Would you break the head or cut open the breast to look for the brains or the heart, you would only show your ignorance and destroy the workmanship. This has often made me compare the virtues of great men to your large China jars: they make a fine show, and are ornamental even to a chimney; one would, by the bulk they appear in and the value that is set upon them, think they might be very useful, but look into a thousand of them, and you will find nothing in them but dust and cobwebs. . . .

[The Violence of Luxury]

If we trace the most flourishing nations in their origin, we shall find, that in the remote beginnings of every society, the richest and most considerable men among them were a great while destitute of a great many comforts of life that are now enjoyed by the meanest and most humble wretches: so that many things which were once looked upon as the invention of luxury are now allowed even to those that are so miserably poor as to become the objects of public charity, nay, counted so necessary, that we think no human creature ought to want them.

In the first ages, man, without doubt, fed on the fruits of the earth without any previous preparation, and reposed himself naked like other animals on the lap of their common parent. Whatever has contributed since to make life more comfortable, as it must have been the result of thought, experience, and some labour, so it more or less deserves the name of luxury, the more or less trouble it required, and deviated from the primitive simplicity. Our admiration is extended no farther than to what is new to us, and we all overlook the excellency of things we are used to, be they never so curious. A man would be laughed at that should discover luxury in the plain dress of a poor creature that walks along in a thick parish gown and a coarse shirt underneath it; and yet what a number of people, how many different trades, and what a variety of skill and tools must be employed to have the most ordinary Yorkshire cloth? What depth of thought and ingenuity, what toil and labour, and what length of time must it have cost before man could learn from a seed to raise and prepare so useful a product as linen.

Must that society not be vainly curious, among whom this admirable commodity, after it is made, shall not be thought fit to be used even by the poorest of all before it is brought to a perfect whiteness, which is not to be procured but by the assistance of all the elements joined to a world of industry and patience? I have not done yet: can we reflect not only on the cost laid out upon this luxurious invention, but likewise on the little time the whiteness of it continues, in which part of its beauty consists, that every six or seven days at farthest it wants cleaning, and while it lasts is a continual charge to the wearer;

can we, I say, reflect on all this and not think it an extravagant piece of nicety that even those who receive alms of the parish should not only have whole garments made of this operose [18] manufacture, but likewise that as soon as they are soiled, to restore them to their pristine purity, they should make use of one of the most judicious as well as difficult compositions that chemistry can boast of; with which, dissolved in water by the help of fire, the most detersive and yet innocent lixivium [19] is prepared that human industry has hitherto been able to invent?

It is certain, time was that the things I speak of would have bore those lofty expressions, and in which everybody would have reasoned after the same manner; but the age we live in would call a man fool who should talk of extravagance and nicety if he saw a poor woman, after having wore her crown cloth smock a whole week, wash it with a bit of stinking soap of a groat a pound. . . .

In what concerns the fashions and manners of the ages men live in, they never examine into the real worth or merit of the cause and generally judge of things not as their reason but custom direct them. Time was when the funeral rites in the disposing of the dead were performed by fire and the cadavers of the greatest emperors were burnt to ashes. Then burying the corpse in the ground was a funeral for slaves or made a punishment for the worst of male-factors. Now nothing is decent or honourable but interring; and burning the body is reserved for crimes of the blackest dye. At some times we look upon trifles with horror, at other times we can behold enormities without concern. . . .

I have often thought, if it was not for this tyranny which custom usurps over us, that men of any tolerable good-nature could never be reconciled to the killing of so many animals for their daily food, as long as the bountiful earth so plentifully provides them with varieties of vegetable dainties. I know that reason excites our compassion but faintly, and therefore I would not wonder how men should so little commiserate such imperfect creatures as crayfish, oysters, cockles, and indeed all fish in general. . . . But in such perfect animals as sheep and oxen, in whom the heart, the brain and nerves differ so little from ours, and in whom the separation of the spirits from the blood, the organs of sense, and consequently feeling itself, are the same as they are in human creatures; I cannot imagine how a man not hardened in blood and massacre is able to see a violent death, and the pangs of it, without concern.

In answer to this, most people will think it sufficient to say that all things being allowed to be made for the service of man, there can be no cruelty in putting creatures to the use they were designed for; but I have heard men make this reply while their nature within them has reproached them with the falsehood of the assertion. There is of all the multitude not one man in ten but what will own (if he was not brought up in a slaughter-house) that of all trades he could never have been a butcher; and I question whether ever anybody so much as killed a chicken without reluctancy the first time. Some

18. Laborious.
19. A lye solution used as a detergent ("detersive")

people are not to be persuaded to taste of any creatures they have daily seen and been acquainted with while they were alive; others extend their scruple no further than to their own poultry and refuse to eat what they fed and took care of themselves; yet all of them will feed heartily and without remorse on beef, mutton, and fowls when they are bought in the market. In this behaviour, methinks, there appears something like a consciousness of guilt; it looks as if they endeavoured to save themselves from the imputation of a crime (which they know sticks somewhere) by removing the cause of it as far as they can from themselves; and I can discover in it some strong remains of primitive pity and innocence, which all the arbitrary power of custom and the violence of luxury have not yet been able to conquer. . . .

[The Dream of Simplicity]

When people have small comings in and are honest withal, it is then that the generality of them begin to be frugal, and not before. Frugality in ethics is called that virtue from the principle of which men abstain from superfluities and, despising the operose contrivances of art to procure either case of pleasure, content themselves with the natural simplicity of things and are carefully temperate in the enjoyment of them, without any tincture of covetousness. Frugality thus limited is perhaps scarcer than many may imagine; but what is generally understood by it is a quality more often to be met with, and consists in a medium between profuseness and avarice, rather leaning to the latter. As this prudent economy, which some people call saving, is in private families the most certain method to increase an estate, so some imagine that whether a country be barren or fruitful, the same method, if generally pursued (which they think practicable), will have the same effect upon a whole nation, and that, for example, the English might be much richer than they are if they would be as frugal as some of their neighbours. This, I think, is an error. . . .

Experience teaches us first that as people differ in their views and perceptions of things, so they vary in their inclinations; one man is given to covetousness, another to prodigality, and a third is only saving. Secondly, that men are never, or at least, very seldom, reclaimed from their darling passions, either by reason or precept, and that if anything ever draws them from what they are naturally propense to, it must be a change in their circumstances or their fortunes. If we reflect upon these observations, we shall find that to render the generality of a nation lavish, the product of the country must be considerable in proportion to the inhabitants, and what they are profuse of cheap; that, on the contrary, to make a nation generally frugal, the necessaries of life must be scarce, and consequently dear; and that, therefore, let the best politician do what he can, the profuseness or frugality of a people in general must always depend upon and will, in spite of his teeth, be ever proportioned to the fruitfulness and product of the country, the number of inhabitants, and the taxes they are to bear. If anybody would refute what I have said, let them only prove from history that there ever was in any country a national frugality without a national necessity.

Let us examine then what things are requisite to aggrandize and enrich a nation. The first desirable blessings for any society of men are a fertile soil, and a happy climate, a mild government, and more land than people. These things will render man easy, loving, honest, and sincere. In this condition they may be as virtuous as they can, without the least injury to the public, and consequently as happy as they please among themselves. But they shall have no arts or sciences or be quiet longer than their neighbours will let them; they must be poor, ignorant, and almost wholly destitute of what we call the comforts of life, and all the cardinal virtues together won't so much as procure a tolerable coat or a porridge-pot among them; for in this state of slothful ease and stupid innocence, as you need not fear great vices, so you must not expect any considerable virtues. Man never exerts himself but when he is roused by his desires; while they lie dormant, and there is nothing to raise them, his excellence and abilities will be forever undiscovered, and the lumpish machine, without the influence of his passions, may be justly compared to a huge windmill without a breath of air.

Would you render a society of men strong and powerful, you must touch their passions. Divide the land, though there be never so much to spare, and their possessions will make them covetous; rouse them, though but in jest, from their idleness with praises, and pride will set them to work in earnest; teach them trades and handicrafts, and you will bring envy and emulation among them; to increase their numbers, set up a variety of manufactures and leave no ground uncultivated; let property be inviolably secured and privileges equal to all men; suffer nobody to act but what is lawful and everybody to think what he pleases; for a country where everybody may be maintained that will be employed, and the other maxims are observed, must always be thronged and can never want people, as long as there is any in the world. Would you have them bold and warlike, turn to military discipline, make good use of their fear, and flatter their vanity with art and assiduity; but would you, moreover, render them an opulent, knowing, and polite nation, teach them commerce with foreign countries, and, if possible, get into the sea, which to compass spare no labour nor industry, and let no difficulty deter you from it; then promote navigation, cherish the merchant, and encourage trade in every branch of it; this will bring riches, and where they are, arts and sciences will soon follow; and by the help of what I have named and good management, it is that politicians can make a people potent, renowned, and flourishing.

But would you have a frugal and honest society, the best policy is to preserve men in their native simplicity, strive not to increase their numbers; let them never be acquainted with strangers or superfluities, but remove and keep from them everything that might raise their desires or improve their understanding.

Great wealth and foreign treasure will ever scorn to come among men, unless you'll admit their inseparable companions, avarice and luxury; where trade is considerable, fraud will intrude. To be at once well-bred and sincere is no less than a contradiction; and therefore, while man advances in knowledge and his manners are polished, we must expect to see, at the same time, his desires enlarged, his appetites refined, and his vices increased. . . .

                                                                    1714, 1723

DANIEL DEFOE
c. 1660–1731

From The Fortunes and Misfortunes of the Famous Moll Flanders [1]

I went out now by daylight, and wandered about I knew not whither, and in search of I knew not what, when the devil put a snare in my way of a dreadful nature indeed, and such a one as I have never had before or since. Going through Aldersgate Street, there was a pretty little child who had been at a dancing-school, and was going home, all alone; and my prompter, like a true devil, set me upon this innocent creature. I talked to it, and it prattled to me again, and I took it by the hand and led it along till I came to a paved alley that goes into Bartholomew Close, and I led it in there. The child said that was not its way home. I said, 'Yes, my dear, it is; I'll show you the way home.' The child had a little necklace on of gold beads, and I had my eye upon that, and in the dark of the alley I stooped, pretending to mend the child's clog that was loose, and took off her necklace, and the child never felt it, and so led the child on again. Here, I say, the devil put me upon killing the child in the dark alley, that it might not cry, but the very thought frighted me so that I was ready to drop down; but I turned the child about and bade it go back again, for that was not its way home. The child said, so she would, and I went through into Bartholomew Close, and then turned round to another passage that goes into Long Lane, so away into Charterhouse Yard and out into St. John Street; then, crossing into Smithfield, went down Chick Lane and into Field Lane to Holborn Bridge, when, mixing with the crowd of people usually passing there, it was not possible to have been found out; and thus I enterprised my second sally into the world.

The thoughts of this booty put out all the thoughts of the first, and the reflections I had made wore quickly off; poverty, as I have said, hardened my heart, and my own necessities made me regardless of anything. The last affair left no great concern upon me, for as I did the poor child no harm, I only said to myself, I had given the parents a just reproof for their negligence in leaving the poor little lamb to come home by itself, and it would teach them to take more care of it another time.

This string of beads was worth about twelve or fourteen pounds. I suppose it might have been formerly the mother's, for it was too big for the child's wear, but that perhaps the vanity of the mother, to have her child look fine at the dancing-school, had made her let the child wear it; and no doubt the child had a maid sent to take care of it, but she, careless jade, was taken up perhaps with some fellow that had met her by the way, and so the poor baby wandered till it fell into my hands.

However, I did the child no harm; I did not so much as fright it, for I had a great many tender thoughts about me yet, and did nothing but what, as I may say, mere necessity drove me to.

1. The second of Defoe's great novels deals with a woman in reduced circumstances who, after unsuccessful efforts to remarry to advantage, turns to crime, gains notoriety as a thief, and eventually repents and reforms. This episode presents Moll Flanders' second act of theft.

HENRY FIELDING

1707–1754

From A Modern Glossary [1]

ANGEL   The name of a woman, commonly of a very bad one.

BEAR   A country gentleman; or, indeed, any animal upon two legs that doth not make a handsome bow.

BEAUTY   The qualification with which women generally go into keeping.

BRUTE   A word implying plain-dealing and sincerity, but more especially applied to a philosopher.

CAPTAIN ⎫   Any stick of wood with a head to it, and a piece of black
COLONEL ⎭   ribband upon that head.

COXCOMB   A word of reproach, and yet, at the same time, signifying all that is most commendable.

DEATH   The final end of man; as well of the *thinking part of the body* as of all the other parts.

DRESS   The principal accomplishment of men and women.

DULNESS   A word applied by all writers to the wit and humour of others.

EATING   A science.

FINE   An adjective of a very peculiar kind, destroying, or, at least, lessening the force of the substantive to which it is joined: as *fine* gentlemen, *fine* lady, *fine* house, *fine* clothes, *fine* taste;—in all which *fine* is to be understood in a sense somewhat synonymous with useless.

GALLANTRY   Fornication and adultery.

GREAT   Applied to a thing, signifies bigness; when to a man, often littleness, or meanness.

HONOUR   Duelling.

LOVE   A word properly applied to our delight in particular kinds of food; sometimes metaphorically spoken of the favourite objects of all our *appetites.*

MARRIAGE   A kind of traffic carried on between the two sexes, in which both are constantly endeavouring to cheat each other, and both are commonly losers in the end.

MODESTY   Awkwardness, rusticity.

NOBODY   All the people in Great Britain, except about 1200.

PATRIOT   A candidate for a place at court.

POLITICS   The art of getting such a place.

RELIGION   A word of no meaning; but which serves as a bugbear to frighten children with.

RICHES   The only thing upon earth that is really valuable or desirable.

ROGUE ⎫
RASCAL ⎭   A man of a different party from yourself.

SUNDAY   The best time for playing at cards.

SHOCKING   An epithet which fine ladies apply to almost everything. It is, indeed, an interjection (if I may so call it) of delicacy.

1. See note 1 on Fielding to the selection from Fielding's *Jonathan Wild* that follows John Gay's *The Beggar's Opera.* This comes from his later journalism, written after the last of his novels, *Amelia,* had appeared (1751).

TASTE   The present whim of the town, whatever it be.

VIRTUE ⎱
VICE   ⎰   Subjects of discourse.

[From *The Covent-Garden Journal*, No. 4, January 14, 1752]

JAMES BOSWELL
1740–1795

Boswell's father was the eighth Laird of Auchinleck, a distinguished jurist, and a man with a strong feeling for the continuity of his family. His eldst son James resisted a legal career but agreed to prepare for the bar before going to London to obtain a commission in a fashionable regiment. Self-indulgent, capricious, and eager for literary fame, James Boswell danced at the end of a tether. His efforts to obtain a commission failed, and he won only a deferment of his legal career in the form of a grand tour of the Continent. Before he left London, however, he met Samuel Johnson, to whom he turned as a more tolerant and affectionate paternal authority. Johnson's influence re-inforced, even if it moderated, his father's, and Boswell—in spite of an early literary success with his *Account of Corsica* (1768), based on a visit to the heroic defender of liberty, General Paoli—settled into a legal career in Scotland, breaking out of its confinement only in bouts of self-indulgence and, more important, in the remarkable journal he kept with Johnson's approval. The extracts from the journal show him in his early London years, in his swaggering but somewhat timid visit to Rousseau, and in a typically reflective moment during a darker and later phase. But the journals were also to yield the brilliant account of his 1773 tour of the Hebrides with Johnson, and the success of its publication the year after Johnson's death encouraged him to complete the great *Life* four years before his own death.

It is only in recent years, since the discovery and publication of his journals, that Boswell has come to be recognized as a major literary artist. His openness to every nuance of feeling, his delicacy in capturing (with something of Sterne's skill) fugitive sentiments and revealing gestures, his comic self-regard and (at times) self-contempt—all these have transformed the earlier view of Boswell as alternately a servile buffoon and a mere camera eye. Clearly he induced Johnson's characteristic postures and declarations just as he induced his own, with bold experimental curiosity and a willingness to record what others repress. At times he may have lived in order to record and acted in order to be able to study himself; his journal, as Frederick Pottle has shown, is a fascinating compromise between the freshness of emerging experience and the ironic hindsight of a recorder who (with the advantage of a few days' delay and a concealed knowledge of what will ensue) can intensify naïve expectation and the shock of the real.

From the *Life* a number of extracts have been chosen to illustrate the range of techniques (as well as to suggest the dimensions of the Johnson who is, however real, a work of Boswell's imagination): the reconstruction of Johnson's early life, the dramatic encounters which Boswell attended, the final retrospective view (of which an earlier version had appeared in the Hebrides *Tour*).

From The Journals [1]
[1762–63: Farewell to Louisa]

Wednesday 22 December I stood and chatted a while with the sentries before Buckingham House. One of them, an old fellow, said he was in all the last war. 'At the battle of Dettingen,' said he, 'I saw our cannon make a lane through the French army as broad as that' (pointing to the Mall), 'which was filled up in as short time as I'm telling you it.' They asked me for a pint of beer, which I gave them. I talked on the sad mischief of war and on the frequency of poverty. 'Why, Sir,' said he, 'GOD made all right at first when he made mankind. ('I believe,' said the other, 'he made but few of them.') But, Sir, if GOD was to make the world today, it would be crooked again tomorrow. But the time will come when we shall all be rich enough. To be sure, salvation is promised to those that die in the field.' I have great pleasure in conversing with the lower part of mankind, who have very curious ideas.

This forenoon I went to Louisa's [2] in full expectation of consummate bliss. I was in a strange flutter of feeling. I was ravished at the prospect of joy, and yet I had such an anxiety upon me that I was afraid that my powers would be enervated. I almost wished to be free of this assignation. I entered her apartment in a sort of confusion. She was elegantly dressed in the morning fashion, and looked delightfully well. I felt the tormenting anxiety of serious love. I sat down and I talked with the distance of a new acquaintance and not with the ease and ardour of a lover, or rather a gallant. I talked of her lodgings being neat, opened the door of her bedchamber, looked into it. Then sat down by her in a most melancholy plight. I would have given a good deal to be out of the room.

We talked of religion. Said she, 'People who deny that, show a want of sense.' 'For my own part, Madam, I look upon the adoration of the Supreme Being as one of the greatest enjoyments we have. I would not choose to get rid of my religious notions. I have read books that staggered me. But I was glad to find myself regain my former opinions.' 'Nay, Sir, what do you think of the Scriptures having stood the test of ages?' 'Are you a Roman Catholic, Madam?' 'No, Sir. Though I like some parts of their religion, in particular, confession; not that I think the priest can remit sins, but because the notion that we are to confess to a decent clergyman may make us cautious what we do.' 'Madam,' said I, 'I would ask you to do nothing that you should be sorry to confess. Indeed I have a great deal of principle in matters of gallantry, and never yet led any woman to do what might afterwards make her uneasy. If she thinks it wrong, I never insist.' She asked me some questions about my intrigues, which I nicely eluded.

1. Boswell's journals, which have been recovered only in the 20th century, provide an extraordinary record of a man of intense sensibility and remarkable candor of self-analysis. The first excerpt is from the London Journal, which records Boswell's futile quest for a commission, his first meeting with Johnson, and his eventual departure for Holland. The second excerpt, drawn from the record of the grand tour, records Boswell's visit to Rousseau in Switzerland. The third, which takes us beyond the time of the tour of the Hebrides, shows a typical instance of the metaphysical concerns that troubled him throughout his life.
2. Louisa was Mrs. Lewis, an actress, of whom little is known but her relationship with Boswell.

I then sat near her and began to talk softly, but finding myself quite dejected with love, I really cried out and told her that I was miserable; and as I was stupid, would go away. I rose, but saluting her with warmth, my powers were excited, I felt myself vigorous. I sat down again. I beseeched her, 'You know, Madam, you said you was not a Platonist. I beg it of you to be so kind. You said you are above the finesse of your sex.' (Be sure always to make a woman better than her sex.) 'I adore you.' 'Nay, dear Sir' (I pressing her to me and kissing her now and then), 'pray be quiet. Such a thing requires time to consider of.' 'Madam, I own this would be necessary for any man but me. But you must take my character from myself. I am very good-tempered, very honest, and have little money. I should have some reward for my particular honesty.' 'But, Sir, give me time to recollect myself.' 'Well then, Madam, when shall I see you?' 'On Friday, Sir.' 'A thousand thanks.' I left her and came home and took my bread and cheese with great contentment. . . .

Thursday 20 January   I then went to Louisa.[3] With excellent address did I carry on this interview, as the following scene, I trust, will make appear.

LOUISA   My dear Sir! I hope you are well today.

BOSWELL   Excessively well, I thank you. I hope I find you so.

LOUISA   No, really, Sir. I am distressed with a thousand things. (Cunning jade, her circumstances!) I really don't know what to do.

BOSWELL   Do you know that I have been very unhappy since I saw you?

LOUISA   How so, Sir?

BOSWELL   Why, I am afraid that you don't love me so well, nor have not such a regard for me, as I thought you had.

LOUISA   Nay, dear Sir! (Seeming unconcerned.)

BOSWELL   Pray, Madam, have I no reason?

LOUISA   No, indeed, Sir, you have not.

BOSWELL   Have I no reason, Madam? Pray think.

LOUISA   Sir!

BOSWELL   Pray, Madam, in what state of health have you been in for some time?

LOUISA   Sir, you amaze me.

BOSWELL   I have but too strong, too plain reason to doubt of your regard. I have for some days observed the symptoms of disease, but was unwilling to believe you so very ungenerous. But now, Madam, I am thoroughly convinced.

LOUISA   Sir, you have terrified me. I protest I know nothing of the matter.

BOSWELL   Madam, I have had no connection with any woman but you these two months. I was with my surgeon this morning, who declared I had got a strong infection, and that she from whom I had it could not be ignorant of it. Madam, such a thing in this case is worse than from a woman of the town, as from her you may expect it. You have used me very ill. I did not deserve it. You know you said where there was no confidence, there was no breach of trust. But surely I placed some confidence in you. I am sorry that I was mistaken.

---

3. On January 18 Boswell first discovers "a little heat in the members of my body sacred to Cupid," and on January 19, "Too, too plain was Signor Gonorrhoea."

LOUISA   Sir, I will confess to you that about three years ago I was very bad. But for these fifteen months I have been quite well. I appeal to GOD Almighty that I am speaking true; and for these six months I have had to do with no man but yourself.

BOSWELL   But by G—D, Madam, I have been with none but you, and here am I very bad.

LOUISA   Well, Sir, by the same solemn oath I protest that I was ignorant of it.

BOSWELL   Madam, I wish much to believe you. But I own I cannot upon this occasion believe a miracle.

LOUISA   Sir, I cannot say more to you. But you will leave me in the greatest misery. I shall lose your esteem. I shall be hurt in the opinion of everybody, and in my circumstances.

BOSWELL   (to himself) What the devil does the confounded jilt mean by being hurt in her circumstances? This is the grossest cunning. But I won't take notice of that at all.—Madam, as to the opinion of everybody, you need not be afraid. I was going to joke and say that I never boast of a lady's *favours*. But I give you my word of honour that you shall not be discovered.

LOUISA   Sir, this is being more generous than I could expect.

BOSWELL   I hope, Madam, you will own that since I have been with you I have always behaved like a man of honour.

LOUISA   You have indeed, Sir.

BOSWELL   (rising) Madam, your most obedient servant.

During all this conversation I really behaved with a manly composure and polite dignity that could not fail to inspire an awe, and she was pale as ashes and trembled and faltered. Thrice did she insist on my staying a little longer, as it was probably the last time that I should be with her. She could say nothing to the purpose. And I sat silent. As I was going, said she, 'I hope, Sir, you will give me leave to inquire after your health.' 'Madam,' said I, archly, 'I fancy it will be needless for some weeks.' She again renewed her request. But unwilling to be plagued any more with her, I put her off by saying I might perhaps go to the country, and left her. I was really confounded at her behaviour. There is scarcely a possibility that she could be innocent of the crime of horrid imposition. And yet her positive asseverations really stunned me. She is in all probability a most consummate dissembling whore.

Thus ended my intrigue with the fair Louisa, which I flattered myself so much with, and from which I expected at least a winter's safe copulation. It is indeed very hard. I cannot say, like young fellows who get themselves clapped in a bawdy-house, that I will take better care again. For I really did take care. However, since I am fairly trapped, let me make the best of it. I have not got it from imprudence. It is merely the chance of war.

I then called at Drury Lane for Mr. Garrick.[4] He was vastly good to me. 'Sir,' said he, 'you will be a very great man. And when you are so, remember the year 1763. I want to contribute my part towards saving you. And pray, will you fix a day when I shall have the pleasure of treating you with tea?' I

---

4. David Garrick (1717–79), Johnson's former pupil who was recognized early as the finest actor in England.

fixed next day. 'Then, Sir,' said he, 'the cups shall dance and the saucers skip.'

What he meant by my being a great man I can understand. For really, to speak seriously, I think there is a blossom about me of something more distinguished than the generality of mankind. But I am much afraid that this blossom will never swell into fruit, but will be nipped and destroyed by many a blighting heat and chilling frost. Indeed, I sometimes indulge noble reveries of having a regiment, of getting into Parliament, making a figure, and becoming a man of consequence in the state. But these are checked by dispiriting reflections on my melancholy temper and imbecility [5] of mind. Yet I may probably become sounder and stronger as I grow up. Heaven knows. I am resigned. I trust to Providence. I was quite in raptures with Garrick's kindness —the man whom from a boy I used to adore and look upon as a heathen god —to find him paying me so much respect! How amiable is he in comparison of Sheridan! [6] I was this day with him what the French call *un étourdi*.[7] I gave free vent to my feelings. Love [8] was by, to whom I cried, 'This, Sir, is the real scene.' And taking Mr. Garrick cordially by the hand, 'Thou greatest of men,' said I, 'I cannot express how happy you make me.' This, upon my soul, was no flattery. He saw it was not. And the dear great man was truly pleased with it. This scene gave me a charming flutter of spirits and dispelled my former gloom.

[1764: The Visit to Rousseau [9]]

Monday 3 December   To prepare myself for the great interview, I walked out alone. I strolled pensive by the side of the river Reuse in a beautiful wild valley surrounded by immense mountains, some covered with frowning rocks, others with clustering pines, and others with glittering snow. The fresh, healthful air and the romantic prospect around me gave me a vigorous and solemn tone. I recalled all my former ideas of J. J. Rousseau, the admiration with which he is regarded over all Europe, his *Héloïse, his Émile:* in short, a crowd of great thoughts. This half hour was one of the most remarkable that I ever passed.

I returned to my inn, and the maid delivered to me a card with the following answer from Monsieur Rousseau: 'I am ill, in pain, really in no state to receive visits. Yet I cannot deprive myself of Mr. Boswell's, provided that out of consideration for the state of my health, he is willing to make it short.'

My sensibility dreaded the word 'short.' But I took courage, and went im-

5. Stupefaction.
6. Thomas Sheridan (1719–88), actor and teacher of elocution.
7. A giddy creature.
8. James Love, an English actor who had given Boswell lessons in elocution.
9. Jean Jacques Rousseau was at the height of his fame, but he was under steady pressure from authority. Having left Paris to settle in Switzerland, he found that the Genevan authorities sought his expulsion; he took refuge in the mountain village of Môtiers in the independent territory of Neuchâtel. He was living in retirement when Boswell visited him, attended by Rousseau's mistress Thérèse Le Vasseur (then 43, in spite of Boswell's impression). (For excerpts from Rousseau's posthumously published *Confessions*, see below, Sense and Sensibility.) The text of Boswell's conversation was written in his journal in French, and this translated text (in large part the work of Geoffrey Scott) is reprinted from the edition of Frederick A. Pottle.

mediately. I found at the street door Mademoiselle Le Vasseur waiting for me. She was a little, lively, neat French girl and did not increase my fear. She conducted me up a darkish stair, then opened a door. I expected, 'Now I shall see him'—but it was not so. I entered a room which serves for vestibule and for kitchen. My fancy formed many, many a portrait of the wild philosopher. At length his door opened and I beheld him, a genteel black man in the dress of an Armenian. I entered saying, 'Many, many thanks.' After the first looks and bows were over, he said, 'Will you be seated? Or would you rather take a turn with me in the room?' I chose the last, and happy I was to escape being formally placed upon a chair. I asked him how he was. 'Very ill. But I have given up doctors.' 'Yes, yes; you have no love for them.' As it is impossible for me to relate exactly our conversation, I shall not endeavour at order, but give sentences as I recollect them.

BOSWELL. 'The thought of your books, Sir, is a great source of pleasure to you?' ROUSSEAU. 'I am fond of them; but when I think of my books, so many misfortunes which they have brought upon me are revived in my memory that really I cannot answer you. And yet my books have saved my life.' He spoke of the Parlement of Paris: 'If any company could be covered with disgrace, that would be. I could plunge them into deep disgrace simply by printing their edict against me on one side, and the law of nations and equity on the side opposite. But I have reasons against doing so at present.' BOSWELL. 'We shall have it one day, perhaps?' ROUSSEAU. 'Perhaps.'

I was dressed in a coat and waistcoat, scarlet with gold lace, buckskin breeches, and boots. Above all I wore a greatcoat of green camlet [10] lined with fox-skin fur, with the collar and cuffs of the same fur. I held under my arm a hat with a solid gold lace, at least with the air of being solid. I had it last winter at The Hague. I had a free air and spoke well, and when Monsieur Rousseau said what touched me more than ordinary, I seized his hand, I thumped him on the shoulder. I was without restraint. When I found that I really pleased him, I said, 'Are you aware, Sir, that I am recommended to you by a man you hold in high regard?'

ROUSSEAU. 'Ah! My Lord Marischal?' [11] BOSWELL. 'Yes, Sir; my Lord furnished me with a note to introduce me to you.' ROUSSEAU. 'And you were unwilling to take advantage of it?' BOSWELL. 'Nay, Sir; I wished to have proof of my own merits.' ROUSSEAU. 'Sir, there would have been no kind of merit in gaining access to me by a note of Lord Marischal's. Whatever he sends will always find a welcome from me. He is my protector, my father; I would venture to say, my friend.' One circumstance embarrassed me a little: I had forgotten to bring with me from Neuchâtel my Lord's billet. But a generous consciousness of innocence and honesty gives a freedom which cannot be counterfeited. I told Monsieur Rousseau, 'To speak truly, I have forgotten to bring his letter with me; but you accept my word for it?'

10. A costly fabric of satin weave, originally of angora wool. (For Boswell in this costume see Fig. 34.)

11. George Keith, 10th Earl Marischal of Scotland (d. 1778); a distinguished soldier and disenchanted Jacobite, he served Frederick the Great of Prussia; as governor of Neuchâtel he became a friend and protector of Rousseau. Boswell had traveled with him in Germany earlier in the year.

ROUSSEAU. 'Why, certainly. Numbers of people have shown themselves ready to serve me in their own fashion; my Lord Marischal has served me in mine. He is the only man on earth to whom I owe an obligation.' He went on, 'When I speak of kings, I do not include the King of Prussia. He is a king quite alone and apart. That force of his! Sir, there's the great matter, to have force—revenge, even. You can always find stuff to make something out of. But when force is lacking, when everything is small and split up, there's no hope. The French, for example, are a contemptible nation.' BOSWELL. 'But the Spaniards, Sir?' ROUSSEAU. 'Yes, you will find great souls in Spain.' BOSWELL. 'And in the mountains of Scotland. But since our cursed Union,¹² ah—' ROUSSEAU. 'You undid yourselves. . . .'

'Sir, you don't see before you the bear you have heard tell of. Sir, I have no liking for the world. I live here in a world of fantasies, and I cannot tolerate the world as it is.' BOSWELL. 'But when you come across fantastical men, are they not to your liking?' ROUSSEAU. 'Why, Sir, they have not the same fantasies as myself.—Sir, your country is formed for liberty. I like your habits. You and I feel free to stroll here together without talking. That is more than two Frenchmen can do. Mankind disgusts me. And my housekeeper tells me that I am in far better humour on the days when I have been alone than on those when I have been in company.' BOSWELL. 'There has been a great deal written against you, Sir.' ROUSSEAU. 'They have not understood me. As for Monsieur Vernet at Geneva, he is an Arch-Jesuit, that is all I can say of him.'

BOSWELL. 'Tell me, Sir, do you not find that I answer to the description I gave you of myself?' ROUSSEAU. 'Sir, it is too early for me to judge. But all appearances are in your favour.' BOSWELL. 'I fear I have stayed too long. I shall take the honour of returning tomorrow.' ROUSSEAU. 'Oh, as to that, I can't tell.' BOSWELL. 'Sir, I shall stay quietly here in the village. If you are able to see me, I shall be enchanted; if not, I shall make no complaint.' ROUSSEAU. 'My Lord Marischal has a perfect understanding of man's feelings, in solitude no less than in society. I am overwhelmed with visits from idle people.' BOSWELL. 'And how do they spend their time?' ROUSSEAU. 'In paying compliments. Also I get a prodigious quantity of letters. And the writer of each of them believes that he is the only one.' BOSWELL. 'You must be greatly surprised, Sir, that a man who has not the honour of your acquaintance should take the liberty of writing to you?' ROUSSEAU. 'No. I am not at all surprised. For I got a letter like it yesterday, and one the day before yesterday, and others many times before that.' BOSWELL. 'Sir, your very humble servant.—What, you are coming further?' ROUSSEAU. 'I am not coming with you. I am going for a walk in the passage. Good-bye.'

I had great satisfaction after finding that I could support the character which I had given of myself, after finding that I should most certainly be regarded by the illustrious Rousseau. I had a strange kind of feeling after having at last seen the author of whom I had thought so much.

Wednesday 5 December   When I waited upon Monsieur Rousseau this morning, he said, 'My dear Sir, I am sorry not to be able to talk with you as I would wish.' I took care to waive such excuses, and immediately set conversation a-going. I told him how I had turned Roman Catholic and had intended

---

12. The union of England and Scotland under one parliament in 1707.

to hide myself in a convent in France. He said, 'What folly! I too was Catholic in my youth.[13] I changed, and then I changed back again. I returned to Geneva and was readmitted to the Protestant faith. I went again among Catholics, and used to say to them, "I am no longer one of you"; and I got on with them excellently.' I stopped him in the middle of the room and I said to him, 'But tell me sincerely, are you a Christian?' I looked at him with a searching eye. His countenance was no less animated. Each stood steady and watched the other's looks. He struck his breast, and replied. 'Yes. I pique myself upon being one.' BOSWELL. 'Sir, the soul can be sustained by nothing save the Gospel.' ROUSSEAU. 'I feel that. I am unaffected by all the objections. I am weak; there may be things beyond my reach; or perhaps the man who recorded them made a mistake. I say, God the Father, God the Son, God the Holy Ghost.'

BOSWELL. 'But tell me, do you suffer from melancholy?' ROUSSEAU. 'I was born placid. I have no natural disposition to melancholy. My misfortunes have infected me with it.' BOSWELL. 'I, for my part, suffer from it severely. And how can I be happy, I, who have done so much evil?' ROUSSEAU. 'Begin your life anew. God is good, for he is just. Do good. You will cancel all the debt of evil. Say to yourself in the morning, "Come now, I am going to *pay off* so much evil." Six well-spent years will pay off all the evil you have committed.' BOSWELL. 'But what do you think of cloisters, penances, and remedies of that sort?' ROUSSEAU. 'Mummeries, all of them, invented by men. Do not be guided by men's judgments, or you will find yourself tossed to and fro perpetually. Do not base your life on the judgments of others; first, because they are as likely to be mistaken as you are, and further, because you cannot know that they are telling you their true thoughts; they may be impelled by motives of interest or convention to talk to you in a way not corresponding to what they really think.' BOSWELL. 'Will you, Sir, assume direction of me?' ROUSSEAU. 'I cannot. I can be responsible only for myself.' BOSWELL. 'But I shall come back.' ROUSSEAU. 'I don't promise to see you. I am in pain. I need a chamber-pot every minute.'[14] BOSWELL. 'Yes, you will see me.' ROUSSEAU. 'Be off; and a good journey to you.'

About six I set out.

[1776: Reflections on Man]

Sunday 31 December   (I am now writing on Tuesday 2 January 1776.) My cold and sprained ankle were worse. I lay in bed but did not enjoy that tranquillity which I have formerly done in that state of indolence. I read in *The Critical Review* an account of Priestley's edition of Hartley's *Observations on Man*[15] with some essays of his own relative to the subject of that book. While

13. For Rousseau's conversion, see the Headnote to his *Confessions* in Sense and Sensibility; of Boswell's nothing is known. While he was in Holland, Boswell had found relief from some of his own Calvinistic severities of self-reproach in reading Rousseau's "Creed of a Savoyard Vicar," in *Émile*.

14. Rousseau was suffering from a congestion or constriction of the urethra.

15. David Hartley (1705–57) was trained in both medicine and divinity although he did not take either a medical degree or holy orders; his *Observations on Man* (1749) derived all religious and moral ideas from association of sense perceptions, and all thought processes from mechanical vibrations in the nerves and brain. While Hartley denied free will he claimed not to be a materialist and remained a devout Christian. Joseph Priestley abridged his work in 1775, omitting the theory of vibrations as too obscure, and gained great popularity for Hartley (whose influence on Coleridge and Wordsworth was great).

I was carried into metaphysical abstraction, and felt that *perhaps* all our thinking of every kind was only a variety of modification upon matter, I was in a sort of amaze; but I must observe that it did not affect me with 'that secret dread and inward horror' [16] which it has occasioned at other times. There is no accounting for our feelings, but certain it is that what strikes us strongly at one time will have little influence at another. Speculation of this kind relieved me from the vexation of family differences, by changing objects and by making me consider, 'If all thought and all volition and all that we denominate spirit be only properties of matter, why should I distress myself at present, while in full consciousness, about eventual successions of machines?' I however thought that philosophical theories were transient, whereas feudal principles remained for ages. In truth the mortality or immortality of the soul can make no difference on the enthusiasm for supporting a family, for, in either case, the matter must be of no moment to those who have departed this life. If they have ceased to exist, they know nothing of it. If they exist in another state, they perhaps even then know not what passes here, and, if they do, it is perhaps as trifling in their eyes as our childish concerns are in ours when we have arrived at manhood. How strange is it, then, that a man will toil all his life and deny himself satisfactions in order to aggrandize his posterity after he is dead. It is, I fancy, from a kind of delusion in the imagination, which makes us figure ourselves contemplating for ages our own magnificence in a succession of descendants. So strong is this delusion with me that I would suffer death rather than let the estate of Auchinleck be sold; and this must be from an enthusiasm for an *idea* for *the Family*.[17] The founder of it I never saw, so how can I be zealous for his race? and were I to be a martyr, I should only be reckoned a madman. But an *idea* will produce the highest enthusiasm. Witness the ardour which the individuals at the time have for the glory of their regiment, though they have no line of connexion with it, being picked out from all parts of the kingdom. The officers and soldiers of the Scots Greys boast that '*We* were never known to fly.'—'*We* gained distinguished honour at such a battle.' Yet the officers and soldiers under that *name* at former periods were as different from its officers and soldiers now as the Romans were. I don't mean that they were different in body or in mind, in any remarkable degree, but that there is not a trace of identity, unless that there is always a remain of a regiment to communicate the same discipline and gallantry of sentiment to those who come into it, so that *l'esprit du corps*, like the fire of Vesta,[18] is kept incessantly burning, though the materials are different. I thought for a little that a man should place his pride and his happiness in his own individuality, and endeavour to be as rich and as renowned and as happy as he can. I considered that Dr. Johnson is as well as if he belonged to a *family*. Priestley's *material* system affected me less that he declared his belief in Christianity, which teaches us that GOD bestows a future life. However, I thought myself strongly conscious of an immaterial something—of a soul. I read a pamphlet today, which I remember having looked at about twenty years ago: *The Trial of the Witnesses for the Resurrection of Jesus*.[19] I found it to be a

16. "Whence this secret dread, and inward horror, of falling into naught?" Addison, *Cato* V.i.4–5.
17. Perhaps "an *idea* of the *Family*" or "for an *idea*, for the *Family*."
18. Whose perpetual flame was kept by the Vestal Virgins in her temple at Rome.
19. (1729) by Thomas Sherlock, later Bishop of London.

piece of very good argument which confirmed me in my faith; but I was a little disgusted with its author's affecting a sort of easy smartness of dialogue in some places. . . .

Wednesday 3 January. . . . My state of mind today was still affected by Hartley and Priestley's metaphysics, and was continually trying to perceive my faculties operating as machinery. My animal spirits were so light now that such sort of thinking did not distress me as it has done when I was more atrabilious.[20] I felt an easy indifference as to what was my mental system. I liked present consciousness. Man's continuation of existence is a flux of ideas in the same body, like the flux of a river in the same channel. Even our bodies are perpetually changing. What then is the subject of praise or blame upon the whole? what of love or hatred when we are to contemplate a character? There *must* be *something,* which we understand by a *spirit* or a *soul,* which is permanent. And yet I must own that except the sense or perception of identity, I cannot say that there is any sameness in my soul now and my soul twenty years ago, or surely none thirty years ago. Though souls may be in a flux, each may have a distinct character as rivers have: one rapid, one smooth, etc. I read a little of Lord Hailes's *Annals.* . . .

Tuesday 9 January   In the intervals while Mr. Lawrie copied passages, I read *The Monthly Review* on Priestley's edition of Hartley, and found his *material* system refuted with ability and spirit. I was much pleased, and wished to be acquainted with the writer of the article. I could not but think what a strange life a man would lead who should fairly act according to metaphysical conviction or impression at the time. What inconsistency and extravagance should we find! Sometimes he would be rigidly virtuous, at other times abandoned to extreme licentiousness; and at both times acting from *principle.* I have thought of writing a kind of novel to show this: 'Memoirs of a Practical Metaphysician.' I remember I mentioned this to Dr. Reid,[21] who writes on the mind according to common sense. He told me the same thought had occurred to him. Maclaurin observed very well, when he was last with me, that thinking metaphysically destroys the principles of morality; and indeed when a man analyses virtues and vices as a chemist does material substances, they lose their value as well as their odiousness. . . .

From The Life of Samuel Johnson, LL.D.

[1729: "Morbid Melancholy"]

The 'morbid melancholy,' which was lurking in his constitution, and to which we may ascribe those particularities, and that aversion to regular life, which, at a very early period, marked his character, gathered such strength in his twentieth year, as to afflict him in a dreadful manner. While he was at Lich-

20. Afflicted by black bile or melancholy.
21. Dr. Thomas Reid (1710–96), Professor of Moral Philosophy at the University of Glasgow, a leader of the Common Sense school of philosophy and an opponent of David Hume; his *Inquiry into the Human Mind* (1764) had freed Boswell from the "sceptical cobweb" of Hume during Boswell's stay in Berlin.

field, in the college vacation of the year 1729, he felt himself overwhelmed with an horrible hypochondria, with perpetual irritation, fretfulness, and impatience; and with a dejection, gloom, and despair, which made existence misery. From this dismal malady he never afterwards was perfectly relieved; and all his labours, and all his enjoyments, were but temporary interruptions of its baleful influence. How wonderful, how unsearchable are the ways of GOD! Johnson, who was blest with all the powers of genius and understanding in a degree far above the ordinary state of human nature, was at the same time visited with a disorder so afflictive, that they who know it by dire experience, will not envy his exalted endowments. That it was, in some degree, occasioned by a defect in his nervous system, that inexplicable part of our frame, appears highly probable. He told Mr. Paradise that he was sometimes so languid and inefficient, that he could not distinguish the hour upon the town-clock.

Johnson, upon the first violent attack of this disorder, strove to overcome it by forcible exertions. He frequently walked to Birmingham and back again,[1] and tried many other expedients, but all in vain. His expression concerning it to me was, 'I did not then know how to manage it.' His distress became so intolerable, that he applied to Dr. Swinfen, physician in Lichfield, his god-father, and put into his hands a state of his case, written in Latin. Dr. Swinfen was so much struck with the extraordinary acuteness, research, and eloquence of this paper, that in his zeal for his godson he showed it to several people. His daughter, Mrs. Desmoulins, who was many years humanely supported in Dr. Johnson's house in London, told me that upon his discovering that Dr. Swinfen had communicated his case, he was so much offended, that he was never afterwards fully reconciled to him. He indeed had good reason to be offended; for though Dr. Swinfen's motive was good, he inconsiderately betrayed a matter deeply interesting and of great delicacy, which had been entrusted to him in confidence; and exposed a complaint of his young friend and patient, which, in the superficial opinion of the generality of mankind, is attended with contempt and disgrace.

But let not little men triumph upon knowing that Johnson was an HYPO-CHONDRIAC, was subject to what the learned, philosophical, and pious Dr. Cheyne has so well treated under the title of 'The English Malady.'[2] Though he suffered severely from it, he was not therefore degraded. The powers of his great mind might be troubled, and their full exercise suspended at times; but the mind itself was ever entire. As a proof of this, it is only necessary to consider, that, when he was at the very worst, he composed that state of his own case, which showed an uncommon vigour, not only of fancy and taste, but of judgement. I am aware that he himself was too ready to call such a complaint by the name of *madness*; in conformity with which notion, he has traced its gradations, with exquisite nicety, in one of the chapters of his *Rasselas*. But there is surely a clear distinction between a disorder which affects only the imagination and spirits, while the judgement is sound, and a disorder by which the judgement itself is impaired. . . .

. . . To Johnson, whose supreme enjoyment was the exercise of his reason,

1. Thirty-two miles in all.
2. Dr. George Cheyne (1671–1743), *The English Malady, or a Treatise of Nervous Diseases of All Kinds* (1733), a book Johnson twice recommended to Boswell.

the disturbance or obscuration of that faculty was the evil most to be dreaded. Insanity, therefore, was the object of his most dismal apprehension; and he fancied himself seized by it, or approaching to it, at the very time when he was giving proofs of a more than ordinary soundness and vigour of judgement. That his own diseased imagination should have so far deceived him is strange; but it is stranger still that some of his friends should have given credit to his ground-less opinion when they had such undoubted proofs that it was totally fallacious; though it is by no means surprising that those who wish to depreciate him should, since his death, have laid hold of his circumstance and insisted upon it with very unfair aggravation.

Amidst the oppression and distraction of a disease which very few have felt in its full extent, but many have experienced in a slighter degree, Johnson, in his writings, and in his conversation, never failed to display all the varieties of intellectual excellence. In his march through this world to a better, his mind still appeared grand and brilliant, and impressed all around him with the truth of Virgil's noble sentiment—

Igneus est ollis vigor et cœlestis origo.[3]

The history of his mind as to religion is an important article. I have men-tioned the early impressions made upon his tender imagination by his mother, who continued her pious care with assiduity, but, in his opinion, not with judge-ment. 'Sunday (said he) was a heavy day to me when I was a boy. My mother confined me on that day, and made me read "The Whole Duty of Man,"[4] from a great part of which I could derive no instruction. When, for instance, I had read the chapter on theft, which from my infancy I had been taught was wrong, I was no more convinced that theft was wrong than before; so there was no accession of knowledge. A boy should be introduced to such books by having his attention directed to the arrangement, to the style, and other excellencies of composition; that the mind being thus engaged by an amusing variety of objects, may not grow weary.'

He communicated to me the following particulars upon the subject of his religious progress. 'I fell into an inattention to religion, or an indifference about it, in my ninth year. The church at Lichfield, in which we had a seat, wanted reparation, so I was to go and find a seat in other churches; and having bad eyes, and being awkward about this, I used to go and read in the fields on Sunday. This habit continued till my fourteenth year; and still I find a great reluctance to go to church. I then became a sort of lax *talker* against religion, for I did not much *think* against it; and this lasted till I went to Oxford, where it would not be *suffered*. When at Oxford, I took up Law's *Serious Call to a Holy Life*,[5] expecting to find it a dull book (as such books generally are), and perhaps to laugh at it. But I found Law quite an over-match for me; and this was the first occasion of my thinking in earnest of religion, after I became

3. "Quick in these seeds is might of fire and birth of heavenly place" (*Aeneid*, Morris trans., VI.730).
4. The popular moral work attributed to Dr. Richard Allestree (1619–81).
5. For William Law, see the selections from Edward Gibbon's *Memoirs* in Sense and Sensi-bility. Law's work had great influence upon both John Wesley and George Whitefield, the founders of Methodism.

capable of rational inquiry.' From this time forward religion was the predominant object of his thoughts; though, with the just sentiments of a conscientious Christian, he lamented that his practice of its duties fell far short of what it ought to be. . . .

How seriously Johnson was impressed with a sense of religion, even in the vigour of his youth, appears from the following passage in his minutes kept by way of diary: Sept. 7, 1736. I have this day entered upon my twenty-eighth year. 'Mayest thou, O God, enable me, for Jesus Christ's sake, to spend this in such a manner that I may receive comfort from it at the hour of death, and in the day of judgement! Amen.'

The particular course of his reading while at Oxford, and during the time of vacation which he passed at home, cannot be traced. Enough has been said of his irregular mode of study. He told me that from his earliest years he loved to read poetry, but hardly ever read any poem to an end; that he read Shakespeare at a period so early, that the speech of the ghost in Hamlet terrified him when he was alone; that Horace's Odes were the compositions in which he took most delight, and it was long before he liked his Epistles and Satires. He told me what he read *solidly* at Oxford was Greek; not the Grecian historians, but Homer and Euripides, and now and then a little Epigram; that the study of which he was the most fond was Metaphysics, but he had not read much, even in that way. I always thought that he did himself injustice in his account of what he had read, and that he must have been speaking with reference to the vast portion of study which is possible, and to which a few scholars in the whole history of literature have attained; for when I once asked him whether a person, whose name I have now forgotten, studied hard, he answered 'No, Sir; I do not believe he studied hard. I never knew a man who studied hard. I conclude, indeed, from the effects, that some men have studied hard, as Bentley and Clarke.' [6] Trying him by that criterion upon which he formed his judgement of others, we may be absolutely certain, both from his writings and his conversation, that his reading was very extensive. Dr. Adam Smith,[7] than whom few were better judges on this subject, once observed to me that 'Johnson knew more books than any man alive.' He had a peculiar facility in seizing at once what was valuable in any book, without submitting to the labour of perusing it from beginning to end. He had, from the irritability of his constitution, at all times, an impatience and hurry when he either read or wrote. A certain apprehension, arising from novelty, made him write his first exercise at College twice over; but he never took that trouble with any other composition; and we shall see that his most excellent works were struck off at a heat, with rapid exertion.

Yet he appears, from his early notes or memorandums in my possession, to have at various times attempted, or at least planned, a methodical course of study, according to computation, of which he was all his life fond, as it fixed

6. Richard Bentley (1662–1742), the great classical scholar attacked by Swift in *The Battle of the Books* and Pope in *The Dunciad* IV; Samuel Clarke (1675–1729), distinguished metaphysician and moral philosopher, who gave the Boyle Lectures in 1704–1705 and engaged in a celebrated correspondence with Leibnitz.

7. Adam Smith (1723–90), the Scottish professor of logic and moral philosopher, now best known for his work of economics, *The Wealth of Nations* (1776).

his attention steadily upon something without, and prevented his mind from preying upon itself. Thus I find in his handwriting the number of lines in each of two of Euripides' Tragedies, of the Georgics of Virgil, of the first six books of the Aeneid, of Horace's Art of Poetry, of three of the books of Ovid's Metamorphosis, of some parts of Theocritus, and of the tenth Satire of Juvenal; and a table, showing at the rate of various numbers a day (I suppose verses to be read), what would be, in each case, the total amount in a week, month, and year.

No man had a more ardent love of literature, or a higher respect for it than Johnson. His apartment in Pembroke College was that upon the second floor, over the gateway. The enthusiasts of learning will ever contemplate it with veneration. One day, while he was sitting in it quite alone, Dr. Panting, then master of the College, whom he called 'a fine Jacobite fellow,' overheard him uttering this soliloquy in his strong, emphatic voice: 'Well, I have a mind to see what is done in other places of learning. I'll go and visit the Universities abroad. I'll go to France and Italy. I'll go to Padua.—And I'll mind my business. For an *Athenian* blockhead is the worst of all blockheads.'

Dr. Adams told me that Johnson, while he was at Pembroke College, 'was caressed and loved by all about him, was a gay and frolicsome fellow, and passed there the happiest part of his life.' But this is a striking proof of the fallacy of appearances, and how little any of us know of the real internal state even of those whom we see most frequently; for the truth is, that he was then depressed by poverty, and irritated by disease. When I mentioned to him this account as given me by Dr. Adams, he said, 'Ah, Sir, I was mad and violent. It was bitterness which they mistook for frolic. I was miserably poor, and I thought to fight my way by my literature and my wit; so I disregarded all power and all authority.'

[1754: The *Dictionary* and Lord Chesterfield]

The *Dictionary*, we may believe, afforded Johnson full occupation this year. As it approached to its conclusion, he probably worked with redoubled vigour, as seamen increase their exertion and alacrity when they have a near prospect of their haven.

Lord Chesterfield, to whom Johnson had paid the high compliment of addressing to his Lordship the *Plan* of his *Dictionary*, had behaved to him in such a manner as to excite his contempt and indignation. The world has been for many years amused with a story confidently told, and as confidently repeated with additional circumstances, that a sudden disgust was taken by Johnson upon occasion of his having been one day kept long in waiting in his Lordship's antechamber, for which the reason assigned was, that he had company with him; and that at last, when the door opened, out walked Colley Cibber; [8] and that Johnson was so violently provoked when he found for whom he had been so long excluded, that he went away in a passion, and never would return . . . but Johnson himself assured me, that there was not the least foundation for it.

8. Colley Cibber (1671–1757), dramatist and actor, poet laureate 1730–57, the mock-hero of Pope's revised *Dunciad;* Johnson scorned his ignorance and "impenetrable impudence."

He told me, that there never was any particular incident which produced a quarrel between Lord Chesterfield and him; but that his Lordship's continued neglect was the reason why he resolved to have no connection with him. When the *Dictionary* was upon the eve of publication, Lord Chesterfield, who, it is said, had flattered himself with expectations that Johnson would dedicate the work to him, attempted, in a courtly manner, to soothe, and insinuate himself with the Sage, conscious, as it should seem, of the cold indifference with which he had treated its learned author; and further attempted to conciliate him, by writing two papers in *The World*, in recommendation of the work; and it must be confessed, that they contain some studied compliments, so finely turned, that if there had been no previous offence, it is probable that Johnson would have been highly delighted. Praise, in general, was pleasing to him; but by praise from a man of rank and elegant accomplishments, he was peculiarly gratified. . . .

This courtly device failed of its effect. Johnson, who thought that 'all was false and hollow,' despised the honeyed words, and was even indignant that Lord Chesterfield should, for a moment, imagine that he could be the dupe of such an artifice. His expression to me concerning Lord Chesterfield, upon this occasion, was, 'Sir, after making great professions, he had, for many years, taken no notice of me; but when my *Dictionary* was coming out, he fell a scribbling in *The World* about it. Upon which, I wrote him a letter expressed in civil terms, but such as might show him that I did not mind what he said or wrote, and that I had done with him.'

This is that celebrated letter of which so much has been said, and about which curiosity has been so long excited, without being gratified. . . .

'*To* The Right Honourable the Earl of Chesterfield
'My Lord,   February 1755
'I have been lately informed, by the proprietor of *The World*, that two papers, in which my Dictionary is recommended to the public, were written by your Lordship. To be so distinguished, is an honour, which, being very little accustomed to favours from the great, I know not well how to receive, or in what terms to acknowledge.

'When, upon some slight encouragement, I first visited your Lordship, I was overpowered, like the rest of mankind, by the enchantment of your address; and could not forbear to wish that I might boast myself *Le vainqueur du vainqueur de la terre;* [9]—that I might obtain that regard for which I saw the world contending; but I found my attendance so little encouraged, that neither pride nor modesty would suffer me to continue it. When I had once addressed your Lordship in public, I had exhausted all the art of pleasing which a retired and uncourtly scholar can possess. I had done all that I could; and no man is well pleased to have his all neglected, be it ever so little.

'Seven years, my Lord, have now past, since I waited in your outward rooms, or was repulsed from your door; during which time I have been pushing on my work through difficulties, of which it is useless to complain, and have brought it, at last, to the verge of publication, without one act of assistance,

---

9. "The conqueror of the conqueror of the earth."

one word of encouragement, or one smile of favour. Such treatment I did not expect, for I never had a Patron before.

'The shepherd in Virgil grew at last acquainted with Love, and found him a native of the rocks.[10]

'Is not a Patron, my Lord, one who looks with unconcern on a man struggling for life in the water, and, when he has reached ground, encumbers him with help? The notice which you have been pleased to take of my labours, had it been early, had been kind; but it has been delayed till I am indifferent, and cannot enjoy it; till I am solitary, and cannot impart it; [11] till I am known, and do not want it. I hope it is no very cynical asperity not to confess obligations where no benefit has been received, or to be unwilling that the Public should consider me as owing that to a Patron which Providence has enabled me to do for myself.

'Having carried on my work thus far with so little obligation to any favourer of learning, I shall not be disappointed though I should conclude it, if less be possible, with less; for I have been long wakened from that dream of hope, in which I once boasted myself with so much exultation, my Lord, your Lordship's most humble, most obedient servant,

SAM. JOHNSON.'

. . . There is a curious minute circumstance which struck me, in comparing the various editions of Johnson's imitations of Juvenal. In the tenth Satire, one of the couplets upon the vanity of wishes even for literary distinction stood thus:

> Yet think what ills the scholar's life assail,
> Pride, envy, want, the *garret*, and the jail.

But after experiencing the uneasiness which Lord Chesterfield's fallacious patronage made him feel, he dismissed the word *garret* from the sad group, and in all the subsequent editions the line stands

> Toil, envy, want, the *Patron*, and the jail.[12]

[1763: The Meeting with Boswell]

. . . Mr. Davies [13] recollected several of Johnson's remarkable sayings, and was one of the best of the many imitators of his voice and manner, while relating them. He increased my impatience more and more to see the extraordinary man whose works I highly valued, and whose conversation was reported to be so peculiarly excellent.

At last, on Monday the 16th of May, when I was sitting in Mr. Davies's back-parlour, after having drunk tea with him and Mrs. Davies, Johnson unexpectedly came into the shop; and Mr. Davies having perceived him through the glass door in the room in which we were sitting, advancing towards us,—he an-

---

10. *Eclogues* VIII.43: "I know thee, Love; in deserts thou wast bred" (Dryden trans.).
11. Referring to the death of his wife, March 17, 1752.
12. In his *Dictionary* Johnson defined *patron* as "commonly a wretch who supports with insolence and is paid with flattery."
13. Thomas Davies, actor and bookseller, "a man of good understanding and talents, with the advantage of a liberal education"; "a friendly and very hospitable man" whom Johnson visited freely.

nounced his aweful approach to me, somewhat in the manner of an actor in the part of Horatio, when he addresses Hamlet on the appearance of his father's ghost, 'Look, my Lord, it comes.' I found that I had a very perfect idea of Johnson's figure from the portrait of him painted by Sir Joshua Reynolds soon after he had published his *Dictionary*, in the attitude of sitting in his easy chair in deep meditation. . . . Mr. Davies mentioned my name, and respectfully introduced me to him. I was much agitated; and recollecting his prejudice against the Scotch, of which I had heard much, I said to Davies, 'Don't tell where I come from.'—'From Scotland,' cried Davies roguishly. 'Mr. Johnson, (said I) I do indeed come from Scotland, but I cannot help it.' I am willing to flatter myself that I meant this as light pleasantry to soothe and conciliate him, and not as an humiliating abasement at the expence of my country. But however that might be, this speech was somewhat unlucky; for with that quickness of wit for which he was so remarkable, he seized the expression 'come from Scotland,' which I used in the sense of being of that country, and, as if I had said that I had come away from it, or left it, retorted, 'That, Sir, I find, is what a very great many of your countrymen cannot help.' This stroke stunned me a good deal; and when we had sat down, I felt myself not a little embarrassed, and apprehensive of what might come next. He then addressed himself to Davies: 'What do you think of Garrick? [14] He has refused me an order for the play for Miss Williams,[15] because he knows the house will be full, and that an order would be worth three shillings.' Eager to take any opening to get into conversation with him, I ventured to say, 'O, Sir, I cannot think Mr. Garrick would grudge such a trifle to you.' 'Sir, (said he, with a stern look,) I have known David Garrick longer than you have done: and I know no right you have to talk to me on the subject.' Perhaps I deserved this check; for it was rather presumptuous in me, an entire stranger, to express any doubt of the justice of his animadversion upon his old acquaintance and pupil. I now felt myself much mortified, and began to think that the hope which I had long indulged of obtaining his acquaintance was blasted. And, in truth, had not my ardour been uncommonly strong, and my resolution uncommonly persevering, so rough a reception might have deterred me for ever from making any further attempts. Fortunately, however, I remained upon the field not wholly discomfited; and was soon rewarded by hearing some of his conversation, of which I preserved the following short minute, without marking the questions and observations by which it was produced.

'People (he remarked) may be taken in once, who imagine that an author is greater in private life than other men. Uncommon parts require uncommon opportunities for their exertion.

'In barbarous society, superiority of parts is of real consequence. Great strength or great wisdom is of much value to an individual. But in more polished times there are people to do every thing for money; and then there are a number of other superiorities, such as those of birth and fortune, and

14. David Garrick, the great actor, had been a pupil of Johnson in his school at Edial (1736–37).
15. Anna Williams (1706–83), Johnson's friend and protégée, for whom David Garrick gave a benefit at Drury Lane.

rank, that dissipate men's attention, and leave no extraordinary share of respect for personal and intellectual superiority. This is wisely ordered by Providence, to preserve some equality among mankind.

'Sir, this book (*The Elements of Criticism*,[16] which he had taken up,) is a pretty essay, and deserves to be held in some estimation, though much of it is chimerical.'

Speaking of one [17] who with more than ordinary boldness attacked public measures and the royal family, he said,

'I think he is safe from the law, but he is an abusive scoundrel; and instead of applying to my Lord Chief Justice to punish him, I would send half a dozen footmen and have him well ducked.'

'The notion of liberty amuses the people of England, and helps to keep off the *tædium vitæ*. When a butcher tells you that *his heart bleeds for his country*, he has, in fact, no uneasy feeling.

'Sheridan [18] will not succeed at Bath with his oratory. Ridicule has gone down before him, and, I doubt, Derrick is his enemy.

'Derrick may do very well, as long as he can outrun his character; but the moment his character gets up with him, it is all over.'

It is, however, but just to record, that some years afterwards, when I reminded him of this sarcasm, he said, 'Well, but Derrick has now got a character that he need not run away from.'

I was highly pleased with the extraordinary vigour of his conversation, and regretted that I was drawn away from it by an engagement at another place. I had, for a part of the evening, been left alone with him, and had ventured to make an observation now and then, which he received very civilly; so that I was satisfied that though there was a roughness in his manner, there was no ill-nature in his disposition. Davies followed me to the door, and when I complained to him a little of the hard blows which the great man had given me, he kindly took upon him to console me by saying, 'Don't be uneasy. I can see he likes you very well.'

A few days afterwards I called on Davies, and asked him if he thought I might take the liberty of waiting on Mr. Johnson at his Chambers in the Temple. He said I certainly might, and that Mr. Johnson would take it as a compliment. So upon Tuesday the 24th of May, after having been enlivened by the witty sallies of Messieurs Thornton, Wilkes, Churchill [19] and Lloyd, with whom I had passed the morning, I boldly repaired to Johnson. His Chambers were on the first floor of No. 1, Inner-Temple-lane, and I entered them with

16. By Henry Home, Lord Kames, published in Edinburgh in 1762.

17. John Wilkes (1727–97), in 1762 founded *The North Briton*, a journal in which he attacked the ministry of Lord Bute. He was prosecuted for libel and, as a result of an obscene article, expelled from Commons and declared an outlaw. He fled to Paris and returned in 1768 to resume his parliamentary career. His famous meeting with Johnson took place in 1776, two years after he served as Lord Mayor of London.

18. Thomas Sheridan (1719–88), actor, author, father of the playwright, and lecturer on elocution—at the moment at Bath, where Samuel Derrick was Master of Ceremonies, "or as the phrase is, King" (Boswell).

19. Charles Churchill (1731–64), the satiric poet, who had attacked Johnson "violently" (in Boswell's view).

an impression given me by the Reverend Dr. Blair, of Edinburgh,[20] who had been introduced to him not long before, and described his having 'found the Giant in his den'; an expression, which, when I came to be pretty well acquainted with Johnson, I repeated to him, and he was diverted at this picturesque account of himself. Dr. Blair had been presented to him by Dr. James Fordyce. At this time the controversy concerning the pieces published by Mr. James Macpherson, as translations of *Ossian*, was at its height. Johnson had all along denied their authenticity; and, what was still more provoking to their admirers, maintained that they had no merit. The subject having been introduced by Dr. Fordyce, Dr. Blair, relying on the internal evidence of their antiquity, asked Dr. Johnson whether he thought any man of a modern age could have written such poems? Johnson replied, 'Yes, Sir, many men, many women, and many children.' Johnson, at this time, did not know that Dr. Blair had just published a *Dissertation*, not only defending their authenticity, but seriously ranking them with the poems of Homer and Virgil; and when he was afterwards informed of this circumstance, he expressed some displeasure at Dr. Fordyce's having suggested the topic, and said, 'I am not sorry that they got thus much for their pains. Sir, it was like leading one to talk of a book when the author is concealed behind the door.'

He received me very courteously; but, it must be confessed, that his apartment, and furniture, and morning dress, were sufficiently uncouth. His brown suit of clothes looked very rusty; he had on a little old shrivelled unpowdered wig which was too small for his head; his shirt-neck and knees of his breeches were loose; his black worsted stockings ill drawn up; and he had a pair of unbuckled shoes by way of slippers. But all these slovenly particularities were forgotten the moment that he began to talk. Some gentlemen, whom I do not recollect, were sitting with him; and when they went away, I also rose; but he said to me, 'Nay, don't go.' 'Sir, (said I,) I am afraid that I intrude upon you. It is benevolent to allow me to sit and hear you.' He seemed pleased with this compliment, which I sincerely paid him, and answered, 'Sir, I am obliged to any man who visits me.' I have preserved the following short minute of what passed this day:—

'Madness frequently discovers itself merely by unnecessary deviation from the usual modes of the world. My poor friend Smart showed the disturbance of his mind, by falling upon his knees, and saying his prayers in the street, or in any other unusual place. Now although, rationally speaking, it is greater madness not to pray at all, than to pray as Smart did, I am afraid there are so many who do not pray, that their understanding is not called in question.'

Concerning this unfortunate poet, Christopher Smart, who was confined in a mad-house, he had, at another time, the following conversation with Dr.

20. Dr. Hugh Blair (1718–1800), a clergyman well known for his sermons and a critic of rhetoric and literature; introduced to Johnson by his friend the physician Fordyce. The controversy concerning Macpherson's alleged translations from Ossian was settled by a committee that, after his death, declared them in part free versions of traditional poems with much original matter added. The Ossianic poems, purporting to be Gaelic epics, gained enormous vogue throughout Europe and were highly esteemed by Goethe among others. William Blake insisted upon their authenticity; Dr. Johnson remarked in 1783, "Sir, a man might write such stuff for ever, if he would *abandon* his mind to it."

Burney: [21]—B U R N E Y . 'How does poor Smart do, Sir; is he likely to recover?' J O H N S O N . 'It seems as if his mind had ceased to struggle with the disease; for he grows fat upon it.' B U R N E Y . 'Perhaps, Sir, that may be from want of exercise.' J O H N S O N . 'No, Sir; he has partly as much exercise as he used to have, for he digs in the garden. Indeed, before his confinement, he used for exercise to walk to the ale-house; but he was *carried* back again. I did not think he ought to be shut up. His infirmities were not noxious to society. He insisted on people praying with him; and I'd as lief pray with Kit Smart as any one else. Another charge was, that he did not love clean linen; and I have no passion for it.'—Johnson continued. 'Mankind have a great aversion to intellectual labour; but even supposing knowledge to be easily attainable, more people would be content to be ignorant than would take even a little trouble to acquire it.'

'The morality of an action depends on the motive from which we act. If I fling half a crown to a beggar with intention to break his head, and he picks it up and buys victuals with it, the physical effect is good; but, with respect to me, the action is very wrong. So, religious exercises, if not performed with an intention to please GOD, avail us nothing. As our Saviour says of those who perform them from other motives, "Verily they have their reward.". . .' [22]

When I rose a second time he again pressed me to stay, which I did.

He told me, that he generally went abroad at four in the afternoon, and seldom came home till two in the morning. I took the liberty to ask if he did not think it wrong to live thus, and not make more use of his great talents. He owned it was a bad habit. On reviewing, at the distance of many years, my journal of this period, I wonder how, at my first visit, I ventured to talk to him so freely, and that he bore it with so much indulgence.

Before we parted, he was so good as to promise to favour me with his company one evening at my lodgings; and, as I took my leave, shook me cordially by the hand. It is almost needless to add, that I felt no little elation at having now so happily established an acquaintance of which I had been so long ambitious. . . .

I did not visit him again till Monday, June 13, at which time I recollect no part of his conversation, except that when I told him I had been to see Johnson ride upon three horses,[23] he said, 'Such a man, Sir, should be encouraged; for his performances show the extent of the human powers in one instance, and thus tend to raise our opinion of the faculties of man. He shows what may be attained by persevering application; so that every man may hope, that by giving as much application, although perhaps he may never ride three horses at a time, or dance upon a wire, yet he may be equally expert in whatever profession he has chosen to pursue.'

He again shook me by the hand at parting, and asked me why I did not come oftener to him. Trusting that I was now in his good graces, I answered, that he had not given me much encouragement, and reminded him of the check I had received from him at our first interview. 'Poh, poh! (said he, with

21. Dr. Charles Burney (1726–1814), musician and historian of music, who helped raise a subscription for Smart during his final confinement in 1771.
22. Matthew 6:16.
23. A famous exhibition of riding by a Johnson of whom only the last name is known.

a complacent smile,) never mind these things. Come to me as often as you
can. I shall be glad to see you.'

[1776: The Meeting with Wilkes]

I am now to record a very curious incident in Dr. Johnson's Life, which fell
under my own observation; of which *pars magna fui*,[24] and which I am persuaded will, with the liberal-minded, be much to his credit.

My desire of being acquainted with celebrated men of every description, had
made me, much about the same time, obtain an introduction to Dr. Samuel
Johnson and to John Wilkes, Esq. Two men more different could perhaps not
be selected out of all mankind. They had even attacked one another with some
asperity in their writings; yet I lived in habits of friendship with both. I could
fully relish the excellence of each; for I have ever delighted in that intellectual
chemistry, which can separate good qualities from evil in the same person. . . .

Notwithstanding the high veneration which I entertained for Dr. Johnson, I
was sensible that he was sometimes a little actuated by the spirit of contradiction, and by means of that I hoped I should gain my point. I was persuaded
that if I had come upon him with a direct proposal, 'Sir, will you dine in
company with Jack Wilkes?' he would have flown into a passion, and would
probably have answered, 'Dine with Jack Wilkes, Sir! I'd as soon dine with Jack
Ketch.' [25] I therefore, while we were sitting quietly by ourselves at his house
in an evening, took occasion to open my plan thus:—'Mr. Dilly,[26] Sir, sends his
respectful compliments to you, and would be happy if you would do him the
honour to dine with him on Wednesday next along with me, as I must soon go
to Scotland.' J O H N S O N . 'Sir, I am obliged to Mr. Dilly. I will wait upon
him—' B O S W E L L . 'Provided, Sir, I suppose, that the company which he is
to have is agreeable to you.' J O H N S O N . 'What do you mean, Sir? What do
you take me for? Do you think I am so ignorant of the world, as to imagine that
I am to prescribe to a gentleman what company he is to have at his table?'
B O S W E L L . 'I beg your pardon, Sir, for wishing to prevent you from meeting
people whom you might not like. Perhaps he may have some of what he calls
his patriotic[27] friends with him.' J O H N S O N . 'Well, Sir, and what then? What
care *I* for his *patriotic friends*? Poh!' B O S W E L L . 'I should not be surprised
to find Jack Wilkes there.' J O H N S O N . 'And if Jack Wilkes *should* be there,
what is that to *me*, Sir? My dear friend, let us have no more of this. I am
sorry to be angry with you; but really it is treating me strangely to talk to me
as if I could not meet any company whatever, occasionally.' B O S W E L L .
'Pray forgive me, Sir: I meant well. But you shall meet whoever comes, for me.'
Thus I secured him, and told Dilly that he would find him very well pleased to
be one of his guests on the day appointed. . . .

When we entered Mr. Dilly's drawing room, he found himself in the midst
of a company he did not know. I kept myself snug and silent, watching how

---

24. "I was a great part," *Aeneid* II.5.
25. That is, the hangman.
26. Edward Dilly (1732–79), the bookseller.
27. Referring to the government opposition; in 1773 Johnson added a new definition of
patriot: "It is sometimes used for a factious disturber of the government."

he would conduct himself. I observed him whispering to Mr. Dilly, 'Who is that gentleman, Sir?'—'Mr. Arthur Lee.'—J O H N S O N. 'Too, too, too,' (under his breath,) which was one of his habitual mutterings. Mr. Arthur Lee could not but be very obnoxious to Johnson, for he was not only a *patriot* but an *American*. He was afterwards minister from the United States at the court of Madrid. 'And who is the gentleman in lace?'—'Mr. Wilkes, Sir.' This information confounded him still more; he had some difficulty to restrain himself, and taking up a book, sat down upon a window-seat and read, or at least kept his eye upon it intently for some time, till he composed himself. His feelings, I dare say, were awkward enough. But he no doubt recollected his having rated me for supposing that he could be at all disconcerted by any company, and he, therefore, resolutely set himself to behave quite as an easy man of the world, who could adapt himself at once to the disposition and manners of those whom he might chance to meet.

The cheering sound of 'Dinner is upon the table,' dissolved his reverie, and we *all* sat down without any symptom of ill humour. There were present, besides Mr. Wilkes, and Mr. Arthur Lee, who was an old compaion of mine when he studied physic at Edinburgh, Mr. (now Sir John) Miller, Dr. Lettsom, and Mr. Slater the druggist. Mr. Wilkes placed himself next to Dr. Johnson, and behaved to him with so much attention and politeness that he gained upon him insensibly. No man eat [28] more heartily than Johnson, or loved better what was nice and delicate. Mr. Wilkes was very assiduous in helping him to some fine veal. 'Pray give me leave, Sir:—It is better here—A little of the brown— Some fat, Sir—A little of the stuffing—Some gravy—Let me have the pleasure of giving you some butter—Allow me to recommend a squeeze of this orange; —or the lemon, perhaps, may have more zest.'—'Sir, Sir, I am obliged to you, Sir,' cried Johnson, bowing, and turning his head to him with a look for some time of 'surly virtue,' [29] but, in a short while, of complacency.

Foote [30] being mentioned, Johnson said, 'He is not a good mimic.' One of the company added, 'A merry Andrew, a buffoon.' J O H N S O N. 'But he has wit too, and is not deficient in ideas, or in fertility and variety of imagery, and not empty of reading; he has knowledge enough to fill up his part. One species of wit he has in an eminent degree, that of escape. You drive him into a corner with both hands; but he's gone, Sir, when you think you have got him—like an animal that jumps over your head. Then he has a great range for his wit; he never lets truth stand between him and a jest, and he is sometimes mighty coarse. Garrick is under many restraints from which Foote is free.' W I L K E S. 'Garrick's wit is more like Lord Chesterfield's.' J O H N S O N. 'The first time I was in company with Foote was at Fitzherbert's. Having no good opinion of the fellow, I was resolved not to be pleased; and it is very difficult to please a man against his will. I went on eating my dinner pretty sullenly, affecting not to mind him. But the dog was so very comical, that I was obliged to lay down my knife and fork, throw myself back upon my chair, and fairly laugh it out.

28. "Eat" (pronounced *ett*) was a standard past form.
29. Boswell cites Johnson's *London*, ll. 144–45: "How, when competitors like these contend, / Can surly virtue hope to fix a friend?"
30. Samuel Foote (1720–77), actor and dramatist, of whom Johnson said, "For loud obstreperous broadfaced mirth, I know not his equal."

No, Sir, he was irresistible. He upon one occasion experienced, in an extraordinary degree, the efficacy of his powers of entertaining. Amongst the many and various modes which he tried of getting money, he became a partner with a small-beer [31] brewer, and he was to have a share of the profits for procuring customers amongst his numerous acquaintance. Fitzherbert was one who took his small-beer; but it was so bad that the servants resolved not to drink it. They were at some loss how to notify their resolution, being afraid of offending their master, who they knew liked Foote much as a companion. At last they fixed upon a little black boy, who was rather a favourite, to be their deputy, and deliver their remonstrance; and having invested him with the whole authority of the kitchen, he was to inform Mr. Fitzherbert, in all their names, upon a certain day, that they would drink Foote's small-beer no longer. On that day Foote happened to dine at Fitzherbert's, and this boy served at table; he was so delighted with Foote's stories, and merriment, and grimace, that when he went down stairs, he told them, "This is the finest man I have ever seen. I will not deliver your message. I will drink his small-beer." '

Somebody observed that Garrick could not have done this. W I L K E S. 'Garrick would have made the small-beer still smaller. He is now leaving the stage; but he will play *Scrub* all his life.' [32] I knew that Johnson would let nobody attack Garrick but himself, as Garrick once said to me, and I had heard him praise his liberality; so to bring out his commendation of his celebrated pupil, I said, loudly, 'I have heard Garrick is liberal.' J O H N S O N. 'Yes, Sir, I know that Garrick has given away more money than any man in England that I am acquainted with, and that not from ostentatious views. Garrick was very poor when he began life; so when he came to have money, he probably was very unskilful in giving away, and saved when he should not. But Garrick began to be liberal as soon as he could; and I am of opinion, the reputation of avarice which he has had, has been very lucky for him, and prevented his having many enemies. You despise a man for avarice, but do not hate him. Garrick might have been much better attacked for living with more splendour than is suitable to a player: if they had had the wit to have assaulted him in that quarter, they might have galled him more. But they have kept clamouring about his avarice, which has rescued him from much obloquy and envy.' . . .

Mr. Arthur Lee mentioned some Scotch who had taken possession of a barren part of America, and wondered why they should choose it. J O H N S O N. 'Why, Sir, all barrenness is comparative. The *Scotch* would not know it to be barren.' B O S W E L L. 'Come, come, he is flattering the English. You have now been in Scotland, Sir, and say if you did not see meat and drink enough there.' J O H N S O N. 'Why yes, Sir; meat and drink enough to give the inhabitants sufficient strength to run away from home.' All these quick and lively sallies were said sportively, quite in jest, and with a smile, which showed that he meant only wit. Upon this topic he and Mr. Wilkes could perfectly assimilate; here was a bond of union between them, and I was conscious that as

31. A weak or inferior beer.
32. Scrub is the servant to Sullen in George Farquhar's comedy *The Beaux' Stratagem* (1707); he has a different duty each day (that of butler on Sundays) and supplies a full staff in himself.

both of them had visited Caledonia, both were fully satisfied of the strange narrow ignorance of those who imagine that it is a land of famine. But they amused themselves with persevering in the old jokes. When I claimed a superiority for Scotland over England in one respect, that no man can be arrested there for a debt merely because another swears it against him; but there must first be the judgement of a court of law ascertaining its justice; and that a seizure of the person, before judgement is obtained, can take place only, if his creditor should swear that he is about to fly from the country, or, as it is technically expressed, is in *meditatione fugæ*: [33] W I L K E S. 'That, I should think, may be safely sworn of all the Scotch nation.' J O H N S O N. (to Mr. Wilkes,) 'You must know, Sir, I lately took my friend Boswell and showed him genuine civilised life in an English provincial town. I turned him loose at Lichfield, my native city, that he might see for once real civility: for you know he lives among savages in Scotland and among rakes in London.' W I L K E S. 'Except when he is with grave, sober, decent people like you and me.' J O H N S O N. (smiling,) 'And we ashamed of him.'

They were quite frank and easy. Johnson told the story of his asking Mrs. Macaulay to allow her footman to sit down with them,[34] to prove the ridiculousness of the argument for the equality of mankind; and he said to me afterwards, with a nod of satisfaction, 'You saw Mr. Wilkes acquiesced.' Wilkes talked with all imaginable freedom of the ludicrous title given to the Attorney-General, *Diabolus Regis;* [35] adding, 'I have reason to know something about that officer; for I was prosecuted for a libel.' Johnson, who many people would have supposed must have been furiously angry at hearing this talked of so lightly, said not a word. He was now, *indeed,* 'a good-humoured fellow.' . . .

This record, though by no means so perfect as I could wish, will serve to give a notion of a very curious interview, which was not only pleasing at the time, but had the agreeable and benignant effect of reconciling any animosity, and sweetening any acidity, which in the various bustle of political contest, had been produced in the minds of two men, who though widely different, had so many things in common—classical learning, modern literature, wit, and humour, and ready repartee—that it would have been much to be regretted if they had been for ever at a distance from each other.

Mr. Burke gave me much credit for this successful *negotiation;* and pleasantly said, that 'there was nothing to equal it in the whole history of the *Corps Diplomatique.*' . . .

On the evening of the next day I took leave of him, being to set out for Scotland. I thanked him with great warmth for all his kindness. 'Sir, (said he,) you are very welcome. Nobody repays it with more.'

How very false is the notion which has gone round the world of the rough, and passionate, and harsh manners of this great and good man. That he had occasional sallies of heat of temper, and that he was sometimes, perhaps, too

33. "Meditating flight."
34. That proposal silenced the "great republican" but, Johnson reported, "She has never liked me since. Sir, your levellers wish to level *down* as far as themselves; but they cannot bear levelling *up* to themselves."
35. "The King's Devil."

'easily provoked' by absurdity and folly, and sometimes too desirous of triumph in colloquial contest, must be allowed. The quickness both of his perception and sensibility disposed him to sudden explosions of satire; to which his extraordinary readiness of wit was a strong and almost irresistible incitement. To adopt one of the finest images in Mr. Home's *Douglas,*

> On each glance of thought
> Decision followed, as the thunderbolt
> Pursues the flash! [36]

I admit that the beadle [37] within him was often so eager to apply the lash, that the Judge had not time to consider the case with sufficient deliberation.

That he was occasionally remarkable for violence of temper may be granted: but let us ascertain the degree, and not let it be supposed that he was in a perpetual rage, and never without a club in his hand, to knock down every one who approached him. On the contrary, the truth is, that by much the greatest part of his time he was civil, obliging, nay, polite in the true sense of the word; so much so, that many gentlemen, who were long acquainted with him, never received, or even heard a strong expression from him.

[1777: The Fear of Death]

I mentioned to Dr. Johnson, that David Hume's persisting in his infidelity, when he was dying, shocked me much.[38] J o h n s o n. 'Why should it shock you, Sir? Hume owned he had never read the New Testament with attention. Here then was a man, who had been at no pains to inquire into the truth of religion, and had continually turned his mind the other way. It was not to be expected that the prospect of death would alter his way of thinking, unless God should send an angel to set him right.' I said, I had reason to believe that the thought of annihilation gave Hume no pain. J o h n s o n. 'It was not so, Sir. He had a vanity in being thought easy. It is more probable that he should assume an appearance of ease, than that so very improbable a thing should be as a man not afraid of going (as, in spite of his delusive theory, he cannot be sure but he may go,) into an unknown state, and not being uneasy at leaving all he knew. And you are to consider, that upon his own principle of annihilation he had no motive to speak the truth.' The horror of death which I had always observed in Dr. Johnson, appeared strong tonight. I ventured to tell him, that I had been, for moments in my life, not afraid of death; therefore I could suppose another man in that state of mind for a considerable space of time. He said, 'he never had a moment in which death was not terrible to him.' He added, that it had been observed, that scarce any man dies in public, but with apparent resolution; from that desire of praise

36. *Douglas* was the very popular tragedy by John Home (1722–1808), dramatist and friend of the poet William Collins.
37. A minor official who keeps order.
38. Boswell had an interview with Hume seven weeks before his death in 1776 and wrote an account of his own sense of danger in the face of Hume's obdurate disbelief in personal immortality ("But I maintained my faith"); still, Boswell admits that Hume was so good-humored that "Death for the time did not seem dismal."

which never quits us. I said, Dr. Dodd [39] seemed to be willing to die, and full of hopes of happiness. 'Sir, (said he,) Dr. Dodd would have given both his hands and both his legs to have lived. The better a man is, the more afraid he is of death, having a clearer view of infinite purity.' He owned, that our being in an unhappy uncertainty as to our salvation, was mysterious; and said, 'Ah! we must wait till we are in another state of being to have many things explained to us.' Even the powerful mind of Johnson seemed foiled by futurity. But I thought, that the gloom of uncertainty in solemn religious speculation, being mingled with hope, was yet more consolatory than the emptiness of infidelity. A man can live in thick air, but perishes in an exhausted receiver.

Dr. Johnson was much pleased with a remark which I told him was made to me by General Paoli: [40]—'That it is impossible not to be afraid of death; and that those who at the time of dying are not afraid, are not thinking of death, but of applause, or something else, which keeps death out of their sight: so that all men are equally afraid of death when they see it; only some have a power of turning their sight away from it better than others.' . . .

Some ladies, who had been present yesterday when I mentioned his birthday, came to dinner today, and plagued him unintentionally, by wishing him joy. I know not why he disliked having his birthday mentioned, unless it were that it reminded him of his approaching nearer to death, of which he had a constant dread.

I mentioned to him a friend of mine who was formerly gloomy from low spirits, and much distressed by the fear of death, but was now uniformly placid, and contemplated his dissolution without any perturbation. 'Sir, (said Johnson,) this is only a disordered imagination taking a different turn.' . . .

He observed, that a gentleman of eminence in literature [41] had got into a bad style of poetry of late. 'He puts (said he,) a very common thing in a strange dress till he does not know it himself, and thinks other people do not know it.' B o s w e l l. 'That is owing to his being so much versant in old English poetry.' J o h n s o n. 'What is that to the purpose, Sir? If I say a man is drunk, and you tell me it is owing to his taking much drink, the matter is not mended. No, Sir,——has taken to an odd mode. For example, he'd write thus:

> Hermit hoar, in solemn cell,
> Wearing out life's evening gray.

Gray evening is common enough; but *evening gray* he'd think fine.[42]—Stay;— we'll make out the stanza:

39. Dr. William Dodd (1729–77), king's chaplain and a popular preacher, forged a bond in the name of Lord Chesterfield, his former pupil; before his execution for this crime, Johnson did much for him and wrote several documents for him, including a "last solemn declaration." Dodd wrote Johnson at the very last: "Admitted, as I trust I shall be, to the realms of bliss before you, I shall hail *your* arrival there with transport. . . ."
40. General Pasquale Paoli (1725–1807), the Corsican general and patriot who had found asylum in England.
41. Thomas Warton (1728–90), who had just published a volume of poems.
42. Writing later in his life of Collins, Johnson complained of similar affectations in Warton's friend: "he puts his words out of the common order, seeming to think . . . that not to write prose is certainly to write poetry."

> Hermit hoar, in solemn cell,
>> Wearing out life's evening gray;
> Smite thy bosom, sage, and tell,
>> What is bliss? and which the way?

B o s w e l l. 'But why smite his bosom, Sir?' J o h n s o n. 'Why, to show he was in earnest,' (smiling.)—He at an after period added the following stanza:

> Thus I spoke; and speaking sighed;
>> —Scarce repressed the starting tear;—
> When the smiling sage replied—
>> —Come, my lad, and drink some beer.

I cannot help thinking the first stanza very good solemn poetry, as also the three first lines of the second. Its last line is an excellent burlesque surprise on gloomy sentimental enquirers. And, perhaps, the advice is as good as can be given to a low-spirited dissatisfied being:—'Don't trouble your head with sickly thinking: take a cup, and be merry.'

[The Character of Samuel Johnson]

The character of Samuel Johnson has, I trust, been so developed in the course of this work, that they who have honoured it with a perusal, may be considered as well acquainted with him. As, however, it may be expected that I should collect into one view the capital and distinguishing features of this extraordinary man, I shall endeavour to acquit myself of that part of my biographical undertaking, however difficult it may be to do that which many of my readers will do better for themselves.

His figure was large and well formed, and his countenance of the cast of an ancient statue; yet his appearance was rendered strange and somewhat uncouth by convulsive cramps, by the scars of that distemper [43] which it was once imagined the royal touch could cure, and by a slovenly mode of dress. He had the use only of one eye; yet so much does mind govern and even supply the deficiency of organs that his visual perceptions, as far as they extended, were uncommonly quick and accurate. So morbid was his temperament that he never knew the natural joy of a free and vigorous use of his limbs: when he walked, it was like the struggling gait of one in fetters; when he rode, he had no command or direction of his horse, but was carried as if in a balloon. That with his constitution and habits of life he should have lived seventy-five years, is a proof that an inherent *vivida vis* [44] is a powerful preservative of the human frame.

Man is, in general, made up of contradictory qualities; and these will ever show themselves in strange succession, where a consistency in appearance at least, if not in reality, has not been attained by long habits of philosophical discipline. In proportion to the native vigour of the mind, the contradictory qualities will be the more prominent, and more difficult to be adjusted; and, therefore, we are not to wonder, that Johnson exhibited an eminent example of

43. Scrofula.
44. Lively force.

this remark which I have made upon human nature. At different times, he seemed a different man, in some respects; not, however, in any great or essential article upon which he had fully employed his mind and settled certain principles of duty, but only in his manners and in the display of argument and fancy in his talk. He was prone to superstition, but not to credulity. Though his imagination might incline him to a belief of the marvellous and the mysterious, his vigorous reason examined the evidence with jealousy. He was a sincere and zealous Christian, of high Church-of-England and monarchical principles, which he would not tamely suffer to be questioned; and had, perhaps, at an early period, narrowed his mind somewhat too much, both as to religion and politics. His being impressed with the danger of extreme latitude in either, though he was of a very independent spirit, occasioned his appearing somewhat unfavourable to the prevalence of that noble freedom of sentiment which is the best possession of man. Nor can it be denied that he had many prejudices; which, however, frequently suggested many of his pointed sayings, that rather show a playfulness of fancy than any settled malignity. He was steady and inflexible in maintaining the obligations of religion and morality; both from a regard for the order of society, and from a veneration for the Great Source of all order; correct, nay stern in his taste; hard to please, and easily offended; impetuous and irritable in his temper, but of a most humane and benevolent heart, which showed itself not only in a most liberal charity, as far as his circumstances would allow, but in a thousand instances of active benevolence. He was afflicted with a bodily disease which made him often restless and fretful; and with a constitutional melancholy, the clouds of which darkened the brightness of his fancy and gave a gloomy cast to his whole course of thinking: we, therefore, ought not to wonder at his sallies of impatience and passion at any time; especially when provoked by obtrusive ignorance or presuming petulance; and allowance must be made for his uttering hasty and satirical sallies, even against his best friends. And, surely, when it is considered, that, 'amidst sickness and sorrow,' he exerted his faculties in so many works for the benefit of mankind, and particularly that he achieved the great and admirable DICTIONARY of our language, we must be astonished at his resolution. The solemn text, 'of him to whom much is given, much will be required,' [45] seems to have been ever present to his mind, in a rigorous sense, and to have made him dissatisfied with his labours and acts of goodness, however comparatively great; so that the unavoidable consciousness of his superiority was, in that respect, a cause of disquiet. He suffered so much from this, and from the gloom which perpetually haunted him and made solitude frightful, that it may be said of him, 'If in this life only he had hope, he was of all men most miserable.' [46] He loved praise, when it was brought to him; but was too proud to seek for it. He was somewhat susceptible of flattery. As he was general and unconfined in his studies, he cannot be considered as master of any one particular science; but he had accumulated a vast and various collection of learning and knowledge, which was so arranged in his mind, as to be ever in readiness to be brought forth. But his superiority over other learned men consisted chiefly in what may be called the art of

45. A close paraphrase of Luke 12:48.
46. Adapting I Corinthians 15:19.

thinking, the art of using his mind; a certain continual power of seizing the useful substance of all that he knew and exhibiting it in a clear and forcible manner; so that knowledge, which we often see to be no better than lumber in men of dull understanding, was, in him, true, evident, and actual wisdom. His moral precepts are practical; for they are drawn from an intimate acquaintance with human nature. His maxims carry conviction; for they are founded on the basis of common sense, and a very attentive and minute survey of real life. His mind was so full of imagery that he might have been perpetually a poet; yet it is remarkable that, however rich his prose is in this respect, his poetical pieces, in general, have not much of that splendour, but are rather distinguished by strong sentiment and acute observation, conveyed in harmonious and energetic verse, particularly in heroic couplets. Though usually grave, and even awful, in his deportment, he possessed uncommon and peculiar powers of wit and humour; he frequently indulged himself in colloquial pleasantry; and the heartiest merriment was often enjoyed in his company; with this great advantage, that as it was entirely free from any poisonous tincture of vice or impiety, it was salutary to those who shared in it. He had accustomed himself to such accuracy in his common conversation, that he at all times expressed his thoughts with great force, and an elegant choice of language, the effect of which was aided by his having a loud voice and a slow deliberate utterance. In him were united a most logical head with a most fertile imagination, which gave him an extraordinary advantage in arguing: for he could reason close or wide, as he saw best for the moment. Exulting in his intellectual strength and dexterity, he could, when he pleased, be the greatest sophist that ever contended in the lists of declamation; and, from a spirit of contradiction and a delight in showing his powers, he would often maintain the wrong side with equal warmth and ingenuity; so that when there was an audience, his real opinions could seldom be gathered from his talk; though when he was in company with a single friend, he would discuss a subject with genuine fairness: but he was too conscientious to make error permanent and pernicious by deliberately writing it; and, in all his numerous works, he earnestly inculcated what appeared to him to be the truth; his piety being constant, and the ruling principle of all his conduct.

Such was SAMUEL JOHNSON, a man whose talents, acquirements, and virtues, were so extraordinary, that the more his character is considered, the more he will be regarded by the present age, and by posterity, with admiration and reverence.

1791

From The Journal of a Tour to the Hebrides with Samuel Johnson, LL.D.

Wednesday, 1st September, 1773   I awaked very early. I began to imagine that the landlord,[1] being about to emigrate, might murder us to get our money, and lay it upon the soldiers in the barn. Such groundless fears will arise in the

1. This was written of the stay at Anoch in Glenmorison, the occasion for Johnson's description of the Highlands in his *Journey* (see The Garden and the Wild).

mind, before it has resumed its vigour after sleep! Dr. Johnson had had the same kind of ideas; for he told me afterwards, that he considered so many soldiers, having seen us, would be witnesses, should any harm be done, and that circumstance, I suppose, he considered as a security. When I got up, I found him sound asleep in his miserable sty, as I may call it, with a coloured handkerchief tied round his head. With difficulty could I awaken him. It reminded me of Henry the Fourth's fine soliloquy on sleep; for there was here as *uneasy a pallet* as the poet's imagination could possibly conceive.[2]

A redcoat of the 15th regiment, whether officer or only sergeant I could not be sure, came to the house in his way to the mountains to shoot deer, which it seems the Laird of Glenmorison does not hinder anybody to do. Few, indeed, can do them harm. We had him to breakfast with us. We got away about eight. M'Queen[3] walked some miles to give us a convoy. He had, in 1745, joined the Highland army at Fort Augustus, and continued in it till after battle of Culloden.[4] As he narrated the particulars of that ill-advised but brave attempt, I could not refrain from tears. There is a certain association of ideas in my mind upon that subject, by which I am strongly affected. The very Highland names, or the sound of a bagpipe, will stir my blood, and fill me with a mixture of melancholy and respect for courage; with pity for the unfortunate, and superstitious regard for antiquity, and thoughtless inclination for war; in short, with a crowd of sensations with which sober rationality has nothing to do.

We passed through Glensheal, with prodigious mountains on each side. We saw where the battle was fought in the year 1719.[5] Dr. Johnson owned he was now in a scene of as wild nature as he could see; but he corrected me sometimes in my inaccurate observations.—'There (said I) is a mountain like a cone.'—*Johnson.* 'No, sir. It would be called so in a book; and when a man comes to look at it, he sees it is not so. It is indeed pointed at the top; but one side of it is larger than the other.'—Another mountain I called immense.— *Johnson.* 'No; it is no more than a considerable protuberance.'

Sunday, 12th September . . . We spoke of Death. Dr. Johnson on this subject observed, that the boastings of some men as to dying easily were idle talk, proceeding from partial views. I mentioned Hawthornden's Cypress-grove,[6] where it is said that the world is a mere show; and that it is unreasonable for a man to wish to continue in the show-room, after he has seen it. Let him go cheerfully out, and give place to other spectators.—*Johnson.* 'Yes, sir, if he is sure he is to be well, after he goes out of it. But if he is to grow blind after he goes out of the show-room, and never to see any thing again; or if he does not know whither he is to go next, a man will not go cheerfully out of a show-room. No wise man will be contented to die, if he thinks he is to go into

---

2. See II *Henry IV* III.i for the soliloquy.
3. The landlord at Anoch.
4. The decisive defeat, April 16, 1746, of the Highlanders under the Jacobite Prince Charles Edward by the English troops under the Duke of Cumberland.
5. The battle of Glensheal (or Glenshiel) was lost to the British by a Jacobite force of Highlanders and Spaniards.
6. "The Cypress Grove" was a prose meditation on death by William Drummond of Hawthornden (1585–1649). For similar reflections by Johnson, see the passage from Boswell's *Life* for 1777 given above.

a state of punishment. Nay, no wise man will be contented to die, if he thinks he is to fall into annihilation: for however unhappy any man's existence may be, he yet would rather have it, than not exist at all. No; there is no rational principle by which a man can die contented, but a trust in the mercy of GOD, through the merits of Jesus Christ.'—This short sermon, delivered with an earnest tone, in a boat upon the sea, which was perfectly calm, on a day appropriated to religious worship, while every one listened with an air of satisfaction, had a most pleasing effect upon my mind.

Pursuing the same train of serious reflection, he added, that it seemed certain that happiness could not be found in this life, because so many had tried to find it, in such a variety of ways, and had not found it. . . .

Monday and Tuesday, September 13–14 . . . We arrived at Dunvegan late in the afternoon. The great size of the castle, which is partly old and partly new, and is built upon a rock close to the sea, while the land around it presents nothing but wild, moorish, hilly, and craggy appearances, gave a rude magnificence to the scene. . . . We were introduced into a stately dining-room, and received by Lady Macleod,[7] mother of the laird, who, with his friend Talisker, having been detained on the road, did not arrive till some time after us.

We found the lady of the house a very polite and sensible woman, who had lived for some time in London, and had there been in Dr. Johnson's company. . . .

Dr. Johnson said in the morning, 'Is not this a fine lady?'—There was not a word now of his 'impatience to be in civilized life';—though indeed I should beg pardon,—he found it here. We had slept well, and lain long. After breakfast we surveyed the castle, and the garden. . . . M'Leod started the subject of making women do penance in the church for fornication.—*Johnson.* 'It is right, sir. Infamy is attached to the crime, by universal opinion, as soon as it is known. I would not be the man who would discover it, if I alone knew it, for a woman may reform; nor would I commend a parson who divulges a woman's first offence; but being once divulged, it ought to be infamous. Consider of what importance to society the chastity of women is. Upon that all the property in the world depends. We hang a thief for stealing a sheep; but the unchastity of a woman transfers sheep, and farm and all, from the right owner. I have much more reverence for a common prostitute than for a woman who conceals her guilt. The prostitute is known. She cannot deceive: she cannot bring a strumpet into the arms of an honest man, without his knowledge.'—*Boswell.* 'There is, however, a great difference between the licentiousness of a single woman and that of a married woman.'—*Johnson.* 'Yes, sir; there is a great difference between stealing a shilling and stealing a thousand pounds; between simply taking a man's purse, and murdering him first, and then taking it. But when one begins to be vicious, it is easy to go on. Where single women are licentious, you rarely find faithful married women.'— *Boswell.* 'And yet we are told that in some nations in India, the distinction is strictly observed.'—*Johnson.* 'Nay, don't give us India. That puts me in mind of

---

7. John McLeod (d. 1786) was 9th Laird of Raasay; his son, Colonel John McLeod (1718–98), and the latter's wife also entertained Boswell and Johnson.

Montesquieu,[8] who is really a fellow of genius too in many respects; whenever he wants to support a strange opinion, he quotes you the practice of Japan or of some other distant country, of which he knows nothing. To support po lygamy, he tells you of the island of Formosa, where there are ten women born for one man. He had but to suppose another island, where there are ten men born for one woman, and so make a marriage between them.'

At supper, Lady M'Leod mentioned Dr. Cadogan's book on the gout.[9] Lady M'Leod objected that the author does not practice what he teaches.— *Johnson.* 'I cannot help that, madam. That does not make his book the worse. People are influenced more by what a man says if his practice is suitable to it,—because they are blockheads. The more intellectual people are, the readier will they attend to what a man tells them. If it is just, they will follow it, be his practice what it will. No man practises so well as he writes. I have, all my life long, been lying till noon; yet I tell all young men, and tell them with great sincerity, that nobody who does not rise early will ever do any good. Only consider! You read a book; you are convinced by it; you do not know the author. Suppose you afterwards know him, and find that he does not practise what he teaches; are you to give up your former conviction? At this rate you would be kept in a state of equilibrium, when reading every book, till you knew how the author practised.'—'But,' said Lady M'Leod, 'you would think better of Dr. Cadogan, if he acted according to his principles.'—*Johnson.* 'Why, madam, to be sure, a man who acts in the face of light is worse than a man who does not know so much; yet I think no man should be the worse thought of for publishing good principles. There is something noble in publishing truth, though it condemns one's self.'—I expressed some surprize at Cadogan's recommending good humour, as if it were quite in our own power to attain it. —*Johnson.* 'Why, sir, a man grows better humoured as he grows older. He improves by experience. When young, he thinks himself of great consequence, and every thing of importance. As he advances in life, he learns to think himself of no consequence, and little things of little importance; and so he becomes more patient, and better pleased. All good-humour and complaisance are acquired. Naturally a child seizes directly what it sees, and thinks of pleasing itself only. By degrees, it is taught to please others, and to prefer others; and that this will ultimately produce the greatest happiness. If a man is not convinced of that, he never will practise it. Common language speaks the truth as to this: we say, a person is well *bred.* As it is said, that all material motion is primarily in a right line, and is never *per circuitum,* never in another form, unless by some particular cause; so it may be said intellectual motion is.' —Lady M'Leod asked, if no man was naturally good?—*Johnson.* 'No, madam, no more than a wolf.'—*Boswell.* 'Nor no woman, sir?'—*Johnson.* 'No, sir.'— Lady M'Leod started at this, saying, in a low voice, 'This is worse than Swift.'

Tuesday, October 19 . . . We continued to coast along Mull, and passed

8. Referring to the use of comparative evidence (such as had earlier been made by John Locke) by the Baron de Montesquieu (1689–1755) in *The Spirit of Laws* (1748); here a probable allusion to XVI.iv.
9. *A Dissertation on the Gout* (1771), a very popular work (nine printings in its first year). Dr. Cadogan was believed (perhaps falsely) to drink more than he could recommend in his book.

by Nuns' Island, which, it is said, belonged to the nuns of Icolmkill, and from which, we were told, the stone for the buildings there was taken. As we sailed along by moonlight, in a sea somewhat rough, and often between black and gloomy rocks, Dr. Johnson said, 'If this be not *roving among the Hebrides,* nothing is.'—The repetition of words which he had so often previously used, made a strong impression on my imagination; and, by a natural course of thinking, led me to consider how our present adventures would appear to me at a future period.

I have often experienced, that scenes through which a man has passed, improve by lying in the memory: they grow mellow. *Acti labores sunt jucundi.*[10] This may be owing to comparing them with present listless ease. Even harsh scenes acquire a softness by length of time; and some are like very loud sounds, which do not please, or at least do not please so much, till you are removed to a certain distance. They may be compared to strong coarse pictures, which will not bear to be viewed near. Even pleasing scenes improve by time, and seem more exquisite in recollection than when they were present; if they have not faded to dimness in the memory. Perhaps, there is so much evil in every human enjoyment when present,—so much dross mixed with it, that it requires to be refined by time; and yet I do not see why time should not melt away the good and the evil in equal proportions;—why the shade should decay, and the light remain in preservation.

After a tedious sail, which, by our following various turnings of the coast of Mull, was extended to about forty miles, it gave us no small pleasure to perceive a light in the village at Icolmkill, in which almost all the inhabitants of the island live, close to where the ancient buildings stood. As we approached the shore, the tower of the cathedral, just discernible in the air, was a picturesque object.

When we had landed upon the sacred place, which, as long as I can remember, I had thought on with veneration, Dr. Johnson and I cordially embraced. We had long talked of visiting Icolmkill; and, from the lateness of the season, were at times very doubtful whether we should be able to effect our purpose. To have seen it, even alone, would have given me great satisfaction; but the venerable scene was rendered much more pleasing by the company of my great and pious friend, who was no less affected by it than I was; and who has described the impressions it should make on the mind, with such strength of thought, and energy of language, that I shall quote his words, as conveying my own sensations much more forcibly than I am capable of doing:

'We were now treading that illustrious Island, which was once the luminary of the Caledonian regions, whence savage clans and roving barbarians derived the benefits of knowledge, and the blessings of religion. To abstract the mind from all local emotion would be impossible, if it were endeavoured, and would be foolish, if it were possible. Whatever withdraws us from the power of our senses, whatever makes the past, the distant, or the future, predominate over the present, advances us in the dignity of thinking beings. Far from me, and from my friends, be such frigid philosophy as may conduct us indifferent and

---

10. "Past labors are sweet," Cicero, *De Finibus* II.32.

unmoved over any ground which has been dignified by wisdom, bravery, or virtue. That man is little to be envied, whose patriotism would not gain force upon the plain of *Marathon*, or whose piety would not grow warmer among the ruins of *Iona!*" [11]

1773   1785

SAMUEL JOHNSON
1709–1784

Samuel Johnson dominates the English literary scene of the later eighteenth century and has, as well, become one of the mythical heroes of British common sense. Because of Boswell's remarkable *Life* we know him in more vividly intimate detail than most men of any age, and we are rarely without a sense of his personal presence as we read his works. While the range of Johnson's work is great, it has remarkable unity; for, whatever the stretch of his mind into natural science, philology, or history, it returns insistently to central moral themes, and notably to his favorite one, the efforts of the mind to escape the limitations of the actual. Whether in stupor or fantasy, in self-deception or in distraction, the mind seeks to elude that reality that stands outside it and rebuffs its systems. We see this in Johnson's attack upon the rules by which Shakespeare was foolishly judged, but we see it also in his identification of Shakespeare's "fatal Cleopatra" (an uncontrolled indulgence in verbal play). We see it ironically presented in Rasselas's fruitless quest for an ideal "choice of life," or in Johnson's acknowledgment of man's need for hope, however delusive. We see it in the "vanity" that overleaps the given, in the easy consolation that mistakes intention for act, in idleness and the fear of the self that seeks refuge in procrastination.

Johnson was born the son of a Lichfield bookseller, attended Oxford, and set up as a schoolmaster upon his marriage to Elizabeth Jervis Porter. In 1737 he went to London with his pupil David Garrick and began a literary career of translation, scholarship, and journalism. Among his remarkable feats was the reconstruction from notes of parliamentary debates for the *Gentleman's Magazine* (1741–44). His career was marked by three great projects. The first was the *Dictionary of the English Language* (1755), the second the edition of Shakespeare with preface and notes (1765), the third the *Lives of the Poets* written to accompany a printing of their works. But these projects were accompanied as well by the remarkable poems; the extensive series of essays that filled the *Rambler* twice a week (1750–52), and later *The Adventurer* (1753) and the *Idler* (1758–60); and the philosophical tale *Rasselas* (1759). In 1763 he met James Boswell and ten years later toured Scotland and the Hebrides with him producing the *Journey to the Western Islands of Scotland* in 1775.

Johnson became the center of a group that included David Garrick, Edmund Burke, Sir Joshua Reynolds, Oliver Goldsmith, and others; and he often contributed encouragement, advice, and even revisions to the works of his contemporaries—notably Goldsmith, Reynolds, and Crabbe. In his conversation as well as his writing, Johnson exhibits different aspects, or perhaps different degrees of intensity. He could, with a strong histrionic sense and the levity of a debater, adopt an outrageous stance and

11. "Had our tour produced nothing but this sublime passage, the world must have acknowledged that it was not made in vain." (Boswell)

win the pleasures of domination; Johnson's nature demanded power, and he never questioned its appeal. He could, at other times, show a more defensive assertiveness, a bravado, in the face of his own doubts or fears, which insisted upon what he needed to believe in defiance of what, at a deeper level, he genuinely could. But more impressive than either is the empiricism that can be called common sense but is in fact something more radical: a recognition of the reality of the actual and a refusal to let it be dissolved in theory or masked in convention. "Liberty is the birthright of man, and where obedience is compelled, there is no liberty." This he takes to be the argument of the American revolutionaries. "The answer is equally simple. Government is necessary to man, and where obedience is not compelled, there is no government." This positivistic recognition of the fact of power is typical: "It is not infallible, for it may do wrong; but it is irresistible, for it can be resisted only by rebellion, by an act which makes it questionable what shall be thenceforward the supreme power." These three stances—the histrionic, the defensive, and the empirical—are hard to separate, and Johnson's tone must always be considered. He is a great ironist, and yet he is not the kind of skeptic who can remain uncommitted; he asserts with absoluteness what must not be ignored, however easily or little it can be wedded with its contraries or reconciled with our desires.

The Vanity of Human Wishes

Like Pope's Horatian imitations, Johnson's is a free adaptation of Juvenal's poem to his own time and to his own frame of thought. This is nowhere clearer than in the closing lines, where Juvenal writes, "You would have no divinity if there were wisdom; it is we who make a goddess of you, Fortune, and place you in the heavens." Johnson sees instead the force of "celestial wisdom" saving man from himself, making the good fortune ("happiness") man cannot create for himself or even ask for properly. We have contemporary reactions to the difficulty of Johnson's condensed verse; David Garrick judged it "as hard as Greek." Johnson found in Juvenal a "mixture of gaiety and stateliness, of pointed sentences" (i.e. *sententiae* or maxims) "and declamatory grandeur." His version is more formal and austere than Dryden's, using the spacious generalization to indicate the ludicrous folly, as in the brilliant lines on the displaced favorite, whose image has lost its goodness with its greatness. The removal of the portrait is not presented dramatically or pictorially but in all the irony of its elaborate rationalization: "The form distorted justifies the fall, / And detestation rids the indignant wall." It is as if the very wall cannot bear his presence, as if his distortion of form is so strikingly evident to all that it cannot expect a moment's further tolerance; such, Johnson implies, is the cost of losing power in a world that knows no other standard. One can see "gaiety" in this rendering of lunacy as well as "stateliness" in the solemn recording of its pretexts, and even more in the deeper sense of its universal prevalence. The density of Johnson's diction is best seen in such compressed phrases, from which numerous particulars can be surmised, as "The general massacre of gold" or "dubious title shakes the madded land."

The Vanity of Human Wishes

The Tenth Satire of Juvenal Imitated

Let observation with extensive view,
Survey mankind, from China to Peru;
Remark each anxious toil, each eager strife,
And watch the busy scenes of crowded life;
Then say how hope and fear, desire and hate,
O'erspread with snares the clouded maze of fate,
Where wavering man, betrayed by venturous pride,
To tread the dreary paths without a guide,
As treacherous phantoms in the mist delude,
10   Shuns fancied ills, or chases airy good;
How rarely reason guides the stubborn choice,
Rules the bold hand, or prompts the suppliant voice;
How nations sink, by darling schemes oppressed,
When vengeance listens to the fool's request.°
Fate wings with every wish the afflictive dart,°
Each gift of nature, and each grace of art,
With fatal heat impetuous courage glows,
With fatal sweetness elocution flows,
Impeachment° stops the speaker's powerful breath,
20   And restless fire precipitates° on death.
But scarce observed, the knowing and the bold
Fall in the general massacre of gold;
Wide-wasting pest! that rages unconfined,
And crowds with crimes the records of mankind;
For gold his sword the hireling ruffian draws,
For gold the hireling judge distorts the laws;
Wealth heaped on wealth, nor truth nor safety buys,
The dangers gather° as the treasures rise.
Let history tell where rival kings command,
30   And dubious title shakes the madded land,
When statutes glean the refuse of the sword,°
How much more safe the vassal than the lord;
Low skulks the hind° beneath the rage of power,
And leaves the wealthy traitor° in the Tower,
Untouched his cottage, and his slumbers sound,

When vengeance . . . request i.e. the harshest vengeance is to give what the fool seeks, here a favorite ("darling") scheme
Fate wings . . . dart i.e. the dart is given flight (feathered) by every wish, gift, or "grace of art"
Impeachment public accusation
precipitates rushes or falls headlong; with perhaps the chemical sense of falling to the bottom as a sediment (the opposite of chemical sublimation)
The dangers gather Cf. Matthew 24:28: "For wheresoever the carcass is, there will the eagles be gathered together"; cf. the "vultures" of l. 36.

When statutes . . . sword i.e. when new laws undo those spared by open conflict; cf. l. 59
hind peasant
wealthy traitor perhaps the overthrown leader, now declared a "traitor" and imprisoned in the Tower of London, as Robert Harley, Earl of Oxford, chief minister of Queen Anne, was upon the accession of George I and Whig power in 1714 (see l. 130 below). More recent instances were the imprisonment and execution of Scottish lords after the Jacobite rising of 1745, and Johnson had originally written "bonny traitor."

Though confiscation's vultures hover round.
   The needy traveller, serene and gay,
Walks the wild heath, and sings his toil away.
Does envy seize thee? crush the upbraiding joy,
Increase his riches and his peace destroy;
Now fears in dire vicissitude invade,
The rustling brake° alarms, and quivering shade,
Nor light nor darkness bring his pain relief,
One shows the plunder, and one hides the thief.
   Yet still one general cry the skies assails,
And gain and grandeur load the tainted gales;°
Few know the toiling statesman's fear or care,
The insidious rival and the gaping heir.
   Once more, Democritus,° arise on earth,
With cheerful wisdom and instructive mirth,
See motley° life in modern trappings dressed,
And feed with varied fools the eternal jest:
Thou who couldst laugh where want enchained caprice,
Toil crushed conceit,° and man was of a piece;
Where wealth unloved without a mourner died,
And scarce a sycophant was fed by pride;
Where ne'er was known the form of mock debate,
Or seen a new-made mayor's unwieldy state;°
Where change of favorites made no change of laws,
And senates heard before they judged a cause;
How wouldst thou shake at Britain's modish tribe,
Dart the quick taunt, and edge the piercing gibe,
Attentive truth and nature to descry,
And pierce each scene with philosophic eye.
To thee were solemn toys or empty show
The robes of pleasure and the veils of woe:
All aid the farce, and all thy mirth maintain,
Whose joys are causeless or whose griefs are vain.
   Such was the scorn that filled the sage's mind,
Renewed at every glance on humankind;
How just that scorn ere yet thy voice declare,
Search every state, and canvass every prayer.
   Unnumbered suppliants crowd Preferment's gate,°
Athirst for wealth, and burning to be great;
Delusive Fortune hears the incessant call,
They mount, they shine, evaporate, and fall.
On every stage the foes of peace attend,

40
50
60
70

---

brake thicket
tainted gales breezes carrying the scent of the
hunted quarry
Democritus (*c.* 460–370 B.C.) known as the
"laughing philosopher." Robert Burton wrote as
Democritus Junior in *The Anatomy of Melancholy* (1621), one of Johnson's favorite books.
motley of various colors, like the traditional
Fool's costume
conceit imagination
unwieldy state referring to the gilt coach and
elaborate rituals of the Lord Mayor's procession
Preferment's gate the gate of a lord who can
grant posts of office

Hate dogs their flight, and insult mocks their end.
Love ends with hope, the sinking statesman's door
80 Pours in the morning worshipper° no more;
For growing names the weekly scribbler° lies,
To growing wealth the dedicator flies,
From every room descends the painted face,
That hung the bright Palladium° of the place,
And smoked in kitchens, or in auctions sold,
To better features yields the frame of gold;
For now no more we trace in every line
Heroic worth, benevolence divine:
The form distorted justifies the fall,
90 And detestation rids the indignant wall.
    But will not Britain hear the last appeal,
Sign her foes' doom, or guard her favourites' zeal?
Through Freedom's sons no more remonstrance° rings,
Degrading nobles and controlling kings;
Our supple tribes repress their patriot throats,
And ask no questions but the price of votes;
With weekly libels and septennial ale,°
Their wish is full to riot and to rail.
    In full-blown dignity, see Wolsey° stand,
00 Law in his voice, and fortune in his hand:
To him the church, the realm, their powers consign,
Through him the rays of regal bounty shine,
Turned by his nod the stream of honour flows,
His smile alone security bestows:
Still to new heights his restless wishes tower,
Claim leads to claim, and power advances power;
Till conquest unresisted ceased to please,
And rights submitted left him none to seize.
At length his sovereign frowns—the train of state
10 Mark the keen glance and watch the sign to hate.
Where'er he turns he meets a stranger's eye,
His suppliants scorn him and his followers fly;
At once is lost the pride of awful state,
The golden canopy, the glittering plate,
The regal palace, the luxurious board,

morning worshipper the assiduous attendant at levees (or morning receptions)
the weekly scribbler in the political journals
Palladium the statue of Pallas Athena that supposedly conferred safety upon the city of Troy and was stolen by Diomedes so that Troy might be taken. The portrait which served this protective purpose has now been banished to the smoky kitchen or sold off and only the frame preserved.
remonstrance alluding to the Grand Remonstrance of 1641 demanding that Charles I's council be chosen from men approved by Parliament

septennial ale provided at parliamentary elections (held at least every seven years) to attract votes, as were more substantial bribes and the demagoguery of newspaper campaigns ("weekly libels"). Thus parliamentary "questions" and debate give way, through corruption, to demonstrations and slanderous railing.
Wolsey Thomas Wolsey (c. 1475–1530), cardinal and Lord Chancellor of Henry VIII, replacing Juvenal's Sejanus, the favorite of the emperor Tiberius

The liveried army° and the menial lord.
With age, with cares, with maladies oppressed,
He seeks the refuge of monastic rest.
Grief aids disease, remembered folly stings,
120   And his last sighs reproach the faith of kings.
    Speak thou, whose thoughts at humble peace repine,
Shall Wolsey's wealth with Wolsey's end be thine?
Or livest thou now, with safer pride content,
The wisest justice on the banks of Trent?°
For why did Wolsey near the steeps of fate,
On weak foundations raise the enormous weight?
Why but to sink beneath misfortune's blow,
With louder ruin to the gulfs below?
    What gave great Villiers° to the assassin's knife,
130   And fixed disease on Harley's° closing life?
What murdered Wentworth, and what exiled Hyde,°
By kings protected, and to kings allied?
What but their wish indulged in courts to shine,
And power too great to keep, or to resign?
    When first the college rolls receive his name,
The young enthusiast quits his ease for fame;
Through all his veins the fever of renown
Burns from the strong contagion of the gown;°
O'er Bodley's dome° his future labours spread,
140   And Bacon's mansion° trembles o'er his head.
Are these thy views? proceed, illustrious youth,
And virtue guard thee to the throne of Truth!
Yet should thy soul indulge the generous heat,
Till captive Science yields her last retreat;
Should Reason guide thee with her brightest ray,
And pour on misty Doubt resistless day;°
Should no false Kindness lure to loose delight,
Nor Praise relax, nor Difficulty fright;
Should tempting Novelty thy cell refrain,
150   And Sloth effuse her opiate fumes in vain;
Should Beauty blunt on fops her fatal dart,
Nor claim the triumph of a lettered heart;
Should no Disease thy torpid veins invade,

liveried army an army of servants, or officers behaving as servants
on the banks of Trent any provincial scene, but here referring to Johnson's own birthplace, Lichfield
great Villiers George Villiers, 1st Duke of Buckingham, favorite of James I and Charles I, murdered in 1628
Harley's See above l. 34 and note; Harley later suffered bad health, perhaps because of his confinement in the Tower.
Wentworth . . . Hyde Thomas Wentworth, Earl of Strafford, advisor of Charles I, impeached and executed in 1641; Edward Hyde, Earl of Clarendon, Lord Chancellor to Charles II but impeached and banished in 1667 ("to

kings allied" as father-in-law of James II and grandfather of Queen Mary and Queen Anne)
the strong . . . gown with the suggestion of Nessus' shirt, the poisoned robe that caused Hercules so much torture that he tore away his flesh in trying to remove it
Bodley's dome the Bodleian Library at Oxford; "dome" is used in the sense of a building
Bacon's mansion referring to the tradition that the study of Roger Bacon, the medieval Oxford philosopher and scientist, built on an arch over a bridge, would fall when a greater man than Bacon passed under it
resistless day Cf. Pope, Essay on Criticism, ll. 211–12.

Nor Melancholy's phantoms haunt thy shade;
Yet hope not life from grief or danger free,
Nor think the doom of man reversed for thee:
Deign on the passing world to turn thine eyes,
And pause awhile from letters to be wise;
There mark what ills the scholar's life assail,
160 Toil, envy, want, the patron,° and the jail.
See nations slowly wise, and meanly just,
To buried merit raise the tardy bust.°
If dreams yet flatter, once again attend,
Hear Lydiat's life, and Galileo's end.°

     Nor deem, when learning her last prize bestows,
The glittering eminence exempt from foes;
See when the vulgar 'scape, despised or awed,
Rebellion's vengeful talons seize on Laud.°
From meaner minds, though smaller fines content,
170 The plundered palace or sequestered rent;°
Marked out by dangerous parts he meets the shock,
And fatal Learning leads him to the block:
Around his tomb let Art and Genius weep,
But hear his death, ye blockheads, hear and sleep.

     The festal blazes, the triumphal show,
The ravished standard, and the captive foe,
The senate's thanks, the gazette's° pompous tale,
With force resistless o'er the brave prevail.
Such bribes the rapid Greek° o'er Asia whirled,
180 For such the steady Romans shook the world;°
For such in distant lands the Britons° shine,
And stain with blood the Danube or the Rhine;
This power has praise that virtue scarce can warm,
Till fame supplies the universal charm.
Yet Reason frowns on War's unequal game,
Where wasted nations raise a single name,
And mortgaged states their grandsires' wreaths regret,°
From age to age in everlasting debt;

patron For this substitution for "garret" see
James Boswell's *Life of Johnson* on the publication of the *Dictionary*, where a patron is defined as "commonly a wretch who supports with
insolence and is paid with flattery."
tardy bust e.g. that of John Milton, not placed
in Westminster Abbey until 1737; but also late
monuments to Dryden (1720), Samuel Butler
(1721), and Shakespeare (1741)
Lydiat's . . . end Thomas Lydiat (1572–
1646), a brilliant scholar ranked with Francis
Bacon in his day but poor and forgotten at the
time of his death. Galileo (1564–1642) was
declared a heretic and imprisoned by the Inquisition in 1633 and later became blind (Mrs.
Piozzi recorded that Johnson "burst into a passion of tears" one day as he read aloud this
passage on the scholar's life).
Laud William Laud, Archbishop of Canterbury
under Charles I, was executed by Parliament in

1645; Johnson attributes his high-church policies to his "Learning" and his gifts ("parts").
sequestered rent confiscated income, sufficient
to "content" the persecutors of lesser men
gazette's official court record
rapid Greek Alexander the Great
shook the world perhaps evoking the famous
long marches of the Roman legions
Britons referring to the Duke of Marlborough's
campaigns in Austria and Bavaria, particularly
the great victory of Blenheim (1704) in the
War of the Spanish Succession
mortgaged states . . . regret Cf. Swift in *The
Conduct of the Allies* (1711): "It will, no
doubt, be a mighty comfort to our grandchildren, when they see a few rags hang up in
Westminster Hall which cost an hundred millions, whereof they are paying the arrears, and
boasting, as beggars do, that their grandfathers
were rich and great."

Wreathes which at last the dear-bought right convey
190   To rust on medals, or on stones decay.
　　On what foundation stands the warrior's pride,
How just his hopes let Swedish Charles° decide;
A frame of adamant, a soul of fire,
No dangers fright him, and no labours tire;
O'er love, o'er fear, extends his wide domain,
Unconquered lord of pleasure and of pain;
No joys to him pacific sceptres yield,
War sounds the trump, he rushes to the field;
Behold surrounding kings their power combine,
200   And one capitulate, and one resign;°
Peace courts his hand, but spreads her charms in vain;
'Think nothing gained,' he cries, 'till nought remain,
On Moscow's walls till Gothic° standards fly,
And all be mine beneath the polar sky.'
The march begins in military state,
And nations on his eye suspended wait;
Stern Famine guards the solitary coast,
And Winter barricades the realms of Frost;
He comes, not want and cold his course delay;—
210   Hide, blushing Glory, hide Pultowa's day:°
The vanquished hero leaves his broken bands,
And shows his miseries in distant lands;
Condemned a needy supplicant to wait,
While ladies interpose, and slaves debate.
But did not Chance at length for error mend?
Did no subverted empire mark his end?
Did rival monarchs give the fatal wound?
Or hostile millions press him to the ground?
His fall was destined to a barren strand,
220   A petty fortress, and a dubious hand;°
He left the name, at which the world grew pale,
To point a moral, or adorn a tale.
　　All times their scenes of pompous woes afford,
From Persia's tyrant to Bavaria's lord.
In gay hostility, and barbarous pride,
With half mankind embattled at his side,
Great Xerxes° comes to seize the certain prey,
And starves exhausted regions in his way;
Attendant Flattery counts his myriads o'er,
230   Till counted myriads soothe his pride no more;
Fresh praise is tried till madness fires his mind,

Swedish Charles Charles XII of Sweden (1682–1718), replacing Juvenal's Hannibal
one capitulate . . . resign Frederick IV of Denmark in 1700 and Augustus II of Poland in 1704
Gothic Swedish
Pultowa's day the defeat by Peter the Great in

1709 at Poltava in Russia, followed by Charles's flight to Turkey
dubious hand Charles was killed in Norway, perhaps by the hand of his own officer.
Xerxes who invaded Greece and was defeated at the sea battles at Salamis in 480 B.C.

The waves he lashes, and enchains the wind;
New powers are claimed, new powers are still bestowed,
Till rude resistance lops the spreading god;°
The daring Greeks deride the martial show,
And heap their valleys with the gaudy foe;
The insulted sea with humbler thoughts he gains,
A single skiff to speed his flight remains;
The incumbered oar scarce leaves the dreaded coast
240   Through purple billows and a floating host.°
    The bold Bavarian,° in a luckless hour,
Tries the dread summits of Cesarean power,
With unexpected legions bursts away,
And sees defenceless realms receive his sway;
Short sway! fair Austria spreads her mournful charms,
The queen, the beauty, sets the world in arms;
From hill to hill the beacons' rousing blaze
Spreads wide the hope of plunder and of praise;
The fierce Croatian, and the wild Hussar,°
250   And all the sons of ravage crowd the war;
The baffled prince in honour's flattering bloom
Of hasty greatness finds the fatal doom,
His foes' derision, and his subjects' blame,
And steals to death from anguish and from shame.
    'Enlarge my life with multitude of days,'
In health, in sickness, thus the suppliant prays;
Hides from himself his state, and shuns to know,
That life protracted is protracted woe.
Time hovers o'er, impatient to destroy,
260   And shuts up all the passages of joy:
In vain their gifts the bounteous seasons pour,
The fruit autumnal, and the vernal flower,
With listless eyes the dotard views the store,
He views, and wonders that they please no more;
Now pall the tasteless meats and joyless wines,
And Luxury with sighs her slave resigns.
Approach, ye minstrels, try the soothing strain,
Diffuse the tuneful lenitives° of pain:
No sounds, alas, would touch the impervious ear,
270   Though dancing mountains witnessed Orpheus° near;
Nor lute nor lyre his feeble powers attend,
Nor sweeter music of a virtuous friend,
But everlasting dictates crowd his tongue,

---

lops . . . god i.e. as the branches of an over-
arching tree
The incumbered . . . host This account of
Xerxes' flight through a sea dyed with blood and
thick with corpses was reported to be Johnson's
own favorite couplet.
bold Bavarian Charles Albert, Elector of Bavaria, claimed the Holy Roman Empire against

Maria Theresa ("fair Austria"); he was crowned
Charles VII (1742) but became a puppet of
his allies and died in 1745.
Hussar Hungarian light-horseman; like the
Croatian, recruited in Austria's defense
lenitives easers, anodynes
Orpheus the legendary Greek bard whose music
made mountains dance

Perversely grave, or positively° wrong.
The still returning tale and lingering jest
Perplex the fawning niece and pampered guest,
While growing hopes scarce awe the gathering sneer,
And scarce a legacy can bribe to hear;
The watchful guests still hint the last offence,
280   The daughter's petulance, the son's expense,
Improve° his heady rage with treacherous skill,
And mould his passions till they make his will.
    Unnumbered maladies his joints invade,
Lay siege to life, and press the dire blockade;
But unextinguished Avarice still remains,
And dreaded losses aggravate his pains;
He turns, with anxious heart and crippled hands,
His bonds of debt and mortgages of lands;
Or views his coffers with suspicious eyes,
290   Unlocks his gold, and counts it till he dies.
    But grant, the virtues of a temperate prime
Bless with an age exempt from scorn or crime;
An age that melts with unperceived decay,
And glides in modest innocence away;
Whose peaceful day Benevolence endears,
Whose night congratulating Conscience cheers;
The general favourite as the general friend:
Such age there is, and who shall wish its end?
    Yet even on this her load Misfortune flings,
300   To press the weary minutes' flagging wings:
New sorrow rises as the day returns,
A sister sickens, or a daughter mourns.
Now kindred Merit fills the sable bier,
Now lacerated Friendship claims a tear.
Year chases year, decay pursues decay,
Still drops some joy from withering life away;
New forms arise, and different views engage,
Superfluous lags the veteran on the stage,
Till pitying Nature signs the last release,
310   And bids afflicted worth retire to peace.
    But few there are whom hours like these await,
Who set unclouded in the gulfs of fate.
From Lydia's monarch° should the search descend,
By Solon cautioned to regard his end,
In life's last scene what prodigies surprise,
Fears of the brave, and follies of the wise?
From Marlborough's° eyes the streams of dotage flow,

positively peremptorily, in strong terms
Improve increase
Lydia's monarch Croesus, warned by Solon to consider no man happy while he was living

Marlborough John Churchill (1650–1722), 1st Duke of Marlborough, the great military leader and victor of Blenheim, suffered paralytic strokes in his last years.

And Swift° expires a driveller and a show.
        The teeming mother, anxious for her race,
320 Begs for each birth the fortune of a face:
Yet Vane° could tell what ills from beauty spring;
And Sedley° cursed the form that pleased a king.
Ye nymphs of rosy lips and radiant eyes,
Whom Pleasure keeps too busy to be wise,
Whom Joys with soft varieties invite,
By day the frolic, and the dance by night,
Who frown with vanity, who smile with art,
And ask the latest fashion of the heart,
What care, what rules your heedless charms shall save,
330 Each nymph your rival, and each youth your slave?
Against your fame with fondness hate combines,
The rival batters, and the lover mines.
With distant voice neglected Virtue calls,
Less heard and less, the faint remonstrance falls;
Tired with contempt, she quits the slippery reign,
And Pride and Prudence take her seat in vain.
In crowd at once, where none the pass defend,
The harmless freedom and the private friend.
The guardians yield, by force superior plied;
340 By Interest, Prudence; and by Flattery, Pride.
Now Beauty falls betrayed, despised, distressed,
And hissing Infamy proclaims the rest.
        Where then shall Hope and Fear their objects find?
Must dull Suspense° corrupt the stagnant mind?
Must helpless man, in ignorance sedate,
Roll darkling down the torrent of his fate?
Must no dislike alarm, no wishes rise,
No cries attempt the mercies of the skies?
Enquirer, cease, petitions yet remain,
350 Which heaven may hear; nor deem religion vain.
Still raise for good the supplicating voice,
But leave to heaven the measure and the choice,
Safe in his power, whose eyes discern afar
The secret ambush° of a specious prayer.
Implore his aid, in his decisions rest,
Secure whate'er he gives, he gives the best.
Yet when the sense of sacred presence fires,
And strong devotion to the skies aspires,
Pour forth thy fervours for a healthful mind,

Swift Swift's final madness (he was placed under the care of guardians from 1741 until his death in 1745) was "compounded of rage and fatuity"; except for a few intervals, he "sunk into lethargic stupidity, motionless, heedless, and speechless" (Johnson, *Life of Swift*).
Vane Anne Vane, mistress of Frederick, Prince of Wales, who deserted her

Sedley Catherine Sedley, mistress to the Duke of York, but abandoned when he became James II
Suspense i.e. a suspension of all moral choice, producing stagnancy
Sedley Catherine Sedley, mistress to the Duke through avowed sincerity

360   Obedient passions, and a will resigned;
     For love, which scarce collective man can fill;°
     For patience sovereign o'er transmuted° ill;
     For faith, that panting for a happier seat,
     Counts death kind Nature's signal of retreat:
     These goods for man the laws of heaven ordain,
     These goods he grants, who grants the power to gain;
     With these celestial wisdom calms the mind,
And makes the happiness she does not find.°
1748   1749

On the Death of Dr. Robert Levet°

Condemned to hope's delusive mine,
     As on we toil from day to day,
By sudden blasts, or slow decline,
     Our social comforts drop away.

Well tried through many a varying year,
     See Levet to the grave descend;
Officious,° innocent, sincere,
     Of every friendless name the friend.

Yet still he fills affection's eye,
10   Obscurely wise and coarsely kind;
Nor, lettered Arrogance, deny
     Thy praise to merit unrefined.

When fainting Nature called for aid,
     And hovering Death prepared the blow,
His vigorous remedy displayed
     The power of art without the show.

In misery's darkest caverns known,
     His useful care was ever nigh,
Where hopeless Anguish poured his groan,
20   And lonely Want retired to die.

No summons mocked by chill delay,
     No petty gain disdained by pride,
The modest wants of every day
     The toil of every day supplied.

For love . . . fill Cf. Pope, *Essay on Man* IV. 369–70: "Wide and more wide, the o'erflowings of the mind / Take every creature in, of every kind."
transmuted i.e. altered or transformed by the very patience that meets it, as in the next lines
makes . . . find i.e. once absorbed into the mind, such wisdom has the power to create its own happiness by seeking only those objects which (in Johnson's words) are "always to be obtained"
On . . . Levet Levet (1705–82) lived as part of Johnson's household for many years, a poor man without a medical degree, somewhat stiff and silent in manner, but generous in treating others for little or no money.
Officious full of good offices

His virtues walked their narrow round,
 Nor made a pause, nor left a void;
And sure the Eternal Master found
 The single talent well employed.

The busy day, the peaceful night,
 Unfelt, uncounted, glided by;
His frame was firm, his powers were bright,
 Though now his eightieth year was nigh.

30

Then with no throbbing fiery pain,
 No cold gradations of decay,
Death broke at once the vital chain,
 And freed his soul the nearest way.

1782   1782

The History of Rasselas, Prince of Abyssinia

This Oriental tale was written "in the evenings of one week" to defray the expense of Johnson's mother's funeral and to pay off her few small debts. Its elevated, highly formalized narrative is always tinged with an ironic sense of the ludicrous, and its hero—the young Prince Rasselas—is a solemn, rather priggish idealist who seeks to make "the choice of life." A prisoner in the Happy Valley of Abyssinia, which none can leave once they enter it (or re-enter once they leave), the prince becomes restless with the sheer banality of its serene pleasures, and he devises a plan to escape. Before he does so, he encounters the poet Imlac and asks countless questions about the world outside. "The poet pitied his ignorance and loved his curiosity"; and his narrative—with Rasselas's naïvely incredulous interruptions—follows. In later chapters, the prince Rasselas and his sister Nekayah, accompanied by Imlac and by the princess's companion Pekuah, traverse the scenes of man, never finding the ideal "choice of life" in a world of mixed blessings. "There are goods so opposed that we cannot seize both, but, by too much prudence, may pass between them at too great distance to enjoy either," Nekayah concludes. "Of the blessings set before you, make your choice and be content." To Rasselas's desire to find a happiness that is "solid and permanent, without fear and without uncertainty" is opposed Imlac's wry observation, "Very few live by choice," or Nekayah's sense of the impossibility of clear choice: "Marriage has many pains, but celibacy has no pleasures." The narrative ends with a "conclusion, in which nothing is concluded," with each of its participants making resolutions he will probably not be able to achieve, and with all returning to Abyssinia and surrendering the quest. Johnson's sad comedy was written at almost the same time as a work in a different spirit but with similar conclusions, Voltaire's *Candide*.

From The History of Rasselas, Prince of Abyssinia

Chapter VIII: The History of Imlac

The close of the day is, in the regions of the torrid zone, the only season of diversion and entertainment, and it was therefore midnight before the music ceased, and the princesses retired. Rasselas then called for his companion, and required him to begin the story of his life.

'Sir,' said Imlac, 'my history will not be long: the life that is devoted to knowledge passes silently away, and is very little diversified by events. To talk in public, to think in solitude, to read and to hear, to inquire and answer inquiries, is the business of a scholar. He wanders about the world without pomp or terror, and is neither known nor valued but by men like himself.

'I was born in the kingdom of Goiama,[1] at no great distance from the fountain of the Nile. My father was a wealthy merchant, who traded between the inland countries of Africk and the ports of the Red Sea. He was honest, frugal, and diligent, but of mean sentiments and narrow comprehension: he desired only to be rich, and to conceal his riches, lest he should be spoiled[2] by the governors of the province.'

'Surely,' said the prince, 'my father must be negligent of his charge, if any man in his dominions dares take that which belongs to another. Does he not know that kings are accountable for injustice permitted as well as done? If I were emperor, not the meanest of my subjects should be oppressed with impunity. My blood boils when I am told that a merchant durst not enjoy his honest gains, for fear of losing them by the rapacity of power. Name the governor who robbed the people, that I may declare his crimes to the emperor.'

'Sir,' said Imlac, 'your ardour is the natural effect of virtue animated by youth: the time will come when you will acquit your father, and perhaps hear with less impatience of the governor. Oppression is, in the Abyssinian dominions, neither frequent nor tolerated; but no form of government has been yet discovered, by which cruelty can be wholly prevented. Subordination supposes power on one part, and subjection on the other; and if power be in the hands of men, it will sometimes be abused. The vigilance of the supreme magistrate may do much, but much will still remain undone. He can never know all the crimes that are committed, and can seldom punish all that he knows.'

'This,' said the prince, 'I do not understand; but I had rather hear thee than dispute. Continue thy narration.'

'My father,' proceeded Imlac, 'originally intended that I should have no other education, than such as might qualify me for commerce; and discovering in me great strength of memory and quickness of apprehension, often declared his hope that I should be some time the richest man in Abyssinia.'

'Why,' said the prince, 'did thy father desire the increase of his wealth,

---

1. "One of the most fruitful provinces of all the Abyssinian dominions"; Johnson had in 1735 translated from the French the *Voyage to Abyssinia* by the Portuguese Jesuit Father Jerome Lobo (1595–1678), and many of his geographical references derive from that work.
2. Despoiled, plundered.

when it was already greater than he durst discover or enjoy? I am unwilling to doubt thy veracity, yet inconsistencies cannot both be true.'

'Inconsistencies,' answered Imlac, 'cannot both be right, but, imputed to man, they may both be true. Yet diversity is not inconsistency. My father might expect a time of greater security. However, some desire is necessary to keep life in motion; and he whose real wants are supplied, must admit those of fancy.'

'This,' said the prince, 'I can in some measure conceive. I repent that I interrupted thee.'

'With this hope,' proceeded Imlac, 'he sent me to school; but when I had once found the delight of knowledge, and felt the pleasure of intelligence and the pride of invention,[3] I began silently to despise riches, and determined to disappoint the purpose of my father, whose grossness of conception raised my pity. I was twenty years old before his tenderness would expose me to the fatigue of travel, in which time I had been instructed, by successive masters, in all the literature of my native country. As every hour taught me something new, I lived in a continual course of gratification; but, as I advanced towards manhood, I lost much of the reverence with which I had been used to look on my instructors; because when the lesson was ended, I did not find them wiser or better than common men.

'At length my father resolved to initiate me in commerce, and opening one of his subterranean treasuries, counted out ten thousand pieces of gold. "This, young man," said he, "is the stock with which you must negotiate. I began with less than the fifth part, and you see how diligence and parsimony have increased it. This is your own to waste or to improve. If you squander it by negligence or caprice, you must wait for my death before you will be rich; if in four years you double your stock, we will thenceforward let subordination cease, and live together as friends and partners; for he shall always be equal with me, who is equally skilled in the art of growing rich."

'We laid our money upon camels, concealed in bales of cheap goods, and travelled to the shore of the Red Sea. When I cast my eye on the expanse of waters, my heart bounded like that of a prisoner escaped. I felt an unextinguishable curiosity kindle in my mind, and resolved to snatch this opportunity of seeing the manners of other nations, and of learning sciences unknown in Abyssinia.

'I remembered that my father had obliged me to the improvement of my stock, not by a promise which I ought not to violate, but by a penalty which I was at liberty to incur; and therefore determined to gratify my predominant desire, and, by drinking at the fountains of knowledge, to quench the thirst of curiosity.

'As I was supposed to trade without connexion with my father, it was easy for me to become acquainted with the master of a ship, and procure a passage to some other country. I had no motives of choice to regulate my voyage; it was sufficient for me that, wherever I wandered, I should see a country which I had not seen before. I therefore entered a ship bound for Surat,[4] having left a letter for my father declaring my intention.

3. Imagination.
4. Indian seaport 150 miles north of Bombay.

Chapter IX: The History of Imlac Continued

'When I first entered upon the world of waters, and lost sight of land, I looked round about me with pleasing terror, and thinking my soul enlarged by the boundless prospect, imagined that I could gaze round for ever without satiety; but in a short time I grew weary of looking on barren uniformity, where I could only see again what I had already seen. I then descended into the ship, and doubted for awhile whether all my future pleasures would not end like this, in disgust and disappointment. Yet, surely, said I, the ocean and the land are very different; the only variety of water is rest and motion, but the earth has mountains and valleys, deserts and cities; it is inhabited by men of different customs and contrary opinions; and I may hope to find variety in life, though I should miss it in nature.

'With this thought I quieted my mind; and amused myself during the voyage, sometimes by learning from the sailors the art of navigation, which I have never practised, and sometimes by forming schemes for my conduct in different situations, in not one of which I have been ever placed.

'I was almost weary of my naval amusements when we landed safely at Surat. I secured my money, and purchasing some commodities for show, joined myself to a caravan that was passing into the inland country. My companions, for some reason or other, conjecturing that I was rich, and, by my inquiries and admiration, finding that I was ignorant, considered me as a novice whom they had a right to cheat, and who was to learn at the usual expense the art of fraud. They exposed me to the theft of servants and the exaction of officers, and saw me plundered upon false pretences, without any advantage to themselves but that of rejoicing in the superiority of their own knowledge.'

'Stop a moment,' said the prince. 'Is there such depravity in man, as that he should injure another without benefit to himself? I can easily conceive that all are pleased with superiority; but your ignorance was merely accidental, which, being neither your crime nor your folly, could afford them no reason to applaud themselves; and the knowledge which they had, and which you wanted, they might as effectually have shown by warning, as betraying you.'

'Pride,' said Imlac, 'is seldom delicate, it will please itself with very mean advantages; and envy feels not its own happiness, but when it may be compared with the misery of others. They were my enemies, because they grieved to think me rich; and my oppressors, because they delighted to find me weak.'

'Proceed,' said the prince: 'I doubt not of the facts which you relate, but imagine that you impute them to mistaken motives.'

'In this company,' said Imlac, 'I arrived at Agra, the capital of Indostan, the city in which the great Mogul [5] commonly resides. I applied myself to the language of the country, and in a few months was able to converse with the learned men; some of whom I found morose and reserved, and others easy and communicative; some were unwilling to teach another what they had with difficulty learned themselves; and some showed that the end of their studies was to gain the dignity of instructing.

'To the tutor of the young princes I recommended myself so much, that I

5. The ruler of the Mohammedan empire established in India by Akbar the Great; his capital was at Agra.

was presented to the emperor as a man of uncommon knowledge. The emperor asked me many questions concerning my country and my travels; and though I cannot now recollect any thing that he uttered above the power of a common man, he dismissed me astonished at his wisdom, and enamoured of his goodness.

'My credit was now so high, that the merchants with whom I had travelled, applied to me for recommendations to the ladies of the court. I was surprised at their confidence of solicitation, and gently reproached them with their practices on the road. They heard me with cold indifference, and showed no tokens of shame or sorrow.

'They then urged their request with the offer of a bribe; but what I would not do for kindness, I would not do for money, and refused them, not because they had injured me, but because I would not enable them to injure others; for I knew they would have made use of my credit to cheat those who should buy their wares.

'Having resided at Agra till there was no more to be learned, I travelled into Persia, where I saw many remains of ancient magnificence, and observed many new accommodations of life. The Persians are a nation eminently social, and their assemblies afforded me daily opportunities of remarking characters and manners, and of tracing human nature through all its variations.

'From Persia I passed into Arabia, where I saw a nation at once pastoral and warlike; who live without any settled habitation; whose only wealth is their flocks and herds; and who have yet carried on through all ages an hereditary war with all mankind, though they neither covet nor envy their possessions.'

Chapter X: Imlac's History Continued. A Dissertation upon Poetry

'Wherever I went, I found that poetry was considered as the highest learning, and regarded with a veneration somewhat approaching to that which man would pay to the angelic nature. And yet it fills me with wonder, that, in almost all countries, the most ancient poets are considered as the best: whether it be that every other kind of knowledge is an acquisition gradually attained, and poetry is a gift conferred at once; or that the first poetry of every nation surprised them as a novelty, and retained the credit by consent, which it received by accident at first; or whether, as the province of poetry is to describe nature and passion, which are always the same, the first writers took possession of the most striking objects for description, and the most probable occurrences for fiction, and left nothing to those that followed them but transcription of the same events, and new combinations of the same images:—whatever be the reason, it is commonly observed that the early writers are in possession of nature, and their followers of art; that the first excel in strength and invention, and the latter in elegance and refinement.

'I was desirous to add my name to this illustrious fraternity. I read all the poets of Persia and Arabia, and was able to repeat by memory the volumes that are suspended in the mosque of Mecca.[6] But I soon found that no man was ever great by imitation. My desire of excellence impelled me to transfer

6. Illuminated manuscripts, chiefly of the *Koran* and other religious books, hung as sacred texts.

my attention to nature and to life. Nature was to be my subject, and men to be my auditors: I could never describe what I had not seen; I could not hope to move those with delight or terror, whose interests and opinions I did not understand.

'Being now resolved to be a poet, I saw everything with a new purpose; my sphere of attention was suddenly magnified; no kind of knowledge was to be overlooked. I ranged mountains and deserts for images and resemblances, and pictured upon my mind every tree of the forest and flower of the valley. I observed with equal care the crags of the rock and the pinnacles of the palace. Sometimes I wandered along the mazes of the rivulet, and sometimes watched the changes of the summer clouds. To a poet nothing can be useless. Whatever is beautiful, and whatever is dreadful, must be familiar to his imagination: he must be conversant with all that is awfully [7] vast or elegantly little. The plants of the garden, the animals of the wood, the minerals of the earth, and meteors of the sky must all concur to store his mind with inexhaustible variety: for every idea is useful for the enforcement or decoration of moral or religious truth; and he who knows most, will have most power of diversifying his scenes, and of gratifying his reader with remote allusions and unexpected instruction.

'All the appearances of nature I was therefore careful to study; and every country which I have surveyed has contributed something to my poetical powers.'

'In so wide a survey,' said the prince, 'you must surely have left much unobserved. I have lived, till now, within the circuit of these mountains, and yet cannot walk abroad without the sight of something which I had never beheld before, or never heeded.'

'The business of a poet,' said Imlac, 'is to examine, not the individual, but the species; to remark general properties and large appearances. He does not number the streaks of the tulip, or describe the different shades in the verdure of the forest: he is to exhibit in his portraits of nature such prominent and striking features, as recall the original to every mind; and must neglect the minuter discriminations, which one may have remarked, and another have neglected, for those characteristics which are alike obvious to vigilance and carelessness.

'But the knowledge of nature is only half the task of a poet: he must be acquainted likewise with all the modes of life. His character requires that he estimate the happiness and misery of every condition, observe the power of all the passions in all their combinations, and trace the changes of the human mind as they are modified by various institutions and accidental influences of climate or custom, from the sprightliness of infancy to the despondence of decrepitude. He must divest himself of the prejudices of his age and country; he must consider right and wrong in their abstracted and invariable state; he must disregard present laws and opinions, and rise to general and transcendental truths, which will always be the same. He must therefore content himself with the slow progress of his name, contemn the applause of his own

---

7. Awe-inspiringly; cf. Burke's work on the Sublime, which had been published two years earlier than *Rasselas*.

time, and commit his claims to the justice of posterity. He must write as the interpreter of nature, and the legislator of mankind, and consider himself as presiding over the thoughts and manners of future generations; as a being superior to time and place.

'His labour is not yet at an end; he must know many languages and many sciences; and, that his style may be worthy of his thoughts, must, by incessant practice, familiarise to himself every delicacy of speech and grace of harmony.'

Chapter XI: Imlac's Narrative Continued. A Hint on Pilgrimage

Imlac now felt the enthusiastic fit, and was proceeding to aggrandize his own profession, when the prince cried out, 'Enough! thou hast convinced me that no human being can ever be a poet. Proceed with thy narration.'

'To be a poet,' said Imlac, 'is indeed very difficult.'

'So difficult,' returned the prince, 'that I will at present hear no more of his labours. Tell me whither you went when you had seen Persia.'

'From Persia,' said the poet, 'I travelled through Syria, and for three years resided in Palestine, where I conversed with great numbers of the northern and western nations of Europe; the nations which are now in possession of all power and all knowledge; whose armies are irresistible, and whose fleets command the remotest parts of the globe. When I compared these men with the natives of our own kingdom, and those that surround us, they appeared almost another order of beings. In their countries it is difficult to wish for anything that may not be obtained: a thousand arts, of which we never heard, are continually labouring for their convenience and pleasure; and whatever their own climate has denied them is supplied by their commerce.'

'By what means,' said the prince, 'are the Europeans thus powerful; or why, since they can so easily visit Asia and Africa for trade or conquest, cannot the Asiatics and Africans invade their coasts, plant colonies in their ports, and give laws to their natural princes? The same wind that carries them back, would bring us thither.'

'They are more powerful, sir, than we,' answered Imlac, 'because they are wiser; knowledge will always predominate over ignorance, as man governs the other animals. But why their knowledge is more than ours, I know not what reason can be given, but the unsearchable will of the Supreme Being.'

'When,' said the prince with a sigh, 'shall I be able to visit Palestine, and mingle with this mighty confluence of nations? Till that happy moment shall arrive, let me fill up the time with such representations as thou canst give me. I am not ignorant of the motive that assembles such numbers in that place, and cannot but consider it as the centre of wisdom and piety, to which the best and wisest men of every land must be continually resorting.'

'There are some nations,' said Imlac, 'that send few visitants to Palestine; for many numerous and learned sects in Europe concur to censure pilgrimage as superstitious, or deride it as ridiculous.'

'You know,' said the prince, 'how little my life has made me acquainted with diversity of opinions; it will be too long to hear the arguments on both sides; you, that have considered them, tell me the result.'

'Pilgrimage,' said Imlac, 'like many other acts of piety, may be reasonable or superstitious, according to the principles upon which it is performed. Long journeys in search of truth are not commanded. Truth, such as is necessary to the regulation of life, is always found where it is honestly sought. Change of place is no natural cause of the increase of piety, for it inevitably produces dissipation of mind. Yet, since men go every day to view the fields where great actions have been performed, and return with stronger impressions of the event, curiosity of the same kind may naturally dispose us to view that country whence our religion had its beginning; and I believe no man surveys those awful scenes without some confirmation of holy resolutions. That the Supreme Being may be more easily propitiated in one place than in another is the dream of idle superstition; but that some places may operate upon our own minds in an uncommon manner is an opinion which hourly experience will justify. He who supposes that his vices may be more successfully combatted in Palestine, will, perhaps, find himself mistaken; yet he may go thither without folly: he who thinks they will be more freely pardoned dishonours at once his reason and religion.'

'These,' said the prince, 'are European distinctions. I will consider them another time. What have you found to be the effect of knowledge? Are those nations happier than we?'

'There is so much infelicity,' said the poet, 'in the world, that scarce any man has leisure from his own distresses to estimate the comparative happiness of others. Knowledge is certainly one of the means of pleasure, as is confessed by the natural desire which every mind feels of increasing its ideas. Ignorance is mere privation, by which nothing can be produced: it is a vacuity in which the soul sits motionless and torpid for want of attraction; and, without knowing why, we always rejoice when we learn and grieve when we forget. I am therefore inclined to conclude, that if nothing counteracts the natural consequence of learning, we grow more happy as our minds take a wider range.'

'In enumerating the particular comforts of life, we shall find many advantages on the side of the Europeans. They cure wounds and diseases with which we languish and perish. We suffer inclemencies of weather which they can obviate. They have engines for the despatch of many laborious works which we must perform by manual industry. There is such communication between distant places, that one friend can hardly be said to be absent from another. Their policy removes all public inconveniences; they have roads cut through their mountains, and bridges laid upon their rivers. And, if we descend to the privacies of life, their habitations are more commodious, and their possessions are more secure.'

'They are surely happy,' said the prince, 'who have all these conveniences, of which I envy none so much as the facility with which separated friends interchange their thoughts.'

'The Europeans,' answered Imlac, 'are less unhappy than we; but they are not happy. Human life is every where a state in which much is to be endured, and little to be enjoyed.'

Chapter XII: The Story of Imlac Continued

'I am not yet willing,' said the prince, 'to suppose that happiness is so parsimoniously distributed to mortals; nor can believe but that, if I had the choice of life, I should be able to fill every day with pleasure. I would injure no man, and should provoke no resentment; I would relieve every distress, and should enjoy the benedictions of gratitude. I would choose my friends among the wise, and my wife among the virtuous; and therefore should be in no danger from treachery or unkindness. My children should, by my care, be learned and pious, and would repay to my age what their childhood had received. What would dare to molest him who might call on every side to thousands enriched by his bounty, or assisted by his power? And why should not life glide quietly away in the soft reciprocation of protection and reverence? All this may be done without the help of European refinements, which appear by their effects to be rather specious than useful. Let us leave them, and pursue our journey.'

'From Palestine,' said Imlac, 'I passed through many regions of Asia; in the more civilized kingdoms as a trader, and among the barbarians of the mountains as a pilgrim. At last I began to long for my native country, that I might repose, after my travels and fatigues, in the places where I had spent my earliest years, and gladden my old companions with the recital of my adventures. Often did I figure to myself those with whom I had sported away the gay hours of dawning life, sitting round me in its evening, wondering at my tales, and listening to my counsels.

'When this thought had taken possession of my mind, I considered every moment as wasted which did not bring me nearer to Abyssinia. I hastened into Egypt, and notwithstanding my impatience, was detained ten months in the contemplation of its ancient magnificence, and in inquiries after the remains of its ancient learning. I found in Cairo a mixture of all nations; some brought thither by the love of knowledge, some by the hope of gain, and many by the desire of living after their own manner without observation, and of lying hid in the obscurity of multitudes: for in a city, populous as Cairo, it is possible to obtain at the same time the gratifications of society, and the secrecy of solitude.

'From Cairo I travelled to Suez, and embarked on the Red Sea, passing along the coast till I arrived at the port from which I had departed twenty years before. Here I joined myself to a caravan, and re-entered my native country.

'I now expected the caresses of my kinsmen, and the congratulations of my friends, and was not without hope that my father, whatever value he had set upon riches, would own with gladness and pride a son who was able to add to the felicity and honour of the nation. But I was soon convinced that my thoughts were vain. My father had been dead fourteen years, having divided his wealth among my brothers, who were removed to some other provinces. Of my companions, the greater part were in the grave; of the rest, some could with difficulty remember me, and some considered me as one corrupted by foreign manners.

'A man used to vicissitudes is not easily dejected. I forgot, after a time, my disappointment, and endeavoured to recommend myself to the nobles of the kingdom; they admitted me to their tables, heard my story, and dismissed me. I opened a school, and was prohibited to teach. I then resolved to sit down in the quiet of domestic life, and addressed a lady that was fond of my conversation but rejected my suit because my father was a merchant.

'Wearied at last with solicitation and repulses, I resolved to hide myself for ever from the world, and depend no longer on the opinion or caprice of others. I waited for the time when the gate of the *happy valley* should open, that I might bid farewell to hope and fear: the day came; my performance was distinguished with favour; and I resigned myself with joy to perpetual confinement.' [8]

'Hast thou here found happiness at last?' said Rasselas. 'Tell me without reserve; art thou content with thy condition? or, dost thou wish to be again wandering and inquiring? All the inhabitants of this valley celebrate their lot, and at the annual visit of the emperor, invite others to partake of their felicity.'

'Great prince,' said Imlac, 'I shall speak the truth; I know not one of all your attendants, who does not lament the hour when he entered this retreat. I am less unhappy than the rest, because I have a mind replete with images, which I can vary and combine at pleasure. I can amuse my solitude by the renovation of the knowledge which begins to fade from my memory, and by recollection of the incidents of my past life. Yet all this ends in the sorrowful consideration, that my acquirements are now useless, and that none of my pleasures can be again enjoyed. The rest, whose minds have no impression but of the present moment, are either corroded by malignant passions, or sit stupid in the gloom of perpetual vacancy.'

'What passions can infest those,' said the prince, 'who have no rivals? We are in a place where impotence precludes malice, and where all envy is repressed by community of enjoyments.'

'There may be community,' said Imlac, 'of material possessions, but there can never be community of love or of esteem. It must happen that one will please more than another; he that knows himself despised will always be envious; and still more envious and malevolent, if he is condemned to live in the presence of those who despise him. The invitations by which they allure others, to a state which they feel to be wretched, proceed from the natural malignity of hopeless misery. They are weary of themselves and of each other, and expect to find relief in new companions. They envy the liberty which their folly has forfeited, and would gladly see all mankind imprisoned like themselves.

'From this crime, however, I am wholly free. No man can say that he is wretched by my persuasion. I look with pity on the crowds who are annually soliciting admission to captivity, and wish that it were lawful for me to warn them of their danger.'

'My dear Imlac,' said the prince, 'I will open to thee my whole heart. I have long meditated an escape from the *happy valley*. I have examined the mountains on every side, but find myself insuperably barred: teach me the way to break my prison; thou shalt be the companion of my flight, the guide of my rambles, the partner of my fortune, and my sole director in the *choice of life.*'

'Sir,' answered the poet, 'your escape will be difficult, and, perhaps, you may soon repent your curiosity. The world, which you figure to yourself smooth and quiet as the lake in the valley, you will find a sea foaming with tempests, and boiling with whirlpools: you will be sometimes overwhelmed by the waves of

8. The gates of the Happy Valley were opened once each year for the Emperor's visit, and only those were admitted for permanent residence "whose performance was thought able to add novelty to luxury." Once admitted, one could remain; but once one left one could never re-enter.

violence, and sometimes dashed against the rocks of treachery. Amidst wrongs and frauds, competitions and anxieties, you will wish a thousand times for these seats of quiet, and willingly quit hope to be free from fear.'

'Do not seek to deter me from my purpose,' said the prince; 'I am impatient to see what thou hast seen; and, since thou art thyself weary of the valley, it is evident that thy former state was better than this. Whatever be the consequence of my experiment, I am resolved to judge with mine own eyes of the various conditions of men, and then to make deliberately my *choice of life.*'

'I am afraid,' said Imlac, 'you are hindered by stronger restraints than my persuasions; yet, if your determination is fixed, I do not counsel you to despair. Few things are impossible to diligence and skill.'

1759

From The Rambler

Quis scit, an adjiciant hodiernae crastina summae Tempora Dî superi!   HORACE, *Odes,* IV.7.17–18

Who knows if Heaven, with ever-bounteous power, Shall add tomorrow to the present hour?
(trans. FRANCIS)

I sat yesterday morning employed in deliberating on which, among the various subjects that occurred to my imagination, I should bestow the paper of today. After a short effort of meditation by which nothing was determined, I grew every moment more irresolute, my ideas wandered from the first intention, and I rather wished to think, than thought, upon any settled subject; till at last I was awakened from this dream of study by a summons from the press: the time was come for which I had been thus negligently purposing to provide, and, however dubious or sluggish, I was now necessitated to write.

Though to a writer whose design is so comprehensive and miscellaneous that he may accommodate himself with a topic from every scene of life, or view of nature, it is no great aggravation of his task to be obliged to a sudden composition, yet I could not forbear to reproach myself for having so long neglected what was unavoidably to be done, and of which every moment's idleness increased the difficulty. There was however some pleasure in reflecting that I, who had only trifled till diligence was necessary, might still congratulate myself upon my superiority to multitudes, who have trifled till diligence is vain; who can by no degree of activity or resolution recover the opportunities which have slipped away; and who are condemned by their own carelessness to hopeless calamity and barren sorrow.

The folly of allowing ourselves to delay what we know cannot be finally escaped, is one of the general weaknesses, which, in spite of the instruction of moralists, and the remonstrances of reason, prevail to a greater or less degree in every mind: even they who most steadily withstand it, find it, if not the most violent, the most pertinacious of their passions, always renewing its attacks, and though often vanquished, never destroyed.

It is indeed natural to have particular regard to the time present, and to be most solicitous for that which is by its nearness enabled to make the strongest impressions. When therefore any sharp pain is to be suffered or any formidable danger to be incurred, we can scarcely exempt ourselves wholly from the seducements of imagination; we readily believe that another day will bring some support or advantage which we now want; and are easily persuaded that the moment of necessity which we desire never to arrive is at a great distance from us.

Thus life is languished away in the gloom of anxiety, and consumed in collecting resolutions which the next morning dissipates; in forming purposes which we scarcely hope to keep, and reconciling ourselves to our own cowardice by excuses, which, while we admit them, we know to be absurd. Our firmness is by the continual contemplation of misery hourly impaired; every submission to our fear enlarges its dominion; we not only waste that time in which the evil we dread might have been suffered and surmounted, but even where procrastination produces no absolute encrease of our difficulties, make them less superable to ourselves by habitual terrors. When evils cannot be avoided, it is wise to contract the interval of expectation; to meet the mischiefs which will overtake us if we fly; and suffer only their real malignity without the conflicts of doubt and anguish of anticipation.

To act is far easier than to suffer, yet we every day see the progress of life retarded by the *vis inertiae*,[1] the mere repugnance to motion, and find multitudes repining at the want of that which nothing but idleness hinders them from enjoying. The case of Tantalus, in the region of poetic punishment, was somewhat to be pitied, because the fruits that hung about him retired from his hand;[2] but what tenderness can be claimed by those who though perhaps they suffer the pains of Tantalus will never lift their hands for their own relief?

There is nothing more common among this torpid generation than murmurs and complaints; murmurs at uneasiness which only vacancy[3] and suspicion expose them to feel, and complaints of distresses which it is in their own power to remove. Laziness is commonly associated with timidity. Either fear originally prohibits endeavours by infusing despair of success; or the frequent failure of irresolute struggles, and the constant desire of avoiding labour, impress by degrees false terrors on the mind. But fear, whether natural or acquired, when once it has full possession of the fancy, never fails to employ it upon visions of calamity, such as if they are not dissipated by useful employment, will soon overcast it with horrors, and imbitter life not only with those miseries by which all earthly beings are really more or less tormented, but with those which do not yet exist, and which can only be discerned by the perspicacity of cowardice.

Among all who sacrifice future advantage to present inclination, scarcely any gain so little as those that suffer themselves to freeze in idleness. Others are corrupted by some enjoyment of more or less power to gratify the passions; but to neglect our duties, merely to avoid the labour of performing them, a labour which is always punctually rewarded, is surely to sink under weak temptations. Idleness never can secure tranquillity; the call of reason and of conscience will pierce the closest pavilion of the sluggard, and, though it may not have force

1. "Force of inertia."
2. Tantalus was tortured when the fruit receded, as he advanced his hand, and the water as he advanced his lips.
3. Idleness.

to drive him from his down,[4] will be loud enough to hinder him from sleep. Those moments which he cannot resolve to make useful by devoting them to the great business of his being, will still be usurped by powers that will not leave them to his disposal; remorse and vexation will seize upon them, and forbid him to enjoy what he is so desirous to appropriate.

There are other causes of inactivity incident to more active faculties and more acute discernment. He to whom many objects of pursuit arise at the same time, will frequently hesitate between different desires, till a rival has precluded him, or change his course as new attractions prevail, and harass himself without advancing. He who sees different ways to the same end, will, unless he watches carefully over his own conduct, lay out too much of his attention upon the comparison of probabilities and the adjustment of expedients, and pause in the choice of his road till some accident intercepts his journey. He whose penetration extends to remote consequences and who, whenever he applies his attention to any design, discovers new prospects of advantage and possibilities of improvement, will not easily be persuaded that his project is ripe for execution; but will superadd one contrivance to another, endeavour to unite various purposes in one operation, multiply complications, and refine niceties, till he is entangled in his own scheme, and bewildered in the perplexity of various intentions. He that resolves to unite all the beauties of situation in a new purchase, must waste his life in roving to no purpose from province to province. He that hopes in the same house to obtain every convenience, may draw plans and study Palladio,[5] but will never lay a stone. He will attempt a treatise on some important subject, and amass materials, consult authors, and study all the dependent and collateral parts of learning, but never conclude himself qualified to write. He that has abilities to conceive perfection, will not easily be content without it; and since perfection cannot be reached, will lose the opportunity of doing well in the vain hope of unattainable excellence.

The certainty that life cannot be long, and the probability that it will be much shorter than nature allows, ought to awaken every man to the active prosecution of whatever he is desirous to perform. It is true that no diligence can ascertain success; death may intercept the swiftest career; but he who is cut off in the execution of an honest undertaking has at least the honour of falling in his rank, and has fought the battle, though he missed the victory. [No. 134, Saturday, June 29, 1751]

> *Nulla fides regni sociis, omnisque potestas*
> *Impatiens consortis erat.*   LUCAN, I.92–93

> No faith of partnership dominion owns;
> Still discord hovers o'er divided thrones.

The hostility perpetually exercised between one man and another is caused by the desire of many for that which only few can possess. Every man would be rich, powerful, and famous; yet fame, power, and riches, are only the names of relative conditions, which imply the obscurity, dependence, and poverty of greater numbers.

4. That is, from his pillow.
5. Andrea Palladio, the influential Italian Renaissance architect; cf. Pope, *Epistle to Burlington.*

This universal and incessant competition, produces injury and malice by two motives, interest and envy; the prospect of adding to our possessions what we can take from others, and the hope of alleviating the sense of our disparity by lessening others, though we gain nothing to ourselves.

Of these two malignant and destructive powers, it seems probable at the first view that interest has the strongest and most extensive influence. It is easy to conceive that opportunities to seize what has been long wanted may excite desires almost irresistible; but surely, the same eagerness cannot be kindled by an accidental power of destroying that which gives happiness to another. It must be more natural to rob for gain than to ravage only for mischief.

Yet I am inclined to believe that the great law of mutual benevolence is oftener violated by envy than by interest, and that most of the misery which the defamation of blameless actions or the obstruction of honest endeavours brings upon the world is inflicted by men that propose no advantage to themselves but the satisfaction of poisoning the banquet which they cannot taste, and blasting the harvest which they have no right to reap.

Interest can diffuse itself but to a narrow compass. The number is never large of those who can hope to fill the posts of degraded power, catch the fragments of shattered fortune, or succeed to the honours of depreciated beauty. But the empire of envy has no limits, as it requires to its influence very little help from external circumstances. Envy may always be produced by idleness and pride, and in what place will not they be found?

Interest requires some qualities not universally bestowed. The ruin of another will produce no profit to him who has not discernment to mark his advantage, courage to seize, and activity to pursue it; but the cold malignity of envy may be exerted in a torpid and quiescent state, amidst the gloom of stupidity, in the coverts of cowardice. He that falls by the attacks of interest is torn by hungry tigers; he may discover and resist his enemies. He that perishes in the ambushes of envy is destroyed by unknown and invisible assailants, and dies like a man suffocated by a poisonous vapour, without knowledge of his danger or possibility of contest.

Interest is seldom pursued but at some hazard. He that hopes to gain much has commonly something to lose, and when he ventures to attack superiority, if he fails to conquer, is irrecoverably crushed. But envy may act without expence or danger. To spread suspicion, to invent calumnies, to propagate scandal, requires neither labour nor courage. It is easy for the author of a lie, however malignant, to escape detection, and infamy needs very little industry to assist its circulation.

Envy is almost the only vice which is practicable at all times and in every place; the only passion which can never lie quiet for want of irritation; its effects therefore are everywhere discoverable, and its attempts always to be dreaded.

It is impossible to mention a name which any advantageous distinction has made eminent, but some latent animosity will burst out. The wealthy trader, however he may abstract himself from public affairs, will never want those who hint, with Shylock,[6] that ships are but boards. The beauty, adorned only with the unambitious graces of innocence and modesty, provokes whenever

6. Shakespeare, *Merchant of Venice* I.iii.20.

she appears a thousand murmurs of detraction. The genius, even when he endeavours only to entertain or instruct, yet suffers persecution from innumerable critics whose acrimony is excited merely by the pain of seeing others pleased, and of hearing applauses which another enjoys.

The frequency of envy makes it so familiar that it escapes our notice; nor do we often reflect upon its turpitude or malignity till we happen to feel its influence. When he that has given no provocation to malice, but by attempting to excel, finds himself pursued by multitudes whom he never saw with all the implacability of personal resentment; when he perceives clamour and malice let loose upon him as a public enemy, and incited by every stratagem of defamation; when he hears the misfortunes of his family, or the follies of his youth exposed to the world; and every failure of conduct, or defect of nature aggravated and ridiculed; he then learns to abhor those artifices at which he only laughed before, and discovers how much the happiness of life would be advanced by the eradication of envy from the human heart.

Envy is, indeed, a stubborn weed of the mind, and seldom yields to the culture [7] of philosophy. There are, however, considerations, which if carefully implanted and diligently propagated, might in time overpower and repress it, since no one can nurse it for the sake of pleasure, as its effects are only shame, anguish, and perturbation.

It is above all other vices inconsistent with the character of a social being, because it sacrifices truth and kindness to very weak temptations. He that plunders a wealthy neighbour gains as much as he takes away, and may improve his own condition in the same proportion as he impairs another's; but he that blasts a flourishing reputation must be content with a small dividend of additional fame, so small as can afford very little consolation to balance the guilt by which it is obtained.

I have hitherto avoided that dangerous and empirical morality, which cures one vice by means of another. But envy is so base and detestable, so vile in its original, and so pernicious in its effects, that the predominance of almost any other quality is to be preferred. It is one of those lawless enemies of society against which poisoned arrows may honestly be used. Let it, therefore, be constantly remembered that whoever envies another, confesses his superiority, and let those be reformed by their pride who have lost their virtue.

It is no slight aggravation of the injuries which envy incites that they are committed against those who have given no intentional provocation; and that the sufferer is often marked out for ruin, not because he has failed in any duty, but because he has dared to do more than was required.

Almost every other crime is practised by the help of some quality which might have produced esteem or love if it had been well employed; but envy is mere unmixed and genuine evil; it pursues a hateful end by despicable means, and desires not so much its own happiness as another's misery. To avoid depravity like this, it is not necessary that any one should aspire to heroism or sanctity, but only that he should resolve not to quit the rank which nature assigns him, and wish to maintain the dignity of a human being. [No. 183, Tuesday, December 17, 1751]

7. Cultivation (in its literal sense; a metaphor pursued in the next sentence).

From The Idler

Among the innumerable mortifications that waylay human arrogance on every side may well be reckoned our ignorance of the most common objects and effects, a defect of which we become more sensible by every attempt to supply it. Vulgar and inactive minds confound familiarity with knowledge, and conceive themselves informed of the whole nature of things when they are shown their form or told their use; but the speculatist, who is not content with superficial views, harasses himself with fruitless curiosity, and still as he enquires more perceives only that he knows less.

Sleep is a state in which a great part of every life is passed. No animal has been yet discovered whose existence is not varied with intervals of insensibility; and some late philosophers have extended the empire of sleep over the vegetable world.

Yet of this change so frequent, so great, so general, and so necessary, no searcher has yet found either the efficient or final cause; [8] or can tell by what power the mind and the body are thus chained down in irresistible stupefaction; or what benefits the animal receives from this alternate suspension of its active powers.

Whatever may be the multiplicity or contrariety of opinions upon this subject, nature has taken sufficient care that theory shall have little influence on practice. The most diligent enquirer is not able long to keep his eyes open; the most eager disputant will begin about midnight to desert his argument, and once in four and twenty hours, the gay and the gloomy, the witty and the dull, the clamorous and the silent, the busy and the idle, are all overpowered by the gentle tyrant, and all lie down in the equality of sleep.

Philosophy has often attempted to repress insolence by asserting that all conditions are levelled by death; a position which, however it may deject the happy, will seldom afford much comfort to the wretched. It is far more pleasing to consider that sleep is equally a leveller with death; that the time is never at a great distance when the balm of rest shall be effused alike upon every head, when the diversities of life shall stop their operation, and the high and the low shall lie down together.

It is somewhere recorded of Alexander, that in the pride of conquests and intoxication of flattery, he declared that he only perceived himself to be a man by the necessity of sleep.[9] Whether he considered sleep as necessary to his mind or body it was indeed a sufficient evidence of human infirmity; the body which required such frequency of renovation gave but faint promises of immortality; and the mind which, from time to time, sunk gladly into insensibility had made no very near approaches to the felicity of the supreme and self-sufficient nature.

I know not what can tend more to repress all the passions that disturb the peace of the world than the consideration that there is no height of happiness or honour from which man does not eagerly descend to a state of unconscious repose; that the best condition of life is such that we contentedly quit its good

8. That is, that which brings it about or the end it may be supposed to serve.
9. In Plutarch's life, XXII.3–4; Johnson refers to Alexander's conviction of his divine origin (see Dryden, *Alexander's Feast*).

to be disentangled from its evils; that in a few hours splendour fades before the eye and praise itself deadens in the ear; the senses withdraw from their objects, and reason favours the retreat.

What then are the hopes and prospects of covetousness, ambition and rapacity? Let him that desires most have all his desires gratified, he never shall attain a state which he can, for a day and a night, contemplate with satisfaction, or from which, if he had the power of perpetual vigilance, he would not long for periodical separations.

All envy would be extinguished if it were universally known that there are none to be envied, and surely none can be much envied who are not pleased with themselves. There is reason to suspect that the distinctions of mankind have more show than value when it is found that all agree to be weary alike of pleasures and of cares, that the powerful and the weak, the celebrated and obscure, join in one common wish, and implore from nature's hand the nectar of oblivion.

Such is our desire of abstraction from ourselves that very few are satisfied with the quantity of stupefaction which the needs of the body force upon the mind. Alexander himself added intemperance to sleep, and solaced with the fumes of wine the sovereignty of the world. And almost every man has some art by which he steals his thoughts away from his present state.

It is not much of life that is spent in close attention to any important duty. Many hours of every day are suffered to fly away without any traces left upon the intellects. We suffer phantoms to rise up before us, and amuse ourselves with the dance of airy images, which after a time we dismiss for ever, and know not how we have been busied.

Many have no happier moments than those that they pass in solitude, abandoned to their own imagination, which sometimes puts sceptres in their hands or mitres on their heads, shifts the scene of pleasure with endless variety, bids all the forms of beauty sparkle before them, and gluts them with every change of visionary luxury.

It is easy in these semi-slumbers to collect all the possibilities of happiness, to alter the course of the sun, to bring back the past, and anticipate the future, to unite all the beauties of all seasons, and all the blessings of all climates, to receive and bestow felicity, and forget that misery is the lot of man. All this is a voluntary dream, a temporary recession from the realities of life to airy fictions; an habitual subjection of reason to fancy.

Others are afraid to be alone, and amuse themselves by a perpetual succession of companions, but the difference is not great; in solitude we have our dreams to ourselves, and in company we agree to dream in concert. The end sought in both is forgetfulness of ourselves. [No. 32, Saturday, November 25, 1758]

Respicere ad longae jussit spatia ultima vitae.
JUVENAL, X.275 [10]

Much of the pain and pleasure of mankind arises from the conjectures which every one makes of the thoughts of others; we all enjoy praise which we do not

10. "Bidden to look at the last lap of a long life."

hear, and resent contempt which we do not see. The Idler may therefore be forgiven if he suffers his imagination to represent to him what his readers will say or think when they are informed that they have now his last paper in their hands.

Value is more frequently raised by scarcity than by use. That which lay neglected when it was common rises in estimation as its quantity becomes less. We seldom learn the true want of what we have till it is discovered that we can have no more.

This essay will, perhaps, be read with care even by those who have not yet attended to any other; and he that finds this late attention recompensed will not forbear to wish that he had bestowed it sooner.

Though the Idler and his readers have contracted no close friendship they are perhaps both unwilling to part. There are few things not purely evil of which we can say, without some emotion of uneasiness, 'this is the last.' Those who never could agree together shed tears when mutual discontent has determined them to final separation; of a place which has been frequently visited, though without pleasure, the last look is taken with heaviness of heart; and the Idler, with all his chillness of tranquillity, is not wholly unaffected by the thought that his last essay is now before him.

This secret horror of the last is inseparable from a thinking being whose life is limited, and to whom death is dreadful. We always make a secret comparison between a part and the whole; the termination of any period of life reminds us that life itself has likewise its termination; when we have done anything for the last time, we involuntarily reflect that a part of the days allotted us is past, and that as more is past there is less remaining.

It is very happily and kindly provided that in every life there are certain pauses and interruptions, which force consideration upon the careless and seriousness upon the light; points of time where one course of action ends and another begins; and by vicissitude of fortune, or alteration of employment, by change of place, or loss of friendship, we are forced to say of something, 'this is the last.'

An even and unvaried tenor of life always hides from our apprehension the approach of its end. Succession is not perceived but by variation; he that lives today as he lived yesterday, and expects that, as the present day is, such will be the morrow, easily conceives time as running in a circle and returning to itself. The uncertainty of our duration is impressed commonly by dissimilitude of condition; it is only by finding life changeable that we are reminded of its shortness.

This conviction, however forcible at every new impression, is every moment fading from the mind; and partly by the inevitable incursion of new images, and partly by voluntary exclusion of unwelcome thoughts, we are again exposed to the universal fallacy; and we must do another thing for the last time, before we consider that the time is nigh when we shall do no more.

As the last *Idler* is published in that solemn week [11] which the Christian world has always set apart for the examination of the conscience, the review of life, the extinction of earthly desires and the renovation of holy purposes, I

---

11. On Holy Saturday of Easter week.

hope that my readers are already disposed to view every incident with seriousness and improve it by meditation; and that when they see this series of trifles
brought to a conclusion, they will consider that by outliving the *Idler* they have
past weeks, months, and years which are now no longer in their power; that an
end must in time be put to everything great as to everything little; that to
life must come its last hour, and to this system of being its last day, the hour
at which probation ceases, and repentance will be vain; the day in which every
work of the hand and imagination of the heart shall be brought to judgment,
and an everlasting futurity shall be determined by the past. [No. 103, Saturday,
April 5, 1760]

From The Preface to Shakespeare [1]

Nothing can please many, and please long, but just representations of general
nature. Particular manners can be known to few, and therefore few only can
judge how nearly they are copied. The irregular combinations of fanciful invention may delight awhile by that novelty of which the common satiety of life
sends us all in quest; but the pleasures of sudden wonder are soon exhausted,
and the mind can only repose on the stability of truth.

Shakespeare is, above all writers, at least above all modern writers, the poet
of nature, the poet that holds up to his readers a faithful mirror of manners and
of life. His characters are not modified by the customs of particular places,
unpractised by the rest of the world; by the peculiarities of studies or professions which can operate but upon small numbers; or by the accidents of
transient fashions or temporary opinions: they are the genuine progeny of
common humanity, such as the world will always supply, and observation will
always find. His persons act and speak by the influence of those general passions and principles by which all minds are agitated and the whole system of
life is continued in motion. In the writings of other poets a character is too
often an individual; in those of Shakespeare it is commonly a species.

It is from this wide extension of design that so much instruction is derived.
It is this which fills the plays of Shakespeare with practical axioms and domestic
wisdom. It was said of Euripides that every verse was a precept; [2] and it may
be said of Shakespeare that from his works may be collected a system of civil
and economical prudence. Yet his real power is not shown in the splendour of
particular passages, but by the progress of his fable and the tenor of his dia-

---

1. The Preface and Notes to Shakespeare are part of an edition Johnson undertook almost
a decade earlier and finally completed in 1765. It need hardly be said that Johnson was
not the first in his age to denounce the "rules" (in this case, the unity of time and place)
derived on slender grounds from Aristotle. Addison had written a half-century before:
"There is sometimes a greater judgment shown in deviating from the rules of art than in
adhering to them" (*Spectator* No. 592). But Johnson uses his discussion to explore, as
Dryden had before and Reynolds was to do in his thirteenth Discourse (1786), the nature of
art and illusion; and he provides the most telling discussion before (or even including) Coleridge of the "willing suspension of disbelief." In his appeal from art to nature (i.e. from
rules to experience) and in his notes on characters, Johnson shows the moral centrality of
his literary criticism, the constant inquiry as to what human ends art can be said to serve.
2. By Cicero, *Familiar Letters* XVI.8.

logue; and he that tries to recommend him by select quotations will succeed like the pedant in Hierocles,[3] who, when he offered his house to sale, carried a brick in his pocket as a specimen.

It will not easily be imagined how much Shakespeare excels in accommodating his sentiments to real life but by comparing him with other authors. It was observed of the ancient schools of declamation that the more diligently they were frequented, the more was the student disqualified for the world, because he found nothing there which he should ever meet in any other place.[4] The same remark may be applied to every stage but that of Shakespeare. The theatre, when it is under any other direction, is peopled by such characters as were never seen, conversing in a language which was never heard, upon topics which will never arise in the commerce of mankind. But the dialogue of this author is often so evidently determined by the incident which produces it, and is pursued with so much ease and simplicity, that it seems scarcely to claim the merit of fiction, but to have been gleaned by diligent selection out of common conversation and common occurrences.

Upon every other stage the universal agent is love, by whose power all good and evil is distributed and every action quickened or retarded. To bring a lover, a lady, and a rival into the fable; to entangle them in contradictory obligations, perplex them with oppositions of interest, and harass them with violence of desires inconsistent with each other; to make them meet in rapture and part in agony, to fill their mouths with hyperbolical joy and outrageous sorrow, to distress them as nothing human ever was distressed, to deliver them as nothing human ever was delivered, is the business of a modern dramatist. For this, probability is violated, life is misrepresented, and language is depraved. But love is only one of many passions; and as it has no great influence upon the sum of life, it has little operation in the dramas of a poet who caught his ideas from the living world and exhibited only what he saw before him. He knew that any other passion, as it was regular or exorbitant, was a cause of happiness or calamity.

Characters thus ample and general were not easily discriminated and preserved, yet perhaps no poet ever kept his personages more distinct from each other. I will not say with Pope that every speech may be assigned to the proper speaker,[5] because many speeches there are which have nothing characteristical; but, perhaps, though some may be equally adapted to every person, it will be difficult to find any that can be properly transferred from the present possessor to another claimant. The choice is right, when there is reason for choice.

Other dramatists can only gain attention by hyperbolical or aggravated characters, by fabulous and unexampled excellence or depravity, as the writers of barbarous romances invigorated the reader by a giant and a dwarf; and he that should form his expectations of human affairs from the play, or from the tale, would be equally deceived. Shakespeare has no heroes; his scenes are occupied only by men, who act and speak as the reader thinks that he should

3. Hierocles was an Alexandrian of the 5th century A.D.; his "jests" were freely translated in 1741, possibly by Johnson.
4. Petronius, *Satyricon* I.i.
5. In his Preface to Shakespeare (1725).

himself have spoken or acted on the same occasion. Even where the agency is supernatural, the dialogue is level with life. Other writers disguise the most natural passions and most frequent incidents; so that he who contemplates them in the book will not know them in the world. Shakespeare approximates the remote and familiarizes the wonderful; the event which he represents will not happen, but, if it were possible, its effects would probably be such as he has assigned; and it may be said that he has not only shown human nature as it acts in real exigences, but as it would be found in trials to which it cannot be exposed.

This, therefore, is the praise of Shakespeare, that his drama is the mirror of life; that he who has mazed his imagination in following the phantoms which other writers raise up before him, may here be cured of his delirious ecstasies by reading human sentiments in human language, by scenes from which a hermit may estimate the transactions of the world and a confessor predict the progress of the passions.

. . .

Shakespeare's plays are not in the rigorous and critical sense either tragedies or comedies, but compositions of a distinct kind; exhibiting the real state of sublunary [6] nature, which partakes of good and evil, joy and sorrow, mingled with endless variety of proportion and innumerable modes of combination; and expressing the course of the world, in which the loss of one is the gain of another; in which, at the same time, the reveller is hasting to his wine, and the mourner burying his friend; in which the malignity of one is sometimes defeated by the frolic of another; and many mischiefs and many benefits are done and hindered without design.

Out of this chaos of mingled purposes and casualties the ancient poets, according to the laws which custom had prescribed, selected some the crimes of men, and some their absurdities; some the momentous vicissitudes of life, and some the lighter occurrences; some the terrors of distress, and some the gaieties of prosperity. Thus rose the two modes of imitation, known by the names of *tragedy* and *comedy*, compositions intended to promote different ends by contrary means, and considered as so little allied that I do not recollect among the Greeks or Romans a single writer who attempted both.

Shakespeare has united the powers of exciting laughter and sorrow not only in one mind but in one composition. Almost all his plays are divided between serious and ludicrous characters, and, in the successive evolutions of the design, sometimes produce seriousness and sorrow, and sometimes levity and laughter.

That this is a practice contrary to the rules of criticism will be readily allowed; but there is always an appeal open from criticism to nature. The end of writing is to instruct; the end of poetry is to instruct by pleasing. That the mingled drama may convey all the instruction of tragedy or comedy cannot be denied, because it includes both in its alternations of exhibition and approaches nearer than either to the appearance of life, by showing how great machinations and slender designs may promote or obviate one another, and the high and the low cooperate in the general system by unavoidable concatenation.

It is objected that by this change of scenes the passions are interrupted in

6. That is, beneath the celestial realms; on earth.

their progression, and that the principal event, being not advanced by a due gradation of preparatory incidents, wants at last the power to move, which constitutes the perfection of dramatic poetry. This reasoning is so specious [7] that it is received as true even by those who in daily experience feel it to be false. The interchanges of mingled scenes seldom fail to produce the intended vicissitudes of passion. Fiction cannot move so much but that the attention may be easily transferred; and though it must be allowed that pleasing melancholy be sometimes interrupted by unwelcome levity, yet let it be considered likewise that melancholy is often not pleasing, and that the disturbance of one man may be the relief of another; that different auditors have different habitudes; and that, upon the whole, all pleasure consists in variety.

. . .

Shakespeare with his excellencies has likewise faults, and faults sufficient to obscure and overwhelm any other merit. I shall show them in the proportion in which they appear to me, without envious malignity or superstitious veneration. No question can be more innocently discussed than a dead poet's pretensions to renown; and little regard is due to that bigotry which sets candour [8] higher than truth.

His first defect is that to which may be imputed most of the evil in books or in men. He sacrifices virtue to convenience and is so much more careful to please than to instruct that he seems to write without any moral purpose. From his writings indeed a system of social duty may be selected, for he that thinks reasonably must think morally; but his precepts and axioms drop casually from him; he makes no just distribution of good or evil, nor is always careful to show in the virtuous a disapprobation of the wicked; he carries his persons indifferently through right and wrong and at the close dismisses them without further care and leaves their examples to operate by chance. This fault the barbarity of his age cannot extenuate; for it is always a writer's duty to make the world better, and justice is a virtue independent on time or place.

The plots are often so loosely formed that a very slight consideration may improve them, and so carelessly pursued that he seems not always fully to comprehend his own design. He omits opportunities of instructing or delighting which the train of his story seems to force upon him, and apparently rejects those exhibitions which would be more affecting, for the sake of those which are more easy.

. . .

It is incident to him to be now and then entangled with an unwieldy sentiment, which he cannot well express and will not reject; he struggles with it a while, and, if it continues stubborn, comprises it in words such as occur and leaves it to be disentangled and evolved by those who have more leisure to bestow upon it.

Not that always where the language is intricate the thought is subtle, or the image always great where the line is bulky; the equality of words to things is very often neglected, and trivial sentiments and vulgar ideas disappoint the attention to which they are recommended by sonorous epithets and swelling figures.

7. Plausible.
8. Sympathy, kindness.

But the admirers of this great poet have most reason to complain when he approaches nearest to his highest excellence and seems fully resolved to sink them in dejection [9] and mollify them with tender emotions by the fall of greatness, the danger of innocence, or the crosses of love. What he does best, he soon ceases to do. He is not long soft and pathetic without some idle conceit or contemptible equivocation.[10] He no sooner begins to move than he counteracts himself; and terror and pity, as they are rising in the mind, are checked and blasted by sudden frigidity.

A quibble is to Shakespeare what luminous vapours are to the traveller; he follows it at all adventures; it is sure to lead him out of his way and sure to engulf him in the mire. It has some malignant power over his mind, and its fascinations are irresistible. Whatever be the dignity or profundity of his disquisition, whether he be enlarging knowledge or exalting affection, whether he be amusing attention with incidents or enchaining it in suspense, let but a quibble spring up before him, and he leaves his work unfinished. A quibble is the golden apple [11] for which he will always turn aside from his career or stoop from his elevation. A quibble, poor and barren as it is, gave him such delight that he was content to purchase it by the sacrifice of reason, propriety, and truth. A quibble was to him the fatal Cleopatra for which he lost the world and was content to lose it.

It will be thought strange that in enumerating the defects of this writer, I have not yet mentioned his neglect of the unities, his violation of those laws which have been instituted and established by the joint authority of poets and of critics.

For his other deviations from the art of writing, I resign him to critical justice, without making any other demand in his favour than that which must be indulged to all human excellence: that his virtues be rated with his failings. But from the censure which this irregularity may bring upon him, I shall, with due reverence to that learning which I must oppose, adventure to try how I can defend him.

His histories, being neither tragedies nor comedies, are not subject to any of their laws; nothing more is necessary to all the praise which they expect than that the changes of action be so prepared as to be understood, that the incidents be various and affecting, and the characters consistent, natural, and distinct. No other unity is intended, and therefore none is to be sought.

In his other works he has well enough preserved the unity of action. He has not, indeed, an intrigue regularly perplexed and regularly unravelled; he does not endeavour to hide his design only to discover it, for this is seldom the order

9. While Johnson sees this power as a strength, he associates it with a sense of justice ("which all reasonable beings naturally love") and cannot condone the death of Cordelia. He cites the version of Nahum Tate which permits her survival: "In the present case the public has decided. Cordelia, from the time of Tate, has always retired with victory and felicity. And, if my sensations could add anything to the general suffrage, I might relate that I was many years ago so shocked by Cordelia's death that I know not whether I ever endured to read again the last scenes of the play till I undertook to revise them as an editor."
10. On the "conceit," see Johnson on the Metaphysical poets in the *Life of Cowley;* by "equivocation" he means pun or quibble (the latter defined by him as "a low conceit depending on the sound of words; a pun").
11. Referring to Atalanta, the fleet princess who was overtaken when Meleager (or Melanion) cast a golden apple in her path.

of real events, and Shakespeare is the poet of nature; but his plan has commonly, what Aristotle requires, a beginning, a middle, and an end; one event is concatenated with another, and the conclusion follows by easy consequence. There are perhaps some incidents that might be spared, as in other poets there is much talk that only fills up time upon the stage; but the general system makes gradual advances, and the end of the play is the end of expectation.

To the unities of time and place he has shown no regard; and perhaps a nearer view of the principles on which they stand will diminish their value and withdraw from them the veneration which, from the time of Corneille,[12] they have very generally received, by discovering that they have given more trouble to the poet than pleasure to the auditor.

The necessity of observing the unities of time and place arises from the supposed necessity of making the drama credible. The critics hold it impossible that an action of months or years can be possibly believed to pass in three hours; or that the spectator can suppose himself to sit in the theatre while ambassadors go and return between distant kings, while armies are levied and towns besieged, while an exile wanders and returns, or till he whom they saw courting his mistress shall lament the untimely fall of his son. The mind revolts from evident falsehood, and fiction loses its force when it departs from the resemblance of reality.

From the narrow limitation of time necessarily arises the contraction of place. The spectator, who knows that he saw the first act at Alexandria, cannot suppose that he sees the next at Rome, at a distance to which not the dragons of Medea [13] could, in so short a time, have transported him; he knows with certainty that he has not changed his place; and he knows that place cannot change itself; that what was a house cannot become a plain; that what was Thebes can never be Persepolis.

Such is the triumphant language with which a critic exults over the misery of an irregular poet and exults commonly without resistance or reply. It is time, therefore, to tell him by the authority of Shakespeare that he assumes, as an unquestionable principle, a position which, while his breath is forming it into words, his understanding pronounces to be false. It is false, that any representation is mistaken for reality; that any dramatic fable in its materiality was ever credible, or, for a single moment, was ever credited.

The objection arising from the impossibility of passing the first hour at Alexandria and the next at Rome, supposes that when the play opens the spectator really imagines himself at Alexandria and believes that his walk to the theatre has been a voyage to Egypt and that he lives in the days of Antony and Cleopatra. Surely he that imagines this may imagine more. He that can take the stage at one time for the palace of the Ptolemies may take it in half an hour for the promontory of Actium. Delusion, if delusion be admitted, has no certain limitation; if the spectator can be once persuaded that his old acquaintance are Alexander and Caesar, that a room illuminated with candles is the plain of Pharsalia or the bank of Granicus,[14] he is in a state of

---

12. Pierre Corneille in the 1660 edition of his plays included a discourse on the unities and also *examens* of each of his plays in which he discussed such problems.

13. They draw the chariot in which she flees from Corinth after killing Jason's new wife Creusa and her own children.

14. Alexander fought a battle near the river Granicus, Caesar on the plains of Pharsalia.

elevation above the reach of reason or of truth, and from the heights of empyrean poetry may despise the circumscriptions of terrestrial nature. There is no reason why a mind thus wandering in ecstasy should count the clock, or why an hour should not be a century in that calenture [15] of the brains that can make the stage a field.

The truth is that the spectators are always in their senses and know, from the first act to the last, that the stage is only a stage, and that the players are only players. They come to hear a certain number of lines recited with just gesture and elegant modulation. The lines relate to some action, and an action must be in some place; but the different actions that complete a story may be in places very remote from each other; and where is the absurdity of allowing that space to represent first Athens and then Sicily which was always known to be neither Sicily nor Athens, but a modern theatre.

By supposition, as place is introduced, time may be extended; the time required by the fable elapses for the most part between the acts; for, of so much of the action as is represented, the real and poetical duration is the same. If in the first act preparations for war against Mithridates are represented to be made in Rome, the event of the war may, without absurdity, be represented in the catastrophe as happening in Pontus; we know that there is neither war nor preparation for war; we know that we are neither in Rome nor Pontus; that neither Mithridates nor Lucullus are before us.[16] The drama exhibits successive imitations of successive actions; and why may not the second imitation represent an action that happened years after the first, if it be so connected with it that nothing but time can be supposed to intervene? Time is, of all modes of existence, most obsequious [17] to the imagination; a lapse of years is as easily conceived as a passage of hours. In contemplation we easily contract the time of real actions and therefore willingly permit it to be contracted when we only see their imitation.

It will be asked how the drama moves if it is not credited. It is credited with all the credit due to a drama. It is credited, whenever it moves, as a just picture of a real original; as representing to the auditor what he would himself feel if he were to do or suffer what is there feigned to be suffered or to be done. The reflection that strikes the heart is not that the evils before us are real evils, but that they are evils to which we ourselves may be exposed. If there be any fallacy, it is not that we fancy the players, but that we fancy ourselves, unhappy for a moment; but we rather lament the possibility than suppose the presence of misery, as a mother weeps over her babe when she remembers that death may take it from her. The delight of tragedy proceeds from our consciousness of fiction; if we thought murders and treasons real, they would please no more.

Imitations produce pain or pleasure, not because they are mistaken for realities, but because they bring realities to mind. When the imagination is recreated [18] by a painted landscape, the trees are not supposed capable to

15. Fever.
16. Mithridates the Great (c. 130–63 B.C.), ruler of Pontus and conqueror of much of the rest of Asia Minor; attacked with temporary success by the Romans under Lucullus (73–66 B.C.) and finally defeated by the forces of Pompey.
17. Yielding, submissive.
18. Gratified.

give us shade, or the fountains coolness; but we consider how we should be pleased with such fountains playing beside us and such woods waving over us. We are agitated in reading the history of *Henry the Fifth,* yet no man takes his book for the field of Agincourt. A dramatic exhibition is a book recited with concomitants that increase or diminish its effect. Familiar comedy is often more powerful in the theatre than on the page; imperial tragedy is always less. The humour of Petruchio may be heightened by grimace; but what voice or what gesture can hope to add dignity or force to the soliloquy of Cato? [19]

A play read affects the mind like a play acted. It is therefore evident that the action is not supposed to be real; and it follows that between the acts a longer or shorter time may be allowed to pass, and that no more account of space or duration is to be taken by the auditor of a drama than by the reader of a narrative, before whom may pass in an hour the life of a hero or the revolutions of an empire.

. . .

He that, without diminution of any other excellence, shall preserve all the unities unbroken deserves the like applause with the architect who shall display all the orders of architecture in a citadel without any deduction from its strength; but the principal beauty of a citadel is to exclude the enemy, and the greatest graces of a play are to copy nature and instruct life.

Perhaps what I have here not dogmatically but deliberatively written may recall the principles of the drama to a new examination. I am almost frighted at my own temerity and, when I estimate the fame and the strength of those that maintain the contrary opinion, am ready to sink down in reverential silence; as Aeneas withdrew from the defence of Troy when he saw Neptune shaking the wall and Juno heading the besiegers.[20]

Those whom my arguments cannot persuade to give their approbation to the judgement of Shakespeare will easily, if they consider the condition of his life, make some allowance for his ignorance.

Every man's performances, to be rightly estimated, must be compared with the state of the age in which he lived and with his own particular opportunities; and though to the reader a book be not worse or better for the circumstances of the author, yet as there is always a silent reference of human works to human abilities, and as the inquiry how far man may extend his designs, or how high he may rate his native force, is of far greater dignity than in what rank we shall place any particular performance, curiosity is always busy to discover the instruments as well as to survey the workmanship, to know how much is to be ascribed to original powers and how much to casual and adventitious help. The palaces of Peru or Mexico were certainly mean and incommodious habitations if compared to the houses of European monarchs; yet who could forbear to view them with astonishment who remembered that they were built without the use of iron? . . .

19. Referring to Joseph Addison's tragedy of 1713.
20. *Aeneid* II.610–14.

From The Notes to Shakespeare

[Falstaff]

But Falstaff, unimitated, unimitable Falstaff, how shall I describe thee? Thou compound of sense and vice; of sense which may be admired but not esteemed, of vice which may be despised but hardly detested. Falstaff is a character loaded with faults, and with those faults which naturally produce contempt. He is a thief and a glutton, a coward and a boaster, always ready to cheat the weak and prey upon the poor; to terrify the timorous and insult the defenceless. At once obsequious and malignant, he satirizes in their absence those whom he lives by flattering. He is familiar with the prince only as an agent of vice, but of this familiarity he is so proud as not only to be supercilious and haughty with common men but to think his interest of importance to the Duke of Lancaster. Yet the man thus corrupt, thus despicable, makes himself necessary to the prince that despises him, by the most pleasing of all qualities, perpetual gaiety, by an unfailing power of exciting laughter, which is the more freely indulged as his wit is not of the splendid or ambitious kind but consists in easy escapes and sallies of levity, which make sport but raise no envy. It must be observed that he is stained with no enormous or sanguinary crimes, so that his licentiousness is not so offensive but that it may be borne for his mirth.

The moral to be drawn from this representation is that no man is more dangerous than he that, with a will to corrupt, hath the power to please; and that neither wit nor honesty ought to think themselves safe with such a companion when they see Henry seduced by Falstaff.

[Polonius]

The commentator makes the character of Polonius a character only of manners, discriminated by properties superficial, accidental, and acquired. The poet intended a nobler delineation of a mixed character of manners and of nature. Polonius is a man bred in courts, exercised in business, stored with observation, confident of his knowledge, proud of his eloquence, and declining into dotage. His mode of oratory is truly represented as designed to ridicule the practice of those times, of prefaces that made no introduction, and of method that embarrassed rather than explained. This part of his character is accidental, the rest is natural. Such a man is positive and confident, because he knows that his mind was once strong and knows not that it is become weak. Such a man excels in general principles but fails in the particular application. He is knowing in retrospect and ignorant in foresight. While he depends upon his memory and can draw from his repositories of knowledge, he utters weighty sentences and gives useful counsel; but as the mind in its enfeebled state cannot be kept long busy and intent, the old man is subject to sudden dereliction of his faculties, he loses the order of his ideas and entangles himself in his own thoughts, till he recovers the leading principle and falls again into his former train. This idea of dotage encroaching upon wisdom will solve all the phenomena of the character of Polonius.

[Lady Macbeth]

. . . The arguments by which Lady Macbeth persuades her husband to commit the murder afford a proof of Shakespeare's knowledge of human nature. She urges the excellence and dignity of courage, a glittering idea which has dazzled mankind from age to age and animated sometimes the housebreaker and sometimes the conqueror; but this sophism Macbeth has for ever destroyed, by distinguishing true from false fortitude, in a line and a half; of which it may almost be said that they ought to bestow immortality on the author, though all his other productions had been lost;

> I dare do all that may become a man,
> Who dares do more, is none.

This topic, which has been always employed with too much success, is used in this scene with peculiar propriety, to a soldier by a woman. Courage is the distinguishing virtue of a soldier, and the reproach of cowardice cannot be borne by any man from a woman, without great impatience.

She then urges the oaths by which he had bound himself to murder Duncan, another art of sophistry by which men have sometimes deluded their consciences and persuaded themselves that what would be criminal in others is virtuous in them; this argument Shakespeare, whose plan obliged him to make Macbeth yield, has not confuted, though he might easily have shown that a former obligation could not be vacated by a latter; that obligations laid on us by a higher power could not be overruled by obligations which we lay upon ourselves.

1765

The Lives of the Poets

Johnson had planned biographical studies of English writers for many years, but the enterprise was given shape by an agreement with thirty-six London booksellers to supply lives to accompany the selections from fifty-two poets (from Cowley to Gray) who were no longer alive. The first four volumes appeared in 1779, the remaining six in 1781; the lives were collected in the latter year and have since acquired the unofficial but familiar title given above. The *Life of Cowley* provided Johnson with an occasion for a general discussion of the Metaphysical poets, given below. All the lives contain a balance, usually clearly demarcated, of biographical and critical writing; but in both, Johnson remains a profound, acutely aphoristic moralist.

From The Lives of the Poets

[Cowley and the Metaphysical Poets [1]]

The metaphysical poets were men of learning, and to show their learning was their whole endeavour; but, unluckily resolving to show it in rhyme, instead of writing poetry they only wrote verses, and very often such verses as stood the

---

1. Johnson used the *Life of Cowley* as an occasion for reviewing the methods of all the Metaphysical poets. While he cited many of the excesses of John Donne, whose work he knew well, the most outrageous instances are cited from such late Metaphysical poets as

trial of the finger better than of the ear; for the modulation was so imperfect, that they were only found to be verses by counting the syllables.

If the father of criticism has rightly denominated poetry τέχνη μιμητική, *an imitative art*,[2] these writers will, without great wrong, lose their right to the name of poets, for they cannot be said to have imitated anything; they neither copied nature nor life, neither painted the forms of matter, nor represented the operations of intellect.

Those, however, who deny them to be poets, allow them to be wits. Dryden confesses of himself and his contemporaries, that they fall below Donne in wit, but maintains that they surpass him in poetry.[3]

If wit be well described by Pope, as being 'that which has been often thought, but was never before so well expressed,'[4] they certainly never attained, nor ever sought it; for they endeavoured to be singular in their thoughts, and were careless of their diction. But Pope's account of wit is undoubtedly erroneous: he depresses it below its natural dignity, and reduces it from strength of thought to happiness[5] of language.

If by a more noble and more adequate conception that be considered as wit which is at once natural and new, that which, though not obvious, is, upon its first production, acknowledged to be just; if it be that which he that never found it wonders how he missed, to wit of this kind the metaphysical poets have seldom risen. Their thoughts are often new, but seldom natural; they are not obvious, but neither are they just; and the reader, far from wondering that he missed them, wonders more frequently by what perverseness of industry they were ever found.

But wit, abstracted from its effects upon the hearer, may be more rigorously and philosophically considered as a kind of *discordia concors;* a combination of dissimilar images, or discovery of occult resemblances in things apparently unlike. Of wit, thus defined, they have more than enough. The most heterogeneous ideas are yoked by violence together; nature and art are ransacked for illustrations, comparisons, and allusions; their learning instructs, and their subtlety surprises; but the reader commonly thinks his improvement dearly bought, and, though he sometimes admires, is seldom pleased.

From this account of their compositions it will be readily inferred that they were not successful in representing or moving the affections. As they were wholly employed on something unexpected and surprising, they had no regard to that uniformity of sentiment which enables us to conceive and to excite the pains and the pleasure of other minds: they never inquired what, on any occasion, they should have said or done, but wrote rather as beholders than

---

Cowley and John Cleveland. By Johnson's day these poets (whom Coleridge later called "witty logicians") had fallen greatly in reputation; we can see that decline begin with Dryden's remarks on Cleveland and continue in Pope's censure of those who pursue "conceit alone" (*Essay on Criticism*, ll.289 ff.). When Pope "versified" two of Donne's satires, he demonstrated by his changes his own definition of "true Wit": "a justness of thought and a facility of expression, or (in the midwives' phrase) a perfect conception with an easy delivery."

2. Aristotle in the *Poetics*.
3. In *Of Dramatic Poesy: An Essay;* see above, the section Dryden's Critical Prose.
4. Paraphrased from the *Essay on Criticism*, ll. 297–98.
5. Felicity; implying chance as well as success.

partakers of human nature; as beings looking upon good and evil, impassive and at leisure; as Epicurean deities, making remarks on the actions of men and the vicissitudes of life, without interest and without emotion. Their courtship was void of fondness, and their lamentation of sorrow. Their wish was only to say what they hoped had been never said before.

Nor was the sublime more within their reach than the pathetic; for they never attempted that comprehension and expanse of thought which at once fills the whole mind, and of which the first effect is sudden astonishment, and the second rational admiration.[6] Sublimity is produced by aggregation, and littleness by dispersion. Great thoughts are always general, and consist in positions not limited by exceptions, and in descriptions not descending to minuteness. It is with great propriety that subtlety, which in its original import means exility [7] of particles, is taken in its metaphorical meaning for nicety of distinction. Those writers who lay on the watch for novelty could have little hope of greatness; for great things cannot have escaped former observation. Their attempts were always analytic; they broke every image into fragments; and could no more represent, by their slender conceits and laboured particularities, the prospects of nature, or the scenes of life, than he who dissects a sunbeam with a prism can exhibit the wide effulgence of a summer noon.

What they wanted however of the sublime, they endeavoured to supply by hyperbole; their amplification had no limits; they left not only reason but fancy behind them; and produced combinations of confused magnificence, that not only could not be credited, but could not be imagined.

Yet great labour, directed by great abilities, is never wholly lost: if they frequently threw away their wit upon false conceits, they likewise sometimes struck out unexpected truth; if their conceits were far-fetched, they were often worth the carriage. To write on their plan, it was at least necessary to read and think. No man could be born a metaphysical poet, nor assume the dignity of a writer, by descriptions copied from descriptions, by imitations borrowed from imitations, by traditional imagery, and hereditary similes, by readiness of rhyme, and volubility of syllables.

In perusing the works of this race of authors, the mind is exercised either by recollection or inquiry; either something already learned is to be retrieved, or something new is to be examined. If their greatness seldom elevates, their acuteness often surprises; if the imagination is not always gratified, at least the powers of reflection and comparison are employed; and in the mass of materials which ingenious absurdity has thrown together, genuine wit and useful knowledge may be sometimes found buried perhaps in grossness of expression, but useful to those who know their value; and such as, when they are expanded to perspicuity, and polished to elegance, may give lustre to works which have more propriety though less copiousness of sentiment.

[Milton [8]]

His political notions were those of an acrimonious and surly republican, for which it is not known that he gave any better reason than that *a popular gov-*

6. See below, Burke's *Enquiry* of 1757.
7. Smallness of number, meagerness.
8. These paragraphs, however unfair, are refreshing in an age of "candour" (to use the term, as Johnson does, in opposition to "truth") and highly characteristic of their author.

ernment was the most frugal; for the trappings of a monarchy would set up an ordinary commonwealth. It is surely very shallow policy that supposes money to be the chief good; and even this, without considering that the support and expense of a court is, for the most part, only a particular kind of traffic, for which money is circulated without any national impoverishment.

Milton's republicanism was, I am afraid, founded in an envious hatred of greatness, and a sullen desire of independence; in petulance impatient of control, and pride disdainful of superiority. He hated monarchs in the State, and prelates in the Church; for he hated all whom he was required to obey. It is to be suspected that his predominant desire was to destroy rather than establish, and that he felt not so much the love of liberty as repugnance to authority.

It has been observed that they who most loudly clamour for liberty do not most liberally grant it. What we know of Milton's character in domestic relations is that he was severe and arbitrary. His family consisted of women; and there appears in his books something like a Turkish contempt of females, as subordinate and inferior beings. That his own daughters might not break the ranks, he suffered them to be depressed by a mean and penurious education. He thought woman made only for obedience, and man only for rebellion.

[Richard Savage [9]]

Such were the life and death of Richard Savage, a man equally distinguished by his virtues and vices, and at once remarkable for his weaknesses and abilities.

He was of a middle stature, of a thin habit of body, a long visage, coarse features, and melancholy aspect; of a grave and manly deportment, a solemn dignity of mien, but which, upon a nearer acquaintance, softened into an engaging easiness of manners. His walk was slow, and his voice tremulous and mournful. He was easily excited to smiles, but very seldom provoked to laughter.

His mind was in an uncommon degree vigorous and active. His judgment was accurate, his apprehension quick, and his memory so tenacious that he was frequently observed to know what he had learned from others in a short time, better than those by whom he was informed, and could frequently recollect incidents, with all their combination of circumstances, which few would have regarded at the present time, but which the quickness of his apprehension impressed upon him. He had the art of escaping from his own reflections, and accommodating himself to every new scene.

. . .

His method of life particularly qualified him for conversation, of which he knew how to practise all the graces. He was never vehement or loud, but at once modest and easy, open and respectful; his language was vivacious or elegant, and equally happy upon grave and humorous subjects. He was generally censured for not knowing when to retire; but that was not the defect of his judgment, but of his fortune; when he left his company, he was frequently to spend the remaining part of the night in the street, or at least was abandoned

9. Richard Savage (1697–1743) was a close friend of Johnson, and his is the fullest and most intimate of all the *Lives;* originally composed and published in 1744.

to gloomy reflections, which it is not strange that he delayed as long as he could; and sometimes forgot that he gave others pain to avoid it himself.

It cannot be said that he made use of his abilities for the direction of his own conduct: an irregular and dissipated manner of life had made him the slave of every passion that happened to be excited by the presence of its object, and that slavery to his passions reciprocally produced a life irregular and dissipated. He was not master of his own motions, nor could omission promise anything for the next day.

With regard to his economy, nothing can be added to the relation of his life. He appeared to think himself born to be supported by others, and dispensed from all necessity of providing for himself; he therefore never prosecuted any scheme of advantage, nor endeavoured even to secure the profits which his writings might have afforded him. His temper was, in consequence of the dominion of his passions, uncertain and capricious; he was easily engaged, and easily disgusted; but he is accused of retaining his hatred more tenaciously than his benevolence.

He was compassionate both by nature and principle, and always ready to perform offices of humanity; but when he was provoked (and very small offences were sufficient to provoke him), he would prosecute his revenge with the utmost acrimony till his passion had subsided.

His friendship was therefore of little value; for though he was zealous in the support or vindication of those whom he loved, yet it was always dangerous to trust him, because he considered himself as discharged by the first quarrel from all ties of honour or gratitude, and would betray those secrets which in the warmth of confidence had been imparted to him. This practice drew upon him an universal accusation of ingratitude: nor can it be denied that he was very ready to set himself free from the load of an obligation; for he could not bear to conceive himself in a state of dependence, his pride being equally powerful with his other passions, and appearing in the form of insolence at one time, and of vanity at another. Vanity, the most innocent species of pride, was most frequently predominant: he could not easily leave off when he had once begun to mention himself or his works; nor ever read his verses without stealing his eyes from the page, to discover in the faces of his audience how they were affected with any favourite passage.

.   .   .

For his life, or for his writings, none, who candidly consider his fortune, will think an apology either necessary or difficult. If he was not always sufficiently instructed in his subject, his knowledge was at least greater than could have been attained by others in the same state. If his works were sometimes unfinished, accuracy cannot reasonably be exacted from a man oppressed with want, which he has no hope of relieving but by a speedy publication. The insolence and resentment of which he is accused were not easily to be avoided by a great mind, irritated by perpetual hardships, and constrained hourly to return the spurns of contempt, and repress the insolence of prosperity; and vanity surely may be readily pardoned in him to whom life afforded no other comforts than barren praises, and the consciousness of deserving them.

Those are no proper judges of his conduct who have slumbered away their time on the down of plenty; nor will any wise man easily presume to say, 'Had

I been in Savage's condition, I should have lived or written better than Savage.'

[Dryden and Pope [10]]

Integrity of understanding and nicety of discernment were not allotted in a less proportion to Dryden than to Pope. The rectitude of Dryden's mind was sufficiently shown by the dismission of his poetical prejudices, and the rejection of unnatural thoughts and rugged numbers.[11] But Dryden never desired to apply all the judgment that he had. He wrote, and professed to write, merely for the people; and when he pleased others, he contented himself. He spent no time in struggles to rouse latent powers; he never attempted to make that better which was already good, nor often to mend what he must have known to be faulty. He wrote, as he tells us, with very little consideration; when occasion or necessity called upon him, he poured out what the present moment happened to supply, and, when once it had passed the press, ejected it from his mind; for when he had no pecuniary interest, he had no further solicitude.

Pope was not content to satisfy; he desired to excel, and therefore always endeavoured to do his best: he did not court the candour, but dared the judgment of his reader, and, expecting no indulgence from others, he showed none to himself. He examined lines and words with minute and punctilious observation, and retouched every part with indefatigable diligence, till he had left nothing to be forgiven.

For this reason he kept his pieces very long in his hands, while he considered and reconsidered them. The only poems which can be supposed to have been written with such regard to the times as might hasten their publication were the two satires of *Thirty-eight;* [12] of which Dodsley [13] told me that they were brought to him by the author, that they might be fairly copied. 'Almost every line,' he said, 'was then written twice over; I gave him a clean transcript, which he sent some time afterwards to me for the press, with almost every line written twice over a second time.'

His declaration that his care for his works ceased at their publication was not strictly true. His parental attention never abandoned them; what he found amiss in the first edition, he silently corrected in those that followed. He appears to have revised the Iliad, and freed it from some of its imperfections; and the *Essay on Criticism* received many improvements after its first appearance. It will seldom be found that he altered without adding clearness, elegance, or vigour. Pope had perhaps the judgment of Dryden; but Dryden certainly wanted the diligence of Pope.

In acquired knowledge, the superiority must be allowed to Dryden, whose education was more scholastic, and who before he became an author had been allowed more time for study, with better means of information. His mind has a larger range, and he collects his images and illustrations from a more

10. This method of comparison is to be seen in Dryden's discussion of Shakespeare and Jonson or Horace and Juvenal; another example, Pope's comparison of Homer and Virgil, is given below.
11. Harsh versification.
12. Later entitled the *Epilogue to the Satires.*
13. Robert Dodsley (1703–64), the publisher.

extensive circumference of science. Dryden knew more of man in his general nature, and Pope in his local manners. The notions of Dryden were formed by comprehensive speculation, and those of Pope by minute attention. There is more dignity in the knowledge of Dryden, and more certainty in that of Pope.

Poetry was not the sole praise of either; for both excelled likewise in prose; but Pope did not borrow his prose from his predecessor. The style of Dryden is capricious and varied; that of Pope is cautious and uniform. Dryden observes the motions of his own mind; Pope constrains his mind to his own rules of composition. Dryden is sometimes vehement and rapid; Pope is always smooth, uniform, and gentle. Dryden's page is a natural field, rising into inequalities, and diversified by the varied exuberance of abundant vegetation; Pope's is a velvet lawn, shaven by the scythe, and levelled by the roller.

Of genius, that power which constitutes a poet; that quality without which judgment is cold, and knowledge is inert; that energy which collects, combines, amplifies, and animates; the superiority must, with some hesitation, be allowed to Dryden. It is not to be inferred that of this poetical vigour Pope had only a little, because Dryden had more; for every other writer since Milton must give place to Pope; and even of Dryden it must be said, that, if he has brighter paragraphs, he has not better poems. Dryden's performances were always hasty, either excited by some external occasion, or extorted by domestic necessity; he composed without consideration, and published without correction. What his mind could supply at call, or gather in one excursion, was all that he sought, and all that he gave. The dilatory caution of Pope enabled him to condense his sentiments, to multiply his images, and to accumulate all that study might produce or chance might supply. If the flights of Dryden therefore are higher, Pope continues longer on the wing. If of Dryden's fire the blaze is brighter, of Pope's the heat is more regular and constant. Dryden often surpasses expectation, and Pope never falls below it. Dryden is read with frequent astonishment, and Pope with perpetual delight.

This parallel will, I hope, when it is well considered, be found just; and if the reader should suspect me, as I suspect myself, of some partial fondness for the memory of Dryden, let him not too hastily condemn me; for meditation and inquiry may, perhaps, show him the reasonableness of my determination.

1779–81

Pope on Homer and Virgil

. . . Nothing is more absurd or endless than the common method of comparing eminent writers by an opposition of particular passages in them and forming a judgment from thence of their merit upon the whole. We ought to have a certain knowledge of the principal character and distinguishing excellence of each; it is in *that* we are to consider him, and in proportion to his degree in *that* we are to admire him. No author or man ever excelled all the world in more than one faculty, and as Homer has done this in invention, Virgil has in judgment. Not that we are to think Homer wanted judgment because Virgil had it in a more eminent degree, or that Virgil wanted invention because

Homer possessed a larger share of it: each of these great authors had more of both than perhaps any man besides, and are only said to have less in comparison with one another. Homer was the greater genius, Virgil the better artist. In one we most admire the man, in the other the work. Homer hurries and transports us with a commanding impetuosity, Virgil leads us with an attractive majesty. Homer scatters with a generous profusion, Virgil bestows with a careful magnificence. Homer, like the Nile, pours out his riches with a sudden overflow; Virgil, like a river in its banks, with a gentle and constant stream. When we behold their battles, methinks the two poets resemble the heroes they celebrate: Homer, boundless and irresistible as Achilles, bears all before him, and shines more and more as the tumult increases; Virgil, calmly daring like Aeneas, appears undisturbed in the midst of the action, disposes all about him, and conquers with tranquillity. And when we look upon their machines, Homer seems like his own Jupiter in his terrors, shaking Olympus, scattering the lightnings, and firing the Heavens; Virgil, like the same power in his benevolence, counselling with the gods, laying plans for empires, and regularly ordering his whole creation. [From Preface to the translation of the *Iliad*, 1715]

EDWARD GIBBON
1737–1794

The great historian of the fall of the Roman empire and the triumph over it of "barbarism and religion" was a small, plump, extremely elegant man, whose irony concealed from some his capacity for concentrated study and his intense devotion to political liberty. At Oxford Gibbon spent, he wrote later, "the fourteen months the most idle and unprofitable of my whole life." From that scene of indolence Gibbon absented himself often "without once hearing the voice of admonition, without once feeling the hand of control." It was, however, at Oxford that he was converted to Roman Catholicism, and he was sent to Lausanne in Switzerland to study privately and to recover from this "error." Having returned by 1752 to Protestantism, Gibbon "suspended" his "religious inquiries, acquiescing with implicit belief in the tenets and mysteries" common to all churches.

Before he found his great subject, Gibbon, like Milton before him, contemplated others, among them a life of Sir Walter Ralegh, a history of the liberty of the Swiss, and a history of Florence under the Medici. Gibbon meditated in his journal upon the last two: "the one a poor, warlike, virtuous republic, which emerges into glory and freedom; the other, a commonwealth, soft, opulent, and corrupt, which, by just degrees, is precipitated from the abuse to the loss of her liberty; both lessons are, perhaps, equally instructive." In the fall of the republic of Florence an important role would have been given to Savonarola and to "enthusiasm" as "the most formidable weapon" of the Medicis' adversaries. These plans of 1762 reveal those moral themes that engaged Gibbon's feelings most deeply and govern his history of the Roman empire.

The first volume of the *History* (1776) created some scandal by its ironical treatment of Christianity but won immediate respect for its artistry and learning. Gibbon completed his plan by 1788 with the fall of the Byzantine empire and the revival of learning in Rome. In 1783 Gibbon left England behind and moved permanently to Lausanne. Upon his death, his *Memoirs* were left in several overlapping drafts, begun as early as 1788, and they were first edited by his friend Lord Sheffield. The manuscripts survive and have been published; each reading-text is necessarily an eclectic selection from them. (For excerpts, see below, in the section entitled Sense and Sensibility.)

The style of his abortive account of the Swiss, written in French, was (in Gibbon's own words) "above prose and below poetry," and had "degenerated into a verbose and turgid declamation." Gibbon worked hard to find a style for his *History* that would "hit a middle tone between a dull chronicle and a rhetorical declamation." What gives Gibbon's achieved style its peculiar energy is his ironic respect for the pretensions he exposes. He rarely descends to explicit judgment, and the generality of his terms disdains to name what it so clearly suggests. Writing of the advancement of Christianity from an underground messianic faith to a worldly power, he traces the corresponding changes in its spiritual vision: "A garden of Eden, with the amusements of a pastoral life, was no longer suited to the advanced state of society which prevailed under the Roman Empire. A city was therefore erected of gold and precious stones, and a supernatural plenty of corn and wine was bestowed on the adjacent territory, in the free enjoyment of whose spontaneous productions the happy and benevolent people was never to be restrained by any jealous laws of exclusive property." Or writing of the self-indulgence of a Roman emperor (the younger Gordianus): "Twenty-two acknowledged concubines, and a library of sixty-two thousand volumes, attested the variety of his inclinations, and from the productions which he left behind him, it appears that the former as well as the latter were designed for use rather than ostentation." With the same splendid aloofness he can show how powerful an instrument of conquest intolerant zeal becomes in the early history of the Christians; or, in the third chapter, given below, the process by which Augustus undermines Roman liberties while preserving their forms—until we dramatically find ourselves at the close in a vast prison built of cunning and acquiescence. This chapter, which professes to deal with Roman institutions, is in fact a profound drama of ideas, and ideas for Gibbon are scarcely extricable from motives and passions (not least what he calls "the dexterity of self-love").

From The History of the Decline and Fall of the Roman Empire

Chapter III: Of the Constitution of the Roman Empire, in the Age of the Antonines

The obvious definition of a monarchy seems to be that of a state in which a single person, by whatsoever name he may be distinguished, is intrusted with the execution of the laws, the management of the revenue, and the command of the army. But unless public liberty is protected by intrepid and vigilant guardians, the authority of so formidable a magistrate will soon degenerate into despotism. The influence of the clergy, in an age of superstition, might be usefully employed to assert the rights of mankind; but so intimate is the connexion between the throne and the altar, that the banner of the church has very seldom been seen on the side of the people. A martial nobility and stubborn commons, possessed of arms, tenacious of property, and collected into constitutional assemblies, form the only balance capable of preserving a free constitution against enterprises of an aspiring prince.

Every barrier of the Roman constitution had been levelled by the vast ambition of the dictator; every fence had been extirpated by the cruel hand of the triumvir.[1] After the victory of Actium, the fate of the Roman world depended on the will of Octavianus, surnamed Caesar by his uncle's adoption, and afterwards Augustus, by the flattery of the senate.[2] The conqueror was at the head of forty-four veteran legions, conscious of their own strength and of the weakness of the constitution, habituated during twenty years' civil war to every act of blood and violence, and passionately devoted to the house of Caesar, from whence alone they had received and expected the most lavish rewards. The provinces, long oppressed by the ministers of the republic, sighed for the government of a single person, who would be the master, not the accomplice, of those petty tyrants. The people of Rome, viewing with a secret pleasure the humiliation of the aristocracy, demanded only bread and public shows, and were supplied with both by the liberal hand of Augustus. The rich and polite Italians, who had almost universally embraced the philosophy of Epicurus,[3] enjoyed the present blessings of ease and tranquillity, and suffered not the pleasing dream to be interrupted by the memory of their old tumultuous freedom. With its power, the senate had lost its dignity; many of the most noble families were extinct. The republicans of spirit and ability had perished in the field of battle, or in the proscription. The door of the assembly had been designedly left open for a mixed multitude of more than a thousand persons, who reflected disgrace upon their rank, instead of deriving honour from it.[4]

The reformation of the senate was one of the first steps in which Augustus laid aside the tyrant and professed himself the father of his country. He was

---

1. The first triumvirate was that of Julius Caesar, Pompey, and Crassus; the second, that of Octavianus (later Augustus), Mark Antony, and Lepidus.

2. Augustus was born Gaius Octavius in 63 B.C.; upon his adoption by his great uncle, he became G. Julius Caesar Octavianus; the title Augustus was given to him by the Senate in 27 B.C. Upon the assassination of his uncle in 44 B.C. he joined the republican party and forced Antony to flee. Thereupon he compelled the Senate to elect him consul and later became reconciled to Antony, forming the second triumvirate with him and Lepidus. Their proscriptions led to the death of 2000 *equites* (or knights) and 300 senators, among them Cicero. Antony, who had married Octavia, the sister of Augustus, repudiated her for Cleopatra and, in the war of Rome against Egypt that followed, was defeated in the naval battle of Actium, 31 B.C. At this point Augustus assumed full power but refused (for reasons Gibbon explores) any honors that might recall kingship.

3. Epicurus (341–270 B.C.) founded the philosophy transmitted by Lucretius and others. His atomic philosophy attributed to chance whatever design we can find in nature or in man, and his ethics were based upon pleasure and pain. He urged man to increase his pleasures to the utmost and to prefer higher pleasures to lower; the pleasures of mind—and particularly peace of mind—are highest of all. The Epicurean placed a much lower value upon active citizenship than the Stoic; personal "ease and tranquillity" tended to replace any sense of social engagement.

4. "Julius Caesar introduced soldiers, strangers, and half-barbarians into the Senate. . . . The abuse became still more scandalous after his death." (Gibbon)

elected censor; [5] and, in concert with his faithful Agrippa, he examined the list of the senators, expelled a few members whose vices or whose obstinacy required a public example, persuaded near two hundred to prevent the shame of an expulsion by a voluntary retreat, raised the qualification of a senator to about ten thousand pounds, created a sufficient number of patrician families, and accepted for himself the honourable title of Prince of the Senate, which had always been bestowed by the censors on the citizen the most eminent for his honours and services. But, whilst he thus restored the dignity, he destroyed the independence, of the senate. The principles of a free constitution are irrecoverably lost when the legislative power is nominated by the executive.

Before an assembly thus modelled and prepared, Augustus pronounced a studied oration, which displayed his patriotism and disguised his ambition. 'He lamented, yet excused, his past conduct. Filial piety had required at his hands the revenge of his father's murder; the humanity of his own nature had sometimes given way to the stern laws of necessity, and to a forced connexion with two unworthy colleagues: as long as Antony lived, the republic forbade him to abandon her to a degenerate Roman and a barbarian queen. He was now at liberty to satisfy his duty and his inclination. He solemnly restored the senate and people to all their ancient rights; and wished only to mingle with the crowd of his fellow-citizens and to share the blessings which he had obtained for his country.'

It would require the pen of Tacitus [6] (if Tacitus had assisted at this assembly) to describe the various emotions of the senate; those that were suppressed and those that were affected. It was dangerous to trust the sincerity of Augustus; to seem to distrust it was still more dangerous. The respective advantages of monarchy and a republic have often divided speculative inquirers; the present greatness of the Roman state, the corruption of manners, and the licence of the soldiers, supplied new arguments to the advocates of monarchy; and these general views of government were again warped by the hopes and fears of each individual. Amidst this confusion of sentiments, the answer of the senate was unanimous and decisive. They refused to accept the resignation of Augustus; they conjured him not to desert the republic which he had saved. After a decent resistance the crafty tyrant submitted to the orders of the senate; and consented to receive the government of the provinces, and the general command of the Roman armies, under the well-known names of PROCONSUL and IMPERATOR.[7] But he would receive them only for ten years. Even before the expiration of that period, he hoped that the wounds of civil discord would be completely healed, and that the republic, restored to its pristine health and vigour,

5. Originally appointed to take the census, the censor gained additional powers in time: stigmatizing any citizen for a moral offense which was not punishable by law, expelling men from the Senate or the equestrian order, and transferring men from one tribe to another (thus affecting their voting power).

6. Tacitus (d. c. 117), the great Roman historian, first promoted by Vespasian and active through the reign of Trajan; a writer of deep moral integrity with a close, difficult, epigrammatic style.

7. A proconsul assumed the consular power, that of supreme magistrate, combining military and judicial power, outside Rome. The title of *imperator* originally meant "general" and was conferred with a military triumph; Augustus made it part of his name, replacing Gaius.

would no longer require the dangerous interposition of so extraordinary a magistrate. The memory of this comedy, repeated several times during the life of Augustus, was preserved to the last ages of the empire by the peculiar pomp with which the perpetual monarchs of Rome always solemnized the tenth years of their reign.

Without any violation of the principles of the constitution, the general of the Roman armies might receive and exercise an authority almost despotic over the soldiers, the enemies, and the subjects of the republic. With regard to the soldiers, the jealousy of freedom had, even from the earliest ages of Rome, given way to the hopes of conquest and a just sense of military discipline. The dictator, or consul, had a right to command the service of the Roman youth, and to punish an obstinate or cowardly disobedience by the most severe and ignominious penalties, by striking the offender out of the list of citizens, by confiscating his property, and by selling his person into slavery. The most sacred rights of freedom, confirmed by the Porcian and Sempronian laws,[8] were suspended by the military engagement. In his camp the general exercised an absolute power of life and death; his jurisdiction was not confined by any forms of trial or rules of proceeding, and the execution of the sentence was immediate and without appeal. The choice of the enemies of Rome was regularly decided by the legislative authority. The most important resolutions of peace and war were seriously debated in the senate, and solemnly ratified by the people. But when the arms of the legions were carried to a great distance from Italy, the generals assumed the liberty of directing them against whatever people, and in whatever manner, they judged most advantageous for the public service. It was from the success, not from the justice, of their enterprises that they expected the honours of a triumph. In the use of victory, especially after they were no longer controlled by the commissioners of the senate, they exercised the most unbounded despotism. When Pompey[9] commanded in the East, he rewarded his soldiers and allies, dethroned princes, divided kingdoms, founded colonies, and distributed the treasures of Mithridates. On his return to Rome he obtained, by a single act of the senate and people, the universal ratification of all his proceedings. Such was the power over the soldiers, and over the enemies of Rome, which was either granted to, or assumed by, the generals of the republic. They were, at the same time, the governors, or rather monarchs, of the conquered provinces, united the civil with the military character, administered justice as well as the finances, and exercised both the executive and legislative power of the state.

From what has been already observed in the first chapter of this work, some notion may be formed of the armies and provinces thus intrusted to the ruling hand of Augustus. But, as it was impossible that he could personally command the legions of so many distant frontiers, he was indulged by the senate, as

8. The Porcian law (197 B.C.) ruled that a Roman citizen should not be scourged or put to death; the Sempronian law (123 B.C.) that no judgment involving the life or freedom of a citizen should be valid without the assent of the Roman people.

9. Pompey was appointed to this command in 66 B.C. and returned to Italy four years later, entering Rome in triumph in 61 B.C. During his defeat of Mithridates, King of Pontus and conqueror of much of Asia Minor, Pompey (as Gibbon indicates) assumed vast powers and, after the siege of Jerusalem in 63, entered the sanctuary of the holy temple.

Pompey had already been, in the permission of devolving the execution of his great office on a sufficient number of lieutenants. In rank and authority these officers seemed not inferior to the ancient proconsuls; but their station was dependent and precarious. They received and held their commissions at the will of a superior, to whose *auspicious* influence the merit of their action was legally attributed.[10] They were the representatives of the emperor. The emperor alone was the general of the republic, and his jurisdiction, civil as well as military, extended over all the conquests of Rome. It was some satisfaction, however, to the senate that he always delegated his power to the members of their body. The imperial lieutenants were of consular or praetorian dignity; the legions were commanded by senators, and the praefecture of Egypt was the only important trust committed to a Roman knight.[11]

Within six days after Augustus had been compelled to accept so very liberal a grant, he resolved to gratify the pride of the senate by an easy sacrifice. He represented to them that they had enlarged his powers, even beyond that degree which might be required by the melancholy condition of the times. They had not permitted him to refuse the laborious command of the armies and the frontiers; but he must insist on being allowed to restore the more peaceful and secure provinces to the mild administration of the civil magistrate. In the division of the provinces Augustus provided for his own power and for the dignity of the republic. The proconsuls of the senate, particularly those of Asia, Greece, and Africa, enjoyed a more honourable character than the lieutenants of the emperor, who commanded in Gaul or Syria. The former were attended by lictors, the latter by soldiers.[12] A law was passed that, wherever the emperor was present, his extraordinary commission should supersede the ordinary jurisdiction of the governor; a custom was introduced that the new conquests belonged to the imperial portion; and it was soon discovered that the authority of the *Prince*, the favourite epithet of Augustus, was the same in every part of the empire.

In return for this imaginary concession, Augustus obtained an important privilege, which rendered him master of Rome and Italy. By a dangerous exception to the ancient maxims, he was authorized to preserve his military command, supported by a numerous body of guards, even in time of peace, and in the heart of the capital. His command, indeed, was confined to those citizens who were engaged in the service by the military oath; but such was the propensity of the Romans to servitude, that the oath was voluntarily taken by the magistrates, the senators, and the equestrian order, till the homage of flattery was insensibly converted into an annual and solemn protestation of fidelity.

Although Augustus considered a military force as the firmest foundation,

10. Auguries of success had to be officially taken before every public act, and the power of the augury was tied to the power of the official taking the auspices; hence an "auspicious influence" was a claim of responsibility or merit.

11. The knights (or *equites* and thus the "equestrian order") were originally a military rank, but by 123 B.C. they had become a third class between the Senate and the people, their standing based upon income; Augustus removed most of the legal status of the class but employed its members in important and confidential posts.

12. The proconsuls, like the consul, had twelve lictors with bundles of rods and axes; they executed punishments and exacted proper obeisance. These become empty rituals as Augustus shifts authority from the civil governors to imperial jurisdiction.

he wisely rejected it as a very odious instrument, of government. It was more agreeable to his temper, as well as to his policy, to reign under the venerable names of ancient magistracy, and artfully to collect in his own person all the scattered rays of civil jurisdiction. With this view, he permitted the senate to confer upon him, for his life, the powers of the consular and tribunitian offices, which were, in the same manner, continued to all his successors. The consuls had succeeded to the kings of Rome and represented the dignity of the state. They superintended the ceremonies of religion, levied and commanded the legions, gave audience to foreign ambassadors, and presided in the assemblies both of the senate and people. The general control of the finances was intrusted to their care; and, though they seldom had leisure to administer justice in person, they were considered as the supreme guardians of law, equity, and the public peace. Such was their ordinary jurisdiction; but, whenever the senate empowered the first magistrate to consult the safety of the commonwealth, he was raised by that decree above the laws, and exercised, in the defence of liberty, a temporary despotism. The character of the tribunes was, in every respect, different from that of the consuls. The appearance of the former was modest and humble; but their persons were sacred and inviolable. Their force was suited rather for opposition than for action. They were instituted to defend the oppressed, to pardon offences, to arraign the enemies of the people, and, when they judged it necessary, to stop, by a single word, the whole machine of government. As long as the republic subsisted, the dangerous influence which either the consul or the tribune might derive from their respective jurisdiction was diminished by several important restrictions. Their authority expired with the year in which they were elected; the former office was divided between two, the latter among ten, persons; and, as both in their private and public interest they were adverse to each other, their mutual conflicts contributed, for the most part, to strengthen rather than to destroy the balance of the constitution. But when the consular and tribunitian powers were united, when they were vested for life in a single person, when the general of the army was, at the same time, the minister of the senate and the representative of the Roman people, it was impossible to resist the exercise, nor was it easy to define the limits, of his imperial prerogative.

To these accumulated honours the policy of Augustus soon added the splendid as well as important dignities of supreme pontiff, and of censor. By the former he acquired the management of the religion, and by the latter a legal inspection over the manners and fortunes, of the Roman people. If so many distinct and independent powers did not exactly unite with each other, the complaisance [13] of the senate was prepared to supply every deficiency by the most ample and extraordinary concessions. The emperors, as the first ministers of the republic, were exempted from the obligation and penalty of many inconvenient laws: they were authorized to convoke the senate, to make several motions in the same day, to recommend candidates for the honours of the state, to enlarge the bounds of the city, to employ the revenue at their discretion, to declare peace and war, to ratify treaties; and, by a most comprehensive clause, they were empowered to execute whatsoever they should

13. Readiness to oblige, compliance.

judge advantageous to the empire, and agreeable to the majesty of things private or public, human or divine.

When all the various powers of executive government were committed to the *Imperial magistrate,* the ordinary magistrates of the commonwealth languished in obscurity, without vigour and almost without business. The names and forms of the ancient administration were preserved by Augustus with the most anxious care. The usual number of consuls, praetors, and tribunes were annually invested with their respective ensigns of office, and continued to discharge some of their least important functions. Those honours still attracted the vain ambition of the Romans; and the emperors themselves, though invested for life with the powers of the consulship, frequently aspired to the title of that annual dignity which they condescended to share with the most illustrious of their fellow-citizens. In the election of these magistrates, the people, during the reign of Augustus, were permitted to expose all the inconveniences of a wild democracy. That artful prince, instead of discovering the least symptom of impatience, humbly solicited their suffrages for himself or his friends, and scrupulously practised all the duties of an ordinary candidate. But we may venture to ascribe to his councils the first measure of the succeeding reign, by which the elections were transferred to the senate. The assemblies of the people were for ever abolished, and the emperors were delivered from a dangerous multitude, who, without restoring liberty, might have disturbed, and perhaps endangered, the established government.

By declaring themselves the protectors of the people, Marius and Caesar [14] had subverted the constitution of their country. But as soon as the senate had been humbled and disarmed, such an assembly, consisting of five or six hundred persons, was found a much more tractable and useful instrument of dominion. It was on the dignity of the senate that Augustus and his successors founded their new empire; and they affected, on every occasion, to adopt the language and principles of Patricians. In the administration of their own powers, they frequently consulted the great national council, and *seemed* to refer to its decision the most important concerns of peace and war. Rome, Italy, and the internal provinces were subject to the immediate jurisdiction of the senate. With regard to civil objects, it was the supreme court of appeal; with regard to criminal matters, a tribunal, constituted for the trial of all offences that were committed by men in any public station, or that affected the peace and majesty of the Roman people. The exercise of the judicial power became the most frequent and serious occupation of the senate; and the important causes that were pleaded before them afforded a last refuge to the spirit of ancient eloquence. As a council of state and as a court of justice, the senate possessed very considerable prerogatives; but in its legislative capacity, in which it was supposed virtually to represent the people, the rights of sovereignty were acknowledged to reside in that assembly. Every

14. Gaius Marius (157–86 B.C.) began his rise to dictatorial power as tribune of the people and enemy of the aristocracy; so, too, Julius Caesar (102–44 B.C.) was brought into the popular party through his aunt's marriage with Marius and his own to the daughter of Marius' chief supporter. The Senate, which had been a formidable if unsuccessful enemy in the past, is now turned by Augustus into an "instrument," and he is careful to show verbal respect for the patrician order (from which alone, until about 350 B.C., the Senate was drawn).

power was derived from their authority, every law was ratified by their sanction. Their regular meetings were held on three stated days in every month, the Calends, the Nones, and the Ides.[15] The debates were conducted with decent [16] freedom; and the emperors themselves, who gloried in the name of senators, sat, voted, and divided with their equals.

To resume, in a few words, the system of the Imperial government, as it was instituted by Augustus, and maintained by those princes who understood their own interest and that of the people, it may be defined an absolute monarchy disguised by the forms of a commonwealth. The masters of the Roman world surrounded their throne with darkness, concealed their irresistible strength, and humbly professed themselves the accountable ministers of the senate, whose supreme decrees they dictated and obeyed.

The face of the court corresponded with the forms of the administration. The emperors, if we except those tyrants whose capricious folly violated every law of nature and decency, disdained that pomp and ceremony which might offend their countrymen but could add nothing to their real power. In all the offices of life, they affected to confound themselves with their subjects, and maintained with them an equal intercourse of visits and entertainments. Their habit, their palace, their table, were suited only to the rank of an opulent senator. Their family, however numerous or splendid, was composed entirely of their domestic slaves and freedmen.[17] Augustus or Trajan would have blushed at employing the meanest of the Romans in those menial offices which, in the household and bedchamber of a limited monarch, are so eagerly solicited by the proudest nobles of Britain.

The deification of the emperors is the only instance in which they departed from their accustomed prudence and modesty. The Asiatic Greeks were the first inventors, the successors of Alexander the first objects, of this servile and impious mode of adulation. It was easily transferred from the kings to the governors of Asia; and the Roman magistrates very frequently were adored as provincial deities, with the pomp of altars and temples, of festivals and sacrifices. It was natural that the emperors should not refuse what the proconsuls had accepted; and the divine honours which both the one and the other received from the provinces attested rather the despotism than the servitude of Rome. But the conquerors soon imitated the vanquished nations in the arts of flattery; and the imperious spirit of the first Caesar too easily consented to assume, during his life time, a place among the tutelar deities of Rome. The milder temper of his successor declined so dangerous an ambition, which was never afterwards revived, except by the madness of Caligula and Domitian.[18] Augustus permitted indeed some of the provincial cities to erect temples to his honour, on condition that they should associate the worship of

15. The days corresponding, originally, to the first appearance of the new moon, the first quarter, and the full moon.
16. Decorous, restrained.
17. "A weak prince will always be governed by his domestics. The power of slaves aggravated the shame of the Romans; and the Senate paid court to a Pallas or a Narcissus. There is a chance that a modern favourite may be a gentleman." (Gibbon)
18. Caligula, 12–41 A.D., and Domitian, 51–96 A.D., both notoriously vicious and uncontrolled emperors; Caligula claimed the honors paid to Apollo, Mars, and Jupiter, and built a temple to his own divinity; Domitian assumed the titles of Lord and God and claimed to be the son of Minerva.

Rome with that of the sovereign; he tolerated private superstition, of which he might be the object; but he contented himself with being revered by the senate and people in his human character, and wisely left to his successor the care of his public deification. A regular custom was introduced that, on the decease of every emperor who had neither lived nor died like a tyrant, the senate by a solemn decree should place him in the number of the gods; and the ceremonies of his apotheosis were blended with those of his funeral. This legal and, as it should seem, injudicious profanation, so abhorrent to our stricter principles, was received with a very faint murmur by the easy nature of Polytheism; but it was received as an institution not of religion, but of policy. We should disgrace the virtues of the Antonines by comparing them with the vices of Hercules or Jupiter.[19] Even the characters of Caesar or Augustus were far superior to those of the popular deities. But it was the misfortune of the former to live in an enlightened age, and their actions were too faithfully recorded to admit of such a mixture of fable and mystery as the devotion of the vulgar requires. As soon as their divinity was established by law, it sunk into oblivion, without contributing either to their own fame or to the dignity of succeeding princes.

In the consideration of the Imperial government, we have frequently mentioned the artful founder, under his well-known title of Augustus, which was not however conferred upon him till the edifice was almost completed. The obscure name of Octavianus he derived from a mean family in the little town of Aricia. It was stained with the blood of the proscription; and he was desirous, had it been possible, to erase all memory of his former life. The illustrious surname of Caesar he had assumed as the adopted son of the dictator; but he had too much good sense either to hope to be confounded, or to wish to be compared, with that extraordinary man. It was proposed in the senate to dignify their minister with a new appellation; and, after a very serious discussion, that of Augustus was chosen, among several others, as being the most expressive of the character of peace and sanctity which he uniformly affected. *Augustus* was therefore a personal, *Caesar* a family, distinction. The former should naturally have expired with the prince on whom it was bestowed; and, however the latter was diffused by adoption and female alliance, Nero was the last prince who could allege any hereditary claim to the honours of the Julian line. But, at the time of his death, the practice of a century had inseparably connected those appellations with the Imperial dignity, and they have been preserved by a long succession of emperors,—Romans, Greeks, Franks, and Germans,—from the fall of the republic to the present time. A distinction was, however, soon introduced. The sacred title of Augustus was always reserved for the monarch, whilst the name of Caesar was more freely communicated to his relations; and, from the reign of Hadrian at least, was appropriated to the second person in the state, who was considered as the presumptive heir of the empire.

The tender respect of Augustus for a free constitution which he had de-

---

19. Hercules was regarded not only as a hero but as a god, and there were temples to him in Rome; among the vices ascribed to him in legend, as well as to Jupiter, are cruelty and sexual profligacy. For the admirable lives of the Antonines, see notes 31 and 32 below.

stroyed can only be explained by an attentive consideration of the character of that subtle tyrant. A cool head, an unfeeling heart, and a cowardly disposition prompted him at the age of nineteen to assume the mask of hypocrisy, which he never afterwards laid aside. With the same hand, and probably with the same temper, he signed the proscription of Cicero and the pardon of Cinna.[20] His virtues, and even his vices, were artificial; and according to the various dictates of his interest, he was at first the enemy, and at last the father, of the Roman world. When he framed the artful system of the Imperial authority, his moderation was inspired by his fears. He wished to deceive the people by an image of civil liberty, and the armies by an image of civil government.

I. The death of Caesar was ever before his eyes. He had lavished wealth and honours on his adherents; but the most favoured friends of his uncle were in the number of the conspirators. The fidelity of the legions might defend his authority against open rebellion, but their vigilance could not secure his person from the dagger of a determined republican; and the Romans, who revered the memory of Brutus,[21] would applaud the imitation of his virtue. Caesar had provoked his fate as much by the ostentation of his power as by his power itself. The consul or the tribune might have reigned in peace. The title of king had armed the Romans against his life.[22] Augustus was sensible that mankind is governed by names; nor was he deceived in his expectation that the senate and people would submit to slavery, provided they were respectfully assured that they still enjoyed their ancient freedom. A feeble senate and enervated people cheerfully acquiesced in the pleasing illusion as long as it was supported by the virtue, or by even the prudence, of the successors of Augustus. It was a motive of self-preservation, not a principle of liberty, that animated the conspirators against Caligula, Nero, and Domitian. They attacked the person of the tyrant, without aiming their blow at the authority of the emperor.

There appears, indeed, *one* memorable occasion, in which the senate, after seventy years of patience, made an ineffectual attempt to reassume its long-forgotten rights. When the throne was vacant by the murder of Caligula, the consuls convoked that assembly in the Capitol, condemned the memory of the Caesars, gave the watchword *liberty* to the few cohorts who faintly adhered to their standard, and during eight and forty hours, acted as the independent chiefs of a free commonwealth. But while they deliberated, the praetorian guards [23] had resolved. The stupid Claudius, brother of Germanicus, was already in their camp, invested with the Imperial purple, and prepared to support his election by arms. The dream of liberty was at an end; and the senate awoke

20. Marcus Tullius Cicero (106–43 B.C.), the orator, statesman, and philosopher, was proscribed by order of the first triumvirate and put to death near Caieta. Gaius Cornelius Cinna was, in contrast, pardoned by Augustus for alleged conspiracy (*c.* 16–13 B.C.).
21. "'Two centuries after the establishment of monarchy, the emperor Marcus Antoninus recommends the character of Brutus as the perfect model of Roman virtue." (Gibbon)
22. That Julius Caesar secretly sought, and might accept, the crown was the fear that led to his assassination.
23. The praetorian guards were the bodyguard of the emperor; when Claudius was discovered in hiding after the murder of Caligula, the guards saluted him as emperor (41 A.D.); his brother Germanicus, an impressive military leader, had died about twenty years earlier.

to all the horrors of inevitable servitude. Deserted by the people, and threatened by a military policy, that feeble assembly was compelled to ratify the choice of the praetorians, and to embrace the benefit of an amnesty, which Claudius had the prudence to offer, and the generosity to observe.

II. The insolence of the armies inspired Augustus with fears of a still more alarming nature. The despair of the citizens could only attempt what the power of the soldiers was, at any time, able to execute. How precarious was his own authority over men whom he had taught to violate every social duty! He had heard their seditious clamours; he dreaded their calmer moments of reflection. One revolution had been purchased by immense rewards; but a second revolution might double those rewards. The troops professed the fondest attachment to the house of Caesar; but the attachments of the multitude are capricious and inconstant. Augustus summoned to his aid whatever remained in those fierce minds of Roman prejudices; enforced the rigour of discipline by the sanction of law; and, interposing the majesty of the senate between the emperor and the army, boldly claimed their allegiance as the first magistrate of the republic.

During a long period of two hundred and twenty years, from the establishment of this artful system to the death of Commodus, the dangers inherent to a military government were, in a great measure, suspended. The soldiers were seldom roused to that fatal sense of their own strength and of the weakness of the civil authority, which was, before and afterwards, productive of such dreadful calamities. Caligula and Domitian were assassinated in their palace by their own domestics: the convulsions which agitated Rome on the death of the former were confined to the walls of the city. But Nero involved the whole empire in his ruin. In the space of eighteen months four princes perished by the sword; and the Roman world was shaken by the fury of the contending armies. Excepting only this short, though violent, eruption of military licence, the two centuries from Augustus to Commodus passed away unstained with civil blood, and undisturbed by revolutions. The emperor was elected by the *authority of the senate* and *the consent of the soldiers*. The legions respected their oath of fidelity; and it requires a minute inspection of the Roman annals to discover three inconsiderable rebellions, which were all suppressed in a few months, and without even the hazard of a battle.

In elective monarchies, the vacancy of the throne is a moment big with danger and mischief. The Roman emperors, desirous to spare the legions that interval of suspense, and the temptation of an irregular choice, invested their designed successor with so large a share of present power as should enable him, after their decease, to assume the remainder without suffering the empire to perceive the change of masters. Thus Augustus, after all his fairer prospects had been snatched from him by untimely deaths, rested his last hopes on Tiberius, obtained for his adopted son [24] the censorial and tribunitian powers, and dictated a law, by which the future prince was invested with an authority equal to his own over the provinces and the armies. Thus Vespasian subdued the generous mind of his eldest son. Titus was adored by the eastern legions, which, under his command, had recently achieved the conquest of Judea. His

---

24. Tiberius, who ruled from 14 to 37 A.D., was the son of Livia, whom Augustus had married; in 4 A.D. Augustus adopted him as a son and placed him in charge of the Roman armies.

power was dreaded, and, as his virtues were clouded by the intemperance of youth, his designs were suspected. Instead of listening to such unworthy suspicions, the prudent monarch associated Titus to the full powers of the Imperial dignity; and the grateful son ever approved himself the humble and faithful minister of so indulgent a father.[25]

The good sense of Vespasian engaged him indeed to embrace every measure that might confirm his recent and precarious elevation. The military oath, and the fidelity of the troops, had been consecrated, by the habits of an hundred years, to the name and family of the Caesars; and, although that family had been continued only by the fictitious rite of adoption, the Romans still revered, in the person of Nero, the grandson of Germanicus, and the lineal successor of Augustus. It was not without reluctance and remorse that the praetorian guards had been persuaded to abandon the cause of the tyrant. The rapid downfall of Galba, Otho, and Vitellius, taught the armies to consider the emperors as the creatures of *their* will, and the instruments of *their* licence.[26] The birth of Vespasian was mean; his grandfather had been a private soldier, his father a petty officer of the revenue, his own merit had raised him, in an advanced age, to the empire; but his merit was rather useful than shining, and his virtues were disgraced by a strict and even sordid parsimony. Such a prince consulted his true interest by the association of a son whose more splendid and amiable character might turn the public attention from the obscure origin to the future glories of the Flavian house. Under the mild administration of Titus, the Roman world enjoyed a transient felicity, and his beloved memory served to protect, above fifteen years, the vices of his brother Domitian.

Nerva[27] had scarcely accepted the purple from the assassins of Domitian before he discovered that his feeble age was unable to stem the torrent of public disorders which had multiplied under the long tyranny of his predecessor. His mild disposition was respected by the good; but the degenerate Romans required a more vigorous character, whose justice should strike terror into the guilty. Though he had several relations, he fixed his choice on a stranger. He adopted Trajan, then about forty years of age, and who commanded a powerful army in the Lower Germany; and immediately, by a decree of the senate, declared him his colleague and successor in the empire. It is sincerely to be lamented that, whilst we are fatigued with the disgustful relation of Nero's crimes and follies, we are reduced to collect the actions of Trajan from the glimmerings of an abridgement or the doubtful light of a panegyric. There remains, however, one panegyric far removed beyond the suspicion of

25. Vespasian, emperor 70–79 A.D., shared a triumph with his son Titus and gave him the title of Caesar; Titus lived to succeed his father for a reign of two years, after which his brother Domitian became emperor.
26. Servius Sulpicius Galba was raised to the throne by the praetorian guards in 68 A.D. and assassinated by them the following year; they then elevated Marcus Salvius Otho, who ruled for the first three months of 69 A.D. and committed suicide during the rebellion of Aulus Vitellius. He ruled a comparably short while before his murder and the succession of Vespasian.
27. Nerva succeeded to the empire in 96 A.D., when Domitian was murdered by a conspiracy of praetorian guards and court officials; while he restored many Roman liberties, his advanced age (66 at accession) and his lack of military support made his short reign insecure. He was succeeded by Trajan in 98 A.D.

flattery. Above two hundred and fifty years after the death of Trajan, the senate, in pouring out the customary acclamations on the accession of a new emperor, wished that he might surpass the felicity of Augustus and the virtue of Trajan.

We may readily believe that the father of his country hesitated whether he ought to intrust the various and doubtful character of his kinsman Hadrian with sovereign power. In his last moments, the arts of the empress Plotina either fixed the irresolution of Trajan, or boldly supposed a fictitious adoption, the truth of which could not be safely disputed; and Hadrian was peaceably acknowledged as his lawful successor.[28] Under his reign, as has been already mentioned, the empire flourished in peace and prosperity. He encouraged the arts, reformed the laws, asserted military discipline, and visited all his provinces in person. His vast and active genius was equally suited to the most enlarged views and the minute details of civil policy. But the ruling passions of his soul were curiosity and vanity. As they prevailed, and as they were attracted by different objects, Hadrian was, by turns, an excellent prince, a ridiculous sophist, and a jealous tyrant. The general tenor of his conduct deserved praise for its equity and moderation. Yet, in the first days of his reign, he put to death four consular senators, his personal enemies, and men who had been judged worthy of empire; and the tediousness of a painful illness rendered him, at last, peevish and cruel. The senate doubted whether they should pronounce him a god or a tyrant; and the honours decreed to his memory were granted to the prayers of the pious Antoninus.

The caprice of Hadrian influenced his choice of a successor. After revolving in his mind several men of distinguished merit, whom he esteemed and hated, he adopted Aelius Verus, a gay and voluptuous nobleman, recommended by uncommon beauty to the lover of Antinous.[29] But, whilst Hadrian was delighting himself with his own applause and the acclamations of the soldiers, whose consent had been secured by an immense donative,[30] the new Caesar was ravished from his embraces by an untimely death. He left only one son. Hadrian commended the boy to the gratitude of the Antonines. He was adopted by Pius; and, on the accession of Marcus, was invested with an equal share of sovereign power. Among the many vices of this younger Verus, he possessed one virtue—a dutiful reverence for his wiser colleague, to whom he willingly abandoned the ruder cares of empire. The philosophic emperor dissembled his follies, lamented his early death, and cast a decent veil over his memory.

As soon as Hadrian's passion was either gratified or disappointed, he resolved to deserve the thanks of posterity by placing the most exalted merit on the Roman throne. His discerning eye easily discovered a senator about fifty years of age, blameless in all the offices of life; and a youth of about seventeen, whose riper years opened the fair prospect of every virtue: the elder of these was

28. Trajan's adoption of Hadrian (emperor, 117–138 A.D.) was announced after his death, and, as Gibbon indicates, was suspected as a fiction.
29. Antinous, the Greek youth whose beauty and grace won Hadrian's love, was drowned in the Nile before he was twenty; he was deified and was represented in many statues, some of them highly influential on Renaissance sculpture. "The deification of Antinous, his medals, statues, temple, city, oracles, and constellation, are well known and still dishonour the memory of Hadrian. Yet we may remark that of the first fifteen emperors Claudius was the only one whose taste in love was entirely correct." .(Gibbon)
30. A gift from public funds.

declared the son and successor of Hadrian, on condition, however, that he himself should immediately adopt the younger. The two Antonines [31] (for it is of them that we are now speaking) governed the Roman world forty-two years with the same invariable spirit of wisdom and virtue. Although Pius had two sons, he preferred the welfare of Rome to the interest of his family, gave his daughter Faustina in marriage to young Marcus, obtained from the senate the tribunitian and proconsular powers, and, with a noble disdain, or rather ignorance, of jealousy, associated him to all the labours of government. Marcus, on the other hand, revered the character of his benefactor, loved him as a parent, obeyed him as a sovereign, and, after he was no more, regulated his own administration by the example and maxims of his predecessor. Their united reigns are possibly the only period of history in which the happiness of a great people was the sole object of government.

Titus Antoninus Pius has been justly denominated a second Numa. The same love of religion, justice, and peace, was the distinguishing characteristic of both princes. But the situation of the latter opened a much larger field for the exercise of those virtues. Numa could only prevent a few neighbouring villages from plundering each other's harvests. Antoninus diffused order and tranquillity over the greatest part of the earth. His reign is marked by the rare advantage of furnishing very few materials for history; which is, indeed, little more than the register of the crimes, follies, and misfortunes of mankind. In private life he was an amiable as well as a good man. The native simplicity of his virtue was a stranger to vanity or affectation. He enjoyed with moderation the conveniences of his fortune and the innocent pleasures of society; and the benevolence of his soul displayed itself in a cheerful serenity of temper.

The virtue of Marcus Aurelius Antoninus was of a severer and more laborious kind.[32] It was the well-earned harvest of many a learned conference, of many a patient lecture, and many a midnight lucubration. At the age of twelve years he embraced the rigid system of the Stoics, which taught him to submit his body to his mind, his passions to his reason; to consider virtue as the only good, vice as the only evil, all things external as things indifferent. His Meditations, composed in the tumult of a camp, are still extant; and he even condescended to give lessons on philosophy, in a more public manner than was perhaps consistent with the modesty of a sage or the dignity of an emperor. But his life was the noblest commentary on the precepts of Zeno.[33] He was severe to himself, indulgent to the imperfection of others, just and beneficent to all mankind. He regretted that Avidius Cassius, who excited a rebellion in

---

31. Antoninus Pius (86–161 A.D.) virtually ruled during Hadrian's final illness and argued successfully for that emperor's consecration. He ruled in his own name from 138 to 161 and was called a "second Numa" after the second King of Rome, Numa Pompilius (c. 715–c. 673 B.C.), of whom legends report that he ruled ably through the counsel of the nymph Egeria.

32. Marcus Aurelius Antoninus, emperor from 161 to 180, was charged by his enemies with hypocrisy. Gibbon notes, "This suspicion, unjust as it was, may serve to account for the superior applause bestowed upon personal qualifications in preference to the social virtues. . . . The wildest scepticism never insinuated that Caesar might possibly be a coward or Tully a fool. Wit and valour are qualifications more easily ascertained than humanity or the love of justice." Marcus Aurelius' *Meditations* (the written version of his "midnight lucubration") remains a classic of Roman Stoicism.

33. Zeno (335–263 B.C.), founder of the Stoic school, wished, however, to teach only true philosophers rather than the general public.

Syria, had disappointed him, by a voluntary death, of the pleasure of converting an enemy into a friend; and he justified the sincerity of that sentiment by moderating the zeal of the senate against the adherents of the traitor. War he detested, as the disgrace and calamity of human nature; but when the necessity of a just defence called upon him to take up arms, he readily exposed his person to eight winter campaigns on the frozen banks of the Danube, the severity of which was at last fatal to the weakness of his constitution. His memory was revered by a grateful posterity, and above a century after his death many persons preserved the image of Marcus Antoninus among those of their household gods.

If a man were called to fix the period in the history of the world during which the condition of the human race was most happy and prosperous, he would, without hesitation, name that which elapsed from the death of Domitian to the accession of Commodus.[34] The vast extent of the Roman empire was governed by absolute power under the guidance of virtue and wisdom. The armies were restrained by the firm but gentle hand of four successive emperors whose characters and authority commanded involuntary respect. The forms of the civil administration were carefully preserved by Nerva, Trajan, Hadrian, and the Antonines, who delighted in the image of liberty and were pleased with considering themselves as the accountable ministers of the laws. Such princes deserved the honour of restoring the republic, had the Romans of their days been capable of enjoying a rational freedom.

The labours of these monarchs were over-paid by the immense reward that inseparably waited on their success; by the honest pride of virtue, and by the exquisite delight of beholding the general happiness of which they were the authors. A just but melancholy reflection embittered, however, the noblest of human enjoyments. They must often have recollected the instability of a happiness which depended on the character of a single man. The fatal moment was perhaps approaching when some licentious youth, or some jealous tyrant, would abuse, to the destruction, that absolute power which they had exerted for the benefit, of their people. The ideal restraints of the senate and the laws might serve to display the virtues but could never correct the vices, of the emperor. The military force was a blind and irresistible instrument of oppression; and the corruption of Roman manners would always supply flatterers eager to applaud, and ministers prepared to serve, the fear or the avarice, the lust or the cruelty, of their masters.

These gloomy apprehensions had been already justified by the experience of the Romans. The annals of the emperors exhibit a strong and various picture of human nature, which we should vainly seek among the mixed and doubtful characters of modern history. In the conduct of those monarchs we may trace the utmost lines of vice and virtue; the most exalted perfection and the meanest degeneracy of our own species. The golden age of Trajan and the Antonines had been preceded by an age of iron. It is almost superfluous to enumerate the unworthy successors of Augustus. Their unparalleled vices, and the splendid theatre on which they were acted, have saved them from oblivion. The dark

---

34. That is, 96–180 A.D. Commodus, the older son of Marcus Aurelius, succeeded for a reign of twelve years during which he became increasingly mad with power, regarding himself as the Roman incarnation of Hercules; he was finally assassinated as he played the gladiator.

unrelenting Tiberius, the furious Caligula, the stupid Claudius, the profligate and cruel Nero, the beastly Vitellius,[35] and the timid inhuman Domitian are condemned to everlasting infamy. During fourscore years (excepting only the short and doubtful respite of Vespasian's reign), Rome groaned beneath an unremitting tyranny, which exterminated the ancient families of the republic and was fatal to almost every virtue and every talent that arose in that unhappy period.

Under the reign of these monsters the slavery of the Romans was accompanied with two peculiar circumstances, the one occasioned by their former liberty, the other by their extensive conquests, which rendered their condition more wretched than that of the victims of tyranny in any other age or country. From these causes were derived, 1. The exquisite sensibility of the sufferers; and 2. The impossibility of escaping from the hand of the oppressor.

I. When Persia was governed by the descendants of Sefi, a race of princes whose wanton cruelty often stained their divan, their table, and their bed with the blood of their favourites, there is a saying recorded of a young nobleman, that he never departed from the sultan's presence without satisfying himself whether his head was still on his shoulders. The experience of every day might almost justify the scepticism of Rustan.[36] Yet the fatal sword, suspended above him by a single thread, seems not to have disturbed the slumbers, or interrupted the tranquillity, of the Persian. The monarch's frown, he well knew, could level him with the dust; but the stroke of lightning or apoplexy might be equally fatal; and it was the part of a wise man to forget the inevitable calamities of human life in the enjoyment of the fleeting hour. He was dignified with the appellation of the king's slave; had, perhaps, been purchased from obscure parents, in a country which he had never known; and was trained up from his infancy in the severe discipline of the seraglio. His name, his wealth, his honours, were the gift of a master, who might, without injustice, resume what he had bestowed. Rustan's knowledge, if he possessed any, could only serve to confirm his habits by prejudices. His language afforded not words for any form of government except absolute monarchy. The history of the East informed him that such had ever been the condition of mankind. The Koran, and the interpreters of that divine book, inculcated to him that the sultan was the descendant of the prophet, and the viceregent of heaven; that patience was the first virtue of a Mussulman, and unlimited obedience the great duty of a subject.

The minds of the Romans were very differently prepared for slavery. Oppressed beneath the weight of their own corruption and of military violence, they for a long while preserved the sentiments, or at least the ideas, of their freeborn ancestors. The education of Helvidius and Thrasea, of Tacitus and Pliny, was the same as that of Cato and Cicero.[37] From Grecian philosophy

---

35. "Vitellius consumed in mere eating at least six millions of our money in about seven months. It is not easy to express his vices with dignity, or even decency." (Gibbon)

36. The young Persian cited in Sir John Chardin's account of that nation's tyranny.

37. Thrasea Paetus (d. 66 A.D.) was a Stoic who modeled himself on Cato and held republican sympathies; he was condemned by the emperor Nero and forced to commit suicide. His son-in-law Helvidius Priscus, also a Stoic, was exiled but returned to lead the opposition, as a more and more outright republican, to Vespasian (by whom he was executed c. 75 A.D.).

they had imbibed the justest and most liberal notions of the dignity of human nature and the origin of civil society. The history of their own country had taught them to revere a free, a virtuous, and a victorious commonwealth; to abhor the successful crimes of Caesar and Augustus; and inwardly to despise those tyrants whom they adored with the most abject flattery. As magistrates and senators, they were admitted into the great council which had once dictated laws to the earth, whose name gave still a sanction to the acts of the monarch, and whose authority was so often prostituted to the vilest purposes of tyranny. Tiberius, and those emperors who adopted his maxims, attempted to disguise their murders by the formalities of justice, and perhaps enjoyed a secret pleasure in rendering the senate their accomplice as well as their victim. By this assembly the last of the Romans were condemned for imaginary crimes and real virtues. Their infamous accusers assumed the language of independent patriots, who arraigned a dangerous citizen before the tribunal of his country; and the public service was rewarded by riches and honours. The servile judges professed to assert the majesty of the commonwealth, violated in the person of its first magistrate, whose clemency they most applauded when they trembled the most at his inexorable and impending cruelty. The tyrant beheld their baseness with just contempt, and encountered their secret sentiments of detestation with sincere and avowed hatred for the whole body of the senate.

II. The division of Europe into a number of independent states, connected, however, with each other, by the general resemblance of religion, language and manners, is productive of the most beneficial consequences to the liberty of mankind. A modern tyrant who should find no resistance either in his own breast or in his people, would soon experience a gentle restraint from the example of his equals, the dread of present censure, the advice of his allies, and the apprehension of his enemies. The object of his displeasure, escaping from the narrow limits of his dominions, would easily obtain, in a happier climate, a secure refuge, a new fortune adequate to his merit, the freedom of complaint, and perhaps the means of revenge. But the empire of the Romans filled the world, and, when that empire fell into the hands of a single person, the world became a safe and dreary prison for his enemies. The slave of Imperial despotism, whether he was condemned to drag his gilded chain in Rome and the senate, or to wear out a life of exile on the barren rock of Seriphus or the frozen banks of the Danube, expected his fate in silent despair.[38] To resist was fatal, and it was impossible to fly. On every side he was encompassed with a vast extent of sea and land, which he could never hope to traverse without being discovered, seized, and restored to his irritated master. Beyond the frontiers, his anxious view could discover nothing except the ocean, inhospitable deserts, hostile tribes of barbarians, of fierce manners and unknown language, or dependent kings, who would gladly purchase the emperor's protection by the sacrifice of an obnoxious fugitive. 'Wherever you are,' said Cicero to the exiled Marcellus, 'remember that you are equally within the power of the conqueror.'

1776

---

38. "Seriphus was a small rock island in the Aegean Sea, the inhabitants of which were despised for their ignorance and obscurity" (Gibbon). The poet Ovid was exiled by Augustus in 8 A.D. to a frontier fortress on the Black Sea and lived there for his last ten years.

From *Chapter XVI: The Conduct of the Roman Government Towards
the Christians, from the Reign of Nero to That of Constantine* [1]

In this general view of the persecution, which was first authorized by the
edicts of Diocletian, I have purposely refrained from describing the particular
sufferings and deaths of the Christian martyrs. It would have been an easy
task, from the history of Eusebius,[2] from the declamations of Lactantius,[3] and
from the most ancient acts, to collect a long series of horrid and disgustful
pictures, and to fill many pages with racks and scourges, with iron hooks and
red-hot beds, and with all the variety of tortures which fire and steel, savage
beasts and more savage executioners, could inflict on the human body. These
melancholy scenes might be enlivened by a crowd of visions and miracles
destined either to delay the death, to celebrate the triumph, or to discover the
relics of those canonized saints who suffered for the name of Christ. But I
cannot determine what I ought to transcribe till I am satisfied how much I
ought to believe. The gravest of the ecclesiastical historians, Eusebius himself,
indirectly confesses that he has related whatever might redound to the glory,
and that he has suppressed all that could tend to the disgrace, of religion.
Such an acknowledgment will naturally excite a suspicion that a writer who
has so openly violated one of the fundamental laws of history has not paid a
very strict regard to the observance of the other; and the suspicion will derive
additional credit from the character of Eusebius, which was less tinctured with
credulity, and more practised in the arts of courts, than that of almost any
of his contemporaries. On some particular occasions, when the magistrates were
exasperated by some personal motives of interest or resentment, when the zeal
of the martyrs urged them to forget the rules of prudence, and perhaps of
decency, to overturn the altars, to pour out imprecations against the emperors,
or to strike the judge as he sat on his tribunal, it may be presumed that every
mode of torture, which cruelty could invent or constancy could endure, was
exhausted on those devoted victims. Two circumstances, however, have been
unwarily mentioned, which insinuate that the general treatment of the Christians who had been apprehended by the officers of justice was less intolerable
than it is usually imagined to have been. 1. The confessors who were condemned to work in the mines were permitted, by the humanity or the negligence
of their keepers, to build chapels and freely to profess their religion in the
midst of those dreary habitations. 2. The bishops were obliged to check and to
censure the forward zeal of the Christians, who voluntarily threw themselves

1. This passage from the close of Chapter XVI shows Gibbon's ironic questioning of the
claims of Christianity. In Chapter XV he presents the march of Christianity to power, stressing those qualities in it which made for worldly success; in this chapter he presents its
gradual conquest of the Roman empire and he examines the cost at which this was
obtained. The dry use of statistics is deliberately set against the sanctity of the martyrs
and cool calculation against their righteousness. In this Gibbon's method may be compared
with Swift's ironic use of statistics. Swift uses them to stress the inhumanity implicit in
such calculation. Gibbon uses them to undercut zealous pretensions and then, shockingly,
to measure the true, unacknowledged inhumanity of that zeal.
2. The Christian scholar (c. 260–340 A.D.) of Caesarea in Palestine, where he witnessed
the persecution, 303–10; after the toleration in 311, he was named bishop.
3. The "Christian Cicero," 250?–317? A.D., a professor of rhetoric who became a
Christian in his mature years and wrote of the persecutions of Diocletian (emperor 284–
305).

into the hands of the magistrates. Some of these were persons oppressed by poverty and debts, who blindly sought to terminate a miserable existence by a glorious death. Others were allured by the hope that a short confinement would expiate the sins of a whole life; and others, again, were actuated by the less honourable motive of deriving a plentiful subsistence, and perhaps a considerable profit, from the alms which the charity of the faithful bestowed on the prisoners. After the church had triumphed over all her enemies, the interest as well as vanity of the captives prompted them to magnify the merit of their respective suffering. A convenient distance of time or place gave an ample scope to the progress of fiction; and the frequent instances which might be alleged of holy martyrs whose wounds had been instantly healed, whose strength had been renewed, and whose lost members had miraculously been restored, were extremely convenient for the purpose of removing every difficulty and of silencing every objection. The most extravagant legends, as they conduced to the honour of the church, were applauded by the credulous multitude, countenanced by the power of the clergy, and attested by the suspicious evidence of ecclesiastical history.

The vague descriptions of exile and imprisonment, of pain and torture, are so easily exaggerated or softened by the pencil [4] of an artful orator that we are naturally induced to inquire into a fact of a more distinct and stubborn kind: the number of persons who suffered death, in consequence of the edicts published by Diocletian, his associates, and his successors. The recent legend-aries [5] record whole armies and cities which were at once swept away by the undistinguishing rage of persecution. The more ancient writers content them-selves with pouring out a liberal effusion of loose and tragical invectives, with-out condescending to ascertain the precise number of those persons who were permitted to seal with their blood their belief of the gospel. From the history of Eusebius, it may however be collected that only nine bishops were punished with death; and we are assured, by his particular enumeration of the martyrs of Palestine, that no more than ninety-two Christians were entitled to that honourable appellation. As we are unacquainted with the degree of episcopal zeal and courage which prevailed at that time, it is not in our power to draw any useful inferences from the former of these facts; but the latter may serve to justify a very important and probable conclusion. According to the distribu-tion of Roman provinces, Palestine may be considered as the sixteenth part of the Eastern empire; and since there were some governors who, from a real or affected clemency, had preserved their hands unstained with the blood of the faithful, it is reasonable to believe that the country which had given birth to Christianity produced at least the sixteenth part of the martyrs who suffered death within the dominions of Galerius and Maximin; the whole might conse-quently amount to about fifteen hundred: a number which, if it is equally divided between the ten years of the persecution, will allow an annual con-sumption of one hundred and fifty martyrs. Allotting the same proportion to the provinces of Italy, Africa, and perhaps Spain, where, at the end of two or three years, the rigour of the penal laws was either suspended or abolished,

4. Paintbrush; here pictorial power.
5. Modern ecclesiastical historians.

the multitude of Christians in the Roman empire on whom a capital punishment was inflicted by a judicial sentence will be reduced to somewhat less than two thousand persons. Since it cannot be doubted that the Christians were more numerous, and their enemies more exasperated, in the time of Diocletian than they had ever been in any former persecution, this probable and moderate computation may teach us to estimate the number of primitive saints and martyrs who sacrificed their lives for the important purpose of introducing Christianity into the world.

We shall conclude this chapter by a melancholy truth which obtrudes itself on the reluctant mind; that even admitting, without hesitation or inquiry, all that history has recorded or devotion has feigned on the subject of martyrdoms, it must still be acknowledged that the Christians, in the course of their intestine [6] dissensions, have inflicted far greater severities on each other than they had experienced from the zeal of infidels. During the ages of ignorance which followed the subversion of the Roman empire in the West, the bishops of the Imperial city extended their dominion over the laity as well as clergy of the Latin church. The fabric of superstition which they had erected, and which might long have defied the feeble efforts of reason, was at length assaulted by a crowd of daring fanatics, who, from the twelfth to the sixteenth century, assumed the popular character of reformers. The church of Rome defended by violence the empire which she had acquired by fraud; a system of peace and benevolence was soon disgraced by proscriptions, wars, massacres, and the institution of the holy office.[7] And, as the reformers were animated by the love of civil, as well as of religious, freedom, the Catholic princes connected their own interest with that of the clergy, and enforced by fire and the sword the terrors of spiritual censures. In the Netherlands alone, more than one hundred thousand of the subjects of Charles the Fifth are said to have suffered by the hand of the executioner; and this extraordinary number is attested by Grotius,[8] a man of genius and learning, who preserved his moderation amidst the fury of contending sects, and who composed the annals of his own age and country at a time when the invention of printing had facilitated the means of intelligence and increased the danger of detection. If we are obliged to submit our belief to the authority of Grotius, it must be allowed that the number of Protestants who were executed in a single province and a single reign far exceeded that of the primitive martyrs in the space of three centuries and of the Roman empire. But, if the improbability of the fact itself should prevail over the weight of evidence; if Grotius should be convicted of exaggerating the merit and sufferings of the Reformers; we shall be naturally led to inquire what confidence can be placed in the doubtful and imperfect monuments of ancient credulity; what degree of credit can be assigned to a courtly bishop and a passionate declaimer, who, under the protection of Constantine, enjoyed the exclusive privilege of recording the persecutions inflicted on the Christians by the vanquished rivals or disregarded predecessors of their gracious sovereign.

1776

6. Internal.

7. The Inquisition, the tribunal established in the 13th century for the discovery and suppression of heretics.

8. Hugo Grotius (1583–1645), Dutch statesman and jurist.

EDMUND BURKE
1729–1797

Burke's political eloquence has obscured his important early work in aesthetics; it is a matter for regret that he did not follow Edmond Malone's advice of 1789 to "revise and enlarge his admirable book on the *Sublime and Beautiful,* which the experience, reading, and observation of thirty years could not but enable him to improve considerably." Burke seems to have been occupied with aesthetic problems as early as 1744, when he entered Trinity College, Dublin, at fifteen. At Trinity he read the classical treatise of the so-called Longinus (fl. first century A.D.) on the sublime (which had entered English criticism once it had been translated into French by Boileau in 1674), and he seems to have drafted the earliest version of his *Enquiry* in 1747. In the year immediately following, Burke edited and largely wrote a journal, *The Reformer,* in Dublin and in 1750 entered the Middle Temple in London to study law. The *Enquiry* was published with success in 1757 but amplified and revised for a second edition two years later.

Burke entered politics in 1759, and by 1765 he became private secretary to the Marquess of Rockingham and a leader of the liberal Whigs. His famous speech on conciliation with the American colonies was published in 1775, and in the next decade he was deeply involved in prosecuting the charges of corruption he brought against Warren Hastings, Governor General of India. The greatest concern of his career, however, was embodied in his *Reflections on the Revolution in France* (1790), an attack upon the "grave, demure, insidious, spring-nailed, velvet-pawed, green-eyed philosophers, whether going upon two legs or upon four," and, it might be added, in England or in France. These phrases come from the vehement *Letter to a Noble Lord* (1796), both an eloquent apology for himself and a renewed attack upon the theoretical planners and dehumanized metaphysicians he saw at work in France.

In opposition to those who would frame a new state and abolish the past, Burke asserted a redefinition of that social contract Rousseau had made a rallying cry:

> Each contract of each particular state is but a clause in the great primaeval contract of eternal society, linking the lower with the higher natures, connecting the visible and invisible world, according to a fixed compact sanctioned by the inviolable oath which holds all physical and all moral natures, each in their appointed place. . . . It is the first and supreme necessity only, a necessity that is not chosen but chooses . . . which alone can justify a resort to anarchy.

In his great lament for the persecution of Marie Antoinette, Burke wrote memorably:

> But the age of chivalry is gone. That of sophisters, economists, and calculators has succeeded; and the glory of Europe is extinguished forever. . . . It is gone, that sensibility of principle, that chastity of honour, which felt a stain like a wound, which inspired courage whilst it mitigated ferocity, which ennobled whatever it touched, and under which vice itself lost half its evil by losing all its grossness.

Burke's words may seem at times to have a ferocity of their own, but we have Gibbon's tribute: "I admire his eloquence; I approve his politics; I adore his chivalry; and I can almost excuse his reverence for church establishments."

The young Burke was far more theoretical than he later became. Following the patterns we can see in Addison and others, he transformed Longinus' concern with the sublime as an elevation of style that corresponds to a nobility of spirit into a psychophysical analysis of the mechanism of our response to the grand and terrible in nature and in art. The physiological explanation is omitted here, and only the central discussion of the sublime is given. Burke's treatise is at once a symptom of the literary tendencies of his age (such as we can see in James Thomson, Gray, and Collins) —not least its new responsiveness to Milton—and at the same time a stimulus to those tendencies. Burke is not much concerned with the moral implications of the sublime, as others had been and were to be; and his views are reconcilable with those, like Blake's, that repudiate conventional moral categories in their celebration of energy. One of Burke's most interesting contributions is his analysis of the language of poetry, which tries to come to terms with the way in which poetry transcends the merely visual or imagistic; he comes close to a doctrine of words conveying the contagion of emotion, and he opens up important issues (such as the function of imagery in poetry or its hypnotic and incantatory power) that are still with us.

A Philosophical Enquiry into the Origin of Our Ideas of the Sublime and Beautiful

[*From* Part II]

The passion caused by the great and sublime in *nature*, when those causes operate most powerfully, is Astonishment; and astonishment is that state of the soul, in which all its motions are suspended, with some degree of horror. In this case the mind is so entirely filled with its object, that it cannot enter-tain any other, nor by consequence reason on that object which employs it. Hence arises the great power of the sublime, that far from being produced by them, it anticipates our reasonings and hurries us on by an irresistible force. Astonishment, as I have said, is the effect of the sublime in its highest degree; the inferior effects are admiration, reverence and respect.

No passion so effectually robs the mind of all its powers of acting and reason-ing as fear. For fear being an apprehension of pain or death, it operates in a manner that resembles actual pain. Whatever therefore is terrible, with regard to sight, is sublime too, whether this cause of terror be endued with greatness of dimensions or not; for it is impossible to look on any thing as trifling or contemptible that may be dangerous. There are many animals, who though far from being large, are yet capable of raising ideas of the sublime, because they are considered as objects of terror. As serpents and poisonous animals of almost all kinds. And to things of great dimensions, if we annex an adventi-tious idea of terror, they become without comparison greater. A level plain of a vast extent on land, is certainly no mean idea; the prospect of such a plain may be as extensive as a prospect of the ocean; but can it ever fill the mind with any thing so great as the ocean itself? This is owing to several causes, but it is owing to none more than this, that the ocean is an object of no small terror. Indeed terror is in all cases whatsoever, either more openly or latently the ruling principle of the sublime. . . .

To make any thing very terrible, obscurity seems in general to be necessary. When we know the full extent of any danger, when we can accustom our eyes to it, a great deal of the apprehension vanishes. Every one will be sensible of this, who considers how greatly night adds to our dread, in all cases of danger, and how much the notions of ghosts and goblins, of which none can form clear ideas, affect minds, which give credit to the popular tales concerning such sorts of beings. Those despotic governments, which are founded on the passions of men, and principally upon the passion of fear, keep their chief as much as may be from the public eye. The policy has been the same in many cases of religion. Almost all the heathen temples were dark. Even in the barbarous temples of the Americans at this day, they keep their idol in a dark part of the hut, which is consecrated to his worship. For this purpose too the druids performed all their ceremonies in the bosom of the darkest woods, and in the shade of the oldest and most spreading oaks.

No person seems better to have understood the secret of heightening, or of setting terrible things, if I may use the expression, in their strongest light by the force of a judicious obscurity, than Milton. His description of Death in the second book is admirably studied; it is astonishing with what a gloomy pomp, with what a significant and expressive uncertainty of strokes and colouring he has finished the portrait of the king of terrors.

> The other shape,
> If shape it might be called that shape had none
> Distinguishable in member, joint, or limb;
> Or substance might be called that shadow seemed,
> For each seemed either; black he stood as night;
> Fierce as ten furies; terrible as hell;
> And shook a deadly dart. What seemed his head
> The likeness of a kingly crown had on.[1]

In this description all is dark, uncertain, confused, terrible, and sublime to the last degree.

It is one thing to make an idea clear, and another to make it *affecting* to the imagination. If I make a drawing of a palace, or a temple, or a landscape, I present a very clear idea of those objects; but then (allowing for the effect of imitation which is something) my picture can at most affect only as the palace, temple, or landscape would have affected in the reality. On the other hand, the most lively and spirited verbal description I can give, raises a very obscure and imperfect *idea* of such objects; but then it is in my power to raise a stronger *emotion* by the description than I could do by the best painting. This experience constantly evinces. The proper manner of conveying the *affections* of the mind from one to another, is by words; there is a great insufficiency in all other methods of communication; and so far is a clearness of imagery from being absolutely necessary to an influence upon the passions, that they may be considerably operated upon without presenting any image at all, by certain sounds adapted to that purpose; of which we have a sufficient proof in the acknowledged and powerful effects of instrumental music. In reality a great clearness helps but little towards affecting the passions, as it is in some sort an enemy to all enthusiasms whatsoever.

---

1. *Paradise Lost* II.666–73; Burke misquotes: for "he stood" read "it stood"; for "deadly dart" read "dreadful dart."

. . . Among the common sort of people, I never could perceive that painting had much influence on their passions. It is true that the best sorts of painting, as well as the best sorts of poetry, are not much understood in that sphere. But it is most certain, that their passions are very strongly roused by a fanatic preacher, or by the ballads of Chevy Chase, or the Children in the Wood, and by other little popular poems and tales that are current in that rank of life. I do not know of any paintings, bad or good, that produce the same effect. So that poetry with all its obscurity, has a more general as well as a more powerful dominion over the passions than the other art. And I think there are reasons in nature why the obscure idea, when properly conveyed, should be more affecting than the clear. It is our ignorance of things that causes all our admiration, and chiefly excites our passions. Knowledge and acquaintance make the most striking causes affect but little. It is thus with the vulgar, and all men are as the vulgar in what they do not understand. The ideas of eternity, and infinity, are among the most affecting we have, and yet perhaps there is nothing of which we really understand so little, as of infinity and eternity. We do not anywhere meet a more sublime description than this justly celebrated one of Milton, wherein he gives the portrait of Satan with a dignity so suitable to the subject.

> He above the rest
> In shape and gesture proudly eminent
> Stood like a tower; his form had yet not lost
> All her original brightness, nor appeared
> Less than archangel ruined, and the excess
> Of glory obscured: as when the sun new risen
> Looks through the horizontal misty air
> Shorn of his beams; or from behind the moon
> In dim eclipse disastrous twilight sheds
> On half the nations; and with fear of change
> Perplexes monarchs.[2]

Here is a very noble picture; and in what does this poetical picture consist? in images of a tower, an archangel, the sun rising through mists, or in an eclipse, the ruin of monarchs, and the revolutions of kingdoms. The mind is hurried out of itself, by a crowd of great and confused images; which affect because they are crowded and confused. For separate them, and you lose much of the greatness, and join them, and you infallibly lose the clearness. The images raised by poetry are always of this obscure kind; though in general the effects of poetry are by no means to be attributed to the images it raises; which point we shall examine more at large hereafter. But painting, when we have allowed for the pleasure of imitation, can only affect simply by the images it presents; and even in painting a judicious obscurity in some things contributes to the effect of the picture; because the images in painting are exactly similar to those in nature; and in nature dark, confused, uncertain images have a greater power on the fancy to form the grander passions than those have which are more clear and determinate. . . .

2. *Paradise Lost* I.589–99.

I am sensible that this idea has met with opposition, and is likely still to be rejected by several. But let it be considered that hardly anything can strike the mind with its greatness, which does not make some sort of approach towards infinity; which nothing can do whilst we are able to perceive its bounds; but to see an object distinctly, and to perceive its bounds, is one and the same thing. A clear idea is therefore another name for a little idea. There is a passage in the book of Job amazingly sublime, and this sublimity is principally due to the terrible uncertainty of the thing described. *In thoughts from the visions of the night, when deep sleep falleth upon men, fear came upon me and trembling, which made all my bones to shake. Then a spirit passed before my face. The hair of my flesh stood up. It stood still,* but I could not discern the form thereof; *an image was before mine eyes; there was silence; and I heard a voice,—Shall mortal man be more just than God?* [3] We are first prepared with the utmost solemnity for the vision; we are first terrified, before we are let even into the obscure cause of our emotion; but when this grand cause of terror makes its appearance, what is it? is it not, wrapt up in the shades of its own incomprehensible darkness, more awful, more striking, more terrible, than the liveliest description, than the clearest painting could possibly represent it? . . .

Besides these things which *directly* suggest the idea of danger, and those which produce a similar effect from a mechanical cause, I know of nothing sublime which is not some modification of power. And this branch rises as naturally as the other two branches, from terror, the common stock of every thing that is sublime. The idea of power at first view, seems of the class of these indifferent ones, which may equally belong to pain or to pleasure. But in reality, the affection arising from the idea of vast power, is extremely remote from that neutral character. For first, we must remember, that the idea of pain, in its highest degree, is much stronger than the highest degree of pleasure; and that it preserves the same superiority through all the subordinate grada- tions. From hence it is, that where the chances for equal degrees of suffering or enjoyment are in any sort equal, the idea of the suffering must always be prevalent. And indeed the ideas of pain, and above all of death, are so very affecting, that whilst we remain in the presence of whatever is supposed to have the power of inflicting either, it is impossible to be perfectly free from terror. Again, we know by experience, that for the enjoyment of pleasure, no great efforts of power are at all necessary; nay we know, that such efforts would go a great way towards destroying our satisfaction: for pleasure must be stolen, and not forced upon us; pleasure follows the will; and therefore we are generally affected with it by many things of a force greatly inferior to our own. But pain is always inflicted by a power in some way superior, because we never submit to pain willingly. So that strength, violence, pain and terror, are ideas that rush in upon the mind together.

Look at a man, or any other animal of prodigious strength, and what is your idea before reflection? Is it that this strength will be subservient to you, to your ease, to your pleasure, to your interest in any sense? No; the emotion you feel is, lest this enormous strength should be employed to the purposes of rapine and destruction. That power derives all its sublimity from the terror with

3. Job 4: 13–17.

which it is generally accompanied, will appear evidently from its effect in the very few cases, in which it may be possible to strip a considerable degree of strength of its ability to hurt. When you do this, you spoil it of everything sublime, and it immediately becomes contemptible. An ox is a creature of vast strength; but he is an innocent creature, extremely serviceable, and not at all dangerous; for which reason the idea of an ox is by no means grand. A bull is strong too; but his strength is of another kind; often very destructive, seldom (at least amongst us) of any use in our business; the idea of a bull is therefore great, and it has frequently a place in sublime descriptions, and elevating comparisons.

Let us look at another strong animal in the two distinct lights in which we may consider him. The horse in the light of an useful beast, fit for the plough, the road, the draft, in every social useful light the horse has nothing of the sublime; but is it thus that we are affected with him, *whose neck is clothed with thunder, the glory of whose nostrils is terrible, who swalloweth the ground with fierceness and rage, neither believeth that it is the sound of the trumpet?* [4] In this description the useful character of the horse entirely disappears, and the terrible and sublime blaze out together. We have continually about us animals of a strength that is considerable, but not pernicious. Amongst these we never look for the sublime: it comes upon us in the gloomy forest, and in the howling wilderness, in the form of the lion, the tiger, the panther, or rhinoceros. Whenever strength is only useful, and employed for our benefit or our pleasure, then it is never sublime; for nothing can act agreeably to us, that does not act in conformity to our will; but to act agreeably to our will, it must be subject to us; and therefore can never be the cause of a grand and commanding conception. . . .

The power which arises from institution in kings and commanders, has the same connection with terror. Sovereigns are frequently addressed with the title of *dread majesty*. And it may be observed that young persons little acquainted with the world, and who have not been used to approach men in power, are commonly struck with an awe which takes away the free use of their faculties. *When I prepared my seat in the street* (says Job) *the young men saw me, and hid themselves.*[5] Indeed so natural is this timidity with regard to power, and so strongly does it inhere in our constitution, that very few are able to conquer it, but by mixing much in the business of the great world, or by using no small violence to their natural dispositions. I know some people are of opinion, that no awe, no degree of terror, accompanies the idea of power, and have hazarded to affirm, that we can contemplate the idea of God himself without any such emotion. . . . Now, though in a just idea of the Deity, perhaps none of his attributes are predominant, yet to our imagination, his power is by far the most striking. Some reflection, some comparing is necessary to satisfy us of his wisdom, his justice, and his goodness; to be struck with his power, it is only necessary that we should open our eyes. But whilst we contemplate so vast an object, under the arm, as it were, of almighty power, and invested upon every side with omnipresence, we shrink into the minuteness of

4. Job 39: 19, 20, 24 (somewhat misquoted, as are most of Burke's quotations, but they have not been altered here).
5. Job 29: 7, 8.

our own nature, and are, in a manner, annihilated before him. And though a consideration of his other attributes may relieve in some measure our apprehensions; yet no conviction of the justice with which it is exercised, nor the mercy with which it is tempered, can wholly remove the terror that naturally arises from a force which nothing can withstand. If we rejoice, we rejoice with trembling; and even whilst we are receiving benefits, we cannot but shudder at a power which can confer benefits of such mighty importance. When the prophet David contemplated the wonders of wisdom and power, which are displayed in the economy of man, he seems to be struck with a sort of divine horror, and cries out, *fearfully and wonderfully am I made!* [6]. . . The Psalms and the prophetical books are crouded with instances of this kind. *The earth shook* (says the psalmist) *the heavens also dropped at the presence of the Lord.*[7] And what is remarkable, the painting preserves the same character, not only when he is supposed descending to take vengeance upon the wicked, but even when he exerts the like plenitude of power in acts of beneficence to mankind. *Tremble, thou earth! at the presence of the Lord; at the presence of the God of Jacob; which turned the rock into standing water, the flint into a fountain of waters!*[8] It were endless to enumerate all the passages both in the sacred and profane writers, which establish the general sentiment of mankind, concerning the inseparable union of a sacred and reverential awe, with our ideas of the divinity. . . . Thus we have traced power through its several gradations unto the highest of all, where our imagination is finally lost; and we find terror quite throughout the progress, its inseparable companion, and growing along with it, as far as we can possibly trace them. Now as power is undoubtedly a capital source of the sublime, this will point out evidently from whence its energy is derived, and to what class of ideas we ought to unite it. . . .

[*From* Part III: The Sublime and Beautiful Compared]

On closing this general view of beauty, it naturally occurs, that we should compare it with the sublime; and in this comparison there appears a remarkable contrast. For sublime objects are vast in their dimensions, beautiful ones comparatively small; beauty should be smooth, and polished; the great, rugged and negligent; beauty should shun the right line, yet deviate from it insensibly; the great in many cases loves the right line, and when it deviates, it often makes a strong deviation; beauty should not be obscure; the great ought to be dark and gloomy; beauty should be light and delicate; the great ought to be solid, and even massive. They are indeed ideas of a very different nature, one being founded on pain, the other on pleasure; and however they may vary afterwards from the direct nature of their causes, yet these causes keep up an eternal distinction between them, a distinction never to be forgotten by any whose business it is to affect the passions. In the infinite variety of natural combinations we must expect to find the qualities of things the most remote imaginable from each other united in the same object. We must expect

6. Psalms 139: 14.
7. Psalms 68: 8.
8. Psalms 114: 7–8.

also to find combinations of the same kind in the works of art. But when we consider the power of an object upon our passions, we must know that when anything is intended to affect the mind by the force of some predominant property, the affection produced is like to be the more uniform and perfect, if all the other properties or qualities of the object be of the same nature, and tending to the same design as the principal;

> If black, and white blend, soften, and unite,
> A thousand ways, are there no black and white? [9]

If the qualities of the sublime and beautiful are sometimes found united, does this prove that they are the same, does it prove that they are any way allied, does it prove even that they are not opposite and contradictory? Black and white may soften, may blend, but they are not therefore the same. Nor when they are so softened and blended with each other, or with different colours, is the power of black as black, or of white as white, so strong as when each stands uniform and distinguished.

[*From* Part V]

. . . In reality poetry and rhetoric do not succeed in exact description so well as painting does; their business is to affect rather by sympathy than imitation; to display rather the effect of things on the mind of the speaker, or of others, than to present a clear idea of the things themselves. This is their most extensive province, and that in which they succeed the best.

Hence we may observe that poetry, taken in its most general sense, cannot with strict propriety be called an art of imitation. It is indeed an imitation so far as it describes the manners and passions of men which their words can express. . . . But *descriptive* poetry operates chiefly by *substitution;* by the means of sounds, which by custom have the effect of realities. Nothing is an imitation further than as it resembles some other thing; and words undoubtedly have no sort of resemblance to the ideas for which they stand.

Now, as words affect, not by any original power, but by representation, it might be supposed, that their influence over the passions should be but light; yet it is quite otherwise; for we find by experience that eloquence and poetry are as capable, nay indeed much more capable of making deep and lively impressions than any other arts, and even than nature itself in very many cases. And this arises chiefly from these three causes. First, that we take an extraordinary part in the passions of others, and that we are easily affected and brought into sympathy by any tokens which are shown of them; and there are no tokens which can express all the circumstances of most passions so fully as words; so that if a person speaks upon any subject, he can not only convey the subject to you, but likewise the manner in which he is himself affected by it. Certain it is, that the influence of most things on our passions is not so much from the things themselves, as from our opinions concerning them; and these again depend very much on the opinions of other men, conveyable for the most part by words only. Secondly; there are many things of

---

9. Pope, *Essay on Man* II.213–14; properly "If white and black blend, soften, and unite / A thousand ways, is there no black or white?"

a very affecting nature, which can seldom occur in the reality, but the words which represent them often do; and thus they have an opportunity of making a deep impression and taking root in the mind, whilst the idea of the reality was transient; and to some perhaps never really occurred in any shape, to whom it is notwithstanding very affecting, as war, death, famine, etc. Besides, many ideas have never been at all presented to the senses of any men but by words, as God, angels, devils, heaven and hell, all of which have however a great influence over the passions. Thirdly; by words we have it in our power to make such *combinations* as we cannot possibly do otherwise. By this power of combining we are able, by the addition of well-chosen circumstances, to give a new life and force to the simple object.

In painting we may represent any fine figure we please; but we never can give it those enlivening touches which it may receive from words. To represent an angel in a picture, you can only draw a beautiful young man winged; but what painting can furnish out any thing so grand as the addition of one word, 'the angel of the *Lord*.' It is true, I have here no clear idea, but these words affect the mind more than the sensible image did, which is all I contend for. . . . As a further instance, let us consider those lines of Milton, where he describes the travels of the fallen angels through their dismal habitation,

> ———O'er many a dark and dreary vale
> They passed, and many a region dolorous;
> O'er many a frozen, many a fiery Alp;
> Rock, caves, lakes, fens, bogs, dens and shades of death,
> A universe of death.[10]

Here is displayed the force of union in

> Rocks, caves, lakes, dens, bogs, fens and shades;

which yet would lose the greatest part of their effect, if they were not the

> Rocks, caves, lakes, dens, bogs, fens and shades———
> ———of *Death*.

This idea or this affection caused by a word, which nothing but a word could annex to the others, raises a very great degree of the sublime; and this sublime is raised yet higher by what follows, a '*universe of Death.*'

Here are again two ideas not presentable but by language; and an union of them great and amazing beyond conception; if they may properly be called ideas which present no distinct image to the mind;—but still it will be difficult to conceive how words can move the passions which belong to real objects, without representing these objects clearly. This is difficult to us, because we do not sufficiently distinguish, in our observations upon language, between a clear expression and a strong expression. These are frequently confounded with each other, though they are in reality extremely different. The former regards the understanding; the latter belongs to the passions. The one describes a thing as it is; the other describes it as it is felt. Now, as there is a moving tone of voice, an impassioned countenance, an agitated gesture,

10. *Paradise Lost* II.618–22.

which affect independently of the things about which they are exerted, so there are words, and certain dispositions of words, which being peculiarly devoted to passionate subjects and always used by those who are under the influence of any passion; they touch and move us more than those which far more clearly and distinctly express the subject matter. We yield to sympathy, what we refuse to description. The truth is, all verbal description, merely as naked description, though never so exact, conveys so poor and insufficient an idea of the thing described that it could scarcely have the smallest effect, if the speaker did not call in to his aid those modes of speech that mark a strong and lively feeling in himself. Then, by the contagion of our passions, we catch a fire already kindled in another, which probably might never have been struck out by the object described. Words, by strongly conveying the passions, by those means which we have already mentioned, fully compensate for their weakness in other respects. It may be observed that very polished languages, and such as are praised for their superior clearness and perspicuity, are generally deficient in strength. The French language has that perfection, and that defect. Whereas the oriental tongues, and in general the languages of most unpolished people, have a great force and energy of expression; and this is but natural. Uncultivated people are but ordinary observers of things, and not critical in distinguishing them; but, for that reason, they admire more, and are more affected with what they see, and therefore express themselves in a warmer and more passionate manner. If the affection be well conveyed, it will work its effect without any clear idea; often without any idea at all of the thing which has originally given rise to it.

1747–57?   1759

SIR JOSHUA REYNOLDS
1723–1792

"He possessed the theory as perfectly as the practice of his art. To be such a painter, he was a profound and penetrating philosopher." So Edmund Burke wrote in Reynolds's obituary. Boswell, dedicating to Reynolds his *Life of Johnson*, paid tribute to his "equal and placid temper," his "variety of conversation," his "true politeness," and the hospitality which made Reynolds's house "a common centre of union for the great, the accomplished, the learned, and the ingenious." Reynolds achieved greater prestige and wealth than any English painter had before him, and he achieved them early and easily.

Born in Devonshire, he went to London in 1740 to study with the portrait painter Thomas Hudson, and after seven years of practice spent two years in Italy studying the "grand style" of his predecessors. Within two or three years of his return, he became the most successful portrait painter in England. In 1764 he helped form the Literary Club, which gave Johnson, Burke, Goldsmith, and others an occasion for weekly conversations. Four years later he helped organize the Royal Academy and became its president for the rest of his life, giving in all fifteen presidential lectures to the students. These discourses, which show at least some influence of Johnson, are a fine statement of principles, shifting, within a consistent system, to a greater and greater stress upon those qualities that go beyond imitation and beyond narrowly rational limits. In the thirteenth discourse, especially, Reynolds insists upon the artifice of all art and yet relates that artifice to the demands of the imagination, much as Johnson does in his repudiation of rationalistic rules that might delimit the full illusion of dramatic art.

In his own painting Reynolds did not so much achieve the grand style as constantly allude to it: through "borrowings" from classical and Renaissance works of art; through the mock-heroic device of placing children in heroic poses; through allusions that set up ironies, such as that of David Garrick laughingly divided between the appeals of Comedy and Tragedy in the pose of Hercules at the Crossroads, choosing between Virtue and Vice. (See examples of Reynolds's paintings in illustration section.)

From Discourses

[The Grand Style]

It is not easy to define in what this great style [1] consists; nor to describe, by words, the proper means of acquiring it, if the mind of the student should be at all capable of such an acquisition. Could we teach taste or genius by rules, they would be no longer taste and genius. But though there neither are, nor can be, any precise invariable rules for the exercise, or the acquisition, of these great qualities, yet we may truly say that they always operate in proportion to our attention in observing the works of nature, to our skill in selecting, and to our care in digesting, methodizing, and comparing our observations. There are many beauties in our art, that seem, at first, to lie without the reach of precept, and yet may easily be reduced to practical principles. Experience is all in all; but it is not every one who profits by experience; and most people err, not so much from want of capacity to find their object, as from not knowing what object to pursue. This great ideal perfection and beauty are not to be sought in the heavens, but upon earth. They are about us, and upon every side of us. But the power of discovering what is deformed in nature, or in other words, what is particular and uncommon, can be acquired only by experience; and the whole beauty and grandeur of the art consists, in my opinion, in being able to get above all singular forms, local customs, particularities, and details of every kind.

All the objects which are exhibited to our view by nature, upon close examination will be found to have their blemishes and defects. The most beautiful forms have something about them like weakness, minuteness, or

---

1. That style which receives its perfection "from an ideal beauty, superior to what is found in individual nature." Reynolds mocks the "splendour of figurative declamation" (largely Platonic or neoplatonic) used to describe this style and tries to give it a humbler and more accessible guise. Here he offers an empirical approach to the "perfect state of nature," a method of discerning through "sober" study the tendencies that actual nature strives to realize but always falls short of attaining. This conception of Nature as a form that can be glimpsed or (more properly) surmised through its imperfect embodiment in individuals underlies Aristotle's theory of poetry (and particularly his view that poetry is more philosophical than history since it can depart from the actual and realize the latent tendency). Reynolds avoids any mystical effort to achieve an ecstatic vision of the ideal form in its nakedness and immediacy.

imperfection. But it is not every eye that perceives these blemishes. It must be an eye long used to the contemplation and comparison of these forms; and which, by a long habit of observing what any set of objects of the same kind have in common, has acquired the power of discerning what each wants in particular. This long laborious comparison should be the first study of the painter, who aims at the greatest style. By this means, he acquires a just idea of beautiful forms; he corrects nature by herself, her imperfect state by her more perfect. His eye being enabled to distinguish the accidental deficiencies, excrescences, and deformities of things, from their general figures, he makes out an abstract idea of their forms more perfect than any one original; and what may seem a paradox, he learns to design naturally by drawing his figures unlike to any one object. This idea of the perfect state of nature, which the artist calls the ideal beauty, is the great leading principle, by which works of genius are conducted. By this Phidias acquired his fame. He wrought upon a sober principle what has so much excited the enthusiasm of the world; and by this method you, who have courage to tread the same path, may acquire equal reputation.

This is the idea which has acquired and which seems to have a right to the epithet of *divine;* as it may be said to preside, like a supreme judge, over all the productions of nature; appearing to be possessed of the will and intention of the Creator as far as they regard the external form of living beings. When a man once possesses this idea in its perfection, there is no danger but that he will be sufficiently warmed by it himself, and be able to warm and ravish every one else.

Thus it is from a reiterated experience, and a close comparison of the objects in nature, than an artist becomes possessed of the idea of that central form, if I may so express it, from which every deviation is deformity. [From *Discourse III*, 1770]

[Poetic and Literal Truth]

The great end of the art is to strike the imagination. The painter is therefore to make no ostentation of the means by which this is done; the spectator is only to feel the result in his bosom. An inferior artist is unwilling that any part of his industry should be lost upon the spectator. He takes as much pains to discover, as the greater artist does to conceal, the marks of his subordinate assiduity. In works of the lower kind, everything appears studied and encumbered; it is all boastful art and open affectation. The ignorant often part from such pictures with wonder in their mouths and indifference in their hearts.[2]

But it is not enough in invention that the artist should restrain and keep under all the inferior parts of his subject; he must sometimes deviate from vulgar and strict historical truth, in pursuing the grandeur of his design.

How much the great style exacts from its professors to conceive and represent their subjects in a poetical manner, not confined to mere matter of fact,

2. One may compare Dryden on the false wit of such poets as Cleveland, Pope on false wit in the *Essay on Criticism* and the *Epistle to Burlington,* and Johnson on the Metaphysical poets.

may be seen in the cartoons of Raffaelle.³ In all the pictures in which the painter has represented the apostles, he has drawn them with great nobleness; he has given them as much dignity as the human figure is capable of receiving; yet we are expressly told in scripture they had no such respectable appearance; and of St. Paul in particular, we are told by himself, that his *bodily* presence was *mean*. Alexander is said to have been of a low stature: a painter ought not so to represent him. Agesilaus was low, lame, and of a mean appearance: none of these defects ought to appear in a piece of which he is the hero.⁴ In conformity to custom, I call this part of the art history painting; it ought to be called poetical, as in reality it is.

All this is not falsifying any fact; it is taking an allowed poetical licence. A painter of portraits retains the individual likeness; a painter of history shows the man by showing his actions. A painter must compensate the natural deficiencies of his art. He has but one sentence to utter, but one moment to exhibit. He cannot, like the poet or historian, expatiate, and impress the mind with great veneration for the character of the hero or saint he represents, though he lets us know at the same time that the saint was deformed or the hero lame. The painter has no other means of giving an idea of the dignity of the mind but by that external appearance which grandeur of thought does generally, though not always, impress on the countenance; and by that correspondence of figure to sentiment and situation, which all men wish, but cannot command. The painter, who may in this one particular attain with ease what others desire in vain, ought to give all that he possibly can, since there are so many circumstances of true greatness that he cannot give at all. He cannot make his hero talk like a great man; he must make him look like one. For which reason, he ought to be well studied in the analysis of those circumstances which constitute dignity of appearance in real life. [From *Discourse IV*, 1771]

[The Pleasures of the Mind]
He who thinks nature, in the narrow sense of the word, is alone to be followed, will produce but a scanty entertainment for the imagination: everything is to be done with which it is natural for the mind to be pleased, whether it proceeds from simplicity or variety, uniformity or irregularity; whether the scenes are familiar or exotic; rude and wild, or enriched and cultivated; for it is natural for the mind to be pleased with all these in their turn. In short, whatever pleases has in it what is analogous to the mind, and is therefore, in the highest and best sense of the word, natural.⁵

3. The Raphael cartoons are full-scale tapestry designs; the seven that survive were in Hampton Court during much of the 18th century; they are now at the Victoria and Albert Museum in London.
4. II Corinthians 10:10, "his bodily presence is weak, and his speech contemptible." Alexander the Great (356–323 B.C.) became the subject of heroic legends even during his lifetime. Agesilaus (c. 444–360 B.C.) was King of Sparta, renowned as a conqueror of both Persians and fellow Greeks, celebrated by Xenophon and Plutarch.
5. Compare Addison's papers on "The Pleasures of the Imagination" (see The Garden and the Wild). Reynolds is psychologizing the idea of nature; in *Discourse III* it is approached empirically through outward or objective natural forms, but here it is sought in "what is analogous to the mind." One can see a similar tendency in Johnson's treatment of "general nature" in the Preface to Shakespeare.

It is the sense of nature or truth which ought more particularly to be cultivated by the professors of art; and it may be observed, that many wise and
learned men, who have accustomed their minds to admit nothing for truth but
what can be proved by mathematical demonstration, have seldom any relish
for those arts which address themselves to the fancy, the rectitude and truth
of which is known by another kind of proof: and we may add, that the
acquisition of this knowledge requires as much circumspection and sagacity,
as is necessary to attain those truths which are more capable of demonstration.
Reason must ultimately determine our choice on every occasion; but this
reason may still be exerted ineffectually by applying to taste principles which,
though right as far as they go, yet do not reach the object. No man, for
instance, can deny that it seems at first view very reasonable . . . that a
statue which is to carry down to posterity the resemblance of an individual,
should be dressed in the fashion of the times, in the dress which he himself
wore: this would certainly be true if the dress were part of the man; but after
a time, the dress is only an amusement for an antiquarian; and if it obstructs
the general design of the piece, it is to be disregarded by the artist. Common
sense must here give way to a higher sense. In the naked form, and in the
disposition of the drapery, the difference between one artist and another is
principally seen. But if he is compelled to exhibit the modern dress, the naked
form is entirely hid, and the drapery is already disposed by the skill of the
tailor. Were a Phidias to obey such absurd commands, he would please no
more than an ordinary sculptor; since in the inferior parts of every art, the
learned and the ignorant are nearly upon a level. [From *Discourse VII*, 1776]

[Minute Particulars]
. . . At the same time I do not forget, that a painter must have the power of
contracting as well as dilating his sight; because, he that does not at all
express particulars, expresses nothing; yet it is certain, that a nice discrimination of minute circumstances, and a punctilious delineation of them, whatever
excellence it may have (and I do not mean to detract from it), never did
confer on the artist the character of genius.

Beside those minute differences in things which are frequently not observed
at all, and, when they are, make little impression, there are in all considerable
objects great characteristic distinctions which press strongly on the senses, and
therefore fix the imagination. These are by no means, as some persons think,
an aggregate [6] of all the small discriminating particulars; nor will such an
accumulation of particulars ever express them. These answer to what I have
heard great lawyers call the leading points in a case, or the leading cases
relative to those points.

The detail of particulars which does not assist the expression of the main
characteristic is worse than useless; it is mischievous as it dissipates the attention and draws it from the principal point. It may be remarked that the
impression which is left on our mind, even of things which are familiar to us,
is seldom more than their general effect; beyond which we do not look in
recognising such objects. To express this in painting, is to express what is

6. Reynolds contrasts the mere "aggregate" with the "general effect of the whole" or the
"great characteristic distinctions," implying in the latter terms a principle of unity.

congenial and natural to the mind of man, and what gives him by reflection his own mode of conceiving. The other presupposes *nicety* and *research*, which are only the business of the curious and attentive, and therefore does not speak to the general sense of the whole species; in which common, and, as I may so call it, mother tongue, every thing grand and comprehensive must be uttered.

I do not mean to prescribe what degree of attention ought to be paid to the minute parts; this it is hard to settle. We are sure that it is expressing the general effect of the whole which alone can give to objects their true and touching character; and wherever this is observed, whatever else may be neglected, we acknowledge the hand of a master. We may even go further, and observe, that when the general effect only is presented to us by a skilful hand, it appears to express the object represented in a more lively manner than the minutest resemblance would do. [From *Discourse XI*, 1782]

[Art and Illusion]

I observe, as a fundamental ground, common to all the arts with which we have any concern in this discourse, that they address themselves only to two faculties of the mind, its imagination and its sensibility.

All theories which attempt to direct or control the art upon any principles falsely called rational, which we form to ourselves upon a supposition of what ought in reason to be the end or means of art, independent of the known first effect produced by objects on the imagination, must be false and delusive. For though it may appear bold to say it, the imagination is here the residence of truth. If the imagination be affected, the conclusion is fairly drawn; if it be not affected, the reasoning is erroneous, because the end is not obtained; the effect itself being the test, and the only test, of the truth and efficacy of the means.

There is in the commerce of life, as in art, a sagacity which is far from being contradictory to right reason, and is superior to any occasional exercise of that faculty, which supersedes it; and does not wait for the slow progress of deduction, but goes at once, by what appears a kind of intuition, to the conclusion. A man endowed with this faculty feels and acknowledges the truth though it is not always in his power, perhaps, to give a reason for it; because he cannot recollect and bring before him all the materials that gave birth to his opinion; for very many and very intricate considerations may unite to form the principle, even of small and minute parts involved in, or dependent on, a great system of things: though these in process of time are forgotten, the right impression still remains fixed in his mind.

This impression is the result of the accumulated experience of our whole life, and has been collected, we do not always know how or when. But this mass of collective observation, however acquired, ought to prevail over that reason which, however powerfully exerted on any particular occasion, will probably comprehend but a partial view of the subject; and our conduct in life as well as in the arts is, or ought to be, generally governed by this habitual reason: it is our happiness that we are enabled to draw on such funds. If we were obliged to enter into a theoretical deliberation on every occasion, before we act, life would be at a stand, and art would be impracticable.

It appears to me therefore, that our first thoughts, that is, the effect which

anything produces on our minds on its first appearance, is never to be forgotten; and it demands for that reason, because it is the first, to be laid up with
care. If this be not done, the artist may happen to impose on himself by
partial reasoning; by a cold consideration of those animated thoughts which
proceed, not perhaps from caprice or rashness (as he may afterwards conceit [7]), but from the fullness of his mind, enriched with the copious stores
of all the various inventions which he had ever seen or had ever passed in his
mind. These ideas are infused into his design without any conscious effort; but
if he be not on his guard, he may reconsider and correct them till the whole
matter is reduced to a commonplace invention.

This is sometimes the effect of what I mean to caution you against; that is to
say, an unfounded distrust of the imagination and feeling in favour of narrow,
partial, confined, argumentative theories; and of principles that seem to apply
to the design in hand; without considering those general impressions on
the fancy in which real principles of *sound reason,* and of much more weight
and importance, are involved and, as it were, lie hid under the appearance of
a sort of vulgar sentiment.

Reason, without doubt, must ultimately determine every thing; at this
minute it is required to inform us when that very reason is to give way to
feeling.

Though I have often spoke of that mean conception of our art which
confines it to mere imitation, I must add that it may be narrowed to such
a mere matter of experiment as to exclude from it the application of science,
which alone gives dignity and compass to any art. But to find proper foundations for science is neither to narrow or to vulgarise it; and this is sufficiently
exemplified in the success of experimental philosophy. It is the false system
of reasoning grounded on a partial view of things against which I would most
earnestly guard you. And I do it the rather, because those narrow theories,
so coincident with the poorest and most miserable practice, and which are
adopted to give it countenance, have not had their origin in the poorest
minds, but in the mistakes, or possibly in the mistaken interpretations, of
great and commanding authorities. We are not therefore in this case misled by
feeling, but by false speculation.

. . . For this reason I shall beg leave to lay before you a few thoughts on
this subject; to throw out some hints that may lead your minds to an opinion
(which I take to be the truth) that painting is not only not to be considered as an imitation, operating by deception, but that it is, and ought to
be, in many points of view and strictly speaking, no imitation at all of
external nature. Perhaps it ought to be as far removed from the vulgar idea
of imitation, as the refined civilized state in which we live is removed from
a gross state of nature; and those who have not cultivated their imaginations,
which the majority of mankind certainly have not, may be said, in regard
to arts, to continue in this state of nature. Such men will always prefer
imitation to that excellence which is addressed to another faculty that they
do not possess; but these are not the persons to whom a painter is to look,

7. Imagine.

any more than a judge of morals and manners ought to refer controverted points upon those subjects to the opinions of people taken from the banks of the Ohio, or from New Holland.[8]

. . .

Poetry addresses itself to the same faculties and the same dispositions as painting, though by different means. The object of both is to accommodate itself to all the natural propensities and inclinations of the mind. The very existence of poetry depends on the licence it assumes of deviating from actual nature, in order to gratify natural propensities by other means which are found by experience full as capable of affording such gratification. It sets out with a language in the highest degree artificial, a construction of measured words, such as never is, nor ever was used by man. Let this measure be what it may, whether hexameter or any other metre used in Latin or Greek,—or rhyme, or blank verse varied with pauses and accents, in modern languages,—they are all equally removed from nature, and equally a violation of common speech. When this artificial mode has been established as the vehicle of sentiment, there is another principle in the human mind, to which the work must be referred, which still renders it more artificial, carries it still further from common nature, and deviates only to render it more perfect. That principle is the sense of congruity, coherence, and consistency, which is a real existing principle in man; and it must be gratified. Therefore having once adopted a style and a measure not found in common discourse, it is required that the sentiments also should be in the same proportion elevated above common nature, from the necessity of there being an agreement of the parts among themselves, that one uniform whole may be produced.

To correspond therefore with this general system of deviation from nature, the manner in which poetry is offered to the ear, the tone in which it is recited, should be as far removed from the tone of conversation, as the words of which that poetry is composed. This naturally suggests the idea of modulating the voice by art, which I suppose may be considered as accomplished to the highest degree of excellence in the recitative of the Italian opera; as we may conjecture it was in the chorus that attended the ancient drama. And though the most violent passions, the highest distress, even death itself, are expressed in singing or recitative, I would not admit as sound criticism the condemnation of such exhibitions on account of their being unnatural.

. . . Shall reason stand in the way, and tell us we ought not to like what we know we do like, and prevent us from feeling the full effect of this complicated exertion of art? This is what I would understand by poets and painters being allowed to dare everything; for what can be more daring, than accomplishing the purpose and end of art, by a complication of means, none of which have their archetypes in actual nature?

So far therefore is servile imitation from being necessary, that whatever is familiar, or in any way reminds us of what we see and hear every day, perhaps does not belong to the higher provinces of art, either in poetry or painting.

---

8. Presumably a reference to the natives rather than the colonists of America and Australia.

The mind is to be transported, as Shakespeare expresses it, 'beyond the ignorant present,' to ages past. Another and a higher order of beings is supposed; and to those beings every thing which is introduced into the work must correspond. Of this conduct, under these circumstances, the Roman and Florentine schools afford sufficient examples. Their style by this means is raised and elevated above all others; and by the same means the compass of art itself is enlarged.

We often see grave and great subjects attempted by artists of another school; who, though excellent in the lower class of art, proceeding on the principles which regulate that class, and not recollecting, or not knowing, that they were to address themselves to another faculty of the mind, have become perfectly ridiculous.

The picture which I have at present in my thoughts is a sacrifice of Iphigenia, painted by Jan Steen . . . even in this picture, the subject of which is by no means adapted to his genius, there is nature and expression; but it is such expression, and the countenances are so familiar, and consequently so vulgar, and the whole accompanied with such finery of silks and velvet, that one would be almost tempted to doubt, whether the artist did not purposely intend to burlesque his subject.

Instances of the same kind we frequently see in poetry. Parts of Hobbes's translation of Homer are remembered and repeated merely for the familiarity and meanness of their phraseology, so ill corresponding with the ideas which ought to have been expressed, and, as I conceive, with the style of the original.[9]

. . .

If we suppose a view of nature represented with all the truth of the *camera obscura*,[10] and the same scene represented by a great artist, how little and mean will the one appear in comparison of the other. . . . With what additional superiority then will the same artist appear when he has the power of selecting his materials as well as elevating his style? Like Nicolas Poussin, he transports us to the environs of ancient Rome, with all the objects which a literary education make so precious and interesting to man: or, like Sebastian Bourdon, he leads us to the dark antiquity of the pyramids of Egypt; or, like Claude Lorrain, he conducts us to the tranquillity of Arcadian scenes and fairy land.[11]

Like the history-painter, a painter of landscapes in this style and with this conduct, sends the imagination back into antiquity; and, like the poet, he makes the elements sympathise with his subject: whether the clouds roll in volumes like those of Titian or Salvator Rosa,[12]—or, like those of Claude, are gilded with the setting sun; whether the mountains have sudden or bold

9. Hobbes's lame translations of the *Odyssey* and the *Iliad* appeared in 1673 and 1676.
10. The *camera obscura* was an optical device for producing an image on the wall of a darkened room; it was used as an aid by painters such as Vermeer, but it would have in itself only such weight as a documentary photograph might have in relation to a painting.
11. Nicolas Poussin (1594–1665), important French painter resident in Rome for most of his career; Sebastian Bourdon (1616–71), an imitator of Poussin among others; Claude Lorrain (1600–1682), the landscape painter—all painters of "ideal" landscapes.
12. Titian (c. 1490–1576), the great Venetian painter; Salvator Rosa (1615–73), known especially for landscapes of wild and savage scenes, much admired in the 18th century.

projections, or are gently sloped; whether the branches of his trees shoot out abruptly in right angles from their trunks, or follow each other with only a gentle inclination. All these circumstances contribute to the general character of the work whether it be of the elegant or of the more sublime kind. If we add to this the powerful materials of lightness and darkness, over which the artist has complete dominion, to vary and dispose them as he pleases; to diminish, or increase them as will best suit his purpose, and correspond to the general idea of his work: a landscape thus conducted, under the influence of a poetical mind, will have the same superiority over the more ordinary and common views, as Milton's 'Allegro' and 'Penseroso' have over a cold prosaic narration or description; and such a picture would make a more forcible impression on the mind than the real scenes, were they presented before us.

. . .

The theatre, which is said 'to hold the mirrour up to nature,'[13] comprehends both those ideas. The lower kind of comedy, or farce, like the inferior style of painting, the more naturally it is represented, the better; but the higher appears to me to aim no more at imitation, so far as it belongs to any thing like deception, or to expect that the spectators should think that the events there represented are really passing before them, than Raffaelle in his cartoons, or Poussin in his sacraments,[14] expected it to be believed, even for a moment, that what they exhibited were real figures.

For want of this distinction, the world is filled with false criticism. Raffaelle is praised for naturalness and deception, which he certainly has not accomplished, and as certainly never intended; and our late great actor, Garrick, has been as ignorantly praised by his friend Fielding; who doubtless imagined he had hit upon an ingenious device, by introducing in one of his novels (otherwise a work of the highest merit) an ignorant man, mistaking Garrick's representation of a scene in Hamlet, for reality.[15] A very little reflection will convince us, that there is not one circumstance in the whole scene that is of the nature of deception. The merit and excellence of Shakespeare, and of Garrick, when they were engaged in such scenes, is of a different and much higher kind. But what adds to the falsity of this intended compliment is that the best stage-representation appears even more unnatural to a person of such a character, who is supposed never to have seen a play before, than it does to those who have had a habit of allowing for those necessary deviations from nature which the art requires.

. . .

Though I have no intention of entering into all the circumstances of unnaturalness in theatrical representations, I must observe that even the expression of violent passion is not always the most excellent in proportion as it is the most natural: so great terror and such disagreeable sensations

13. *Hamlet* III.ii.24.
14. Poussin did two sets of paintings of the Seven Sacraments; one now hangs in the National Gallery of Scotland.
15. Partridge's response in *Tom Jones* (1749) XVI.xv is that of the naïve spectator who responds to a performance of *Hamlet* as if it were reality; later he sneers at the praise of David Garrick's performance: "I am sure, if I had seen a ghost, I should have looked in the very same manner, and done just as he did."

may be communicated to the audience that the balance may be destroyed by which pleasure is preserved and holds its predominancy in the mind: violent distortion of action, harsh screamings of the voice, however great the occasion, or however natural on such occasion, are therefore not admissible in the theatric art. Many of these allowed deviations from nature arise from the necessity which there is that everything should be raised and enlarged beyond its natural state; that the full effect may come home to the spectator, which otherwise would be lost in the comparatively extensive space of the theatre. Hence the deliberate and stately step, the studied grace of action, which seems to enlarge the dimensions of the actor, and alone to fill the stage. All this unnaturalness, though right and proper in its place, would appear affected and ridiculous in a private room. . . .

So also gardening, as far as gardening is an art, or entitled to that appellation, is a deviation from nature; for if the true taste consists, as many hold, in banishing every appearance of art, or any traces of the footsteps of man, it would then be no longer a garden. Even though we define it, 'Nature to advantage dressed,' [16] and in some sense it is such, and much more beautiful and commodious for the recreation of man; it is however, when so dressed, no longer a subject for the pencil [17] of a landscape-painter, as all landscape-painters know, who love to have recourse to nature herself, and to dress her according to the principles of their own art; which are far different from those of gardening,[18] even when conducted according to the most approved principles, and such as a landscape-painter himself would adopt in the disposition of his own grounds, for his own private satisfaction.

. . .

The great end of all those arts is, to make an impression on the imagination and the feeling. The imitation of nature frequently does this. Sometimes it fails, and something else succeeds. I think therefore the true test of all the arts, is not solely whether the production is a true copy of nature, but whether it answers the end of art, which is to produce a pleasing effect upon the mind.

It remains only to speak a few words of architecture, which does not come under the denomination of an imitative art. It applies itself, like music (and I believe we may add poetry), directly to the imagination, without the intervention of any kind of imitation.

. . .

To pass over the effect produced by that general symmetry and proportion, by which the eye is delighted, as the ear is with music, architecture certainly possesses many principles in common with poetry and painting. Among those which may be reckoned as the first, is, that of affecting the imagination by means of association of ideas. Thus, for instance, as we have naturally a veneration for antiquity, whatever building brings to our remembrance ancient

16. Pope on true wit, *Essay on Criticism*, l. 297.
17. Paintbrush.
18. Although in fact efforts were made to reproduce the effects of landscape painting in gardening, and the theory of the Picturesque sought to achieve in gardening the complexity of painted landscapes by Poussin, Claude, and Salvator Rosa. (See Figs. 21–23 for the example of Stourhead.)

customs and manners, such as the castles of the barons of ancient chivalry, is sure to give this delight. Hence it is that 'towers and battlements' [19] are so often selected by the painter and the poet, to make a part of the composition of their ideal landscape; and it is from hence in a great degree, that in the buildings of Vanbrugh,[20] who was a poet as well as an architect, there is a greater display of imagination, than we shall find perhaps in any other; and this is the ground of the effect which we feel in many of his works, notwithstanding the faults with which many of them are justly charged. For this purpose, Vanbrugh appears to have had recourse to some principles of the Gothic architecture; which, though not so ancient as the Grecian, is more so to our imagination, with which the artist is more concerned than with absolute truth.

. . .

It may not be amiss for the architect to take advantage *sometimes* of that to which I am sure the painter ought always to have his eyes open, I mean the use of accidents; to follow when they lead, and to improve them, rather than always to trust to a regular plan. It often happens that additions have been made to houses, at various times, for use or pleasure. As such buildings depart from regularity, they now and then acquire something of scenery by this accident, which I should think might not unsuccessfully be adopted by an architect, in an original plan, if it does not too much interfere with convenience. Variety and intricacy is a beauty and excellence in every other of the arts which address the imagination; and why not in architecture?

The forms and turnings of the streets of London, and other old towns, are produced by accident, without any original plan or design; but they are not always the less pleasant to the walker or spectator, on that account. On the contrary, if the city had been built on the regular plan of Sir Christopher Wren,[21] the effect might have been, as we know it is in some new parts of the town, rather unpleasing; the uniformity might have produced weariness, and a slight degree of disgust.

. . .

Upon the whole, it seems to me, that the object and intention of all the arts is to supply the natural imperfection of things, and often to gratify the mind by realising and embodying what never existed but in the imagination.

It is allowed on all hands, that facts, and events, however they may bind the historian, have no dominion over the poet or the painter. With us, history is made to bend and conform to this great idea of art. And why? Because these arts, in their highest province, are not addressed to the gross senses, but to the desires of the mind, to that spark of divinity which we have within, impatient of being circumscribed and pent up by the world which is about us.

---

19. " 'Towers and battlements it sees / Bosomed high in tufted trees,' Milton, *L'Allegro*" (Reynolds); ll. 77–78.

20. Sir John Vanbrugh (1664–1726), who turned to architecture after a successful career as playwright.

21. Wren's plan for rebuilding the city of London after the Great Fire of 1666 was a centralized baroque one; Reynolds's stress upon the value of accident and of the unplanned anticipates later Picturesque theories of Sir Uvedale Price and Richard Payne Knight.

Just so much as our art has of this, just so much of dignity, I had almost said of divinity, it exhibits; and those of our artists who possessed this mark of distinction in the highest degree, acquired from thence the glorious appellation of Divine. [From *Discourse XIII*, 1784]

1769–90?   1790

THE GARDEN AND THE WILD

The question this section raises is how one gets from the formal, geometric gardens of the seventeenth century to the mountain scenes of Wordsworth's Lake Country. It is a question that involves more than landscape, for the landscape is the outward and correspondent form of the mind that regards it (and in imagination creates it). Therefore the emergence of the natural scene becomes at the same time the discovery of new metaphors for the powers of mind.

This double movement is reflected in the forms it inspires. On the one hand there is a search for authentic images of nature, too vast or free to be controlled by human art, and corresponding to the native grandeur of untutored genius; on the other, there is the deliberate cultivation of an art that will be reflexive, that is, will reveal the processes of mind, more an expression of creative process than a finished and self-subsistent achievement. The first gives us new response to Alpine scenery, a passion for those ruins that show art being overwhelmed by nature, the love of broad prospects in space and deep recessions in time (through such monuments as Stonehenge or the ruins of ancient abbeys and castles). The second gives us artfully designed garden landscapes (with "follies," those architectural stage-props meant to be seen at a distance; miniature temples or shrines; vistas closed with emblematic statues) that are meant to evoke a carefully orchestrated set of associations, the sedulous creation (sometimes through sheer forgery) of primitive works (the Ossianic poems, the pseudo-medieval ballads of Thomas Chatterton), the whole pattern of revivals and exoticism that meant the trying on of costumes and roles. It is easy to mock the Pindarique and the Gothick, but giving them their eighteenth-century spelling only reminds us how much a creation of their time they were. What functions did they serve? (For examples of garden architecture and artificial ruins see Figs. 17, 18, 20, 21–23, 52, 55, 56.)

The movement away from a poetry of social reality is a movement toward more mysterious and less conscious aspects of mind, both grandeur and terror. The first effort to evoke these forces has a histrionic and melodramatic quality; men play at being bards or seers or ogres. Such play-acting is an effort to induce feelings that seem to have been buried, repressed, or brought into daylight only to be denounced and exorcised. Gray's creation of a Bard of more than human dimensions, placed in a landscape of extremes, delivering chant-like and magical prophecies—all this marks a shift from the clear, sharp image to the larger half-spectral fantasy that reminds us of our own part in creating it.

Two themes are conspicuous in many of these passages. The first is that man's process of perception creates the beauty he thinks he finds. While, as Addison makes clear, this emphasis is furthered by Locke's empirical philosophy, it lends itself to neoplatonic concern with the forming power of mind; and throughout the century one can see a division between those who stress the passive process of perception and those who stress the inherent shaping powers of mind. We can see the testing of these powers as they are made to embrace the most disorderly and extreme of natural scenes (as in Thomson's treatment of the blaze of summer noon or the turbulence of winter storms). Such scenes elicit an imaginative effort to capture their vivid concreteness and yet to order them as well within the larger harmony of nature. Such an effort, once rewarded, breeds impatience with easier forms of beauty that neither challenge our powers of response nor awaken them to self-awareness.

If the typical response to such challenge is exultation in the powers it summons up, what Johnson calls "a flattering notion of self-sufficiency," the alternative, as confidence ebbs, is a sense of human limitation. As Thomson pushes the winter scene into the far north of Lapland or Siberia, life subsides to mere grim and mindless survival; the sense of liberty and severe grandeur fades into chilling desperation as the more benign latitudes are too far exceeded. Johnson, typically enough, stresses the dark obverse of the tribute to man's intrinsic goodness or power, in the description of the Highlands as he does in *Rasselas*.

SIR WILLIAM TEMPLE
1628–1699

From Upon the Gardens of Epicurus [1]

What I have said of the best forms of gardens is meant only of such as are in some sort regular; for there may be other forms wholly irregular that may, for aught I know, have more beauty than any of the others; but they must

1. This essay was written after Sir William Temple's retirement in 1681 from a distinguished parliamentary and diplomatic career (during which he was ambassador to Holland and became a trusted adviser of William of Orange). While the essay includes a famous account of Moor Park in Hertfordshire (for which Temple named his own estate in Surrey), its most prophetic element is the account which follows of Chinese gardens, one of the earliest tributes in the age to irregularity. For while Temple claimed that Moor Park followed nature ("which I take to be the great rule in this, and perhaps everything else, as far as the conduct not only of our lives but our governments"), his account of it reveals a largely formal garden with a small, defined area that was "very wild, shady, and adorned with rough rock-work and fountains."

The source of the word *sharawadgi* is not known, although it bears some relationship (as has been suggested by Y. Z. Chang) to Chinese words that taken together might mean the "quality of being impressive or surprising through careless or unorderly grace." At any rate, Temple's knowledge of Chinese gardens may have come from printed reports of missionaries or travelers; from direct conversation with them; or from Chinese paintings, prints, and decorations in English collections.

Later Horace Walpole, in *The History of the Modern Taste in Gardening* (1771), reprinted this passage with adverse comments on the naturalness of Chinese gardens: "They are as whimsically irregular as European gardens are formally uniform and unvaried—but with regard to nature, it seems as much avoided as in the squares and oblongs and straight lines of our ancestors." The Chinese "have passed to one extremity of absurdity as the French and all antiquity had advanced to the other, both being equally remote from nature. . . ." But Walpole was writing after the vogue of the "natural garden" had established itself, and, as we see in Addison's *Spectator* No. 414, Temple's essay was illuminating and influential. Twenty years earlier (in 1750) Walpole himself had written with enthusiasm of the *sharawadgi*: "you will be pleased with the liberty of taste into which we are struck, and of which you can have no idea!"

owe it to some extraordinary dispositions of nature in the seat, or some great race of fancy or judgment in the contrivance, which may reduce many disagreeing parts into some figure, which shall yet, upon the whole, be very agreeable. Something of this I have seen in some places, but heard more of it from others who have lived much among the Chinese, a people whose way of thinking seems to lie as wide of ours in Europe, as their country does. Among us, the beauty of building and planting is placed chiefly in some certain proportions, symmetries, or uniformities; our walks and our trees ranged so as to answer one another, and at exact distances. The Chinese scorn this way of planting, and say, a boy that can tell an hundred may plant walks of trees in straight lines, and over against one another, and to what length and extent he pleases. But their greatest reach of imagination is employed in contriving figures where the beauty shall be great and strike the eye, but without any order or disposition of parts that shall be commonly or easily observed. And, though we have hardly any notion of this sort of beauty, yet they have a particular word to express it, and, where they find it hit their eye at first sight, they say the *sharawadgi* is fine or is admirable, or any such expression of esteem. And whoever observes the work upon the best India gowns or the painting upon their best screens or porcelains will find their beauty is all of this kind (that is) without order. But I should hardly advise any of these attempts in the figure of gardens among us; they are adventures of too hard achievement for any common hands; and, though there may be more honour if they succeed well, yet there is more dishonour if they fail, and 'tis twenty to one they will; whereas, in regular figures, 'tis hard to make any great and remarkable faults.

1685?   1690

ALEXANDER POPE

The Gardens of Alcinous°

Close to the gates a spacious garden lies,
From storms defended, and inclement skies:
Four acres was the allotted space of ground,
Fenced with a green enclosure all around.
Tall thriving trees confessed the fruitful mould;
The redening apple ripens here to gold,
Here the blue fig with luscious juice o'erflows,
With deeper red the full pomegranate glows,
Then branch here bends beneath the weighty pear,
10   And verdant olives flourish round the year.
The balmy spirit of the western gale
Eternal breathes on fruits untaught to fail:

The Gardens of Alcinous This translation from *Odyssey* VII was first published in *Guardian*, No. 173 and later included in the full translation of 1725 as VII.142–75. It represents one of the chief classical counterparts of the garden of Eden; it is various and fruitful but also significantly orderly, like Milton's version of Eden in *Paradise Lost* IV.

Each dropping pear a following pear supplies,
On apples apples, figs on figs arise:
The same mild season gives the blooms to blow,°
The buds to harden, and the fruits to grow.
   Here ordered vines in equal ranks appear
With all the united labours of the year;
Some to unload the fertile branches run,
20 Some dry the blackening clusters in the sun,
Others to tread the liquid harvest join,
The groaning presses foam with floods of wine.
Here are the vines in early flower descried,
Here grapes discoloured on the sunny side,
And there in autumn's richest purple dyed.
   Beds of all various herbs, forever green,
In beauteous order terminate the scene.
   Two plenteous fountains the whole prospect
      crowned;
This through the gardens leads its streams around,
30 Visits each plant, and waters all the ground:
While that in pipes beneath the palace flows,
And thence its current on the town bestows;
To various use their various streams they bring,
The people one, and one supplies the King.

1713

From Windsor Forest°

   The groves of Eden,° vanished now so long,
Live in description, and look green in song:
These, were my breast inspired with equal flame,
10 Like them in beauty, should be like in fame.
Here hills and vales, the woodland and the plain,
Here earth and water seem to strive again;
Not chaos-like together crushed and bruised,
But, as the world, harmoniously confused:°
Where order in variety we see,
And where, though all things differ, all agree.
Here waving groves a chequered scene display,
And part admit and part exclude the day;
As some coy nymph her lover's warm address

---

blow blossom
Windsor Forest This poem treats the Forest
("At once the Monarch's and the Muse's seats")
not merely as a royal forest preserve but as a
center of England's natural beauty and its culture; in the early section given below, Pope
creates an example of "picturesque" landscape,
that is, a landscape seen as it might be in a
painting, with interwoven colors and well-
defined receding space.

groves of Eden an evocation of Milton, *Paradise
Lost* IV
harmoniously confused echoing Ovid's *discors
concordia* (*Metamorphoses* I.433), anticipating
the larger cosmic application of the theme in
the *Essay on Man:* "But all subsists by elemental
strife" (I.169); "the lights and shades, whose
well accorded strife / Gives all the strength and
colour of our life" (II.121–22); "All nature's
difference keeps all nature's peace" (IV.56)

20 Nor quite indulges, nor can quite repress.°
There, interspersed in lawns and opening glades,
Thin trees arise that shun each other's shades.
Here in full light the russet plains extend:
There wrapped in clouds the bluish hills ascend.
Even the wild heath displays her purple dyes,
And midst the desert° fruitful fields arise,
That crowned with tufted trees and springing corn,
Like verdant isles the sable waste adorn.
Let India boast her plants, nor envy we
30 The weeping amber or the balmy tree,°
While by our oaks° the precious loads are borne,
And realms commanded which those trees adorn.
Not proud Olympus° yields a nobler sight,
Though gods assembled grace his towering height,
Than what more humble mountains offer here,
Where, in their blessings,° all those gods appear.
See Pan° with flocks, with fruits Pomona° crowned,
Here blushing Flora paints the enamelled ground,°
Here Ceres' gifts° in waving prospect stand,
40 And nodding tempt the joyful reaper's hand;
Rich Industry° sits smiling on the plains,
And peace and plenty tell, a Stuart reigns.
1704–13   1713

ANTHONY ASHLEY COOPER,
THIRD EARL OF SHAFTESBURY
1671–1713

The Moralists

The third Earl of Shaftesbury was the grandson of the Whig statesman whom Dryden portrayed as Achitophel, and he had as his tutor the philosopher John Locke. Shaftesbury was himself a Whig in sentiment, dedicated to the idea of liberty, and radically distrustful of church doctrines. His own system builds upon classical sources, particularly Stoic and neoplatonic. He stresses the orderliness and artistry of the universe; it is a work of mind, and the divine mind is present everywhere as

Nor quite . . . repress Cf. John Keats's "Ode on a Grecian Urn": "Bold lover, never, never canst thou kiss, / Though winning near the goal . . ."; or "Ode to Psyche": "Their lips touched not, but had not bade adieu."
desert barrenness, wild (cf. "waste" in l. 28)
weeping . . . tree Cf. *Paradise Lost* IV.248: "Groves whose rich trees wept odorous gums and balm."
oaks in the form of ships of trade or war
Olympus the Greek mountain where the gods had their home
in their blessings in the form of their natural gifts

Pan as shepherd
Pomona as goddess of orchards and fruit
blushing Flora . . . ground The goddess of flowers, herself suffused with their color, paints the earth as if it were a painter's surface, prepared with a "ground" or coating of paint.
Ceres' gifts grain
Industry Here Pope turns Virgil's account of the Golden Age in *Eclogue* IV to a vision of English life in a time of peace, newly realized with Stuart Queen Anne's Peace of Utrecht (1713), which ended the War of the Spanish Succession begun under William III in 1701.

form. Man must be educated into an awareness of this form as he must be educated into a sense of form in the arts. Shaftesbury has no trust in the naïve or spontaneous as such, but he sees it as preferable to the fashionable miseducation offered by a sensual and materialistic world. (In this respect Shaftesbury recalls those paradoxes of Restoration wit by which the libertine is shown to be at least more natural than the primly repressed or the deviously respectable.)

Shaftesbury's typical literary form is the dialogue, wherein the man of imperfect awareness is drawn upward through the confusion of awakened consciousness to a full vision of the difficult truth; here Theocles plays a role like that of Diotima in Plato's *Symposium*, leading Philocles from love of the external to love of the ordering mind. Along the way, however, they move from the formal garden to the wild, from a stinted and limited art of man to the more authentic art of God in nature. The wild is not to be a resting place; it frees man of the false idols of society, but it must lead him farther to the creative power itself. In the same process, man comes to free himself of his devotion to worldly honors or to mere physical pleasures and to recognize his own god-like powers as a Prometheus or "second maker under Jove." Shaftesbury is therefore important in two ways: he provides a philosophic ground for the love of wild nature and for the visionary ascent beyond nature; and he secularizes this experience so that it need not be—as it tends still to be in Addison— governed by a Christian final cause, that is, existing in order to draw man to God. Shaftesbury strikes a note, not necessarily opposed to Christianity but moving in another direction, of the divine in man which must be released and given full confidence; it gains this confidence through discovery of itself in those sublime forms of nature that alone are adequate counterparts of the energy, reason, and creativity of man.

The Moralists is one of six treatises that were finally in 1711 collected by Shaftesbury under the title *Characteristics of Man, Manners, Opinions, Times,* and a book that had enormous European influence in the eighteenth century.

From The Moralists

A Philosophical Rhapsody

. . . But do you expect I should imitate the poet's god you mentioned,[1] and sing 'the rise of things from atoms, the birth of order from confusion, and the origin of union, harmony, and concord from the sole powers of chaos and blind chance'? The song indeed was fitted to the god. For what could better suit his jolly character than such a drunken creation, which he loved often to celebrate by acting it to the life? But even this song was too harmonious for the night's debauch. Well has our poet made it of the morning when the god was fresh; for hardly should we be brought ever to believe that such harmonious numbers could arise from a mere chaos of the mind. But we must hear our poet speaking in the mouth of some soberer demi-god or hero. He then presents us with a different principle of things, and in a more proper order of precedency gives thought the upper hand. He makes mind originally to have governed

---

1. Silenus, the shaggy, bearded god with horse's ears, knew important secrets of nature, and in Virgil's Sixth Eclogue he is made to reveal them in mythological form to two shepherds; what he presents is an Epicurean view of nature derived from Lucretius (see note 12 below).

body, not body mind; for this had been a chaos everlasting, and must have
kept all things in a chaos-state to this day, and for ever, had it ever been. But

> This active mind, infused through all the space,
> Unites and mingles with the mighty mass;
> Hence men and beasts.[2]

Here, Philocles, we shall find our sovereign genius, if we can charm the genius
of the place [3] (more chaste and sober than your Silenus) to inspire us with a
truer song of Nature, teach us some celestial hymn, and make us feel divinity
present in these solemn places of retreat.

Haste then, I conjure you, said I, good Theocles, and stop not one moment
for any ceremony or rite. For well I see, methinks, that without any such
preparation some divinity has approached us and already moves in you. We are
come to the sacred groves of the Hamadryads,[4] which formerly were said to
render oracles. We are on the most beautiful part of the hill, and the sun, now
ready to rise, draws off the curtain of night and shows us the open scene of
Nature in the plains below. Begin: for now I know you are full of those divine
thoughts which meet you ever in this solitude. Give them but voice and accents;
you may be still as much alone as you are used, and take no more notice of
me than if I were absent.

Just as I had said this, he turned away his eyes from me, musing awhile by
himself; and soon afterwards, stretching out his hand, as pointing to the objects
round him, he began:—

'Ye fields and woods, my refuge from the toilsome world of business, receive
me in your quiet sanctuaries and favour my retreat and thoughtful solitude. Ye
verdant plains, how gladly I salute ye! Hail all ye blissful mansions! known
seats! delightful prospects! majestic beauties of this earth, and all ye rural
powers and graces! Blessed be ye chaste abodes of happiest mortals, who here
in peaceful innocence enjoy a life unenvied, though divine; whilst with its
blessed tranquillity it affords a happy leisure and retreat for man, who, made
for contemplation, and to search his own and other natures, may here best
meditate the cause of things, and, placed amidst the various scenes of Nature,
may nearer view her works.

'O glorious nature! supremely fair and sovereignly good! all-loving and all-
lovely, all-divine! whose looks are so becoming and of such infinite grace; whose
study brings such wisdom, and whose contemplation such delight; whose every
single work affords an ampler scene, and is a nobler spectacle than all which
ever art presented! O mighty Nature! wise substitute of Providence! impowered
creatress! [5] Or thou impowering Deity, supreme creator! Thee I invoke and thee
alone adore. To thee this solitude, this place, these rural meditations are sacred;
whilst thus inspired with harmony of thought, though unconfined by words,

---

2. Virgil, *Aeneid* VI.726–28 (*Dryden's trans.*, VI.984–86), where Anchises speaks.
3. The tutelary spirit or deity that protects the place.
4. Wood nymphs.
5. Pope, in *The Dunciad* IV.487–90, invokes this speech and, in order to use it as a
specimen of Deism, cites it selectively in his original note, omitting the following clause.
Shaftesbury was often accused of a deistic worship of a God who behaves according to
rational laws, makes nature self-sufficient, and has no direct communion with his creatures;
but in fact, while Shaftesbury is hostile to the church and its doctrines of man's weak and
sinful nature, he regards himself as a theist.

and in loose numbers,[6] I sing of Nature's order in created beings, and celebrate the beauties which resolve in thee, the source and principle of all beauty and perfection.

'Thy being is boundless, unsearchable, impenetrable. In thy immensity all thought is lost, fancy gives over its flight, and wearied imagination spends itself in vain, finding no coast nor limit of this ocean, nor, in the widest tract through which it soars, one point yet nearer the circumference than the first centre whence it parted. Thus having oft essayed, thus sallied forth into the wide expanse, when I return again within myself, struck with the sense of this so narrow being and of the fulness of that immense one, I dare no more behold the amazing depths nor sound the abyss of Deity.

'Yet since by thee, O sovereign mind, I have been formed such as I am, intelligent and rational, since the peculiar dignity of my nature is to know and contemplate thee, permit that with due freedom I exert those faculties with which thou hast adorned me. Bear with my venturous and bold approach. And since nor vain curiosity, nor fond conceit, nor love of aught save thee alone inspires me with such thoughts as these, be thou my assistant and guide me in this pursuit, whilst I venture thus to tread the labyrinth of wide Nature and endeavour to trace thee in thy works.'

Here he stopped short, and starting as out of a dream: now, Philocles, said he, inform me, how have I appeared to you in my fit? Seemed it a sensible kind of madness, like those transports which are permitted to our poets? or was it downright raving?

. . .

. . . Philocles, the cold indifferent Philocles, is become a pursuer of the same mysterious beauty.

'Tis true, said I, Theocles, I own it. Your genius, the genius of the place, and the Great Genius have at last prevailed. I shall no longer resist the passion growing in me for things of a natural kind, where neither art nor the conceit or caprice of man has spoiled their genuine order by breaking in upon that primitive state. Even the rude rocks, the mossy caverns, the irregular unwrought grottos and broken falls of waters, with all the horrid graces of the wilderness itself, as representing Nature more, will be the more engaging, and appear with a magnificence beyond the formal mockery of princely gardens. . . . But tell me, I entreat you, how comes it that, excepting a few philosophers of your sort, the only people who are enamoured in this way, and seek the woods, the rivers, or seashores, are your poor vulgar lovers?

Say not this, replied he, of lovers only. For is it not the same with poets, and all those other students in nature and the arts which copy after her? In short, is not this the real case of all who are lovers either of the Muses or the Graces?

However, said I, all those who are deep in this romantic way are looked upon, you know, as a people either plainly out of their wits, or overrun with melancholy and enthusiasm. We always endeavour to recall them from these solitary places. And I must own that often when I have found my fancy run this way, I have checked myself, not knowing what it was possessed me, when I was passionately struck with objects of this kind.

---

6. In free measures, somewhat as in the Pindaric ode.

No wonder, replied he, if we are at a loss when we pursue the shadow for the substance. For if we may trust to what our reasoning has taught us, whatever in Nature is beautiful or charming is only the faint shadow of that first beauty. So that every real love depending on the mind, and being only the contemplation of beauty either as it really is in itself or as it appears imperfectly in the objects which strike the sense, how can the rational mind rest here, or be satisfied with the absurd enjoyment which reaches the sense alone?

From this time forward then, said I, I shall no more have reason to fear those beauties which strike a sort of melancholy, like the places we have named, or like these solemn groves. No more shall I avoid the moving accents of soft music or fly from the enchanting features of the fairest human face.

If you are already, replied he, such a proficient in this new love that you are sure never to admire the representative beauty except for the sake of the original, nor aim at other enjoyment than of the rational kind, you may then be confident. I am so, and presume accordingly to answer for myself. However, I should not be ill satisfied if you explained yourself a little better as to this mistake of mine you seem to fear. Would it be any help to tell you, 'That the absurdity lay in seeking the enjoyment elsewhere than in the subject loved'? The matter, I must confess, is still mysterious. Imagine then, good Philocles, if being taken with the beauty of the ocean, which you see yonder at a distance, it should come into your head to seek how to command it, and, like some mighty admiral, ride master of the sea, would not the fancy be a little absurd?

Absurd enough, in conscience. The next thing I should do, 'tis likely, upon this frenzy, would be to hire some bark and go in nuptial ceremony, Venetian-like, to wed the gulf, which I might call perhaps as properly my own.

Let who will call it theirs, replied Theocles, you will own the enjoyment of this kind to be very different from that which should naturally follow from the contemplation of the ocean's beauty. The bridegroom-Doge, who in his stately Bucentaur [7] floats on the bosom of his Thetis, has less possession than the poor shepherd, who from a hanging rock or point of some high promontory, stretched at his ease, forgets his feeding flocks, while he admires her beauty. But to come nearer home, and make the question still more familiar. Suppose (my Philocles) that, viewing such a tract of country as this delicious vale we see beneath us, you should, for the enjoyment of the prospect, require the property or possession of the land.

The covetous fancy, replied I, would be as absurd altogether as that other ambitious one.

O Philocles! said he, may I bring this yet a little nearer, and will you follow me once more? Suppose that, being charmed as you seem to be with the beauty of those trees under whose shade we rest, you should long for nothing so much as to taste some delicious fruit of theirs; and having obtained of Nature some certain relish by which these acorns or berries of the wood became as palatable as the figs or peaches of the garden, you should afterwards, as oft as you revisited these groves, seek hence the enjoyment of them by satiating yourself in these new delights,

7. The wedding of the Doge of Venice with the sea, ("his Thetis") was celebrated in a pageant each year on Ascension Day with the casting of a ring into the Adriatic from the special gondola called Bucentaur.

The fancy of this kind, replied I, would be sordidly luxurious, and as absurd, in my opinion, as either of the former.

Can you not then, on this occasion, said he, call to mind some other forms of a fair kind among us, where the admiration of beauty is apt to lead to as irregular a consequence?

I feared, said I, indeed, where this would end, and was apprehensive you would force me at last to think of certain powerful forms in human kind which draw after them a set of eager desires, wishes, and hopes; no way suitable, I must confess, to your rational and refined contemplation of beauty. The proportions of this living architecture, as wonderful as they are, inspire nothing of a studious or contemplative kind. The more they are viewed, the further they are from satisfying by mere view. Let that which satisfies be ever so disproportionable an effect, or ever so foreign to its cause, censure it as you please, you must allow, however, that it is natural. So that you, Theocles, for aught I see, are become the accuser of Nature by condemning a natural enjoyment.

Far be it from us both, said he, to condemn a joy which is from Nature. But when we spoke of the enjoyment of these woods and prospects, we understood by it a far different kind from that of the inferior creatures, who, rifling in these places, find here their choicest food. Yet we too live by tasteful food, and feel those other joys of sense in common with them. But 'twas not here (my Philocles) that we had agreed to place our good, nor consequently our enjoyment. We who were rational, and had minds, methought, should place it rather in those minds which were indeed abused and cheated of their real good, when drawn to seek absurdly the enjoyment of it in the objects of sense and not in those objects they might properly call their own, in which kind, as I remember, we comprehended all which was truly fair, generous, or good.

So that beauty, said I, and good with you, Theocles, I perceive, are still one and the same.

'Tis so, said he. And thus are we returned again to the subject of our yesterday's morning conversation. Whether I have made good my promise to you in showing the true good, I know not. But so, doubtless, I should have done with good success had I been able in my poetic ecstasies, or by any other efforts, to have led you into some deep view of Nature and the sovereign genius. We then had proved the force of divine beauty and formed in ourselves an object capable and worthy of real enjoyment.

O Theocles! said I, well do I remember now the terms in which you engaged me that morning when you bespoke my love of this mysterious beauty. You have indeed made good your part of the condition and may now claim me for a proselyte. If there be any seeming extravagance in the case I must comfort myself the best I can, and consider that all sound love and admiration is enthusiasm: 'The transports of poets, the sublime of orators, the rapture of musicians, the high strains of the virtuosi—all mere enthusiasm! Even learning itself, the love of arts and curiosities, the spirit of travellers and adventurers, gallantry, war, heroism—all, all enthusiasm!' [8] 'Tis enough; I am content to be this new enthusiast in a way unknown to me before.

8. Shaftesbury is citing his own *Letter Concerning Enthusiasm*, where a false, hysterical religious enthusiasm (such as Butler and Swift satirize in *Hudibras* and *A Tale of a Tub*) is condemned but a "reasonable ecstasy" is celebrated instead.

And I, replied Theocles, am content you should call this love of ours enthusiasm, allowing it the privilege of its fellow-passions. For is there a fair and plausible enthusiasm, a reasonable ecstasy and transport allowed to other subjects, such as architecture, painting, music; and shall it be exploded here? Are there senses by which all those other graces and perfections are perceived, and none by which this higher perfection and grace is comprehended? Is it so preposterous to bring that enthusiasm hither, and transfer it from those secondary and scanty objects to this original and comprehensive one? Observe how the case stands in all those other subjects of art or science. What difficulty to be in any degree knowing! How long ere a true taste is gained! How many things shocking, how many offensive at first, which afterwards are known and acknowledged the highest beauties! For 'tis not instantly we acquire the sense by which these beauties are discoverable. Labour and pains are required, and time to cultivate a natural genius ever so apt or forward. But who is there once thinks of cultivating this soil, or of improving any sense or faculty which Nature may have given of this kind? And is it a wonder we should be dull then, as we are, confounded and at a loss in these affairs, blind as to this higher scene, these nobler representations? Which way should we come to understand better? which way be knowing in these beauties? Is study, science, or learning necessary to understand all beauties else? And for the sovereign beauty, is there no skill or science required? In painting there are shades and masterly strokes which the vulgar understand not, but find fault with; in architecture there is the rustic; in music the chromatic kind and skilful mixture of dissonancies: [9] and is there nothing which answers to this in the whole?

I must confess, said I, I have hitherto been one of those vulgar who could never relish the shades, the rustic, or the dissonancies you talk of. I have never dreamt of such masterpieces in Nature. 'Twas my way to censure freely on the first view. But I perceive I am now obliged to go far in the pursuit of beauty, which lies very absconded [10] and deep; and if so, I am well assured that my enjoyments hitherto have been very shallow. I have dwelt, it seems, all this while upon the surface, and enjoyed only a kind of slight superficial beauties, having never gone in search of beauty itself, but of what I fancied such. Like the rest of the unthinking world, I took for granted that what I liked was beautiful, and what I rejoiced in was my good. I never scrupled [11] loving what I fancied and aiming only at the enjoyment of what I loved; I never troubled myself with examining what the subjects were, nor ever hesitated about their choice.

Begin then, said he, and choose. See what the subjects are and which you would prefer, which honour with your admiration, love, and esteem. For by these again you will be honoured in your turn. Such, Philocles, as is the worth of these companions, such will your worth be found. As there is emptiness or

9. For an attack upon the "chromatic," see Pope, The Dunciad IV.54–58, on opera. Here Shaftesbury is insisting upon the educated taste required to respond to a "difficult" beauty, which includes apparent disorder or disharmony, as in the "rustic" or harsh and seemingly unfinished elements in architecture. The analogy with the rustic or wild in the natural landscape is clear.
10. Hidden, as God in his mysteriousness is called Deus absconditus.
11. Questioned.

fulness here, so will there be in your enjoyment. See therefore where fulness is and where emptiness. See in what subject resides the chief excellence, where beauty reigns, where 'tis entire, perfect, absolute; where broken, imperfect, short. View these terrestrial beauties and whatever has the appearance of excellence and is able to attract. See that which either really is, or stands as in the room of fair, beautiful, and good. 'A mass of metal, a tract of land, a number of slaves, a pile of stones, a human body of certain lineaments and proportions.' Is this the highest of the kind? Is beauty founded then in body only, and not in action, life, or operation? . . .

Hold! hold! said I, good Theocles, you take this in too high a key above my reach. If you would have me accompany you, pray lower this strain a little, and talk in a more familiar way.

Thus then, said he (smiling), whatever passion you may have for other beauties, I know, good Philocles, you are no such admirer of wealth in any kind as to allow much beauty to it, especially in a rude heap or mass. But in medals, coins, embossed work, statues, and well-fabricated pieces, of whatever sort, you can discover beauty and admire the kind. True, said I, but not for the metal's sake. 'Tis not then the metal or matter which is beautiful with you? No. But the art? Certainly. The art then is the beauty? Right. And the art is that which beautifies? The same. So that the beautifying, not the beautified, is the really beautiful? It seems so. For that which is beautified is beautiful only by the accession of something beautifying, and by the recess or withdrawing of the same it ceases to be beautiful? Be it. In respect of bodies therefore, beauty comes and goes? So we see. Nor is the body itself any cause either of its coming or staying? None. So that there is no principle of beauty in body? None at all. For body can no way be the cause of beauty to itself? No way. Nor govern nor regulate itself? Nor yet this. Nor mean nor intend itself? [12] Nor this neither. Must not that, therefore, which means and intends for it, regulates and orders it, be the principle of beauty to it? Of necessity. And what must that be? Mind, I suppose, for what can it be else?

. . .

If brutes, therefore, said he, be incapable of knowing and enjoying beauty, as being brutes, and having sense only (the brutish part) for their own share, it follows 'that neither can man by the same sense or brutish part conceive or enjoy beauty; but all the beauty and good he enjoys is in a nobler way, and by the help of what is noblest, his mind and reason.' Here lies his dignity and highest interest, here his capacity toward good and happiness. His ability or incompetency, his power of enjoyment or his impotence, is founded in this alone. As this is sound, fair, noble, worthy, so are its subjects, acts, and employments. For as the riotous mind, captive to sense, can never enter in competition or contend for beauty with the virtuous mind of reason's culture; so neither can the objects which allure the former compare with those which attract and charm the latter. And when each gratifies itself in the enjoyment and possession of its object, how evidently fairer are the acts which join the latter pair, and give a soul the enjoyment of what is generous and good? This at least, Philocles,

12. Shaftesbury is attacking the Epicurean doctrine that form arises from the chance collocation of atoms and that it emerges from body; he insists instead upon a universe governed by mind or intelligence.

you will surely allow, that when you place a joy elsewhere than in the mind, the enjoyment itself will be no beautiful subject, nor of any graceful or agreeable appearance. But when you think how friendship is enjoyed, how honour, gratitude, candour, benignity, and all internal beauty; how all the social pleasures, society itself, and all which constitutes the worth and happiness of mankind; you will here surely allow beauty in the act, and think it worthy to be viewed and passed in review often by the glad mind, happily conscious of the generous part, and of its own advancement and growth in beauty.

Thus, Philocles (continued he, after a short pause), thus have I presumed to treat of beauty before so great a judge, and such a skilful admirer as yourself. For, taking rise from Nature's beauty, which transported me, I gladly ventured further in the chase, and have accompanied you in search of beauty, as it relates to us and makes our highest good in its sincere and natural enjoyment. And if we have not idly spent our hours, nor ranged in vain through these deserted regions, it should appear from our strict search that there is nothing so divine as beauty, which belonging not to body nor having any principle or existence except in mind and reason, is alone discovered and acquired by this diviner part when it inspects itself, the only object worthy of itself. For whatever is void of mind is void and darkness to the mind's eye. This languishes and grows dim whenever detained on foreign subjects, but thrives and attains its natural vigour when employed in contemplation of what is like itself. 'Tis thus the improving mind, slightly surveying other objects and passing over bodies and the common forms (where only a shadow of beauty rests), ambitiously presses onward to its source and views the original of form and order in that which is intelligent. And thus, O Philocles, may we improve and become artists in the kind; learning 'to know ourselves, and what that is, which by improving, we may be sure to advance our worth and real self-interest.' For neither is this knowledge acquired by contemplation of bodies, or the outward forms, the view of pageantries, the study of estates and honours; nor is he to be esteemed that self-improving artist who makes a fortune out of these, but he (he only) is the wise and able man, who with a slight regard to these things, applies himself to cultivate another soil, builds in a different matter from that of stone or marble; and having righter models in his eye, becomes in truth the architect of his own life and fortune by laying within himself the lasting and sure foundations of order, peace, and concord. . . . But now 'tis time to think of returning home. The morning is far spent. Come! let us away and leave these uncommon subjects, till we retire again to these remote and unfrequented places.

At these words Theocles, mending his pace, and going down the hill, left me at a good distance, till he heard me calling earnestly after him. Having joined him once again, I begged he would stay a little longer, or if he were resolved so soon to leave both the woods and that philosophy which he confined to them, that he would let me, however, part with them more gradually, and leave the best impression on me he could against my next return. For as much convinced as I was, and as great a convert to his doctrine, my danger still, I owned to him, was very great, and I foresaw that when the charm of these places and his company was ceased, I should be apt to relapse and weakly yield to that too powerful charm, the world. Tell me, continued I, how is it possible to hold out against it and withstand the general opinion of mankind, who have so different a notion of that which we call good? Say truth now, Theocles, can anything be more odd or dissonant from the common voice of the world than what we have determined in this matter?

Whom shall we follow, then? replied he. Whose judgment or opinion shall we take concerning what is good, what contrary? If all or any part of mankind are consonant with themselves, and can agree in this, I am content to leave philosophy and follow them. If otherwise, why should we not adhere to what we have chosen? . . .

1705   1711

JOSEPH ADDISON
1672–1719

[The Pleasures of the Imagination]

Joseph Addison attended Oxford and studied on the Continent thereafter (1699–1703), composing his rhymed *Letter from Italy,* prose *Remarks on Several Parts of Italy,* and a *Dialogue on Medals.* His first great literary success was *The Campaign* (1705), a poem in celebration of the Duke of Marlborough's victories. He held public office and served in Parliament from 1708, and he became a prominent dispenser of Whig patronage to writers. In 1709 he began to aid Sir Richard Steele in the writing of the *Tatler,* and two years later they joined as full collaborators in the *Spectator.* Addison's tragedy *Cato* (1713) was one of the best-known plays of the century.

In eleven papers on "The Pleasures of the Imagination," which appeared as *Spectator* Nos. 411–21, Addison explores the principal aesthetic questions of the day. He distinguishes among the great, the new (or uncommon), and the beautiful in ways that look ahead to later categories of Sublime, Picturesque, and Beautiful. From this discussion, passages on the Great or Sublime have been chosen as instances of growing interest in the wild as opposed to the garden (the residence of the beautiful). In No. 413 Addison pursues the problem of primary and secondary qualities, adapting John Locke's epistemology to the uses of aesthetics and religion. Locke tried to distinguish between those qualities which were constant because located "in" the objects and those that were relative because dependent upon our perception of objects. The primary qualities (e.g. bulk, figure) are "in the things themselves, whether they are perceived or not"; and upon their different modifications the secondary qualities (e.g. color, warmth, smell) depend, arising as they do from man's own contributory response.

By *greatness* I do not only mean the bulk of any single object, but the largeness of a whole view, considered as one entire piece. Such are the prospects of an open champaign [1] country, a vast uncultivated desert, of huge heaps of mountains, high rocks and precipices, or a wide expanse of waters, where we are not struck with the novelty or beauty of the sight, but with that rude kind of magnificence which appears in many of these stupendous works of nature.

1. Of flat fields.

Our imagination loves to be filled with an object, or to grasp at anything that is too big for its capacity. We are flung into a pleasing astonishment at such unbounded views and feel a delightful stillness and amazement in the soul at the apprehension of them. The mind of man naturally hates everything that looks like a restraint upon it and is apt to fancy itself under a sort of confinement when the sight is pent up in a narrow compass, and shortened on every side by the neighbourhood of walls or mountains. On the contrary, a spacious horizon is an image of liberty, where the eye has room to range abroad, to expatiate at large on the immensity of its views, and to lose itself amidst the variety of objects that offer themselves to its observation. Such wide and undetermined prospects are as pleasing to the fancy as the speculations of eternity or infinitude are to the understanding. But if there be a beauty or uncommonness joined with this grandeur, as in a troubled ocean, a heaven adorned with stars and meteors, or a spacious landscape cut out into rivers, woods, rocks, and meadows, the pleasure still grows upon us, as it arises from more than a single principle. [From *Spectator* No. 412, June 23, 1712]

Final causes [2] lie more bare and open to our observation, as there are often a great variety that belong to the same effect; and these, though they are not altogether so satisfactory, are generally more useful than the other, as they give us greater occasion of admiring the goodness and wisdom of the First Contriver.

One of the final causes of our delight in anything that is *great* may be this: the Supreme Author of our being has so formed the soul of man that nothing but Himself can be its last, adequate, and proper happiness. Because, therefore, a great part of our happiness must arise from the contemplation of His Being, that He might give our souls a just relish of such a contemplation, He has made them naturally delight in the apprehension of what is great or unlimited. Our admiration,[3] which is a very pleasing motion of the mind, immediately arises at the consideration of any object that takes up a great deal of room in the fancy, and by consequence, will improve into the highest pitch of astonishment and devotion when we contemplate His nature, that is neither circumscribed by time nor place, nor to be comprehended by the largest capacity of a created being.

.   .   .

. . . He has given almost everything about us the power of raising an agreeable idea in the imagination, so that it is impossible for us to behold His works with coldness or indifference, and to survey so many beauties without a secret satisfaction and complacency. Things would make but a poor appearance to the eye if we saw them only in their proper figures and motions. And what reason can we assign for this exciting in us many of those ideas, which are different from anything that exists in the objects themselves (for such are light and colours), were it not to add supernumerary ornaments to the universe and make it more agreeable to the imagination? We are everywhere entertained with pleasing shows and apparitions: we discover imaginary glories in the heavens and in the earth, and see some of this visionary beauty

2. That is, explanation by the end or object which a thing serves or for which it is made.
3. Wonder, awe.

poured out upon the whole creation; but what a rough, unsightly sketch of nature should we be entertained with, did all her colouring disappear and the several distinctions of light and shade vanish? [4] In short, our souls are at present delightfully lost and bewildered in a pleasing delusion; and we walk about like the enchanted hero of a romance, who sees beautiful castles, woods, and meadows, and at the same time hears the warbling of birds and the purling of streams; but upon the finishing of some secret spell, the fantastic scene breaks up, and the disconsolate knight finds himself on a barren heath or in a solitary desert. It is not improbable that something like this may be the state of the soul after its first separation [5] in respect of the images it will receive from matter, though indeed the ideas of colours are so pleasing and beautiful in the imagination that it is possible the soul will not be deprived of them, but perhaps find them excited by some other occasional cause, as they are at present by the different impressions of the subtle matter on the organ of sight.

I have here supposed that my reader is acquainted with that great modern discovery which is at present universally acknowledged by all the inquirers into natural philosophy—namely, that light and colours as apprehended by the imagination are only ideas [6] in the mind and not qualities that have any existence in matter. As this is a truth which has been proved incontestably by many modern philosophers, and is indeed one of the finest speculations in that science, if the English reader would see the notion explained at large, he may find it in the eighth chapter of the second book of Mr. Locke's *Essay on Human Understanding*. [From *Spectator No 413*, June 24, 1712]

If we consider the works of nature and art as they are qualified to entertain the imagination, we shall find the last very defective in comparison of the former, for though they may sometimes appear as beautiful or strange, they can have nothing in them of that vastness and immensity which afford so great an entertainment to the mind of the beholder. The one may be as polite and delicate as the other, but can never show herself so august and magnificent in the design. There is something more bold and masterly in the rough, careless strokes of nature than in the nice touches and embellishments of art. The beauties of the most stately garden or palace lie in a narrow compass: the imagination immediately runs them over, and requires something else to gratify her; but in the wide fields of nature, the sight wanders up and down without confinement, and is fed with an infinite variety of images, without any certain stint or number. For this reason we always find the poet in love with a country life, where nature appears in the greatest perfection, and furnishes out all those scenes that are most apt to delight the imagination. . . .

We have before observed that there is generally in nature something more grand and august than what we meet with in the curiosities of art. When, therefore, we see this imitated in any measure, it gives us a nobler and more exalted kind of pleasure than what we receive from the nicer and more accurate productions of art. On this account, our English gardens are not so entertaining to the fancy as those in France and Italy, where we see a large extent of ground covered over with an agreeable mixture of garden and forest, which

4. See Swift, *A Tale of a Tub* IX, on the pleasures of the senses.
5. From the body in death, thus losing the sense organs.
6. Images.

represent everywhere an artificial rudeness much more charming than that neatness and elegancy which we meet with in those of our own country. It might, indeed, be of ill consequence to the public, as well as unprofitable to private persons, to alienate so much ground from pasturage and the plough in many parts of a country that is so well peopled and cultivated to a far greater advantage. But why may not a whole estate be thrown into a kind of garden by frequent plantations that may turn as much to the profit as the pleasure of the owner? A marsh overgrown with willows or a mountain shaded with oaks are not only more beautiful but more beneficial than when they lay bare and unadorned. Fields of corn make a pleasant prospect, and if the walks were a little taken care of that lie between them, if the natural embroidery of the meadows were helped and improved by some small additions of art, and the several rows of hedges set off by trees and flowers that the soil was capable of receiving, a man might make a pretty landscape of his own possessions.

Writers who have given us an account of China [7] tell us the inhabitants of that country laugh at the plantations of our Europeans, which are laid by the rule and line, because, they say, anyone may place trees in equal rows and uniform figures. They choose rather to show a genius in works of this nature, and therefore always conceal the art by which they direct themselves. They have a word, it seems, in their language by which they express the particular beauty of a plantation that thus strikes the imagination at first sight without discovering what it is that has so agreeable an effect. Our British gardeners, on the contrary, instead of humouring nature, love to deviate from it as much as possible. Our trees rise in cones, globes, and pyramids. We see the marks of the scissors upon every plant and bush. I do not know whether I am singular in my opinion, but for my own part, I would rather look upon a tree in all its luxuriancy and diffusion of boughs and branches than when it is thus cut and trimmed into a mathematical figure, and cannot but fancy that an orchard in flower looks infinitely more delightful than all the little labyrinths of the most finished parterre. [From *Spectator* No. 414, June 25, 1712]

HORACE WALPOLE AND THOMAS GRAY

[Crossing the Alps, 1739 [1]]

Precipices, mountains, torrents, wolves, rumblings, Salvator Rosa [2]——the pomp of our park and the meekness of our palace! Here we are, the lonely lords of glorious desolate prospects. . . .

. . . Did you ever see anything like the prospect we saw yesterday? I never

7. Notably Sir William Temple in *Upon the Gardens of Epicurus*, who cites the word *sharawadgi*.

1. These excerpts are from letters sent by Walpole and Gray during their grand tour to their schoolmate and friend Richard West (see the Headnote to Thomas Gray). They are among the best and earliest expressions of feeling for the sublime landscape; Gray was to write in a similar vein years later in the Lake Country.

2. The Neapolitan satirist and painter (1615–73), highly esteemed in England for his paintings of wild and turbulent landscape (often inhabited by bandits); here he is aligned with the mountain scene in opposition to cultivated parks or man-made palaces (a similar contrast is used by Gray).

did. We rode three leagues to see the Grande Chartreuse; [3] expected bad roads and the finest convent in the kingdom. We were disappointed pro and con. The building is large and plain and has nothing remarkable but its primitive simplicity: they entertained us in the neatest manner, with eggs, pickled salmon, dried fish, conserves, cheese, butter, grapes and figs, and pressed us mightily to lie there. We tumbled into the hands of a lay-brother, who, unluckily having the charge of the meal and bran, showed us little besides. . . . —But the road, West, the road! winding round a prodigious mountain, and surrounded with others, all shagged with hanging woods, obscured with pines or lost in clouds! Below, a torrent breaking through cliffs, and tumbling through fragments of rocks! Sheets of cascades forcing their silver speed down channelled precipices, and hasting into the roughened river at the bottom! Now and then an old foot-bridge, with a broken rail, a leaning cross, a cottage, or the ruin of an hermitage! This sounds too bombast and too romantic to one that has not seen it, too cold for one that has. If I could send you my letter post between two lovely tempests that echoed each other's wrath, you might have some idea of this noble roaring scene as you were reading it. Almost on the summit, upon a fine verdure, but without any prospect, stands the Chartreuse. We stayed there two hours, rode back through this charming picture, wished for a painter, wished to be poets! [From a letter of September 28–30, 1739, from Horace Walpole to Richard West]

. . . The palace here in town is the very quintessence of gilding and looking-glass; inlaid floors, carved panels, and painting wherever they could stick a brush. I own I have not, as yet, anywhere met with those grand and simple works of Art that are to amaze one, and whose sight one is to be the better for: but those of Nature have astonished me beyond expression. In our little journey up to the Grande Chartreuse, I do not remember to have gone ten paces without an exclamation that there was no restraining: not a precipice, not a torrent, not a cliff, but is pregnant with religion and poetry. There are certain scenes that would awe an atheist into belief without the help of other argument. One need not have a very fantastic imagination to see spirits there at noonday. You have Death perpetually before your eyes, only so far removed as to compose the mind without frighting it. . . . The week we have since passed among the Alps has not equalled the single day upon that mountain, because the winter was rather too far advanced, and the weather a little foggy. However, it did not want its beauties; the savage rudeness of the view is inconceivable without seeing it: I reckoned in one day, thirteen cascades, the least of which was, I dare say, one hundred feet in height. . . . Mont Cenis, I confess, carries the permission mountains have of being frightful rather too far; and its horrors were accompanied with too much danger to give one time to reflect upon their beauties.[4] [From letter of November 16, 1739, from Thomas Gray to Richard West]

3. The motherhouse of the Carthusian order of monks, in the mountains near Grenoble, France, about 3000 feet above sea level. The monks were expelled in 1793 and allowed to return in 1816, and the Chartreuse is the subject of several 19th-century English poets, notably Wordsworth and Arnold.
4. Gray raises an issue to be dealt with later by Burke in his *Enquiry* on the sublime (see above).

JAMES THOMSON
1700–1748

The Seasons°

From Summer

'Tis raging noon; and, vertical, the sun
Darts on the head direct his forceful rays.
O'er heaven and earth, far as the ranging eye
Can sweep, a dazzling deluge reigns; and all
From pole to pole is undistinguished blaze.
In vain the sight dejected to the ground
Stoops for relief; thence hot ascending steams
And keen reflection pain. Deep to the root
440 Of vegetation parched, the cleaving fields
And slippery lawn an arid hue disclose,
Blast fancy's blooms and wither even the soul.
Echo no more returns the cheerful sound
Of sharpening scythe: the mower, sinking, heaps
O'er him the humid hay, with flowers perfumed;
And scarce a chirping grasshopper is heard
Through the dumb mead. Distressful nature pants.
The very streams look languid from afar,
Or, through the unsheltered glade, impatient seem
450 To hurl into the covert of the grove.
    All-conquering heat, oh, intermit thy wrath!
And on my throbbing temples potent thus
Beam not so fierce! Incessant still you flow,
And still another fervent flood succeeds,
Poured on the head profuse. In vain I sigh,
And restless turn, and look around for night:
Night is far off; and hotter hours approach.
Thrice happy he, who on the sunless side
Of a romantic mountain, forest-crowned,
460 Beneath the whole collected shade reclines;
Or in the gelid caverns, woodbine-wrought
And fresh bedewed with ever-spouting streams,
Sits coolly calm; while all the world without,
Unsatisfied and sick, tosses in noon.
Emblem instructive of the virtuous man,

The Seasons James Thomson was the son of a Scottish minister and came to London for a literary career, publishing the first version of *Winter* the year after his arrival (1726), and the full *Seasons* in 1730. He wrote several plays and two other long poems, *Liberty* and (in Spenserian stanzas and allegorical mode) *The Castle of Indolence*. Thomson was probably as well known throughout Europe as any English poet of his age; his descriptive poetry, carrying a weight of moral and philosophical suggestion, had enormous influence. In the spirit of Shaftes- bury, Thomson explored those areas (of climate, of weather, of moral choice) where order was threatened and yet could be shown, in a larger frame, to have survived; in doing so, he studied natural phenomena with a new closeness and a new feeling for their sublimity, and the result was the displacement of epic action by a descriptive counterpart. *The Seasons* underwent extensive revision and reordering throughout Thomson's career, and the last version is given here.

Who keeps his tempered mind serene and pure,
And every passion aptly harmonized
Amid a jarring world with vice inflamed.
    Welcome, ye shades! ye bowery thickets, hail!
470   Ye lofty pines! ye venerable oaks!
Ye ashes wild, resounding o'er the steep!
Delicious is your shelter to the soul
As to the hunted hart the sallying spring
Or stream full-flowing, that his swelling sides
Laves as he floats along the herbaged brink.
Cool through the nerves your pleasing comfort glides;
The heart beats glad; the fresh-expanded eye
And ear resume their watch; the sinews knit;
And life shoots swift through all the lightened limbs
480   Around the adjoining brook, that purls along
The vocal grove, now fretting o'er a rock,
Now scarcely moving through a reedy pool,
Now starting to a sudden stream, and now
Gently diffused into a limpid plain,
A various group the herds and flocks compose,
Rural confusion! On the grassy bank
Some ruminating lie, while others stand
Half in the flood and, often bending, sip
The circling surface. In the middle droops
490   The strong laborious ox, of honest front,
Which incomposed° he shakes; and from his sides
The troublous insects lashes with his tail,
Returning still. Amid his subjects safe
Slumbers the monarch-swain, his careless arm
Thrown round his head on downy moss sustained;
Here laid his scrip° with wholesome viands filled,
There, listening every noise, his watchful dog.
    Light fly his slumbers, if perchance a flight
Of angry gad-flies fasten on the herd,
500   That startling scatters from the shallow brook
In search of lavish stream. Tossing the foam,
They scorn the keeper's voice, and scour the plain
Through all the bright severity of noon;
While from their labouring breasts a hollow moan
Proceeding runs low-bellowing round the hills.
    Oft in this season too, the horse, provoked,
While his big sinews full of spirits swell,
Trembling with vigour, in the heat of blood
Springs the high fence, and, o'er the field effused,°
510   Darts on the gloomy flood with steadfast eye
And heart estranged to fear: his nervous chest,
Luxuriant and erect, the seat of strength,

incomposed disturbed   **effused** streaming, rushing
scrip satchel or bag

Bears down the opposing stream; quenchless his thirst,
He takes the river at redoubled draughts,
And with wide nostrils, snorting, skims the wave.
    Still let me pierce into the midnight depth
Of yonder grove, of wildest largest growth,
That, forming high in air a woodland quire,°
Nods o'er the mount beneath. At every step,
520   Solemn and slow the shadows blacker fall,
And all is awful listening gloom around.
    These are the haunts of meditation, these
The scenes where ancient bards the inspiring breath
Ecstatic felt, and, from this world retired,
Conversed with angels and immortal forms,
On gracious errands bent—to save the fall
Of virtue struggling on the brink of vice;
In waking whispers and repeated dreams
To hint pure thought, and warn the favoured soul,
530   For future trials fated, to prepare;
To prompt the poet, who devoted gives
His muse to better themes; to soothe the pangs
Of dying worth, and from the patriot's breast
(Backward to mingle in detested war,
But foremost when engaged) to turn the death;
And numberless such offices of love,
Daily and nightly, zealous to perform.

. . .

From Winter

    When from the pallid sky the sun descends,°
With many a spot, that o'er his glaring orb
120   Uncertain wanders, stained; red fiery streaks
Begin to flush around. The reeling clouds
Stagger with dizzy poise, as doubting yet
Which master to obey; while, rising slow,
Blank in the leaden-coloured east, the moon
Wears a wan circle round her blunted horns.
Seen through the turbid, fluctuating air,
The stars obtuse° emit a shivering ray;
Or frequent seem to shoot athwart the gloom,
And long behind them trail the whitening blaze.
130   Snatched in short eddies, plays the withered leaf;
And on the flood the dancing feather floats.
With broadened nostrils to the sky upturned,

quire i.e. the natural counterpart in trees of
the Gothic piers of a church choir

When . . . descends This account of the storm
echoes Virgil, *Georgics* I.351–92.
obtuse dulled

The conscious° heifer snuffs the stormy gale.
Even, as the matron, at her nightly task,
With pensive labour draws the flaxen thread,
The wasted taper° and the crackling flame
Foretell the blast. But chief the plumy race,
The tenants of the sky, its changes speak.
Retiring from the downs, where all day long
140   They picked their scanty fare, a blackening train
Of clamorous rooks thick-urge their weary flight,
And seek the closing shelter of the grove.
Assiduous, in his bower, the wailing owl
Plies his sad song. The cormorant on high
Wheels from the deep, and screams along the land.
Loud shrieks the soaring hern;° and with wild wing
The circling sea-fowl cleave the flaky clouds.
Ocean, unequal pressed, with broken tide
And blind commotion heaves; while from the shore,
150   Eat° into caverns by the restless wave,
And forest-rustling mountain comes a voice
That, solemn-sounding, bids the world prepare.
Then issues forth the storm with sudden burst,
And hurls the whole precipitated air
Down in a torrent. On the passive main
Descends the ethereal force, and with strong gust
Turns from its bottom the discoloured deep.
Through the black night that sits immense around,
Lashed into foam, the fierce-conflicting brine
160   Seems o'er a thousand raging waves to burn.
Meantime the mountain-billows, to the clouds
In dreadful tumult swelled, surge above surge,
Burst into chaos with tremendous roar,
And anchored navies from their stations drive
Wild as the winds, across the howling waste
Of mighty waters: now the inflated wave
Straining they scale, and now impetuous shoot
Into the secret chambers of the deep,
The wintry Baltic thundering o'er their head.
170   Emerging thence again, before the breath
Of full-exerted heaven they wing their course,°
And dart on distant coasts—if some sharp rock
Or shoal insidious break not their career,
And in loose fragments fling them floating round.
    Nor less at land the loosened tempest reigns.
The mountain thunders, and its sturdy sons°
Stoop to the bottom of the rocks they shade.
Lone on the midnight steep, and all aghast,

---

conscious alert, responsive
wasted taper guttering and running candle
hern heron
Eat eaten, eroded

wing their course i.e. the sailing vessels, seen as birds
sturdy sons great trees

The dark wayfaring stranger breathless toils,
180 And, often falling, climbs against the blast.
Low waves the rooted forest, vexed, and sheds
What of its tarnished honours° yet remain—
Dashed down and scattered, by the tearing wind's
Assiduous fury, its gigantic limbs.
Thus struggling through the dissipated° grove,
The whirling tempest raves along the plain;
And, on the cottage thatched or lordly roof
Keen-fastening, shakes them to the solid base.
Sleep frighted flies; and round the rocking dome,°
190 For entrance eager, howls the savage blast.
Then too, they say, through all the burdened air
Long groans are heard, shrill sounds, and distant sighs,
That, uttered by the demon of the night,
Warn the devoted° wretch of woe and death.
　　Huge uproar lords it wide. The clouds, commixed
With stars swift-gliding, sweep along the sky.
All Nature reels: till Nature's King, who oft
Amid tempestuous darkness dwells alone,
And on the winds of the careering° wind
200 Walks dreadfully serene, commands a calm;°
Then straight air, sea, and earth are hushed at once.

1726–46

EDWARD YOUNG
1683–1765

The Complaint; or, Night Thoughts
on Life, Death, and Immortality °

From *Night I*

How poor, how rich, how abject, how august,
How complicate, how wonderful, is man!
70 How passing wonder He, who made him such!
Who centred in our make such strange extremes!

tarnished honours faded foliage
dissipated ravaged, scattered
dome building
devoted doomed
careering wildly rushing; cf. Psalms 104:3:
"who walketh upon the wings of the wind"
commands a calm Cf. "Then he arose, and re-
buked the winds and the sea; and there was a
great calm" (Matthew 8:26).
The　Complaint . . . Immortality　Young's
Night Thoughts became one of the most popular
poems of the age both in England and abroad,
and Boswell could declare it "a mass of the
grandest and richest poetry that human genius
has ever produced." Johnson was cooler: "Let
burlesque go beyond him," he remarked of
Young's extended conceits. By the time he wrote

Night Thoughts Young had achieved a distinguished career as a satirist. This poem, with its
graveyard imagery, is an implicit reply to
Pope's *Essay on Man;* it dramatizes the emptiness of any quest for happiness in the world and
urges on man his power of flight above the
claims of the world. In this last, Young becomes
an enthusiastic celebrant of the latent divinity in
man and seeks to induce a flight into those
realms of infinity that the soul must find its
congenial climate. His tactics, in his constant
rebuke to the young libertine Lorenzo, are
those of shock and witty paradox, and he was
later denounced by George Eliot for his "radical
insincerity as a poetic artist"; but, at least in the
passage quoted from Night VI, he could anticipate and appeal to Wordsworth.

From different natures marvelously mixed,
Connexion exquisite of distant worlds!
Distinguished link in being's endless chain!
Midway from nothing to the deity!
A beam ethereal, sullied, and absorpt!
Though sullied and dishonoured, still divine!
Dim miniature of greatness absolute!
An heir of glory! A frail child of dust!
80   Helpless immortal! Insect infinite!
A worm! a god!—I tremble at myself,
And in myself am lost! At home, a stranger,
Thought wanders up and down, surprised, aghast,
And wondering at her own: How reason reels!
O what a miracle to man is man,
Triumphantly distressed! what joy, what dread!
Alternately transported, and alarmed!
What can preserve my life? or what destroy?
An angel's arm can't snatch me from the grave,
90   Legions of angels can't confine me there . . .

1742

From *Night VI*

.   .   .

Where, thy true treasure? Gold says, 'Not in me:'
And, 'Not in me,' the diamond. Gold is poor;
India's insolvent: Seek it in thyself,
Seek in thy naked self, and find it there;
In being so descended, formed, endowed;
Sky-born, sky-guided, sky-returning race!
Erect, immortal, rational, divine!
420   In senses, which inherit earth and heavens,
Enjoy the various riches nature yields;
Far nobler! *give* the riches they enjoy;
Give taste to fruits and harmony to groves;
Their radiant beams to gold, and gold's bright fire;
Take in, at once, the landscape of the world,
At a small inlet, which a grain might close,
And half create the wondrous world they see.
Our senses, as our reason, are divine.
But for the magic organ's powerful charm,
430   Earth were a rude, uncoloured chaos still.
Objects are but the occasion; ours the exploit;
Ours is the cloth, the pencil, and the paint°
Which nature's admirable picture draws;
And beautifies creation's ample dome.
Like Milton's Eve,° when gazing on the lake,

the cloth . . . paint i.e. the canvas, brush, and paint
Milton's Eve *Paradise Lost* IV.456–71, where

Eve unknowingly beholds her own reflection in the water

Man makes the matchless image man admires:
Say then, shall man his thoughts all sent abroad,
Superior wonders in himself forgot,
His admiration waste on objects round,
440   When heaven makes him the soul of all he sees?
Absurd; not rare! so great, so mean, is man.

      .   .   .

  What wealth in souls that soar, dive, range around,
Disdaining limit, or from place or time;
And hear at once, in thought extensive, hear
The almighty fiat and the trumpet's sound!°
Bold, on creation's outside walk, and view
What was, and is, and more than e'er shall be;
Commanding, with omnipotence of thought,
Creations new in fancy's field to rise!
470   Souls, that can grasp whate'er the Almighty made,
And wander wild through things impossible!
What wealth, in faculties of endless growth,
In quenchless passions violent to crave,
In liberty to choose, in power to reach,
And in duration (how thy riches rise!)
Duration to perpetuate——boundless bliss!

      .   .   .

1746

SAMUEL JOHNSON

From A Journey to the Western Islands [1]

. . . We were now in the bosom of the Highlands, with full leisure to contemplate the appearance and properties of mountainous regions, such as have been, in many countries, the last shelters of national distress, and are every where the scenes of adventures, stratagems, surprises and escapes.

    Mountainous countries are not passed but with difficulty, not merely from the labour of climbing; for to climb is not always necessary: but because that which is not mountain is commonly bog, through which the way must be picked with caution. Where there are hills, there is much rain, and the torrents pouring down into the intermediate spaces, seldom find so ready an outlet, as not to stagnate, till they have broken the texture of the ground.

    Of the hills, which our journey offered to the view on either side, we did

fiat . . . sound i.e. the first (Creation) and
last (Judgment)

1. This is from Johnson's record of the tour that was also recorded by Boswell in his
Tour to the Hebrides with Samuel Johnson (published after Johnson's death). Johnson's
imagination had been stirred by the Hebrides in his boyhood reading of Martin Martin's
Description of the Western Islands of Scotland (1703), and he spent a hundred days on
the tour with Boswell in the autumn of 1773. This section comes from the account of the
mainland of Scotland and describes the area near Anoch in Glenmorison.

not take the height, nor did we see any that astonished us with their loftiness. Towards the summit of one, there was a white spot, which I should have called a naked rock, but the guides, who had better eyes, and were acquainted with the phenomena of the country, declared it to be snow. It had already lasted to the end of August, and was likely to maintain its contest with the sun, till it should be reinforced by winter.

The height of mountains philosophically considered is properly computed from the surface of the next sea; but as it affects the eye or imagination of the passenger, as it makes either a spectacle or an obstruction, it must be reckoned from the place where the rise begins to make a considerable angle with the plain. In extensive continents the land may, by gradual elevation, attain great height, without any other appearance than that of a plane gently inclined, and if a hill placed upon such raised ground be described, as having its altitude equal to the whole space above the sea, the representation will be fallacious.

These mountains may be properly enough measured from the inland base; for it is not much above the sea. As we advanced at evening towards the western coast, I did not observe the declivity to be greater than is necessary for the discharge of the inland waters.

We passed many rivers and rivulets, which commonly ran with a clear shallow stream over a hard pebbly bottom. These channels, which seem so much wider than the water that they convey would naturally require, are formed by the violence of wintry floods, produced by the accumulation of innumerable streams that fall in rainy weather from the hills, and bursting away with resistless impetuosity, make themselves a passage proportionate to their mass.

Such capricious and temporary waters cannot be expected to produce many fish. The rapidity of the wintry deluge sweeps them away, and the scantiness of the summer stream would hardly sustain them above the ground. This is the reason why in fording the northern rivers, no fishes are seen, as in England, wandering in the water.

Of the hills many may be called with Homer's Ida 'abundant in springs,' but few can deserve the epithet which he bestows upon Pelion by 'waving their leaves.' [2] They exhibit very little variety; being almost wholly covered with dark heath, and even that seems to be checked in its growth. What is not heath is nakedness, a little diversified by now and then a stream rushing down the steep. An eye accustomed to flowery pastures and waving harvests is astonished and repelled by this wide extent of hopeless sterility. The appearance is that of matter incapable of form or usefulness, dismissed by nature from her care and disinherited of her favours, left in its original elemental state, or quickened only with one sullen power of useless vegetation.

It will very readily occur, that this uniformity of barrenness can afford very little amusement to the traveller; that it is easy to sit at home and conceive rocks and heath, and waterfalls; and that these journeys are useless labours, which neither impregnate the imagination, nor enlarge the understanding. It is true that of far the greater part of things, we must content ourselves with such knowledge as description may exhibit, or analogy supply; but it is true likewise,

2. Cf. Homer, *Iliad* XXIII.117 and II.757.

that these ideas are always incomplete, and that at least, till we have compared them with realities, we do not know them to be just. As we see more, we become possessed of more certainties, and consequently gain more principles of reasoning, and found a wider basis of analogy.

Regions mountainous and wild, thinly inhabited, and little cultivated, make a great part of the earth, and he that has never seen them, must live unacquainted with much of the face of nature, and with one of the great scenes of human existence.

As the day advanced towards noon, we entered a narrow valley not very flowery, but sufficiently verdant. Our guides told us, that the horses could not travel all day without rest or meat, and entreated us to stop here, because no grass would be found in any other place. The request was reasonable and the argument cogent. We therefore willingly dismounted and diverted ourselves as the place gave us opportunity.

I sat down on a bank, such as a writer of romance might have delighted to feign. I had indeed no trees to whisper over my head, but a clear rivulet streamed at my feet. The day was calm, the air soft, and all was rudeness,[3] silence, and solitude. Before me, and on either side, were high hills, which by hindering the eye from ranging, forced the mind to find entertainment for itself. Whether I spent the hour well I know not; for here I first conceived the thought of this narration.

We were in this place at ease and by choice, and had no evils to suffer or to fear; yet the imaginations excited by the view of an unknown and untravelled wilderness are not such as arise in the artificial solitude of parks and gardens, a flattering notion of self-sufficiency, a placid indulgence of voluntary delusions, a secure expansion of the fancy, or a cool concentration of the mental powers. The phantoms which haunt a desert are want, and misery, and danger; the evils of dereliction rush upon the thoughts; man is made unwillingly acquainted with his own weakness, and meditation shews him only how little he can sustain, and how little he can perform. There were no traces of inhabitants, except perhaps a rude pile of clods called a summer hut, in which a herdsman had rested in the favourable seasons. Whoever had been in the place where I then sat, unprovided with provisions and ignorant of the country, might, at least before the roads were made, have wandered among the rocks, till he had perished with hardship, before he could have found either food or shelter. Yet what are these hillocks to the ridges of Taurus,[4] or these spots of wildness to the deserts of America? . . .

1775

WILLIAM COLLINS
1721–1759

Collins formed part of a group of poets of the mid-century who, in Johnson's words, were "eminently delighted with those flights of imagination which pass the bounds of nature"—Joseph and Thomas Warton and Mark Akenside among them. Collins came

3. Wildness.
4. The great mountain chain in southern Turkey.

to know Joseph Warton at Winchester School, and they later planned a joint volume of odes. While that plan, like most that Collins entertained, was never realized, their work shows common impulse and mutual influence. Collins's *Odes on Several Descriptive and Allegoric Subjects,* dated 1747 and published on December 20, 1746, followed Warton's volume by a few weeks; but it had little success. The last decade of Collins's life was spent in depression and eventual madness.

The Wartons' father, Thomas Warton the Elder (1688–1745), had already attempted imitations of Chaucer, Spenser, and Milton and had written two "Scandinavian" odes; he transmitted to his sons the new enthusiasms of the age, and in *The Enthusiast* (1744) of Joseph and *The Pleasures of Melancholy* (1747) of the younger Thomas we can see the cultivation of wild nature, of primitive energy, and of moral rigor such as had characterized the work of James Thomson. The new literary movement had its manifesto in Joseph Warton's *Essay on the Genius and Writings of Pope* (of which the first volume appeared in 1756). Warton there distinguishes sharply between the poetry of "familiar life" and true poetry, which embodies a "creative and glowing imagination" of "exalted and very uncommon character," a power that typically aspires (as Pope, Warton felt, did not) to the "transcendently sublime and prophetic." Such aspiration seeks to achieve visionary power in the revival of romance, in the enraptured transcendence of the visible, in the power to excite man to a full sense of his own divinity. As Akenside writes, we become God-like through imagination: "we feel within ourselves / His energy divine; he tells the heart, / He meant, he made us to behold and love / What he beholds and loves / . . . to be great like Him, beneficent and active . . ." (*The Pleasures of the Imagination,* 1743, III.624–29). As he turns to nature, the poet seeks to "behold in lifeless things, / The inexpressive resemblance of himself, / Of thought and passion" (III.284–86); for "mind alone / . . . The living fountains in itself contains / Of beauteous and sublime" (I.481–83). This drive toward the imaginative sometimes puts excessive stress upon the merely imaginary. As Johnson said of Collins, he "delighted to rove through the meanders of enchantment, to gaze on the magnificence of golden palaces, to repose by the waterfalls of Elysian gardens." But we can also find an effort to generate myth, to inform the natural scene with visionary presences, and—in Collins's late ode—to recover the creative power that is native to the popular mind and the folk imagination. In these efforts the imaginary achieves the release of an internal power too easily suppressed in "familiar life."

Ode on the Poetical Character °

I

As once—if not with light regard
I read aright that gifted bard°
(Him whose school above the rest

Ode on the Poetical Character This is one of Collins's most difficult poems, and it shows an emergent power of myth-making in its condensation of images and themes. The Poetical Character becomes a divine gift difficult to merit; it is a power akin to God's own creative energies and has been realized only by such committed and heroic bards as Milton. There is a sense of poetry as a sacred power, terrifying in its demands and yet compelling in its claims; and this poem seems to mark Collins's ascent from the eclogue to the far greater and more exacting odes.

that gifted bard Edmund Spenser, whose subject was the Elfin (or Faerie) Queen and whose school (such poets as Edward Fairfax, Giles and Phineas Fletcher, Michael Drayton, and to a degree John Milton) is mentioned below

His loveliest Elfin queen has blessed)—
One, only one, unrivalled fair,
Might hope the magic girdle° wear,
At solemn tourney hung on high,
The wish of each love-darting eye;

Lo! to each other nymph in turn applied,°
10   As if, in air unseen, some hovering hand,
Some chaste and angel friend to virgin fame,
      With whispered spell had burst the starting band,
It left unblessed her loathed dishonoured side;
      Happier, hopeless fair, if never
Her baffled hand with vain endeavour
Had touched that fatal zone to her denied!
Young Fancy° thus, to me divinest name,
To whom, prepared and bathed in Heaven,
The cest of amplest power is given,
20 To few the godlike gift assigns
To gird their blessed prophetic loins
And gaze° her visions wild and feel unmixed her flame!

        II

The band, as fairy legends say,
Was wove on that creating day,
When He who called with thought to birth
Yon tented° sky, this laughing° earth,
And dressed° with springs and forests tall,
And poured the main engirting all,
Long by the loved Enthusiast° wooed,
30 Himself in some diviner mood,°
Retiring, sate with her alone,
And placed her on his sapphire throne,°
The whiles, the vaulted shrine around,
Seraphic wires were heard to sound,
Now sublimest triumph swelling,
Now on love and mercy dwelling;
And she, from out the veiling cloud,

the magic girdle The girdle (or zone) called
Cestus (thus "cest" in l. 19) that belonged to
Florimel could be worn only by a virtuous
woman; "But whosoever contrarie doth prove, /
Might not the same about her middle weare,
/ But it would loose, or else a sunder teare"
(Spenser, *The Faerie Queene* IV.v.3, ll. 3–5).
applied tried on, brought into contact
Fancy the counterpart, in Collins's myth, of
Florimel
gaze gaze upon, be inspired by
tented tent-like
laughing pleasant, fertile
dressed adorned; the metaphor carried on in
the "engirting" ocean of the next line
Enthusiast Fancy; possessed by God, as in ll.
17–22; cf. Milton's invocation to Urania in

Paradise Lost VII.8–12: "Before the hills appeared or fountain flowed, / Thou with Eternal
wisdom didst converse. / Wisdom the sister,
and with her didst play / In presence of the
Almighty Father, pleased / With thy celestial
song."
diviner mood Cf. Dryden, *Absalom and Achitophel*, ll. 19–20: "Whether, inspired by some
diviner lust, / His father got him with a greater
gust."
sapphire throne Cf. Milton, *At a Solemn Music*,
where before the "sapphire-coloured throne" of
God, "the bright seraphim in burning row /
Their loud up-lifted angel trumpets blow, /
And the cherubic host in thousand choirs /
Touch their immortal harps of golden wires
. . . " (ll. 10–13).

Breathed her magic notes aloud:
And thou, thou rich-haired Youth of Morn,°
40 And all thy subject life was born!
The dangerous Passions kept aloof,
Far from the sainted growing woof,°
But near it sate ecstatic Wonder,
Listening the deep applauding thunder,
And Truth, in sunny vest arrayed,
By whose the tarsel's° eyes were made;
All the shadowy tribes of Mind
In braided° dance their murmurs joined,
And all the bright uncounted Powers
50 Who feed on Heaven's ambrosial flowers.
Where is the bard whose soul can now
Its high presuming hopes avow?
Where he who thinks, with rapture blind,
This hallowed work° for him designed?

III

High on some cliff, to Heaven up-piled,°
Of rude access, of prospect wild,
Where, tangled round the jealous steep,
Strange shades o'erbrow the valleys deep,
And holy genii guard the rock,
60 Its glooms embrown, its springs unlock,
While on its rich ambitious head
An Eden, like his own, lies spread,
I view that oak,° the fancied glades among,
By which as Milton lay, his evening ear,
From many a cloud that dropped ethereal dew,
Nigh sphered in Heaven, its native strains could hear;
On which that ancient trump° he reached was hung.
　　Thither oft, his glory greeting,
　　From Waller's myrtle shades° retreating,

Youth of Morn the sun, Apollo, who was also the god of poetry; perhaps poetry itself as well **sainted . . . woof** the sacred fabric (either of the "subject life" of the Sun, or, more aptly, here, of the "cest" of Fancy; both may be implied, for the Sun and the poet seem fused in the "Youth of Morn")
tarsel's the male hawk's
braided interweaving (but carrying on the metaphor of the "woof")
hallowed work the cest of Fancy, i.e. the high task of poetic creation as the analogy of God's creation of the world
High on . . . up-piled In the following section Collins seems to fuse the mount of poetry itself (traditionally the resort of the Muses, Mt. Parnassus); the "steep savage hill" on which Eden is situated in *Paradise Lost* IV.134–37: "the champaign head / Of a steep wilderness, whose hairy sides / With thicket overgrown, grotesque and wild, / Access denied"; the towering

ascent, difficult of access by imitation, of Milton's own poetic powers (as one who wore the "cest").
that oak In *Il Penseroso*, ll. 59–60, Milton describes himself as listening to the nightingale's "even-song" near "the accustomed oak"; with possible overtones of the sacred oak of the Druids and the oak tree at the ancient oracle of Dodona, in the rustling of whose leaves the will of Zeus was revealed; at any rate, the scene is one of inspired listening to the "strains," whether "native" to Heaven or to Milton's own exalted spirit.
ancient trump presumably the epic voice or power
Waller's . . . shades the myrtle as sacred to Venus and an emblem of love, appropriate to the amorous lyrics of Edmund Waller (1606–87), as opposed to the heroic strain of Spenser and Milton

70 With many a vow from Hope's aspiring tongue,
My trembling feet his guiding steps pursue;
　　In vain—such bliss to one alone,
　　Of all the sons of soul was known,
　　And Heaven and Fancy, kindred powers,
　　Have now o'erturned the inspiring bowers,°
Or curtained close such scene from every future view.

Ode to Evening°

If aught of oaten stop° or pastoral song
May hope, chaste Eve, to soothe thy modest ear,
　　Like thy own solemn springs,°
　　Thy springs and dying gales,

O nymph reserved, while now the bright-haired sun°
Sits in yon western tent, whose cloudy skirts,°
　　With brede° ethereal wove,
　　O'erhang his wavy bed°—

Now air is hushed, save where the weak-eyed bat,
10 With short shrill shriek, flits by on leathern wing;°
　　Or where the beetle winds
　　His small but sullen horn,°

As oft he rises 'midst the twilight path,
Against the pilgrim° borne in heedless hum—
　　Now teach me, maid composed,
　　To breathe some softened strain,

o'erturned . . . bowers suggesting Guyon's destruction of the Bower of Bliss (*The Faerie
Queene* II.xii) but also the closing of Eden to
the fallen Adam, repeating the theme of the in-
accessibility of Eden (ll. 55 ff.) but now with
a new note of despair
Ode to Evening The meter and unrhymed
stanza were, as Collins's friend Thomas Warton
pointed out, based on Milton's in his translation of Horace's Pyrrha ode (I.v) and were
used by Warton as well. The 1748 text, which is
used here, contains revisions, and one in particular of special interest. Lines 29–32 originally read as follows:
　　Then let me rove some wild and
　　　　heathy scene,
　　Or find some ruin midst its dreary
　　　　dells,
　　Whose walls more awful nod
　　　　By thy religious gleams.
　　　　　　　1746
In the later version printed below, the light of
Evening is diffused and reflected in the landscape, so that the lake holds the light and casts
it in turn upon the "time-hallowed pile." The
traditional personification of Evening tends to

give way to an immanent presence, absorbed
into the landscape rather than acting upon it;
and this looks ahead to those underpresences
of Romantic poetry such as Wordsworth's.
oaten stop Cf. Milton, *Comus*, l. 345: "Or sound
of pastoral reed with oaten stops."
solemn springs originally "brawling springs";
suggesting that "springs" refers to brooks; interestingly altered to the less specific and more
complex "solemn" in revision
bright-haired sun Cf. the "rich-haired Youth of
Morn" in "Poetical Character," l. 39.
skirts the edges of clouds; with suggestion of
canopy and curtains
brede braid; implying interweaving of colors as
in a rainbow, here in sunset clouds
wavy bed Cf. Milton, Nativity ode, ll. 229–31:
"So when the sun in bed, / Curtained with
cloudy red, / Pillows his chin upon an orient
wave . . . "
leathern wing a phrase to be found in Spenser,
Shakespeare, Pope, and Gay
sullen horn Cf. Milton, *Lycidas*, l. 28: "What
time the gray-fly winds her sultry horn."
pilgrim wanderer, traveler

Whose numbers,° stealing through thy darkening vale,
May not unseemly with its stillness suit,
 As musing slow, I hail
 Thy genial loved return!

20

For when thy folding-star° arising shows
His paly circlet,° at his warning lamp
 The fragrant Hours, and elves
 Who slept in flowers the day,

And many a nymph who wreathes her brows with sedge,
And sheds the freshening dew, and, lovelier still,
 The pensive Pleasures sweet
 Prepare thy shadowy car.°

Then lead, calm votaress, where some sheety lake
Cheers the lone heath, or some time-hallowed pile°
 Or upland fallows gray
 Reflect its last cool gleam.

30

But when chill blustering winds or driving rain
Forbid my willing feet, be mine the hut
 That from the mountain's side
 Views wilds and swelling floods,°

And hamlets brown, and dim-discovered spires,
And hears their simple bell, and marks o'er all
 Thy dewy fingers draw
 The gradual dusky veil.

40

While Spring shall pour his showers, as oft he wont,
And bathe thy breathing° tresses, meekest Eve;
 While Summer loves to sport
 Beneath thy lingering light;

While sallow Autumn fills thy lap with leaves;
Or Winter, yelling through the troublous air,
 Affrights thy shrinking train,
 And rudely rends thy robes;

So long, sure-found beneath the sylvan shed,
Shall Fancy, Friendship, Science,° rose-lipped Health,
 Thy gentlest influence own,
 And hymn thy favourite name!

50

1748

numbers verses
folding-star the Evening Star, which arises at
the time to put sheep in their fold or pen
paly circlet Cf. Milton, *Paradise Lost* V.169
for the Morning Star's "bright circle."
car chariot

pile building, ancient and probably Gothic
floods rivers
breathing emitting fragrance
Science learning, study; there is in the four per-
sonifications a mixture of private and social,
intellectual and physical

Ode on the Popular Superstitions of the Highlands of Scotland°

Considered as the Subject of Poetry

I

H[ome], thou returnest from Thames,° whose Naiads long
    Have seen thee lingering, with a fond delay,
    Mid those soft friends whose hearts, some future day,
Shall melt, perhaps, to hear thy tragic song.
Go, not unmindful of that cordial youth
    Whom, long endeared, thou leavest by Lavant's side;°
Together let us wish him lasting truth,
    And joy untainted with his destined bride.
Go! nor regardless, while these numbers boast
10   My short-lived bliss, forget my social name;
But think, far off, how, on the southern coast,
    I met thy friendship with an equal flame!
Fresh to that soil thou turnest, whose every vale
    Shall prompt° the poet, and his song demand;
To thee thy copious subjects ne'er shall fail;
    Thou needest but take the pencil° to thy hand,
And paint what all believe who own° thy genial land.

II

There must thou wake perforce thy Doric quill;°
    'Tis Fancy's land to which thou settest thy feet;
20   Where still, 'tis said, the fairy people meet,
Beneath each birken° shade, on mead or hill.
There each trim lass that skims the milky store
    To the swart tribes their creamy bowls allots;°
By night they sip it round the cottage door,
    While airy minstrels warble jocund notes.
There every herd° by sad experience knows
    How, winged with fate, their elf-shot arrows fly,
When the sick ewe her summer food foregoes,

Ode . . . Highlands of Scotland This ode was addressed to John Home (1727–1808), a Scottish clergyman who later achieved fame as the author of the tragedy *Douglas* (1756). The ode was seen by the Wartons in 1754 and mentioned, on Joseph Warton's report, by Johnson in his life of Collins. This led to Alexander Carlyle's discovery of a defective draft of the poem he remembered having seen among his papers. A more complete text appeared in print in London (1788), but its authenticity was questioned by many, including Wordsworth, and it now seems to have been a forgery. Interestingly, Home later encouraged James Macpherson in his Gaelic forgeries of Ossian, and Collins's interest in folk materials may have been a stimulus to their fabrication.
from Thames The ode was presumably written upon his return to Scotland.

by Lavant's side in Chichester ("on the southern coast"), where Home's friend Thomas Barrow probably introduced him to Collins (Barrow had just been married there)
prompt inspire
pencil paintbrush
own acknowledge as their own
Doric quill rustic pipe or reed; cf. Milton, *Lycidas*, ll. 188–89: "He touched the tender stops of various quills, / With eager thought warbling his Doric lay"
birken birch's (in a Northern form)
swart tribes . . . allots The "swart tribes" are Brownies, who helped with the farmwork in return for a reward but made the animals sick (with "elf-shot arrows") if they were neglected.
herd herdsman

651

Or, stretched on earth, the heart-smit heifers lie.
30 Such airy beings awe the untutored swain,
   Nor thou, though learnèd, his homelier thoughts neglect;
Let thy sweet Muse the rural faith sustain:
   These are the themes of simple, sure effect,
   That add new conquests to her boundless reign,
     And fill, with double force, her heart-commanding strain.

III

E'en yet preserved, how often mayst thou hear,
   Where to the pole the boreal° mountains run,
   Taught by the father to his listening son,
Strange lays, whose power had° charmed a Spenser's ear.
40 At every pause, before thy mind possessed,°
   Old Runic° bards shall seem to rise around,
   With uncouth lyres, in many-coloured vest,°
Their matted hair with boughs fantastic crowned:
   Whether thou biddest the well-taught hind° repeat
   The choral dirge that mourns some chieftain brave,
When every shrieking maid her bosom beat,
   And strewed with choicest herbs his scented grave;
Or whether, sitting in the shepherd's shiel,°
   Thou hearest some sounding° tale of war's alarms;
50 When at the bugle's call, with fire and steel,
   The sturdy clans poured forth their bonny° swarms,
And hostile brothers met to prove each other's arms.

IV

'Tis thine to sing how, framing hideous spells,°
   In Skye's lone isle, the gifted wizard seer,
   Lodged in the wintry cave with [   ]
Or in the depth of Uist's dark forests dwells:
   How they whose sight such dreary dreams engross
With their own visions oft astonished droop,
   When o'er the watery strath° or quaggy moss°
60 They see the gliding ghosts unbodied troop;
   Or, if in sports, or on the festive green,
   Their [   ] glance some fated youth descry,

---

boreal northern
had would have
possessed i.e. by vision; spellbound
Runic ancient Scottish (transferred from Scandinavian)
vest garment, dress
hind peasant
shiel "a kind of hut built every summer for . . . milking the cattle" (Collins); i.e. in distant pastures
sounding resounding
bonny MS. reads "bony" and could mean big-boned, of large frame, but "bonny," i.e. good-looking, is more likely.

hideous spells An account of "second sight," the faculty of perceiving apparitions connected with future disasters; during the vision, the seer is entirely in the control of what he beholds; later reported by Boswell and Johnson in their tour of the Hebrides (of which Skye and two islands of Uist are part). In lines 65 ff. Collins seems to imply, in contradiction of his sources, that the seers have power over the spirits.
strath stretch of flat land beside water
quaggy moss muddy bog

Who now perhaps in lusty vigour seen,
And rosy health, shall soon lamented die.
  For them the viewless° forms of air obey,
Their bidding heed, and at their beck repair;
  They know what spirit brews the stormful day,
And, heartless,° oft like moody madness stare
To see the phantom train their secret work prepare.

    v [missing]

    vi [eight lines missing]
What though far off, from some dark dell espied,
  His glimmering mazes cheer the excursive° sight,
Yet turn, ye wanderers, turn your steps aside,
  Nor trust the guidance of that faithless light;°
For, watchful, lurking mid the unrustling reed,
100   At those mirk° hours the wily monster° lies,
And listens oft to hear the passing steed,
  And frequent round him rolls his sullen eyes,
If chance his savage wrath may some weak wretch surprise.

    VII
Ah, luckless swain, o'er all unblessed indeed!
  Whom late bewildered in the dank, dark fen,
  Far from his flocks and smoking hamlet then,
To that sad spot [   ]
  On him, enraged, the fiend, in angry mood,
Shall never look with pity's kind concern,
110   But instant, furious, raise the whelming flood
O'er its drowned bank, forbidding all return.
  Or, if he meditate his wished escape
To some dim hill, that seems uprising near,
  To his faint eye the grim and grisly shape,
In all its terrors clad, shall wild appear.
  Meantime the watery surge shall round him rise,
Poured sudden forth from every swelling source.
  What now remains but tears and hopeless sighs?
His fear-shook limbs have lost their youthly force,
120 And down the waves he floats, a pale and breathless corse!

    VIII
For him in vain his anxious wife shall wait,
  Or wander forth to meet him on his way;
For him in vain at to-fall° of the day,

viewless invisible
heartless dismayed, stupefied
excursive ranging, wandering
faithless light the wildfire or will-o'-the-wisp;
cf. Milton, *Paradise Lost* IX.634–42

mirk dark, murky
wily monster the kelpie or water spirit (cf. l.
137)
to-fall the close

His babes shall linger at the unclosing gate!
Ah, ne'er shall he return! Alone, if night
   Her travelled° limbs in broken slumbers steep,
With dropping° willows dressed his mournful sprite°
   Shall visit sad, perchance, her silent sleep;
Then he, perhaps, with moist and watery hand,
130   Shall fondly seem to press her shuddering cheek,
And with his blue-swoln face before her stand,
   And, shivering cold, these piteous accents speak:
'Pursue, dear wife, thy daily toils pursue,
   At dawn or dusk, industrious as before;
Nor e'er of me one hapless thought renew,
   While I lie weltering° on the osiered shore,
Drowned by the kelpie's wrath, nor e'er shall aid thee more!'

IX

Unbounded is thy range: with varied style
   Thy Muse may, like those feathery tribes which spring
140   From their rude rocks, extend her skirting wing
Round the moist marge of each cold Hebrid isle,
   To that hoar pile which still its ruins shows;
In whose small vaults a pigmy-folk is found,°
   Whose bones the delver with his spade upthrows,
And culls them, wondering, from the hallowed ground!
Or thither where, beneath the showery West,
   The mighty kings of three fair realms are laid;°
Once foes, perhaps, together now they rest;
   No slaves revere them, and no wars invade:
150   Yet frequent now, at midnight's solemn hour,
   The rifted mounds their yawning cells unfold,
And forth the monarchs stalk with sovereign power,
   In pageant robes, and wreathed with sheeny gold,
And on their twilight tombs aërial council hold.

X

But O! o'er all, forget not Kilda's race,°
   On whose bleak rocks, which brave the wasting tides,
   Fair Nature's daughter, Virtue, yet abides.
Go, just, as they, their blameless manners trace!
   Then to my ear transmit some gentle song
160   Of those whose lives are yet sincere and plain,
   Their bounded walks the ragged cliffs along,

travelled travailed, wearied
dropping dripping
sprite spirit
weltering tossed about by the waters
a pigmy-folk is found Small bones, discovered in the Flannan Islands and in a stone vault on Benbecula, gave rise to the conjecture that a race of pygmies had once lived there.

thither where . . . are laid Iona, where kings of Scotland, Ireland, and Norway were supposed to lie buried together
Kilda's race the people of St. Kilda, the outermost of the Hebrides, celebrated for simple, stoical virtues as of the Golden Age

And all their prospect but the wintry main.
  With sparing temperance, at the needful time,
They drain the sainted spring; or, hunger-pressed.
  Along the Atlantic rock undreading climb,
And of its eggs despoil the solan's° nest.
  Thus blessed in primal innocence they live,
  Sufficed and happy with that frugal fare
    Which tasteful toil and hourly danger give.
170 Hard is their shallow soil, [   ] and bare;
    Nor ever vernal bee was heard to murmur there!

      XI
Nor needest thou blush that such false themes engage
  Thy gentle° mind, of fairer stores possessed;
  For not alone they touch the village breast,
But filled in elder time, the historic page.
  There Shakespeare's self, with every garland crowned,
  In musing hour his Wayward Sisters° found,
And with their terrors dressed the magic scene.
  From them he sung, when, mid his bold design,
180 Before the Scot, afflicted and aghast,
    The shadowy kings of Banquo's fated line
Through the dark cave in gleamy pageant passed.°
  Proceed, nor quit the tales which, simply told,
  Could once so well my answering bosom pierce;
  Proceed—in forceful sounds and colours bold
The native legends of thy land rehearse;
  To such adapt thy lyre, and suit thy powerful verse.

      XII
In scenes like these, which, daring to depart
  From sober truth,° are still to Nature true,
190 And call forth fresh delight to Fancy's view,
    The heroic muse employed her Tasso's art!°
  How have I trembled, when at Tancred's stroke,
  Its gushing blood the gaping cypress poured;
  When each live plant with mortal accents spoke,
And the wild blast upheaved the vanished sword!
  How have I sat, where piped the pensive wind,
  To hear his harp by British Fairfax strung;

solan's a goose or gannet
gentle cultivated
Wayward Sisters the Witches in Macbeth,
"wayward" in their supernatural power over
fate
in . . . passed Macbeth IV.i
daring . . . truth Cf. Dryden, "Of Heroic
Plays: An Essay" (1672), where he cites,
among other inventions, the Enchanted Wood
in Tasso and the Bower of Bliss in Spenser: "an

heroic poet is not tied to a bare representation
of what is true, or exceeding probable but
. . . he may let himself loose to visionary objects and to the representation of such things as
. . . may give him a freer scope for imagination."
Tasso's art Edward Fairfax's translation (1600)
of *Jerusalem Delivered* (where Tancred appears) was reprinted in 1749, shortly before
Collins wrote the poem.

Prevailing° poet! whose undoubting mind
Believed the magic wonders which he sung!
200   Hence, at each sound, imagination glows;
    Hence his warm lay with softest sweetness flows;
Melting it flows, pure, numerous,° strong, and clear,
And fills the impassioned heart and lulls the harmonious° ear.

XIII

All hail, ye scenes that o'er my soul prevail,
Ye [   ] firths° and lakes, which, far away,
    Are by smooth Annan filled or pastoral Tay,
Or Don's romantic springs; at distance, hail!
The time shall come, when I, perhaps, may tread
    Your lowly glens, o'erhung with spreading broom;
210   Or, o'er your stretching heaths, by Fancy led;
Then will I dress once more the faded bower,
    Where Jonson° sat in Drummond's [   ] shade;
Or crop, from Tiviot's dale,° each [   ]
    And mourn, on Yarrow banks,° [   ]
Meantime, ye Powers, that on the plains which bore
    The cordial youth,° on Lothian's plains, attend,
Where'er he dwell, on hill or lowly muir,°
    To him I lose, your kind protection lend,
220   And, touched with love like mine, preserve my absent friend.
1749–50   1788

THOMAS GRAY
1716–1771

Gray's production was more slender than his talent, but his rather neurasthenic temperament would permit no more. Most of his life was spent at Cambridge, where he finally became Regius Professor of Modern History three years before his death (always planning but never giving a lecture). At Eton he became a close friend of Horace Walpole and Richard West, and this friendship continued at Cambridge. Having planned a legal career, he gave it up and returned to Cambridge within a few months after the early death of West; he quarreled with Walpole during their grand tour, but they were finally reconciled after more than four years (1741–45), and Walpole remained an enthusiastic patron and supporter of his poetry, printing the two great odes on his

Prevailing powerful
numerous musical
harmonious filled with harmony
firths arms of the sea, into which some of the rivers named below empty
Jonson Ben Jonson walked in Scotland in 1619 to visit William Drummond at his estate at Hawthornden near Edinburgh, and Drummond published the record of their conversations; Collins may see himself as Jonson to Home's Drummond.

Tiviot's dale probably a reference to the Border Ballads set there, particularly *Chevy Chase*
Yarrow banks referring to the ballad *The Braes of Yarrow* by William Hamilton of Bangour (1704–54), whose poems were first collected in 1748
cordial youth here Home, in Edinburgh ("on Lothian's plains")
muir moor

own press. Gray was a formidable scholar—called by one friend "the most learned man in Europe"—and was open to many of the new literary influences of his day; in addition to classical models he turned to newly discovered Welsh and Norse poetry, and he was greatly interested in the supposed works of Ossian that Dr. Johnson helped expose as a forgery. His travel letters are among the earliest to record the new enthusiasm for the sublimities of the Alps and, later, of the Lake Country and Scotland. He was somewhat affected, delicate, and mincing in manner, especially (as his friend and editor William Mason put it) "before those whom he did not wish to please." They seem to have been many, and they included his Cambridge enemy Christopher Smart. That Gray aspired to more generosity than he sometimes achieved in life is clearest in the *Elegy*.

Gray wrote early to his friend West that "the language of the age is never the language of poetry," and he created a fabric of heightened "poetic diction," sometimes deliberately allusive and sometimes faintly evocative, from reminiscences of classical and earlier English poetry—notably Spenser, Shakespeare, and Milton—as well as of Dryden and Pope. This diction could be used with great subtlety to frame in the Eton ode an ironic and self-critical nostalgia, to give lapidary form in the *Elegy* to sentiments which (as Johnson said) each reader "persuades himself that he has always felt," or in *The Bard* to produce a visionary intensity that renders English history with the sublime terror and radiance of prophecy.

Ode on a Distant Prospect of Eton College°

Ἄνθρωπος · ἱκανὴ πρόφασις εἰς τὸ δυστυχεῖν.
MENANDER°

Ye distant spires, ye antique towers,
That crown the watery glade,
Where grateful Science° still adores
Her Henry's holy shade;°
And ye, that from the stately brow
Of Windsor's heights° the expanse below
Of grove, of lawn, of mead survey,
Whose turf, whose shade, whose flowers among
Wanders the hoary Thames along
10   His silver-winding way:

Ode . . . Eton College Among the sorrows that lie behind the poem are the death of Gray's schoolmate and friend Richard West; Gray's quarrel with his friend Horace Walpole; and perhaps the fall from power of Walpole's father, Sir Robert. In a letter to West of May 27, 1742, Gray contemplates the aging of his old schoolmates into husbands, fathers, statesmen. "Do not you remember them dirty boys playing at cricket?" he writes. "As for me, I am never a bit older, nor the bigger, nor the wiser than I was then; no, not for having been beyond sea." The "dirty boys" become figures of Eden or a golden age; the world Gray recalls is cut

off as by the distance of the prospect; and the poem evokes a poignant double view, pivoting sharply on the phrase "the little victims" (l. 52). For Edward Gibbon's view of the poem, see the Headnote to the section Sense and Sensibility. Menander a fragment: "I am a man, a sufficient excuse for being unhappy."
Science knowledge in general
Henry's . . . shade Eton was founded in the 15th century by Henry VI, sometimes called the "martyr king."
Windsor's heights The towers of Windsor Castle stand across the Thames from Eton.

Ah happy hills, ah pleasing shade,
Ah fields beloved in vain,°
Where once my careless childhood strayed,
A stranger yet to pain!
I feel the gales° that from ye blow
A momentary bliss bestow,
As, waving fresh their gladsome wing,
My weary soul they seem to soothe,
And, redolent° of joy and youth,
20   To breathe a second spring.

Say, Father Thames, for thou hast seen
Full many a sprightly race°
Disporting on thy margent green
The paths of pleasure trace,
Who foremost now delight to cleave
With pliant arm thy glassy wave?
The captive linnet which enthrall?
What idle progeny succeed
To chase the rolling circle's° speed,
30   Or urge the flying ball?

While some on earnest business bent
Their murmuring labours° ply
'Gainst graver hours, that bring constraint
To sweeten liberty;
Some bold adventurers disdain
The limits of their little reign,
And unknown regions dare descry;
Still as they run they look behind,
They hear a voice in every wind,
40   And snatch a fearful joy.

Gay hope is theirs by fancy fed,
Less pleasing when possessed;
The tear forgot as soon as shed,
The sunshine of the breast;
Their buxom° health of rosy hue,
Wild wit, invention ever new,
And lively cheer of vigour born;
The thoughtless day, the easy night,
The spirits pure, the slumbers light,
50   That fly the approach of morn.

in vain stressing the distance in time as well as space, the painful irreversibility of the past
gales breezes
redolent smelling sweetly
race generation
rolling circle's hoop's (Gray's use of formalized "poetic diction" with its stately and periphrastic —i.e. roundabout—terms for familiar objects is related to earlier mock-heroic diction; here it acquires a peculiar sense of distance, a mockery of naïve innocence, and some genuine acknowledgment of the heroic nature of that golden age of youth)
Their . . . labours presumably studying and memorizing, repeating softly to themselves what they will present to their teachers in "graver hours"
buxom lively

Alas, regardless° of their doom,
The little victims play!
No sense have they of ills to come,
Nor care beyond today:
Yet see how all around 'em wait
The ministers of human fate,
And black Misfortune's baleful train!
Ah, show them where in ambush stand
To seize their prey the murtherous band!
60   Ah, tell them, they are men!

These shall the fury Passions tear,
The vultures of the mind;
Disdainful Anger, pallid Fear,
And Shame that skulks behind;
Or pining Love shall waste their youth,
Or Jealousy with rankling tooth,
That inly gnaws the secret heart,
And Envy wan, and faded Care,
Grim-visaged comfortless Despair,
70   And Sorrow's piercing dart.

Ambition this shall tempt to rise,
Then whirl the wretch from high,
To bitter Scorn a sacrifice,
And grinning Infamy.
The stings of Falsehood those shall try,
And hard Unkindness' altered eye,
That mocks the tear it forced to flow;
And keen Remorse with blood defiled,
And moody Madness laughing wild
80   Amid severest woe.

Lo, in the vale of years beneath
A grisly troop are seen,
The painful family° of Death,
More hideous than their queen:
This racks the joints, this fires the veins.
That every labouring sinew strains,
Those in the deeper vitals rage;
Lo, Poverty, to fill the band,
That numbs the soul with icy hand,
90   And slow-consuming Age.

To each his sufferings; all are men,
Condemned alike to groan:
The tender for another's pain,
The unfeeling for his own.

regardless heedless, unaware   family household, tribe

Yet, ah! why should they know their fate?
Since sorrow never comes too late,
And happiness too swiftly flies.
Thought would destroy their paradise.
No more: where ignorance is bliss,
100 'Tis folly to be wise.

1742   1747

Ode on the Death of a Favourite Cat, Drowned in a Tub of Gold Fishes°

'Twas on a lofty vase's side,°
Where China's gayest art had dyed
    The azure flowers that blow;°
Demurest of the tabby kind,
The pensive Selima reclined,
    Gazed on the lake below.

Her conscious tail her joy declared;
The fair round face, the snowy beard,
    The velvet of her paws,
10 Her coat, that with the tortoise vies,
Her ears of jet, and emerald eyes,
    She saw; and purred applause.°

Still had she gazed; but 'midst the tide
Two angel forms were seen to glide,
    The genii° of the stream:
Their scaly armour's Tyrian° hue
Through richest purple to the view
    Betrayed a golden gleam.

The hapless nymph with wonder saw:
20 A whisker first and then a claw,
    With many an ardent wish,
She stretched in vain to reach the prize.
What female heart can gold despise?
    What cat's averse to fish?

Ode on the Death . . . Gold Fishes Gray wrote this at Horace Walpole's request as an epitaph for one of his cats. It takes the form of an animal fable with appropriate moral, but its mock-heroic idiom carefully evokes—through echoes of Pope and Dryden—Homer's Helen and Virgil's Camilla, as well as Milton's Eve. One might compare Chaucer's *Nun's Priest's Tale* for similar interplay between high diction and obtrusive animal details (e.g. l. 8).
'Twas . . . side Cf. the opening of John Dryden's *Alexander's Feast.*
blow bloom, blossom. Dr. Johnson remarks on "how resolutely a rhyme is sometimes made when it cannot easily be found," but the pointlessness of the emphasis may be meant to set the comic tone.
purred applause Selima's narcissism may be meant to suggest Eve in Milton, *Paradise Lost* IV.456–66, where she first beholds her reflection and feels "sympathy and love" for the fair stranger, even pining "with vain desire."
genii guardian spirits, as in the "genius of the place"
Tyrian Tyre in Phoenicia was an ancient source of purple dye.

Presumptuous maid! with looks intent
Again she stretched, again she bent,
   Nor knew the gulf between.
(Malignant Fate sat by and smiled)
The slippery verge° her feet beguiled,
30   She tumbled headlong in.

Eight times emerging from the flood
She mewed to every watery god,
   Some speedy aid to send.
No dolphin° came, no Nereid° stirred;
Nor cruel Tom nor Susan° heard.
   A favourite has no friend!

From hence, ye beauties, undeceived,
Know, one false step is ne'er retrieved,
   And be with caution bold.
Not all that tempts your wandering eyes
And heedless hearts is lawful prize.
   Nor all that glisters, gold.°
1747   1748

Elegy Written in a Country Churchyard°

The curfew tolls the knell of parting day,
  The lowing herd wind slowly o'er the lea,
The ploughman homeward plods his weary way,
  And leaves the world to darkness and to me.

Now fades the glimmering landscape on the sight,
  And all the air a solemn stillness holds,
Save where the beetle wheels his droning flight,
  And drowsy tinklings lull the distant folds;

---

verge bank, rim
dolphin such as rescued the drowning musician Arion by carrying him to safety on its back
Nereid sea nymph
Tom . . . Susan servants
all . . . gold a proverbial phrase, perhaps best known in Shakespeare's *Merchant of Venice* II. vii.65
Elegy . . . Churchyard When Gray began to write this poem, whose earlier manuscript title was *Stanza's Wrote in a Country Church-Yard*, is hard to determine; his friend (as of 1747) William Mason dated its beginning in 1742, but other evidence suggests a real commencement some three or more years later. At any rate, it was completed and seen by Horace Walpole in 1750. The poem had great and immediate success, which Gray was inclined to attribute to its subject; while it had been pre-

ceded by such "graveyard" poems as Edward Young's *Night Thoughts* (1742–45) and Robert Blair's *The Grave* (1743), it is far more restrained and classical in spirit. Where, however, the *Stanza's* originally concluded with a generalized moral statement of serene endurance ("But through the last sequestered vale of life / Pursue the silent tenor of thy doom"), the *Elegy* has created, through a double distancing, the swain's account of the poet and finally the epitaph (presumably of the poet's own composition). In the epitaph we see the problem of self-fulfillment (treated earlier in the village poor) translated into the capacity for feeling and the reward of a friend. From that tribute to personal feeling one can look back to the "wonted fires" of l. 92 for the claims that Gray's poem is written both to recognize and to meet.

Save that from yonder ivy-mantled tower
10   The moping owl does to the moon complain
Of such, as wandering near her secret bower,
        Molest her ancient solitary reign.

Beneath those rugged elms, that yew-tree's shade,
        Where heaves the turf in many a mouldering heap,
Each in his narrow cell forever laid,
        The rude forefathers° of the hamlet sleep.

The breezy call of incense-breathing morn,
        The swallow twittering from the straw-built shed,
The cock's shrill clarion or the echoing horn,°
20   No more shall rouse them from their lowly bed.

For them no more the blazing hearth shall burn,
        Or busy housewife° ply her evening care;
No children run to lisp their sire's return,
        Or climb his knees the envied kiss to share.

Oft did the harvest to their sickle yield;
        Their furrow oft the stubborn glebe° has broke;
How jocund did they drive their team afield!
        How bowed the woods beneath their sturdy stroke!

Let not Ambition mock their useful toil,
30   Their homely° joys and destiny obscure;
Nor Grandeur hear with a disdainful smile
        The short and simple annals° of the poor.

The boast of heraldry, the pomp of power,
        And all that beauty, all that wealth e'er gave,
Awaits alike the inevitable hour:
        The paths of glory lead but to the grave.

Nor you, ye proud, impute to these the fault,
        If Memory o'er their tomb no trophies° raise,
Where through the long-drawn aisle and fretted° vault
40   The pealing anthem° swells the note of praise.

Can storied° urn or animated° bust
        Back to its mansion call the fleeting breath?
Can Honour's voice provoke° the silent dust,
        Or Flattery soothe the dull cold ear of Death?

---

rude forefathers humble (uneducated) ancestors
horn of the hunter
housewife pronounced "hussif"
glebe field
homely simple, domestic (originally, "rustic")
annals year-by-year life records, as opposed to the more expansive "histories" of nations or "lives" of great men

trophies carved memorials; literally symbols of victory, as here over the blankness of death
fretted decorated with patterns of carving
pealing anthem Cf. Milton, *Il Penseroso*, ll. 161, 163: "There let the pealing organ blow / . . . In service high and anthems clear."
storied having stories represented upon it
animated as if breathing
provoke rouse up

Perhaps in this neglected spot is laid
    Some heart once pregnant with celestial fire;
Hands that the rod of empire might have swayed,
    Or waked to ecstasy the living lyre.

But Knowledge to their eyes her ample page,
50   Rich with the spoils of time, did ne'er unroll;
Chill Penury repressed their noble rage,°
    And froze the genial current° of the soul.

Full many a gem of purest ray serene,°
    The dark unfathomed caves of ocean bear;
Full many a flower is born to blush unseen,
    And waste its sweetness on the desert air.

Some village Hampden,° that with dauntless breast
    The little tyrant of his fields withstood;
Some mute inglorious Milton here may rest,
60   Some Cromwell, guiltless of his country's blood.

The applause of listening senates to command,
    The threats of pain and ruin to despise,
To scatter plenty o'er a smiling land,
    And read their history in a nation's eyes,

Their lot forbade; nor circumscribed alone°
    Their growing virtues, but their crimes confined.
Forbade to wade through slaughter to a throne,
    And shut the gates of mercy on mankind;

The struggling pangs of conscious truth to hide,
70   To quench the blushes of ingenuous shame,°
Or heap the shrine of Luxury and Pride
    With incense kindled at the Muse's flame.

Far from the madding crowd's ignoble strife,
    Their sober wishes never learned to stray;
Along the cool sequestered vale of life
    They kept the noiseless tenor of their way.

Yet even these bones from insult to protect,
    Some frail memorial° still erected nigh,
With uncouth rhymes and shapeless sculpture decked,
80   Implores the passing tribute of a sigh.

---

rage rapture, ardor
genial current creative energies
serene clear, bright (as in Latin *serenus*); with possible overtones of calm and quiet as well
Hampden John Hampden (1594–1643), who refused to submit to a special tax levied by Charles I in 1636 and as a member of Parliament defended the rights of the people; originally "Cato" (for the Roman senator who championed republican rights), as "Milton" was "Tully" (Cicero) and "Cromwell" was "Caesar"
nor . . . alone i.e. not only
ingenuous shame natural (or innately noble) honor
frail memorial presumably the simple tombstones in the churchyard as opposed to the monumental tombs within the church

Their name, their years, spelt by the unlettered Muse,
    The place of fame and elegy° supply;
And many a holy text around she strews,
    That teach the rustic moralist to die.

For who, to dumb forgetfulness a prey,
    This pleasing anxious being e'er resigned,
Left the warm precincts of the cheerful day,
    Nor cast one longing lingering look behind?

On some fond breast the parting soul relies,
90   Some pious drops° the closing eye requires;
Even from the tomb the voice of Nature cries,
    Even in our ashes live their wonted fires.

For thee,° who mindful of the unhonoured dead
    Dost in these lines their artless tale relate;
If chance,° by lonely contemplation led,
    Some kindred spirit shall inquire thy fate,

Haply some hoary-headed swain may say,
    'Oft have we seen him at the peep of dawn
Brushing with hasty steps the dews away
100   To meet the sun upon the upland lawn.

'There at the foot of yonder nodding beech
    That wreathes its old fantastic roots so high,
His listless length at noontide would he stretch,
    And pore upon the brook that babbles by.

'Hard by yon wood, now smiling as in scorn,
    Muttering his wayward fancies he would rove;
Now drooping, woeful-wan, like one forlorn,
    Or crazed with care, or crossed in hopeless love.

'One morn I missed him on the customed hill,
110   Along the heath and near his favourite tree;
Another came; nor yet beside the rill,
    Nor up the lawn, nor at the wood was he;

'The next, with dirges due, in sad array,
    Slow through the church-way path we saw him borne.
Approach and read (for thou canst read) the lay,
    Graved on the stone beneath yon agèd thorn.'

THE EPITAPH

Here rests his head upon the lap of earth,
    A youth to fortune and to fame unknown;

---

elegy a formal tribute on the monument or elsewhere; supplied for the poor in the churchyard
by this poem (which is also a poetic meditation in the classical sense of "elegy")

drops mourner's tears
thee the poet's own self
chance i.e. by chance

Fair Science° frowned not on his humble birth,
  And Melancholy° marked him for her own.

Large was his bounty and his soul sincere;
  Heaven did a recompense as largely send:
He gave to Misery all he had, a tear;
  He gained from Heaven ('twas all he wished) a friend.

No farther seek his merits to disclose,
  Or draw his frailties from their dread abode,
(There they alike in trembling hope repose)
  The bosom of his Father and His God.
    1742–50   1751

The Bard

Although Gray had begun the ode earlier, he was inspired to resume it by the visit to Cambridge of John Parry, a blind Welsh harper who could perform "tunes of a thousand years old with names enough to choke you." This poem was first printed with its "sister ode," *The Progress of Poesy* by Horace Walpole, and later published by Dodsley. Gray expected the poems to baffle many readers; they outdid expectations and finally were given notes by Gray, although only "out of spite," in 1768. Gray explains in the original Advertisement to the poem that it is "founded on a tradition current in Wales that Edward the First, when he completed the conquest of that country, ordered all the bards that fell into his hands to be put to death." In his Commonplace Book Gray envisages "a venerable figure seated on the summit of an inaccessible rock, who, with a voice more than human, reproaches the king with all the misery and desolation which he had brought on his country" and prophesies that the "noble ardour of poetic genius in this island" will "never be wanting to celebrate true virtue and valour" and to "censure tyranny and oppression." As his song ends, "he precipitates himself from the mountain, and is swallowed up by the river that rolls at its foot."

This Pindaric ode, more authentically regular than Dryden's, brings together various forms of sublime power (the heroic and biblical—Moses and Ezekiel, the Welsh, and Norse) and typical themes (the spirit of liberty, the poet as prophet, the grandeur and wildness of the mountain scene). Dr. Johnson's adverse criticism points to Gray's deliberate effort: "The images are magnified by affectation; the language is laboured into harshness. The mind of the writer seems to work with unnatural violence. . . . He has a kind of strutting dignity, and is tall by walking on tiptoe. His art and struggle are too visible, and there is too little appearance of ease and nature." Yet one may see that "ease" is hardly Gray's object and the very surpassing or transcendence of "nature" in visionary intensity is his goal. William Blake found "weaving the winding sheet of Edward's race by means of spiritual music . . . a bold, daring, and masterly conception." For William Blake's and John Martin's conceptions of Gray's bard, see Figs. 48 and 49 in the illustration section of this volume.

Science knowledge or learning
Melancholy implying a pensiveness and heightened sensibility, with a great capacity for feeling, for others (as we see in his "bounty") as well as for himself

The Bard

A Pindaric Ode
'Ruin seize thee, ruthless King!
Confusion on thy banners wait,°
Though fanned by Conquest's crimson wing
They mock the air with idle state.°
Helm, nor hauberk's° twisted mail,
Nor even thy virtues, tyrant, shall avail
To save they secret soul from nightly fears,
From Cambria's° curse, from Cambria's tears!'
Such were the sounds that o'er the crested pride°
10 Of the first Edward scattered wild dismay,
As down the steep of Snowdon's° shaggy side
He wound with toilsome march his long array.
Stout Gloucester° stood aghast in speechless trance;
'To arms!' cried Mortimer, and couched his quivering lance.

On a rock whose haughty brow
Frowns o'er old Conway's foaming flood,
Robed in the sable garb of woe,
With haggard° eyes the poet stood
(Loose his beard and hoary hair
20 Streamed, like a meteor, to the troubled air),°
And with a master's hand and prophet's fire
Struck the deep sorrows of his lyre:
'Hark, how each giant oak and desert cave
Sighs to the torrent's awful voice beneath!
O'er thee, O King! their hundred arms they wave,
Revenge on thee in hoarser murmurs breathe;
Vocal no more, since Cambria's fatal day,
To high-born Hoel's harp, or soft Llewellyn's lay.°

'Cold is Cadwallo's tongue,
30 That hushed the stormy main;
Brave Urien sleeps upon his craggy bed;
Mountains, ye mourn in vain
Modred, whose magic song

Confusion . . . wait Cf. Shakespeare, *King John* IV.iii.152, 154: "vast confusion waits / . . . The imminent decay of wrested pomp."
They mock . . . state Cf. *King John* V.i.72: "Mocking the air with colours idly spread"; "idle" also implying that the "state" is barren or foredoomed.
hauberk's coat of chain-mail
Cambria's Wales's
crested pride Gray cites "The crested adder's pride" from Dryden, *The Indian Queen* III.i.
Snowdon's the Welsh mountain, known for its eagles (cf. l. 38)
Gloucester like Mortimer one of the border lords who have joined Edward's forces
haggard "a metaphor taken from an unreclaimed hawk, which is called a haggard, and looks wild and *farouche* and jealous of its liberty" (Gray)
Loose . . . air "The image was taken from a well-known picture of Raphael representing the Supreme Being in the vision of Ezekiel" (Gray); "or (if you have been at Parma) you may remember Moses breaking the tables by . . . Parmigianino, which comes still closer to my meaning" (Gray); cf. also Milton, *Paradise Lost* I.537: "Shone like a meteor streaming to the wind."
Hoel's . . . Llewellyn's lay imaginary bards with actual Welsh names, as are those named in the next stanza

Made huge Plinlimmon° bow his cloud-topped head.
On dreary Arvon's° shore they lie,
Smeared with gore, and ghastly pale;
Far, far aloof the affrighted ravens sail;
The famished eagle screams, and passes by.
Dear lost companions of my tuneful art,
40 Dear as the light that visits these sad eyes,
Dear as the ruddy drops that warm my heart,
Ye died amidst your dying country's cries—
No more I weep. They do not sleep.
   On yonder cliffs, a grisly band,
I see them sit; they linger yet,
Avengers of their native land;
With me in dreadful harmony they join,
And weave with bloody hands the tissue of thy line.

' "Weave the warp, and weave the woof,
50 The winding-sheet of Edward's race.°
Give ample room, and verge enough
The characters° of hell to trace.
Mark the year, and mark the night,
When Severn shall re-echo with affright
The shrieks of death through Berkeley's roofs that ring,
Shrieks of an agonizing king!°
She-wolf of France, with unrelenting fangs,
That tearest the bowels of thy mangled mate,
From thee be born, who o'er thy country hangs,
60 The scourge of heaven.° What Terrors round him wait!
Amazement in his van, with Flight combined,
And Sorrow's faded form, and Solitude behind.

' "Mighty victor, mighty lord,
Low on his funeral couch he lies!
No pitying heart, no eye, afford
A tear to grace his obsequies.°
Is the Sable Warrior° fled?
Thy son is gone. He rests among the dead.
The swarm that in thy noontide beam were born?
70 Gone to salute the rising morn.
Fair laughs the morn, and soft the zephyr blows,°

Plinlimmon a high mountain between Cardigan and Glamorgan
Arvon's Caernarvonshire in North Wales
Weave . . . Edward's race "The image is taken from an ancient Scaldic Ode, written in the Old Norwegian tongue about A.D. 1029" (Gray); "the winding-sheet" used to wrap the buried corpse
characters figures, marks
Shrieks . . . king Edward II was painfully killed in Berkeley Castle beside the river Severn (1327) at the instigation of Isabel of Anjou, his adulterous wife.

The scourge of heaven Edward III (1312–77), who conquered much of France
his obsequies death of Edward III, "abandoned by his children and even robbed in his last moments by his courtiers and his mistress" (Gray)
Sable Warrior "Edward, the Black Prince, dead some time before his father" (Gray); the famous victor at Crécy and Poitiers
Fair laughs . . . blows "magnificence of Richard II's reign" (Gray)

While proudly riding o'er the azure realm
In gallant trim the gilded vessel goes;
Youth on the prow, and Pleasure at the helm;
Regardless of the sweeping whirlwind's sway,
That, hushed in grim repose, expects his evening prey.

' "Fill high the sparkling bowl,
The rich repast prepare;
Reft of a crown, he yet may share the feast;
80   Close by the regal chair
Fell Thirst and Famine scowl
A baleful smile upon their baffled guest.°
Heard ye the din of battle° bray,
Lance to lance, and horse to horse?
Long years of havoc urge their destined course,
And through the kindred squadrons mow their way.
Ye towers of Julius, London's lasting shame,°
With many a foul and midnight murther fed,
Revere his consort's faith, his father's fame,
90   And spare the meek usurper's holy head.°
Above, below, the rose of snow,
Twined with her blushing foe, we spread;°
The bristled boar° in infant gore
Wallows beneath the thorny shade.
Now, brothers, bending o'er the accursèd loom,
Stamp we our vengeance deep, and ratify his doom.

' "Edward, lo! to sudden fate
(Weave we the woof: the thread is spun)
Half of thy heart° we consecrate.
100   (The web is wove. The work is done.)"
Stay, oh stay! nor thus forlorn
Leave me unblessed, unpitied, here to mourn:
In yon bright track that fires the western skies,
They melt, they vanish from my eyes.
But oh! what solemn scenes on Snowdon's height,
Descending slow, their glittering skirts° unroll?

baffled guest Richard II was starved to death (1400), according to one historian: served in a royal manner but prevented from eating anything set before him.
din of battle "ruinous civil wars of York and Lancaster" (Gray); the Wars of the Roses
Ye towers . . . shame Henry VI, Edward V, and others of the royal family "believed to be murthered secretly in the Tower of London. The oldest part of that structure is vulgarly attributed to Julius Caesar" (Gray).
the meek . . . head Henry VI "very near being canonized"; his consort "Margaret of Anjou, a woman of heroic spirit, who struggled hard to save her husband and her crown"; her father Henry V, the great victor at Agincourt. Henry VI is called a "usurper" because "the line of Lancaster had no right of inheritance to the crown" (Gray).

Above, below . . . spread "The white and red roses of York and Lancaster" (Gray)
bristled boar Richard III, whose badge was a silver boar, and who wallowed in the blood of his nephews, the infant princes, under the "thorny shade" of the roses—to be intertwined in the marriage of Henry VII (of the house of Lancaster) and Elizabeth of York. Henry VII defeated and killed Richard III at Bosworth Field in 1485.
Half of thy heart Edward I's wife Eleanor of Castile died a few years after the conquest of Wales and was deeply mourned by the king; here she is consecrated or devoted to doom.
skirts Cf. "cloudy skirts," William Collins, *Ode to Evening*, l. 6; the visions are imagined as descending clouds catching the sunset light.

Visions of glory, spare my aching sight;
Ye unborn ages, crowd not on my soul!
No more our long-lost Arthur° we bewail.
All hail, ye genuine kings, Britannia's issue, hail!

10

'Girt with many a baron bold
Sublime their starry fronts° they rear;
And gorgeous dames, and statesmen old
In bearded majesty, appear.
In the midst a form divine!°
Her eye proclaims her of the Briton line;
Her lion-port, her awe-commanding face,
Attempered sweet to virgin-grace.
What strings symphonious tremble in the air,
What strains of vocal transport round her play!
Hear from the grave, great Taliessin,° hear;
They breathe a soul to animate thy clay.
Bright Rapture calls, and soaring, as she sings,
Waves in the eye of Heaven her many-coloured wings.

20

'The verse adorn again
Fierce War, and faithful Love,°
And Truth severe, by fairy Fiction dressed.
In buskined° measures move
Pale Grief, and pleasing Pain,
With Horror, tyrant of the throbbing breast.
A voice, as of the cherub-choir,
Gales from blooming Eden bear;°
And distant warblings lessen on my ear,
That lost in long futurity° expire.
Fond° impious man, thinkest thou yon sanguine cloud,
Raised by thy breath, has quenched the orb of day?
Tomorrow he repairs the golden flood,°
And warms the nations with redoubled ray.
Enough for me: with joy I see
The different doom our Fates assign.
Be thine Despair, and sceptered Care;
To triumph,° and to die, are mine.'
He spoke, and headlong from the mountain's height
Deep in the roaring tide he plunged to endless night.

30

40

1755–57   1757

Arthur "It was the common belief of the Welsh nation that King Arthur was still alive in fairyland and should return again to reign over Britain" (Gray); Welsh rule is restored with the house of Tudor under Henry VII.
fronts brows
form divine Elizabeth I
Taliessin "chief of the bards, flourished in the 6th century" (Gray); here the revival of poetry
Fierce War . . . Love Gray cites Spenser, *The Faerie Queene*, Proem: "Fierce warres and faithfull loves shall moralize my song."

buskined wearing the tragic *cothurnus* or boot of the Greek theater; Shakespeare is implied
from . . . Eden bear Milton's *Paradise Lost*
lost . . . futurity "the succession of poets after Milton's time" (Gray)
Fond foolish; referring to Edward I, whose "sanguine" or crimson cloud of conquest conceals the sun
repairs . . . flood restores his flood of light
triumph in the ultimate restoration of liberty and the revival of poetry

On Lord Holland's Seat near Margate, Kent°

Old, and abandoned by each venal friend,
   Here Holland took the pious resolution
To smuggle some few years, and strive to mend
   A broken character and constitution.

On this congenial spot he fixed his choice,
   Earl Goodwin° trembled for his neighbouring sand;
Here seagulls scream and cormorants rejoice,
   And mariners, though shipwrecked, dread to land.

Here reign the blustering North and blighting East,
10   No tree is heard to whisper, bird to sing.
Yet Nature cannot furnish out the feast;
   Art he invokes new horrors still to bring.

Now mouldering fanes and battlements arise,
   Arches and turrets° nodding to their fall,
Unpeopled palaces delude his eyes,
   And mimic desolation covers all.

'Ah!' said the sighing peer, 'had Bute° been true,
   Nor Shelburne's, Rigby's, Calcraft's friendship vain,
Far other scenes than these had blessed our view,
20   And realized the ruins that we feign.

'Purged by the sword and beautified by fire,
   Then had we seen proud London's hated walls:
Owls might have hooted in St. Peter's choir,
   And foxes stunk and littered in St. Paul's.'°
1768   1769

On Lord . . . Kent Henry Fox (1705–74), 1st Lord Holland, became Paymaster General in 1757 and proceeded to amass a great fortune; as Leader of the House of Commons in Lord Bute's ministry he did much to promote the Peace of Paris (1763). Fox was widely mistrusted as an unscrupulous schemer and self-seeker who resorted to bribery and intimidation; this view emerged only some years after Horace Walpole could write Fox: "I know you think Mr. Gray the greatest poet we have and I know he thinks you the greatest man we have" (1756). Holland in retirement (because of poor health) built a classical villa surrounded by "many fanciful representations of antique and ruined buildings," ironically described by Walpole as resembling "a prospect in some half-civilized island discovered by Captain Cook." The poem was first published without Gray's permission as *Inscription for the Villa of a Decayed Statesman on the Sea Coast*, but Gray refused to allow its republication during his lifetime (or Holland's). It is one of the few sharply satiric poems Gray wrote, very much in the spirit of the age of Pope; it represents a gift that Gray did not sufficiently honor in himself.
Earl Goodwin Goodwin Sands, a dangerous sandbank off the Kent coast, was named for Earl Godwine of the 11th century; as the legendary remains of an island, they are threatened by the grasping presence of Holland.
fanes . . . turrets artificial ruins and fantastic "follies" (as such ornamental architecture, not meant to be lived in but for view, were called); cf. Timon's "laboured quarry" in Pope's *Epistle to Burlington*, ll. 99 ff.
Bute Fox had received a peerage as Baron Holland in 1763, but he claimed betrayal and quarreled over political spoils with the Prime Minister, Lord Bute, and other colleagues named in the next line; he was widely attacked as a "traitor" to England, particularly by the middle-class supporters of the elder Pitt in the City of London, and it is of their ruin that he regretfully dreams.
Owls . . . St. Paul's Cf. Isaiah 13:21: "But wild beasts of the desert shall lie there; and their houses shall be full of doleful creatures; and owls shall dwell there, and satyrs shall dance there"; also Pope, *Windsor Forest*, ll. 70–71: "The fox obscene to gaping tombs retired, / And savage howlings fill the sacred choirs"; with, finally, a play upon Fox's name in the last line ("St. Peter's" refers to Westminster Abbey).

CHRISTOPHER SMART
1722–1771

Smart's brilliant and erratic career at Cambridge ended with heavy debts and Thomas Gray's prophecy that he "must come to a jail or Bedlam, and that without help, almost without pity." Smart's facility in both Latin and English verse had led him to translate Pope's *Essay on Criticism* into Latin with the poet's blessing, and it took him to London with hopes of a literary career. He worked for the publisher John Newbery and married Newbery's stepdaughter in 1752. By then his *Poems on Several Occasions* had appeared, he had been editing the humorous journal *The Midwife* with great success, and he had made a wide range of literary acquaintance, including Johnson and Hogarth. In 1757 Smart was admitted to St. Luke's Hospital for the insane and discharged a year later uncured. He was probably confined somewhere else during the next seven years, and the *Jubilate Agno* was written during that time. Upon his release he wrote and published *A Song to David* (1763), but his reputation for madness affected the reception of much of his later work. This included a remarkable verse paraphrase of the Psalms, a verse translation of Horace (1767), and finally *Hymns for the Amusement of Children* (1770). He died the following year in debtor's prison.

Smart's religious poetry goes back at least to the poems written for the Seaton prize at Cambridge, which he won several times. One, published in 1751, has these images of the sea: "Shrubs of amber from the pearl-paved bottom / Rise richly varied, where the finny race / In blithe security their gambols play." His remarkable diction had biblical sources but took its example in part from Horace, whose "beauty, force, and vehemence of Impression" Smart saw as a "talent or gift of Almighty God by which a genius is impowered to throw an emphasis upon a word or sentence in such wise that it cannot escape any reader of sheer good sense or true critical sagacity."

Smart's diction is one part of his distinctive effect. Another is the mystical geometry of form in *A Song to David*, its stanzas ordered in patterns of threes, sevens, and nines; its variations a constant embellishment of an architectonic frame; its elements elaborately arranged in a celebrative procession one can associate with baroque ceremoniousness. For the poem seems to be a tribute to God as poet of the universe and to that responsive celebration which all creatures, instinct with spirit, pay to Him. Of these David as divine poet is at once the symbol and the highest example.

Jubilate Agno°

From *Fragment B1*

Let Elizure rejoice with the Partridge,° who is a prisoner of state and is proud of his keepers.

For I am not without authority in my jeopardy, which I derive inevitably from the glory of the name of the Lord.

Let Shedeur rejoice with Pyrausta,° who dwelleth in a medium of fire, which God hath adapted for him.

For I bless God whose name is Jealous—and there is a zeal to deliver us from everlasting burnings.

Let Shelumiel rejoice with Olor,° who is of a goodly savour, and the very look of him harmonizes the mind.

For my existimation° is good even amongst the slanderers and my memory shall arise for a sweet savour unto the Lord.

Let Jael rejoice with the Plover, who whistles for his live,° and foils the marksmen and their guns.

For I bless the PRINCE of PEACE and pray that all the guns may be nailed up, save such as are for the rejoicing days.

From *Fragment B2*

For I will consider my Cat Jeoffry.

For he is the servant of the Living God duly and daily serving him.

For at the first glance of the glory of God in the East he worships in his way.

700 For is this done by wreathing his body seven times round with elegant quickness.

For then he leaps up to catch the musk, which is the blessing of God upon his prayer.

For he rolls upon prank to work it in.

Jubilate Agno "Rejoice in the Lamb." This remarkable work was apparently written during Smart's period of madness, and its manuscript survived as an example of poetic mania, interest in it stimulated by the similar case of William Cowper. The poem was written in sections of lines beginning with either *Let* or *For,* and it was clearly based upon theories of the antiphonal or responsive structure of Hebrew poetry, particularly those set forth by Bishop Robert Lowth, who was known to Smart personally as well as through his *De Sacra Poesia Hebraeorum* (1753). Although the *Let* and *For* sections were physically separate, they are joined by connections often ingenious and oblique. The *Let* verses tend toward impersonality, and the *For* verses make some application to Smart's own feeling or state. In the sample given from Fragment B1, the *Let* and *For* verses are placed in alternation in order to show more clearly their relationship.

The second and longer section given, concerning Smart's cat Jeoffry, lacks the *Let* verses.
Partridge here caged
Pyrausta a winged insect said to dwell in the fire
Olor swan; connected with *olere,* to smell of or savor of
existimation from *existimare,* to esteem; hence, reputation
live life

For having done duty and received blessing he begins to consider himself.

For this he performs in ten degrees.

For first he looks upon his fore-paws to see if they are clean.

For secondly he kicks up behind to clear away there.

For thirdly he works it upon stretch with the fore-paws extended.

For fourthly he sharpens his paws by wood.

For fifthly he washes himself.

710   For sixthly he rolls upon wash.

For seventhly he fleas himself, that he may not be interrupted upon the beat.°

For eighthly he rubs himself against a post.

For ninthly he looks up for his instructions.

For tenthly he goes in quest of food.

For having considered God and himself he will consider his neighbour.

For if he meets another cat he will kiss her in kindness.

For when he takes his prey he plays with it to give it a chance.

For one mouse in seven escapes by his dallying.

For when his day's work is done his business more properly begins.

720   For he keeps the Lord's watch in the night against the adversary.

For he counteracts the powers of darkness by his electrical skin and glaring eyes.

For he counteracts the Devil, who is death, by brisking about the life.

For in his morning orisons he loves the sun and the sun loves him.

For he is of the tribe of Tiger.

For the Cherub Cat is a term of the Angel Tiger.

For he has the subtlety and hissing of a serpent, which in goodness he suppresses.

For he will not do destruction if he is well-fed, neither will he spit without provocation.

For he purrs in thankfulness, when God tells him he's a good Cat.

For he is an instrument for the children to learn benevolence upon.

730   For every house is incomplete without him and a blessing is lacking in the spirit.

For the Lord commanded Moses concerning the cats at the departure of the Children of Israel from Egypt.

that he may not . . . beat so that he need not
break off his activities to scratch

For every family had one cat at least in the bag.

For the English Cats are the best in Europe.

For he is the cleanest in the use of his fore-paws of any quadruped.

For the dexterity of his defence is an instance of the love of God to him exceedingly.

For he is the quickest to his mark of any creature.

For he is tenacious of his point.

For he is a mixture of gravity and waggery.

For he knows that God is his Saviour.

740   For there is nothing sweeter than his peace when at rest.

For there is nothing brisker than his life when in motion.

For he is of the Lord's poor and so indeed is he called by benevolence perpetually—Poor Jeoffry! poor Jeoffry! the rat has bit thy throat.

For I bless the name of the Lord Jesus that Jeoffry is better.

For the divine spirit comes about his body to sustain it in complete cat.

For his tongue is exceeding pure so that it has in purity what it wants in music.

For he is docile and can learn certain things.

For he can set up with gravity which is patience upon approbation.

For he can fetch and carry, which is patience in employment.

For he can jump over a stick which is patience upon proof positive.

750   For he can spraggle upon waggle at the word of command.

For he can jump from an eminence into his master's bosom.

For he can catch the cork and toss it again.

For he is hated by the hypocrite and miser.

For the former is afraid of detection.

For the latter refuses the charge.

For he camels his back to bear the first notion of business.

For he is good to think on, if a man would express himself neatly.

For he made a great figure in Egypt for his signal services.

For he killed the Icneumon-rat° very pernicious by land.

Icneumon-rat The icneumon is in fact regarded
as beneficial and kills rats and mice.

760 For his ears are so acute that they sting again.

For from this proceeds the passing quickness of his attention.

For by stroking of him I have found out electricity.

For I perceived God's light about him both wax and fire.

For the electrical fire is the spiritual substance, which God sends from heaven
   to sustain the bodies both of man and beast.

For God has blessed him in the variety of his movements.

For, though he cannot fly, he is an excellent clamberer.

For his motions upon the face of the earth are more than any other quadruped.

For he can tread to all the measures upon the music.

For he can swim for life.

770 For he can creep.

1756–63   1939

A Song to David

David the son of Jesse said, and the man who was raised up on high, the anointed
of the God of Jacob, and the sweet psalmist of Israel, said, 'The Spirit of the Lord
spake by me, and His word was in my tongue.'

II SAMUEL 23:1–2

O thou, that sittest upon a throne,°
With harp of high majestic tone,
   To praise the King of kings;
And voice of heaven-ascending swell,
Which, while its deeper notes excel,
   Clear as a clarion rings:

To bless each valley, grove, and coast,
And charm the cherubs to the post
   Of gratitude in throngs;
10 To keep the days on Zion's mount,
And send the year to his account,
   With dances and with songs;

O Servant of God's holiest charge,
The minister of praise at large,
   Which thou mayst now receive;
From thy blessed mansion hail and hear,
From topmost eminence appear
   To this the wreath I weave.

O thou . . . throne The first three stanzas provide an incantation, and within them we can
see Smart's play with implicit antithesis: David
sits on a royal throne but pays humble praise
as Psalmist (1–3); his voice excels in "deeper

note" but sounds "clear as a clarion" (4–6); he
blesses the earth but charms cherubs from
heaven (7–9); he pays praise and receives it in
turn (13–15); etc.

Great, valiant, pious, good, and clean,
20 Sublime, contemplative, serene,
      Strong, constant, pleasant, wise!
Bright effluence of exceeding grace;
Best man!—the swiftness and the race,
      The peril and the prize!

Great—from the lustre of his crown,
From Samuel's horn° and God's renown,
      Which is the people's voice;
For all the host, from rear to van,
Applauded and embraced the man—
30   The man of God's own choice.

Valiant—the word and up he rose—
The fight—he triumphed o'er the foes
      Whom God's just laws abhor;
And armed in gallant faith he took
Against the boaster, from the brook,
      The weapons of the war.°

Pious—magnificent and grand;
'Twas he the famous temple planned:°
      (The seraph in his soul)
40 Foremost to give his Lord his dues,
Foremost to bless the welcome news,
      And foremost to condole.

Good—from Jehudah's° genuine vein,
From God's best nature good in grain,°
      His aspect and his heart;
To pity, to forgive, to save:
Witness En-gedi's conscious cave,°
      And Shimei's blunted dart.°

Clean—if perpetual prayer be pure,
50 And love, which could itself inure
      To fasting and to fear—
Clean in his gestures, hands, and feet,
To smite the lyre, the dance complete,
      To play the sword and spear.

Samuel's horn "Then Samuel took the horn of oil, and anointed him in the midst of his brethren: and the Spirit of the Lord came upon David from that day forward" (I Samuel 16:13).
weapons of the war Taking "five smooth stones from out the brook" for his sling, David kills the Philistine champion and "boaster" Goliath (I Samuel 17:40).
the famous . . . planned While David had it in his heart to build the temple, the Lord reserved this task ("because thou hast been a man of war, and hast shed blood") for his son Solomon. David proceeded "to bless the welcome news" and give to Solomon "the pattern of all that he had by the Spirit" (cf. the

"Seraph in the soul"). "All this, said David, the Lord made me understand in writing by his hand upon me, even all the works of this pattern" (I Chronicles 28:1–19).
Jehudah's i.e. Judah, the tribe to which David belonged
good in grain good through and through
En-gedi's . . . cave where David spared the life of Saul, who was pursuing him. And Saul said to David, "Thou art more righteous than I: for thou hast rewarded me good, whereas I have rewarded thee evil" (I Samuel 24:17).
Shimei's . . . dart Shimei, "of the family of the house of Saul," stoned and cursed David but was later forgiven (II Samuel 16:5–14; 19:16–23).

Sublime—invention ever young,
Of vast conception, towering tongue,
   To God the eternal theme;
Notes from yon exaltations caught,
Unrivaled royalty of thought,
60   O'er meaner strains supreme.

Contemplative—on God to fix
His musings, and above the six
   The sabbath day he blessed;
'Twas then his thoughts self-conquest pruned,
And heavenly melancholy tuned,
   To bless and bear the rest.

Serene—to sow the seeds of peace,
Remembering, when he watched the fleece,
   How sweetly Kidron° purled—
70 To further knowledge, silence vice,
And plant perpetual paradise
   When God had calmed the world.

Strong—in the Lord, who could defy
Satan, and all his powers that lie
   In sempiternal night;
And hell and horror and despair
Were as the lion and the bear°
   To his undaunted might.

Constant—in love to God the Truth,
80 Age, manhood, infancy, and youth—
   To Jonathan his friend
Constant, beyond the verge of death;
And Ziba and Mephibosheth
   His endless fame attend.°

Pleasant—and various as the year;
Man, soul, and angel, without peer,
   Priest, champion, sage, and boy;
In armour, or in ephod° clad,
His pomp, his piety was glad;
90   Majestic was his joy.

Kidron a brook near Jerusalem, over which David passed in his flight from his rebellious son Absalom (II Samuel 15:23); here associated with his youth as a shepherd and (probably) with Ezekiel's messianic vision of a river flowing from the altar of the temple which will fertilize the desolate land until it "become like the garden of Eden" (Ezekiel 47:1–12; 35:35)
the lion and the bear When Saul fears for David's weakness and youth, David recounts his rescue of his sheep from a lion and a bear, and concludes, "The Lord that delivered me out of the paw of the lion, and out of the paw of the bear, will deliver me out of the hand of this Philistine" (I Samuel 17:37).
To Jonathan . . . attend David restored the land of Saul to Mephibosheth, the son of Jonathan and grandson of Saul, and he made Ziba, Saul's former servant, steward (II Samuel 9).
ephod the priest's vestment, worn by David when he brought the ark of the Lord into Jerusalem and "danced before the Lord with all his might" (II Samuel 6:14)

Wise—in recovery from his fall,°
Whence rose his eminence o'er all,
   Of all the most reviled;
The light of Israel in his ways,
Wise are his precepts, prayer, and praise,
   And counsel to his child.

His Muse, bright angel of his verse,
Gives balm for all the thorns that pierce,
   For all the pangs that rage;
100 Blessed light, still gaining on the gloom,
The more than Michal of his bloom,
   The Abishag° of his age.

He sung of God—the mighty source
Of all things—the stupendous force
   On which all strength depends;
From whose right arm, beneath whose eyes,
All period, power, and enterprise
   Commences, reigns, and ends.

Angels—their ministry and meed,°
110 Which to and fro with blessings speed,
   Or with their citterns° wait;
Where Michael° with his millions bows,
Where dwells the seraph and his spouse,
   The cherub° and her mate.

Of man—the semblance° and effect
Of God and love, the saint elect
   For infinite applause—
To rule the land and briny broad,
To be laborious in his laud,
120   And heroes in his cause.

The world—the clustering spheres° he made,
The glorious light, the soothing shade,
   Dale, champaign, grove, and hill;
The multitudinous abyss,°
Where secrecy remains in bliss,
   And wisdom hides her skill.

---

his fall the stratagem for bringing death to Uriah the Hittite once his wife Bathsheba began to bear David's child (II Samuel 11–12). Smart, following Patrick Delany's *Historical Account of David* (1740–42), takes some of Proverbs as "David's instructions to his son Solomon."
Michal . . . Abishag Michal was David's first wife and Abishag the virgin brought to warm him in old age (I Kings 1–4); both are surpassed by his Muse, the inspirer of the Psalms.
meed gift
citterns stringed instruments

Michael the archangel regarded as patron and guardian of the Hebrews; and later as the leader with his angels of the fight against the dragon (Revelation 12:7); here shown in service or humility
seraph . . . cherub the highest orders of angels
semblance i.e. made in God's image, to praise (l. 119) and serve (l. 120) Him
clustering spheres the concentric spheres of the heavenly bodies
abyss presumably Chaos, or the "deep" of Genesis 1.2, wherein reside the materials not yet given form

Trees, plants, and flowers—of virtuous° root;
Gem° yielding blossom, yielding fruit,
   Choice gums and precious balm;
130 Bless ye the nosegay in the vale,
And with the sweeteners of the gale°
   Enrich the thankful psalm.

Of fowl—e'en every beak and wing
Which cheer the winter, hail the spring,
   That live in peace or prey;
They that make music or that mock,
The quail, the brave domestic cock,
   The raven, swan, and jay.

Of fishes—every size and shape
140 Which nature frames of light escape,
   Devouring man to shun;
The shells are in the wealthy deep,
The shoals° upon the surface leap,
   And love the glancing sun.

Of beasts—the beaver plods his task;
While the sleek tigers roll and bask,
   Nor yet the shades arouse;°
Her cave the mining coney° scoops;
Where o'er the mead the mountain stoops°
150   The kids exult and browse.

Of gems—their virtue and their price,
Which hid in earth from man's device,°
   Their darts of lustre sheathe:
The jasper of the master's stamp,°
The topaz blazing like a lamp
   Among the mines beneath.

Blessed was the tenderness he felt
When to his graceful harp he knelt,
   And did for audience call;
160 When Satan with his hand he quelled,
And in serene suspense he held
   The frantic throes of Saul.°

His furious foes no more maligned
As he such melody divined,°

virtuous medicinal, beneficial
gem bud
gale breeze
shoals schools (of fish)
arouse make terrible
coney rabbit
stoops leans, hangs

device contrivance, design
stamp signet
Saul from whom David drove an "evil spirit"
("Satan") by playing on his harp (I Samuel
16:23)
divined discovered

And sense and soul detained;
Now striking strong, now soothing soft,
He sent the godly sounds aloft,
    Or in delight refrained.

When up to heaven his thoughts he piled,
170 From fervent lips fair Michal° smiled,
    As blush to blush she stood,
And chose herself the queen, and gave
Her utmost from her heart, 'so brave,
    And plays his hymns so good.'

The pillars of the Lord are seven,°
Which stand from earth to topmost heaven;
    His wisdom drew the plan;
His Word accomplished the design,
From brightest gem to deepest mine,
180   From Christ enthroned to man.

Alpha,° the cause of causes, first
In station, fountain, whence the burst
    Of light, and blaze of day;
Whence bold attempt and brave advance
Have motion, life, and ordinance,
    And heaven itself its stay.

Gamma supports the glorious arch
On which angelic legions march,
    And is with sapphires paved;
190 Thence the fleet clouds are sent adrift,
And thence the painted folds, that lift
    The crimson veil, are waved.°

Eta with living sculpture breathes,
With verdant carvings, flowery wreaths
    Of never-wasting bloom;
In strong relief his goodly base
All instruments of labor grace,
    The trowel, spade, and loom.

Next Theta stands to the Supreme—
200 Who formed, in number, sign,° and scheme,
    The illustrious lights that are;

fair **Michal** For her love of David, see I Samuel 18:18–20 (her words are Smart's invention). **The pillars . . . seven** "Wisdom hath builded her house; she hath hewn out her seven pillars" (Proverbs 9:1). Smart fuses these seven pillars (through their carvings) with the seven days of Creation; further implications may be drawn from Masonic symbolism, which is based upon the building of Solomon's temple. The scale of Creation is presented in terms that recall the traditional Great Chain of Being, in which all of God's works are ranged continuously from highest to lowest. **Alpha** God in the creative form of the Son or Word (John 1:1). Here, as in the following stanzas, Smart uses letters of the Greek alphabet, from Alpha (the first) to Omega (the last). **painted folds . . . waved** presumably the clouds that, brilliantly colored ("painted"), reveal the rising sun, like curtains raised or folded back **sign** division of the zodiac; constellation

And one addressed° his saffron robe,
And one, clad in a silver globe,°
   Held rule with every star.

Iota's tuned to choral hymns
Of those that fly, while he that swims
   In thankful safety lurks;
And foot, and chapiter,° and niche,
The various histories enrich
210   Of God's recorded works.

Sigma presents the social droves,
With him that solitary roves,
   And man of all the chief;
Fair on whose face, and stately frame,
Did God impress his hallowed name,
   For ocular belief.

Omega! Greatest and the Best,
Stands sacred to the day of rest,
   For gratitude and thought;
220 Which blessed the world upon his pole,
And gave the universe his goal,
   And closed the infernal draught.°

O David, scholar of the Lord!
Such is thy science, whence reward
   And infinite degree;°
O strength, O sweetness, lasting ripe!
God's harp thy symbol, and thy type°
   The lion and the bee!

There is but One who ne'er rebelled,
230 But One by passion unimpelled,
   By pleasures unenticed;
He from himself his semblance sent,°
Grand object of his own content,
   And saw the God in Christ.

'Tell them I am,' Jehovah said
To Moses; while earth heard in dread,°
   And smitten to the heart,
At once above, beneath, around,
All nature, without voice or sound,
240   Replied, 'O Lord, Thou art.'

one addressed i.e. the sun clad in
one . . . silver globe the moon
chapiter capital of a pillar
draught i.e. closed off the drain of Hell
degree rank, ascent in divine favor
type symbol or emblem, i.e. strength and sweetness, as in the riddle of Samson (who found

honey in the carcass of a lion: "Out of the
strong came forth sweetness," Judges 14:14)
his semblance sent God's creation of the Son
earth . . . dread "And God said unto Moses,
I AM THAT I AM" (Exodus 3:14). The following stanzas embody versions of most of the
Ten Commandments.

Thou art—to give and to confirm
For each his talent and his term;
   All flesh thy bounties share.
Thou shalt not call thy brother fool;°
The porches of the Christian school°
   Are meekness, peace, and prayer.

Open, and naked of offence,
Man's made of mercy, soul, and sense;
   God armed the snail and wilk;°
250 Be good to him that pulls thy plough;
Due food and care, due rest, allow
   For her that yields thee milk.

Rise up before the hoary head,
And God's benign commandment dread,
   Which says thou shalt not die:
'Not as I will, but as thou wilt,'°
Prayed He whose conscience knew no guilt;
   With whose blessed pattern vie.

Use all thy passions!—love is thine,
260 And joy, and jealousy° divine,
   Thine hope's eternal fort;
And care thy leisure to disturb,
With fear concupiscence to curb,
   And rapture to transport.

Act simply, as occasion asks;
Put mellow wine in seasoned casks,
   Till not with ass and bull.
Remember thy baptismal bond;
Keep from commixtures foul and fond,
270   Nor work thy flax with wool.

Distribute: pay the Lord his tithe,
And make the widow's heartstrings blithe;
   Resort° with those that weep;
As you from all and each expect,
For all and each thy love direct,
   And render as you reap.

The slander and its bearer spurn,
And propagating praise sojourn

Thou shalt . . . fool "But I say unto you, that whosoever is angry with his brother without a cause shall be in danger of the judgment . . . but whosoever shall say, Thou fool, shall be in danger of hell fire" (Matthew 5:22).
porches . . . school as opposed to the Stoa of the Greeks; cf. St. Paul's encounter with the Stoics and his preaching at the Areopagus (Acts 17:16–34)

wilk whelk (a shellfish)
Not as I . . . wilt the words of Christ, Matthew 26:39
jealousy zeal; cf. St. Paul: "For I am jealous over you with godly jealousy: for I have espoused you to one husband, that I may present you as a chaste virgin to Christ" (II Corinthians 11:2)
Resort consort

To make thy welcome last;
280 Turn from old Adam to the New;°
By hope futurity pursue;
    Look upwards to the past.

Control thine eye, salute success,
Honour the wiser, happier bless,
    And for thy neighbour feel;
Grutch not of Mammon and his leaven,°
Work emulation up to heaven
    By knowledge and by zeal.

O David, highest in the list
290 Of worthies, on God's ways insist,
    The genuine word repeat:°
Vain are the documents of men,
And vain the flourish of the pen
    That keeps the fool's conceit.

Praise above all—for praise prevails;
Heap up the measure, load the scales,
    And good to goodness add.
The generous soul her Saviour aids,
But peevish obloquy degrades;
300   The Lord is great and glad.

For Adoration all the ranks
Of angels yield eternal thanks,
    And David in the midst;
With God's good poor, which, last and least
In man's esteem, thou to thy feast,
    O blessed bridegroom, bidst.°

For Adoration seasons change,
And order, truth, and beauty range,
    Adjust, attract, and fill:
310 The grass the polyanthus checks;°
And polished porphyry reflects,
    By the descending rill.

Rich almonds colour to the prime
For Adoration; tendrils climb,
    And fruit trees pledge their gems;
And Ivis° with her gorgeous vest
Builds for her eggs her cunning nest,
    And bellflowers bow their stems.

New the New Adam or Christ, who redeems what the Old Adam lost (1 Corinthians 15:22, 45)
Grutch not . . . leaven i.e. do not envy the rich man his gains; a version of the last of the Commandments, "Thou shalt not covet thy neighbour's house . . ." (Exodus 20:17).
genuine . . . repeat "Psalm 119" (Smart)

O blessed . . . bidst "And the Spirit and the bride say, Come . . . And let him that is athirst come. And whosoever will, let him take the water of life freely" (Revelation 22:17).
the polyanthus checks i.e. the polyanthus variegates or decorates
Ivis "hummingbird" (Smart)

With vinous syrup° cedars spout;
320 From rocks pure honey gushing out,°
　　For Adoration springs.
All scenes of painting crowd the map
Of nature; to the mermaid's pap
　　The scalèd infant clings.

The spotted ounce and playsome cubs
Run rustling 'mongst the flowering shrubs,
　　And lizards feed° the moss;
For Adoration beasts embark,°
While waves upholding halcyon's ark
330 　　No longer roar and toss.

While Israel sits beneath his fig,°
With coral root and amber sprig
　　The weaned adventurer° sports;
Where to the palm the jasmine cleaves,
For Adoration 'mongst the leaves
　　The gale his peace reports.

Increasing days their reign exalt,
Nor in the pink and mottled vault
　　The opposing spirits tilt;°
340 And, by the coasting reader° spied,
The silverlings and crusions° glide
　　For Adoration gilt.

For Adoration ripening canes
And cocoa's purest milk detains
　　The western pilgrim's staff;
Where rain in clasping boughs inclosed,
And vines with oranges disposed,
　　Embower the social laugh.

Now labour his reward receives,
350 For Adoration counts his sheaves
　　To peace, her bounteous prince;
The nectarine his strong tint imbibes,
And apples of ten thousand tribes,
　　And quick° peculiar quince.

---

syrup sap
From rocks . . . out "And with honey out of
the rock should I have satisfied thee" (Psalms
81:16)
feed feed upon
beasts embark "There is a large quadruped
that preys upon fish and provides himself with
a large piece of timber for that purpose, with
which he is very handy" (Smart); but the halcyon was believed to build its nest ("ark")
upon the sea and may in turn recall Noah's ark
and its assemblage of beasts

fig fig tree: "But they shall sit every man
under his vine and under his fig tree; and none
shall make them afraid" (Micah 4:4)
weaned adventurer small child
spirits tilt winds or storm clouds rise in conflict
coasting reader someone drifting in a boat while
reading
silverlings and crusions tarpons and carp-like
fish
quick pungent

The wealthy crops of whitening rice,
'Mongst thyine° woods and groves of spice,
    For Adoration grow;
And, marshalled in the fencèd land,
The peaches and pomegranates stand,
50   Where wild carnations blow.

The laurels with the winter strive;
The crocus burnishes alive
    Upon the snow-clad earth,
For Adoration myrtles stay
To keep the garden from dismay,
    And bless the sight from dearth.

The pheasant shows his pompous neck;
And ermine, jealous of a speck,
    With fear eludes offence;
70 The sable, with his glossy pride,
For Adoration is descried,
    Where frosts the wave condense.°

The cheerful holly, pensive yew,
And holy thorn,° their trim renew;
    The squirrel hoards his nuts;
All creatures batten o'er their stores,
And careful nature all her doors
    For Adoration shuts.

For Adoration, David's psalms
80 Lift up the heart to deeds of alms;
    And he who kneels and chants
Prevails his passions to control,
Finds meat and medicine to the soul,
    Which for translation° pants.

For Adoration, beyond match,
The scholar bullfinch° aims to catch
    The soft flute's ivory touch;
And, careless on the hazel spray,
The daring redbreast keeps at bay
90   The damsel's greedy clutch.

For Adoration, in the skies,
The Lord's philosopher espies
    The Dog, the Ram, and Rose;
The planet's ring, Orion's sword;
Nor is his greatness less adored
    In the vile worm° that glows.

thyine scented
condense congeal
holy thorn the hawthorn associated with Christ
and with St. Joseph of Arimathea

translation removal to heaven
scholar bullfinch the bird, taught to imitate a
whistled tune
the vile worm i.e. the glowworm or firefly

For Adoration on the strings°
The western breezes work their wings,
   The captive ear to soothe.
400 Hark! 'tis a voice°—how still and small—
That makes the cataracts to fall,
   Or bids the sea be smooth.

For Adoration, incense comes
From bezoar° and Arabian gums,
   And on the civet's fur.
But as for prayer, or ere it faints,°
Far better is the breath of saints
   Than galbanum° and myrrh.

For Adoration, from the down
410 Of damsons° to the anana's° crown,
   God sends to tempt the taste;
And while the luscious zest invites
The sense, that in the scene delights,
   Commands desire be chaste.

For Adoration, all the paths
Of grace are open, all the baths
   Of purity refresh;
And all the rays of glory beam
To deck the man of God's esteem,
420   Who triumphs o'er the flesh.

For Adoration, in the dome
Of Christ the sparrows find an home,°
   And on his olives perch;
The swallow also dwells with thee,
O man of God's humility,
   Within his saviour Church.

Sweet is the dew that falls betimes,
And drops upon the leafy limes;
   Sweet Hermon's° fragrant air;
430 Sweet is the lily's silver bell,
And sweet the wakeful tapers smell
   That watch for early prayer.

Sweet the young nurse with love intense,
Which smiles o'er sleeping innocence;

---

strings "Aeolian harp" (Smart), played on by
the wind as it hangs in a tree
voice the "still small voice" of God (I Kings
19:12)
bezoar substance found in the stomachs of cows
faints fades
galbanum an aromatic gum used in making
perfume

damsons plums
anana's pineapple's
the sparrows . . . home "Yea, the sparrow
hath found an house, and the swallow a nest for
herself . . . even thine altars, O Lord of hosts"
(Psalms 84:3)
Hermon's a Syrian mountain mentioned in
Psalms 133

Sweet when the lost arrive;
Sweet the musician's ardour beats,
　　While his vague mind's in quest of sweets,
　　　　The choicest flowers to hive.

Sweeter in all the strains of love,
440　The language of thy turtle dove,
　　　　Paired to thy swelling chord;
Sweeter with every grace endued,
The glory of thy gratitude,
　　　　Respired unto the Lord.

Strong is the horse upon his speed;
Strong in pursuit the rapid glede,°
　　　　Which makes at once his game;
Strong the tall ostrich on the ground;
Strong through the turbulent profound
450　　　Shoots xiphias° to his aim.

Strong is the lion—like a coal
His eyeball—like a bastion's mole°
　　　　His chest against the foes;
Strong, the gier-eagle° on his sail,
Strong against tide, the enormous whale
　　　　Emerges as he goes.

But stronger still, in earth and air,
And in the sea, the man of prayer;
　　　　And far beneath the tide;
460　And in the seat to faith assigned,
Where ask is have, where seek is find,
　　　　Where knock is open wide.°

Beauteous the fleet before the gale;
Beauteous the multitudes in mail,
　　　　Ranked arms and crested heads;
Beauteous the garden's umbrage mild,
Walk, water, meditated wild,°
　　　　And all the gloomy beds.

Beauteous the moon full on the lawn;
470　And beauteous, when the veil's withdrawn,
　　　　The virgin to her spouse;
Beauteous the temple decked and filled,
When to the heaven of heavens they build
　　　　Their heart-directed vows.

glede hawk
xiphias "the swordfish" (Smart)
mole heavy wall
gier-eagle vulture

Where knock . . . wide "Ask, and it shall be
given you; seek, and ye shall find; knock, and
it shall be opened unto you" (Matthew 7:7)
meditated wild planned, artificial

Beauteous, yea beauteous more than these,
The shepherd king upon his knees,
   For his momentous trust;
With wish of infinite conceit,°
For man, beast, mute,° the small and great,
480   And prostrate dust to dust.

Precious the bounteous widow's mite;°
And precious, for extreme delight,
   The largess from the churl;°
Precious the ruby's blushing blaze,
And alba's blessed imperial rays,°
   And pure cerulean pearl.

Precious the penitential tear;
And precious is the sigh sincere,
   Acceptable to God;
490 And precious are the winning flowers,
In gladsome Israel's feast of bowers,
   Bound on the hallowed sod.°

More precious that diviner part
Of David, even the Lord's own heart,°
   Great, beautiful, and new;
In all things where it was intent,
In all extremes, in each event,
   Proof—answering true to true.

Glorious the sun in mid-career;
500 Glorious the assembled fires° appear;
   Glorious the comet's train;
Glorious the trumpet and alarm;
Glorious the almighty stretched-out arm;
   Glorious the enraptured main;

Glorious the northern lights astream;
Glorious the song, when God's the theme;
   Glorious the thunder's roar;
Glorious hosanna from the den;°
Glorious the catholic° amen;
510   Glorious the martyr's gore;

---

conceit conception
mute fish
bounteous . . . mite Cf. Mark 12:42–5, where
Jesus esteems the widow's contribution of a
farthing as "more" than all that was given out
of abundance.
churl a reference, as Smart notes, to Nabel, who
is "churlish and evil in his doings" (I Samuel
25)
alba's . . . rays the "white stone" of Revelation 2:17

Bound on . . . sod Cf. the "feast of taber-
nacles" (Leviticus 23:34–44).
the Lord's . . . heart "I have found David
. . . a man after mine own heart, which shall
fufil all my will" (Acts 13:22)
assembled fires stars
den the lion's den where Daniel was preserved
because of his faith (Daniel 6:22–23)
catholic universal

Glorious—more glorious is the crown
Of Him that brought salvation down
   By meekness, called thy Son;
Thou at stupendous truth believed,
And now the matchless deed's achieved,
   Determined, Dared, and Done.

                    1763

OLIVER GOLDSMITH
1730?–1774

The contrast between Goldsmith's writings and his person was so great that some were tempted to call him an "inspired idiot." He was as versatile and accomplished a writer as any of his age, if neither the deepest nor the most imaginative; but he was so eager to claim attention in society, so envious of the praise of others, so "greedy and impatient to speak" (as Reynolds put it) that he would hold the floor with nothing to say and with little skill in making the emptiness diverting. His early life in Ireland, as the son of an Anglican curate, was not such as to assure him of either cultivation or learning; his career at Trinity College, Dublin, was often one of self-display and of dissipation. He turned successively to divinity, law, and medicine, pursuing the last at Edinburgh and Leyden, and ending with a ramble through Europe in 1755. In England he soon abandoned the practice of medicine and supported himself by writing. The range and level of his accomplishment were impressive: the essays in *The Bee* (1759); the satiric letters of a Chinese visitor to England later collected as *The Citizen of the World* (1762); the *Life* of Beau Nash of Bath (1762); a fine novel, *The Vicar of Wakefield* (1766); two plays, one of which (*She Stoops to Conquer*, 1773) is still performed with great success; and two major poems, *The Traveler* (1765) and *The Deserted Village* (1770). As Dr. Johnson exclaimed "with great dignity" at Reynolds's table, "If nobody was suffered to abuse poor Goldy but those who could write as well, he would have few censors."

Whatever the self-defeating forces revealed in his personal manner, Goldsmith could write with singular ease and charm, with elegant irony as well as pathos. *The Deserted Village* is perhaps his most careful composition, and its broad appeal may be taken as an implicit reply to those tendencies Goldsmith had deplored in his age: the "affected obscurity" of Gray's odes, the "tuneless flow of our blank verse, the pompous epithet, laboured diction, and every other deviation from common sense which procures the poet the applause of the month."

The Deserted Village

Sweet Auburn, loveliest village of the plain,
Where health and plenty cheered the labouring swain,
Where smiling spring its earliest visit paid,
And parting summer's lingering blooms delayed;
Dear lovely bowers of innocence and ease,

Seats of my youth, when every sport could please,
How often have I loitered o'er thy green,
Where humble happiness endeared each scene;
How often have I paused on every charm,
10   The sheltered cot,° the cultivated farm,
The never-failing brook, the busy mill,
The decent° church that topped the neighbouring hill,
The hawthorn bush, with seats beneath the shade,
For talking age and whispering lovers made.
How often have I blessed the coming day,
When toil remitting lent its turn to play,
And all the village train, from labour free,
Led up their sports beneath the spreading tree,
While many a pastime circled in the shade,
20   The young contending as the old surveyed;
And many a gambol frolicked o'er the ground,
And sleights of art and feats of strength went round;
And still, as each repeated pleasure tired,
Succeeding sports the mirthful band inspired;
The dancing pair that simply° sought renown,
By holding out to tire each other down;
The swain mistrustless of his smutted face,
While secret laughter tittered round the place;
The bashful virgin's sidelong looks of love,
30   The matron's glance that would those looks reprove:
These were thy charms, sweet village; sports like these,
With sweet succession, taught even toil to please;
These round thy bowers their cheerful influence shed;
These were thy charms—but all these charms are fled.
    Sweet smiling village, loveliest of the lawn,°
Thy sports are fled and all thy charms withdrawn;
Amidst thy bowers the tyrant's hand is seen,
And desolation saddens all thy green;
One only master grasps the whole domain,°
40   And half a tillage° stints thy smiling plain;
No more thy glassy brook reflects the day,
But choked with sedges works its weedy way;
Along thy glades, a solitary guest,
The hollow-sounding bittern guards its nest;
Amidst thy desert walks the lapwing flies,
And tires their echoes with unvaried cries.
Sunk are thy bowers in shapeless ruin all,
And the long grass o'ertops the mouldering wall;

cot cottage
decent becoming, suitable, seemly
simply naïvely, artlessly
lawn plain
One . . . domain Enclosure acts passed in the
18th century permitted the lord of the manor
to enclose the "common" land, forcing the

small farmers to emigrate to cities or colonies;
in his essay "The Revolution in Low Life"
(1762) Goldsmith describes such an enclosure
made for the sake of a pleasure seat for the
landlord, thus introducing the related theme of
luxury.
half a tillage i.e. only half the land is plowed

And, trembling, shrinking from the spoiler's hand,
50 Far, far away thy children leave the land.
     Ill fares the land, to hastening ills a prey,
Where wealth accumulates and men decay;
Princes and lords may flourish or may fade;
A breath can make them as a breath has made;
But a bold peasantry, their country's pride,
When once destroyed, can never be supplied.
     A time there was, ere England's griefs began,
When every rood° of ground maintained its man;
For him light labour spread her wholesome store,
60 Just gave what life required, but gave no more:
His best companions, innocence and health;
And his best riches, ignorance of wealth.
     But times are altered; trade's unfeeling train
Usurp the land, and dispossess the swain;
Along the lawn, where scattered hamlets rose,
Unwieldy wealth and cumbrous pomp repose;
And every want to luxury allied,
And every pang that folly pays to pride.
Those gentle hours that plenty bade to bloom,
70 Those calm desires that asked but little room,
Those healthful sports that graced the peaceful scene,
Lived in each look, and brightened all the green;
These, far departing, seek a kinder shore,
And rural mirth and manners° are no more.
     Sweet Auburn! parent of the blissful hour,
Thy glades forlorn confess the tyrant's power.
Here, as I take my solitary rounds
Amidst thy tangling walks and ruined grounds,
And, many a year elapsed, return to view
80 Where once the cottage stood, the hawthorn grew,
Here, as with doubtful, pensive steps I range,
Trace every scene, and wonder at the change,°
Remembrance wakes with all her busy train,
Swells at my breast, and turns the past to pain.
     In all my wanderings round this world of care,
In all my griefs—and God has given my share—
I still had hopes, my latest hours to crown,
Amidst these humble bowers to lay me down;
My anxious day to husband near the close,
90 And keep life's flame from wasting by repose.
I still had hopes, for pride attends us still,
Amidst the swains to show my book-learned skill,
Around my fire an evening group to draw,
And tell of all I felt, and all I saw;

rood literally a quarter-acre
manners customs

Here . . . change These two lines were omitted
in the fourth edition.

And, as an hare whom hounds and horns pursue,
Pants to the place from whence at first she flew,
I still had hopes, my long vexations past,
Here to return—and die at home at last.
　　O blessed retirement, friend to life's decline,
100　Retreats from care that never must be mine,
How blessed is he who crowns in shades like these
A youth of labour with an age of ease;
Who quits a world where strong temptations try,
And, since 'tis hard to combat, learns to fly.
For him no wretches, born to work and weep,
Explore the mine, or tempt° the dangerous deep;
No surly porter stands in guilty state
To spurn imploring famine from his gate;
But on he moves to meet his latter end,
110　Angels around befriending virtue's friend;
Sinks to the grave with unperceived decay,
While resignation gently slopes the way;
And all his prospects brightening to the last,
His heaven commences ere the world be past!
　　Sweet was the sound, when oft at evening's close
Up yonder hill the village murmur rose;
There, as I passed with careless steps and slow,
The mingling notes came softened from below;
The swain responsive as the milkmaid sung,
120　The sober herd that lowed to meet their young,
The noisy geese that gabbled o'er the pool,
The playful children just let loose from school,
The watchdog's voice that bayed the whispering wind,
And the loud laugh that spoke the vacant° mind;
These all in soft confusion sought the shade,
And filled each pause the nightingale had made.
But now the sounds of population fail,
No cheerful murmurs fluctuate in the gale,
No busy steps the grass-grown footway tread,
130　For all the bloomy flush of life is fled;
All but yon widowed, solitary thing
That feebly bends beside the plashy spring;
She, wretched matron, forced in age, for bread,
To strip the brook with mantling° cresses spread,
To pick her wintry faggot from the thorn,
To seek her nightly shed° and weep till morn;
She only left of all the harmless train,
The sad historian of the pensive° plain.
　　Near yonder copse, where once the garden smiled,

tempt venture on　　　　　　　　　　　shed shelter
vacant carefree　　　　　　　　　　　　pensive melancholy
mantling covering

140 And still where many a garden flower grows wild,
There, where a few torn shrubs the place disclose,
The village preacher's modest mansion rose.
A man he was to all the country dear,
And passing rich with forty pounds a year;
Remote from towns he ran his godly race,
Nor e'er had changed nor wished to change his place;°
Unskillful he to fawn or seek for power,
By doctrines fashioned to the varying hour;
Far other aims his heart had learned to prize,
150 More bent to raise the wretched than to rise.
His house was known to all the vagrant train;
He chid their wanderings, but relieved their pain;
The long remembered beggar was his guest,
Whose beard descending swept his agèd breast;
The ruined spendthrift, now no longer proud,
Claimed kindred there and had his claims allowed;
The broken soldier, kindly bade to stay,
Sate by his fire and talked the night away;
Wept o'er his wounds, or, tales of sorrow done,
160 Shouldered his crutch and showed how fields were won.
Pleased with his guests, the good man learned to glow,
And quite forgot their vices in their woe;
Careless their merits or their faults to scan,
His pity gave ere charity began.
    Thus to relieve the wretched was his pride,
And even his failings leaned to virtue's side;
But in his duty prompt at every call,
He watched and wept, he prayed and felt for all.
And, as a bird each fond endearment tries
170 To tempt its new-fledged offspring to the skies,
He tried each art, reproved each dull delay,
Allured to brighter worlds, and led the way.
    Beside the bed where parting life was laid,
And sorrow, guilt, and pain by turns dismayed,
The reverend champion stood. At his control
Despair and anguish fled the struggling soul;
Comfort came down the trembling wretch to raise,
And his last faltering accents whispered praise.
    At church, with meek and unaffected grace,
180 His looks adorned the venerable place;
Truth from his lips prevailed with double sway,
And fools, who came to scoff, remained to pray.
The service past, around the pious man,
With ready zeal, each honest rustic ran;
Even children followed with endearing wile,

place appointment, church living

And plucked his gown, to share the good man's smile.
His ready smile a parent's warmth expressed,
Their welfare pleased him and their cares distressed;
To them his heart, his love, his griefs were given,
190   But all his serious thoughts had rest in Heaven.
As some tall cliff, that lifts its awful form,
Swells from the vale and midway leaves the storm,
Though round its breast the rolling clouds are spread,
Eternal sunshine settles on its head.
      Beside yon straggling fence that skirts the way,
With blossomed furze unprofitably gay,°
There, in his noisy mansion, skilled to rule,
The village master taught his little school.
A man severe he was, and stern to view;
200   I knew him well, and every truant knew;
Well had the boding tremblers learned to trace
The day's disasters in his morning face;
Full well they laughed with counterfeited glee
At all his jokes, for many a joke had he;
Full well the busy whisper, circling round,
Conveyed the dismal tidings when he frowned;
Yet he was kind, or, if severe in aught,
The love he bore to learning was in fault;
The village all declared how much he knew;
210   'Twas certain he could write and cipher° too;
Lands he could measure, terms° and tides° presage,
And even the story ran that he could gauge;°
In arguing too, the parson owned his skill,
For e'en though vanquished, he could argue still;
While words of learnèd length and thundering sound
Amazed the gazing rustics ranged around;
And still they gazed, and still the wonder grew
That one small head could carry all he knew.
      But past is all his fame. The very spot
220   Where many a time he triumphed is forgot.
Near yonder thorn that lifts its head on high,
Where once the signpost caught the passing eye,
Low lies that house where nut-brown draughts° inspired,
Where graybeard mirth and smiling toil retired,
Where village statesmen talked with looks profound,
And news much older than their ale went round.
Imagination fondly stoops to trace
The parlour splendours of that festive place;
The whitewashed wall, the nicely sanded floor,

---

unprofitably gay grown for ornament
cipher calculate
terms quarter days when rents and wages were
due (based on the church calendar)

tides variable or movable feasts, e.g. Easter
gauge measure the capacity of casks or other
vessels
draughts of ale

30 The varnished clock that clicked behind the door;
The chest contrived a double debt to pay,
A bed by night, a chest of drawers by day;
The pictures placed for ornament and use,
The twelve good rules,° the royal game of goose;°
The hearth, except when winter chilled the day,
With aspen boughs and flowers and fennel gay;
While broken teacups, wisely kept for show,
Ranged o'er the chimney, glistened in a row.
    Vain transitory splendours! Could not all
40 Reprieve the tottering mansion from its fall?
Obscure it sinks, nor shall it more impart
An hour's importance to the poor man's heart;
Thither no more the peasant shall repair
To sweet oblivion of his daily care;
No more the farmer's news, the barber's tale,
No more the woodman's ballad shall prevail;
No more the smith his dusky brow shall clear,
Relax his ponderous strength, and lean to hear;
The host himself no longer shall be found
50 Careful to see the mantling° bliss go round;
Nor the coy maid, half willing to be pressed,
Shall kiss the cup° to pass it to the rest.
    Yes! let the rich deride, the proud disdain,
These simple blessings of the lowly train;
To me more dear, congenial to my heart,
One native charm, than all the gloss of art;
Spontaneous joys, where nature has its play,
The soul adopts and owns their first-born sway;
Lightly they frolic o'er the vacant mind,
60 Unenvied, unmolested, unconfined.
But the long pomp, the midnight masquerade,
With all the freaks of wanton wealth arrayed,
In these, ere triflers half their wish obtain,
The toiling pleasure sickens into pain;
And even while fashion's brightest arts decoy,
The heart distrusting asks if this be joy.
    Ye friends to truth, ye statesmen, who survey
The rich man's joys increase, the poor's decay,
'Tis yours to judge how wide the limits stand
70 Between a splendid and an happy land.
Proud swells the tide with loads of freighted ore,
And shouting Folly hails them from her shore;
Hoards even beyond the miser's wish abound,

twelve good rules those of Charles I, which appeared beneath a woodcut of his execution hung in many houses and including "pick no quarrels," "encourage no vice," and other maxims
royal game of goose a game played on a board
with compartments, through which counters were moved by the throw of dice
mantling frothing
kiss the cup take a sip

And rich men flock from all the world around.
Yet count our gains. This wealth is but a name
That leaves our useful products still the same.
Not so the loss. The man of wealth and pride
Takes up a space that many poor supplied;
Space for his lake, his park's extended bounds,
280   Space for his horses, equipage, and hounds;
The robe that wraps his limbs in silken sloth
Has robbed the neighbouring fields of half their growth;
His seat, where solitary sports are seen,
Indignant spurns the cottage from the green;
Around the world each needful product flies,
For all the luxuries the world supplies;
While thus the land adorned for pleasure all
In barren splendour feebly waits the fall.
　　As some fair female, unadorned and plain,
290   Secure to please while youth confirms her reign,
Slights every borrowed charm that dress supplies,
Nor shares with art the triumph of her eyes;
But when those charms are past, for charms are frail,
When time advances and when lovers fail,
She then shines forth, solicitous to bless,
In all the glaring impotence of dress:
Thus fares the land, by luxury betrayed,
In nature's simplest charms at first arrayed;
But verging to decline, its splendours rise,
300   Its vistas° strike, its palaces surprise;
While scourged by famine from the smiling land,
The mournful peasant leads his humble band;
And while he sinks, without one arm to save,
The country blooms—a garden and a grave.°
　　Where then, ah where, shall poverty reside,
To 'scape the pressure of contiguous pride?°
If to some common's fenceless limits strayed,
He drives his flock to pick the scanty blade,
Those fenceless fields the sons of wealth divide,
310   And even the bare-worn common is denied.
　　If to the city sped—what waits him there?
To see profusion that he must not share;
To see ten thousand baneful arts combined
To pamper luxury, and thin mankind;
To see each joy the sons of pleasure know
Extorted from his fellow-creature's woe.
Here while the courtier glitters in brocade,

---

vistas designed prospects or views at the end
of an avenue of trees
a garden and a grave i.e. improved with elaborate gardens for the rich and thus made a
grave for the poor
contiguous pride neighboring and encroaching
luxury

There the pale artist° plies the sickly trade;
Here while the proud their long-drawn pomps display,
320 There the black gibbet glooms beside the way;
The dome° where Pleasure holds her midnight reign,
Here, richly decked, admits the gorgeous train;
Tumultuous grandeur crowds the blazing square,
The rattling chariots clash, the torches glare:
Sure scenes like these no trouble e'er annoy!
Sure these denote one universal joy!
Are these thy serious thoughts?—Ah, turn thine eyes
Where the poor houseless shivering female lies.
She once, perhaps, in village plenty blessed,
330 Has wept at tales of innocence distressed;
Her modest looks the cottage might adorn,
Sweet as the primrose peeps beneath the thorn;
Now lost to all; her friends, her virtue fled,
Near her betrayer's door she lays her head,
And pinched with cold, and shrinking from the shower,
With heavy heart deplores that luckless hour,
When idly first, ambitious of the town,
She left her wheel° and robes of country brown.
    Do thine, sweet Auburn, thine, the loveliest train,
340 Do thy fair tribes participate her pain?
Even now, perhaps, by cold and hunger led,
At proud men's doors they ask a little bread!
    Ah, no. To distant climes, a dreary scene,
Where half the convex world intrudes between,
To torrid tracts with fainting steps they go,
Where wild Altama° murmurs to their woe.
Far different there from all that charmed before,
The various terrors of that horrid shore;
Those blazing suns that dart a downward ray,
350 And fiercely shed intolerable day;
Those matted woods where birds forget to sing,
But silent bats in drowsy clusters cling;
Those poisonous fields with rank luxuriance crowned
Where the dark scorpion gathers death around;
Where at each step the stranger fears to wake
The rattling terrors of the vengeful snake;
Where crouching tigers° wait their hapless prey,
And savage men more murderous still than they;
While oft in whirls the mad tornado flies,
360 Mingling the ravaged landscape with the skies.
Far different these from every former scene,

artist artisan, workman
dome building
wheel for spinning
Altama the Altamaha River in Georgia, where

Goldsmith's friend General Oglethorpe had
founded a colony in 1735
tigers Goldsmith refers to the cougar or "red
tiger" (also called the "American tiger").

The cooling brook, the grassy-vested green,
The breezy covert of the warbling grove,
That only sheltered thefts of harmless love.
    Good Heaven! what sorrows gloomed that parting day
That called them from their native walks away;
When the poor exiles, every pleasure past,
Hung round their bowers, and fondly looked their last,
And took a long farewell, and wished in vain
370 For seats like these beyond the western main;
And shuddering still to face the distant deep,
Returned and wept, and still returned to weep.
The good old sire the first prepared to go
To new-found worlds, and wept for others' woe;
But for himself, in conscious virtue brave,
He only wished for worlds beyond the grave.
His lovely daughter, lovelier in her tears,
The fond companion of his helpless years,
Silent went next, neglectful of her charms,
380 And left a lover's for her father's arms.
With louder plaints the mother spoke her woes,
And blessed the cot where every pleasure rose,
And kissed her thoughtless babes with many a tear,
And clasped them close, in sorrow doubly dear;
Whilst her fond husband strove to lend relief
In all the decent manliness of grief.
    O Luxury! thou cursed by heaven's decree,
How ill exchanged are things like these for thee!
How do thy potions, with insidious joy,
390 Diffuse their pleasures only to destroy!
Kingdoms by thee, to sickly greatness grown,
Boast of a florid vigour not their own:
At every draught more large and large they grow,
A bloated mass of rank, unwieldy woe;
Till sapped their strength, and every part unsound,
Down, down they sink, and spread a ruin round.
    Even now the devastation is begun,
And half the business of destruction done;
Even now, methinks, as pondering here I stand,
400 I see the rural virtues leave the land:
Down where yon anchoring vessel spreads the sail,
That idly waiting flaps with every gale,
Downward they move, a melancholy band,
Pass from the shore, and darken all the strand.
Contented Toil, and hospitable Care,
And kind connubial Tenderness are there;
And Piety with wishes placed above,
And steady Loyalty, and faithful Love.
And thou, sweet Poetry, thou loveliest maid,

410 Still first to fly where sensual joys invade,
Unfit, in these degenerate times of shame,
To catch the heart, or strike for honest fame;
Dear charming nymph, neglected and decried,
My shame in crowds, my solitary pride;
Thou source of all my bliss and all my woe,
That foundest me poor at first, and keepest me so;
Thou guide by which the nobler arts excel,
Thou nurse of every virtue, fare thee well!
Farewell, and O where'er thy voice be tried,
420 On Torno's° cliffs, or Pambamarca's° side,
Whether where equinoctial fervours° glow,
Or winter wraps the polar world in snow,
Still let thy voice, prevailing over time,
Redress the rigours of the inclement clime;
Aid slighted truth, with thy persuasive strain
Teach erring man to spurn the rage of gain;
Teach him that states of native strength possessed,
Though very poor, may still be very blessed;
That trade's proud empire hastes to swift decay,
430 As ocean sweeps the laboured mole° away;
While self-dependent power can time defy,
As rocks resist the billows and the sky.
1768–70   1770

WILLIAM COWPER
1731–1800

Cowper suffered his first severe attack of melancholy at the age of twenty-one as he settled into the study of law at the Middle Temple. "Day and night," he wrote later, "I was upon the rack, lying down in horrors and rising up in despair." He was called to the bar two years later and in 1759 was appointed Commissioner of Bankrupts; but through need of a greater income he sought a post in the House of Lords. This required a competitive examination, and the strain of anticipation led to his first full attack of insanity in 1763. He experienced a sense of utter damnation, and attempts at suicide only intensified feelings of guilt. During his months in an asylum he underwent a religious conversion that gave him hope and reconciled him to a life of country retirement, which the Unwin family made possible by taking him into their household. Under the influence of John Newton, an evangelical minister, the Unwins (and Cowper with them) moved to Olney, a place (as Cowper described it) "inhabited chiefly by the half-starved and ragged of the earth." In 1773 Cowper proposed marriage to the widowed Mrs. Unwin but lost his sanity again a month or so before the marriage was to take place. In his later years of intermittent serenity, still

Torno's in Lapland
Pambamarca's in Ecuador
equinoctial fervours the intense heat at the Equator

laboured mole the man-built breakwater, as opposed to the "self-dependent power" of natural rocks; the last four lines were written by Dr. Johnson haunted by terrifying dreams and black depression, he translated Homer, edited Milton, and enjoyed the admiration of William Hayley (the poet and insensitive patron of William Blake), who became his literary executor and biographer.

Three of the poems given here show Cowper dealing directly with his sense of damnation, the early *Lines* and the two last poems of his life. His major work, apart from the hymns he wrote with Newton, was *The Task*, begun at the bidding of his neighbor Lady Austen as a distraction, an "assigned" poem about a sofa. But the poem opened into a long meditative and descriptive work, mixing satire upon luxury and urban corruption with georgic celebrations of country life, and resolved itself at last into a vision for which the country scene provided only outward surface. In the sixth and last book, from which selections are given below, the poem moves to the vision of a recovered Eden and to a new poise of self whose dwelling is (at least in its deepest reaches) already there. The section from *The Task* provides a striking counterpoise, in its strong affirmation and its serenity, to the tormented and more powerful poems that came out of his despair.

Lines Written During a Period of Insanity

Hatred and vengeance, my eternal portion,
Scarce can endure delay of execution,
Wait with impatient readiness to seize my
        Soul in a moment.

Damned below Judas; more abhorred than he was,
Who for a few pence sold his holy Master.
Twice-betrayed Jesus me, the last delinquent,
        Deems the profanest.

Man disavows, and Deity disowns me;
10   Hell might afford my miseries a shelter;
Therefore Hell keeps her ever-hungry mouths all
        Bolted against me.

Hard lot! encompassed with a thousand dangers,
Weary, faint, trembling with a thousand terrors,
I'm called, if vanquished, to receive a sentence
        Worse than Abiram's.°

Him the vindictive rod of angry Justice
Sent quick and howling to the centre headlong;
I, fed with judgment,° in a fleshly tomb, am
20   Buried above ground.

1763?   1816

Abiram's Korah, Dathan, and Abiram rebelled against Moses, who brought down upon them a special curse: "If these men die the common death of all men . . . then the Lord hath not sent me. But if the Lord make a new thing, and the earth open her mouth, and swallow them up . . . then ye shall understand that these men have provoked the Lord. And it came to pass . . ." (Numbers 16:29–31). **fed with judgment** Cf. Ezekiel 34:7–16, where God speaks ironically of feeding the wicked ("the fat and the strong") among his flock "with judgment," i.e. with punishment.

On the Ice Islands Seen Floating in the German Ocean°

What portents, from what distant region, ride,
Unseen till now in ours, the astonished tide?
In ages past, old Proteus,° with his droves
Of sea-calves, sought the mountains and the groves:
But now, descending whence of late they stood,
Themselves the mountains seem to rove the flood.
Dire times were they, full-charged with human woes;
And these, scarce less calamitous than those.
What view we now? More wondrous still! Behold!
Like burnished brass they shine, or beaten gold;
And all around the pearl's pure splendour show,
And all around the ruby's fiery glow.
Come they from India? where the burning earth,
All-bounteous, gives her richest treasures birth;
And where the costly gems, that beam around
The brows of mightiest potentates, are found?
No. Never such a countless dazzling store
Had left unseen the Ganges' peopled shore.
Rapacious hands, and ever-watchful eyes,
Should sooner far have marked and seized the prize.
Whence sprang they then? Ejected have they come
From Ves'vius', or from Aetna's burning womb?°
Thus shine they self-illumed, or but display
The borrowed splendours of a cloudless day?
With borrowed beams they shine. The gales that breathe
Now land-ward, and the current's force beneath,
Have borne them nearer: and the nearer sight,
Advantaged more, contèmplates them aright.
Their lofty summits crested high they show,
With mingled sleet and long-incumbent snow.
The rest is ice. Far hence, where, most severe,
Bleak winter well-nigh saddens all the year,
Their infant growth began. He bade arise
Their uncouth forms, portentous in our eyes.
Oft as, dissolved by transient suns, the snow
Left the tall cliff, to join the flood below,

10

20

30

On the Ice Islands . . . Ocean This was written first in Latin, then shortly afterward translated into English, during Cowper's last illness; the English version was completed the day before *The Castaway* was written. The remarkable turn of the last stanza of that poem is diffused through this poem and left more implicit, but surely the icebergs are taken as some aspect of the self—beautiful in a sinister way, rejected by Phoebus Apollo (god of the sun and of poetry alike), unable to be kept in the "Cimmerian darkness" yet unable to survive in the full light of day—a telling contrast to fertile Delos, perhaps its demonic counterpart. **Proteus** the herdsman of the sea cattle, given prophetic powers in return; according to some legends a king of Egypt who took Helen of Troy and her wealth from Paris and kept them for Menelaus; the father of two sons slain by Hercules (perhaps the "human woes" mentioned here) **Ves'vius' . . . Aetna's burning womb** Both volcanoes had undergone spectacular eruptions in modern times as well as in antiquity.

He caught and curdled, with a freezing blast,
The current, ere it reached the boundless waste.
By slow degrees uprose the wondrous pile,
40 And long-successive ages rolled the while;
Till, ceaseless in its growth, it claimed to stand
Tall as its rival mountains on the land.
Thus stood—and, unremovable by skill
Or force of man, had stood the structure still;
But that, though firmly fixt, supplanted yet
By pressure of its own enormous weight,
It left the shelving° beach—and, with a sound
That shook the bellowing waves and rocks around,
Self-launched, and swiftly, to the briny wave,
50 As if instinct with strong desire to lave,
Down went the ponderous mass. So bards of old,
How Delos° swam the Aegean deep, have told.
But not of ice was Delos. Delos bore
Herb, fruit, and flower. She, crowned with laurel, wore,
E'en under wintry skies, a summer smile;
And Delos was Apollo's favorite isle.
But, horrid wanderers of the deep, to you
He deems Cimmerian darkness° only due.
Your hated birth he deigned not to survey,
60 But, scornful, turned his glorious eyes away.
Hence! Seek your home; no longer rashly dare
The darts of Phoebus, and a softer air;
Lest ye regret, too late, your native coast,
In no congenial gulf for ever lost!
1799   1803

The Castaway°

Obscurest night involved the sky,
    The Atlantic billows roared,
When such a destined wretch as I,
    Washed headlong from on board,
Of friends, of hope, of all bereft,
His floating home for ever left.

shelving sloping
Delos the floating island given to Latona as a refuge from persecution; the birthplace of Apollo and Artemis, regarded as sacred in antiquity
Cimmerian darkness the gloomy retreat of a people who dwelt in caves and hid from the light of the sun; associated with hell and the Stygian regions in antiquity and by Milton, *L'Allegro*, l. 10
The Castaway The poem is based upon an incident in Richard Walter's *A Voyage Round the World by George Anson* (1748). Anson, later an admiral, led the expedition against the Spanish; while they were rounding Cape Horn in a storm, one of the seamen was carried overboard: "We perceived that he swam very strong, and it was with the utmost concern that we found ourselves incapable of assisting him; and we were the more grieved at his unhappy fate since we lost sight of him struggling with the waves, and conceived . . . that he might continue sensible for a considerable time longer of the horror attending his irretrievable situation" (I.viii).

No braver chief could Albion boast
   Than he with whom he went,
Nor ever ship left Albion's coast,
10   With warmer wishes sent.
He loved them both, but both in vain,
Nor him beheld, nor her again.

Not long beneath the whelming brine,
   Expert to swim, he lay;
Nor soon he felt his strength decline,
   Or courage die away;
But waged with death a lasting strife,
Supported by despair of life.

He shouted: nor his friends had failed
20   To check the vessel's course,
But so the furious blast prevailed,
   That, pitiless perforce,
They left their outcast mate behind,
And scudded still before the wind.

Some succour yet they could afford;
   And, such as storms allow,
The cask, the coop,° the floated cord,
   Delayed not to bestow.
But he (they knew) nor ship, nor shore,
30   Whate'er they gave, should visit more.

Nor, cruel as it seemed, could he
   Their haste himself condemn,
Aware that flight, in such a sea,
   Alone could rescue them;
Yet bitter felt it still to die
Deserted, and his friends so nigh.

He long survives who lives an hour
   In ocean, self-upheld;
And so long he, with unspent power,
40   His destiny repelled;
And ever, as the minutes flew,
Entreated help, or cried, 'Adieu!'

At length, his transient respite past,
   His comrades, who before
Had heard his voice in every blast,
   Could catch the sound no more.
For then, by toil subdued, he drank
The stifling wave, and then he sank.

---

coop basket used for catching fish, here used
for rescue

No poet wept him: but the page
50   Of narrative sincere,
That tells his name, his worth, his age,
  Is wet with Anson's tear.
And tears by bards or heroes shed
Alike immortalize the dead.

I therefore purpose not, or dream,
  Descanting on his fate,
To give the melancholy theme
  A more enduring date:
But misery still delights to trace
60   Its semblance in another's case.

No voice divine the storm allayed,
  No light propitious shone;
When, snatched from all effectual aid,
  We perished, each alone:
But I beneath a rougher sea,
And whelmed in deeper gulfs than he.
1799   1803

The Task

From *Book VI: The Winter Walk at Noon*
The Lord of all, himself through all diffused,
Sustains, and is the life of all that lives.
Nature is but a name for an effect
Whose cause is God. He feeds the secret fire
By which the mighty process is maintained,
Who sleeps not, is not weary; in whose sight
Slow circling ages are as transient days;
Whose work is without labour; whose designs
No flaw deforms, no difficulty thwarts;
230 And whose beneficence no charge exhausts.
Him blind antiquity profaned, not served,
With self-taught rites, and under various names,
Female and male, Pomona, Pales, Pan,
And Flora, and Vertumnus;° peopling earth
With tutelary goddesses and gods
That were not; and commending, as they would,
To each some province, garden, field, or grove.
But all are under one. One spirit—His
Who wore the platted° thorns with bleeding brows—

Pomona . . . Vertumnus These deities were, respectively, the goddess of gardens and fruit, the goddess of sheepfolds and pastures, the god of shepherds and huntsmen, the goddess of flowers and gardens, and the god of orchards and of the spring.
platted woven; referring to the crown of thorns of the crucified Christ, seen here as the God of Nature

40 Rules universal nature. Not a flower
But shows some touch, in freckle, streak, or stain,
Of his unrivalled pencil.° He inspires
Their balmy odours, and imparts their hues,
And bathes their eyes with nectar, and includes,
In grains as countless as the sea-side sands,
The forms with which he sprinkles all the earth.
Happy who walks with him! whom what he finds
Of flavour or of scent in fruit or flower,
Or what he views of beautiful or grand
50 In nature, from the broad majestic oak
To the green blade that twinkles in the sun,
Prompts with remembrance of a present God!
His presence, who made all so fair, perceived,
Makes all still fairer. As with him no scene
Is dreary, so with him all seasons please.
Though winter had been none, had man been true,
And earth be punished for its tenant's sake,°
Yet not in vengeance; as this smiling sky,
So soon succeeding such an angry night,
60 And these dissolving snows, and this clear stream
Recovering fast its liquid music, prove.
    Who then, that has a mind well strung and tuned
To contemplation, and within his reach
A scene so friendly to his favourite task,
Would waste attention at the chequered board,°
His host of wooden warriors to and fro
Marching and counter-marching, with an eye
As fixt as marble, with a forehead ridged
And furrowed into storms, and with a hand
270 Trembling, as if eternity were hung
In balance on his conduct of a pin?—
Nor envies he aught more their idle sport,
Who pant with application misapplied
To trivial toys, and, pushing ivory balls°
Across a velvet level, feel a joy
Akin to rapture when the bawble finds
Its destined goal, of difficult access.—
Nor deems he wiser him who gives his noon
To miss, the mercer's plague,° from shop to shop
280 Wandering, and littering with unfolded silks
The polished counter, and approving none,
Or promising with smiles to call again.—

pencil paintbrush
Though winter . . . tenant's sake referring to
the doctrine that all Nature fell when man did,
and that the unchanging climate of Eden gave
way to the rotating seasons (cf. Milton, *Paradise
Lost* IX). Cowper's point is that the fall of
Nature was necessary but that its effects are too
beautiful to constitute a mere act of vengeance.
chequered board chess or checker (draughts)
board
ivory balls billiards
miss . . . plague the young woman who
plagues the silk merchant

Nor him who by his vanity seduced,
And soothed into a dream that he discerns
The difference of a Guido° from a daub,
Frequents the crowded auction: stationed there
As duly as the Langford° of the show,
With glass at eye and catalogue in hand,
And tongue accomplished in the fulsome cant
290   And pedantry that coxcombs learn with ease;
Oft as the price-deciding hammer falls
He notes it in his book, then raps his box,
Swears 'tis a bargain, rails at his hard fate
That he has let it pass—but never bids!
    Here, unmolested, through whatever sign°
The sun proceeds, I wander. Neither mist,
Nor freezing sky nor sultry, checking me,
Nor stranger intermeddling with my joy.
Even in the spring and play-time of the year,
300   That calls the unwonted villager abroad
With all her little ones, a sportive train,
To gather king-cups in the yellow mead,
And prink their hair with daisies, or to pick
A cheap but wholesome salad from the brook,
These shades are all my own. The timorous hare,
Grown so familiar with her frequent guest,
Scarce shuns me; and the stock-dove, unalarmed,
Sits cooing in the pine-tree, nor suspends
His long love-ditty for my near approach.
310   Drawn from his refuge in some lonely elm
That age or injury has hollowed deep,
Where, on his bed of wool and matted leaves,
He has outslept the winter, ventures forth
To frisk awhile, and bask in the warm sun,
The squirrel, flippant, pert, and full of play:
He sees me, and at once, swift as a bird,
Ascends the neighbouring beech; there whisks his brush,
And perks his ears, and stamps and scolds aloud,
With all the prettiness of feigned alarm,
320   And anger insignificantly fierce.
    The heart is hard in nature, and unfit
For human fellowship, as being void
Of sympathy, and therefore dead alike
To love and friendship both, that is not pleased
With sight of animals enjoying life,
Nor feels their happiness augment his own.

Guido Guido Reni (1575–1642), the Bolognese painter whose works were held in very high regard in the 17th and 18th centuries

Langford Abraham Langford (1711–74), playwright and the best known auctioneer of the day
sign of the zodiac

The bounding fawn, that darts across the glade
When none pursues, through mere delight of heart,
And spirits buoyant with excess of glee;
330   The horse as wanton, and almost as fleet,
That skims the spacious meadow at full speed,
Then stops and snorts, and, throwing high his heels,
Starts to the voluntary race again;
The very kine° that gambol at high noon,
The total herd receiving first from one
That leads the dance a summons to be gay,
Though wild their strange vagaries and uncouth
Their efforts, yet resolved with one consent
To give such act and utterance as they may
340   To ecstasy too big to be suppressed—
These, and a thousand images of bliss,
With which kind nature graces every scene
Where cruel man defeats not her design,
Impart to the benevolent, who wish
All that are capable of pleasure pleased,
A far superior happiness to theirs,
The comfort of a reasonable joy.

      . . .

Oh scenes surpassing fable, and yet true,
Scenes of accomplished bliss! which who can see,
760   Though but in distant prospect, and not feel
His soul refreshed with foretaste of the joy?
Rivers of gladness water all the earth,
And clothe all climes with beauty; the reproach
Of barrenness is past. The fruitful field
Laughs with abundance; and the land, once lean,
Or fertile only in its own disgrace,°
Exults to see its thistly curse repealed.
The various seasons woven into one,
770   And that one season an eternal spring,
The garden fears no blight, and needs no fence,
For there is none to covet, all are full.
The lion, and the libbard,° and the bear
Graze with the fearless flocks; all bask at noon
Together, or all gambol in the shade
Of the same grove, and drink one common stream.
Antipathies are none. No foe to man
Lurks in the serpent now: the mother sees,
And smiles to see, her infant's playful hand
780   Stretched forth to dally with the crested worm,
To stroke his azure neck, or to receive
The lambent homage of his arrowy tongue.

kine cattle   libbard leopard
fertile . . . disgrace i.e. rank with weeds

All creatures worship man, and all mankind
One Lord, one Father. Error has no place:
That creeping pestilence is driven away;
The breath of heaven has chased it. In the heart
No passion touches a discordant string,
But all is harmony and love. Disease
Is not: the pure and uncontaminate blood
790   Holds its due course, nor fears the frost of age.
One song employs all nations; and all cry,
'Worthy the Lamb, for he was slain for us!'°
The dwellers in the vales and on the rocks
Shout to each other, and the mountain tops
From distant mountains catch the flying joy;
Till, nation after nation taught the strain,
Earth rolls the rapturous hosanna round.
Behold the measure of the promise fill'd;
See Salem° built, the labour of a God!
800   Bright as a sun the sacred city shines;
All kingdoms and all princes of the earth
Flock to that light; the glory of all lands
Flows into her; unbounded is her joy,
And endless her increase. Thy rams are there,
Nebaioth, and the flocks of Kedar° there;
The looms of Ormus, and the mines of Ind,°
And Saba's° spicy groves, pay tribute there.
Praise is in all her gates: upon her walls,
And in her streets, and in her spacious courts,
810   Is heard salvation. Eastern Java there
Kneels with the native of the farthest west;
And Ethiopia spreads abroad the hand,
And worships. Her report has travelled forth
Into all lands. From every clime they come
To see thy beauty and to share thy joy,
O Sion! an assembly such as earth
Saw never, such as heav'n stoops down to see.

        ·   ·   ·

    He is the happy man, whose life even now
Shows somewhat of that happier life to come;
Who, doomed to an obscure but tranquil state,
Is pleased with it, and, were he free to choose,
910   Would make his fate his choice; whom peace, the fruit
Of virtue, and whom virtue, fruit of faith,

Worthy . . . us "Worthy is the Lamb that was slain to receive power, and riches, and wisdom, and strength, and honour, and glory, and bless-ing" (Revelation 5:12)
Salem the New Jerusalem
Nebaioth . . . Kedar "The sons of Ishmael and progenitors of the Arabs, in the prophetic scripture here alluded to, may be reasonably considered as representatives of the Gentiles at large" (Cowper).
ormus . . . Ind Cf. Milton, *Paradise Lost* II.2. Ormus is an island at the mouth of the Persian Gulf and was a rich trading city, coupled by Milton with India for their "wealth."
Saba's Sheba in southwest Arabia

Prepare for happiness; bespeak him one
Content indeed to sojourn while he must
Below the skies, but having there his home.
The world o'erlooks him in her busy search
Of objects more illustrious in her view;
And occupied as earnestly as she,
Though more sublimely, he o'erlooks the world.
She scorns his pleasures, for she knows them not;
920 He seeks not hers, for he has proved them vain.
He cannot skim the ground like summer birds
Pursuing gilded flies; and such he deems
Her honours, her emoluments, her joys.
Therefore in contemplation is his bliss,
Whose power is such, that whom she lifts from earth
She makes familiar with a heaven unseen,
And shows him glories yet to be revealed.
Not slothful he, though seeming unemployed,
And censured oft as useless. Stillest streams
930 Oft water fairest meadows, and the bird
That flutters least is longest on the wing.
Ask him, indeed, what trophies he has raised,
Or what achievements of immortal fame
He purposes, and he shall answer—None.
His warfare is within. There unfatigued
His fervent spirit labours. There he fights,
And there obtains fresh triumphs o'er himself,
And never withering wreaths, compared with which
The laurels that a Caesar reaps are weeds.

.   .   .

So life glides smoothly and by stealth away,
More golden than that age of fabled gold
Renowned in ancient song; not vexed with care
Or stained with guilt, beneficent, approved
Of God and man, and peaceful in its end.
1000 So glide my life away! and so at last,
My share of duties decently fulfilled,
May some disease, not tardy to perform
Its destined office, yet with gentle stroke,
Dismiss me, weary, to a safe retreat,
Beneath the turf that I have often trod. . . .
1783–84   1785

GEORGE CRABBE
1754–1832

After a difficult early life and abortive plans for a medical career, Crabbe gained Edmund Burke's favorable notice of his poetry and through him met Reynolds and Dr. Johnson. The latter helped with the revision of *The Village* and wrote a letter to Reynolds that Crabbe later published in his 1807 preface. Johnson found Crabbe's poem "original, vigorous, and elegant," and, as Boswell tells us, found Crabbe's scorn of "the false notions of rustic happiness and rustic virtue . . . quite congenial with his own." Crabbe served as a curate for a time in his native village of Aldeburgh and held other church livings later in rural areas. He continued to write verse tales in heroic couplets throughout his life, winning from Byron the tribute of "Nature's sternest painter, yet best."

William Hazlitt was to write of Crabbe's almost obsessive concern with "teasing, helpless, unimaginative distress." In fact, Crabbe is always fascinated with the power of repressed or unfulfilled feeling, and he is a remarkably sharp student of the obscure and tortured destinies that were to become the subject of much realistic fiction later. But he also looked back to the example of Pope (particularly the Pope of the satiric portraits), who had, he claimed, "no small portion of this actuality of relation, this nudity of description, and poetry without an atmosphere." In the preface to *The Parish Register* Crabbe provides a good statement of his achievement, the attack upon the conventional forms of romance and pastoral through the patient and often subtle study of mixed motive: "an endeavour . . . to describe village-manners, not by adopting the notion of pastoral simplicity or assuming ideas of rustic barbarity, but by more natural views of the peasantry, considered as a mixed body of persons, sober or profligate, and hence, in a great measure, contented or miserable." *The Parish Register* is divided into three sections, each recording the year's entries under one heading—births, marriages, or deaths—and creating through brief portraits or narratives a rounded picture of parish life. In later works, notably *The Borough* (1810), *Tales in Verse* (1812), and *Tales of the Hall,* he devotes himself more completely to a dry, often witty, narrative verse which deliberately risks self-parody in its willful flatness and bareness.

The Village

> From *Book I*
> The village life, and every care that reigns
> O'er youthful peasants and declining swains;
> What labour yields, and what, that labour past,
> Age, in its hour of languor, finds at last;
> What form the real picture of the poor,
> Demand a song—the Muse can give no more.
>
> Fled are those times when, in harmonious strains,
> The rustic poet praised his native plains.
> No shepherds now, in smooth alternate verse,

10 Their country's beauty or their nymphs' rehearse;
   Yet still for these we frame the tender strain,
   Still in our lays fond Corydons° complain,
   And shepherds' boys their amorous pains reveal,
   The only pains, alas! they never feel.
     On Mincio's banks, in Caesar's bounteous reign,
   If Tityrus found the Golden Age again,
   Must sleepy bards the flattering dream prolong,
   Mechanic echoes of the Mantuan song?
   From Truth and Nature shall we widely stray,
20 Where Virgil, not where Fancy, leads the way?
     Yes, thus the Muses sing of happy swains,
   Because the Muses never knew their pains.
   They boast their peasants' pipes;° but peasants now
   Resign their pipes and plod behind the plough;
   And few, amid the rural-tribe, have time
   To number syllables, and play with rhyme;
   Save honest Duck,° what son of verse could share
   The poet's rapture, and the peasant's care?
   Or the great labours of the field degrade,
30 With the new peril of a poorer trade?
     From this chief cause these idle praises spring,
   That themes so easy few forbear to sing;
   For no deep thought the trifling subjects ask:
   To sing of shepherds is an easy task.
   The happy youth assumes the common strain,
   A nymph his mistress, and himself a swain;
   With no sad scenes he clouds his tuneful prayer,
   But all, to look like her, is painted fair.
     I grant indeed that fields and flocks have charms
40 For him that grazes or for him that farms;
   But, when amid such pleasing scenes I trace
   The poor laborious natives of the place,
   And see the midday sun, with fervid ray,
   On their bare heads and dewy temples play;
   While some, with feebler heads and fainter hearts,
   Deplore their fortune, yet sustain their parts:
   Then shall I dare these real ills to hide
   In tinsel trappings of poetic pride?
     No; cast by fortune on a frowning coast,
50 Which neither groves nor happy valleys boast;
   Where other cares than those the Muse relates,
   And other shepherds dwell with other mates;

Corydons such shepherds as appear in Virgil's
Eclogues (c. 42–37 B.C.), where the poet traditionally is supposed to appear as Tityrus. The
pastoral poems are set in the countryside near
Mantua beside the Mincio River. Of the following lines, 15–18 were written by Dr. Johnson.

pipes the musical reeds of the traditional shep-
herd
Duck Stephen Duck (1705–56), the Thresher
Poet, a fashionable "primitive" whom Queen
Caroline made keeper of her library at Rich-
mond

By such examples taught, I paint the cot,°
As truth will paint it, and as bards will not:
Nor you, ye poor, of lettered scorn complain,
To you the smoothest song is smooth in vain;
O'ercome by labour, and bowed down by time,
Feel you the barren flattery of a rhyme?
Can poets soothe you, when you pine for bread,
By winding myrtles round your ruined shed?
Can their light tales your weighty griefs o'erpower,
Or glad with airy mirth the toilsome hour?

     .   .   .

    Ye gentle souls, who dream of rural ease,
Whom the smooth stream and smoother sonnet please;
Go! if the peaceful cot your praises share,
Go, look within, and ask if peace be there:
If peace be his—that drooping weary sire,
Or theirs, that offspring round their feeble fire;
Or hers, that matron pale, whose trembling hand
Turns on the wretched hearth the expiring brand!°
    Nor yet can Time itself obtain for these
Life's latest comforts, due respect and ease:
For yonder see that hoary swain, whose age
Can with no cares except his own engage;
Who, propped on that rude staff, looks up to see
The bare arms broken from the withering tree
On which, a boy, he climbed the loftiest bough,
Then his first joy, but his sad emblem now.
    He once was chief in all the rustic trade;
His steady hand the straightest furrow made;
Full many a prize he won, and still is proud
To find the triumphs of his youth allowed.
A transient pleasure sparkles in his eyes;
He hears and smiles, then thinks again and sighs:
For now he journeys to his grave in pain;
The rich disdain him, nay, the poor disdain;
Alternate masters now their slave command,
Urge the weak efforts of his feeble hand;
And, when his age attempts its task in vain,
With ruthless taunts, of lazy poor complain.
    Oft may you see him, when he tends the sheep,
His winter-charge, beneath the hillock weep;
Oft hear him murmur to the winds that blow
O'er his white locks and bury them in snow,
When, roused by rage and muttering in the morn,
He mends the broken hedge with icy thorn:—
    'Why do I live, when I desire to be

cot cottage   **brand** coal, ember

At once from life and life's long labour free?
Like leaves in spring, the young are blown away,
Without the sorrows of a slow decay;
I, like yon withered leaf, remain behind,
Nipped by the frost, and shivering in the wind;
There it abides till younger buds come on,
As I, now all my fellow-swains are gone;
Then, from the rising generation thrust,
It falls, like me, unnoticed to the dust.
   'These fruitful fields, these numerous flocks I see,
Are others' gain, but killing cares to me:
To me the children of my youth are lords,
Cool in their looks, but hasty in their words:
Wants of their own demand their care; and who
Feels his own want and succours others too?
A lonely, wretched man, in pain I go,
None need my help, and none relieve my woe;
Then let my bones beneath the turf be laid,
And men forget the wretch they would not aid!'
   Thus groan the old, till, by disease oppressed,
They taste a final woe, and then they rest.

       .   .   .

   Now once again the gloomy scene explore,
Less gloomy now; the bitter hour is o'er,
The man of many sorrows sighs no more.—
Up yonder hill, behold how sadly slow
The bier moves winding from the vale below;
There lie the happy dead, from trouble free,
And the glad parish pays the frugal fee.
No more, O Death! thy victim starts to hear
Churchwarden stern or kingly overseer;
No more the farmer claims his humble bow,
Thou art his lord, the best of tyrants thou!
   Now to the church behold the mourners come,
Sedately torpid and devoutly dumb;
The village children now their games suspend,
To see the bier that bears their ancient friend:
For he was one in all their idle sport,
And like a monarch ruled their little court;
The pliant bow he formed, the flying ball,
The bat, the wicket, were his labours all;
Him now they follow to his grave, and stand
Silent and sad, and gazing, hand in hand;
While bending low, their eager eyes explore
The mingled relics of the parish poor.
The bell tolls late, the moping owl flies round,
Fear marks the flight and magnifies the sound;
The busy priest, detained by weightier care,

Defers his duty till the day of prayer;
And, waiting long, the crowd retire distressed,
To think a poor man's bones should lie unblessed.

1783

The Parish Register

From *Part III: Burials*

There was, 'tis said, and I believe, a time,
When humble Christians died with views sublime;
When all were ready for their faith to bleed,
But few to write or wrangle for their creed;
When lively Faith upheld the sinking heart,
And friends, assured to meet, prepared to part;
When Love felt hope, when Sorrow grew serene,
And all was comfort in the death-bed scene.
   Alas! when now the gloomy king they wait,
'Tis weakness yielding to resistless fate;
Like wretched men upon the ocean cast,
They labour hard and struggle to the last,
'Hope against hope,' and wildly gaze around,
In search of help that never shall be found:
Nor, till the last strong billow stops the breath,
Will they believe them in the jaws of Death!

   When these my records I reflecting read,
And find what ills these numerous births succeed;
What powerful griefs these nuptial ties attend,
With what regret these painful journeys end;
When from the cradle to the grave I look,
Mine I conceive a melancholy book.
   Where now is perfect resignation seen?
Alas! it is not on the village-green:—
I've seldom known, though I have often read,
Of happy peasants on their dying-bed;
Whose looks proclaimed that sunshine of the breast,
That more than hope, that Heaven itself expressed.
   What I behold are feverish fits of strife,
'Twixt fears of dying and desire of life:
Those earthly hopes that to the last endure;
Those fears that hopes superior fail to cure;
At best a sad submission to the doom,
Which, turning from the danger, lets it come.

   Sick lies the man, bewildered, lost, afraid,
His spirits vanquished and his strength decayed;
No hope the friend, the nurse, the doctor lend—
'Call then a priest, and fit him for his end.'

A priest is called; 'tis now, alas! too late,
40 Death enters with him at the cottage-gate;
Or, time allowed, he goes, assured to find
The self-commending, all-confiding mind;
And sighs to hear what we may justly call
Death's common-place, the train of thought in all.
    'True, I'm a sinner,' feebly he begins,
'But trust in Mercy to forgive my sins';
(Such cool confession no past crimes excite;
Such claim on Mercy seems the sinner's right!)
'I know, mankind are frail, that God is just,
50 And pardons those who in his mercy trust;
We're sorely tempted in a world like this;
All men have done, and I like all, amiss;
But now, if spared, it is my full intent
On all the past to ponder and repent:
Wrongs against me I pardon great and small,
And if I die, I die in peace with all.'
    His merits thus and not his sins confessed,
He speaks his hopes, and leaves to Heaven the rest.
Alas! are these the prospects, dull and cold,
60 That dying Christians to their priests unfold?
Or mends the prospect when the enthusiast cries,
'I die assured!' and in a rapture dies?
    Ah, where that humble, self-abasing mind,
With that confiding spirit, shall we find—
The mind that, feeling what repentance brings,
Dejection's terrors and Contrition's stings,
Feels then the hope that mounts all care above,
And the pure joy that flows from pardoning love?
    Such have I seen in death and much deplore,
70 So many dying, that I see no more.
Lo! now my records, where I grieve to trace,
How Death has triumphed in so short a space;
Who are the dead, how died they, I relate,
And snatch some portion of their acts from fate.

    With Andrew Collett we the year begin,
The blind, fat landlord of the Old Crown Inn—
Big as his butt,° and, for the self-same use,
To take in stores of strong fermenting juice.
On his huge chair beside the fire he sate,
80 In revel chief, and umpire in debate;
Each night his string of vulgar tales he told,
When ale was cheap and bachelors were bold:
His heroes all were famous in their days,
Cheats were his boast and drunkards had his praise;

butt ale cask

'One, in three draughts, three mugs of ale took down,
As mugs were then—the champion of the Crown;
For thrice three days another lived on ale,
And knew no change but that of mild and stale;°
Two thirsty soakers watched a vessel's side,
90   When he the tap, with dexterous hand, applied;
Nor from their seats departed, till they found
That butt was out and heard the mournful sound.'
    He praised a poacher, precious child of fun!
Who shot the keeper with his own spring-gun;°
Nor less the smuggler who the exciseman tied,
And left him hanging at the birch-wood side,
There to expire; but one who saw him hang
Cut the good cord—a traitor of the gang.
    His own exploits with boastful glee he told,
100   What ponds he emptied and what pikes° he sold;
And how, when blessed with sight alert and gay,
The night's amusements kept him through the day.
    He sang the praises of those times, when all
'For cards and dice, as for their drink, might call;
When justice winked on every jovial crew,
And ten-pins tumbled in the parson's view.'
    He told, when angry wives, provoked to rail,
Or drive a third-day drunkard from his ale,
What were his triumphs, and how great the skill
110   That won the vexed virago to his will:
Who raving came—then talked in milder strain—
Then wept, then drank, and pledged her spouse again.
Such were his themes: how knaves o'er laws prevail,
Or, when made captives, how they fly from jail;
The young how brave, how subtle were the old;
And oaths attested all that Folly told.
    On death like his what name shall we bestow,
So very sudden! yet so very slow?
'Twas slow:—Disease, augmenting year by year,
120   Showed the grim king by gradual steps brought near.
'Twas not less sudden: in the night he died,
He drank, he swore, he jested, and he lied;
Thus aiding folly with departing breath.—
'Beware, Lorenzo, the slow-sudden death.'°

·   ·   ·

    Down by the church-way walk, and where the brook
Winds round the chancel like a shepherd's crook,
In that small house with those green pales° before,

---

mild and stale two kinds of ale ("stale" is
stronger)
spring-gun concealed gun with a trip-wire
pikes large and valuable fish

Beware . . . death the admonition to the young
libertine in Edward Young, *Night Thoughts*
I.387
pales picket fence

Where jasmine trails on either side the door;
Where those dark shrubs that now grow wild at will,
Were clipped in form and tantalized with skill;
Where cockles blanched and pebbles neatly spread,
Formed shining borders for the larkspurs' bed—
20   There lived a Lady, wise, austere, and nice,
Who showed her virtue by her scorn of vice.
In the dear fashions of her youth she dressed,
A pea-green Joseph° was her favourite vest;
Erect she stood, she walked with stately mien,
Tight was her length of stays, and she was tall and lean.
   There long she lived in maiden-state immured,
From looks of love and treacherous man secured;
Though evil fame (but that was long before)
Had blown her dubious blast at Catherine's door.
30   A Captain thither, rich from India, came,
And though a cousin called, it touched her fame:
Her annual stipend rose from his behest,
And all the long-prized treasures she possessed:—
If aught like joy awhile appeared to stay
In that stern face, and chase those frowns away,
'Twas when her treasures she disposed for view,
And heard the praises to their splendour due;
Silks beyond price, so rich, they'd stand alone,
And diamonds blazing on the buckled zone;°
40   Rows of rare pearls by curious workmen set,
And bracelets fair in box of glossy jet;
Bright polished amber precious from its size,
Or forms the fairest fancy could devise.
Her drawers of cedar, shut with secret springs,
Concealed the watch of gold and rubied rings;
Letters, long proofs of love, and verses fine
Round the pinked rims of crispèd Valentine.
Her china-closet, cause of daily care,
For woman's wonder held her pencilled° ware;
50   That pictured wealth of China and Japan,
Like its cold mistress, shunned the eye of man.
   Her neat small room, adorned with maiden-taste,
A clipped French puppy, first of favourites, graced;
A parrot next, but dead and stuffed with art;
(For Poll, when living, lost the Lady's heart,
And then his life; for he was heard to speak
Such frightful words as tinged his Lady's cheek;)
Unhappy bird! who had no power to prove,
Save by such speech, his gratitude and love.
360   A grey old cat his whiskers licked beside;

Joseph long riding cloak   **pencilled** painted
zone belt

A type of sadness in the house of pride.
The polished surface of an India chest,
A glassy globe, in frame of ivory, pressed;
Where swam two finny creatures: one of gold,
Of silver one, both beauteous to behold.
All these were formed the guiding taste to suit;
The beasts well-mannered and the fishes mute.
A widowed Aunt was there, compelled by need
The nymph to flatter and her tribe to feed;
370   Who, veiling well her scorn, endured the clog,
Mute as the fish and fawning as the dog.
    As years increased, these treasures, her delight,
Arose in value in their owner's sight:
A miser knows that, view it as he will,
A guinea kept is but a guinea still;
And so he puts it to its proper use,
That something more this guinea may produce:
But silks and rings, in the possessor's eyes,
The oftener seen, the more in value rise,
380   And thus are wisely hoarded to bestow
The kind of pleasure that with years will grow.
    But what availed their worth—if worth had they—
In the sad summer of her slow decay?
    Then we beheld her turn an anxious look
From trunks and chests, and fix it on her book—
A rich-bound Book of Prayer the Captain gave,
(Some Princess had it, or was said to have;)
And then once more, on all her stores, look round,
And draw a sigh so piteous and profound,
390   That told, 'Alas! how hard from these to part,
And form new hopes and habits from the heart!
What shall I do,' (she cried,) 'my peace of mind
To gain in dying, and to die resigned?'
    'Hear,' we returned;—'these baubles cast aside,
Nor give thy God a rival in thy pride;
Thy closets shut, and ope thy kitchen's door;
There own thy failings, *here* invite the poor;
A friend of Mammon let thy bounty make;
For widows' prayers thy vanities forsake;
400   And let the hungry of thy pride partake:
Then shall thy inward eye with joy survey
The angel Mercy tempering Death's delay!'
    Alas! 'twas hard; the treasures still had charms,
Hope still its flattery, sickness its alarms;
Still was the same unsettled, clouded view,
And the same plaintive cry, 'What shall I do?'
    Nor change appeared: for when her race was run,
Doubtful we all exclaimed, 'What has been done?'

Apart she lived, and still she lies alone;
410 Yon earthy heap awaits the flattering stone,
On which invention shall be long employed,
To show the various worth of Catherine Lloyd.

.   .   .

Then died a Rambler: not the one who sails
And trucks, for female favours, beads and nails;°
Not one, who posts from place to place—of men
And manners treating with a flying pen;°
Not he, who climbs, for prospects, Snowdon's height,
And chides the clouds that intercept the sight;°
No curious shell, rare plant, or brilliant spar,
510 Enticed our traveller from his home so far;
But all the reason, by himself assigned
For so much rambling, was, a restless mind;
As on, from place to place, without intent,
Without reflection, Robin Dingley went.
Not thus by nature;—never man was found
Less prone to wander from his parish-bound:
Claudian's old Man,° to whom all scenes were new,
Save those where he and where his apples grew,
Resembled Robin, who around would look,
520 And his horizon for the earth's mistook.
To this poor swain a keen Attorney came:—
'I give thee joy, good fellow! on thy name;
The rich old Dingley's dead;—no child has he,
Nor wife, nor will; his ALL is left for thee:
To be his fortune's heir thy claim is good;
Thou hast the name, and we will prove the blood.'
The claim was made; 'twas tried—it would not stand;
They proved the blood, but were refused the land.
Assured of wealth, this man of simple heart,
530 To every friend had predisposed a part:
His wife had hopes indulged of various kind;
The three Miss Dingleys had their school assigned,
Masters were sought for what they each required,
And books were bought and harpsichords were hired:
So high was hope;—the failure touched his brain,
And Robin never was himself again.
Yet he no wrath, no angry wish expressed,
But tried, in vain, to labour or to rest;
Then cast his bundle on his back, and went
540 He knew not whither, nor for what intent.

the one . . . nails an itinerant peddler
one . . . pen *Rambler,* the periodical published
by Dr. Johnson, 1750–52
he . . . sight the mountain climber (Mt. Snowdon is in Wales) and collector of minerals (e.g.
crystal, "spar")

Claudian's old Man the old man of Verona
(who never left his rural home) in the idyll by
the Roman poet of the late 4th and early 5th
century A.D.

Years fled;—of Robin all remembrance past,
When home he wandered in his rags at last.
A sailor's jacket on his limbs was thrown,
A sailor's story he had made his own;
Had suffered battles, prisons, tempests, storms,
Encountering death in all his ugliest forms.
His cheeks were haggard, hollow was his eye,
Where madness lurked, concealed in misery;
Want, and the ungentle world, had taught a part,
550   And prompted cunning to that simple heart:
He now bethought him, he would roam no more,
But live at home and labour as before.
    Here clothed and fed, no sooner he began
To round and redden, than away he ran;
His wife was dead, their children past his aid:
So, unmolested, from his home he strayed.
Six years elapsed, when, worn with want and pain,
Came Robin, wrapt in all his rags, again.—
We chide, we pity;—placed among our poor,
560   He fed again, and was a man once more.
    As when a gaunt and hungry fox is found,
Entrapped alive in some rich hunter's ground;
Fed for the field, although each day's a feast,
Fatten you may, but never *tame* the beast;
A house protects him, savoury viands sustain;
But loose his neck and off he goes again:
So stole our vagrant from his warm retreat,
To rove a prowler and be deemed a cheat.
    Hard was his fare; for, him at length we saw,
570   In cart conveyed and laid supine on straw.
His feeble voice now spoke a sinking heart;
His groans now told the motions of the cart;
And when it stopped, he tried in vain to stand;
Closed was his eye, and clenched his clammy hand;
Life ebbed apace, and our best aid no more
Could his weak sense or dying heart restore:
But now he fell, a victim to the snare
That vile attorneys for the weak prepare—
They who, when profit or resentment call,
580   Heed not the groaning victim they enthrall.

·   ·   ·

1807

ROBERT BURNS
1759–1796

Wordsworth praised Burns as one who "showed my youth / How Verse may build a princely throne / On humble truth." And he paid tribute to Burns's appeal in terms Johnson might have used: "Deep in the general heart of men / His power survives." Burns's public role was in part that of the primitive poet; and his strong, confident personality, given edge by reluctance to defer to rank, contributed to that effect. As the son of an unsuccessful farmer, educated largely at home, working on the farm until his first book achieved fame, and returning later in life to a farm (with as little success as his father), Burns's career was hardly the conventional one of a man of letters. The irregularity of his personal life (which produced nine illegitimate children), his bawdy lyrics in *The Merry Muses of Caledonia,* his support of the French Revolution, his attacks upon the conservative forces in the Presbyterian Scottish Kirk, and his bouts of drunkenness all served to fill out the image of a "natural" man whose poetry was the overflow of a strong, undisciplined personality.

In fact, Burns had begun to write early but found his own idiom through his discovery of the earlier Scots vernacular poetry of the eighteenth century, particularly that of Allan Ramsay and Robert Fergusson. His literary achievement had its traditional basis both in these poets and in the English poets of his century. Recent studies have shown that Burns's use of Scots vernacular is rarely consistent, and he himself sometimes speaks of a "sprinkling" of Scots in his poems. He seems to use Scots or English equivalents interchangeably as they serve his literary purposes, and at times his words may look both ways, achieving double meaning in literal dialect sense and in English suggestion. Raymond Bentman points out that the word "bickering" in *To a Mouse* means "hastening" in Scottish "but also carries the English 'fighting,' 'squabbling,' 'brawling,' and thus conveys antagonism as well as fear in the mouse." So, conversely, the sudden emergence of formal English in "Nature's social union" surrounds the phrase with irony. Examples can be found throughout his work, and they make us aware of the artificial nature of Burns's language (comparable in its invention to Chatterton's medieval English and reminiscent in certain ways of the Augustan interplay of levels of diction in mock-heroic poetry). Burns denounced other kinds of literary artifice: "Darts, flames, Cupids, loves, graces, and all that farrago are just . . . a senseless rabble." His own artifice creates the impression of spontaneity and naturalness, while at the same time gaining subtle literary effects.

To a Mouse

On Turning Her Up in Her Nest with the Plough, November 1785

Wee, sleekit,° cowrin, tim'rous beastie,
O, what a panic's in thy breastie!
Thou need na start awa sae hasty,
        Wi' bickering brattle!°

sleekit sleek

bickering brattle hurrying scamper (but see Headnote)

I wad be laith to rin an' chase thee,
           Wi' murdering pattle!°

I'm truly sorry man's dominion
Has broken Nature's social union,
An' justifies that ill opinion
10   Which makes thee startle
At me, thy poor earth-born companion
          An' fellow-mortal!

I doubt na, whyles,° but thou may thieve;
What then? poor beastie, thou maun° live!
A daimen icker° in a thrave°
          'S a sma' request;
I'll get a blessin wi' the lave,°
          An' never miss't!

Thy wee bit housie, too, in ruin!
20 Its silly wa's° the win's are strewin!
An' naething, now, to big° a new ane,
          O' foggage° green!
An' bleak December's winds ensuin,
          Baith snell° an' keen!

Thou saw the fields laid bare an' waste,
An' weary winter comin fast,
An' cozie here, beneath the blast,
          Thou thought to dwell,
Till crash! the cruel coulter past
30   Out thro' thy cell.

That wee bit heap o' leaves an' stibble
Has cost thee mony a weary nibble!
Now thou's turned out, for a' thy trouble,
          But house or hald,°
To thole° the winter's sleety dribble,
          An' cranreuch° cauld!

But, Mousie, thou art no thy lane,°
In proving foresight may be vain:
The best laid schemes o' mice an' men
40   Gang aft agley.°
An' lea'e us nought but grief an' pain
          For promised joy!

pattle plow staff
whyles sometimes
maun must
daimen icker occasional ear
thrave twenty-four sheaves
lave rest
silly wa's feeble walls

big build
foggage rank grass left after the harvest
snell biting
But . . . hald without house or home (holding)
thole endure
cranreuch hoarfrost
no thy lane not alone
agley awry

Still thou art blest, compared wi' me!
The present only toucheth thee:
But och! I backward cast my e'e
        On prospects drear!
An' forward, tho' I canna see,
        I guess an' fear!
1785   1786

Address to the Deil

O Prince! O Chief of many thronèd powers!
That led the embattled seraphim to war.
                          MILTON°

O thou! whatever title suit thee,
Auld Hornie, Satan, Nick, or Clootie,°
Wha in yon cavern grim an' sootie,
        Closed under hatches,
Spairges° about the brunstane cootie,°
        To scaud° poor wretches!

Hear me, auld Hangie,° for a wee,
An' let poor damnèd bodies be;
I'm sure sma' pleasure it can gie,
        Even to a deil,
To skelp° an' scaud poor dogs like me,
        An' hear us squeel.

Great is thy power, an' great thy fame;
Far kend° an' noted is thy name;
An' tho' yon lowan heugh's° thy hame,
        Thou travels far;
An' faith! thou's neither lag° nor lame,
        Nor blate nor scaur.°

Whyles,° ranging like a roarin lion
For prey, a' holes an' corners tryin;
Whyles on the strong-winged tempest flyin,
        Tirlan the kirks;°
Whyles, in the human bosom pryin,
        Unseen thou lurks.

Milton *Paradise Lost* I.128–29; in a letter of 1787 Burns voices his admiration for Milton's "great personage, Satan": "the dauntless magnanimity, the intrepid unyielding independence, the desperate daring and noble defiance of hardship." But this poem plays between that majestic myth and the homelier figure of folk legends. **Clootie** cloven-hoofed **Spairges** splashes **cootie** basin, tub

scaud scald
Hangie hangman
skelp slap
kend known
lowan heugh's flaming pit's
lag backward
Nor blate nor scaur nor bashful nor afraid
Whyles sometimes
Tirlan the kirks unroofing the churches

I've heard my reverend graunie say,
In lanely glens ye like to stray;
Or where auld ruined castles grey
        Nod to the moon,
Ye fright the nightly wanderer's way,
30   Wi' eldritch croon.°

When twilight did my graunie summon,
To say her prayers, douce,° honest woman!
Aft yont the dyke° she's heard you bumman,°
        Wi' eerie drone;
Or, rustlin, thro' the boortrees° coman,
        Wi' heavy groan.

Ae dreary, windy, winter night,
The stars shot down wi' sklentan° light,
Wi' you mysel I gat a fright
40   Ayont the lough;°
Ye, like a rash-buss° stood in sight
        Wi' waving sugh.°

The cudgel in my nieve° did shake,
Each bristled hair stood like a stake,
When, wi' an eldritch, stoor° quaick, quaick,
        Amang the springs,
Awa ye squattered, like a drake,
        On whistling wings.

Let warlocks grim, an' withered hags,
50 Tell how wi' you on ragweed nags,
They skim the muirs, an' dizzy crags,
        Wi' wicked speed;
And in kirk-yards renew their leagues,
        Owre howcket° dead.

Thence countra wives, wi' toil an' pain,
May plunge an' plunge the kirn° in vain;
For, oh! the yellow treasure's taen
        By witching skill;
An' dawtit, twal-pint Hawkie's° gaen
60   As yell's the bill.°

Thence mystic knots mak great abuse
On young guidmen,° fond, keen, an' crouse;°

eldritch croon ghastly moan
douce prudent
Aft yont the dyke often beyond the wall
bumman humming
boortrees bowertrees, elders
sklentan slanting
Ayont the lough beyond (across) the lake
rash-buss clump of rushes
sugh wind-like rushing sound

nieve fist
stoor harsh
howcket dug up
kirn churn
dawtit . . . Hawkie's the petted twelve-pint
Hawkie (white-faced cow)
As . . . bill as dry as the bull
guidmen newly married men
crouse brisk, confident

When the best wark-lume° i' the house,
       By cantraip wit,°
Is instant made no worth a louse,
       Just at the bit.°

When thowes dissolve the snawy hoord,
An' float the jinglin icy boord,°
Then water-kelpies° haunt the foord,
70   By your direction,
An' nighted travellers are allured
       To their destruction.

An' aft your moss-traversing spunkies°
Decoy the wight that late an' drunk is:
The bleezan,° curst, mischievous monkies
       Delude his eyes,
Till in some miry slough he sunk is,
       Ne'er mair to rise.

When Masons' mystic word an' grip
80 In storms an' tempests raise you up,
Some cock or cat your rage maun° stop,
       Or, strange to tell!
The youngest brother ye wad whip
       Aff straught to hell.

Lang syne,° in Eden's bonie yard,°
When youthfu' lovers first were paired,
An' all the soul of love they shared,
       The raptured hour,
Sweet on the fragrant flowery swaird,
90   In shady bower:

Then you, ye auld, snick-drawing° dog!
Ye cam to Paradise incog,
An' played on man a cursed brogue°
       (Black be you fa'!°),
An' gied the infant warld a shog,°
       'Maist ruin'd a'.

D'ye mind that day, when in a bizz,°
Wi' reekit duds, an' reestit gizz,°

---

wark-lume weaver's loom, tool, or implement
(with sexual suggestion)
cantraip wit magic art
bit nick of time, critical moment
boord surface
water-kelpies mischievous spirits; cf. William
Collins, *Ode on the Popular Superstitions of
the Highlands* vi, viii
moss-traversing spunkies bog-crossing will-o'-
the-wisps
bleezan flaming, blazing

maun must
syne since
yard garden
snick-drawing latch-lifting (trick-contriving)
brogue trick
fa' fortune
shog shake
bizz flurry
Wi' . . . gizz with smoky clothes and singed
wig

Ye did present your smoutie phiz
100   'Mang better folk,
An' sklented° on the man of Uz°
          Your spitefu' joke?

An' how yet gat him i' your thrall,
An' brak him out o' house an' hal',
While scabs an' botches° did him gall
          Wi' bitter claw,

An' lowsed° his ill-tongued, wicked scawl,°
          Was warst ava?

But a' your doings to rehearse,
110 Your wily shares an' fechtin° fierce,
Sin' that day Michael did you pierce,°
          Down to this time,
Wad ding° a' Lallan° tongue, or Erse,°
          In prose or rhyme.

An' now, auld Cloots,° I ken ye're thinkan,
A certain Bardie's rantin, drinkin,
Some luckless hour will send him linkan,°
          To your black pit;
But faith! he'll turn a corner jinkan,°
120   An' cheat you yet.

But fare you weel, auld Nickie-ben!
O wad ye tak a thought an' men'!°
Ye aiblins° might—I dinna ken—
          Still hae a stake:°
I'm wae° to think upo' yon den,
          Even for your sake!
1785–86   1786

sklented shot, cast
man of Uz Job
botches boils
lowsed loosed
scawl scold (i.e. his wife)
fechtin fighting
did you pierce Cf. *Paradise Lost* VI.320–34 for
Michael's cleaving of Satan.
ding beat
Lallan Lowland

Erse Gaelic, still spoken in the Highlands of
Burns's day
Cloots hoofs
linkan skipping
jinkan dodging
men' mend
aiblins perhaps
stake gambler's chance
wae filled with woe; cf. Dryden's "hope, with
Origen, that the Devil himself may, at last, be
saved" (Preface to *Absalom and Achitophel*)

Holy Willie's Prayer°

And send the godly in a pet to pray.
POPE°

O Thou, wha in the heavens dost dwell,
Wha, as it pleases best thysel,
Sends ane to heaven an' ten to hell,°
A' for thy glory,
And no for ony guid or ill
They've done afore thee!

I bless and praise thy matchless might,
Whan thousands thou hast left in night,
That I am here afore thy sight,
For gifts an' grace
A burnin an' a shinin light,°
To a' this place.

What was I, or my generation,°
That I should get sic° exaltation?
I, wha deserved most just damnation
For broken laws
Five thousand years 'fore my creation,
Thro' Adam's cause!

When from my mither's womb I fell,
Thou might hae plunged me deep in hell,
To gnash my gums and weep and wail,
In burnin lakes,
Where damnèd devils roar and yell,
Chained to their stakes.

Yet I am here, a chosen sample,
To show thy grace is great an' ample;
I'm here a pillar in thy temple,

Holy Willie's Prayer This mock-prayer or dramatic monologue is composed as if by William Fisher (1737–1809), a Calvinistic elder in the parish of Mauchline. Gavin Hamilton, a lawyer and both friend and patron of Burns (who dedicated his 1786 *Poems* to Hamilton), was cited for neglecting church attendance and for traveling on Sunday. In an appeal to the Synod, Hamilton was successfully defended by another of Burns's friends and patrons, Robert Aiken. Burns explains the situation in a headnote: "Holy Willie was a rather oldish bachelor elder . . . much and justly famed for that polemical chattering which ends in tippling orthodoxy, and for that spiritualized bawdry which refines to a liquorish devotion" (that is, lecherous one). "Holy Willie and his priest, Father Auld . . . came off second best" in the hearing of the Presbytery of Ayr, "owing partly to the oratorical powers of Mr. Robert Aiken . . . but chiefly to Mr. Hamilton's being one of the most irreproachable and truly respectable characters in the country." As for Holy Willie, on "losing his process, the Muse overheard him at his devotions," in the poem that follows. Burns writes a compound of colloquial Scots and biblical English that was characteristic of the evangelical Presbyterian, and he attributes to Willie the intensity of a faith at once prostrate and vindictive.

Pope *The Rape of the Lock* IV.64

ane . . . hell The Calvinistic doctrine of the elect, by which God judges according to his foreordained will rather than the good works men may have performed; the arbitrariness of God's will reveals his power, incommensurate with human understanding.

burnin . . . light "He was a burning and a shining light . . ." (John 5:35)

generation ancestry, birth

sic such

Strong as a rock,
A guide, a buckler, and example
30   To a' thy flock.

O Lord, thou kens what zeal I bear,
When drinkers drink, an' swearers swear,
And singin here and dancin there,
                    Wi' great an' sma':
For I am keepit by thy fear
                    Free frae them a'.

But yet, O Lord! confess I must,
At times I'm fashed° wi' fleshy lust;
An' sometimes too, in warldly trust,°
40   Vile self gets in;
But thou remembers we are dust,
                    Defiled wi' sin.

O Lord! yestreen,° thou kens, wi' Meg—
Thy pardon I sincerely beg;
O! may't ne'er be a livin plague°
                    To my dishonour,
An' I'll ne'er lift a lawless leg
                    Again upon her.

Besides I farther maun° allow,
50 Wi' Leezie's lass, three times I trow—
But, Lord, that Friday I was fou,°
                    When I cam near her,
Or else, thou kens, the servant true
                    Wad ne'er hae steered° her.

May be thou lets this fleshly thorn
Beset thy servant e'en and morn
Lest he owre high and proud should turn,
                    Cause he's sae gifted;°
If sae, thy han' maun e'en be borne,
60   Until thou lift it.

Lord, bless thy chosen in this place,
For here thou hast a chosen race;
But God confound their stubborn face,
                    And blast their name,
Wha bring thy elders to disgrace
                    An' public shame!

fashed troubled
warldly trust Willie was responsible for valuation and arbitration in parish farming.
yestreen last night
livin plague i.e. by pregnancy

maun must
fou drunk
steered roused
gifted i.e. with grace, as one of the elect (cf. "thy chosen" in l. 61)

Lord, mind Gau'n Hamilton's deserts,
He drinks, an' swears, an' plays at cartes,
Yet has sae mony takin arts
Wi' great and sma',
Frae God's ain priest the people's hearts
He steals awa'.

An' when we chastened him therefore,
Thou kens how he bred sic a splore°
As set the warld in a roar
  O' laughin at us;
Curse thou his basket and his store,°
Kail° an' potatoes.

Lord, hear my earnest cry an' prayer,
Against that Presbyt'ry o' Ayr;
Thy strong right hand, Lord, mak it bare°
Upo' their heads;
Lord, weigh it down, and dinna spare,
For their misdeeds!

O Lord my God, that glib-tongued Aiken,
My vera heart and saul are quakin,
To think how we stood sweatin, shakin,
An' pissed wi' dread,
While he, wi' hingin lips and snakin,°
Held up his head.

Lord, in thy day of vengeance try him;
Lord, visit him wha did employ him,
And pass not in thy mercy by them,
Nor hear their prayer;
But, for thy people's sake, destroy them,
And dinna spare!

But, Lord, remember me and mine
Wi' mercies temp'ral and divine,
That I for grace an' gear° may shine
Excelled by nane;
And a' the glory shall be thine,
Amen, Amen!

1785   1789

Line numbers: 70, 80, 90, 100

splore frolic, riot
Curse . . . store "Cursed shall be thy basket
and thy store" (Deuteronomy 28:17).
Kail cabbage (the vast and terrible curse
threatened by Jehovah is aimed rather narrowly
and spitefully by Willie, as again in the next
stanza)
mak it bare "The Lord hath made bare his holy
arm in the eyes of all the nations . . ." (Isaiah
52:10)

snakin curling. Other versions have Willie turn
upon Father Auld in exasperated disloyalty:
"While Auld wi' hingin lip gaed sneaking / And
hid his head!"
gear wealth (not orthodox Calvinism but a frequent misinterpretation of election among Puritans; cf. Dryden, Absalom and Achitophel, ll.
535–36)

Tam O' Shanter°

Of Brownyis and of Bogillis full in this Buke.
GAVIN DOUGLAS°

When chapman billies° leave the street,
And drouthy° neebors, neebors meet,
As market days are wearing late,
An' folk begin to tak the gate;°
While we sit bousing at the nappy,°
An' getting fou° and unco° happy,
We think na on the lang Scots miles,°
The mosses, waters, slaps, and styles,°
That lie between us and our hame,
Whare sits our sulky, sullen dame,
Gathering her brows like gathering storm,
Nursing her wrath to keep it warm.
This truth fand honest Tam o' Shanter,
As he frae Ayr ae° night did canter,
(Auld Ayr, wham ne'er a town surpasses
For honest men and bonie lasses).
O Tam! hadst thou but been sae wise,
As taen thy ain wife Kate's advice!
She tauld thee weel thou was a skellum,°
A bletherin,° blusterin, drunken blellum;°
That frae November till October,
Ae market-day thou was nae sober;
That ilka melder,° wi' the miller
Thou sat as lang as thou had siller;°
That every naig was ca'd a shoe on,°
The smith and thee gat roarin fou on;
That at the Lord's house, even on Sunday,

Tam O' Shanter Burns regarded this as "his own favourite poem . . . an essay in a walk of the Muses entirely new to him." Thomas Carlyle (1828) felt that Burns "had not gone back . . . into that dark, earnest wondering age, when the tradition was believed," and thus "the tragedy of the adventure becomes a mere drunken phantasmagoria, painted on ale-vapours, and the farce alone has any reality." This Romantic response to Burns's irony seems to blame him for not recovering the attitude of William Collins, who was celebrating the "popular superstitions" as a source and even a form of poetic power. Burns could in fact share this view; he tells us that an old family servant with a great repertory of folk tales and songs cultivated in him "the latent seeds of poesy; but had so strong an effect on my imagination that, to this hour, in my nocturnal rambles I sometimes keep a sharp look-out in suspicious places; and though nobody could be more sceptical in these matters than I, yet it often takes an effort of philosophy to shake off these idle terrors" (letter of 1787). In this poem Burns is not mocking superstitions but rather the literal-minded Tam, who seems less capable of awe than of simple fear and appetite (or thirst); the moralizing narration is mock-solemn (like the heroic similes and other occasional "literary" forms), striking a note that seems pointedly inappropriate to Tam's own consciousness.
Gavin Douglas (1474?–1522), from the prologue, l. 18, to the sixth book of his translation of Virgil, *Eneados* ("bogillis" would be spirits)
chapman billies peddlers or market-stall keepers
drouthy thirsty
gate road
nappy ale
fou drunk
unco very
Scots miles about two hundred yards more than the English or American
mosses . . . styles bogs, pools, hedge (or wall) openings, stiles
ae one
skellum wretch
bletherin babbling
blellum chatterbox, idler
ilka melder every time you brought oats to be ground
siller silver, money
ca'd a shoe on shod

Thou drank wi' Kirkton Jean° till Monday.
She prophesied that, late or soon,
30 Thou would be found deep drowned in Doon;°
Or catched wi' warlocks in the mirk,°
By Alloway's auld, haunted kirk.
    Ah, gentle dames! it gars me greet°
To think how mony counsels sweet,
How mony lengthened sage advices,
The husband frae the wife despises!
    But to our tale: ae market night,
Tam had got planted unco right;
Fast by an ingle,° bleezing° finely,
40 Wi' reamin swats,° that drank divinely;
And at his elbow, Souter° Johnie,
His ancient, trusty, drouthy crony;
Tam lo'ed him like a vera brither;
They had been fou for weeks thegither.
The night drave on wi' sangs and clatter;
And ay° the ale was growing better:
The landlady and Tam grew gracious,
Wi' secret favours, sweet and precious:
The souter tauld his queerest stories;
50 The landlord's laugh was ready chorus:
The storm without might rair and rustle,
Tam did na mind the storm a whistle.
    Care,° mad to see a man sae happy,
E'en drowned himsel amang the nappy.
As bees flee hame wi' lades o' treasure,
The minutes winged their way wi' pleasure;
Kings may be blest, but Tam was glorious,
O'er a' the ills o' life victorious!
    But pleasures are like poppies spread,
60 You seize the flower, its bloom is shed;
Or like the snow falls in the river,
A moment white—then melts for ever;
Or like the borealis race,°
That flit ere you can point their place;
Or like the rainbow's lovely form
Evanishing amid the storm—
Nae man can tether time or tide;
The hour approaches Tam maun° ride;
That hour, o' night's black arch the key-stane,

Kirkton Jean who with her sister kept an ale-
house
Doon a river that flows by Alloway Kirk (i.e.
church)
mirk murk, dark
gars me greet makes me weep
ingle fireplace
bleezing blazing

reamin swats foaming new ale
Souter Cobbler
ay ever
Care a sudden use of personification, a mocking
reference to a more formal mode
borealis race northern lights
maun must

70 That dreary hour, he mounts his beast in;
And sic° a night he taks the road in
As ne'er poor sinner was abroad in.
  The wind blew as 'twad° blawn its last;
The rattling showers rose on the blast;
The speedy gleams the darkness swallowed;
Loud, deep, and lang, the thunder bellowed:
That night, a child might understand,
The Deil° had business on his hand.
  Weel mounted on his grey mare, Meg,
80 A better never lifted leg,
Tam skelpit° on thro' dub° and mire,
Despising wind, and rain, and fire;
Whiles° holding fast his guid blue bonnet;
Whiles crooning o'er some auld Scots sonnet;°
Whiles glowering round wi' prudent cares,
Lest bogles° catch him unawares:
Kirk-Alloway was drawing nigh,
Whare ghaists and houlets° nightly cry.
  By this time he was cross the ford,
90 Where in the snaw the chapman smoored;°
And past the birks° and meikle° stane,
Where drunken Charlie brak's neck-bane;
And thro' the whins,° and by the cairn
Where hunters fand the murdered bairn;
And near the thorn,° aboon° the well,
Where Mungo's mither hanged hersel.
Before him Doon pours all his floods;
The doubling storm roars thro' the woods;
The lightnings flash from pole to pole;
100 Near and more near the thunders roll:
When, glimmering thro' the groaning trees,
Kirk-Alloway seemed in a bleeze;
Thro' ilka bore° the beams were glancing,
And loud resounded mirth and dancing.
  Inspiring bold John Barleycorn!
What dangers thou canst make us scorn!
Wi' tippenny,° we fear nae evil;
Wi' usquebae° we'll face the devil!
The swats sae reamed in Tammie's noddle,
110 Fair play,° he cared na deils a boddle.°

sic such	**birks** birches
'twad if it would have	**meikle** great, huge
Deil Devil	**whins** furze, gorse
skelpit hurried	**thorn** hawthorn tree
dub puddle	**aboon** above
Whiles sometimes	**ilka bore** every chink
sonnet song	**tippenny** twopenny ale
bogles spirits, ghosts, bogies	**usquebae** whisky
houlets owls	**Fair play** in justice to him
smoored smothered	**boddle** halfpenny (actually a fraction of that)

But Maggie stood right sair° astonished,
Till, by the heel and hand admonished,
She ventured forward on the light;
And, vow! Tam saw an unco° sight!
    Warlocks and witches in a dance;
Nae cotillon brent new° frae France,
But hornpipes, jigs, strathspeys,° and reels,
Put life and mettle in their heels.
A winnock-bunker° in the east,

20 There sat auld Nick, in shape o' beast;
A towzie tyke,° black, grim, and large!
To gie them music was his charge:
He screwed the pipes and gart them skirl,°
Till roof and rafters a' did dirl.°
Coffins stood round like open presses,°
That shawed the dead in their last dresses;
And, by some devilish cantraip sleight,°
Each in its cauld hand held a light,
By which heroic Tam was able

30 To note upon the haly table
A murderer's banes in gibbet-airns;°
Twa span-lang,° wee, unchristened bairns;
A thief new-cutted frae a rape,°
Wi' his last gasp his gab° did gape;
Five tomahawks, wi' blude red-rusted;
Five scymitars, wi' murder crusted;
A garter which a babe had strangled;
A knife a father's throat had mangled,
Whom his ain son o' life bereft,

40 The grey hairs yet stack to the heft;
Wi' mair of horrible and awefu',
Which even to name wad be unlawfu'.
    As Tammie glowred,° amazed and curious,
The mirth and fun grew fast and furious:
The piper loud and louder blew,
The dancers quick and quicker flew,
They reeled, they set, they crossed, they cleekit,°
Till ilka carlin° swat and reekit,
And coost her duddies to the wark,°

50 And linket° at it in her sark!°

sair sore	**airns** irons
unco strange, prodigious	**span-lang** as long as the span of a hand
brent new brand new	**rape** rope
strathspeys dances of couples (or their music)	**gab** mouth
winnock-bunker (on a) window-seat	**glowred** stared
towzie tyke shaggy dog	**cleekit** hooked arms
He . . . skirl he squeezed the bagpipes and	**ilka carlin** each witch or hag
made them squeal	**And . . . wark** and threw off her clothes to
dirl rattle	dance better (for the sake of the work)
presses clothes cupboards, wardrobes	**linket** tripped along
cantraip sleight magic trick	**sark** shift

Now Tam, O Tam! had thae been queans,°
A' plump and strapping in their teens;
Their sarks, instead o' creeshie° flannen,
Been snaw-white seventeen hunder° linen!
Thir breeks° o' mine, my only pair,
That ance were plush, o' guid blue hair,
I wad hae gi'en them off my hurdies,°
For ae blink o' the bonie burdies!°
But withered beldams, auld and droll,
160   Rigwoodie° hags wad spean° a foal,
Louping and flinging on a crummock,°
I wonder did na turn thy stomach!
But Tam kend what was what fu' brawlie:°
There was ae winsome wench and wawlie°
That night enlisted in the core°
(Lang after kend on Carrick shore;
For mony a beast to dead she shot,
And perished mony a bonie boat,
And shook° baith meikle corn and bear,°
170   And kept the country-side in fear),
Her cutty sark,° o' Paisley harn,°
That while a lassie she had worn,
In longitude tho' sorely scanty,
It was her best, and she was vauntie.°
Ah! little kend thy reverend grannie
That sark she coft° for her wee Nannie
Wi' twa pund Scots° ('twas a' her riches)
Wad ever graced a dance of witches!
But here my Muse her wing maun cour;°
180   Sic flights are far beyond her power:
To sing how Nannie lap and flang,°
(A souple jad she was, and strang),
And how Tam stood, like ane bewitched,
And thought his very een enriched;
Even Satan glowred, and fidged fu' fain,°
And hotched° and blew wi' might and main:
Till first ae caper, syne° anither,
Tam tint° his reason a' thegither,

queans young girls	**bear** barley
creeshie greasy	**cutty sark** short shift
seventeen hunder finely woven	**Paisley harn** linen made at Paisley (rather than
Thir breeks those breeches	woven at home)
hurdies buttocks	**vauntie** boastful, proud of it
burdies lasses	**coft** bought
Rigwoodie rough, ropy	**pund Scots** The Scots pound was worth one-
spean wean (by causing fright)	twelfth of the English.
Louping . . . crummock leaping and capering	**cour** curb
with a crooked staff	**lap and flang** leapt and flung herself about
brawlie well	**fidged fu' fain** fidgeted very eagerly
wawlie ample	**hotched** wriggled
core corps	**syne** then
shook scattered, destroyed	**tint** lost

And roars out, 'Weel done, Cutty-sark!'
190 And in an instant all was dark,
And scarcely had he Maggie rallied,
When out the hellish legion sallied.
    As bees bizz out wi' angry fyke,°
When plundering herds° assail their byke;°
As open° pussie's° mortal foes,
When, pop! she starts before their nose;
As eager runs the market-crowd,
When 'Catch the thief!' resounds aloud;
So Maggie runs; the witches follow,
200 Wi' mony an eldritch° skriech and hollo.
    Ah, Tam! ah, Tam! thou'll get thy fairin!°
In hell they'll roast thee like a herrin!
In vain thy Kate awaits thy comin!
Kate soon will be a woefu' woman!
Now do thy speedy utmost, Meg,
And win the key-stane o' the brig;°
There at them thou thy tail may toss,
A running stream they dare na cross.
But ere the key-stane she could make,
210 The fient a° tail she had to shake;
For Nannie, far before the rest,
Hard upon noble Maggie prest,
And flew at Tam wi' furious ettle;°
But little wist she Maggie's mettle!
Ae spring brought off her master hale,
But left behind her ain grey tail:
The carlin claught° her by the rump,
And left poor Maggie scarce a stump.
    Now, wha this tale o' truth shall read,
220 Ilk man and mother's son, take heed:
Whene'er to drink you are inclined,
Or cutty-sarks run in your mind,
Think! ye may buy the joys o'er-dear;
Remember Tam o' Shanter's mare.
1790   1791

fyke fret
herds herdsmen
byke hive
open bay (in following a scent)
pussie's the hare's
eldritch ghastly, unearthly

fairin just deserts
brig bridge
The fient a the devil a
ettle purpose
claught clutched

Green Grow the Rashes°

Green grow the rashes, O;
  Green grow the rashes, O;
The sweetest hours that e'er I spend,
  Are spent amang the lasses, O!

There's nought but care on every han',
  In every hour that passes, O;
What signifies the life o' man,
  An' 'twere na for the lasses, O.

The warly° race may riches chase,
10   An' riches still may fly them, O;
An' tho' at last they catch them fast,
  Their hearts can ne'er enjoy them, O.

But gie me a canny° hour at e'en,
  My arms about my dearie, O;
An' warly cares, an' warly men,
  May a' gae tapsalteerie,° O!

For you sae douce,° ye sneer at this,
  Ye're nought but senseless asses, O;
The wisest man° the warl' e'er saw,
20   He dearly loved the lasses, O.

Auld Nature swears, the lovely dears
  Her noblest work she classes, O;
Her prentice han' she tried on man,
  An' then she made the lasses, O.
  1784?   1787

Ae Fond Kiss

Ae° fond kiss, and then we sever;
Ae fareweel and then for ever!
Deep in heart-wrung tears I'll pledge thee,
Warring sighs and groans I'll wage thee.
Who shall say that fortune grieves him
While the star of hope she leaves him?
Me, nae cheerfu' twinkle lights me;
Dark despair around benights me.

Green . . . Rashes That is, rushes; the first stanza is a refrain repeated after every other stanza. Burns offered the song as "the genuine language of my heart," as "one who spends the hours and thoughts which the vocations of the day can spare with Ossian, Shakespeare, Thomson, Shenstone, Sterne, etc., or, as the maggot takes him, a gun, a fiddle, or a song to make or mend; and at all times some hearts-dear bonny lass in view." He doubts whether such a life is "more inimical to the sacred interests of piety and virtue than . . . bustling and straining after the world's riches and honours."
warly worldly
canny pleasant
tapsalteerie topsy-turvy
douce sober, prudent
wisest man Solomon
Ae one

I'll ne'er blame my partial fancy,
10   Naething could resist my Nancy:
But to see her was to love her,
Love but her, and love for ever.
Had we never loved sae kindly,
Had we never loved sae blindly,
Never met, or never parted,
We had ne'er been broken-hearted.

Fare thee weel, thou first and fairest!
Fare thee weel, thou best and dearest!
Thine be ilka° joy and treasure,
20   Peace, enjoyment, love, and pleasure!
Ae fond kiss, and then we sever;
Ae fareweel, alas! for ever!
Deep in heart-wrung tears I'll pledge thee,
Warring sighs and groans I'll wage thee.
1791   1792

A Red, Red Rose°

O my luve's like a red, red rose,
     That's newly sprung in June;
O my luve's like the melodie
     That's sweetly played in tune.

As fair art thou, my bonie lass,
     So deep in luve am I;
And I will luve thee still, my dear,
     Till a' the seas gang dry.

Till a' the seas gang dry, my dear,
10   And the rocks melt wi' the sun;
And I will luve thee still, my dear,
     While the sands o' life shall run.

And fare thee weel, my only luve!
     And fare thee weel a while!
And I will come again, my luve,
     Tho' it were ten thousand mile!
                              1794

ilka every
A Red, Red Rose James Kinsley suggests that
this may be a song Burns simply collected—without even reconstructing. Burns spoke of it as "a
simple old Scots song which I had picked up";
and he remarked, "What to me appears the
simple and the wild . . . will be looked on as
the ludicrous and the absurd" by others. It has,
at any rate, been widely regarded in terms like
those of Thomas Crawford: "a lyric of genius,
made out of the common inherited material of
folk-song."

Scots Wha Hae

Robert Bruce's Address to His Army,
Before the Battle of Bannockburn°

Scots, wha hae wi' Wallace bled,
Scots, wham Bruce has aften led,
Welcome to your gory bed,
    Or to victorie.

Now's the day, and now's the hour;
See the front o' battle lour;
See approach proud Edward's power—
    Chains and slaverie!

Wha will be a traitor knave?
10 Wha can fill a coward's grave?
Wha sae base as be a slave?
    Let him turn and flee!

Wha for Scotland's king and law
Freedom's sword will strongly draw,
Freeman stand, or freeman fa'?
    Let him follow me!

By oppression's woes and pains!
By your sons in servile chains!
We will drain our dearest veins,
20   But they *shall* be free!

Lay the proud usurpers low!
Tyrants fall in every foe!
Liberty's in every blow!
    Let us do—or die!
   1793   1794

For A' That and A' That°

Is there, for honest poverty,
    That° hings his head, and a' that;
The coward-slave, we pass him by,
    We dare be poor for a' that!

Bannockburn Robert the Bruce won independence for Scotland and became its king by defeating the forces of Edward II on June 13–14, 1314. In this imaginary address, he calls to mind the heroic struggle of Sir William Wallace (c. 1272–1306) against Edward I of England. While the Scottish war of independence always stirred Burns's feelings, he is here associating it, as he put it in a letter of 1793, "with the glowing ideas of some other struggles of the same nature, *not quite so ancient,*" i.e. the French Revolution.

For A' That and A' That Based on an old tune, this poem was inspired by the French Revolution and perhaps influenced by Thomas Paine's *The Rights of Man* (1791–92), e.g. "The artificial noble shrinks into a dwarf before the noble of nature."

That one that

For a' that, and a' that,
    Our toils obscure, and a' that,
The rank is but the guinea's stamp,
    The man's the gowd° for a' that.

What though on hamely fare we dine,
10   Wear hoddin-grey,° and a' that;
Gie fools their silks, and knaves their wine,
    A man's a man for a' that.
        For a' that, and a' that,
        Their tinsel show, and a' that;
        The honest man,° tho' e'er sae poor,
        Is king o' men for a' that.

Ye see yon birkie,° ca'd a lord,
    Wha struts, and stares, and a' that;
Tho' hundreds worship at his word,
20   He's but a coof° for a' that.
        For a' that, and a' that,
        His ribband, star,° and a' that,
        The man of independent mind,
        He looks and laughs at a' that.

A prince can mak a belted° knight,
    A marquis, duke, and a' that;
But an honest man's aboon° his might,
    Guid faith, he mauna fa'° that!
        For a' that, and a' that,
30   Their dignities, and a' that,
        The pith o' sense, and pride o' worth,
        Are higher rank than a' that.

Then let us pray that come it may,
    As come it will for a' that,
That sense and worth, o'er a' the earth,
    Shall bear the gree,° and a' that.
        For a' that and a' that,
        It's coming yet, for a' that,
        That man to man, the warld o'er,
40   Shall brothers be for a' that.
    1794   1795

---

gowd gold; cf. William Wycherley, *The Plain Dealer* (1677) I.i: "I weigh the man, not his title; 'tis not the King's stamp can make the metal better or heavier"
hoddin-grey natural, undyed wool
honest man alluding to the 17-century celebration of the *honnête homme*, comparable to the Augustan celebration of "goodness" as opposed to "greatness" (cf. Henry Fielding, *Jonathan Wild*, excerpt above, and Pope, *Essay on Man*

IV.248, "An honest man's the noblest work of God")
birkie fellow
coof blockhead
star order of knighthood
belted distinguished, decorated
aboon above
mauna fa' must not claim
gree prize, first place

SENSE AND SENSIBILITY

In both the literature and painting of the later eighteenth century there is a marked strain of the sentimental. This was not so much a cozy celebration of middle-class delicacy or of working-class nobility, as it came to be later. Instead, it was a vehement, often defiant assertion of the value of man's feelings; in fact, it was often a claim that his feelings were his essential strength and the source of his great imaginative powers. The vehemence of the assertion made for theatricality in the display of emotion; it was exhibited in its extremes and at times with a self-congratulatory sense of the nobility it betokened. At the same time, there was a skeptical counter-current of thought that saw these emotions not so much as the highest reaches of the spirit but as the mechanical expression of physical states. In one view man's emotion revealed him as saintly; in the other as a puppet of blind impulses (like the hero that Dryden showed under the power of Timotheus' music in *Alexander's Feast*).

The sensitivity that revealed an honest and generous heart by its free responsiveness came to be considered a gift of sensibility. To those who saw it only as self-indulgence or as merely a low threshold of irritability, and who prized man's common sense and objectivity of response, sensibility (or its kindred excess, sentimentality) became an object of scornful laughter. At a deeper level one can see a division between those who trust the natural goodness of man's feelings and those who stress his fallibility and self-deception. Of those who stand for trust in man's feelings Rousseau is perhaps the key figure; at once notorious and sanctified, loathed and worshiped, his influence became a European phenomenon. If any one man can be said to have invented Romanticism (or even modern childhood) by creating the imaginative forms and the vision of the self which it required, it was he; and in Boswell we can see one of the earliest instances of his influence.

"My nerves are not tremblingly alive, and my literary temper is so happily framed that I am less sensible of pain than of pleasure." Gibbon's sentence sets him apart from Rousseau and from many of his English contemporaries. A German traveler of the 1780's tells us that when he came to England "what is called *sentimental* was the hobby-horse of many moral writers and of such persons as pretended to have finer feelings, and tenderer moral nerves, than others, though"—he adds dryly—"they contradicted it frequently by their actions." By the time he wrote, a certain contempt had arisen for "everything which appears to come under the denomination of sentimental." A satirical Sensibility Academy, somewhat earlier, offered to turn out "such a tribe of snivellers, whimperers, sobbers, and blubberers at funerals, charity sermons, hanging bouts, and tragedies as shall raise a very sentimental uproar through his majesty's three kingdoms." As Vicesimus Knox put it (1779), the "sentimental manner has given an amiable name to vice and has obliquely excused the extravagance of the passions by representing them as the effect of lovely sensibility. . . ." One may cite the instance of James Boswell, who wrote with pride in Turin (1765): "Never was mind so formed as that of him who now recordeth his own transactions. I was now in a fever of love for an abandoned being whom multitudes had often treated like a a very woman of the town." But when his advances were curtly refused by the "abandoned being," Boswell "saw that amongst profligate wretches a man of sentiment could only expose himself."

More interesting is that sense of uniqueness we see in Boswell, or in Rousseau at the opening of *Confessions;* each sees himself as mysterious and inexhaustible, and with reason. In contrast, there is Gibbon's account of awakening to erotic awareness: "a very interesting moment of our lives . . . it less properly belongs to the memoirs of an individual than to the natural history of the species." Or, describing his parents' attachment: "Such is the beginning of a love tale at Babylon or at Putney." In a related way, it is significant that Rousseau (whose most satisfying intimacy was to be treated as an only child) keeps his earliest sentiments "tremblingly alive," rejoicing in recovering them in all their immediacy and freshness after decades. Gibbon, on the other hand, rejoices no less in "autumnal felicity" and disengaged retrospection; and he mocks the nostalgia of Gray's ode on Eton College:

> My name, it is most true, could never be enrolled among the sprightly race, the idle progeny of Eton or Westminster, who delight to cleave the water with pliant arm, to urge the flying ball, and to chase the speed of the rolling circle. But I would ask the most active hero of the play field whether he can seriously compare his childish with his manly enjoyments; whether he does not feel as the most precious attribute of his existence, the vigorous maturity of sensual and spiritual powers which Nature has reserved for the age of puberty. A state of happiness arising only from the want of foresight and reflection shall never provoke my envy; such degenerate taste would tend to sink us in the scale of beings from a man to a child, a dog, and an oyster; till we had reached the confines of brute matter, which cannot suffer because it cannot feel. . . . Freedom is the first wish of our heart; freedom is the first blessing of our nature; and unless we bind ourselves with the voluntary chains of interest or passion, we advance in freedom as we advance in years.

One of the questions that vexes Boswell and Rousseau is the need to feel to the utmost the sentiment of being, to be assured that one has a soul. We can see the same problem in Sterne's account of his heroes, as they prove their authentic existence in self-forgetful spontaneity. Yet they are never quite self-forgetful, or at least they cannot be for longer than it takes to attend to and prize that moment. Sterne is full of an ironic awareness of the excesses of sentiment even as he prizes it; and, like Boswell, he tends both to feel deeply and to study himself while feeling, always aware of the conflict and exploiting its incongruity.

EDWARD GIBBON
1737–1794

From Memoirs of My Own Life [1]
[Aunt Hester and William Law]

Of my two wealthy aunts on the father's side, Hester persevered in a life of celibacy, while Catherine became the wife of Mr. Edward Elliston, a captain

---

1. Gibbon's memoirs consist of six overlapping and partial drafts written between 1788 and 1793; they were left to his literary executor Lord Sheffield, who edited a connected version for publication in 1796. It was only a hundred years later that the original manuscripts were edited and published by John Murray. While Lord Sheffield's version has gained currency through frequent reprintings, it is marked by serious deletions as well as ingenious conflation. Any single text of the memoirs must be an eclectic one, and the following excerpts are drawn as indicated from the various manuscripts in Murray's edition.

in the service of the East India Company. . . . These two ladies are described by Mr. Law under the names of Flavia and Miranda, the pagan and Christian sister.[2] The sins of Flavia, which excluded her from the hope of salvation, may not appear to our carnal apprehension of so black a dye. Her temper was gay and lively; she followed the fashion in her dress and indulged her taste for company and public amusements. But her expense was regulated by economy; she practised the decencies of religion; nor is she accused of neglecting the essential duties of a wife or a mother.

The sanctity of her sister, the original or the copy of Miranda, was indeed of a higher cast. By austere penance Mrs. Hester Gibbon laboured to atone for the faults of her youth, for the profane vanities into which she had been led or driven by authority or example.[3] But no sooner was she mistress of her own actions and plentiful fortune than the pious virgin abandoned forever the house of a brother from whom she was alienated by the interest of this world and of the next. With her spiritual guide, and a widow lady of the name of Hutchinson, she retired to a small habitation at Cliffe, in Northamptonshire, where she lived almost half a century, surviving many years the loss of her two friends.

It is not my design to enumerate or extenuate the Christian virtues of Miranda as they were described by Mr. Law. Her charity, even in its excess, commands our respect. 'Her fortune,' says the historian, 'is divided between herself and several *other* poor people, and she has only her part of relief from it.' The sick and lame, young children and aged persons, were the first object of her benevolence. But she seldom refused to give alms to a common beggar, 'and instead'—I resume Mr. Law's words—'of driving him away as a cheat because she does not know him, she relieves him because he *is* a stranger and unknown to her. Excepting her victuals, she never spent ten pounds a year upon herself. If you was to see her, you would wonder what poor body it was that was so surprisingly neat and clean. She eats and drinks only for the sake of living, and with so regular an abstinence that every meal is an exercise of self-denial, and she humbles her body every time she is forced to feed it.'

Her only study was the Bible, with some legends and books of piety which she read with implicit faith; she prayed five times each day; and as singing, according to the *Serious Call,* is an indispensable part of devotion, she rehearsed

---

2. William Law (1686–1761) took a degree at Cambridge and became a fellow of Emmanuel College; but he refused, on the accession of George I, to take an oath of allegiance to the new monarch and abjuring all support of the Stuart Pretender. As a Nonjuror he resigned his fellowship and turned to controversial writing. In 1723 he joined the Gibbon household as a tutor to Gibbon's undistinguished father and became a "spiritual director of the whole family." Law's greatest work was *A Serious Call to a Devout and Holy Life* (1729); it had a strong influence upon Samuel Johnson and John Wesley. Later Law turned to the mystical writings of Jacob Boehme and formed a religious household with two ladies, one of them Hester Gibbon. In the *Serious Call* Law presented the exemplary cases of Flavia and Miranda, based upon the Gibbon sisters. Of Flavia he wrote that "the poor, vain turn of mind, the irreligion, the folly, and vanity . . . is all owing to the manner of using her estate."

3. "While she was under her mother, she was forced to be genteel, to live in ceremony . . . to be in every polite conversation, to hear profaneness at the playhouse and wanton songs and love intrigues at the opera, to dance at public places that fops and rakes might admire the fineness of her shape and the beauty of her motions." (Law, *Serious Call* VII)

the psalms and hymns of thanksgiving which she now, perhaps, may chant in a full chorus of saints and angels. Such is the portrait and such was the life of that holy virgin who by gods was Miranda called, and by men Mrs. Hester Gibbon. Of the pains and pleasures of a spiritual life I am ill-qualified to speak, yet I am inclined to believe that her lot, even on earth, has not been unhappy. Her penance was voluntary and, in her own eyes, meritorious; her time was filled by regular occupations; and instead of the insignificance of an old maid, she was surrounded by dependents, poor and abject as they were, who implored her bounty and imbibed her lessons. . . .

At an advanced age, about the year 1761, Mr. Law died in the house, I may not say in the arms, of his beloved Miranda. In our family he has left the reputation of a worthy and pious man, who believed all that he professed, and practised all that he enjoined. The character of a Nonjuror, which he main-tained to the last, is a sufficient evidence of his principles in church and state; and the sacrifice of interest to conscience will be always respectable.

His theological writings, which our domestic connection has tempted me to peruse, preserve an imperfect sort of life, and I can pronounce with more con-fidence and knowledge on the merits of the author. His last compositions are darkly tinctured by the incomprehensible visions of Jacob Behmen,[4] and his discourse on the absolute unlawfulness of stage entertainments[5] is sometimes quoted for a ridiculous intemperance of sentiment and language: 'The actors and spectators must all be damned; the playhouse is the porch of Hell, the place of the Devil's abode, where he holds his filthy court of evil spirits; a play is the Devil's triumph, a sacrifice performed to his glory, as much as in the heathen temples of Bacchus or Venus, etc. etc.'

But these sallies of religious frenzy must not extinguish the praise which is due to Mr. William Law as a wit and a scholar. His argument on topics of less absurdity is specious[6] and acute, his manner is lively, his style forcible and clear; and had not his vigorous mind been clouded by enthusiasm, he might be ranked with the most agreeable and ingenious writers of the times. While the Bangorian controversy[7] was a fashionable theme, he entered the lists on the subject of Christ's Kingdom and the authority of the priesthood. Against the plain account of the sacrament of the Lord's Supper he resumed the combat with Bishop Hoadley, the object of Whig idolatry and Tory abhorrence; and at every weapon of attack and defence the Nonjuror, on the ground which is common to both, approves[8] himself at least equal to the prelate. On the ap-

---

4. Or Jacob Boehme (1575–1624), the German mystic who wrote under the influence of Paracelsus, and whose work was translated into English (by Law among others) and had considerable influence from the late 17th century on.
5. Written in 1726 (Gibbon quotes imprecisely, probably from memory).
6. Plausible.
7. Benjamin Hoadley (1676–1761), Bishop of Bangor, in reply to those who wished to involve the church in political factions, preached before George I in 1717 the doctrine that the church was not of this world and that Christ had not delegated his authority to any representatives. This was severely attacked in the Convocation of the clergy, which the king then dismissed. Later, in 1735, Hoadley aroused new controversy by his interpretation of the sacrament of communion, in a work much praised by Henry Fielding's Parson Adams (in *Joseph Andrews*, 1742).
8. Proves.

pearance of the *Fable of the Bees*,[9] he drew his pen against the licentious doctrine that private vices are public benefits; and morality as well as religion must join in his applause.

Mr. Law's masterwork, the *Serious Call*, is still read as a popular and powerful book of devotion. His precepts are rigid, but they are founded on the Gospel; his satire is sharp, but it is drawn from the knowledge of human life; and many of his portraits are not unworthy of the pen of La Bruyère.[10] If he finds a spark of piety in his reader's mind, he will soon kindle it to a flame, and a philosopher must allow that he exposes, with equal severity and truth, the strange contradiction between the faith and practice of the Christian world. Hell-fire and eternal damnation are darted from every page of the book, and it is indeed somewhat whimsical that the fanatics who most vehemently inculcate the love of God should be those who despoil him of every amiable attribute. [From *Memoir F*]

[His Conversion to Roman Catholicism]

It might at least be expected that an ecclesiastical school [11] should inculate the orthodox principles of religion. But our venerable mother had contrived to unite the opposite extremes of bigotry and indifference. An heretic or unbeliever was a monster in her eyes; but she was always, or often, or sometimes remiss in the spiritual education of her own children. . . . Without a single lecture, either public or private, either Christian or Protestant, without any academical subscription, without any episcopal confirmation, I was left by the dim light of my catechism to grope my way to the chapel and communion table, where I was admitted without a question how far, or by what means, I might be qualified to receive the sacrament.

Such almost incredible neglect was productive of the worst mischiefs. From my childhood I had been fond of religious disputation. My poor aunt had been often puzzled by the mysteries which she strove to believe, nor had the elastic spring been totally broken by the weight of the atmosphere of Oxford. The blind activity of idleness urged me to advance without armour into the dangerous mazes of controversy, and at the age of sixteen I bewildered myself in the errors of the Church of Rome.

The progress of my conversion may tend to illustrate at least the history of my own mind. It was not long since Dr. Middleton's [12] free inquiry had sounded an alarm in the theological world. Much ink and much gall had been spilled in the defence of the primitive miracles, and the two dullest of their champions were crowned with academic honours by the University of Oxford. The name of Middleton was unpopular, and his proscription very naturally led me to peruse his writings and those of his antagonists. His bold criticism,

---

9. When Mandeville published an expanded version of his work (see above, The Urban Scene) in 1723, Law wrote one of the ablest of the many attacks.

10. Jean de La Bruyère (1645–96), French translator and imitator of Theophrastus' *Characters*, an acute and witty moralist.

11. Gibbon was enrolled in Magdalen College at Oxford: "To the University of Oxford I acknowledge no obligation, and she will as cheerfully renounce me for a son as I am willing to disclaim her for a mother."

12. Conyers Middleton (1683–1750) in his *Free Enquiry* (1749) attacked the evidence for widespread miracles in the primitive church after the days of the Apostles.

which approaches the precipice of infidelity, produced on my mind a singular effect, and had I persevered in the communion of Rome, I should now apply to my own fortune the prediction of the Sibyl:

. . . via prima salutis
Quod minimum reris, Graia pandetur ab urbe [13]

The elegance of style and freedom of argument were repelled by a shield of prejudice. I still revered the character, or rather the names, of the saints and fathers whom Dr. Middleton exposes, nor could he destroy my implicit belief that the gift of miraculous powers was continued in the Church during the first four or five centuries of Christianity. But I was unable to resist the weight of historical evidence that within the same period most of the leading doctrines of popery were already introduced in theory and practice. Nor was my conclusion absurd that miracles are the test of truth, and that the church must be orthodox and pure which was so often approved by the visible interposition of the Deity. The marvelous tales which are so boldly attested by the Basils and Chrysostoms, the Augustines and Jeromes,[14] compelled me to embrace the superior merits of celibacy, the institution of the monastic life, the use of the sign of the cross, of holy oil, and even of images, the invocation of saints, the worship of relics, the rudiments of purgatory in prayers for the dead, and the tremendous mystery of the sacrifice of the body and blood of Christ, which insensibly swelled into the prodigy of Transubstantiation.[15]

In these dispositions, and already more than half a convert, I formed an unlucky intimacy with a young gentleman of our college whose name I shall spare. With a character less resolute, Mr.   had imbibed the same religious opinions, and some popish books, I know not through what channel, were conveyed into his possession. I read; I applauded; I believed. The English translations of two famous works of Bossuet, Bishop of Meaux, the *Exposition of the Catholic Doctrine* and the *History of the Protestant Variations*, achieved my conversion, and I surely fell by a noble hand. . . .

No sooner had I settled my new religion than I resolved to profess myself a Catholic. Youth is sincere and impetuous, and a momentary glow of enthusiasm had raised me above all temporal considerations. . . . My father was neither a bigot nor a philosopher, but his affection deplored the loss of an only son, and his good sense was astonished at my strange departure from the religion of my country. In the first sally of passion he divulged a secret which prudence might have suppressed, and the gates of Magdalen College were forever shut against my return. Many years afterward, when the name of

---

13. *Aeneid* VI.96–97: "The dawnings of thy safety shall be shown, / From whence thou least shall hope, a Grecian town" (Dryden trans., VI.145–46).
14. The Church Fathers whose testimony Middleton reviewed.
15. That is, the supreme wonder of Christ's body and blood being present in the bread and wine of the Eucharist. Later, as Gibbon tells us, he felt "solitary transport at the discovery of a philosophical argument against the doctrine of transubstantiation: that the text of Scripture which seems to inculcate the real presence is attested only by a single sense, our sight; while the real presence itself is disproved by three of our senses, the sight, the touch, and the taste. The various articles of the Romish creed disappeared like a dream, and, after a full conviction, on Christmas Day 1754, I received the sacrament in the Church of Lausanne."

Gibbon was become as notorious as that of Middleton, it was industriously whispered at Oxford that the historian had formerly 'turned papist.' My character stood exposed to the reproach of inconstancy, and this invidious topic would have been handled without mercy by my opponents could they have separated my cause from that of the university. For my own part, I am proud of an honest sacrifice of interest to conscience. I can never blush if my tender mind was entangled in the sophistry that seduced the acute and manly understandings of Chillingworth and Bayle, who afterward emerged from superstition to scepticism.[16] [From *Memoir B*]

[Gibbon in Love]

I hesitate, from the apprehension of ridicule, when I approach the delicate subject of my early love. By this word I do not mean the polite attention of the gallantry, without hope or design, which has originated from the spirit of chivalry and is interwoven with the texture of French manners. I do not confine myself to the grosser appetite which our pride may affect to disdain because it has been implanted by nature in the whole animal creation: *amor omnibus idem*.[17] The discovery of a sixth sense, the first consciousness of manhood, is a very interesting moment of our lives, but it less properly belongs to the memoirs of an individual than to the natural history of the species. I understand by this passion the union of desire, friendship, and tenderness which is inflamed by a single female, which prefers her to the rest of her sex, and which seeks her possession as the supreme or the sole happiness of our being. I need not blush at recollecting the object of my choice, and though my love was disappointed of success, I am rather proud that I was once capable of feeling such a pure and exalted sentiment.

The personal attractions of Mademoiselle Susanne Curchod were embellished by the virtues and talents of the mind. Her fortune was humble, but her family was respectable. Her mother, a native of France, had preferred her religion to her country. The profession of her father did not extinguish the moderation and philosophy of his temper, and he lived content with a small salary and laborious duty in the obscure lot of minister of Crassy, in the mountains that separate the Pays de Vaud from the county of Burgundy. In the solitude of a sequestered village he bestowed a liberal, and even learned, education on his only daughter. She surpassed his hopes by her proficiency in the sciences and languages, and in her short visits to some relations at Lausanne, the wit, the beauty, and erudition of Mademoiselle Curchod were the theme of universal applause.

The report of such a prodigy awakened my curiosity; I saw and loved. I found her learned without pedantry, lively in conversation, pure in sentiment, and elegant in manners; and the first sudden emotion was fortified by the habits and knowledge of a more familiar acquaintance. She permitted me to make her two or three visits at her father's house. I passed some happy days

16. William Chillingworth (1602–44) was converted to Catholicism in 1630 but later became an Anglican priest. His *The Religion of Protestants* (1638) is one of the great theological works of the age: a defense of the sole authority of the Bible and of the freedom of each individual to interpret it. Pierre Bayle (1647–1706) was a French philosopher and author of a famous biographical dictionary. Gibbon quotes Bayle: "I am most truly a protestant; for I protest indifferently against all systems and all sects."
17. "Love is the same for all" (Virgil, *Georgics* III.124).

in the mountains of Burgundy, and her parents honourably encouraged a connection which might raise their daughter above want and dependence. In a calm retirement the gay vanity of youth no longer fluttered in her bosom: she listened to the voice of truth and passion, and I might presume to hope that I had made some impression on a virtuous heart.

At Crassy and Lausanne I indulged my dream of felicity; but on my return to England, I soon discovered that my father would not hear of this strange alliance, and that without his consent I was myself destitute and helpless. After a painful struggle I yielded to my fate; the remedies of absence and time were at length effectual; and my love subsided in friendship and esteem.[18] [From *Memoir B*]

[His Italian Tour]

I shall advance with rapid brevity in the narrative of my Italian tour, in which somewhat more than a year (April 1764–May 1765) was agreeably employed. Content with tracing my line of march, and slightly touching on my personal feelings, I shall waive the minute investigation of the scenes which have been viewed by thousands, and described by hundreds, of our modern travelers. ROME is the great object of our pilgrimage; and i, the journey; ii, the residence, and iii, the return, will form the most proper and perspicuous division.

i I climbed Mont Cenis, and descended into the plain of Piedmont, not on the back of an elephant, but on a light osier seat in the hands of the dextrous and intrepid chairmen of the Alps. The architecture and government of Turin presented the same aspect of tame and tiresome uniformity, but the court was regulated with decent and splendid economy; and I was introduced to his Sardinian majesty Charles Emmanuel, who, after the incomparable Frederick, held the second rank (*proximus longo tamen intervallo*) among the kings of Europe.[19] The size and populousness of Milan could not surprise an inhabitant of London; the Dome [20] or cathedral is an unfinished monument of Gothic superstition and wealth. But the fancy is amused by a visit to the Boromean Islands, an enchanted palace, a work of the fairies in the midst of a lake encompassed with mountains, and far removed from the haunts of men.

I was less amused by the marble palaces of Genoa than by the recent memorials of her deliverance (in December 1746) from the Austrian tyranny, and I took a military survey of every scene of action within the enclosure of her double walls. My steps were detained at Parma and Modena by the precious relics of the Farnese and Este collections, but, alas! the far greater part had been already transported, by inheritance or purchase, to Naples and Dresden. By the road of Bologna and the Apennine I at last reached Florence, where I reposed from June to September, during the heat of the summer months. In the gallery, and especially in the Tribune, I first acknowledged, at the feet of the Venus of Medicis, that the chisel may dispute the pre-eminence

---

18. *Memoir C* contains the memorable passage: "I sighed as a lover: I obeyed as a son: my wound was insensibly healed by time, absence, and the habits of a new life; and my cure was accelerated by a faithful report of the tranquillity and cheerfulness of the lady herself."

19. "Next, however, by a long interval" (Virgil, *Aeneid* V.320) after Frederick the Great of Prussia.

20. That is, *duomo* (cathedral).

with the pencil,[21] a truth in the fine arts which cannot on this side of the Alps be felt or understood. At home I had taken some lessons of Italian; on the spot I read with a learned native the classics of the Tuscan idiom. But the shortness of my time, and the use of the French language, prevented my acquiring any facility of speaking, and I was a silent spectator in the conversations of our envoy, Sir Horace Mann, whose most serious business was that of entertaining the English at his hospitable table. After leaving Florence I compared the solitude of Pisa with the industry of Lucca and Leghorn, and continued my journey through Siena to Rome, where I arrived in the beginning of October.

ii My temper is not very susceptible of enthusiasm, and the enthusiasm which I do not feel I have ever scorned to affect. But at the distance of twenty-five years I can neither forget nor express the strong emotions which agitated my mind as I first approached and entered the *Eternal City*. After a sleepless night I trod with a lofty step the ruins of the Forum; each memorable spot where Romulus stood, or Tully spoke, or Caesar fell, was at once present to my eye, and several days of intoxication were lost or enjoyed before I could descend to a cool and minute investigation. . . .

Six weeks were borrowed for my tour of Naples, the most populous of cities relative to its size, whose luxurious inhabitants seem to dwell on the confines of paradise and hell-fire.[22] I was presented to the boy king [23] by our new envoy, Sir William Hamilton, who, wisely diverting his correspondence from the Secretary of State to the Royal Society and British Museum, has elucidated a country of such inestimable value to the naturalist and antiquarian. On my return I fondly embraced, for the last time, the miracles of Rome, but I departed without kissing the foot of Rezzonico (Clement XIII), who neither possessed the wit of his predecessor Lambertini, nor the virtues of his successor Ganganelli.

iii In my pilgrimage from Rome to Loreto I again crossed the Apennine. From the coast of the Adriatic I traversed a fruitful and populous country, which would alone disprove the paradox of Montesquieu that modern Italy is a desert. Without adopting the exclusive prejudice of the natives, I sincerely admire the paintings of the Bologna school. I hastened to escape the sad solitude of Ferrara, which in the age of Caesar was still more desolate. The spectacle of Venice afforded some hours of astonishment and some days of disgust; the university of Padua is a dying taper; but Verona still boasts her amphitheater; and his native Vicenza is adorned by the classic architecture of Palladio. The road of Lombardy and Piedmont (did Montesquieu find them without inhabitants?) led me back to Milan, Turin, and the passage of Mont Cenis, where I again crossed the Alps in my way to Lyons.

. . .

[The Ideal Traveler]

He should be endowed with an active, indefatigable vigour of mind and body, which can seize every mode of conveyance, and support with a careless smile every hardship of the road, the weather, or the inn. I must stimulate him

21. The Venus de Medici in the Tribune of the Uffizi Gallery; the "pencil" is the paint-brush.
22. Referring to the climate and the proximity of the volcano Vesuvius.
23. Ferdinand IV (1751–1825).

with a restless curiosity, impatient of ease, covetous of time, and fearless of danger, which drives him forth at any hour of the day or night to brave the flood, to climb the mountain, or to fathom the mine on the most doubtful promise of entertainment or instruction. The arts of common life are not studied in the closet. With a copious stock of classical and historical learning, my traveler must blend the practical knowledge of husbandry and manufactures. He should be a chemist, a botanist, and a master of mechanics. A musical ear will multiply the pleasures of his Italian tour; but a correct and exquisite eye, which commands the landscape of a country, discerns the merit of a picture, and measures the proportions of a building, is more closely connected with the finer feelings of the mind; and the fleeting image should be fixed and realized by the dexterity of the pencil.

I have reserved for the last a virtue which borders on a vice—the flexible temper which can assimilate itself to every tone of society from the court to the cottage, the happy flow of spirits which can amuse and be amused in every company and situation. With the advantage of an independent fortune and the ready use of national and provincial idioms, the traveler should unite the pleasing aspect and decent familiarity which makes every stranger an acquaintance, and the art of conversing with ignorance and dullness on some topic of local and professional information. The benefits of foreign travel will correspond with the degrees of these qualifications. But in this sketch of ideal perfection, those to whom I am known will not accuse me of framing my own panegyric.

Yet the historian of the decline and fall must not regret his time or expense, since it was the view of Italy and Rome which determined the choice of the subject. It was at Rome, on the 15th of October 1764, as I sat musing amid the ruins of the Capitol, while the barefooted friars were singing vespers in the temple of Jupiter, that the idea of writing the decline and fall of the city first started to my mind.[24] But my original plan was circumscribed to the decay of the city rather than of the empire, and though my reading and reflections began to point toward that object, some years elapsed, and several avocations intervened, before I was seriously engaged in the execution of that laborious work. [From *Memoir C*]

[A Retrospective View]
When I contemplate the common lot of mortality, I must acknowledge that I have drawn a high prize in the lottery of life. The far greater part of the globe is overspread with barbarism or slavery; in the civilized world the most numerous class is condemned to ignorance and poverty; and the double fortune of my birth in a free and enlightened country, in an honourable and wealthy family, is the lucky chance of a unit against millions. The general probability is about three to one that a newborn infant will not live to complete his fiftieth year. I have now passed that age, and may fairly estimate the present value of my existence in the threefold division of mind, body, and estate.

i The first indispensable requisite of happiness is a clear conscience, unsullied by the reproach or remembrance of an unworthy action.

24. This memorable sentence actually appears in *Memoir E* and is here substituted for its weaker counterpart in *Memoir C*.

Hic murus aheneus esto,
Nil conscire sibi, nulla pallescere culpa.[25]

I am endowed with a cheerful temper, a moderate sensibility, and a natural disposition to repose rather than to action; some mischievous appetites and habits have perhaps been corrected by philosophy or time. The love of study, a passion which derives fresh vigour from enjoyment, supplies each day, each hour, with a perpetual source of independent and rational pleasure, and I am not sensible of any decay of the mental faculties. The original soil has been highly improved by labour and manure,[26] but it may be questioned whether some flowers of fancy, some grateful errors, have not been eradicated with the weeds of prejudice.

ii Since I have escaped from the long perils of my childhood, the serious advice of a physician has seldom been requisite. 'The madness of superfluous health' [27] I have never known; but my tender constitution has been fortified by time; the play of the animal machine still continues to be easy and regular, and the inestimable gift of the sound and peaceful slumbers of infancy may be imputed both to the mind and body. About the age of forty I was first afflicted with the gout, which in the space of fourteen years has made seven or eight different attacks. Their duration, though not their intensity, appears to encrease, and after each fit I rise and walk with less strength and agility than before. But the gout has hitherto been confined to my feet and knees; the pain is never intolerable; I am surrounded by all the comforts that art and attendance can bestow; my sedentary life is amused with books and company; and in each step of my convalescence I pass through a progress of agreeable sensations.

iii I have already described the merits of my society and situation, but these enjoyments would be tasteless and bitter if their possession were not assured by an annual and adequate supply. . . . According to the scale of Switzerland I am a rich man, and I am indeed rich, since my income is superior to my expense, and my expense is equal to my wishes. My friend Lord Sheffield has kindly relieved me from the cares to which my taste and temper are most adverse. The economy of my house is settled without avarice or profusion; at stated periods all my bills are regularly paid, and in the course of my life I have never been reduced to appear, either as plaintiff or defendant, in a court of justice. Shall I add that, since the failure of my first wishes, I have never entertained any serious thoughts of a matrimonial connection?

I am disgusted with the affectation of men of letters who complain that they have renounced a substance for a shadow and that their fame (which sometimes is no insupportable weight) affords a poor compensation for envy, censure, and persecution.[28] My own experience, at least, has taught me a very

25. Horace, *Epistles* I.i.60–61: "Let this be a man's brazen wall, to be conscious of no ill, to turn pale with no guilt."
26. Cultivation.
27. Pope, *Essay on Man* III.3.
28. "Mr. d'Alembert relates that, as he was walking in the gardens of Sans Souci with the King of Prussia, Frederick said to him, 'Do you see that old woman, a poor weeder, asleep on that sunny bank? She is probably a more happy being than either of us.' The King and the philosopher may speak for themselves; for my part I do not envy the old woman." (Gibbon)

different lesson. Twenty happy years have been animated by the labour of my *History*, and its success has given me a name, a rank, a character in the world, to which I should not otherwise have been entitled. The freedom of my writings has indeed provoked an implacable tribe; but as I was safe from the stings, I was soon accustomed to the buzzing of the hornets. My nerves are not tremblingly alive, and my literary temper is so happily framed that I am less sensible of pain than of pleasure.

The rational pride of an author may be offended rather than flattered by vague indiscriminate praise, but he cannot, he should not, be indifferent to the fair testimonies of private and public esteem. Even his social sympathy may be gratified by the idea that now, in the present hour, he is imparting some degree of amusement or knowledge to his friends in a distant land, that one day his mind will be familiar to the grandchildren of those who are yet unborn.[29] I cannot boast of the friendship or favour of princes. The patronage of English literature has long since been devolved on our booksellers, and the measure of their liberality is the least ambiguous test of our common success. Perhaps the golden mediocrity [30] of my fortune has contributed to fortify my application. Few books of merit and importance have been composed either in a garret or a palace. A gentleman possessed of leisure and competency may be encouraged by the assurance of an honourable reward; but wretched is the writer, and wretched will be the work, where daily diligence is stimulated by daily hunger.

The present is a fleeting moment; the past is no more; and our prospect of futurity is dark and doubtful. This day may *possibly* be my last, but the laws of probability, so true in general, so fallacious in particular, still allow me about fifteen years, and I shall soon enter into the period which, as the most agreeable of his long life, was selected by the judgment and experience of the sage Fontenelle. His choice is approved by the eloquent historian of nature, who fixes our moral happiness to the mature season in which our passions are supposed to be calmed, our duties fulfilled, our ambition satisfied, our fame and fortune established on a solid basis.[31]

I am far more inclined to embrace than to dispute this comfortable doctrine. I will not suppose any premature decay of the mind or body, but I must reluctantly observe that two causes, the abbreviation of time and the failure of hope, will always tinge with a browner shade the evening of life.

i The proportion of a part to the whole is the only standard by which we can measure the length of our existence. At the age of twenty, one year is a tenth, perhaps, of the time which has elapsed within our consciousness and memory. At the age of fifty it is no more than the fortieth, and this relative value continues to decrease till the last sands are shaken by the hand of

29. "In the first of ancient or modern romances (*Tom Jones* XIII.i) this proud sentiment, this feast of fancy is enjoyed by the genius of Fielding: 'Foretell me that some future maid whose grandmother is yet unborn etc.' But the whole of this beautiful passage deserves to be read" (Gibbon). Fielding had written "tender maid."

30. *Aurea mediocritas* or golden mean (from Horace).

31. The opinion of Bernard de Fontenelle (1657–1757) was recorded by the Comte de Buffon (1707–88): "In private conversation that great and amiable man added the weight of his own experience; and this autumnal felicity might be exemplified in the lives of Voltaire, Hume, and many other men of letters." (Gibbon)

death. This reasoning may seem metaphysical, but on a trial it will be found satisfactory and just.

ii The warm desires, the long expectations of youth, are founded on the ignorance of themselves and of the world. They are gradually damped by time and experience, by disappointment or possession; and after the middle season the crowd must be content to remain at the foot of the mountain, while the few who have climbed the summit aspire to descend or expect to fall. In old age the consolation of hope is reserved for the tenderness of parents, who commence a new life in their children; the faith of enthusiasts, who sing hallelujahs above the clouds; and the vanity of authors, who presume the immortality of their name and writings. [From *Memoir E*]

JEAN JACQUES ROUSSEAU
1712–1778

The *Confessions* were undertaken probably early in 1765. As the title suggests, the book looks back to the work of St. Augustine, but it sets itself in opposition through Rousseau's questioning of the doctrine of original sin and his different conception of the "justice and goodness of the Supreme Being." The *Confessions* were published posthumously, Books I–IV in 1781 and VII–XII in 1788. Rousseau was born in Geneva, the son of a watchmaker; his mother died in childbirth. At sixteen he left home to wander on his own; and he became a Catholic convert (he was to revert to Protestantim in 1754 to gain Genevan citizenship). From 1731 he spent ten years with his patroness, Mme de Warens ("Maman," as he called her), the last of those years at her house Les Charmettes (near Chambéry). In 1742 he reached Paris and entered literary and musical circles. At this time began his lifelong liaison with Thérèse Levasseur, a half-literate servant girl (who bore him five children, Rousseau later confessed, that were placed in the Foundling Hospital). His great works began to appear in the 1750's, particularly the *Discourse on Inequality* (1754), *The Social Contract* (1752), *La Nouvelle Héloïse* (1751), and *Émile* (1752). Persecuted for offensive religious statements, he fled to Switzerland and finally found refuge on the small island of Saint-Pierre. When that refuge was denied him by local ecclesiastical authorities, he accepted David Hume's invitation to stay in England, where he was given a small government pension. But he became deeply suspicious of Hume (as of almost everyone else) and returned to France after eighteen months. His final years—until almost the very end of his life—were darkened by both poverty and paranoid rage.

The English text given here is the work of an anonymous nineteenth-century translator.

From The Confessions

I am commencing an undertaking, hitherto without precedent, and which will never find an imitator. I desire to set before my fellows the likeness of a man in all the truth of nature, and that man myself.

Myself alone! I know the feelings of my heart, and I know men. I am not made like any of those I have seen; I venture to believe that I am not made like any of those who are in existence. If I am not better, at least I am different. Whether Nature has acted rightly or wrongly in destroying the mould in which she cast me, can only be decided after I have been read.

Let the trumpet of the Day of Judgment sound when it will, I will present myself before the Sovereign Judge with this book in my hand. I will say boldly: 'This is what I have done, what I have thought, what I was. I have told the good and the bad with equal frankness. I have neither omitted anything bad, nor interpolated anything good. If I have occasionally made use of some immaterial embellishments, this has only been in order to fill a gap caused by lack of memory. I may have assumed the truth of that which I knew might have been true, never of that which I knew to be false. I have shown myself as I was: mean and contemptible, good, high-minded and sublime, according as I was one or the other. I have unveiled my inmost self, even as Thou hast seen it, O Eternal Being. Gather round me the countless host of my fellow men; let them hear my confessions, lament for my unworthiness, and blush for my imperfections. Then let each of them in turn reveal, with the same frankness, the secrets of his heart at the foot of the Throne, and say, if he dare, "*I was better than that man!*" '

[His Aunt Suzon]

I was brought into the world in an almost dying condition; little hope was entertained of saving my life. I carried within me the germs of a complaint which the course of time has strengthened, and which at times allows me a respite only to make me suffer more cruelly in another manner. One of my father's sisters, an amiable and virtuous young woman, took such care of me that she saved my life. At this moment, while I am writing, she is still alive, at the age of eighty, nursing a husband younger than herself but exhausted by excessive drinking. Dear aunt, I forgive you for having preserved my life; and I deeply regret that, at the end of your days, I am unable to repay the tender care which you lavished upon me at the beginning of my own.[1] My dear old nurse Jacqueline is also still alive, healthy and robust. The hands which opened my eyes at my birth will be able to close them for me at my death.

I felt before I thought: this is the common lot of humanity. I experienced it more than others. I do not know what I did until I was five or six years old. I do not know how I learned to read; I only remember my earliest reading, and the effect it had upon me; from that time I date my uninterrupted self-consciousness. My mother had left some romances behind her, which my father and I began to read after supper. At first it was only a question of

1. Suzanne Rousseau (1682–1775) was married late (1730) to Isaac Henri Gonceru. In 1768 Rousseau settled a small annual pension on her.

practising me in reading by the aid of amusing books; but soon the interest became so lively, that we used to read in turns without stopping, and spent whole nights in this occupation. We were unable to leave off until the volume was finished. Sometimes, my father, hearing the swallows begin to twitter in the early morning, would say, quite ashamed, 'Let us go to bed; I am more of a child than yourself.'

In a short time I acquired, by this dangerous method, not only extreme facility in reading and understanding what I read, but a knowledge of the passions that was unique in a child of my age. I had no idea of things in themselves, although all the feelings of actual life were already known to me. I had conceived nothing, but felt everything. These confused emotions, which I felt one after the other, certainly did not warp the reasoning powers which I did not as yet possess; but they shaped them in me of a peculiar stamp, and gave me odd and romantic notions of human life, of which experience and reflection have never been able wholly to cure me.

. . .

. . . Except during the time I spent in reading or writing in my father's company, or when my nurse took me for a walk, I was always with my aunt, sitting or standing by her side, watching her at her embroidery or listening to her singing; and I was content. Her cheerfulness, her gentleness and her pleasant face have stamped so deep and lively an impression on my mind that I can still see her manner, look, and attitude; I remember her affectionate language: I could describe what clothes she wore and how her head was dressed, not forgetting the two little curls of black hair on her temples, which she wore in accordance with the fashion of the time.

I am convinced that it is to her I owe the taste, or rather passion, for music, which only became fully developed in me a long time afterwards. She knew a prodigious number of tunes and songs which she used to sing in a very thin, gentle voice. This excellent woman's cheerfulness of soul banished dreaminess and melancholy from herself and all around her. The attraction which her singing possessed for me was so great, that not only have several of her songs always remained in my memory, but even now, when I have lost her, and as I grew older, many of them, totally forgotten since the days of my childhood, return to my mind with inexpressible charm. Would anyone believe that I, an old dotard, eaten up by cares and troubles, sometime find myself weeping like a child, when I mumble one of those little airs in a voice already broken and trembling? . . . I ask, where is the affecting charm which my heart finds in this song? it is a whim, which I am quite unable to understand; but, be that as it may, it is absolutely impossible for me to sing it through without being interrupted by my tears . . . but I am almost certain that the pleasure which I feel in recalling the air would partly disappear, if it should be proved that others besides my poor aunt Suzon have sung it.

[Life with Mme de Warens]
It is sometimes said that the sword wears out the scabbard. That is my history. My passions have made me live, and my passions have killed me. What passions? will be asked. Trifles, the most childish things in the world, which, however, excited me as much as if the possession of Helen or the

throne of the universe had been at stake. In the first place—women. When I possessed one, my senses were calm; my heart, never. The needs of love devoured me in the midst of enjoyment; I had a tender mother,[2] a dear friend; but I needed a mistress. I imagined one in her place; I represented her to myself in a thousand forms, in order to deceive myself. If I had thought that I held mamma in my arms when I embraced her, these embraces would have been no less lively, but all my desires would have been extinguished; I should have sobbed from affection, but I should never have felt any enjoyment. Enjoyment! Does this ever fall to the lot of man? If I had ever, a single time in my life, tasted all the delights of love in their fulness, I do not believe that my frail existence could have endured it; I should have died on the spot.

Thus I was burning with love, without an object; and it is this state, perhaps, that is most exhausting. I was restless, tormented by the hopeless condition of poor mamma's affairs, and her imprudent conduct, which were bound to ruin her completely at no distant date. My cruel imagination, which always anticipates misfortunes, exhibited this particular one to me continually, in all its extent and in all its results. I already saw myself compelled by want to separate from her to whom I had devoted my life, and without whom I could not enjoy it. Thus my soul was ever in a state of agitation; I was devoured alternately by desires and fears.

Music was with me another passion, less fierce, but no less wasting, from the ardour with which I threw myself into it, from my persistent study of the obscure treatises of Rameau, from my invincible determination to load my rebellious memory with them, from my continual running about, from the enormous heap of compilations which I got together and often spent whole nights in copying. But why dwell upon permanent fancies, while all the follies which passed through my inconstant brain—the transient inclinations of a single day, a journey, a concert, a supper, a walk to take, a novel to read, a comedy to see, everything that was entirely unpremeditated in my pleasure or business, became for me so many violent passions, which, in their ridiculous impetuosity, caused me the most genuine torment? The imaginary sufferings of Cleveland,[3] which I read of with avidity and constant interruption, have, I believe, afflicted me more than my own.

.   .   .

At this period commences the brief happiness of my life; here approach the peaceful, but rapid moments which have given me the right to say, *I have lived*. Precious and regretted moments! begin again for me your delightful course; and, if it be possible, pass more slowly in succession through my memory than you did in your fugitive reality. What can I do to prolong, as I should like, this touching and simple narrative, to repeat the same things over and over again, without wearying my readers by such repetition, any

2. Louise Elénore de Warens (1700–1762), born at Vevey in Switzerland, was employed by the clergy of Savoy in the conversion of Protestants from Geneva, and she seems also to have engaged in some political espionage; she was Rousseau's protectress from 1729 to 1742.

3. The hero of *The English Philosopher, or The History of Mr. Cleveland* (1732–39; an illegitimate son of Oliver Cromwell) in the novel by the Abbé Prévost (1697–1763), translator of Samuel Richardson and best known for *Manon Lescaut*.

more than I was wearied of them myself, when I recommenced the life again and again? If all this consisted of facts, actions, and words, I could describe, and in a manner, give an idea of them; but how is it possible to describe what was neither said nor done, nor even thought, but enjoyed and felt, without being able to assign any other reason for my happiness than this simple feeling? I got up at sunrise and was happy; I walked, and was happy; I saw mamma, and was happy; I left her, and was happy; I roamed the forests and hills, I wandered in the valleys, I read, I did nothing, I worked in the garden, I picked the fruit, I helped in the work of the house, and happiness followed me everywhere—happiness, which could not be referred to any definite object, but dwelt entirely within myself, and which never left me for a single instant.

Nothing that occurred to me during that delightful period, nothing that I did, said, or thought, during all the time it lasted, has escaped my memory. Preceding and subsequent periods only come back to me at intervals; I recall them unequally and confusedly; but I recall this particular period in its entirety, as if it still existed. My fancy, which, during my youth, always looked ahead, and now always looks back, compensates me by these charming recollections for the hope which I have lost for ever. I no longer see anything in the future to tempt me; only the reminiscences of the past can flatter me, and these reminiscences of the period of which I speak, so vivid and so true, often make my life happy, in spite of my misfortunes.

I will mention one single instance of these recollections, which will enable the reader to judge of their liveliness and accuracy. The first day we set out to pass the night at Les Charmettes, mamma was in a sedan-chair, and I followed on foot. The road was somewhat steep, and, being rather heavy and afraid of tiring her bearers, she got down about half-way, intending to finish the rest of the journey on foot. During the walk, she saw something blue in the hedge, and said to me, 'Look! there is some periwinkle still in flower.' I had never seen any periwinkle, I did not stoop down to examine it, and I am too near-sighted to distinguish plants on the ground, when standing upright. I merely cast a passing glance at it, and nearly thirty years passed before I saw any periwinkle again, or paid any attention to it. In 1764, when I was at Cressier with my friend Du Peyrou, we were climbing a hill, on the top of which he has built a pretty *salon*, which he rightly calls Belle-Vue. I was then beginning to botanise a little. While ascending the hill, and looking amongst the bushes, I exclaimed with a cry of joy, 'Ah! there is some periwinkle!' as in fact it was. Du Peyrou observed my delight, without knowing the cause of it; he will learn it, I hope, one day, when he reads these words. The reader may judge, from the impression which so trifling a circumstance made upon me, of the effect produced by everything which has reference to that period.

.   .   .

. . . I repeat, true happiness cannot be described; it can only be felt, and felt the more, the less it can be described, since it is not the result of a number of facts, but is a permanent condition. I often repeat myself, but I should do so still more if I said the same thing as often as it occurs to me. When my frequently-changed manner of life had at last adopted a regular course, it was distributed as nearly as possible in the following manner.

I got up every day before sunrise; I climbed through a neighbouring orchard to a very pretty path above the vineyard which ran along the slope as far as Chambéry. During my walk I offered a prayer, which did not consist merely of idle, stammering words, but of a sincere uplifting of the heart to the Creator of this delightful Nature, whose beauties were spread before my eyes. I never like to pray in a room: it has always seemed to me as if the walls and all the petty handiwork of man interposed between myself and God. I love to contemplate Him in His works, while my heart uplifts itself to Him. My prayers were pure, I venture to say, and for that reason deserved to be heard. I only asked for myself and for her, who was inseparably associated with my wishes, an innocent and peaceful life, free from vice, pain, and distressing needs; the death of the righteous, and their lot in the future. For the rest, this act of worship consisted rather of admiration and contemplation than of requests, for I knew that the best means of obtaining the blessings which are necessary for us from the giver of all true blessings, was to deserve, rather than to ask for, them. My walk consisted of a tolerably long round, during which I contemplated with interest and pleasure the rustic scenery by which I was surrounded, the only thing of which heart and eye never tire. From a distance I looked to see if it was day with mamma. When I saw shutters open, I trembled with joy and ran towards the house; if they were shut, I remained in the garden until she awoke, amusing myself by going over what I had learned the evening before, or by gardening. The shutters opened, I went to embrace her while she was still in bed, often still half asleep; and this embrace, as pure as it was tender, derived from its very innocence a charm which is never combined with sensual pleasure.

[The Roman Past]
. . . I had been told to go and see the Pont du Gard,[4] and did not fail to do so. It was the first Roman work that I had seen. I expected to see a monument worthy of the hands which had erected it; for once, and for the only time in my life, the reality surpassed the expectation. Only the Romans could have produced such an effect.

The sight of this simple, yet noble, work produced the greater impression upon me, as it was situated in the midst of a desert, where silence and solitude bring the object into greater prominence, and arouse a livelier feeling of admiration; for this pretended bridge was nothing but an aqueduct. One naturally asks what strength has transported these enormous stones so far from any quarry, and united the arms of so many thousands of men in a spot where not one of them dwells. I went through the three storeys of this superb building, within which a feeling of respect almost prevented me from setting foot. The echo of my footsteps under these immense vaults made me imagine that I heard the sturdy voices of those who had built them. I felt myself lost like an insect in this immensity. I felt, in spite of my sense of littleness, as if my soul was somehow or other elevated, and I said to myself with a sigh, 'Why was I not born a Roman?' I remained there several hours in rapturous contemplation. . . .

---

4. The great Roman aqueduct near Nîmes in southern France.

[The Island of Saint-Pierre]

I have always been passionately fond of the water, and the sight of it throws me into a delightful state of dreaminess, although often without any definite object. When it was fine weather, I always hastened to the terrace as soon as I was up, to inhale the fresh and healthy morning air, and let my eyes roam over the horizon of this beautiful lake, the shores of which, surrounded by mountains, formed an enchanting prospect. I can think of no worthier homage to the Divinity than the mute admiration which is aroused by the contemplation of his works, and does not find expression in outward acts. I can understand how it is that the inhabitants of cities, who see nothing but walls, streets and crimes, have so little religious belief; but I cannot understand how those who live in the country, especially in solitude, can have none. How is it that their soul is not lifted up in ecstasy a hundred times a day to the Author of the wonders which strike them? As far as I am concerned, it is especially after rising, weakened by a night of sleeplessness, that I am led by long-standing habit to those upliftings of the heart, which do not impose upon me the trouble of thinking. But, for this to take place, my eyes must be smitten by the enchanting spectacle of nature. In my room, my prayers are not so frequent or so fervent; but, at the sight of a beautiful landscape, I feel myself moved without knowing why. I remember reading of a wise bishop, who, during a visit to his diocese, came upon an old woman who, by way of prayer, could say nothing but 'Oh!' 'Good mother,' said the bishop, 'continue to pray in this manner; your prayer is better than ours.' This better prayer is also mine.

After breakfast I hastily wrote a few miserable letters, with a sulky air, longing eagerly for the happy moment when I need write no more. I bustled about my books and papers for a few moments . . . after which I became tired of the task, and spent the three or four remaining hours of the morning in the study of botany. . . .

In the afternoon I abandoned myself entirely to my idle and careless disposition, and followed, without any system, the impulse of the moment. Frequently, when the weather was calm, immediately after dinner, I jumped by myself into a little boat, which the receiver had taught me how to manage with a single oar, and rowed out into the middle of the lake. The moment at which I left the bank, I felt ready to leap for joy. It is impossible for me to explain or understand the reason of this feeling, unless it was a secret self-congratulation on being thus out of the reach of the wicked. I rowed by myself all over the lake, sometimes near the bank, but never landing. Frequently, leaving my boat at the mercy of the wind and water, I abandoned myself to aimless reveries, which, although foolish, were none the less delightful. I sometimes exclaimed with emotion, 'O Nature! O my mother! behold me under thy protection alone! Here there is no cunning or knavish mortal to thrust himself between me and thee.' In this manner I got out half a league from land. I could have wished that this lake had been the ocean. However, in order to please my poor dog, who was not so fond of long excursions on the water as I was, as a rule I followed a definite plan. I landed on the small island, walked about for an hour or two, or stretched myself on the grass at the top of the rising ground, to sate myself with the pleasure of admiring this lake and its surroundings, to examine and anatomise all the plants within my reach, and to build for myself, like a second Robinson,[5] an imaginary dwelling in this little island. I became passionately attached to this hillock. When I was able to take Thérèse, the receiver's wife, and her sisters, for a walk there, how proud I felt to be their pilot and their guide! We solemnly took some rabbits to it, to stock it. Another gala for Jean Jacques! This colony made the little island still more interesting to me. I visited it more frequently and with greater pleasure from that time, to look for signs of the progress of the new inhabitants.

To these amusements I united another, which reminded me of the delightful life at Les Charmettes, and for which the season was particularly suitable. This was the occupations of a country life; and we gathered in the fruit and vegetables, which Thérèse and myself were delighted to share with the receiver and his family. I remember that a Bernese, named M. Kirchberger, when he came to see me, found me perched on the branches of a tall tree, with a bag tied round my waist, so full of apples that I could not move. I was not at all sorry that he and others should find me thus. I hoped that the Bernese, seeing how I employed my leisure time, would no longer think about disturbing its tranquillity, and would leave me in peace in my solitude. I should have preferred to be shut up there by their will than by my own; for, in that case, I should have felt more certain of not seeing my rest disturbed.

I am now again coming to one of those confessions, in regard to which I feel sure beforehand that those readers will be incredulous, who are always determined to judge me by their own standard, although they have been compelled to see, throughout the whole course of my life, a thousand inner emotions which have not the least resemblance to their own. The most extraordinary thing is that, while denying to me all the good or indifferent feelings which they do not themselves possess, they are always ready to attribute to me others so utterly bad that they could not even enter into the heart of a man. They find it perfectly simple to put me into contradiction with nature, and to make me out a monster such as cannot possibly exist. No absurdity appears incredible to them, if only it is calculated to blacken me; nothing that is at all out of the common seems to them possible, if only it is calculated to bring honour upon me.

But, whatever they may believe or say, I will none the less continue faithfully to set forth what Jean Jacques Rousseau was, did, and thought, without either explaining or justifying the singularity of his sentiments and ideas, or inquiring whether others have thought as he. I took such a fancy to the island of Saint-Pierre, and was so comfortable there, that, from continually concentrating all my desires upon this island, I formed the design of never leaving it. The visits which I had to pay in the neighbourhood, the excursions which I should have been obliged to make to Neufchâtel, Bienne, Yverdun, and Nidau, already wearied me in imagination. A day to be spent out of the island seemed to me a curtailment of my happiness; and to go beyond the circumference of the lake was, for me, to leave my element. Besides, my experi-

5. Robinson Crusoe, of Defoe's novel of 1719.

ence of the past had made me timid. It only needed something to make me happy and soothe my heart, to make me expect to lose it; and my ardent desire of ending my days in this island was inseparably united with the fear of being compelled to leave it. I was in the habit of going every evening to sit upon the shore, especially when the lake was rough. I felt a singular pleasure in seeing the waves break at my feet. They represented to me the tumult of the world and the peacefulness of my own abode; and I was sometimes so touched by this delightful idea, that I felt the tears trickling down from my eyes. This repose, which I passionately enjoyed, was only troubled by the apprehension of losing it; but this feeling of uneasiness spoilt its charm. I felt my position to be so precarious, that I could not reckon upon its continuance. Ah! said I to myself, how gladly would I exchange the permission to leave the island, for which I do not care at all, for the assurance of being able to remain there always! Instead of being allowed here by sufferance, why am I not kept here by force? Those who only leave me here on sufferance, can drive me away at any moment; can I venture to hope that my persecutors, seeing me happy here, will allow me to continue to be so? It is little enough that I am permitted to live here; I could wish to be condemned, to be forced to remain in this island, so as not to be forced to leave it. . . .

Tormented, buffeted by storms of every kind, worn out by journeys and persecutions for many years past, I strongly felt the need of the repose of which my barbarous enemies, by way of amusing themselves, deprived me. I sighed more than ever for the delightful idleness, for the sweet repose of body and soul, which I had so longed for, to which the supreme happiness of my heart, now cured of its idle dreams of love and friendship, was limited. I only regarded with alarm the task which I was on the point of undertaking, the stormy life to which I proposed to abandon myself; and if the greatness, the beauty, and the usefulness of the object in view inspired my courage, the impossibility of exposing myself to risk with any chance of success completely deprived me of it. Twenty years of profound and solitary meditation would have been less painful to me than six months of an active life in the midst of men and public affairs, with the certainty of failure.

1765–70   1781–88

LAURENCE STERNE
1713–1768

Tristram Shandy and A Sentimental Journey

Tristram Shandy interrupts the comic and rather bawdy account of his Uncle Toby's amours, i.e. his feckless courtship of the Widow Wadman, with this tale, which is derived from his own travels in France (mostly recounted in Book VII). Sterne may have introduced the tale as a counter-thrust to the ill-tempered *Travels Through France and Italy* of Tobias Smollett (1766), and also as a foretaste of his own *Sentimental*

Journey. At any rate, there is a delicate mixture of pathos and humor in both narratives. Tristram cannot resist the unseasonable jest, and he closes with a seemingly
unfooling tribute to the inn; Yorick, Tristram's clergyman friend (and clearly in some
measure a self-portrait of Sterne), becomes comparably involved in the business of
the handkerchief. In each case Sterne is exquisite in catching the tones of feeling,
self-consciously adroit in representing them, and theoretically concerned with the
meaning of "sensibility," that sensitivity of response that becomes in his view one
of man's highest powers. But he is no less aware of the presence of the physical
and commonplace that sensibility, in its very intensity, tends to overlook; and the
humor of Sterne fuses the detachment of someone like Gibbon (who can see himself
from the outside or from a distance) with the rather humorless, if often exquisitely
delicate, sensitivity of Rousseau.

The Life and Opinions of Tristram Shandy, Gentleman

From *Volume IX, Chapter XXIV*

—For my uncle Toby's amours running all the way in my head, they had
the same effect upon me as if they had been my own—I was in the most
perfect state of bounty and good-will; and felt the kindliest harmony vibrating
within me, with every oscillation of the chaise alike; so that whether the roads
were rough or smooth, it made no difference; every thing I saw or had
to do with, touched upon some secret spring either of sentiment or rapture.

—They were the sweetest notes I ever heard; and I instantly let down
the fore-glass to hear them more distinctly—'Tis Maria; said the postillion,[1]
observing I was listening——Poor Maria, continued he (leaning his body on
one side to let me see her, for he was in a line betwixt us), is sitting upon
a bank playing her vespers upon her pipe, with her little goat beside her.

The young fellow uttered this with an accent and a look so perfectly in
tune to a feeling heart, that I instantly made a vow, I would give him a
four-and-twenty sous piece, when I got to Moulins——

——And who is poor Maria? said I.

The love and pity of all the villages around us; said the postillion—it is but
three years ago, that the sun did not shine upon so fair, so quick-witted and
amiable a maid; and better fate did Maria deserve than to have her banns
forbid, by the intrigues of the curate of the parish who published them—

He was going on, when Maria, who had made a short pause, put the pipe
to her mouth, and began the air again—they were the same notes; yet were
ten times sweeter: It is the evening service to the Virgin, said the young man—
but who has taught her to play it—or how she came by her pipe, no one
knows; we think that heaven has assisted her in both; for ever since she has
been unsettled in her mind, it seems her only consolation—she has never once
had the pipe out of her hand, but plays that service upon it almost night
and day.

1. The driver of the carriage or post-chaise.

The postillion delivered this with so much discretion and natural eloquence, that I could not help deciphering something in his face above his condition, and should have sifted out his history, had not poor Maria taken such full possession of me.

We had got up by this time almost to the bank where Maria was sitting: she was in a thin white jacket, with her hair, all but two tresses, drawn up into a silk-net, with a few olive leaves twisted a little fantastically on one side—she was beautiful; and if ever I felt the full force of an honest heart-ache, it was the moment I saw her—

—God help her! poor damsel! above a hundred masses, said the postillion, have been said in the several parish churches and convents around, for her,— but without effect; we have still hopes, as she is sensible for short intervals, that the Virgin at last will restore her to herself; but her parents, who know her best, are hopeless upon that score, and think her senses are lost for ever.

As the postillion spoke this, Maria made a cadence so melancholy, so tender and querulous, that I sprung out of the chaise to help her, and found myself sitting betwixt her and her goat before I relapsed from my enthusiasm.

Maria looked wistfully for some time at me, and then at her goat—and then at me—and then at her goat again, and so on, alternately—

—Well, Maria, said I softly—What resemblance do you find?

I do entreat the candid reader to believe me, that it was from the humblest conviction of what a beast man is,—that I asked the question; and that I would not have let fallen an unseasonable pleasantry in the venerable presence of misery, to be entitled to all the wit that ever Rabelais [2] scattered— and yet I own my heart smote me, and that I so smarted at the very idea of it, that I swore I would set up for wisdom, and utter grave sentences the rest of my days—and never—never attempt again to commit mirth with man, woman, or child, the longest day I had to live.

As for writing nonsense to them—I believe, there was a reserve [3]—but that I leave to the world.

Adieu, Maria!—adieu, poor hapless damsel!—some time, but not now, I may hear thy sorrows from thy own lips—but I was deceived; for that moment she took her pipe and told me such a tale of woe with it, that I rose up, and with broken and irregular steps walked softly to my chaise.

——What an excellent inn at Moulins!

1757

---

2. François Rabelais (c. 1490–c. 1554), the French monk and author of *Gargantua* and *Pantagruel*, upon whose work Sterne modeled his own in some degree.
3. Reservation.

From A Sentimental Journey Through France and Italy by Mr. Yorick

Moulines

I never felt what the distress of plenty was in any one shape till now—to travel it through the Bourbonnois, the sweetest part of France—in the hey-day of the vintage, when Nature is pouring her abundance into every one's lap, and every eye is lifted up—a journey through each step of which Music beats time to Labour, and all her children are rejoicing as they carry in their clusters—to pass through this with my affections flying out, and kindling at every group before me—and every one of them was pregnant with adventures.

Just Heaven!—it would fill up twenty volumes—and alas! I have but a few small pages left of this to crowd it into—and half of these must be taken up with the poor Maria my friend Mr. Shandy met with near Moulines.

The story he had told of that disordered maid affected me not a little in the reading; but when I got within the neighbourhood where she lived, it returned so strong into my mind, that I could not resist an impulse which prompted me to go half a league out of the road, to the village where her parents dwelt, to enquire after her.

'Tis going, I own, like the Knight of the Woeful Countenance, in quest of melancholy adventures [1]—but I know not how it is, but I am never so perfectly conscious of the existence of a soul within me,[2] as when I am entangled in them.

The old mother came to the door, her looks told me the story before she opened her mouth—She had lost her husband; he had died, she said, of anguish, for the loss of Maria's senses, about a month before.—She had feared at first, she added, that it would have plundered her poor girl of what little understanding was left—but, on the contrary, it had brought her more to herself—still she could not rest—her poor daughter, she said, crying, was wandering somewhere about the road—

—Why does my pulse beat languid as I write this? and what made La Fleur,[3] whose heart seemed only to be tuned to joy, to pass the back of his hand twice across his eyes, as the woman stood and told it? I beckoned to the postillion to turn back into the road.

When we got within half a league of Moulines, at a little opening in the road leading to a thicket, I discovered poor Maria sitting under a poplar—she was sitting with her elbow in her lap, and her head leaning on one side within her hand—a small brook ran at the foot of the tree.

1. Don Quixote.
2. Cf. James Boswell's meditations in his journal of December 27, 1775, where his reading about Hartley and Priestley makes him entertain a mechanistic view of man but also stirs him to protest that he has a soul; this theme of authenticating one's belief in one's soul is a characteristic one in 18th-century skepticism. Sterne in his *Sermons* cites Epicurus' testimony that benevolence contributes to the health of the body and that "the very mechanical motions which maintain life" are better performed by a benevolent man than by "a poor, sordid, selfish wretch. . . ." Again, "What divines say of the mind, naturalists have observed of the body; that there is no passion so natural to it as love, which is the principle of doing good. . . ."
3. Yorick's traveling companion and servant.

I bid the postillion go on with the chaise to Moulines—and La Fleur to bespeak my supper—and that I would walk after him.

She was dressed in white, and much as my friend described her, except that her hair hung loose, which before was twisted within a silk net.—She had, superadded likewise to her jacket, a pale green ribband, which fell across her shoulder to the waist; at the end of which hung her pipe.—Her goat had been as faithless as her lover: and she had got a little dog in lieu of him, which she had kept tied by a string to her girdle: as I looked at her dog, she drew him towards her with the string.—'Thou shalt not leave me, Sylvio,' said she. I looked in Maria's eyes, and saw she was thinking more of her father than of her lover or her little goat; for as she uttered them, the tears trickled down her cheeks.

I sat down close by her; and Maria let me wipe them away as they fell, with my handkerchief.—I then steeped it in my own—and then in hers—and then in mine—and then I wiped hers again—and as I did it, I felt such undescribable emotions within me, as I am sure could not be accounted for from any combinations of matter and motion.

I am positive I have a soul; nor can all the books with which materialists have pestered the world ever convince me to the contrary.

When Maria had come a little to herself, I asked her if she remembered a pale thin person of a man, who had sat down betwixt her and her goat about two years before? She said she was unsettled much at that time, but remembered it upon two accounts—that ill as she was, she saw the person pitied her; and next, that her goat had stolen his handkerchief, and she had beat him for the theft—she had washed it, she said, in the brook, and kept it ever since in her pocket to restore it to him in case she should ever see him again, which, she added, he had half promised her. As she told me this, she took the handkerchief out of her pocket to let me see it; she had folded it up neatly in a couple of vine-leaves, tied round with a tendril—on opening it, I saw an S marked in one of the corners.

She had since that, she told me, strayed as far as Rome, and walked round St. Peter's once—and returned back—that she found her way alone across the Apennines—had travelled over all Lombardy without money—and through the flinty roads of Savoy without shoes—how she had borne it, and how she had got supported, she could not tell—but God tempers the wind, said Maria, to the shorn lamb.

Shorn indeed! and to the quick, said I; and wast thou in my own land, where I have a cottage, I would take thee to it and shelter thee: thou shouldst eat of my own bread and drink of my own cup—I would be kind to thy Sylvio—in all thy weaknesses and wanderings I would seek after thee and bring thee back—when the sun went down I would say my prayers; and when I had done thou shouldst play thy evening song upon thy pipe, nor would the incense of my sacrifice be worse accepted for entering heaven along with that of a broken heart.

Nature melted within me as I uttered this; and Maria observing, as I took out my handkerchief, that it was steeped too much already to be of use, would

needs go wash it in the stream.—And where will you dry it, Maria? said I.—
I'll dry it in my bosom, said she—'twill do me good.

And is your heart still so warm, Maria? said I.

I touched upon the string on which hung all her sorrows—she looked with
wistful disorder for some time in my face; and then, without saying any
thing, took her pipe, and played her service to the Virgin—The string I had
touched ceased to vibrate—in a moment or two Maria returned to herself—
let her pipe fall—and rose up.

And where are you going, Maria? said I.—She said, to Moulines—Let us go,
said I, together.—Maria put her arm within mine, and lengthening the string,
to let the dog follow—in that order we entered Moulines.

Though I hate salutations and greetings in the marketplace,[4] yet when we got
into the middle of this, I stopped to take my last look and last farewell of
Maria.

Maria, though not tall, was nevertheless of the first order of fine forms—
affliction had touched her looks with something that was scarce earthly—still
she was feminine—and so much was there about her of all that the heart
wishes, or the eye looks for in woman, that could the traces be ever worn
out of her brain, and those of Eliza out of mine,[5] she should not only eat of
my bread and drink of my own cup, but Maria should lie in my bosom, and
be unto me as a daughter.

Adieu, poor luckless maiden!—Imbibe the oil and wine which the compassion of a stranger, as he journeyeth on his way, now pours into thy
wounds [6]—the Being who has twice bruised thee can only bind them up
for ever.

The Bourbonnois [7]

There was nothing from which I had painted out for myself so joyous a riot of
the affections, as in this journey in the vintage, through this part of France;
but pressing through this gate of sorrow to it, my sufferings have totally
unfitted me: in every scene of festivity I saw Maria in the background of the
piece, sitting pensive under her poplar; and I had got almost to Lyons before
I was able to cast a shade across her.

—Dear sensibility! source inexhausted of all that's precious in our joys,
or costly in our sorrows! thou chainest thy martyr down upon his bed of
straw—and 'tis thou who liftest him up to Heaven—eternal fountain of our
feelings!—'tis here I trace thee—and this is thy 'divinity which stirs within
me'—not that in some sad and sickening moments, 'my soul shrinks back

4. Cf. Mark 12:38, where the Scribes and Pharisees "love salutations in the marketplace."
5. Mrs. Elizabeth Sclater Draper, whom Sterne had met in 1767, while her husband was
serving in India as an official of the East India Company. She left to join her husband
about three months after Sterne met her, and both his letters and *Journal to Eliza* convey
Sterne's affection for her. The *Journal* is extremely tender and lachrymose as well as somewhat histrionic; here Eliza is more lightly mentioned, somewhat as the mysterious "Jenny"
is in *Tristram Shandy*.
6. Cf. Luke 10: 33–34 on the Good Samaritan: "and when he saw him, he had compassion on him, And went to him, and bound up his wounds, pouring in oil and wine."
7. That is, the Bourbonnais, a province on the border of Burgundy.

upon herself, and startles at destruction'[8]—mere pomp of words!—but that I feel some generous joys and generous cares beyond myself—all comes from thee, great—great Sensorium of the world![9] which vibrates, if a hair of our heads but falls upon the ground, in the remotest desert of thy creation— Touched with thee, Eugenius draws my curtain when I languish—hears my tale of symptoms, and blames the weather for the disorder of his nerves.[10] Thou givest a portion of it sometimes to the roughest peasant who traverses the bleakest mountains—he finds the lacerated lamb of another's flock— This moment I beheld him leaning with his head against his crook, with piteous inclination looking down upon it!—Oh! had I come one moment sooner!—it bleeds to death—his gentle heart bleeds with it—

Peace to thee, generous swain!—I see thou walkest off with anguish—but thy joys shall balance it—for happy is thy cottage—and happy is the sharer of it—and happy are the lambs which sport about you.

1768

8. Cf. Addison's *Cato* (1713) V.i.2–7: "whence this pleasing hope . . . / This longing after immortality? / Or whence this secret dread, and inward horror / Of falling into nought? Why shrinks the soul / Back on herself, and startles at destruction? / 'Tis the divinity that stirs within us. . . ." Sterne insists upon man's generous emotions rather than his fears as evidence of the divine soul within.

9. The *sensorium* was regarded as the center to which all sensations are transmitted by the nerves. Hartley devised, in his *Observations on Man* (1749), a materialistic account of this transmission by a series of vibrations, and Sterne plays upon this in his discussion of "strings" that vibrate. Here he alludes to God as all-knowing and all-caring, and he evokes Sir Isaac Newton's vision of God as a Divine intelligence within the *sensorium* of infinite space; that is, a God for whom (in Addison's words) "infinite space gives room to infinite knowledge and is, as it were, an organ to omniscience." (*Spectator*, No. 565) Cf. Matthew 10:29–31: "Are not two sparrows sold for a farthing? and one of them shall not fall on the ground without your Father. But the very hairs of your head are all numbered. Fear ye not therefore, ye are of more value than many sparrows."

10. Eugenius, the friend of Yorick, who covers his own emotion by ascribing it to the weather, or (perhaps) seriously ascribes it to material causes.

Glossary

A Commentary on Selected Literary and Historical Terms

Airs (1) Songs, or tunes in general. (2) The songs for solo voice with lute accompaniment, as opposed to the polyphonic madrigals (*q.v.*) of the late 16th and early 17th centuries. Airs were strophic, and the successive strophes, or stanzas, of a poem were set to the same melody.

Alchemy The predecessor of chemistry, based upon classical and medieval mythological notions of the structure of matter; it was a study that nevertheless produced a great deal of practical chemical knowledge. Believing in the ancient notion of the relative nobility of metals—for example, from gold down to "baser" substances like lead—alchemists sought to discover a mysterious *philosopher's* (i.e. "scientist's") *stone* enabling them to perform transmutations of baser metals into gold. Since it thus constituted reversing a natural order, it could be thought of as theologically subversive. Alchemists themselves were by way of being practitioners of a hermetic (*q.v.*) religion, and transmuting metals was by no means their sole aim. Alchemical theory employed what would be today regarded as poetic concepts; e.g. sexual combination for chemical compounding, where today one might think of valence or charge. During the 17th century, when chemistry evolved as a science, alchemical lore and language, alluded to in poetry, became part of the body of myth, like Ptolemaic astronomy and the astrological theory it supported.

Allegory Literally, "other reading"; originally a way of interpreting a narrative or other text in order to extract a more general, or a less literal, meaning from it, e.g. reading Homer's *Odyssey* as the universal voyage of human life—with Odysseus standing for all men—which must be made toward a final goal. In the Middle Ages allegory came to be associated with ways of reading the Bible, particularly the Old Testament in relation to the New. In addition, stories came to be written with the intention of being interpreted symbolically; thus e.g. the *Psychomachia* or "battle for the soul" of Prudentius (b. 348 A.D.) figured the virtues and vices as contending soldiers in a battle (see *Personification*). There is allegorical lyric poetry and allegorical drama as well as allegorical narrative. In works such as Spenser's *The Faerie Queene* and Bunyan's *Pilgrim's Progress* allegory becomes a dominant literary form. See also *Dream Vision; Figure; type.*

Alliteration   A repeated initial consonant in successive words. In Old English verse, any vowel alliterates with any other, and alliteration is not an unusual or expressive phenomenon but a regularly recurring structural feature of the verse, occurring on the first and third, and often on the first, second, and third, primary-stressed syllables of the four-stressed line. Thus, from "The Seafarer":

> hreran mid hondum hrimcælde sæ
> ("to stir with his hand the rime-cold sea")

In later English verse tradition, alliteration becomes expressive in a variety of ways. Spenser uses it decoratively, or to link adjective and noun, verb and object, as in the line: "Much daunted with that dint, her sense was dazed." In the 18th and 19th centuries it becomes even less systematic and more "musical."

Amplificatio, Amplifying   The rhetorical enlargement of a statement or dilation of an argument, especially used in tragedy or epic (*q.v.*) poetry or in mock-heroic (*q.v.*). Language and stylistic ornament are deployed so as to increase the importance of a subject or to raise the level of its treatment.

Assonance   A repeated vowel sound, a part-rhyme, which has great expressive effect when used internally (within lines), e.g. "An old, mad, blind, despised and dying king,—" (Shelley, "Sonnet: England in 1819").

Astronomy and Astrology   Astrology may be regarded as an earlier phase or state of the science of astronomy—with an added normative provision in the notion that the *apparent* positions of the heavenly bodies, when viewed from a central earth about which all were thought to move, determined the shape of human life. (See *Zodiac.*) The geocentric astronomy of Ptolemy, wrong as it was about the relation between what was seen by an observer on earth and what caused him to see what he saw, nevertheless enabled men to predict with some accuracy events such as eclipses. In the microcosmic-macrocosmic world-view of the Middle Ages and the Renaissance, in which perspective the microcosm, or little world of man, constituted a miniature version of the whole cosmos, the relations between patterns discernible in the heavens and those of the four elements (*q.v.*), or the humors of the human constitution (*q.v.*), came to have great meaning. Specifically, the stars (meaning sun, moon, planets, fixed stars) were thought to radiate non-material substances called influences (literally, "in flowings") that beamed down to earth and affected human lives. Although the new astronomy of Copernicus, Kepler, and Galileo helped to destroy the conceptual basis for the belief in stellar influence, it is improper to think of a 16th- or 17th-century intellectual (and far less, a medieval man of letters and learning) as being superstitious in his use of astrological lore that was losing its centrality only with acceptance of the new ideas.

Aubade   The French form of the Provençal *alba* ("dawn"), the morning song complementary to the evening *serenade;* it took its name from the word *alba* in the refrain (e.g. that of a famous anonymous poem, *L'alba, l'alba, oc l'alba, tan tost ve* ("the dawn, the dawn, o the dawn, it comes too soon"). In English such a song as Shakespeare's "Hark, hark, the lark / At heaven's gate sings" (from *Cymbeline*) exemplifies this tradition.

Aureate   Literally, "golden"; used of the poetic and sometimes the prose language of 14th- and 15th-century England and Scotland; an idiom highly wrought and specializing in vernacular coinages from Latin.

Baroque   (1) Originally (and still), an oddly shaped rather than a spherical pearl, and hence something twisted, contorted, involuted. (2) By a complicated analogy, a term designating stylistic periods in art, music, and literature during the 16th and 17th centuries in Europe. The analogies among the arts are frequently strained, and the stylistic periods by no means completely coincide. But the relation between the poetry of Richard Crashaw in English and Latin, and the sculpture and architecture of Gianlorenzo Bernini (1598–1680), is frequently taken to typify the spirit of the baroque. (See Wylie Sypher, *Four Stages of Renaissance Style,* 1955.)

Balade, Ballade   The dominant lyric form in French poetry of the 14th and 15th centuries; a strict form consisting of three stanzas of eight lines each, with an *envoi* (*q.v.*), or four-line conclusion, addressing either a person of importance or a personification. Each stanza, including the *envoi*, ends in a refrain.

Ballad Meter   Or *common meter;* four-lined stanzas, rhyming *abab,* the first and third lines in iambic tetrameter (four beats), and the second and fourth lines in iambic trimeter (three beats). See *Meter.*

Blazon, Blason (*Fr.*)   A poetic genre cataloguing the parts or attributes of an object in order to praise it (or, in its satirical form, to condemn it). The first type, most influential chiefly on English Renaissance poetry, had its origin in a poem by Clément Marot in 1536 in praise of a beautiful breast. The English verb, *to blazon,* thus came to mean to catalogue poetically.

Bob and Wheel   The bob (usually consisting of a two-syllable line) and the wheel (a brief set of short lines) are used either singly or together as a kind of *envoi* (*q.v.*) or comment on the action of the stanza preceding them. See *Sir Gawain and the Green Knight* for a prime example.

Calvin, Calvinist   John Calvin (1509–64), French organizer of the strict religious discipline of Geneva (Switzerland), and author of its *Institutes* (1st ed., 1536). Calvin's teachings include among other things, the doctrine of Scripture as the sole rule of faith, the denial of free will in fallen man, and God's absolute predestination of every man, before his creation, to salvation or to damnation. There are Calvinist elements in the Thirty-Nine Articles (1563) of the Church of England, but the English (as opposed to the Scottish) tradition modified the rigor of the doctrine; Milton passed through a phase of strict Calvinism into greater independence and a rejection of absolute predestination.

Carol, Carole   Originally (apparently) a song sung to an accompaniment of dance, and often set out in ballad meter and uniform stanzas of which the leader probably sang the verse and the dancers a refrain; later, generally, a song of religious joy, usually rapid in pace.

Carpe Diem   Literally, "seize the day"; from Horace's Ode I.xi, which ends, *Dum loquimur, fugerit invida / aetas: carpe diem, quam minimum credula postero* ("Even while we're talking, envious Time runs by: seize the day, putting a minimum of trust in tomorrow"). This became a standard theme of Renaissance erotic verse, as in Robert Herrick's "Gather ye rosebuds while ye may."

Cavalier Designating the supporters of Charles I and of the Anglican church establishment, in opposition to the Puritans, or Roundheads, during the English Civil War. In a literary context, the lyric poetry of some of these so-named soldier-lover-poets (e.g. Thomas Carew, Richard Lovelace) is implied with its elegant wit (*q.v.*) and grace. (See *Civil War.*)

Chanson d'aventure A French poetic form describing a conversation about love or between lovers, and represented as overheard by the poet.

Civil War The struggle between Charles I and his Parliament came to a head in 1641, when the King tried forcibly to arrest five dissident members of Parliament. He failed, and in April 1642 raised his standard at Northampton, intending to advance on London. For some time there was a military deadlock, but in January 1644 the Parliamentary forces, allied with the Scots, defeated the King at Marston Moor. The Parliament men now controlled the North, but not until they instituted major military reforms did they overcome the King decisively at Naseby in June 1645. Charles became the captive of Parliament in January 1647 and was executed two years later. In 1653 Oliver Cromwell expelled the "Rump" of the Long Parliament (*q.v.*), which had survived since 1640, and became Lord Protector.

The terms "Cavalier" and "Roundhead," implying respectively aristocratic dash and middle-class puritanism, are not wholly misleading as descriptive of the Royalist and Parliamentary sides in the war; but the fact of new money and religious fervor on the winning side was not the whole story. The split between "Presbyterian" and "Independent" in the Parliament faction was partly religious, partly a division between the affluent and the enthusiastic; and with the victory of the "monied" interest the Revolution itself became conservative. But the execution of the King was an event that for a century or more resonated throughout the course of English history, and, as Marvell understood (see his "Horation Ode"), ended a whole phase of civilization.

Complaint Short poetic monologue, expressing the poet's sorrow at unrequited love or other pains and ending with a request for relief from them.

Complexion See *Temperaments*.

Conceit From the Italian *concetto*, "concept" or "idea"; used in Renaissance poetry to mean a precise and detailed comparison of something more remote or abstract with something more present or concrete, and often detailed through a chain of metaphors or similes (see *Rhetoric*). In Petrarchan (*q.v.*) poetry, certain conceits became conventionalized and were used again and again in various versions. The connection between the Lady's eyes and the Sun, so typical of these, was based on the proportion *her gaze : love's life and day :: sun's shining: world's life and daylight.* Conceits were closely linked to emblems (*q.v.*), to the degree that the verbal connection between the emblem picture and its *significatio,* or meaning, was detailed in an interpretive conceit. See also *Personification*.

Contemptus Mundi Contempt for the world, i.e. rejection of temporal and transitory pleasures and values in favor of the spiritual and eternal.

Contraries See *Qualities*.

Courtly Love   Modern scholarship has coined this name for a set of conventions around which medieval love-poetry was written. It was essentially chivalric and a product of 12th-century France, especially of the troubadours. This poetry involves an idealization of the beloved woman, whose love, like all love, refines and ennobles the lover so that the union of their minds and/or bodies—a union that ought not to be apparent to others—allows them to attain excellence of character.

Dance of Death   Poem accompanied by illustrations on the inevitability and universality of death, which is shown seizing men and women of all ranks and occupations, one after the other.

Decorum   Propriety of discourse; what is becoming in action, character, and style; the avoidance of impossibilities and incongruities in action, style, and character: "the good grace of everything after his kind" and the "great masterpiece to observe." More formally, a neoclassical doctrine maintaining that literary style—grand, or high, middle, and low—be appropriate to the subject, occasion, and genre. Thus Milton, in *Paradise Lost* (I.13–14), invokes his "adventurous song, / That with no middle flight intends to soar. . . ." See also *Rhetoric*.

Digressio   Interpolated story or description in a poem or oration, introduced for ornamentation or some structural purpose.

Dissenters   In England, members of Protestant churches and sects that do not conform to the doctrines of the established Church of England; from the 16th century on, this would include Baptists, Puritans of various sorts within the Anglican Church, Presbyterians, Congregationalists, and (in the 18th century) Methodists. Another term, more current in the 19th century, is *Nonconformist*.

Dream Vision, Dream Allegory   A popular medieval poetic form. Its fictional time is usually Spring; as the poet falls asleep in some pleasant place—a wood or garden—to the music of a stream and the song of birds, he dreams of "real" people or personified abstractions, who illuminate for him the nature of some aspect of knowledge, mode of behavior, or social or political question. See also *Allegory*.

Elegy   Originally, in Greek and Latin poetry, a poem composed not in the hexameter lines of epic (*q.v.*) and, later, of pastoral, but in the elegiac couplets consisting of one hexameter line followed by a pentameter. Elegiac poetry was amatory, epigrammatic. By the end of the 16th century, English poets were using heroic couplets (*q.v.*), to stand for both hexameters and elegiacs; and an elegiac poem was any serious meditative piece. Perhaps because of the tradition of the pastoral elegy (*q.v.*), the general term "elegy" came to be reserved, in modern terminology, for an elaborate and formal lament, longer than a *dirge* or *threnody*, for a dead person. By extension, "elegiac" has come to mean, in general speech, broodingly sad.

Elements   In ancient and medieval science, the four basic substances of which all matter was composed: earth, water, air, fire—in order of density and heaviness. They are often pictured in that order in diagrams of the universe. All four elements, being material, are below the sphere of the moon (above, there is a fifth: the quintessence). The elements are formed of combinations of the

Qualities (*q.v.*) or Contraries: the union of hot and dry makes fire; of hot and moist, air; of cold and moist, water; of cold and dry, earth.

Emblem A simple allegorical picture, or *impresa*, labeled with a motto to show its significance, and usually accompanied by a poetic description that connects the picture or "device" with the meaning, frequently by means of elaborate conceits (*q.v.*), sometimes with more obvious moralizing. Many Renaissance paintings are emblems, without the text. The first Renaissance emblem book was that of the Venetian lawyer Andrea Alciati, in 1531; for the next century and one-half, the pictures and verses were copied, translated, expanded upon, added to, and adapted in French, Dutch, Spanish, German, and Italian as well as his original Latin. Famous English books of emblems were those of Geoffrey Whitney (1586), Henry Peacham (*Minerva Brittana, or A Garden of Heroical Devices,* 1612), George Wither (1635), and Francis Quarles (1635). Based originally on classical mythography, an interest in ancient coins and statuary, as well as "hieroglyphics" in all ancient art, emblem traditions generally divided, in the 17th century, into "Jesuitical" types (involving precise and intense images such as tears, wings, hearts, and classical Cupids signifying not *amor,* but *caritas*), and more pragmatic Protestant emblems (particularly in the Dutch tradition), which tend toward genre scenes of everyday life illustrating proverbs in the text. In the Renaissance, pictures were to be *read* and understood, like texts; and this kind of reading of hieroglyphics extends, in a writer like Sir Thomas Browne, to all of creation:

> The world's a book in folio, printed all
> With God's great works in letters capital:
> Each creature is a page, and each effect
> A fair character, void of all defect.

These lines of Joshua Sylvester are a commonplace. See also *Conceit; Symbolism;* and Figs. 16–21 in illustrations for the Renaissance section of this Anthology.

Enjambment The "straddling" of a clause or sentence across two lines of verse, as opposed to closed, or end-stopped, lines. Thus, in the opening lines of Shakespeare's *Twelfth Night:*

> If music be the food of love, play on!
> Give me excess of it, that, surfeiting
> The appetite may sicken and so die . . .

the first line is stopped, the second enjambed. When enjambment becomes strong or violent, it may have an ironic or comic effect.

The Enlightenment A term used very generally, to refer to the late 17th and the 18th century in Europe, a period characterized by a programmatic rationalism—i.e. a belief in the ability of human reason to understand the world and thereby to transform whatever in it needed transforming; an age in which ideas of science and progress accompanied the rise of new philosophies of the relation of man to the state, an age which saw many of its hopes for human betterment fulfilled in the French Revolution.

Envoi, Envoy Short concluding stanza found in certain French poetic forms and their English imitations, e.g. the *ballade* (*q.v.*). It serves as a dedicatory postscript, and a summing up of the poem of which it repeats the refrain.

Epic   Or, *heroic poetry;* originally, oral narrative delivered in a style different from that of normal discourse by reason of verse, music, and heightened diction, and concerning the great deeds of a central heroic figure, or group of figures, usually having to do with a crisis in the history of a race or culture. Its setting lies in this earlier "heroic" period, and it will often have been written down only after a long period of oral transmission. The Greek *Iliad* and *Odyssey* and the Old English *Beowulf* are examples of this, in their narration mixing details from both the heroic period described and the actual time of their own composition and narration. What is called *secondary* or *literary* epic is a long, ambitious poem, composed by a single poet on the model of the older, primary forms, and of necessity being more allusive and figurative than its predecessors. Homer's poems lead to Virgil's *Aeneid,* which leads to Milton's *Paradise Lost,* in a chain of literary dependency. Spenser's *Faerie Queene* might be called *romantic epic* of the secondary sort, and Dante's *Divine Comedy* might also be assimilated to post-Virgilian epic tradition.

Epic Simile   An extended comparison, in Homeric and subsequently in Virgilian and later epic poetry, between an event in the story (the *fable*) and something in the experience of the epic audience, to the effect of making the fabulous comprehensible in terms of the familiar. From the Renaissance on, additional complications have emerged from the fact that what is the familiar for the classical audience becomes, because of historical change, itself fabled (usually, pastoral) for the modern audience. Epic similes compare the fabled with the familiar usually with respect to one property or element; thus, in the *Odyssey,* when the stalwart forward motion of a ship in high winds is described, the simile goes:

> And as amids a fair field four brave horse
> Before a chariot, stung into their course
> With fervent lashes of the smarting scourge
> That all their fire blows high, and makes them rise
> To utmost speed the measure of their ground:
> So bore the ship aloft her fiery bound
> About whom rushed the billows, black and vast
> In which the sea-roars burst . . .
> (*Chapman translation*)

Notice the formal order of presentation: "even as . . .": *the familiar event, often described in detail;* "just so . . .": *the fabled one.*

Epicureanism   A system of philosophy founded by the Greek Epicurus (342–270 B.C.), who taught that the five senses are the sole source of ideas and sole criterion of truth, and that the goal of human life is pleasure (i.e. hedonism), though this can be achieved only by practicing moderation. Later the term came to connote bestial self-indulgence, which Epicurus had clearly rejected.

Exclamatio   Rhetorical figure representing a cry of admiration or grief.

Exemplum   A short narrative used to illustrate a moral point in didactic literature (especially sermons) or in historical writing. Its function is to recommend or dissuade from a particular course of conduct.

Fabliau   A short story in verse, comic in character, its subject matter often indecent, and the joke hinging on sex or excretion. The plot usually involves a witty turn or practical joke, the motive of which is love or revenge. See The Miller's Tale of Chaucer.

Fathers of the Church   The earliest Christian theologians and ecclesiastical writers (also referred to as "patristic"), flourishing from the late 1st century through the 8th, composing severally in Greek or Latin. Well-known "Fathers" are St. Augustine, St. Jerome, Tertullian.

Feudal System   The system of land tenure and political allegiance characteristic of Europe during the Middle Ages. The king, as owner of all land, gives portions of it to his vassals, by whom it can be passed on to heirs, in return for their pledge of loyalty and of specified military service. These nobles divide their land among their followers, the subdivision continuing until it reaches the serfs, who cultivate the land but must hand over most of their produce to the lord.

Figurative Language   In a general sense, any shift away from a literal meaning of words, brought about by the use of tropes (*q.v.*) or other rhetorical devices. See *Rhetoric*.

Figure   As defined by Erich Auerbach in his essay "Figura," a mode of interpretation establishing a connection between two events or persons, the first of which signifies both itself and the second, while the second encompasses or fulfills the first—e.g. the Eucharist, which is the "figure" of Christ. See *Allegory*.

Free Verse, Vers Libre   Generally, any English verse form whose lines are measured neither by the number of 1) stressed syllables (see *Meter* §3, accentual verse), 2) alternations of stressed and unstressed syllables (§4, accentual-syllabic verse), nor syllables alone (§2, syllabic verse). The earliest English free verse —that of Christopher Smart in *Jubilate Agno* (18th century)—imitates the prosody of Hebrew poetry (reflected also in the translation of the English Bible), in maintaining unmeasured units marked by syntactic parallelism. While many free-verse traditions (e.g. that of Walt Whitman) remain close to the impulses of this biblical poetry, yet others, in the 20th century, have developed new *ad hoc* patternings of their own. *Vers libre* usually refers to the experimental, frequently very short unmeasured lines favored by poets of the World War I period, although the term, rather than the form, was adopted from French poetry of the 19th century.

Gothic   Term (originally pejorative, as alluding to the Teutonic barbarians) designating the architectural style of the Middle Ages. The revival of interest in medieval architecture in the later 18th century produced not only pseudo-Gothic castles like Horace Walpole's "Strawberry Hill", and more modest artificial ruins on modern estates, but also a vogue for atmospheric prose romances set in medieval surroundings and involving improbable terrors, and known as Gothic novels. The taste for the Gothic, arising during the Age of Sensibility (*q.v.*), is another reflection of a reaction against earlier 18th-century neoclassicism (*q.v*).

Hermetic, Hermeticism, Hermetist   Terms referring to a synthesis of Neoplatonic and other occult philosophies, founded on a collection of writings attributed to Hermes Trismegistus ("Thrice-greatest Hermes"—a name given the Egyptian god Thoth), but which in fact date from the 2nd and 3rd centuries A.D. An important doctrine was that of correspondences between earthly and heavenly things. By studying these correspondences, a man might "walk to the sky" (in the words of Henry Vaughan) in his lifetime. Hermetic tradition favored *esoteric* or forbidden knowledge, over what could be more publicly avowed.

Heroic Couplet   In English prosody, a pair of rhyming, iambic pentameter lines, used at first for closure—as at the end of the Shakespearean sonnet (*q.v.*)— or to terminate a scene in blank-verse drama; later adapted to correspond in English poetry to the elegiac couplet of classical verse as well as to the heroic, unrhymed, Greek and Latin hexameter. Octosyllabic couplets, with four stresses (eight syllables) to the line, are a minor, shorter, jumpier form, used satirically unless in implicit allusion to the form of Milton's "Il Penseroso," in which they develop great lyrical power. (See *Meter.*)

Humors   The combinations, in men and women (the *microcosm*) of the qualities (*q.v.*), or contraries. In primitive physiology, the four principal bodily fluids in their combinations produce the temperaments (*q.v.*) or "complexions" These "humors," with their properties and effects—at least in the Middle Ages—are, respectively: Blood (hot and moist)—cheerfulness, warmth of feeling; Choler (hot and dry)—a quick, angry temper; Phlegm (cold and moist)—dull sluggishness; Melancholy (cold and dry)—fretful depression. The Renaissance introduced the concept of "artificial" humors—e.g. scholars' and artists' melancholy, creative brooding. The humors, the temperaments, and the four elements (*q.v.*) of the macrocosm, or universe, were all looked upon as interrelated. See *Renaissance Psychology.*

Irony   Generally, a mode of saying one thing to mean another. *Sarcasm*, in which one means exactly the opposite of what one says, is the easiest and cheapest form; thus, e.g. "Yeah, it's a *nice day!*" when one means that it's a miserable one. But serious literature produces ironies of a much more complex and revealing sort. *Dramatic irony* occurs when a character in a play or story asserts something whose meaning the audience or reader knows will change in time. Thus, in Genesis when Abraham assures his son Isaac (whom he is about to sacrifice) that "God will provide his own lamb," the statement is lighted with dramatic irony when a sacrificial ram is actually provided at the last minute to save Isaac. Or, in the case of Sophocles' *Oedipus,* when almost everything the protagonist says about the predicament of his city is hideously ironic in view of the fact (which he does not know) that he is responsible therefor. The ironies generated by the acknowledged use of non-literal language (see *Rhetoric*) and fictions in drama, song, and narrative are at the core of imaginative literature.

Judgment   In Catholic doctrine, God's retributive judgment, which decides the fate of rational creatures according to their merits and faults. Particular judgment is the decision about the eternal destiny of each soul made immediately after death; General (Last) Judgment is at the Second Coming of Christ as God and Man, when all men will be judged again in the sight of all the world. See Fig. 50 in illustrations for the Medieval section of this anthology.

Kenning   An Old Norse form designating, strictly, a condensed simile or metaphor of the kind frequently used in Old Germanic poetry; a figurative circumlocution for a thing not actually named—e.g. "swan's path" for sea; "world-candle" or "sky-candle" for sun. More loosely, often used to mean also a metaphorical compound word or phrase such as "ring-necked" or "foamy-necked" for a ship, these being descriptive rather than figurative in character.

Lancastrians   See *Wars of the Roses.*

Locus Amoenus   Literally, "pleasant place"; a garden, either Paradise, the most perfect of all gardens, or its pagan equivalent, or the later literary garden that was a figure (*q.v.*) of Paradise. See *Topos.*

Long Parliament   The Parliament summoned by Charles I on November 3, 1640; the last remnant, not dissolved until 1660, opposed the King and brought about his downfall and execution. See *Civil War.*

Macaronic   Verse in which two languages are mingled, usually for burlesque purposes.

Machiavelli, Niccolò   Italian diplomat, historian, and political theorist (1469–1527), whose chief work, *Il Principe* (*The Prince*, 1513), based in part on the career of Cesare Borgia, outlines a pragmatic rule of conduct for a ruler; thus, politics should have nothing to do with morality; the prince should be an exponent of ruthless power in behalf of his people. In England his theories were put into practice by Thomas Cromwell in the reign of Henry VIII; his writings, however, were not translated until the 17th century, and his image in England, based on rumor and the reports of his adversaries, fostered a myth of the evil "Machiavel" as he appears in Marlowe (*Titus Andronicus*) and Shakespeare (*Richard III*).

Madrigal   Polyphonic setting of a poem, in the 16th and 17th centuries, for several voice parts, unaccompanied or with instruments. Because of the contrapuntal texture, the words were frequently obscured for a listener, though not for the performers.

Meter   Verse may be made to differ from prose and from ordinary speech in a number of ways, and in various languages these ways may be very different. Broadly speaking, lines of verse may be marked out by the following regularities of pattern:

1. *Quantitative Verse,* used in ancient Greek poetry and adopted by the Romans, used a fixed number of what were almost musical measures, called *feet;* they were built up of long and short syllables (like half- and quarter-notes in music), which depended on the vowel and consonants in them. *Stress accent* (the *word* stress which, when accompanied by vowel reduction, distinguishes the English noun "*content*" from the adjective "*content*") did not exist in ancient Greek, and played no part in the rhythm of the poetic line. Thus, the first line of the *Odyssey: Andra moi ennepe mousa, polytropon hos mala polla* ("Sing me, O muse, of that man of many resources who, after great hardship . . .") is composed in *dactyls* of one long syllable followed by two shorts (but, as in musical rhythm, replaceable by two longs, a *spondee*).

With six dactyls to a line, the resulting meter is called *dactylic hexameter* (*hexameter*, for short), the standard form for epic poetry. Other kinds of foot or measure were: the *anapest* (∪ ∪ —); the *iamb* (∪ —); the *trochee* (— ∪); and a host of complex patterns used in lyric poetry. Because of substitutions, however, the number of syllables in a classical line was not fixed, only the number of measures.

2. *Syllabic Verse*, used in French, Japanese, and many other languages, and in English poetry of the mid-20th century, measures only the *number* of syllables per line with no regard to considerations of *quantity* or *stress*. Because of the prominence of stress in the English language, two lines of the same purely syllabic length may not necessarily sound at all as though they were in the same meter, e.g.:

> These two incommensurably sounding
> Lines are both written with ten syllables.

3. *Accentual Verse*, used in early Germanic poetry, and thus in Old English poetry, depended upon the number of strong *stress accents* per line. These accents were four in number, with no fixed number of unstressed. Folk poetry and nursery rhymes often preserve this accentual verse, e.g.:

> Sing, sing, what shall I sing?
> The cat's run away with the pudding-bag string

The first line has six syllables, the second, eleven, but they sound more alike (and not merely by reason of their rhyme) than the two syllabic lines quoted above.

4. *Accentual-Syllabic Verse*, the traditional meter of English poetry from Chaucer on, depends upon both numbered *stresses* and numbered *syllables*, a standard form consisting of ten syllables alternately stressed and unstressed, and having five stresses; thus it may be said to consist of five syllable pairs.

For complex historical reasons, accentual-syllabic groups of stressed and unstressed syllables came to be known by the names used for Greek and Latin feet—which can be very confusing. The analogy was made between *long* syllables in the classical languages, and *stressed* syllables in English. Thus, the pair of syllables in the adjective "content" is called an *iamb*, and in the noun "content," a *trochee*; the word "classical" is a *dactyl*, and the phrase "of the best," an *anapest*. When English poetry is being discussed, these terms are always used in their adapted, accentual-syllabic meanings, and hence the ten-syllable line mentioned earlier is called "iambic pentameter" in English. The phrase "high-tide" would be a *spondee* (as would, in general, two monosyllables comprising a proper name, e.g. "John Smith"); whereas compound nouns like "highway" would be *trochaic*. In this adaptation of classical nomenclature, the terms *dimeter, trimeter, tetrameter, pentameter, hexameter* refer not to the number of quantitative feet but to the number of syllable-groups (pairs or triplets, from one to six) composing the line. Iambic pentameter and tetrameter lines are frequently also called *decasyllabic* and *octosyllabic* respectively.

5. *Versification.* In verse, lines may be arranged in patterns called *stichic*

or *strophic,* that is, the same linear form (say, iambic pentameter) repeated without grouping by rhyme or interlarded lines of another form, or varied in just such a way into *stanzas* or *strophes* ("turns"). Unrhymed iambic pentameter, called *blank verse,* is the English stichic form that Milton thought most similar to classic hexameter or *heroic* verse. But in the Augustan period iambic pentameter rhymed pairs, called heroic couplets (*q.v.*), came to stand for this ancient form as well as for the classical elegiac verse (*q.v.*). Taking couplets as the simplest strophic unit, we may proceed to *tercets* (groups of three lines) and to *quatrains* (groups of four), rhymed *abab* or *abcb,* and with equal or unequal line lengths. Other stanzaic forms: *ottava rima,* an eight-line, iambic pentameter stanza, rhyming *ababbcc; Spenserian stanza,* rhyming *ababbcbcc,* all pentameter save for the last line, an iambic hexameter, or *alexandrine.* There have been adaptations in English (by Shelley, notably, and without rhyme by T. S. Eliot) of the Italian *terza rima* used by Dante in *The Divine Comedy,* interlocking tercets rhyming *aba bcb cdc ded,* etc. More elaborate stanza forms developed in the texts of some Elizabethan songs and in connection with the ode (*q.v.*).

Microcosm Literally, "the small world"—man. For fuller explanation see selections of Walter Ralegh and Thomas Browne on this theme. See also *Astronomy, Astrology; Humors; Qualities.*

Mirror for Princes A treatise setting out the education necessary to make a ruler and the modes of mental, moral, and physical activity that befitted him.

Mock-heroic, Mock-epic The literary mode resulting when low or trivial subjects are treated in the high, artificial literary language of classical epic (*q.v.*) poetry. The point of the joke is usually to expose not the inadequacies of the style but those of the subject, although occasionally the style may be caricatured, and the joke made about decorum (*q.v.*) itself. Alexander Pope's *The Rape of the Lock* is a famous example.

Music of the Spheres The ancient fiction held that the celestial spheres made musical sounds, either by rubbing against the ether, or because an angel— the Christian replacement for the Intelligence which in Plato's *Timaeus* guided each one—sang while riding on his charge. The inaudibility of this music was ascribed by later Platonism (*q.v.*) to the imprisonment of the soul in the body, and by Christian writers, to man's fallen state. Frequent attempts were made to preserve some meaning for this beautiful idea: thus, Aristotle's conclusion that the continuous presence of such sounds would make them inaudible to habituated ears (a sophisticated prefiguration of the modern notion of background noise). And thus the belief of the Ptolemaic astronomy that at a certain point the ratios of the diameters of the spheres of the various heavenly bodies were "harmonious" in that they would generate the overtone series. Even Kepler, who demonstrated that the planetary orbits, let alone non-existent spheres, could not be circular, suggested that the ratios of the angular velocities of the planets would generate a series of melodies; he then proceeded to put them together contrapuntally. See *Astronomy and Astrology.*

Myth A primitive story explaining the origins of certain phenomena in the world and in human life, and usually embodying gods or other supernatural forces, heroes (men who are either part human and part divine, or are placed between an ordinary mortal and a divine being), men, and animals. Literature continues to incorporate myths long after the mythology (the system of stories containing them) ceases to be a matter of actual belief. Moreover, discarded beliefs of all sorts tend to become myths when they are remembered but no longer literally clung to, and are used in literature in a similar way. The classical mythology of the Greeks and Romans was apprehended in this literary, or interpreted, way, even in ancient times. The gods and heroes and their deeds came to be read as allegory (q.v.). During the Renaissance, *mythography*—the interpretation of myths in order to make them reveal a moral or historical significance (rather than merely remaining entertaining but insignificant stories)—was extremely important, both for literature and for painting and sculpture. In modern criticism, mythical or *archetypal* situations and personages have been interpreted as being central objects of the work of the imagination.

Neoclassicism (1) In general the term refers to Renaissance and post-Renaissance attempts to model enterprises in the various arts on Roman and Greek originals—or as much as was known of them. Thus, in the late Renaissance, the architectural innovations of Andrea Palladio may be called "neoclassic," as may Ben Jonson's relation, and Alexander Pope's as well, to the Roman poet Horace. The whole Augustan period in English literary history (1660–1740) was a deliberately neoclassical one.

(2) More specifically, neoclassicism refers to that period in the history of all European art spanning the very late 18th and early 19th century, which period may be seen as accompanying the fulfillment, and the termination, of the Enlightenment (q.v.). In England such neoclassic artists as Henry Fuseli, John Flaxman, George Romney, and even, in some measure, William Blake, are close to the origins of pictorial and literary Romanticism itself.

Neoplatonism See *Platonism.*
Nonconformist See *Dissenters.*

Octosyllabic Couplet See *Heroic Couplet; Meter.*
Ode A basic poetic form, originating in Greek antiquity. The *choral ode* was a public event, sung and danced, at a large ceremony, or as part of the tragic and comic drama. Often called *Pindaric ode,* after a great Greek poet, the form consisted of *triads* (groups of three sections each). These were units of song and dance, and had the form *aab*—that is, a *strophe* (or "turn"), an *antistrophe* (or "counter-turn"), and an *epode* (or "stand"), the first two being identical musically and metrically, the third different. In English poetry, the Pindaric ode form, only in its metrical aspects, became in the 17th century a mode for almost essayistic poetic comment, and was often used also as a kind of cantata libretto, in praise of music and poetry (the so-called *musical ode*). By the 18th century the ode became the form for a certain kind of personal, visionary poem, and it is this form that Wordsworth and Coleridge transmitted to Romantic tradition. A second English form, known as *Horatian ode,* was based on the lyric (not choral) poems of Horace, and is written in *aabb* quatrains, with the last two lines shorter than the first two by a pair of syllables or more.

Oral Formula   A conventional, fossilized phrase common in poetry composed as it was recited, or composed to be recited, and repeated frequently in a single poem. It serves as either a means of slowing or even stopping the action momentarily, or of filling out a verse: e.g. "Beowulf, son of Ecgtheow," or "go or ride"—i.e. "whatever you do."

Paradox   In logic, a self-contradictory statement, hence meaningless (or a situation producing one), with an indication that something is wrong with the language in which such a situation can occur, e.g. the famous paradox of Epimenedes the Cretan, who held that all Cretans are liars (and thus could be lying if—and only if—he wasn't), or that of Zeno, of the arrow in flight: since at any instant of time the point of the arrow can always be said to be at one precise point, therefore it is continually at rest at a continuous sequence of such points, and therefore never moves. In literature, however, particularly in the language of lyric poetry, paradox plays another role. From the beginnings of lyric poetry, paradox has been deemed necessary to express feelings and other aspects of human inner states, e.g. Sappho's invention of the Greek word *glykypikron* ("bittersweet") to describe love, or her assertion that she was freezing and burning at the same time. So too the Latin poet Catullus, in his famous couplet

> I'm in hate and I'm in love; why do I? you may ask.
> Well, I don't know, but I feel it, and I'm in agony.

may be declaring thereby that true love poetry must be illogical.

In Elizabethan poetry, paradoxes were frequently baldly laid out in the rhetorical form called *oxymoron* (see *Rhetoric*), as in "the victor-victim," or across a fairly mechanical sentence structure, as in "My feast of joy is but a dish of pain." In the highest poetic art, however, the seeming self-contradiction is removed when one realizes that either, or both, of the conflicting terms is to be taken figuratively, rather than literally. The apparent absurdity, or strangeness, thus gives rhetorical power to the utterance. Elaborate and sophisticated paradoxes, insisting on their own absurdity, typify the poetic idiom of the tradition of John Donne.

Pastoral   A literary mode in which the lives of simple country people are celebrated, described, and used allegorically by sophisticated urban poets and writers. The *idylls* of Sicilian poet Theocritus (3rd century B.C.) were imitated and made more symbolic in Virgil's *eclogues;* shepherds in an Arcadian landscape stood for literary and political personages, and the Renaissance adapted these narrative and lyric pieces for moral and aesthetic discussion. Spenser's *Shepheardes Calendar* is an experimental collection of eclogues involving an array of forms and subjects. In subsequent literary tradition, the pastoral imagery of both Old and New Testaments (Psalms, Song of Songs, priest as *pastor* or shepherd of his flock, and so on) joins with the classical mode. Modern critics, William Empson in particular, have seen the continuation of pastoral tradition in other versions of the country-city confrontation, such as child-adult and criminal-businessman. See *Pastoral Elegy.*

Pastoral Elegy   A form of lament for the death of a poet, originating in Greek bucolic tradition (Bion's lament for Adonis, a lament for Bion by a fellow poet, Theocritus' first idyll, Virgil's tenth eclogue) and continued in use by Renaissance poets as a public mode for the presentation of private, inner, and even coterie matters affecting poets and their lives, while conventionally treating questions of general human importance. At a death one is moved to ask, "Why this death? Why now?" and funeral elegy must always confront these questions, avoiding easy resignation as an answer. Pastoral elegy handled these questions with formal mythological apparatus, such as the Muses, who should have protected their dead poet, local spirits, and other presences appropriate to the circumstances of the life and death, and perhaps figures of more general mythological power. The end of such poems is the eternalization of the dead poet in a monument of myth, stronger than stone or bronze: Spenser's *Astrophel*, a lament for Sir Philip Sidney, concludes with an Ovidian change—the dead poet's harp, like Orpheus' lyre, becomes the constellation Lyra. Milton's *Lycidas* both exemplifies and transforms the convention. Later examples include Shelley's *Adonais* (for Keats), Arnold's *Thyrsis* (for Clough), and Swinburne's *Ave Atque Vale* (for Baudelaire).

Penance   In Catholic doctrine, the moral virtue by which a sinner is disposed to hate his sin as an offense against God; and the sacrament, of which the outward signs are the acknowledgment of sin, self-presentation of the sinner to priest to confess his sins, the absolution pronounced by the priest, and the satisfaction (penance) imposed on the sinner by the priest and to be performed before the sinner is delivered from his guilt. See Figs. 32 and 52 in illustrations for the Medieval section of this Anthology.

Peroration   Final part of an oration, reviewing and summarizing the argument, often in an impassioned form. (See also *Rhetoric*.)

Personification   Treating a thing or, more properly, an abstract quality, as though it were a person. Thus, "Surely *goodness* and *mercy* shall follow me all the days of my life" tends to personify the italicized terms by reason of the metaphoric use of "follow me." On the other hand, a conventional, complete personification, like *Justice* (whom we recognize by her *attributes*—she is blindfolded, she has scales and a sword) might also be called an *allegorical figure* in her own right, and her attributes *symbols* (blindness = impartiality; scales = justly deciding; sword = power to mete out what is deserved). Often the term "personification" applies to momentary, or *ad hoc*, humanizations.

Petrarch, Petrarchan   Francesco Petrarca (1304–74), the Italian founder of humanistic studies, with their revival of Greek and Latin literature, was influential in Renaissance England chiefly for his *Rime sparse*, the collection of love sonnets in praise of his muse, Laura. These poems, translated and adapted in England from the 1530's on, provided not only the sonnet (*q.v.*) form but also many devices of imagery widely used by English poets of the 16th and 17th centuries.

Physiognomics   The "art to read the mind's complexion in the face." From ancient times to the Renaissance, it was believed possible to gauge a person's character precisely from his outward appearance and physical characteristics.

Platonism   The legacy of Plato (429–347 B.C.) is virtually the history of philosophy. His *Timaeus* was an important source of later cosmology; his doctrine of ideas is central to Platonic tradition. His doctrine of love (especially in the *Symposium*) had enormous influence in the Renaissance, at which time its applicability was shifted to heterosexual love specifically. The *Republic* and the *Laws* underlie a vast amount of political thought, and the *Republic* contains also a philosophical attack on poetry (fiction) which defenders of the arts have always had to answer. Neoplatonism—a synthesis of Platonism, Pythagoreanism, and Aristotelianism—was dominant in the 3rd century A.D.; and the whole tradition was revived in the 15th and 16th centuries. The medieval Plato was Latinized, largely at second-hand; the revival of Greek learning in the 15th century led to another Neoplatonism: a synthesis of Platonism, the medieval Christian Aristotle, and Christian doctrine. Out of this came the doctrines of love we associate with some Renaissance poetry; a sophisticated version of older systems of allegory and symbol; and notions of the relation of spirit and matter reflected in Marvell and many other poets.

Prayer Book   The Book of Common Prayer, containing the order of services in the Church of England. Based on translations from medieval service books, it first appeared in 1549, under the direction of Thomas Cranmer (1489–1556), Archbishop of Canterbury. It was much revised, partly to meet Puritan complaints, but in 1662 achieved the form it has since kept, with only slight alteration.

Purgatory   According to Catholic doctrine, a place or condition of temporal punishment for those who die in the grace of God, but without having made full satisfaction for their transgressions. In Purgatory they are purified so as to be fit to come into God's presence.

Quadrivium   The second division of the seven liberal arts, which together with the trivium (*q.v.*) comprised the full course of a medieval education and fitted a man to study theology, the crown of the arts and sciences. The quadrivium consisted of music, arithmetic, geometry, and astronomy.

Qualities Or contraries; the properties of all material things, the various combinations of which were held to determine their nature. They were four in number, in two contrasting pairs: hot and cold; moist and dry. See *Elements; Humors; Temperaments.*

Recusant   Literally, "refuser"; in the Elizabethan period, anyone who refused to join the Church of England—although now the term is commonly used to allude to "popish recusants," i.e. Roman Catholics, and "recusancy," to English writings of certain Catholics during the late 16th century.

Renaissance Psychology   Poetic language, particularly that of lyric poetry, is always implicitly raising assumptions about inner states of people who have feelings and who wish to express them. In the Renaissance, several informal ways coexisted of talking about the relation which we now see as one of mind and body. From Aristotelian tradition the concept of three orders of soul was maintained: in ascending order these were the *vegetable* (the "life," immobile and inactive, of plants), the *animal* (accounting for the behavior of beasts), and the *rational* (the power of reason, often associated with language as well as thought, in men). On the other hand, *wit* (*q.v.*) meant intellect, and in Elizabethan language, the conflict of *wit* and *will* correspond roughly, but not precisely, to a modern opposition of reason and emotion. Physical, as well as psychological, human diversity was explained by the theory of the humors and temperaments (*qq.v.*). On the other hand, there were mysterious entities called *spirits* (associated with the Latin root, meaning "breath," and its application to alcoholic fluids: waters that "breathe" and "burn"). Spirits were fine vapors mediating between the body and the soul, and patching up a connection which scientific psychology is still trying to make. *Natural spirits* came from the liver and circulated through the veins. *Vital spirits* came from the heart and circulated arterially. *Animal spirits* were distilled from the vital spirits (which can be associated with blood) and went to the brain through the nerves, which were thought to be conducting vessels. (See the selection from Burton's *Anatomy of Melancholy*.) Other faculties of the soul included the power of *fancy* or *fantasy* (the word "imagination" most often referred to something imagined, rather than to a faculty).

Reverdie   Old French dance poem imitated in other languages, usually consisting of five or six stanzas without refrain, in joyful celebration of the coming of Spring.

Rhetoric   In classical times, rhetoric was the art of persuading through the use of language. The major treatises on style and structure of discourse—Aristotle's *Rhetoric*, Quintilian's *Institutes of Oratory*, the *Rhetorica ad Herrenium* ascribed for centuries to Cicero—were concerned with the "arts" of language in the older sense of "skills." In the Middle Ages the *trivium* (*q.v.*), or program that led to the degree of Bachelor of Arts, consisted of grammar, logic, and rhetoric, but it was an abstract study, based on the Roman tradition. In the Renaissance, classical rhetorical study became a matter of the first importance, and it led to the study of literary stylistics and the application of principles and concepts of the production and structure of eloquence to the higher eloquence of poetry.

Rhetoricians distinguished three stages in the production of discourse: *inventio* (finding or discovery), *dispositio* (arranging), and *elocutio* (style). Since the classical discipline aimed always at practical oratory (e.g. winning a case in court, or making a point effectively in council), *memoria* (memory) and *pronuntiatio* (delivery) were added. For the Renaissance, however, rhetoric became the art of writing. Under the heading of *elocutio,* style became stratified into three levels, *elevated* or high, *elegant* or middle, and *plain* or low. The proper fitting of these styles to the subject of discourse comprised the subject of decorum (*q.v.*).

Another area of rhetorical theory was concerned with classification of devices of language into *schemes, tropes,* and *figures.* A basic but somewhat confused distinction between figures of speech and figures of thought need not concern us here, but we may roughly distinguish between schemes (or patterns) of words, and tropes as manipulations of meanings, and of making words non-literal.

Common Schemes

anadiplosis   repeating the terminal word in a clause as the start of the next one: "Pleasure might cause her read; reading might cause her know; / Knowledge might pity win, and pity grace obtain" (Sidney, *Astrophel and Stella*).

anaphora   the repetition of a word or phrase at the openings of successive clauses, e.g. "The Lord sitteth above the water floods. The Lord remaineth King forever. The Lord shall give strength unto his people. The Lord shall give his people the blessing of peace."

chiasmus   a pattern of criss-crossing a syntactic structure, whether of noun and adjective, e.g. "Empty his bottle, and his girlfriend gone," or of a reversal of normal syntax with similar effect, e.g. "A fop her passion, and her prize, a sot," reinforced by assonance (*q.v.*). Chiasmus may even extend to assonance, as in Coleridge's line "In Xanadu did Kubla Khan."

Common Tropes

metaphor and simile   both involve comparison of one thing to another, the difference being that the *simile* will actually compare, using the words "like" or "as," while the metaphor identifies one with the other, thus producing a non-literal use of a word or attribution. Thus, Robert Burns's "O, my love is like a red, red rose / That's newly sprung in June" is a simile; had Burns written, "My love, thou art a red, red rose . . .", it would have been a metaphor—and indeed, it would not mean that the lady had acquired petals. In modern critical theory, *metaphor* has come to stand for various non-expository kinds of evocative signification. I. A. Richards, the modern critic most interested in a general theory of metaphor in this sense, has contributed the terms *tenor* (as in the case above, the girl) and *vehicle* (the rose) to designate the components. See also *Epic Simile.*

metonymy   a trope in which the vehicle is closely and conventionally associated with the tenor, e.g. "crown" and "king," "pen" and "writing," "pencil" and "drawing," "sword" and "warfare."

synecdoche   a trope in which the part stands for the whole, e.g. "sail" for "ship."

hyperbole   intensifying exaggeration, e.g. the combined synecdoche and hyperbole in which Christopher Marlowe's Faustus asks of Helen of Troy "Is this the face that launched a thousand ships / And burned the topless towers of Ilium?"

oxymoron   literally, sharp-dull; a figure of speech involving a witty paradox, e.g. "sweet harm"; "darkness visible" (Milton, *Paradise Lost* I.63).

Rhyme Royal   See *Troilus stanza.*

Right Reason   A natural faculty of intelligence in man, his capability of choosing between moral alternatives. In the humanism of the Renaissance, Aristotle's term, *orthos logos,* associated with the Latin word *ratio,* was thought of as having preceded the fallen knowledge acquired in Paradise by Adam and Eve's first sin.

Romance   (1) A medieval tale of chivalric or amorous adventure, in prose or verse, with the specification that the material be fictional. Later on, there developed cycles of stories, such as those involving Arthurian material or the legends of Charlemagne. Many of these, particularly the Arthurian, came to involve the theme of courtly love (*q.v.*)

(2) In the Renaissance, romance becomes more complex and literary, involving some degree of consciousness on the part of the author that he was reworking medieval materials (Spenser's *Faerie Queene,* of Arthurian legends; Ariosto's *Orlando Furioso,* of Charlemagne's heroic knight; Tasso's *Gerusalemme Liberata,* of stories of the Crusades).

(3) Prose romance, the 19th-century outgrowth of earlier essays into the

Gothic (*q.v.*) tale, represents a poetic kind of narrative to be clearly distinguished (in England if not in America) from the mode of the novel (e.g. Mary Shelley's *Frankenstein* and Hawthorne's *The Scarlet Letter* are both prose romance).

Rondeau, Roundel A strict French poetic form, thirteen lines of eight to ten syllables, divided into stanzas of five, three, and five lines, using two rhymes only and repeating the first word or first few words of line one after the second and third stanzas. The two terms are used interchangeably in the Middle Ages.

Satire A literary mode painting a distorted verbal picture of part of the world in order to show its true moral, as opposed merely to its physical, nature. In this sense, Circe, the enchantress in Homer's *Odyssey* who changed Odysseus' men into pigs (because they made pigs of themselves while eating) and would have changed Odysseus into a fox (for he was indeed foxy), was the first satirist. Originally the Latin word *satura* meant a kind of literary grab bag, or medley, and a satire was a fanciful kind of tale in mixed prose and verse; but later a false etymology connected the word with *satyr* and thus with the grotesque. Satire may be in verse or in prose; in the 16th and 17th centuries, the Roman poets Horace and Juvenal were imitated and expanded upon by writers of satiric moral verse, the tone of the verse being wise, smooth, skeptical, and urbane, that of the prose, sharp, harsh, and sometimes nasty. A tradition of English verse satire runs through Donne, Jonson, Dryden, Pope, and Samuel Johnson; of prose satire, Addison, Swift, and Fielding.

Scholasticism, Schoolmen Scholasticism is the term used for the philosophy and theology of the Middle Ages. This consisted of rational inquiry into revealed truth; for it was important to understand what one believed. This technique of disposition was developed by the Schoolmen over a long period, reaching its perfection in Peter Abelard (1079–1142). In the 13th century it absorbed the newly discovered Aristotelian philosophy and method. In this phase its greatest exponent was St. Thomas Aquinas (*c.* 1225–74), who became the chief medieval philosopher and theologian; his authority, challenged in the 16th century, was more seriously contested in the 17th century by the adherents of the "new science."

Seneca Lucius Annaeus Seneca (4 B.C.–65 A.D.) was an important source of Renaissance stoicism (*q.v.*), a model for the "closet" drama of the period, and an exemplar for the kind of prose that shunned the Ciceronian loquacity of early humanism and cultivated terseness. He was Nero's tutor; in 62 A.D. he retired from public life, and in 65 was compelled to commit suicide for taking part in a political conspiracy. He produced writings on ethics and physics, as well as ten tragedies often imitated in the Renaissance.

Sensibility (1) In the mid-18th century, the term came to be used in a literary context to refer to a susceptibility to fine or tender feelings, particularly involving the feelings and sorrows of others. This became a quality to be cultivated in despite of stoical rejections of unreasonable emotion which the neoclassicism (*q.v.*) of the earlier Augustan age had prized. The meaning of the word blended easily into "sentimentality"; but the literary period in England characterized by the work of writers such as Sterne, Goldsmith, Gray, Collins, and Cowper is often called the Age of Sensibility.

(2) A meaning more important for modern literature is that of a special kind of total awareness, an ability to make the finest discriminations in its perception of the world, and yet at the same time not lacking in a kind of force by the very virtue of its own receptive power. The varieties of awareness celebrated in French literature from Baudelaire through Marcel Proust have been adapted by modernist English critics, notably T. S. Eliot, for a fuller extension of the meaning of *sensibility*. By the term "dissociation of sensibility," Eliot implied the split between the sensuous and the intellectual faculties which he thought characterized English poetry after the Restoration (1660).

Sententia   A wise, fruitful saying, functioning as a guide to morally correct thought or action.

Sestina   Originally a Provençal lyric form supposedly invented by Arnaut Daniel in the 12th century, and one of the most complex of those structures. It has six stanzas of six lines each, folllowed by an *envoi* (*q.v.*) or *tornada* of three lines. Instead of rhyming, the end-words of the lines of the first stanza are all repeated in the following stanzas, but in a constant set of permutations. The *envoi* contains all six words, three in the middle of each line. D. G. Rossetti, Swinburne, Pound, Auden, and other modern poets have used the form, and Sir Philip Sidney composed a magnificent double-sestina, "Ye Goat-herd Gods."

Skepticism   A philosophy that denies the possibility of certain knowledge, and, although opposed to Stoicism and Epicureanism (*q.v.*), advocated *ataraxy*, imperturbability of mind. Skepticism originated with Pyrrhon (*c.* 360–270 B.C.), and its chief transmitter was Sextus Empiricus (*c.* 200 B.C.). In the Renaissance, skepticism had importance as questioning the power of the human mind to know truly (for a classic exposition see Donne's *Second Anniversary*, ll. 254–300), and became a powerful influence in morals and religion through the advocacy of Montaigne.

Sonnet   A basic lyric form, consisting of fourteen lines of iambic pentameter rhymed in various patterns. The *Italian* or *Petrarchan* sonnet is divided clearly into *octave* and *sestet,* the first rhyming *abba abba* and the second in a pattern such as *cdc dcd.* The *Shakespearean* sonnet consists of three quatrains followed by a couplet: *abab cdcd efef gg.* In the late 16th century in England, sonnets were written either independently as short epigrammatic forms, or grouped in sonnet sequences, i.e. collections of upwards of a hundred poems, in imitation of Petrarch, purportedly addressed to one central figure or muse—a lady usually with a symbolic name like "Stella" or "Idea." Milton made a new kind of use of the Petrarchan form, and the Romantic poets continued in the Miltonic tradition. Several variations have been devised, including the addition of "tails" or extra lines, or the recasting into sixteen lines, instead of fourteen.

Stoicism, Stoics   Philosophy founded by Zeno (335–263 B.C.), and opposing the hedonistic tendencies of Epicureanism (*q.v.*). The Stoics' world-view was pantheistic: God was the energy that formed and maintained the world, and wisdom lay in obedience to this law of nature as revealed by the conscience. Moreover, every man is free because the life according to nature and conscience is available to all; so too is suicide—a natural right. Certain Stoics saw the end of the world as caused by fire. In the Renaissance, Latin Stoicism, especially that of Seneca (*q.v.*), had a revival of influence and was Christianized in various ways.

Strong Lines   The term used in the 17th century to refer to the tough, tense conceit (*q.v.*)-laden verse of Donne and his followers.

Style   See *Decorum*.

Sublime   "Lofty"; as a literary idea, originally the basic concept of a Greek treatise (by the so-called "Longinus") on style. In the 18th century, however, the *sublime* came to mean a loftiness perceivable in nature, and sometimes in art—a loftiness different from the composed vision of landscape known as the *picturesque*, because of the element of wildness, power, and even terror. The *beautiful*, the picturesque, and the sublime became three modes for the perception of nature.

Symbolism   (1) Broadly, the process by which one phenomenon, in literature, stands for another, or group of others, and usually of a different sort. Clear-cut cases of this in medieval and Renaissance literature are *emblems* or *attributes* (see *Personification; Allegory*). Sometimes conventional symbols may be used in more than one way, e.g. a mirror betokening both truth and vanity. See also *Figure; Emblem*.

(2) In a specific sense (and often given in its French form, *symbolisme*), an important esthetic concept for modern literature, formulated by French poets and critics of the later 19th century following Baudelaire. In this view, the literary symbol becomes something closer to a kind of commanding, central metaphor, taking precedence over any more discursive linguistic mode for poetic communication. The effects of this concept on literature in English have been immense; and some version of the concept survives in modern notions of the poetic *image*, or *fiction*.

Temperaments   The balance of combinations of humors (*q.v.*) which in the medieval and Renaissance periods was believed to determine the psychosomatic make-up or "complexion" of a man or a woman. See *Renaissance Psychology*.

Topographical Poem   A descriptive poem popular in the 17th and 18th centuries and devoted to a specific scene or landscape with the addition (in the words of Samuel Johnson in 1799) of "historical retrospection or incidental meditation." Sir John Denham's "Cooper's Hill" (1642) is an influential example of the tradition (which includes also Pope's "Windsor Forest") and sometimes blends with the genre of a poem in praise of a particular house or garden.

Topos   Greek for "place," commonplace; in rhetoric (*q.v.*), either a general argument, description, or observation that could serve for various occasions; or a method of inventing arguments on a statement or contention. It is often used now to mean a basic literary topic (either a proposition such as the superiority of a life of action to that of contemplation, or vice versa; of old age vs. youth; or a description, such as that of the *locus amoenus* (*q.v.*), the pleasant garden place, Paradise, which allows many variations of thought and language.

Trivium   The course of study in the first three of the seven liberal arts—grammar, rhetoric, and logic (or dialectic): the basis of the medieval educational program in school and university. See also *Quadrivium*.

Troilus stanza   Or *rhyme royal;* iambic pentameters in stanzas of seven lines, rhyming *ababbcc,* popularized by Chaucer in his poem *Troilus and Criseyde* and called *rhyme royal* supposedly on account of its use by James I of Scotland, king and poet.

Trope   (1) See *Rhetoric.* (2) In the liturgy of the Catholic Church, a phrase, sentence, or verse with its musical setting, introduced to amplify or embellish some part of the text of the mass or the office (i.e. the prayers and Scripture readings recited daily by priests, religious, and even laymen) when chanted in choir. Tropes of this second kind were discontinued in 1570 by the authority of Pope Pius V. Troping new material into older or conventional patterns seems to have been, in a general way, a basic device of medieval literature, and was the genesis of modern drama.

Type, Typology   (1) Strictly, in medieval biblical interpretation, the prefiguration of the persons and events of the New Testament by persons and events of the Old, the Old Testament being fulfilled in, but not entirely superseded by, the New. Thus, the Temptation and Fall of Man were held to prefigure the first Temptation of Christ, pride in each case being the root of the temptation, and a warning against gluttony the moral lesson to be drawn from both. The Brazen Serpent raised up by Moses was held to prefigure the crucifixion of Christ; Isaac, as a sacrificial victim ("God will provide his own Lamb," says Abraham to him) is a *type* of Christ. The forty days and nights of the Deluge, the forty years of Israel's wandering in the desert, Moses' forty days in the desert are all typologically related.

(2) In a looser sense, a person or event seen as a model or paradigm. See also *Figure.*

Ubi Sunt . . .   A motif introducing a lament for the passing of all mortal and material things: e.g. *"Ubi sunt qui ante nos in mundo fuere?"* (Where are they who went before us in this world?), or "Where are the snows of yesteryear?" (Swinburne's translation from the French of Villon's *ballade*).

Virelay   A French poetic form, a dance song; short, with two or three rhymes, and two lines of the first stanza as a refrain.

Wars of the Roses   Series of encounters between the house of Lancaster (whose emblem was the red rose) and the house of York (whose emblem was the white), which took place between 1455 and 1485 to decide the right of possession of the English throne. At the Battle of Bosworth Field in 1485 the Lancastrian Henry Tudor defeated the Yorkist Richard III and was proclaimed king as Henry VII. He married Elizabeth of York, daughter of King Edward IV.

Worthies, Nine   Nine exemplary heroes, three from the Bible (Joshua, David, Judas Maccabaeus); three from pagan antiquity (Hector of Troy, Alexander the Great, Julius Caesar), and three from "Christian" romance (King Arthur, the Emperor Charlemagne, and Godfrey of Bouillon, a leader of the First Crusade and King of Jerusalem). They were favorite figures for tapestries (see Fig. 46 in illustrations for the Medieval section of this Anthology) and pageants.

Wit (1) Originally, "intellect," "intelligence"; later, "creative intelligence," or poetical rather than merely mechanical intellectual power. Thus, during the age of Dryden and Pope, a poet might be called a wit without any compromising sense. In the 19th century, "wit" came to mean verbal agility or cleverness, as opposed to the more creative powers of the mind. (2) More specifically, in literary history, as characterizing the poetic style of John Donne and his 17th-century followers. The Augustan age would contrast this with the "true wit" of *neoclassical* (*q.v*) poetry.

Yorkists See *Wars of the Roses.*

Zodiac In astrology, a belt of the celestial sphere, about eight or nine degrees to either side of the ecliptic (the apparent orbit of the sun), within which the apparent motions of the sun, moon, and planets take place. It is divided into twelve equal parts, the signs, through each of which the sun passes in a month. Each division once coincided with one of the constellations after which the signs are named: Aries (Ram)—in Chaucer's time the sun entered this sign on 12 March; Taurus (Bull); Gemini (Twins); Cancer (Crab); Leo (Lion); Virgo (Virgin); Libra (Scales); Scorpio; Sagittarius (Archer); Capricornus (Goat); Aquarius (Water-Carrier); Pisces (Fishes). Each zodiacal sign was believed to govern a part of the human body. See *Astronomy and Astrology.*

Suggestions for Further Reading

Social and Political History   Three volumes of the Oxford History of England cover this period: Sir George Clark, *The Later Stuarts 1660–1714*, 2nd ed., 1956; Basil Williams, *The Whig Supremacy 1714–1760*, 2nd ed. revised by C. H. Stuart, 1961; and J. Steven Watson, *The Reign of George III 1760–1815*, 1960. For the earlier period see also J. R. Western, *Monarchy and Revolution: The English State in the 1680s*, 1972; J. H. Plumb, *The Growth of Political Stability in England 1675–1725*, 1967; David Ogg, *England in the Reign of Charles II*, 2nd ed., and *England in the Reigns of James II and William III*, 1955; and the three volumes by G. M. Trevelyan, *England under Queen Anne*, 1930–34. For the later period see the important biography by J. H. Plumb, *Sir Robert Walpole*, 1956; Caroline Robbins, *The Eighteenth-Century Commonwealthman*, 1959; Isaac Kramnick, *Bolingbroke and His Circle: The Politics of Nostalgia in the Age of Walpole*, 1968; R. J. White, *The Age of George III*, 1968.

For social history, see M. Dorothy George, *London Life in the Eighteenth Century*, 1925; Dorthy Marshall, *English People in the Eighteenth Century*, 1969; A. S. Turberville ed., *Johnson's England* (excellent essays on all aspects of English life), 1933; A. R. Humphreys, *The Augustan World*, 1954; J. L. Clifford ed., *Man versus Society in Eighteenth-Century Britain*, 1968. On political radicalism, see George Rudé, *Wilkes and Liberty*, 1962; S. Maccoby, *English Radicalism 1762–1785*, 1935; H. Butterfield, *George III, Lord North, and the People 1779–80*, 1949; Carl B. Cone, *The English Jacobins*, 1968.

Literary History   George Sherburn, "The Restoration and Eighteenth Century," in A. C. Baugh ed., *A Literary History of England*, 1948; two volumes of The Oxford History of English Literature, both of which contain substantial bibliographies: James Sutherland, *English Literature of the Late Seventeenth Century*, 1969, and Bonamy Dobrée, *English Literature in the Early Eighteenth Century*, 1959; and the fourth volume in the Sphere History of Literature in the English Language, *Dryden to Johnson*, ed. Roger Lonsdale, 1971. Valuable for reference is George Watson ed., *The New Cambridge Bibliography of English Literature*, Vol. II, *1660–1800*, 1971; and still useful is Leslie Stephen's *History of English Thought in the Eighteenth Century*, two vols., 1876.

Critical Studies (General)   There is a good collection of recent work in James L. Clifford ed., *Eighteenth Century English Literature: Modern Essays in Criticism*, 1959. For introduction to the literary forms of the age, see James Sutherland, *A*

Preface to Eighteenth Century Poetry, 1948; Ian Jack, *Augustan Satire*, 1952; R. P. Bond, *English Burlesque Poetry 1700–1750*, 1932; Donald Davie, *Purity of Diction in English Verse*, 1952. For critical thought of the period, see the collection by Scott Elledge, *Eighteenth Century Critical Essays*, two vols., 1961, and the following studies: W. J. Bate, *From Classic to Romantic*, 1946; S. H. Monk, *The Sublime*, 1935; M. H. Abrams, *The Mirror and the Lamp*, 1953; P. W. R. Stone, *The Art of Poetry 1750–1820*, 1967; Lawrence Lipking, *The Ordering of the Arts in Eighteenth-Century England*, 1970; René Wellek, *A History of Modern Criticism*, Vol. I, 1955.

For thematic studies relating literary forms to ideas of the period, see Paul Fussell, *The Rhetorical World of Augustan Humanism*, 1965; Martin Price, *To the Palace of Wisdom: Studies in Order and Energy from Dryden to Blake*, 1964; J. W. Johnson, *The Formation of Neo-Classical Thought*, 1967 (particularly concerned with ideas of history); Patricia M. Spacks, *The Poetry of Vision*, 1967 (on Thomson, Collins, Gray, Smart, and Cowper); and the collection of essays in honor of F. A. Pottle, *From Sensibility to Romanticism*, ed. F. W. Hilles and Harold Bloom, 1965.

On the relations of poetry and the arts in the age, see Jean H. Hagstrum, *The Sister Arts*, 1958; Edward Malins, *English Landscaping and Literature, 1660–1840*, 1966; on related arts, see Sir John Summerson, *Architecture in Britain, 1530 to 1830*, 1953; Ellis K. Waterhouse, *Painting in Britain, 1530 to 1790*, 1953; M. D. Whinney, *Sculpture in Britain, 1530–1830*, 1964; M. D. Whinney and Oliver Millar, *English Art 1625–1714*, 1957; David G. Irwin, *English Neoclassical Art*, 1966.

The Novel   The best introduction is A. D. McKillop's *The Early Masters of English Fiction*, 1956. Important general studies are Ian Watt, *The Rise of the Novel*, 1957 (particularly good on the realism of Defoe and Richardson), and Ronald Paulson, *Satire and the Novel in Eighteenth-Century England*, 1967. There are valuable sections in Dorothy Van Ghent, *The English Novel*, 1953, and Wayne C. Booth, *The Rhetoric of Fiction*, 1961.

The Drama   For history, Allardyce Nicoll, *A History of English Drama*, Vols. I–III, 1952; for records of performances, and other data, *The London Stage 1660–1800*, ed. W. Van Lennep, E. L. Avery, A. H. Scouten, G. W. Stone, C. B. Hogan, eleven vols., 1960–68.

On the relation of the drama to the times, see two works by John Loftis, *Comedy and Society from Congreve to Fielding*, 1959, and *The Politics of Drama in Augustan England*, 1963.

On the heroic plays of the Restoration, see Arthur C. Kirsch, *Dryden's Heroic Drama*, 1965, and two works by Eugene M. Waith, *The Herculean Hero*, 1962, and *Ideas of Greatness: Heroic Drama in England*, 1971.

On Restoration comedy, see especially Thomas H. Fujimura, *The Restoration Comedy of Wit*, 1952; Norman H. Holland, *The First Modern Comedies*, 1959, and, particularly for its general introductory chapters, Dale Underwood, *Etherege and the Seventeenth-Century Comedy of Manners*, 1957. For the later period, there is F. W. Bateson, *English Comic Drama 1700–50*, 1929.

SAMUEL BUTLER

The standard editions are *The Complete Works*, ed. A. R. Waller and R. Lamar, 1905–28; and *Hudibras*, ed. John Wilders, 1967. For critical discussion and historical setting see E. A. Richards, *Hudibras and the Burlesque Tradition*, 1937, and, under Critical Studies (General), Bond and Jack.

JOHN BUNYAN

Among editions *Grace Abounding and The Pilgrim's Progress*, ed. Roger Sharrock, 1966, is recent and good. For biographical and critical studies see Roger Sharrock, *John Bunyan*, 1954; Henri Talon, *John Bunyan: The Man and the Work*, 1951; and U. M. Kaufmann, *The Pilgrim's Progress and Traditions in Puritan Meditation*, 1966.

GEORGE SAVILE, MARQUESS OF HALIFAX

The newest (at this writing) and best edition is the *Complete Works*, ed. J. P. Kenyon, 1969. The life, included with a good edition, by H. C. Foxcroft, 1898, was brought up to date in her *A Character of the Trimmer*, 1946.

JOHN WILMOT, EARL OF ROCHESTER

The best edition is now *Complete Poems*, ed. David Vieth, 1968. For a biographical study see V. deSola Pinto, *Enthusiast in Wit*, 1962, and, for wider milieu, J. H. Wilson, *The Court Wits of the Restoration*, 1948.

JOHN DRYDEN

Editions   The best complete edition of the poetry is by James Kinsley, four vols., 1958. In process is the careful and richly annotated edition of all the works, known as the California Dryden, ed. E. N. Hooker, H. T. Swedenberg, and others, from 1956. For the critical essays the once-standard edition of W. P. Ker (1900, 1926) is now superseded by that of George Watson, *Of Dramatic Poetry and Other Critical Writings*, two vols., 1962.

Critical Studies   Louis I. Bredvold's *The Intellectual Milieu of Dryden's Thought*, 1934, is corrected and amplified by Philip Harth, *Contexts of Dryden's Thought*, 1968 (on the religious thought). The first modern critical study of the poetry, by Mark Van Doren (1920), has been succeeded by recent works of importance: William Frost, *Dryden and the Art of Translation*, 1955; A. W. Hoffman, *Dryden's Imagery*, 1962; A. H. Roper, *Dryden's Poetic Kingdoms*, 1965; and Earl Miner, *Dryden's Poetry*, 1967.

Biography   The standard life (1961) is that of C. E. Ward, who also edited the *Letters*, 1952.

WILLIAM CONGREVE

Standard editions include *Complete Plays*, ed. Herbert Davis, 1967; *Complete Works*, ed. M. Summers, 1923; *Congreve: Letters and Documents*, ed. J. C. Hodges, 1964. There is a critical study by W. Van Voris, *The Cultivated Stance*, 1966; see also, under The Drama (General), Fujimura, Loftis, and Holland. The standard biography is J. C. Hodges, *Congreve the Man*, 1941.

JONATHAN SWIFT

Editions   *Prose Works,* ed. Herbert Davis, 1939–68; *Poems,* ed. Harold Williams, 1937 (rev. 1958); *Correspondence,* ed. Harold Williams, 1963–65; *A Tale of a Tub* [and shorter prose works], ed. A. C. Guthkelch and D. N. Smith, 1920 (rev. 1958); *Gulliver's Travels,* in various editions by Harold Williams (1926), A. E. Case (1936), L. A. Landa (1960).

Critical Studies   Kathleen Williams, *Swift and the Age of Compromise,* 1958; Martin Price, *Swift's Rhetorical Art,* 1953; W. B. Ewald, *The Masks of Jonathan Swift,* 1954; Ronald Paulson, *Theme and Structure in Swift's Tale of a Tub,* 1960; Edward R. Rosenheim, *Swift and the Satirist's Art,* 1965. Important works on Swift's thought are Ricardo Quintana, *The Mind and Art of Jonathan Swift,* 1936 (rev. 1953); Miriam Starkman, *Swift's Satire on Learning in A Tale of a Tub,* 1950; and Philip Harth, *Swift and Anglican Rationalism,* 1961. There is a survey of recent studies in M. Voigt, *Swift and the Twentieth Century,* 1964, and among collections of essays is *The World of Jonathan Swift,* ed. Brian Vickers, 1968.

Biography   Irvin Ehrenpreis, *Swift: The Man, His Works, and the Age* (to be completed in three volumes, 1962–   ), L. Landa, *Swift and the Church of Ireland,* 1954.

ALEXANDER POPE

Editions   Standard for the poetry, including the translations, is the Twickenham Edition, ed. John Butt and others, 1940–67. The *Correspondence* is well edited by George Sherburn, 1956; and there is a useful collection of the *Literary Criticism,* ed. B. A. Goldgar, 1965.

Critical Studies   Among the best are Geoffrey Tillotson, *On the Poetry of Pope,* 1938 (rev. 1950); Reuben A. Brower, *Alexander Pope: The Poetry of Allusion,* 1959; T. R. Edwards, *This Dark Estate,* 1963; and Aubrey Williams, *Pope's Dunciad,* 1955.

Biography   The standard account to 1728 is George Sherburn, *The Early Career of Alexander Pope,* and there is a valuable record of the poet in Joseph Spence's *Observations, Anecdotes, and Characters of Books and Men,* ed. J. M. Osborn, 1966. These may be supplemented by Robert W. Rogers, *The Major Satires of Alexander Pope,* 1955 (in large part biographical), and Maynard Mack, *The Garden and the City,* 1970 (a searching study of Pope's imagination).

JOHN GAY

Standard is the *Poetical Works,* ed. G. C. Faber, 1926. For *The Beggar's Opera,* see the Regents edition by E. V. Roberts (1969), and the forthcoming scholarly edition by Yvonne Noble Davies, as well as the historical study by W. E. Schulz, *Gay's Beggar's Opera,* 1923. The best critical study is Patricia M. Spacks, *John Gay,* 1965. For biography see W. H. Irving, *John Gay: Favorite of the Wits,* 1940.

JAMES BOSWELL

Miscellaneous writings are collected in *Private Papers,* ed. Geoffrey Scott and F. A. Pottle, 1928–34; and *The Yale Editions of the Private Papers,* ed. F. A. Pottle and others, from 1950 (the Research Edition began to appear in 1966). For biography see

F. A. Pottle, *James Boswell: The Earlier Years*, 1966 (to be completed in a second volume); Farnk Brady, *Boswell's Political Career*, 1965.

SAMUEL JOHNSON

Editions *Works* (The Yale Edition), ed. A. T. Hazen and others, 1958– ; *Letters*, ed. R. W. Chapman, 1952. For Boswell's *Life*, the standard edition is the revision of G. B. Hill by L. F. Powell, 1934–64; this may be supplemented by J. L. Clifford, *Young Sam Johnson* (up to 1749), 1955, and two penetrating general studies, W. J. Bate, *The Achievement of Samuel Johnson*, 1955, and B. H. Bronson, *Johnson and Boswell*, 1944.

Special Topics Richard Voitle, *Johnson the Moralist*, 1961; Arieh Sachs, *Passionate Intelligence: Imagination and Reason in the Work of Samuel Johnson*, 1967; J. H. Hagstrum, *Samuel Johnson's Literary Criticism*, 1952; D. J. Greene, *The Politics of Johnson*, 1960; and a masterful study by W. K. Wimsatt, *The Prose Style of Samuel Johnson*, 1941. A useful index and collection is *The Critical Opinions of Samuel Johnson*, ed. J. E. Brown, 1926.

EDWARD GIBBON

There are editions of *The History of the Decline and Fall of the Roman Empire* by J. B. Bury, 1896–1900 (rev. 1909–14); of *Memoirs*, by John Murray, 1896 (supplying all manuscript fragments) and by G. A. Bonnard, 1966; *Letters*, ed. J. E. Norton, 1956. The best biography is by D. M. Low, *Edward Gibbon*, 1937, and there is critical discussion in Harold L. Bond, *The Literary Art of Gibbon*, 1960.

EDMUND BURKE

The *Philosophical Enquiry* is well edited by J. T. Boulton, 1958; there are various collections of the works, of which the most helpful is *Select Works*, ed. E. J. Payne, 1874–78. *The Correspondence* has been edited by Thomas Copeland and others, 1958   . There are important essays in Thomas Copeland, *Our Eminent Friend Edmund Burke*, 1949. Of value also are Carl B. Cone, *Burke and the Nature of Politics*, two vols., 1957–64, and B. T. Wilkins, *The Problem of Burke's Political Philosophy*, 1967.

SIR JOSHUA REYNOLDS

The *Discourses* have been carefully edited by R. P. Wark, 1959; and the *Portraits* (manuscript essays) by F. W. Hilles, 1952. Hilles has also edited the *Letters*, 1929, and is the author of *The Literary Career of Sir Joshua Reynolds*, 1936. For biography, se Derek Hudson, *Reynolds: A Personal Study*, 1958; for a catalogue and study of the paintings, Ellis K. Waterhouse, *Reynolds*, 1941 (rev. 1973).

WILLIAM COLLINS

The best edition of his *Poems* (with those of Gray and Goldsmith) is by Roger Lonsdale, 1969. See, under Critical Studies (General), Hagstrum, Spacks, Hilles and Bloom.

For biography see E. G. Ainsworth, *Poor Collins*, 1937, and for a general study, O. F. Sigsworth, *William Collins*, 1965.

THOMAS GRAY

Standard editions include *Complete Poems*, ed. H. W. Starr and J. R. Hendrickson, 1966; *Poems*, superbly annotated and edited by Roger Lonsdale (Collins and Goldsmith are in this volume also), 1969; *Correspondence*, ed. P. Toynbee and L. Whibley, 1935. See under Critical Studies (General) Spacks, and, for three important essays on the *Elegy*, Hilles and Bloom. The best biography is by R. W. Ketton-Cremer, 1955.

CHRISTOPHER SMART

The writings are published in *Collected Poems*, ed. Norman Callan, 1949; *Poems*, ed. R. E. Brittain, 1956 (a selection with good commentary); *Jubilate Agno*, ed. W. H. Bond, 1954. For criticism see Moira Dearnley, *The Poetry of Christopher Smart*, 1968, as well as, under Critical Studies (General), the fine study by Spacks. For biography see Arthur Sherbo, *Christopher Smart: Scholar of the University*, 1967.

OLIVER GOLDSMITH

Standard is the *Collected Works*, ed. Arthur Friedman, 1966; the *Poems* are well edited by Roger Lonsdale (with Gray and Collins), 1969. For biography see Ralph Wardle, *Oliver Goldsmith*, 1967; and for recent criticism, Ricardo Quintana, *Goldsmith*, 1967, and R. H. Hopkins, *The True Genius of Goldsmith*, 1969.

WILLIAM COWPER

Editions   *Poetical Works*, ed. H. S. Milford and N. H. Russell, 1967; *Correspondence*, ed. T. Wright, 1904; *Unpublished and Uncollected Letters*, ed. T. Wright, 1925.

Critical Studies   R. Huang, *William Cowper: Nature Poet*, 1957, and Norman Nicholson, *William Cowper*, 1951. See also, under Critical Studies (General), Davie and Spacks.

Biography   David Cecil, *The Stricken Deer*, 1929; M. J. Quinlan, *Cowper: A Critical Life*, 1953; and Charles Ryskamp, *William Cowper of the Inner Temple, Esq.*, 1959 (on the early years).

GEORGE CRABBE

Editions   *Poetical Works*, ed. A. J. and R. M. Carlyle, 1914; *Poems*, ed. A. W. Ward, 1905–7; *Tales and Miscellaneous Poems*, ed. H. Mills, 1967.

Critical Studies: O. F. Sigsworth, *Nature's Sternest Painter*, 1965; L. Haddakin, *The Poetry of Crabbe*, 1955; and a section of John Speirs, *Poetry into Novel*, 1971.

Author and Title Index

First-Line Index